IT WASN'T SO JOLLY

The Story of the Jolly Rogers and the James Horner Crew

Front cover, top, the B-24 "Boise Bronc" of the Jolly Rogers' 320th Squadron. Bottom: the James Horner crew in the summer of 1944 on Biak Island.

Back cover, upper left, Col. Art Rogers. Lower right: Charles Lindbergh, also photographed on Biak Island in 1944.

IT WASN'T SO JOLLY

The Story of the Jolly Rogers and the James Horner Crew

Copyright ©2018 by
Thomas A. Baker

Copyright © 2018 by Thomas A. Baker

All rights reserved. This book, or any portion thereof, may not be reproduced or used in any manner without the express written permission of the publisher or author except for the use of brief quotations in a book review or scholarly journal.

First Printing: 2018

ISBN 978-0-692-16026-8

U.S. trade bookstores or wholesalers:
Please contact Tom Baker, e-mail tbaker@nmia.com

Also by Tom Baker:

Never Say Can't, The Memoirs of Orville E. Dickerhoof
The story of an American aviation pioneer

Above the Thunder, Reminiscences of a Field Artillery Pilot in WWII
by Raymond C. Kerns, edited & annotated by Tom Baker

For all those who went out to the Pacific war and never came back.

Table of Contents

Preface i
Introduction iv

Part One

The Jolly Rogers

1. The Formation of the 90th Bomb Group 1
2. Arthur H. Rogers 13
3. The Move to Hawaii 35
4. The Move to Australia 44
5. The 90th Joins the 5th Air Force 48
6. Iron Range 54
7. The 90th Prepares for Combat 66
8. The 90th Bomb Group's First Combat Mission 70
9. The 90th's Second Combat Mission: Rabaul 78
10. Staying the Course 90
11. Col. Rogers Arrives at Iron Range 98
12. Col. Rogers' First Combat Mission 101
13. The Crosson Crew's Odyssey 118
14. Casualties Mount 127
15. Taking Turns at Port Moresby 136
16. The Loss of General Walker 142
17. Another Convoy Attack 148
18. Lt. McMurria is Shot Down 155
19. The B-24 Gets a Nose Turret 173
20. The 319th Goes to Darwin 180
21. The 90th Moves to Port Moresby 188
22. The Loss of General Ramey 197
23. No Rest for the Weary 200
24. Cannibals 209
25. The Battle of the Bismarck Sea 219
26. Rogers' Flight to Prove the B-24 Nose Turret 240

27. Col. Rogers Skip-Bombs a Ship 254
28. The 90th Bomb Group Becomes the Jolly Rogers 269
29. The Loss of Capt. Lark Martin 279
30. The Drive on Salamaua and Lae 288
31. Wewak Attacked, Lae and Nadzab Captured 302
32. Bridge Busting 324
33. The Big Strike on Rabaul 330
34. More Losses at Wewak 346
35. Cape Gloucester Gets "Gloucesterized" 365
36. Col. Art Rogers Leaves the Jolly Rogers 375
37. Japanese Airpower in New Guinea Smashed 381
38. The Jolly Rogers Move to Nadzab 398

Part Two

The Horner Crew

39. Into Uniform 407
40. Crew Training at March Field, California 453
41. The Flight to the Pacific 468
42. Port Moresby to Nadzab 490
43. Wakde Island 510
44. Charles Lindbergh Flies Shotgun for the Jolly Rogers 578
45. The Move to Biak Island 598
46. Life on Biak Island 642
47. The Move to the Philippines 696
48. The Horner Crew Returns Home 729
49. The End of the War 734
50. The Jolly Rogers Disband 750
Epilogue 758
Chapter Notes 775
Acknowledgments 785
Bibliography 788
Index 794

PREFACE

A few years ago, my wife Lee and I taught an American history class to a group of home-schooled students of high school age. When we took up the subject of World War II, the mother of one of the students told us that she knew a deacon in her church who had served as a gunner on a bomber in the Pacific, and he might be willing to come to the class and describe his experiences to us.

The man turned out to be Mr. Jaime Baca, known to most of his friends and all of his church associates as Deacon Baca, and he kindly consented to come to our class and speak to our students. He gave the class a fascinating description of the America of the Great Depression and World War II, and spoke of his experiences as a crewmember of a B-24 bomber. He informed us that a B-24 had a crew of ten, and the crewmen trained together and stayed together during the war. Mr. Baca and his crew had flown dozens of combat missions and had had some remarkable experiences, which it seemed to me ought to be preserved in writing. I also wondered whether we might be able to find any more members of this crew and acquire their reminiscences as well. Since Mr. Baca was then in his late eighties, it seemed likely that some of the other crew members, being of similar ages, had passed away, and in fact this proved to be the case. Most of our searches for other crewmembers led only to their newspaper obituaries on the Internet.

However, we were able to track down two more members of the crew, the pilot, Mr. James Horner, who lives in Florida, and the navigator, Mr. Tom Theobald, in Iowa. The story of this crew, and the bomb group known as the Jolly Rogers to which they belonged, seemed so remarkable to me that I decided it might become the subject of a book, and this book is the result.

The young men who flew America's warplanes during World War II were young indeed. Many were in their late teens and early twenties. They came straight from high school or college, from the farms, offices, and byways of America. Most had never been in an airplane before, and they had to grow up fast in the deadly kill-or-be-killed environment of aerial warfare. After a year or so of training in the States they embarked on a combat tour either in Europe or in the Pacific. Whether they flew in fighter planes, bombers, or transports, they continued to fly until they either completed their combat tour, were injured too badly to continue (or, in the Pacific, were struck down by malaria or other tropical diseases), or were shot down and killed or taken prisoner.

Each young man racked up hundreds of combat hours in the course of flying many sorties, and none of them knew for sure, when they embarked on any combat mission, whether they would return. Many were sustained by the optimism of youth and its sense of invulnerability, and the feeling that the bad stuff always happens to the other guy, but many tragically learned otherwise and came home maimed, or in a coffin, or went missing and never came home at all. Others came to realize full well when the odds were stacked against their survival but still summoned the courage to continue flying dangerous missions. The bones of many are still out there in the Pacific, in the jungles and under the sea, along with the wreckage of their aircraft. Thousands remain missing, their fates unknown for the last 70-plus years, and perhaps forever.

As I write this, World War II is nearly three quarters of a century behind us and fast receding into history. The numbers of the men who participated in the war and witnessed it firsthand are dwindling. The three men who contributed their memories to this book are all in their mid-90s now. James Horner was twenty-two years old when, after only a year's training, he became a bomber pilot entrusted with the command of a four-engine B-24 and the lives of the nine other young men who formed its crew (in keeping with the convention of the times, in which a crew was named after its pilot, this was the Horner crew). One of those men was Jaime Baca, twenty years old, who manned a machine gun in an open window in the waist section of the plane as a defense against enemy fighter planes. Tom Theobald, twenty-one, was the airplane's navigator, who from his station in the nose of the plane with his maps, charts, and plotting instruments, directed the bomber's course wherever it flew.

Today James Horner is 97 and living at his home in Florida, while both Jaime Baca (95) and Tom Theobald (97) reside in assisted-living facilities, the former in New Mexico and the latter in Iowa. Men of this age today were the youngest of the men who fought World War II. Their superior officers, the men higher up the chain of command, who were naturally older than they were, are nearly all gone now. These were the young men who were actually tasked with the fighting, the ones "on the tip of the spear," who can provide eyewitness accounts of the historical events in which they participated.

The details of the stories that these three men related for this book sometimes differ, even when they describe the same incident, and in such cases I have either provided all versions of the event or the one best supported by the evidence. The crew's copilot, Lt. Allan Cooper, who died in 1981, kept a small pocket diary in which he recorded all the missions in which he participated. This little notebook, plus Lt. Cooper's flight logbook, which were both made available to me by his son Michael, have clarified many of the incidents with respect to time, place, the objective of missions, and things that occurred during the flights.

PREFACE

Part I of this book is a history of the 90th Bomb Group, known as the Jolly Rogers, of which these men were members. It follows the history of the Group from its formation in January of 1942, after the Pearl Harbor attack, up to the point where the Horner crew joined it in the spring of 1944. Part II describes the backgrounds and training of the three men, their flight from San Francisco across the Pacific to the war zone, and then their assignment to the Jolly Rogers. From that point the stories of the Jolly Rogers the Horner crew merge, and continue together to the end of the crew's combat tour and the end of the war.

I have tried to let the principal figures in the story speak for themselves wherever possible. In the case of men who have passed away since the war, I have quoted from their letters, journals, and diary entries. I have quoted long passages verbatim from the unpublished war memoirs of Col. Art Rogers (for whom the Group was named), which was kindly provided to me by his sons, Buck and Bob Rogers.

In order that the reader may check the sources of information and quotes, if he cares to, there are small reference numbers embedded throughout the text of each chapter referring to that chapter's end notes, which are listed in an appendix at the back of the book. My academic training was in archaeology, so the reader will also have to excuse or (if it doesn't interest him) ignore my occasional digressions into such things as where a crashed aircraft happens to lie today, or what is left today (if anything) of a formerly important airbase.

One thing that surprised me as I did the research for this book was how many families still mourn the loss of a relative in that seemingly long-ago war. The parents and siblings of the men who were killed or went missing in action may be gone by now, but younger family members still search for information concerning the circumstances of their family member's loss, or in the case of those still missing, where their remains might now lie, and whether they can be recovered and brought home.

There are stacks of history books all around me as I write this, books that I have read in order to gain enough knowledge of the Pacific air war and the history of the Jolly Rogers to be able to write about them. History books sometimes give the impression that World War II happened a very long time ago. However, the fact that I can pick up a telephone right now and talk to men who were in the midst of all this wartime activity, and can give me eyewitness accounts of events described in those books, shows that these events did not really happen all that long ago, after all.

Tom Baker
Tijeras, New Mexico
17 May 2018

INTRODUCTION

The Pacific war: setting the stage

World War II was fought on two sides of the world: Europe and the Pacific. Germany and Japan, simply put, were twin pinnacles of evil, and their governments were profoundly malevolent dictatorships. By 1941 Hitler was the undisputed dictator of Germany, and his followers idolized him with an almost religious fervor. Japan was ruled by a hereditary emperor, and the Japanese worshiped him with an actual religious fervor, for the Emperor of Japan was in the same position as a Pharaoh of ancient Egypt—both the ancient Egyptians and the Japanese of this time worshiped their leader as a god. Many Japanese believed that to look directly at their divine emperor would cause blindness, and they considered his decrees to be divine edicts. No one was permitted to hear the Emperor's voice except those of his inner circle, including the military cabal that had taken control of Japan and acted as the Emperor's advisors and, many would say, his controllers, since by many accounts he was a weak and easily swayed leader.

All Japanese individuals, as subjects of their Emperor, believed that they possessed no rights whatever except what he allowed them, their fate subject to his whims. He was a divinity to whom every Japanese owed unquestioning obedience. Their ultimate purpose in life was to serve him, and to die for him in military service, if necessary, was considered an honor and a duty. All Japanese schoolchildren bowed to a photograph of the Emperor every morning, and were indoctrinated into the emperor cult from birth.

A political system of this type is as old as humanity: countless times in the dim past a powerful warrior would take control of a society by force and proclaim himself divine, with all his descendants becoming hereditary rulers by divine right. Nearly all governments in ancient times were in this mold, as were the monarchies of more recent times (though the latter, in the Western world at least, abandoned claims of divinity).

By the 20th century there had still been no intellectual Enlightenment in Japan, nor for that matter anywhere else in the Orient, as had occurred in Western Civilization. The Orient had no equivalent of ancient Greece or Rome where concepts regarding personal liberty and the importance and dignity of the individual had arisen, and ultimately influenced the shape of governments and

INTRODUCTION

their relationship with the governed. The idea that every person had inherent God-given rights and freedoms, as declared in the American Declaration of Independence and Constitution, had never entered Japanese (nor any other Oriental) culture and was entirely foreign to it.

The feudal Japanese political system, with its all-powerful emperor/dictator, was susceptible to takeover by evil and ambitious men, claiming to speak and act for the emperor, and that is exactly what happened in the early 20th century when a cabal of militarists hijacked the Japanese government, with the weak-willed Emperor's acquiescence. To Americans, the face of this rogue government was Hideki Tojo, Prime Minister of Japan from October of 1941 to July of 1944.

Prime Minister Hideki Tojo was the face of Japanese militarism for most Americans.

By the early 1930s an evil of a most virulent nature had infected the soul of the Japanese nation, arising from the morally bankrupt political and military culture that had inserted itself between the Emperor and the populace. This was a group of fanatics with a twisted belief in the Shinto religion and the Bushido warrior code. Japan by this time had industrialized itself on the Western model to the point of having an army and navy more powerful than any other nation in the Far East, and the militarists decided to exploit this power, backed by the divine authority of the Emperor, to promote an ambitious program to conquer and enslave all the other nations in the region and thereby create a Japanese Empire.

This sort of thing, too, is nothing new in human history, and Japanese leaders might have succeeded in their ambitions had they confined their aggression to the other countries of the Pacific Rim and not foolishly provoked a war with the United States of America. Leaving aside matters of right and wrong, good and evil, and considering only the raw wellsprings of military power, Japan simply did not have the population, a large enough industrial base, nor the resources on hand to defeat the U. S. The Japanese would learn this lesson the hard way.

The military junta that served as Japan's wartime government was a criminal enterprise, repressive enough toward its own people, but viciously brutal and depraved toward the peoples it conquered. Statistics on deaths caused by Japan's military aggression are hard to come by, and the numbers vary widely, but from the invasion of China in 1937 to the end of World War II, as many as 10,000,000 people died, including 6,000,000 Chinese, Indonesians, Koreans, Filipinos, and Indochinese. Against the Chinese the Japanese practiced the most brutal aggression imaginable. Japan's invasion and takeover of the other countries of the Pacific, and its attempt to defend its short-lived empire, also resulted in the deaths of over two and a half million of its own people. Additionally, over 100,000 Americans would lose their lives in the Pacific war.

The people of Japan obediently followed their Emperor and his military clique into their war of conquest, and, after its initial successes, backed it willingly, even enthusiastically. Their leaders' assertions that the Japanese were a superior race destined to rule the Pacific by divine right was heady wine, and seemed confirmed by the ease of the early victories. The few members of the Japanese government or intelligentsia who objected to the war were persecuted and imprisoned or driven underground by the militarists. An Anglican priest named James Benson (whom we will hear more of in later chapters), who had run a mission at the village of Gona on the northeast coast of New Guinea before the war, was taken prisoner by the Japanese when they invaded New Guinea in the first few months of 1942. As a captive, Benson met one of these Japanese dissenters, a war correspondent named Seizo Okada who wrote for Japan's leading newspaper, *Ashai Shimbun*. Benson later recounted a conversation that he'd had with Okada:

> I had been talking to Okada only a little while before he said, quite unexpectedly: "I feel it is impossible for Japan to win the war; and what a horrible prospect it would be for the world if she did!"
>
> I replied cautiously, uncertain of how far I could trust him. He noticed this, and said:
>
> "Please believe that what I say is genuine. I am no secret police spy. I am an honest man, a writer, who hates all that militarism stands for. Militarism must go."
>
> I told him I had always believed that militarism was part and parcel of Japanese Shintoism and emperor worship.
>
> "All that must go too!" he replied at once. "We of the intelligentsia will stand for it no longer!"
>
> He told me that his newspaper really held the most liberal ideals, although it was now muzzled by the militarists.
>
> "But the day of freedom will come," he said, "and what a day! I shall be able to speak and write what I feel in my heart... But see what is around us now. The world is full of filth and evil, hate and blood, mud and sorrow and pain; yet if we wanted to we could fill it with things that are lovely, beautiful and true. That is where Buddhism is such a help to us. In Japan," he went on, "we are all Buddhists at

heart, but our leaders have twisted the Master's teaching."

"I thought," I said, "that you were largely Shinto."

"Shinto," said Okada, "is no religion at all; it is a hodgepodge of fables and legends, demigods and spirits. It's true there's a tendency for the young people to be taken in by it. But when a Japanese grows old, he attends a Buddhist temple to prepare for death.

Then he said something rather significant:

"Actually, you Christians, with your great doctrine of the brotherhood of man, have the solution to all the world's problems. But you never try to put the idea into practice."

I countered his remark with Chesterton's famous dictum that "Christianity has not been tried and found wanting; it has been found difficult and not tried." To which he replied:

"Probably you are right. Mankind takes what it thinks is the easy way, and it proves the hardest."[1]

The roots of Japan's hatred of America

Throughout human history greed and the lust for power have always been sufficient motivation for wars of conquest, and this one was no different in that respect, but there were some additional factors unique to Japanese culture and history that intensified Japan's antagonism toward America, and made a Japanese attack on the U. S. practically inevitable.

Often overlooked by historians is what Japan perceived as an old insult by the U. S., in which Japanese leaders felt that they had lost honor and prestige. This was the forceful opening up of Japan's xenophobic society to the West by Admiral Matthew Perry in 1853. Just as Germans sought revenge for the humiliation of the Versailles Treaty of 1918, which ended their World War One aggression, so did the Japanese, with the long memory of an Oriental culture, seek revenge for what they saw as America's disrespect and humiliation of Japan over three-quarters of a century before.

Up until 1853, Japan had been firmly and deliberately closed to the outside world for 250 years, and its leaders had intended to keep it that way. All through the 17th and 18th centuries the Japanese had seen how easily Western powers with their superior technology had dominated Eastern countries such as China, and how they had established colonies anywhere they chose to in the Pacific. As a result the Japanese had decided to keep the West at arm's length, wanting no part of European cultural or religious influences. Prior to 1853, anyone from the West who visited Japan, or even accidentally entered Japanese waters through shipwreck, was imprisoned or killed by the Japanese. Any Christian missionaries who dared to enter Japan were murdered in horrible ways, in order to convey and emphasize the message that no Westerners, Western ideas, or Western religions were welcome in Japan.

The insult of Uraga Harbor

However, America's navy saw Japan as a potentially well-positioned coaling station for the resupply of its new steam-powered ships, and also possessed of ports that would be useful to American whaling ships operating in the area, not to mention the possibilities of commercial trade with the Japanese. So America, the brash new country and newcomer on the Pacific scene, took a more direct approach to opening up diplomatic and trade relations with Japan than had other Western nations—On July 14, 1853, Admiral Perry had simply sailed into Japan's Uraga Harbor, at the entrance to Tokyo Bay, with five big, black-painted warships loaded with cannon and Marines, and put an end to the country's self-imposed isolationism by threat of force. He would brook no refusal. It was classic gunboat diplomacy.

Perry's demands on the Japanese were ironclad. Backed by 200 United States Marines, whom he paraded ashore, he insisted on an audience with the Japanese Emperor and his advisers, and would not take no for an answer. Here was the origin of Japanese antipathy towards America. First and foremost the Japanese resented their divine leader being dominated and ordered around by a foreigner, even if at the meeting Perry also gave the Emperor gifts and presented him with a letter of friendship from President Millard Fillmore. Perry demonstrated to the Japanese the benefits of modern technology and the industrial revolution that was then sweeping America and the West. He brought to the Japanese working models of useful machines and samples of the products of industry. He gave them a functional telegraph, a camera, a telescope, maps and charts, and firearms: rifles and Colt revolvers, and showed them how to use them. He spoke of the benefits of trade and of friendship with America.

All of what Perry said about the advantages of embracing Western technology and culture was true, but having Western ways forced upon them in this manner created lasting resentment among Japanese leaders. Most Japanese considered Perry's actions to be condescending, overbearing, humiliating, and had caused them to "lose face." And in the Oriental culture of the time (and in some respects even today), losing face was considered a fate worse than death. The arrogance and obvious technical superiority of the Americans (and Europeans) was bitterly resented by the Japanese. Then there were the racial overtones: white men had once again demonstrated their superiority over the peoples of the Orient, and this, perhaps, was the greatest humiliation of all.

Having Western culture shoved in their faces with demands to adopt it, in compliance with American wishes, had caused the Japanese, in their own eyes, to suffer a loss of dignity and honor. They had been shown to be inferior and treated in a way that a teacher behaves toward a recalcitrant student.

It took the Japanese 87 years of diligent work, employing the Western industry and technology that they had been obliged to adopt, but among other goals they avenged the humiliation of Uraga Harbor in 1853 with the attack on Pearl Harbor in 1941. In discussing the basic causes of the Japanese attack on America and the European colonies in the Pacific in 1941, this motive of asserting racial pride and avenging the old insult of Perry's visit is laid out by M. G. Sheftall in his book *"Blossoms in the Wind"*:

> The goal, really, had always been, first and foremost, to humble the West—to daub the teacher's face with mud—by kicking the white man out of Asia and bringing about the end, once and for all, win or lose, of what former Prime Minister Konoe had so aptly termed Anglo-Saxon global hegemony. The Caucasian bogeyman—and the unspeakable fear that he might really be the superior being he seemed to think himself—had whispered in the ear and haunted the nightmares of the Japanese psyche for the last ninety years, ever since Commodore Matthew C. Perry's Black Ships first fouled the waters of Uraga Bay, humiliating the nation by forcing it to accommodate the Americans and their insulting demands. Whipping Russia [in the Russo-Japanese war of 1904-5] had been a promising start toward righting old wrongs, but holy war with the United States—inevitable, really, since that dark day at Uraga in 1853—had given Japan the chance to silence the unsettling murmurs in the nation's troubled conscience and the mocking laughter of that blue-eyed blight once and for all. The white man had been swallowing cultures and civilizations for too long. Now it was time for him to choke on one.[2]

The Japanese had always been an energetic and adaptable people, and after being forced, however unwillingly and resentfully, out of their feudal past and onto the road of modernization by America, they opened relations with European nations and embarked on a program of Western-style industrialization that they calculated would make them the dominant power in the Orient. They would build a naval power of their own to rival that of the hated Americans and the British. Always ardent imitators of anything they admired, they adopted as their model the navy of another island people who had built a worldwide empire with it, the British, and they set about imitating it in every detail.

Japan established a naval academy at Eta Jima that meticulously reproduced the British training academy at Dartmouth, right down to the smallest detail. Eta Jima's elegant Georgia-style main building was imported, brick by carefully-wrapped brick, from Britain and reassembled in Japan. A lock of Admiral Lord Nelson's hair was kept there as a sacred relic.[3] Japanese sailors were taught to use British nautical terms. Japanese naval officers ate with knives and forks instead of chopsticks, and they dined off copies of British china. If painstaking imitation of British naval traditions could have brought victory to the Japanese, then the Japanese navy would have been invincible. Unfortunately for them, it didn't work out that way.

Japanese ambivalence about the West

The Japanese people had had a love-hate relationship with the Western world ever since Admiral Perry's visit, and for Japanese politicians and military men, it was mostly hate, even though their society as a whole had embraced many aspects of Western culture, such as clothing styles and music. During WWII, when Saburo Saki, a Japanese fighter ace, was granted leave to visit his fiancé in Tokyo, she didn't dress in a kimono and play a koto for him; she wore a skirt and sat down at a grand piano and played Beethoven's Moonlight Sonata, and neither one of them considered it unusual.

When Saki's squadron relaxed after combat flights at Lae, in New Guinea, they broke out harmonicas, guitars, and accordions. Japanese diplomats wore Western suits, ties, and top hats in their own home offices. Many aspects of Western culture had been absorbed into Japanese life, but there was still that humiliating feeling of inferiority, both cultural and racial, that had to be expunged, and defeating the Americans in war, and driving them and the European colonists back to their own side of the world would accomplish that while also providing the Japanese with an empire.

Dreams of empire

By the 1930s, having established a world-class navy, the Japanese determined to do with it just what the British had done with theirs: establish an empire. Even if it would not be so large an empire that the sun never set on it, it would still be large enough to make Japan the most powerful country on its own side of the world. It was, Japanese leaders felt, their turn to have an empire; European countries had been creating them for centuries. Japan therefore set out to establish what its propaganda termed the Greater East Asia Co-Prosperity Sphere, in which the hated Western powers would play no part, and all the peoples of the Pacific would prosper under the wise and benevolent leadership of Japan. So the story went.

What Japanese propaganda did not say was that some countries would be more equal than others, with the Japanese being the most equal of all. Japan intended to control all industry and agriculture in this Pacific co-op from Tokyo, while the conquered nations would participate according to what the Japanese judged to be their abilities. China's teeming millions, under Japanese direction, would provide manual labor and perhaps some light industry. Korea would become a vast rice paddy to provide the co-op with food, and the inhabitants of Manchuria would practice animal husbandry.[4] All the inhabitants of the Pacific Rim would be under the authority of Japan's military cabal, nominally ruled by its divine emperor. The Japanese Empire and the British Empire would be equals, and the arrogant Americans (whom Japanese leaders often compared to the gangsters of American crime movies), indeed all white men, would be banished from the Pacific Sphere and humbled at last.

Throughout history white men had come to the Pacific in their ships, flaunting their superior technology, and had laid claim to Pacific islands and territories in the names of their home countries (in fact Britain had taken over entire countries such as India). This had been a longstanding humiliation to all Oriental peoples that would now be avenged by the Japanese. There would be no more Dutch East Indies, no British Singapore, no American (formerly Spanish) Philippines, and no Australian influences allowed in New Guinea or other Pacific islands. Australia itself would be invaded and "ethnically cleansed" i.e. all the detestable Caucasians would be either killed or driven off to their own side of the world. All European influences in the Pacific would be swept away and replaced by superior Japanese management and culture.

As the Japanese army advanced through China, however, it quickly became obvious that the only country that was intended to benefit from all this reorganization and unification of Pacific nations into a prosperous confederation was Japan. Japanese brutality, cruelty, and in fact wholesale slaughter in China demonstrated to the world that after Japanese takeover the subject countries would be little better than slave states whose only purpose would be to provide labor and natural resources for Japan. The Oriental solidarity and equality promised for the so-called Greater East Asia Co-Prosperity Sphere was a lie; Japan's murderous regime would reign supreme, and whatever Japan decreed would be law throughout its empire, ruthlessly enforced.

Another "master race"

Like the Nazis on the other side of the world, the Japanese fell under the delusion that they were a superior race of people, if not in stature (since the Japanese man is on the average 15% smaller than the average Caucasian) at least morally and spiritually. In some ways they did consider themselves to be superior physically; for example when the Japanese first heard of the Anglo-American invention of radar, they believed that they didn't need it because they had superior eyesight. They could even see better at night, they thought, and so trained for night naval battles.[5] Mainly, the righteous and irresistible Japanese fighting spirit would sweep away any opposition that arose from the decadent and immoral Western world.

Japan's defeat of the Russian military forces in the Russo-Japanese War of 1904-5, and especially its naval victory in the Battle of Tushima Strait in 1905, only reinforced the belief of the Japanese in their military, cultural, and racial superiority. They had demonstrated to themselves that they could beat the hated white man on his own terms. This racial element in Japan's motivations is not often mentioned by historians but was quite real.

The Japanese had begun the Russo-Japanese war with a surprise attack by torpedo boats on the Russian Pacific fleet in its home harbor, Port Arthur, without first making any declaration of war, just as they would do thirty-six years later to the American Pacific fleet at Pearl Harbor (which gives the lie to those who say that the Japanese had intended to declare war before the attack but that there was some mixup in the timing). The 1905 attack on the Russian fleet at Port Arthur had had an intimidating effect on the Russian naval commanders, who responded half-heartedly and were eventually defeated. Japanese warlords hoped that a sneak attack on Pearl Harbor would similarly demoralize the Americans. By the time they repeated their hit-and-run tactic at Pearl Harbor in 1941, airplanes had come into use, and the Japanese carried out their sucker punch with torpedo bombers instead of torpedo boats.

The timing seemed providential

To Japanese planners, the war that had broken out in Europe provided them with an excellent opportunity to pursue their goal of establishing a Pacific empire. Hitler had started things off in 1939 by invading Poland, and by 1941 the European countries had become so preoccupied with the war on their own doorstep that they could not defend their far-off Pacific colonies against Japanese invasion; in fact the Dutch had surrendered to Hitler in 1940 and were powerless to defend their Dutch East Indies. Britain was under assault by the German Blitz and was expecting an invasion by Germany at any time, and thus could not extend any help to its colonies at Singapore, Hong Kong, or Borneo, nor could it defend its commonwealth of Australia. The Australians had sent their soldiers to Britain and North Africa to help their mother country, and had never had any significant navy or air force, so Australia was practically defenseless. France had also surrendered to the Germans in June of 1940, and thus French Indochina and the French protectorate (island) of New Caledonia were up for grabs. By early December of 1941 Germany, Japan's Axis partner, had reached the gates of Moscow, and it looked like Russia would soon be knocked out of the war as well.

In other words, if ever there was an opportune time for Japan to launch its quest to seize and dominate all the countries of the Pacific sphere, including all the European colonies encompassed therein, 1941 was that time. Only the Americans, who were not yet at war with anyone, still posed any significant threat to their schemes, since they had a Pacific Fleet and might try to defend their Philippine protectorate with it, or provide aid to Australia (an ally if they entered the European war), or they might simply pursue a policy of inhibiting Japanese aggression in the Pacific for political purposes or on moral grounds. Hence Japan's preemptive, surprise strike on the U. S. Pacific Fleet on December 7, 1941, in what was intended to be a knockout blow. Interestingly, the dishonorable act of striking a nation with which it professed to be at peace, without warning, seems to have bothered no one in a nation supposedly concerned with honor. The Japanese leadership apparently had a very elastic definition of honor.

The Pearl Harbor attack: a fatal mistake for Japan

There has never been any question that starting a war with America in 1941 was a mortal error on the part of the Japanese. Had they simply left America alone, they may have gotten away with their schemes of conquest and dreams of empire. The U. S. had been bound to enter the European war on the side of its ally, Britain, in the fight against Hitler, and once it was in the war America would have been fully engaged there. Had Japan simply let the "sleeping giant" lie, and pursued its Pacific conquests without antagonizing the U. S., by the time the European war concluded and America's attention turned to the Pacific, Japan might have faced a war-weary nation with no appetite for further losses in yet another war. Japan's conquest of the Pacific may then have been successful and permanent. As James Holmes, a Professor of Strategy at the Naval War College put it:

> **Rather than the vengeful America that Japan faced by the evening of December 7, it may have faced a relatively halfhearted America, war-weary from fighting in Europe. By consolidating and fortifying the islands it had wrested from their inhabitants, and by electing to protect a shorter island defense perimeter, it may have imposed higher costs on the United States than Americans were willing to bear. Washington may have accepted some sort of negotiated settlement that left Japan supreme in East Asia. Tokyo should have been patient, exercised self-restraint, and stuck with its prewar game plan. Interceptive operations held far more promise than a one-off preemptive strike into the Eastern Pacific.**[6]

Some say America may have gone to war with Japan to reclaim its Philippine territory, inherited from Spain after the Spanish American War, but in fact America had been planning to grant independence to the Philippines in 1946 and had no overriding interest in defending it.

Japan apparently found irresistible the opportunity to strike at the hated country of Admirable Perry and demonstrate its military superiority at a moment when it seemed advantageous to do so. After all, the strategy had worked before: the Russians had practically folded up after such an attack in 1905. However, The dynamic America of 1940 was not the declining empire of the Czar in 1905. Far from demoralizing the "sleeping giant" that was America, as the Japanese had hoped, the Pearl Harbor attack awakened that giant, enraged him, and filled him with a "terrible resolve" for revenge and retaliation that the nascent Japanese Empire could never hope to survive. Only a delusional government such as the one in Tokyo could refuse to admit the inevitability of defeat after provoking war with the United States.

Japan's Admiral Isoroku Yamamoto, wiser than most Japanese leaders, warned his superiors of what would happen if they attacked America, but he was overruled by the Emperor and his warmongering cabal. Yamamoto, who had been a naval attaché in Washington in the 1920s, had no illusions about the outcome of a war with America. Only ten weeks before the Pearl Harbor attack, on September 29, 1940, he had written to the chief of the Japanese Naval General Staff that if they went to war with America, the U. S. would never stop fighting until Japan was crushed. "We would not be able to escape defeat," he wrote, and added that "as a result of this war, the people of this nation [will] be reduced to absolute poverty." His advice was dismissed, and he was ordered to prepare for war with the U. S. Obediently, he then laid the plans for the Pearl Harbor attack.

Admiral Isoroku Yamamoto, architect of the Pearl Harbor attack. Medals and braid notwithstanding, his planning of the attack was inept, leaving all the fuel reserves of the U. S. Pacific Fleet and its logistical support untouched.

There is a popular misconception that Japan had been backed into a corner by U. S. embargoes, especially of oil (at one time Japan imported 80 percent of its oil from America), and thus had no choice but to go to war with America in order to survive. The U. S., in other words, had set out to provoke a war with Japan instead of the other way around, and got what it asked for. This is patently false. America instituted its embargoes only to show its disapproval of Japanese aggression toward China and Southeast Asia by freezing Japanese assets in the U. S. and blocking Japanese imports of American raw materials, in an attempt to restrict Japan's ability to continue its warmaking.

In truth, the Japanese knew full well that the large, oil-rich island of Borneo, a British possession, was theirs for the taking. Borneo, southwest of the Philppines, contained the vast oilfields of Balikpapan, the "Ploesti of the Pacific," and there were other oil-producing areas that Japan intended to seize. Japan could have pursued its aims perfectly well without oil from America.

Japanese military incompetence

Not only was it a mistake for Japan to attack America at Pearl Harbor, but once it had decided to do so, it made a poor job of it. In concentrating their bombs and torpedoes on only the largest American warships, the Japanese ignored the dry docks that could repair the battleships and left them unmolested. They did not bomb any of the fleet's oiler ships, nor any destroyer or seaplane tenders. In short, they left the American fleet's logistical support untouched, and only went after the battleships themselves, which could be repaired or replaced. Worst of all, they left intact the fleet's huge fuel storage tanks adjacent to the harbor. Ships cannot steam without fuel oil; airplanes cannot fly without aviation fuel; sailors can't eat without long-distance transportation of their supplies. All these things require fuel. Yet when the last of the Japanese planes receded from view at the end of the attack, all of the fleet's stored fuel, and the giant, vulnerable tank farm in which it was stored, had been left untouched.

General George C. Kenney, MacArthur's air chief, after waging war with Japanese air power for several months and seeing how poorly the Japanese used their air assets, declared that they were "not big league players." One military historian writes that Japan was ready for a battle, not a war.[7] In fact, throughout the war the Japanese clung to the notion that they would defeat the Americans in one big decisive naval battle, and based their strategy on preparing for that battle and bringing it about under conditions favorable to themselves. However, whenever sizable Japanese and American naval forces of approximately equal strength did meet and give battle, the Americans did not prove so easy to defeat as the Japanese had imagined. The Americans had also broken the communication codes that Tokyo used to direct its forces in the field, and thus were able to thwart Japanese plans even before they went into effect.* The Battle of Midway between the U.S. and Japanese navies was fought only six months after the Pearl Harbor attack and was a decisive defeat for Japan.

The Japanese had other problems besides their ineptitude in handling their air, naval, and ground forces. Their army and navy were bitter rivals, often unwilling to cooperate or share information until compelled to do so. They would pay dearly for this lack of cooperation throughout the war. The Japanese navy also failed to adequately protect the supply ships bringing raw materials from newly conquered areas of the Japanese empire to the home islands. Although Japan had to import most of its raw materials in order to make war, and ships carrying these supplies to Japan were vital to its warmaking industries, convoy

---

* That was, in fact, how Admiral Yamamoto died. The Americans intercepted a coded radio message that he was going to visit a certain Japanese garrison on an island near Bougainville, and would be flown there in a twin-engine transport plane on April 18, 1943. The Americans ambushed him in the air with P-38 fighter planes and shot his airplane down.

duty was considered unmanly and degrading by Japanese warship captains. Thus no effective convoy protection strategy was developed, and as a result many supply ships carrying oil, rubber, metal, and other vital resources to Japan fell prey to American submarines. One by one, sinking after sinking, American submarines cut the sinews of Japanese industrial power, until near the end of the war Japan was desperate to replace ships and planes but lacked the raw materials to build them, or the fuel to power what assets remained.

Japan's barbaric military culture

The military machine that Japan fielded for World War II was one of the most evil and barbaric forces in the history of mankind. It is unfashionable today, in an age of moral equivalence, to refer to any country or any army as "evil;" in fact President Ronald Reagan invoked a great deal of scorn and ridicule from America's intellectual "elite" when he called the Soviet Union an "evil empire" in a speech in 1983. But if ever a military force deserved the label evil, it was the Japanese army, navy, and air forces of World War II. When Japan invaded China, it brutalized and murdered millions of Chinese civilians in shockingly cruel and sadistic ways. In what has been called the Rape of Nanking alone, 200,000 to 300,000 civilians were butchered. The Japanese army had a fetish for cold steel, and they beheaded Chinese by the thousands with swords, mounting the severed heads on pikes along the roadsides. People were buried alive in mass graves, used for bayonet practice; babies were ripped from their mothers' arms and tossed into the air to be caught on bayonets (see a photo of this on page 772). In the first six months of Japan's rampage across the Pacific, it spread its hellish barbarism over one-fourth of the globe.

After its war with America began, and Japan captured the Philippines, the Bataan Death March was just the beginning of thousands of war crimes that the Japanese would perpetrate against any Americans and their allies unfortunate enough to fall into their hands. Any impartial record of the Pacific war, either in the books of historians or the letters and diaries of eyewitnesses, contains a long and sickening litany of Japanese atrocities committed against Allied civilians (planters, missionaries, civil administrators, hospital workers) and military prisoners of war. Brutality was ingrained in Japanese military culture. Japanese soldiers and sailors themselves were often beaten savagely by their own officers and noncoms. The entire Japanese military was a study in depravity and fanaticism. In this book the reader will repeatedly encounter eyewitness accounts of Japanese fighter plane pilots machine-gunning helpless Allied pilots and air crewmen as they hung in their parachute harnesses or floated in life rafts after ditching their planes in the sea.

Another feature of the Japanese military was that it had no concept of individual merit or achievement within its ranks. Although the admirals and generals covered themselves with medals, ordinary soldiers, airmen, and sailors were treated as faceless drones, and received no recognition for valor, no medals or commendations of any kind. Nor were any efforts made by the Japanese commanders to recover their downed airmen or stranded soldiers, considering it not worth the effort. If a pilot made a successful ditching and got into a life raft, he had no hope or expectation of rescue. No one would come looking for him, for there was no Japanese search-and-rescue service such as the Americans had. If he didn't make it back to base on his own, he was simply written off. Soldiers bypassed on islands by the American advance were left to their fate and were expected by their superiors to either die fighting or commit suicide. To a Japanese, death was always preferable to surrender.

The Pacific battleground

The Southwest Pacific war theater was about 3,000 miles wide by 2,500 miles deep, encompassing 45 degrees of longitude by 30 degrees of latitude on the globe, though the fighting on the islands was often measured in deadly feet and yards on beaches and in dense jungles. Warfare in the Pacific did not involve large masses of land on which opposing armies could maneuver against each other as they did in Europe. There were no "Battles of the Bulge" in the Pacific, just slugging matches between small infantry units over small pieces of territory, either small islands or small parts of large islands, and the fights were always over airfields, or sites where airfields could be built. The Japanese had three million troops scattered across China and the Pacific islands by the time the Allies, chiefly the Americans, set out to evict them, either by killing them (since in most cases they refused to surrender) or by driving them back to their home islands.

Air Superiority was everything in World War II

The war in the Pacific was fought to either seize or defend airfields—it's as simple as that. In most cases the Americans did the seizing and the Japanese, since they had gotten there first, did the defending. In World War II airpower came into its own, and air superiority quickly became the main determinant of either victory or defeat, on land or sea. In World War One, aviation had been in its infancy; there had been no aircraft capable of carrying large loads of heavy bombs or torpedoes, nor were the airplanes of that day armed with multiple machine guns and cannon. Between the wars all these things were developed, and by the Second World War they were all a reality. As usual, the military minds of the old order were slow to accept this at first. In the 1920s Gen. Billy Mitchell had had a hard time convincing American military leaders that a bomber could sink a large ship. He had to demonstrate it on an old captured German warship, and the lesson still didn't really sink in.

Not until the American Pacific Fleet at Pearl Harbor had been damaged by a Japanese air attack, and a few days later the great battleship *HMS Prince of Wales* and the battlecruiser *Repulse*, mighty symbols of British seapower, had been sunk off the coast of Malaya near Singapore by Japanese dive and torpedo bombers, did the lesson really strike home that it was no longer the great battleships that would determine the outcome of sea battles. Ships could no longer safely sail without air cover above them, and soon aircraft carriers came to be more valuable than battleships.

The Battle of the Coral Sea, fought between the American and Japanese navies in May of 1942, was the first sea battle in history in which the opposing ships never even saw each other—all the attacking and sinking of ships was done by planes launched from aircraft carriers.

Lieutenant General George Kenney, commander of the U. S. Army Air Corps' Fifth Air Force, knew that the war in the Pacific was all about air superiority: the nation that owned the air would win the war. The main American offensive weapon was the heavy bomber, first the B-17, then the B-24, and finally the B-29, which fire-bombed Japanese cities to ashes and dropped the atomic bombs that ended the war.

Kenney called his bombers "flying artillery." In a letter to his superior, General Henry "Hap" Arnold, in the fall of 1942, General Kenney put it this way:

Lt. Gen. George C. Kenney, commander of the U. S. 5th Air Force in the Pacific theater.

> The artillery in this theater flies... In the Pacific we have a number of islands garrisoned by small forces. These islands are nothing more or less than aerodromes or aerodrome areas from which modern firepower is launched. Sometimes they are true islands like Wake or Midway, sometimes they are localities on large land masses. Port Moresby, Lae and Buna are all on the island of New Guinea, but the only practical way to get from one to the other is by air or by water: they are all islands as far as warfare is concerned. Each is garrisoned by a small force, and each can be taken by a small force once local air control is secured. Every time one of these islands is taken, the rear is better secured and the emplacements for the flying artillery are advanced closer and closer to Japan itself.[8]

Part I

The Story of the 90th Bomb Group, the Jolly Rogers

Jolly Rogers leather jacket patch painted by
Lt. Allan G. Cooper, copilot of the Horner crew
and former Disney artist.

Chapter One

THE FORMATION OF THE 90TH BOMB GROUP

The Jolly Rogers was the nickname given in the summer of 1943 to the 90th Bombardment Group (Heavy)* of the U. S. 5th Air Force, which operated B-24 bombers (like the one pictured below) in the Pacific theater of World War II against the forces of Imperial Japan between 1942 and 1945. The 90th was one of several bomb groups under the control of the Air Force's V (Fifth) Bomber Command. Since the Group did not acquire the nickname "The Jolly Rogers" until July of 1943, it will be referred to here as the 90th Bomb Group (or just "the 90th") until Chapter

A B-24 bomber of the 90th Bomb Group, the Jolly Rogers, with the Group's famous skull and crossed bombs symbol on its tail, 1944.

28, wherein the circumstances of the Group's acquiring that nickname, and its origin, are explained.

---

* "Heavy" refers to the size of the bombers, in this case the nineteen-ton (empty) four-engine B-24 Liberator. American heavy bomb groups flew either the B-24 or the (also four-engine) B-17 Flying Fortress, while medium bomb groups flew smaller twin-engine bombers (B-25, B-26, A-20, etc.).

The 90th Bomb Group was equipped with the Consolidated B-24 Liberator four-engine bomber from its inception, and continued to use this aircraft, with its various modifications, throughout the war. The Group had forty-eight B-24s when it arrived in the Pacific theater in late 1942 (twelve for each of its four squadrons), and continued to operate approximately that number of planes throughout the war, although due to operational losses, mechanical problems, or just routine maintenance it could rarely put that many into the air all at the same time.

The beginnings of the 90th Bomb Group, spring, 1942

The shock of the sneak attack by Japan on the American Pacific Fleet at Pearl Harbor on December 7, 1941, followed only four days later by the declaration of war against the United States by Japan's ally, Germany, left America scrambling to create ground and air forces to meet the challenge of powerful enemies on both sides of the world. The 90th Bomb Group came into being, on paper at least, at Kay Army Airfield in Mississippi in late January of 1942, less than two months after the Pearl Harbor attack. But it takes time for a concept on paper to become a reality, and four months went by before the group actually began to materialize.

The 90th Bomb Group was laid out with four squadrons: the 319th, the 320th, the 321st, and (through some quirk of military numbering) the 400th. The new group began assembling at Barksdale Field, Louisiana, in May of 1942, where Lt. Colonel Eugene P. Mussett assumed command.[1] However, he had precious little to command at first. The Group started out with just two officers and ninety enlisted men, and no airplanes or pilots at all.[2] But from that sketchy beginning it grew steadily, soon acquiring aircraft, aircrews, mechanics, and administrative staff. It was a functioning bomb group by June.

After a mere three months of training as a group in the B-24, the 90th left the United States for the Southwest Pacific in early September, flying 48 bombers, and after a stopover in Hawaii arrived in Australia in October. It flew its first combat mission against the Japanese from Australia on November 15th. Thus the Group went from a concept on paper to actually bombing the enemy within a time span of just 9 1/2 months in 1942. All this will be taken up in detail in the chapters that follow.

The Consolidated B-24 Liberator heavy bomber

Throughout its existence, the 90th Bomb Group flew the B-24 bomber exclusively. At Barksdale Field the group received its first twenty-four planes, six per squadron. These were the early D models with the glass "greenhouse"

1. THE FORMATION OF THE 90TH BOMB GROUP

nose, later replaced by a nose turret.* The big aircraft had a wingspan of 110 feet, was 64 feet long from nose to tail, weighed 19 tons empty, 28 tons fully loaded with fuel, bombs, and crew, and was powered by four turbocharged

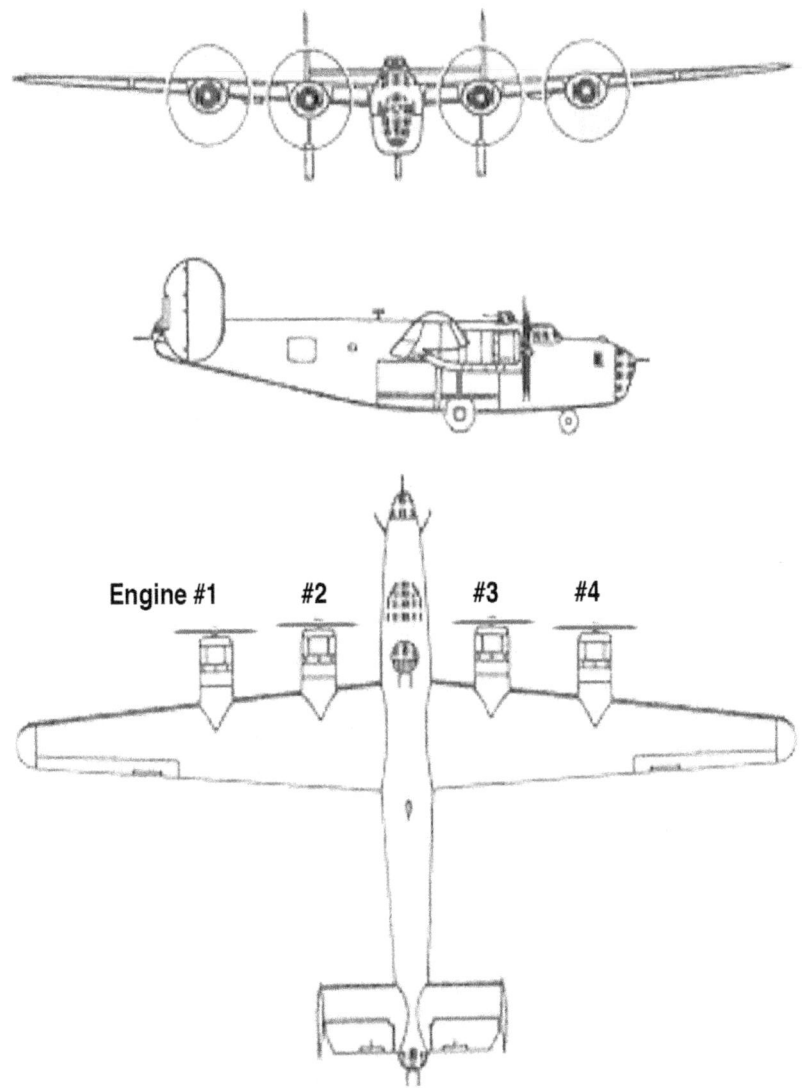

Three views of the B-24 Liberator bomber, the plane flown by the 90th Bomb Group, the Jolly Rogers, throughout the war. This is the early D model with the "greenhouse" plexiglass nose. Later versions had a powered gun turret on the nose similar to the one on the tail. The numbering of the engines is useful to keep in mind, since throughout this book individual engines are referred to by their numbers.

---

*The B-24 underwent continual modification throughout the war, so that there was a B-24D, B-24J, B-24L, etc.

Pratt & Whitney air-cooled radial engines of 1,200 horsepower each. Cruising speed over the ground, as with any aircraft, varied with the altitude at which the airplane flew.* Mr. Horner, the pilot of the B-24 crew whose story is covered in Part 2, remembers that he normally cruised the airplane with 155 mph on the airspeed indicator. As all pilots learn, indicated speeds shown on an airplane's instrument panel result in actual speeds across the ground that vary with such factors as altitude, winds encountered (headwinds or tailwinds), the temperature and density of the air being flown through, and other factors.

Performance specifications on the B-24 vary somewhat depending on the source of information,† and what version of the plane is under discussion, but as a general rule it is common to see ground speeds of from 180 to 215 mph claimed when the aircraft was cruised at between 10,000 and 20,000 feet ASL (Above Sea Level) in calm air, and one source claims that a ground speed of around 278 mph was possible with the aircraft flown at 25,000 feet, rising to 300 mph at 30,000 feet. It would have been unusual to fly a B-24 at its top speed, however, owing to excessive strain on the engines and high fuel consumption.

The B-24 had a double bomb bay (one bay in front of the other) in which a total of four tons of bombs could be carried in various combinations (aerial bombs came in sizes ranging from 100 to 2,000 pounds). A great asset of this bomber was its range: with a 5,000-pound bomb load it could fly 1,700 miles in around 7 hours at an altitude of 20,000 feet. It could also hold a tremendous amount of fuel: 2,364 gallons in the main wing tanks, 450 gallons in auxiliary wing tanks, and up to 800 gallons in optional tanks carried in the bomb bays (at the expense of some of the bomb load, of course). With the auxiliary fuel the range could be increased to 3,000 miles. Although the recommended take-off weight when loaded for combat was 56,000 pounds, in the Pacific B-24s were routinely loaded to over 70,000 pounds, which could make for some very exciting (and sometimes disastrously unsuccessful) takeoffs on short island runways.

The B-24 carried a crew of ten men: the pilot, copilot, bombardier, navigator, flight engineer, nose gunner, radio operator, ball turret gunner (in Europe only; the heavy ball turret was eliminated in the Pacific and its weight replaced with bombs or fuel, owing to the vast distances it was necessary to fly on missions), two waist gunners, and a tail gunner. The radioman and engineer could fill in at other positions (the engineer, for example, also manned the top turret).

The name Liberator has been credited to the English governess of the children of Reuben H. Fleet, the president of Consolidated Aircraft, who wrote to

---

*Aircraft fly faster at high altitudes because the air is thinner and offers less resistance.

† The B-24 specs in this chapter are from the book *Aircraft Anatomy of World War II*, p. 29.

1. THE FORMATION OF THE 90TH BOMB GROUP

the British Purchasing Commission in October of 1940 to suggest that the new bomber be named the Liberator because "this airplane can carry destruction to the heart of the Hun, and thus help you and us to liberate those nations temporarily finding themselves under Hitler's yoke." The name was adopted.[3]

Receiving B-24s instead of B-17s was a disappointment to many of the men in the 90th Bomb Group, since the famous Boeing B-17, known as the Flying Fortress, had been the standard bomber in service up to that time, and was widely considered to be the best heavy bomber in the world.

Beauty is in the eye of the beholder

Most people agree that the B-17 was the better looking of the two heavy bombers. The eye loves graceful curves, and the slim-waisted B-17 provided plenty of them, all blending smoothly into one another, while the ungainly looking, twin-tailed, slab-sided B-24 was often sneered at as "the pregnant cow," or "the box the B-17 came in."

Although the B-24 also had rounded surfaces, their function definitely took precedence over form, resulting in a rather ungainly overall appearance. Aside from its better looks, the B-17 was also considered by most people to be the better-built bomber. From early on in the war the public had seen B-17s in newsreels and newspaper photos that had been shot to tatters, sometimes with large pieces blown off, that still brought their crews home, whereas in early 1942, when the 90th received its B-24s, the Liberator had yet to prove itself in combat and its durability was open to question.

Although the long, narrow, shoulder-mounted wing of the B-24 was somewhat less sturdy than the thick, wide wing of the B-17, in due time the B-24 would prove itself nearly as durable as the B-17, although a B-24 definitely tended to break apart more easily than a B-17 when it was ditched in the sea, a fairly common occurrence in the Pacific. In the European theater, German fighter plane pilots were said to prefer attacking the B-24s as the easier of the two American four-engine bombers to shoot down.

The B-24 had a wingspan six feet longer than the B-17, but its total wing area was 25% less, owing to its higher aspect ratio (long length and narrow width), and the B-24's wing consequently bore more weight per square foot. With respect to battle damage, the B-24's narrower, thinner wings proved unable to take as much punishment from flak* as a B-17's wider, thicker ones. However, because of its highly efficient airfoil, developed by aeronautical engineer David R. Davis of Consolidated Aircraft, the newer† B-24 was the better

---

* "Flak," from the German FLiegerAbwehrKanone (aircraft defense cannon), was the name given to air-bursting artillery shells fired by antiaircraft guns on the ground, also known as "Ack-Ack" or AA (both derived from anti-aircraft). The shells had timed fuses.

† The first B-17 flew in July of 1935; the first B-24 in December of 1939.

The squat, pudgy B-24 Liberator was often referred to as the "pregnant cow" or the "flying boxcar," but despite its bulky looks it could fly faster, farther, and carry a bigger payload than its more attractive cousin, the B-17 (below).

The rugged B-17 Flying Fortress built by Boeing was all graceful curves.

1. THE FORMATION OF THE 90TH BOMB GROUP

B-24 wings were believed by many to be more fragile than a B-17's. Here a B-24 of 464th Bombardment Group rolls over and goes down after taking a fatal flak hit in the left wing over Lugo, Italy, on April 10, 1945. Only one member of the crew was able to bail out and survive.

performing of the two bombers, able to fly faster and farther with a bigger bomb load (each of the B-24's twin bomb bays was as large as the B-17's single one).

The Davis wing had proven itself an excellent performer on Consolidated's Model 31 flying boat, so it was re-used on the B-24. At this period in the development of aviation, less than four decades after the Wright brothers' first flight in 1903, it was considered better to rely on proven, real-world results than to try to design and test yet another new wing for the new bomber. There hadn't been time for that anyway—Consolidated had been racing to meet a government deadline for submitting its new bomber design. Along with the Davis wing, the B-24 got the twin tail of the Model 31, and it shared the oval-shaped cowlings of Consolidated's PBY Catalina flying boat.

It was the B-24's longer range that made it the preferred bomber in the Pacific war theater, where vast distances over water had to be covered to reach targets. Although the war began with two B-17 groups already in the Pacific

Another B-24 hit by flak loses half its left wing.

Not all flak hits to a B-24's wing were fatal. This bomber continued to fly with a large section of its right wing blown off because the main wing spars (the lengthwise structural beams in the wings) remained intact. The plane was hit by flak while bombing a target in southern France, and was able to make it back to its base in Italy.

1. THE FORMATION OF THE 90TH BOMB GROUP

(the 19th and 43rd), by the end of 1943 all B-17s had been phased out in combat roles and the Pacific was an all-B-24 show until near the end of the war when the newer B-29 Superfortress went into service.

One measure of the B-24's success is the fact that over 18,400 of them were built during the war, more than any other type of warplane, in fact more than any other military airplane ever built at any time (for comparison, the total number of B-17s built was about 12,700).

Both American four-engine bombers were conceived as flying forts

Like the B-17 Flying Fortress, the B-24 Liberator had been designed to be a bomber capable of defending itself independently against enemy fighter planes whenever friendly fighter escort was not available, such as when the bombers went on missions that exceeded the range of the fighter planes. For that purpose both the B-17 and the B-24 bristled with machine guns from nose to tail. On both bombers there were machine guns mounted in the nose, on the tail, on either side of the waist section of the fuselage, and on the top and bottom of the fuselage, with gunners trained specifically to operate them.

In theory, with all these defensive guns, either bomber was a "flying fortress" that could shoot down attacking fighters approaching it from any direction. In practice, however, neither bomber's self-defenses turned out to be quite as effective as had been hoped, owing mostly to the blazing speed of attacking fighter planes, which often flashed past before the bomber gunners could get them in their gunsights. The gunners were also faced with the problems of aiming accurately when both they and their target were moving at different speeds and in different directions (which in some cases required a gunner to aim *behind* a fighter plane to hit it—see the gunnery aiming diagram on page 19).

Nevertheless the American bombers were formidable opponents for enemy fighter planes, especially when they flew tight formations so that each bomber was covered by the guns of several others as well as its own, greatly multiplying the firepower. German pilots called a formation of American bombers, bristling with guns, a "flying porcupine" and approached it with considerable respect.

When B-17s were first encountered by Japanese Zero fighter pilots (during their attack on the Philippines, beginning the day after the Pearl Harbor attack) the Japanese soon recognized that they were dealing with much more powerful and durable bombers than they had encountered in China, or anywhere else for that matter. Masatake Okumiya, a high-level planner of Japanese air tactics throughout the war, wrote in the book *Zero*:

> **It was not long before the Zero pilots realized that they were confronted with an enemy plane well capable of defending itself,**

and one which could survive tremendous damage from the guns and cannon of the Zeros. On numerous occasions the Boeings flew undaunted on their bombing and reconnaissance missions despite the attacks of Zero fighters which swarmed about them and which the enemy's heavy machine guns too often destroyed... The B-17s and B-24s seemed almost to ignore the intercepting Zeros as they flew into any area of their choice...

Although the B-24 lacked the protection of the B-17 in total number of defending guns and other characteristics, the two airplanes were unique in their ability to defeat enemy fighter attacks. Neither Britain, Germany, nor Japan produced bombers capable of protecting themselves as well as the Fortresses and Liberators.

We believed that the heavy American bombers, with their great defensive power and amazing aggressiveness in battle, stemming from a great national strength and a national policy which at all times proved itself to be aggressive, were fundamentally responsible for the defeat of Germany and Japan.[4]

Long-range reconnaissance: a crucial role of heavy bombers in the Pacific

As noted earlier, American B-24s (and B-17s) were designed with large gas tanks that gave them a tremendous flying range. The B-24 cruised about ten mph faster than the B-17, giving it the greatest range, but both bombers could range out a thousand miles or more before returning to base. B-24s in the Pacific routinely flew round-trip missions of 2,400 miles, staying aloft from 14 to 17 hours. No other aircraft in the world could match that range until the American B-29 came into service late in the war.

Such long range allowed the bombers to fly deep into enemy territory to bomb important targets in both theaters of the war, but in the Pacific it also gave the Americans a vital advantage over the Japanese: long-range reconnaissance capability. Knowing where the enemy was, and what he was up to, was at least as important as bombing him, and often more important. The Japanese keenly felt the disadvantage of having their activities constantly exposed to the prying eyes and cameras of American reconnaissance bombers, while having no comparable aircraft to gather similar information about the Americans. This contributed in large measure to the downfall of the Japanese in the Pacific war. As Okumiya put it:

> Flying Fortresses on reconnaissance discovered the Japanese invasion convoy headed for Port Moresby in May of 1942; this led directly to the savagely fought Coral Sea Battle [which turned back the Japanese invasion]. Without the B-17's tremendous range, many of our operations would have been successfully executed without encountering enemy interference.

1. THE FORMATION OF THE 90TH BOMB GROUP

> The Midway sea battle of June, 1942, was also due to the far-reaching B-17s, which scoured the ocean surface in search of our invasion fleet and radioed the position of our ships to powerful American bombing forces. In the Guadalcanal campaign, the movement of our forces was constantly exposed to the prying eyes of B-17 crewmen. We came to learn that it was almost impossible to conceal our activities within seven hundred nautical miles [805 statute miles] of any base which might harbor Flying Fortresses, and within eight hundred nautical miles [920 statute miles] of bases from which Consolidated-Vultee B-24 Liberator bombers might take off.
>
> Sun, the great Chinese strategist, once wisely said: "those who know the enemy as well as they know themselves never suffer defeat." This historical statement was never proved truer than by the probing missions of the B-17 and B-24 bombers, which endowed the Americans with a tremendous advantage in the far-flung Pacific war.
>
> For years the Japanese navy had followed a strategic concept laid down by tradition: that a small Japanese force could achieve victory over superior enemy strength only so long as we were informed of the enemy's strength and movement, while ours remained hidden. With the B-17s and B-24s thundering constantly over our ships, airfields, and staging areas, the situation was reversed. We were in the position of the traditional enemy and handicapped by the same limitations we had always regarded as the opponent's weakness.
>
> Placed in the uncomfortable position of having our every movement fully known to the enemy, we were compelled to discard plans long prepared and resort to the application of mass strength and force in battle. The [American] strength of quantity could well outweigh the value of [Japanese] quality in a modern war...
>
> By September of 1942 the reconnaissance-mission-flying B-17s and B-24s had become a grave problem, and the Japanese Navy tried every possible means of destroying the troublesome raiders. With the Guadalcanal battle in full swing, our fighter pilots became desperate, but failed to achieve any notable advance in increasing the number of destroyed American bombers. Only overwhelming numbers of Zero fighters could destroy the enemy marauders, and there was little hope that we might acquire fighter planes with heavier firepower than that of the Zero.[5]

As we shall see in later chapters, long-range reconnaissance flights conducted by the Jolly Rogers also paid huge dividends. The pivotal Battle of the Bismarck Sea (Chapter 25), in which the Japanese lost an entire convoy of troops and supplies headed from New Britain to New Guinea, occurred after a Jolly Rogers B-24 from Port Moresby spotted the convoy about halfway to its destination. This battle between Japanese warships and American land-based aircraft heralded the end of Japanese control over New Guinea.

However, long-distance flying in the Pacific involved its own set of hazards, quite apart from the Japanese. As we shall also see, many Jolly Rogers bombers simply disappeared on lone reconnaissance flights, their fates never learned. More bombers fell victim to the terrible Pacific storms, navigation errors, or mechanical failures than to enemy action.

The B-24 (above) had a slab-sided fuselage with high-mounted wings, while the B-17 (below) had a round fuselage with the wings mounted low. The B-24 also had a nosewheel and sat level on the ground, while the B-17 had a tailwheel and sat nose-high.

Chapter Two

ARTHUR H. ROGERS

Present in the 90th Bomb Group from its inception at Barksdale Field, Louisiana, was Major (later Colonel) Arthur H. Rogers, age 33 in 1942, from Greenville, South Carolina, a family man with a wife and small son. He was the man whose name would eventually (in 1943) give the 90th Bomb Group its nickname, the Jolly Rogers.

Art Rogers had joined the Army Air Corps in the early 1930s and earned his wings in 1935. He had begun his Air Corps career flying Keystone B-6 twin-engine biplane bombers, an aircraft design from an earlier era. He had married his highschool sweetheart, Miss Elsie Hunt, in 1936.

Maj. (later Col.) Arthur H. Rogers

By 1937 Rogers was flying B-17s at Langley Field, Virginia. After the Pearl Harbor attack he was one of the officers called upon to form the new 90th Bomb Group, and he took command of one of the Group's four squadrons, the 319th, and began flying the Group's new B-24s.

Although Major Rogers had never flown a bomber in combat, he knew that the key to any bomber's survival in confrontations with enemy fighter planes would be the skill and efficiency of its gunners. He was impressed with the B-24's three powered gun turrets: one on the top of the fuselage, just aft of the cockpit, a ball turret on the belly, and another on the tail, each firing twin .50-caliber machine guns. All the turrets were either electrically or hydraulically operated, depending on the model of the B-24 or the factory that built it. The Emerson version of the tail turret had electric power, while the versions built by Motor Products and Consolidated were hydraulic. Both types were fast and responsive, and could track an incoming fighter plane with great speed.

"Even though I had never been in combat," Rogers wrote, "I realized that it was the gunners who actually [would be] responsible for seeing whether their airplane returned to its base after a combat mission."[1] And he was certain that powered turrets were the best means of defense. The B-24's designers had put turrets everywhere they felt they could mount them, but the waist guns—single .50-cal. machine-guns mounted on swivels and firing through large openings or windows in the sides of the fuselage, and the nose guns—also single guns shooting through "eyeball sockets" in the plexiglass nose, were still hand operated. And of course none of these single, hand-swung guns packed the firepower of the double guns in the powered turrets.

Rogers discovered to his chagrin that the first gunners sent to his squadron from the Army gunnery schools were woefully undertrained, having been rushed through their training in the first hurried efforts to create an air force to oppose the Axis Powers.* When he put his gunners into the B-24s' turrets to see how well they operated them, he was further dismayed to discover that many of them didn't even know how to turn the power on. Even those who did manage to operate the turrets showed little skill at tracking moving targets with them. Rogers had no confidence that any of these men would be able to defend their bombers or shoot down enemy fighter planes. If the effectiveness of a bomber's gunners would determine whether the plane would return from a mission or be shot down by enemy fighters, then he felt his squadron's planes would stand little chance of survival in combat with gunners such as these.

Rogers decided to start his gunners' training over from scratch, as well as recruit new ones from any enlisted men in his bomb group who might show an aptitude for shooting. He would train them himself, and use them as his squadron's gunners. In casting about for likely prospects, he reasoned that experienced hunters, men already accustomed to shooting guns at moving targets, would be the most suitable candidates.

"It was my belief," he wrote, "that this country has the greatest number of the world's finest potential aerial gunners, since many of our farm lads and mountaineers have spent a large portion of their lives hunting for rabbits, squirrels, birds, and deer." But how and where to find such men? Everyone in the 90th Bomb Group already had an assigned job, an MOS (Military Occupational Specialty), and to take any of them out of those jobs to retrain them as gunners would cause turmoil in the organization. And as anyone who has been in the military can attest, rocking the boat is not popular with superior officers.

---

* The Axis Powers (sometimes called just "the Axis") was a military alliance of Germany, Italy, and Japan, who joined forces during the 1930s in something called the Tripartite Pact. They became known as the "Axis Powers" after a spokesman for the pact declared that the world would soon rotate on the "Rome-Berlin-Tokyo axis."

Where, then, to find available men with natural ability as gunners? As if on cue, fifty new men, all buck privates, arrived at the 90th Bomb Group to perform what was termed "garrison work," army jargon for menial tasks such as street cleaning, garbage collection, kitchen chores (KP), and other unskilled work. These were men who had scored low on army IQ and aptitude tests, and such work was all they were thought capable of—they represented the bottom of the barrel. Some had never attended school beyond the third grade. However, they had one thing going for them, as far as Major Rogers was concerned: they were not assigned to any particular duty and were available for any kind of training.

Does poor education and low IQ mean a man can't shoot well, Rogers wondered? He suspected—correctly as it turned out—that many of these rough, unlettered men knew their way around a gun. "I received permission to interview the fifty privates," he wrote, "and as I expected, I found that over eighty-five percent of them had spent most of their lives hunting, farming and bootlegging. These men offered to me what I considered the ideal solution if I could arrange to qualify them as gunners."

Rogers, a sportsman himself, happened to be an expert skeet shooter, and Barksdale Field, an old established army post, had a skeet shooting range. Rogers took his motley mob of "hunters, farmers, and bootleggers" to the skeet range to give each man a chance to show what he could do with a shotgun. As he had guessed, although most of the men were familiar with guns, none of them knew anything about skeet shooting, and he had to explain to them what it was all about.

After the fifty bemused gunner candidates had hopped down out of the trucks that had transported them to the skeet range and fallen into line, wondering just what was going to happen next, Rogers, holding a 12-gauge shotgun, addressed them. "See that little booth over there on the right?" he said. "A small clay disc is going to come flying out of that little house at about 45 miles an hour. I want you to try to shoot that disc as it goes by." Then, one by one, each man was given his turn with the shotgun, while the others watched with interest, but no one with more interest than Major Rogers.

The results of this experiment both amazed and delighted him. Once they understood the game, and without any coaching as to proper skeet shooting technique, many of the men were happily breaking one clay pigeon after another, a task they found much more to their liking than garbage collecting or picking up cigarette butts. They soon had impromptu competitions going, jeering good-naturedly at the missed shots, and cheering each other on. Garrison duty had never been this much fun.

"To be a professional skeet shooter," Rogers wrote, "one must have a set form, and follow through as in golf... [yet] without any definite form these men . . . to my amazement, broke the majority of clay pigeons that flew out of the house."

Rogers also figured that since most of his natural shooters had been hunters and had killed game, they were probably immune to "buck fever," the tendency of a shooter to get so excited when confronted by a live target that he flinches and misses it. Rogers had seen too many champion skeet shooters get rattled on a hunt and botch shots at live game. But these rough men had done plenty of shooting at live targets (in the case of the bootleggers, it was probably best not to inquire what they'd been shooting at) and could be expected to have no such problems when confronted with fighter planes flown by live pilots coming at them.

"My theory was [that] I had rather be flying an airplane with good hunters for my gunners than to have a man who had a high IQ and a lot of theories on how to shoot, but who may develop buck fever when the chips are down."

Skeet shooting with a bomber turret

After determining that he had a crop of promising shooters on his hands, the next question for Rogers was whether the men could be trained to hit targets while operating the power turrets of a B-24. There was no time or opportunity for him to send these men off to Army gunnery schools to get proper training in shooting from turrets. Rogers realized that he would have to improvise the turret gunner training himself. Fortunately, improvisation was something he

The top turret of a B-24. Maj. Rogers removed one of these turrets and used it to train his gunners by shooting skeet with it.

was good at. If the men were already good at shooting skeet in the normal manner, he reasoned, why not challenge them further and have them shoot skeet with a turret?

With Col. Mussett's permission, Rogers removed a top turret from a B-24 and converted it into a portable gunnery trainer. He replaced the turret's twin machine guns with a single, semi-automatic* twelve-gauge shotgun, a weapon for which there was plentiful ammunition, mounting it where the right-hand machine gun had been. Unsurprisingly, no one had ever tried to shoot clay pigeons from a bomber turret before, and many of those who heard about the project thought it not only impossible but downright goofy. Rogers soon became aware that he was becoming the butt of a lot of jokes.

"While in the process of doing this [mounting a shotgun in the turret] I found that I had become the laughingstock of the Group among the younger officers and enlisted men. It was being said that even if I got the contraption to work, no gunner would ever be able to hit a small clay pigeon from a turret . . . [and] I was even beginning to doubt it myself." After the device was assembled, Rogers took it to the skeet range to give it a try. "Being an excellent skeet shot myself," he wrote, "I realized that if I was unable to hit a clay pigeon from the turret I needn't expect my gunners to."

Just in case his detractors proved to be right, and it was impossible to hit clay targets from a turret, Rogers waited until the post's skeet range was empty before he gave turret skeet shooting a try, not wishing to provide anyone with eyewitness proof of his folly. With only his armament officer and a sergeant on hand to help him, his first attempts to break the flying clay discs with the turret-mounted shotgun were disappointing. He moved the turret too jerkily, and he couldn't seem to get the clay disc in the shotgun's sights. Maybe, he thought, his critics were right—shooting skeet from a turret was impossible.

But he continued to try, and it wasn't long before things began looking up (so to speak). After missing the first ten clay pigeons, Rogers began to hit a few. "The eleventh and twelfth clay pigeons . . . I broke in midair," he wrote, "and shouts of joy were heard from my two colleagues. With a standard box of twenty-five shells, I ended up breaking six clay pigeons. I found that my trouble had been caused by the jerky motion of the turret, due to the fact that I had to think of every movement of the controls ahead of time."

What Rogers was discovering was that, just like driving a car with a stick shift, in which the movements of the hand on the shifting lever have to be coordinated with those of the foot on the clutch pedal, operating a power turret took multiple, coordinated actions to get results. The shooter had to swing the turret

---

*Semi-automatic means the gun held several shells and fired every time the trigger was pulled, with no reloading or re-cocking required.

at the right speed to track the target, while simultaneously aiming the gun, and then fire the gun at the proper instant to hit the target.

Turning a good skeet shooter into a successful turret gunner thus proved to be simply a matter of practice. And Rogers decided that the coordinated skills required were best practiced separately before trying to merge them. The first thing to learn was simply to follow the target with the turret, never mind the shooting. Rogers took his turret into a darkened hangar and had each of his new gunners practice tracking the beam of a flashlight across the hangar wall with it, until he could follow the spot of light smoothly wherever it went. It was not an easy thing to do. He found that it took about fifteen hours per man to reach that point.

"After they had mastered [the] smooth movement of the turret," Rogers wrote, "I allowed them to shoot at the clay pigeons on the skeet range. I set up a requirement of sixteen clay pigeons to be broken out of twenty-five . . . and to my satisfaction every gunner in my squadron met these qualifications. . . [In fact] the accuracy in breaking clay pigeons so increased with our new gunners that many of them were breaking 23 to 24 out of 25 pigeons."

Just out of curiosity, Rogers had some of his gunners get out of the turret and try shooting from the shoulder again, to see how well they would do, and found that most of them couldn't hit as many clay pigeons freehand as they could with the turret.

Although his gunners became skilled at turret skeet shooting, it was later found that shooting skeet well did not automatically translate into success against enemy fighter planes. Shooting from a stationary turret on the ground proved to be a different matter from shooting from a turret mounted on a moving aircraft, in which the movement of that aircraft also had to be considered. Rogers, and apparently many other gunnery instructors at the beginning of the war, had yet to learn that in actual combat, the relative speeds of both the bomber and the attacking fighter had to be taken into account when aiming.

To hit the fighter, the gunner didn't always lead the target as in skeet shooting. In fact, with an enemy fighter plane passing a bomber from rear to front, or approaching directly from the side (as in the diagram opposite), it was often necessary for a gunner to aim *behind* a fighter plane to hit it, in order to compensate for the forward motion of his own aircraft. But this would become evident later on, and would eventually be incorporated into all aerial gunnery training. Skilled bomber gunners would eventually learn when to lead a fighter, when to shoot directly at it, and when to shoot behind it to hit it.

A nose turret for the B-24

Although he was not an aircraft designer, and had not yet been in combat, as a practical layman Major Rogers took a critical look at the B-24 to see how its defenses might be improved. What mainly caught his eye was the bomber's insufficient firepower to the front, which consisted, originally, of a single flexibly-mounted machine-gun sticking forward through a socket in the glass "greenhouse" nose. It was obvious to Rogers that the gunner in the nose of a B-24 was inadequately equipped, just as it would soon become evident to enemy fighter plane pilots in the air. His solution, given his predilection for power turrets, was to put a turret on the nose just like the one on the tail.

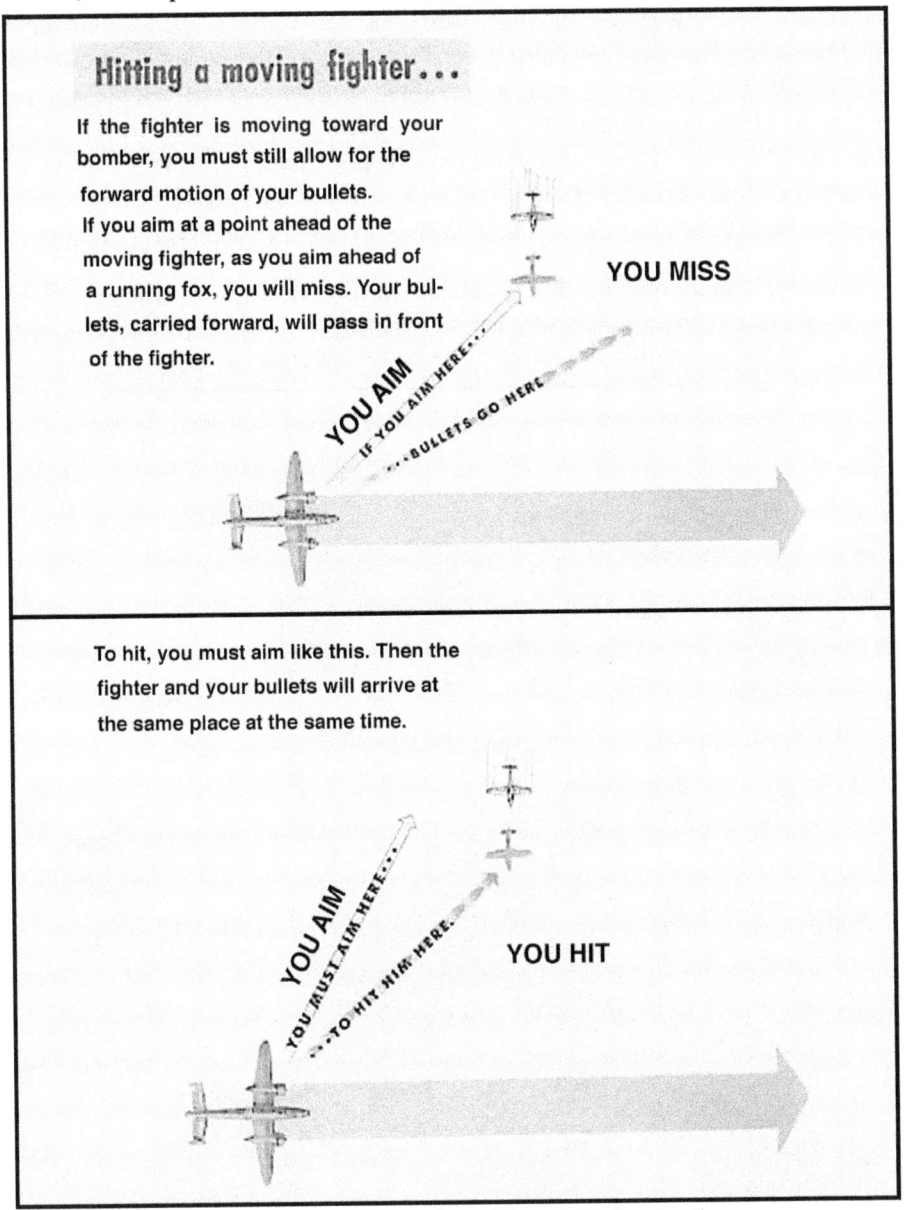

Hitting a moving fighter...

If the fighter is moving toward your bomber, you must still allow for the forward motion of your bullets.

If you aim at a point ahead of the moving fighter, as you aim ahead of a running fox, you will miss. Your bullets, carried forward, will pass in front of the fighter.

YOU MISS

To hit, you must aim like this. Then the fighter and your bullets will arrive at the same place at the same time.

YOU HIT

An Air Corps gunnery school diagram from May 1944 showing how gunners sometimes had to shoot behind an approaching enemy fighter plane in order to hit it.

"I came to the conclusion," he wrote, "that if we were ever attacked from the front, our flexible gun in the nose could not adequately protect us. . . . [Then] an inspiration hit me—why not put a tail turret in the nose? In fact I ran and got a steel tape and started measuring."

As the B-24 Liberator bomber came from the factory in 1942, it had a smoothly rounded, aerodynamically shaped nose covered with clear plexiglass panels, like window panes, and there were one or more hand-operated machine guns shooting through "eyeball sockets" in some of the panes. The original design called for just one flexible gun pointed straight forward, but this was so obviously inadequate that in production two more guns were added, one on either side of the first. However, the famous aviator Charles Lindbergh, who had been hired by the Ford bomber factory as a consultant on aircraft design, considered the two side guns to be practically useless, and wrote in his journal:

> I found one of the engineers in the nose-gun mock-up, puttering around in an attempt to find some way of following out the last order that has come through, demanding the installation of three .50-cal. pivot guns in the nose. A "four-star general" is reported to have given the order, so—good or bad—it must

Early D-model B-24s had a "greenhouse" of 24 transparent plastic panes on the nose, with machine guns sticking out through "eyeball sockets" everywhere. This plane has four.

Inside the "greenhouse" nose of a B-24D like the one in the photo at left. The nose gunner has three machine-guns on pivots, one aimed forward and one each to left and right, and the crowding is obvious. The distracted bombardier, kneeling in front of his bombsight, is trying to go about his business with his head up against the center gun. The gunner is aiming the right gun, with his hip against the left one behind him. While the guns were being fired they would also spew red-hot cartridge cases all over the bombardier. This was obviously a very impractical arrangement, although the first B-24s went to war this way.

Section II
Group Assembly Parts List

RESTRICTED
AN 01-5E-4
ARMAMENT

Figure 88 — Nose Gun Instal

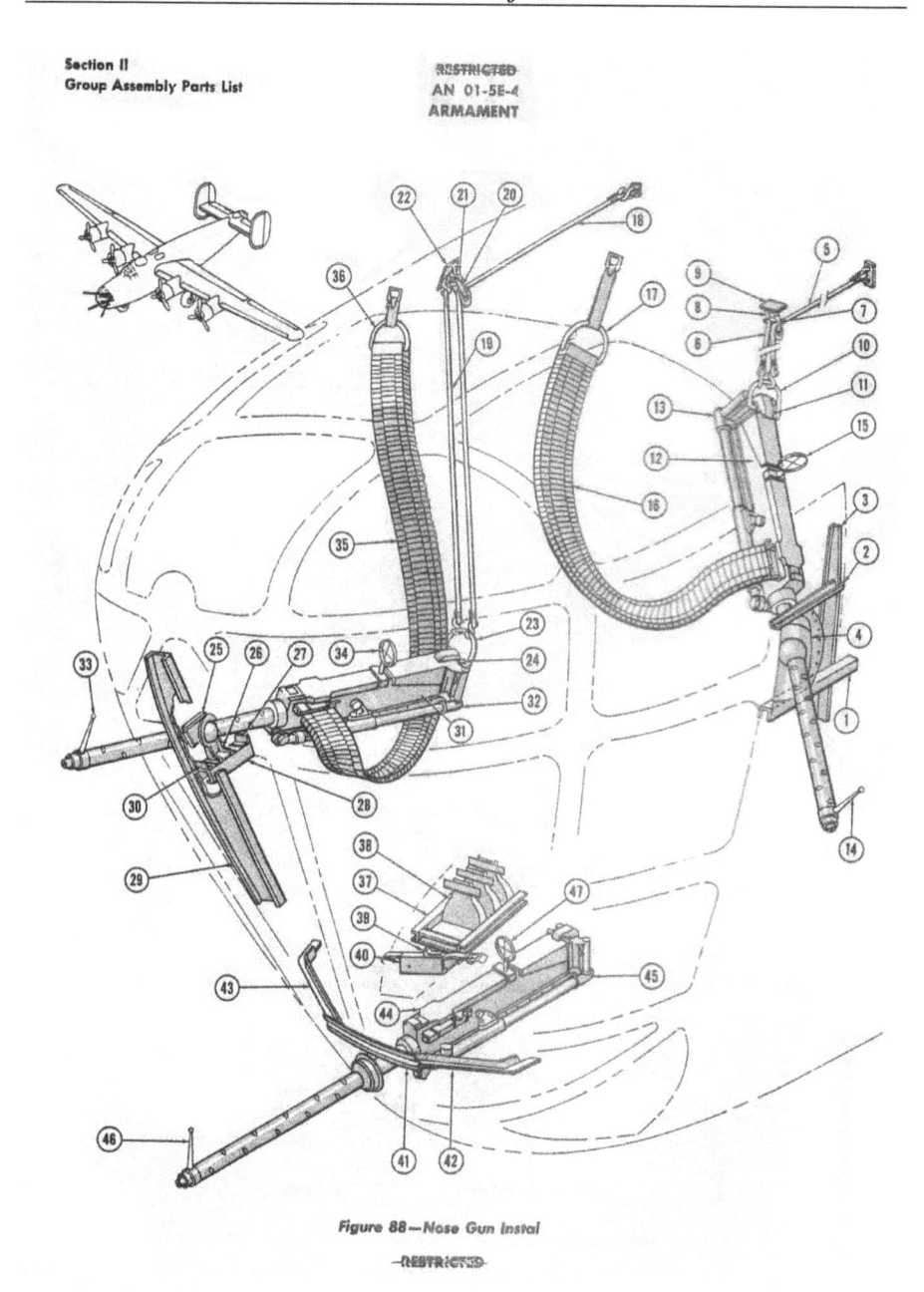

RESTRICTED

A diagram showing how four .50-cal. machine-guns were to be mounted in the "greenhouse" nose of a B-24D (the fourth gun, on the other side of the nose, is omitted from the drawing for clarity). This arrangement can be seen in the photo of the bomber on page 20. The crowdedness and impracticality of this setup was obvious to Charles Lindbergh and other engineers in the Willow Run factory, but this was what the Army Air Corps ordered, based on the simple and naive idea that "the more guns the better."

The tail turret of a B-24 with its twin .50-caliber machine guns.

be carried out. He was terribly discouraged when I talked to him; said the two side guns would spoil the effectiveness of the nose gun installation we have about completed and so crowd the bomber's [bombardier's] compartment that it would interfere with the bombing, while the guns themselves would get so much in each other's way that they would be practically useless. Just one more impractical and little-thought-about idea, he felt. . .[2]

The truth of Lindbergh's statement can be seen in the photo on page 21. The multiple independent guns in the B-24D's nose, plus their belted ammunition, crowded the bombardier's compartment to the point where the bombardier could barely function. Each of the nose guns had limited traverse because of the sockets through which it pivoted, and the gunner could only fire one gun at a time. The guns were awkward to handle and difficult to aim in such a confined space, with the gunner having to jump from one gun to another as an enemy fighter plane passed by.

As the diagram on the opposite page (which shows the mounting of *four* nose guns) shows, the ammunition belts for all the guns were suspended all over the place, and when the gunner fired, the hot empty shell casings cascaded down over the bombardier. A bombardier with a red-hot piece of brass down the back of his neck was not likely to be an accurate bombardier. As Lindbergh wrote, and as Major Rogers realized, this nose gun arrangement was practically useless. Combat experience would prove them right, and Japanese fighter pilots would use it to their advantage.

Major Rogers' idea of putting a power turret on the nose identical to the one on the tail would solve all the problems, and would give the B-24 two fast-acting, widely traversing guns aimed forward. The turret would also put the gunner in his own compartment, ahead of the bombardier's station and separated from it, leaving the bombardier in the clear, free to use his bombsight without hindrance or distraction. This would increase his efficiency, and dropping bombs accurately on the enemy was the whole purpose of a bomber. In short, it would be the ideal setup. The question was, could a turret be mounted on the nose of a B-24? Major Rogers decided that it could. He wrote:

> After about two hours of measuring and rechecking measurements, I was sure there was a chance to make this installation possible. It meant a slight change in the design of the nose, which would naturally have some effects on the flying characteristics, since it [the heavy turret] would move a good deal more weight forward of the center of gravity. It also would change the flow of air. These two unknown quantities had me worried, but I was positive that the movement of the weight forward would help this airplane, since to me the Liberator had always flown tail-heavy... My plan was to get the front end of an old cracked-up Liberator out of the salvage dump at Barksdale to make a mock-up and prove the feasibility of the idea. However, while I was negotiating to get the cracked-up fuselage, we were ordered to leave.

The 90th Bomb Group had been ordered to a new, partially completed airbase at Greenville, South Carolina. This was in the middle of June, 1942. It was a pleasant move for Major Rogers, however, since his home was in Greenville and he was able to visit his wife and young son near the base. The field was not really ready for heavy bombers, though, since it had only a single runway that was only half paved, and one unhappy member of the Group claimed that with all the construction work going on, and in rainy weather to boot, it was "the only place in the world where you could stand in mud up to your knees while dust blew in your face."[3] Despite the disadvantages, the bomber crews began flying their new B-24s from this field, familiarizing themselves with the plane, practicing cross-country flying, simulating bombing missions, and learning to fly in tight formations.

They also experienced their first fatalities when one of their B-24s, piloted by 2nd Lt. Earl M. Hobson, with a crew of four, encountered a thunderstorm twenty miles southwest of Chattanooga, Tennessee, and dove into the ground, killing all aboard. The cause of the crash may have been structural failure of the plane's tail, due to the stresses imposed on the aircraft either by the storm or by the pilot losing control in the storm. For whatever reason, the twin-tail assembly appeared to have been wrenched off the airplane. An eyewitness said he saw the tail come off the bomber before it crashed, and in fact the plane's complete tail assembly was found 500 feet away from the rest of the wreckage. At that time only four bolts held the twin tail onto the fuselage of a B-24, and this evidently did not provide enough strength to withstand the stresses of severe weather or violent maneuvering (the factories building the bomber later doubled the number of bolts).[4] These five deaths were the 90th Bomb Group's first, and by the end of the war there would be over eight hundred more.

After only two months at Greenville, the 90th moved again, this time to an airfield right beside Ford's Willow Run B-24 bomber plant at Ypsilanti, Michigan, about 30 miles west of Detroit. This move may have been as much political as practical; there had been worker strikes at the Willow Run factory, and apparently someone in authority thought that if the striking plant workers could actually see the men they were building the bombers for, and see them flying and training in the planes daily, their patriotic feelings would kick in and they'd buckle down and work without complaint. If that was indeed the motive behind the move, the ploy apparently worked, since no further mention of strikes entered the record from that time onward.

The B-24 plant at Willow Run, Michigan

The Willow Run bomber plant was built in 1941, and the first B-24 rolled out the doors in Sept. of 1942. Willow Run became one of five factories in the U. S. building the B-24 bomber,[*] and it was the largest of them — in fact it was the biggest single building in the United States. The main factory building was an amazing one mile long, a quarter-mile wide, and contained 70 assembly lines — the largest enclosed space under one roof in the world.

Within this monumental structure 42,000 employees, working in shifts, labored 24 hours a day, seven days a week, turning out, at the height of production, an astonishing one bomber every hour. In late 1944 the factory was producing 650 of the big four-engine aircraft per month, and again, this was only one of five factories producing the plane. And this particular warplane was only one of many types being turned out by hundreds of other aircraft factories all over America. And these were only the aircraft factories; there were thousands of other factories, large and small, turning out a myriad of other kinds of war matériel, from pistols to aircraft carriers, demonstrating

---

[*]The other four B-24 factories were the Consolidated factories at San Diego, California and Forth Worth, Texas, the Douglas plant at Tulsa, Oklahoma, and the North American plant at Dallas, Texas.

At the height of its B-24 production in 1944 the mile-long Willow Run plant was turning out an astonishing one bomber per hour, around the clock.

the stupendous industrial capacity of the United States.

Each B-24 produced consisted of fifteen tons of aluminum alone, and was made up of 30,000 individually machined parts assembled over a period of 20,000 man-hours,[5] many of them more accurately described as woman-hours, since thousands of women were employed in the assembly process in order to free men for wartime service (the female riveters were represented in song, poster, and prose as Rosie the Riveter, the lady welders by Acetylene Annie). Of a total of more than eighteen thousand B-24s built during the war, over 8,600 were built in the Willow Run plant.

The 90th Bomb Group, by this time 1,500 men strong and growing steadily,

A government poster encouraging women to work in war factories.

took up residence in a large airplane hangar next to the Willow Run B-24 plant on August 9, 1942. Their aircraft (whose numbers continued to grow until the Group had 48, with crews to man them) were parked around the airfield adjacent to the factory, from whose runway new bombers fresh off the assembly line were test-flown, and then flown away to airbases around the country. Some of these deliveries were made by women pilots, as another way to free men for combat.

The women delivery pilots were known as Women's Airforce Service Pilots (WASPs), and during the war there were over a thousand of them delivering every type of warplane from the factories where they were made to the bases where they went into service. Many servicemen at these bases were amazed (and enchanted) when the pilot of a newly-arrived four-engine bomber got down out of the cockpit and took off her helmet to allow a cascade of feminine hair fall over her shoulders.

At Willow Run the men's cots were set up side-by-side down the length of the hangar, but despite the great size of the building the facilities proved to be inadequate for so many men. It was hard for them to sleep when every little sound was magnified and echoed throughout the cavernous hangar, food had to be served and eaten outdoors, and the latrines were too small and too few.

Four WASPs (Women's Airforce Service Pilots) who have just delivered a B-17 to a four-engine training school at Lockbourne Army Airfield, in Ohio. Left to right: Frances Green, Margaret Kirchner, Ann Waldner and Blanche Osborn.

Henry Ford's son Edsel, who was in charge of the Ford company at the time,[*] tried to make the accommodations more comfortable by providing the men with gas-burning stoves and bus service to town when they were off duty. He also gave the men a clubhouse and installed a piano in it.[6]

Charles Lindbergh meets the 90th Bomb Group

At Willow Run the members of the 90th Bomb Group also met Charles A. Lindbergh, the aviator who had become the most famous man in the world after he flew the Atlantic solo in 1927 in a Ryan monoplane that he named the *Spirit of St. Louis*.[†] Lindbergh was working at the factory as a consultant on aircraft design. He had been an ardent isolationist, and as World War II approached he had been touring the country giving speeches as a member of an organization called America First, whose goal was to keep the U. S. out of the war. His speeches had angered President Franklin Roosevelt, and when Roosevelt attacked Lindbergh in the press, Lindbergh responded by resigning his commission as a colonel in the Air Corps.

After Japan's attack on Pearl Harbor had made all arguments for isolationism moot, Lindbergh requested that his commission be restored so that he could participate in the war as a military officer. Roosevelt spitefully refused to reinstate him. Denied a place in the armed forces, Lindbergh decided to do what he could for the war effort as a consultant for aircraft factories, assisting in the design and testing of warplanes. Ford had hired him in that capacity at Willow Run, and he became a great friend of Henry Ford, who shared his political views.

When Lindbergh flew a B-24 to evaluate its performance, he was not impressed with the bomber. "There are many improvements which can and should be made before American fliers are sent out to fight in these ships," he wrote. "I found the controls to be the stiffest and heaviest I have ever handled."[7] The controls of a B-24 were so stiff because the control surfaces of the big bomber, like those of a tiny Piper Cub, were operated by cables and pulleys alone, with no power assistance. The pilot moved them by sheer muscle power. In the case of the little Cub or other small planes, that is not a problem, since moving their small, lightweight control surfaces takes little effort, but the large control surfaces of the bomber required considerable strength to deflect, especially at high speed with the push-back of wind resistance. Since the pilot's left hand and arm were on the control yoke most of the time, while his right hand

---

[*] Edsel Ford was actually seriously ill at this time and would die of stomach cancer nine months later, in May of 1943.

[†] The airplane was named the *Spirit of St. Louis* because Lindbergh's financial backers were all St. Louis businessmen.

operated throttles and switches, it was said that you could spot an experienced B-24 pilot by the overdeveloped muscles of his left arm.

Lindbergh also wrote, ominously, "I would certainly hate to be in a bomber of this type if a few pursuit [fighter] planes caught up with it." Many young American men would find themselves in exactly that position over the next few years, although the bomber would not prove to be as vulnerable to fighter planes as Lindbergh imagined, especially when the bombers were flown in tight formations so that the firepower of all the gunners could be combined, as mentioned earlier.

The relatively lightly-armed Japanese Zero fighter planes found the B-24 (as well as the B-17) particularly difficult to deal with, and having no armor or self-sealing gas tanks they were especially vulnerable to the bombers' guns. After the war, Japanese Lieutenant Commander Mitsugu Kofukuda of the Imperial Japanese Navy's 6th Air Group would write:

> The four engine B-17 and B-24 bombers were, generally speaking, the most difficult enemy aircraft for the Zeros to shoot down. Because of their excellent self-sealing fuel tanks, they were extremely difficult to set afire with the Zero's 20mm cannon shells. Our fighter pilots soon learned that the B-17s and B-24s could rarely be destroyed unless the pilots or vital parts of the aircraft were hit and rendered useless. The fierce resistance with which the heavy American bombers opposed our fighters, unlike that of our own land-based medium attack bombers which too often fell easy prey to enemy fighters, was a most serious problem. In my opinion, which is shared by many Japanese combat officers, the ability of the B-17 and B-24 to defend themselves and carry out their intended missions despite enemy fighter opposition was a deciding factor in the final outcome of the war.[8]

At Willow Run, Major Art Rogers resumed his quest to get a tail turret mounted on the nose of a B-24, to demonstrate the advantages. When one day he found himself talking to Edsel Ford, he realized that fate had placed him in exactly the right place to pursue this goal. Ford, after all, was the man in charge of the largest plant that was building the B-24. In Rogers' own words:

> While talking with Mr. Ford, he asked me how I liked the new Liberator they were building. This gave me the opening I had longed for, since I saw a possible chance to get some help on my plan for the nose turret. I told him of my idea and explained to him the difficulties I expected would be encountered. He was very encouraging and directed me to see the Technical Adviser for the plant. After discussing the problem further a program was set up, the expense of which was completely covered by the Ford Motor Company, to

make a complete mock-up and compute the flying characteristics of the airplane with a nose turret in it. Our operations officer, Colonel Marion Unruh, had become as enthusiastic about the installation as I was. We both spent many hours showing the crew how we wanted the installation made on the mock-up. To our satisfaction and the company's, the figures indicated that the plane would fly better.

Major Rogers could have asked for nothing more. He had also brought his skeet-shooting training turret up to Willow Run and demonstrated it to the officials at the factory. Lindbergh was one of the witnesses, and afterward wrote in his journal:

> Maj. Rogers is a young man in his early thirties—alert, able, active, with a somewhat Southern voice. . . In order to train his gunners Major Rogers has removed a Martin top turret from one of his bombers, removed the .50-cal. machine-guns, and installed a twelve-gauge shotgun in place of the right-hand machine-gun. With this arrangement his gunners shoot clay pigeons for practice. And they break up to twenty out of twenty-five birds when experienced! Rogers said he ran into great opposition from his higher officers when he applied for permission to mount a shotgun in a turret and finally had to go ahead on his own authority and at the risk of being court-martialed. He is now trying to put a tail turret in the nose of the B-24 and again is being discouraged and told it is no use. . . I told Major Rogers I would try to get some help for him on the turret. He has been revising the tail turret from one of his planes; but has had to do the work somewhere it would not be noticed by his higher-ranking officers, who say that such things should be done at experimental stations. (They should, but they aren't—at least in time.)[9]

Meanwhile training flights continued from the airfield beside the Willow Run factory, the new young pilots and crews flying the Group's bombers day and night, both locally and on cross-country flights.

On August 14 [1942] another 90th B-24 encountered a thunderstorm and crashed, this time in a cornfield near Hastings, Michigan. The pilot, 2nd Lt. Eugene B. King, and his crew of eight were all killed. Lindbergh was distressed by the news. He had been an airmail pilot in the 1920s, and had often found it necessary to fly in bad weather himself. With long experience at flying in storms (he had more than once bailed out of storm-crippled planes), he wrote critically in his journal of an Air Corps' B-24 training regime that put young, inexperienced pilots fresh out of flight school in charge of huge four engine aircraft and their crews, and then sent them out on missions in all kinds of weather. Of this crash he wrote:

> I found the pilot had been out of flying school for only a few months and had less than 500 hours' total flying time; yet he was the captain of a four-engine bomber and sent out through a stormy night to carry on a practice mission![10]

These training flights often encountered thunderstorms that experienced pilots would have carefully avoided, but the young Air Corps novices in their giant, powerful B-24s, with the confidence of youth and inexperience, would try to bore right through, with sometimes fatal results. The unbelievably powerful and wildly swirling winds within a thunderstorm, which include updrafts and downdrafts moving at hundreds of miles an hour (often right next to each other) can toss even the largest plane out of control, tear it apart, or encrust it with so much ice that it can't fly.* To Lindbergh's disgust, the Air Corps seemed to accept these training accidents and deaths as unavoidable in wartime.

The 90th is alerted for Pacific duty

The seemingly chaotic creation and juggling of air groups around the country following the Pearl Harbor attack continued, and the 90th Bomb Group was in the thick of it. Consistent with Army logic, after the Group's weathermen had been thoroughly briefed on the climate and weather of England and the European continent, the Group was informed that it would be going to the Pacific.[11] The men had only arrived at Willow Run on August 9 [1942], and had barely had time to settle in there when they were informed by Third Air Force Command on Aug. 23 that they would be moving again, this time to San Francisco, the jumping-off place for the Pacific war zone.

The original purpose of moving the 90th Bomb Group and its B-24s to Willow Run, which had been to drive home to the balky factory workforce the purpose and importance of their work, had been accomplished in less than a month. Now, despite their short training period, it was time for the 90th to go to war, even though some of the pilots did not even have complete crews yet (more men from the Air Corps' training schools around the country were being assigned to the Group all the time). Lindbergh, again, considered such haste to be dangerous folly and wrote, "What possible good can come from pushing men so fast? First, this B-24 squadron [group] is organized of young and inexperienced officers; then it is sent for training to a field [Greenville] with the concrete runways uncompleted; then it is ordered for the combat zone

---

* Ice accumulation is doubly deadly to an aircraft, sometimes building up such great weight that the airplane becomes too heavy to fly, or changing the shape of the wings so that they lose their aerodynamic (lifting) qualities, or both simultaneously. Ironically, by the time accident investigators arrive at the scene of a crash caused by ice buildup, the ice has often melted away, leaving no clue as to what happened.

'in one month,' untrained, unequipped, and without having had a single round of .50-caliber ammunition with which to train its gunners."[12] (Apparently the only shooting practice that many of the 90th's gunners had had was the skeet shooting that Major Rogers had conducted at Barksdale Field back in May and early June.)

Lindbergh also sympathized with the non-pilot crewmen assigned to the bombers, whose lives were being placed in the hands of new, inexperienced pilots. These crewmen had no say in the matter and just had to take their chances with whatever pilot they were assigned to. He wrote in his journal:

> Army pilots, some of them with little over 200 hours' previous experience, are trained to handle four-engine equipment. It is no wonder we are having so many crashes these days. The training of pilots is being pushed too fast for safety, and I think too fast even for the maximum effectiveness in war. I cannot help feeling sorry for the crews of these planes. If a pilot crashes, he has at least had his life in his own hands; but these crew members have to go up with any pilot who is authorized to fly the plane, no matter how good or bad he may be. And they grow to know very well when a pilot is inexperienced and handles his plane poorly. I heard a general say, "None of these 200-hour pilots for me." But the members of a crew say nothing; they simply go when they are called.[13]

Major Rogers agreed that men were being made into B-24 pilots too fast, noting that before the war it took seven years before an army pilot was entrusted with the controls of a four-engine bomber, and even then he was considered a novice. Now young men who had never flown any type of airplane before entering the Air Corps were becoming B-24 pilots with only several months of training. And an entire group of such pilots, the 90th Bomb Group, had been formed in only three months. Major Rogers wrote of this:

> The Group we were to form at Barksdale Field, La., early in 1942 had [only] eight enlisted men and four officers with more than three years service, and we were to organize a group of approximately 2,500 men to fight the Japs. These four officers and eight enlisted men were expected to organize a hard-hitting combat group in three months, using airplanes larger and heavier and harder to fly than the famous Flying Fortresses.[14]

Yet Rogers was not as pessimistic as Lindbergh was about the outcome. He believed that it could be done, and that it was in fact necessary under the circumstances. He also wrote of his amazement at the rapid conversion of "shoe store clerks" into bomber mechanics, with credit for success going to the older and more experienced NCOs (non-commissioned officers), the men who form the backbone of all armies:

> Our mechanics were enlisted men who'd had a six month course in an Army Airplane Mechanics School. Many of these boys had never held a wrench in their hands before they entered this school. It is very easy to cover the theory of internal combustion engines in a period of six months, but it is an almost impossible task to turn out a mechanic capable of maintaining and repairing a complex twelve hundred horsepower engine, let alone maintaining an immense bomber weighing sixty thousand pounds with many miles of wiring, hydraulic lines and cables. In my squadron I had one old-timer mechanic who had a world of knowledge and the patience of Job. He started a school which had to be practical since the students were required to maintain the airplanes that our young pilots were flying day and night. It would surprise me when at one o'clock at night I would enter the hangar after making a night flight with one of my pilots, to find this 50-year-old sergeant patiently explaining to a young mechanic, who only six months before was probably a shoe clerk, how to install a complicated turbocharger. To my amazement the next morning at daybreak when our flying started I would find this same old man on the line instructing his young mechanics how to warm up and make their daily checks on the airplanes that must be kept flying.[15]

If Lindbergh made any of his criticisms of the rushed and inadequate training of air groups known to the powers that be, they fell on deaf ears. The newly organized and barely trained 90th Bomb Group would now be going off to the Pacific war, its mission to deliver opposition to the Japanese forces that at this time were rampaging practically unchecked southward from their home islands through the Dutch East Indies and New Guinea toward Australia. The 90th's bombers would soon be headed to McClellan Field at Sacramento, California, 75 miles northeast of San Francisco, where the Group's long overwater journey to the other side of the world would begin.

With the Group's departure from Willow Run, the nose turret modification for the B-24 was again shelved. The pressure to turn out bombers rapidly in quantity overrode the prospect of making a major modification to the plane's design that would have held up the assembly lines while the changes were adopted. As a result, the first B-24s would go into combat with insufficient forward firepower, which enemy fighter pilots would exploit, and American airmen would die, but the cruel priorities of war dictated getting as many bombers into the air as possible at this time. The reasoning was that changes to the aircraft's design could be made later, after there was a proven need for them.

As for Lindbergh, neither he nor anyone else could know that two years hence he would encounter the 90th Bomb Group again, out in the Pacific, when he would fly fighter escort for the 90th's bombers on some of their bombing missions. For Lindbergh was destined to become, of all the improbable things, a civilian fighter plane pilot, and we will meet him again in that role in later chapters.

The 90th Bomb Group's ground contingent embarked by rail for California on August 23, 1942, and on Sept. 9 the Group's 48 bombers took off from Willow Run to follow them. The young men on the five-day train ride marveled at the scenery passing outside the car windows. Many boys raised during the Depression had never been far from home, and the changing scenes, from the Great Plains to the Rocky Mountains and the picturesque Southwestern deserts of New Mexico and Arizona, were a revelation to them. They had never realized that their country contained such diverse landscapes.

Along with the sightseeing, their time was taken up with the nonstop card and dice games that were usual on troop trains, along with conversations about what might lie ahead for them in the Pacific, and the reading of books and magazines. Two of the Group's bombardiers risked getting into trouble when they decided to hone their aiming skills by tossing empty beer bottles at passing railroad signal lights, but they got away with it.[16]

The 90th's new, temporary quarters were at Camp Stoneman near San Francisco, where both air and ground crews were issued equipment and supplies, got their immunization shots, were encouraged to make and sign wills, and made other preparations for overseas war duty. Last leaves to home were taken and relatives bidden farewell in person when possible. Some men who could not get leave to say goodbye to their loved ones simply took it anyway, unofficially. Wiley Woods, the Group's historian, wrote:

> **Shortly after arrival [at Camp Stoneman], Russ Whitcomb recalled, "Friday afternoon I signed a statement saying I realize being AWOL* in time of war was punishable by death, climbed over the fence and hitchhiked home." The men were informed they would be entitled to one five-hour pass, but many took French leave to avoid the formalities of requesting a pass.**[17]

Those who took such informal passes all returned to the Group before it left for overseas. Many of the Group's men spent their few last nights in the States in San Francisco nightspots, where "every night was Saturday night"[18] during the war. They all knew that this would be their last big-city experience in America until they returned, and some feared that they might not return at all, so everyone set out to make the most of it.

---

*AWOL = Absent Without Leave.

CHAPTER THREE

THE MOVE TO HAWAII

At this period in the Pacific War, Japan, having put America's Pacific Fleet temporarily out of action in the Pearl Harbor attack nine months previously, had used the time to rampage practically unopposed across the Pacific nearly as far south as Australia, and in fact there were fears that Australia was next on its list of countries to invade. Australia, then, would be the ultimate destination of the 90th Bomb Group, but it was over seven thousand miles from the west coast of America, and the journey would have to be taken in stages. The first leg would be to Hawaii, 2,400 miles southwest of San Francisco.

Once again the Group's ground detachment, around 1,500 men, went ahead of its aircraft, boarding a troopship named the *U.S.A.T.** *Republic* on Sept. 3 [1942]. The ship set out on the week-long voyage to Hawaii in a small convoy consisting of the *Republic*, four merchantmen, and two destroyers. On their way out of San Francisco Bay the 90th's young men saw the famous prison island of Alcatraz drift by, then passed under the majestic Golden Gate Bridge, which many of them would not see again for years, and finally, with mixed feelings, watched the shore of their homeland fade from sight behind them. A Navy airship ("blimp") accompanied the convoy on its first day at sea, keeping aerial watch for Japanese submarines, then turned back to San Francisco after dark, since its range was limited.

Most of the youngsters had never been on a ship before, and in fact many of them had never seen an ocean. Now they found themselves surrounded by water out to the horizon in all directions. One young corporal filled his diary with ecstatic descriptions of the brilliant stars glittering overhead "like jewels" during the nights at sea, while many of his comrades were too seasick to care whether the sky had any stars in it at all.[1]

As on most troopships, nonstop games of dice, poker, and cribbage broke out immediately after leaving port and continued throughout the voyage. The ship docked in Honolulu on the 12th of September, and the men disembarked to the music of an army band welcoming them with Hawaiian music and pop-

---
* U.S.A.T. = U. S. Army Transport

ular songs of the day. Since the Group's bombers had not yet arrived, and in fact would not even depart San Francisco for another three days, they took up quarters at Hickam and Wheeler airfields and passed the time surveying their exotic new Pacific island surroundings.

Meanwhile the B-24s that the Group had flown from Willow Run to Sacramento were exchanged for forty-eight brand new B-24Ds, fresh from the San Diego factory, that had auxiliary gas tanks installed in their forward bomb bays to provide extra fuel for the approximately fourteen-hour flight to Hawaii. These planes were without the ball turret usually seen on the belly of a B-24, which had been removed to save weight on long overwater flights. In fact it had been decided that no Liberators sent to the Pacific would have belly turrets. The turret was replaced by either one gun or a pair of guns on a ring mount, pointing down through the hole in the floor where the turret used to be.* No one had much confidence that this arrangement was anywhere near as effective as a belly turret, and many thought it useless because it was so difficult to see down through the hole in the plane's belly to shoot at anything.

The aircrews spent several days at Sacramento looking over their new airplanes and getting familiar with them. Some of the crews personalized their planes with impromptu modifications. First Lieutenant Charles P. Whitlock felt that the three machine guns in the nose of his plane were not enough, so he crammed in two more, procured and installed somehow by the Sacramento Air Depot. How his poor bombardier was supposed to get to his bombsight, let alone operate it, among this thicket of guns is not recorded. Still not satisfied, Whitlock added yet another gun on the catwalk in one of the bomb bays, aimed down through the bay, which he intended for his navigator to use during bomb runs while the bomb bay doors were open (perhaps not considering the possibility that the navigator might shoot a falling bomb, or fall out of the bomb bay himself, since the catwalk was only six inches wide).[2] Apparently convinced that the more guns his plane carried, the better his crew's chances of survival in combat, it's surprising that Whitlock didn't try to add a couple more guns in the cockpit for himself and the copilot to shoot.

The crews then flew their new planes from Sacramento to Hamilton Field near San Francisco, the jumping-off spot for Hawaii, and spent a few days there testing out all the systems of their aircraft, calibrating the compasses and radios, and becoming familiar with the planes' flight characteristics on short local flights. And since theirs would be the first B-24s ever seen in Hawaii, they also filled their planes with spare B-24 parts which might not be immedi-

---

*This belly gun was called a "tunnel gun," possibly because that section of the plane's fuselage, just forward of the waist gunners and behind the bomb bays, was similar to a tunnel. The belly gun did not have a full-time gunner assigned to it; instead it was to be manned by the radio operator when he was not needed at his radio.

ately available there. With all the gasoline, people, and parts crammed aboard the aircraft, these were going to be some heavily loaded bombers at takeoff time. Fortunately Hamilton Field's runway was a long one.

Meanwhile each crew's navigator nervously looked over his charts and worried how well his newly learned navigational skills would measure up to a journey of this magnitude—2,400 miles across a featureless ocean with no landmarks anywhere for guidance. To date, none of the 90th's crews had ever flown over any body of water wider than the Mississippi River. As with the ground contingent on their troopship, many of the men had never even seen an ocean before they'd arrived at San Francisco.

Major Rogers now became Lt. Col. Rogers, promoted to Deputy Group Commander, second-in-command of the Group under Col. Mussett. He also retained his command of the 319th Squadron. Rogers, too, was worried about flying over so much water with inexperienced navigators. Of the day before the flight he later wrote:

> For a wartime Group, after seeing others that were in our same predicament preparing for overseas, we considered ourselves as well trained as many others. But when the task of flying the B-24s from San Francisco to Hawaii was faced, even the four officers with experience carried many doubts which we could not express to our eager bunch of cubs. No B-24 had ever made this flight, and accurate range data was not at hand to give us the confidence we badly needed...
>
> None of the navigators had navigated over water and they were none too confident of their ability. It is doubtful whether any of the Group got much sleep that night.

Although no B-24 had ever flown to Hawaii before, it was not expected to be too serious a problem since B-17s had been doing it routinely since before the beginning of the war (some, in fact, had actually flown right into the middle of the Japanese attack on Pearl Harbor), and the B-24s would be carrying extra gas in their auxiliary bomb bay tanks to extend their range and provide a safety factor. Some of the 90th's new bombers turned out to have minor mechanical problems that would take a few days to sort out, so Rogers and Mussett decided to split the Group in half, the first half leaving on schedule on the 15th of September, and the second half following on the 19th, after all its planes were in flying order.

Col. Rogers described the morning of the takeoff to Hawaii:

> Colonel Mussett and I decided we would fly in the same airplane so that one of us could be checking the navigator's work while the other was flying. Our plan was to take off just at dawn and circle the airdrome until our young fledglings were all in sight of us, then strike out for the long distant island twenty-four-hundred miles

away. To execute this plan we had a great deal to do beforehand, such as briefing our pilots on the takeoff procedure, the altitudes at which we could find favorable winds, emergency procedures in case of engine trouble, radio communications, and recognition signals necessary to approach the Islands of Hawaii. This, in addition to seeing that all the airplanes were properly serviced and a final check on the engines, carried us late into the night.

When the alarm clock sounded at four AM I was still awake, and though I had not slept I was too excited to be tired. I jumped out of bed anxious to be off. After our crowd had eaten breakfast, and lunches were packed, we had a final briefing of all our crews that were to make the flight. We decided it would be necessary to top up all our fuel tanks since it would cost us approximately fifty gallons of gasoline to warm up our engines, and we knew that every drop would be precious if we were running short at the other end. Every crew was dispatched to its airplane and Mussett and I departed for ours. In addition to our normal combat crew we carried along our flight surgeon, Captain Mitchell, as an extra passenger.

Due to a dry cigarette lighter belonging to Captain Mitchell, I received one of the most exciting moments of my life. All the crew were at their stations, and I was checking my radio to see if I had contact with the tower. The big four-thousand-gallon gasoline truck was filling all of our tanks, which held thirty-one hundred gallons of hundred-octane gasoline, and filling them to overflowing. All of a sudden the darkness was broken by a flash of light and I heard the screaming of our aerial engineer that the airplane was on fire.

Until you have been sitting on thirty-one hundred gallons of hundred-octane gasoline and heard the word "FIRE!" shouted, you can never know the feeling that all of us had. We all made a mad rush to jump out of the bomb-bay doors, [but] flames were coming from the concrete as though it were burning and the flames were filling the expanse in which the bombs were usually stored. We all dove headlong through the flames, which by this time were dying down some as the fire extinguishers had been put into action. This made our escape possible with only a few singes.

Once on the outside we saw gas burning under the wings and right up to the nozzle of the gasoline truck. We all grabbed emergency fire extinguishers and soon put the fire out. As soon as the last flame was extinguished, everyone with one accord said, "How in the hell did the fire start?" Our medical officer, with a sheepish expression on his face, stepped forward and said in a meek voice, "Sir, I did it with this blasted cigarette lighter. It was dry, and the overflowing gasoline was dripping off the wing, and I decided to fill it. When I opened the lighter a spark came from the flint and the next thing I knew flames were running up the wing."

3. THE MOVE TO HAWAII

There is one thing that can be said for the medical officer: after he had started the fire his reaction time was perfect since he had the fire extinguisher playing on the flames a split second after the fire started. I am sure all of our crew can credit him with our lives for his quick thinking. It was indeed a shaky crew that went back to their stations just as the first streaks of dawn came over the horizon. We started our four powerful twelve-hundred-horsepower engines, and the roaring was reassuring as we taxied down to the end of the runway for takeoff.

On checking with the tower, we received our clearance along with good wishes for a safe flight. We shoved the four throttles forward and the great props started biting into the air with a forward acceleration that threw us back in our seats. The Group Commander and I were both wondering if she would get into the air with such a tremendous load, but neither of us expressed our fears to the other. We barely cleared a little rise in the ground at the end of the runway as we became airborne.

In a short time we were cruising over the Golden Gate Bridge, preparing to circle back over the field according to our plans to wait for the other airplanes. On our return to the field we could see three of our planes already in the air, but after circling for fifteen minutes over the field, no other planes took off. We started calling the tower, since any great loss in time might mean we would not have enough gasoline to make Hawaii. We were notified by the tower that one of our planes had taxied out for a takeoff and had electrical trouble. They were towing him off the runway and another airplane was taking his place.

Forty-five minutes after our takeoff the last airplane was in the air, but we were afraid to have them close in to a tight formation since all the pilots were having trouble keeping the planes flying with such a heavy load. We just called the pilots and told them to close in to a reasonable distance but not attempt to get too close, because if they got into a skid they might crash into one another.

About this time Mussett let out a scream, and I glanced up just in time to see a huge bomber descending on us at a terrific speed. It looked as though it were going to dive into the middle of our airplane. The only thing that flashed into my mind was that one of the pilots had probably lost complete control of his plane and that maybe someday somebody would fish our bodies out of the Bay. Just as I had given up hope, the airplane missed us by a few feet and pulled up into a climb in a chandelle maneuver. Over the radio came a cheery goodbye, and I knew then that this was a stunt being pulled by an old classmate of mine, Lt. Col. Red Elkins, who had taken off before we did and had checked to see if the weather was okay, and had flown out to give us a special send-off. This second fright began to tell on my exhausted nerves, and I felt plenty weak in the knees.

It could hardly be said it was a formation leaving San Francisco, but at least the planes were in sight of each other.

For the next six hours, the flight of 24 bombers droned on peacefully across the ocean, flying at 11,000 feet, making good time, keeping each other in sight, with all the navigators cross-checking each other's computations and comparing notes over the radio. Then, as if Col. Rogers' nerves weren't frayed enough, he got another severe shock. While he was switching the fuel flow to the bomber's engines from its wing tanks to its auxiliary bomb bay tank, something went wrong and the flow stopped entirely. Suddenly, and nearly simultaneously, all four of the bomber's engines quit, starved for gas, their steady drone replaced by an appalling silence.

As the overloaded bomber slowed and lost momentum, Rogers found it necessary to point its nose steeply downward in order to keep up its airspeed and prevent the wings from stalling. In the process he was practically diving straight for the sea. As the altimeter rapidly wound down, with crew members scrambling into their life jackets, anticipating a landing at sea, the flight engineer, working frantically at the fuel transfer valves, was able to get the gas flowing again. "At 4,000 feet," Rogers wrote, "three of our engines came back in with a roar, and a few minutes later the fourth one caught, and we sat weak from excitement while many of the other airplanes called to see if we were okay."

After a fire, a near-midair collision, and a near-ditching at sea, on top of having had no sleep the night before, no one was happier than Col. Rogers to see the distinctive shape of Diamond Head on the Hawaiian island of Oahu rise up on the horizon some hours later. The navigators had performed flawlessly, the winds had been favorable, and they had made good time, 2,400 miles in 13 hours for an average speed of 185 mph. All the bombers landed safely at Hickam Field beside Pearl Harbor, each plane with hundreds of gallons of fuel to spare, and the utterly spent Col. Rogers parked his airplane and tottered off to find a bed somewhere to collapse into.

Four days later, on Saturday, Sept. 19th, the second half of the 90th's bombers left Hamilton Field in California and struck out for Hawaii. This group of 24 was led by Lt. Col. Unruh, with Maj. Harry Bullis as his copilot, and the flight did not begin well. Two of the bombers had problems, one before takeoff and one just after. A bomber piloted by Lt. James McMurria (of whom we will hear more later) sprang a fuel leak on the runway that forced him to remain on the ground. Only minutes after the takeoff of a bomber piloted by Lt. John Davis, of Col. Rogers' 319th Squadron, with eight other men aboard, the plane had a fuel flow problem similar to what Col. Rogers had experienced halfway to Hawaii, but this time, with the plane at a low altitude, the trouble could not be corrected in time to prevent a crash.

Only about 20 miles from Hamilton Field, with two of his engines cutting out for lack of fuel, Lt. Davis was forced to set the plane down in San Francisco Bay near Angel Island, not even having made it as far as the Golden Gate Bridge. This was the Group's first ditching, and there would be many more before the war was over. The B-24's tendency to break up in a water landing was now witnessed by the Group for the first time: on contact with the water the plane broke in half just behind the wing. It sank in less than two minutes, taking Lt. William R. Gunther down with it. An army launch from Ft. McDowell on Angel Island quickly picked up the other eight men, who were floating in the water in their life vests. Lt. Gunther became the Group's 15th fatality. The other 22 bombers of the second contingent reached Hawaii without incident, and with their arrival the 90th Bomb Group was once again intact, with its headquarters now established at Hickam Field.

The bomber that had been left behind at Hamilton Field because of a fuel leak, piloted by Lt. McMurria, required two days for repairs. When it was ready to fly again McMurria was sent back east to Patterson Field, Ohio to pick up some additional supplies that the Group would need overseas. The trip gave him a chance to see his fiancé, Mary Francis Smith, one last time before he left for the Pacific. He would not see her again for three years, and when he returned to her it would be as the emaciated survivor of three years of horror in a Japanese prison camp.

In Hawaii, the 90th Bomb Group came under the authority of the 7th Air Force, commanded by Major General Willis H. Hale. Like Charles Lindbergh, Gen. Hale felt that the Group had not yet had sufficient training to be plunged straight into the war, so he decided to keep it in Hawaii a month or so for further training before sending it on to Australia. Of this Col. Rogers wrote:

> **The High Command realized that we had not been fully trained due to the few months since the Group had been activated and our numerous moves. Therefore we were assigned to patrol five hundred miles out daily in protection of the Hawaiian Islands. This gave our navigators a great deal of experience in overwater flying and helped our pilots to accustom themselves to their new equipment.**

In addition to the offshore patrols, during the month that it spent in Hawaii the Group flew practice bombing missions, dropping dummy bombs on uninhabited islands in the area. The crews also bombed sea sleds towed by navy ships, since one of their anticipated tasks in combat would be to bomb Japanese shipping at sea. The gunners were given air-to-air gunnery practice by shooting at cloth sleeves towed on ropes behind small planes. The Group also conducted search missions for missing aircraft out to 900 miles from the islands, which gave the navigators yet more valuable experience at plotting courses over long stretches of water, as well as accustoming the crews to extended hours in the air.

At this time many members of the 90th were still complaining that they would rather be flying the more popular and (they believed) better-built B-17 Flying Fortress instead of their B-24 Liberators. A B-17, it was said (with some truth), did not break up when it was ditched like Lt. Davis' B-24 had done, and they felt that Lt. Gunther would probably still be alive if he'd been in a B-17 when his plane crash-landed in San Francisco Bay, since the plane would have remained intact and floated for a while, giving everybody time to get out.

The B-17 also had a belly turret to ward off enemy fighter planes attacking it from below, while the belly turrets of their B-24s had been removed at the factory to lighten the plane so that it could carry more fuel and bombs.

Gen. H. H. (Hap) Arnold, Commanding General of all the U. S. Army Air Forces, passed through Hawaii on an inspection tour just after the 90th Bomb Group arrived there, and he became aware of many of the men's worries about their B-24s. He was alarmed at this attitude and wrote to Gen. Hale demanding that something be done to correct it, as though the men's lack of confidence in the plane could be banished by an order or two.

"Your quick and careful attention must be given to the requirement that this popular notion of the inferiority of the B-24 shall not be reflected in the personnel of the 90th Bombardment Group. . ." Arnold wrote. "[I]t must be perfectly evident to you that the result might approach disaster if the 90th moves into Australia . . . with the belief that their airplane is an inferior weapon."

For no apparent reason, except possibly to make it look like he was taking action to comply with the order, Gen. Hale replaced the perfectly capable Col. Mussett as commander of the 90th with Col. Arthur W. Meehan, an officer who had been in Hawaii flying B-17s since before the attack on Pearl Harbor. Whatever the motive for the switch, the 38-year-old Meehan was a good choice, an energetic West Pointer (class of 1928), an accomplished athlete (he quarterbacked Army's football team and later coached it) and a proven leader. Meehan and his wife Lucy, with their two small daughters, had found themselves in the midst of the Japanese attack on Pearl Harbor on Dec. 7, but had escaped without injury. Five days later, on Dec. 12, Meehan wrote a letter to his parents in the States to assure them that he and his family were well:

> Dear Folks,
>
> Since the surprise visit we received from our small yellow friends last Sunday I've been too busy to write. I knew how worried you would be, but I hoped that you would work on the old theory that "no news is good news."
>
> When the raid hit I hurried to my office and I've been on duty ever since. All of the families were evacuated from Hickam and oth-

er fields as soon as the first raid was quieted. Lucy left me a note telling me approximately where she was headed for. I finally located her late that night. She and Mrs. Lewis (another officer's wife) had moved in with their total of four kids on some people they knew in a peaceful valley. It is a lovely home and they are safe and comfortable. I don't know whether they will be allowed back to Hickam Field or not. I imagine that families may be evacuated to the mainland if safe passage can be arranged. Much as I hate the thought of separation, I'll be more relaxed about the whole thing when Lucy is safe somewhere in the U. S. A. . . .

Col. Art Meehan

Christmas is going to seem funny this year, but we'll celebrate it somehow. To show how Americans work, a load of Christmas trees from the mainland arrived yesterday—and they are selling like hotcakes. A gift I bought for Lucy—a very fetching evening gown—arrived on the same boat. I'll feel silly giving it to her now with a blackout on every night.

I'll try to write as often as I can, but if letters are scarce don't worry. The mail will be irregular from now on. Best to everyone—and tell them that our chins are up, and out.   Love,

Arthur.[3]

Less than a year later, on Nov. 16, 1942, Meehan would vanish without a trace on the second combat mission flown by the 90th Bomb Group.

At Hickam Field, Cols. Rogers and Unruh resumed their project of mounting a tail turret on the nose of a B-24, hoping that once they demonstrated its feasibility, the factories building the B-24 would adopt the modification. This time Unruh took the lead, since Rogers was too busy with his duties with the Group to be able to contribute much time to it, though he followed the progress closely. "With the pictures and a few sketches of our original mock-up at the Willow Run plant, and many hours of work by Col. Unruh and a crew at the depot," Rogers wrote, "the installation was progressing rapidly."

However, as had become frustratingly normal for the turret project, before the design could be finalized Rogers and the 90th Bomb Group were off again on their way to Australia, where they would be going into combat against the Japanese. Rogers would go with the Group, but Unruh was transferred out of the 90th and remained in Hawaii, where he was able to continue working on the nose turret project.

Chapter Four

THE MOVE TO AUSTRALIA

The 90th would fly to Australia in two groups of 24 bombers each, the same way it had flown from California to Hawaii. The 5,375-mile route from Hawaii to Australia would use a series of Pacific islands as stepping stones for the crossing, with the planes refuelling and spending the night at each stop (see map 4-1, opposite). From Hawaii the planes would fly first to Christmas Island, then to Canton Island, both tiny dots in the vast Pacific Ocean, then to Nandi in the Fiji Islands, then to the island of New Caledonia, and finally to the continent of Australia, landing at Amberly Field, 20 miles west of Brisbane.

Finding such miniscule islands as Christmas and Canton would be considerably more difficult than finding Hawaii had been on their flight out from California, but thanks to their month-long training in Hawaii, the 90th's navigators were much more confident about navigating long distances over water, and felt that they could locate all the islands on the route without undue difficulty, and in fact did so. Every plane made the trip from Hawaii to Australia successfully.

This time the air echelon went ahead of the Group's ground contingent, the opposite situation from the last two moves. Once again the planes were loaded up with spare B-24 parts, since they would be the first B-24s ever seen in Australia, and parts for them would be scarce there at first. This time they also took along as many mechanics and crew chiefs as they could, since they would have to operate there without the rest of their ground personnel until the latter's ship arrived. For the men traveling by ship, it was a long, slow trip of 16 days at sea, with the continual worry of being attacked by Japanese submarines.

The first half of the 90th Bomb Group's planes (two squadrons, or 24 aircraft) set out on the 1,330-mile journey to Christmas Island on the 19th of October [1942]. They were led by Col. Meehan, who said goodbye to his wife Lucy and his two little girls just before taking off. They would never see him again.

Col. Rogers wrote:

> **Colonel Mussett, our Group Commander, who was beloved by the entire Group, remained in Hawaii in quite an important job and**

4. THE MOVE TO AUSTRALIA

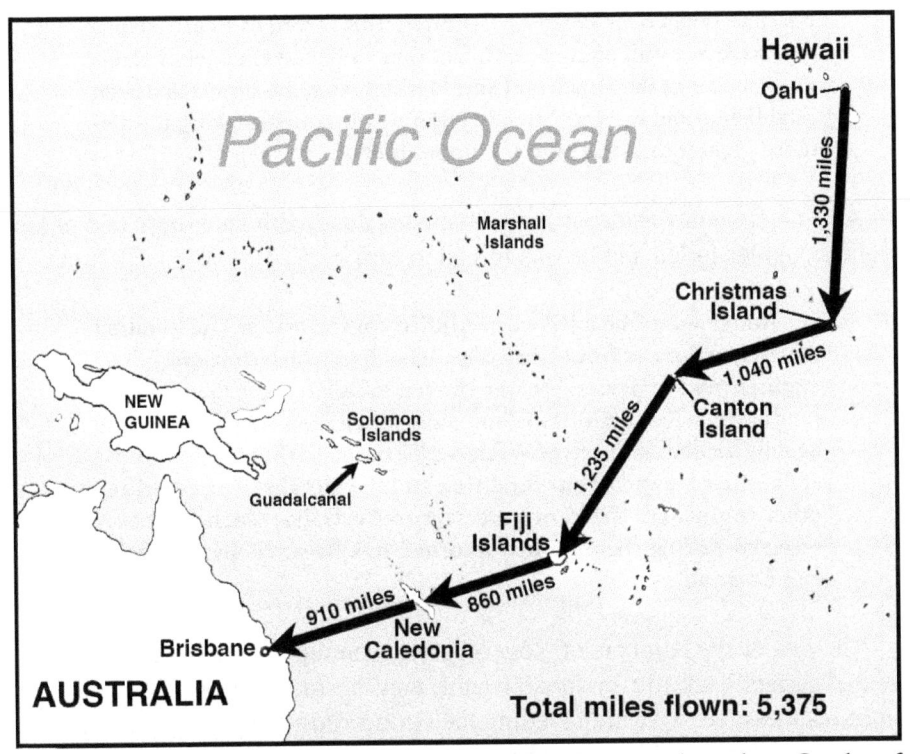

Map 4-1. The route flown by the 90th Bomb Group from Hawaii to Australia in October of 1942. With an overnight stop at each island, the 5,375-mile trip took five days.

another Group Commander, Colonel Art W. Meehan, was appointed to take us to the South or Southwest Pacific. The Group was split into halves. The Commander [Meehan] was to take the first half and the following day I was to follow with the second half. I told Art and the two squadrons goodbye... We shook hands and wished each other the best of luck. This happened to be the last time I ever saw him, as he was lost on his first [actually his second] combat mission.

The next day I prepared the two squadrons I was leading and during the briefing, which covered weather, course and possible enemy interception, we were forced to consider the fact that the little islands we were to land on might be taken by the enemy before we could arrive. Our stops were to be Christmas Island, a little speck in the Pacific and at the time none too well guarded, then Canton, another small island with about the same amount of defense as Christmas Island, then on to New Caledonia...

At that time very little or no rescue service had been set up and it was expected that a good number of planes would be lost trying to fly the huge expanse of the Pacific. The prewar route flown by the Clipper Ships [flying-boat airliners] could not be flown by us since the

Japs had taken over Wake and Midway. This forced us to use islands that were not well equipped. In fact they only had emergency strips prepared since the attack on Pearl Harbor. No radio beams had been established and we were forced to fly a zigzag course making the distance greater than the prewar Clipper route.

As Col. Rogers was departing Christmas Island with his group, one of his plane's engines failed and he was forced to turn back.

> Things went fine until we had flown approximately one hundred and fifty miles out from Christmas Island, at which time one of our engines went to pieces. We were forced to full-feather the propeller [and] return to Christmas Island on three engines with the airplane heavily loaded. We arrived safely on Christmas Island and immediately wired Hawaii of our condition and the fact that we needed another engine. We also sent a message to Australia, which was never received, telling them we had returned to Christmas Island due to engine trouble.

The rest of the bombers of Rogers' group continued on to Australia. After he had turned back to Christmas Island, they heard no more from him, and since his message to Australia letting the Group know that he was detained on Christmas Island, waiting for a replacement engine from Hawaii, was never received, he was feared lost at sea.

While Rogers and his crew were cooling their heels on Christmas Island, with nothing much to do after they had removed the damaged engine from the airplane (using a block and tackle furnished by the men who garrisoned the island), he noted how lonely the few men who manned this transient facility were:

> While at Christmas Island we realized that people could go what is known as 'rock happy' in not too long a time. A few members of this servicing base were willing to pay as high as $100 for a quart of whiskey, and I am sure the sight of any kind of a woman would probably have caused heart failure. These poor lonesome boys were far from home, with no decent food, and wondering when the Japs might come and take their little sand island, which they knew was not too well defended.
>
> However, they were proud of one fact, and that was that they had quite a few palm trees on Christmas Island. One of the men said to me before I left, "Just you wait until you land on Canton. There is only one tree on that whole Island, and so many of the crews going through have taken a branch for a souvenir that a guard has been posted in a roost. He not only protects the tree, but it's the highest point on the Island, and he stands watch for any sign of the enemy."

4. THE MOVE TO AUSTRALIA

[Later] when we landed on Canton Island, I found it just as the man had told me, and there was a sentry posted in the tree guarding the prize possession of the little Island of Canton. Fresh meat and any luxuries of life were not to be found at this time on these little islands. Men actually considered Spam a delicacy when it could be gotten.

Without these little sand islands, and men with courage to hold them, it would have been impossible to reinforce the Solomons or Australia, whose air strength at that time was almost completely depleted.

When the replacement engine for Rogers' plane arrived from Hawaii in a cargo plane, it was found to be dismantled, and would have to be put together before it could be mounted on the bomber. No one stationed on the island knew anything about B-24 engines, so it was up to Rogers and his single mechanic, with help from the rest of the crew, to assemble it themselves. Working out in the open under the hot tropical sun, with sand blowing in their eyes as well as into the engine, they managed to put the complex powerplant together using the few tools available. When it was all assembled, they realized that it was probably too full of sand to run, so they repeatedly flushed it out with gasoline until it seemed clean inside. After they mounted it on the airplane and installed the propeller, Rogers wrote that "to the amazement of all, including the mechanic, it ran..."

Canton Island's lone palm tree with its guard and lookout on duty, sitting on a platform built onto the trunk.

Nearly six weeks after the rest of the 90th Bomb Group had reached Australia, Rogers and his crew finally took off from Christmas Island to follow them.

Chapter Five

THE 90ᵀᴴ JOINS THE 5ᵀᴴ AIR FORCE

When the 90th Bomb Group arrived in Australia with its 48 bombers, 1,407 enlisted men, and 289 officers, it became a part of the U. S. Fifth Air Force, which controlled all Army Air Corps aircraft in the Southwest Pacific Area (SWPA). All members of the Group soon had the 5th Air Force patch sewn onto their uniforms.

The head of the Fifth Air Force, General George C. Kenney, welcomed the men of the Group to the theater, and he was exceedingly glad to have them. The Fifth Air Force had been operating on a shoestring ever since the Japanese had run it out of the Philippines at the beginning of the war, and Kenney needed every airplane he could get, especially heavy bombers, the Air Corps' foremost offensive weapon.

All members of the 5th Air Force wore this symbol as a patch on their uniforms. The 5 was yellow, the stars white, and the background blue.

The lack of Allied war matériel in the Pacific theater was due to the fact that at the beginning of the war, U. S. President Franklin D. Roosevelt and British Prime Minister Winston S. Churchill had made an agreement that the United States would give priority to the defeat of Hitler and the Nazis, and therefore most American manpower and weaponry were going to Europe. The war with Japan in the Pacific was placed on the back burner, as something to be dealt with later on, after Germany was defeated.

General Douglas MacArthur, who had been placed in charge of Allied forces in the Southwest Pacific, with his headquarters in Australia, was told to simply do whatever he could with the limited means available to him to contain the Japanese advance. MacArthur, however, refused to sit passively on the defensive in Australia and went over to the offense, despite having little to work with, and thereafter spent much of the war trying to persuade the U. S. Joint Chiefs of Staff to send him more men and arms as he first checked the advance of the Japanese forces and then pushed them back to the north. It was MacArthur's pleading for aircraft that had resulted in the 90th

5. THE 90TH JOINS THE 5TH AIR FORCE

V Fighter Command	Night Fighter Units	V Bomber Command	Photo Reconnaissance	54th Troop Carrier Wing
3d ACG (P-51, C-47)	418th NFS	3d BG (L) (B-25, A-20)	6th RG (F-5, F-7)	2d CCG
8th FG (P-40, P-38)	421st NFS	22d BG (M/H) (B-26 – B-24)	71st RG (B-25)	317th TCG
35th FG (P-47, P-51)	547th NFS	38th BG (M) (B-25)		374th TCG (1943 only)
49th FG (P-40, P-47, P-38)		43d BG (H) (B-24)		375th TCG
58th FG (P-47)		90th BG (H) (B-24)		433d TCG
348th FG (P-47, P-51)		312th BG (L) (A-20)		
475th FG (P-38)		345th BG (M) (B-25)		
		380th BG (H) (B-24)		
		417th BG (L) (A-20)		

LEGEND: ACG – Air Commando Group, FG – Fighter Group, NFS – Night Fighter Squadron, BG (L) – Light Bomb Group, BG (M) – Medium Bomb Group, BG (H) – Heavy Bomb Group, RG – Reconnaissance Group, CCG – Combat Cargo Group, TCG – Troop Carrier Group

Above: the table of organization of the U. S. Fifth Air Force, commanded by General George C. Kenney, who in turn reported to overall Southwest Pacific Area (SWPA) commander General Douglas MacArthur. The 90th Bomb Group (circled) came under the control of V (Fifth) Bomber Command.

Bomb Group going to the Pacific instead of to Europe.

The Fifth Air Force

MacArthur had been appointed Commander-in-Chief of the Southwest Pacific Area in April of 1942, a month after his escape from the Japanese siege of Corregidor Island in the Philippines (described in greater detail in later chapters).

The Southwest Pacific Area was comprised of Australia and islands to the north of it, including New Guinea, the western part of the Solomon Islands, the Philippines, the Dutch East Indies, and Borneo (see map 5-1 on the next page). The fighting forces under MacArthur's command were mainly American and Australian, but there were some British, Dutch, and Filipino elements as well.

62-year-old Gen. Douglas MacArthur was the Commander of all Allied forces in the Southwest Pacific Area.

MacArthur was no expert on the use of air forces, and in fact had managed the 5th Air Force badly in the Philippines, allowing many of its aircraft to be

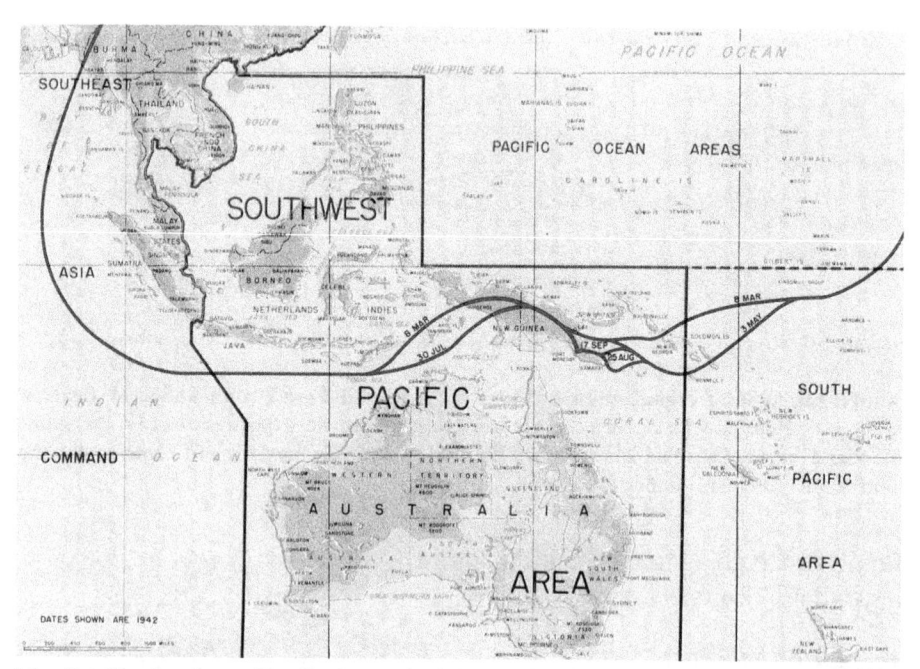

Map 5-1. The Southwest Pacific Area, which was under the command of General Douglas MacArthur. This was the area in which the 90th Bomb Group would conduct most of its operations during the war. The wavy lines indicate the limits of the Japanese advance before they were beaten back.

caught and destroyed on the ground at Clark Field, near Manila. MacArthur needed an air specialist to run the 5th Air Force for him, under his direction.

General George C. Kenney, MacArthur's Air Chief

53-year-old Major General George Kenney managed all Army Air Corps affairs for General MacArthur from August of 1942 onward, working with MacArthur at his headquarters in a hotel in Brisbane. The headquarters remained at Brisbane until August of 1944, when MacArthur moved it to Hollandia, on the north coast of New Guinea, following the advances of his troops toward the Philippines and Japan.

Within the 5th Air Force, the bombers were controlled by V (Fifth) Bomber Command, the fighters by V Fighter Command, etc. (see the 5th Air Force's table of organization on the previous page).

General Kenney was a short (five-foot-six) bulldog of a man, a former World War One pilot. He had replaced the original 5th Air Force commander, Lt. General George Brett, in early August of 1942, only two and a half months before the 90th Bomb Group arrived in Australia.

General Brett had not gotten along well with General MacArthur, and a large part of the problem had been MacArthur's arrogant and self-important

Chief of Staff, Maj. Gen. Richard K. Sutherland, who kept inserting himself between Brett and MacArthur. Sutherland also interfered with Brett's decisions and was continually dictating to him how the air force should be run. Kenney wrote in his memoirs:

> **Brett told me of his troubles with Sutherland... [He] said he had so much trouble getting past Sutherland to see MacArthur that he hadn't seen the General for weeks, and he just talked to Sutherland on the telephone when he had to.[1]**

When Kenney took over from Brett, it appeared that he was in for the same treatment from Sutherland,* so he decided to nip it in the bud. He went to Sutherland's office, where he picked up a blank piece of paper and a pencil off his desk, drew a dot in the center of the paper, and showed it to Sutherland. "That dot represents what you know about running an air force," he said. "The rest of the paper represents what I know. Now, how about we go see Gen. MacArthur right now and find out which one of us he wants to be his air chief?" Sutherland backed down, and Kenney had no more trouble with him.[2]

In Kenney's first meeting with MacArthur, the Supreme Commander gave him a lecture on the substandard performance of the 5th Air Force in the SWPA up to that time, and enumerated its many shortcomings as he saw them. Kenney heard him out, then stood up and told him that

53-year-old General George C. Kenney was the Commander of the 5th Air Force from August 1942 to the end of the war.

---

* General Sutherland eventually fell out of favor with MacArthur when he persisted in bringing his mistress, an Australian woman officer, along with him to wherever MacArthur moved his headquarters, despite MacArthur's orders to leave her behind in Australia. When MacArthur was informed in late 1944 that Sutherland had brought the woman all the way up to the Philippines and installed her in her own cottage near his headquarters, MacArthur flew into a rage and told Sutherland, essentially, that he had no further use for him.[3]

General George Churchill Kenney took command of the Allied Air Forces in the Southwest Pacific Area in August of 1942 and continued in that capacity to the end of the war. The Jolly Rogers (90th Bomb Group) was one of the groups under his command. Upper left: Gen. Kenney receives a decoration in the field from his boss General Douglas MacArthur, the overall commander of all Allied forces in the Southwest Pacific.

he (Kenney) thought he knew what needed to be done with the 5th Air Force, and if MacArthur didn't agree with his methods he would just pack up and go home. According to Kenney, MacArthur immediately softened his attitude, put his arm around him and said, "George, I think we're going to get along together all right."[4]

In fact they did get along exceedingly well throughout the war, and MacArthur left nearly all the details of air force operations in Kenney's hands. Kenney later proudly recalled one of MacArthur's press conferences:

> One of the correspondents said, "General, what is the air force doing today?" General MacArthur said, "Oh, I don't know. Go ask General Kenney." The newspaper man said, "General, do you mean to say you don't know where the bombs are falling?" MacArthur turned to him, grinned, and said, "Of course I know where they're falling. They're falling in the right place. Go ask General Kenney where it is."[5]

The aggressive and innovative Kenney was able to achieve highly effective results with what few men and planes he had to work with for most of the war.

Kenney needed the 90th Bomb Group to replace the worn-out 19th Bomb Group that had been battling the Japanese with its B-17s since the first day of the war. The 19th had initially been based in the Philippines, and for them the war had begun only hours after the Pearl Harbor attack, when the oncoming Japanese tide had destroyed sixteen of their thirty-three B-17 bombers on the ground in a bombing and strafing attack on Clark Field. The remaining bombers of the 19th had struck back as best they could at the Japanese invasion fleet, but had been overwhelmed by superior numbers of Japanese aircraft and were unable to do much damage. The surviving bombers retreated to Australia.

A couple of the 19th's bombers had been able to slip back from Australia to the Philippines to rescue General MacArthur and his family and staff after their escape from Corregidor in PT boats. The 19th then attempted to defend Java, but again were overpowered by superior Japanese numbers and once again driven back to Australia. In the spring of 1942, while the 90th Bomb Group was still being formed in the States, the 19th Bomb Group flew 18 strikes from Australia against the Japanese stronghold of Rabaul on the island of New Britain, and had suffered more losses in the process. In March of 1942 they had also bombed a Japanese force that was invading the town of Lae on New Guinea's north coast. By the fall of 1942 they were worn out and dispirited.

Now, as the fresh and untried 90th was coming in to Australia to enter the fray, the war-weary 19th was being relieved and sent home to the States. The two bomb groups passed each other going and coming, and when they temporarily shared the same Australian airfield at Brisbane, members of the battered (and somewhat embittered) 19th Bomb Group had only pessimistic things to tell the newcomers about what they would be up against when they went into action against the Japanese.

And one thing they told the men of the 90th was that their B-24s would not be up to the task, being an inferior bomber to the B-17, confirming what many of them already feared. The pilots and crews of the 90th therefore felt a lot of anxiety about their upcoming combat missions. Until the B-24s entered combat, no one would know how they would measure up.

Chapter Six

IRON RANGE

General Kenney had a decision to make: where should he base the newly arrived 90th Bomb Group? It had to be a place from which it could conduct combat operations against the Japanese, but not so close to any Japanese airbases that it would be easy for them to retaliate. At this time the Japanese had air superiority everywhere north of Australia, while Allied air assets and defenses in the theater were meager. The most forward airbase to which Kenney could have sent the 90th was Port Moresby on the southern coast of New Guinea, an Australian outpost town 350 miles across the Coral Sea from the northern tip of Australia (see map 6-3 on page 59).

Port Moresby had some long dirt runways a few miles east of town that heavy bombers could use, and there were already American and Australian troops established at the town and airfields, so it would have been a good place to send the 90th if it hadn't been so close to Japanese airbases in New Guinea, particularly the one at Lae (map 6-1, opposite). In fact Japanese air raids on Port Moresby from Lae were frequent—by January of 1943 the town and airfield would suffer nearly 100 bombing raids.

Kenney didn't want his valuable heavy bombers to be caught and destroyed on the ground, as had happened to many of the B-17s based in the Philippines at the outset of the war. It would be wise therefore to keep them a safe distance back, away from the Japanese, at least to begin with, and the long range of the B-24s would allow him to do that. But again, where to put them?

By mid-1942 the Japanese had occupied the entire length of New Guinea's north coastline and controlled all of the island except for Port Moresby on the south coast, which they intended to capture next by amphibious assault and use as a base for a possible invasion of Australia. Their airbase at Lae was only 185 miles north of Moresby, across the Owen Stanley Mountain range which runs like a spine down the center of the island between its north and south coasts.

In 1942 twin-engine Japanese Mitsubishi "Betty" bombers from Lae were a frequent sight in the skies over Port Moresby, coming across the mountains in V-shaped formations like flights of fat metal geese to drop bombs on Moresby's airfields and harbor. In addition, gaggles of Zero fighters, also from

6. IRON RANGE

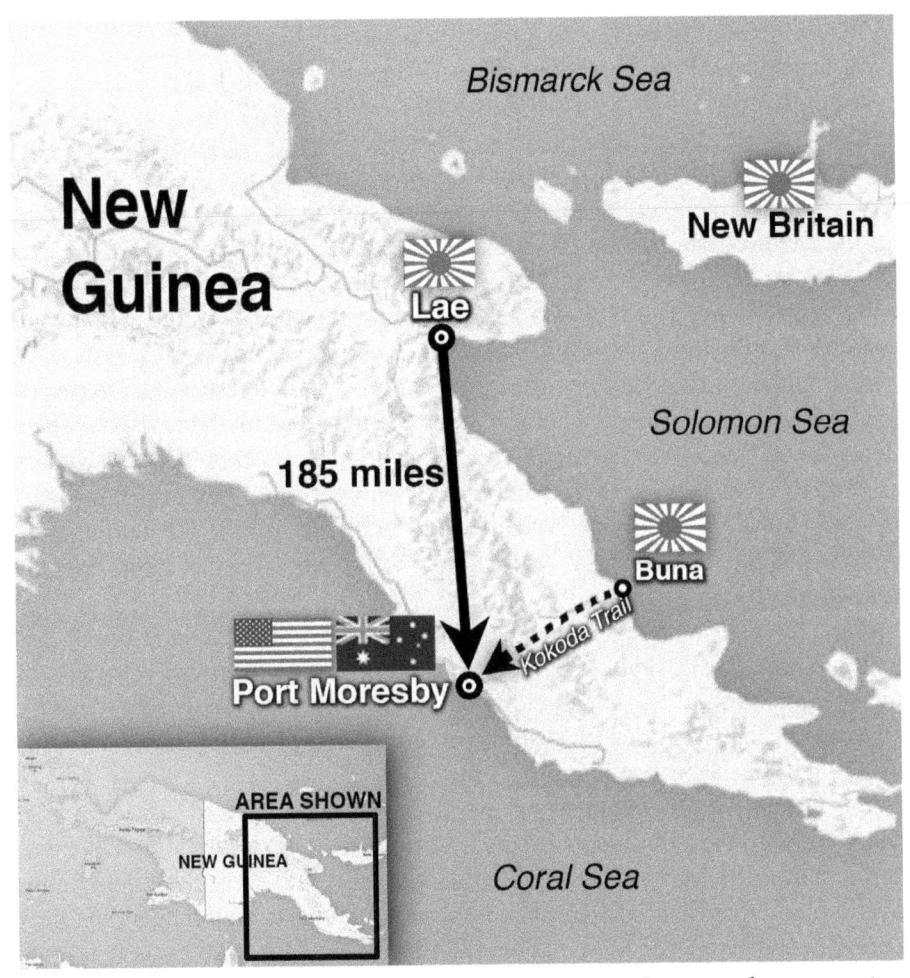

Map 6-1. Port Moresby was a dangerous place to be in 1942. Japanese planes operating from Lae, only 185 miles to the north, didn't have far to fly to bomb it, and they did so frequently. The Japanese also made an overland attempt to capture Port Moresby across the Kokoda Trail in July of 1942. For those reasons, Port Moresby was considered too risky a place to base the 90th Bomb Group when they first arrived in the Pacific war theater.

Lae, would suddenly appear over the nearby mountains and swoop down on Port Moresby with guns blazing to conduct strafing attacks at treetop level.

As if that wasn't bad enough, starting in July of 1942, only three months before the 90th Bomb Group arrived in Australia, the Japanese had launched an attempt to capture Port Moresby from the landward side.* An invasion force of the Japanese army started out from the village of Buna, on the north coast

---

*A planned Japanese amphibious assault on Port Moresby had been turned back by the American navy in the Battle of the Coral Sea in May, 1942.

of the island, and trekked across the Owen Stanley Mountains on the Kokoda Trail headed for Port Moresby (Map 6-1 again). They had gotten within 32 miles of the town—so close that they could see the searchlights of its airfields at night—before they were halted on September 16 by tough Australian troops of the 7th Division, fresh from fighting Rommel in North Africa, who then slowly pushed them all the way back over the mountains to their starting point on the north coast. The Battle of the Kokoda Trail would be a slow, vicious slugging match over the steep, swampy, miserable mountainous jungle track, and it would not end until November, but the battle was still in full swing when the 90th Bomb Group arrived in Australia in mid-October.

For all these reasons Port Moresby was out of the question as a base for the 90th, at least for the time being. General Kenney decided that the next best thing would be to base the bombers in Australia, but as close to New Guinea as possible. Owing to their great range, the bombers could take off from somewhere in northern Australia, fly across the Coral Sea to strike Japanese targets in New Guinea, New Britain, or the Solomon Islands, and then return to their base in Australia.

Port Moresby would still be available for the bombers to land briefly for help with mechanical problems, to get gas, take refuge from bad weather, get medical attention for wounded crewmen, or any other reason, before scooting back across the Coral Sea to Australia at the earliest opportunity to avoid getting caught in a Japanese bombing raid.

As time went on, missions by the 90th would be "staged" through Port Moresby, with the outbound bombers landing there to take aboard fuel, bombs, and ammunition that were stockpiled at Moresby, and sometimes remaining overnight so that they could launch a mission before dawn the next day, thus saving the 350 miles of flying across the Coral Sea.

Iron Range: a strategically located hellhole

The location picked to build an airbase for the 90th Bomb Group in northern Australia was a place deep in the jungle wilderness on Australia's Cape York Peninsula, which on a map looks like a finger pointing straight at New Guinea (Maps 6-2, opposite, and 6-3, page 59). There, only 150 miles from the northernmost tip of the Australian continent, American engineers hacked out an airbase from dense jungle growth amid 50-foot tall trees. They bulldozed three dirt runways, one of them 7,000 feet long, and they also graded a winding, 29-mile road northeastward from the airfields to the nearest location on the coast that had a jetty for unloading cargo, a spot known as Portland Roads, so that supplies could be brought up to the airbase by ship.

This primitive airbase in the jungle became known as Iron Range, named after some small iron mines in the nearby mountains. In the first week of

6. IRON RANGE
57

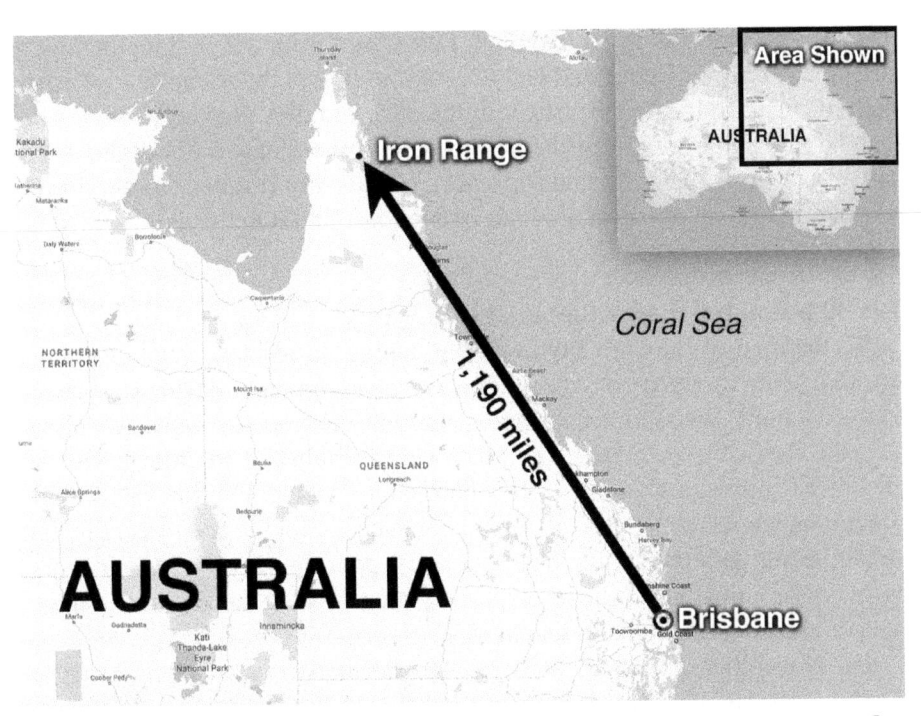

Map 6-2. After arriving in Brisbane, Australia from Hawaii, the 90th Bomb Group flew 1,190 miles up to their new base at Iron Range on the Cape York Peninsula. Japanese air superiority over New Guinea meant that the 90th would have to remain on the Australian continent for a while.

November, 1942, the 90th Bomb Group flew its Liberators up from Brisbane to Iron Range, a distance of 1,190 miles, (map, above). Landing on a dirt runway in the middle of a virgin jungle was something of a shock for the young American pilots, who up to this time had always operated their big bombers from paved runways in civilized surroundings.

Iron Range, by contrast, was about as miserable and primitive a place as can be imagined, far from any Australian towns, villages, or ranches. The nearest Australian settlement was 400 miles away. Seen from the air, the reddish soil of the airfield's main runway looked like a small red streak in the vast jungle cover. This airbase was so remote and difficult to spot that it was hoped the Japanese would never find it to bomb it, and in fact they never did, although they bombed Australian towns farther down the coast. Nor did some American and other Allied pilots find Iron Range on their first try, even though they had been told where it was and had it marked on their maps.

When approaching Iron Range, a pilot had to make a close examination of the jungle, especially when visibility was poor owing to bad weather, to confirm that the relatively small clearing in the jungle canopy really was an airfield. And that was in the daytime. Pilots who went out on long bombing missions from Iron Range and had to return to it at night often found it especially difficult to locate the airfield in the dark and then land on it, even with searchlights shining up into the sky to help guide them in (the lights were hard to see in rain, clouds, and fog). Several tragedies resulted from trying to take off or land on this field at night, or even just find it in the dark, as will be related shortly.

The 90th Bomb Group settles in at Iron Range

To the men of the 90th Bomb Group, taking up residence at Iron Range was like being dropped onto the set of a *Tarzan of the Apes* movie. All it needed was Johnny Weissmuller swinging through the trees on vines, yodeling, to make the scene complete. The vines were certainly there, along with all the other features of a classic Hollywood jungle, including primeval swamps containing giant crocodiles and a superabundance of reptile and insect life that would, along with the stifling heat, humidity, pouring rains, and tropical diseases, make living there pure misery. The young men from America had never seen or experienced anything like this.

On November 20, 1942, a Royal Australian Air Force pilot, Lt. Alan Randal, flying a DC-2 cargo plane, landed at Iron Range to refuel on his way up to Port Moresby. He was surprised to find so many Americans living in the jungle under such primitive conditions, and wrote afterward in his diary:

> From the air the place looked no more than a landing strip with a few men in control, but when shown around we were simply amazed at the magnitude of this U. S. base. It was surrounded by a veritable jungle with lianas hanging from the treetops like giant ropes and the gnarled and twisted trunks of the beech trees. In this maze lived four and a half thousand U. S. troops, like little dwarves in a wood, living as near to nature as a human being can. The shipping was a few miles north at Portland Roads and supplies were constantly being unloaded there... All this activity was carried out under the cover of the jungle and was a wonderful camouflage to enemy aircraft.[1]

On December 2 Lt. Randal again flew up to Iron Range from Townsville, this time bringing with him great joy for the Americans in the form of hundreds of pounds of mail from home that had finally arrived in Australia. Randal and his crew arrived at Iron Range while the 90th Bomb Group was busy setting out on a bombing mission against a Japanese convoy that had been sighted off the north coast of New Guinea (this was Col. Art Rogers' first combat mission, described in detail in Chapter 12). Randal wrote:

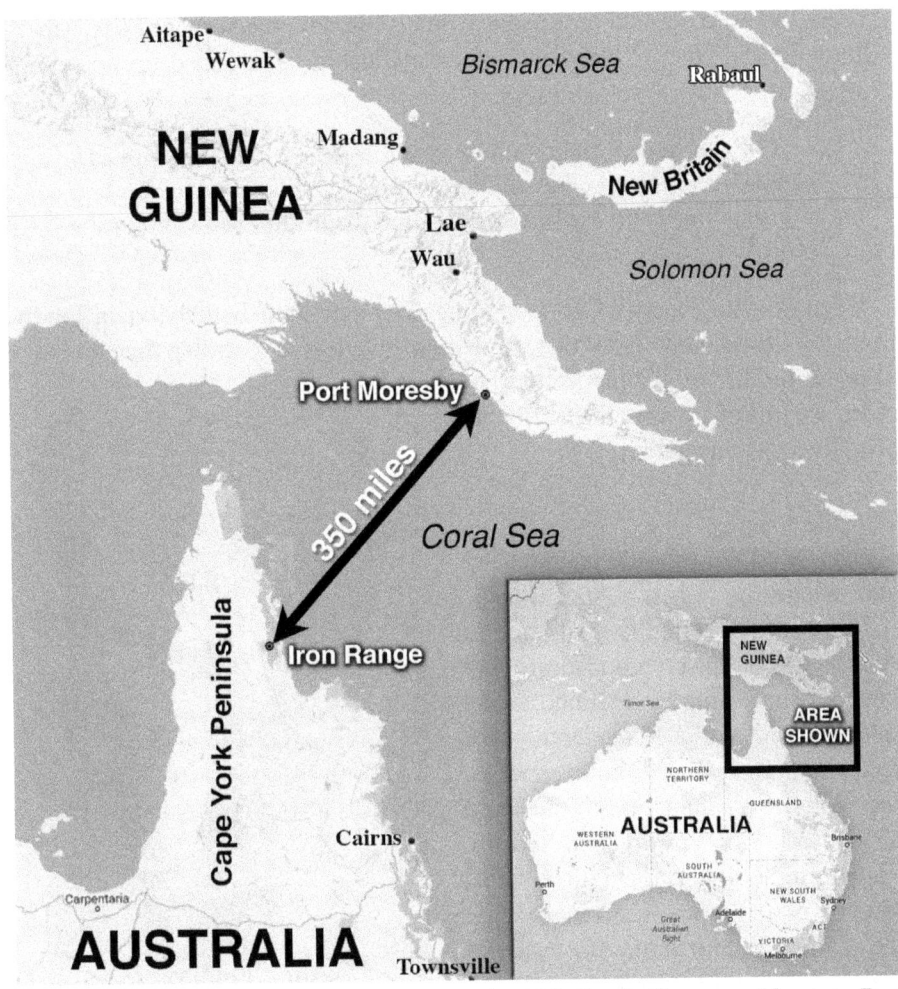

Map 6-3. Iron Range was about as close as the 90th Bomb Group could get to Port Moresby while still remaining on the Australian continent. The distance across the Coral Sea was 350 miles.

We landed at Iron Range three and a half hours out of Townsville and received a great welcome. We had over one and a half thousand pounds of mail for the troops. It gives them great cheer and in my opinion is just as necessary as food for them in these remote areas.

We had to wait two hours to be refueled but were quite happy when informed that the fueling tankers were busy refuelling the giant Liberators which were about to go out on a big raid against the Japs. We saw half a dozen of these great bombers leaving on their mission, each with 16 X 500-lb. death-dealing bombs.[2]

On a sad note, Randal returned to Townsville with the bodies of five Americans who had tried to brew their own moonshine and ended up poisoning themselves:

> On the return flight to Townsville we carried five lead-lined coffins with Yankee bodies, soldiers who had died as a result of drinking alcoholic brew made in a 44-gallon drum that had contained leaded fuel.[3]

Seen from any perspective, Iron Range was a hellhole both to live in and fly from, and it was no wonder that some men were trying to drown their sorrows in home-brewed alcoholic drinks. The camp conditions were indescribably primitive and miserable.

Wildlife woes

The 90th Bomb Group's young men from the farms, small towns, and cities of America, accustomed to at least decent accommodations and fresh air in a camp, now found themselves living in the fetid depths of a wet, steaming jungle amid snakes, scorpions, ants, and clouds of flies and mosquitoes. They were tortured by ringworm, hookworm, chiggers, fleas, leeches and many other insects that the soldiers had no names for. Anthills twenty feet high spewed out millions of the biting little pests.

One of the snakes they killed was a python 33 feet long. The men avoided the snakes as much as possible, but the snakes did not always avoid the men.

Shades of Bela Lugosi! Giant bats were another feature of the jungle at Iron Range.

On one bombing mission, one of the Group's bombardiers was making his bomb run when he realized that there was a deadly cobra coiled two feet from his bombsight. He ignored the snake as best he could and was careful to make no sudden movements. After "bombs away" he pulled out his jungle knife and hacked the snake to pieces (fortunately it had been rendered sluggish by the high-altitude cold). It may be safely said that trouble of this type was seldom encountered by bombardiers in Europe.[4]

6. IRON RANGE

Snakes came in all sizes at Iron Range. The one above was fifteen feet long, and one over twice as long was reported. Smaller ones like those below, including deadly cobras, liked to join the men in their cots at night to enjoy the warmth of their bodies.

Disease and bad food

Such a perpetually hot, wet environment is the best breeding ground in the world for microorganisms, and it spawned such a variety of diseases that the American doctors had never encountered some of them, and of course the American boys had little resistance to them.

Weakened by substandard food (mostly corned beef, dehydrated eggs, potatoes, Spam, and goulash) and by overwork, many of the men had to go about their jobs while suffering from dysentery or worse. The atabrine tablets that everyone took daily to try to ward off malaria turned their skin a sickly orange-yellow. The men often had to pick insects out of their tasteless meals of reconstituted food, since both the cooks and the diners were constantly enveloped in clouds of flies, mosquitoes, and other flying insects.

One of the men was delighted when the cooks presented him with what he took to be fresh-baked raisin bread, until he realized that what he was looking at were not raisins:

> **It was raisin bread, or it looked like raisin bread with whole wheat flour. Closer examination revealed the "raisins" to be rather large insects baked into the bread and the "whole wheat" was smaller versions of flying insects. . . Our initial reaction, when we discovered these now-cooked bugs, was to pick the biggest ones out of the slices of bread before eating. So many big bugs were baked into the bread, however, that we finally gave up our "picking" in the bigger problem of getting something to eat. We accepted our lot with the hope that the insects were all properly cooked in the baking process and maybe added some protein to our lousy diet.**[5]

In climbing into his cot one night, one man found it swarming with ants that had established a colony in it during the day. Another man who used a piece of a tree stump as a chair during a card game in a tent suddenly leapt into the air with a whoop when a six-inch-long centipede a half-inch in diameter stung him in a tender place.[6]

No one dared to get into his cot without first examining it for snakes, stinging insects, or other wildlife, nor could a man safely put on his shoes without checking them for scorpions. Mosquito nets tucked tightly around cots were absolutely necessary if the men were to get any sleep at all. In the perpetually wet environment the canvas of the tents soon rotted, letting in the rain, and the entire camp smelled of mildew.[7] It became impossible to keep cots, clothing, or anything else dry. One man wrote:

> **One of the problems with eating was the very holey tarpaulin that covered what we called our "mess hall." This mess hall had no tables or benches—just some boards that were attached to posts for stand-up dining (this word is used very loosely!). The incessant rains leaked through the rotted tarp and splashed into our mess kits of food. We quickly learned to keep from eating watered-down meals by putting our raincoats over our heads and bending over the food at an angle sufficient to ward off the dripping water.**[8]

The long, drenching tropical rains at Iron Range created mud so deep that even jeeps could not power through it. To try to firm up the roadbeds around the airfield, the engineers cut down hundreds of small-diameter trees, trimmed off the branches, and laid the trunks across the roads. These rough but solid corduroy roads worked for a time, until the rains grew so heavy that the logs simply floated away. When the mud got so deep that the bombers could not taxi out to the runways, or even move from their parking spaces among the trees, bombing missions had to be canceled. At times there was a foot of standing water on the runways.

On rare occasions when the rains paused long enough for the mud to dry out, the propellers of the bombers threw up such clouds of thick red dust with each takeoff and landing that the grit got sucked into the bombers' engines to create problems for the mechanics, not to mention the visibility problems it created for the pilots.

Just trying to endure life under such conditions was difficult, but the men also had to carry out the strenuous work of maintaining and flying their forty-eight B-24s. Only the strength and resilience of youth can explain how so many of the young men of the 90th were able to endure the hardships of Iron Range.

Lt. James McMurria of the 319th Squadron, the pilot who had been left behind in California because of a fuel leak in his bomber when the second group of 90th planes had left for Hawaii, noted in his diary that the only thing he could find pleasing about Iron Range was the beauty of the jungle birds:

> There are many wild boar, crocodiles and pythons all around us, but to reconcile that fact I have seen some of the most beautiful birds in the world. Their whistles and calls make the place a little more livable.[9]

There were also humans living in these jungles: Australian Aborigines. Of them McMurria wrote:

> Northern Australia is very primitive and the Aborigines are so black they're almost blue. The most surprising thing in the world is to hear one of them open his mouth and speak with an almost Eton accent. The ones with the bushy hair, incidentally, were originally headhunters but are now quite friendly. Nevertheless I have so far avoided the bushy-headed type.[10]

Morale craters

Beautiful birds notwithstanding, the men who took up residence at Iron Range beside the primitive airstrip in the jungle were soon discouraged and disillusioned by the situation in which they found themselves, and the loss of lives that would accompany the Group's first combat missions would only deepen the gloom.

The excitement and glamor of war that many of the young men had imagined they were headed for overseas had failed to materialize. They were far from home and loved ones, in dank, squalid surroundings in one of the most isolated places in the world, enduring every sort of deprivation, with no relief in sight. As their morale sank, they tried to keep up their spirits by spending long hours discussing what they would do when they got back home.

Among the aircrews, another way of bolstering sagging morale was thinking up names to give their bombers, then finding men in the Group with enough artistic talent to paint those names, sometimes with artwork to match, on the sides of their planes.* Some of the names that the crews bestowed on their bombers were "Hellzapoppin," "Little Eva" (named for a huge barmaid in Greenville, South Carolina), "Pride of the Yanks," "8-Ball," "Cowtown's Revenge," "Bombs to Nippon," "The Condor," "50 Cal. Gal," "Dirty Gertie," "Change O'Luck," "Punjab," "Patches," "Big Emma," "Roarin' Rosie," "Pelly-Can," "Aincha Sorry," and "Lady Beverly." Some of these planes were destined to have short lives.

Mail from home, one of the main boosters of morale, arrived rarely and unpredictably in this remote place, adding to the general atmosphere of despondency. In the world we live in today, in which instantaneous worldwide messaging between individuals is taken for granted, it's hard to imagine the world of 1942 when a letter or package from home took weeks to reach a soldier in a war zone, if it ever got to him at all.

Artwork painted on the side of a B-24D of the 90th Bomb Group's 400th Squadron at Iron Range. Everyone at Iron Range was certainly hoping for a change of luck.

On Christmas Eve of 1942, Lt. McMurria finally received some mail from his family and his fiancé back home that they had sent him nearly two months before. He wrote in his diary:

> Today is Christmas Eve and I've just been told by the dentist, Joe Black, that I have a wisdom tooth that is frightening. Don't know why he should be frightened. To compensate for this bad news some mail has just come in. Two letters from Mother and one from Mary Frances, all dated Oct. 28. Mary Frances also sent

---

*The Army Air Corps realized the morale value of allowing fliers to decorate their planes with whimsical names and art, whereas the Navy and Marines did not usually allow airmen to customize their airplanes.

me a leather cigarette case that matches the billfold she sent me in Hawaii. That's my sweetie! Wish I had a picture of her—a big one. Mother's letters were newsy and encouraging. I seem to want to choke up on them a little though.[11]

A few portable wind-up phonographs were in evidence at Iron Range, brought along from the States, and the records were played constantly, the songs a link to the world back home. This was what is today called the Big Band era, and the most popular singers on the records at Iron Range were the Andrews Sisters, Bing Crosby, and a popular black foursome called the Ink Spots, who sang *Someone's Rocking My Dream Boat*, *Just As Though You Were Here*, and *This Is Worth Fighting For*, among other hits. The top instrumental tune at this time was *The Jersey Bounce* by Benny Goodman's band.

There were also radios in some of the squadron tents that could pick up Japanese propaganda broadcasts from Tokyo. McMurria wrote:

> The Tokyo Radio is a scream. Last night they mentioned that they hadn't forgotten about us at Iron Range... After their fantastic news report they always play "Home Sweet Home" sung in Japanese and let some of their prisoners of war speak to their folks back home. They all have to say they were torpedoed by an Allied sub and were picked up by a Japanese vessel. The girl that sings "Home Sweet Home" sounds like an amateur playing a saw. It's very pathetic and I know Steven [sic] Foster would object. I know I do.[12]

The Japanese obviously knew about the Iron Range airbase, though they never bombed it, probably because it was in such an out-of-the-way place, so far from their own airbases, and so difficult for bomber pilots to locate.

The Japanese spy network was extensive, and it was often startling how much they knew. For example, in 1944, after General MacArthur reached the Philippines, he stayed for a time in a private residence in the town of Tacloban on Leyte Island. A Radio Tokyo broadcast reported:

> General MacArthur and his staff and General Kenney have established their headquarters in the Price house, right in the center of the town. Our brave aviators will soon take care of that situation.*[13]

Another broadcast advised a bomber squadron at Port Moresby that the clock in its headquarters tent was ten minutes slow—and it was.

---

*MacArthur dismissed the threat as so much hot air, like most of Radio Tokyo's broadcasts.

Chapter Seven

THE 90ᵀᴴ PREPARES FOR COMBAT

During the second week of November, 1942, as the 90th Bomb Group prepared for its first combat mission, it had been about eleven months since the Japanese had bombed Pearl Harbor to start the war. The Group had only been flying its aircraft for about six months, and it had been a remarkable achievement to create, equip, and field a heavy bomb group in so short a time.

However, the flight crews' lack of experience, plus the exceptional hazards of flying in the Pacific environment, would soon take a heavy toll of the Group's men and aircraft. On top of the normal dangers of flying in this theater would be the difficulties of operating under such primitive conditions as existed at Iron Range. If someone had deliberately set out to find the worst possible place on earth for a new bomb group to begin operations from, he could hardly have made a better choice than Iron Range. But it was from this place, unfortunately, that the young men of the 90th would have to gain their first combat experience.

Deadly risks at Iron Range

Since most of the Japanese targets to be bombed were so far away from Iron Range, and it would often take ten or twelve hours to reach them and return, the bombers would have to take off at night in order to get back to the field and land in daylight.

Aside from the difficulty of even finding the Iron Range airbase at night, it was difficult and dangerous to land on the narrow, jungle-bordered runway in the dark, with 50-foot high trees crowding in all around, and the few small lights that lined the sides of the runways difficult to see. Night approaches would have to be made extremely carefully, and would be hazardous, but nevertheless there would be times when it was necessary for bombers returning from long missions to land at night. This was war, and risks had to be taken.

One pilot remembered that the runway lights (which were strung down both sides of the runway) for night takeoffs and landings were powered by a little generator that often faltered, causing the lights to flicker and dim, and they were none too bright to begin with, especially when obscured by clouds of dust kicked up by the propellers of planes landing or taking off.

Pacific weather: the worst enemy of all

Adding night flying to the typically bad Pacific weather set up challenges for these new and relatively inexperienced pilots that even seasoned airline pilots would have found daunting. Owing to bad weather and darkness, and often both together, the pilots would frequently have to fly blindly (i. e. on instruments alone) for hours at a time, which required sustained concentration by the pilots as well as putting the navigators in doubt as to where exactly they were, since they could not see any landmarks below. When clouds hid the moon and stars, the bombers just seemed to be enveloped by and suspended motionless in a black void.

Throughout the war, the combination of mountains, jungle, wide expanses of ocean, terrible tropical weather, inaccurate charts, and relatively inexperienced pilots and navigators would cause the loss of many aircraft and crews. Most pilots in the Pacific said that the weather, the ocean, and the mountains were their main enemies, not the Japanese.

General Kenney described a typical bombing mission in the Pacific thus:

> **This job calls for night takeoffs with maximum loads and often with crosswinds, climbing [blindly] through overcasts to fifteen and sometimes twenty thousand feet to get on top in order to navigate. It is then normally necessary to come on down to see the target under a ceiling that may range from two thousand to ten thousand feet, pulling back on up [through the overcast] after the attack to navigate home and on arrival... breaking through again to land.**[1]

What he was describing was a lot of blind flying in clouds, relying on instruments alone to maintain altitude and course, sometimes for considerable lengths of time, which even veteran pilots can find challenging. Frequent, violent storms in the Pacific made instrument flying even more difficult by tossing the airplanes around, sometimes tumbling the gyroscopes in the instruments, rendering them useless and disorienting the pilots.

A pilot flying blind must trust his instruments implicitly, staking his life on their accuracy, since vertigo caused by sensations of the inner ear can make it seem as though an airplane is going through all sorts of maneuvers when in fact it is flying straight and level. Disbelieving his instruments and responding to these false feelings can be fatal to a pilot and his crew, and this was likely often the case for these new B-24 pilots in Pacific storms.

As Gen. Kenney described, a bomber pilot often had to descend blindly through cloud layers over his target, or what his navigator believed to be the target area, not knowing where the bottom of the overcast was, nor whether the clouds extended all the way to the sea or ground. If the cloud or fog did go all the way to the surface, a descending bomber could crash into the ocean, the jungle, or smash against the side of some remote, uncharted mountain, and many planes did in fact end up that way, never to be heard from again.

All this blind flying made things equally tough and sometimes impossible for the navigators. Navigating an aircraft as it was done in WWII depended on knowing where you were at least part of the time, but blind flying in clouds and darkness for hours on end could turn a navigator's job into more guesswork than calculation. Winds that either sped up or slowed down the aircraft's groundspeed, as well as blowing it far off course, could go undetected during long bouts of instrument flying. Add inaccurate charts of vast areas of unfamiliar terrain and you have some of the reasons why so many planes took off on missions never to be seen again.

Sink or swim

The 90th's new pilots would gain their experience the hard way, and would either survive, along with their crews, or not. The non-pilot crewmen, as Charles Lindbergh had noted, were mostly just helpless passengers, their fates entirely dependent on the skill and judgment of their pilots.

As one historian of the 90th Bomb Group described the dilemma of these young Americans:

> [They were], in retrospect, green kids with only the haziest conception of the hard realities of modern aerial warfare, or of the primitive, demanding conditions under which they would ply their trade. In fact, their Stateside training had scarcely begun to equip them with the skills and discipline which they would require to survive and effectively carry the war to the enemy. It was one thing to take off and land from a long, concrete runway at Barksdale, Greenville, or Willow Run; to navigate across the well-charted, familiar and relatively tame surface of the United States; and to blaze away at sedately moving target sleeves or even at skeet targets. It was quite another to lift a heavily laden B-24 from a narrow, darkened strip lined with gum trees; to fly hundreds of miles across featureless expanses of ocean and between the peaks of towering mountains; to be mercilessly thrown about in massive tropical storms; and to bomb a target defended by flak and scores of fighters which hurtled and twisted in from all directions, pouring forth lethal streams of machine-gun and cannon fire. It was enough to make corpses, or seasoned veterans (or both) out of very young men in a very short while.[2]

7. THE 90TH PREPARES FOR COMBAT

The early missions of the 90th would also be characterized by only minimal knowledge of the targets to be bombed and the weather conditions en route. One member of the Group wrote later:

> [At this time] the 90th Bomb Group was operating when the only requisites for a bombing mission were an airplane that had a good chance of getting off the ground with sufficient gasoline and a load of bombs with which to strike the target. Briefing consisted of handing the pilot and navigator a map, which was often inaccurate . . . and wishing them luck. Information about the possible target was [often] nonexistent. . . Weather data could be found only one way, by going up and trying to get through it.[3]

All these problems were recipes for disaster, and as we shall see, the 90th Bomb Group would suffer many losses during its operations in the Southwest Pacific. Over 800 men would die before the war ended.

The 90th's first combat mission, in the middle of November, 1942, would provide the young men with a taste of things to come.

B-24s of the 90th Bomb Group parked on a dirt taxiway at Iron Range, Australia. When they start their engines they'll be enveloped in the same kind of dust cloud that the jeep is kicking up at right, but at least on this day they won't be stuck in the mud, as so often happened during the incessant rains.

Chapter Eight

THE 90ᵀᴴ BOMB GROUP'S FIRST COMBAT MISSION

The 90th's first combat mission was flown on Nov. 15, 1942, and the assignment was to attack a concentration of Japanese shipping that had been spotted by aerial reconnaissance in the Buin-Faisi anchorage on the southern tip of Bougainville Island, 925 miles to the northeast of Iron Range (Map 8-1, opposite). Nine bombers from the 319th and 320th Squadrons were assigned to the strike. Because of the long distance to the target, they would have auxiliary fuel tanks installed in their forward bomb bays, leaving only the rear bays for bombs and effectively cutting their bomb-carrying capacity in half. However, they would still be able to carry 4,000 pounds of bombs in the rear bay, in this case four 1,000-pounders, each one capable of sinking a ship if it hit it in the right place.

General Kenney had decided that until the 90th Bomb Group gained some combat experience, all of its targets would be bombed at night to give them cover from defending Japanese fighter planes and antiaircraft gunners. But in this case, since the enemy ships that were being targeted would also have been invisible to the bombers at night, it was planned for them to arrive over the area in the twilight before dawn, when they would be able to spot and bomb the ships, but still be able to escape before it was fully light.*

Since the target was so far away from Iron Range, the mission would be staged through Port Moresby, 350 miles away, across the Coral Sea. The nine bombers would land there, take aboard the bombs and top up their fuel tanks, then take off again during the night at exactly the right time (it was hoped) to arrive over Bougainville just before sunup.

On the afternoon of 14 November 1942 the bombers took off from Iron Range with the 90th Bomb Group's commander, Col. Art Meehan, leading the way in a bomber piloted by Maj. Harry Bullis, with Meehan flying as the co-pilot. The planes flew across the Coral Sea, landed at Port Moresby's Jackson Field, and waited there until after midnight while their gas tanks were topped up, four 1,000-pound bombs were loaded into each plane's bomb bay, and the crews attended a briefing on the upcoming mission. The fatherly and experi-

---

*Bombing raids could also be successfully conducted by the light of a full or near-full moon, but apparently there was no such moon at the time of this mission.

8. THE 90TH'S FIRST COMBAT MISSION

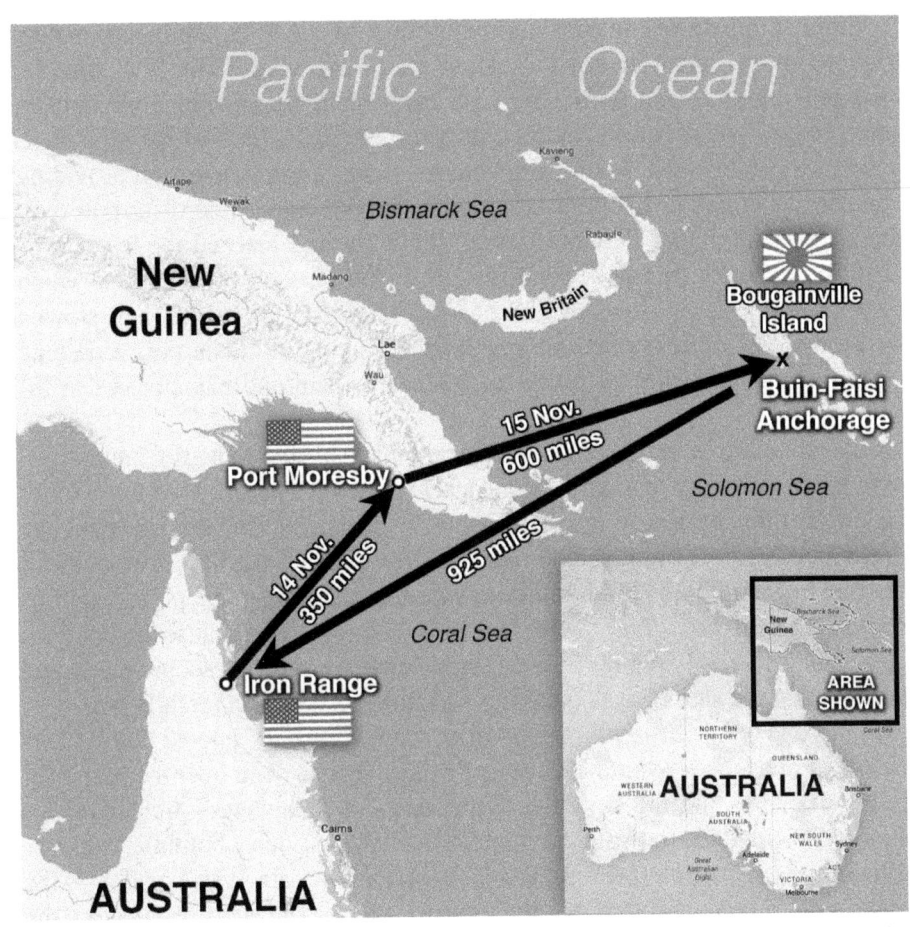

Map 8-1. The 90th Bomb Group's first combat mission, on Nov. 15, 1942, was a strike against Japanese shipping in the Buin-Faisi anchorage of Bougainville Island. The mission was staged through Port Moresby, as shown, but the return was direct to Iron Range, 925 miles.

enced* Col. Meehan projected a reassuring aura of competence, which had a calming effect on his novice crews, as he had intended; nevertheless a strong undercurrent of excitement and anticipation gripped the young airmen under his command, mixed with a certain amount of gut-wrenching fear of the unknown. This first combat mission would be the real-world life-or-death event that they had all been thinking about since the beginning of their flight training in the States, and no one knew what to expect. If it turned out that their B-24s really could not defend themselves against any Japanese fighter planes they might encounter, this could easily be their first and last combat mission.

---

*Col. Meehan had been awarded the Distinguished Flying Cross for a 2,300-mile (round-trip) strike against the Japanese on Wake Island in June of 1942, flying from Midway Island.

In the darkness of the early morning hours of the 15th, the nine bombers took off from Port Moresby's Jackson Field and headed for Bougainville, now 600 miles to the northeast, with each plane proceeding individually, since no sort of formation could be flown in the dark. Each of the nine navigators was on his own, studying his charts, plotting his course, and providing compass headings to his pilot along with the estimated time of arrival over the target. The planes flew on through the night and reached the target area at different times, most of them, as it transpired, well after sunrise when they could easily be seen by the enemy. They had probably been slowed by headwinds. They spotted several Japanese ships in the harbor, and some patrolling Japanese fighter planes also spotted them and maneuvered to intercept.

Each bomber pilot picked out a ship and made his bombing run on it, dropping his four bombs "entrain," or one after the other. The ships were at anchor and were thus stationary targets, unable to maneuver, but the inexperience of the bombardiers on their first real bombing runs was on full display as all but one of their bombs fell harmlessly into the sea; in fact one plane's bombs missed the ship they were intended for by over two miles, because the bombardier had accidentally put his bombsight's viewfinder into telescopic mode and thought that the ship he was bombing was much closer than it really was.

Only one bomb, dropped by a bomber named "8-Ball," piloted by Lt. Clarence A. Eckert, was seen to hit a ship. "8-Ball" had arrived over the harbor in full daylight to find the sky filled with Japanese floatplanes—fighter planes equipped with floats for water landings. Eckert made a quick bombing run over a Japanese cruiser at 8,000 feet, and his bombardier's aim was excellent—the plane's tail gunner reported that the first two bombs fell short of the ship, the third one fell on the deck, and the fourth fell into the water just beyond it.

A ship hit squarely by a one-thousand pound bomb may well have sunk, but Lt. Eckert didn't hang around to witness the outcome. The instant his bombs were gone he was diving away toward the sea to protect what he considered his plane's most vulnerable spot—its belly—from the enemy fighter planes that were suddenly swarming all around him. Like most of the other inexperienced bomber pilots, Eckert felt that his B-24, having no belly turret, had no defense against fighter planes attacking from below (and there was some validity to this view in the case of a lone bomber, flying as he was without the cover of other planes in a formation). Eckert figured that if he flew his bomber down close enough to the sea, no fighter plane would have the room to get underneath him.

During the dive, fighter planes came at "8-Ball" from several directions with their guns blazing, but one of them was taken under fire from more than one of the bomber's gunners, burst into flames, and went down, the first fighter

8. THE 90TH'S FIRST COMBAT MISSION

plane kill for the 90th Bomb Group in the war, and a great reassurance to those who had worried that B-24s would prove easy meat for enemy fighters.[1]

All nine of the bombers on the mission managed to drop their bombs and get away from the target area, some of them after taking battle damage from the bullets of the fighter planes or antiaircraft fire from the ships. Eight of the nine bombers made it back to Australia, but one B-24 had sustained too much damage to make it home. This one was named "Lady Beverly,"* a bomber of the 319th Squadron flown by 1st Lt. John H. Werner.

Werner had picked out a Japanese ship to drop his bombs on but found it necessary to make two passes over it, because his bombs failed to release on the first run. Bomb rack trouble would plague B-24s throughout the war, and in this case it ended up causing the loss of the plane and the lives of most of its crewmen by making a second bombing run necessary. The Japanese warship had been caught by surprise on the first pass and had not put up any defensive fire at all, but on the second run, with the bomber flying at only 6,000 feet, its antiaircraft gunners were fully alerted and firing everything they had.

Like most navy antiaircraft gunners, either Japanese or American (as opposed to the ground-based gunners of either army, who generally received less training), they were deadly shots, and at 6,000 feet "Lady Beverly" was not a difficult target to hit (as the war went on, American bombers learned to bomb ships from at least 9,000 feet, and preferably higher, anything lower than that being considered too dangerous).

"Lady Beverly's" bombs released on the second try, but by that time the bomber was taking hits all over from antiaircraft shells bursting near it, and in all the excitement of their first experience under fire, distracted by the loud airbursts all around them, no crewman noticed where the plane's bombs fell. At least the fighter planes had failed to spot "Lady Beverly," or else were too busy chasing the other bombers, for the plane was not attacked from the air. After he had flown out of range of the ship's guns, Lt. Werner took stock of the damage to his bomber and realized that the situation was serious.

In fact it would prove fatal. No member of the crew was hurt, but fuel was leaking from holes in the auxiliary gas tank in the bomb bay, and the explosive fumes were filling up the airplane. Werner reopened the bomb bay doors to try to suck the liquid gas and vapors out into the slipstream. The two engines on the right wing were damaged so badly that they both soon quit, one after the other, leaving only the two left engines running. Werner and his copilot, 2nd Lt. Edward J. Devine, then had to deal with the asymmetrical thrust.† Only one

---

* Wiley O. Woods, historian of the 90th Bomb Group, recorded the airplane's name as "Miss Beverly" rather than "Lady Beverly."

† With only the two left engines pulling, the plane would tend to veer to the right, and only by strenuous manipulation of the flight controls could the pilots counteract this.

of the two big propellers on the dead engines could be feathered (turned edge-on to the airstream to reduce air drag); the other one dragged in the wind and made handling the plane even more difficult.

Lt. Werner steered a course for Milne Bay, at the extreme east or tail end of the buzzard-shaped island of New Guinea (see Map 8-2 on page 76), the nearest place that had an allied-held airfield where he might be able to land, and about the only place in New Guinea besides Port Moresby that wasn't under Japanese control.* As the plane struggled along on its two left engines only, fighting the air drag caused by the open bomb bay and the unfeathered propeller, it was slowly but steadily losing altitude. "Lady Beverly's" bad luck continued when the area around Milne Bay was found to be shrouded in clouds so that the airfield could not be seen.

Lt. Werner's next hope was to make Port Moresby, and he crossed over the narrow neck of land separating the north and south coasts of New Guinea at this location and started up the southern coastline for Moresby. By this time the crippled bomber had been flying for over three hours and had covered an amazing 500 miles on just two engines. It was eight o'clock in the morning, and they were still 175 miles from Port Moresby when Lt. Werner realized that his plane was losing altitude at such a rate that it was not going to be able to continue much farther. They were not going to make Moresby.

With this grim fact evident, Werner polled his crew over the intercom: would they prefer to bail out over the New Guinea jungle, or (since the beach along the coastline was too narrow to set a plane down on) ditch the plane in the sea just offshore? They chose to ditch, and by this time the plane may have been too low for anyone to jump safely anyway. The radio operator, S/Sgt. William Gregory, sent a message out to Port Moresby giving their approximate location and predicament. Then the bomb bay doors were closed to prevent an inrush of water, and everyone braced for a landing in the sea.

Lining up parallel with the ocean swells, Werner set the plane down on the water about a half mile offshore, but it bounced, slammed into a tall wave with a terrific jolt, and, as B-24s tended to do in water landings, broke apart (just as Lt. Davis' plane had done in San Francisco Bay two months before). The broken plane sank so fast that not a single member of the crew was able to escape before it went under.

After a minute, only two men surfaced amidst all the floating debris and burning fuel on the water: 2nd Lt. Walter C. Seidel and S/Sgt. Albert L. But-

---

*The Japanese had tried to seize the Milne Bay airfields earlier in the year, landing a battalion-sized force along with two tanks on Aug. 25, 1942, but they were beaten off by the mostly Australian garrison (with some Americans) defending the fields. The Japanese withdrew after heavy casualties on Sept. 7, and the Battle of Milne Bay was the first decisive defeat for the Japanese army in the Pacific war, followed shortly thereafter by the Battle of the Kokoda Trail, which ended in another disaster for Japan.

8. THE 90TH'S FIRST COMBAT MISSION

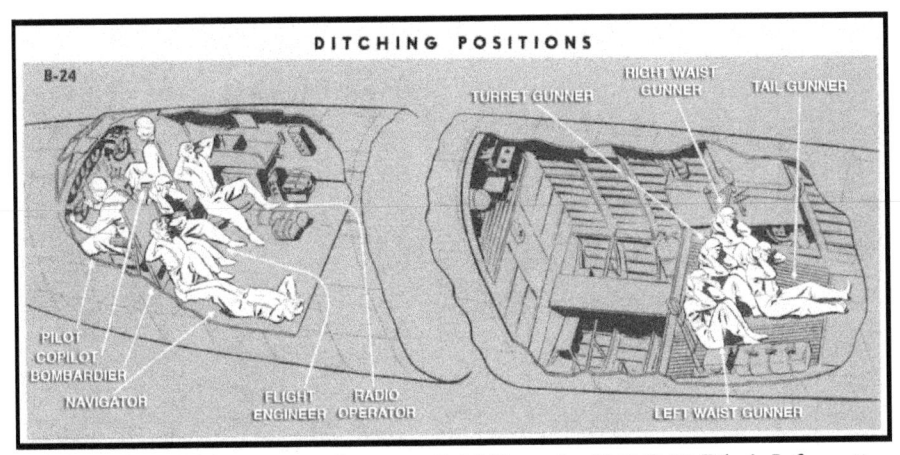

Ditching positions for crewmembers in a B-24 (from the 1943 B-24 Pilot's Information Manual). Only the pilots had seats to strap into; everyone else had to brace against some part of the aircraft's structure such as a bulkhead.

terfield. The other eight men, including Lt. Werner, had been unable to free themselves from the wreckage before they drowned. Those who died were:

> 1st Lt. John H. Werner (from Wisconsin)
> 2nd Lt. Edward J. Devine (from California)
> 1st Lt. Edward J. Walpole (from Illinois)
> S/Sgt. William B. Gregory (from California)
> Cpl. John J. Glenn (home state not listed)
> Cpl. Harold L. Williams (from Nebraska)
> Cpl. Raymond J. Slazas (from Pennsylvania)
> Pvt. Claude J. Semler (from Iowa)

The two survivors were soon rescued by natives who had seen the crash and paddled out from shore in canoes to pick them up. The bodies of two more of the crew, Lt. Devine and Cpl. Glenn, washed ashore the next day and were buried by the natives.

Their radio message had been heard, however, and Lt. Seidel and Sgt. Butterfield were rescued by a boat that took them up to Port Moresby, where they reported what had happened. The wreckage of the plane, possibly still containing the remains of John Werner and six other crewmen, lies today on the sea floor in fairly shallow water near tiny Baibara Island, just offshore from the New Guinea mainland* (see Map 8-2, next page).

Another of the bombers on this first mission was named "The Condor," piloted by Capt. Dale J. Thornhill. After he dropped his bombs (with no hits),

---
* In 2005 the wreckage of "Lady Beverly" was reported by a helicopter pilot to be lying on the sea floor near Baibara Island, but it has not been investigated as of this writing (2018).[2]

Map 8-2. The remains of Lt. Werner and six men of his crew lie today on the sea bottom off the south coast of New Guinea in the wreckage of their bomber "Lady Beverly."

Thornhill set a course back to Iron Range, since he knew he had enough fuel left to make the Australian base. However, as he neared the Australian coastline, he ran into the B-24 bugaboo of stuck fuel tank valves, and was unable to transfer fuel from his bomb bay tank to the engines. There was still a chance he could make it to the airfield, but he knew it was going to be a near thing. The plane was within sight of Iron Range, but still over the water, when the wing tanks ran dry and all four engines quit. Thornhill managed to land the bomber wheels-up on the beach, intact, with no fatalities and only one man injured (with a wrenched back), but "The Condor" would never fly again.

In the days that followed, mechanics from Iron Range drove to the crash site in trucks and stripped "The Condor" of its engines and all other useful parts, leaving it an empty hulk on the beach, where it still sits today, although now mostly under sand.[3]

8. THE 90TH'S FIRST COMBAT MISSION

The remaining seven bombers on the mission made it safely back to Iron Range, where everyone examined the bullet and flak holes in the bombers with great interest, having never before seen any battle damage. The ground crews then set about making repairs.

This first bombing mission thus cost the 90th Bomb Group two bombers and eight men killed, in exchange for negligible damage done to the enemy.[4] The eight men of the Werner crew who were killed in the ditching of their bomber were the 90th's first battle deaths, and their loss sent a message to all the young men of the Group that this war was a deadly serious business, without any of the romance and glamour that many had imagined when they had first joined the Air Corps.

Lt. McMurria, the young pilot who had been admiring the colorful birds in the jungle around Iron Range, was particularly hard hit by the loss of his good friend Eddie Devine, the copilot of Werner's crew. McMurria could scarcely believe that his high-spirited friend, who'd always shown such a zest for life, was gone. He wrote in his diary:

> Just heard, but refuse to believe, that only two of Werner's crew got out alive. They say Eddie Devine is buried on the beach near Bougainville Island. [Actually his body had washed ashore on the New Guinea coast near Baibara Island.] It just can't be. Seems like he ought to be bringing us watermelon or a keg of beer or something right now. I'm not going to say anything about Eddie. There's too much to say because there was so much to him. He was all heart.[5]

The casualties of the Werner crew were shortly afterward declared officially dead, and back in the States their families received the dreaded telegrams from the War Department informing them that their loved ones had been killed in action. Their grief would be repeated in the homes of over a hundred thousand other families of American men killed in the Pacific during the four years it took to rid the world of the obscene scourge on humanity known as Imperial Japan.

"The Condor" shortly after its crash-landing on a remote Australian beach, 15 November 1942. It lies there still.

Chapter Nine

THE 90ᵀᴴ'S SECOND COMBAT MISSION: RABAUL

The Group's second combat mission was carried out the day after the first one, or rather the night—the night of 16-17 November 1942. This time fourteen of the Group's bombers would participate in the strike, and the result would be more tragic loss of life, once again with little damage done to the Japanese. It was a strike against the big Japanese stronghold of Rabaul* on the north end of the island of New Britain, 850 miles northeast of Iron Range (Map 9-1, opposite).

Rabaul was originally a German colonial town, described as a tropical paradise in the early 1900s, a German-neat little settlement filled with elegant homes, a hospital, shops, shade trees, and flower gardens. After Germany's defeat in World War I, Rabaul came under Australian rule, and the Germans were largely replaced by Australians, but the town's character changed little.

The settlement boasted a movie house, a golf course, a cricket field, a baseball diamond, a concrete swimming pool, and an airfield visited by a weekly mail plane from Australia. It had an ice-making and cold storage plant, a library, pubs, social clubs, a gas station for motorists, and a printing office. By the late 1930s the town contained about 800 Europeans and a thousand or so Orientals, mostly Chinese who ran small shops and a few swank hotels. There were also about three thousand native islanders living on the outskirts of town, many of them employed by the townspeople for menial tasks.

In the 1920s Rabaul's pubs were frequented by a young adventurer from Australia by the name of Errol Flynn,† when he wasn't prospecting in the goldfields of New Guinea. The town was (and still is) surrounded by active volcanoes, and it overlooks a large deepwater anchorage known as Simpson Harbor (which is actually the water-filled crater of an ancient volcano). Trading

---

* "Rabaul" means "place of the mangroves" in one of the local languages.

† After Flynn migrated to England and then America in pursuit of an acting career, he became the swashbuckling star of many Hollywood adventure films, including *Captain Blood, The Adventures of Robin Hood, The Charge of the Light Brigade,* and he was the heartthrob of millions of female moviegoers. Flynn was born in Tasmania, an island state of Australia. Despite his many athletic movie roles, Flynn was declared physically unfit for service in WWII.

9. SECOND COMBAT MISSION: RABAUL

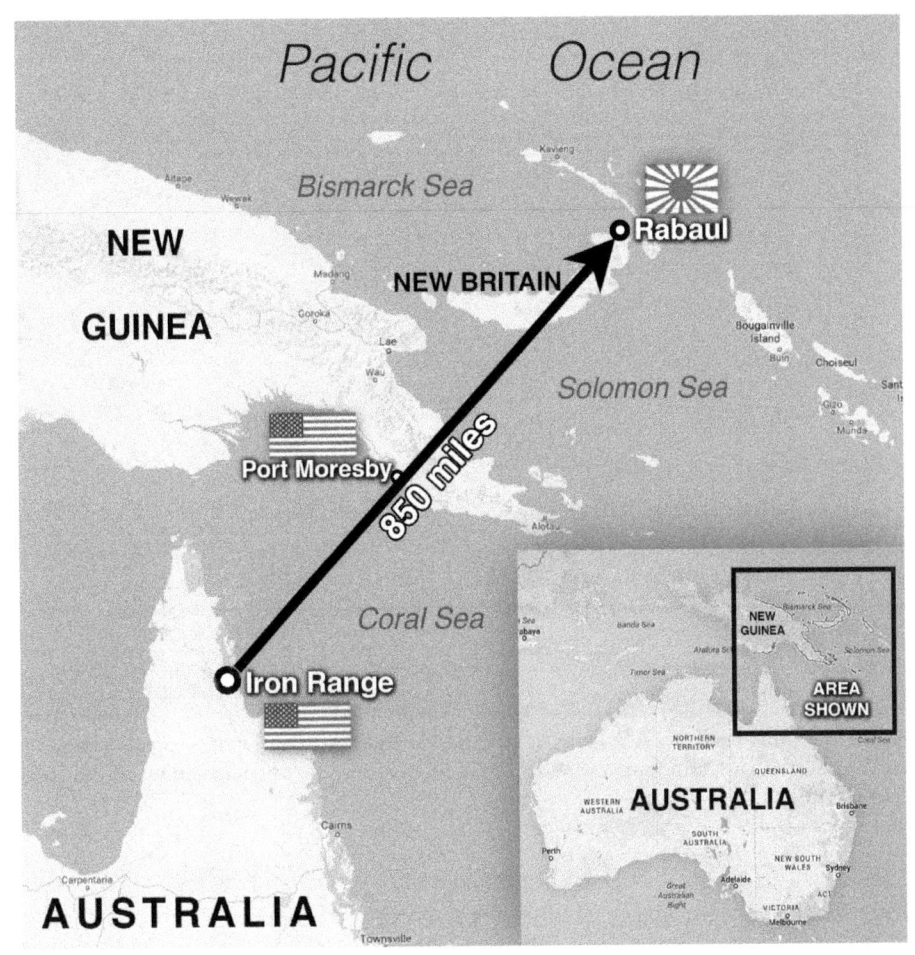

Map 9-1. The second combat mission of the 90th Bomb Group, on the night of 16-17 November, 1942, was a strike against the Japanese stronghold of Rabaul, 850 miles northeast of Iron Range on the northern tip of New Britain Island.

companies had constructed several wharves, piers, and warehouses around the harbor to benefit the local plantation owners and dealers in trade goods.[1]

After the invading Japanese, attracted by the fine deepwater harbor, captured this orderly and cosmopolitan town at the beginning of 1942, they developed it into a powerful military base, the hub of Japanese power in the Southwest Pacific. Over 100,000 Japanese troops were shipped in and stationed there, and Simpson Harbor was often filled with Japanese warships, troopships, and freighters.

The Japanese built additional piers and installed floating cranes to load and unload ships. The once-picturesque town was soon submerged in Oriental

Aerial view of Rabaul, New Britain, in 1942 beside Simpson Bay. Japanese installations in and around Rabaul, and Japanese ships in the harbor, became frequent targets of the 90th Bomb Group.

military squalor, built over with ramshackle barracks and storage sheds, with an official army brothel staffed by slave women kidnapped from other parts of the new Japanese Empire, and a brutal prisoner-of-war camp where Allied prisoners were starved, tortured, beaten, and worked to death. The Japanese established five airfields around Rabaul, widely dispersed and with enough revetments to accommodate over four hundred aircraft.

Flashback: the Japanese invasion of Rabaul and subsequent war crimes

Rabaul was invaded by the Japanese on January 23, 1942, when they killed, captured, or drove into the jungle the 1,400 men of the Australian 22nd Battalion (known as Lark Force) that were stationed there and had tried to defend the town. Japanese fighter planes easily shot down the few hopelessly obsolete Australian air force airplanes based on the town's airfield. Like the American defenders of the Philippines, to whom America had been unable to send any aid, the vastly outnumbered and outgunned Australians at Rabaul had resisted the Japanese to the best of their ability without hope of assistance from Australia. The Australian commander of Rabaul's pathetic little air force, as he was on the verge of being overwhelmed by Japanese bombers and fighters, had

9. SECOND COMBAT MISSION: RABAUL

Gen. George Kenney, head of the 5th Air Force, studies a model of the Japanese stronghold of Rabaul and its harbor.

radioed to Port Moresby the words of the ancient Roman gladiators: "We who are about to die salute you."

After losing the lopsided battle to the Japanese invaders, groups of surviving Australian soldiers and civilians fled into the jungles of New Britain, into some of the most rugged terrain in the world, hoping to find ways to escape the island and reach Australia or Port Moresby. Very few succeeded in getting away or being rescued. In their desperate flight they had to cope with all the usual dangers of the jungle plus exhaustion and starvation. In the end only a few managed to escape in small boats. Most of the fugitives either died in the jungle or were captured by the Japanese patrols that pursued them.

On February 4, 1942, a group of 160 ragged and exhausted Australian soldiers found themselves surrounded by a large Japanese force at a place called Tol Plantation. After the Japanese commander assured them that they would be treated humanely as prisoners of war, the Australians surrendered.

Surrendering to the Japanese in WWII was always a very bad move, and this case was no exception. After the Australians had laid down their arms, the loathsome troops of Imperial Japan behaved as they always did toward enemies of their emperor, especially white men. In truth the Japanese had no concept of prisoners of war, and only kept prisoners alive if they could be useful for some purpose. As one historian put it, "The concept of surrender was so alien to the Japanese that they treated their own captives with absolute contempt. A man who willingly capitulated was as good as dead. . . [The Japanese] deeply loathed Caucasians but abhorred the concept of surrender even more."[2]

Site of the Tol Plantation Massacre, photographed after the war (Australian War Memorial photo).

Disregarding their pledge to take the Australians prisoner, the Japanese trussed the men together in groups and then tortured, bayoneted, beheaded, and shot them to death in cold blood. A few badly wounded Australians managed to survive by feigning death amid the piles of their murdered comrades. After the Japanese left, the survivors slipped away into the jungle and lived to tell the tale of what became known as the Tol Plantation Massacre, one of many similar slaughters of helpless groups of people that the Japanese carried out throughout the Pacific, throughout the war. Two of the men who escaped were captured again later by the Japanese and sadistically burned alive by being smeared with pig grease and set afire.*

Parties of Japanese troops were also sent out from Rabaul to arrest any white plantation owners and their families on New Britain who had been foolish enough to remain at their homes when the Japanese invaded. One such family, that of Ted Harvey and his wife Marjorie, with their 11-year-old son Richard, were taken to Rabaul, then transported to a site outside town near the town dump, at the foot of one of the volcanoes, where they were stood before a ditch that would become their grave.

Holding hands, the father and mother, with their little boy between them, were then shot dead by a Japanese firing squad. Such murders at this particular site near Rabaul, of both civilians and Allied prisoners, would be repeated many times during the war. It was an out-of-the-way location where there were no witnesses to Japanese war crimes and the soft volcanic ash made it easy to dig graves.[3]

11-year-old Richard Harvey was shot to death along with his parents by a Japanese firing squad at Rabaul on June 5, 1942.

The Japanese reign of terror on New Britain would continue to the end of the war, since the island ended up being bypassed by the Americans as they advanced toward Japan, and Rabaul remained in Japanese hands until their emperor surrendered in the summer of 1945.

General MacArthur realized that it would be necessary to neutralize Rabaul, however, before American forces could move past it toward Japan. He was committed to bypassing Japanese strongholds wherever possible, but an enemy force as large as the one at Rabaul could not safely be left in his rear until it had been rendered incapable of interfering with Allied activities. General Kenney intended to simply bomb the place into submission, and had been hitting it with

---

*The Australian government, ashamed that it had not made a greater effort to rescue its troops and other refugees after the fall of Rabaul, suppressed public knowledge of the Tol Plantation Massacre until 1988, 46 years after it occurred. In 2015 there were calls to the government by relatives of the dead to find and identify the bodies of family members who still lay unburied in the jungle where they fell that day, and to set up a memorial in their memory. A small stone marker now marks the spot of the massacre.

the 19th and 43rd Heavy Bomb Groups before the 90th arrived from America. Now that the 19th had returned to America, the 90th would shoulder the task.

The 90th's turn in the lion's den

Rabaul was a difficult and dangerous target for bombers, especially at this stage of the war, when its defenses were at full strength. There were often over 300 Japanese aircraft based on Rabaul's five airfields, many of them fighter planes, and the town and harbor were ringed with 360 antiaircraft guns, supplemented by the guns of whatever warships happened to be in the harbor during an attack. Therefore this second bombing mission of the 90th Bomb Group was scheduled to take place under cover of darkness, between 3:55 and 6 AM on November 17 [1942]. The reasoning was that even if Rabaul was largely invisible in the dark, the place was so thick with military targets that any bombs dropped on the town were likely to hit something of value to the Japanese. Sunrise would occur during the return trip, and then the bombers would be able to navigate home to land at Iron Range in daylight.

To reach Rabaul, the bombers once again had to fly the 350 miles across the Coral Sea to the south coast of New Guinea, then 100 more miles across the rugged, 13,000-foot-high Owen Stanley Mountains to the north coast of the island, then 210 miles across the Solomon Sea to the island of New Britain, and finally another 190 miles up the full length of that island to where Rabaul sits at its northern tip, 850 miles in all, as shown on Map 9-1 (page 79). All this distance would be flown in darkness and the usual bad tropical weather, a daunting challenge to the Group's navigators. Since the bombers would not be able to see each other in the dark, no sort of formation could be flown, and again each plane would fly and bomb on its own. Strict radio silence would be observed, since the Japanese monitored the radio channels.

Given the conditions, and the inexperience of the pilots and navigators, it's not surprising that multiple misfortunes attended the Group's second combat mission. The fourteen B-24s assigned to the strike were scheduled to begin taking off from Iron Range at 11 PM on the 16th, each plane carrying eight 500-pound bombs to drop on Rabaul's airfields, harbor facilities, or any ships that they might be able to spot in the harbor (and as before, this was only half a bomb load, the rest of the weight being taken up by auxiliary gas tanks in the bomb bays). There would be no stop at Port Moresby this time—the route would be direct to the target and back, a total of 1,700 miles. Once again Col. Art Meehan, the Group's commander, led the way, flying as copilot in the first plane to take off, a bomber named "Punjab." The pilot was Maj. Raymond S. Morse, commander of the Group's 320th Squadron. "Punjab" lifted off of Iron Range's main dirt runway just before midnight and set course for Rabaul.

No order, rule or tradition demanded that a group commander fly missions, but the 38-year-old Meehan believed in leading from the front, and setting an example to his young pilots to help them gain confidence and experience. As mentioned in the last chapter, he himself had already earned the Distinguished Flying Cross five months earlier in June of 1942, when he volunteered to fly the longest overwater bombing mission ever flown up to that time: 1,190 miles from Midway Island to bomb Japanese Installations on Wake Island. On that occasion he had flown an earlier version of the B-24, the LB-30. He thus had considerable experience with the B-24, and he wanted to pass it on to his cubs personally. Although there would be no communication between bombers during the outbound phase of the mission, due to radio silence, Meehan planned to discuss the lessons learned during the strike in a debriefing to be held the next day.

But it was not to be. After Meehan's plane took off and faded into the night, it was never seen or heard from again. It was the first of the group's bombers to vanish utterly, and there would be many more before the end of the war. Somewhere along the 850 miles between Iron Range and Rabaul, some fatal crisis must have arisen in the bomber "Punjab," or it may have simply run into a mountain in the dark or been destroyed in a storm. Its wreckage may lie today in some remote corner of the Owen Stanley Mountains, where it might yet be found, or it may rest somewhere in the depths of the Pacific Ocean, where it will likely never be found. Unless the wreckage of the airplane is someday discovered, no one will ever have a clue as to what happened to Col. Meehan and his crew on that fateful night.

This mission thus brought an end to the illustrious and promising military career of Col. Art W. Meehan. His wife Lucy and their two little girls would never know what happened to their husband and father, nor would the families of the nine other men aboard the plane ever know where or how their men met their fate.* The other crewmen were:

> Maj. Raymond S. Morse, from Oklahoma
> 1st Lt. Wallace S. Sorensen, from Indiana
> 1st Lt. John K. Booroojy, from New Jersey
> 1st Lt. Robert I. Kinsella, from Texas
> S/Sgt. William J. Whiteman, from Oklahoma
> Sgt. Vico W. Jordan, from Illinois
> Sgt. Jimmie M. Nayfa, from Oklahoma
> Cpl. Albert J. Pyron, from Washington, DC
> Cpl. Forest C. Schooler, from Ohio

The loss of Meehan and his crew would not be the only tragedy attending this mission. The runway at Iron Range was dry that night as the bombers lined

---

* In 1947 Lucy Meehan was presented with the Purple Heart medal from President Truman in memory of her husband, along with a personal letter of condolence.

up to take off, and the propellers of Col. Meehan's B-24, with its engines at full throttle, kicked up a terrific dust storm during its takeoff run, blinding all the bombers behind it. Meehan had used his landing lights to see down the runway and stay aligned with it as he took off, but the planes behind him found that their lights revealed only swirling clouds of dust. The small perimeter lights strung down both sides of the runway were too widely spaced, too dim, and now too obscured by the dust to be seen.

Murphy's Law, which decrees that everything that can go wrong will go wrong, seemed to be in full effect during the takeoff phase of this second mission. There was no ground controller directing the bombers, some of the pilots were not ready to go when it was their turn to take off, others didn't want to start blindly into the dust cloud, no one seemed to be sure where his place in the line was, and in short, mass confusion reigned in the dark on the airfield.

Lt. Leroy C. Iverson, the pilot of a plane named "Big Emma," discovered when he got ready to taxi that he couldn't close his bomb bay doors. It was found that the auxiliary gas tank in the front bomb bay was interfering with one of the doors and had jammed it. "Big Emma" was therefore scratched from the mission and never left the parking area. Iverson and his crew climbed back out of their airplane and stood beside it to watch the other planes take off. Since there were no revetments in the jungle for the planes to park in, "Big Emma" and all the other bombers that were not assigned to this mission were lined up along the sides of the runway, an additional hazard to the planes taking off.

After Col. Meehan's bomber took off, the pilot of the second plane in line had to wait fourteen minutes before the dust settled down enough for him to see the runway lights. His takeoff was successful, but his propeller wash once again enveloped the airfield in boiling clouds of dust. It was obvious that if a quarter of an hour were to elapse between all takeoffs it would require hours for the twelve remaining bombers to get into the air, and they'd end up bombing Rabaul in broad daylight. The planes would just have to risk taking off at closer intervals under the low-visibility conditions. The pilots would have to trust their compasses to stay aligned with the runway and hope for glimpses of the faintly visible runway lights as they made their takeoff runs.*

Eight planes following the first two managed to get up in the air successfully this way, but luck ran out for the ninth, a bomber named "Bombs To Nippon" of the 400th Squadron, piloted by Lt. Paul R. Larson. As Larson started his takeoff run under the near-blind conditions, he must have become disoriented, for his bomber did not go straight down the runway but angled off toward a line of parked bombers. One of these was "Big Emma" with her

---

* Pilots in England were taking off this way in fog, with the pilot closely watching his compass while the copilot kept his head in the plexiglass bubble in the window beside his seat, watching for the runway lights and calling out corrections to the pilot as he saw them.[6]

stuck bomb bay door, and Lt. Iverson and his crew standing beside her. With disbelief at first, and then horror, the Iverson crew saw Lt. Larson's plane become misaligned with the runway and begin turning toward them, with all four engines bellowing at full takeoff power. Realizing what was about to happen, they dashed madly into the jungle to get clear of the crash—one man ran into a small tree so hard that he tore it out by the roots.

Lt. Larson's bomber only grazed "Big Emma," its right wing wiping off the navigator's glass dome and pitot tubes, but then the fully loaded, 35-ton bomber plowed through the noses of three other bombers parked beside "Emma." Sgt. Claude D. Red, who had been assigned to guard the parked bombers and was sitting on the wing of one of them, couldn't get out of the way fast enough and was struck and killed by Lt. Larson's bomber as it careened past. Sgt. Red had reported for duty with the 90th Bomb Group only that afternoon, and thus had been with the Group for only a few hours before he was killed.[4]

Another aircrewman who was not assigned to fly that night was sitting inside one of the parked bombers on the navigator's table, idly dangling his shoes on the ends of his toes, when one of the huge propellers of Larson's plane sliced through the fuselage and batted one of the shoes away. The shocked man scrambled to the rear of the plane and escaped injury.[5]

After crashing through the parked bombers, Larson's plane exploded, its thousands of gallons of aviation fuel turning the flames into an inferno that lit up the night like the fires of hell, with the flames reflecting off the thick, churning dust. Because of the intense heat no one could get near the wreckage to try to save the crew. The only survivor of the crash was Capt. Robert S. Holt, an intelligence officer who had decided to go along on the mission at the last minute and had hopped aboard Larson's plane. Holt had been standing on the catwalk in the bomb bay between the bombs, and by some miracle he came staggering out of the flames alive, with only minor injuries.

Lt. Larson and his crew were all killed along with Sgt. Red, making eleven deaths in all.* A parked B-17 of the 43rd Bomb Group was destroyed, and two B-24s had their noses smashed, along with the minor damage to "Big Emma." Fragments of wreckage from Larson's plane lay scattered across the runway, preventing three bombers still waiting in line from taking off.

The crewmen who died in this crash were:

> 1st Lt. Paul R. Larson, pilot, from Illinois
> 2nd Lt. Herbert R. Bassman, copilot, from Mississippi
> 2nd Lt. David D. Muething, bombardier, from Ohio
> 2nd Lt. William F. Sipple, Jr., navigator (home state not listed)

---

* Today a memorial plaque at the Iron Range airfield (now called Lockhart River Airport) commemorates the men who died in this crash, and the loss of Col. Meehan's plane and crew.

Sgt. Ernest I. Irving, flight engineer, from Massachusetts
Sgt. Axel J. Halgren, radio operator, (home state not listed)
Sgt. William J. Dee, assistant radio operator, from Illinois
Cpl. Lewis A. Diotti, assistant flight engineer, from West Virginia
Cpl. Harold L. Patty, tail gunner, from Pennsylvania
Cpl. Lester L. Picker, gunner, from Indiana

The ten bombers that made it into the air that night headed for Rabaul, and it is a tribute to the skill of the navigators that any of them were able to fly 850 miles in the dark, over mountains and sea, to find the place, especially with their inadequate maps and their inability to see any landmarks, not to mention the fact that the Japanese had Rabaul blacked out. The confusion has penetrated even the historical records, which state that four planes turned back before reaching the target, while other accounts say that nine of the ten planes arrived over Rabaul around 4 AM and dropped their bombs.

Some bombs fell on the wharf area of the harbor, some exploded on one of the Japanese airfields, and one was thought to have hit a ship in the harbor. Regardless of how many bombers actually made it to Rabaul and dropped their bombs, once again only minor damage was done to the Japanese. Meehan's plane was the only one that did not return.

One of the bombers had an engine failure on the return trip and landed at Port Moresby for repairs (fortunately, as Map 9-1 on page 79 shows, Moresby was directly on the route both going and coming from Rabaul). All the rest of the planes, except for Meehan's, arrived back at Iron Range beginning around 9 AM on the morning of the 17th and landed safely. The returning crews, seeing all the damage to the airfield from Larson's wreck, assumed that the Japanese had bombed the place while they were gone, until they were told what had happened.

As the day of November 17 wore on, and the men sadly cleaned up the wreckage of the planes and performed the gruesome task of gathering up the remains of the dead, the depressing reality set in that not only were the men of Larson's crew gone forever but their commanding officer, Col. Meehan, was also not coming back. Gone with him was Maj. Morse, the commander of the 320th Squadron, along with the men they flew with. The Group had now flown only two combat missions and had lost four bombers and thirty men. Before that, the Deputy Commander of the 90th, Col. Art Rogers, had also vanished, on the flight over from Hawaii. Morale at Iron Range sank even lower than it had been, if that were possible.

In the following days, planes from the 90th Bomb Group took off and searched the first half of the route from Iron Range to Rabaul without finding any trace of Col. Meehan's plane, and eventually the search was abandoned. General Kenney appointed 40-year-old Col. Ralph E. ("Zipper") Koon as the

9. SECOND COMBAT MISSION: RABAUL

new commander of the Group. Koon had been a classmate of Meehan's at West Point.

(Above and below) two of the parked bombers that had their noses wiped off by Lt. Larson's out-of-control plane on the night of 16-17 November, 1942.

Chapter Ten

STAYING THE COURSE

Dispirited as they were after the losses suffered during their first two bombing missions, the young men of the 90th Bomb Group were determined to carry on. These men had come of age during America's Great Depression, had already endured many hardships and deprivations while growing up, and they were made of stern stuff. It's no wonder that Americans born after the war would look back on them as the "Greatest Generation." The men of the 90th, although discouraged, took their losses, kept their chins up, and stayed the course. No one was defeatist or ready to quit. Many adopted the attitude that things could only get better from here.

General Kenney realized that the first couple of missions he'd assigned to the 90th had been tough ones, perhaps too tough for an inexperienced bomb group fresh from the States, and he could see how the losses they'd sustained had disheartened them and that their morale was low. He decided to dial back his demands on the Group a little until they gained more experience, and give them easier tasks if circumstances allowed. He wrote:

> I'm trusting that the tactical situation, the weather, and other factors give me a chance to nurse them [the 90th Bomb Group] along for a while before I have to push them too hard.[1]

On the 27th of November, 1942, he assigned them a fairly easy task, to be flown in full daylight, which was to bomb a stationary shipwreck off the northern coast of New Guinea near Buna, where the Americans (the 32nd and 41st Infantry Divisions) and Australians (7th Division) were locked in a bloody battle with the Japanese after the Australians had pushed them back over the Kokoda Trail to their starting point at Buna Village (Map 10-1, opposite). At Buna the Japanese had dug into the dense, swampy jungle to create an extensive network of hidden bunkers and camouflaged fortifications. Digging them out of these defensive works was a brutal job that was costing the Allies a lot of casualties, so many in fact that some historians today refer to this battle as "Bloody Buna," with nearly 2,000 Allied troops and 4,000 Japanese killed.

During this battle Japanese ships from Rabaul tried to reinforce their troops, and one of these ships had been sunk just offshore from Buna. The sea was

10. STAYING THE COURSE 91

Map 10-1. The Japanese attempted to capture Port Moresby by sending an army across the Owen Stanley Mountains on the Kokoda Trail (dotted line) from the village of Buna on the north coast, but they were stopped and slowly beaten back to their starting point by the Australians, then besieged by both the Americans and the Australians at Buna. The Battle of Buna, although nearly forgotten today, was one of the bloodiest fights of World War II.

so shallow where it sank, however, that much of it remained above water. It was suspected that there were still Japanese aboard the wreck, using it as an observation post from which to direct artillery fire by radio onto the American and Australian troops. Being a stationary target, and quite a durable one, it was decided that heavy bombers might be able to destroy the half-sunken ship with their large, powerful demolition bombs. It was deemed worth a try.

Accordingly, six bombers of the 90th Bomb Group's 320th Squadron set out from Iron Range, again carrying eight 500-pound high-explosive bombs each. After crossing the Coral Sea, passing over the Owen Stanley Mountains, and arriving over Buna, the crews scanned the sky warily for Japanese fighter planes, and seeing none, lined up to make individual bombing runs on the wrecked ship. Each bomber dropped only a bomb or two on each pass until all of its eight bombs were gone.

As usual, some of the bombers had their bombs hang up in their bomb bays and refuse to release, others dropped their bombs close to the target but missed, and only one bomber, piloted by Lt. Robert N. McWilliams, actually hit the ship. In fact, McWilliams' bombardier, Sgt. Jay B. Parsons, hit it three times, showing either extraordinary luck or (more likely) what could be done by a man who really knew how to use the Norden bombsight. The bomb explosions caused a fire to break out on the wreck, and from that time forward no more radio transmissions were heard from it. The six bombers returned safely to Iron Range, having suffered no damage and gained some valuable experience in navigating and bombing. Things were finally looking up a little.

However, six B-24s bombing a *stationary* ship under ideal bombing conditions and getting only three hits out of 48 bombs showed just how difficult it was to hit a ship, or any such small target, with a heavy bomber, or for that matter any kind of a bomber that was bombing level (i. e. flying horizontally above its target rather than diving directly down on it like a dive bomber).

The Americans learn skip-bombing

The 43rd Bomb Group, flying B-17s, had arrived in Australia from the States in February of 1942, eight months ahead of the 90th, and had accumulated considerable combat experience by this time. General Kenney, therefore, chose the 43rd to try out a different kind of bombing against Japanese ships, a method he had experimented with years before, in peacetime: skip-bombing. In skip-bombing, a bomber flew at very low altitude straight at the side of a ship and released its bombs short of it so that they skipped across the surface of the water to strike the ship in the side. This worked against any target on (or adjacent to) water—the British would use skip-bombing in May of 1943 to blow up hydroelectric dams in Germany's Ruhr Valley.*

There was a rusty old freighter stranded on a reef near Port Moresby known as the Moresby Wreck,† and Kenney had the 43rd's pilots practice skip-bombing on it. They found that the technique worked very well once they got the hang of it, and they were soon slinging bomb after bomb into the sides of the old hulk. General Kenney rode along with them himself to observe the practice, and wrote:

> I spent the morning with Bill Benn, playing with skip-bombing on the old wreck on the reef outside Port Moresby Harbor. The lads were doing quite well. A nice looking lad named Captain Ken McCullar was especially good. He tested ten shots and put six of them up against the wreck.[2]

---

* It was called Operation Chastise, later the subject of a 1955 movie called *The Dam Busters*.

† The 400-foot-long ship known as the Moresby Wreck was the British merchant ship *SS Pruth*, which had been driven up onto the reef by a storm in 1924, and had sat there, abandoned, ever since. Because it was sitting upright on the reef, looking for all the world like a ship just sailing up the coast, the Japanese had occasionally bombed it (which made it an equal-opportunity target, bombed by both sides, one for practice and the other by mistake). In 1934 the wreck had been used as a backdrop for the Hollywood movie *Red Morning*.

10. STAYING THE COURSE

Compared to bombing from altitude, which as we have seen could rarely hit a target so small as a ship, skip-bombing got a hit nearly every time. The big drawback to skip-bombing, of course, was that it required the bomber to approach a ship at such a low altitude that it made a big target for the ship's antiaircraft gunners, especially a plane as large as a four-engine bomber. Skip-bombing was thus a very exciting, and very dangerous, business.

General Kenney was well aware of the dangers that a bomber faced when skip-bombing, hence he planned to have his B-17s do it at night, when there was enough moonlight to see the ships, but (it was hoped) the shipboard gunners would find it hard to see the bombers coming. However, the fact remained that if a bomber pilot could see a ship well enough to skip-bomb it, there was always a chance that the ship's gunners might also be able to see the bomber well enough to shoot at it. Kenney therefore decided that he needed to create a diversion for the ships' gunners before his skip-bombers went in.

Capt. Kenneth McCullar and several other pilots of the 43rd Bomb Group had practiced skip-bombing on the Moresby Wreck with their B-17s until they were expert at it, and on the night of the 23rd of October [1942] Kenney employed their skill in an attack on Japanese shipping in Rabaul Harbor. He wrote:

> We put over another trick on the Nips on the night of the 23rd. Twelve B-17s went over Rabaul Harbor after air reconnaissance the day before had reported a concentration of shipping that looked worthwhile. The first six bombers were from the newly organized 64th Squadron of the 43rd Group. They bombed from 10,000 feet and, while the Jap searchlights lit up the sky and the antiaircraft guns blazed away, the other six bombers from the 63rd Squadron came in at 100-feet altitude and introduced skip-bombing to the Nips. Captain Ken McCullar, whose airplane already had been credited with sinking or damaging four Jap vessels, sank a Jap destroyer with two direct hits amidships. Captain Green scored direct hits on a light cruiser or large destroyer, a small cargo vessel, and a medium-sized one. The crew reported that the cruiser had her stern underwater and was on fire all over when they left. The cargo vessels were both sunk. A lieutenant named Hustad hit another cargo vessel, estimated at 10,000 tons, setting fire to it. Hustad reported that she was blazing nicely and listing a little when he left, but he could not claim the vessel as definitely destroyed. The six planes from the 64th claimed damaging four other vessels with hits or near misses.[3]

Kenney never required the pilots of the 90th Bomb Group to learn skip-bombing, probably because he came to realize that 4-engine bombers were too large and slow to do it in daylight without a good chance of being shot down. Within a year skip-bombing would become the specialty of much smaller and speedier twin-engine bombers, such as the A-20 Havoc and B-25 Mitchell, that Kenney had specially modified for the task, the actual work being done by his mechanical wizard Paul I. "Pappy" Gunn. Gunn added several heavy machine-guns to the noses of the bombers to sweep the decks of the ships as they were beginning their skip-bombing runs, in order to neutralize the antiaircraft gunners on the way in. We shall see in Chapter 25 how effectively these planes performed during the Battle of the Bismarck Sea.

Some B-24 pilots chose to learn skip-bombing on their own, anyway, including Col. Art Rogers, who also honed his skills on the Moresby Wreck. One of Rogers' skip-bombing adventures was written up by a correspondent for the *Saturday Evening Post*, and the article is reproduced in Chapter 27.

Different fuses for different uses

Aerial bombs could be detonated with a variety of fuse types, from instantaneous detonation on contact with the ground (or other target) to a delay of several hours after being dropped. Fuses for skip-bombing and fuses for horizontal bombing required different timing. Fuses for skip-bombing had to be set for a three- to five-second delay, for two reasons: first to give the bomber time to get clear of the explosion, and second so that the bomb would penetrate a ship's side and explode inside of it, ideally blowing out the bottom of its hull. Pilots could argue whether the shorter or longer delay was best, but all agreed that there had to be some delay.

Fusing for bombs dropped on ships by horizontal bombing from high altitude were a different matter; they could either be set to explode instantly on contact or set for a slight delay, and once again there were differing views on which was better. General Kenney and General Kenneth Walker, whom Kenney had appointed Commander of V Bomber Command, took opposite sides on the question. Walker wanted to use delayed-action fuses to allow a bomb a split-second to penetrate the deck of a ship before exploding. Kenney, however, argued that since most bombs dropped from altitude missed the ships they were aimed at, and detonated in the water nearby, instantaneous fuses would at least allow them to do some damage.

An instantaneous fuse that detonated the bomb on contact with the water would still hurl metal through the air to strike and damage a ship despite a miss, he asserted, whereas a delayed-action fuse would cause the bomb to explode underwater, muffling or eliminating its effectiveness altogether.

Kenney decided to settle his dispute with Walker and prove his point by having some bombs with instantaneous fuses dropped close to the Moresby Wreck, and then examining the results. As he wrote in his memoirs:

I told Ken [Walker] to have somebody go out and drop about

four bombs on the old wreck on the reef outside Moresby and that we would then go out and inspect it.

After lunch we took a motorboat out as close as we could get to the wreck and a corporal rowed Ken and me about a mile the rest of the way. The evidence was there. The bombs had missed the vessel by twenty-five to seventy-five yards, and yet fragments had torn holes all through it. Some of them were two to four square feet in area. I showed Ken the nice clean edges as compared with the rusty edges of holes and gashes made by previous practice bombings. Ken finally said, "Okay, you win, I'm convinced." I turned to the corporal and said, "Corporal, come back here and sit in the stern with me. General Walker is rowing us back to the motorboat."

Ken didn't say a word (except for a few of three or four letters when his oarsmanship went wrong) all the way back. I didn't kid him any more, so after a couple of drinks up at [Gen.] Whitehead's before dinner, Ken thawed out. Ken was okay.[4]

The Moresby Wreck provided bombing and gunnery practice to hundreds of Allied aircrews during the war. Twenty airmen are known to have died in accidents while bombing or shooting it up. In one incident, a B-25 flew so close to the ship that one of its wings was sheared off by a mast, and the crew was killed in the crash. Today the sea floor around what remains of the old ship is littered with the wreckage of various types of aircraft, along with various kinds of ordnance, both spent and live.[*]

The 90th goes after its first Japanese convoy

Japanese supply convoys, which consisted of cargo ships often escorted by warships, usually destroyers, were dangerous targets for bombers, not only because of the antiaircraft fire from the warships but because convoys often also had a protective umbrella of fighter planes. General Kenney had not wanted to send the 90th Bomb Group against a convoy so soon after its arrival in Australia, but on the morning of November 29th [1942] a reconnaissance plane spotted a group of several Japanese ships headed south out of Rabaul into the Solomon Sea, their destination no doubt either Buna or Lae. With the 43rd Bomb Group occupied elsewhere, Kenney felt that he had no choice but to assign the job of bombing it to the 90th.

The Group was ordered to attack this convoy immediately, and Col. Koon soon had six bombers of the 319th Squadron on the way, their crews all nervously keyed up for a fight. The men who had been convinced by members

---

[*] After the war the *Pruth* was salvaged for scrap metal down to the waterline, but its boilers can still be seen today sticking up out of the water at low tide, and its outline is still visible from the air. Today it's a popular wreck for recreational scuba diving, although divers are cautioned to leave old bombs and bullets alone.

of the departing 19th Bomb Group that their B-24s would be easy prey for Japanese Zeros were wondering whether they were going to survive this mission. No doubt to the great relief of many of the crewmen, when the bombers arrived over the area south of New Britain where the ships had been reported, the sea was empty, and there was not enough daylight left to conduct a search. Five of the six bombers then jettisoned their bombs into the sea and headed back to Iron Range, the pilots now faced with a new worry: would they be able to find their airfield in the darkness? It was, after all, a hard enough place to locate in daylight. And after they found it, would they be able to see it well enough to land on it?

Meanwhile the pilot of the sixth bomber, Lt. Edward R. DeFreitas, decided (probably much to the disgust of his crew) that he didn't want to waste his bombs, so he broke from the formation and angled west a couple hundred miles to Lae, where he dropped the bombs on Lae's airfield, even though his bombardier was only barely able to make it out in the twilight. Fortunately they were unopposed by any Japanese fighter planes. Satisfied that he had probably done some damage to the enemy, DeFreitas took up a compass heading for Iron Range given to him by his navigator (whose name is not recorded) and climbed up to a safe altitude to clear the unseen peaks of the Owen Stanley Mountains in the dark.

An hour or so ahead of him, the other five bombers of his squadron, in a loose formation and with their navigators all checking each others' computations over their planes' radios, managed to find Iron Range in the dark. Col. Koon assisted them by lighting up the airfield so far as he was able, with searchlights aimed upward to attract their attention, and all the planes spotted the field and managed to land safely.

Now it was up to DeFreitas' navigator to get his plane home too, if he could, all by himself. It was an appalling situation for a navigator. Lae was 500 miles from Iron Range, with first the towering Owen Stanley Mountains and then the Coral Sea in between (see Map 12-1 on p. 102 for the route between Lae and Iron Range), and all the flying would be in darkness. He had no way of knowing whether there were any winds aloft blowing him off course, nor whether any head or tailwinds would cause the plane to get to Iron Range either sooner or later than his estimate.

After a few hours of blind flying, the navigator announced that they were probably in the general vicinity of Iron Range, but being unable to see anything below, it was about all he could say. DeFreitas' copilot, Lt. Donald L. Sanxter, later recorded in his journal what happened next:

> Our plane and crew became detached from the formation of planes [while] bombing Lae, New Guinea. After the bomb run we headed back to Iron Range, Australia, over the Owen Stanley

10. STAYING THE COURSE

Mountains of New Guinea. The mountains were topped by the usual foul weather, which resulted in 2 to 3 hours of scared flying.

Finally we came into the calmer weather of Australia, but the sky was still a blanket of clouds. In attempting to determine our location, we concluded that we were lost and didn't know where we were. We took a consensus of opinions and decided that we were *probably* west of our intended course and that we *probably* had reached some part of Australia, but we had nothing to support those conclusions.

Nevertheless, we headed our plane in a southeasterly direction, hoping to spot some form of civilization or landmark. We flew for an hour and a half, and as our fuel was now running low, we began to doubt our choice of the course we had been following. But it was too late to do anything other than to prepare to leave our plane and parachute to earth.

Lt. Edward DeFreitas, from Portland, Oregon landed his crew safely at Iron Range on the night of Nov. 9, 1942. Forty days later, on 19 December, he was killed on another bombing mission when Japanese fighters attacked his bomber. His plane has never been found, and he remains missing. He was 22 years old.[6]

With thirty minutes of fuel left, we all donned parachutes and prepared to bail out. DeFreitas gave the word to bail out, then canceled the order a second later. A light was spotted dead ahead; then another—and yet another —and then a lot more lights! Lucky us, it was an airstrip's lights, but would our fuel last long enough to bring our plane in?

Droning ahead we made our descent and approach straight, lowering the landing gear at the last moment to avoid drag. We touched down and as we completed our rollout, the number 4 engine quit from lack of fuel. As we tumbled out of our plane, we were greeted by our ground crews who were sweating us out. We had stumbled onto—and were now safe on—our own Iron Range airstrip![5]

It had been a very close call. Only through pure luck, and an abundance of it, had DeFreitas made it home. Map 13-1 on p. 121 shows where DeFrietas made his lucky turn toward the airfield. Three days later another of the 90th's bomber crews would find itself in exactly the same situation, lost over the Cape York Peninsula in the dark, searching for Iron Range, but they would not make any such lucky turn, and as we shall see, the outcome would be disastrous.

Chapter Eleven

COL. ROGERS ARRIVES AT IRON RANGE

When the 90th flew its first combat missions, Col. Art Rogers was still stuck on Christmas Island with a blown engine on his bomber. As noted earlier, he had wired Hawaii for a new engine and also sent a message to Australia letting the Group know that he was temporarily stranded, but for some reason the message was never received. Everyone in Australia therefore assumed that Rogers had gone down at sea and been lost. Since it had been necessary for him and his crew to put the replacement engine together when it finally arrived from Hawaii in pieces, and then mount it on the airplane themselves, Rogers didn't show up at Iron Range until the 29th of November, 1942, forty days after he'd been left behind during the ocean crossing from Hawaii to Australia.[1]

When he reached Brisbane, Rogers learned where the 90th was based, marked the location of Iron Range on his map, and took off headed north on the 1,200 mile flight to the field. When he arrived where he thought Iron Range should be, he had the usual first-timer's trouble finding it, even though it was full daylight, because the airfield blended into the jungle so well. He wrote:

> We overshot Iron Range, but knowing its approximate location we started a square search and finally spotted a big red streak in the middle of the jungle. The runway was constructed of red soil and gravel. I could not visualize this being an airdrome and therefore flew over it in hopes of seeing some airplanes belonging to our group. Sure enough, tucked away in crude revetments, I recognized the Liberator, and knowing that ours was the only group of Liberators at that time in the entire theater it definitely settled any doubts I might have had.
>
> As I came in to land over the tops of fifty-foot trees, which were on all sides of the strip, I wondered how we could operate long out of this place without having a high casualty list due to takeoff and landing accidents. I landed and taxied to a parking place where I was signaled by one of our crew chiefs.[2]

A jeep drove Rogers into the jungle to the tent of Col. Koon, whom he had known from prior assignments in the States, and whom he called by his

Col. Ralph Koon (left), Commander of the 90th Bomb Group after the loss of Col. Meehan, with Lt. Col. Art Rogers, the Group's Deputy Commander, at Iron Range, Australia.

nickname, "Zipper." After Koon got over his surprise at seeing Rogers, a man everyone had thought dead, he warned Rogers that the Group was very dispirited as a result of the primitive living conditions and the losses the men had incurred on their first missions. The first thing Rogers did was go looking for the men of his 319th Squadron, all of whom he knew well since he had been their squadron commander from the very beginning of the Group's formation. He still commanded their squadron, in fact, even though he had also been promoted to Deputy Group Commander just before the 90th left the States for Hawaii. Rogers remembered:

> After crossing a stream on a crudely made bridge, I came to the campsite of my old outfit. When I walked in, you would have thought a ghost had walked into the midst of the camp, but soon you could hear the cheers and such expressions as, "We thought you had gone down!" "How did you ever find us?" and "Gee, Colonel, but it's good to see you!"

Rogers found, as Col. Koon had warned him, that the morale of the 90th Bomb Group was near rock bottom. As he put it later in his memoirs, "their spirit was broken." Many of the 319th's bomber crewmen had not yet gone out on a combat mission, and a lot of them didn't expect to survive one. Rogers soon heard about what the 19th Bomb Group had told his men before they left for the States: that they were in for serious trouble when they went up against the Japanese Zero. Rogers wrote:

> This group [the 19th] had taken too many beatings to have a very optimistic outlook in regards to fighting the Japs. They had immediately told our boys that they would all be shot down, since in their opinion the Liberator could not match their Flying Fortresses. They explained to the young pilots that since the Liberators had no bottom turrets the Jap Zero would come right up underneath them and shoot them out of the sky the very first thing.
>
> In fact once I had broken the ice the young pilots poured out all their troubles and their disbelief in their equipment, as if by so doing they could relieve themselves of their worries and fears. They kept saying, "Colonel, the first time we engage those Zeros we haven't got a chance, they're going to shoot us to pieces."
>
> I tried to tell them that they had heard a group of officers talk who knew nothing of the Liberator. I told them that I had flown the Flying Fortress for four years and knew it to be a wonderful airplane, but that in my opinion it could not excel the Liberator.
>
> Even though I had never been in combat, I told them that I was ready to prove my statement. I said, "If you will remember at our pilots' meeting when we were activated I told you then that I would be in the lead plane when my squadron engaged the enemy, and that is just what I intend to do."

But Rogers could tell that he hadn't really convinced anyone. The young men knew that he'd had no combat experience, and he also had no answer to all the vacant bunks that had appeared throughout the camp after the Group's first missions.

But only two days after Rogers arrived at Iron Range, the opportunity arose for him to fly his first combat mission, and demonstrate to his men (and himself) the validity of his claims. On the morning of Dec. 1, 1942, a reconnaissance plane spotted a convoy of four Japanese destroyers headed south out of Rabaul into the Solomon Sea and down the south coast of New Britain. This convoy was obviously headed for either Lae or the battle in progress at Buna, probably carrying troops, supplies, or both.

General Kenney received this intelligence at his headquarters in Brisbane and immediately ordered the 90th Bomb Group at Iron Range to intercept and bomb the convoy. The ships were reported to have about forty Zeros flying protective cover over them. The question of whether B-24s could defend themselves against Japanese Zeros was about to be settled.

Chapter Twelve

COL. ROGERS' FIRST COMBAT MISSION

Each of the 90th Bomb Group's four squadrons would furnish six bombers for this mission, and each bomber would carry twelve 500-pound demolition bombs. The twenty-four bombers would thus be dropping a total of 288 bombs on four Japanese warships.

At the pre-mission briefing, Rogers told all the crews the location of the convoy, its composition, and the number of enemy fighter planes believed to be flying cover for it. He would lead the Group with his 319th squadron, and the three other squadrons would follow at short intervals.

Aware that it was difficult to hit targets as small as ships, especially ships in motion, from ten thousand feet, the altitude from which he planned to make the attack, Rogers had decided that their best chance to do damage to the convoy would be for each squadron's six planes, flying in formation, to release all their bombs at once in a form of saturation bombing. With any reasonable accuracy by the bombardiers, some of the ships should be caught in the bomb patterns. Each squadron's six planes would form a triangle, and all planes in the triangle would drop their bombs on the cue of the lead plane's bombardier. Rogers wrote:

> I explained to the crews that our method of attacking would consist of two runs. We would drop six of the five-hundred pound bombs entrain on the first run at intervals of every twenty-five feet. All the airplanes would drop their bombs simultaneously on the leader so that the bombs hitting would make a pattern the same width as the formation of the six ships [planes][*] which were being flown in a triangle.
>
> This triangle would consist of a big five-ship V with one airplane in the slot to close the triangle. Due to the bombs dropping at twenty-five foot intervals, the pattern would be one hundred and twenty-five feet long. The second run was to be the same as the first. I explained to them that the Jap fighters would probably come out

---

[*] Pilots in World War II (and aviators before that) often referred to their planes as "ships," which causes confusion today when both aircraft and real (seagoing) ships are referred to in the same paragraphs, as here.

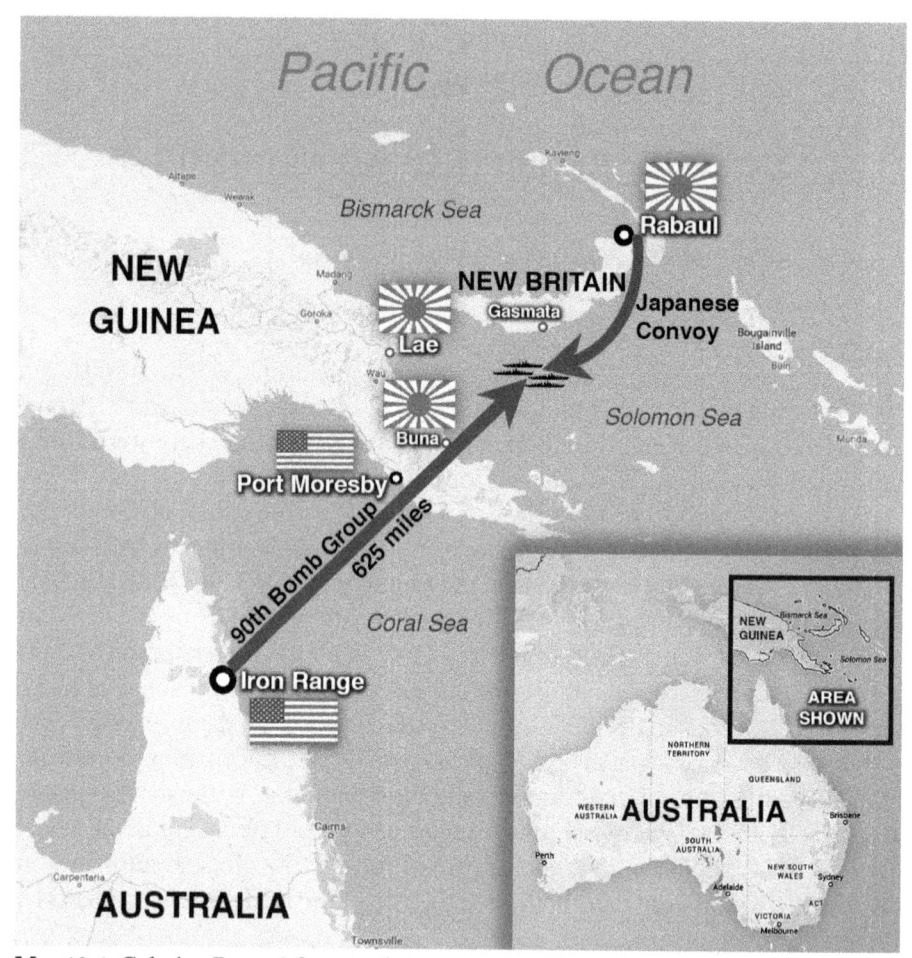

Map 12-1. Col. Art Rogers' first combat mission, on Dec. 1, 1942, was to intercept and bomb a convoy of four Japanese destroyers in the Solomon Sea south of Gasmata, New Britain. The convoy was probably headed for either Lae or the ongoing battle at Buna. The upper arrow represents the route of the Japanese convoy, the lower one the route of the American bombers intercepting it.

and intercept us fifteen to twenty minutes before we reached the convoy, and since it would take us a few more minutes to maneuver into position to begin our run, it meant that we would be under constant attack.

With no friendly fighter planes available to accompany the bombers and take on the Japanese fighters, the bombers' only defense would be their gunners. The squadrons would therefore have to fly tight formations to concentrate the fire of all the gunners and increase the effectiveness of the defense:

12. COL. ROGERS' FIRST COMBAT MISSION

I warned them that our only chance to return home lay in our ability to remain in formation during the entire attack. I explained to them that in case any airplane of the formation had an engine shot out, they were to notify the leader of their squadron immediately, so that he could slow down enough to allow the plane to stay in formation with three engines. I told the squadron commanders that unless they stayed on the alert to do this, they would surely lose one or more of their flight if the engine of a plane was knocked out.

A number of the pilots questioned the wisdom of making two bombing runs over the ships, since it would double their exposure to the ships' antiaircraft fire, not to mention giving the enemy fighters twice as long to try to shoot them down:

> There was opposition over the method of attack from the three other squadron commanders, since they felt that we had very little chance to come back after engaging forty Zeros and the many batteries of ack-ack on the destroyers even if we made only one pass. But two passes they considered would double our chances of not getting back.
>
> To attack a convoy with any chance of success involved making a two to three minute bombing run maintaining a constant altitude and speed. This allows the bombardier to synchronize his sight on the target. To maneuver the organization into position to make this three minute run often takes fifteen minutes after sighting the target. To make two runs over a convoy would probably mean your formation would be under constant attack by the enemy fighters for approximately thirty minutes or more. It would also involve the formation flying through the flak twice.
>
> I realized all this, but I also knew that our chances of hitting would be doubled also. I could not see the percentage of dropping all twelve bombs in one pass, because if the bombardier's sighting was inaccurate it might mean the loss of many of our airplanes without doing any damage to the enemy. I explained all this to them, but I could see that everyone was jittery and there was more fear than belief.
>
> As the meeting broke up, I heard one of the officers state on his way out of the tent that chances were we would all be shot down, exactly like John Doe of the 19th Group had stated. He said the Zeros would come from the rear and underneath us, allowing their gunfire to enter the bellies of our bombers. I still had confidence that since the guns in our rear turret could deflect sixty-five degrees [downward] it would be practically impossible for the Zeros to get underneath us without being shot to pieces first.
>
> Since our bombardiers had had very little experience practicing the dropping of bombs with their pilots, I knew their chances of hit-

> ting a rapidly moving and maneuvering target were slim, and this was another reason I had decided on two runs... I was confident that the Japs would know they had been in a fight when we were through with them. Without this implicit confidence I am sure I would have been more shaky than any man in the flight.

Since this would be Rogers' first combat mission, and his views were untested, he knew that his credibility was on the line. This mission could either make or break his reputation as a leader. He wrote:

> I was under a terrific strain myself, as I realized the success of this mission was a lot more than sinking a destroyer or two, since the morale of the organization and my word was at stake. Since my arrival, I had continually assured the men that we could lick the hell out of three times our number of Jap fighters anytime, and I would prove it to them.
>
> If our losses on this mission were too great it would be a definite proof to these men that their equipment was unable to cope with the Jap Zero, and they would not be able to defend themselves on future missions.
>
> It also meant that my leadership was definitely in the balance. If my prophecy regarding my gunners and tail turrets did not pan out, I knew these men would no longer feel that I was competent to be their Deputy Group Commander and [the] Operations Officer who planned their missions.

With the Japanese convoy making good time along the south coast of New Britain that day, there was little time to lose in launching the strike. Rogers and the other five pilots of his squadron cranked up their engines at 1:30 in the afternoon (Dec. 1, 1942) and lined up for takeoff on the rough, unpaved runway of Iron Range, with the other three squadrons starting up their engines to go right behind them. Each engine's propeller threw up a cloud of dust behind it as it fired up, and the individual clouds soon blended until dust was swirling all over the noisy Iron Range airfield, and the air was filled with the thunder of ninety-six big radial engines.

The bombers would not reach the convoy until late in the afternoon, and after bombing it they would be faced with returning to Iron Range after nightfall. The risk of not being able to find the field in the darkness would have to be taken, along with the dangers of landing on the primitive runway at night.

> The plan was for each squadron commander to take off and assemble his six ships in their triangle formation while circling the airdrome and then to depart for the target. This meant that there would be, if everything worked out right, an interval of two or three minutes between flights [squadrons]...I taxied out and

took off with each of my six airplanes taking off at forty-five-second intervals.

The six bombers of Rogers' flight joined up over the airfield, with him in the lead, and he set a course for New Guinea with the planes flying in a loose formation (a tight formation required close concentration by the pilots, causing fatigue, as well as using up extra gas, and was avoided until necessary).[1] From Iron Range the Group would fly across the Coral Sea, pass by Port Moresby on the south coast of New Guinea, and continue on across the Owen Stanley Mountains to the north coast of the island and into the Solomon Sea beyond (see Map 12-1 on page 102). For Rogers, who had never yet flown across the Coral Sea, this would be his first look at the great island of New Guinea, the second largest island in the world.

> As we flew over the Coral Sea, I was wondering how New Guinea would look... I had heard many tales about the unmapped Owen Stanley Range and its dense jungles. Soon the coastline was sighted, and my navigator was trying to determine our exact position in relation to a big cove we were approaching. He finally decided that we had drifted approximately a mile off to the right of our course. For the past hour I had been climbing the formation

A loose formation of 90th Bomb Group bombers headed for a target.

to gain altitude, as I knew the point at which we were to cross the Owen Stanley Range was thirteen thousand feet high.

As soon as Rogers sighted the majestic mountain range, he also saw the high, dense cloud formations billowing up above it. Such storms formed over the Owen Stanley Mountains every afternoon, and would be the nemesis of all American airmen in New Guinea during the war. The storms would prove fatal to many pilots who became lost and disoriented within them, and ended up crashing on a mountainside, or whose airplanes were torn apart by the vicious air turbulence. Wreckage of the many aircraft that vanished over this mountain range during the war continues to be found today.

> In flying over the green matted jungle far below us, I could see the mountains rising in the distance ahead, and above these mountains were huge cumulus clouds towering up another fifteen thousand feet. I could see by now that my course would take me right into these thunderheads. Knowing the almost impossibility of flying even one airplane through such clouds, I knew I must change my course to go through a broken area in the clouds, which appeared fifteen to twenty miles to the right, if we were to stay in formation. As we went through this break in the clouds I began to worry, wondering whether this break would also close in before we could return. I knew that we would have to cross the range on our way back, since at this time the only airdromes that we could return to were either our own at Iron Range or the one at Port Moresby.
>
> My mind could not dwell upon this unpleasant subject long, however, because within the next two hours I knew we would be engaging a tremendous [enemy] force greatly outnumbering any three to one ratio, for our other squadrons were nowhere in sight. As we topped the range of mountains, the Bismarck [Solomon] Sea could be seen clearly ahead. We were definitely in enemy territory now, where at any time a scouting force of Zeros might be lurking. I called all the airplanes and cautioned their commanders to keep their gunners on alert and ready for any interception.

After the bomber formation passed through the cloud gap over the mountains, the air became clear, with unlimited visibility ahead. The six bombers, now on high alert, tightened up their formation, and the pilots and bombardiers studied the horizon, trying to catch sight of the Japanese convoy, while the gunners nervously scanned the skies in all directions for enemy fighter planes.

First the convoy came into view on the sea ahead of them. And then, suddenly, Japanese fighter planes appeared overhead.

90th Bomb Group bombers in a tight defensive formation, as viewed from the right waist gun window of the bomber from which the photo was snapped.

[N]o sooner had we sighted the convoy than approximately forty Zeros passed over our formation about four thousand feet higher than we were.[2] The Japs had a big surprise in store for them, since they had never encountered a Liberator before, even though they thought they had. The LB-30*, that was originally designed for the British, was a parent ship of the Liberator and built by the same company. During the evacuation of Java many of our pilots were shot down while flying the LBs due to the fact that they were so poorly armed. There were many differences in the parent ship and our Liberator which were not visible to the Japs, the main one being [that] the LB did not have a tail turret with two .50-caliber machine guns in it. The Japs' ignorance was proven when their entire formation squared off to make an attack. They were coming in from above and on our tails. This meant that our top turrets and also our tail turrets would have them directly in the line of our fire all the way in on their attack.

The gunners in the bombers were now seeing enemy fighter planes coming at them for the first time, and their adrenalin levels were running high. In view

---
* LB stood for Land Bomber.

of their inexperience, it was only natural that they would begin firing before the Zeros were within range of their guns.

> They were still a good two miles out, coming at us like hell, when our nervous gunners opened fire. Even though the Japs were out of range, it was only seconds before they had entered the deadly cone of fire on their death dives, since eight of the lot kept right on diving into the ocean. After this first disastrous attack the Japs pulled off just out of range of our guns to look us over.
>
> My gunners were still firing at them even though they were out of range, and I was forced to call the planes and order the gunners not to fire unless the Japs were in range, or else we would be out of ammunition before the fight was over...
>
> I was watching the Japs as they sported their little fighters in a difficult maneuver known as a slow roll, just out of our range of fire, and I couldn't help but admire their airplane and their ability to fly it.

Numerous other accounts by American airmen mention the tendency of Japanese fighter pilots to break into aerobatic maneuvers at odd times and for no apparent reason. Whether the Japanese pilots were just showing off, or hoping to "psych out" their opponents, or had some other reason for doing this is not known. Perhaps it was just some Oriental proclivity for embellishing a fight, like a Samurai swordsman waving his sword around in fancy arabesques in an attempt to intimidate an opponent.

Lt. James McMurria of the 90th's 319th Squadron also saw this on several occasions and wrote:

> The Zeros came in from everywhere and their acrobatics are a sight to behold. A couple of them will just get out of range and put on an aerial show.[3]

On September 15, 1942, B-25 pilot Garrett Middlebrook's bomber formation was attacked by a pair of Zeros, and he wrote afterward:

> Just as the two planes cleared our formation, they did a perfect slow roll in absolute unison. I was amazed that they performed such a maneuver while still under fire of our guns... I could reach no other conclusion except that they were showing us that they were skilled pilots... [A]s time passed I witnessed other grandstand maneuvers, which were equally inexplicable.[4]

Joe Foss, a Marine fighter pilot, commented:

> "Oh, they put on lots of acrobatics, slowovers, loops. The only reason that we could figure out for their doing all those stunts,

they wanted to show us just how 'hot' they were. So, we showed them how hot we were and shot them down."[5]

Suburo Sakai, Japan's highest-scoring fighter pilot to survive the war, displayed the same exhibitionist tendencies in his Zero. He wrote that on May 16, 1942, after making a strafing attack on the American airfields at Port Moresby, he and two other Zero pilots performed a series of loops over the Americans' heads, apparently just to taunt them. They did it "for fun," he said.[6]

This inclination of Japanese fighter pilots to show off could also be linked to a collective Japanese inferiority complex in the presence of Allied opponents—demonstrating their skill to the Westerners to "prove" that they were just as good at flying as they were, like children showing off in front of adults. In that case it was just the aerial version of the exaggerated swaggering that so many Allied prisoners reported in the behavior of their Japanese captors.

As Col. Rogers led his six B-24s toward the Japanese convoy, the fighter planes resumed their attacks, trying to break up the formation and prevent the Americans from bombing the ships. The speedy little Zeros could run rings around the big lumbering American bombers, like sports cars cavorting around 18-wheel trucks on a highway, only in three dimensions, and the fighters could attack the bombers from any angle while the B-24s could take no evasive action in their tight defensive formation.

Rogers' longstanding worries about the poor forward firepower of the B-24D bomber now proved to be well founded. The Japanese pilots soon realized this weakness in the plane's defense and switched to frontal attacks.

> [I]t did not take [the enemy pilots] but a few seconds to recognize the one weak spot on our airplane, which was the nose. They pulled out ahead of us approximately five miles and [then] turned directly into us on a head-on attack just as we were beginning our first run on their convoy. The rate of closure was about 500 miles per hour, head-on, and a collision looked inevitable unless one or the other of us changed our altitude. I was determined to hold mine, since my bombing run had commenced.
>
> I knew the Japs were making a desperate effort to break up our bombing run and scatter the formation so we would be easy pickings. I called the pilots and told them to hold their formation, and with what few [forward-firing] guns we could maneuver into position we started firing on them.
>
> The entire wings of the attacking Zeros appeared to be on fire from their blazing machine guns ... we could see their tracer bullets either hitting our planes or passing over or under us. Their head-on collision course was maintained until they were a few hundred yards from us, at which time they rolled over on their backs and continued to fire at us until you could actually see the

The famous Japanese Mitsubishi A6M "Zero" fighter plane was of fragile construction but was light and highly maneuverable. It was hard to beat at the beginning of the war, but by 1944 American fighter designs were outclassing it. The Zero was actually the navy (carrier-based) version of the plane. The land-based ones were known as the "Oscar." However, Allied pilots tended to call any radial-engine Japanese fighter a Zero.

writing on their airplanes. Then they completed a half roll which brought them out ahead of us again allowing them to make the same attack over and over again.

The Japs came in one at a time in a string formation. The fourth plane in the string had his elevation high as his tracer bullets were passing just above my cabin by a few feet. I watched him as his nose dropped and naturally expected to meet my Maker. However, as his nose dropped he had commenced to roll over on his back, causing his fire to hit my wing instead, and at this exact time my nose gunner poured a burst of fifty-caliber shots into his belly, which resembled that of a shark. As he rolled out ahead of us we could see flames coming out of his cockpit as he made his last dive and crashed into the ocean.

As the bombers neared the convoy, the Japanese antiaircraft gunners on the ships below opened up on them, and the explosions of the shells in the sky around them added to the din of roaring engines and chattering machine guns. The Japanese fighter planes pulled off to the sides to get out of the flak from their ships and waited nearby for the bombers to pass through the antiaircraft fire. The flak explosions roiled the air around the bombers and made the planes jump and wobble "like corks bobbing in rough water," Rogers wrote.

Ever since I had been in the Air Corps I had wondered how it would feel to see huge shells exploding around a fragile airplane two miles up in the air. I can say right now from actual experience that it is not a pleasant feeling.

12. COL. ROGERS' FIRST COMBAT MISSION 111

Since the bombs of the six-plane formation would all be released on the cue of the lead bombardier in Rogers' plane, the other five bombardiers in the formation were now watching the lead plane closely, their fingers ready on their bomb release switches. The lead bombardier thus had a lot of pressure on him, and Rogers sympathized with his difficulties. Not only was this his first bomb run in combat, with all the other bombers in the squadron cueing on him, but he was also sitting out front in the glass nose of the plane feeling very vulnerable to the Japanese fighter planes, with their tracer bullets zipping all around him. He could also see quite clearly all the flak shells bursting noisily nearby.

It took a lot of willpower for a bombardier to concentrate on lining up a target in his bombsight under these conditions. A bombardier also had control of his plane's flight path through his bombsight, which was linked to the plane's autopilot system, and the pilot relinquished control to his bombardier during the bombing run. Rogers called his bombardier over the intercom to ask how things were going, but got no reply—the young man was obviously too preoccupied to talk.

As the bomber formation passed directly over the convoy, Rogers saw the light flicker on his instrument panel indicating that the bombs had been released, and a split-second later all the other bombers added their bombs to his. Thirty-six 500-pound bombs, half of the bombs the squadron was carrying, were on their way toward the convoy below. Rogers took control of the bomber again and waited for a report on where the bombs hit, since he could not see downward and rearward from his cockpit. Less than a minute later the tail gunner reported that all the bombs had missed the convoy, doing nothing more than raising big waterspouts near the ships.

Rogers then got a call over the command radio that one of the other bombers had taken a flak hit and lost an engine. He immediately called for all the other bombers in the formation to throttle back and reduce speed so that the disabled bomber could keep up with them. Everyone knew that a straggler would immediately be pounced on by the enemy fighter planes. Rogers now led his formation, with the crippled plane setting the pace, in a wide sweeping turn back over the convoy to make the second bombing run, at the same time dropping to a lower altitude to make it more difficult for the Japanese gunners below to determine their altitude and fuse their shells accurately.

This second run over the convoy was the situation that all the pilots and crews had dreaded, and with the formation flying more slowly now to allow the cripple to keep up, they were even more vulnerable to the antiaircraft fire than before. At this point, Rogers remembered, the sky was "black with flak."

As we maneuvered in for the second run I called the bombardier and told him for God's sake to calm down and pay attention to

what he was doing. By this time he must have begun to take a little courage, because I got a reply and my bomb indicator was being operated more smoothly. Another airplane reported that they had lost an engine from Zero fire, and that another engine was smoking, and it meant a possibility of fire.

The bomb light flashed again, and I said a little prayer for success this time as these were our last six bombs. The flak was even more intense now than before, if this could be possible. It may have been because they had set up on our altitude better, even though I had changed altitude for the second run, or maybe it was due to the fact that it took us longer to get through their range of fire as we were having to fly considerably slower as a result of two damaged planes.

I heard a jubilant cry, "We've hit them this time, we've hit them!" This raised my spirits, even though I saw we were still being attacked by the remaining Zeros. They continued to attack my limping formation for another fifteen minutes. We had cost them twelve airplanes and probably a destroyer, and yet all of us were still in formation and on our weary way home.

As soon as the last attack was made by the Zeros, I called the two pilots of the damaged planes and asked for a report on their condition. The airplane that was smoking reported that no fire had developed and the smoke was decreasing. The other airplane reported that one of his remaining three good engines was running awfully hot, and he felt positive that he would be unable to make it back to Iron Range.

Since I had many holes in my plane, I requested each airplane commander to check in with me, and was not at all surprised to find the remaining three planes had many holes in their fuselages, but the damage was not serious.

Even better was the news that no one was hurt. As the formation made its slow way back over the mountains, Rogers made a slight course adjustment to head for Port Moresby so that the two damaged bombers could land there, since it was doubtful that they could make it across the Coral Sea to Australia and Iron Range. Fortunately Moresby was only slightly west of their course home.

Rogers began to breathe easier after the strain of the bombing runs, but not for long. Suddenly his radio crackled with the news that another formation of planes had been sighted dead ahead, heading straight at them.

After this terrible nervous strain I felt quite weak and exhausted, and just as I was attempting to relax a bit, by turning over my airplane to my co-pilot, I heard an excited announcement over the radio that a formation of airplanes were attacking us head-on.

Well off in the distance I could see a formation of planes, but as yet could not recognize what type they were. It was almost dusk and they were hard to spot. I immediately thought that the Japs had called for reinforcements from Lae or Madang, since they were coming from that general direction. Knowing that our ammunition was running low, and with two damaged planes we would be in desperate straits, I cautioned our gunners to hold their fire until the last second, and then only fire very short bursts.

In the meantime the airplanes were getting nearer, and I noticed they were larger than fighters would be at that distance. It wasn't long before I saw that they were Liberators, and I realized that the planes were our other three squadrons... I called the leader of the first squadron and told him that we had been attacked by approximately forty Zeros and had shot down twelve. I gave him the exact location of the convoy and wished him the best of luck.

Rogers then continued on toward Port Moresby, calling ahead to inform the lookouts on the field that the six-plane formation that they would shortly see coming into their view were American bombers, not Japanese, since the airbase had suffered so many Japanese air raids that its antiaircraft gunners might get trigger-happy at the sight of incoming planes.

When they arrived over Port Moresby Rogers got his first view of the airfield complex where the 90th would be based later on, after the threat of Japanese bombings had sufficiently diminished. He waited until his two damaged B-24s had entered the landing pattern for Jackson Drome before leading the other three planes off across the Coral Sea on a heading back to Iron Range.

Tropical darkness fell swiftly as the four planes headed out over the sea, a darkness so black that Rogers had to turn on his landing lights so that the three planes following him could keep him in sight and stay with him. "I have seen many dark nights," he wrote, "but [this one] was blacker than the inside of an ink bottle." With nothing to see outside his cockpit window he was forced to fly on instruments. A high overcast prevented any of the navigators from taking star shots to fix their position, so they just had to rely on dead reckoning and hope for the best.

By the time the formation arrived in the area where they calculated Iron Range should be, the four planes were running low on gas, and no one was able to spot the airfield anywhere in the darkness below. In fact they could not even be sure that they were over land (Iron Range was about ten miles inland from the Australian coastline, at the angle they were approaching it). Rogers' flight engineer, Sgt. Jake Seper, informed him that only enough fuel remained in their tanks for about 45 more minutes of flying, and tension began rising steadily as the minutes ticked by.

Knowing that the airfield would be lit up for their return, so far as it was able to be, every crewman in the four planes strained his eyes peering out into the blackness hoping to see a light, or any other sign of human life. Then Rogers saw a flash in his peripheral vision.

> While staring out into the cold black night I saw a flash slightly behind us and off to the left. I kept my eyes glued to the spot and sure enough I saw it again. It was high in the sky and in some respects looked like lightning, yet it did not cover enough area for lightning. All of a sudden I realized that it was our searchlights from Iron Range. Later I found out that there was a light layer of mist below us that we could not see. Zipper [Col. Koon] had become worried for fear we might fly past without seeing any signs of the airdrome, so he had ordered the powerful batteries of searchlights to scan the horizon with the idea that the light would shine through the thin layer of mist and we might see it.
> I turned the formation toward the light, and called our ground station and requested the height of the cloud layer. I knew we would have to go [down] through this, and I did not want to collide with some 1,500-foot hills about ten miles from the airdrome. I wanted to make sure that we had enough clearance underneath the mist so that we could let down. We were told that we had a ceiling of one thousand feet, and our best approach was to go out over the water and let down under the mist, and then we could see the searchlights clearly and perhaps could also see our emergency runway lights.

As he maneuvered the squadron into position and lined up on the field for landing, Rogers tried to lower his landing gear, but discovered that the plane's nosewheel was jammed in the up position.

> The two main wheels went down, but one little red light burned indicating that our nosewheel had failed to lower into position. Not wanting to hold up the rest of the formation, since I did not know the exact trouble, I told them to go ahead and land while my aerial engineer crawled down into the nosewheel compartment to see if he could correct the trouble.
> After we had circled the airdrome for about fifteen minutes he finally came back and told me that our nosewheel gear had been damaged by the explosion of a Jap 20mm cannon shell. He had tried to shove the wheel into place but with no success. I ordered my co-pilot to go down and check and see if he could determine the damage. He returned to tell me that the gear itself had not been damaged, but the hinges were twisted all out of shape and this had jammed the doors and prevented the nose wheel from lowering.
> I instructed my aerial engineer to go back and try to force the doors open, and if he did not have any success for him to use his forty-five automatic and shoot the hinges off, which would release

12. COL. ROGERS' FIRST COMBAT MISSION 115

> the doors from the fuselage. This was not necessary as he used a long screwdriver as a lever and forced the battered doors open.
>
> A good landing was made, considering that the lights were not adequate on the runway. . . As we taxied into our parking place and attempted to cut our engines, we found that the two left engines would not quit running when we advanced our idle cut-off lever. Since this was the only method other than full feathering the props to stop an engine, we were forced to full feather [i. e. turn the propeller blades edge-on to the front, so that they resisted spinning].

Col. Rogers climbed stiffly from his plane and was immediately surrounded by ground personnel, mechanics, the flight surgeon, Maj. James King, and Col. Koon, all of whom had been anxiously watching the landings and wanted to know how the mission had gone. The mechanics soon explained why Rogers had been unable to shut off his two left engines: a Japanese shell had severed the cut-off controls in the left wing.

Looking over the aircraft by flashlight, they found numerous holes in the fuselage made by bullets and flak, which meant that lethal fragments of metal must have been flying around inside the airplane during the battle, but amazingly not one of the ten crewmen had so much as a scratch on him.

Koon told Rogers that he'd received a radio message from Port Moresby letting him know that the two damaged bombers had made it down safely there. The other three squadrons had reported that they were on their way back and had lost no aircraft over the convoy while bombing it, and had scored a hit on a ship.

Col. Rogers and the crews of his four bombers were, as was to be expected, utterly worn out.

> Our flight surgeon [Maj. King] had brought out his medical whiskey, which he measured out two ounces to each man. Many of the crew complained that this was not near enough, and Jimmie immediately agreed after he saw how high-strung and exhausted the men were. On my way back I had made up my mind that when we got to Iron Range the case of whiskey that I had personally brought from Hawaii would be opened up and shared by all. We gathered the crews of each ship together and departed for the squadron area where we assembled in the largest tent to relax and talk over the mission.

To his great satisfaction, Col. Rogers found that the former pessimism of his crews had completely vanished in the wake of this mission. In fact, many of the men were jubilant. Their six bombers had been under attack by forty enemy fighter planes for the better part of an hour, and not only had none of the bombers been shot down, but they had shot down several of their attackers and the squadron had also scored a bomb hit on an enemy ship. Predictions by members of the 19th Bomb Group that B-24s would be easily shot down by Japanese fighter planes had been proven utterly false. Col. Rogers' views were vindicated, and feelings of relief and optimism pervaded the tent.

> Even though everyone was excited and tired, I was pleased because the bull session started out with one of the men saying, "We gave the Japs such a licking that I'm all for going back tomorrow and giving them another dose." I was doubly grateful as this was the same officer who had made the remark that we were all going out and get shot down.
> There was no question that these men were proud of the job they had done, and they no longer lacked confidence in themselves or their airplane. . . Later on in the night the other three squadrons returned, and we rushed down to find out the results of their mission. To our amazement, they had not been engaged by any enemy fighters. This was probably due to the long engagement we had had with the Zeros, and they probably [had been] running short of ammunition and gasoline at the completion of the fight. They also must have thought our six ships were the only striking force we had, as darkness was near and no other planes were in sight when we departed.
> They [the other three squadrons] had a destroyer to their credit,* and they were very eager to find out the results of our fight. You could see confidence mixed with recklessness written all over their faces as [our squadron's] pilots and gunners described the Zeros burning and going into the ocean. Everyone agreed that the Japs' frontal attack was vicious, and due to our poor firepower forward something would have to be done about it or our losses would be terrific.
> This brought back the problem I had been working and worrying over, trying to get a nose turret installed.

Rogers' quest to get a nose turret on the B-24 was on again.

The three squadrons returning behind Rogers that night had had the same trouble he'd experienced in finding their airfield; in fact they had flown right past Iron Range in the dark and kept on going for a considerable distance. Their estimated time of arrival at Iron Range had been 10:30 PM, and by midnight their navigators were certain that they had overshot the airfield and told the pilots to turn around. On the backtrack they had finally spotted the field's searchlights and landed, nearly out of gas.

---

* Lt. Thomas F. Doyle, the bombardier on Lt. McMurria's crew, reported that his bombs hit the stern of one of the Japanese destroyers.[7]

All of the Group's bombers had returned safely to Iron Range by 1:30 AM except for one, a plane of the 321st Squadron named "Little Eva,"* piloted by Lt. Norman R. Crosson. While the other ground crews looked over their planes, assessing battle damage, "Little Eva's" ground crew sat beside the runway in their jeeps, waiting for their bomber, scanning the pitch-dark sky for its landing lights, listening for the sound of its engines. The searchlights on the field continued to shine upward into the low cloud layer to guide Crosson in.

Not far from where they sat, the ground crewmen could hear the babble of animated conversation, punctuated by an occasional loud laugh or shout, as the tired aircrews unwound from the tremendous tensions of the day, drank Col. Rogers' liquor and raucously relived the details of the day's battle in their tents.

"Little Eva's" ground crew would wait for her in vain. None of them would ever see the airplane again. Her fate is the subject of the next chapter.

Ground crewmen wait beside the runway for their bomber to return. Sometimes, as in the case of "Little Eva," a ground crew waited in vain.

---

* Little Eva was the name of a 300-pound barmaid who kept order in a restaurant and lounge named Shorty's at Greenville, South Carolina, that had been a favorite haunt of 90th Bomb Group personnel when they were stationed there. She had once thrown an unruly customer through a glass door, and the sight of Eva riding a motorcycle was said to be something to remember. Little Eva had been so popular among the men of the Group that two of their bombers were named after her.

Chapter Thirteen

THE CROSSON CREW'S ODYSSEY

During the attack on the convoy that afternoon, Crosson's bomber "Little Eva" had had bomb rack trouble and had been unable to release its bombs, a maddeningly common problem with B-24s, especially the early models. After three unsuccessful tries to drop his bombs on the ships,[*] and probably feeling that he'd pushed his luck about far enough amid the cloud of deadly flak being thrown up by the warships, Crosson left the squadron formation and headed for the Group's secondary target, Lae[1] (see Map 13-1 on page 121).

This was exactly what Lt. DeFreitas had done three days before when his squadron had not been able to locate the convoy they were searching for. Crosson's mission was turning into a carbon copy of DeFreitas', but unfortunately it would have a much different ending.

In hindsight (always 20-20), Crosson should have stuck with his squadron, but like DeFreitas he was determined to hit the Japanese somewhere if he couldn't drop on the convoy, and he took his bombs to Lae, about 250 miles to the west. His crew was not happy with the decision to leave the formation, and with good reason, as it would turn out; Crosson's zeal to hit the Japanese would end up costing the lives of seven members of his crew.

Over Lae Crosson finally managed to release his bombs,[†] and may have done some damage to the enemy airfield (no one could be sure in the twilight), but now the bomber was separated from the squadron, night was falling, and the crew was alone in a hostile sky and in an unfamiliar area. Now, like DeFreitas three days earlier, Crosson had to make his way back to Iron Range alone and in the dark.

---

[*] The entire 321st Squadron also made three bomb runs over the convoy, because the squadron commander's plane, with the lead bombardier aboard, also had his bombs hang up the first two times, and since he didn't drop, no one else did either. The third try was successful and all the squadron's bombs released except Crosson's.

[†] One source states that Crosson saw a lightning storm ahead of him before he reached Lae and aborted his attack, jettisoning his bombs into the sea and heading for Iron Range, while the 90th's Bomb Group's historian Wiley O. Woods wrote that Crosson dropped his bombs on Lae. With all the crewmen now deceased, there is no way to know which version is correct.

13. THE CROSSON CREW'S ODYSSEY

The problem of finding the way home now fell squarely on the shoulders of Crosson's navigator, Lt. John D. Dyer, who like the rest of the crew was on his first bombing mission. Dyer was now faced with about as daunting a task as any navigator ever could be: he had to plot a course of nearly 500 miles back to Iron Range, over the towering Owen Stanley Mountains and across the Coral Sea to Australia, all in pitch darkness, over unfamiliar territory, with charts of doubtful accuracy, to find an airfield situated in dense jungle that was not easy to spot even in daylight. It was the stuff of nightmares.

The darkness would prevent Dyer from seeing any landmarks on the way, so his navigation would have to be by dead reckoning, which in this case was another way of saying informed guesswork, complicated by the usual storms over the Owen Stanleys and the unpredictable winds aloft. Crosson would have to fly on instruments, out of visual contact with the world just like his navigator. There were of course no radio navigation aids to assist them, and they might as well have been navigating across the surface of Mars.

Since getting home now was the job of the pilot and navigator, with possibly some help from the radioman, the rest of the crewmembers were just nervous passengers on this part of the mission, with nothing to do but hope for the best.

After departing Lae, Crosson put the bomber into a climb to gain the necessary height to clear the mountain peaks. As they were passing over the mountains, they struck a storm so violent that Crosson and his copilot, 2nd Lt. Arthur N. Speltz, lost control of the airplane and the huge bomber went whirling down toward the ground. The terrified crew could only hang on and pray. Miraculously, Crosson managed to regain control of the plane before it struck a mountainside to become just one more bomber that mysteriously failed to return from a mission. Once he had the plane back under control, Crosson climbed to regain the lost altitude and resumed the compass heading provided by Dyer, a course that everyone fervently hoped would take them back to Iron Range.

Adding to an already dismal situation came bad luck: the plane ran into a second storm over the Coral Sea and its radios failed, leaving Crosson unable to contact Iron Range or any of the other aircraft of his squadron that might still have been in the air on their way back to base that night.

After all the other bombers of the Group were back on the ground at Iron Range, and the crews were celebrating their successful mission with Col. Rogers, the Crosson crew was still in the air, searching for the airfield.

Sometime before midnight, Crosson's bomber flew past Iron Range, passing about 40 miles to the northwest of it, still headed southwest (see Map 13-1 again). When DeFreitas had been in the same situation three nights before, he and his crew had made a nearly random decision to turn southeast, hoping to spot any sign of civilization in that direction before they ran out of gas and had to jump, and by the most amazing good luck they had run straight into the lights of Iron Range just as they were on the verge of bailing out.

Such luck would not attend Crosson's flight, however; he never deviated from his southwest heading, and without being aware of it in the dark he flew across the entire Cape York Peninsula and into the Gulf of Carpentaria, making landfall again on a wild and desolate stretch of northern Australian wilderness. As the flight neared its inevitable end, Crosson was unable to tell in the dark whether he was over land or water. As the gas gauges dropped toward empty, he took the bomber up to 9,000 feet and told his crew to get their parachutes on and get ready to bail out.

The men were now faced with a new nightmare: the prospect of jumping into an inky black void over an unknown location. As far as they knew they could have been over jungle, mountains, or sea; there was no way of knowing. Just in case they happened to be over water, they all put on their inflatable life vests.

At about 2:30 AM, as the bomber's engines began to stutter for lack of fuel, Crosson opened the bomb bay doors and gave the order to jump. In the rear of the plane, one of the gunners, Sgt. Charles B. Workman, made the mistake of trying to jump from the left waist window. Jumping from the waist windows of a B-24 was not recommended because they were right in front of the bomber's tail, and the jumper could be struck by the tail or get snagged on it. The approved method of exiting the aircraft in this part of the plane was through a camera hatch in the floor, which put the jumper beneath the tail. A bomb bay was always the best place to jump from, but for some reason Workman chose not to go forward to the bomb bays but to jump from a window instead.

The worst happened: as Workman jumped, his parachute opened prematurely and the shroud lines snagged on something on the lower window sill, probably the gun mount, and he was caught, his body flopping around outside in the slipstream, banging against the fuselage and tail. The other three men in the rear of the plane, Sgt. James B. Hilton, Sgt. Edward J. McKeen, and Cpl. John Geydos, Jr., realized Workman's predicament and, working together, tried desperately to free him.

Lt. Crosson and the six men in the front of the plane were unaware of this drama going on back in the waist and they jumped, one after the other, from the bomb bay. Crosson thought he was the last man to leave, and before he jumped he throttled back the engines and put the plane into a glide, hoping that if they were over land it might make a decent wheels-up landing and stay intact, to be found by him and the others later. An intact bomber could be used as a shelter, a refuge from the sun and rain, and it would contain emergency food and medical supplies, weapons, and survival equipment. If the radio and

13. THE CROSSON CREW'S ODYSSEY 121

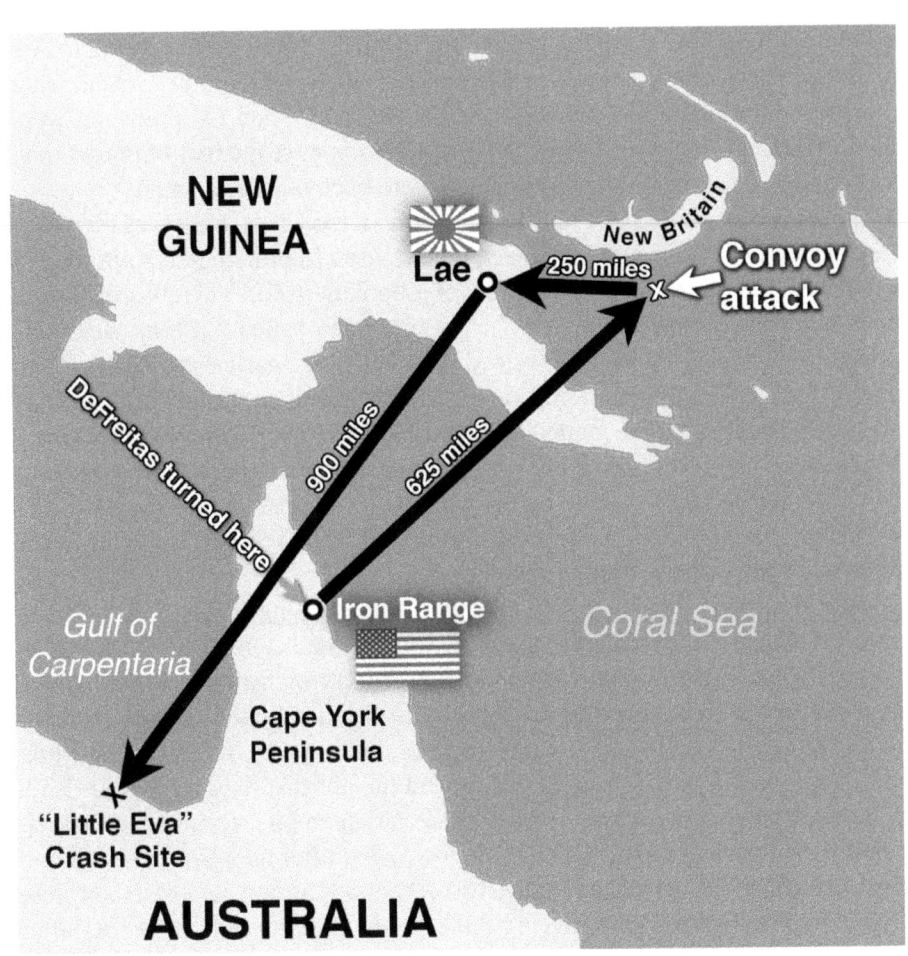

Map 13-1. The route of the Crosson bomber, "Little Eva," on the night of Dec. 1-2, 1942. The short gray arrow shows where the DeFreitas crew, in the same situation as Crosson's crew three nights previously, had made a lucky turn to the southeast and found Iron Range. Crosson did not turn, but held his course all the way across the Cape York Peninsula and the Gulf of Carpentaria and into the wilderness beyond, crashing in the remote Australian outback at the location shown when the bomber ran out of gas.

batteries survived the crash-landing, the radio might be able to send messages, and the flare guns could be used to catch the attention of searching, or just passing, aircraft. An intact aircraft would be a treasure chest for men trying to survive in a wilderness.

The three men back in the waist area of the plane, still working frantically to free Workman, could not tell how close to the ground they were in the darkness, and they waited too long to jump. The bomber struck the ground hard on its belly and burst into flames, the impact and fire killing all four of them. The burning bomber slid along the ground for some distance before coming to rest in an open area of scrub grass and brush only about fifteen miles inland from the coast. The plane had actually been over water when the crewmen were putting on their life vests, but by the time Crosson gave the bail-out order they had crossed the Australian coastline and were back over land again.

The odyssey of the surviving six members of the Crosson crew as they subsequently trekked through the barren wilderness of northern Australia toward what they hoped was rescue is worthy of a book in itself.* There is only space here to record the bare facts: Of the six men who bailed out (and were surprised to land on solid ground instead of water in the darkness), Crosson and one of the crew's gunners, Sgt. Loy L. Wilson, found each other after sunrise and hiked to the airplane, guided to it by the smoke rising from the smoldering wreckage. They found the body of Sgt. Workman lying beside the bomber's tail, still attached to the plane by his parachute shrouds, and looking over the wreckage they saw three more bodies, charred beyond recognition, lying in the remains of the waist section of the plane.

After failing to locate the four men who were missing, Crosson and Wilson set off walking to the northeast, the direction they had come from in the plane, hoping to encounter some sign of human activity or habitation. For twelve days the two walked together through the wild, uninhabited outback, a landscape of open grasslands with scattered trees, finding very little to eat or drink, until they were so weak from exposure and hunger that they were near death when they were spotted by two Australian cattlemen on December 14 [1942]. They were taken to a hospital at Burketown, and after they had been fed and rested (the heavily-built Crosson had lost 50 pounds during the hike) they were flown back to Iron Range, arriving there on the 27th, over three weeks after the crash. Their friends were shocked to see them alive, since the whole crew had been given up for lost, and they hardly recognized Crosson with his new, slim figure.

Lt. McMurria got Crossons' story from him and wrote in his diary:

> I had a long talk with [Crosson]. He was lost 13 days during which time he had two mussels, some grass, and some dysentery medicine for food. He and his radio operator wandered around the first two days without knowing each others' names and thinking there were three of them along. They swam rivers the natives would not even get near because of sharks and crocodiles. At night they covered themselves with mud to keep off the mosquitoes. They traveled through country that the blacks say has never been trav-

---

*In fact a book was written about the Crosson crew's trek, titled *Savage Wilderness: The Epic Outback Search for the Crew of Little Eva*, by Barry Ralph, University of Queensland Press, 2004.

eled by a white man. After 13 days of it, one morning they dropped off to sleep and were awakened by some shouting. It was a white man and an Aborigine. They [Crosson and Wilson] started yelling their heads off and scared the two men on horses. They went the other way, thinking that Crosson might be Japanese. When they finally saw they weren't armed they picked them up and led them to the ranch. Crosson had to cut his socks off. He went from 205 pounds down to 155 in those 13 days.[2]

The four other crewmen who had bailed out, Grady Gaston, Arthur Speltz, Dale Grimes, and John Dyer, joined up and walked north until they reached the shore of the Gulf of Carpentaria, without having seen any sign of human presence anywhere. They had the idea that they were on the Cape York Peninsula, hundreds of miles to the east of where they really were, and thought they had reached the Coral Sea. They decided that the city of Cairns must be to the north of them, so they turned northwest up the coastline, which actually took them deeper into the wilderness. Ironically, the settlement of Burketown was only a few days' walking distance down the coast in the opposite direction. The crew's bad luck just never let up.

On about the 28th of December (the men had lost track of time, after jumping on the 2nd), while trying to swim a river, Grimes was carried out to sea by the current and drowned. The other three men, so weak by this time that they could barely walk, decided that their best move would be to stay put in the shelter of a small, abandoned cattleman's shack they had run across, and try to attract the attention of airplanes that occasionally passed overhead. By that time they had walked over 100 miles.

Weeks passed, and the young men managed to stay alive by eating berries, carrion, and anything else they could find in the vicinity of the shack, but they all grew steadily weaker. Dyer faded away and died of starvation on February 10, followed by Speltz on the 25th. Over two months later, on April 21 [1943], on the 141st day since he had bailed out of "Little Eva," Gaston was feebly searching for something to eat near the shack when he was discovered and rescued by an Australian cowboy out searching for stray cattle. By that time he was only barely alive, his weight down to 80 pounds.

Thus only three men of Crosson's ten-man crew survived their first combat mission.

"Little Eva" and the "Lady Be Good"

There are striking parallels between the story of "Little Eva's" crash in the Australian wilderness on December 2, 1942, and that of the bomber

The wreckage of the bomber "Lady Be Good" lying where it was found in the Libyan desert in 1958. As usual in hard landings, the B-24 had snapped in half just behind the wing.

named "Lady Be Good"* that crashed five months later on April 4, 1943 in the North African desert on the other side of the world, in the European theater of the war.

Both of these crews were flying B-24D bombers, and both had been on their first combat missions (the "Lady Be Good" flying from North Africa across the Mediterranean Sea to bomb Naples, Italy and return). Both bombers got separated from their formations during the strikes, both returned from their missions across an ocean (the Coral Sea; the Mediterranean), both planes overshot their airfields in the dark and flew hundreds of miles beyond them into wilderness. Both crews bailed out of their aircraft around 2 AM wearing life jackets, thinking they were probably over water when they were not.

---

*The bomber "Lady Be Good" was named after the 1941 movie and song of the same name.

13. THE CROSSON CREW'S ODYSSEY 125

The wreckage of the B-24 "Little Eva" still lies today in the Australian wilderness where it crashed on Dec. 2, 1942. The plane landed more gently than the "Lady Be Good" and remained intact until it caught fire and burned.

Eight of the nine crewmen of the "Lady Be Good" survived their jumps and joined up on the ground (the ninth man was killed when his parachute failed to open). They never located their bomber, and all of them died about eight days later when they ran out of water in the scorching desert heat while trying to walk out to civilization. A diary kept by one of the men recorded their agonizing ordeal day by day, right up to the last.

While the men of the "Lady Be Good" were walking lost in the Libyan desert, Sgt. Grady Gaston of "Little Eva" was still lost in the Australian wilderness, after Lts. Dyer and Speltz had died, so that the time periods of the two bomber tragedies even overlap.

The public's interest in the "Lady Be Good" story began when the bomber was discovered in the Libyan desert in May of 1958 by a British oil exploration team. What they had run across appeared to be a "ghost bomber," lying alone and empty on the desert floor, its guns and radio still operable, coffee in thermoses inside the plane still drinkable, but with no trace of the crew.

A year later a joint Army/Air Force search team picked up the trail that the "Lady Be Good's" crewmen had left as they tried to walk out of the desert, finding equipment and clothing that the men had discarded as they walked, and marker arrows they had made by weighing down parachutes with rocks to guide anyone who might come searching for them. The bone-dry desert had preserved all these items as though they had been left there only yesterday, and the marker arrows performed their intended function, guiding the searchers to the crewmen, but far too late—by then the men had all been dead for over fifteen years.

Most of the men's bodies, along with the diary, were found 85 miles from where the men had assembled after bailing out, but one man had left the group after it had halted and continued walking until he had covered an amazing 132 miles across the desert from his starting point. The body of another man who had also kept walking after the main group gave up has never been found.

Sgt. Grady Gaston recuperating in the hospital after his 141-day ordeal in the Australian wilderness.

In the years since the discovery of the "ghost bomber" in the desert, the saga of the "Lady Be Good's" crew has been told in books, magazine articles, television shows (including an episode of *The Twilight Zone*), a movie, a permanent Air Force monument and museum exhibit, and there was even a song written about it. The terrible odyssey of "Little Eva's" crew, by contrast, is practically unknown today.

Since three men of "Little Eva's" crew survived their ordeal and lived to tell the tale, the element of mystery that so fascinated the world in the case of the "Lady Be Good" was absent from the "Little Eva" story. Nevertheless the men who hiked through the Australian wilderness showed the same grit, endurance, and determination as those who trekked through the African desert, and they should be remembered for it as well.

The charred remains of "Little Eva" still lie today in the remote Australian outback, visited only by an occasional hunter or cattleman.*

---

* In 1974 one of the bomber's engines, a landing gear leg, and some other parts were removed from the wreckage and are now on display in a museum in Mareeba, Queensland.[3]

CHAPTER FOURTEEN

CASUALTIES MOUNT

The morale in the 90th Bomb Group improved greatly with the reappearance of Col. Rogers and the successful battle with Japanese fighter planes during the bombing of the Japanese convoy on Dec. 1 [1942]. However, as time went on, further losses of planes and men sobered the young men's outlook again, and showed them just what sort of a war they were fighting in this remote and primitive part of the world.

In the first six months after the Group came overseas, the 90th would lose 24 bombers and their crews. Only five of them were shot down by the Japanese. Five more were lost to accidents, such as Lt. Larson's takeoff crash on Nov. 16. All the rest were bombers that went out on missions and simply failed to return, their fates unknown.[1] Col. Meehan's disappearance on the same date as Lt. Larson's crash was only the first of these, and aircraft and men would continue to vanish throughout the war. The wreckage of some of the 90th's missing planes has been discovered in the postwar years, but many more are yet to be found, along with hundreds of other lost American aircraft.

This would be a war in which the long distances to be flown, the flying at night over rugged and remote territory, and especially the weather, the terrible tropical weather, would pose more danger than the human enemy.

Deadly Weather

Many of the 90th's losses can be blamed on the weather patterns in the Southwest Pacific. The weather region around the equator is known today as the Intertropical Convergence Zone, where trade and equatorial winds collide and interact with solar heating. This and other complex meteorological conditions in the tropics produce extremely violent thunderstorms that often tower 40,000 feet or more above the sea, far above the altitude that a B-24 or any other World War II airplane could fly. Modern weather satellites show this zone as a band of clouds, often thunderstorms, circling the equator.

During World War II, bombers confronted by these monster storms on the way to their targets either had to abort their missions and return to base, or accept the risks (which was the normal course of action in war) and try to bore through them, enduring turbulence that could cause the pilot to lose control or even tear his airplane to pieces. Flying blindly in the dark under instrument conditions, pilots sometimes had no idea what sort of weather they were heading into, unless increasing air turbulence and flashes of lightning gave them warning. Killer storms were without a doubt the cause of many of the unsolved disappearances of American aircraft during the Pacific war.

Many who encountered the Pacific's deadly weather never lived to tell the tale, while others survived, often only by pure luck, to describe the experience. 1st Lt. Everett Wood was one of the latter. He was flying a new bomber up to Iron Range from Brisbane on December 18, 1942 when he ran into thick clouds. As he wrote later in his diary:

> Passing Townsville we encountered bad weather, so I dropped down to sea level in an attempt to fly along the coast, but the visibility was zero, and there were so many mountains to the left of us that I decided to head out to sea. At 3000' I leveled off, not wishing to get too far from shore, and took up my old heading. Twenty minutes passed (blind) when my navigator screamed into the interphone that we had just missed a mountain on our right. This meant that for twenty minutes I had been flying over land that was covered with 4000' hills, while I was flying at 3000'. I immediately hit the throttles, increased the RPM, and climbed out of danger expecting at each moment to crash into an unseen mountain.[2]

Lt. Wood made it safely to Iron Range, but Lady Luck is fickle, and another 90th bomber flying on that same day, in the same area, did not experience such good fortune. Lt. James E. Gumaer, Jr. took off from Townsville and also headed north for Iron Range. As would frequently be the case on ferry missions throughout the war, Gumaer was carrying a number of hitchhikers who had taken the opportunity to hop aboard a bomber going their way for a quick lift. Some members of a coastal artillery unit stationed near Iron Range needed to return to their station and bummed a ride on Gumaer's plane, and other men joined them who were returning to Iron Range from leave or business in Sydney. One of the passengers was a civilian representative of the Pratt and Whitney Engine Corporation, going up to Iron Range to evaluate how the company's engines were performing under combat conditions.

Since this was not a combat mission, Gumaer wasn't carrying any gunners, so there were only six crewmen aboard, making more room for the seven hitchhikers. Gumaer left Townsville at 8:15 in the morning and almost immediately flew into the same low clouds that Lt. Wood had encountered, so that he was likewise flying blind. Then, 70 miles north of Townsville, Gumaer barreled straight into the heart of an embedded thunderstorm.

Residents of the town of Ingham heard the bomber circling overhead in the storm, and then around 9 AM, only 45 minutes after Gumaer had taken

14. CASUALTIES MOUNT

off, witnesses reported seeing a flash on the face of Mt. Stralock, one of the mountains on Hitchinbrook Island just offshore. Searches in subsequent days failed to locate the plane, but in late1943 some Australian Aborigines reported finding wreckage on the mountain that turned out to be parts of Gumaer's plane. He had flown blindly into the face of a cliff, and all 13 men aboard the bomber had been killed instantly.[3]

Reconnaissance missions take their toll

The 90th's bomber crews took turns going out on lone reconnaissance missions, since it was imperative for MacArthur's headquarters to know what the enemy was up to. How badly these reconnaissance flights hurt the Japanese can be seen in Masatake Okumiya's statement on pages 10-11. Sometimes a plane would be sent to examine and photograph a specific location, such as an enemy airfield, in advance of a bombing mission by the Group; at other times a reconnaissance bomber would just fly an assigned route, looking for any signs of enemy activity in a particular area. If an enemy convoy was spotted, its position would be immediately reported back to base by radio, and then the bomber would shadow the convoy for as long as its fuel allowed, or until another bomber arrived to take over. With one bomber continually handing off to another, a convoy could be kept under surveillance until headquarters sent out a strike force.

Often a reconnaissance plane carried bombs (in which case it was called an "armed reconnaissance") that could be used to attack targets of opportunity. The great range of the B-24 allowed the airmen to keep watch over wide swaths of enemy territory many hundreds of miles from their base. However, many planes failed to return from these "recon" missions, and disappeared without a clue as to what had happened, or where or how the airplane and crew met their fate. The finding of wreckage in the years since the war has solved some of the mysteries.

On December 20, 1942, only two days after Lt. Gumaer's collision with a mountain on a ferry flight up to Iron Range from Townsville, Lt. John Rafferty and his crew took off from Iron Range and flew north across the Coral Sea to conduct a lone reconnaissance mission on the north coast of New Guinea near the Japanese airbase at Wewak. Night fell and Rafferty was on his way back, not sure where he was in the darkness, when he decided it would be better to land at Port Moresby than to recross the Coral Sea and try to find Iron Range at night. As he crossed back over the Owen Stanley Mountains he evidently thought he had cleared the peaks and was on the downslope toward Moresby, with nothing below him but low foothills.

Perhaps a headwind had slowed his progress, or his navigator had made an error, but for whatever reason he was actually still over the mountains when he began his descent to the airfield. He radioed ahead asking for Moresby's searchlights to be turned on to guide him in to the field, obviously thinking he was much closer to it than he was, and that was the last that was ever heard from him.

In the spring of 1984 the wreckage of Lt. Rafferty's bomber was found 200 miles north of Port Moresby on the 60-degree slope of a mountain in the Owen Stanley range. Like Gumaer, Rafferty had flown straight into the side of a mountain. The crew's remains were recovered from the wreck site and in 1990, forty-seven years after the crash, they were interred in a ceremony at Arlington National Cemetery.[4]

On the afternoon of 19 February, 1943, Lt. Howard F. Carlson and his crew took off from Ward's Field at Port Moresby to fly a reconnaissance mission up to the south coast of New Britain. An hour after takeoff a radio message came back that they were encountering bad weather on the northeast coast of New Guinea. Then another message was received saying that they'd spotted a four-ship Japanese convoy near Gasmata on New Britain's south coast. After that, no further word was heard, and no trace of the plane has ever been found.[5]

Of such flights Staff Sgt. Gordon Bixler, a gunner in the 90th's 320th Squadron, wrote:

> Recon missions were in some ways the most difficult. In fact, we may have lost more planes on recons than on strikes. Too often some crew would fly out in the morning and that would be the last anyone heard of them... All in all, our young pilots and navigators were not that experienced. In addition, there certainly were no [radio] flying aids for us. Some simply got lost, ran out of gas, and crashed. Others no doubt got shot down. And some simply ran into a cloud and didn't come out the other side. The weather often wasn't the best, and the Japs certainly didn't broadcast weather bulletins.[6]

The 43rd Bomb Group, nicknamed "Ken's Men," was the friendly rival of the 90th, and bombers from the two groups often operated side-by-side from the same airfields and flew joint missions throughout the war. Ralph K. DeLoach of the 43rd remembered how several of his group's crews also simply vanished on reconnaissance missions:

> They just went out and that was the end of it. There was never another word... A crew would go out and not come back, and we never had any idea of whether the cannibals had put them in their pots... or whether the sharks had eaten them, or whether the Japanese had captured them.[7]

43rd Pilot James L. Harrow recalled:

We lost a lot of airplanes in the swampy areas and up in the mountains. I got into a big thunderstorm one night near the Owen Stanley Mountains, and we went up and down. We'd lose about three or four thousand feet, and then go shooting up. I think we went over the mountains on our back. The navigator seemed to think so—but the copilot and I were quite busy. When we finally recovered and came back to Port Moresby, the navigator got out of the airplane and kissed the dirt...

Too many crews were less fortunate. The slopes of the Owen Stanley Mountains are strewn with scores of wrecked aircraft, many of them still undiscovered.[8]

Disappearances during bombing missions

Planes also disappeared during group bombing missions. On 18 December five bombers of the 90th flew a mission from Iron Range to attack yet another Japanese convoy consisting of warships and troop transports that had been reported moving along the northern coast of New Guinea. As they flew across New Guinea from the south coast to the north, the bombers ran into the usual rotten weather over the Owen Stanley Mountains.

After entering the storm clouds they were tossed about by extreme turbulence that scattered the formation as the pilots fought for control in the wild air currents. They aborted the mission and returned to Iron Range, except for a plane piloted by 1st Lt. Harold M. Adams.[9] No one had seen Adams' bomber crash, but the other pilots had been too busy with their own problems in the storm to keep track of any other planes. The fate of Adams and his crew remained unknown until 1944, when the wreckage of their bomber was found on a mountainside by an Australian army patrol, and the remains of the crew were recovered and returned to their families in the U. S. for burial.

The next day, 19 December [1942], another five B-24s of the 90th flew out from Iron Range to attack the same convoy, which was now just above Alexishafen on New Guinea's north coast, between the small volcanic islands of Bagabag and Karkar. The Japanese ships had fighter plane coverage, and the Zeros intercepted the bombers as they made their bomb runs. In the heat of the battle, a plane piloted by 22-year-old Capt. Elmo L. Patterson was last seen diving toward the sea, apparently out of control. No one saw the plane hit the water, but presumably it did since it was never heard from again either.[10] This bomber's wreckage has never been found, but probably lies today on the sea floor between the two small islands.

Takeoff and landing accidents

Accidents on the airfields, especially on takeoff with the heavily loaded (and often overloaded) bombers, took a continual toll on the 90th's aircraft

Seven members of Lt. Eugene Straw's crew died when their plane crashed on takeoff just moments before this picture was taken (note the fire still burning on the wing).

and men throughout the war.[11]* The first was the night-takeoff crash of Lt. Paul Larson's bomber on November 17, 1942, at Iron Range that was covered in Chapter 9. Then on the day after Christmas another bomber taking off from Iron Range in the dark, on another mission to Rabaul, veered off the runway just as Lt. Larson's had done. Barely airborne, it plowed through the branches of the trees on one side of the runway, burst into flame, and fell to the ground where it exploded and burned. The pilot, Lt. Roy A. Kendrick, and everyone else aboard the plane was killed.[11]

Six days later, on the 1st of January [1943] at Port Moresby, Lt. Eugene W. Straw was taking off in the predawn darkness when his bomber strayed off the runway and hit rocks and other debris. The bomber skidded across the ground, clipped a parked truck, broke apart, and caught fire. Straw and two others managed to get out of the burning wreckage and survived, but the other seven crewmembers died in the fire (photo above).

In 1944, when the 90th was based at Nadzab, New Guinea, Sgt. John F. Heyn of the 3rd (Light) Bomb Group's photo section remembered:

> The one event that sticks very prominently in my mind was not a pleasant one. The 90th Bomb Gp. (H) [Heavy] was also stationed

---
* Major Kenneth D. McCullar, the swashbuckling B-17 pilot who specialized in skip-bombing and was a favorite of General Kenney, was killed along with all his crew when his bomber reportedly struck a wallaby that ran across the runway at Port Moresby, the animal bouncing up into an engine supercharger and setting off a chain of failures on the plane that caused it to crash in flames just after it lifted off.

14. CASUALTIES MOUNT

The crew of this bomber survived when the plane lost its brakes on landing, overshot the runway, and ran off an embankment into a river. The fuselage of the plane is still there today.

> at Nadzab with their B-24's. There was about a six day stretch when you could almost set your watch at 7:00 AM by an explosion. It would be a B-24 fully loaded with bombs and fuel, exploding on take-off. Never did hear what the problem was, but they made a hell of a racket and a hell of a crater in the runway. And that was a hell of a way for those poor guys to go—but then there ain't no easy way.[12]

And so it went, over and over again on every airfield occupied by the 90th throughout the war. Sometimes the pressures of war caused men to simply demand more than the laws of physics would allow, trying to get aircraft to fly that were just too heavy to get off the ground on the length of runway available. At other times mechanical failures during takeoff, the most critical time of a loaded bomber's flight, caused crashes. Tire blowouts and engine failures caused planes to veer off the runway and crash. In still other cases the bombers struck something on the runway, such as a pile of gravel or sand washed onto the field by rain, unseen in the dark.

Coming to grips with death

Some of the anguish of losing friends in a bomber that failed to return from a mission, or that was shot down in combat, or crashed on takeoff, is evident in a diary entry of Lt. Charles Rolph, navigator on the crew of Lt. "Hoot" Basset of the 90th Bomb Group. Rolph wrote:

> It is with great sadness that I write this as we lost one of our crews today. You just can't believe that it happens. It comes like a shot out of the blue and you tell yourself it can't be true, it's impossible, but then you see it is true because they are not around.[13]

Another 90th pilot, Capt. Henry C. Holliday, lost a good friend, Lt. Louis Wells, in a takeoff accident and poured out his grief in his diary, in the form of a letter to his dead friend:

> My Dear Louis: This I dedicate to you and hope and pray you have found everlasting happiness. Your death, the death of a dear friend, has left a scar on me that will never be erased. We had become lifelong friends in such a short time. . . Do you remember the night before you died, we signed each other's Short Snorters, gabbed and had a beer? Then you had to turn in as you were flying early next morn, your last flight. If only we would have known! Louis, I pray for your soul. You know the value and depth of friendship between men. That is why your death has knocked the heart out of me. . . To you Louis I have this to say: through knowing you I have gained in wealth of friendship a thousand-fold. . . I'm talking to you across the space. You've gone but yet you are still here. . . Don't feel badly old man. Life is short for all of us. . . You are out of the turmoil and strife but I still carry on. Mine is the hardships and the heartbreak to face. The sorrow is mine but there is that one beautiful tomorrow coming. . . Goodbye and good luck buddy. I'll be seeing you.[14]

In another diary entry Holliday wrote:

> This steady progression of friends into the unknown—so swift—leaves little time for a full measure of sorrow. One discovers a deadening of the finer senses with the passing of each one. The act is so sudden that the loss is not fully realized until a long period of time has elapsed.[15]

Mr. Jaime Baca, one of the waist gunners on the crew of Lt. James Horner, whose story will be told in Part 2, told the author that although he and all the other men on his crew were always scared on bombing missions, when it came right down to it they believed that bad things would only happen to "the other guy," the other plane, the other crew. "All young men have that feeling of being indestructible," he said. "Without it we couldn't have gone on."

However, there were times when it was driven home to some young men, when they lost close friends, that death could very well claim them too.

Sgt. Carl Camp was a gunner on one of the 90th's bombers and wrote:

> We had already seen flak and fighters trying to kill us and had not felt much fear, but the loss of friends had pushed us over the invisible line. Then we knew we could die also. We didn't know or believe that until then. That was what made us older suddenly, and different looking—and feeling. . . The first time the message gets through to us, that is the real blow. . .
>
> I suppose, too, we grieved for them because they were dead for all time and would never be able to do any of the things we all talked about doing "when the war was over." We all expected to return to a life of unadulterated peace after suffering a lot or a little to bring it about, but our friends would never glean any of the rewards. One can very quickly project such thoughts to oneself. . . That is why we never spent much time after that grieving for the dead. It affects one's efficiency too much and hurts like hell. Then, after a few months, when one became rather inured to it all, it didn't hurt at all. We sort of buried any memories of home and any hopes of returning. It seemed like we had been there in New Guinea forever and would be forever, one way or another.[16]

A kind of fatalism set in among many of the men, an emotional numbness, exemplified by another gunner's attitude:

> We had seen dead men hauled out of the bombers and we had seen a few go down over the target, but mostly we had aged from the constant shock of seeing crews go out and just never come home. A lot of people we met on our first days were with us no longer. It no longer chilled us as it had at first. We were numb, having already acquired that nonchalant regard of other peoples' deaths the older ones had startled us with upon our arrival.
>
> Nothing seemed to matter very much anymore. Everything in the jungle seemed of gray hue. It was hard to enthuse over anything, even [leave to] Sydney. We were suspended in limbo, doing a required task enough times until we earned redemption to the States. . .We gloomily supposed we wouldn't live that long anyway.[17]

The 90th Bomb Group's depressing litany of losses from various causes would continue month by month until the end of the war, as hundreds of fine young men from America met their deaths in remote places on the opposite side of the world from their homes, places that they had never heard of or imagined that they would ever see, let alone die in. The remains of many of them, along with their aircraft, still lie scattered throughout the Southwest Pacific today. Families in America grieve for them still.

Chapter Fifteen

TAKING TURNS AT PORT MORESBY

During December of 1942, a particularly sopping wet month at Iron Range, an area of Australia that has been known to get 100 inches of rain in a single month, the problems with basing a heavy bomber group in so primitive a place, and one so far away from the enemy, became increasingly apparent. Not only did flying from Iron Range across the Coral Sea add 350 miles each way to bombing missions against the Japanese on New Guinea and surrounding islands, but the mud on Iron Range's unpaved runways and taxiways during the rainy season (not to mention the thick dust on the rare times the airfield was dry), along with the 50-foot trees crowding the field on all sides, made landings and takeoffs exceptionally hazardous, as Col. Art Rogers had predicted on the first day he landed there.

The first solution tried was to have the 90th's four squadrons take turns being based at Port Moresby for a week each, and fly bombing missions from there, despite the Japanese air raids on the Moresby airfields. Thus, while one squadron of (nominally) twelve bombers was actively flying strikes against the Japanese from Moresby, the other three squadrons of the Group would remain safely at Iron Range and stand down except for any "maximum effort" missions that would require them to fly also. This policy of rotating squadrons through Port Moresby would continue for about six weeks, until General Kenney felt it was safe enough to bring the entire 90th Bomb Group up to Port Moresby and base it there in February.

At the beginning of January 1943, it had been six weeks since the 90th Bomb Group's first combat mission—the strike at Bougainville's Faisi-Buin harbor on November 15, and during those six weeks the group had lost 11 bombers and had 84 crewmen killed. The losses exceeded replacements from the States, since new aircraft and crews arrived only sporadically, in a trickle, and that situation would continue until near the end of the war when the Germans were finally defeated in Europe. Most of the output of America's war industries continued to go to Europe to fight Hitler, and Europe was where the attention of the Joint Chiefs of Staff in Washington remained centered. Men and supplies seemed to be sent to the Pacific only as afterthoughts. Generals MacArthur and Kenney's continual requests for more men and matériel often seemed to fall on deaf ears. Kenney made more than one trip from Australia to Washington to plead in person for aircraft and pilots.

Only two new bombers were received by the 90th in the entire month of December, 1942.

On-the-job training

Meanwhile, as the weeks went by and the missions began piling up, the young men of the 90th, along with all other American airmen sent to the Pacific, were learning their deadly trade of fighting the Japanese with their aircraft on-the-job. There had been no way to simulate the horrible conditions of Pacific combat flying in Stateside training; in fact many of the problems had not even been foreseen. As the 90th's historian wrote:

> The men had no experienced personnel in the art of combat flying and their experience was gained only as they faced the enemy. They had proven that the B-24 Liberator was a dependable bomber, but they were also learning its limitations. It was not an ideal bombing platform against ships at high altitude, since they [the ships] could take evasive action after the bombs were dropped. The men of the 90th were also doing much of the reconnaissance and would continue to do so until reconnaissance squadrons arrived in the theater. Fighter escort over long missions was not available, but the 90th had well protected itself in most of the encounters with Jap fighters.[1]

The 90th's bombing missions against such Japanese strongholds as Rabaul and Lae were still mostly being conducted at night, to try to remain unseen by Japanese fighter planes and flak guns. Sometimes the bombers went out on strikes in formations of several planes, while at other times they went singly. One of the lone flights, a mission that met with yet another tragic ending, is well documented: an attack on Rabaul by a bomber named "Crosair."*

The last flight of the bomber "Crosair"

On the first day of the new year 1943, Maj. Philip J. Kuhl and his crew flew a lone night mission to Rabaul, taking off from Port Moresby shortly after midnight in a bomber with the name "Crosair." The nine men aboard were:

Maj. Phillip J. Kuhl, the pilot, from Chicago, Illinois
2nd Lt. Charles F. Boster, copilot, from San Francisco, California
2nd Lt. John Perakos, bombardier, from New Britain, Connecticut
1st Lt. Alonzo D. Alexander, navigator, from Marrowbone, Kentucky

---

*The name was probably supposed to be "Corsair," but the artist who painted it on the side of the airplane misspelled it.

S/Sgt. Harold H. Helzer, flight engineer, from Lincoln, Nebraska
T/Sgt. Earnest R. Rhodes, radio operator, from Wewoka, Oklahoma
S/Sgt. Fred T. Diggs, waist gunner, from Johnson City, Tennessee
Sgt. Theodore N. Elias, waist gunner, from Los Angeles, California
Sgt. Carol E. Domer, tail gunner, from Centralia, Kansas

"Crosair" took off from Jackson Field just after midnight and was soon crossing the Owen Stanley Mountains on a heading for Rabaul. On this night the mountain range served up its usual smorgasbord of bad weather, and Kuhl ran into rain, snow, sleet, and lightning. Determined to carry out his mission, he decided to try to go up over the top of the storm, so everyone put on oxygen masks and up they went, but the storm clouds were still thick at 32,000 feet, which was as high as the airplane could go. Kuhl then just punched through the storm, giving everybody aboard a wild ride for a while, but they finally made it through into smooth air.

Once they reached Rabaul, Kuhl found the town and harbor concealed by an undercast, so he circled around dropping flares through the clouds, trying to illuminate the target area well enough to bomb something, and finally ended up dropping his bombs on Vunakanau, one of the Japanese airfields near Rabaul. Kuhl then withdrew to the east and flew through St. George's Channel to reach the south side of New Britain Island, and turned southwest across the Solomon Sea on a course back to Port Moresby (Map 15-1, opposite).

At 6:45 AM, without warning, the bomber's number four engine (the outboard engine on the right wing) quit, and could not be restarted. A little while later the inboard engine on the same wing (number three) also suddenly stopped. "Crosair" nearly snap-rolled when the second engine quit, but Kuhl caught it and got it back under control, then did his best to fly the plane on its two left engines only. He found that he could only keep it under good control by flying with the right wing high. As the plane was flying along in this tilted attitude, Kuhl ordered the crew to throw out everything loose inside the plane to lighten it and try to keep it in the air.

Maj. Kuhl thus found himself in the same situation that Lt. Werner had been in on the Group's very first combat mission on Nov. 15, 1942, i. e. his two right engines dead and the plane difficult to control, and flying over the Solomon Sea a long ways from land. Werner had decided to make for the nearest Allied airfield, which was at Milne Bay, and Kuhl did the same. Making it back to Port Moresby was out of the question, since the plane would never be able to climb over the mountains on two engines. Kuhl turned southeast for Milne Bay.

Werner had managed to fly 500 miles from Bougainville Island back to the southern New Guinea coast on two engines before he'd had to ditch,* but Kuhl

---

*And as we shall see shortly, another B-24 made 600 miles on only two engines, but it

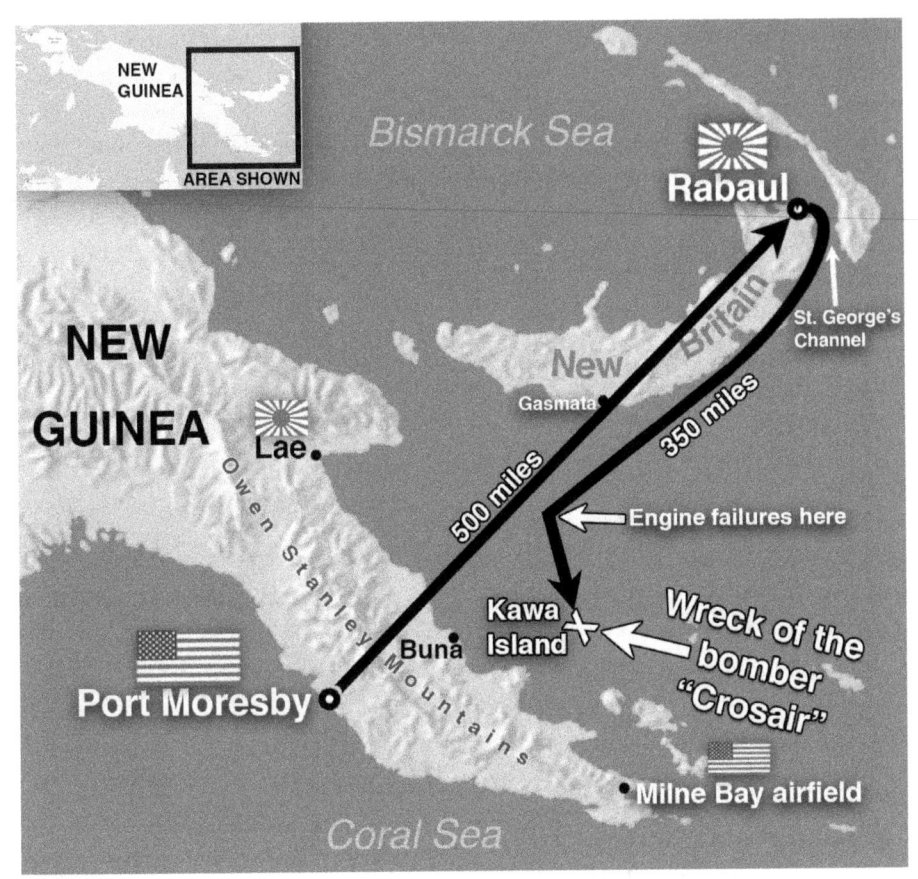

Map 15-1. On January 1, 1943, Maj. Philip J. Kuhl flew a lone night bombing mission from Port Moresby to Rabaul in a B-24D named "Crosair." After losing two engines on the way back he ditched near tiny Kawa Island.

only covered about 50 miles, while the plane slowly descended from 9,000 to only 500 feet above the sea, before he could go no further. He was pushing the two left engines hard, and the strain finally told on them: the propeller speed governors failed, allowing the engines to run wild and causing the plane to vibrate violently. Kuhl then had no choice but to chop the throttles and set the plane down on the water right where they were, which happened to be near little Kawa Island, one of the many small islets and reefs off the northeast coast of New Guinea known as the Trobriand Island Group.

By this time it was daylight, so that Kuhl was able to see the ocean and set up his water landing. He skimmed the bomber along just above the surface of the sea as it slowed to stall speed, then raised the nose so that the tail touched the water first, trying to make the landing as gentle as possible. However, the

---

was one engine on each wing, not both on one side as in Werner's case.

plane's tail could not stand the strain of being dragged through the water, and it snapped loose and folded up over the fuselage. Then the bulk of the plane plowed into the water and began sinking rapidly.

When the tail folded over, one of the gunners in the rear of the plane, Sgt. Carol Domer, was thrown deep into the bomb bay, where he became trapped in the wreckage. Sgt. Fred Diggs, standing near him, was also badly hurt. As the bomber was sinking, Sgt. Ted Elias did his best to free Domer, but was unsuccessful, and Domer went down with the plane. The two life rafts deployed, and Sgts. Ernest Rhodes and Harold Helzer were able to pull the badly injured Sgt. Diggs into the raft before the plane went down. All eight survivors got into the two rafts.

Natives on Kawa Island had seen the big airplane splash into the water and sink, and they paddled out in canoes to help. They towed the two rafts to the island, where the crew was met by some Australian army coastwatchers. The Australians put the crew into a motor launch and headed for Kiriwina Island, about fifty miles to the east. Sgt. Diggs died in the launch.

Sgt. Carol E. Domer went down with the wreckage of the bomber "Crosair."

Before the boat reached Kiriwina, it was spotted by a big four-engine flying boat named "Camilla," a former British Airways amphibious airliner that the Australians had pressed into wartime service for air-sea rescue. "Camilla" had been alerted to "Crosair's" ditching by radio and had come out to search for the crew. The big seaplane landed on the water near the motor launch and took the Americans aboard, including Diggs' body, and flew them to the Milne Bay airfield that Maj. Kuhl had hoped to reach in "Crosair."[2] Later they were flown back to Port Moresby.

In 2002 the wreckage of the bomber "Crosair" was spotted resting on the white, sandy bottom of the Solomon Sea in only 100 feet of water, in good condition. The tail is still folded over the rear part of the fuselage, but otherwise it appears as though it had only recently landed there. Photographs taken by divers revealed that there are still machine guns protruding from the bomber's nose, showing that the crew had not been able to jettison all their guns in their attempt to lighten the plane. The open waist windows where Sgts. Diggs and Elias once manned their guns now stare blankly out at the schools of fish passing by. Presumably the remains of Sgt. Domer are still present in the bomb bay.

In 2016 the family of Sgt. Domer enlisted the help of their congressman, Sen. Jerry Moran, to authorize a government-funded effort to recover Domer's remains from the submerged plane, hoping to bury him in his hometown cemetery in Centralia, Kansas, with his sister (then 98 years old) attending the funeral. This has not been accomplished as of 2018.

Rescuing aircrews downed at sea

Although the crew of "Crosair" was picked up by a four-engined flying boat, more often crews were rescued by twin-engine PBY Catalinas. During bomber strikes against Japanese targets, Catalinas and sometimes U. S. submarines in the area would be alerted and placed on standby to rescue any crews that had to ditch. These efforts to rescue downed crews at sea mystified the Japanese, who made no effort whatever to rescue their own downed aviators— they were simply left to die if they couldn't save themselves.

At Chichi Jima, a small island near Iwo Jima, on Sept. 2, 1944, Japanese soldiers on the island saw an American dive bomber shot down by their flak crash in the sea offshore. Of the three-man crew, only the pilot survived. To the amazement of the watching Japanese, an American submarine surfaced and took the pilot aboard. No Japanese submarine captain would ever have risked his sub to do such a thing.

"We were supposed to die for the Emperor," said Masaji Ozawa, a Japanese soldier on Chichi Jima. "We were small things, like bugs to be squashed."[3] Japan's fighting men expected no individual recognition, and they received none. If the Emperor and his warlords considered their own soldiers as only "bugs to be squashed," their attitude toward the peoples of the countries they conquered, as demonstrated by all the the mindless brutality and countless atrocities they condoned, makes sense. It was an emperor and an empire without a trace of humanity, a government obsessed with power and greed—in other words, the very definition of evil.

The dive-bomber pilot who was rescued by a submarine that day was Lt. George H. W. Bush, who 45 years later would become the 41st president of the United States.

The Japanese who were so astounded that an American sub would pick up a downed aviator would have been shocked to the core to learn that Admiral Halsey had once diverted an entire task force of many ships toward an area where a few downed American airmen had been reported to be floating in rafts, hoping to spot and rescue them.

Chapter Sixteen

THE LOSS OF GENERAL WALKER

On 3 September, 1942, General Kenney appointed Brigadier General Kenneth N. Walker to be the head of 5th Bomber Command, which was the controlling authority for all bomb groups in the 5th Air Force area of operation, including the 90th Bomb Group. In January of 1943 Walker established his headquarters at Port Moresby, the most forward base for Allied bombers at the time. Kenney himself remained with General MacArthur at his headquarters in Brisbane, Australia, sending orders up to Walker from there.

Kenneth Walker was another officer who, like Col. Meehan, Col. Rogers, and nearly every other U. S. military commander of WWII, believed in leading from the front and sharing the dangers of the men under his command. Flying bombing missions at the head of his men cost Col. Meehan his life, and it would cost Gen. Walker his. Only by the greatest good fortune did Col. Rogers, who could always be found in the lead bomber on the most dangerous of missions, survive the war.

On average Walker went out on one bombing mission per week with his bomber crews, until General Kenney got wind of it and ordered him to stop flying combat and remain on the ground. Kenney was mainly afraid of what would happen if Walker was shot down and captured by the Japanese. With Walker's rank and his knowledge of American air operations, the Japanese would do their best to torture the information out of him, and, Kenney felt, would likely succeed.

As Kenney wrote in his journal:

> I gave Walker and [Brig. Gen. Ennis] Whitehead a lecture ... and ordered them to stop flying combat missions. Walker had come back the night before from a reconnaissance mission with three feet gone from the left wingtip of the B-17 he was flying in. Flying under the low clouds in the dark looking for Jap barges along the coast, they had just got too low passing over a point of land and hooked the wing on a tree. They were lucky to get the plane back home. Walker had been over Rabaul several times already on the excuse that he thought he should go along once in a while to see how his crews were doing. I told him that from then on I wanted him to run his command from his headquarters. In the airplane he was just extra baggage. He was probably not as

16. THE LOSS OF GENERAL WALKER

good in any job on the plane as the man already assigned to it. In fact, in case of trouble, he was in the way. On the other hand, he was the best bombardment commander I had and I wanted to keep him so that the planning and direction would be good and his outfit take minimum losses in the performance of their missions. One of the big reasons for keeping him home was that I would hate to have him taken prisoner by the Japs. They would have known that a general was bound to have access to a lot of information and there was no limit to the lengths they would go to extract that knowledge from him. We had plenty of evidence that the Nips had tortured their prisoners until they either died or talked. After the prisoners talked they were beheaded anyhow, but most of them had broken under the strain. I told Walker that frankly I didn't believe he could take it without telling everything he knew, so I was not going to let him go on any more combat missions.[1]

Walker ordered a dozen or so bombers of the 43rd Bomb Group to be based continually at Port Moresby, and the 90th would soon follow, coming up from Iron Range in February. The 43rd's bombers were conducting missions against the same targets as the 90th's, and the two groups would often combine forces and fly together on the same missions, although at this time the 43rd was still flying the slower B-17 (they would switch to B-24s later).

One of these joint missions was flown on the 5th of January, 1943. It was yet another strike at the Japanese stronghold of Rabaul, and this time the target would be a large concentration of transports and warships that aerial reconnaissance had spotted in Simpson Harbor and Blanche Bay. It was no doubt a convoy in the making that would soon be heading south to reinforce and supply the Japanese garrisons in New Guinea, and this was a chance to hit and disrupt it at its source, while it was sitting stationary and concentrated.

Twenty-one bombers would fly the mission, making this a big raid by Pacific war standards.* As usual there would be no Allied fighter escort for the bombers, since the American fighters in use at this time didn't have the range to fly that far (the distance to Rabaul and back from Port Moresby was a thousand miles—see Map 16-1 on page 145).

Ignoring Kenney's orders not to fly, Gen. Walker decided to lead the mission himself, riding along in a B-17 named "San Antonio Rose." Kenney had ordered the strike to be carried out at dawn, when the approach of the bombers would be covered by darkness, but Walker disregarded that order too and changed the time of the attack to noon, reasoning that in daylight all

---

*In Europe at this time it was not unusual for the U. S. 8th Air Force to send hundreds of bombers at a time on missions from England to bomb targets in Nazi-occupied Europe. For example, on 17 August, 1943, 230 bombers made a daylight raid on Schweinfurt, Germany.

the planes would be able to see each other and remain together, operating more as a unit instead of flying through darkness separately to arrive over Rabaul individually at dawn.

Thus on the morning of the 5th, around 9 AM, six B-24s of the 90th Bomb Group's 400th Squadron that were temporarily based at Port Moresby, plus six B-17s from the Moresby-based 43rd Bomb Group, took off from Jackson Field and headed for Rabaul. As usual when Liberators flew with Fortresses, the six B-24s of the 90th had to throttle back and slow down to stay in formation with the slower B-17s so that they would all arrive over the target together.[2]

Nine more of the 90th's B-24s were supposed to fly up from Iron Range to participate in this mission, but they had not been able to take off from their muddy airfield and so remained on the ground. The mission thus proceeded with twelve bombers only.

When the American planes arrived over Simpson Harbor at noon, the Japanese were caught by surprise, being accustomed by now to night or dawn raids. The Japanese fighter planes were nearly all sitting on the ground, and there was not even any antiaircraft fire at first. Whether Walker had anticipated this, or it was just a lucky break, is impossible to say, but whatever the case, the noon attack time had worked out excellently.

Brigadier General Kenneth N. Walker (above and below), lost while leading a combat mission over Rabaul, 5 January 1943, for which he was awarded the Medal of Honor.

The dozen bombers spread out over the harbor, their bombardiers picking their targets, and practically simultaneously dropped their bombs on individual ships from around 5,000 feet. They were able to work without much hindrance, sinking two ships and doing serious damage to several others, while the enemy fighters were still scrambling to get into the air and the flak gunners were running to man their guns.

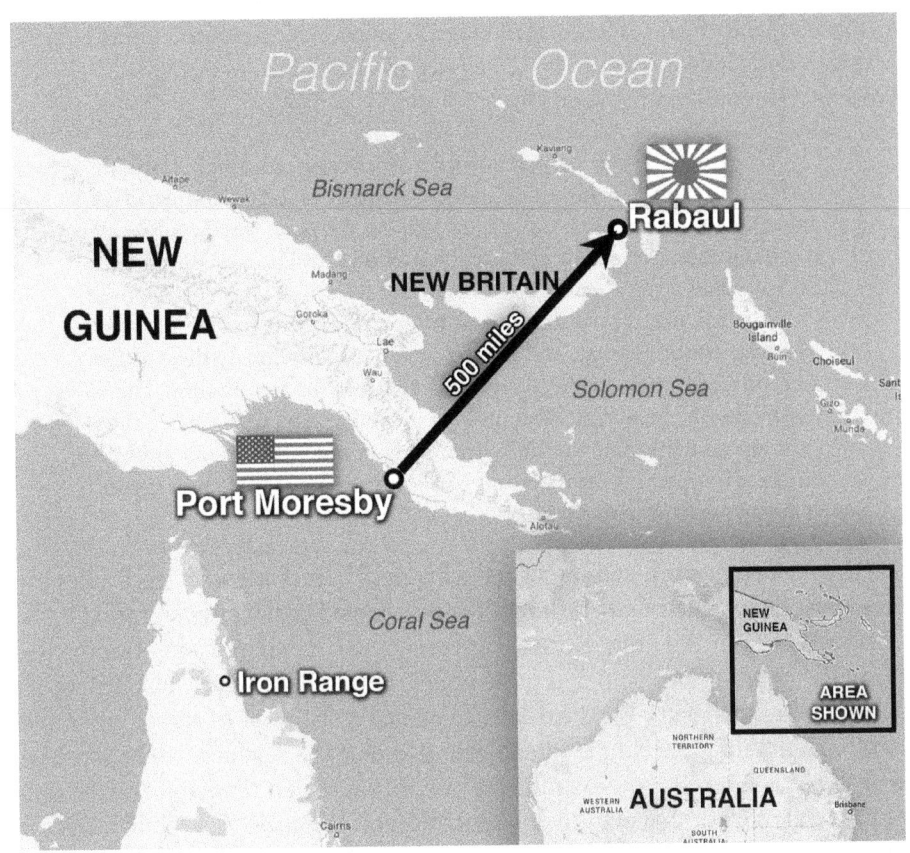

Map 16-1. Gen. Walker's mission to Rabaul, 5 Jan. 1943. Walker led six B-24s of the 90th Bomb Group, along with six B-17s from the 43rd, to bomb Japanese shipping in Rabaul's harbor. He did not return.

The pilot of one of the 90th's bombers was Lt. James McMurria, the 319th Squadron pilot mentioned in earlier chapters, who had flown up to Port Moresby from Iron Range and had been temporarily attached to the 400th for this mission. "You never saw so many ships in one harbor," McMurria wrote in his diary that night.[3] Lt. William L. Whitacre of the 400th Squadron remembered, "We went in over the harbor to bomb ships and could see the aerodrome with Zeros taking off to come up and get us, and bombers taking off to keep from being bombed."

The bombardier aboard Lt. Henry Chovanec's plane reported that his bombs hit and sank a 10,000-ton transport ship, and Lt. Whitacre saw at least three other ships on fire as the bombers turned for home.[4] One Japanese cargo ship split in half when bombs straddled it and buckled its hull in on both sides.[5]

Probably encouraged by the initial lack of opposition, Gen. Walker's bomber was seen circling the harbor, likely taking photos of the damage done to the ships. But he lingered too long. A swarm of Japanese fighters soon pounced on "San Antonio Rose." The pilot of one of the departing B-17s, Fred Wesche, remembered the scene in an interview in 2001:

> We had to break formation over the target to bomb individually, and then we were supposed to form up immediately after crossing the target, but no sooner had we dropped our bombs and my tail gunner says, "Hey, there's somebody in trouble behind us." So we made a turn and looked back and here was an airplane, one of our airplanes, going down, smoking and on fire, not necessarily fire, but smoke anyway, and headed down and obviously headed for a cloud bank with a whole cloud of fighters on top of him. There must have been about fifteen or twenty fighters. Of course, they gang up on a cripple, you know, polish that one off with no trouble, but he disappeared into a cloud bank and we never saw him again. It turns out it was the general.[6]

The desperate maneuvering of the damaged "San Antonio Rose" under attack must have ended in a crash, but the wreckage has never been found.

Two of "San Antonio Rose's" crewmen, the copilot, Capt. Benton H. Daniel, and an officer who had gone along on the flight with Gen. Walker as an observer, Maj. Jack W. Bleasdale, managed to bail out of the bomber and landed in the jungle. Had they been able to evade the Japanese and somehow return to Port Moresby or Australia they could have shed some light on the fate of General Walker, but they were captured and imprisoned at Rabaul. Then they too vanished, no doubt murdered like so many other prisoners of the Japanese.[*]

One other B-17 on the raid was shot up and lost on this strike, ditching on the way home, but its crew was recovered. The other four B-17s and all six of the 90th Bomb Group's B-24s made it back to Port Moresby.

Gen. Kenney was furious when he heard that Gen. Walker had personally led another bombing mission against his orders, and that his worst fear had been realized and Walker had been shot down. He told Gen. MacArthur that if Walker were found and rescued he would reprimand him and temporarily relieve him of command. MacArthur agreed, but said that if Walker were not found then he (MacArthur) would recommend him for the Congressional Medal of Honor.

Gen. Walker's fate remained (and remains to this day) a mystery, and the Medal of Honor award went through. President Roosevelt presented the medal to Walker's teenage son in the Oval Office. General Kenney happened to be in

---

[*] The Japanese on Rabaul destroyed all their prisoner records before surrendering in 1945, no doubt hoping to avoid being charged with war crimes.

16. THE LOSS OF GENERAL WALKER

Washington at the time on one of his visits to plead for more aircraft to be sent to the Pacific, and he went to the White House to attend the ceremony, writing afterward:

> The kindly, fatherly way the President handled the situation, putting young Walker, who was about seventeen, at ease and sending him away with his eyes shining with pride over the nice things F. D. R. had said about his father, was something to watch and listen to. The Roosevelt charm was no myth. He did a swell job.[7]

Gen. Walker's replacement as Commander of 5th Bomber Command was Gen. Howard K. Ramey. Ironically, Ramey, too, would soon be lost without a trace in a B-17, as will be described in Chapter 22.

Today (2018) Douglas Walker, Gen. Walker's son who accepted the Congressional Medal of Honor for his father from President Roosevelt, is petitioning Congress to authorize a search for the wreckage of the B-17 "San Antonio Rose," hoping to recover the remains of his father and the other men aboard the plane. Witnesses in other planes had all agreed that Walker's bomber was headed toward the land, not the sea, as it was going down (and the two men who parachuted out of it landed in the jungle, not the ocean). Its wreckage therefore may lie somewhere in the rugged and remote Tor mountains of New Britain near Rabaul. Perhaps the bomber will yet be found.

The last picture ever taken of Gen. Walker shows him in front of his tent at Port Moresby.

Chapter Seventeen

ANOTHER CONVOY ATTACK

The supply convoy that the Japanese had been assembling in Rabaul's harbor, preparing for a run to New Guinea, turned out to have been in a different part of the harbor from where Walker's bombers attacked that morning, and its ships were unscathed. The convoy got underway the next day, 6 January [1943], running down the south coast of New Britain, headed for Lae. It consisted of five transports, four destroyers, and two cruisers, with ten to fifteen Zeros flying protective cover over it.

The convoy was spotted that morning by a 90th Bomb Group plane piloted by Lt. Frank D. Dowie, Jr. that was out on reconnaissance, and its location was radioed back to Port Moresby. Dowie followed the convoy, staying in clouds most of the time for concealment, and kept Port Moresby updated on the convoy's position until his bomber's fuel ran low and he had to head for home.

At Port Moresby, 321st Squadron pilot Lt. Walter E. Higgins and his crew were briefed on the location and composition of the convoy, and they took off at noon in a bomber named "Cowtown's Revenge," flying alone, to take over shadowing duties from Dowie and continue reporting the convoy's position until it could be attacked in force. Higgins had a load of bombs aboard and planned to drop them on the ships if he got the chance. The nine crewmen of "Cowtown's Revenge" were:

> 1st Lt. Walter E. Higgins, Pilot
> 2nd Lt. Lyle Schoenaue, Copilot
> 2nd Lt. Robert Paviour, Bombardier
> Lt. George W. Sellmer, Navigator
> Cpl. Ralph N. Wolf, Radio Operator
> T/Sgt. Neil J. Gaudet, Flight Engineer
> Sgt. Louis C. Izzo, Gunner
> S/Sgt. Henry W. Satterfield, Gunner
> Sgt. Edward A. Leonard, Gunner

"Cowtown's Revenge" found the enemy ships at 2 PM, still moving southwestward off the southern coast of New Britain, but the bomber was spotted by three Zeros that immediately attacked. Higgins dove his plane into a cloud-

17. ANOTHER CONVOY ATTACK

bank to hide, and escaped undamaged, and then by ducking in and out of the clouds for the next hour as Dowie had done he was able to shadow the convoy, unmolested, radioing position reports to Port Moresby.

Then he decided to drop his bombs on the convoy, even though it would require his bomber to be completely exposed to the Zeros as well as to the ships' antiaircraft guns. It was a bold move, and it proved a foolhardy one. From 11,500 feet Higgins dove down to 9,500, leveled off, and started his bomb run. As he neared the ships he handed control of the plane off to his bombardier, Lt. Paviour, who picked out a ship and lined up his Norden bombsight on it.

The Japanese ships and the Zeros all saw the American bomber coming, and the six warships sent up a tremendous barrage of flak while nine Zeros dove on it, flying right into their own flak cloud to press their attacks. Paviour stayed concentrated on his bomb run and let his bombs go. The first one of the string was seen to hit the side of a destroyer, but later no one could remember where the rest of them went because everybody suddenly became too busy trying to fight off the Japanese fighter planes to watch bomb hits. The bomber's gunners were all firing away at the Zeros, and Sgt. Leonard riddled one and saw it go down.

A flak burst then hit the bomber's number one engine (the outboard engine on the left wing), causing it to burst into flames, but the internal fire extinguisher in the wing was able to suppress the fire. The Zero pilots, seeing that the bomber was damaged, sensed a kill and attacked with even greater determination. Gunner Sgt. Louis C. Izzo hit another Zero and sent it down out of control. Radio operator Sgt. Wolf manned one of the gun positions and managed to hit a third Zero, which veered off smoking.

Flight Engineer Sgt. Gaudet was in the upper turret firing at the fighters when Lt. Higgins called him down to shut off the fuel to the dead engine. While Gaudet was doing this, the navigator, Lt. George W. Sellmer, climbed up into the turret to take his place and drove off a Zero that was attacking from above. Gaudet then resumed his place in his turret.

With the bombs gone, Lt. Higgins turned the bomber toward home and the Zeros finally broke off their attacks in order to remain over the convoy. Probably doubting that his crippled bomber could make it back over the Owen Stanleys to Port Moresby, Higgins steered a course for the Allied airfield at Milne Bay. The bomber had not gone many miles, however, before the dead engine burst back into flame again, and this time the fire could not be extinguished. Higgins watched the fire spreading along the wing and knew it was useless to try to fly any farther, so he told his crew to brace for a ditching.

As the plane descended toward the sea, navigator Sellmer gave radio operator Wolf their approximate position in the Solomon Sea, about 50 miles north of Goodenough Island off the north coast of New Guinea, and by coincidence only about fifteen miles from where Maj. Kuhl had ditched "Crosair" five days before on January 1st (see Map 17-1, opposite). Wolf successfully transmitted the ditching location to Port Moresby before they hit the water.

Higgins made such a good water landing that the bomber remained intact, but the impact of the thirty-ton aircraft against the sea tore off the bomb bay doors and allowed the plane to quickly fill with water. Both of the plane's life rafts deployed successfully, and as the men escaped from the sinking plane they swam over and climbed into them. One of the gunners, Sgt. Satterfield, had been thrown against some part of the plane's internal structure during the landing and was badly injured. He was pulled aboard one of the rafts unconscious.

The jolt of hitting the sea had also knocked the top turret off its mount and it had pinned Sgt. Gaudet in the plane. The other members of the crew could only watch helplessly as "Cowtown's Revenge" sank out of sight with Gaudet trapped inside, just as Sgt. Domer had been trapped and gone down a few days earlier in the bomber "Crosair." After the plane sank, the men began paddling toward a small island called Islet Island (known today as Lifaba Island). By the time they beached their rafts, Satterfield had died, and the crew buried him on the island.[*1]

The bomber "Cowtown's Revenge" now lies intact on the floor of the Solomon Sea somewhere near tiny Lifaba Island.

"Cowtown's Revenge" thus lies intact today on the sea floor somewhere near Lifaba Island, with the remains of Sgt. Gaudet still aboard. Unlike "Crosair," it has not yet been found.

Lt. Higgins and the other survivors of the crew set up camp on the island and waited for rescue, hoping that Sgt. Wolf's radio message to Port Moresby giving their position had been received and that rescue was on the way. The message had been received, all right, but the location had not been very accurate. After all the wild combat maneuvering, and then navigating across the Solomon Sea by dead reckoning, navigator Sellmer had not been exactly sure where they were when they ditched, and thus had only been able to provide the approximate location. Rescue was far from certain.

---

* Sgt. Satterfield's body was recovered after the war by the American Graves Registration Service and transported to Manila where he was buried in the American Manila Cemetery.

17. ANOTHER CONVOY ATTACK 151

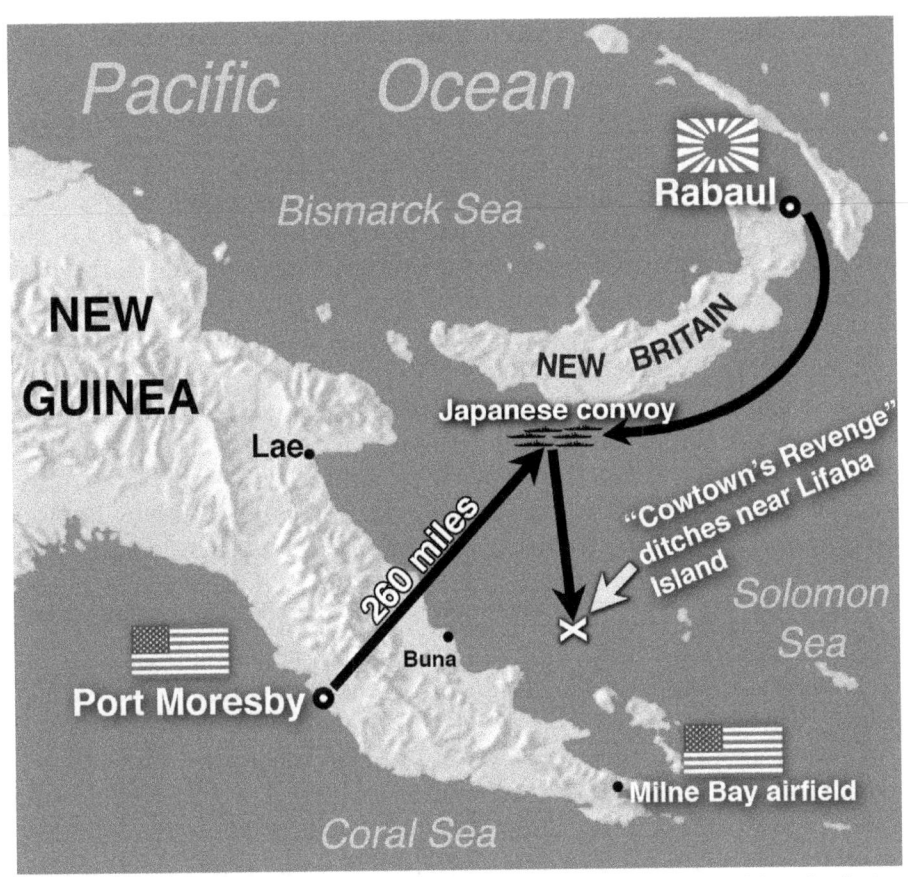

Map 17-1. Lt. Higgins ditched his bomber "Cowtown's Revenge" near Lifaba Island after bombing a convoy off the southern coast of New Britain.

The same day that Higgins attacked the convoy and subsequently ditched his plane, the 90th sent out another bomber from the 321st Squadron, piloted by Lt. George M. Rose, to search for General Walker's plane. This became yet another unexplained flight into eternity, for Rose and his crew were never heard from again, nor has their plane been found.

The next day, the 7th of January [1943], Lt. McMurria and his crew also went out searching, this time not only for Gen. Walker but for Lts. Rose and Higgins as well. McMurria recorded in his diary:

> Higgins had sent in a report of his approximate position just before he crashed so I got busy on it and searched the area north of Goodenough Island. It was the greatest mission I've ever been on—we found them on Islet Island. Eight of the ten [actually seven of nine] survived. We dropped them water, food, blankets and mosquito nets, then went back to Milne Bay and got the Catalina

out there in a hurry. It was a magnificent feeling to save someone's life.[2]

The Japanese convoy that Gen. Walker had tried to attack in the Rabaul harbor, and that Lt. Higgins had attacked at sea, continued on its way to Lae, but Gen. Kenney was determined to destroy it. He sent out one strike after another against it, so that the Japanese ships were hit by more B-24s, B-25s, and B-17s escorted by P-38 fighters. The convoy took more losses as a result, and became scattered at sea; nevertheless most of the ships made it to Lae. Kenney continued sending strikes at them even after they had anchored in the harbor and were unloading.

On 8 January more bombers from the 90th Bomb Group sank a large transport vessel and several barges in Lae's harbor. Again the Japanese defended the ships with both Zeros, these from Lae's airfield, and the antiaircraft fire from the warships as well as flak guns onshore. A bomber piloted by Lt. Paul W. Gottke was hit in the waist section by a flak burst that killed two men, S/Sgt. Clarence S. Utne and Capt. Robert S. Holt. Capt. Holt, from New Jersey, was the Intelligence Officer of the 320th Squadron who had miraculously survived the flaming crash of Lt. Larson's bomber on takeoff at Iron Range on 16 November, 1942 (page 87), and he had been the only man to survive that crash.

Holt, 42, was a courageous man whose job as an intelligence officer did not require him to fly at all, but who preferred to see things for himself rather than hear only second-hand reports from returning crewmen. He made it his habit to supplement his usual sources of information with personal examination of enemy installations and operations from the air, regardless of the hazards involved. He had been hitching a ride with Larson to do just that on the night that Larson crashed on takeoff, and he had continued hitching rides on so many of the 90th's missions that he was said to have flown as much as any pilot in the squadron.

But on this day over Lae harbor, Holt's luck ran out. After his death, Lt. Charles P. Whitlock,[*] a pilot in the 320th Squadron, wrote in his journal that Holt had been beloved by everyone in the squadron, and he wrote a letter to Holt's widow and two teen-aged children to let them know that, and he provided them with the circumstances of their husband and father's death.[3] Holt's grave is in the National Memorial Cemetery of the Pacific in Honolulu, Hawaii, known as the "Punchbowl" (photo, opposite).

Ships of the Japanese convoy continued to straggle toward Lae, and reconnaissance aircraft continued to report their locations. On January 9, 1943, a B-24D of the 90th Bomb Group's 320th Squadron piloted by 2nd Lt. Day-

---

[*]The same Whitlock who had added all the extra machine guns to his bomber back in San Francisco, before the 90th Bomb Group left for Hawaii (page 36).

ton S. Altman was on patrol in the area and picked up a radio report giving the position of some of the Japanese ships still at sea. Altman's navigator, Lt. William Hoyt, plotted a course to that location and Altman set out to intercept them. He was flying the second of the 90th's bombers to be named "Little Eva" in honor of the large barmaid in Greenville, South Carolina (the first "Little Eva," as you recall, was now lying wrecked in the Australian outback where Lt. Crosson crashed it on 2 December 1942).

Capt. Holt's gravestone today in the "Punchbowl" cemetery in Honolulu, Hawaii.

Altman was flying at 7,000 feet among broken clouds when he reached the area where the Japanese ships had been reported, and he was over them before he realized it. His first indication that he'd found the ships was when a flight of eight Zeros zipped across his bow, setting up their attack on him. Altman then saw the vessels below him and set up a bombing run on them. However, his bombardier, Lt. Herbert Gardner, never got a chance to complete the run.

Just as they had done on Col. Rogers' strike against another convoy on Dec. 2, 1942, the Zeros pulled a few miles out in front of the bomber and then turned to make head-on attacks, obviously aware that the weakest defensive position on a B-24D was the nose. This time they attacked in pairs, and after seven or eight firing passes the guns in the bomber's nose fell silent. Records do not provide the name of the crewman who was manning the nose guns, but whoever he was, he had apparently been wounded or killed.

At the same time that the nose gun stopped firing, Lt. Altman was hit in the head by a bullet, and the radioman, T/Sgt. Francis H. Brigham, who was sitting behind him, was struck in the shoulder by the same slug. Altman was still alive but only barely conscious as his copilot, Lt. Norman D. Smith, took over the controls and dove the plane down to 2000 feet where he'd spotted a cloudbank to hide in. The Zeros followed "Little Eva" down, firing at her all the way, and further riddled the bomber with machine gun and cannon fire.

The bomber's number three engine, just outside Smith's cockpit window,[*] was hit and caught fire. He activated the internal fire extinguisher on that engine and the fire went out. Then Smith noticed Altman weakly holding up two fingers, and realized that he was trying to convey to him that the number two

---

[*] The copilot in a B-24 (or any other aircraft with a copilot) sat in the cockpit's right seat, while the pilot occupied the left seat.

engine (which Smith could not see from where he sat) was also on fire. Smith used the engine's internal fire extinguisher to put out that fire too. But the two remaining engines were not putting out full power, and the bomber was losing altitude at a rate of 500 feet per minute. It was not going to stay in the air much longer. Smith called the rest of the crew over the intercom and told everyone to come up onto the flight deck with him, since he figured it would be the best place to survive a ditching. No one answered him. Lt. Altman, still only partly conscious, realized what was happening and tried to help Smith with the water landing. "Little Eva" hit the water with a bad jolt, and as usual in B-24 ditchings snapped in two behind the wing. By the time the plane came to a stop, its nose was already underwater and the cockpit was filling up fast.

Lt. Smith unhooked his seat belt and squirmed out through the right cockpit window. Once he was outside the sinking plane he shouted for anyone else who might have escaped, but again got no answer. Everyone else in the bomber had been either too injured to get out, like Lt. Altman, or was already dead. Smith saw that both the plane's life rafts had automatically deployed and swam over to one and got aboard. From the other raft he took the survival kit. The bomber then sank out of sight and he was alone in the raft, surrounded by floating debris. He was lucky that the Zeros were nowhere to be seen, since their normal habit was to shoot up Americans in life rafts.

Nine days later Smith, weak, hungry, and sunburned, made land on the coast of New Guinea and was taken by natives to Zaca Mission, eight miles southeast of the town of Morobe, where Australian coastwatchers took him in and radioed to Port Moresby that he had been found. For several weeks Smith was moved around the area to avoid Japanese patrols, but was finally picked up by a light plane from a small airstrip and returned to Port Moresby on 15 February, thirty-seven days after the ditching. Until he had been found, and was able to report the fate of "Little Eva," the bomber had been consigned to the category of those many lone recon missions that went out and were never heard from again.[4]

The eight men who died aboard the second "Little Eva" (whose remains, along with the wreckage of their plane, have not yet been located) were:

  2nd Lt. Dayton S. Altman, Jr., pilot, from South Carolina
  2nd Lt. William H. Hoyt, Jr., navigator, from Tennessee
  2nd Lt. Herbert H. Gardner, bombardier, from Georgia
  T/Sgt. Freddie K. Affeld, flight engineer, from Indiana
  T/Sgt. Francis H. Brigham, radio operator, from Connecticut
  S/Sgt. Vincent H. Calise, gunner, from New York
  S/Sgt. John F. Ratliff, gunner, from Virginia
  S/Sgt. Francis H. Bogucki, gunner, from Connecticut

Chapter Eighteen

LT. McMURRIA IS SHOT DOWN

As mentioned earlier, whenever a bomber crew failed to return from a lone mission, or otherwise went down with no witnesses (i. e. became separated from a formation and lost), the crewmen would often never be heard from again, usually because the bomber crashed into the sea or some remote part of the mountains or jungle. Often the entire crew was killed when a plane went down, but should any men survive a crash by parachuting or other means, they might still die trying to walk out of the jungle in this wild and largely uncharted part of the world, or if they were on a raft at sea, they might never make land and die of exposure. If survivors of a crash were captured by the Japanese, and for some reason kept alive until the end of the war (the Japanese usually murdered their prisoners unless they could serve some useful purpose), then their fate, and the fate of their vanished bomber, would only be learned after the war, when they were liberated from Japanese prison camps.

Into the latter category falls the case of pilot James A. McMurria and his crew. Lt. McMurria was the young pilot of the 319th Squadron who had been left behind in San Francisco when his bomber had sprung a fuel tank leak on the runway. He had eventually rejoined the Group in Hawaii, and then moved with it to Australia and Iron Range. He kept a sporadic diary that reflected the misery and disillusionment of life at Iron Range, and in which he recorded his fear that it was only a matter of time before he, like so many of his friends, would fail to return from a mission, his fate unknown and perhaps never learned by his loved ones.

McMurria's own first mission with his squadron, on 23 November, 1942, had been to bomb Lae on New Guinea's north coast. He'd taken off from Iron Range in the dark at 1:30 AM, and upon reaching Lae had found that he couldn't drop his bombs because his bomb bay doors were stuck shut. After finally getting the doors to open and dropping the bombs (all the while dodging flak from Japanese antiaircraft guns on the ground) he'd gotten lost on the return trip owing to a 20-degree error in his aircraft's compass. Fortunately, unlike Lts. DeFreitas and Crosson, he got lost over the Australian jungle in daylight, and was able to search for Iron Range, find it, and land before he ran out of fuel.[1]

McMurria had also been on the Group mission to bomb a Japanese convoy of four destroyers off the south coast of New Britain on Dec. 1-2, which had been Col. Rogers' first combat mission (Chapter 12). On that strike he had dropped his bombs on the convoy independently of his squadron and had seen two of them hit the stern of a Japanese destroyer, which was either remarkably good bombing, or good luck, or both.

He had been part of the returning group of bombers that had overshot Iron Range in the dark, but had turned around while they still had enough fuel and found the airfield by spotting its searchlights.

By the time the new year 1943 arrived, McMurria had flown sixteen missions. He had lost several good friends among the more than 80 crewmen of the 90th who were either missing or known to be dead up to that time. McMurria had a premonition that his luck was about to run out too, and wrote in his diary:

Lt. James A. McMurria

> Just realized that myself and Crawford, Shaffer, and Higgins are the only four officers [left] of the original 321st Bomber Squadron... Shaffer and I went over to the 319th area last night to visit the boys. Muscatel wine sure makes you sing. An Aussie taught us a song called "Waltzing Matilda." Everybody is singing it today. It sure looked bad though last night in their club to see all those new faces. They realize it as much as we do that they're replacements for some of the best guys I've ever known. Please Lord don't make it necessary to put anyone in my place.[2]

But his prayer, like his family's prayers for his safety, and the prayers of thousands of other families in the States to keep their young men safe in the Pacific, would not be answered. McMurria, realizing the likelihood that he would soon die in combat like so many of his friends, sought solace in the idea of being reborn into another life on earth after death:

> I've thought a lot about reincarnation lately. It seems so useless to live just the short while I've lived. There are so many things

to live for when you sit down and count them. But if I should go, I'd like to think I have another chance to come back and live life in its entirety.[3]

McMurria's fiancé, Mary Francis Smith, the young woman he had left in Greenville, South Carolina (and would one day marry) dominated his thoughts, but the lack of communication with her, and with his family, owing to the long waits for mail from home, was frustrating.

One bright note appeared when McMurria's squadron commander decided that in order to raise his men's morale he would send one crew back to Sydney every ten days for two weeks of R & R.* The crew that would be eligible to go each time would be the one that had completed the most combat missions up to that time.

At the time that this was decided, the four squadrons of the 90th Bomb Group were taking turns being temporarily based at Port Moresby and flying bombing missions from there. It so happened that it was the 319th Squadron's turn to operate from Port Moresby, and they flew up there from Iron Range on the 19th of January, 1943. On that same day McMurria participated in a mission to bomb the Japanese airbase at Wewak, which he described afterward as a "milk run," since they had found no fighter planes on the field to oppose them, the flak had been light, and all the planes had dropped their bombs and returned without incident. There had also been no ships in Wewak's harbor.

Lt. McMurria shortly before his ill-fated Jan. 20, 1943 mission to Wewak.

After that mission McMurria realized that he was in a tie with another crew in his squadron for the highest number of missions flown up to then: nineteen. If he flew one more mission to break the tie, his would be the first crew to get two weeks' leave in Sydney. He decided to do so immediately, and volunteered for a lone reconnaissance mission scheduled for the next day, January 20. He wrote:

> One more mission would put me clearly ahead in the race and I need not apologize for accepting the award that could be mine without argument. So for my crew it's off to the northwest

---
* Rest & Recreation, sometimes referred to by the men as "belles and bars."

> Japanese shipping lanes covering Finschaffen, Wewak, Admiralty Island, back down New Britain's coast, through the Vitiaz Straits, over the [Owen Stanley] mountains and back to Moresby in about 10 hours. If, if, if and all goes well—look out Sydney and here comes a ravenous crew![4]

But all would not go well. His earlier premonition that it might soon be his turn to disappear on a mission as so many of his friends had done would prove well founded. This mission, McMurria's 20th, would turn out to be one more lone reconnaissance flight in which the plane did not return, and nothing was known of its fate.

The members of McMurria's ten-man crew (including himself) were:

> 1st Lt. James A. McMurria, pilot, from Columbus, Georgia
> 2nd Lt. Robert R. Martindale, copilot, from Texas
> 2nd Lt. Thomas F. Doyle, bombardier (home state not listed)
> 2nd Lt. Alston F. Sugden, navigator (home state not listed)
> T/Sgt. Leslie H. Burnette, flight engineer, from North Carolina
> S/Sgt. Fred Stephen Engel, radio operator, from Illinois
> S/Sgt. Frank O. Wynne, Jr., tail gunner, from Mississippi
> Sgt. Raymond J. Farnell, Jr., gunner (home state not listed)
> Pfc. Walter R. Erskine, gunner, from Oregon
> Pfc. Patsy F. Grandolfo, waist gunner, from Ohio

The mission was jinxed from the beginning. McMurria, in his haste to get going, disregarded a forecast of bad weather and tried to take off from Jackson Field around 4 AM in darkness and rain, intending to reach the north coast of New Guinea by daybreak. The sides of the runway were dimly marked with little flickering flames from smudge pots. On the takeoff run, halfway down the field the plane's landing lights revealed a mass of sand, mud, and gravel that had been washed onto the runway by the rain, and when the bomber's wheels hit this loose material it swerved and lost takeoff speed. The two pilots immediately chopped the throttles and stood up on the brakes, but the plane still ran off the end of the runway and fifty feet beyond, where its nosewheel became entangled in a barbed wire fence that marked the airfield boundary.

Unfazed by this setback, and with visions of the delights of Sydney dancing in their heads, the crew extricated their bomber from the fence by the light of flashlights, got it turned around, and McMurria taxied it back onto the runway for another try. Before he could make the second run, however, he saw headlights approaching and an officer came speeding up in a jeep, waving a flashlight. McMurria unstrapped himself from his seat, opened the bomb bay doors, and climbed down out of the plane to ask the man what he wanted.

18. LT. McMURRIA IS SHOT DOWN

Standing in the dark beside the bomber with its big engines rumbling at idle, they held a conference. The officer argued that for safety reasons the flight should be delayed until later in the morning, after sunrise, when the runway could be cleared of debris. McMurria would have none of it. He insisted that by hugging one side of the runway he could steer around the worst of the detritus, now that he knew where it was, and it would be no hindrance.

The officer finally gave in and drove his jeep down the runway where he parked it off to one side, with its headlights illuminating the worst of the mud and gravel so that McMurria could see it better. For the second takeoff try, McMurria put the bomber's wing flaps in their full down position, to provide maximum lift, then held the bomber's brakes and revved the engines up to full power. "With full flaps and maximum mercury," he wrote, "I unleashed the brakes of the shuddering plane, skirted down the left side [of the runway], and with great relief of tension became airborne." Easing up the flaps, he then flew northwest up the southern coastline of New Guinea, angling inland to set a direct course for Wewak on the island's north coast, climbing to get enough altitude to cross safely over the Owen Stanley Mountains (see map 18-1 on page 162).

As dawn broke, McMurria saw that they were coming up behind Wewak, and since on the previous day he had seen no enemy fighter planes on the field and no ships in the harbor, he didn't expect to encounter any trouble there.

However, on this day things were different—much different, in fact: as they neared Wewak, the crew counted twenty-seven Japanese fighter planes on the airfield, and the harbor was filled with ships, whose antiaircraft guns were even then opening up on their bomber. They couldn't know it, but the fighter planes had been flown in by crack Japanese pilots who were veterans of years of combat flying in China. McMurria had unwittingly flown into a hornet's nest. His bombardier, Lt. Tom Doyle, called frantically from his position in the bomber's glass nose to say that they should dump their bombs immediately and get out of there in a hurry. McMurria emphatically agreed.

Doyle salvoed the bombs to lighten the plane and McMurria stood the big bomber on its right wing in the tightest turn he'd ever made. The bombs fell short of the airfield and did no damage to it, but no one cared about that now—their only thought was to put as much distance as they could between themselves and Wewak in the shortest possible time. As luck would have it, at that moment the bomber took a flak hit in its number three engine, which began smoking and soon had to be shut down. Just when they needed all possible speed, their bomber had lost an engine and began slowing down.

The fighters on the airfield raced into the air one after the other, and they were so much faster than the huge, lumbering bomber, especially since it was now flying on only three engines, that within a few minutes they had caught up to it and swarmed all over it, making firing passes from all directions.

With every gunner aboard his airplane firing desperately at the attackers, McMurria headed for some storm clouds that he spotted some 20 miles offshore in hopes of hiding in them. But when he reached the clouds they turned out to be so thin that they were useless for concealment.

Above him, through the plexiglass panels in his cockpit roof, McMurria saw two Zeros flying level and parallel to his course, one to his left and one to his right, and they began dropping aerial bombs that they were carrying under their wings. When he turned to the left, the left fighter dropped a bomb, and when he turned right the other one did. Fortunately the bombs, with timed fuses, exploded harmlessly below the bomber.

There were too many enemy planes for the bomber's gunners to deal with, but they kept up a continual fire at the ones that came nearest. Several Zeros began making head-on passes, their pilots aware, or sensing, as Col. Rogers had long feared, that the firepower in the B-24's nose was weak. McMurria remembered afterward:

> **Head-on passes were the most frightening for me because I could see all the action... The Japs would fly directly at you, firing from a thousand yards out before they rolled over and split-S'ed out, barely clearing my bomb bay.**[5]

They were doing exactly the same thing as the fighters that had attacked Col. Rogers on his first mission, which had had Rogers fervently wishing for a nose turret. Pvt. Patsy Grandolfo at the left waist gun and Lt. Tom Doyle up in the nose both announced over the intercom that they had shot down Zeros, but it made little difference with so many of them attacking. An aerial cannon shell tore a large hole in the bomber's nose and sliced through Doyle's left shoulder and leg, putting him out of action. Pvt. Walter Erskine took over the nose gun position and kept the guns firing.

Another of the bomber's engines was soon shot out, and the situation was approaching critical. McMurria felt his controls becoming increasingly sluggish as the wings and tail were being riddled by bullets. Flying on only two engines, the plane slowed further, and its interior filled with smoke. The smell of cordite from all the guns firing was stifling, and the flight deck was awash in empty .50-caliber shell casings cascading down from the top turret above and behind the pilots.

The plane was steadily losing altitude as well as speed, and McMurria warned his crew that it was only a matter of minutes before they'd have to ditch. He told them to get their life jackets on—at this point the gunbattle was over and they'd lost; now it was time to save themselves, if they could. He called to the three men who were down in the nose to come up onto the flight deck where they'd have a better chance of getting out of the plane after it hit the water.

The bombardier, Doyle, came up, with a big flap of his skin hanging loose from his bloody shoulder, and navigator Lt. Fred Sugden appeared, but the nose gunner, Erskine, refused to budge and stuck grimly to his gun, firing at the Japanese fighters all the way down. Choosing to remain at his station in the nose would cost him his life.

Sgt. Leslie Burnette, the flight engineer, got ready to deploy the bomber's two life rafts as soon as the plane came to rest in the water. Someone told McMurria that Pvt. Grandolfo was down in the bomb bay putting on heavy high-altitude flight clothing as fast as he could, to cushion himself from the shock that he expected would come when the plane hit the sea.

Now all the attacking fighter planes were shooting at them from above, since the bomber was getting so close to the water that none of them could get below it anymore. McMurria could see their machine gun bullets stitching rows of splashes in the water all around them. As they neared touchdown, McMurria told everyone to get braced for a jolt. The bomber slowed to near its 120 mph stall speed, and just as it was about to contact the water McMurria hauled up the nose and gave the two remaining engines full power to try to slow their descent and make the impact as gentle as possible. The maneuver did little good, however; the bomber behaved as B-24s usually did in ditchings and broke in two behind the wing. McMurria would write of it later:

> The guys on the flight deck [including himself], because of the heavy engines, took a nose dive straight for the bottom of the ocean. The rear section of the plane apparently floated for a couple of minutes because when I crawled out of the window, from 30 or 40 feet underwater, and finally surfaced, I saw a small portion of the vertical stabilizers still above water but going down fast. The front half of the plane was near the bottom by this time, I'm sure.[6]

Gunner Erskine had been trapped in the nose and had gone down with the plane. Waist gunner Patsy Grandolfo may also have been trapped in the wreckage, or he may have found himself unable to swim with all the extra flight clothing he'd put on; either way, he also went down. The other eight men of the crew all managed to get out of the plane and up to the surface of the water. Only one of the life rafts had ejected, however, and it was still tied to the plane by a rope, standing up on end and just about to be dragged under.

Radio operator Sgt. Fred Engel swam quickly over to the upended raft and reached for the jungle knife that he always carried on his belt, to cut the rope and free the raft, but discovered that the knife was missing. He shouted to Lt. Doyle to give him his knife, but Doyle found his gone, too. Then Doyle re-

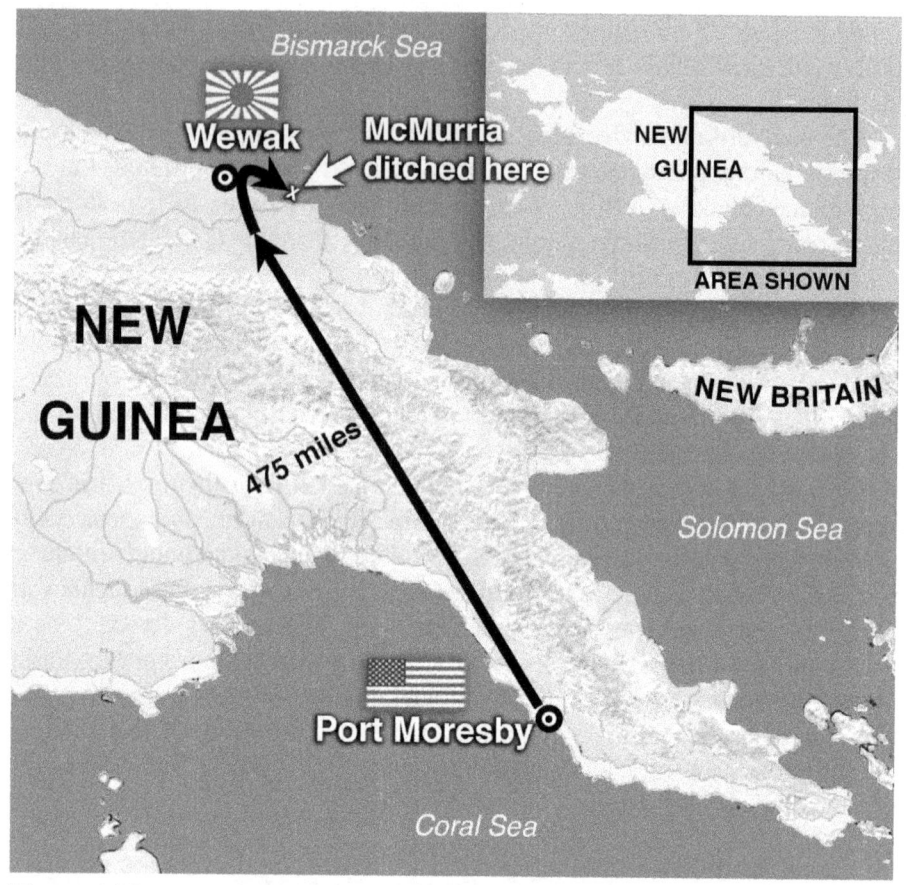

Map 18-1. The route of Lt. McMurria's ill-fated reconnaissance flight to Wewak on 20 January, 1943, showing approximately where he ditched his bomber.

membered a little penknife on a keychain that he kept in his pocket. He fished it out and tossed it twenty feet across the water to Engel, who deftly caught it one-handed and used it to cut the raft free. Months later McMurria was still having nightmares about what would have happened if Engel had not caught that little knife—the raft would have gone down with the plane, and it was the raft that would save them all.

After the bomber sank, three of the Japanese fighter planes circled the men and their raft for a few minutes, then made a low pass at them. "Here it comes," thought McMurria, expecting to be machine-gunned in the water, as the Japanese nearly always did to helpless men in either the water or descending in parachutes. But for some reason, perhaps because they had used up all their ammunition, the Japanese pilots merely looked them over and then flew off, headed back to Wewak.

18. LT. McMURRIA IS SHOT DOWN

After the fighter planes departed, McMurria was struck by the silence that had suddenly descended upon the scene. Only minutes earlier they'd been in the midst of a deafening bedlam of roaring engines, chattering machine guns, and shouting men, and now there was only the quiet, gentle motion of the sea, the waves lapping against the raft, and the sound of their own voices as the men took stock of their situation.

In one thing they were fortunate: the water temperature. On the other side of the world, in the European theater of war, American bomber crews who ditched in the North Sea and ended up floating in its frigid waters could freeze to death in minutes. On this side of the globe, however, where the war was being fought down near the equator, the water was warm, and a man could float in it comfortably for as long as he had to. On the minus side, there were the sharks.

The sea was calm and the water warm, but the raft was only big enough to hold four men, so for the rest of the day the eight men took turns in and out of it, four men lying in the raft while the other four clung to its sides. All of them were injured to some extent, several were bleeding, and since they were floating in some of the most shark-infested waters in the world, they wondered how long it would take the sharks to sense their blood and begin attacking them from below. It was a well-founded fear. Many aircrewmen or sailors floating in Pacific waters had been dragged under and killed by sharks.

Zero pilot Saburo Sakai had seen American bomber crewmen attacked by sharks after they had ditched in this same area. After he shot down a B-26 Marauder near Lae, Sakai saw four crewmen bail out, land in the water, and inflate a raft. Then, as he circled them, he saw sharks attack them. He wrote afterward:

> As I circled the raft, I saw that the men clung to its sides. Since they were only two miles from the Lae airbase, it was only a matter of time before a boat would pick them up and make them prisoners.
>
> Suddenly one of the men thrust his hands high above his head and disappeared. The others were beating fiercely at the water and trying to get into the raft. Sharks! It seemed that there were thirty or forty of them; the fins cut the water in erratic movements all about the raft. Then the second man disappeared. I circled lower and lower, and nearly gagged as I saw the flash of teeth which closed on the arm of the third man. The lone survivor, a big, bald-headed man, was clinging to the raft with one hand and swinging wildly with a knife in the other. Then he, too, was gone.
>
> When the men on the speedboat returned to Lae, they reported that they had found the raft empty and bloodstained. Not even a shred of the men was visible.[7]

McMurria and his crewmen saw fins cutting the water all around them and fervently prayed that they were dolphins, not sharks. Whatever they were, the men's luck held and they were not attacked.

Because McMurria had flown so far out to sea to try to hide in clouds offshore, they were floating out of sight of land and could only hope to drift back to either the New Guinea mainland or to one of the small islands in the area. With no water to drink, and the tropical sun blazing down on them, the men were all soon suffering from thirst. Hours later, when the sun went down and things cooled off, they felt a little better.

There was no moon that night, and the sea rose. In the pitch-black darkness the men lying in the raft, and the ones clinging to its sides, rode the waves like a roller coaster all night and tried to keep the raft from overturning. After the sun rose the next day a storm blew up that not only mercifully blotted out the hot sun for a while but dropped some rain that the men were able to catch in the raft and drink.

They were hoping to be spotted by a search plane from Port Moresby, since planes were always sent out looking for crews that did not return to base, and in fact a B-24 piloted by Lt. Scott L. Regan was sent out the next day (January 22) on another reconnaissance mission to Wewak with instructions to look for McMurria's crew. However, Regan's plane also failed to return to Port Moresby, and he was never heard from again. Regan probably ran into the same horde of Zeros defending Wewak that McMurria had, and he and his crew likely suffered a similar fate, but with no survivors. Regan's story will never be known, and McMurria's would only become known after the war, because there would be survivors to tell what happened.

The day after Regan's plane vanished, a pair of the 90th's bombers were sent out from Port Moresby to look for both missing crews. Perhaps Gen. Ramey or Col. Koon had decided that two planes should go out together this time, since they were disappearing when they went out singly. If two went, maybe at least one would return. It was a wise decision, as it turned out, because they too would be attacked by the Japanese fighters, and although one bomber would end up with two of its engines shot out, it was covered and defended by the other one, which shielded it from further damage and likely saved it from going down. The plane that was reduced to flying on two engines was piloted by the skilled and recklessly courageous Capt. Lark Martin, known as "the Lark," whom we will meet again in Chapter 29. Historian Andrew Lord wrote:

> [O]n January 23, 1943, operating from Moresby, Lt. [actually Capt.] Lark Martin of the 400th Squadron, accompanied by Lt. Paul Johnson, whose plane and crew were attached from the 319th Squadron, took off on an armed reconnaissance and search for the missing ship flown by Lt. Regan, which was lost on January 22 in the

18. LT. McMURRIA IS SHOT DOWN

vicinity of Wewak... Lt. Regan's ship was the second to be lost there in as many days, Lt. McMurria having disappeared in the same area the day before Regan.

Two and a half hours after take-off, Martin and Johnson, approaching Wewak, sighted a convoy consisting of three transports, one light cruiser, and one destroyer. It was decided to report the position of the convoy, then to withdraw and shadow it while continuing the search for Regan. So the two planes turned back toward Keul Island, where they were intercepted by approximately 18 Zekes [Zeke was another name for the Zero]. The Zekes, gray with black rings around their fuselages, attacked at first from the nose and above, sometimes descending in their passes to within fifty feet of the sea. Later attacks were made principally on the tail of Lt. Martin's ship, whose rear turret had been shot out.

The action was fought down the coast to Nubia and thence inland to the vicinity of Bena Bena. The Zekes attacked persistently until they were apparently out of ammunition, concentrating chiefly on Lt. Martin's badly crippled plane, which was limping along on two engines, numbers three and four having been shot out early in the fight. Seeing the plight of his comrade, Lt. Johnson dropped back to cover him, remaining close by for the duration of the two-hour engagement, and on the return flight to Moresby.

Both crews distinguished themselves by their determination and valor in the face of severe damage to both personnel and equipment. Lt. Johnson and crew were credited with two Zekes destroyed and one probably destroyed, while Lt. Martin and crew were credited with four Zekes destroyed and three probably destroyed. Five men were wounded during the engagement, none fatally.

Lt. Martin's ship [named "Mission Belle"] reached its base with more than four hundred bullet and cannon holes in it, looking something like a flying sieve. It landed with no mercury, with two engines going out, and on only one good tire, which blew out on touching the ground.

Lt. Johnson's plane was in only slightly better condition, having the tail turret out, one engine smoking badly, ailerons ripped, and holes all over the ship.

When the weary crews of the two riddled Liberators told their surprising stories to the Intelligence Officer, it wasn't difficult to guess why Lt. Regan and Lt. McMurria had gone out and never come back. The Rising Sun of Nippon was reaching its zenith at Wewak.[8]

As McMurria and the survivors of his crew floated in the sea the day after ditching their plane, the storm that had brought the welcome rain increased in intensity, and became so violent that they were soon riding mountainous waves amid deafening peals of thunder and flashes of lightning. After riding out this terrible storm and enduring another night at sea, the men were elated when the sun came up to reveal a couple of islands on the horizon.

Hours of paddling with their hands brought them close to one of the islands, but they could see that getting ashore was not going to be an easy task. There was no smooth, sandy beach to land on. The surf was crashing against rocks and reefs and shooting jets of spray hundreds of feet into the air, and it would have been suicide to try to land at such a place. After a few more hours of paddling along the shoreline they found a somewhat protected cove, and although it was still rocky, they decided to try their luck there.

The first wave of the surf capsized the raft and hurled the four men lying in it into the sea, and then the waves raked all eight men back and forth across the sharp coral reef before they all managed to stagger up onto the shore, bruised and bleeding, to collapse into an exhausted sleep just beyond the reach of the waves.

There is not space here to relate all the wanderings and hardships of the McMurria crew in the weeks that followed. For a detailed account of their experiences the reader is referred to McMurria's own book, *Fight for Survival!*[*] Only a bare outline of the story can be presented here.

Being young and strong, all in their early to mid-twenties, the eight men were naturally resilient and optimistic. They hoped, foolishly, to walk the 400 miles back to Port Moresby, despite being separated from it by wide rivers, vast swamps, and the immense jungle-covered peaks and gorges of the Owen Stanley Mountains.

The group was soon discovered and aided by friendly natives who fed the men, treated their wounds, and shepherded them from village to village, and then from island to island in outrigger canoes, trying to move them in the direction they wanted to go while hiding them from the Japanese who held the area.

One of the native chiefs told McMurria about a missionary named Father Manion, an American citizen and the head of Saint John's Catholic Mission on the island of Kairiru, just off the coast of New Guinea, who might be able to help them. McMurria scribbled a note to Manion that was delivered to the priest by a native courier. But the Japanese somehow got wind of the communication and rounded up Father Manion and all the other people at his mission station, men, women, and children, some of them orphans in the care of the

---

[*] *Fight for Survival! An American Bomber Pilot's 1,000 Days as a P. O. W. of the Japanese*, by James A. McMurria, Honoribus Press, 2005.

missionaries, forty-two people in all. They were put aboard the destroyer *Akikaze*, which set a course for Rabaul.

Once the ship was at sea, the Japanese committed yet another of their countless horrible war crimes. The sailors erected a wooden scaffold on the stern of the ship with a hoisting device above it, and then, one by one, they hoisted each one of the men, women, and children into the air, riddled them with bullets, and dumped their bodies into the sea in the ship's wake. The smaller children and babies were simply hurled into the ocean to drown, not being considered worth a bullet.[9]

It's a wonder that the Japanese bothered to take the missionaries aboard a ship to murder them, since their usual practice was to just kill them on the spot wherever they found them, often torturing them first.* For example, when the Japanese landed at Buna in August of 1942, they simply rounded up all the men, women, and children of Buna Mission, dragged them down to the beach, and slaughtered them with swords and bayonets. All these missionaries had foolishly thought that the Japanese, being from a supposedly civilized nation, would see the good works they were doing among the natives, consider them no threat, and leave them in peace, and they had therefore stayed at their missions instead of fleeing to safety in Australia. By the time they realized their mistake it was too late.

The Japanese hated Christian missionaries both because they were white and because they taught the natives that there was a God other than their emperor.[10] When Rev. James Benson of the Buna mission was taken prisoner in 1942, during the first flush of Japanese victories all over the Pacific, he was interrogated by a Japanese army major who exhibited the same Japanese inferiority complex seen in most of the soldiers of Japan:

> He told me England and Australia were begging for mercy. "No longer are you the haughty and proud White race," he gibed. "The yellow races are the finest people now."[11]

Benson believed that this new feeling of racial superiority and righteous vengeance explained the "swashbuckling arrogance" exhibited by most of the Japanese soldiers he met. Their early success in the war had served to inflate their fragile egos, always so obsessed with maintaining "face."[12] He was told that "no white man may go free in this country [New Guinea]."[13] Any whites encountered by the Japanese during their invasion of the Pacific islands, whether they were missionaries, gold miners, plantation owners, government

---

* It's possible that for so heinous a crime as this they wanted no non-Japanese witnesses, and therefore carried it out at sea. Word got out anyway.

Francis May Hayman and Rev. Vivian Redlich operated the Buna mission on New Guinea's north coast. They were engaged to be married when the Japanese captured and brutally murdered them both (Miss Hayman was bayoneted through the throat, while Rev. Redlich was beheaded). It was typical of Japanese treatment of white missionaries on all the Pacific islands they invaded. Missionaries especially incurred the wrath of the Japanese because they taught that there was a God other than their emperor.

administrators, or traders, were usually murdered as a matter of course, killed without mercy simply because they were of the hated white race.

Although some white missionaries were spared and allowed to live near Rabaul, in a secluded area outside the town where they tried to grow their own food, the Japanese mistreated them continually, especially the Catholic nuns, whom they repeatedly assaulted sexually and tortured. After Fr. Benson was transported to Rabaul, to eventually become part of this persecuted religious community, he wrote:

> Several times Mother Cecilia and some of the senior Sisters were tortured by the Japanese . . . indeed Mother Cecilia's pitiable lameness was caused by the stick torture. In this, the victim must kneel down; then a bush stick is laid across his or her leg just on the calf behind the knee. Two Japanese soldiers then stand, one on each end of the stick, and rock it up and down like a see-saw until the victim either says what they want to be said or faints from agony. This, and the water torture, and many other abominations

18. LT. McMURRIA IS SHOT DOWN

had these brave and simple women suffered in three years of exile, hardship, and near-starvation.[14]

Another group of missionaries tried to flee from Buna into the jungle, led by a Lt. Louis Austin, but they were caught by the Japanese and everyone in the party murdered, as recounted by ABC war correspondent Raymond Paul:

> The rapid [Japanese] advance inland trapped many of the Europeans at the hospitals, missions and plantations on the Buna coast. Few succeeded in eluding the enemy and crossing the [Owen Stanley] mountains to the south coast. Lieut. Louis Austin and an Anglican mission party traveling from Ioma to Tufi were betrayed to the Japanese by the natives of Perembata village. [The group consisted of] Miss Margaret Branchley, Miss Lillian Lashman, the Rev. Henry Holland, the Rev. Vivian Redlich, Mr. John Duffill, two half-caste mission workers, Louise Artango and Anthony Gore, and Gore's six-year-old son.
> At Buna, on 12th August, 1942, outside the headquarters of the Sasebo No. 5 Special Naval Landing Party, the entire group was beheaded one by one with the sword, the boy last of all.[15]

While the Japanese were massacring the missionaries and other workers of St. John's Catholic Mission at sea, McMurria and his men managed to reach the mainland of New Guinea, near the mouth of the Sepik River, about 60 miles southeast of Wewak. There they hoped to begin their long trek to Port Moresby, which was still 425 miles away over some of the roughest terrain in the world. Had they connected with any of the Australian coastwatchers in the area somewhere along their journey, the latter might have arranged a boat pick-up for them by radio, or even air evacuation as would be done for Lt. Norman Smith, who at this time was also on the run from the Japanese (although in the care of Australian coastwatchers) after surviving the ditching of the B-24 "Little Eva" on 9 January [1943], as related in the previous chapter.

But we will never know what might have been for the McMurria crew, for at the Sepik River one of the natives betrayed them to the Japanese, probably for the rewards that the Japanese frequently offered for the capture of Allied airmen (on New Britain, the payment to a native for turning in a downed Allied flier was 500 Japanese cigarettes).[16]

Asleep on a beach early one morning, McMurria's party awoke to find themselves surrounded by Japanese soldiers, vicious little men in brown uniforms who threatened them with bayonets attached to ridiculously long rifles. Looking them over, McMurria reflected that it probably hadn't been long since these ignorant, brutish peasant soldiers had been tending water buffalo in some Japanese rice paddy.

The soldiers bound the men's hands and feet so tightly that their arms and legs swelled to three times their normal size, then tied ropes around their knees and chests, inserted poles through the ropes, and carried the Americans like captured animals to the local Japanese headquarters, where their long ordeal as slave laborers began.

The men were first brutally abused while employed in Japanese work projects, and then in May of 1943 they were transported to Rabaul, where over the next three years McMurria would survive savage beatings, starvation, disease, and medical experiments carried out on him by the Japanese, while he was forced to labor at such tasks as unloading cargo ships and digging air raid shelters. His weight dropped from 180 to less than 100 pounds.[*]

During his time in captivity McMurria and other American prisoners often subsisted on a single six-ounce ball of dirty rice each day, sleeping on the hard floor of their filthy cell, and were barely kept alive. Sometimes days passed without the prisoners being given any food or water at all. The sick and injured got no medical attention. McMurria saw other American prisoners brought in from time to time, usually captured airmen, and many who were weak or injured either died on the cell floors from neglect or were dragged outside and murdered. In November of 1943 four members of McMurria's crew, Martindale, Burnette, Engle, and Wynne were taken by ship from Rabaul to Japan, where they were found alive in a prison camp near Tokyo after the war.

McMurria, Doyle, Sugden, and Farnell, Jr. remained imprisoned at Rabaul, and on March 3, 1944 all except McMurria were taken to the outskirts of Rabaul and beheaded in one of the many Japanese orgies of killing that occurred from time to time, without apparent rhyme or reason, or perhaps whenever the Japanese simply felt that they had too many non-Japanese mouths to feed. The March 3 massacre occurred the day after a heavy American bombing raid on Rabaul, and it's possible that the Japanese considered the killings to be retribution for the raid. Some of the murdered prisoners had their livers cut out and ritually eaten by Japanese officers, who believed that they gained spiritual

---

[*] In Europe any captured airman, British or German, was given medical attention and in many cases even taken to a hospital if he had wounds needing treatment, after which he was placed in a prisoner-of-war camp where he was reasonably well treated, fed, and housed, with a camp doctor overseeing his recovery. The Germans and the Allies had an unspoken agreement that each side would treat the other's prisoners of war humanely, and honored the terms of the 1929 Geneva Convention. The barbaric Japanese, by contrast, had no conception of a prisoner of war; Japan had rejected the rules for the treatment of prisoners set forth in the Geneva Convention and cared nothing for any of their own men who fell into Allied hands. They considered any prisoner, even one of their own people captured by the Allies, to be contemptible and only worthy of death, since a Japanese soldier was expected to die fighting or commit suicide rather than surrender. Japan usually only kept prisoners alive for use as slave labor, as in this case with the McMurria crew.

power by such cannibalism.[17] Why McMurria was not killed along with his crewmen is not known.

Father James Benson was initially spared from death by the Japanese in order to serve as a translator between themselves and the natives. Two British women who worked with Fr. Benson at Buna mission, another missionary and a nurse, were taken down to the beach and bayoneted to death.

Eventually, and probably inevitably, the Rev. Benson was accused of being an Allied spy and sent to the prison camp at Rabaul where McMurria and other captured American aviators were being held. He was thrown into a cell occupied by two American airmen, a pilot, Capt. Alexander R. Berry, and his gunner, Cpl. Cephas L. Kelly, who had been captured when their Navy TBF Avenger torpedo bomber was shot down on Feb. 28, 1943. In his memoirs Benson wrote:

> The elder, whom I guessed to be Berry, had a rough bandage on his left leg, otherwise he looked tolerably well, though hungry and desperately tired. The youngster [Kelly, 18 years old] looked pretty sick. . . [T]hey had been dreadfully tortured . . . but with magnificent courage they were holding out. Kelly . . . was desperately ill. It was ten days before I had a chance to whisper to Berry. He was in considerable pain. "Beat up every day," he whispered; "hung up by the feet. They want information." "Can't you give them false information?" I asked. "Won't do. They spot it. Then it's worse." Surely, I thought, there was no greater courage than this; the courage of men who, having faced the perils and dangers of combat in the air, must now suffer this inhuman torture. A few words would ease them of this daily pain, but they never spoke. And theirs was an ordeal that went on and on. When I left the prison in late June [1943] they had been tortured almost every day. Berry was standing up to it magnificently. But poor young Kelly was nearing the end of his tether, but he too was holding out, and I doubt if he could have lived many more days. I repeat that surely such persistent, continual courage is far greater than that of the bravest soldier in action. . . I feel that some kind of official recognition should surely be made for such supreme devotion, which is quite beyond the call of normal duty.[18]

The heroism of these young Americans and many others like them in the face of Japanese savagery should never be forgotten. Cpl. Kelly was shipped to Japan and survived the war in a prison camp in Tokyo, but Capt. Berry was among a group of Allied prisoners who were taken to Talili Bay near Rabaul and, in what became known as the Talili Massacre, were murdered by their Japanese captors on 15 March, 1944, twelve days after three survivors of McMurria's crew had suffered the same fate.

Rabaul was eventually pounded into impotence by American airpower and bypassed by American naval and ground forces on their advance toward Japan. The town thus remained in Japanese hands until the end of the war. Allied commanders knew that there were many thousands of Japanese at Rabaul who were prepared to resist to the death any invasion behind carefully prepared defenses, and deemed it not worth the cost to invade, preferring instead to let the isolated garrison "wither on the vine."

There had been 126 known Allied prisoners at Rabaul, most of them captured American aviators, but by war's end only seven were left alive, one of them being Lt. James McMurria. All the others had either died of overwork, malnutrition, lack of medical care, medical experiments carried out on them, or had simply been murdered by the Japanese. Thirty-five were known to have been killed on March 5, 1944 alone.

To sum up the fate of the ten men of the McMurria crew, then: two died in the ditching of the bomber, three were murdered by the Japanese after capture, and five, including McMurria, survived the war in prison camps. The siren call of two weeks' leave in Sydney had led five of the men to their deaths and the other five to years of torture and deprivation at the hands of the enemy.

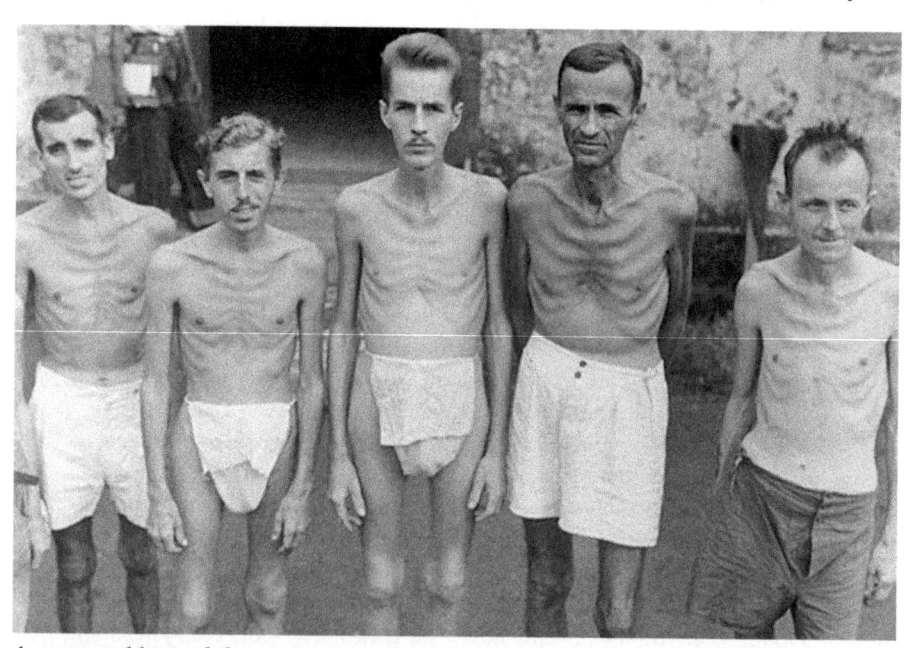

Americans liberated from a Japanese prison camp after the war. Of hundreds of Allied prisoners held at Rabaul, only Lt. McMurria and six others survived; all the rest were killed.

CHAPTER NINETEEN

THE B-24 GETS A NOSE TURRET

When the monsoon season began at Iron Range in late January of 1943, bringing torrents of rain such as few of the Americans there had ever seen before, bombing missions had to be scrubbed because the bombers (which weighed over thirty tons loaded with bombs and gas) couldn't taxi through the deep mud without getting stuck, nor could they have taken off from the muddy runway with such heavy loads even if they had managed to reach it.

With operations slowed down, and the Group unable to fly missions until conditions improved, Col. Art Rogers saw an opportunity to get the ball rolling again on his nose turret project. On his combat missions he had seen firsthand how Japanese fighter planes took advantage of the B-24's insufficient firepower in the nose by attacking mostly from the front, and he convinced Col. Koon of the necessity of getting a power turret with twin machine guns onto the noses of the Group's bombers as soon as possible. It was, he emphasized, literally a matter of life and death. Lt. Altman's bomber "Little Eva," as noted in Chapter 17, had literally been shot to pieces by Zeros attacking it mostly from the front, and it was becoming a common occurrence.

Koon gave Rogers permission to take one of the Group's B-24s down to the aircraft service depot at Brisbane to see if a turret installation could be undertaken there. If it proved successful, then perhaps all the Group's bombers could be retrofitted with nose turrets. By removing as much weight as possible from one of the B-24s, Rogers managed to take it off from the mud of Iron Range and fly it down to 5th Air Force headquarters at Brisbane to plead his case. He wrote:

> Upon arriving at Brisbane, I contacted the Air Service Command, which normally is in charge of all repairs and installation work, and was pleasantly surprised to find the general in charge to be General Carl Connell, a former commanding officer of mine. He was eager and willing to help us make the installation. He arranged appointment for me to see General Kenney, our Air Force Commander, and after explaining to General Kenney the difficulties we were encountering he also agreed that all haste should be made to get the turret installed and into combat.[1]

(Left to right): Col. Ralph Koon, Commander of the 90th Bomb Group, Gen. George Kenney, Commander of the 5th Air Force, and Col. Art Rogers, Deputy Commander of the 90th Bomb Group (early 1943).

Luck was with Rogers, for George Kenney was just the man to whom to propose such a project. During World War One Kenney had been much like Rogers himself, a pilot always looking for ways to improve his aircraft, or find new ways to use them (in the present war, his skip-bombing innovation for bombers has already been mentioned). In another example, Kenney had been

19. THE B-24 GETS A NOSE TURRET

The nose of a B-24D being prepared for the mounting of a turret.

convinced during World War One that it would be better to put machine-guns on the wings of a fighter plane rather than on the fuselage, where they had to shoot through the propeller arc. The idea was a sound one, although it would have been difficult to accomplish with the aircraft technology and fragile wood-and-fabric wings of the day.

After the war Kenney had continued advocating that the guns of fighter planes be mounted in their wings, and rapid advancements in aircraft design soon made it possible, so that by WWII most American fighter planes carried them there.[*] In the Southwest Pacific, Kenney had his "Special Projects Officer," Paul I. "Pappy" Gunn, a self-taught mechanical genius and innovator, modifying B-25s to take several heavy machine guns in the nose, and these custom strafer/bombers would figure prominently in the destruction of Japanese airplanes parked on airfields and in sinking ships at sea.

Kenney had also invented the parachute or "parafrag" bomb that would soon wreak havoc on Japanese airfields in the Southwest Pacific.

---

[*] Twin-engine warplanes such as the P-38 fighter and the modified Mitchell medium strafer/bombers did have guns on their noses rather than their wings, since their engines were on their wings.

Nose turret being lifted into place.

Col. Marion Unruh had continued working on the B-24 nose turret installation in Hawaii after Col. Rogers and the 90th Bomb Group had left there for Australia in October of 1942, and Unruh had actually succeeded in getting a turret installed and working on one bomber. The airplane had shortly afterward been lost at sea while returning from a mission, but Unruh sent Rogers the blueprints he'd developed for the nose modification. Rogers remembered:

> I had received a complete report from Colonel Unruh, whom we had left in Hawaii, on the installation that was made there. The airplane had been lost on its way back from a combat mission, and it was known that it had not been destroyed by ack-ack or fighter planes since the radio message giving the location on the way home indicated that it was completely out of the zone of enemy interception. No word was ever heard of the plane after this message, and many people suspected that the nose turret had twisted off due to the fact that the fuselage had not been designed for the additional weight. This had discouraged a modification in Hawaii, but I was sure that this claim was false and went ahead with another installation with a few minor changes which I considered improvements.
>
> Without [having] good shops, and working with unskilled Australian labor, every piece had to be cut and recut many times

19. THE B-24 GETS A NOSE TURRET

before it could actually be fitted into the jigsaw puzzle. Without any aeronautical engineers ... to figure the exact stress and strain that would be brought on the fuselage, we were left to use common horse sense in the judgment of this matter. It is probably true that our structure was crude, and maybe heavier than necessary, but when it was finished I did not hesitate to climb in and take the plane off for its first flight.

Skeptics had predicted that the performance of the B-24 would suffer with the additional weight and extra air drag of a nose turret, since the original plexiglass nose had been much more aerodynamically streamlined (see illustration at right). To Col. Rogers' delight,

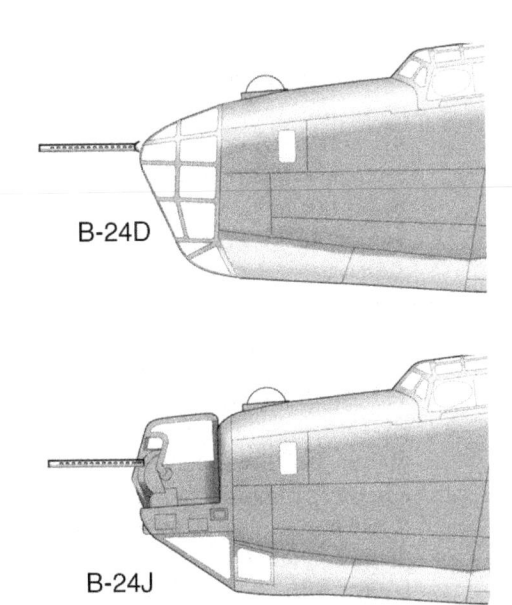

Nose comparison: the early B-24D with its "greenhouse" nose (top) and individual hand-operated guns, and the B-24J with twin guns in a powered nose turret. All guns were .50-cal. machine-guns.

however, not only was there no performance penalty with the nose turret, but the airplane actually flew better and faster:

> I was pleased to note that the airplane had actually picked up from eight to twelve miles per hour. . . This had been due to the shifting forward of the center of gravity, which made the airplane fly on an even keel. Before this, the plane had been tail-heavy, and had a tendency to fly nose-up, which increased the [air] resistance and slowed down the speed. After completing these tests, I was anxious to get back up north into the combat zone to actually find out the results of the nose turret against the Japs' head-on attacks.

In honor of General Connell, who had provided such enthusiastic help on the project, Rogers named this first B-24 to carry a nose turret the "Connell's Special," and had the name painted prominently on the nose of the plane. This bomber, incidentally, was one of those that had had its nose practically wiped off by the takeoff crash of Lt. Larson's bomber on the night of November 16, 1942, so the nose turret installation was actually its second nose rebuild.

General Kenney remembered the nose turret project this way:

> The forward gun protection in the B-24 turned out to be quite unsatisfactory. The Jap fighters found out about it and we were getting the airplanes shot up badly every time we got intercepted. There were four .50-caliber guns in the nose of the B-24, but as they shot through individual "eyeball" sockets, only one could be fired at a time. It was a clumsy arrangement and didn't give the protection we needed, so I started Lieutenant Colonel Art Rogers of the 90th Bombardment Group installing a turret, which we took off the tail of a wrecked B-24, in the nose. This would give us a pair of power-operated .50-calibers and should surprise the Nip the next time he tried a head-on attack against a B-24 so equipped. Rogers said the Air Depot in Hawaii had been working out something along this line when he left there a month previously and he knew how to do it. He said that when he had made the installation he would like to take the plane to New Guinea and hunt up a fight to try the scheme out. I gave him the go-ahead and told Connell to give him all the help he needed to expedite the job.[2]

After the turret was installed, Rogers had a gunner fire thousands of rounds of ammunition through the twin .50s to see if any problems arose from the vibrations and recoil of the guns (none did). Once he was satisfied that the turret was in good working order, ready to be taken into combat, he flew the "Connell's Special" back up to Iron Range, where the new nose turret created a sensation among the aircrews:

> When I landed my plane with the new nose turret at our airdrome, the news spread like wildfire that I was back, and from the crowd that gathered one would have thought that none of the men had ever seen an airplane before... Questions were flying from every angle, and when I told them that we had fired over ten thousand rounds of ammunition with even more success than we had expected, everyone was jubilant.

But whether or not the factories that made the B-24 would start putting nose turrets on them was still a question. The installation had not yet been proven to be practical and effective in combat. Rogers wanted to immediately take the airplane out on a combat mission and provoke a fight with Japanese fighter planes to show what the turret could do. He was quite confident that when the Zeros made their usual frontal attacks they'd fly straight into a hail of bullets and suffer the consequences.

19. THE B-24 GETS A NOSE TURRET

But Col. Koon informed Rogers that because of all the problems the Group was experiencing trying to operate from Iron Range, especially with the monsoon rains and the waterlogged runways, he had finally received permission from Gen. Kenney to move the 90th Bomb Group up to Port Moresby, and the move would be the first priority. The turret would have to be tested out in combat after the move.

Bomber crewmen examine the nose turret installation on the B-24 "Connell's Special."

Chapter Twenty

THE 319TH GOES TO DARWIN

But not all four squadrons of the 90th Bomb Group would be making the move to Port Moresby, at least not to begin with. In early January of 1943 the 319th Squadron was temporarily detached from the Group and sent 800 miles west of Iron Range to Batchelor and Fenton airfields near Darwin, Australia, to counter Japanese activities in the Dutch East Indies area (Map 20-1 below). During the nearly six months that the squadron operated from there it would be under Australian control.

The 319th would not rejoin the 90th Bomb Group at Port Moresby until July of 1943, after it was replaced at Darwin by the 380th Bomb Group, a new group that arrived from the States.[1] While the 319th was flying from Fenton, it flew 238 bombing missions and reconnaissance flights. The targets were Japanese installations on Bali (of romantic fame), on Macassar in the Celebes Islands, Java, Manokwari in northeastern New Guinea, and Ambon Island (the former spice trade center made famous by Marco Polo, and which

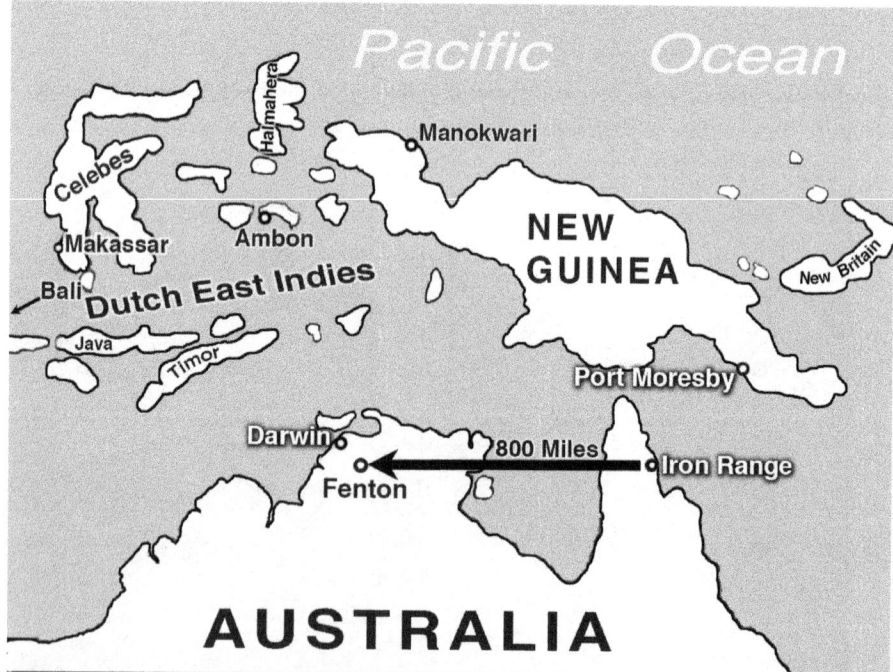

Map 20-1. The 319th Squadron moved from Iron Range to Fenton in January of 1942 (black arrow).

20. THE 319TH GOES TO DARWIN

had lured Magellan around the world). Someone counted 208 Japanese fighter plane interceptions during these missions, with the bombers always heavily outnumbered, and 45 of the Japanese interceptors were confirmed to have been shot down.

None of these bombing missions were accompanied by Allied fighter planes, since Allied fighters had such limited range at the time; the fighters were left behind to defend the Darwin airfields from Japanese bombers.[2] Interestingly, some of the fighters used in this part of Australia were British Spitfires sent over from England, planes only rarely seen on American airfields in the Pacific.

The 319th lost five bombers and their crews on these missions.[3] One of the bombers lost was flown by the commander of the 319th Squadron, Capt. Charles E. Jones, and another one by his successor, Capt. Roy W. Olsen.

The loss of Capt. Charles Jones, 16 March 1943

Capt. Jones was lost while flying a bomber named "Dirty Gertie" on a two-plane reconnaissance flight on March 16, 1943. The planes were flying along the south coast of New Guinea, between Kaiman and Timuka (see Map 20-2 on page 187), looking for Japanese shipping or other enemy activity when Jones' bomber mysteriously exploded in mid-air.

The crew of the other B-24, which was flying above and behind Jones' bomber, piloted by Lt. Harold G. Hevener, witnessed the explosion. Jones was in the midst of speaking to Hevener over the radio[*] when the blast suddenly blew "Dirty Gertie" apart. The explosion was centered in the bomb bay, just behind the wing, and it broke the bomber in two.

As Hevener's crew looked on in horror, the front half of Jones' bomber, on fire and with all four propellers still turning, fell nose first into the sea and sank instantly, leaving a 100-yard wide pool of burning gasoline and oil. The rear half of the fuselage, with the tail still attached, spiraled down into the inferno and also disappeared beneath the waves. There were no survivors, and in a few moments only an oil slick marked the spot

Capt. Charles E. Jones, commander of the 90th Bomb Group's 319th Squadron, was killed on March 16, 1943 along with his crew when his bomber "Dirty Gertie" mysteriously exploded during a routine reconnaissance mission.

---

[*] One source says that Jones realized the bomber was about to blow up and told Hevener over the radio, "Get away from me!"[4]

The crew of the bomber "Dirty Gertie" all died on 16 March, 1943 when their plane mysteriously exploded in mid-air. Back row, left to right: Lt. Daniels, bombardier; Lt. Munker, navigator; unidentified major; Capt. Charles E. Jones, pilot; Lt. Habein, copilot; T/Sgt. Hamby, flight engineer. Front row: left to right, Sgt. Willie Hicks, waist gunner; Cpl. Baker, nose gunner; S/Sgt. William Simon, waist gunner; S/Sgt. Alphonso Mascaskas, assistant engineer; S/Sgt. John Salemi, radio operator; S/Sgt. Smeade, tail gunner; Sgt. Wyatt, gunner. An Australian photographer, Cpl. Darcy A. J. Sharland of the RAAF, not pictured, was also aboard the plane.

where ten young men had been suddenly whisked off to eternity. Today the location of this bomber's wreckage on the sea floor is only vaguely known, and it will likely never be found.

Capt. Jones, a 1941 graduate of West Point, had been an outstanding commander and was popular with everyone in his squadron. On the day that he died, he was expecting to hear at any moment that his wife Mary Ann had given birth to their first child back in the States. Instead, on March 16, 1943, Mary Ann Jones became yet another young wife who would never see her husband again, with a child who would never know its father.

"Dirty Gertie" had been considered by many members of the squadron to be a jinxed plane. A crew chief at Fenton who had worked on it said it "had always been a lemon of the worst sort," with all sorts of mysterious problems cropping up all the time. Another pilot, Lt. William L. Whitacre, wrote in his diary, "'Dirty Gertie' was always acting up with gas line trouble," and on a previous flight in the plane Capt. Jones had experienced a fuel leak so serious that he'd had to open the cockpit windows to avoid passing out from the fumes. It seems likely that another such leak occurred on Jones' last flight, and this time some source of ignition detonated the explosive vapors.[5]

Dangerous fuel leaks were a known hazard in all B-24s, especially when they were equipped with the temporary auxiliary tanks in the bomb bays. The fuel line connections and valves were often unreliable, and when they leaked, any sort of a spark could trigger an explosion or fire. Leaks were often encountered in the process of trying to transfer fuel from the bomb bay tank to the plane's wing tanks. As one historian noted:

> A troublesome fuel transfer system and wing tanks in the wing center section caused fuel to seep into the bomb bays where explosive mixtures were often created. The electric hydraulic pump was situated in the bomb bay and is suspected of causing a number of fatal explosions. Bomb bays were often left partly open for ventilation.[6]

With the death of Capt. Jones, Capt. Roy W. Olsen became the commander of the 319th Squadron, but not for long. Only three months later Olsen and his crew were also killed on a mission, and the manner of their death taught the men of the 319th just how fanatical the Japanese were in the service of their "divine" emperor.

The loss of Capt. Roy Olsen, 23 June 1943

The 380th Bomb Group arrived at Darwin in June of 1943 to take over from the 319th Squadron of the 90th. On the 23rd of June the 380th sent fourteen bombers to bomb the harbor and piers of the port city of Makassar in the Celebes Islands, a 2000-mile round trip of 13 hours in the air (see Map 20-2, p. 187). Capt. Olsen decided to fly one last mission from Fenton and accompany the 380th's bombers with three planes of the 319th. It was a fatal decision, as events turned out.

As the bombers neared their target, about ten miles southeast of Makassar, a lone Japanese plane appeared, an obsolete fighter plane with a fixed landing gear called a Nate. One of the American bombers fired on the plane and hit it. The pilot of the Nate then dove on Capt. Olsen's bomber and deliberately rammed it, shearing off the number four engine and a large part of the right wing, and knocking the bomber into a flat spin. As the bomber whirled down toward the sea, its crew was apparently trapped inside by centrifugal forces and unable to get out, for no parachutes were seen. The bomber struck the ocean with such force that it's unlikely anyone inside could have survived. The Nate also spun into the sea.

Capt. Roy Olsen's crew, all killed when a Japanese suicide pilot rammed their bomber on 23 June, 1943, near Makassar in the Celebes Islands. The crewmen in this photo are not individually identified, but they were, in addition to Capt. Olsen, 1st Lt. Thomas H. Durkin, 2nd Lt. Kenneth F. Strong. 2nd Lt. Russell R. Setterblade, T/Sgt. Robert F. Cole, T/Sgt. Robert K. Enders, S/Sgt. Frank A. Hudspeth, S/Sgt. Harold Muscato, and S/Sgt. William C. Simon. An Australian, Sgt. John Alexander of the Royal Australian Air Force flew with the crew on this mission and was killed along with them.

The bomber sank quickly and no survivors were seen in the water.[7] Ten more young Americans were suddenly gone, ten more families back home soon to be stricken with lifelong grief. The crews of the other bombers were so stunned that they could hardly believe what they had just seen, but they carried on and completed their mission, dropping their bombs on the harbor at Makassar, where they hit a Japanese cruiser amidships with two 500-pound bombs and started fires among the warehouses on the wharf. They then made their sad way back to Fenton Field in Australia, a flight of over six hours, thinking of Capt. Olsen and the men on his crew, whom they would never see again.[8]

A 319th bomber flies 600 miles on two engines

Some people wondered how well or how far a B-24 could fly on just two of its four engines, if it had to. A mission flown by the 319th Squadron on 22 June [1943] provided some idea. The strike was flown from Fenton against a Japanese seaplane base on the island of Taberfane (see Map 20-2 again). The Taberfane seabase was home to Japanese floatplane fighters known by the Allied code names Nates, Petes, and Rufes.[*]

---

[*] The Nate was the Nakajima Ki-27, called by the Japanese the Army Type 97 fighter. It was used in China as the main Japanese fighter plane until around 1940 when it was su-

20. THE 319TH GOES TO DARWIN

The mission was flown in collaboration with some Royal Australian Air Force (RAAF) Beaufort twin-engine fighter planes. The plan was for three B-24s of the 319th Squadron to precede the Beauforts and bomb the seabase, then descend to a low altitude so that the gunners on the bombers could shoot up the base and any floatplanes that might be caught sitting on the water.

It was expected that at least some of the enemy fighters would rise to engage the bombers, so the bombers would have to defend themselves until they were able to make their escape. Thirty minutes after the three American bombers departed, several RAAF Beaufort fighters were to come in at low level to catch the Japanese planes refueling and destroy them on the water.

The three bombers of the 319th Squadron on this mission were piloted by Lieutenants Charles Hess, Alden Currie, and Hal Hevener.[*] Hevener was flying a B-24D named "Alley Oop," with the cartoon caveman's picture painted on the side (photo, p. 187). After the 600-mile flight from Fenton to Taberfane they caught the Japanese seabase by surprise and dropped their bombs, then turned back and made strafing passes, shooting up Japanese floatplanes on the water and some on the beach. They destroyed one floatplane as it was trying to take off, but others managed to get into the air and attack the bombers.

Lts. Hess and Currie then turned for home, their jobs done, but Lt. Hevener was all keyed up and decided to go back for one more strafing pass. It was not a wise move, for by that time the hornet's nest was fully stirred up, and several floatplane fighters pounced on the B-24.

In Hevener's own words:

> Four Rufes and one Pete jumped me, with the Pete doing most of the damage. The Pete was using 20mm and put one into number four [engine], then into number one, then into my trim cables in the tail. While he is chopping me up, the Rufes are sprinkling me from one end to the other. We take "Alley Oop" into the cloud cover, which is too thin to hide in. I know because they are still shooting and we can't see anything but their tracers coming at us from a lot of different directions. I decide to put "Alley Oop" just below the clouds in the clear so at least we can make a fight of it. Number four [engine] is feathered, number one has a smashed rocker-arm box and is spouting oil, and [Lt. John H.] Heath has his feet braced on the dash helping me keep the nose up when number two [engine] quits.

---

perseded by the Zero (it was a Nate that deliberately crashed into Capt. Olsen's bomber on 23 June 1943). The Pete was a two-seat biplane floatplane, a Mitsubishi F1M, and the Rufe was a variant of the Zero on floats.

[*]Lt. Hevener is the pilot who saw Capt. Jones bomber "Dirty Gertie" mysteriously explode on a reconnaissance mission in March.

We drop from 3000 feet to 200 in nothing flat, but I stop it with takeoff power on number three and 2300 rpm on number one. We throw out everything that is not nailed down! I cut number three to 2300 rpm and number one to 1800 rpm. With ten degrees of flaps down, we are only able to maintain our 200 feet. One Rufe, obviously out of ammo, pulls alongside on our starboard wing and flies formation with me for another 30 minutes. I know what he is waiting on and it isn't a "probable!"

I had radioed Darwin our position, course, A/S [airspeed]110 mph, and I would call every 30 minutes if still in the air. Darwin answered that they were dispatching a Walrus to intercept us. They never reached us! We could see nothing wrong with number two, so we restarted it. It would run roughly for about 10 to 20 minutes in auto-rich and then quit—a real mystery!

Finally Darwin and a straight-in approach with cylinder-head temps in the red. I made no power corrections for fear of losing the two engines that seemed to be working, although number one was black with oil. The gear came down and locked at ten feet, I chopped the throttles and it sat right down. Number one quit, number three caught fire, and they had to come out and tow us off the runway. When I took a look at number two, the mystery was explained, because a shell fragment from the 20mm in the top of number one had knocked a hole in the carburetor of number two. "Alley Oop" will never fly again![9]

The bomber "Alley Oop" had flown nearly 600 miles back to Australia on mostly two engines, and one of them was damaged. The crew's navigator, Lt. Fran Milder, remarked, "If anyone says a 24 can't fly on two engines I'll dispute it, as we did it for nearly 600 miles!"[10]

A Walrus floatplane was sent out from Darwin to intercept Lt. Hevener's crippled B-24 but failed to make contact with it. Fortunately Hevener didn't need rescuing this day.

20. THE 319TH GOES TO DARWIN

Lt. Hevener (left) and the other three officers of the crew of "Alley Oop." Hevener flew the bomber nearly 600 miles on only two engines. The other three men are (left to right) Lt. Barney E. Trainor, Lt. John H. Heath, and Lt. Fran G. Milder.

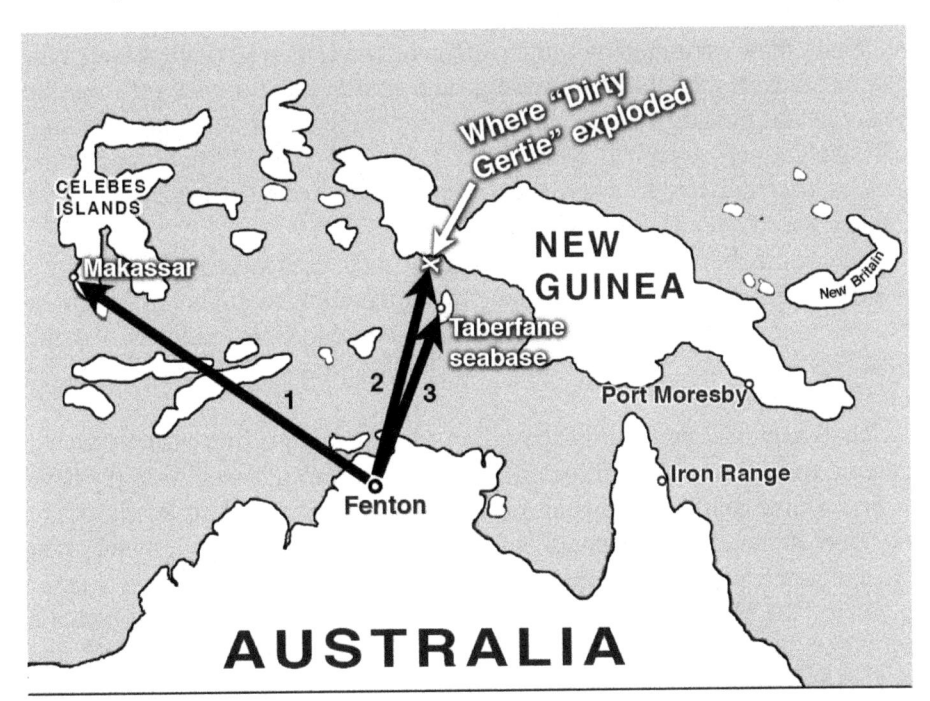

Map 20-2. The three missions of the 319th Squadron flown from Fenton, Australia described in this chapter. #1: the mission to Macassar during which a Japanese fighter plane crashed into the bomber of Capt. Roy Olsen. #2: the location where Capt. Charles Jones' bomber "Dirty Gertie" mysteriously exploded during a reconnaissance flight. #3: the mission to the Japanese seaplane base at Taberfane, from which the bomber "Alley Oop" returned 600 miles on two engines.

Chapter Twenty-One

THE 90ᵀᴴ MOVES TO PORT MORESBY

The 90th Bomb Group made the move from Iron Range to Port Moresby starting in early February of 1943.* Between February 1st and 10th, the 320th, the 321st, and 400th Squadrons† of the Group flew their bombers up from Iron Range, across the Coral Sea (see Map 6-3 on page 59), to Port Moresby in a permanent change of base, or at least as permanent as any base would be as the American war effort moved relentlessly forward toward Japan over the next two and a half years. The Group would be based at Port Moresby for ten months, until January of 1944, when they would move across the Owen Stanley Mountains to Dobodura.[1]

While they were making the move, since the Group's bombers were still getting stuck in the mud at Iron Range and couldn't taxi or take off from the soggy field if they carried much weight, most of the Group's equipment, along with the ground personnel, were driven down the muddy 29-mile road to the jetty at Portland Roads where they were loaded aboard a Liberty ship for transport across the Coral Sea to Port Moresby.

The bombers, carrying little more than their crews, flew to Moresby's Ward's Field, a runway scraped out of the scrubby foothills of the Owen Stanley range five miles east of the town of Port Moresby (which is why the field was also known as "Five-Mile Field"). The move was complete by the middle of February.

The Japanese were still bombing Port Moresby at this time, as they would continue to do throughout the spring of 1943, but the raids would simply have to be endured until American air power grew strong enough to dominate the sky over the area. Gen. Kenney was beginning to receive the airplanes that Washington had promised him, and more American fighter groups were coming in to Port Moresby all the time. The 348th Fighter Group, flying Republic P-47 Thunderbolts, arrived in Australia in June of 1943 and took up residence at Port Moresby in July. The 475th Fighter Group was activated in Australia

---

* The last combat mission flown from Iron Range by the 90th Bomb Group was on the 6th of February, 1943.[2]

† The 319th Squadron was still being temporarily based at Fenton, Australia.

21. THE 90ᵀᴴ MOVES TO PORT MORESBY

Aerial view of Ward's Field at Port Moresby, where the 90th Bomb Group took up residence in Feb. of 1943 after moving up from Iron Range. This was one of several airfields at Moresby.

in May and would be ready for combat at Port Moresby in August with one hundred twin-engine Lockheed P-38s.

These fighters took up continual patrols over the Moresby airbase and started making it hot for the Japanese bombers and their escorting Zeros whenever they came over from Lae or Wewak. But at this time no Allied fighter plane was the equal of the agile, lightweight Japanese Zero in maneuverability, so the American pilots often got the worst of it when they challenged Zeros in close dogfights. Through experience, they found it safer to dive on Zeros from above with guns blazing (American planes had more firepower than the Japanese) and then continue diving right past them, using their superior diving speed to escape, and then maneuver back into position for another pass, if necessary, rather than trying to out-turn them at close quarters.

General Kenney would also be receiving some light and medium bomber groups flying A-20s and B-25s, respectively, in July. The 345th Bomb Group (Medium) would be used as low-level strafer/bombers, and would specialize in skip-bombing Japanese ships. The four-engine heavy bombers (which flew at 150 mph, or about half the speed of the smaller twin-engine bombers) would no longer be assigned skip-bombing missions, but instead would bomb from high altitudes, flying level, as they had been trained to do in the States.

The pilots of the big B-17s and B-24s were not forbidden to skip-bomb Japanese ships on their own initiative, however, and occasionally did so if a

American B-17 bombers parked in protective earth revetments at 7-Mile Field (Jackson Field) at Port Moresby, New Guinea, in April of 1943.

pilot saw the opportunity and thought it worth the risk; in fact Col. Art Rogers made a specialty of it, although he usually skip-bombed transport ships rather than the much better-armed warships.

The 345th with its B-25s had been headed to England, but the success of B-25s used as skip-bombers and strafers in the Battle of the Bismarck Sea in March (which will be covered in Chapter 25) convinced the Joint Chiefs of Staff in Washington that they would be better employed in the Pacific, and General Kenney was elated to get them. With these medium bombers, plus the heavy bombers of the 90th and 43rd Groups, Kenney could carry the war to the Japanese and destroy their aircraft on their home airfields.

American engineers were also busy at Port Moresby's airfields building air raid shelters for the men and protected parking spots (revetments) for the aircraft, to minimize the effects of Japanese bombing. By the time the 90th moved to Moresby, most aircraft were being parked in these high-walled and widely dispersed dirt revetments that had been bulldozed up to shield them from bomb fragments and bullets (see photos above and opposite). This made it difficult for the Japanese to do much damage with their bombs unless they could score an almost direct hit on a bomber.

21. THE 90TH MOVES TO PORT MORESBY

90th Bomb Group B-24s parked in "horseshoe" revetments at Ward's Field, Port Moresby to provide them with some protection from Japanese bombs and bullets.

Moving the 90th Bomb Group to Port Moresby's airfields not only got the bombers out of the primitive runways of Iron Range, but it removed the men from the hardships of jungle life, since the Port Moresby airfield complex was on fairly open terrain, with only scattered, scrubby trees, in the foothills of the Owen Stanley Mountains. The move also based the bombers closer to their targets, since they would no longer have to cross the 350 miles of the Coral Sea to reach New Guinea and beyond.

As sparse as the living was at Port Moresby's Ward's Field, it seemed like a wonderful place to the men who had lately lived in the dark, dank jungles of Iron Range, and Group morale rose accordingly. Anyone coming out of hell would undoubtedly consider purgatory a fine improvement in his surroundings, but life in New Guinea, even away from the jungle, was never any picnic—far from it. Col. Art Rogers wrote:

> Just prior to the war, I had heard that a survey was made relative to living conditions in New Guinea, and the report that the committee made was that the one place on the face of the Earth where a white man could not live long was New Guinea. This I heartily agree with. Even if malaria, typhus, dengue fever, dysentery and all the parasitic diseases were completely blotted out, I still believe that the intense heat and miserable humidity would sap the strength of a white man in a few short years.

In early August of 1942 General Kenney flew up to Port Moresby to have a look at the place, and arrived just in time to experience a Japanese air raid. As he remembered it:

> Around noon the Japs raided Seven Mile [Jackson Field] with twelve bombers covered by fifteen fighters which came in at twenty thousand feet and laid a string of bombs diagonally across one end of the runway and into the dispersal area where our fighters and a few A-24 dive bombers were parked. A couple of damaged P-39s didn't need any more work done on them, three A-24s were burned up, and a few drums of gasoline were set on fire, shooting up huge flames which probably encouraged the Jap pilots to go home and turn in their usual report of heavy damage to the place. . . . I had a grandstand seat from a slit trench on the side of a small hill just off the edge of and overlooking Seven Mile, although I did not enjoy the spectacle as much as I might have under better conditions. The trench was full of muddy water and there were at least six too many people in with me.[3]

Some of the bombs the Japanese dropped had delayed-action fuses that didn't set them off for several hours. Kenney went on:

> I noticed a soldier on a bulldozer pushing dirt along to surround something or build a circular wall around it. I stopped and asked him what he was doing. He stopped the bulldozer and said, "Oh, we got one of them delay-action bombs down there in the ground about ten feet that ain't gone off yet. The engineers have dehorned most of the others, but this one is a new breed that they don't know about, so I'm just pushing dirt around her so she'll just fizz straight up when she goes off." I thanked him for the information. He wiped the sweat off his forehead and calmly went on with his job. The bomb went off that night about eight o'clock. As he had predicted, "She just fizzed straight up." It made quite a lot of noise and a lot of dirt went up in the air, but no damage was done.[4]

Kenney then inspected the camp next to the airfield and was informed that tropical diseases were running rampant among the Americans there:

> [T]he malaria and dysentery rates were so high that two months' duty in New Guinea was about all that the units could stand before they had to be relieved and sent back to Australia. Everyone spoke of losing fifteen to thirty pounds of weight during a two months' tour in Port Moresby. . . . Swarms of flies competed with you for your food, and unless you kept one hand busy waving them off as you ate, you were liable to lose the contest. Even while walking around, the pests worked on you and it didn't take long to figure out what the kids meant when they referred to the constant movement of your hands as "the New Guinea salute."

21. THE 90TH MOVES TO PORT MORESBY

The mosquito problem was not being taken care of, with the result that the malaria rate was appalling. Most of the men had mosquito netting, but a large percentage of it was torn in places or full of holes and afforded little protection. They really had big mosquitoes up there. Big ones that dwarfed the famous New Jersey variety.[5]

One young airman (Kenney called all his fliers his "kids") told the general that the mosquitoes were so large around Jackson Field that a few nights earlier one of them had landed on the end of the runway in the dark, and the night crew had filled it with 20 gallons of gasoline before they realized it wasn't a fighter plane. Gen. Kenney allowed as how there may have been some exaggeration in this claim.

The fact that the approximately 2,500 men of the 90th Bomb Group viewed New Guinea as a great improvement over Iron Range only underlines how terrible life had been at Iron Range. Anyone who joined the 90th Bomb Group after it left Iron Range was apt to grow tired of hearing how awful conditions had been there, and how easy he and all other newcomers had it by comparison. It could get so annoying that Lt. Allan Cooper, the copilot on the Horner crew and a former Disney artist, would draw a cartoon in 1944 in which even the Japanese were telling one another how tough the Americans had had it at Iron Range (right).

Lt. Allan Cooper, copilot of the Horner crew and a former Disney artist, grew so tired of hearing from the veteran members of the Group how easy he had it compared to their time at Iron Range that he drew this cartoon about it. In his cartoon, even the Japanese are still talking about Iron Range.

At Port Moresby, Col. Rogers picked a campsite for the Group high up on a hillside above Ward's Field, where he hoped breezes might somewhat alleviate the stifling heat and so that rainwater would run downhill away from their tents. The Group also set up a little store where the men could buy razor blades, toothpaste, toothbrushes, shaving cream, and other necessities. At times this PX* also sold candy, peanuts, chewing gum and other scarce luxuries, when it could get them. Rogers wrote:

> A Coca-Cola would have easily brought a dollar a bottle in the camp from most anyone.† The only form of recreation that could be offered to the men was the movies. We picked a site that was a natural amphitheater and set up a small projection house and screen (photo, p. 377). The men would attend our three showings a week regardless of how poor the picture was, if they were not on a mission, and would spend an hour and a half in a world of make-believe.

Another lifter of morale was pets. A number of dogs had been smuggled through the inspections of bombers being flown out to the Pacific, and had made it all the way from the States to Port Moresby. In addition, some men captured jungle birds and made pets of them. Col. Rogers had three large white cockatoos in a cage outside his tent, and whenever a Japanese air raid occurred the birds would screech, "Damn the Japs!" in imitation of their owner.

> As any group of men will invariably have pets and mascots [Rogers wrote], ours was no exception. There were hundreds of dogs, thoroughbreds and otherwise, that would line up at the mess hall for their daily rations just as the men would.
>
> With each incoming airplane and crew our doctors would call my attention to the fact that we would

Cockatoos were a favorite pet of many of the men in New Guinea. Col. Art Rogers had three.

---
* PX stands for Post Exchange.

† A dollar in 1943 was the equivalent of $14.25 today (2018).

receive one or two more mongrel dogs. This was a threat to the sanitation of the camp, because typhus fever is carried by fleas on rats which might transfer to the dogs and infect the entire camp. We had had very few cases of typhus fever [however], and being a dog lover myself, I could not see stooping low enough to issue an order to have all dogs disposed of.

To see a lonesome boy caressing his dog, that he had stowed away through three inspections at San Francisco, Hawaii and Australia, where airplanes were searched to prevent any pets being brought in to Australia, touched my heart. This was the only direct contact a lonesome boy would have with the life he knew back home, and it also amazed me how anyone could contrive to smuggle these little stowaways through all the inspections.

Many of the men had captured parrots, parakeets and beautiful white cockatoos of the jungle as their pets. I was one of the bird admirers, for I had three cockatoos in a cage in front of my tent. The sulfur-crested cockatoo is one of the most beautiful birds in the world, and is by far the best talker. He even seems to have intelligence, and at times can carry on a reasonable conversation with you. Chuck [Rawlings] and I enjoyed spending a good deal of our leisure time trying to teach the birds new words.

The life in a bomber camp becomes very tense just before a mission. Men very seldom smile, and they seem to be eager to get off on their mission and get it over with. But our many pets did a good deal to relax the men upon their return, and would give a lighter side to the grim war they were in.

A puppy mascot gets a bath at Port Moresby.

Capt. Norman Lawler and furry friend. Lawler preserved a large collection of Jolly Rogers photographs and passed them down to his grandson, Robert Tupa, who made them available for this book.

It was common for a bomber crew to adopt a dog as its mascot. While the crewmen were off on a mission, their dog anxiously awaited their return. When a crew did not return, their dog was often heartbroken. The historian of the Jolly Rogers wrote of a crew at Port Moresby that had a cocker spaniel named Flaps. When his crew was killed trying to land in fog after a mission, Flaps was inconsolable, and pined away until he died.[6]

Music soothes the nerves, bagpipes excepted

The popularity of wind-up phonographs in the camp (as in the photo below) has already been mentioned, but live music could also be heard. Col. Rogers helped the Group Chaplain, William H. Beeby, to form a choir that sang at religious services on Sundays, and both Rogers and Beeby were choir members. Rogers recorded that choir practice sessions held in the evenings were themselves a boost to morale, as the clear young voices harmonized in the stillness of the tropical night, singing songs familiar to all the boys.

Some of the Group's members had also managed to bring their own musical instruments all the way from the States, and played them in their tents. This too was a spirit lifter, except in the case of bagpipes. Lt. Harold Hevener, the pilot who had flown a damaged B-24 600 miles on two engines (pages 185-6), had brought his bagpipe from home, and played it frequently until a delegation of enlisted men visited him one day to ask that he please cease and desist. The starting up of the bagpipe, they told him, sounded so much like the startup of the airfield's air raid siren that they were getting tired of leaping from their cots to dash for the air raid shelters, only to realize that they were just hearing a bagpipe. Hevener reluctantly put his instrument away.[7]

Wind-up phonographs with a collection of records were prized in the 90th Bomb Group's camps. Here members of the Group introduce a couple of New Guinea natives to recorded music.

CHAPTER TWENTY-TWO

THE LOSS OF GENERAL RAMEY

Less than three months after he had been appointed the Commander of Fifth Bomber Command, following the loss of Gen. Walker on a bombing mission to Rabaul, Gen. Ramey too went out on a mission and never returned. On 26 March, 1943, Ramey took off from Jackson Field in a B-17 named "Pluto" and headed west on what was to have been a routine seven-hour reconnaissance of the Torres Strait, flying a triangular route from Port Moresby westward to Merauke on the south coast of New Guinea, thence south across the Torres Strait to Horn Island, and back to Port Moresby (see Map 22-1 on page 199). Why Gen. Ramey wanted to conduct this reconnaissance flight personally has not been recorded. He was a pilot, though, and perhaps just wanted to get out of headquarters for a few hours and get in some flying time.

Brigadier General Howard Ramey, lost on a lone reconnaissance mission on 26 March 1943.

Twenty minutes after Ramey's bomber took off, its radio operator made a routine call to Port Moresby, checking in, and that was the last that was ever heard from the plane. An extensive air search of the route the next day found no sign of the bomber or the twelve men aboard. Examination of Japanese records after the war showed that no American aircraft had been encountered by the Japanese in this area on that day, so it is unlikely the bomber was shot down. It was more likely the victim of bad weather or some sort of mechanical failure, or possibly some kind of pilot error.

Like Col. Meehan, who had disappeared without a trace on a combat mission from Iron Range to Rabaul five months earlier in November of 1942, Gen. Ramey left behind a wife and two daughters in the States who never knew the cause of his disappearance, nor where his mortal remains lie today.

The men who died on this mission were:

Brig. Gen. Howard K. Ramey of Waynesboro, Mississippi
Lt. Colonel Harold N. Chaffin from Arkansas
Capt. Stanley A. Loewenberg, of Brooklyn, New York
Commander Ferdinand D. Mannoccir, II, USN, from California
Capt. James R. Griffin from Texas
2nd Lt. William Lief from New York
M/Sgt. James D. Collier, Jr., from Louisiana
T/Sgt. Ortis L. Quaal from South Dakota
S/Sgt. Robert R. Stith from Oklahoma
S/Sgt. Harry A. Johnson from New York
Sgt. Marvin Berkowitz from New York
Pfc. George T. Hopfield from Ohio

Since B-17s did not often break up on water landings as B-24s tended to do, Ramey's bomber may today lie intact, like a time capsule, somewhere on the sea bottom in the Torres Strait between Australia and New Guinea.

With the loss of Gen. Ramey, Gen. Kenney appointed Gen. Ennis Whitehead (photo below), his Deputy Commander, as head of Fifth Bomber Command.

Left to right: Capt. John Clyer, Lee Van Atta, and Major General Ennis Whitehead, standing in front of a B-17. After Gen. Ramey was lost, Gen. Kenney appointed Whitehead to replace him as head of 5th Bomber Command.

22. THE LOSS OF GENERAL RAMEY

As time went on, Whitehead proved to be so able an air commander that Kenney delegated much of the running of bomber operations to him for the rest of the war, and rarely disagreed with his decisions. According to General Kenney, one of the big disadvantages the Japanese had during the war was that "they didn't have a Whitehead to run things for them."

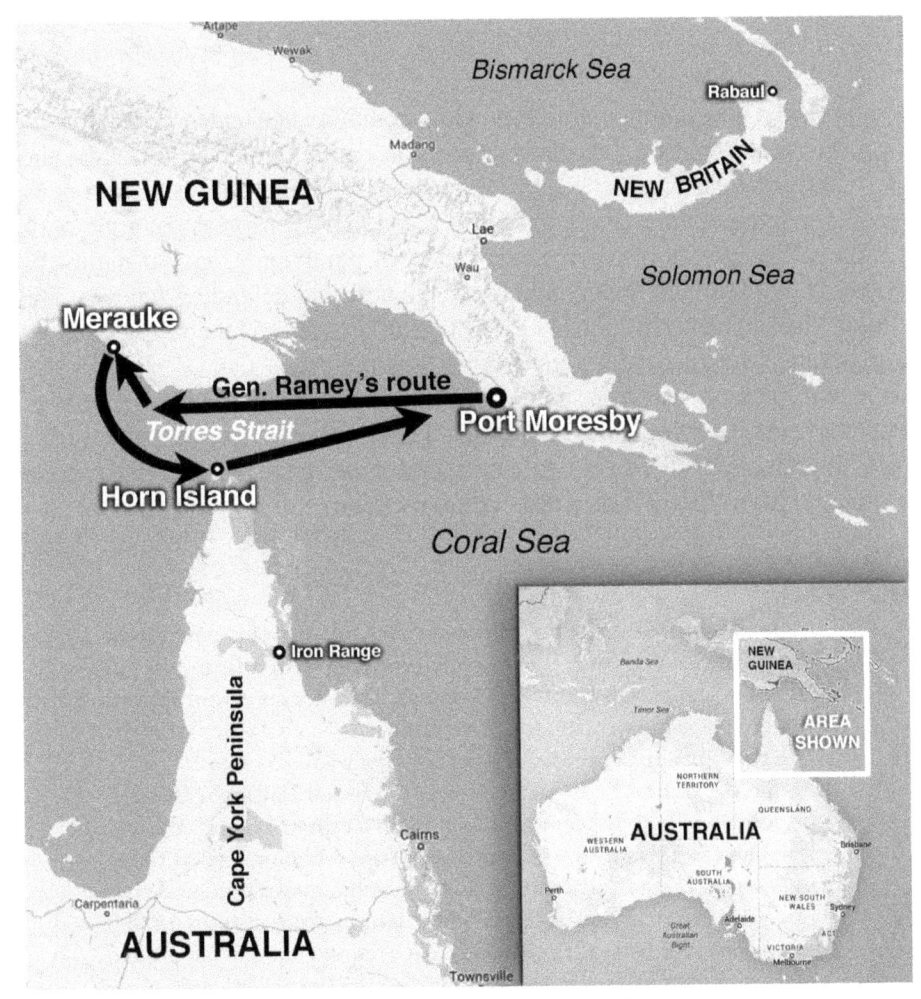

Map 22-1. On 26 March, 1943, General Ramey set off as the pilot on a reconnaissance mission from Port Moresby westward to Merauke, New Guinea, thence across the Torres Strait to Horn Island, Australia, and back to Port Moresby, as shown by the black arrows on this map. For unknown reasons his B-17 vanished without a trace somewhere along this route.

Chapter Twenty-Three

NO REST FOR THE WEARY

As Japanese air power in New Guinea diminished under the steady and increasing pressure of the American bombing of their airfields, and as the Americans stiffened their defense of Port Moresby with newly-arrived fighter planes, the Japanese took to bombing Moresby at night only, for the same reasons the Americans had been bombing Rabaul at night: the darkness cloaked them from antiaircraft gunners and defending fighters. The Americans had no night fighters at this stage of the war, and the Japanese could night-bomb Moresby from high altitude without much risk on nights when there was enough moonlight to see the American airfields. The Americans at Port Moresby, like the Japanese at Rabaul, had searchlights that they used to try to illuminate bombers for their antiaircraft guns, but even a brightly spotlit airplane at high altitude was a difficult target to hit.

Captain Garrett Middlebrook of the 38th Bomb Group (Medium) flying B-25s was at Port Moresby at this time and remembered:

> The Japs bombed the Port Moresby area on an average of at least three nights out of four. Most of the time they sent a formation of only three planes, but from time to time as many as six would appear. Almost invariably we withstood two attacks on each particular night when they did appear, the first flight arriving within 15 minutes of 11 PM and the second flight arrived over us between 1:30 and 2:30 AM.
>
> Occasionally they became lucky and hit a valuable target. We lost a few planes, the runways of our three strips were hit several times and once there was quite a bit of damage at the motor pool at Seven Mile Strip. They always dropped their bombs from around 18,000 feet and at night from that altitude their accuracy was only sporadic.
>
> They surely must have known that the effectiveness of their raids was minimal, which caused all of us, high officials, air crews, and line mechanics alike, to assume they had another purpose for this eternal procedure ... to harass us and disturb our sleep.[1]

Night bombing of Port Moresby was undoubtedly intended mainly to disturb the Americans' rest, since the men had to leap from their cots and jump into foxholes or slit trenches with each raid. It got to the point where many of the exhausted men became fatalistic about the raids and just remained in their cots. Art Rogers wrote:

> During many of the night bombing raids by the Japs, many of our men would refuse to leave their cots and the protection of their mosquito nets to jump into a foxhole often times half full of water, to be eaten up by mosquitoes. You couldn't blame them, since they were forced to work from sunup to sundown under heat that was stifling. This is bad enough for men in excellent health and high spirits, but it becomes almost an impossibility when the men are half sick and so underweight.

Rogers could see the mental and physical toll that the punishing pace and strain of combat missions was taking on the 90th Bomb Group:

> For an entire year, the grueling day-in and day-out strikes had cost its share of lives and equipment. The last few months we had been averaging three to four Group strikes per week, not counting individual reccos [reconnaissance flights]. This kept the entire organization beaten down physically, and it was very noticeable on days that missions were not scheduled how the combat crewmen stayed in their cots getting "bunk fatigue" as daylight rest is known in the Air Corps. Dr. Sanderson, one of my flight surgeons, pointed out that these men were carrying all the load that could be expected of them physically, since it was not normal for an eighteen or nineteen year old boy to spend all of his leisure time sleeping.

The Group's flight surgeons could see that members of some of the most veteran crews were getting close to cracking under the stress. However, from the first combat missions at Iron Range in November of 1942 onward through the fall of 1943 at Port Moresby, there was no policy in place regarding the number of missions or combat hours an airman had to fly before he could be rotated back to the States, and having no definite goal to strive toward and look forward to added to the strain on the men.

In May of 1943 the 90th Bomb Group's surgeons took it upon themselves to ground some of these exhausted crews for what was termed "flying fatigue," and recommended to headquarters that they be relieved of duty and either sent on leave in Australia to recuperate or returned to the States. However, having these doctors ground his men without his permission did not sit well with General Whitehead, who felt that there were too few bomber crews on hand as it was, and if the men were physically capable of flying then they must do so, regardless of their mental state. Replacement crews from the States were so scarce at this time, with nearly all new crews being sent to Europe, that the Pacific veterans could not be relieved or replaced and would just have to continue flying.

The upshot was that Whitehead dismissed all of the 90th Bomb Group's doctors and reassigned them elsewhere, sending some to other bomber or fighter groups and some down to Australia. New medical officers were brought in to replace the ones sent away, and they were warned to adhere to this policy of keeping worn-out men on the job. And so the weary bomber crews slogged valiantly on, resigned to their fate but determined to see it through.[2]

According to the Group's records, by Sept. of 1943, ten months after they had flown their first combat mission on 15 November, 1942, the 90th Bomb Group had flown over a thousand combat missions and dropped 3,800 tons of bombs. The results had been good, however: the Group had destroyed 218 Japanese aircraft on the ground and sunk 41 Japanese ships, with many more damaged. General Kenney had awarded 1,400 decorations to the Group's men, including the Silver Star, Distinguished Flying Cross, Purple Heart, Soldier's Medal and the Air Medal.

Interestingly, on the enemy side, the number of medals awarded to Japanese airmen during the entire war came to a grand total of exactly zero, since the Japanese never acknowledged any valorous deeds or notable achievements of their pilots and crews, just as they never bothered to search for, or make any attempt to rescue, their downed airmen. And any Japanese pilot or crewman who became too weary to carry out his duties was simply beaten until he showed more zeal for his work. Far from rotating weary men back to the homeland to recuperate or train new airmen, the Japanese policy was simply "fly-'till-you-die." There was a grim joke among Japanese airmen that the only way for a man to be sent home was to be killed, at which time his bones or ashes (if perchance recovered) might, if he was lucky, be sent back to Japan in a wooden box to be interred in the Yasukuni Shrine to the war dead in Tokyo.

Finally, in October of 1943, General Kenney enacted a schedule for rotation of bomber crews home, something that alleviated a lot of the stress on the crewmen, who now had something to strive toward. He announced that after a bomber crewman had logged 300 hours of combat flying, he would be relieved of flight duties and would be sent back to the States as soon as a replacement for him was available. As the war went on, the requirements for rotation home would change, switching from the number of hours flown to the number of combat missions flown, and finally to a point system, with points being awarded for each hour flown, each month spent overseas, and other criteria (more on this in a later chapter).

Based on his experience with his bomber groups thus far, in the fall of 1943 Kenney also recorded his expectations regarding the attrition rate of bombers and crews. He expected that his two heavy bomber groups in New Guinea, the

Medics of the Jolly Rogers' 320th Squadron in front of their Dodge ambulance truck.

90th and the 43rd, would each lose seven bombers and their crews (about 70 men) per month to combat flying, three more crews to sickness, wounds, or "war weariness" (a. k. a. "flying fatigue," or what some ground soldiers called "shell-shock"), while twelve other crews would reach the 300-combat-hour limit and become eligible for return home.

As it turned out, few of these 300-hour crews would be able to return to the States immediately. A crew eligible for rotation home would remain with its group in a nonflying status until it was replaced by a new crew from the States. This was done in order to keep on hand the number of men required by the Group's Table of Organization, and presumably these nonflying crews would also be available should some emergency arise that required all available crews to fly. Thus there were always crews in the camp who had completed their combat tours, and were no longer flying, but couldn't go home until their replacements arrived from the States.

The 90th's heroic Medical Officers

Like the mechanics who somehow managed to keep the bombers of the 90th Bomb Group in the air under abysmal working conditions, the Group's medical doctors and the medics who assisted them were a band of unsung heroes. They had to cope with men who came down with not only malaria and many other known tropical diseases, but with illnesses unknown to medical science, collectively referred to as "jungle fevers."

Many kinds of diseases were spawned in the ultra-fertile Petri dish of the hot, wet equatorial jungles, a never-ending process of disease propagation in a part of the world where there is no winter to cause an annual pause in their development. Unlike the native peoples of the Pacific, who had developed immunities to most tropical diseases over a time span of thousands of years, the white men's immune systems were unable to cope with the invisible microbial onslaught.

The Group's doctors raced to the runway to meet returning bombers that had wounded aboard.

On top of all the illnesses, the doctors had to deal with battle injuries, not only bullet wounds but bodies shredded and torn by flak, the 20mm cannon of Japanese fighter planes, and the burns and manglings caused by airplane crashes. They also saw the psychological effects of combat stress on the aircrewmen, and when a doctor felt that some man had reached his mental breaking point he took him off flying status for a short while as a hazard to himself and others. After General Whitehead's decree that until replacements were sent out from the States such men must be retained and kept on duty, a brief rest period in the camp was the best he could do for him.

Col. Rogers wrote of the Group's medical staff:

> Our small medical staff of five doctors in my Group [i.e. one doctor for each of the four squadrons, plus an overall Group surgeon] proved their worth over and over again. They not only advised me and my squadron commanders as to when a combat crewman had reached the ragged edge of endurance, but also met our returning airplanes to minister to the men who at times would have been bleeding for a period of three hours or more.
>
> Airplanes carrying wounded crewmen were given first priority on landing on their return from a mission, and the signal given by an airplane in the air should his radio be shot out was that of burning his bright landing lights. As soon as the plane stopped rolling, an ambulance swung alongside and our doctors would crawl into the bomber to examine the injured and dead crewmen before they were moved. Many men were saved by blood transfusions and minor operations that took place right inside the airplanes.
>
> One remarkable operation was performed right in front of an airplane, when a dazed crewman, after a ten-hour mission in which

the airplane had been shot pretty much to pieces, stepped in front of a revolving propeller before the pilot had killed the engines. This young officer was a navigator, and had been on a long flight out of Darwin on an attack on Ambon [Island].

The airplane had been jumped by twelve or fifteen fighters, and after shooting four or five of them down they had run out of ammunition and were shot to pieces by the pursuing fighters, who dogged them until the fighters themselves had run out of ammunition. With one engine shot completely out of commission, they had returned on three engines.

During the running fight the pilot kept maneuvering so as to prevent the Japs' fire from being too effective. This threw a tremendous strain on the navigator, who was attempting to keep up with their position out over the ocean. He knew that their gasoline was limited, and also knew that if he were unable to navigate the airplane directly back, that even though the Japs didn't get them the sharks would. Upon landing, it was easy to understand the dazed mental condition of this young navigator.

The rotating propeller split his skull open, allowing his brains to come out, and almost cut his hand off. The doctor who performed this miraculous operation, right on the field, was the same doctor who had set fire to my airplane before our takeoff from San Francisco with his cigarette lighter, Captain W. S. Mitchell, known as Mitch to the boys, and the operation was so successful that in time it allowed this young officer to be normal mentally and he had partial use of his hand.

Our doctors, who had been trained to work under ideal conditions and with known diseases, were forced to act as sanitary engineers, advanced psychologists, and experts in unknown jungle diseases. They had to know each individual crewman thoroughly, so as to be able to detect the dreaded thing known as flying fatigue.

This is noted in a personality change, and oftentimes the man himself does not know he is in a serious condition and refuses to tell his closest friends of his inner nervousness and fears. I am positive that our doctors saved many lives by grounding these men at the proper time. Many wives, mothers, and sweethearts can thank these doctors for their untiring efforts in carrying out their job.

One popular medical officer in the 90th Bomb Group was Capt. Richard J. "Doc" Sanderson, originally assigned to the 400th Squadron but eventually appointed to be the overall Group flight surgeon. Sanderson was well-liked by all members of the 90th for his informal manner and extreme competence. He was always addressed by everyone, of any rank, as "Doc," and he liked it that way.

Sanderson made daily rounds of the 90th's encampments, visiting in turn the mechanics, supply men, armaments and ordnance crews, cooks, motor pool men, headquarters personnel, and of course the airmen, to find out if anyone required his services. Any medical complaints that he heard from anyone—and there were many in a zone of operations so fraught with disease and dangerous occupations—were dealt with immediately and effectively. He also did his best to see that every member of the Group took his daily anti-malarial atabrine tablet, and he could tell at a glance when a man had been doing so from the yellow-orange color of his skin.

Anyone with a medical condition or injury too serious for "Doc" to handle in his field hospital was stabilized and sent off by air express in a transport plane to a hospital in Australia that had the proper facilities to deal with it.

After one of the takeoff crashes at Iron Range, in May of 1943, Sanderson had rushed into the burning wreckage to pull survivors to safety. For this he was awarded a Soldier's Medal for bravery. Ever modest, whenever he was asked about the medal he claimed that it had been awarded to him for being seen in the vicinity of a crash, but only because he was the slowest runner in the Group and had been unable catch up to all the other people running away from it.[3]

An airman with battle wounds that only required some time off to heal before he could return to duty was sometimes sent down to Sydney on leave during his recuperation period. Aircrewmen knew that "Doc" Sanderson had the authority to do this, and always hoped that if they got wounded their injuries would be only just serious enough to earn them a trip to Sydney to experience the delights of civilization for a little while, not to mention the company of sympathetic Australian ladies who (they hoped) would want to show their appreciation for their heroism.

"Doc" once treated the navigator of Art Rogers' crew, Lt. Phil Conti, when Conti came to him after a combat mission with his head and face covered in blood, dramatically pleading with "Doc" to save his life. After Sanderson got Conti cleaned up, he searched through his hair and found a small sliver of shrapnel from a flak burst embedded in his scalp, which he deftly plucked out with tweezers. Conti insisted that the only way he could possibly recover from such severe trauma would be to be sent on leave to Sydney. Sanderson told him it wasn't quite so serious a wound as that, but he could have a couple of days of rest in his tent. "Nice try, though, Phil," he said.[4]

Sanderson was often seen dispensing the customary two ounces of liquor to bomber crewmen upon their return from a mission (photo, opposite), and most of the men looked forward to it. S/Sgt. Maston "Harry" Clay, one of the Goup's aerial photographers (who would fly 42 combat missions with the 90th

23. NO REST FOR THE WEARY

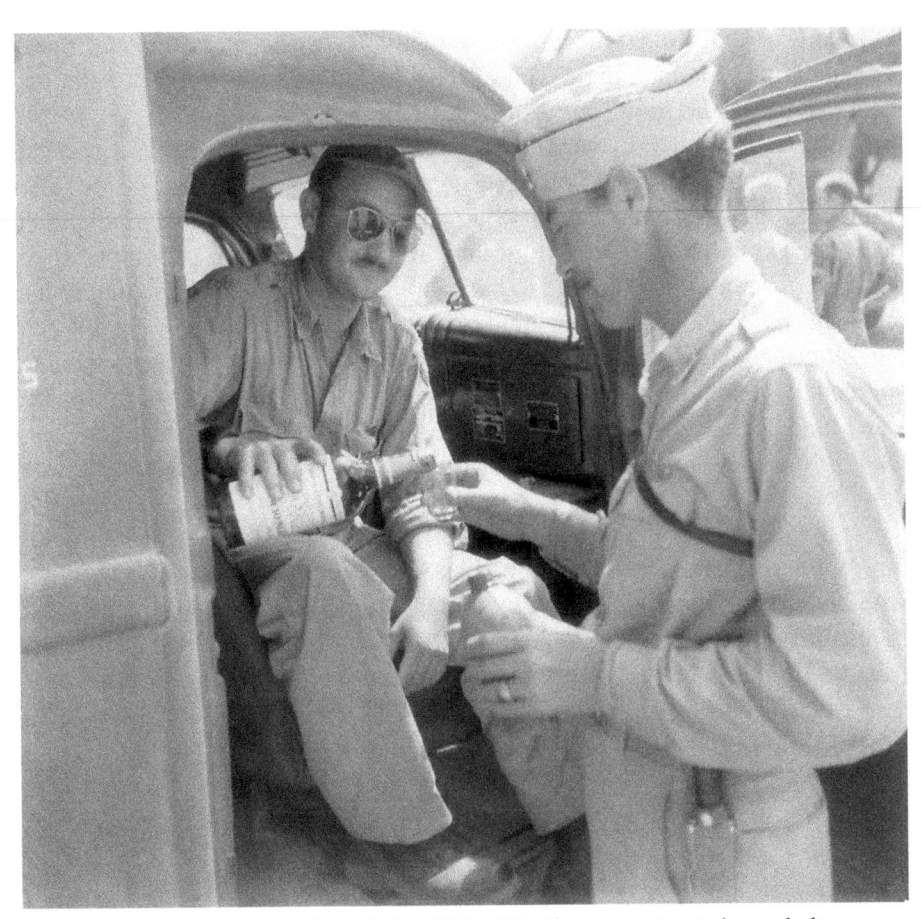

Jolly Rogers' flight surgeon Capt. Richard "Doc" Sanderson, sitting in his ambulance near the flight line, dispenses to Col. Rogers the customary two ounces of whiskey allotted to each bomber crewman upon return from a combat mission. Like many of the men, Rogers is saving his share for later in a canteen. Nondrinkers generally accepted the liquor and later used it as trading material.

by war's end) made the mistake of mentioning this after-mission bracer in a letter to his mother back home in the States.

Mrs. Stella Clay, who held strict views on the evils of drink, was horrified to hear that her son was being proffered a medicinal tot of spirits after his missions and wrote an indignant letter to President Roosevelt expressing her outrage that the Army Air Corps should contribute to the moral downfall of the nation's sons in this manner. She wrote that she had been a nurse in the First World War and knew full well from experience that a candy bar was a perfectly good stimulant after a hard day's work.

Letters to the government were actually read in this earlier and more conscientious time in America, and Mrs. Clay's letter was referred from the White House to the Joint Chiefs of Staff, thence to MacArthur's headquarters in Brisbane, Australia, and on down the Fifth Air Force chain of command until it eventually reached Col. Art Rogers, Deputy Commander of the 90th Bomb Group. The result was that one day after a hard mission, as the men of Harry Clay's crew were getting their well-earned dollop of liquor, when Clay's turn came the medic said to him (to both Clay's surprise and that of his crewmates), "Well, Harry, what'll it be, a Hershey bar or a Baby Ruth?" When the astonished man asked what was going on, he was told (with his crew as an appreciative audience), "Your mother doesn't want you drinking any liquor, Harry, and neither Col. Rogers, General Kenney, General MacArthur, or President Roosevelt wants to go against her wishes. So, what kind of candy bar do you prefer?"

At this Sgt. Clay unleashed such a torrent of abuse on all the military authority figures that, after all, only had his best interests at heart in complying with his mother's wishes, topped by threats of bodily harm to the medic, that he finally got his two ounces of liquor, along with a lot of ribbing from his friends. He had a hard time living it down, and from that time forward was very careful about what he wrote home to his mother.[5]

Tent hospital at Port Moresby, 1943, with the Coral Sea in the background.

Chapter Twenty-Four

CANNIBALS

The Pacific war held some dangers for an aviator that were seldom encountered in the European war theater, one being the extreme violence of the weather, as already mentioned, and another the possibility that after a man bailed out or crash-landed, he might be eaten.

Many native tribes in the more remote parts of the New Guinea highlands had never seen a white man before, and for those who ate human flesh, having these strange white people and their metal machines drop from the sky into their midst must have seemed like supernatural gifts. Given the number of aircraft on both sides that vanished in New Guinea, there were likely quite a few airmen eaten by cannibals. Metal and other materials salvaged from crashed airplanes could also be useful to Stone Age people—for example an arrowhead made of metal is much more durable than one made of stone or bone.

Besides aviators, defeated Japanese soldiers who fled inland from the coastal battles no doubt also ran into cannibals and were devoured. Many Japanese became cannibals themselves when their supplies were cut off and they could get no other food. This was well documented during the Battle of the Kokoda Trail, when captured Japanese diaries revealed the practice, one diarist writing that the bodies of Australians killed on the battlefield were better tasting than the bodies of his own (starved) countrymen.

At least one of the 90th Bomb Group's crews had a tragic encounter with native New Guinea cannibals. This was the crew of Lt. Hank Chovanec of the 321st Squadron. Chovanec, like Art Rogers, had become an expert at sinking Japanese shipping, and he and his crew had sunk more ships than any other crew in the Group by both skip-bombing them on the surface and level bombing from altitude.[1] They flew a bomber that they had named "Czech'em," a reference to Chovanec's Slavic ancestry.

Lt. Hank Chovanec of Fayetteville, Texas, pilot of the bomber "Czech 'em."

Lt. Hank Chovanec (standing, second from right) and his crew in front of their B-24D bomber named "Czech 'em." This bomber actually had two names; the other one was "The Falcon." Behind Chovanec's head can be seen the wings of a falcon painted on the side of the plane.

The Chovanec crew had just completed 50 combat missions and was scheduled to return to the States when they decided to fly one last mission, an armed reconnaissance from Port Moresby to Wewak. On the return trip they were to make a supply drop to some Australian troops operating against the Japanese in the jungle. The date was 30 April, 1943.

Flying with the crew was a well-known Australian coastwatcher, Flight Lt. Leigh Grant Vial, known as "Golden Voice" Vial for his clear, calm voice over the radio as he reported the movements of Japanese troops, ships, and aircraft from his observation posts in the Lae/Salamaua area.* Vial was familiar with the area where the supplies were to be dropped and went along as an adviser. An Army photographer also joined the group, which, with the regular crew of ten, made twelve men in the bomber.

The plane left Port Moresby with the supplies and did not return, and was not heard from again. Two days later a search plane flying their route spotted the wreckage of the bomber in the Owen Stanley Mountains sixteen miles from a village in the central highlands of New Guinea known as Bena Bena (see Map 24-1 on page 217). It was a remote area known to be inhabited by cannibals. As the plane flew over the wreckage, signal flares rose up from the ground, showing that someone had survived the crash.[2]

---

* It was a high-pressure job. The Japanese were constantly searching for him, using direction-finding equipment to home in on his radio broadcasts. A Japanese patrol once passed right beneath the branches of a tree in which he was hiding with his radio.

24. CANNIBALS 211

Members of the rescue party photographed near Bena Bena just before setting off to find the wreck site of Lt. Chovanec's bomber. Back row, left to right: Lt. Bandy of 5th Bomber Command, Maj. Imperato of the 54th Troop Carrier Wing, and Lt. Norman Wilde of the Royal Australian Air Force. Front row, left to right: Sgt. "Jock" Essen of the Australian army, Lt. "Spiffy" Wells of 5th Bomber Command, Capt. Eugene Straw, and Capt. Frank McLaughlin, the latter two of the 90th Bomb Group.

A rescue party was immediately organized, comprised of five members of 5th Bomber Command plus an Australian Air Force officer. They landed in a C-47 on a small grass airfield near Bena Bena that had been used by gold miners before the war, and made contact with local Australian army forces. Sgt. Jock Essen of the Australian army volunteered to accompany the group and act as their guide, and with his knowledge of local languages he would also be their interpreter in any encounters with the natives. For their protection, the seven white men were accompanied by ten black native policemen who had been trained and armed by the Australians. Seventy-eight native carriers were hired to transport the expedition's provisions and equipment.

To reach the wreck site, the party would have to pass through uncharted jungle known to be inhabited by hostile tribes, and it was also territory under the control of the Japanese. As they made their way through the rainforest on native trails, signal drums could be heard around them in the distance

Ten native policemen accompanied the rescue party as bodyguards.

announcing their coming, and an occasional arrow or spear came whizzing out of the jungle from unseen foes. It was a scene that would have fitted perfectly into an Indiana Jones movie.

After five days of hard uphill trekking into the uplands of the Owen Stanley Mountains, the expedition reached the spot where the bomber "Czech'em" had crashed. It was obvious that the plane had come down at a steep angle

Very little remained intact of the bomber "Czech 'em" at the crash site.

and struck the ground with tremendous force, for there was little left of it but scattered piles of twisted wreckage. The mangled bodies of nine of the twelve men aboard were found in and around the wreckage, leaving three men unaccounted for. The tail of the bomber had separated from the rest of the plane, apparently before it hit the ground, and was found separately, the only piece of wreckage left intact. There were indications that someone, possibly the survivors of the crash, had used it for a shelter, presumably the same men who had fired signal flares at the search plane. But the question was, where were these men now? There was no sign of them around the crash site.

Because of the extreme violence of the crash, the bodies of the men extricated from the wreckage could not be individually identified. The remains were collected, separated as well as possible, and buried in nine graves marked with crude wooden crosses. A military funeral was conducted that included a rifle salute by the ten native policemen. As this ceremony was concluding, a horde of armed natives appeared on a hillside above the expedition members, advancing toward them with evidently hostile intentions. These natives were not accompanied by any women, an ominous sign (for even savages do not risk their women on a battlefield).

As the tribesmen moved menacingly down the hill, the members of the rescue party took up defensive positions. Then a couple of the native policemen boldly dashed forward and seized a tribal chieftain, dragging him back within their group and holding him hostage. This act threw the hostiles into confusion, and they halted, hesitated, and then retreated. In the uneasy truce that followed, both sides came warily together again, and Sgt. Essen, speaking through a native interpreter whom he had brought with him (for he did not know this tribe's dialect himself), interrogated some of the natives about the whereabouts of the three missing airmen.

Essen[*] had been the owner of a plantation on New Britain, and he had been out working in his fields when the Japanese invaders attacked and burned his home. They had carried off his wife and daughter, whom he never saw again, nor had he ever been able to learn their fate. He then volunteered to become a coastwatcher, and served as a sergeant in the Australian army for the duration of the war. He was familiar with the ways of New Guinea natives and spoke some of their dialects (no one could learn them all, for there were at least 800).

It was quite obvious that these upland natives were cannibals, just from a glance at their body ornaments, which were made from human body parts. Under persistent questioning, the tribesmen finally admitted that there had been three survivors of the plane crash, but they had captured, killed, and eaten them. Sgt. Essen was unable to determine exactly which tribesmen had

---

[*] In some accounts spelled Esson or Elston

Sgt. Jock Essen interrogates the cannibals about the three missing bomber crewmen. The tribesmen finally confessed that they had killed and eaten them.

perpetrated the killings, but it really made no difference. Being heavily outnumbered, the white men were in no position to punish anyone without starting a war with these natives, a war they might not survive. Capt. Frank McLaughlin said later, in a tape-recorded interview:

> The natives said that all of the crew members were killed when the ship crashed except for three, and they were injured, but they escaped into the jungle, but they were followed and caught—and they [the cannibals] had a feast. The tribe that we had, they insisted that they didn't have the feast; it was another tribe, so our police boys rounded up some from the second tribe and they admitted that there had been a feast, but they didn't do it—it was another tribe. So the police boys rounded up some from the third tribe and they . . . said it was the first tribe. So we never could determine—Sgt. Essen couldn't—what tribe it was, but they did admit there had been a feast and they claimed the white [man] was all the same as pig meat.[3]

24. CANNIBALS 215

Sullen cannibals being questioned at the Chovanec crash site. The man at left, glaring at the cameraman (Capt. Frank McLaughlin), wears a neck ornament made of a human jawbone, and his ears are decorated with severed human fingers. The man at right with the rifle, who is keeping a wary eye on the cannibal, is one of the ten native New Guinea policemen who accompanied the rescue expedition as bodyguards.

There were hundreds of hostile cannibals gathered around the rescue party during these interrogations, and it wouldn't have taken much provocation to trigger a fight with them. The expedition members realized that they were in

Capt. McLaughlin's camera recorded the tense standoff with the cannibals. The native in the foreground at right is a member of the rescue party.

a precarious position, for although these were primitive Stone Age people, armed with only clubs, spears, and bows and arrows, they outnumbered the white men and their native allies by at least ten to one, and in a pitched battle the rescue party would no doubt have been overwhelmed by sheer numbers.

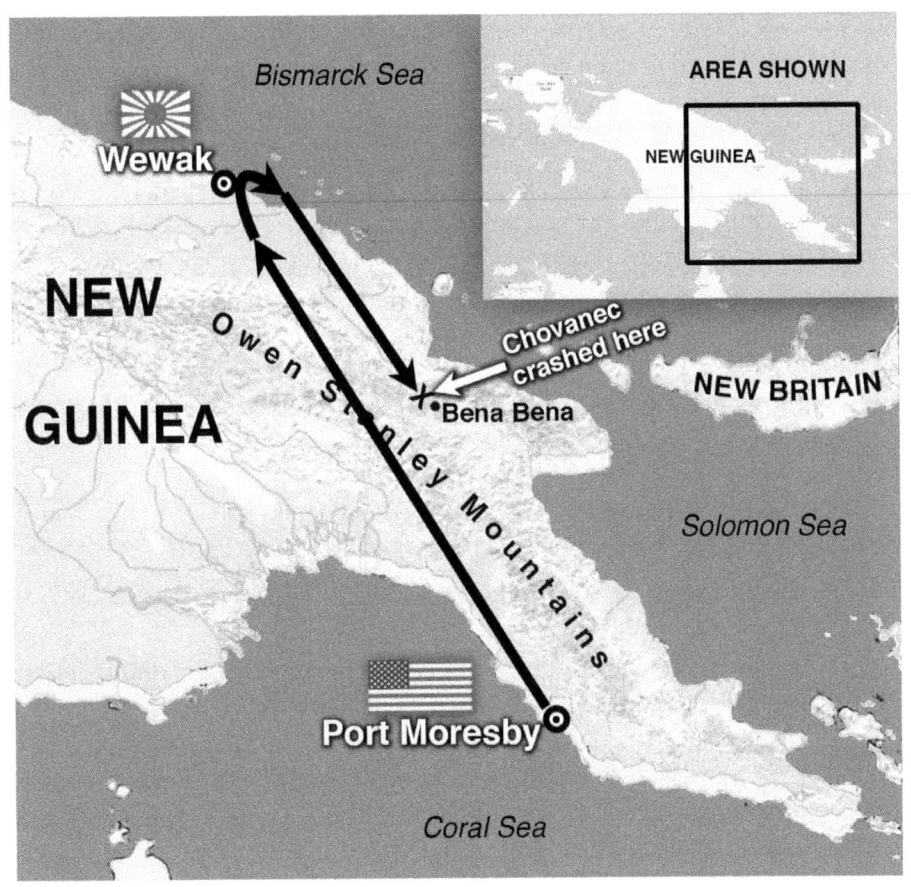

Map 24-1. Lt. Chovanec crashed near Bena Bena in the Owen Stanley Mountains.

Not wanting to risk becoming the main course of another cannibal feast, Essen and the others decided that discretion would be the better part of valor and set out on the return trip to Bena Bena with all possible haste. The cannibals followed them, running along the ridge tops on either side of them for miles, hurling taunts and insults at them. Under this pressure the expedition took a faster but more dangerous route back to Bena Bena, passing through an area where Japanese patrols were known to be frequent, but fortunately they did not encounter any. At Bena Bena the C-47 took the rescue party back to Port Moresby.

The expedition had taken twelve days. Back at 5th Bomber Command headquarters the men reported the sad fate of Lt. Chovanec and his crew. The fact that three of the men aboard the bomber had survived the crash, only to be killed and eaten by cannibals, was not made public. Although it was not known which three of the twelve men had suffered this fate, the fact that some of them had was probably considered too horrible for any of the families of the men to bear. The telegrams to their relatives in the States stated only that their loved ones had been killed in action.*

The men who died when the bomber "Czech'em" went down were:

1st Lt. Jindrich "Henry" L. Chovanec, pilot, of Fayetteville, Texas
2nd Lt. Henry C. Hansen, copilot, from California
2nd Lt. Eugene B. Brown Jr., navigator, from Santa Barbara, California
2nd Lt. Edwin B. Smith, bombardier, from Pointe Coupee, Louisiana
T/Sgt. Clarence W. Boyer from Los Angeles, California
T/Sgt. William C. Lowther (home state not listed)
S/Sgt. Robert P. Nix of Illinois
S/Sgt. Ernest E. Hansen of Michigan
S/Sgt. Robert A. Ratliff of Missouri
S/Sgt. Henry S. Simons of Crawford, Georgia
Cpl. Chester O. Coggin, photographer (home state not listed)
Passenger: Flight Lt. Leigh Grant Vial, RAAF, from East St. Kilda, Victoria, Australia.

Lt. Chovanec was mourned by his parents, three brothers, and three sisters. Lt. Vial left a wife, a son, and two daughters in Australia.

Another picture of the Chovanec crew. Lt. Chovanec is standing on the left.

*The son of Governor Nelson Rockefeller of New York was killed and eaten by cannibals in 1961 while on an expedition to New Guinea to collect primitive tribal art, showing that some of these tribes have been reluctant to give up the practice, and there are reports of cannibalism in New Guinea today.

Chapter Twenty-Five

THE BATTLE OF THE BISMARCK SEA

General Kenney had been hitting one Japanese convoy after another with American airpower as they came down from Rabaul to supply the Japanese garrisons on the north coast of New Guinea. He'd been damaging them and sinking some of the ships but not stopping them. The Japanese in New Guinea desperately needed these troops and supplies.

By November of 1942 the Australian 7th Infantry Division, starting from Port Moresby, had pushed the Japanese invasion force back over the Kokoda Trail all the way to their starting point at Buna Village on the north coast of New Guinea, thus defeating the Japanese attempt to capture Port Moresby by land. MacArthur had then sent in the American 32nd Division and parts of the 41st to join the Australians in the battle at Buna,* where after horribly difficult and bloody jungle fighting, much of it in swamps, they had finally wiped out the Japanese forces there by the end of January, 1943.†

The next step for the Allies was to drive farther up the coast to capture the former Australian towns of Salamaua and Lae (see Map 25-1, next page). Australian forces began pushing through the jungle toward Salamaua and were making good progress. General MacArthur began preparations for amphibious landings at Lae and other Japanese bases still further up the coast. In the summer, the decision would be made to bypass Rabaul, after it had been isolated and cut off by the capture of the islands around it.

The Japanese plan to stop (and, they hoped, reverse) the Allied advance up the New Guinea coast depended on getting reinforcements—they desperately needed more men and supplies in New Guinea, and they could only get them from Rabaul, where they had 70,000 to 100,000 troops to draw from along with plenty of arms, ammunition, and aviation fuel that had been brought in by their navy and stockpiled there. The Japanese high command therefore decided

---

* General Kenney airlifted many of the troops into the battle zone from Australia in C-47 cargo planes, and even borrowed some civilian DC-3 airliners, in one of the first ever large-scale movements of troops by air.

† Some disorganized bands of Japanese survivors from Buna fled north through the jungle toward other Japanese garrisons farther up the coast. Most never made it, succumbing to disease, starvation and the Allied troops pursuing them.

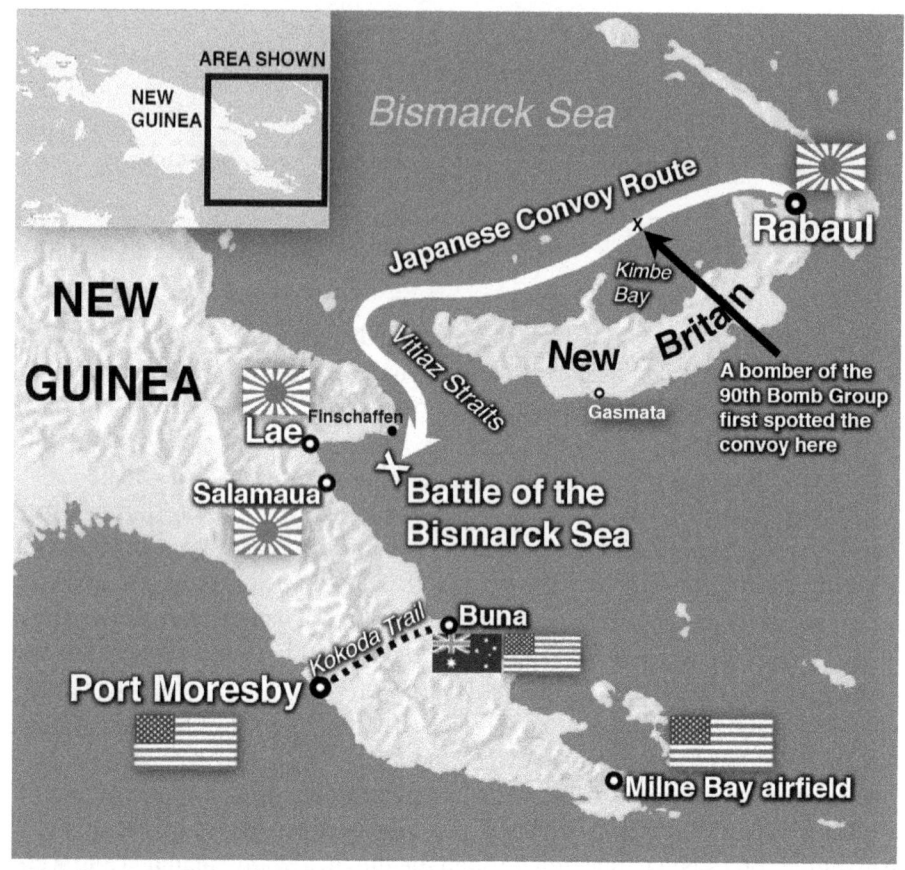

Map 25-1. The Battle of the Bismarck Sea, March 2-4, 1943, was fought between a Japanese convoy from Rabaul and American airpower, and was a decisive defeat for the Japanese.

to send a large convoy, carrying both troops and supplies, escorted by warships (destroyers) from Rabaul to Lae, a distance of about 500 miles by ship.*

American codebreakers in Hawaii had been able to read encrypted Japanese radio messages well enough to be aware that the Japanese were planning a large-scale reinforcement of New Guinea from Rabaul sometime in late February or early March, but they didn't know exactly when. General Kenney therefore kept reconnaissance planes, often the B-24s of the 90th Bomb Group, out continually watching the sea lanes on the north and south sides of New Britain. This was the situation at the end of February, 1943.

In the early morning hours of February 28, by order of Admiral Isoroku Yamamoto, the architect of the Pearl Harbor attack, a convoy of eight transport ships jam-packed with anywhere from six to nine thousand troops (depending

---

*The Japanese never had any kind of air transport system for troops as the Americans did, so all their troop movements had to be made by sea.

25. THE BATTLE OF THE BISMARCK SEA

on the source), along with many tons of weapons and supplies, including one ship loaded with 1,650 drums of fuel for Japanese aircraft and ground vehicles, set out from Simpson Harbor at Rabaul, headed for Lae.*

It was a sixteen-vessel convoy: eight transport ships escorted by eight destroyers. Since there was bad weather on the north side of New Britain at this time, the convoy was directed to run along the northern coast of the island toward Lae so that the rain squalls would, it was hoped, cloak the convoy from the prying eyes of American reconnaissance planes. The convoy would then swing south through the Vitiaz Straits to Lae (see Map 25-1 again, opposite). The convoy sailed undetected all day on the 28th.

On the morning of March 1, 1943, the 90th Bomb Group had a reconnaissance plane out in the area, a B-24D named "Miss Deed," piloted by Lt. Walter Higgins of 321st Squadron, the same pilot who had ditched the bomber "Cowtown's Revenge" on January 6th after an attack on another convoy. Higgins' assignment on this day was to fly from Port Moresby up the north coast of New Guinea past Salamaua and Lae, then cross the Vitiaz Straits to the south coast of New Britain and fly up that coastline toward Rabaul. Before he got to Rabaul, however, he was to turn left (north) and cross the island to its northern coast, then run down that coast on his way back to Port Moresby, all the while scanning the shipping lanes for any sign of Japanese sea traffic.

This was the type of long, lone reconnaissance missions from which so many 90th bomber crews mysteriously failed to return. Higgins and his crew may not have returned either, had he boldly tried to penetrate a 40,000-foot-tall tropical thunderstorm that reared up in front of him as he was running up the south coast of New Britain towards Rabaul, but the young pilots of the 90th were beginning to wise up by this time and backed away from such meteorological monsters whenever they could. Lt. Higgins decided to adopt the attitude of veteran pilots everywhere who said, wisely, that "there are old pilots, and there are bold pilots, but there are no old, bold pilots."

Higgins wisely chose a non-bold strategy of reversing course in the face of the storm and backtracking down New Britain's south coastline, looking for some other place to cross the island to its north coast, someplace free of clouds. Near the town of Gasmata, he saw the gap in the clouds he was looking for and swung north. This brought him out over Kimbe Bay in the Bismarck Sea on the island's north coastline. It also, by pure chance, took him right over the top of the big Japanese convoy that was headed for Lae.

The first crewman to spot the convoy was the navigator, Lt. George W. Sellmer, who had climbed up on the flight deck to stand between the pilot and copilot and make small talk. It was about 4:30 in the afternoon, and glancing out and down through the cockpit windshield, Sellmer suddenly shouted, "My

---
*Yamamoto gave this maneuver the inspiring name of "Operation 81."

God, look at all the ships!" The rest of the crewmen, hearing this over the intercom, were instantly up and scanning the sea below from anyplace in the bomber from which they could see downward. The waist gunners opened up their windows, and through the roaring rush of wind gazed downward at the amazing sight of so many ships.

The bombardier, Lt. Robert Paviour, up in the bomber's glass "greenhouse" nose, had a panoramic view of the scene below him and counted fourteen ships, missing two that were probably hidden under the scattered rain squalls. The radioman sent this number, along with the convoy's location, off to Port Moresby, instantly triggering much excitement there and at General Kenney's headquarters in Brisbane—this had to be the convoy that they had been anticipating.[1]

Thus was the stage set for the Battle of the Bismarck Sea. It would be a disastrous defeat for the Japanese, and as a result would be the last time they ever tried to reinforce their New Guinea forces by means of ship convoys. Like all of MacArthur's battles in the Pacific, it was a small-scale affair compared to battles in Europe, with around 175 Allied aircraft pitted against fewer than two dozen Japanese ships, but it was of paramount importance in this theater.

Confusion over the facts of the battle persist even after all these years, but various sources state that anywhere between 136 and 178 Allied aircraft took part in the fight, and the number of Japanese ships in the convoy vary in the records from fourteen to twenty-two, partly due to the fact that the number changed as ships joined or left the convoy during the battle. There was no ship in this convoy larger than a destroyer (in other words, no cruisers or battleships).

No ships of the American navy were involved in this battle, since they were nowhere near the area. Admiral Nimitz had his own war going down in the Solomon Islands around Guadalcanal, 850 miles to the southeast. The Bismarck Sea battle was fought between Allied land-based aircraft and Japanese shipping only,[*] except for a few small American PT boats that ventured into the area toward the end of the battle to finish off a damaged Japanese ship with torpedoes.

Radiomen in the Japanese convoy had heard "Miss Deed's" radio transmission to Port Moresby, and the convoy's commander, Admiral Masatomi Kimura, knew he'd been spotted. He could only hope that some especially foul

---

[*] This battle vindicated Maj. Gen. William "Billy" Mitchell, a controversial aviation visionary of the 1920s who declared that America should build air fleets instead of more battleships, and who predicted that land-based aircraft could defeat naval forces. His highly publicized assertion that air power would come to dominate sea power rankled the military brass, especially of course the Navy, who ridiculed his ideas and eventually drove him from the service. Today Mitchell is regarded by many as the father of the United States Air Force, and during World War II the B-25 Mitchell bomber was named for him.

weather that the convoy was entering at this time would conceal it from further view in rain and fog. Port Moresby radioed instructions back to Higgins to stick with the convoy until a replacement plane could come out and take over shadowing the ships. From this point on, the 90th's bombers would conduct tag-team reconnaissance, always keeping a bomber near the convoy.

Higgins had a load of bombs aboard his plane, but this time he thought better of trying to attack a convoy all by himself, especially one this size. Aside from all the antiaircraft guns on the warships, there was bound to be a protective umbrella of Zeros above the convoy somewhere nearby. His lone attack on a convoy in the bomber "Cowtown's Revenge" a month earlier was no doubt still fresh in his mind. That attempt, thwarted by covering Zeros, had cost him the bomber and two of his crew dead. This time, Higgins decided to just stay high above the ships and out of sight in clouds as much as possible.

On this day, with its speed set by the slowest ship, the Japanese convoy was moving at an agonizingly slow pace of only 7 knots (about 8 mph). Higgins circled slowly above the convoy, ducking in and out of clouds for concealment, until his dwindling fuel necessitated "Miss Deed's" return to Port Moresby. He turned for home and jettisoned his bombs into the sea. As he started back across the Owen Stanley Mountains he saw his replacement, another 90th bomber piloted by Lt. George W. Shaffer, heading in the opposite direction to take his place.

When the Higgins crew got back to Moresby, the men underwent a debriefing by the 90th Bomb Group's Intelligence Section that was more intense than any they'd ever experienced. The intelligence men wanted to know every little detail of what they'd seen, and even a Navy officer and a group of news reporters got in on the interrogation. This convoy was a serious concern, since if it succeeded in resupplying and reinforcing the Japanese in the Lae area, the American and Australian troops battling their way north toward that region would have a real problem on their hands. Before long they might be confronted by an overwhelming number of fresh Japanese troops from Rabaul, and lose everything they had gained since the Battle of Buna. Thus, whether or not this convoy reached Lae could make a crucial difference in the course of the war in the Southwest Pacific.

Lt. Shaffer, following the directions given to him by the departing Lt. Higgins, found the Japanese ships just before dark, around 8:30 PM, and seeing no enemy fighter planes around, dropped his bombs on them in the twilight and rain without being able to tell whether he hit anything. He then remained over the convoy throughout most of the night, until handing off in the early morning hours to another of the 90th's B-24s named "The Butcher Boy," flown by Lt. Archie B. Browning from the 320th Squadron.[2] During the night a Catalina flying boat of the RAAF also came out and followed the convoy by using an early form of radar to maintain contact with it.

By sunrise on March 2, 1943, the convoy was fifty miles north of the southern tip of New Britain (Cape Gloucester), headed south toward the Vitiaz Straits with Lt. Browning and his crew in "Butcher Boy" still orbiting above it, popping in and out of clouds to stay hidden from Japanese fighters, and keeping Port Moresby updated on its position by radio.

General Whitehead first sent out seven B-17s of the 43rd Bomb Group to bomb the convoy, and Browning guided them in by radio before heading back to Moresby. Just before 10 AM the Fortresses dropped their bombs on the ships from 6,500 feet, in heavy rain, undeterred by flak thrown up by the warships and attacks by covering Zeros.

The artwork on the nose of Lt. Browning's bomber, "The Butcher Boy," turned out to be perfect for the occasion, considering the reception that General Kenney's Fifth Air Force was preparing for the Japanese convoy.

Only one of the ships, a large transport, was struck by any of the bombs, but the hits to it were fatal. The vessel emitted a great puff of smoke and boiling spray, was wracked by internal explosions, caught fire, and sank before noon. Many Japanese troops must have gone down with it, but two of the destroyers picked up several hundred survivors in the water and took them straight to Lae at high speed, where they put the men ashore and then turned around and rejoined the convoy.

Not much more happened for the rest of that day, and during the night of 2-3 March the convoy was harassed, but not hurt, by some Australian Beaufort torpedo bombers from the Milne Bay airbase that dropped flares to illuminate the ships and then launched torpedoes at them. All missed. The Australian Catalina returned in the dark and dropped some bombs that also missed the ships. The weather continued to be atrocious and made air attack difficult.

During that night the convoy drew close enough to Lae to have made it into the harbor under cover of darkness and begun unloading, and perhaps even gotten most, if not all, of the troops and cargo ashore before daylight and the inevitable Allied air attacks. However, Admiral Kimura made a fatal error. He evidently thought that the rain squalls would shield his convoy from further Allied attacks, and probably figured that even if he was attacked at daylight, he was so close to the Lae airfields now that his convoy would surely be protected by their Zeros. He therefore decided not to put into Lae's harbor during the night, but instead kept the convoy out to sea, the ships circling slowly and waiting for the dawn. Kimura intended to enter the harbor after sunrise so that the ships' captains could see what they were doing, and avoid confusion. As a result, the next morning, the 3rd of March, the rising sun found the ships of the Rising Sun at sea about seven miles south of Finschaffen and still nearly sixty miles from Lae's harbor (see again Map 25-1 on page 220).

General Kenney was determined not to let this convoy of troops and supplies reach Lae. He had struck at previous convoys piecemeal, and usually done them some damage, but had never been able to entirely stop one. This time it would be different, for this time Kenney had a couple of aces up his sleeve. He had already discovered that skip-bombing at very low altitudes by fast twin-engine medium and light bombers was the most effective way to sink ships, but there had been a drawback to this method: when it was carried out in daylight, it also gave the ship's antiaircraft gunners good close targets as the skip-bombers approached them.

To solve that problem, Kenney and his wizard aircraft modifier, Paul I. "Pappy" Gunn, had altered a dozen standard B-25 bombers into potent strafer/bombers by putting several heavy machine-guns on their noses in place of the original "greenhouses." These multiple guns were intended to silence a ship's antiaircraft guns as the plane approached it by sweeping its decks with a hurricane of .50-cal. bullets. Kenney wrote:

> I sent word to Major Pappy Gunn at Brisbane to pull the bombardier and everything else out of the nose of a B-25 medium bomber and fill it full of .50-caliber guns, with 500 rounds of ammunition per gun. I told him I wanted him then to strap some more on the sides of the fuselage to give all the forward firepower possible. I suggested four guns in the nose, two on each side of the fuselage, and three underneath. If, when he had made the installation, the airplane still flew and the guns would shoot, I figured I'd have a skip-bomber that could overwhelm the deck defenses of a Jap vessel as the plane came in for the kill with its bombs. With a commerce destroyer as effective as I believed this would be, I'd be able to maintain an air blockade on the Japs anywhere within the radius of action of the airplane.[3]

A stock B-25 as it came from the factory had a nose covered with glass panes similar to that of a B-24D, and just as Col. Rogers had removed a B-24's "greenhouse" and substituted a gun turret, Gunn did the same to twelve B-25s at Brisbane and stuffed their noses full of .50-cal. machine-guns, as Kenney had requested (photos on next page). There had been some initial problems with this: the vibration and recoil of all the guns firing together had sometimes

Top and bottom: General Kenney and his mechanical wizard Paul I. "Pappy" Gunn modified stock B-25 medium bombers like the one seen in the top photo into strafer/bombers, or what Kenney called "commerce destroyers," by eliminating the factory "greenhouse" nose and replacing it with the banks of machine-guns seen in the lower photo. On some planes Gunn also added machine-guns packs on the sides of the nose below the cockpit, called "cheek guns" (these can be seen on the B-25 in the photo on p. 310). Most strafers got six to eight forward-firing .50-caliber machine-guns. These custom-made strafer/bombers played a decisive role in the complete destruction of a Japanese convoy in the Battle of the Bismarck Sea. Note in the lower photo the native children helping the plane's mechanic rotate the propeller.

25. THE BATTLE OF THE BISMARCK SEA

The twin-engine Lockheed P-38 fighter plane was the first American fighter capable of seriously challenging the Japanese Zero in performance. Thirty-eight of these planes took part in the Battle of the Bismarck Sea, flying cover for the bombers.

popped rivets and seams on the B-25s, so "Pappy" had beefed up the aircrafts' structures and added some felt cushioning between the overlapping aluminum panels to absorb shock. For the smaller A-20 light bombers, Gunn mounted four machine-guns in the nose.

There had been some concern over whether all these heavy guns and their belts of ammunition added to their noses would render the aircraft difficult to control, by moving the fore-and-aft balance point (known as the center of gravity, or CG for short) too far forward. When someone asked "Pappy" about the CG, he replied, "Oh, I threw that out to save weight." In the end, the nose-heaviness was compensated for by adding some lead ballast in the tail to restore proper balance.

And then the strafer/bomber pilots had gone out and practiced skip-bombing against the Moresby Wreck until they could bounce a bomb into it nearly every time. Now Kenney had a dozen each of these lethal B-25s and A-20s ready to go, and the pilots were champing at the bit to sink ships.

The other ace up Kenney's sleeve was the long-range, twin-engine P-38 fighter plane (photo above), the first American fighter that could seriously challenge the Japanese Zero, which had finally begun to arrive in the Southwest Pacific in sufficient numbers to make a difference. Thirty-eight of them would be thrown into this battle, along with 16 American fighters of other types (54 fighters total), their job being to keep the Zeros protecting the convoy too busy to interfere with the Allied bombers.

The Royal Australian Air Force (RAAF) would contribute some twin-engine Beaufighters, plus some Bostons (the British name for the American A-20) and Beauforts to attack the ships at low altitude along with the B-25s and A-20s.

Kenney had been waiting for the right moment to unleash this powerful force on a Japanese convoy, and with this large one now coming down from Rabaul, the time was at hand. All pilots were alerted and informed that this was the big show that they had been waiting and training for. During the night of March 2-3, while the reconnaissance aircraft followed the convoy, generator-powered spotlights burned all around the Allied airfields as bombers and fighters at Moresby and the Milne Bay airfields were being armed and fueled, the engines run up and tested by the mechanics, and everything readied for the big battle at daylight.

As morning dawned on March 3, 1943, General Kenney sent in everything in his aerial arsenal to destroy the Japanese convoy. Heavy, medium, and light bombers lifted off the runways followed by the fighter planes. Approximately 100 Zeros from both Rabaul, Lae, and other nearby Japanese airbases took up station over the convoy to protect it as it turned for the harbor. The stage was now set for the mayhem and carnage to follow.

There had been a plan of coordination between all the different kinds of aircraft in the Allied attacking force, so that they would come in from different altitudes (high, medium, low, and very low) and various directions on a precise time schedule, but like so many plans in wartime it all fell apart in the event and all the Allied aircraft ended up just swarming the Japanese convoy, with the four-engine bombers dropping their bombs on the ships from high altitude at the same time that the twin-engine medium bombers were skip-bombing them right on the deck. The attack was perhaps all the more effective for all the confusion, for the Japanese ships found themselves being hit from everywhere at once and found it difficult to take evasive action or defend themselves.

The battle was joined at daylight on the 3rd and lasted all that day and into the next. The convoy was attacked by B-17s from the 43rd Bomb Group, by B-25 and A-20 strafer/skip bombers from the 38th and 89th Bomb Squadrons (respectively), accompanied by some twin-engine Bristol Beauforts and Beaufighters of the RAAF, while the American fighters took on the Zeros, though outnumbered by them two-to-one. The 90th Bomb Group sent out some B-24s from the 321st Squadron, but as it turned out there were more B-17s than B-24s in this battle. Gen. Kenney was betting heavily on his modified B-25s and A-20s, and not so much on the four-engine bombers, which had always found it difficult to hit ships from high up.

The 90th and 43rd Groups' heavy bombers dropped their bombs from five thousand feet and above, not getting many hits on the convoy, again underscoring the difficulty of hitting ships maneuvering on the sea while bombing level from altitude, while the light and medium bombers raced in practically at wavetop height. It was the low-altitude attacks that sealed the convoy's fate. Within fifteen or twenty minutes of the start of the skip-bombing, most of the convoy's ships were shattered wrecks, while not a single one of the skip-bombers was seriously damaged.

In their skip-bomb attacks, each B-25 or A-20 descended to just a few feet above the sea and accelerated to 250-275 mph straight at the side of a ship, while the pilot triggered the multiple machine guns in the plane's nose to rake the ship's decks and suppress antiaircraft fire. Then the bombs were released at just the right instant to ricochet along the surface of the water until they struck the ship in the side while the plane pulled up and over it at masthead height. The bombs had fuses with a three to five-second delay so that the bombers were well out of the way before the bombs exploded. It was deadly, dangerous, dramatic work that required precise timing. And it worked extremely well.

When a B-25 pilot triggered the multiple machine guns in his bomber's nose, the entire front of the plane erupted in a volcano of fire, sending out a thick stream of thousands of rounds of heavy .50-cal. slugs. Earlier that morning, thinking that they were safe from air attack, the troop ships had brought their soldiers up on deck where their officers had been giving them instructions

Photo 1 of 3: A B-25 Mitchell bomber with a ferocious hobgoblin face painted on its nose pulls up after releasing its bomb in front of a Japanese destroyer.

Photo 2 of 3: The bomb skips across the water into the side of the ship.

Photo 3 of 3: Japanese sailors cling to the shattered hull and flounder in sea as their ship rolls over and goes down.

for disembarking. Now many of those troops were caught on deck in the murderous fire of the strafers. Capt. Garrett Middlebrook was a copilot on one of the B-25s, and he later wrote:

In a dramatic photo shot by the tail camera of another plane, an American A-20 Havoc light bomber that has just released its bomb (note the open bomb bay doors) passes just over the masts of a Japanese transport ship. An instant later the bomb skipped into the side of the ship and exploded.

> The A-20s went in first, and then the strafers of the 30th Bomb Group arrived. They went in and hit this troop ship. What I saw looked like little sticks, maybe a foot long or something like that, or splinters flying up off the deck of the ship; they'd fly all around . . . and twist crazily in the air and fall out in the water. I thought, "What could that be? They must have some peculiar cargo on that vessel." Then I realized what I was watching were human beings. . . I was watching hundreds of those Japanese just blown off the deck by those machine guns. They just splintered around in the air like sticks in a whirlwind and they'd fall in the water.[4]*

---

* Middlebrook also wrote that he was glad that he was the copilot that day and not the pilot, because it gave him a better chance to look around at what was happening during the battle. "Without having to concentrate on flying the ship," he wrote, "I had the opportunity to see a war drama of great magnitude unfold. I saw a historical event . . . which will live probably for centuries in history books around the world."[5] Yet it's probably safe to say that very few people today have ever heard of the Battle of the Bismarck Sea. (Pictures of Capt. Middlebrook are on pages 292-3.)

Another Japanese destroyer takes an American skip-bomb in its side.

Once the battle began, the Japanese convoy was under almost continual attack from the 5th Air Force for the rest of that day and part of the next, although some historians believe that the battle was won in the first fifteen minutes after the skip-bombers began their work. It took them less than an hour to turn the transport ships filled with troops into shattered hulks and spill their human cargo into the sea.

Capt. Paul C. Kendall, piloting a 90th Bomb Group B-24 of the 321st Squadron named "Star Duster," reported afterwards that he and his crew were awed by the number of Japanese soldiers and sailors in the water. They saw what appeared to be thousands of heads bobbing about amid the wreckage of the ships, many of the swimmers engulfed in heavy black oil slicks.

The ships fought back with their antiaircraft guns while Japanese fighter planes went after the bombers, and the P-38 fighter planes in turn engaged the Zeros. In the midst of this melee a B-17 named "Double Trouble," piloted by 1st Lt. Woodrow W. Moore, took fatal hits from bullets and cannon fire from

25. THE BATTLE OF THE BISMARCK SEA

A Japanese transport ship sitting dead in the water has been hit squarely amidships by a skip-bomb while other bombs dropped from above explode in the water nearby in the Battle of the Bismarck Sea. Note the ship's caved-in side where the bomb struck it, and the huge plume of flame and smoke billowing from its stern. At upper left a motor launch can be seen making its escape, probably carrying officers abandoning ship. This ship went to the bottom shortly after this picture was taken.

the defending Zeros, or flak from the ships, or both—as usual, eyewitness accounts differed.

What happened next to the crew of this bomber gave the Americans a much better idea of what kind of an enemy they were dealing with, and ended up making the defeat even worse for the Japanese. Sgt. Gordon Manuel, the bombardier of another B-17 that was flying in formation with Moore's, was an eyewitness to the incident and wrote afterward:

> A fortress from the 63rd Squadron [of the 43rd Bomb Group] was hit by flak. The flak just blew the tail off the ship and she started down. There was no saving her. It was dreadful to watch. Then six of her boys jumped. Their chutes opened and they started to float down. From nowhere, like vultures leaping on a wounded rabbit, the Zeros dove. They had been hiding up above in the clouds. They didn't aim at us or any of the other Forts but at the six men in chutes. They killed them, all right. I watched that, feeling cold and sick, and I said to myself, 'That's all, brother, that's all. Now I know. I know what we're fighting now... My hands were

A wildly maneuvering Japanese ship is finally caught in a cluster of American bomb bursts.

> clenched and I was digging my fingernails into my palms until my hands were white. The Japs murdered those Americans. They didn't kill them in combat. They just murdered them. They had no chance to fight back, hanging there in their chutes... It was like stepping on little birds.
>
> No one can ever give me any sweet talk about the enemy after that... From now on all I wanted was to kill the enemy.[6]

General Kenney heard the story slightly differently from other pilots after the battle, and wrote:

> Our formation was intercepted by thirty Jap fighters. One of our B-17s, piloted by Lt. Moore, was hit and set on fire as he was coming in on his bombing run. With one wing enveloped in flames, Moore flew steadily on to the bomb-release point, but just as the bombs came out of the bomb-bay, the B-17 lost its wing and plunged into the ocean. Seven of the nine-man crew bailed out, but about ten Jap fighters dove down and shot all seven as they were hanging in their parachutes. The P-38s were heavily engaged up above with the Jap fighters, trying to keep them off the bombers. Captain Ferrault and two wingmen, Lieutenant Easton and Lieutenant Schifflett, pulled out of combat and went down after

the Nips that were shooting up the B-17 crew. The three P-38s were shot down and we lost all three pilots, but they took five Japs along with them.[7]

The ugly brutality and merciless cruelty of the Japanese military toward its adversaries, civilian or military, in this war had been known to the bomber crews from hearsay, but now they were eyewitnesses to it, and it would be the end of any mercy they may have been willing to show their enemy from this time onward. The war now became very personal and bitter to the Americans of the 5th Air Force. Sgt. Manuel continued:

> In the beginning there were rules, and we played 'em. We were trained to play them and we didn't break them. They did. If you want to pin me down about the Japs, I'll tell you about the six men that they strafed in the Bismarck Sea Battle—six men who bailed out of a Fortress and were coming down in the silk. Well, the Nips in the Zeros broke off their attack on us, circled around our boys lazily, giving it to them as their chutes floated downward. I'm talking of things my gang and I saw. We all heard the stories of the Death March from Bataan long before you did; we heard what happened to the boys who bailed out over Japan in the Tokyo raid; we had actually seen what they had done to pilots and Marines they had captured. After that, you say, "That's all, brother."
>
> The motto of my outfit, which was the 64th Squadron of the 43rd Bomb Group, was "Our greatest joy in living is sending Japs to Hell." We weren't a bunch of killers. We even went to church every time the padre held services, and we didn't care much what church he belonged to. We were normal guys who said our prayers at night, even though we might not admit it out loud, and we believed in God. But that was our motto, and we thought we had a pretty good reason for it. Believe me, we didn't start out that way, but things happened.[8]

For the rest of the day, March 3, word of how the Japanese fighter pilots had cold-bloodedly killed American men dangling in their parachutes spread quickly around Port Moresby as the bombers returned to base and crewmen related what they'd seen. One historian wrote:

> As soon as the bomber crews returned to Port Moresby, word of the atrocity began to spread. On flight lines, in mess halls, in operation shacks and tent cities, the story of the men who were machine-gunned in their parachutes was told again and again. Men who had never heard of Double Trouble or met any of the crew were suddenly gripped by a seething hatred for the Japanese. Most were already familiar with the horror stories coming out of the jungles around Buna and Kokoda, where undeni-

able evidence of war crimes and even cannibalism by Japanese soldiers was being discovered.

Emotions boiled over. The airmen wanted retribution.[9]

Some of the American airmen in action that day were so enraged by what they'd seen that after they returned to base they couldn't wait to seek revenge, and as soon as they could get their aircraft re-armed and refueled they turned right around and took off again and headed back to the battle. When they returned to the scene in the early afternoon they found five Japanese transport ships listing and burning in the water, surrounded by thousands of Japanese soldiers and sailors floating in the ocean in their lifebelts, or clinging to debris, or in small boats.

Of the eight Japanese destroyers, only two remained on the scene. One of them was an abandoned hulk; the other one was picking up survivors in the water until it saw the American aircraft returning. Then it immediately turned north and tried to get away, with its decks packed with as many as 500 survivors it had plucked from the water. But there was no escape from the American planes—once again the hurricanes of .50-caliber machine gun slugs from the noses of the B-25 strafers shattered men and blew them off the destroyer's deck to tumble high in the air, and in a few minutes skip-bombing had transformed the fleeing destroyer into another burning, listing wreck.

That night the American fliers were still anxious to go back and add to the carnage. Sgt. Manuel wrote:

> We got back to the base and everybody knew what had happened to the six boys from the 63rd Squadron. We ate dinner and nobody said much. We were all burning. We couldn't wait until the next day when we might have another crack at those rats. It seems to me that when something big grips you, like fear or anger, it hits you in the stomach. I know I couldn't eat much that night. I looked around and none of the boys were eating much. My stomach was tied up in a knot, and it wasn't from anything but hatred. At last war had become a personal thing to all of us. I went to my bunk and tried to sleep, but I couldn't. I wanted to kill the enemy. I wanted to kill a thousand of them. I couldn't rest until I had. That's how I felt that night, and I'm not making any apology for it—I'm just telling you that's how I felt. I guess I fell asleep about five, and then at six they woke us and we were briefed again. This was a different kind of briefing. No one laughed or kidded . . . and even at six AM we were all tense and still mad. This convoy was steaming toward its objective, which was Lae. We had sunk five ships, but there were still seventeen left. We started out, and Olsen didn't do any kidding over the intercom. None of us was in any mood for kidding.

> We found the convoy again and this time the weather was good. We had a lot of B-25s with us and they went in low—very low. They were trying something which General Kenney had developed called skip bombing. It's been used in all theaters of war since then, but this was the first time I ever saw it tried. . .
>
> We had orders to stay on top, around eight thousand feet, and drop our stuff from there. We weren't kidding today. . . We were going to hit a Nip ship—or else.
>
> By the time we made our run it looked like the 25s and the 17s that had gone in ahead of us had cleaned up the whole convoy. Wherever you looked there were Jap ships leaning over in the water with smoke coming up from them. I kept looking for one that was intact. The skipper yelled into the intercom, "Pick your ship, Gordie!" I kept looking. I wanted a big fat one full of Japs—that's what I wanted. I spotted a destroyer that seemed to be going around in circles. Maybe it had been hit before. I didn't know and didn't care. That was my baby, I told the skipper. We were still flying in what we call elements of three. He leveled off, and the destroyer seemed to sense that we were after it, because it veered sharply to port. . .
>
> "That louse is trying to get away from us," I said in the intercom to Chic Olsen.
>
> "Don't lose him," the skipper said.
>
> I let him have it when two 25s [B-25 Mitchells] hit him too. They gave it to him very nicely. The skipper said, "Let's go down and look it over." We went down to the deck. It was nice to watch. The day before, this convoy had held ships with about fifteen thousand men. Now the sea, as far as you could look, was nothing but wreckage. We had hit every ship. I looked down and saw dark little dots in the water—thousands of Japs were floating around. I started to talk to them. I said, "You're the dirty rats who murdered six Americans yesterday." I said a lot of other things. My hand unconsciously reached for the gun we have in the bombardier's cabin of a Fort.
>
> Let's skip the next half hour.[10]

There were seven B-17 Flying Fortresses of the 43rd Bomb Group—Lt. Moore's group—in the air over the scene, all of them filled with furious American airmen out to avenge the deaths of the Moore crewmen. Crewmen who had been seething with anger all night in their cots vented their fury with their guns. After dropping their bombs on the drifting shipwrecks, the B-17s descended to just above the sea and slowly circled the scene while their gunners sprayed the Japanese in the water with their machine-guns.

The B-25 strafer/bombers also joined in with this strafing. Of the gunners on his bomber Garrett Middlebrook wrote:

> No one told them to fire and no one told them to withhold their fire. It was all a spontaneous beginning and ending. At the [preflight] briefing, Australian officers had told us we must not permit a single enemy to reach the shores of New Guinea. They explained the suffering, agony, and loss by our troops in having to hunt down and kill a suicidal Jap. No one ever gave an order nor issued a policy memorandum telling us that we should or should not strafe helpless Japs in the water. I had always believed that the generals purposely avoided the question. I believed they preferred to leave the responsibility to each airman, and at that point it was left. . . Only God knows if we were justified in what we did. We were lowly aircrews trying to end the war. Soldiers did not declare war; they just fought it.[11]

Thus did Allied pilots debate the necessity and morality of killing helpless enemies. It is safe to say that there were no such debates among the Japanese—they killed the helpless, civilian or military, man, woman, or child, as a matter of course. That is why most Americans who witnessed Japanese war crimes in World War II came to think of the enemy as vicious automatons; evil, loathsome creatures only worthy of extermination. The British General William Slim, fighting in Burma, characterized the Japanese soldier as "the most formidable fighting insect in history."[12] Like fighting ants, Japanese troops fought viciously, mindlessly, and remorselessly until they either prevailed or were killed. Mercy or compassion were unknown to them.

During the Battle of the Bismarck Sea, the ocean turned red in places with Japanese blood, attracting sharks that added to the horror of the scene. By the end of the action against the Japanese convoy, all eight of the transport ships and four of the eight destroyers had been sunk. This was an Allied naval victory won entirely by air power. How many Japanese troops may have survived the debacle varies according to the source. Perhaps 900 were later rescued by the remaining four destroyers and delivered to Lae minus their much-needed weapons and supplies. General Kenney wrote afterwards:

> The final result of the air combat was that we lost a B-17 and three P-38s, with a total of twelve men, and a gunner was killed on one of Ed Larner's B-25s which was so badly shot up that it collapsed on landing at the home airdrome, luckily with no one else hurt. Of the thirty Jap fighters that had intercepted, twenty-two were definitely destroyed, two probably destroyed, and four damaged.[13]

Another source's final tally from the Battle of the Bismarck Sea was all eight Japanese transports and four destroyers sunk, fifteen to twenty Japanese aircraft shot down, and close to 3,000 soldiers and sailors killed, in exchange for one Allied bomber and three American fighters shot down. Put another way, in the Battle of the Bismarck Sea the Americans lost a dozen or so men and a few aircraft while the Japanese lost thousands of men and many ships and aircraft. Such lopsided victories in favor of the Allies would become typical of Pacific battles to the end of the war.

Gen. MacArthur called the Battle of the Bismarck Sea "the decisive aerial engagement in the Southwest Pacific Area."[14] Never again would the Japanese dare to send troops and supplies to New Guinea by convoy.

Masatake Okumiya, an air staff officer at Rabaul, recorded how Admiral Yamamoto received the news of the outcome of his "Operation 81:"

> The effectiveness of enemy air strength was brought to [Admiral Yamamoto] with the news of a crushing defeat which, if similar events were permitted to occur in the future, promised terrifying disasters for Japan... Our losses for this single battle were fantastic... We knew that we could no longer run cargo ships or even fast destroyer transports to any front on the north coast of New Guinea, east of Wewak. Our supply operation to northeastern New Guinea became a scrabbler's run of barges, small craft, and submarines.[15]

From that time on, troops and supplies would be moved only at night, on barges or small boats sneaking furtively along the New Britain coastlines, with quick nighttime dashes across the open water of the Vitiaz Straits to New Guinea. During the daytime the barges were laid up and hidden under camouflage along the shores. Hunting camouflaged Japanese barges along the coastlines would become a common task for aircraft of the 5th Air Force throughout the rest of the war in the Southwest Pacific. After the war, Japanese officials at Rabaul estimated that 20,000 troops had been lost at sea in transit from Rabaul to the New Guinea area in all types of vessels.[16]

From the Battle of the Bismarck Sea onward, the Japanese were on the defensive, and MacArthur and his air chief Kenney continued to deliver blow after telling blow to their air power as the Americans began advancing up the north coast of New Guinea towards the Philippines. Seven months later Lae would fall to the Allies. The 90th Bomb Group flew mission after punishing mission against the Japanese airfields at Rabaul, Lae, and Wewak, while the B-25 and A-20 strafer/bombers went in at low level to clean up what was left on the ground. Along with the Marines advancing up the central Pacific island by island, fighting one bloody battle after another against the "fighting insects" of Japan, the Japanese were now beginning to reap what they had so foolishly sown at Pearl Harbor.

Chapter Twenty-Six

ROGERS' FLIGHT TO PROVE THE B-24 NOSE TURRET

There were thousands of B-24s being flown in combat all over the world at this time, but there was only one that had a gun turret on the nose: the one flown by Col. Art Rogers of the 90th Bomb Group of the 5th Air Force in the Southwest Pacific. After the 90th Bomb Group had set up its camp at Port Moresby in February of 1943, Col. Rogers was determined to prove the value of his B-24's new nose turret in combat, to bolster his argument that every B-24 should have a nose turret, right out of the factory. He wanted to provide a compelling demonstration of the value of the turret that would convince the factories back in the States to go through the time-consuming and expensive process of redesigning the front end of the aircraft, revamping their assembly lines, and start putting nose turrets on production bombers.

His first idea, which he and Col. Koon presented to Gen. Howard Ramey, the Commanding Officer of 5th Bomber Command at the time, was to lead a six-plane daylight mission to bomb Rabaul. Missions to Rabaul usually got a hot reception from the many Japanese fighter planes based there, and these would provide plenty of targets for the nose turret. However, Ramey pointed out that by going to Rabaul in daylight with only six planes Rogers might be biting off more than he could chew, since at the time there were an estimated 300 Japanese fighter planes on the five airfields there—far too many for only six American bombers to handle, and only one of the six would have a nose turret.

On reflection, Rogers agreed, and then suggested that he go to the next strongest Japanese base: Wewak, on the north coast of New Guinea, where only 50 Zeros were thought to reside at the time. Ramey approved that plan, and Rogers and Koon scheduled the mission to take place two days later. The next day, however, General Ramey took off on his ill-fated reconnaissance flight to the west of Port Moresby in a B-17 and was never seen again, his plane and crew vanishing without a trace.

Brigadier General Ennis Whitehead then took command of 5th Air Force operations at Port Moresby, and he disapproved of Rogers' plan. Frustrated, Rogers then asked Whitehead if he might take just his own B-24, with a picked volunteer crew, to Wewak to test the nose turret in combat. Whitehead replied that if Rogers was fool enough to go to Wewak alone, looking for trou-

26. ROGERS' FLIGHT TO PROVE THE B-24 NOSE TURRET 241

The four officers of "Connell's Special's" crew planning their flight. Left to right: "Big Ben" Bennett Browder, copilot; Philip Conti, navigator; Art Rogers, pilot; George "Ace" Dunmore, bombardier.

ble with enemy fighter planes, it was up to him, but he would probably just end up killing himself and his crew. So the mission was on again, but this time only for "Connell's Special." Col. Koon decided to go along as an observer, so that he could deliver his own opinion on the value of the nose turret after seeing it in action.

Rogers assembled a volunteer crew from men of the 90th Bomb Group whom he considered to be the best at their particular crew positions. He wrote in his memoirs:

> My co-pilot, Lt. Ben Browder, was a huge Texan with arms as big as an average man's legs. He had an unquestioning faith in our nose turret and gunners. My navigator, Lt. Phil Conti, was a curly-headed Italian from Vermont who was known in his college days as a superman in the football line. He not only had muscles but a brilliant mind.
>
> Lt. George "Ace" Dunmore, from California, was I believe the coolest, calmest, and best bombardier in the entire Air Force, and he never showed the least sign of excitement or fear in any of our thirty-eight missions together.

Art Rogers with his copilot "Big Ben" Browder in front of their bomber "Connell's Special."

>Sgt. Seper, my aerial engineer, who had had his front teeth knocked out by a piece of flak, was a happy-go-lucky boy who could handle his guns and knew his airplane. In addition to being the aerial engineer, who was responsible for the mechanical operations of the aircraft while in flight, he had the duty of operating the top turret.

For gunners, Rogers chose men who had impressed him with their shooting skills clear back in the days of shooting clay pigeons at Barksdale Field, Louisiana, ten months before.

>My tail gunner was Sgt. Stephens, a small, nervous, but not excitable gunner who could break twenty-four out of twenty-five clay pigeons thrown from any angle and was also a good combat gunner with three airplanes to his credit.
>One of my waist gunners, Sgt. Riley, had been a staff car driver in the city of Brisbane before he convinced me he came over to fight Japs and not to drive colonels around. When I asked him

where he came from he replied, "Out of a coon hollow in Tennessee." He told me he had hunted and shot guns all his life and had volunteered . . . to come over and fight Japs.

My other waist gunner, Sgt. Hodges, was a boy from my home state, Greensboro, North Carolina. He was a quiet chap, but with a great deal of courage, and he was an excellent shot.

My radio operator, Sgt. Robertson, of Texas, had been in the Philippines and was run out of Java and Darwin, and had had an opportunity to go home, but still hadn't had enough. He was one of the best radio operators in the entire group. Not only could he operate his radio, but in a pinch he was an excellent gunner. Oftentimes he manned our bottom two .50-caliber guns which we had installed on a ring in the bottom of our airplane to handle any fighter planes that might break through the fire of our tail or nose turrets. This installation was made at the same time as the nose turret.

For his nose gunner, the most important position as far as this flight was concerned, the man who would be tasked with demonstrating the value of a nose turret on a B-24, Rogers chose someone whose description could have fit a Mafia hit-man:

> The man who held the key position in this flight was a cool, calm, cold blooded killer, my nose turret operator, Sgt. Harold Pierce, from the state of Washington. He was one of my original gunners that I had trained from basic at Barksdale Field. . . At the time of this flight he had already shot down five Zeros. He was a man of very few words, and his only apparent outlet of emotion was the flipping of a large coin, usually a fifty-cent piece. At times I felt as if this man must have ice water running through his veins instead of blood. . . I was not worried for fear he would get excited even if we were attacked by the entire Japanese air force. . .
>
> Every gunner and crew member knew what was expected of him and what we were going up against, but since the crew had been hand picked by me from all four squadrons for their ability and courage, I had the utmost confidence that with any break at all we could handle up to twenty fighters and return home.

Rogers didn't care how his crewmen dressed for missions, with the result that they wore clothing as diverse as their personalities:

> Looking at the average [bomber crewman] you would think he was an old-time buccaneer pirate, as every man carries a pistol. Some use a shoulder holster and others a hip holster.

> Many of the crew members removed the standard hand grips on their pistols and replaced them with plexiglass ones so that their sweetheart or pin-up girl's picture could be inserted underneath. Some carried long jungle knives on their hips and others short hunting knives. . . Many wore leather jackets, others gabardine and even a few fur jackets might be seen, others wore gabardine flying suits. Many different types of caps were worn.

On the 27th of March, 1943, Rogers took off with his motley crew of air pirates from Port Moresby's Jackson Field in the darkness before dawn, with the B-24's bomb bay loaded with twelve 500-pound bombs. He may have been mainly looking for a gunfight, but he was determined to do some damage with his bombs as well. The heavily-loaded bomber flew sluggishly after takeoff and climbed slowly, so Rogers flew northwest, parallel to the Owen Stanley Mountains, until he had gained enough altitude to climb over them, just as Lt. McMurria had done on his ill-fated flight of 20 January. Rogers was flying the same route to Wewak that McMurria had flown, but whereas McMurria had hoped to find no Japanese fighters at Wewak, Rogers was hoping for exactly the opposite.

Navigator Phil Conti set Rogers a course that would bring them out inland of Wewak on the north coast of the island (see Map 26-1 on page 249). The Japanese airbase was on the shoreline (as were most, since that's where the ground was flattest) with its runways practically at the water's edge, and it had a small harbor formed by an indentation in the coast.

Wewak was nearly always well defended by Japanese fighter planes, and Rogers expected them to make their usual frontal attacks against his B-24. This time, however, they would be flying right into his new nose turret and its deadeye gunner, Hal Pierce. During the three hours it took to reach Wewak, the crew relaxed, smoked cigarettes, and made small talk as the bomber droned its way north over the mountains. The waist gunners kept their windows shut against the high-altitude cold. There was nothing to see outside in the dark anyway.

"Ace" Dunmore, the bombardier, came up on the flight deck and stood with Col. Koon between the two pilots, and they discussed the coming attack. The most recent aerial reconnaissance photos of Wewak had shown a couple of Japanese cargo ships in the harbor. If no fighter planes happened to be in the air to challenge them when they arrived there, Rogers intended to bomb the ships, which he figured would bring fighters swarming up off the airfield to defend them.

When he estimated they were about half an hour from the target, Dunmore left the flight deck and crawled back down the passage in the nose to his "office," where he took up his station behind his bombsight. On bombing runs

Dunmore would be in control of the airplane, flying it through his bombsight,* and he intended for his bombs to hit whatever target Rogers might choose. He was hoping that the reported ships were still in the harbor. If they were, he told Conti, he'd bet him a box of cigars that he'd sink one. Conti, knowing how difficult it was to hit such a small target, accepted the bet, and word of the wager spread throughout the crew.

Wewak came into view just as the sun was breaking the surface of the ocean in a magnificent tropical sunrise, spreading liquid gold across the Bismarck Sea ahead and to their right, and for a time sun and water appeared to be merged. It was a beautiful sight, but the crew of the bomber were too intent on their target and too keyed up to fully appreciate the beauty of the scene. The waist gunners raised the hinged hatches that covered their windows and latched them to the ceiling, then pushed out the air deflectors in front of their windows and swung out their guns, ready for business. They began scanning the sky for enemy fighter planes.

Down on the ground at Wewak the Japanese were now beginning to hear the unmistakable, spine-chilling rumble of an approaching B-24, the synchronized growl of its four big engines growing louder by the second. Some of them would be dashing for shelter, while others ran to man antiaircraft guns that were housed in circular gun pits ranged around the airfield and harbor. They could not know it, but one very dangerous B-24 was approaching them in the dawn light and it was spoiling for a fight.

Rogers looked ahead and saw two ships moored in Wewak's harbor. Ace Dunmore saw them too, and called up over the intercom to say that he would like to take the ship on the left as his first target. The gunners reported no fighter planes in sight, so far, and of the few Zeros that were parked on the airfield below, none were moving yet, so it appeared that "Connell's Special" was free to make a bomb run unmolested.

Rogers had been descending ever since they'd crossed the mountains, but was not yet down to the altitude that Dunmore had requested for his bombing run, so he banked to the left, which put the harbor on their right, and continued to bleed off altitude while flying up the coast as though his intention was to bomb Wewak's airfield on the shoreline. The Japanese antiaircraft gunners began firing, but their shells were exploding above the bomber.

When his plane was just opposite the harbor, Rogers made a 90-degree turn to the right to line up on the leftmost ship anchored there, leveled off at the prearranged altitude of 5,100 feet, and announced over the intercom, "All yours, Ace." Dunmore now took control of the bomber's flight path and Rogers opened the bomb bay doors. Col. Koon, who as an observer had no crew

---

*The bombsight was connected to the flight controls through the plane's autopilot.

duties, went to the rear of the flight deck and lay down on his stomach where he could see down through the open bomb bay.

The Japanese gunners below were frantically trying to follow the maneuvers of the bomber, and their next salvo of flak burst above and to the right of it. Lt. Ben Browder, "Big Ben," the copilot, kept an eye on the flak bursts outside his window on the right side of the cockpit. Another salvo exploded, this time at the correct altitude, but still to the bomber's right. The gunners were making their corrections, and the next group of bursts might be right on target. But the bomb run had commenced, and no evasive action could be taken until after the bombs were gone. The seconds ticked by, and the pilots and the rest of the crew were feeling the suspense.

"I sure wish those damn bombs would fall before they get us," Browder remarked, and just then lights on the instrument panel flickered to indicate that the first six bombs had gone. Rogers instantly banked the plane hard left while lowering its nose and pushing the throttles forward to enter a shallow power dive, heading out to sea. The next salvo of flak burst behind them and just about where they would have been if the bomb run had lasted a few seconds longer.

Col. Koon stood up again and tapped Rogers on the shoulder. "I saw the bombs hit the ship," he said. "Looks like Ace collects his bet." Dunmore's voice came over the intercom, "Colonel, we've got one ship to our credit, now let's get the other one before the fighters bother us."

But strangely, there were still no fighter planes in the air. The sky remained mysteriously empty except for themselves, and the few fighter planes on the airfield remained stationary. Rogers then swung the plane around to set up a bomb run on the second ship, making a climbing 180-degree turn back toward the harbor and leveling off at 7,500 feet. This time there would be no doubt among the Japanese below what the target would be, and there was no way to fool them again as to their intentions.

6,100 feet had been agreed upon for this bomb run, and Rogers entered a shallow dive down to that altitude and leveled off there. Once again Dunmore took control of the bomber, and Rogers and the rest of the crew could feel him making slight adjustments to their flight path as he lined up and zeroed in on the second ship.

Flak began bursting all around them now, and close, the explosions roiling the air and causing the bomber to bounce around. Just as Dunmore let the bombs go, all six of them at once in a salvo, the plane lurched so violently from a close flak explosion that Rogers nearly lost control for a moment. He knew that a flak burst that close may have riddled the plane with shrapnel and done some damage somewhere, or wounded someone. As he was banking the plane over into another sharp diving turn to get out of the flak cloud, Rogers got on the intercom: "Anybody hurt?" A chorus of "No, sirs" assured him that all was well, at least with the crew.

The plane, however, had not been so lucky. Sgt. Seper, the flight engineer, came over the intercom to report that a piece of shrapnel had holed the main hydraulic reservoir, and most of the fluid had already leaked out. The wing flaps, landing gear, and brakes were all hydraulically operated, and they wouldn't work without enough fluid in the lines. The flaps and landing gear could be operated by hand cranks in an emergency, but not the brakes. A lack of brakes could make the landing back at Port Moresby a problem, but there was no time to worry about that now, with everyone still expecting a gaggle of Japanese Zeros to pounce on them.

Yet there was still no sign of enemy planes. Since the whole point of this mission was to prove the effectiveness of the nose turret against fighter plane attacks, Rogers was getting frustrated. He turned northwest away from the harbor, directly toward the Wewak airbase, trying to provoke a response, but still no Zeros appeared. After they passed over the nearest of the Wewak airfields, named But, he made a right turn back out over the ocean, mystified and somewhat at a loss for what to do next.

Lt. McMurria and other 90th bomber crews had flown to Wewak on reconnaissance or bombing missions hoping to encounter no fighter planes, and had been swarmed by them. McMurria had been shot down amid a cloud of Zeros, and Regan, who had gone looking for him, vanished without a trace but probably met the same fate. Rogers had flown to Wewak for the express purpose of dueling with Zeros, doing everything he could to provoke a fight, and couldn't find a single one. Murphy's Law was working quite well on this day.

Col. Koon suggested that they turn back to the harbor, staying out of flak range this time, just to see what sort of effect their twelve 500-pound bombs had had against the two ships. As they were making the turn in that direction, Pierce, the nose turret gunner, called up to the cockpit to say that he could see another cargo ship about five miles offshore, heading in toward the harbor.

Here was a fine new target approaching, Rogers reflected, an ideal one for skip-bombing, and all their bombs were gone. He continued back toward the harbor where they saw the second ship they'd hit just disappearing below the surface of the sea, while the first one was ablaze and going down by the stern. This was a satisfying situation, but Rogers was still unhappy that the new nose turret's guns had not even been fired yet.

Rogers then suggested to Koon that even if they couldn't bomb the ship that was approaching the harbor, they could still get a little action out of the nose turret if they made a low pass at it and let Pierce and the other gunners work it over. Koon agreed, and Rogers banked the bomber toward the ship, at the same time starting a shallow dive toward the sea. He called Pierce in the turret to tell him that they were going to fly directly at the side of the ship at mast height, and would then pass above it with about twenty feet to spare. Could Pierce clear the ship's deck as they approached, to suppress any anti-aircraft fire from it? The laconic Pierce replied with his usual, "Yes, sir."

As they bored in at the side of the ship at 150 mph, Rogers wondered what might be going through the minds of the Japanese onboard as the huge B-24 came thundering down on them, completely unopposed by any of the fighter planes from Wewak that were supposed to be protecting them. At a thousand yards, Pierce opened up with his twin .50-caliber machine-guns and expertly raked the ship's deck from bow to stern and back again, the big tracer and incendiary slugs ripping up the deck and superstructure and throwing debris high in the air.

He continued his murderous fire until the bomber was too close to the ship for his guns to depress any further and he had to cease fire. As the plane passed over the ship the radio operator, Sgt. Robertson, sent a quick burst of fire straight down onto the deck from the two downward-pointing "tunnel guns" in the floor behind the bomb bay. Then the tail gunner, Sgt. Stephens, took over and saturated the ship with gunfire as they raced away from it, and he continued firing until they were out of range.

As Rogers banked the bomber around for another pass at the ship, he could see flames erupting all over its deck and swirling up toward the sky. He had to gain some altitude to avoid flying through the inferno on the second pass, and as they roared over the ship the second time the gunners gave it another lashing that sealed its fate. However, on this pass a few bullet holes appeared in the plane's bomb bay, indicating that despite the flames engulfing the ship some determined Japanese sailor down there was still manning a gun.

Rogers flew back toward Wewak's harbor, once again staying out of range of the harbor's and airfield's flak guns, and was gratified to see that now only the bow of the sinking ship remained above the water, and soon it would disappear too. They were three-for-three on the ships they'd attacked this day.

By this time they had been in the area for three-quarters of an hour and there were still no Japanese fighter planes in sight. Evidently there was not going to be any enemy air interception today. Disappointed, Rogers instructed Conti to set a course for home, and as he put the plane into a climb toward the Owen Stanley Mountains he began to think about the lack of hydraulic fluid that would probably result in a landing at Port Moresby without brakes. The thirty-ton bomber was liable to roll the entire length of the runway and off into the boondocks before coming to a stop, and it might break up in the process.

Rogers asked Sgt. Seper if there might not be some way to plug the hole in the hydraulic reservoir and then find some more fluid somewhere to fill it up again. Seper thought a tapered wooden plug hammered into the hole might

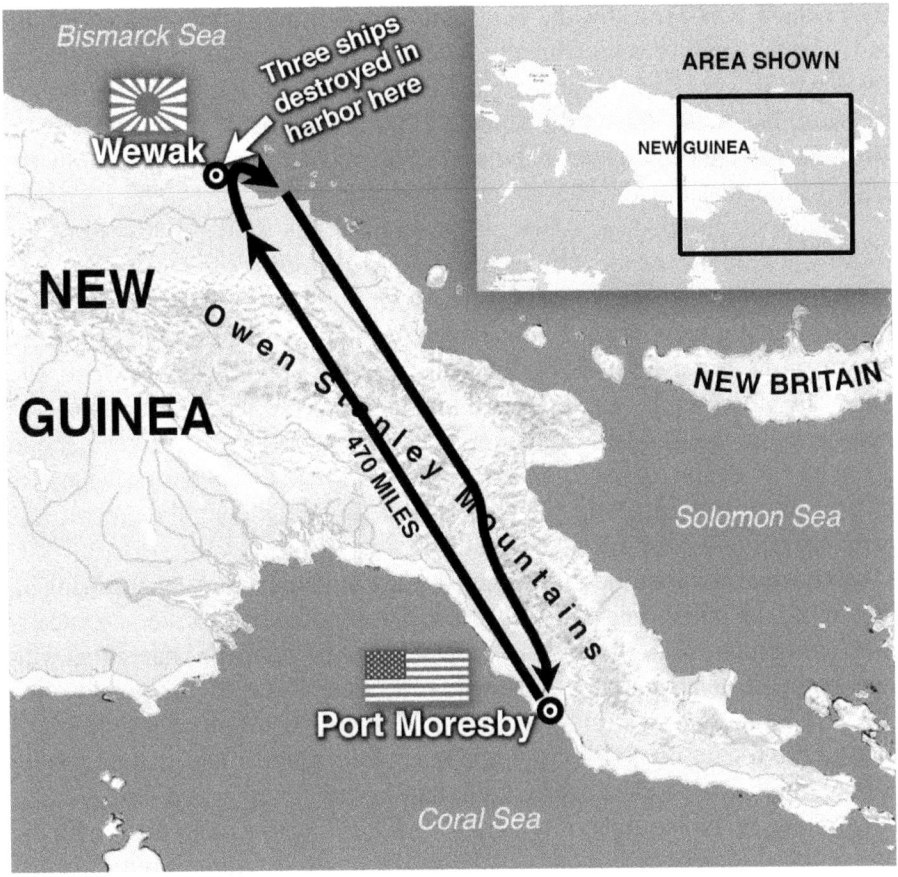

26. ROGERS' FLIGHT TO PROVE THE B-24 NOSE TURRET 249

Map 26-1. Col. Rogers' flight to Wewak and back to prove the new nose turret in combat, March 27, 1943.

do the trick of sealing it, if they could improvise one. About three gallons of hydraulic fluid had leaked out. A search of the plane failed to turn up any containers of spare fluid. Lt. Browder took over the controls while Rogers himself whittled out a wooden peg, and Seper tapped it into place. Rogers then remembered that the nose and tail turrets on the bomber were also hydraulically operated, and since their systems were not connected with the landing gear and flap systems, their reservoirs would still be full. Seper drained the fluid out of the turrets and added it to the main reservoir, but found that it only replaced about half what they'd lost; they were still about a gallon and a half short.

While all this was going on, Col. Koon instructed the radio operator, Sgt. Robertson, to send a message ahead to Port Moresby to let the base know that "Connell's Special" was inbound and might be landing without brakes. The field should have crash trucks and medics standing by during the landing. As they neared Port Moresby, the emergency hand-crank system was employed to lower the landing gear, which took about fifteen minutes of hard cranking by Seper. Rogers hoped that they had enough hydraulic fluid for the brakes to work, but Seper thought it unlikely. On the approach to the runway Lt. Browder used the emergency handle to pump down the wing flaps to slow the plane as much as possible before touchdown.

Rogers set the bomber down on its main wheels on the threshold of the runway at around a hundred miles per hour. As the nose of the plane settled to the runway, the nose gear took the weight only briefly before folding under, so that the bomber's nose continued sinking until it was scraping along the runway—the nosewheel had failed to lock in the down position. Conti and Dunmore, down in the nose, realized that the floor of their compartment was being ground away beneath them and scrambled up onto the flight deck to stand behind the pilots with Col. Koon. Rogers found that although his brakes did not work, the friction of the plane's nose dragging along the ground was acting as a pretty good substitute for them.

As the bomber went skidding down the dirt and gravel runway, throwing up clouds of dust in its wake and slowly losing speed, the bombardier's compartment was ground almost completely away. In the process, the plane filled with dust that resembled smoke, setting everyone's nerves on edge, since fire was the greatest fear of an aircrew in a crash. The big plane slid over a thousand feet before finally coming to rest, and when it stopped at last, the crew went scrambling out the escape hatches, still fearing fire. There was none.

Looking at the sad sight of "Connell's Special" resting on its nose, with the bombardier's compartment ground off (photo, opposite), Rogers reflected that this was the worst damage he'd ever done to an airplane. His only consolation was that the nose turret installation, sitting up high, had not been harmed. But it would take at least a few weeks for damage of this magnitude to be repaired, and until then the turret would remain unproven against enemy fighter planes. Rogers was disgusted, but Col. Koon told him that he had seen how much damage the nose turret had done to the Japanese ship and was convinced of its effectiveness. He told Rogers that he was going to make a recommendation to Bomber Command and General Kenney that all the Group's B-24s now be retrofitted with nose turrets.

Back in camp, the mystery of why "Connell's Special" had encountered no fighter opposition at Wewak was solved by the Group's intelligence officer. The Japanese had sent some ships north to Kavieng that day, covered by many Zeros that must have come from Wewak. The numerous fighter planes that had been seen on the ground at Wewak the day before by a reconnaissance plane must have all been sent out to cover the ships early that morning before Rogers' bomber arrived there. The few fighters the crew had seen on the

"Connell's Special" after its nose gear collapsed on landing at Port Moresby, 27 March, 1943. The bombardier's compartment has been ground away by friction with the runway, but the new nose turret installation is undamaged.

ground were evidently out of commission. The Americans had unknowingly caught the Japanese flat-footed, on the one time that they didn't want to.

Shortly thereafter General Kenney approved the installation of nose turrets on all Liberators in the Pacific theater. Since only seven turrets salvaged from wrecked planes were on hand at the Brisbane repair depot, Kenney requested that more turrets be shipped over from the States. Within months the 90th Bomb Group's bombers were equipped with nose turrets almost a year ahead of those in the European theater. The bombers that were modified to take a nose turret in the field were designated the B-24D-1. The modifications were immediately adopted by the factories back in the States, and all Liberators coming out of the factories from that time forward would be equipped with nose turrets and designated the B-24J. The 90th Bomb Group received their first J-model from the factory in January of 1944.[1]

After his successful nose turret installation on the B-24, Rogers continued thinking up ways to improve the performance of the bomber. Since any airplane's performance can be improved by making it lighter—removing weight—in December of 1943 Rogers decided to strip all the olive drab camouflage paint off of "Connell's Special," leaving only the shiny bare aluminum. Because of the B-24s great size and long wingspan, and correspond-

The navigator's compartment of Connell's Special under reconstruction after it was ground away against the runway in the landing without a nosewheel. A tarpaulin protects the undamaged nose turret.

ingly great surface area, removing the paint actually eliminated about 400 pounds of weight. Rogers didn't think the olive drab paint provided much camouflage anyway.

Before doing this Rogers should have asked for permission in writing, "through the proper channels," but he knew from long experience with the Army that his request would have been tied up in red tape forever if he went that route.[2] So he simply ordered it done. He wrote:

> I had the camouflage paint removed from my plane "Connell's Special," and the aluminum surface was polished until she became known as the "Silver Streak." I did this in an effort to prove that our camouflage paint was a detriment instead of an aid in camouflaging the airplane as well as making it heavier, thereby slowing it down. The entire air force had come to the conclusion that it was impracticable to try to camouflage an airplane as large as a Liberator, with an approximately one hundred foot wingspread, while on the ground. I was convinced it could be picked up at high altitudes by ground observers much easier with a dark coat than it could be in its natural aluminum color. Also, since the paint on the planes had begun to crack and peel off as a result of the intense tropical heat, the rough surfaces caused an increased resis-

26. ROGERS' FLIGHT TO PROVE THE B-24 NOSE TURRET 253

"Connell's Special," stripped of its paint and buffed to a shine, soon became known as the "Silver Streak."

tance to the airflow, thereby slowing down the airplane considerably. To prove my point, I took a full load of bombs up to 20,000 feet before removing the paint and timed my maximum climb, then after removing the paint I found that this time was considerably reduced. By flying another Liberator, which was camouflaged, in formation with me over the airdrome at 25,000 feet, observers on the ground reported that the airplane that was camouflaged was much easier spotted, and in fact my silver plane could not be seen at all unless the sun's rays reflected off the shiny surfaces.

Gen. Kenney visited Port Moresby shortly thereafter and noticed the bright silver airplane sitting among the 90th's other bombers. He asked who had authorized the removal of the camouflage paint. Rogers confessed that he was the culprit, but offered his evidence that it had improved the plane's cruising speed and rate of climb. A faster bomber meant a longer range, and longer range was always a major goal in the vast Pacific theater of war. Rogers also asserted to Kenney that as far as camouflage went, a silver B-24 was actually more difficult to see in the air than a painted one, since the shiny metal mirrored the sky like a chameleon. He won Kenney over, and eventually the factories building the B-24 stopped painting the bombers as well, except for their military markings. B-24s from that time forth were all delivered in their bare silver aluminum.

Chapter Twenty-Seven

COL. ROGERS SKIP-BOMBS A SHIP

After the Battle of the Bismarck Sea, the Japanese stopped trying to run convoys anywhere within reach of General Kenney's 5th Air Force in the Southwest Pacific, but individual transport and cargo ships still made furtive attempts to deliver supplies and troops to various Japanese garrisons in the area, hoping not to be spotted by American reconnaissance planes. Rogers flew his share of recon missions and kept an eye out for such ships, and, he wrote in his memoirs, whenever he spotted one he thought about the American airmen he had seen attacked by Japanese fighters as they hung helplessly in their parachutes, or who had been strafed while trying to launch lifeboats after a ditching, and he took grim satisfaction in sending that ship to the bottom with all hands, usually by skip-bombing it.

Rogers' crew had practiced their skip-bombing technique on the Moresby Wreck until they had become quite expert at it. One of the reconnaissance missions in which Rogers skip-bombed a ship, flown on 13 June, 1943, was particularly well documented in both print and photographs because a war correspondent from the *Saturday Evening Post*, Charles A. Rawlings, rode along on the mission to get a story, accompanied by Air Corps photographer Sgt. Stephen J. Novak to provide him with illustrations.

General Kenney's aide, Major "Kip" Chase, also went along as an observer, as he often did with Rogers' crew. The purpose of the reconnaissance mission was to get photographs of a new Japanese airfield on Wakde Island, a small coral island off the northern coast of New Guinea at Maffin Bay that was being used as a waystation and refueling stop for Japanese aircraft that were being ferried down from Japan through the Philippines to New Guinea. The 90th Bomb Group would actually base half their planes on Wakde Island a year later, after the Americans captured the island in May of 1944, but at this time it was still deep in Japanese-controlled territory, over 750 straight-line miles northwest from Port Moresby (see Map 27-1 on page 256).

Allowing for necessary diversions around the peaks of the Owen Stanley Mountains, and the storms that always capped them, this would be a flight of around 2,220 miles, a distance made possible only by the great range of the B-24. Rogers was flying "Connell's Special" as usual, with the same hand-picked crew that he had used on his flight to prove the nose turret on 27 March,

27. COL. ROGERS SKIP-BOMBS A SHIP 255

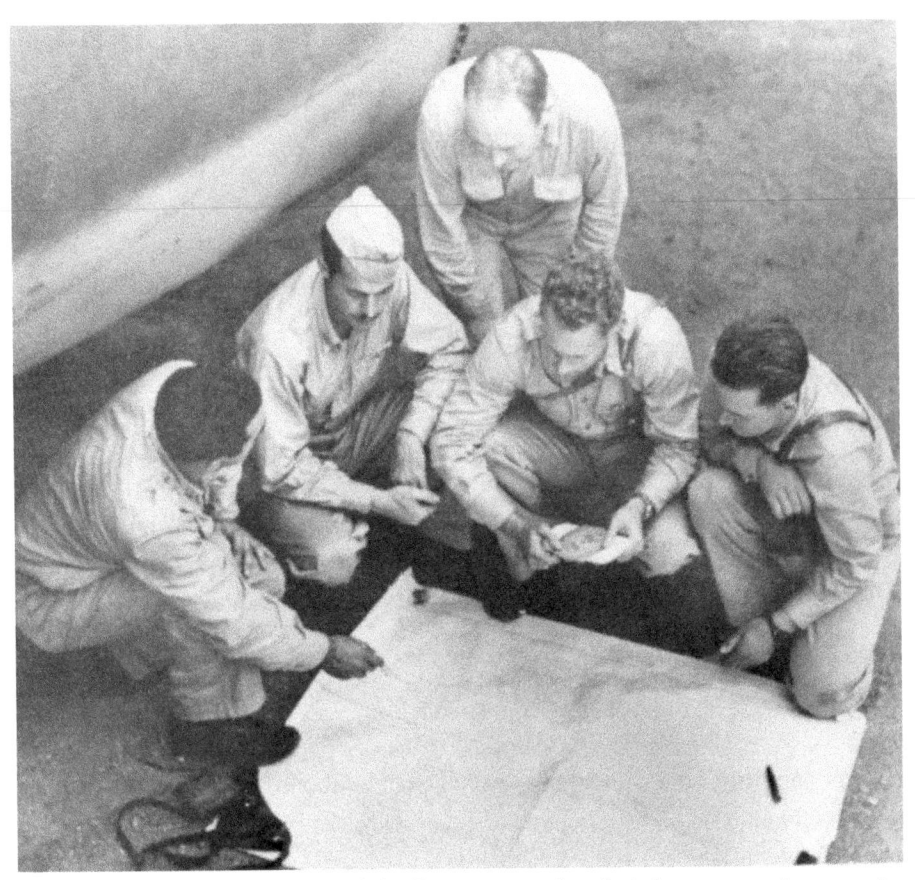

June 13, 1943. The four officers of the Rogers crew plan their lone reconnaissance mission up to Wakde Island on New Guinea's north coast. Col. Rogers is second from left. The man standing at top is Charles Rawlings, the writer for the *Saturday Evening Post Magazine* who accompanied the crew on this flight and wrote the article reproduced in this chapter. The crewman in the center is holding an E6-B manual flight computer, still in use by pilots today.

1943. It was now his regular crew. The plane was loaded with six 500-pound bombs to be used on any targets of opportunity that might be encountered during the flight. Rogers preferred such targets to be Japanese ships.

As Rogers was flying up the north coast of New Guinea, he spotted a 4,000-ton ship sitting a few miles off the coast near the former Dutch administrative town of Hollandia, in Humboldt Bay. It was an unusual-looking ship with some sort of large reed mat or umbrella on its superstructure, amidships, and it was in spic-and-span order and glittering all over with polished brasswork. It was not, in other words, the typical shabby Japanese cargo ship, but rather appeared to be the sort of vessel that might have important officers of the Japanese army or navy aboard, with the awning to provide them with shade.

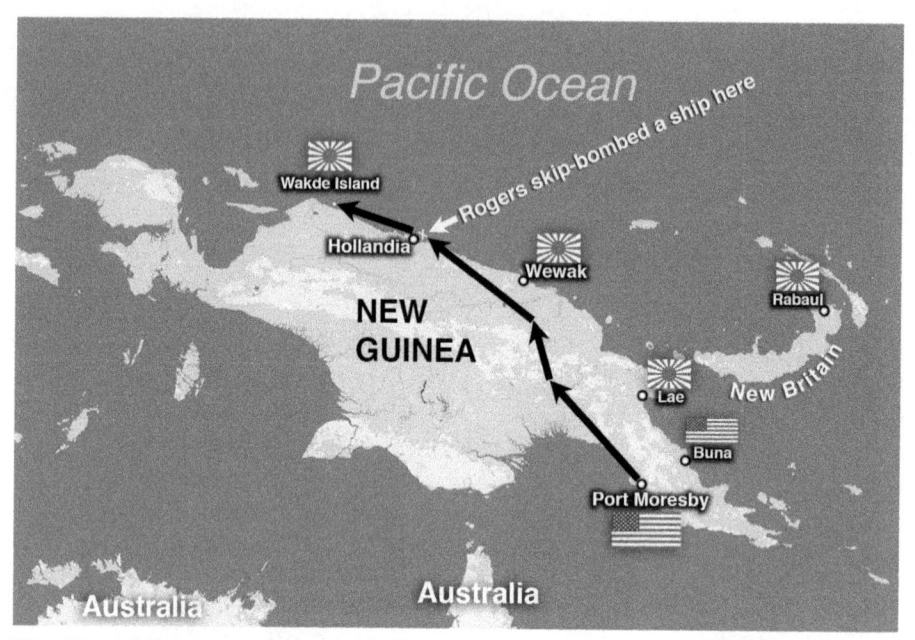

Map 27-1. Col. Rogers' mission to photograph enemy activity on tiny Wakde Island, 2,200 miles out and back from Port Moresby, taking the opportunity to skip-bomb a Japanese ship on the way.

Rogers certainly hoped there were such people aboard the ship, because he intended to sink it.

But let Charles Rawlings of the *Saturday Evening Post*, in his eloquent (or perhaps grandiloquent) writing style, tell the story:*

WE SKIP-BOMB THE JAPS

By Charles A. Rawlings

Somewhere in the South Pacific

New Guinea, that unearthly bright green turkey buzzard of an island roosting where 9 degrees south latitude and 141 east longitude cross to make it a perch, needed a job of long range reconnaissance. Since February, when the bloody struggle at Buna-Gona ended in Allied victories, there had been a lull in the Pacific fighting, and now, in late June, the lull was almost over. We were gathering an offensive stab pointed to the eastward and the ultimate reduction of that volcanic and vital Japanese Gibraltar in New Britain Island, Rabaul.

The contiguous enemy bases in northern and eastern New Guin-

---

*The article appeared in the September 4, 1943 issue of the magazine.

ea, places with names like the fuming of dragons—Lae and Madang and Dagua and Wewak and But—had been "reccoed" many times. But west of But on the northern New Guinea coast, far up on the shoulder of the buzzard—what was there? How had the busy little enemy used the waiting time that was almost over to entrench himself up there? Did he plan to fall back into northwest New Guinea after we had defeated him in the east? There was a rumor of a new Jap 'drome on an island called Wakde, a garrison near Sarmi on the mainland. Now was the time, Lieut. Gen. George C. Kenney decided, to send out a recco and take a long American gander. And while the recco was at it, it might just as well tuck a bomb or two under its wing and sink a boat just to keep the boys from getting ride-weary, just to let Japan know that his boys had been around.

It was an order calling for a good ship and a seasoned one. The course, if everything went well, would log 2,200 miles out and back to base. On a chart it showed a short reach west-northwest down the flat marshes of the south coast of Allied held Papua, then a shift of helm inland up over the Karimji Plateau and the Rubor Range, with 13,000 feet at Mt. Sigul and 12,500 at Mt. Hagan, and then 200 more miles of lonely mountains until the terrain flattened for the north-coast marshes and the enemy. Letting down, there must be a sharp lookout for Zeros that could come in from Boram and Wewak and But. Then, beckoning westward, would be the coast of the Unnamed Sea that washes north New Guinea with its unknown bases and dangers. All that remained of the top half of the gasoline must be used westing down the beach of that Unnamed Sea.

"Maybe we'll gamble a bit more than the top half," said Col. Arthur Rogers. The charts we were studying were his and he was to fly the recco in his heavy bomber named after his long-time friend and flying mate, (General) Connell's Special. "We'll sink our Jap ship early. Two tons of bombs will be gone and we'll be riding light and gay. All we need to do at the end is just bring her home—flank the Zero country again and pick a hole in the cumulus and slide her home for tea."

He smiled, a brown-mustached, good-looking, small, wry smile, knowing better than I did then what "just bring her home" could mean, what cumulus reared up in a barrier could be like. I was fresh up off the sea and cumuli are sail-carrying clouds down there, fair weather, all's-well, summertime clouds.

The colonel is a Carolinian, but his father had come from the fox-hunting Genesee Valley country of upstate New York, a country I knew, and we were good friends. He is a different type of officer from any I had ever sailed with before, a free, easy, Army Air Force hotspur of a guy who loves his wife and longs deeply for his home, yet needs to fly desperate, perfectly planned missions to satisfy his soul. He had had an important role in developing and improving the

Part of the Rogers crew relaxing in a revetment near their bomber, "Connell's Special." In the left foreground is the crew's navigator, Lt. Philip Conti. Sitting behind him, wearing a hat, is the squadron's medical officer, "Doc" Sanderson. Sitting on the ground in the center of the picture is Lt. George "Ace" Dunmore, the bombardier, and behind him is Sgt. Harold Pierce, the crew's nose gunner. Col. Art Rogers is squatting with "Big Ben" Browder, his copilot, on his right. The two men at the right of the photo are unidentified.

B-24 bomber in ways that cannot be told here, and he is famous for the sureness of his flying and the blind following love of his men.

"Commodore," he said to me, "of course the recco is the important part of this mission, but just because all you've ever known is the Navy, poor fellow, and the taint is still strong on you, I hope luck lets us show you how to sink a ship. There'll be one up there. I feel it in my bones. Kip Chase is coming to observe for General Kenney, and we'll have thirteen aboard. That's my lucky number."

The first time one looks at a B-24 bomber asleep on the ground she resembles a prehistoric gargantuan dark brown caterpillar a bit down in the mouth. The nose gunner's windows are vacant eyes, and his guns but dumb antennae and the bombardier's window a mouth ready to drool and her fat round body a slow earth-bound shape. But in a moment, on the strip behind, there is a roar, and over the rim of the revetment where your ship stands cold and inert one of her sisters starts her climb. The clumsy fat landing gear snugs up into her belly* and the slim taut Davis wings use their soaring grace and her tail is up and her guns out her waist windows and you realize she is no caterpillar. She is a killer whale tirelessly dom-

---

*Actually the B-24's main landing gear folded up into the wings.

inating her sea—the cold, blue, fathomless air. On our ship's port-bow cheek her kills were escutcheoned—four stiff, stenciled ships of the watery sea.

The colonel is proud of his gunners. Little Pierce, his nose gunner, a chubby, curly-haired kid, had been a "basic" early in the war. That means he was employed on the base—raking the camp area and cutting and hauling garbage. The first two joints of his right index finger had been missing since boyhood.

Col. Art Rogers in the cockpit window of "Connell's Special."

"I'm looking for someone who has shot birds," the colonel, who had sauntered into the basic quarters, had said one morning. He had a shotgun under his arm. Pierce allowed he had killed a few Oregon partridge. Two weeks later the colonel faced his group doctors.

"I don't see how it matters that this man has lost what used to be called a trigger finger," he said. "My guns have trigger grips. This boy has the makings of the best front gunner in this man's Army. I want him."

Jim Riley, a big pioneer-type lad, had been a staff-car chauffeur at headquarters. He happened to be at the wheel one day to meet the colonel at the airport. Every time thereafter when the colonel called for transportation during his stay there, it was Riley who drove the car.

"Where'd you come from?" the colonel finally asked.

"Out of a 'coon holler in Tennessee, sir," said Riley.

"Where are you going?"

"No'th to Mo'sby to shoot a gun for y'awl if you'll let me," said Riley. "I hunger for some fight."

The port waist gun is the one he mans.

Capt. Philip Conti, who played football for Dartmouth back in the middle 30's, is the colonel's navigator. His forefathers came from the land of the great navigators.

"We'll need a navigator as good as Columbus or Vespucci to bring us back home from this one," said the colonel. "A man who wants to come back home—he makes a good navigator. Conti likes to come back home."

Big, good-natured Ben Browder, from Dallas, and Texas A & M, is copilot. He'd just learned that his girl had married a lawyer at home. His mother had written and told him. "What my philosophy needs just now," he said, "is one more fat Jap ship smokin' and sinkin' under us."

It was a fine crew. It was different from the Navy boatings I had known. The spit-and-polish and discipline was in and about the ship. These men were free men, free as the air they knew.

Chase and I were baggage. I sat on the edge of Conti's navigator's seat. Chase greeted me across the flight deck perched atop the radioman's locker with the parachutes that nobody in his right mind would ever use on the north coast of New Guinea. He'd been working at finance before the war. There is a bank in New York that carries the name of one of his forebears. Now he is aide to a general who is pleased with his staff when they have the courage to fly combat missions. Many missions have weathered his face and made it lean and a bit drawn. It nodded its brown leanness at me and then down at Conti's lap. Both Conti's forefingers were crossed down in his lap.

"Let this be one more good takeoff in the cool New Guinea dawn," the gesture said for all of us. "Let us thunder sixty-two thousand pounds of plane and men and bombs and guns and gasoline safely up into the unimpassioned air."

The Papuan coast slid under us; whitewashed sand and sleepy climbing soapsuds wave. A brown-thatched colony of native huts on stilts cast long, still shadows. The settlement's coconut grove, an orderly stow of fronded green, gave way to the disordered dusty green of jungle, and my ears felt the climb as we left west and turned northwest for the mountains and Japanese country.

Jake Seper, his four Pratt-Whitney engines running with a single synchronized smooth roar and his landing gear up and checked and the gasoline feeds drawing comfortably on the bomb-bay tank and the luncheon sandwiches safe from the gunners, took over the flight deck. Jake is crew chief. That means that he is engineer and top gunner and guardian of generals' aides and war correspondents and watcher of the carpet against cigarette burns and keeper of the sandwiches. He is a gaunt, happy lad with dancing brown eyes and fallen-down socks and a jolly gaping hole where four front upper teeth used to be. He was standing on the catwalk in the open bomb bay in a night strike on Wewak a month or two before, and a big chunk of flak came straight into the bay and knocked the four teeth out as clean as a whistle.

"Had my mouth open, singing," he confided. "Teeth went down leadin' the bombs. Spat 'em down. Got a good bracket."

He stuck a long, greasy-grimed finger into my ribs and grinned widely, exposing the great gap in his dental fence. Inside, his red tongue, clucking and churning as he chuckled wove about like a fat, red puppy bedding down. He climbed into his turret that dominates the flight deck and lit a cigarette. I felt his hand tugging my cap and strained to bring my ear up close to his leaned-down face.

"If this thing"—he patted his gun mount—"gets to shootin', watch out for c'trudges. I rain 'em down. Get a hot one down your collar and you'll dance."

It was five cigarettes across New Guinea, south to north. I smoked the fourth one forward, slouching between the pilot's and copilot's seats. A whole new range of mountains loomed ahead. On the chart—an ancient British survey of the island—we should have been over marsh. Under us and ahead were 11,000-foot peaks instead. Had we been a land expedition the discovery would have upset our timing by weeks. In the air it made little difference. We held the 16,000-foot altitude that had brought us over the charter ranges, and, still on automatic pilot, flew on in fine smooth weather. The mountains—our mountains, if you will—basked under us as they had since time began, as silent and lonely as jungles of the moon. There was a still, round lake as green as jade with slime. Above the lake hung a long raveling of white-lace waterfall that seemed to have no motion.

Suddenly, the colonel pulled his cocked earphones down and listened. "Roger!" he said.

"Better go back and get your mask and get set," he said to me. "The tail turret has sighted a plane."

We saw the plane at last. It was a silver sliver stiff against the purple distance. It was a Jap plane. I went back and sat on the edge of Conti's seat again and watched Jake up in his turret. He had his hands on the gun grips, and the turret kept clicking as he inched it a bit back and forth, holding a bead on the plane. After a time he nodded to himself and relaxed his grip and grinned.

"A Zero?" I stretched up and asked.

"Two-motor job," he said. "Probably a Mitsubishi 97. He was headed to cross us, but he turned around and went the other way. He don't want any." He slouched down in his seat and half-closed his eyes against the glare in the dome and was no longer a killer gunner on the alert, but a deceptively drowsy lookout. He was a very good lookout.

"Coast ahead," he said to me. "It's clear as a bell over the water. Good ship-huntin' day."

Conti, the navigator, came back from forward and got out the chart of the north coast. It was an Australian chart and looked very good. He laid the ruler just east of the bay with a hooked cape for its western promontory and a long spit up inside that made it two bays, an inner and an outer, and drew a pencil line. Humboldt was the bay's name on the chart. I stood and looked out the window and there the bay was. It was uncanny to look at the chart of a wild, lonely place and then look down and see it complete and whole. On the surface of the sea, bays unfold slowly.

Forward, Kip Chase was pointing and gesticulating over the

colonel's shoulder, and Browder was up out of his seat looking down our port side, and when I looked again I saw the ship. It was in Humboldt Bay and was lying very still. It was a fairly big ship with four hatches and two masts and a single funnel. The sea and the bay and the ship and the hills were as peaceful and silent as a painting. The whole world was drenched in sleepy noon. There was, at that moment, no war and no hate.

Fisherman's Luck

But that hung moment did not last long. Below, we could see evidence of a panic. Four spreading fans appeared on the water leading away from the ship. They had seen us and they were getting people ashore to safety.

Kip Chase came aft. "That's an important ship of some sort," he said. "I believe she's got Japanese high command aboard and they're putting them off. Through the binoculars she looks clean and polished. She's a damned important ship."

"We're going to bother with her now, before we've gone up the coast?" I asked him.

"Yes," he said.

As we were speaking, our plane started to swing. It was a slow, remorseless swing, the slow swing of a hunting condor. As we turned, we lost altitude, and I could hear a metallic grinding noise behind me [bomb bay doors opening]. Jake was out of his turret and he lifted the hatch that shut us off from the bomb bay and stepped carefully out into what looked like space. The bomb bay doors were open and I could see the edge of the beach and the beginning of the bay down through the crotch of his pants. Wind whipped at his pants. I peered over and he was standing on the catwalk, a six-inch metal walkway where the keel of a ship's hull would be.

The new light in the bay disclosed the bombs. They were sorrel colored like shotes with mud dried on them sleeping on perches with their noses on their hoofs. Each one had a small prop, like the tin propeller of a child's toy, stuck in its snout.

Jake pulled the cotter pins that kept the props from spinning and put them in his pocket. The bombs had been stored in an outside dump and there was splashed mud on them.

A Game of Tag

There was no excitement in our plane. No one was shrilling or even talking. Kip Chase poked my ankle. He was on the flight deck floor with a movie camera. He motioned me to stretch out beside him and together we hung our heads out the [bomb] bay. We hung there watching the demure blue with just a trace of ripple on it sliding past. Jake tapped my shoulder.

"Dry run," he said. "Plenty of time."

We turned and I pillowed my head in my arms and shut my eyes and withdrew into myself to see how excited I was. I was very excited.

"Here we go," Kip Chase said. "Here's the run."

We waited, he with the camera poised and I with nothing to do but wonder if my hands were too sweaty to grip if there should be sudden pitching. There was a jarring bump that made the plane shudder. It came from the outside. Then there was another, a dull, sickening, jarring bump. I saw a red-hot tracer cutting the air at an angle far beneath us.

"Flak!" Chase said close to my ear. "Three-inch! They've got good ack-ack."

Two bombs went away.

They went away with absolute precision and so swiftly and silently I stiffened, seeing them suddenly, nose first, speeding down the clean blue rectangle of framed sea. They were not rusty pig-iron shotes as they flew, but Roman-gold shapes in the sun, with their yellow painted tailpieces as bright as polished gold. Their drop was the essence of grace, a plummeting of mated golden birds with tight-folded wings.

In a breathless split second, there was the ship. She was not beam-to, as I had expected to see her, but bow-on, with a curved plume of wake astern to show where she had turned into our run. The two plummeting yellow missiles, no bigger than yellow finches now, closed with her so swiftly my eyes lost them for a breath, and then a pair of thousand-fluted petticoats of lace, so laundered and white they were dazzling to look at, blossomed out of the blue water. A miss! Not a bad one—the farthest burst measured eighty-five feet in the picture—but a miss.

I could feel Chase scrambling to his feet beside me, and I struggled up, too, and sat weakly on my scrap of seat. No one was looking at anyone else or speaking. We were in a cloud and the air was gray. Only Jake was still rosy. He stuck his head around the bulkhead and met my eyes. He grasped his nose with grimy forefinger and thumb and made a deep, silent raspberry. Then, to show that defeat is ever a momentary thing, he slid his fingers into a confident OK.

"Watch us this time!" the gesture said.

Chase was going down on his belly again and I joined him. We missed again. The Jap was very good. He was a brilliant helmsman. He had a fast, maneuverable ship. Chase had been right. She was an important ship. This time my brain was cool enough to hold my eyes to the task. The ship's brightwork was varnished and there was a strange great umbrella amidships, made of some kind of reed. An Oriental deck awning to shade officers? She was a coal burner and her fires were smoking madly. She was about 4000 tons. She even had polished brass, I noticed, and it was winking in the sun. Too red a wink for brass—too big a wink. The wink of a gun! Another gun. Why, damn her eyes, she was still shooting up at us defiantly. I drew back and waited. The shells exploding were a faraway "thump—thump-thump." The thumps stopped.

I arose, and as I stood a wave of dejection that was deeper than any I ever remember flowed over me. It was not fear. We were above fear, remote from it. It was a sense of failure, defeat, abysmal loss. It vanished as swiftly as it had come. There was, after all, still a shot left in the locker—several of them.

Chase nodded his well-bred round head and we sank down together on our war's prayer rug, the flight deck's gritty patch of green carpet. This time our plane seemed to be moving swifter and surer. We were nearer the water. The wrinkles of ripple turned into waves with plaster-of-paris whitecaps that stood still. There was a rapping; it was from within our ship—like a brisk tradesman at distant door. It was Pierce, in the nose, strafing with his .50-calibers. We were close enough for machine-gun fire, machine-gun fire down—and up. Very faintly I could hear the Jap's little guns. They crackled like breaking glass. Then his big ones—he had three, bow, stern and amidships—barked. How or where the shells exploded, I do not know, for I did not hear or see them. Our bombs burst white, they were misses again, but this time the after one was so close it threw its lace over the stern of the ship. As we watched it still fountaining upward, a cloud of dirty black smoke or soot reached up and soiled it. We had hit the ship and something had exploded, something was afire on her starboard quarter.

"A fine near-miss," Chase shouted close to my ear. "That hurt him worse than a deck hit. We've got him now."

The temperature inside our cabin said we had him. It was warm and rosy again. Conti was bobbing his head and laughing, leaning down between the colonel and Browder. Chase put his arm around my shoulders and we crowded forward too. The colonel was speaking, using a throat mike.

"Dunmore," he said, "I'm going down and skip him. His steering gear is gone and they're all on deck, fighting a fire. . . . Yes, they've got a big hose. Come up, hey, and change fuses? . . . Aw, g'wan—you didn't let me down. You're doing fine." He pulled off his headset and pushed up out of his seat.

The Last Try

"I'm stretching a leg," he said. "Ben, have everybody keep a sharp lookout for Zeros. There can be a mess of 'em around here out of But [one of the Wewak airfields] anytime now—if they're comin'."

[Photo with labels: "Bomb" and "Splash from skip of bomb"]

Army photographer Sgt. Stephen J. Novak (not Sgt. Riley as Rawlings wrote in his article) aimed his camera down through the bomb bay of "Connell's Special" and snapped the shutter the instant the Japanese ship appeared. The result was this remarkable picture of a 500-pound bomb (circled) a fraction of a second before it penetrated the side of the ship and exploded.

He saw me. "Hey commodore! That last one buckled his plates a bit, hey? We're going down and make a masthead attack and finish him. Glad you're up here instead of down there?"

"Very," I said.

"We'll take a little time," he said, "and let Dunmore get settled down and the gunners all set. Skipping needs organization."

When we came back, Dunmore, the bombardier, was working with electric flashlight and wrenches at the two remaining bombs. Dunmore is a quiet, serious chap from Long Beach, California, who did not look as if he needed quieting down. He grinned, a bit sheepishly, at the colonel.

"Sorry about those first two runs, sir," he said. "This target would not cooperate. He wouldn't stay still like our Moresby practice wreck."

"That last one made up for everything," said the colonel. "Set fuse, and we'll go and get him."

Back in his seat, he pulled on his headset and opened the phone circuit to all hands, his eyes studying the bay below as he talked.

Death Blow

"Roger!" the colonel said. "This time we're going in at two hundred feet. They've shaken a gunboat loose from up the bay and she's closing on our left. I'm going to feint at her. Pierce and Seper, open up on the gunboat at a mile. All I want to do is turn him. Make him think we're coming for him. Then I'll swing into the run on the target. Everybody strafe! Pierce, I'm counting on you to clean that Jap's deck coming in. We're going in at two hundred, and he's got three inch against us. Everybody got everything straight? Report!"

The phone rasped with the different metallic voices.

We came down swiftly in a long banked turn and then leveled the wings and continued to lose altitude in a straight glide. The water came up until the whitecaps on the small summer seas were made of live running spume. Our ship vibrated with short knocking jars as Pierce, in the nose, opened fire. Then Jake's guns directly above my stretched-out legs barked loudly and his cartridge cases pelted my legs in a metallic rain. The reeking fumes of cordite made the air stinking and nauseous. One of the hot cartridges lodged between my locked ankles and scorched until I kicked it away. We were making an even, small turn that straightened and held steady. The faraway crackle of the Japanese guns began. The crazy racket of our guns increased, firing madly, and then, bursting into view, so close it seemed I could reach down and touch her, was the Jap ship and our bombs were flying into her.

One of them hit the water and made a small splash like a clean diver's splash, and then, still like a darting diver's body, sped through the water and into the black ship's side; and then all there was below was black leaping fernlike fingers of explosion, dark red in their core, and a great hot roar of sound that died away and left only the clean "rat—rat-rat-rat-ratttt," of our waist and turret guns shooting astern. They slowed down and stopped, as if content.

The coast to the westward was still peaceful in the noon. We strolled it. Slowly the cordite in our cabin cleared. Our cigarette ashes sifted down on a floor of dirty brass. It was tiled with cartridge cases from Jake's guns. No one bothered to pick them up. They tinkled and made patterns in the vibration of our steady pace. Jake swung down from his turret and with a rapt seriousness on his face stepped out into the bomb bay and disappeared. In a moment he was back with the lunch. It was a pile of sandwiches, Army-cook style, made of slabs of bread as big as floor tiles, crushing between them four small, cold, limp, pink frankfurters.

Japan's evil strategy was under us on the quiet, slumbering coast. Where, and how, is information that must stay where it is for the present—with our reports that are safely locked in Army G-2 files.

Suffice it to say that the atmosphere far up on the shore of that lonely Unnamed Sea is the atmosphere of a new house, carefully and painstakingly built and waiting now for its lord and master and expected tenant—war. From Java Head to the Solomons, Japan waits in a long string of 'dromes and troop areas. She bought them cheaply and put in all modern improvements, and she expects to sell them dear.

"Why," I asked the colonel, "do they let us sail along so insolently and scornfully? They know we're spying. That we have cameras."

"It's my fight," he said. "If they come up against my gunners and my .50-caliber ammunition it means we'll kill two or three Zeros and I can break off at my own time."

"Break off? Where?"

"There!" He waved a hand in over the land.

Reared high was the cumulus. Out at sea we were in clear weather, but New Guinea was wearing her afternoon tea gown of wool-packed clouds. They were beautiful, but there was something in the colonel's eyes that made me sense their terror too. "Cumulus is handy in a fight," he said. "You can slide her into a cloud if you aren't going too fast, and the Zeros turn back. They don't like it inside. We don't either, but we can take it—for awhile. Ask Conti how far to Moresby—going back by Humboldt. We must take a look at our ship."

It was 1,100 miles, Conti said.

There was no ship in Humboldt. There was a large slick of oil, streamed up into the bay by the tide. I looked carefully to see if they had not beached her. I had trouble not feeling traitorously sorry because they had not been able to beach her. She had been a smart little ship. Ships, like music and art, in themselves have no nationality. We made a slow swing over Humboldt and lit a cigarette for home.

Conti brought us home. I have his chart before me. Our morning course in to New Guinea is a straight, confident penciled line, black and bold. Our course out is a series of sharp, angular light lines that dart southwest, south-southwest, west, then back to southwest again and finally one bold last thank-God traverse, due south out of the turbulence and the cumulus into the bright afternoon of the Gulf of Papua. Most of the navigating was done at 27,000 feet with the oxygen flowing and the top of the cloud cover another 12,000 feet above us.

We found a break in the solid wall of cloud and turbulence at 27,000 feet. It was a miraculous meandering channel like the rift in the Red Sea that saved the children of Israel. It saved us from going over the enemy's Wewak and Dagua and trying for a dubious emergency landing at Dobodura, our strip near Buna on the north New Guinea coast. We turned into the break in the wall, a lone blessed canyon in the snarling white land of cloud. It wandered this way and that and like a miracle closed in astern directly we had passed.

There were rifts downward that afforded fleeting glimpses of the terrain. Conti, never off his feet, peering out of one window, then another, found the mountain peaks and river bends and marshes that told him where we were. Over the grotesque oxygen nose cap his big black eyes were intent, suffering with responsibility and the terrible worry that only navigators with ship and men riding their stop watches and their rulers and their decisions can know. Once he smiled. "Two hours' gas?" he asked one of the crew.

"Easy," came the exuberant answer. "Sure?" said Conti.

Jake made an OK with his fingers that vibrated with emphasis. Then he slid across the deck, clasped Conti around the neck and shouted "Yes!" in his ear.

When we reached the Papuan tidal marshes with their thick, brown, sluggish streams that checked our course beyond any doubt, Conti sat down. He did not look around for commendation or applause. He simply sat down, limp and exhausted, his job, his terrifying job, done once more.

Beneath were the gleaming strips and graceful revetments of home. The after crew came forward to give our plane—light as a feather now, with empty tanks and bomb bay—nose trim for the landing. Big Riley grasped my knee.

"Think I got a picture for y'awl," he said. "I'm done strafin'! I pick up the spare camera! I stick her out the waist! I lose my hat! I click her!"

"What do you know about shootin' pictures?" scoffed the radioman.

"Nothin'. I just push buttons," admitted Riley.

The shot of the skip-bombs going home is Riley's picture.

"I wonder," mused Riley, "if that Medical Section guy will be there when we come in with a little shot of good drinkin' liquor? He was when we'uns came back from Wewak."

"If he isn't," said Kip Chase, "I will be. Come over to my car." He turned to me. "A fine mission. I think General Kenney will be very pleased."

"Pleased enough for a medal?" blurted the naive Riley.

The general was that pleased.

Chapter Twenty-Eight

THE 90TH BOMB GROUP BECOMES THE JOLLY ROGERS

Up to the summer of 1943, Lt. Col. Art Rogers had been the Deputy Group Commander, or 2nd-in-command, of the 90th Bomb Group under Col. Koon. On July 11 Koon relinquished command of the Group to Rogers, and Maj. Harry J. Bullis took over the job of Deputy Commander. A few days after Rogers took command, a young officer named Lt. Bernard Stoecklein who worked in Group Headquarters was hosting a couple of war correspondents in his tent one night. One of them was Carl Thusgaard, who worked for *Acme News Pictures,* and the other was an unnamed newsreel photographer. Somebody brought out a bottle of liquor, and after a few drinks Stoecklein declared that the 90th Bomb Group needed a nickname. After all, he pointed out, the 43rd Bomb Group was known as "Ken's Men," named after General Kenney; what name should the 90th Bomb Group adopt?

Since Col. Rogers had just taken command of the Group, someone threw out the name "Jolly Rogers." It struck everyone as appropriate, since one of Col. Rogers' favorite bombing targets was Japanese shipping, and it was said that he prowled the sea lanes preying upon enemy ships like a sea pirate of old. And of course Rogers himself had said that his bomber crews reminded him of "old time buccaneers" in their eccentric ways of dressing.

"Jolly Rogers," therefore, seemed to fit the bill admirably. The pressmen also averred that "the Jolly Rogers" would sound a lot better in their news stories than just "the 90th Bomb Group," which few in the States would remember a few minutes after they read it. Stoecklein became so enthusiastic about the idea that he rushed over to Col. Rogers' tent and woke him up to see what he thought of it. Rogers said he was flattered at the proposal of having his name incorporated into the group's new nickname and gave his approval.[1]

The next day Stoecklein assigned Sgt. Max Baer, a draftsman and amateur cartoonist who worked under him, to come up with an appropriate symbol based on the Jolly Rogers theme. Taking his inspiration from the traditional Jolly Roger pirate flag, a skull over crossed bones, Baer modified the emblem into a grinning skull above crossed bombs.

After Stoecklein approved the design, Baer made a big aluminum template, carried it over to Rogers' B-24, the "Connell's Special," got up on a mechanics' scaffold, and used it to paint the symbol on the outsides of the two vertical rudders, just under the serial numbers. The sight was an immediate hit with other members of the Group, and they decided to put it on all the Group's bombers.[2] Bomber Command made no objections, apparently seeing the whole thing as a morale builder. Within the next few weeks all the bombers of the 90th Bomb Group had the skull and crossed bombs symbol painted on their rudders. Each of the four squadrons of the 90th picked a different background color for the symbol:

        319th Squadron: Blue background
        320th Squadron: Red background
        321st Squadron: Green background
        400th Squadron: Black background

Each squadron also chose a squadron nickname and a squadron symbol:

        319th Squadron   Asterperious*
        320th Squadron   Moby Dick
        321st Squadron   Bombs Away
        400th Squadron   Black Pirates

The squadron symbols were soon being worn as jacket patches. Men on leave in Sydney often had their patches professionally made.

During the war, the Jolly Rogers skull and crossed bombs emblem on the tails of the 90th Bomb Group's B-24s would become nearly as famous as the sharks' mouths of the American Volunteer Group (AVG) of Gen. Chennault in China, the "Flying Tigers."

Col. Rogers wrote in his memoirs that the adoption of the name and symbol was intended not only to boost group morale but to strike fear into the hearts of Japanese fighter plane pilots, and this it no doubt did. On one occasion it also had an unintended benefit after one of the Group's bombers, piloted by Lt. Warren H. Smeltzer, was lost on a bombing mission to New Britain. Rogers wrote:

The Jolly Rogers skull and crossed bombs symbol, adopted in the summer of 1943.

> We knew that the damaged plane had gone down somewhere in the neutral territory between us and the Japanese base at

---

*Asterperious is a made-up word defined as "a superior attitude in an inferior environment."

28. THE 90TH BECOMES THE JOLLY ROGERS

319th Squadron
"Asterperious"

320th Squadron
"Moby Dick"

321st Squadron
"Bombs Away"

400th Squadron
"Black Pirates"

Finschaffen. As a result we sent out armed recco airplanes daily to search for the wreckage of the lost plane. To search over many hundreds of square miles of dense jungle for the sight of a small wreckage is a pretty hopeless job, since the spot of the wreckage is often completely covered by the high dense foliage. Those were the circumstances in this case, and we were forced to give up the search after four days, even though we knew the general area in which the plane was lost.

A few days after this, a formation of our planes, while returning from a mission, were amazed to see a huge skull and crossed bombs in a small clearing two miles below. Underneath our "Jolly Rogers" symbol was the last serial numbers of the lost airplane. One plane of the flight was dispatched to break off from the formation and fly down low over this clearing. When only a few hundred feet above the insignia, they could see it was located in a small native village, and was constructed from the white silk of parachutes, with two black natives squatting on the silk in the

Lt. Smeltzer's crew created a large Jolly Rogers emblem on the ground with their parachutes in hopes of being spotted and rescued. It worked. The crewmen standing around the symbol waving at the photo plane give some idea of its size.

position of the eyes, and one black native lying down to form the mouth. While circling, words began to form underneath the skull in great white letters which spelled out MEDICINE, FOOD, and CIGS. The plane that was dispatched to make these observations was the camera ship for the flight and therefore took beautiful aerial photographs to bring back as proof of the remarkable scene. We knew this was our lost crew.

    The downed crew had been flying a bomber of the 400th Squadron named "Sky Lady" that had gone out on a raid on Rabaul on 18 October 1943. On the way back to Port Moresby an engine had gone out, then the plane's instruments had malfunctioned while they were flying blind in clouds, and without their artificial horizon instrument to refer to, to keep the wings level, the pilots became disoriented and lost control as they approached the Owen Stanley Mountains. The bomber came out of the clouds in a terrifying vertical dive, and the pilots were only barely able to pull out of it before the plane hit the ground.

    However, the violent pullout put such a strain on the bomber that it was damaged; the tail fluttered and the plane bucked uncontrollably. Smeltzer was unable to get the plane to fly straight and level, and he decided it was time for everyone to get out before he lost control again completely. The crew bailed out, suffering only bruises and sprains on landing, except for S/Sgt. George H.

28. THE 90ᵀᴴ BECOMES THE JOLLY ROGERS 273

Col. Rogers stands beside a B-24 rudder with the Jolly Rogers symbol painted on it, illustrating just how large the emblem was.

Hermerding, whose parachute got stuck in a tree. When Hermerding released himself from his harness he fell to the ground and injured his back.

After the men had assembled, they were met by friendly natives who took them to their village and gave them food and shelter. Knowing that there were probably search planes out looking for them, the men got the idea of laying out a giant Jolly Rogers skull and crossed bombs on the ground with their parachutes in a clearing near the village. Luckily a sharp-eyed crewman in a passing Jolly Rogers formation spotted it. Rogers continued:

All the 90th Bomb Group's bombers soon had the Jolly Rogers symbol painted on their tails. Although it is not evident in black and white photos, each squadron had its own background color for the skull and crossed bombs. Since these two B-24s, named "Form 1-A" and "Bad Penny," were bombers of the 319th Squadron, the symbols were painted on a blue background. (Additional information about the bomber "Form 1-A" is on p. 755.)

An airplane returned immediately to the spot to drop the supplies they wanted, and in addition, letters that had been received during the past week from the crew's families in the States. Along with this we dropped a map of the area showing the nearest large village, which was Kerau, some ten days' journey through the jungle. This was the nearest point where a white man was thought to be, since it was known prior to the war that a Catholic priest had been sent to this village to establish a mission. We were all in hopes that the good Father was still alive, and would be able to help our crew on their long journey back to our nearest outpost.

Father A. Wendling was indeed still at the mission, and with his help and that of native guides and porters the crewmen were able to reach his station after eight days of arduous trekking through the jungle. Since Sgt. Hermerding's

28. THE 90TH BECOMES THE JOLLY ROGERS

Members of the 90th Bomb Group with the organization's new symbol: the skull and crossed bombs. The men on either side of the signboard hold jacket patches with the same insignia. The woman is probably a nurse from the Group's hospital at Port Moresby.

injured back prevented him from walking, he was carried the entire distance by the natives on a stretcher.

> The Catholic Father met them with open arms [Rogers went on], and took them to his house where he gave freely of what he had... After the men were safe back in the Group, the pilot stated that the little mission had been completely depleted of its resources in taking care of them, and it would have been impossible for them to have gotten out of the jungle if it had not been for the good priest. He wondered if there was any way that we could repay the little mission with some supplies. I decided to take a quantity of our dried rations and fly over and drop them to the priest to show our appreciation. I am sure this was like manna from heaven to him, as he had not had anything from the outside world in approximately two years.

American aircrewmen might have disputed that anyone could consider their tasteless dehydrated chow "manna from heaven," since to them it seemed

Some of the men even came up with a Jolly Rogers flag to fly near the Group's headquarters building.

more like a product of the infernal regions, but all things are relative and it had to have been better than nothing at all.

The crewmen had been guided to a tiny airstrip in the jungle where they were picked up, one by one, by Australian pilots flying prewar civilian Tiger Moth biplanes, which were able to land and take off from such tight spots. They were flown to a larger airfield from which American C-47 cargo planes could operate, and from there were flown back to Port Moresby. They finally returned to their squadron a full month after they had been lost.

The story of how a bomber crew had been rescued from the New Guinea jungles by creating a large Jolly Rogers insignia from parachutes was picked up by the press and reported in many newspapers in the States, as well as in the 3 January [1944] issue of *Life Magazine*. In the *Life* article one of the rescued men described how he had created a sensation among the New Guinea natives by demonstrating his Zippo cigarette lighter to them. Another crewman, to show his gratitude for the villagers' help, presented his high-altitude electrically-heated flight suit to a tribesman, and was amazed when the man wore the insulated suit full-time from then on, despite the suffocating heat of the jungle.

28. THE 90TH BECOMES THE JOLLY ROGERS

The magazine story also related how S/Sgt. Jack C. Wu, one of the crew's gunners, who was of Chinese ancestry, found it necessary to stay very close to his pilot, Lt. Smeltzer, at all times because the natives had developed a habit of killing Japanese on sight, and Wu looked a little too Japanese to suit them. Any native who was seen staring at Wu for any length of time while fingering his knife was gently shooed away by Smeltzer. When Sgt. Wu got back to Port Moresby he decided to give up flying and switched to permanent ground duties at the airbase.[3]

All this publicity in the States made the Jolly Rogers name and insignia quite well known back home, and the Group's fame only increased as the war went on.

The press in both America and Australia publicized the new Jolly Rogers emblem.

A 90th Bomb Group crew made paper masks and had a little fun with their new Jolly Rogers insignia.

The 320th Squadron emphasized its "Moby Dick" theme by painting sharks' mouths on several of its bombers in addition to the Jolly Rogers emblems on their tails.

The Jolly Rogers laid claim to the title of the "Best Damn Heavy Bomb Group in the World."

Chapter Twenty-Nine

THE LOSS OF CAPT. LARK MARTIN

Ridding the world of barbarous Japanese militarism came at a high cost to America. Many of the nation's finest young men were lost in battles on the land, sea, and air (not to mention illustrious older men such as Col. Meehan and Generals Walker and Ramey). As the Jolly Rogers continued to carry out their combat missions, and more and more aircrews were lost, some of the Group's most talented young leaders were among the fallen.

Col. Rogers eulogized one of them in his memoirs:[1]

Capt. Lark E. Martin

The death of an outstanding hero in the Group, Captain Lark E. Martin Jr., of Fitzgerald, Georgia, had left an empty place in my heart. The Group shared this feeling with me, as Martin had been considered invincible. Of the many heroes our Group had turned out, this young officer represented to me a combination of all the higher ideals that America stands for. To begin with, he was a clean-cut, good looking, dark-curly-haired boy about six feet tall with honest, straightforward eyes. He bubbled over with life, confidence, friendship and courage...

Never was a difficult mission assigned to the Group in which volunteers were asked for than Martin wasn't the first to step forward, whether it was skip-bombing a cruiser, a difficult reconnaissance mission, or leading a low-level attack in an effort to destroy heavy artillery installations. Very seldom would his airplane return from a mission without being shot full of holes.

Capt. Lark Martin's bomber "Mission Belle" with her six enlisted crewmen. They all admired and respected "the Lark," but they also feared that he was going to get them killed.

22-year-old Lark Martin was a cool and effective leader under the stresses of combat, but he had a wild streak in him that would eventually prove his undoing. He had been trained as a fighter plane pilot in Canada before switching to the U. S. Air Corps and bombers, and at times he seemed to forget that he had made the switch. He sometimes flew a bomber as if he were still flying a fighter, also appearing to forget that there were nine other men riding along with him, men who often didn't appreciate the wild rides. Lark's superiors warned him repeatedly that a B-24 was not a stunt plane, and should not be flown at high speeds close to the ground or right down on the surface of the sea just for the thrill of it. Martin agreed, and then went right back to flying his bomber the way he liked.

More than once Col. Rogers saw Martin buzz the airfield on the return from a mission, then go racing up the valley beyond with his propellers nearly trimming the treetops before pulling up into a steep climb and swinging back around for a "hot" show-off landing. Rogers wrote in his memoirs:

> After two or three of these exhibitions, I realized that even though Martin was a good pilot he would certainly not live to be

an old one if this continued. I called him into my office and warned him in a very firm manner that any more acrobatic maneuvers in a B-24, which were prohibited, would be considered grounds for relieving him as a pilot. I told him I knew he was full of life but I had rather he concentrate his ability and energies on fighting the Japs.

Martin professed remorse when reprimanded but kept right on with his exuberant flying. He was utterly fearless in the face of danger and took other risks besides stunting and hedgehopping that his crew often wished that they didn't have to share with him. Still, they appreciated his reputation for sound leadership and courage in combat and were proud to be known as his crew. *Saturday Evening Post* writer Charles Rawlings, the same war correspondent who flew with Col. Rogers when Rogers skip-bombed a Japanese ship (Chapter 27) was in the Jolly Rogers camp at the time, and he wrote of Martin's crew:

> They worshiped him, but they also feared him, because they felt he was going to kill them. They were tremendously proud of flying with him, yet they sweated out missions with drops of pure agony. They appreciated the inherent beauty of the guy, his making a tonic of danger, brushing death's whiskers and zooming away before the old codger could swing his scythe. But they were not made of the eagle stuff the Lark was, and they couldn't stop thinking, the way prosaic mortals do, about the law of averages and the inevitable.[2]

On one night mission to Rabaul, Lark dropped his bombs, but then instead of turning for home immediately, to get out of danger as quickly as possible as his crew expected him to do, he circled the harbor, enchanted by the spectacle of the Japanese searchlights probing the sky for the bombers, the flak exploding like fireworks in the sky, and the bombs of the other Jolly Rogers planes flashing and splashing fire on the darkened ground and ocean below. He paid no attention to his crew's pleading to skip the fireworks display and make a dash for home, and would not leave the area until he had enjoyed the scene to the fullest.

Rawlings got the details of this mission from Martin's crew and wrote:

> It was during the bitterly hard night strikes on Rabaul in the winter and spring of 1943 that I knew Lark and Mission Belle, his plane. There was no formation flying on night strikes in New Guinea, and the planes went off individually, ten minutes apart, and flew alone all the way, in and over and out. There was weather on the Owen Stanley Mountains most of the time to curl your hair—turbulence and icing and lightning and thunder and the terror of the mountains—"hard-centered clouds," the fliers called the jagged 11,000 and 12,000 foot peaks. Rabaul was the toughest spot south of

> Truk then, with flak, night fighters and searchlights... Those lonely planes were small and pitiful against that vast, turbulent sky and the powerful enemy. For most men, those strikes were grim hours of tension and terror all the way. But not for the Lark.
>
> His was one of the early planes over the target... He made his run, and his men heaved a sigh of relief, for the weather under the full moon looked good for once, and all there was left was a quick slide home without oxygen. But the Lark did not go home. He drew off to one side of Simpson Harbor and circled there, watching the beauty of the searchlights, the flak and the bursting 1,000-pound bombs and his brother pilots in their B-24s, silvered in that eerie light, coming in, one after the other, on their runs. He simply did not hear the prayerful beseeching of his crew, they said, to get out and away from danger, so rapt was he in that strange and esoteric beauty.
>
> Sated at last, he swung off and flew home, silent, save for the one remark, "That was quite a picture of war. I hope you guys appreciated it."

Art Rogers recalled another memorable mission flown by Lark Martin. This was the January 23 [1943] two-plane reconnaissance to search for the lost planes of Lts. McMurria and Regan (pages 164-5):

> Martin volunteered to lead an armed reconnaissance flight consisting of two airplanes which were to search for one of our planes lost in the Wewak area. Upon completion of his search he sighted a five-ship convoy approaching Wewak with 18 to 20 Zeros as protection. He proceeded to drop his bombs on the five-ship convoy while being engaged by the entire force of the enemy aircraft. After dropping the bombs, a running fight ensued that lasted for an hour and forty-five minutes.
>
> When Martin's tail turret was shot out, he dove his plane down to 25 to 50 feet over the water, which forced the attacking airplanes to make their attacks from above, so his top turret and waist guns could defend the rear of his airplane. His top turret operator shot down two of the enemy Zeros, and his other gunners divided two more definites with three probables.
>
> When his plane "Mission Belle" returned to our base she had over 400 holes in her. One engine was completely out while two others were running under reduced power. Her gas tanks were leaking, radio shot out, wingtip, ailerons, flap cables, and eight separate control cables in the plane had been damaged. Five separate bullet holes had penetrated his left tire and upon landing his right tire blew out.

Charles Rawlings also wrote of this mission, providing more details:

Lark's was the second ship in a two-plane recco, hunting for a missing bomber down on the sea somewhere off Wewak on the northern New Guinea coast. While flying a hunting grid, a five-ship convoy was sighted and reported. The two bombers shadowed the convoy and hunted for the missing plane at the same time. Eighteen Zeros came out of Wewak. Lark immediately closed with them. As bitter a fight as MacArthur's air had ever seen followed. The Zeros made pass after pass, coming in from forward, on the tail and against both beams. Lark's gunners got four, and the Zeros drew off, cooled their singed wings and talked it over.

Lark claims he knew what they were talking about—a swarming from all sides, including top and bottom—and he dived for the sea and leveled off at fifty feet, making his plane's tender belly safe. The Zeros, as mad as hornets now, buzzed into him from above, and for one hour and forty-five minutes the blazing fight, never more than 200 feet off the sea, went on. It ended when the Zeros broke off, and just in time for Lark. He was down to the very last of his ammunition. The machine gun shells were easier to count than the injuries Mission Belle, his plane, had suffered. They listed one engine shot completely out; two badly damaged, but faltering on; the right tire torn wide open; the hydraulic system punctured and empty of fluid; both ailerons damaged; all fuel tanks hit; radio and interphone communications gone; four crewmen wounded and 400 machine-gun and 20-mm holes in Mission Belle's bones and skin.

All that would have remained to any normal pilot after the tabulation of such a list would have been the first set-down strip possible. Not for the Lark. He hoisted up a few inches in his pilot's seat and took a look at the two limping engines, and decided that one or the other would last long enough. He sent Bomicino, himself wounded in one arm, to check the other wounded.

"See if they're bleeding slow enough to last an hour and thirty minutes," he said. "If they are, I'll get them home."

He brought Mission Belle over the Owen Stanleys, most of the way on two engines. The third lasted just long enough to give him his climb, and he managed to hold just enough of that never-to-be-regained altitude to clear the peaks.

I met him when he rolled to a brakeless, bumping stop on Ward's Drome, Moresby. You could smell Mission Belle from far away; a pungent, hot reek of hydraulic fluid, high-octane gasoline, scorched rubber and blood. She herself seemed to be dripping blood as her bomb bay doors squeaked open and the hydraulic fluid, sloshing about there tinted with a crimson dye to make leaks in the system more easily noticeable, emptied in a big, dark-red puddle on the strip.

The Lark swung out last, squinted down the strip to make sure the ambulances were coming, and then sauntered over to where I stood. He tugged his hat—he always wore a very greasy green G. I. fatigue hat—over his eye in a characteristic gesture and scratched the back of his head.

"How'd you know I was in trouble?" he asked.

"When I saw you circling with landing lights, I knew it was nothing trivial," I said. "What's the story?"

"Oh-h-h," he said. "Lot of shootin'! Lot of shootin'! Nothin' much to it, but a long shootin' fight."

Col. Rogers wrote:

> The entire crew was approaching 300 hours of combat, and the Squadron flight surgeon informed me that Martin's crew as a whole were verging on a serious case of flying fatigue... I called Martin in and had a friendly talk with him, and told him that he and his crew had done enough and I was ready to release them to return to the States.
>
> He stated that he knew the crew was jittery, but unless I ordered him back to the States he had rather stay on a little longer, and insisted I give him a crew to replace his old one. He said he would have a talk with his crew to find out if they wanted to make the mission scheduled for Wewak the next day, to give the Japs something to remember them by. After contacting his crew, he called me back and informed me that his crew was eager to make one more mission before they went home.
>
> The raid on Wewak came just after our first daylight attacks on Rabaul, and top cover was furnished by our Lightnings [P-38 fighters]. Captain Martin was leading the number two element of a formation of six planes led by his Squadron Commander, Maj. Dale Thornhill. The formation was intercepted by 30 enemy fighters, and since our fighters were fully engaged by another formation of the enemy, Maj. Thornhill's squadron was forced to take the brunt of the attack. As the bombs were released, two of his planes had lost one engine each, while his third plane had lost one engine with another smoking and had gotten out of formation. The Japs were concentrating on these three airplanes.
>
> Captain Martin, who was flying in the slot, would fly from one to the other of the two damaged planes trying to stay in formation, depending upon the plane that needed his help the most. Maj. Thornhill, in a desperate effort to prevent the destruction of the plane that had gotten out of formation, turned the other planes over to Martin and went back and proceeded to fly directly over the top of the damaged plane so that all attacks were brought against him instead of his damaged wingman.

> He escorted this damaged plane and destroyed six attacking Zeros until the Jap fighters broke off the engagement. He remained with the crippled plane in an effort to get it back to one of our emergency fields, but about 50 miles out of Wewak eight enemy fighters made a surprise attack, setting fire to the helpless airplane, and after all of Dale's protection there was nothing he could do as the plane nosed over and headed for the ground. He saw six men hit the silk from the flaming plane, but his last vision of the scene was that of the eight Zeros strafing these six men as they floated helplessly to the ground.

The bomber that was shot down was named "Pete the Carrier," piloted by 1st Lt. Alexander F. North, and the date was August 29, 1943. During the fighter attack a fire started in the bomb bay that got out of control and the crew had no choice but to bail out. The copilot, Lt. Leroy Hooper, was last seen slumped over in his seat unconscious as the plane went down. Six or possibly seven parachutes were seen in the wake of the falling bomber. The plane turned into a ball of fire before it hit the ground. What happened to any of the men who may have made it to the ground alive will never be known, for they were never heard from again.*[3] The wreckage of "Pete the Carrier" has not yet been found. The men who died as a result of the loss of this plane were:

> 1st Lt. Alexander F. North, pilot, from California
> 1st Lt. Leroy S. Hooper, copilot, from California
> 2nd Lt. Lawrence D. Jacoby, navigator, from Ohio
> 2nd Lt. Daniel B. Owen, Jr., bombardier, from Virginia
> T/Sgt. John J. Kenny, flight engineer, from California
> T/Sgt. Robert W. Norris, radioman, from Indiana
> S/Sgt. James F. Jaynes, gunner, from Michigan
> S/Sgt. Rowland M. Lewis, Jr., gunner, from New York
> S/Sgt. Joseph J. Maggio, Jr., gunner, from California
> S/Sgt. John Yalch, gunner, from Pennsylvania

Col. Rogers continued:

> In the meantime Martin had successfully defended his crippled planes and had broken off their [the Zeros'] attack. While doing this, a 20mm shell from a Jap fighter exploded in the waist of his airplane, igniting a flare in the racks and shooting out his

---

*A Japanese radio broadcast later stated that two of the men who bailed out, 2nd Lt. Daniel Owen, the crew's bombardier, and T/Sgt. Robert Norris, the radio operator, were prisoners, and their families were notified, but after the war no trace of them or the other men was ever found. It was the same old story of Americans being captured by the Japanese and killed.

hydraulic system. Hydraulic fluid was leaking all over the plane, and with the flare burning, the oil was sure to catch fire unless it could be gotten rid of. Sergeant [Donald] Crandall, a big redheaded waist gunner, with his bare hands grabbed the blazing flare and kicked a hole through the camera door and tossed the flare out. While doing this he received machine-gun wounds in his leg and arm from an oncoming pursuit plane. Even though he was wounded, and his hands severely burned, he proceeded to shoot down another enemy airplane.

Five of Maj. Thornhill's six airplanes arrived at the field shot full of holes and with many wounded men aboard. The Japs had suffered from this formation twelve definite [i.e. planes definitely shot down] and five probables while the entire Group had scored 42 definites and 15 probables. This was one of the bloodiest fights our Group had ever experienced. I congratulated Thornhill, Martin, and their crews on their bravery and ability. I told Martin that he and his crew would be grounded until orders were issued for their return home.

The next day Martin came to my hut and insisted that he was in perfect health, and he wanted a new crew so he could stay on and fight the Japs. I talked to "Sandy" ["Doc" Sanderson] again about his condition, and we were both of the opinion that Martin showed no signs of flying fatigue, and since I considered him excellent material for a squadron commander, I told Martin he could stay on, if that was what he wanted, and that I hoped to give him a squadron to command. However, I did not lift the grounding order that I had issued, since I felt that he should have at least a couple of weeks' rest.

During this two-week period a non-combat pilot was required by his squadron to make a routine test flight to check out one of the planes. As usual, even though grounded for combat duty, Martin volunteered for the flight. What happened on this flight no one will ever know, since all that was ever found of the plane was a tire and wheel that floated up on the beach two days later.

The night before this tragedy Martin had come to my hut for a friendly chat. He told me of his family, and took from his pocket a wallet and proudly exhibited the picture of a pretty girl that he said he intended to marry when he returned home.

Lark Martin's last flight was on Sept. 3, 1943. Martin had also shown pictures of his girl to Charles Rawlings, who remembered:

He had trained with the Canadians before we entered the war, and his girl lived in Ottawa. He loved her very much, and we talked about her... She was a serious, quiet sort of girl, he said, and her pictures looked it. He had two portraits of her that he carried in his back-pocket billfold. One showed a completely self respecting, almost prim face. The other was a snapshot of her trying to pose

> seductively in a bathing suit. It was an abashed and very self-conscious attempt at the pin-up abandon so popular in those days. It always made Lark chuckle.
>
> "She tried to get in the groove, just to please me," he said. "I pretended I thought it was hot stuff, and that's all that mattered to her. That's what is so much fun about this babe. Life's going to be plenty of fun with her. She's OK for me. I'm a screw-up, and she's as steady as porridge, but she kids along with me. I wouldn't let her get hurt for a million dollars. Marry her and take her back to Georgia! I like the sound of that."

The historian of the Jolly Rogers wrote that Martin took a couple of fighter plane pilots with him on his last flight. He was known to let his friends take turns flying the B-24 on such flights, and something may have gone wrong if he did so on this one, or he may have just tried to show the fighter pilots that a four-engine plane could be flown like a fighter, but had not gotten away with it this time. Sadly, the old pilot's adage that "there are no old, bold pilots" was proven true yet again. Col. Rogers wrote of Martin's loss:

> Martin's rugged crew took his death very hard, and two days after the accident they came to my tent to tell me goodbye. The price of war showed on their faces as they bade me farewell. I kept thinking that Martin should have been on his way home with them.

Charles Rawlings wrote of Capt. Lark Martin's last flight:

> His hunger for the sky was what carried him up that last time. He had been grounded for a few days, for no other reason than that the unit's flight surgeon felt that he had been flying too steadily and he needed a rest—or his crew needed one. But there was no rest for the Lark on the dull surface of the earth... Five o'clock came, and he did not come back. At seven o'clock, after Operations had checked all the emergency fields and the 'dromes, the camp stilled in stunned silence. The Lark was down—somewhere—somehow. And because it was Lark, everyone knew that he was not down with some trivial injury and waiting on a shoal or an island beach for rescue. The Lark had spun in. He was gone.

The wreckage of the bomber that Martin flew on his last flight has never been found, and the cause of his disappearance was never determined. Lark Martin had told Rawlings that he wouldn't let his girl get hurt "for a million dollars," and then he hurt her in the worst possible way by continuing to "brush death's whiskers" until the odds came due. Back in Ottawa, she got the word that Martin would not be coming home, and that no one knew what had happened to him. She would never know anything more for the rest of her life.

CHAPTER THIRTY

THE DRIVE ON SALAMAUA AND LAE

After annihilating the Japanese at Buna in January of 1943, the Allies (Australian and American troops) advanced north up the New Guinea coast in a drive on the Japanese-held towns of Salamaua and Lae (Map 30-1, opposite). Both were former gold mining towns that had been frequented by Australian gold prospectors and adventurers before the war, and each possessed its own small airfield that had been built for flying in supplies from Australia to nearby gold mines.* Partly because of its airfield, Lae had been captured by the Japanese in the spring of 1942, during their spree of conquest in the Pacific following the attack on Pearl Harbor, and it had then become a Japanese airbase from which they bombed Port Moresby and parts of the northern coast of Australia.

Salamaua was (and still is) 145 miles up the coastline from Buna, and Lae is twenty miles beyond Salamaua. The pretty and prosperous little Australian town and port of Salamaua had been built on a narrow, curving, sandy neck of land jutting out from the New Guinea mainland (see photo on page 300) and contained a hotel and many private homes with tennis courts and jetties for pleasure boats. Salamaua had become an administrative center as well as a docking place for ships coming up from Australia, bringing in gold miners and supplies for the mines. The owners of Salamaua's homes and businesses had fled at the approach of the Japanese in March of 1942. The Japanese had taken over the town and were using it for a headquarters.

As had happened to the fine, orderly, cosmopolitan community of Rabaul on New Britain, the occupation of Salamaua by the Japanese made it necessary for the Americans to destroy it in order to drive them out of it, and the bombing by the Jolly Rogers did much of the destruction. That spring [1943], Gen. MacArthur began a brilliant series of flanking movements to confuse and disorganize the Japanese in the Salamaua-Lae area. On June 30th American

---

*The town of Lae had achieved brief worldwide fame seven years before as the last place the famous woman flier Amelia Earhart was seen alive. She and her navigator Fred Noonan had taken off from Lae's airfield on July 2, 1937 on one of the final legs of their highly publicized trip to circle the globe by air on a 29,000-mile equatorial route. After they took off from Lae in their twin-engine Lockheed Electra, the plane simply vanished into the vastness of the Pacific Ocean. To this day no one knows what happened to them.

30. THE DRIVE ON SALAMAUA AND LAE 289

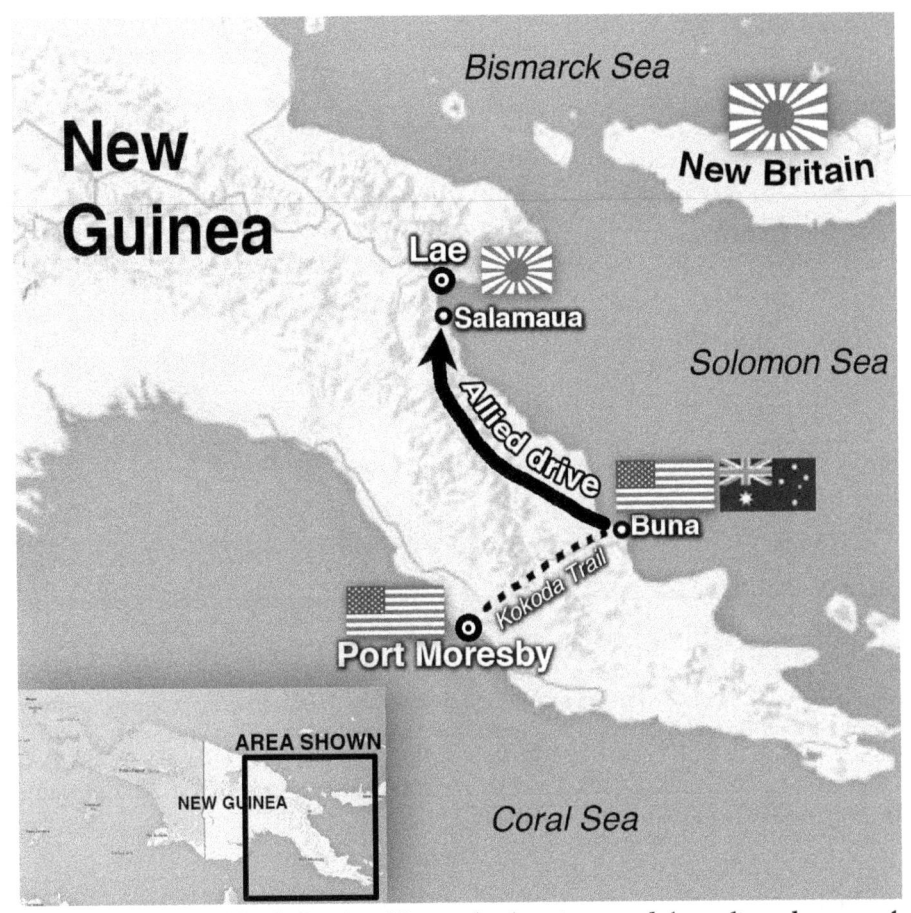

Map 30-1. After the bloody Battle of Buna, the Americans and Australians drove north (black arrow) up the coast through the jungles to take Salamaua and Lae. The Jolly Rogers, flying out of Port Moresby, bombed Japanese positions ahead of them all the way.

troops landed south of Salamaua at Nassau Bay and drove inland to join forces with the Australians coming across the mountains from Wau, and together they advanced on Salamaua.

The Komiatum Ridge

As Australian and American troops battled their way through the jungle toward Salamaua from the southeast, they ran smack up against a tall, steep-sided ridge that stood like a wall between them and the town, and the town's airfield. The airfield that had once been a landing place for cargo planes bringing in gold mining equipment from Australia was now a Japanese airbase, though it had recently been abandoned under American air attacks.

IT WASN'T SO JOLLY

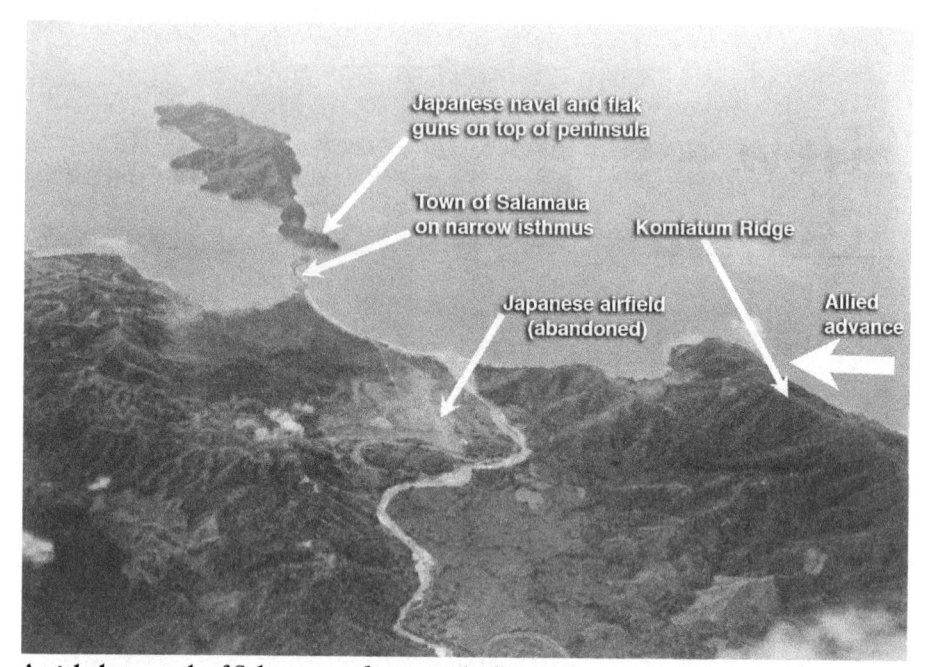

Aerial photograph of Salamaua and vicinity, looking east out to sea from the New Guinea mainland (north is to the left). The Allies were battling their way toward Salamaua from the right (south) in this picture. The Australian colonial town of Salamaua was built on the narrow spit of land separating the mainland from an offshore peninsula. The narrow, steep-sided Komiatum ridge, where the Japanese dug in for a last-ditch stand, and which the Jolly Rogers bombed heavily, is at right.

This natural wall was the Komiatum Ridge, about twelve miles southeast of Salamaua, which rises nearly straight up from the seashore and runs inland for several miles. The Japanese had dug in strongly along the narrow top of this ridge in a determined, last-ditch effort to defend Salamaua at their backs. The top of the ridge was about 400 feet wide at its widest, and from their dugouts and trenches the Japanese were shooting downward and dropping mortar shells onto the Allies trying to battle their way up the steep slope toward them. It was an attacker's nightmare: fighting uphill toward an entrenched enemy, and everything favored the Japanese defenders.

General Kenney decided that his bombers could turn the tide—he would simply bomb and strafe the Japanese off the ridge. Accordingly, Col. Rogers led the Jolly Rogers in several Group missions against the knife-edged spine in August of 1943, and on most of these strikes they used thousand-pound bombs, trying to demolish the Japanese dugouts and trenches. The bombardiers had to be very careful, of course, to place their bombs exactly on top of the ridge, or on its north (Japanese occupied) slope, so as not to hit the Allied troops who were trying to battle their way up the south face. The now-experienced bom-

30. THE DRIVE ON SALAMAUA AND LAE 291

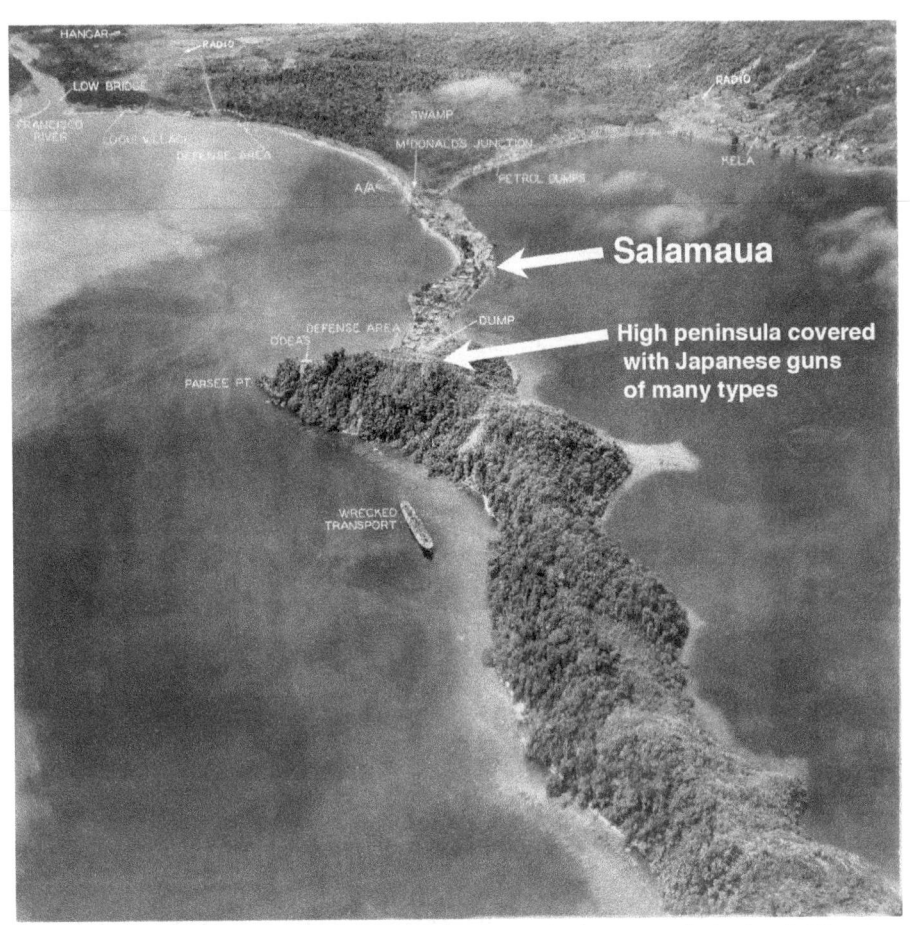

Another aerial photo of Salamaua, looking from the sea toward the land. This is a U. S. military intelligence photo of Japanese-held Salamaua, with the tidy little town undamaged as yet. The Jolly Rogers would soon bomb the Japanese out of the town, but it would be destroyed in the process. The Japanese on the high, jungle-covered peninsula adjacent to the town held out until the Jolly Rogers bombed them out of existence.

bardiers of the Jolly Rogers were equal to the task, and there was not a single Allied ground casualty during the bombing campaign. Rogers wrote:

> Day in and day out we bombed Komiatum Ridge, until there was not a tree left standing. In fact, the bombing was so intense that it caused huge landslides which covered up many large Jap dugouts with thousands of tons of dirt.

Between the air strikes of the Jolly Rogers, General Kenney sent in his B-25 strafer/bombers, in the same one-two punch he was using against Japanese airfields, and had used with such devastating effect on Japanese ships in the Battle of the Bismarck Sea. With the trees all blown off the top of the ridge by the bombs of the Jolly Rogers, the strafers had a clear view of the Japanese fortifications.

The B-25s flew in single file down the length of the narrow ridge top, just a few feet above the ground, firing the multiple machine guns that "Pappy" Gunn had installed in their noses, and dropping smaller (300-pound) bombs on the Japanese trenches and fortifications at close range.

The American and Australian troops who had been halted on the south face of the ridge were warned to take cover whenever either the Jolly Rogers' B-24s or the B-25s went to work on the Japanese positions above them. Each day the infantrymen were

Capt. Garrett E. Middlebrook of Springtown, Texas in the cockpit of his B-25 strafer/bomber.

informed by radio when the bombing would begin, and when it was over they were signaled by a red flare fired from the last bomber.

In streaking down the spine of the ridge on his low-level attacks, flying only 20 feet above the ground at 280 mph, B-25 pilot Capt. Garrett Middlebrook (pictured above) found himself looking straight into the faces of the Japanese in the trenches and dugouts he was shooting up and bombing. The foolish Japanese had not known, or had disregarded, an all-important lesson of trench warfare learned by the Allies and Germans during World War One: never build trenches in long straight lines.

This is why aerial photographs of First World War trench systems look like miles of zig-zags or crenelations running across the landscape. All those angles in the trenches were put there to prevent exactly what Middlebrook and his fellow strafer/bombers were doing: firing straight down the trenches in enfilade, from one end to the other, with nothing to stop their bullets. They killed Japanese by the hundreds. Middlebrook wrote:

> The enemy trenches were directly astride the ridge. I was surprised that they were so straight. . . Neither did I expect that I would be able to enfilade the trenches with my fire. Thus when I was lined up,

30. THE DRIVE ON SALAMAUA AND LAE

I did not weave and turn as usual. Instead I held my fire exactly down the trenches... I saw scores of crouching enemy soldiers in the trenches as I dove lower on my strafing pass. Surely none of them could have lived.[1]

After watching the strafing runs of the other B-25s in his squadron, Middlebrook wrote in his diary:

> The machine-gun fire which erupted from each plane boggled my mind... Donegan and his crew gave us a spectacular show since all his bombs landed directly on target, and upon exploding moved boulders and launched human bodies high into the air before the concussions caused the bodies themselves to disintegrate. He followed the entire length of the trenches with such accuracy that I thought he might have had a track to guide him. About midway, the sides of the trenches had caved in causing the enemy troops to be exposed. His machine-gun fire scattered bodies in all directions, some rolling off the ridge and downhill toward our troops...
>
> The one dugout that I bombed had . . . completely caved in, thereby entombing all the enemy soldiers occupying it... I wondered how a Jap, even had he escaped death or bodily injury, could have fought, because the exploding bombs surely would have left him deaf and senseless.[2]

Capt. Middlebrook (squatting at lower left) and other pilots of his 405th Tactical Bombardment Squadron in front of one of their famous "Green Dragon" B-25 strafer/bombers. The planes had four 50-caliber guns in the nose plus two on each side of the fuselage below the cockpit, for a total of eight forward-firing guns (and if the top turret gunner pointed his twin guns forward there were ten). The pilot operated the fixed guns while the copilot dropped the bombs, often para-frags (see photo of such a drop on p. 312).

Middlebrook was quite right about the effects of bomb concussion on the Japanese troops. Art Rogers received intelligence reports stating that the Jolly Rogers' bombs were having exactly that effect:

A Jolly Rogers B-24 saturates the town of Salamaua with bombs. At upper right in this photo is the peninsula atop which sat many flak guns that the Jolly Rogers also bombed.

A Jolly Rogers Bomber named "Joltin' Janie" is seen just after bombing Japanese positions along the coastline near Salamaua (note smoke rising). The town of Salamaua was built on the narrow, curving neck of land at the upper left of the picture. The Japanese airfield can be seen beneath the bomber, and the Komiatum Ridge that the Jolly Rogers bombed so heavily is at right (just in front of the bomber's nose).

30. THE DRIVE ON SALAMAUA AND LAE

Seen in the air in the previous photo, this was "Joltin' Janie" of the Jolly Rogers' 321st Squadron on the ground between missions. The rabbit painted on the nose was inspired by the Walt Disney animal character "Thumper" in the 1942 animated movie *Bambi*.

> My intelligence officer [Col. Rogers wrote] brought me a report stating that many Jap prisoners were taken alive in these dugouts with blood and pus oozing from their ears, due to busted eardrums from the tremendous concussion caused by our bombs. These Japs just walked around in circles, because they no longer had any equilibrium. By this time there was no question by the line officers as to the effectiveness of our bombing, since Radio Tokyo had begun to scream about inhumane bombing of their troops. This was considered a good sign by our troops, since [usually] the Japs would insist to the last that they were being victorious in every engagement whether on land, sea, or air.

Finally, after about ten days of bombing by both the heavy and medium bombers, in conjunction with determined attacks by the Allied ground troops, the Japanese positions atop the Komiatum Ridge were overrun and captured by the Allies. The Japanese who remained alive retreated down the north slope of the ridge toward their airfield and Salamaua.

Art Rogers wrote:

> After taking the valley and the ridge, our troops came out into a flatland only a few miles from Salamaua [next to the airfield in the photo at left]. The Japs were still in force, barring their approach, and with the assistance of some heavy naval guns which were emplaced on a high peninsula that jutted out from the town of Salamaua, were continuing to hold our troops at bay. I was called into Bomber Headquarters and told that these naval guns must be knocked out, in addition to many ack-ack and artillery guns.

As seen in the aerial photographs (pages 290-1), the curving sandspit of Salamaua ran out to a high, jungle-covered peninsula on which the Japanese had mounted guns of all types, as Rogers noted. Kenney then went to work on these defenses, too.

Garrett Middlebrook flew his B-25 strafer/bomber down the Salamaua isthmus straight at this jungle-covered mound, shooting and bombing it as he had done on the Komiatum Ridge. This time, however, he was unlucky and one of the enemy guns shot out his right engine, forcing him to fly south down the coast to the nearest Allied airfield, Dobodura (next to Buna village), on one engine where he landed safely. The Jolly Rogers then went to work on the peninsula and destroyed every gun on it. They also wrecked the town.

> **We started an all-out effort [Rogers wrote], and after four days of bombing not an ack-ack gun fired at us and not a building was left standing in Salamaua. Since the Bismarck Sea battle the Jap garrisons at Lae and Salamaua had not received any supplies of any kind, and after Salamaua was taken our troops found that the Japs were practically on a starvation diet. I was sure at this time, and it was later proved to be so, that the reason Salamaua was able to offer such a tremendous resistance, even though not receiving any reinforcements or supplies from New Britain, was that the garrison at Lae was being drained of its guns, ammunition, manpower and food to prevent the breakthrough at Salamaua. This was good strategy ... because the Japs knew that if our troops took Salamaua we could start a drive up the coast with an added advantage of being able to supply our troops by water. This would make the Jap position untenable at Lae, since it was impossible for them to get any reinforcements.**

This was exactly General MacArthur's strategy, in fact: to cause the Japanese to send troop reinforcements down from Lae, a larger town and the main Allied objective, to defend the less strategic Salamaua. MacArthur wanted Lae, its harbor and airfield, and the Markham River valley behind it. The village of Nadzab, 20 miles up the river valley from Lae, was on a flat grassy plain that appeared to be an ideal location to build a heavy bomber base, and of course it was the four-engine bombers that were MacArthur's main offensive weapon, and he was constantly striving to move them forward.

His plan worked brilliantly; the Japanese sent so many troops down from Lae to defend Salamaua that they left only 2,500 to hold Lae, while over 8,000 Japanese dug in around Salamaua, mostly on the Komiatum Ridge.

An Australian infantryman's perspective

One of the soldiers battling his way through the jungles toward Salamaua was an Australian private named Peter Pinney. In his diary Pinney described the feelings of many Australian soldiers toward the Japanese. He had seen starving Japanese soldiers resort to cannibalism, eating the corpses of Australian dead on the battlefields, and had witnessed their brutality and savagery toward Allied captives and New Guinea natives alike.

Like Art Rogers and other members of the U. S. Army Air Corps who had observed Japanese atrocities such as shooting helpless men in parachutes or floating in life rafts, Pinney and his fellow soldiers had come to think of the Japanese as less than human and more like vicious animals. Pinney also raged at the senseless waste of life caused by this supremely evil enemy:

> When one of your mates gets knocked [i. e. knocked off— killed] you don't even want to talk about it. You want to remember him in private. But you can hardly see the memories for the rage. It's such unforgivable waste. Who are these rotten mongrels, these jabbering Japs, who come all the way down from Japan by way of burning cities and murdering men and ravaging women and kids, to shoot blokes who've never had a thought of homicide or conquest in their lives?[3]
>
> If Japs are genuinely human, and not some form of mammalian disaster, history still may judge our fight as just, but it may consider our attitudes as malign, vindictive and unfeeling. There is a quality of casual, inanely grinning genocide in the attitude of many of us towards the wretched Japs. Men who, only a year or two before, would have grieved if they had killed a sparrow with an air gun, now shoot or knife or boobytrap these Sons of Heaven with as little compunction as they would crush a roach. . .[4]
>
> They're not fair dinkum humans. . . I don't have to tell you what they do with corpses . . . and buggering piccaninnies to death. They're garbage. Not even the worst animals act like that. They're depraved.[5]

Like General Kenney watching the Japanese high command's bungling of air tactics, Pinney and his Australian comrades fighting in the jungles came to see the Emperor's warriors as practically incompetent unless backed by overwhelming numbers, or strongly dug into defensive positions such as the Komiatum Ridge. Pinney continued:

> A man can't help wondering what kind of peanuts these Orientals are. They can't shoot, they're scared of the dark, they foul their own quarters, and they haven't got the nose of a good sheepdog. They're no good in the scrub, not much better in the open, and seem to do everything arse-about-pig. . .[6] The Japs up here have a woodpecker and light Nambus [machine-guns], but they usually blaze away pretty much at random with the heavier gun and depend on their obliging ancestral spirits to guide the

bullets where they should go. And the Nambus are patterned after a Czech machine-gun, but the Nip is too proud to admit the bipods are not suited to men of small stature, with the result that when they lie prone behind the lighter gun they nearly always fire too high. As you get closer, it gets more dangerous. . .[7]

The way they know this area, after being here so long, they could be causing us merry hell. . . Praise the Lord we're fighting bunnies, not the Huns.[8]

Funny: one of the risks a man runs in this hillbilly feud, at times, is forgetting to be scared. Bully or not we're better fed, better armed, and just plain better fighters than these Japanese, but you have to try and remember to be scared. . . The Nips fire a lot of ammunition, and a bullet is still a bullet, no matter who fires it and if most of them don't even come close, it only takes one to end your game.[9]

You wonder just how much these Japs encountered during their Asian invasion. They have a long history now of ravaging crowded cities and putting peasant armies to flight. . . But nothing they've done so far has worked in the Wau-Salamaua campaign. Their mystique has been shot to hell. They're fine when they send in troops who are all flushed with recent victories, experienced and confident, backed by mortars and machine-gun fire—and by sheer weight of numbers overwhelm raw troops.[10]

It's years since these Nips left Japan; crissakes, they must be homesick! It's said they believe they're already in Australia, that Salamaua is on the Queensland coast. Do they figure these fever-rotten lowlands are worth the crust? Do they want to bring their wife and kids into these miserable, wet, gloomy, stinking bloody hills? This is the kind of place where Happiness goes to die.[11]

Yesterday afternoon, after we'd arrived at Grasstree Camp, thirty-four of their bombers and thirty Zeros bombed and strafed their own troops the length of Salamaua, from the river mouth to Kela Hill. They must have witchetty grubs for brains. Where are these incredible supermen we've heard so much about? . . . Just imagine, though, if we were fighting Germans. If those planes yesterday had been Stukas. For crissakes, there'd be hardly one of us left alive.[12]

We're standing on the very last chunk of dirt that separates the Japs from Australia. If they get New Guinea, there's no barrier left. The fence is down. We're stuffed. You've got a mob of rabid mongrels swarming ashore with no one to stop them because the AIF [Australian Imperial Forces] will all be dead, and what happens to our women, and our kids, is a repetition of Nanking, and Hongkong, and Singapore." [13]

30. THE DRIVE ON SALAMAUA AND LAE

On September 11, 1943, the Allies finally entered what was left of Salamaua.

After the Pearl Harbor attack, as the Japanese juggernaut had rolled south in 1942, seemingly invincible, the fear that Australia's troops in New Guinea would be overwhelmed by superior numbers of Japanese, followed by a Japanese invasion of Australia, had been in the minds of Australian civilians and soldiers alike. Britain, Australia's mother country, was too preoccupied with Hitler and the war in Europe to provide any help to its commonwealth on the other side of the world. The influx of American men and arms into Australia to oppose the Japanese had produced a great feeling of relief and gratitude among the Australians, and it showed in how well Americans were treated in Australia during (and after) the war.

The ground fighting in the Salamaua area, which took place between April and September of 1943, cost the Australians around 1,100 casualties including about 350 killed, and the Americans (the 162nd Regimental Combat Team) had 80 killed and nearly 400 wounded. As usual in the Pacific war, the Japanese fared far worse: over 2,700 killed and 5,300 wounded. Many of the Japanese battle casualties were caused by the bombs dropped on them by the Jolly Rogers, and Allied troop losses would certainly have been far greater without General Kenney's heavy and medium bombers paving the way for them by obliterating Japanese strongholds.

On 11 September, 1943, the Australians finally walked into the ruins of Salamaua (photo above). Allied attention now turned to Lae, the main objective, twenty miles further up the coast (Map 30-1 on page 289).

Today the curved sandspit at Salamaua has a new town built upon it, and visitors can hike from the town up onto the adjacent peninsula to examine the Japanese artillery rusting in the jungle, the gun barrels still pointed in the direction of the Allied advance of 1943. A half-dozen miles to the southeast,

Prewar Salamaua was a pleasant little Australian colonial town and port built on a curving isthmus jutting out from mainland New Guinea. In the 1920s and 30s it was a supply center for gold miners operating in the mountains on the mainland (visible in the distance). Note the tennis court at center right. Screen actor Errol Flynn, the hero of many Hollywood adventure movies of the 1930s and later lived here for a time in his youth. The Japanese seized the town in April of 1942.

30. THE DRIVE ON SALAMAUA AND LAE

By the time the Jolly Rogers bombed the Japanese out of Salamaua in September of 1943, there was little left standing on the sandy isthmus. The Komiatum Ridge is in the far hazy background.

across the swamp that now covers the old airfield, and beyond the Francisco river that contributes its water to the swamp, lies the Komiatum Ridge. There are no roads into the area, and it is as wild a jungle as it was before the war.

For that reason almost no one goes there today, and it is a forgotten battlefield. Anyone who tried to hike to the ridge from Salamaua might contract malaria or worse from mosquito bites on the way, in the swamp. But if anyone did succeed in hiking to the ridge, climbed it, and walked along the ridge top among the large depressions that were once craters created by Jolly Rogers 1,000-pound bombs, before their edges were softened by over 70 years of heavy rains, he would be walking amid a vast graveyard of Japanese troops, many still entombed in their collapsed dugouts beneath his feet—the now-forgotten dead of Imperial Japan.

Chapter Thirty-One

WEWAK ATTACKED, LAE AND NADZAB CAPTURED

During the summer of 1943, photos taken by reconnaissance planes in the vicinity of Lae had shown that the Markham River valley, 20 miles northwest of Lae, near a village called Nadzab (see map, opposite page), had a wide, flat area that was largely free of jungle that would be a good location for a large airbase, on the order of Port Moresby. In fact, much of the valley was covered by only tall kunai grass that could easily be burned off or bulldozed away. The soil was river gravel, part of an old riverbed, which would make a good foundation for runways that could support heavy bombers. The Nadzab area was under Japanese control, but most of the Japanese troops had gone downriver to the defense of Lae.

Kenney and MacArthur together devised a plan for the seizure of the Nadzab area by American paratroopers, in conjunction with the capture of Lae by Australian ground forces. However, reconnaissance photos of Wewak taken on August 16 showed that the Japanese had sent a large number of bombers and fighter planes down from Japan through the Philippines to the four airfields of their Wewak airbase, only 300 miles to the northwest of Nadzab. The photos showed 110 aircraft at Boram, mostly bombers, 35 new fighters at Wewak Central, 60 fighters and bombers at Dagua, and 25 fighters at But, for a total of 230 planes. This was a force to be reckoned with.

The Japanese were obviously planning an air offensive against the Allies, and before any operation to capture Nadzab or Lae could be considered, the threat of these planes would have to be eliminated. Looking at reconnaissance photos on the afternoon of August 16 [1943], General Kenney decided that the time was perfect to catch all these Japanese airplanes sitting on the ground and destroy them in a preemptive strike. He quickly laid a plan for the biggest air strike on the Japanese in the Southwest Pacific since the Battle of the Bismarck Sea, to be carried out immediately, beginning before dawn the next morning.

The Jolly Rogers lead the attack on Wewak

Again the heavy bombers would lead the way, and the Jolly Rogers and Ken's Men were alerted for a mission that same night. Col. Art Rogers got the plan from V Bomber Command and briefed all his squadron leaders, who in turn briefed their crews. Everyone geared up to go. The Jolly Rogers would

31. WEWAK ATTACKED, LAE AND NADZAB CAPTURED 303

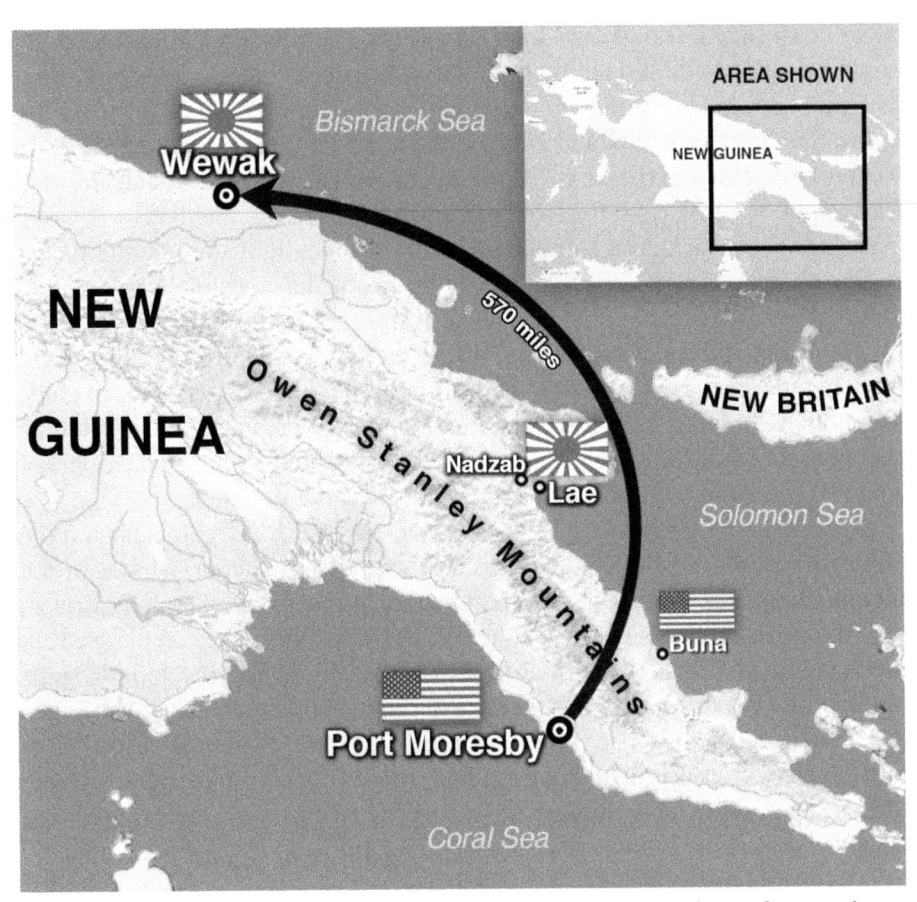

Map 31-1. The route flown by the Jolly Rogers and Ken's Men in the predawn strike on the Japanese airfields at Wewak, 17 August, 1943. The bombers crossed the mountains northeast of Port Moresby and then flew up the coast to Wewak.

put up twenty-five B-24s and Ken's Men would contribute twelve B-17s and twelve B-24s. The heavies would hit the Wewak airfields in the darkness of the early-morning hours, and then the B-25 strafer/bombers of the 38th Bomb Group, fifty-eight of them, would follow up just after dawn, escorted by every long-range fighter plane available.

The thunder of big engines could be heard that night from Jackson and Ward's fields at Port Moresby as the 49 heavy bombers cranked up, lined up, and took off. Taking off at three or four minute intervals, it took three hours for all of them to get into the air. It was a brightly moonlit night with few clouds, so the planes were visible to each other and able to form up in loose formations. Although Wewak was 480 miles to the northwest in a direct line, the bombers first flew north through the Kokoda Pass until they reached the north coast of the island, and then turned left (northwest) and followed the coastline up to Wewak (see map on previous page). The divergence from a straight course added ninety miles to the trip but minimized the flying over the Owen Stanley Mountains and avoided the mountain peaks. One of the Jolly Rogers bombers turned back to Port Moresby with mechanical trouble, leaving forty-eight bombers from the two heavy bomb groups droning their way up to Wewak in loose squadron formations, with the moonlight shimmering on the Pacific Ocean on their right, and the blackness of the coastline and jungle to their left.

The lead bombers of each squadron carried hundreds of four-pound incendiary bombs that it was hoped would start fires on the Wewak airfields to guide in following bombers, a tactic that Allied bombers were using while bombing the cities of Hitler's Europe in darkness. Following bombers carried clusters of small fragmentation bombs intended to destroy parked aircraft.

Around 1 AM, after nearly four hours of flying, the navigators aboard the bombers recognized the distinctive shape of the coastline at Wewak in the moonlight and the leading planes went into their bomb runs. The Jolly Rogers would make their drops from 6,500 feet. One of the first planes on the scene at the Boram and Wewak Central airfields was "Moby Dick," the Jolly Rogers' plane of the 320th Squadron with the grinning shark's mouth that had given the squadron its name. The pilot, Lt. Lionel B. Potter, found the scene below him deceptively peaceful and quiet at first, with no lights or any other signs of life on the ground. This illusion was dispelled when three searchlights were switched on below, followed shortly by five more, and the sky was suddenly filled with searchlight beams. Then the Japanese flak guns opened up, and their aim was good.

While "Moby Dick" rocked and bounced from near flak misses, the bombardier reported over the intercom that the searchlights were blinding him and he couldn't see anything through his bombsight. Lt. Potter replied that he would call the drop himself. Just as what he recalled as "a beautiful string" of tracers from an automatic cannon arced past the bomber's nose, he called for the bomb release, and his load of fragmentation bombs went tumbling down onto the Japanese field and its parked planes below.[1]

Capt. Ellis Brown of the Jolly Rogers' 400th Squadron was in one of the first bombers over the Boram airfield, and his load of 1,500 incendiary bombs ignited fires all over the field and lit it up for the bombers coming up behind him. One of those bombers, named "Yanks From Hell," from the 321st Squadron, piloted by 2nd Lt. Joseph M. Casale, apparently took a direct hit from the antiaircraft fire and was almost instantly ablaze. As the crews of other bombers watched in horror, the burning bomber plummeted down into the black jungle like a comet. Someone noted that the plane's guns were firing all the way down, visible from the tracers. There could have been no survivors from such a crash.

The eleven men who died in the crash of "Yanks From Hell" were:

2nd Lt. Joseph M. Casale, pilot, from South Orange, New Jersey
2nd Lt. Richard T. Dodson, copilot, from San Francisco, California
2nd Lt. Jason V. George, Jr., navigator, from South Carolina
2nd Lt. Valentine B. Kane, Jr., bombardier, from New Jersey
T/Sgt. Oscar R. Jordan, flight engineer, from North Carolina
S/Sgt. Edward S. Meding, gunner, from Ohio
T/Sgt. Raymond L. St. Jeor, from Idaho
S/Sgt. Jack W. Eaton, gunner, from Washington state
S/Sgt. Alfred A. Podesta, gunner, from New York
S/Sgt. Harry M. Manson, gunner, from Massachusetts
M/Sgt. Rupert W. Adams, passenger, from Alabama

When the wreckage of "Yanks From Hell" was found after the war, there were no human remains present (they may have been burned to ashes). The crewmen are memorialized on the Tablets of the Missing at Manila American Cemetery.

Another Jolly Rogers bomber, named "Twin Niftys," of the Jolly Rogers' 400th Squadron, also went down that night, but in the darkness and confusion over the target the eyewitness accounts of what happened to this plane differ. The

Nose art on the Jolly Rogers' 321st Squadron bomber "Yanks from Hell," lost with its crew at Wewak on the night of 16-17 August, 1943.

plane was damaged and did not go down immediately, but continued flying for some distance before crashing. Some believed the bomber was hit by antiaircraft fire, while others said that "Yanks From Hell" collided with "Twin Niftys" on its way down. Captured Japanese documents after the war revealed that the pilot of a Japanese twin-engine night fighter claimed shooting down one American bomber that night, and it may have been "Twin Niftys."

However "Twin Niftys" became damaged, the pilot, Lt. Charles Freas, was able to keep it under control, and it continued to fly, but for some rea-

The bomber "Twin Niftys" of the Jolly Rogers' 400th Squadron, lost with its crew in the night raid on Wewak of August 16-17, 1943. In this picture the bomber did not yet have the big skull and crossed bombs symbol of the Jolly Rogers painted on its rudders.

son, instead of heading back southeast down the coast, Freas steered south-southwest, deeper into the jungle toward the Owen Stanley Mountains. No doubt everyone aboard the plane had hopes that they could somehow make it back to some Allied airfield, or at least get the plane down safely somewhere, but it was not to be. After about 20 minutes of flying, the plane was unable to continue further and Freas attempted to land it in the dark about 40 miles south of Wewak, in a swamp near the Sepik River. There was no chance of a safe landing under those conditions. Villagers in the area reported that they heard an explosion in the night, and the next day they found wreckage and bodies in the swamp. There were no survivors.[2]

Nose art on the Jolly Rogers' bomber "Twin Niftys."

The ten men lost when "Twin Nifys" went down were:

1st Lt. Charles R. Freas, pilot, from Philadelphia, Pennsylvania
1st Lt. Dean P. Hope, copilot, from Glendale, California
2nd Lt. Clifford G. Oskamp, navigator, from Canandaigua, New York
2nd Lt. Joseph Paw, bombardier, from Hamilton, Ohio
T/Sgt. Leo D. Faulk, flight engineer, from Bremerton, Washington

S/Sgt. Kenneth E. Heck, assistant flight engineer, Hastings, W. Virginia
T/Sgt. James A. Bush, radio operator, from Wind Gap, Pennsylvania
S/Sgt. Roland M. Peterson, asst. radio operator, from Campello, Mass.
S/Sgt. Glynn R. Early, waist gunner, from Davenport, Iowa
S/Sgt. John M. Blessing, tail gunner, from Mount Carmel, Pennsylvania

The natives recovered three bodies from the wreckage and buried them near Angoram Mission. They reported that another body had floated away in the swamp before they could recover it. Some villagers also said that one crewman, who was never identified, had bailed out and survived the crash but was later captured by the Japanese and taken to Wewak, never to be seen again. In 1948 the American Graves Registration Service visited the crash site of "Twin Niftys" but was unable to recover any human remains because it was during the wet season and the wreckage was largely underwater. They did exhume the three bodies buried by the villagers at the nearby mission, identified them, and returned them to their relatives in the States. In 2003, during a dry season when the wreck site was more exposed, more remains of the crew were recovered, and today several crew members are buried in a group grave at the Jefferson Barracks National Cemetery in Missouri.

Another of the Jolly Rogers bombers that participated in the Wewak raid that night was named "The Dude," piloted by Lt. Karle W. Yaple, and riding along with Yaple's crew was the photographer Sgt. Stephen J. Novak, the same cameraman who had flown with Col. Art Rogers on the mission that was written up by *Saturday Evening Post* writer Charles Rawlings[*] (Chapter 27). Over Wewak "The Dude" became caught in the beam of several Japanese searchlights, practically blinding the crewmen, but in this case, thanks to Novak, the Americans were able to give as good as they got.

Sgt. Novak heaved a 100-pound flash bomb out one of the bomber's waist windows, to illuminate the landscape below for his camera. This was the first time the Jolly Rogers had ever tried night photography. When the flash bomb ignited, still in the air, it bathed the entire area in a dazzling white light of 500-million candlepower, which probably blinded the Japanese gunners and searchlight operators for the short time that it burned. It certainly blinded Novak, but he aimed his camera downward and triggered it several times, working it by feel. Later in the day, when the pictures were developed, it was found that he had gotten some good photographs of the destruction of the Japanese airfield below.[3]

A third bomber lost on this mission was not a Jolly Rogers plane, and it was not lost through enemy action. It was a B-24 from the 43rd Bomb Group, Ken's Men, piloted by Lt. John T. Parran, which dropped its bombs on Wewak

---

[*] On that occasion he had photographed a bomb skipping into the side of a Japanese ship.

and then simply got lost in the dark on the return trip and was unable to find Port Moresby. Parran flew all the way across the Owen Stanley Mountains to the south coast of New Guinea, where finally, out of gas, he ditched the bomber in the sea on the coastline about 300 miles west of Moresby. As usual with a water landing, the B-24 broke up, and this time four of the crewmen were killed. The survivors hiked to an Australian army outpost that was able to radio for help, and the men were rescued by a PBY Catalina that flew them back to Port Moresby. The wreckage of this plane still lies today in shallow water near Saibai Island in the Torres Straits and is visible at low tide.[4]

Thus, out of the 48 bombers on the mission, three were lost and 25 crewmen killed. The Jolly Rogers had 21 empty bunks in their camp after this raid. When the sun came up on the morning of August 17, aerial photographs of Wewak taken by two high-flying P-38 Lightning photo planes showed 120 freshly wrecked Japanese aircraft on the four airfields.

The photos also showed quite a few intact, flyable aircraft remaining on the fields, but the night attack had only been the first round of General Kenney's plan for Wewak on this day. Unbeknownst to the Japanese, who were busily assessing their losses that morning, and who were also getting ready to launch an air strike against American airfields with their remaining aircraft, the second American blow was about to fall.

The B-25s follow the Jolly Rogers

Even as the last of the Jolly Rogers were landing at Port Moresby after their early-morning strike, forty-nine B-25s modified into strafer/bombers by "Pappy" Gunn were taking off from Port Moresby and Dobodura, heading for a rendezvous with ninety long-range P-38 fighter planes over the village of Bena Bena. Sixteen of them encountered bad weather or had mechanical problems en route to the rendezvous and turned back, aborting the mission.

The remaining thirty-three B-25s picked up their fighter cover and proceeded to Wewak by an overland route, flying just above the treetops and staying far enough back from the coastline to prevent being detected by Japanese coastwatchers. A movie taken from one of the planes of the formation passing low over the jungle shows clouds of white cockatoos rising into the air, frightened into flight by the passing American aircraft.

The Japanese were in for a big surprise on this morning. They had not thought that American twin-engine bombers could reach them at Wewak, nor did they know that the Americans now had long-range fighters (with droppable gas tanks) to accompany them. All of these B-25s were equipped with jury-rigged 400-gallon add-on gas tanks designed and installed by "Pappy" Gunn in place of their belly turrets, and these tanks could be jettisoned after the fuel in them was used up and the plane had been switched back to its regular gas tanks in the wings. "Pappy's" was a simple and rather crude installation: the tanks hung from bomb shackles, and when a B-25 dropped its tank it tore away the fuel hoses, which stank up the interior of the plane with gas fumes for a while and left a breezy gap in the fuselage, but otherwise, like most of "Pappy's" inventions, it worked well.

Japanese documents examined after the war allow us to reconstruct the situation on the Wewak airfields that morning just before the American planes arrived. About seventy Japanese had been killed during the night's raid by the heavy bombers, and after the sun rose the bodies and body parts were being gathered up, and the undamaged aircraft were being prepared for a scheduled strike against the Americans.

At Wewak Central, two planeloads of Japanese senior staff members from Rabaul had arrived the day before, and had survived the night's bombing in deep dugouts that served as air raid shelters for officers, although both of the transport aircraft that had delivered them to Wewak were now smoldering wrecks. Nevertheless, many of the surviving Japanese planes were lined up wingtip-to-wingtip to be inspected by these high-ranking visitors, with their crews standing at attention nearby, while other planes were preparing to take off for the day's raid on American airbases, surrounded by maintenance crews doing last-minute tasks. The flight crews were getting into their aircraft, and some of the planes already had their engines running and were rolling toward the runways.

A Japanese intelligence officer named Akira Yamanaka got a phone call from an outpost at Hansa Bay, about a hundred miles down the coast, telling him that a formation of American planes had just been detected headed toward Wewak from the southeast. It suddenly dawned on Yamanaka what was about to happen, and he realized how vulnerable the planes on the Wewak airbase were to a bombing or strafing attack. Disaster was only twenty minutes away, at most. Last night's bombing, he now understood, was only a preliminary attack. The follow-up strike was nearly on top of them.

Frantically Yamanaka got on the phone and tried to warn the other Wewak airfields, but most of the phone lines were down and he was only able to connect with But, thirty miles up the coast. Then he and several members of his intelligence staff dashed from their headquarters building and began running down the lines of planes, waving their arms and shouting that another American air strike was only minutes away and that everyone should take cover immediately.

It was too late. Behind Yamanaka the first of the American strafer/bombers popped into view over the treetops and came thundering down on them at over 280 mph, descending to just twenty feet above the field. The noses of the American strafers seemed to erupt into flame as each plane cut loose with its eight big Browning .50-caliber machine guns. Together those guns could fire

One of the "Green Dragon" B-25 strafer/bombers of the 38th Bomb Group, 405th Squadron, armed with multiple additional .50-cal. machine guns installed by Maj. Paul I. "Pappy" Gunn in Brisbane, Australia. Thirty-three of these planes wreaked havoc on the Wewak airfields on the morning of Aug. 17, 1943, each plane firing its ten heavy machine guns while dropping hundreds of parafrag bombs.

over a hundred rounds per second, sending out streams of thousands of heavy slugs that began tearing into the rows of parked airplanes.

That morning "Pappy" Gunn's lethal strafer/bombers once again showed what incredible destruction they were capable of inflicting. In the earlier Battle of the Bismarck Sea these massed guns had ripped up the decks of ships and blasted Japanese sailors and soldiers high into the air. Now they were exploding and shredding parked aircraft and any Japanese who were unfortunate enough to be caught in or near them.

Yamanaka dove to the dirt as parts of aircraft and men flew in all directions around him and the fuel tanks of aircraft exploded all up and down the airfield. Drums of fuel that had been left along the edges of the field also blew up. To compound the destruction, the copilot of each B-25 triggered the release of hundreds of parafrag bombs from his plane that drifted to earth under small parachutes in the wake of the strafers and began exploding all over the field (photo on p. 312). Each strafer carried twelve clusters of these 24-pound bombs, and each cluster contained twenty-three bombs, for a total of 276 bombs per plane.

These "parafrags" (short for parachute-retarded fragmentation bombs) were something that General Kenney himself had invented back in the 1920s, but had been little-used until now. In July of 1942, before Kenney had gone to Australia to take up command of the 5th Air Force, he had heard of the shortage of war matériel in the Pacific theater and had scrounged around in the States for anything he might be able to send out to the Pacific to help him pursue the war. He ran across an old store of his parafrag bombs and immediately laid claim to them, writing later:

> While looking around for anything that was not nailed down, I found that there were 3,000 parachute fragmentation bombs in war reserve. No one else wanted them, so they were ordered shipped to Australia on the next boat. Back in 1928, in order to drop bombs in a low-altitude attack without having the fragments hit the airplane, I had put parachutes on the bombs; the parachutes opened as the bombs were released from the airplane. The parachute not only stopped the forward travel of the bomb, but slowly lowered it down to the ground while the airplane got out of range of the fragments by the time the bomb hit the ground and detonated. With a supersensitive fuse, which kicked the thing off instantaneously on contact with anything—even the leaf of a bush, the bomb was a wicked little weapon. It weighed about twenty-five pounds and broke up into around 1,600 fragments the size of a man's little finger. At a hundred yards from the point of impact these fragments could go through a two-inch plank. I had had a hard time getting the Air Corps or the Ordnance Dept. to play with the thing, in spite of a dozen demonstrations I had put on. It was actually 1936 before an order of about 5,000 was made up for a service test. Everyone that used them was enthusiastic, but somehow or other the 3,000 remaining got hidden away in war reserve and people gradually forgot about them. I think the Ordnance Dept. was actually glad to get rid of them. But I was speculating about trying them out on some Jap airdrome and wondering if those fragments would tear airplanes apart—as well as Japs, too, if they didn't get out of the way.[5]

The answer to his question was quick in coming—parafrag bombs worked spectacularly well on parked Japanese aircraft. Their shrapnel riddled and shredded the aluminum airframes, and the bombs were also able to drift straight down into aircraft revetments to defeat those defensive embankments in a way that conventional forward-traveling bombs could not.

The strafer/bombers that hit Wewak on the morning of the 17th had split up as they approached Wewak and made simultaneous attacks on Boram, Wewak Central, and Dagua. The airfield at But was not hit, since the dozen strafers assigned to attack it were among those that had aborted the raid after encountering bad weather. The surprise was complete at all three Japanese airfields, and scores of planes were caught on the ground and destroyed. At Boram alone the strafers found seventy Japanese planes, mostly fighters, neatly lining

Parafrag bombs shower down on Japanese aircraft parked on Wewak's Dagua airfield in the wake of the B-25 strafer/bombers. Photo taken by the tail camera of one of the B-25s.

both sides of the runway, many with their engines running and surrounded by ground crews. The American guns and bombs obliterated them.

Capt. Middlebrook flew one of the B-25s that attacked the Dagua airfield. Like the other attackers, he hugged the treetops all the way in. When the field came into view, the scene that met his eyes, he said later, was "unbelievable," with "at least forty to fifty" twin-engine bombers lined up on the south side of the runway, and several fighter planes on the opposite side. Middlebrook flew down the row of bombers and raked them with his guns from one end to the other. The first "Sally" bomber that his tracers hit exploded. The concussion tossed the one beside it up in the air, and it dropped back to earth in flames.

As he streaked down the row of parked planes with all his guns firing, he saw other bombers shedding their wings and tails as they crumpled up and disintegrated. His stream of bullets struck one bomber just as two Japanese soldiers ran past it headed for refuge in the jungle beyond. The bomber exploded in a fireball that engulfed the two men and seemed to vaporize them as Middlebrook's plane flashed by.[6]

A few Japanese fighter planes managed to take off amidst the chaos, and some evaded the protecting P-38s and attacked the B-25s, but they were unable to shoot any of them down.

General Kenney was elated by the results of this raid and wrote:

31. WEWAK ATTACKED, LAE AND NADZAB CAPTURED   313

> We found out afterward that the Japs referred to the attack as "the Black Day of August 17th" and that they had lost over 150 aircraft, with practically all the flight crews and around three hundred more ground personnel killed. All our P-38s and strafers returned to their home airdromes.[7]

Since reconnaissance photos taken after this raid showed that there were still some aircraft left on the Wewak airfields, Kenney sent a follow-up strike the next day, Aug. 18, 1943. The Jolly Rogers again sent 24 bombers, but several aborted the mission due to mechanical problems and bad weather and returned to Port Moresby. The Jolly Rogers bombed in daylight this time, and they and the low-level strafers hit Wewak nearly simultaneously. The Japanese were on the alert this time, however, and Zeros attacked some of the Jolly Rogers bombers despite a screen of seventy-eight P-38s that were along to protect them, but the bombers defended themselves well and shot down five of their attackers. No Jolly Rogers bombers were lost this day.

One Jolly Rogers crewman, a flight engineer named T/Sgt. William Baker, was on his first combat mission. Sitting in the bomber's top turret, he saw a Zero coming at his plane, and forgetting that gunners were only supposed to fire in short bursts, not continuously (so that the gunbarrels wouldn't become red-hot and warp), he just held the triggers down while keeping the twin guns pointed at the Zero until the fighter exploded. The incident scared him so badly that he wrote home to his parents that night and told them to sell his car, because, he explained, "there's no chance of making it through this mess." (Nevertheless he survived the war).[8]

The sky swirled with dogfights between the P-38s and Japanese fighters. A new fighter pilot named Lt. Thomas B. McGuire, Jr. shot down three of the Japanese planes (two Zekes and a Tony), and within a few days downed two more Zekes to become an "ace" with five kills. McGuire would become a favorite of Gen. Kenney, and would shoot down a total of 38 Japanese aircraft before being killed in a treetop-level stall/spin crash while dogfighting, trying to save another pilot (described on pp. 699-700). He would fly with Charles Lindbergh, as will be related in later chapters, and the Jolly Rogers would move to McGuire Field in the Philippines, named after him, in January of 1944.

Meanwhile, on this day, down at low level, fifty-three B-25 strafer/bombers shot up and parafragged anything left on the Wewak airfields.[9] However, a B-25 piloted by 23-year-old Major Ralph Cheli took hits from either Japanese fighter planes, flak, or both, and one of its engines was set afire. Cheli was leading a formation of strafers in an attack on Dagua airfield, and he continued to lead the attack with his engine streaming flames. Only after all the strafers had finished making their runs did Cheli call for his wingman to take over command, because he was going to have to ditch. He set the crippled plane down in the ocean beyond the surf near the Japanese airfield. Two crewmen went down with the plane, but Cheli and two others were picked up by a Japanese patrol boat.

The Japanese sent Cheli to Rabaul, where he was thrown into a prison cell near Lt. McMurria and other captured American fliers. The other two B-25 crewmen remained at Wewak and were never heard from again, doubtlessly killed by the Japanese. Farther down the coast at Madang, five survivors of two other shot-down B-25s were murdered on August 31, 1943. First the Americans were beaten bloody with clubs and fists, and then three of them were beheaded and the other two used for bayonet practice. Capt. Robert L. Herry, one of the B-25 pilots, was tied between two upright posts before the Japanese went at him with their bayonets.[10]

Maj. Cheli was held at Rabaul along with Lt. McMurria until he too was murdered in yet another massacre of American prisoners, this one on March 6, 1944. His body was found after the war in a mass grave at Rabaul along with several other Americans, their hands tied behind their backs with wire. Cheli was posthumously awarded the Congressional Medal of Honor for continuing to lead his squadron in the attack on Wewak's Dagua airfield despite the fact that his bomber had been fatally hit, was on fire, and was only minutes away from crashing.

After the mid-August aerial assaults on Wewak, the Japanese would continue to restock the fields with aircraft, necessitating more strikes by the Jolly Rogers and Kenney's strafer/bombers later on, but from this time forward Japanese air superiority over New Guinea was ended.

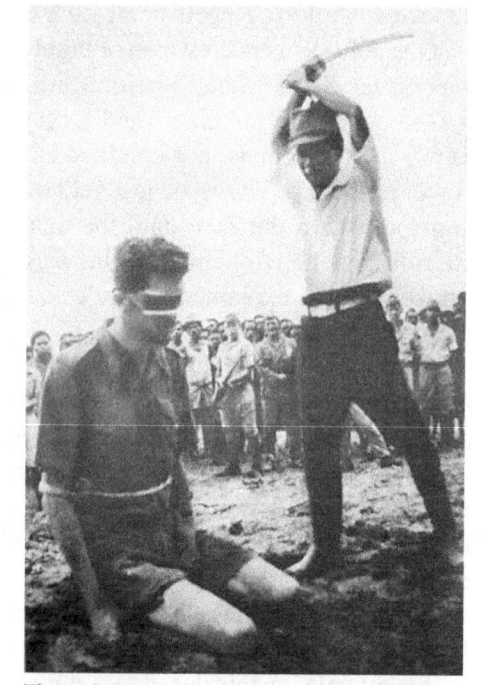

Typical Japanese treatment of a captured Allied airman. The Japanese ignored the rules of the 1929 Geneva Convention regarding the humane treatment of prisoners of war.

The assault on Nadzab and Lae

With the Japanese air threat from Wewak now eliminated, Kenney and MacArthur decided that it was safe to go ahead with the capture of Lae and Nadzab. The Nadzab operation would be the first paratroop assault of the Pacific war. Kenney wanted to watch the

31. WEWAK ATTACKED, LAE AND NADZAB CAPTURED

operation himself from a circling bomber, which he knew was taking a risk, since Japanese fighter planes from Rabaul might try to interfere, and he hoped that General MacArthur would allow him to do it. As it turned out, MacArthur not only allowed it but went along with him. As Kenney remembered it:

> I discussed the details of the plan for covering and supporting the Nadzab operation and casually mentioned that I would be in one of the bombers to see how things went off. General MacArthur said he didn't think I should go. I said I had obeyed his orders to keep out of combat and that, with Wewak's air force out of the picture and a fog stopping the wild eagles* from Rabaul from interfering with the show, I didn't expect any trouble. However, in any case this was to be my big day. If everything went all right, I would still be his Allied Air Force Commander. If the show went sour, I would be what a lot of his staff already thought I was. Furthermore, they were my kids and I was going to see them do their stuff.
>
> The General listened to my tirade and finally said, "You're right, George, we'll both go. They're my kids, too."
>
> "No, that doesn't make sense," I protested. "Why, after living all these years and getting to be the head general of the show, is it necessary for you to risk having some five-dollar-a-month Jap aviator shoot a hole in you?"
>
> General MacArthur looked at me quite seriously and said, "I'm not worried about getting shot. Honestly, the only thing that disturbs me is the possibility that when we hit the rough air over the mountains, my stomach might get upset. I'd hate to get sick and disgrace myself in front of the kids."
>
> It was no use. I gave in and arranged for a "brass hat" flight of three B-17s to fly just above and to one side of the troop carriers as they came into Nadzab for the big parachute jump. I decided to put General MacArthur in one bomber, go in another myself, and have the third handy for mutual protection in case we got hopped. He suggested we go in the same airplane, but I told him that I didn't like to tempt fate by putting too many eggs in one basket. He laughed but agreed.[11]

The plan called for General Kenney's aerial assault on the Nadzab area to coincide with the Allied landings on the coast to capture Lae. Since the two operations were thus tied together, the Lae invasion depended on what day in early September the weather would be clear enough for the airplanes to fly and drop the paratroopers at Nadzab. Kenney had both American and Australian weather forecasters advising him, but to his frustration they couldn't agree on what day the weather might allow the operation. Kenney wrote:

---

*Japanese propagandists referred to their aviators as "wild eagles" in press releases to the Japanese public. Kenney used the term derisively.

> On the morning of September 1st my weather teams were still hopelessly apart. The Aussies still said the 4th and the Americans stuck to the 7th as the proper date. That evening the Americans said that the day's weather data made the picture look a little different and they were willing to gamble on the 5th instead of the 7th. This sounded better but much to my horror the Aussies now said that the 3rd was the best day and that they were not so sure about the 4th as they had been.
>
> I decided that neither of them knew anything about weather, split the difference between the two forecasts, and told General MacArthur we would be ready to go on the morning of the 4th.[12]

MacArthur then scheduled the amphibious landing at Lae for the 4th of September [1943] and the airborne assault on Nadzab for the following day. Australian weathermen were also providing forecasts to the Jolly Rogers crews before their bombing missions, and there was sometimes a bit of confusion owing to differences in the way Americans and Australians pronounced words, as Kenney related:

> The Australian weatherman, in giving the weather conditions along the route and the forecast, mentioned "rine" clouds. I heard one of the youngsters in the back of the room turn to his copilot and say, "What are rine clouds?" The copilot answered, "I think he said 'rime.' Probably the kind of clouds that have rime ice..." Several of the crews who overheard this conversation then became a little worried as they had no de-icing boots on their wings or fluid for the slinger rings to keep ice off the propellers. I relieved their apprehensions by explaining to them that in the Australian accent "rain" became "rine." I then told Whitehead to see that in future an American staff officer was present at all briefings by the Australians.[13]

The seizure of the Markham valley would involve a coordinated effort by heavy, medium, and light bombers to pave the way for the C-47s bringing in the paratroops, with fighters flying cover over the whole operation. General Kenney explained the plan to the air groups involved, and a rehearsal of the operation was held on September 3rd, two days before the actual assault, a short ways up the coast from Port Moresby. The rehearsal went well, and boded well for the real thing.

On the morning of the 5th, Generals MacArthur and Kenney were both on hand at Port Moresby's Jackson airfield (photo on next page) as the 1,700 paratroopers of the 503rd Parachute Regiment boarded their C-47s, which were under the control of the 54th Troop Carrier Wing. To provide some extra firepower to the troops, two Australian artillery officers and thirty men of the

31. WEWAK ATTACKED, LAE AND NADZAB CAPTURED 317

Generals MacArthur and Kenney, at left, hold a last-minute conference at Port Moresby's Jackson Field on the early morning of Sept. 5, 1943 (note the long shadows cast by the rising sun), before boarding their separate B-17s to personally witness the aerial assault on Nadzab. The paratroopers are already aboard the lined-up C-47s at right and ready to go. The airfield's surface is perforated metal Marston matting.

7th Division's 2/4 Field Artillery had volunteered to jump with the Americans, even though none of them had ever made a parachute jump before. General Kenney approved their addition to the paratrooper force and loaded two of their howitzers (short-barreled 25-pounders), in pieces attached to cargo parachutes, into one of the C-47s, to be dropped along with them. The American paratroopers strapped parachutes on the Australians and showed them how to pull the ripcords, and that, along with some verbal instruction, was the full extent of their paratrooper training. Making their first-ever parachute jumps at a dangerously low altitude of 400 to 500 feet onto a battlefield might have seemed like a daunting proposition to many soldiers, but these were the same tough Australians who had driven Rommel's tank corps out of North Africa, then returned to the Pacific to drive the Japanese back over the Kokoda Trail, and it obviously took more than that to faze them.

The plan was for the American paratroopers to seize and hold the site of the airfield, then clear and smooth the ground sufficiently for C-47s to land. Then the Australian 7th Division would be airlifted in and fight its way to Lae.

The capture of Nadzab

The morning of September 5, 1943, fortunately dawned clear over the Markham River valley, and even more fortunately, bad weather over New Britain kept any Japanese fighter planes grounded at Rabaul that might have attempted to interfere with the operation. The Jolly Rogers supported the day's effort with twelve bombers from their 319th and 400th Squadrons, each carrying eight 1,000-pound bombs. Their 96 bombs plastered an area about halfway between Nadzab and Lae known as the Heath Plantation, which was known to be occupied by the Japanese. Other Jolly Rogers bombers were out on reconnaissance, keeping watch for any Japanese aircraft that might be headed for Lae from Rabaul or Wewak. They saw none. The 90th Bomb Group's records state that some of these reconnaissance planes, as an experiment, had twin .50-caliber machine guns mounted in the waist windows instead of the usual single guns, a first, but they must have been found impractical (probably too heavy and cumbersome to aim easily) for they were never used again.[14]

After the C-47s were all in the air, Generals Kenney and MacArthur boarded their separate B-17s and flew above and behind them, as though riding herd on the 96 transport planes and their human cargo as they crossed the Owen Stanley Mountain range headed for Nadzab. On the other side of the mountains, at a rendezvous point above a small Allied airfield at Marilinan, all the other Allied aircraft participating in this operation joined them, and then the great stream of over 300 aircraft proceeded to the Markham River valley.

With so many different kinds of aircraft flying together, from speedy little fighters to the slow, lumbering cargo planes, all with different cruising speeds and converging from several airfields in the Port Moresby and Dobodura areas, timing was crucial. As it turned out, everything went perfectly, probably as a result of the dress rehearsal two days before. Kenney wrote a letter that night to General "Hap" Arnold in Washington describing the operation:

> I will tell you about the show on the 5th September, when we took Nadzab with 1,700 paratroopers and with General MacArthur in a B-17 over the area watching the show and jumping up and down like a kid. I was flying number two in the same flight with him and the operation really was a magnificent spectacle... Three hundred and two airplanes in all, taking off from eight different fields in the Moresby and Dobodura areas, made a rendezvous right on the nose... flying through clouds, passes in the mountains, and over the top. Not a single squadron did any circling or stalling around but all slid into place like clockwork and proceeded on the final flight down into the Watut Valley, turned to the right down the Markham, and went directly to the target.
>
> [T]his was the picture: leading the parade at one thousand feet were six squadrons of B-25 strafers, with the eight .50-caliber guns in the nose and sixty frag bombs in each bomb bay; immediately behind them and about five hundred feet above were six A-20s, flying in pairs—three pairs abreast—to lay smoke as the last frag bomb exploded. At about two thousand feet and directly behind the A-20s came ninety-six C-47s carrying paratroops, supplies, and some artillery. The C-47s flew in three columns of three-plane

31. WEWAK ATTACKED, LAE AND NADZAB CAPTURED

September 5, 1943: the 503rd Parachute Regiment drops on Nadzab behind a smoke screen laid down by six A-20 light bombers. 1,700 paratroopers jumped from ninety-six C-47s within one minute and ten seconds.

elements, each column carrying a battalion set up for a particular battalion dropping ground.

On each side along the column of transports and about one thousand feet above them were the close-cover fighters. Another group of fighters sat at seven thousand feet, and up in the sun, staggered from fifteen to twenty thousand, was still another group. Following the transports came five B-17s, racks loaded with 300-pound packages with parachutes, to be dropped to the paratroopers on call by panel signals as they needed them. This mobile supply unit stayed over Nadzab practically all day serving the paratroops below, dropping a total of fifteen tons of supplies in this manner.

[J]ust behind the five supply B-17s was a group of twenty-four B-24s [including the Jolly Rogers] and four B-17s, which left the column just before the junction of the Watut and the Markham to take out the Jap defensive position at Heath's Plantation, about half way between Nadzab and Lae... The brass-hat flight of three B-17s above the center of the transport column completed the set-up.

The strafers checked in on the target at exactly the time set just prior to take-off. They strafed and frag bombed the whole area in which the jumps were to be made, and then as the last of the bombs exploded the smoke layers went to work. As the streams of smoke were built up, the three columns of transports slid into place, and in one minute and ten seconds from the time the first parachute opened, the last of 1,700 paratroopers had dropped.[15]

The Japanese in the Nadzab area fled under the attack of the strafer/bombers, and by the time the paratroopers landed they met with no opposition. The only Japanese who stood and fought were a few hundred troops on the south side of the river valley at a place called Markham Point, who had previously been surrounded by Australian troops that were moving into the area from Wau to the west. Those Japanese became pinned down under air strikes and posed no threat to the paratroopers.

The only casualties from the jump were three American paratroopers who were killed in accidents; the parachutes of two of them failed to open, and a

General MacArthur (center) poses with the crew of the B-17 that flew him over Nadzab on Sept. 5, 1943 to witness the paratrooper drop (he did not, as he had feared, become airsick). The man at far left is Gen. Roger Ramey of 5th Bomber Command (not to be confused with Gen. Howard Ramey, who was lost on a reconnaissance flight five months earlier).

31. WEWAK ATTACKED, LAE AND NADZAB CAPTURED 321

General Kenney (wearing jacket) poses with the appropriately named B-17 "Cap'n & the Kids" and its crew that flew him above the Nadzab paratrooper operation on September 5, 1943.

third landed in the top of a tree and died when he fell sixty feet to the ground. The novice Australian jumpers landed without any mishap worse than a wrenched shoulder suffered by one of men from a hard landing, and they soon had their artillery pieces assembled and working, ready to head for Lae.

Later in the day, when Generals Kenney and MacArthur landed back at Port Moresby, they were both photographed in front of their B-17s along with the crews that had flown them (left and above).

The capture of Lae

On September 4 [1943], 2,400 men of the 9th Australian Division, commanded by General G. F. Wootten, made an amphibious landing on beaches 17 miles east of Lae, a location chosen because it was out of the range of Japanese artillery in the town. General Kenney sent eight B-25 strafer/bombers up from

Dobodura to shoot up and bomb the beaches ahead of the landing, and Allied fighter planes circled overhead to give both the B-25s and the landing barges cover. This was the first amphibious landing made by Australian troops since their famous landing at Gallipoli in World War One.

The landing did not go without incident. General Kenney wrote later that two Japanese planes (he did not say what type) snuck in under a low layer of haze that prevented the Allied fighter planes higher up from seeing them, and made a quick hit-and-run attack that wrecked one of the smaller landing craft and damaged another. There were no casualties among the men. He speculated that the two planes had been hidden on the airfield at Lae and took off from there that morning. After their attack they fled north toward Madang.

From the landing beach, the Australians started through the jungle for Lae (there was no coastal road) but were slowed by having to cross a series of rain-swollen rivers, as well as fight some Japanese on the way. Meanwhile, at Nadzab, the Australian 7th Division, under General George A. Vasey, had been airlifted into the new partly-constructed airfield at Nadzab in General Kenney's C-47s, and they too advanced toward Lae, so that the Japanese holding the town were subjected to a pincer maneuver, attacked simultaneously from the east by the 9th Division and from the northwest by the 7th. The two Australian generals got a bet going over whose division would be the first to enter Lae, with the loser having to pay twenty cases of whiskey to the winner.

The Jolly Rogers continued to bomb both the town and any Japanese positions that threatened to hold up the Australian advance on either side of the town. Col. Rogers wrote:

> During this time we were carrying out devastating bomb raids on Lae itself. The Jap general and his staff headquarters had been located through our intelligence previously, and at the proper time I was sent in with a large force of bombers to kill the general and his staff so as to add to the chaos the Japs were already in. This we did, destroying their entire headquarters. Lae crumbled up sooner than anyone expected it would; it was only a mere shell of its former self. The Japs fought on doggedly to the last and practically the entire garrison was wiped out.[16]

Both Australian divisions made steady progress, and on 16 September General Vasey's troops were the first to enter the town, winning the competition for the whiskey, but only barely, since Wooten's arrived later the same day. Under the pressure of the pincer movement, the Japanese 18th Army commander, Hatazō Adachi, retreated into the jungle with the disorganized remnants of his troops. With no longer any hope of supply by sea from Rabaul, since the Battle of the Bismarck Sea had rendered this impossible, he found himself in desperate straits. Within a year MacArthur would eventually reduce all Japanese

31. WEWAK ATTACKED, LAE AND NADZAB CAPTURED   323

forces in New Guinea to that same condition. The starving Japanese fled north, hoping to reach other Japanese garrisons farther up the coast. Many died on the trail, and some once again resorted to cannibalism to stay alive.

The first airplane to land at Nadzab after its capture was an L-4, a two-seat Army Piper Cub (like the one in the lower photo on p. 380). In the back seat of the plane was the commander of the local Seabees, who jumped out and began organizing the preparation of the ground so that C-47 cargo planes could land. Although C-47s were landing there the next day, bringing in more troops and supplies, the development of Nadzab into a major airbase that could handle the B-24s of the Jolly Rogers would require the use of heavy earthmoving equipment that was not immediately available, since it was too big and heavy to fit into a C-47. The big graders, bulldozers, and rollers would have to be brought into Lae's harbor by ship, and then driven the 20-miles up to Nadzab over a road that did not yet exist. All this would take weeks to accomplish.

Thus, for the present at least, the Jolly Rogers remained where they were at Port Moresby.

Jeeps, trucks, small bulldozers, fuel drums, and every other kind of supplies were flown into the new Nadzab airstrip in General Kenney's fleet of C-47 cargo planes before a road was built to the site from the harbor at Lae. Two-and-a-half ton trucks were sawn in half and the two halves flown to Nadzab where they were welded back together.

Chapter Thirty-Two

BRIDGE BUSTING

After the Allied capture of Lae, as the remaining Japanese troops retreated to the northwest, up the Ramu River valley, hoping to reach other strongholds such as Madang, Wewak, and Hollandia further up the coast, they made use of existing bridges to cross the numerous rivers and deep ravines in the area. Some of the ravines were so steep-sided, with precipitous drops on either side, that bridges were the only way to cross them. General Kenney directed the Jolly Rogers to bomb and eliminate as many of these bridges as possible in an effort to hamper Japanese mobility.

On July 20, 1943, pilot John B. Willcoxon of the Jolly Rogers' 320th Squadron took off from Ward's Field at Port Moresby on a lone mission to bomb the Gori River Bridge near Madang, about 140 miles northwest of Lae. Previous efforts to bomb this bridge had failed—it was a small target and difficult to hit. Willcoxon made several bomb runs over the bridge that morning, dropping one bomb on each pass, and flying very low to make things easier for his bombardier, Lt. George T. Maher.

They finally succeeded in destroying the bridge, but on their way back to Port Moresby their bomber was set upon by more than a dozen Japanese Tony fighter planes flying out of Wewak. It was the same situation that Lt. McMurria had found himself in six months earlier: one bomber against a multitude of fighter planes, except that Willcoxon's bomber was over land, not the sea. Once again, not only was there an overwhelming number of fighters, but they were flown by elite Japanese navy pilots who showed unusual skill in the attack. The Japanese now considered Wewak as being in their outer ring of defenses, so they were sending their best pilots and planes there.

The Australian 7th Division was advancing through this area at the time, in pursuit of the Japanese retreating from Lae, and that morning the men heard a lot of noise in the sky and looked up to see what was making all the racket. What they saw was an American B-24 bomber zig-zagging full-throttle up the Ramu River valley beset by a swarm of Japanese fighters that were attacking it from all directions. Like Lt. McMurria's bomber, Lt. Willcoxon's plane, named "Virgin III," was being assailed by too many fighters for its gunners to cope with. Lt. E. P. Dunshea of the Australian army later reported that the bomber had nine Japanese fighters attacking it when he first saw it, and shortly afterwards he counted sixteen. Three and possibly four of the Japanese planes were hit by the bomber's gunners and went down in flames, but there were plenty of others to replace them. The aerial battle lasted for about fifteen minutes.

Aboard the bomber was 39-year-old veteran war correspondent Carl Thusgaard, a reporter for Acme News Pictures, who had gone along on the mission to get a news story about the destruction of the bridge. Thusgaard had been one of the visitors to Lt. Stoecklein's tent at Port Moresby on the night when the name "Jolly Rogers" was thought up as a nickname for the 90th Bomb Group; in fact he may have been the one who came up with the name. There is no way to know what was happening in Willcoxon's bomber during the fighter attack, but but in all likelihood Thusgaard was thinking that this was going to make a terrific first-person news story for his readers back in the States: a tale of bridge-busting and aerial combat all combined in one mission. Also aboard the bomber was Cpl. Edwin B. McNaughton Jr., an Air Corps photographer, who had been taking pictures of the bombing of the bridge, both for the records and to illustrate the story that Thusgaard was going to write for his news syndicate. He may also have been trying to photograph the fighter attack.

However, as fate would have it, there would be no first-person eyewitness news report or spectacular photos of this mission. "Virgin III" was taking too many hits from the machine-guns and 20mm cannon of the Japanese fighter planes, and the Australians on the ground saw a fire break out in its bomb bay area—too big a fire for the crew to suppress. The plane trailed smoke for a few moments and then exploded in midair, killing everyone aboard except the nose gunner, Pvt. M. D. Turrentine of San Bernardo, California, who was miraculously blown clear and came down in a parachute. Knocked momentarily unconscious, he did not remember opening the parachute, but he woke up to find himself floating to earth beneath it.

Seeing the American dangling in a parachute, the Japanese fighter pilots followed their usual practice and immediately set out to kill him, making one firing pass after another at him, but Turrentine was leading a charmed life this day and not a single bullet so much as scratched him. Thus did one man of the twelve aboard the bomber live to tell the tale.

The burning fragments of the bomber fell over a wide area in the rugged terrain between Madang and Bena Bena, on the south side of the Ramu River valley. Lt. Dunshea immediately sent a patrol to the scene, but the Australians found nothing but widely scattered bodies and wreckage, except for Pvt. Turrentine, who had taken cover in a ravine and was badly shaken but unhurt. Ultimately, eight of the eleven crewmen's bodies were recovered and returned home for burial after the war, but the remains of the pilot, Lt. Willcoxon, the copilot, Lt. Magness, and war correspondent Thusgaard were never found.

Col. Rogers wrote of this mission:

[M]y Group suffered one of its greatest losses about this time when we lost our operations officer, Lt. John Willcoxon. Johnny got his bombing objective, a bridge, but we did not know it until late in the afternoon when our searching formation sighted its destruction but no sign of Willcoxon or his airplane.

Johnny had volunteered to take a weather recco mission to establish whether the weather was good enough for an entire bomber formation to take off to Madang. He took off three hours before daylight and intended to be over the proposed target at dawn, at which time he would radio back the weather conditions. Upon completing his mission he was to return by the way of Bogadjim Road that the Japs had been using to move supplies along.

There was a small bridge in a high ravine which, if destroyed, would nullify the effects of the road. Many efforts had been made to destroy this bridge, to no avail. Johnny said when he left, "Never you mind, I'll get the bridge," and he did. We carried on the search for him the following day, but still could not see any signs of his bomber on the course from the destroyed bridge that he intended to use on his way home.

However, after returning from our search, we were notified by our ground forces at Bena-Bena that an air battle between sixteen Jap fighters and one Liberator had been sighted by them, and that four Jap fighters had been destroyed before the Liberator exploded in midair. One parachute was observed falling, and an advanced party had been sent to reconnoiter the wreckage area. A full report would be rendered to us as soon as their patrol returned.

We all fervently hoped that most of the ten [actually twelve] men aboard the plane would somehow come out alive, but two days later we received the message, "Wreckage covered twenty acres, one survivor, nose gunner."

Arrangements were made for a small airplane to go into our advanced fighter airdromes, which were under construction in this area, to bring the lone survivor back to the Group so that he could get proper medical attention, and so we could learn the actual details of the encounter. Even before the nose gunner returned, it was not difficult to imagine what had happened, since a [Japanese] force consisting of twenty bombers and approximately thirty fighters from Wewak had attacked our forward airdromes under construction, and had dropped their bombs a few minutes before Johnny should have arrived at this point on his return trip. We figured that the enemy on his way out had sighted the lone Liberator bombing the bridge and had pounced on it in force.

The nose gunner's story was that they had gone down very low into the valley and made three or four bombing runs until the bridge had been completely destroyed. They were apparently on their last run when high in the sky they sighted nine Zeros diving at them.

As soon as Johnny knew of his predicament, he started climbing for altitude so that he would not be hindered by the mountains that surrounded the valley he was in. The gunner stated that at least two or three of the first batch were shot down, and then nine more Zeros joined in the attack...

The explosion in the airplane must have been terrific, because the nose gunner said he was blown completely through the nose and doesn't even remember opening his parachute. It must have been torn open as he went through the wreckage. He was in such an unnerved condition at the time that it was hard to get an accurate account of what had actually happened.

He shuddered as he told us how the Zeros had come at his body hanging from the parachute with all guns blazing, a propeller passing so close to him he had to pull up his feet to keep it from cutting his legs off. He said he finally grabbed his jungle knife and reached up and caught the shroud lines that connected him to his parachute silk with the intention of cutting his body free if another pass was made at him.

By the grace of God he was not riddled full of holes, and struck the ground before another pursuit made a strafing attack on him. He said that he no sooner hit a small opening in the jungle than dirt was flying all around him from bullets of another strafing airplane. He released himself from his parachute harness and dove into a small ravine, where he lay for hours until an advance patrol reached him.

Johnny was one of the most outstanding young officers I have had the opportunity to know. He was full of courage, ambition and determination to see a job well done.[1]

The war correspondent aboard the plane, Danish-born Thusgaard, had emigrated to America and married an American woman before going to work as a writer for *Acme Pictures*. Like the *Saturday Evening Post's* Charles Rawlings (see Chapter 27) he was one of those members of the press with the courage to fly along with bomber crews on combat missions, knowing full well that survival was sometimes only a matter of luck. A Liberty ship was later named in Thusgaard's honor.[*]

In the grim reckoning of war, the lives of eleven young American men had been exchanged for the destruction of one small rustic jungle bridge, the loss of which slowed the retreat of the Japanese in that area and made it easier for the pursuing Australians to overtake and annihilate them, thus speeding up to some small degree the defeat and expulsion of the Japanese from New Guinea.

---

[*] Ten Liberty ships were named in honor of war correspondents who lost their lives reporting the war.

The eleven men killed in the crash were:

    1st Lt. John B. Willcoxon, pilot, from Kansas
    2nd Lt. Thomas M. Magness, copilot, from California
    1st Lt. Irving Adler, navigator, from Massachusetts
    1st Lt. George T. Maher, bombardier, from Texas
    T/Sgt. Howard V. McCalmont, flight engineer, from Pennsylvania
    S/Sgt. John F. Dowd, radio operator, from New York
    S/Sgt. George J. Smith, gunner (home state not listed)
    Sgt. Eugene V. Turner, gunner, from Ohio
    Sgt. John P. Zalic, gunner, from Pennsylvania
    Cpl. Edwin B. McNaughton Jr., photographer, from Pennsylvania
    Carl R. Thusgaard, photojournalist, from New York

Today the wreckage of "Virgin III" still lies scattered over many acres on a mountainous hillside near the New Guinea village of Taru, at an elevation of 2,000 feet above sea level. In 1995 someone walking on the crash site reported seeing a great number of empty .50-cal. cartridge cases scattered about. These would have been from the bomber's machine-guns (and with all guns firing nearly continuously for a quarter of an hour, the interior of the bomber must have been practically awash in spent cartridges by the time it exploded).

Someone else walking on the site in recent years picked up one of the crewmen's .45-cal. pistols, rusted and with the wooden grips rotted away. It is now on display in a small museum in the town of Garoka, 20 miles west of the crash site, which maintains an exhibit of WWII artifacts found in the area.

It was theorized that the three men whose bodies were not found may have been blown to bits in the explosion of the plane, and their remains are therefore non-recoverable. Or, if their remains are intact, they may simply not have been found yet, and may yet lie somewhere on the peaceful slope of a mountain overlooking the Ramu River valley of New Guinea.

The 90th's best bombing mission by a dam site

On September 25, 1943, six Jolly Rogers bombers of the 321st Squadron undertook another bridge-bombing mission in the same area. This bridge spanned a river near the village of Daumoina, near Madang, about halfway between Wewak and Lae. The planes all dropped their bombs together on the cue of the lead bombardier, Lt. Homer F. Little, but he missed the bridge and all the bombs fell on a mountainside nearby.

However, oddly enough, this apparent failure turned out to be a tremendous success in the long run. General Kenney recorded it in his journal:

32. BRIDGE BUSTING

> We had a lucky break on the Bogadjim road. Eight [six] B-24s tried to bomb the biggest bridge along the route, but missed. The bombs, however, struck the side of the mountain rising abruptly from the river and caused a huge landslide, which blocked the road for nearly a mile and dammed up the river to a height of thirty feet above the water. The river rose rapidly, and on September 30th our recco planes reported that the dam had finally burst, washing out several miles of road and taking out the large bridge we were trying to hit and two other good-sized bridges farther downstream.[2]

When Lt. Little was informed of the results of his bombing, he said that of course it had all worked out according to his plan.[*3]

The Jolly Rogers bomber "Pretty Lady" flies through a typical New Guinea skyscape.

---

* Presumably said with a straight face.

CHAPTER THIRTY-THREE

THE BIG STRIKE ON RABAUL

The U. S. Marines and Army troops secured the island of Guadalcanal by early February of 1943. The Americans then began advancing up the Solomon island chain toward Rabaul as part of an Allied strategy code-named Operation Cartwheel, whose goal was to neutralize Rabaul, sometimes called the Japanese Gibraltar of the Southwest Pacific. The plan visualized establishing a ring of Allied airfields on the islands around Rabaul to isolate it, and then taking the town by amphibious assault (although a decision was eventually made by General MacArthur and Admiral Halsey to simply bypass it). The Marine forces coming up from Guadalcanal, 600 miles to the southeast, also wanted airfields near enough to Rabaul that their short-range aircraft, such as dive-bombers, could attack it, escorted by their fighters.

The Japanese-held island of Bougainville, only about 200 miles southeast of Rabaul (Map 33-1, below), fit the bill for a new Allied airbase and was therefore chosen for the next American invasion. Soil tests around

Map 33-1. The big strike on Rabaul on 12 Oct. 1943 by the Jolly Rogers and other bomb groups based in New Guinea was to beat down Japanese airpower to prevent it from interfering with the Marine and Army landings on Bougainville on November 1.

Empress Augusta Bay on the western side of Bougainville Island (conducted by clandestine reconnaissance parties landed by submarine) showed that the ground just inland from the coastline was free of swamps and was flat and firm enough to support airfields. The invasion of Bougainville was therefore scheduled for November 1, 1943. An airfield built at Bougainville would only be 240 miles from Rabaul.

However, the short distance between Rabaul and Bougainville cut both ways; it would also allow Japanese aircraft to easily reach the American landing forces and bomb the beachhead. Therefore General Kenney planned a heavy strike on Rabaul in mid-October to suppress Japanese airpower there and tie it down in defense, so that the U. S. Marines and elements of the Army's 37th Infantry Division could make their landings on Bougainville unmolested.

Col. Art Rogers, the Group Commander, led the Jolly Rogers in the big Oct. 12, 1943 daylight attack on Rabaul. All the B-24s would have nose turrets.

The Jolly Rogers had not hit Rabaul in daylight since January 5, when Gen. Walker, leading the attack in one of the bombers, was shot down and lost, but they would be part of this big daytime strike on Oct. 12, and this time Col. Rogers would lead the Jolly Rogers. And by this time, October of 1943, all the 90th's bombers had nose turrets, installed either at the Repair and Overhaul Depot in Brisbane or in the field at Port Moresby, making them much less vulnerable to fighter plane attacks from the front than they had previously been. Field installation of nose turrets would become unnecessary in 1944 when the new J-model B-24s began arriving with factory-installed nose turrets, thereby fulfilling Col. Rogers' long-sought goal of getting the B-24 redesigned to take a nose turret. Many more bomber crews would survive the war as a result.

Port Moresby was also gaining airpower as more American planes and pilots arrived from the States, as part of the reinforcements that General Ken-

On the 12 Oct. 1943 strike at Rabaul the twin-engine Mitchell B-25 strafer-bombers went in ahead of the heavy bombers at low level and attempted to catch and destroy Japanese fighter planes on the ground. Paul I. "Pappy" Gunn custom-built these strafers from stock B-25s in Brisbane. Most had eight heavy machine guns mounted in the nose, but a few, like this one, carried three 20mm cannon. Not many were fitted with multiple cannon, both because they fired too slowly and the recoil tended to damage the airframes.

ney had been promised by Washington. In mid-June of 1943 the 345th Bomb Group (Medium) had arrived at Port Moresby with the first of its B-25s, which would soon grow to number over a hundred. In July the 348th Fighter Group had arrived at Moresby with thirty-six Republic P-47 Thunderbolt fighters, and in mid-August the 475th came in with forty-four P-38s, General Kenney's favorite fighter, which would soon grow to well over a hundred. And several B-24s and their crews came over from the States to join the Jolly Rogers, replacing some of the veteran crews who were thereby freed to return home. These were not large numbers of aircraft by the standards of the European war, but they were enough to make a significant difference in the Pacific.

The American weathermen predicted clear skies for 12 October, so that was the day chosen for the operation. Aerial photos taken the day before the strike showed 128 Japanese bombers and 145 fighters on Rabaul's four airfields. General Kenney's attack the next day would be the largest airstrike of the Pacific war up to that point. It would be a coordinated strike involving 87 four-engine heavy bombers, both B-24s and B-17s, 114 twin-engine B-25s, 12 Australian Beaufighters, 125 P-38 fighter planes, and various weather and camera aircraft.[1] The low-flying B-25 strafer/bombers would go in first and attempt to surprise and eliminate the Japanese fighter planes on the ground, to reduce opposition to the heavy bombers coming in behind them. Those bombers would have their own fighter cover to deal with any enemy fighters that made it into the air. However, the best laid plans, especially in war, oft go astray, and these plans were among them. As things turned out, the heavy bombers would meet with swarms of enemy fighters anyway.

Each of the Jolly Rogers' four squadrons would contribute six bombers, and General Kenney's personal aide Major "Kip" Chase would fly along with Col. Rogers as an observer, as he so often did. Other observers would be furnished by international press agencies that could find correspondents and photographers brave enough to ride along in some of the other bombers. These included Robert Crombie of the *Chicago Tribune*, flying in a 90th bomber named "Satan's Sister."

The Jolly Rogers bombers would all carry 1,000-pound bombs, eight per plane, and each squadron would concentrate on a different target in and around Rabaul and its harbor. Each squadron's forty-eight high-explosive 1,000-pounders all landing close together on or near a target had a potential to do tremendous damage to it.

When it was announced that Art Rogers would lead the Jolly Rogers in this strike, the first thing his men thought about was that their leader's shiny polished-aluminum bomber, "Connell's Special," being the only plane stripped of its paint at that time, might attract undue attention from Japanese fighter planes, and perhaps get Rogers and his crew killed. The suicidal ramming of Capt. Roy Olsen's bomber by a Japanese plane on June 23rd (p. 183) was still fresh in their minds. Rogers wrote:

> As soon as it became known in the camp that I intended to lead the first big daylight strike on Rabaul, enlisted men and officers began to question me as to whether I intended to fly my "Silver Streak" ["Connell's Special"]. When told that it was my intention, they insisted I had better reconsider, since some slap-happy Jap might decide that an important general was leading the formation, and one would probably pull the same fanatical stunt they had on Captain Olsen and dive right through my plane, thereby assuring himself of a high position in the hereafter.
>
> I had been so busy up until this time that I had really not given it any thought, but after it was brought to my attention, I must admit that it did worry me a little... The question was definitely settled, though, when my four squadron commanders marched into

my office as a unit for the meeting I had called and one of them stepped forward and said, "Colonel, we have decided you will *not* fly "Connell's Special" in the attack tomorrow. We agree with you that without the paint it improves the operation of the plane, but if we can prevent it, no fool Jap is going to dive down through you."

Then another spoke up and said, "We all have an extra airplane in our squadron, and you can have your choice of any one of the four." I was startled at first, for always in the past my squadron commanders had never questioned any of my decisions, and this almost rebellious attitude on my behalf so pleased me that I told them, "Pick the plane you want me to fly, and that will be the one I'll fly tomorrow when we attack Rabaul."

They informed me that the preparations for the strike were progressing as well as could be expected, and we discussed for the next couple of hours the finer details in the method of approach and attack.[2]

The story of this mission is best told in Col. Rogers' own words:

The process of planning this mission, as in all other missions, had taken its normal channel from the Air Force Commander [General George Kenney] down through the Bomber Commander to the Group Commander, then the Squadron Commanders and from the Squadron Commanders to their flight commanders. Then last but most important was our large Group briefing prior to the takeoff when every pilot, copilot, navigator, bombardier, gunner, radio operator and photographer are thoroughly informed as to exactly what our plans would be. As this was the most dangerous mission by far that the Group had undertaken, it brought about a tense air that could not and would not be dispelled until after it was completed. Some of the lights in the tents burned most of the night while the occupants played cards in an effort to

Armorers prepare bombs for loading into a B-24. Tail fins will be attached to the bombs before they are hung in the bomb bay.

keep their minds off tomorrow's mission, while others went to bed early hoping that a good night's sleep would help fortify their courage for the next day's flight.

I have often wondered what passes through the minds of these combat crewmen prior to a mission, but since this is a subject that is never discussed, I never had the courage to ask any of my boys about this feeling. It is true that many nights the entire camp would be awakened by terrible screams caused by some horrible nightmare by one or more of the combat crewmen. Even though a great deal of my religious belief is based on "What is to be will be," it does not prevent the sort of feeling that makes your heart skip a beat when you wonder if your number will be called when you're facing death on tomorrow's mission.

My normal escape from this feeling would be that of sweating out the tactics, their execution, and the eventual success of the mission. This Rabaul raid was no exception, since I had more planning to do than usual, and I was also faced with [giving] the entire crew briefing the next morning. This not only involved explaining the plan of attack but took on the aspects of a pep talk by a coach to his team before a big football game. A lot of this is necessary to add courage to the doubtful minds of many of the crewmen, and I found that it paid big dividends when it was done and done properly.

That night my period of sleep was limited, since I went down to the line after midnight to check on the remaining airplanes that were in the process of being loaded, and to make sure that everything would be ready to go at daylight. Upon returning to my quarters I was so tired that I fell across the bed and was asleep before I knew it. Breakfast was called for three-thirty in the morning, and when the alarm clock went off I could scarcely believe I had been asleep.

I packed my little emergency kit, buckled on my forty-five and holster and went out and crawled into my jeep. As the starter whirled in an effort to get the engine started a loud backfire awakened my large cockatoo who screamed out, "Damn the Japs!" He must have connected this loud noise with the many air raids he had lived through and thought the Japs were at it again. This gave me a good send-off and I considered it a good sign.

Breakfast was over in a hurry, and with a couple of sandwiches stuffed in my pocket for a lunch that I hoped to enjoy on my way back, I headed for the briefing tent that was located on the field. Within a few minutes after I arrived the place was packed and jammed with serious looking young faces. At these briefings it was never necessary to rap for order as very few words were spoken by anyone.

I started off my briefing by telling the men, "Our struggle has been a long, hard uphill grind, and now we have reached the place where we either go over the hump or slide back down the hill, and [the latter] is something we can't allow to happen. Our mission today will give each one of us an opportunity to repay Japan for their treacherous attack on Pearl Harbor, that is, providing every squadron commander, flight commander and bombardier concentrates on sinking the surface vessel assigned as his target."

I then had Big Ben Browder read them the Field Order, which covered the many points I have mentioned before. After the reading of the field order, I explained in detail our method of attack. I told them we would break up into separate elements and approach the target from different angles and at different altitudes, so as to allow each flight leader to concentrate his bombing run on his particular target, and also to diversify the flak. I explained to them that the majority of the Jap fighter planes would be knocked out or on the ground refueling at the time of our attack, but just in case we were intercepted by a small force, we would have some of our own pursuit as fighter protection.

I then had Captain Roy Dye, our intelligence officer, explain to them the location and concentration of the Jap antiaircraft guns. He also outlined the area along the coast of New Britain to make a crash landing if it was necessary, since at this place we hoped to have an American submarine that would endeavor to rescue the unfortunate crew. After Captain Dye finished his briefing, Captain Lindsay, our Weather Officer, covered the forecasted weather on the route out and back. According to the forecast, we were to have the clear skies we had all hoped for. I finished up the briefing with a short pep talk, and a warning to the flight commanders that should one of their wingmen get damaged to immediately throttle back and notify his squadron commander of his difficulties. All crews were sent to their airplanes, and the entire Group was placed on alert status, since the time of our takeoff was set as forty-five minutes after the time of the takeoff of the last Mitchell [B-25] strafer.

While waiting for the takeoff signal, my crew and I were studying the target that I had chosen for our particular element, consisting of six airplanes. The target was a huge destroyer tender which serviced destroyers and submarines, and was loaded down with precision instruments for checking radar and other complicated equipment on these ships. It is virtually a high-powered machine shop, and from the standpoint of cost it equals that of a cruiser. Since precision instruments and machine tools are almost irreplaceable in wartime, this made this one ship a prize target. In addition to this, in the past three days our reconnaissance photographs had shown a minimum of four destroyers tied alongside the tender undergoing repairs.

Ace was licking his chops, and figuring [that] if he could plant our forty-eight one-thousand pound bombs on top of this nest of ships, we could destroy more valuable tonnage than the Japs could replace in months, with our flight of six planes alone. He said, "Colonel, in case we hit the target and live to get back from this raid, what are the chances of the crew taking a week's leave in Sydney?" I had this in mind before he mentioned it, since my crew had been deprived of their normal leave that the other combat crews had enjoyed.

This was due to the fact that Ben, in addition to being my copilot, was Group Operations Officer, and Ace, in addition to being my bombardier, was the Group Bombardiering Officer, and Conti functioned as Group Navigator in addition to being the navigator on my plane. In fact, they made up practically my entire Group Staff, who normally are not used for combat at all. I kiddingly told him, "Ace, your leave depends on whether the bombs hit the target or not." He turned to Conti and said, "In that case, Conti, we'll start packing as soon as we return."

When given the signal by Bomber Command to take off, each plane taxied from its revetment down the taxiway in a long line, with the first airplane taking off on reaching the beginning of the runway, and each successive airplane taking off at intervals of forty-five seconds. A few minutes after the last plane became airborne, we assembled our large formation over the field and departed for the Trobriand Islands,* where we were to pick up the twenty-eight [P-38] fighters which were to act as our defensive cover [map, p. 343].

Upon reaching the Trobriands, our fighter formation was waiting for us and we immediately departed for the target. Since the success of our attack depended a great deal upon radio silence, all crews had been instructed to leave their radios turned off until we were actually in sight of our target. This increased the difficulties in handling such a large formation, and had I known what I found out when I returned to the base, I would have had all the radios on and would have been giving instructions that were actually necessary.

Our flight across the Bismarck [Solomon] Sea was uneventful, with the exception of two airplanes in my formation having to turn back due to engine trouble. Our flight to within one and a half hours of the target had been made at an altitude of approximately 13,000 feet. This was done even though our bombing altitude was set for between 20,000 and 24,000, because a man cannot live above 15,000 feet without oxygen, and our supply of oxygen aboard each plane could not be depended upon for more than three hours.

Our formation was still climbing, and was at around 18,000 feet when we struck the southern coast of New Britain. When our formation was some twenty miles due west of Rabaul harbor, I gave

---

*American ground forces had occupied Kiriwina Island, the largest in the Trobriand Islands group off the north coast of New Guinea, on 30 June, 1943, and the engineers had built a 6000-foot long, 150-foot wide airfield on the island that was used as a forward base for American fighter planes. Flying from this airfield the fighters could escort bombers to and from Rabaul and other targets in the area. No American bombers were based at Kiriwina, but they could use the field for emergency landings.

the visual signal, wobbling my wings to indicate the breaking up of the large formation into smaller formations consisting of elements. Being this far from the target, it allowed each element leader to maneuver his element to the predetermined position he was to start his bombing run from. With the formation spread out into individual elements, it became virtually impossible for the small number of fighters accompanying us to cover more than a very small portion of our formation.

I started my element in on its run towards the target with the sky ahead of us black with bursting three, six and eight-inch shells from the land and naval vessels' guns. Once my run commenced, I kept my eyes on the instruments, which prevented me from seeing the many large flak bursts in and around our formation. I could tell by the indication of my instruments that Ace was making a good bombing run, and as the little light flickered on the instrument panel telling me the bombs were on their way, I had every confidence that they would find their mark.

As I glanced out to see which way to turn to evade the flak, I was amazed and flabbergasted to see, just ahead of us, the biggest swarm of enemy fighters I had ever seen in the air at one time. At about the same time, Ace's voice came clearly over the interphone, "We hit the target, sir." I had no time to congratulate him or anyone else, as there must have been a good 250 to 300 Zeros preparing to attack.[3] They had spotted us, and apparently another one of my elements that was off to the left of us. As we left the target, by actual count made from a window on the right by Maj. Kip Chase, who was riding as an observer, there were eighty-seven individual attacks made by the Jap fighters [on just that side]. There were equally this many made on the left side, not counting the attacks [from] underneath and above.

The Japs would fly by us in formations of twenty-five to thirty airplanes on each side of our formation, just out of reach of our guns, until they were out ahead of us about five miles. Then they would simultaneously turn in from the right and left, and with reference to the nose of our plane, attacks were made from ten o'clock to twelve and from twelve o'clock to three, which is the method we use in reporting positions of attacking airplanes to our gunners. The airplane is considered to be the dial of a clock, with the nose being twelve o'clock, the tail is six o'clock, the right wing being three o'clock and the left wing nine o'clock.

This method of reporting enemy attacks was found to be the simplest, and a gunner never had to hesitate to figure out the exact location the attack was being made from. With all radios on [and] reporting the position of new attacks it sounded like this: "Six airplanes at two o'clock getting in position to attack." "For Christ's sake nose gunners get on that lead plane." "Two more planes coming in at twelve o'clock." "Ten planes coming in at eleven

33. THE BIG STRIKE ON RABAUL

A Mitchell B-25 strafer/bomber races away from Rabaul Harbor after its low-level attack. In the background, white smoke billows from Rabaul's dock facilities while Japanese ships burn in the harbor.

o'clock and from below." "Six ships coming in at twelve o'clock and above." "Nine planes coming in from five o'clock above."

I was on my radio calling for help from our fighters, [but] from their own conversation, it was evident that they were so outnumbered they were having a problem looking out for themselves. As a result, I never saw a one of our fighters after I commenced my bombing run.

I knew now something had gone wrong with the original plans, and I wondered if the Mitchells [B-25s] had been unable to reach their targets, since I could not imagine how it would be possible for the Japs to throw this many fighters at us if they had had a previous engagement. I could see Zeros flying to pieces in front of us as our good old nose turrets rotated to keep the enemy fighters in our gunsights at all times. My plane had received a 20mm shell in the left wing tank, and the hole was so large that the self-sealing material of the tank was allowing the gasoline to seep out. With the exhaust flame not far from the escaping gas, our plane had become a fire hazard.

I had to slow down, since one of my wingmen's engines had been struck and was belching smoke. From radio conversations, the other flight commanders were all having their difficulties, and I began to wonder if any of us would get back. The Japs had followed us out 75 miles, and were still attacking us as fiercely as if the fight had just

> begun. I finally sighted another element of mine just off to the left, with one of his wingmen losing altitude rapidly. Apparently all but one engine had been shot out, and he called his flight commander and stated that he would have to make a forced landing in the ocean.

This was 1st Lt. Hampton E. Rich, flying a bomber from the 321st Squadron named "Pistol Packin' Mama" (photo, opposite). With only one engine still running, Rich had no choice but to make a landing in the sea, and he made an excellent touchdown on the water, alighting so gently that the B-24 remained intact.

> [I]t was well done [Rogers continued], since the airplane did not break up on landing. It had no sooner come to rest, though, before at least twenty Zeros dove down on him, opening their guns up on this defenseless plane and crew seventy-five miles from land. Before the last of the twenty Zeros had passed in their attack, the airplane was seen to burst into flames, and we were positive there would be no survivors of this crash, as the men had not launched their lifeboats or were probably killed in the attempt.

This was the same cowardly and malevolent behavior by Japanese fighter pilots that had been witnessed in the Battle of the Bismarck Sea, described earlier, in which the fighters abandoned shooting at the American bombers that were a threat to them in order to shoot up helpless men in parachutes who were no threat. In this case they were shooting defenseless men who were trying to escape their sinking plane and launch their two rubber rafts.

The men who were killed along with Lt. Rich by the strafing Japanese fighter planes were:[4]

> 2nd Lt. Albert J. Lavedan
> 2nd Lt. Joseph Rothenberg
> 2nd Lt. Frank L. Moss
> T/Sgt. Robert A. Perry
> T/Sgt. Marvin I. Ivie
> T/Sgt. Ellis G. Thomas
> S/Sgt. Eldon M. Flugge
> S/Sgt. Earl T. Post
> S/Sgt. William H. Bowen

Rogers' narrative continues:

> Another wingman in my element reported an engine out, and the air was full of troubles for every flight commander. I kept wondering if these damned pests would ever run out of gas or ammunition, since it looked like this would be the only cause for them

33. THE BIG STRIKE ON RABAUL

This photograph shows eight of the ten men who were killed when their bomber named "Pistol Packin' Mama" went down under attack by Japanese fighter planes after the strike on Rabaul. They successfully ditched their plane in the sea, but were killed when the Japanese pilots repeatedly strafed them as they tried to deploy their rafts.

to leave us alone. They were pressing home their attacks so closely that you could actually see the Jap pilots as they passed just below or above you. It reminded me of a man trying to destroy a hornet's nest by stepping on it. These little Jap hornets were really mad when they realized that not only had their air supremacy been threatened but we had sunk a good share of their most valuable fleet and merchant vessels right in the center of their nest. They seemed to be determined not to let any of us escape to brag about our feat. They became even madder as they saw their own buddies in planes around them disintegrate and fall into the ocean.

With all our airplanes in trouble, I sent out a call to all flight commanders and airplane commanders notifying them to head for the Trobriand Islands, which was our nearest base, and all seriously damaged airplanes were to land there. Other pilots who thought they could make it as far as Buna were to proceed that far and land. I did not want too many damaged planes trying to land at the Trobriands because a crack-up on the runway, which was almost inevitable, might prevent the other planes from coming in.

The Japs continued to dog us until we were 175 miles out. All the planes in my flight had holes in them, but after conferring with the airplane commanders I decided that none of my six planes were damaged to the extent that we could not make it to Buna. Conti was working furiously on his problem of navigation, since I had used many evasive maneuvers during the 175-mile running fight across the Bismarck [Solomon] Sea. He gave me a new course that would bring me into Buna, and after heading on this course for some thirty minutes my aerial engineer [Sgt. Jake Seper] informed me that our gas loss from the damaged wing tank was far greater than I had expected. It was a question then whether I could get to Buna or should I go back to the Trobriand Islands.

As the Jolly Rogers flew on toward home across the Solomon Sea, each pilot was assessing the battle damage to his bomber and making a decision about whether it could make it over the Owen Stanleys to Port Moresby or would have to divert to one of the emergency fields short of the mountains. One of the planes simply disappeared on this flight back. It was seen by other bombers in the loose formation headed for home, but when all the planes were counted at the end of the day it was not among them. This plane was flown by Flight Officer Donald K. McNeff.

Gunners on another bomber had noticed that the waist section of McNeff's plane seemed to be shot up, but all four engines were running when it was last seen at the rear of the formation. However, unnoticed by anyone, it must have dropped back further and gone down into the sea, since it never arrived at Port Moresby. Since no distress calls were heard, the plane's radios may have been inoperative. Search planes that were sent out looking for it in the days that followed found no trace of it. Those who vanished in this plane along with F/O McNeff were:

    2nd Lt. Lester K. Danks
    2nd Lt. Lucien B. Gray
    2nd Lt. William K. Murray
    T/Sgt. John E. Gormley
    S/Sgt. Francis E. Walker
    S/Sgt. John A. Smith
    S/Sgt. Walter E. Kutcha
    S/Sgt. Stephen K. Boes
    S/Sgt. John L. Ford

 I decided to try and make it to Buna [Rogers continued], and we arrived there all right. I notified the control tower to have the fire trucks and ambulance on the alert, since it is impossible to determine how much damage has been done to a plane while it is still in the air. Oftentimes flak will puncture a tire which is retracted up in the wing, cut a hydraulic line, or damage the retracting

33. THE BIG STRIKE ON RABAUL 343

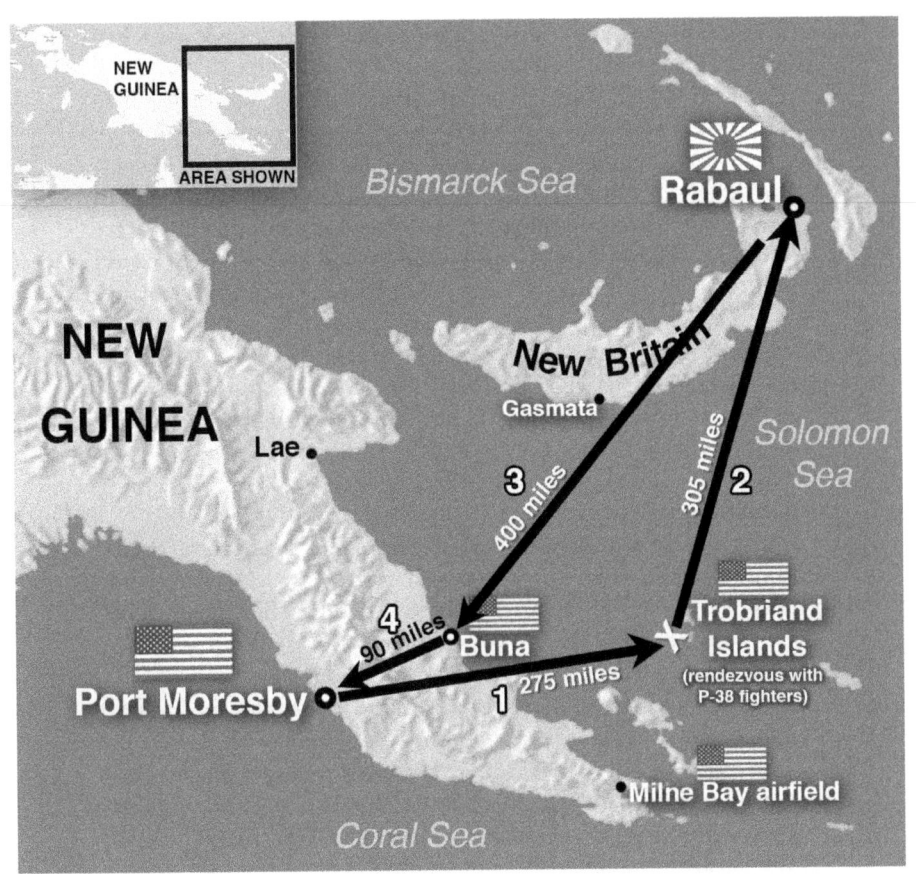

Map 33-2. The route of the 90th Bomb Group's mission to bomb Rabaul on Oct. 12, 1943. Because of battle damage to the bombers from enemy fighter planes, on the return trip Col. Rogers and some of the other pilots landed at Buna instead of trying to make it all the way back across the Owen Stanley Mountains to their base at Port Moresby.

mechanism itself. Some structural member of the plane might have been damaged and so weakened that when subjected to the stress of landing it gives way causing a crash.

On approaching the field, I proceeded straight in to land since my plane was running short of gas. A nice landing was made, but as the plane slowed down to between five and ten miles an hour the nose wheel strut gave way and we stopped just off the edge of the runway on our nose. Everyone crawled out, and after an inspection it was found that a shell had cut through the strut, weakening it, which caused the failure. Other planes landed and it was found necessary to leave two of the planes at Buna for repairs. After servicing the other three, I decided the crew and I would return in one of the other planes and leave the ship I had been flying to be repaired. I was anxious to get back to headquarters to find out how many planes and crews we had actually lost, and what had happened on the Mitchell attack.

As we watched other planes of our Group circling the field to land, all the bombardiers of our flight were congratulating Ace on his beautiful bombing accuracy, and the fact that they saw at least four ships hit. With this good news, and our miraculous escape, all six crews were tired but jubilant, yet within a few minutes they were wondering whether Bill, George, Henry and many others would get through as luckily as we did. We watched about eight planes land, and since no others were in sight, we realized that the rest of the Group must have either gone into the Trobriand Islands or proceeded on in to Port Moresby.

In questioning one of the flight commanders who landed right after we did, we found that he had lost one of his wingmen. He was terribly upset about it, even though I'm sure he did everything he possibly could have done.

Half of my crew got into one of the planes, and the rest of us got into another, and we departed for Port Moresby. Upon arriving, a thorough check was made by radio to determine how many of our planes had landed at the Trobriands and at Buna. We found that there were six Liberators missing [four of them would turn up].

Even though not all the flight commanders had returned to Port Moresby, they had radioed in the results of their bombing, and from all indications, without a thorough interrogation and the developing of photographs, it looked as if the Japs had suffered a heavier blow than we had at Pearl Harbor on December 7th. In all probability the Jap air force and naval commanders at Rabaul would commit hari-kari as the result of this catastrophe, as there was no question that they had not only lost face but their other extremity as well.

After getting the report of our losses, I contacted Bomber Command to find out what had happened to the Mitchell strafing raid. It seems that the Jap radar did not pick up our huge force of airplanes, and the two airdromes the Mitchells strafed had but few of the Jap fighters on them. With the exception of eight or ten planes that finally got off and intercepted our Mitchells on their departure, which were immediately shot down by our heavy fighter cover, there was no other interference.

However, the Jap radar was not fooled into believing that our incoming Liberators were the outgoing Mitchells. In fact, our powerful radios at Port Moresby could hear the Jap ground operations directing their fighters that were in the air, telling them our exact location at least thirty minutes before we got there. Back at our base they knew what trouble we were going into, and we didn't. It was very apparent that the majority of the Jap fighters had been located on the other two airdromes, and these, together with fighters that were not damaged on the airdromes that the Mitchells strafed, took to the air immediately after the Mitchells had departed.

The photographs taken by our airplanes of the bombing, and photographs taken by a recco plane an hour after the bombing, showed the damage to exceed that of our highest expectations.

As usual, the satisfaction of having done great damage to the enemy was tempered by the losses, in this case the twenty young men who crewed the two Jolly Rogers bombers that were lost. Search planes went out looking for them in the days that followed, thinking they may have taken to their life rafts, but no trace of them was ever found.

Aside from the losses, General Kenney was highly pleased with the results of this raid on Rabaul and wrote:

> On October 12th we hit Rabaul with the biggest attack so far in the Pacific... Everything that I owned that was in commission and could fly that far was on the raid.
>
> The B-25s and the Beaufighters opened the attack with simultaneous low-altitude sweeps of the Jap airdromes at Vunakanau, Rapopo, and Tobera and achieved complete surprise, destroying at least 100 airplanes on the ground and badly damaging another fifty-one. Huge fires blazed up from burning fuel dumps, and [there were] heavy explosions at Vunakanau... The B-24s attacked the shipping in Rabaul Harbor, sinking three merchant vessels of between 5,000 and 7,500 tons each, forty-three small merchant ships of 100- to 500-ton size, and seventy small harbor craft. In addition, direct hits were scored, badly damaging five more medium-sized cargo vessels, a destroyer tender [Col. Rogers' chosen target], three destroyers, and a tanker... Our losses were two B-24s, one B-25, and one Beaufighter...
>
> [E]very airplane but one had attacked its assigned target. During the approach to Rabaul Harbor and while still about three miles from the town, one of the B-24s had been knocked almost over on its back by an antiaircraft shell which had burst just under a wing. In order to regain control, the pilot ordered the four-ton load of bombs released. As they hit the ground, a huge explosion occurred and great clouds of smoke billowed up over a huge area. A direct hit had been inadvertently scored on a big Jap fuel dump that we hadn't even known existed. Even Lady Luck was working for us that day.[4]

Chapter Thirty-Four

MORE LOSSES AT WEWAK

Despite the great losses that the Japanese had suffered at their Wewak airbase in the middle of August (Chapter 31), the Japanese high command was nothing if not persistent. Aerial reconnaissance in late November showed that they were once again building up Wewak with an infusion of new fighters and bombers brought down from Japan through the Philippines. High-flying photo planes kept Gen. Kenney's headquarters continually apprised of exactly where everything was on the Wewak airfields: the revetments where the aircraft were parked, the barracks for the personnel, the fuel and ammunition dumps, headquarters buildings, motor parks, and flak gun positions. The Japanese habit of cutting palm fronds and laying them across their aircraft in an attempt to camouflage them fooled no one in Kenney's photo interpretation section. The Japanese at Wewak had no secrets from the Americans.

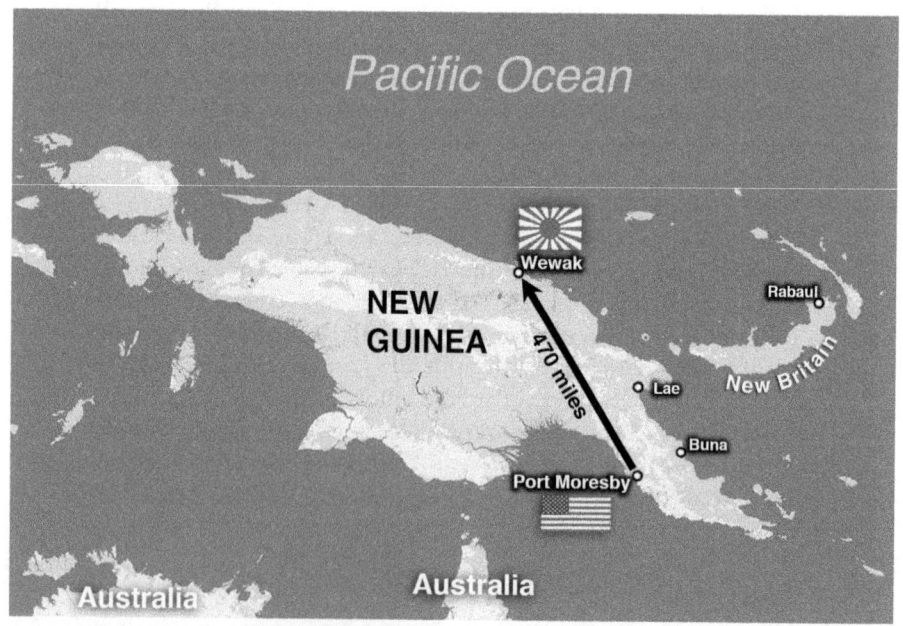

Map 34-1. The route of the Dec. 1, 1943 Jolly Rogers strike on Wewak.

34. MORE LOSSES AT WEWAK

Col. Art Rogers (left) with Capt. Jack Pelander. It was Pelander who (after his promotion to Major) led the Group on the Dec. 1, 1943 strike against Wewak during which three Jolly Rogers bombers were lost, with only six survivors from the three crews.

General Whitehead at 5th Bomber Command was informed by Gen. Kenney that it was time to take out Wewak again, and he assigned the job to the Jolly Rogers. Col. Rogers, the Group Commander, decided to make it a Group effort using six bombers from each of the four squadrons. Rogers did not fly on this raid himself, instead designating Major Jack Pelander [photo above] as the strike leader.

It had been decided that all four squadrons would hit "Wewak Central," the main field of the four-airfield complex, and the one most rich with targets, as shown by aerial photography. Each squadron was assigned to hit a different target on the field. With all four squadrons hitting the same airfield, a plan had been worked out whereby the squadrons would bomb in a certain sequence, coming in from different directions and altitudes to confuse the Japanese flak gunners.

Accordingly, on the 1st of December, 1943, in daylight, so that the bombardiers could see their targets well, the twenty-four bombers took off from Ward's Field at Port Moresby and headed directly northwest across the Owen Stanley Mountains for Wewak (Map 34-1, opposite). Two bombers turned back to base with mechanical problems. No friendly fighter plane cover is

A Jolly Rogers formation headed to a target.

mentioned in the records of this mission, although the bombers certainly could have used some.

The strike did serious damage to the Japanese airfield, with many of its airplanes caught and wrecked on the ground, and buildings, fuel, and ammunition dumps hit and destroyed, but it turned out to be a costly raid for the Americans: three Jolly Rogers bombers were shot down on this day. As noted in earlier chapters, this Japanese stronghold had already claimed Lt. McMurria's bomber, and then the plane of Lt. Regan who had gone there looking for him. Two more of the Group's planes had been lost on the night attack of 16-17 August (Chapter 31), and the losses would continue with subsequent raids. Before the war ended, Wewak would claim a total of eleven Jolly Rogers bombers, while even the raids on heavily defended Rabaul only resulted in the loss of five.[1]

On 1 Dec. 1943, Wewak was strongly defended by fighter planes in the air and many flak guns on the ground. Capt. Lawrence N. Smith of the Group's 320th Squadron was flying a bomber named "Pudgy," with twelve men aboard. In addition to the regular crew of ten, there was a new pilot riding along in the plane as an observer on an orientation flight, as well as a photographer. This would be the new pilot's first and last combat mission.

The men aboard the bomber "Pudgy" were:

    Capt. Lawrence N. Smith, pilot, from Iowa
    1st Lt. George M. Dempster, copilot, from Scotland

34. MORE LOSSES AT WEWAK 349

A nest of Japanese antiaircraft guns in round emplacements at Wewak, in a photograph taken from a low-flying B-25 strafer/bomber.

A closer view shows the details of one of the flak guns.

The bomber "Pudgy" piloted by Capt. Lawrence N. Smith was shot down on the December 1, 1943 raid on Wewak. The bomber's name was obviously meant to describe the B-24 itself, not the female figure painted on its nose. The wreckage of this plane lies today somewhere in a vast swamp forty-five miles southeast of Wewak, New Guinea.

1st Lt. Harry M. Stoll, navigator, from Pennsylvania
1st Lt. Kenneth E. Twitty, bombardier, from Mississippi
F/O Daryl M. Stewart, observer, from South Dakota
T/Sgt. John H. Lenaghan, flight engineer, from Illinois
T/Sgt. Paul D. Waite, radio operator, from Illinois
S/Sgt. William C. Gotcher, gunner, from Tennessee
S/Sgt. Carl A. Canady, gunner, from Arkansas
Sgt. Sidney L. Baggett, gunner, from Louisiana
S/Sgt. William H. Bundy, tail gunner, from Michigan
S/Sgt. Mercy Rendon, Jr., photographer, from Texas

The plan for each of the squadrons to bomb in a certain sequence somehow broke down over the target, and they all ended up attacking more or less at the same time from different altitudes and directions. In all the confusion the 320th Squadron aborted its first bomb run, veered away, and made a second run, prolonging its exposure to the flak guns below. On the second run "Pudgy" took a flak hit in its number two engine, which began trailing smoke, and the plane began slowing down. Capt. Smith called his squadron leader, Capt. Joseph H. Rodenberg, and let him know that he had a problem, so Rodenberg slowed down the other planes of the formation so that Smith could stay with them. Japanese fighter planes then attacked the formation from above, and knowing that they always went after cripples first, some of the other planes in the formation moved over to try to cover Smith's plane.

The formation then entered a slight left turn, but Capt. Smith's bomber did not turn with the others and went straight. Smith was obviously too preoccupied with a fire that had broken out inside his plane to be concerned with trying to stay in formation—the men in the bomber were probably frantically trying to fight the fire. A bomber flying behind Smith's, piloted by Lt. H. C. Mills, passed through the smoke from Smith's number two engine and discovered that it was an oil mist—the oil coated Mills' windshield and prevented him from seeing forward. From then on Mills could only see out his side cockpit window and had trouble keeping formation himself.

Other pilots in the squadron called Capt. Rodenberg to tell him that the formation should turn back to the right to stay with Smith and continue covering for him, but by that time the fire inside Smith's plane had gotten out of control and the plane was too far gone to help. Men began bailing out of the bomber to avoid being burned alive. One was seen to fall from the camera hatch near the tail of the plane without a parachute, and two more jumped from the bomb bay. Someone on the flight deck opened the escape hatch above the pilots, but only flames came out of it. Both engines on the right wing also caught fire.

It appeared that Capt. Smith was keeping control of his burning bomber, holding it straight and level so that his men could jump, despite the inferno that must have been raging around him on the flight deck. Eight parachutes were seen to open before "Pudgy" slammed into a swampy area about 45 miles down the coast from Wewak and exploded (see Map 34-2 on page 362).

The eight men who parachuted from Capt. Smith's bomber before it crashed were never seen or heard from again, which was the norm whenever Americans bailed out near a Japanese base. It is probable that at least some, if not all of the men were captured and killed by the Japanese. A Japanese propaganda broadcast some weeks later mentioned that Flight Officer Daryl Stewart, the new pilot who had gone along on Capt. Smith's bomber as an observer, was a prisoner. Stewart's family in North Dakota, who had already been notified that he was missing in action, was further informed that he had been mentioned in a Japanese radio broadcast as a prisoner of war. This kindled their hopes that he might survive the war in a prison camp, but hope only led to heartbreak when nothing more was ever heard of him, and no trace of him, nor of the oth-

Wewak, 1943. This photo taken during a bombing raid on the Japanese airbase shows how it appeared to the crews aboard the bombers. Bomb explosions are circled. Jolly Rogers bombers are dropping bombs just to the left of the Japanese airfield, possibly targeting an aircraft dispersal area or a fuel dump, although some of the bombs have fallen in the water just offshore. The picture at right shows this same area as it appears today.

er men who had bailed out along with him, was ever found after the war. It is highly likely that they all suffered the fate of most American airmen captured by the Japanese: interrogation, possibly torture, and then death.

The eight men who bailed out of "Pudgy" may have assembled on the ground, may have formulated a plan to evade the Japanese and return to Allied lines, may even have been on the move in

Three Jolly Rogers bombers were named "Pistol Packin' Mama (spelling varied).

34. MORE LOSSES AT WEWAK

Wewak today (2018). In this recent aerial photograph, the same area is circled as in the 1943 photograph at left, and 75 years later the craters made by the bombs, now filled with water, can still be seen (magnified in inset) in an open field back of the beach. The coastal highway in the magnified view provides scale for the size of the craters. The largest one is over sixty feet across. Note that the former Japanese airfield is now built over with postwar structures.

the jungle when, like McMurria's crew, they ran into Japanese patrols, were outnumbered and outgunned (American airmen carried only pistols) and were killed or captured. Whatever happened to these Americans will probably never be known, and their remains are likely buried in unmarked graves somewhere in or around Wewak, New Guinea.

Meanwhile on this day another bomber, this one from the 319th Squadron, was also in trouble. This was another "Pistol Packin' Mamma" (photo, opposite), one of three Jolly Rogers aircraft that carried this name, flown by Lt. Richard A. Adams. The men aboard this bomber were:

        1st Lt. Richard A. Adams, pilot
        1st Lt. John H. Heath, copilot
        1st Lt. Glenn E. Nations, navigator

A crewman aboard another bomber snapped a picture of "Pistol Pakin' Mamma" a few minutes after it ditched in the sea. The rear section of the plane is still afloat, but would go down moments later. When this picture was taken, the four men in this part of the plane may have been struggling to get out, if they hadn't been disabled or killed in the breakup of the plane. In any event they did not get out and went down with the wreckage.

> 1st Lt. Fred H. Blaney, bombardier
> T/Sgt. Joseph H. Hatcher, engineer
> T/Sgt. Lawson M. Johnson, radio operator
> S/Sgt. William D. Ball, gunner
> S/Sgt. Lewis B. Butt, gunner
> S/Sgt. Philip J. LaGarde, Jr., gunner
> S/Sgt. Mitchell E. Balut, gunner

During its bomb run the plane was hit by flak that damaged its number three engine, but Lt. Adams was able to keep his bomber in formation throughout the bomb run; in fact, when the bombardier in the lead plane, whom every other bombardier was cueing on, reported having bombsight trouble, Adams' bombardier, Lt. Blaney, took over for him, and all the planes in the formation dropped when Blaney did.

Then the Japanese flak gunners scored another hit on "Pistol Pakin' Mamma" and set fire to the outer engine on the right wing. Zeros then attacked the plane and did still more damage to it. The internal fire extinguisher was able to put out the engine fire, but the bomber was losing altitude. It was obviously not going to be able to climb over the mountains back to Port Moresby, so Lt.

34. MORE LOSSES AT WEWAK

Adams headed down the coast toward Buna, over 500 miles away, which had an emergency airfield (Dobodura) that could handle heavy bombers.

The crew jettisoned everything loose in the bomber to lighten it and try to keep it in the air, but it was no use; the plane continued losing altitude and was becoming increasingly difficult to control. After flying approximately 250 miles from Wewak, about midway between the town of Saidor on the New Guinea coast and an island called Long Island, 40 miles offshore, it became necessary to ditch (see Map 34-2 on page 362). Lt. Adams and his copilot John Heath managed to set the plane down on the water in a level attitude, but as usual the B-24 broke apart on contact with the water. The four gunners in the waist section of the plane, Sgts. Ball, Butt, Balut, and LaGarde, were unable to get out of the wreckage before it sank and went down with it. The six men on the plane's flight deck were able to escape the sinking wreck, although Lt. Heath later had no memory of how he got out of the cockpit. He had been knocked unconscious on impact with the water and woke up floating in the sea, supported by his Mae West life jacket.

Both of the bomber's life rafts deployed, and the six survivors climbed into them. A bomber piloted by Lt. Stanley Roebeck had accompanied Lt. Adams' crippled bomber down the coastline, keeping it company, and after Adams ditched (and someone aboard Roebeck's plane snapped the picture of "Pistol Pakin' Mamma" at left, just before it sank), Roebeck circled the two

Three crewmen of "Ten Nights in a Bar Room" clowning for the camera. None of these men would survive the Dec. 1, 1943 raid on Wewak.

Three Jolly Rogers B-24s undergoing maintenance in a single revetment at Ward's Field, Port Moresby, New Guinea, in 1943. The bomber "Ten Knights in a Bar Room" can be seen at left.

rafts while his crew dropped all their survival gear to the men in the water, and he continued circling until he was forced to leave when his fuel ran low. He landed at Dobodura and spent the night, and the next day flew back to look for the rafts. After searching the sea for hours, and almost giving up on locating them, he finally found the rafts again, and this time he circled above them for four hours to guide in a Catalina PBY flying boat, which landed near the rafts and took the men aboard.

The third bomber lost by the Jolly Rogers that day was named "Ten Knights in a Bar Room"*and was flown by 1st Lt. Oliver Sheehan. After the 321st Squadron had dropped its bombs and was on its way back to Port Moresby, Sheehan was flying on the far right side of his formation when he was attacked by a lone Japanese Tony fighter plane (photo, opposite). As had happened with Capt. Smith's bomber, a fire broke out inside the fuselage of Lt. Sheehan's plane, and crews of the other planes soon saw intense blue and orange flames

---

*The name is based on a famous temperance novel written in 1854 entitled *Ten Nights in a Bar Room and What I Saw There* by Timothy Shay Arthur.

A Japanese Kawasaki Ki-61 "Tony" fighter plane, the type of plane that reportedly shot down the bomber named "Ten Knights in a Bar Room" on the Dec. 1, 1943 raid on Wewak. The inline engine was a license-built German Daimler-Benz. The Japanese aircraft industry was always more imitative than innovative and relied heavily on its German ally for its new aircraft and engine designs, as formalized in the Nippon-German Technical Exchange Agreement, which gave the Japanese manufacturing rights, blueprints, and in some cases, the actual airframes of German aircraft to copy.

streaming out of the waist gun windows. One of the witnesses felt sure that the oxygen bottles aboard the plane had ruptured and were feeding the flames.[2]

Sheehan must have ordered his crew to bail out, since the bomb bay doors were seen to open to allow them to do so, and soon four parachutes were floating in the plane's wake. The burning bomber entered a shallow dive that became increasingly steep, and then the tail broke off and fell separately. The aircraft continued to disintegrate before slamming into the jungle about 45 miles southeast of Wewak, just a few miles short of the Sepik River (see again Map 34-2, page 362).[3]

Lt. Dustin "Dusty" Swanson was leading the squadron formation when "Ten Knights in a Bar Room" went down, and he wrote in his diary that evening:

> I led the squadron today and we hit Wewak. When we got to the target, things were pretty screwed up and the group leader called up and said to go in one way and then went in a different way himself. That sort of left me out by my lonesome with the squadron, and before I made my run we were hopped by Zeros. I made my run and got the devil out of there.
>
> On the way back, the Zeros got a lucky hit on my number five man [Sheehan] and he burst into flames and went down. We

The crew of the bomber "Ten Knights in a Bar Room," which crashed on Dec. 1, 1943 after a raid on Wewak. Back row, left to right: 1st Lt. Oliver Sheehan, pilot, from Los Angeles, California; 2nd Lt. Robert J. Rothwell, bombardier, from Chicago, Illinois; 2nd Lt. James A. Gebbie, copilot, also from Chicago; 2nd Lt. Wendell P. Rawson, navigator, from Minneapolis, Minnesota. Front row, left to right: T/Sgt. John J. Haggerty, radio operator, from Worcester, Massachusetts; S/Sgt. Rocco W. Bobbora, assistant radio operator, from Chicago; S/Sgt. Thomas D. McNamara, tail gunner, St. Louis, Missouri; T/Sgt. Uhland S. Adair, gunner, from Alabama; S/Sgt. Raymond M. Phillips, waist gunner, from Pittsburgh, Pennsylvania; S/Sgt. Richard D. Wall, gunner, from Nevada.

saw four men bail out. Of course, we were pretty high, and more could have.

They were on us for about thirty minutes, and my tail gunner got one, with the waist getting a probable. When I got back, I found out three planes were shot down out of the group. It was a pretty screwed up deal today... I felt pretty bad about it myself, being I was the leader of the squadron and had one man shot down. I feel a little better now, being that I found out everything was pretty well messed up.[4]

A bomber named "Hot Garters,"* flown by Lt. Bryant E. Poulsen, was flying alongside "Ten Knights in a Bar Room" when it was hit by gunfire from

---

* "Hot Garters" would itself be shot down four months later in April of 1944, over Hansa Bay, New Guinea, with no survivors. The story of this plane and crew is told in Chapter 45.

The headstone of the Sheehan crew's group grave in the Jefferson Barracks National Cemetery in St. Louis, Missouri. The bodies of four of the crewmen were never found, although they are memorialized on the marker.

the Tony. Poulsen's radio operator, T/Sgt. Charles L. Johnson, later wrote in the Missing Aircraft Report (MACR):

> I was manning the left waist gun. The right waist gunner tapped me on the shoulder and pointed to Lt. Sheehan's number two engine. There was smoke coming from it. In a few seconds I could see flames that seemed to cover the whole inside of the gunners' compartment. A second or so after that, the bomb bay doors opened and I saw a few unrecognizable objects fall out. There were also flames shooting out of the bomb bay. The airplane started to lose altitude with flames coming from almost everywhere. The fuselage buckled aft of the rear bomb bay, the wings buckled, and the whole plane seemed to fall apart as it went down.[5]

The flight engineer in "Hot Garters," T/Sgt. Hugh F. Moore, was also watching Lt. Sheehan's plane and wrote:

> A Tony attacked Lt. Sheehan's plane at about two o'clock and his number two engine started to smoke. Almost immediately the fuselage was a mass of flames. For a short time the crippled plane held its original position. Then the tail section broke off the plane, the wings buckled, and the plane went down nose first. The tail section hit the ground about one-half mile from the rest of the plane. The Tony followed the plane down to where it crashed.[6]

The tail gunner in Lt. Swanson's bomber, S/Sgt. James W. Cayten, who was facing to the rear in his tail turret in the lead plane, had a good view of what happened and wrote in the MACR:

> [I] saw Lt. Sheehan attacked by a Tony. The number two engine caught fire. Approximately fifteen seconds after the engine was afire, flames broke out through the bomb bay and waist windows. I saw three chutes open behind the plane. I also saw an object that might have been a man leave the ship; no parachute was seen. I saw two parachutes float with the clouds, and watched the other until out of my view.[7]

In 1969 some native New Guinea children were playing in the jungle near the Sepik River, in an area described as "tropical wet lowland forest" that is rarely visited by people, and they noticed large pieces of metal lying around on the forest floor. They went back to their village, Angoram, and told their schoolteacher about their discovery. He returned to the site with them and confirmed the find, recognizing it as the remains of a WWII aircraft, then notified Australian authorities.

An Australian investigative team found that the children had discovered the wreckage of an American WWII light bomber, an A-20 Havoc, with the remains of the two-man crew still inside. After that crew was recovered, locals informed the Australians of three more wrecks that they knew of in the area, which the Australians investigated the following year (1970). Two of them turned out to be Japanese planes, and the third was a B-24 bomber, scarred by bullets and blackened by fire. Its tail assembly was found a considerable distance away from the main wreckage, and on the vertical fins was a huge skull and crossed bombs symbol painted on a green background. The serial number on the rudders, painted in orange letters, was still legible: 72806.

They had found the wreckage of the B-24 named "Ten Knights in a Bar Room," which had lain undisturbed where it had fallen on Dec. 1, 1943, over 27 years before. In the burned and gutted forward part of the fuselage were found enough scattered bones to represent five men. Four of the five were identified through personal effects: a 1st Lt.'s bar could only have belonged to the pilot, Lt. Oliver Sheehan (the only 1st Lt. aboard the plane), a navigator's pin (with wings emblem) would have been worn by Lt. Wendell P. Rawson, "dog tags"* identified copilot Lt. James Gebbie, and a class ring with initials RJR confirmed the presence of bombardier Lt. Robert J. Rothwell. The fifth man, who would have been one of the crew's six enlisted men, could not be identified by the forensic technology available in the 1970s (DNA testing was

---

*So-called "dog tags" are military-issued aluminum tags with the owner's name and information stamped on them, usually worn around the neck.

Two Jolly Rogers bombers in flight over the seemingly limitless New Guinea jungle. It is easy to see in a picture like this why any bomber that crashed in such a jungle might not be found for years, if ever, and also why any men who survived a crash, or bailed out and tried to walk out, were unlikely to survive (see Fred Miller's comment on trying to survive in such a jungle on p. 511).

not used before 1986). So the crew's four officers, plus one other crewman, had never gotten out of the forward section of the plane before it crashed.

Near the site where the bomber's tail fell, quite some distance from the main wreckage, lay a skeleton still wearing flight boots, the only group of bones that could be attributed to a single man. Among the bones was a wristwatch engraved with the words "From Mom and Dad," and a St. Christopher's medal. The dental work on a jaw fragment matched the records of Sgt. Thomas McNamara (picture on page 358, front row, kneeling, third from left), the bomber's tail gunner, who was a Roman Catholic and would likely have worn the St. Christopher's medal around his neck. McNamara had obviously remained in the detached tail of the bomber all the way to the ground. The skeleton's considerable distance from the bomber's tail led one member of the recovery team to speculate that McNamara had survived the impact with the ground but was fatally injured, and had died while crawling away from the wreckage. Or perhaps he staggered away from the tail, fell down, and never got up. No one will ever know.

The fact that there were no traces of the other four crewmen in or around the wreckage supports the accounts of the witnesses who saw four parachutes in the

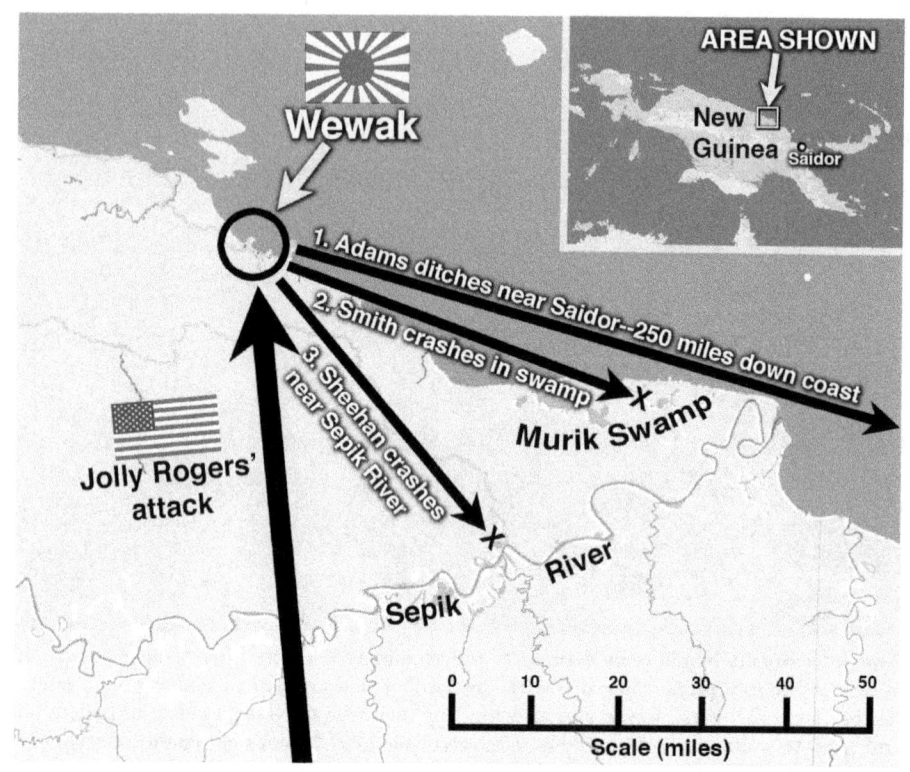

Map 34-2. Three Jolly Rogers bombers were lost on the Dec. 1, 1943 mission against Wewak. Arrow #1: Lt. Adams ditched his damaged bomber named "Pistol Pakin' Mamma" 250 miles down the coast near Saidor (see insert map). Arrow #2: Capt. Smith's bomber "Pudgy" went down somewhere in the vast Murik Swamp near the coast. Arrow #3, Lt. Sheehan's bomber "Ten Knights in a Bar Room" crashed in dense jungle near the Sepik River.

air as the plane was going down. Those four men likely made it to the ground, found each other, and, as Lt. McMurria and his crew had done ten months earlier when they, too were shot down near Wewak, tried to walk out and return to Allied lines. Aside from the danger of unfriendly natives or Japanese patrols, the young Americans probably had no knowledge of how to survive in a jungle (New Guinea jungles are notoriously devoid of edible plants and contain no large game animals). Whatever course of action the four men took must have ended in tragedy, for nothing was ever heard of them and no trace of them has ever been found. Their story, too, will probably never be known.

All the human remains gathered up at the crash site were delivered to the Army's mortuary lab, the Central Identification Laboratory in Hawaii (CIL-HI), which determined that only Sgt. McNamara's bones could be positively identified as all belonging to one person. McNamera's remains, along with his wristwatch, the St. Christopher's medallion, the boots, and a few other small personal effects were returned to his mother, who buried him in a Catholic cemetery in St. Louis in May of 1971.

The lab decided that the remaining bones should represent all the other crewmen, even the four absent ones, and they were interred in a group grave at the Jefferson Barracks National Cemetery in St. Louis, Missouri on June 8, 1971. The headstone over the grave lists all the members of the crew except McNamara, as the photo on page 359 shows.[*]

The funeral was attended by many members of the men's families and made headlines all over the country. These young men, six crewmen of one bomber, had finally come home 28 years after that terrible day, December 1, 1943, when twenty-six young American men were lost.

In 1990 Michael J. Cundiff wrote a book about the bomber named "Ten Knights in a Bar Room"[†] in which he described each crewman's background and prewar activities, and how he came to enlist in the Air Corps and become a bomber crewman. Cundiff was also able to get eyewitness accounts from men aboard other bombers of "Ten Knights in a Bar Room" catching fire and going down. He conducted interviews with the men's relatives and recorded their memories of the shock and grief experienced by the families when their loved ones went missing in action, then the anguish of not knowing anything about their fate for years, and finally the mixed feelings that accompanied the finding of the men's remains and their return for burial at home. The book is an excellent study in the human cost and tragedy of war.

When the Jolly Rogers bombers returned to Port Moresby after the Dec. 1, 1943 Wewak raid, a number of them had been badly shot up by Japanese fighter planes and flak bursts, and several came in to land with their landing lights burning to signal that they had wounded aboard. The Group's doctors and medics, waiting beside the runway in ambulance trucks as usual, raced to the planes as soon as they came to a stop and jumped aboard to tend to the wounded. The most seriously hurt were airlifted to hospitals in Australia.

Later in the day there was a good deal of shock and sadness when it was realized that three of the Group's planes were not coming back. Sgt. Carl Camp, a gunner in the crew of Lt. Carl. H. Vineyard, had friends among Lt. Sheehan's crew and was especially hard hit by their loss. "I was only 17 then," he wrote, "and it was hard, and for a moment I even forgot to be ashamed of crying a little. One gets closer than brothers with the men one flies with, and when they die, the pain is fierce."[8]

---

[*] Many such group burials are located in the Jefferson Barracks cemetery because it is centrally located for visits by family members from all over the country.

[†] *Ten Knights in a Bar Room, Missing in Action in the Southwest Pacific, 1943*, by Michael J. Cundiff, Iowa State University Press, 1990.

After Col. Rogers learned of all the confusion the squadrons had experienced over the target that day, he called a meeting of all the flight leaders the next morning to discuss the problems with the mission. Lt. Swanson wrote in his diary:

> Had a meeting at the Colonel's tent this morning for all flight leaders. He was pretty well pushed out of shape about yesterday's mission and let us know about it.[9]

Wiley O. Woods, the historian of the 90th Bomb Group, wrote:

> Colonel Rogers was very displeased with the performance of the Group on the previous day, not only due to the losses, but also because of the confusion over the target. A meeting was called . . . and the men were read the riot act. Then they were sent aloft for some practice bombing.[10]

An unnamed Jolly Rogers bomber flies in typical New Guinea weather. The waist gunner, with his gun stowed away and both hands on the window sill, watches the cameraman on another bomber take the picture.

Chapter Thirty-Five

CAPE GLOUCESTER GETS "GLOUCESTERIZED"

Map 35-1 below shows the war situation in the Southwest Pacific at the end of September, 1943. Lae had fallen to the Allies on September 15, and the Americans now owned the entire tail of the New Guinea "buzzard," while the Japanese, across the Vitiaz Strait, still controlled

Map 35-1. The situation in the Southwest Pacific in the fall of 1943. In order to ensure complete control of the Vitiaz Strait, the Allies would have to eliminate the three Japanese airbases on New Britain at Cape Gloucester, Arawe Island, and Gasmata. General MacArthur decided to take each one by amphibious assault. Rabaul would be neutralized and bypassed.

all of the island of New Britain. After the big American airstrike on Rabaul on October 12th, in which the Jolly Rogers figured so prominently (covered in Chapter 33), General MacArthur stated his intention to bypass Rabaul after it had been neutralized by further aerial bombardment and move straight up the back of the New Guinea "buzzard" toward the Philippines. Part of the strategy of eliminating opposition from Rabaul in the last months of 1943 was depriving it of its secondary airfields at Cape Gloucester, Arawe, and Gasmata on the southern and western coasts of New Britain. MacArthur decided to take these airfields by amphibious assault.

There was another imperative for capturing these three Japanese airfields. The contingent of the U. S. Navy that was furnishing landing craft and destroyers to MacArthur's amphibious landings did not like the idea of the Japanese having airfields so close to their ships operating along the New Guinea coast, and told General MacArthur that they especially wanted the airfield at Cape Gloucester, on the opposite side of the Vitiaz Straits from Lae, captured and occupied by the Allies. By taking Cape Gloucester, the Americans would own both sides of the Vitiaz Strait, and the Navy would feel more secure passing through it. Capturing Cape Gloucester would also give the Allies an airbase closer to Rabaul from which to strike and neutralize it with American airpower.

Therefore, as part of MacArthur's Operation Cartwheel to eliminate Rabaul as a threat, a campaign was begun to capture Cape Gloucester, along with the smaller Japanese airbases at Arawe (a. k. a. Cape Merkus) and Gasmata farther down the southern coast of the island (refer again to Map 35-1, previous page, and Map 35-2 opposite). MacArthur decided that all three places would have to be taken by amphibious assault, but the Japanese simplified things somewhat in late November when they abandoned their airfield at Gasmata after heavy bombing by the Jolly Rogers. Gasmata had only been a staging base anyway, in support of Yamamoto's "Operation 81," the resupply of Lae by convoy that had resulted in the Battle of the Bismarck Sea.

With Gasmata out of the picture, there was only Cape Gloucester and Arawe to deal with, and of the two, Cape Gloucester and its two airfields was the more important. However, it was hoped that the threat of an assault on Arawe would serve as a diversion from the Cape Gloucester operation and cause the Japanese to send reinforcements to Arawe, thereby weakening their Gloucester defenses. This strategy had already worked well during the Allied drive on Salamaua a few months earlier, when the Japanese sent reinforcements down from Lae to Salamaua, when in fact Lae had been the main objective all along. There was every expectation that they would fall for the same ruse on New Britain, since, as General Kenney was fond of saying, the

35. CAPE GLOUCESTER GETS "GLOUCESTERIZED" 367

Map 35-2. As the U. S. Navy and Marines moved up the Solomon Islands from Guadalcanal to Bougainville (curved white arrow) in November of 1943, the Fifth Air Force, including the Jolly Rogers, pounded Rabaul to keep the Japanese from interfering with the Bougainville beachhead. Navy and Marine aircraft would return the favor in late December, hitting Rabaul while MacArthur invaded Cape Gloucester.

Japanese were "not big league players" when it came to strategy, never seeming to learn from past errors.

At this time the 1st Marine Division was in Melbourne, Australia,[*] recuperating from the battles on Guadalcanal, and since they were in Australia, which was part of the Southwest Pacific Area, they came under the jurisdiction of General MacArthur. These were battle-hardened troops, and he decided to use them in his assault on Cape Gloucester. There was some concern that opposition to the American landings at Cape Gloucester and Arawe might come from Japanese aircraft flying out of Rabaul, but a plan was developed to minimize this threat. Recall that America had two more-or-less independent forces driving northward toward Japan in the Pacific war: Admiral Halsey's South Pacific naval forces, with the Marines, which were island-hopping their way north after their victory at Guadalcanal, and General MacArthur's Southwest Pacific Army forces moving up from Australia through Port Moresby and along the back of the New Guinea "buzzard" toward the Philippines. A plan of cooperation was devised between MacArthur and Halsey that would be of benefit to both.

---

[*] While they were in Australia the 1st Marine Division adopted the Australian folk song "Waltzing Matilda" as its battle hymn.

At this time Admiral Halsey was planning to land Marines on Bougainville Island in the Solomon island chain and establish an airbase there (Map 35-2 above). His chosen landing site, on the western side of the island at Empress Augusta Bay, was only 240 miles from Rabaul, within easy reach of Japanese airpower there. The plan was for MacArthur's 5th Air Force to hammer Rabaul to keep the Japanese off-balance and minimize their threat to the Bougainville landings. Once Halsey's foothold on Bougainville was secure, and Marine aircraft were operating from new airfields there, he would return the favor by pounding Rabaul some more with Navy and Marine aircraft from Bougainville, as well as from aircraft carriers, while MacArthur's Army forces (and his borrowed 1st Marine Division) took Cape Gloucester and Arawe.

MacArthur's invasion plan called for Cape Gloucester and its two Japanese airfields to be taken by the 1st Marine Division at the same time that his Army forces were seizing the Japanese airfield at Arawe. Before the invasions took place the Fifth Air Force would carry out a series of bombings to soften up both places. Gasmata would be bombed as well, to fool the Japanese into thinking that the Americans planned to land there also. The heavy bombers of the Jolly Rogers and Ken's Men would drop their blockbuster 1000 and 2000-lb. bombs from high altitude, and the Fifth's medium and light strafer/bombers and their accompanying fighters would sweep the airfields at treetop height, shooting them up and releasing parafrag bombs, as they had been doing at Wewak and other targets.

By the fall of 1943 General Kenney was much better equipped for such offensive operations than he had been at the beginning of the year. He was now operating with three heavy bomb groups: the 90th (the Jolly Rogers), the 43rd (Ken's Men), both based at Port Moresby, and the 380th (the Flying Circus) based at Darwin, Australia, all three groups now flying B-24 Liberators, and he also had one light bomber group flying A-20 Havocs, three medium bomber groups flying B-25 Mitchells, and five fighter groups flying various types of pursuit planes to protect his bombers and defend his airfields: P-38 Lightnings, P-39 Airacobras, P-40 Warhawks, and P-47 Thunderbolts (and over at Darwin, British Spitfires).

In addition, he had four-and-a-half troop carrier groups flying C-47s with which he could rapidly airlift troops and supplies, plus a photo squadron and a night fighter detachment. Kenney was also anticipating the imminent arrival from the States of a second light bomber group, another fighter group, and another night fighter squadron that had been promised to him by Washington. These were rich resources indeed by Pacific war standards.[1]

The 5th Air Force had been striking Cape Gloucester's airfields and defenses intermittently since December of 1942, as part of a strategy of hitting all Japanese airfields in the area. One such raid was on July 28th, 1943, when

35. CAPE GLOUCESTER GETS "GLOUCESTERIZED"   369

Major Jock Henebry led fifteen B-25s of the Third Attack Group to beat up the two Gloucester airfields and then hunt for Japanese barges along the nearby coastline. Ever since the Battle of the Bismarck Sea in early March, the Japanese had given up trying to resupply their New Guinea garrisons by ship convoys from Rabaul, and instead employed barges, luggers, landing craft, and other small shore-hugging vessels that moved mostly by night. Before dawn these vessels would lay up along the coastlines in sheltered locations and be carefully camouflaged to avoid detection. Barge-hunting became a specialty of Maj. Henebry's B-25s. On this mission the Mitchells were escorted by nine P-38s to deal with any Japanese fighters that might try to interfere.

"Pappy" Gunn, the man who had been converting B-25s into strafer/bombers for General Kenney in Brisbane, Australia, went along with Maj. Henebry's strike force as the pilot of one of the planes, to personally try out a new invention of his: a B-25 with an automatic 75mm cannon in the nose. As they flew up from Port Moresby to Cape Goucester, the other B-25 pilots were happy to let "Pappy" lead the way, being somewhat nervous about getting in front of such an eccentric character with a big cannon at his fingertips. Kenney wrote of Gunn:

> Pappy was a gadgeteer par excellence. He had already developed a package installation of four .50-caliber machine guns that fitted beautifully into the nose of an A-20 with 500 rounds of ammunition per gun. He had learned how to fly with the Navy years ago. No one knew how old he was, but he was probably well over forty, although he looked you straight in the eye and said thirty.
>
> When the war broke out, Pappy was doing civilian flying in the Philippines, so the Army mobilized him and now I had him as a major. It was a private war with him, as he had a wife and four children in [Japanese-held] Manila. He didn't know whether they were still alive or not. Anyhow, he didn't like Japs. . .
>
> [Pappy] was a godsend to me as a super-experimental gadgeteer and all-around fixer. There was absolutely nothing that fazed Pappy. If you asked him to mount a sixteen-inch coastal defense gun in an airplane, Pappy would grin, figure out how to do it, work day and night until the job was finished, and then test the installation by flying it himself against the Japs to see how it worked.[2]

This is what "Pappy" was doing on this day with his new nose-mounted 75-mm cannon—testing it out in combat. When Maj. Henebry's formation of B-25s arrived over Cape Gloucester, they spotted a more interesting target than the airfields: two Japanese destroyers lying just offshore. Seeing the American planes approaching, the destroyers made haste to depart, but of course they could not outrun the American bombers. General Kenney wrote:

Two destroyers just off Cape Gloucester looked to Pappy as if they were placed there for his especial benefit. Picking out the largest of the two vessels, Pappy scored seven hits with his 75-mm cannon, but much to his disgust the destroyer didn't even slow down. A 75-mm gun, which, after all, fires a shell that is only about three inches in diameter, was not enough to worry a destroyer. The two B-25s flying on his wings then told Pappy to please step aside while someone did the job who knew how it should be done. A 1,000-pounder skipped into the Jap warship split her in two. Another 1,000-pounder sank the other destroyer, and the B-25s continued along the New Britain coast looking for barges. They found and sank eight barges and two large motor launches, while the P-38s shot down eight out of fifteen Jap fighters that tried to interfere.

Pappy flew along with the gang, sulking and all mad because they had shown up his pet gun installation. Returning over the Jap airdrome at Cape Gloucester, Pappy looked ahead and saw his chance to redeem himself. Just landing was a Nip two-engined transport airplane. Pappy opened his throttle, pushed ahead of the formation, and fired his two remaining rounds of cannon ammunition at the Jap plane taxiing along the ground. One of the high-explosive shells hit the left engine and the other the pilot's cockpit. The transport literally disintegrated...

We found out afterward that among the fifteen passengers on that Jap plane were two generals and three colonels on their way to a staff conference at Wewak.[3]

After "Pappy's" custom strafer/bombers had proven so effective in the Battle of the Bismarck Sea, General Kenney had written to General "Hap" Arnold in Washington and requested that the extra nose guns be installed at the B-25 factories in the States, so that they would arrive in Australia without needing "Pappy's" attention. However, when the desired modifications were described to factory representatives, they replied that such changes would not be practical, and would adversely affect the balance and flying characteristics of the aircraft. Frustrated, Kenney took up the matter personally with Arnold during a conference in Washington in March of 1943, and afterward wrote:

> I had mailed Arnold a set of drawings showing the changes I had made in the B-25 to make it a skip-bombing, strafing commerce-destroyer. I asked him to have Dutch Kindelberger, who ran the North American factory at Los Angeles and produced the B-25, make these changes in his production and save me the burden that I was forcing on [the] Townsville depot. One day, during a lull in the conferences, Arnold told me to come to his office. On arrival

35. CAPE GLOUCESTER GETS "GLOUCESTERIZED" 371

"Pappy" Gunn in the cockpit of his B-25 test bed, named "Not In Stock."

there I found a battery of engineering experts from Wright Field, who explained to me that the idea was impractical. They tried to prove to me that the balance would be all messed up, the airplane would be too heavy, would not fly properly, and so on.

I listened for a while and then mentioned that twelve B-25s fixed up in this manner had played a rather important part in the Battle of the Bismarck Sea, and that I was remodeling sixty more B-25s right now at Townsville. Arnold glared at his engineering experts and practically ran them out of his office. He told me to send a wire to Pappy Gunn, my uninhibited experimenter, to come back to Los Angeles, report to Dutch Kindelberger, and show him how to do the job.[4]

"Pappy" Gunn dutifully reported to the Los Angeles B-25 factory to show the engineers there how to modify the bombers. Later General Arnold informed Kenney that he would like to keep "Pappy" in the States as a permanent advisor to the factory. Kenney demurred:

> I said his [Pappy's] services were urgently needed in Australia and asked that he be returned as soon as possible. I really needed

A Jolly Rogers bomber over Cape Gloucester, December 1943.

Pappy, but anyhow I had to get him away from that bunch of aeronautical engineers. In a short time they would have either made Pappy scientific, and ruined him, or Pappy would have driven them insane and ruined them and maybe the whole aircraft-production program.[5]

Arnold gave in and allowed Gunn to return to Kenney in Australia.

The American invasions of Cape Gloucester and Arawe were scheduled for the 26th of December, 1943. General Kenney began his pre-invasion bombing campaign at the end of November, and later wrote:

[O]n the 29th I told General MacArthur that I'd like to start working over Gloucester, as our information indicated that the Japs had a garrison there of probably around 5,000 troops, who were building a lot of defensive works and preparing artillery positions which would have to be taken out if we were to go ashore without suffering heavy casualties. I said I wanted to see those Marines go ashore with their rifles on their backs, and that I believed the bombs could make it possible if I put enough of them in there. He said to go ahead...

Between the 1st and the 12th of December, Gloucester really

35. CAPE GLOUCESTER GETS "GLOUCESTERIZED"   373

took a beating. Over 1,100 tons of bombs were poured into the target area during twelve straight days of attacks that plastered the Jap air facilities, camps, artillery and machine-gun positions, and supply dumps.[6]

The Jolly Rogers bombed Cape Gloucester day after day, with at least 24 bombers each time, six planes from each of the Group's four squadrons. Col. Art Rogers led many of these Group strikes himself. The antiaircraft fire from the ground diminished with every bombing session as one flak gun after another was silenced by the bombs.

The bomb trains delivering bombs from Port Moresby's supply dumps to the bombers were working overtime during December of 1943 as the Jolly Rogers pulverized the Japanese installations on Cape Gloucester.

At the conclusion of each raid a photo aircraft took pictures of the airbase to see what Japanese defenses remained, and any sort of installation that seemed intact on the photos became the next day's target.

By the 7th of December, Pearl Harbor Day of 1943, the bombers were not fired upon at all from the ground. The thousand-pound bombs that they had been dropping by the score had blasted the Japanese guns and just about everything else on Cape Gloucester to scrap metal and rubble.

No Japanese fighters had challenged the Jolly Rogers during this bombing campaign, so that the aircrews came to view the final days of the Cape Gloucester missions as "gravy runs" that increased their total combat hours without much risk, as every crewman aimed for the magic 300 hours that made him eligible for rotation back to the States.

On December 14th the Jolly Rogers were able to get 28 bombers into the air, with Col. Rogers leading them, and on that day they switched from Cape Gloucester to Arawe and gave that Japanese airfield the Gloucester treatment. The pilots and bombardiers were at the top of their form that day—their bombing was so accurate, and the target so saturated with bombs, that after intelligence officers examined the post-mission photographs, Fifth Bomber Command sent Col. Rogers a note of congratulations, which he passed on to the rest of the Group.[7] Since Rogers would say his farewell to the Group only three days later, it was a fitting conclusion to his service in the Pacific war.

By the day of the Marine invasion of Cape Gloucester, 26 December 1943, over 4,000 tons of bombs had been dropped on the place. The Jolly Rogers had pulverized Cape Gloucester sixteen times in December alone, leaving parts of the landscape covered with overlapping craters that made it look like the surface of the moon. A pre-landing bombardment by the big guns of Navy warships churned the moonscape still further, and then the Marines went ashore and occupied the beachhead with no resistance, and with their rifles slung on their backs (photo below). From that time forward, whenever General MacArthur wanted a target thoroughly obliterated by American bombers, he told General Kenney, "Gloucesterize the place."

The 1st Marine Division going ashore at Cape Gloucester on 26 Dec. 1943, with their rifles slung. Their battles with the Japanese would be in the jungles farther inland.

Chapter Thirty-Six

COL. ART ROGERS LEAVES THE JOLLY ROGERS

Rogers' career with the 90th Bomb Group deserves a book of its own. It is enough to say here that he fearlessly flew scores of dangerous combat missions at the head of his Group and was lucky to survive them all.

By the winter of 1943, after Rogers had been flying combat missions for nearly a year, General Kenney could see that Rogers was showing the strain and getting tired, both mentally and physically. Many men who had flown far fewer combat missions had been diagnosed with "flying fatigue" and been grounded for a rest, or rotated back to the States to undergo a recovery period and be given less strenuous duties. Kenney decided that it was time for Rogers do the latter. He wrote in his memoirs:

Col. Arthur H. Rogers, Commander of the 90th Bomb Group, the Jolly Rogers.

> Colonel Art Rogers, then commanding the group, had done an exceptionally good job for nearly a year but was worn out and I intended to send him home... Rogers had flown over 500 combat hours already, and 300 was about the number that the average man could take without cracking. Three hundred hours of flying during which you live in constant expectation of having someone shoot at you, is a lot of time.[1]

Kenney sent a message to Gen. Whitehead telling him that he wanted to see Rogers and let him know that it was time for him to go back to the States for a rest. Rogers got the word and later wrote:

> He [Whitehead] told me General Kenney wanted me to report to his headquarters in Australia as soon as possible. My airplane ["Connell's Special"] was the oldest plane in combat service in the Group, and it had reached the stage where it could no longer be considered a first-class fighting plane. General Whitehead, knowing my deep feeling toward the old standby, asked me if I would like to fly her back to the States. He said he felt sure that General Kenney would approve it.[2]

On 17 December, 1943, at Port Moresby, Col. Rogers called his men together in the small open-air theater where movies were shown (photo, opposite) and made a farewell address. He thanked the men for their efforts and told them that they would now have to carry on without him. He remembered it thus:

> Even though only three of the original combat crews remained in the Group, I still had a large ground force of loyal, hardworking men who had come overseas with the organization, and also new crews who had become a part of my heart and Group that I must face with the news that I was going home. I had watched the birth of this organization from the time the Group Commander was handed a blank book and the necessary paper orders giving him the authority to create a new Group.
>
> I had been with them through their struggles of training, their periods of doubt in flying the Pacific, the time that their morale had reached such a low ebb that they no longer had confidence in their ability or equipment, all the way through to the present time when they were the outstanding bombing group of the world... My farewell talk at the theatre to the entire Group could not be classified as a celebration. I tried to give them a pep talk as I had on many other occasions, even though my heart was heavy.

After saying goodbye to the Group at Port Moresby, Rogers flew "Connell's Special" down to Brisbane to say goodbye to General Kenney. Actually, no one in the 5th Air Force who was passing through Brisbane on his way to the States would leave without first saying goodbye to Kenney, regardless of rank. Rogers wrote:

> It had become a well-known custom that no officer nor enlisted man in the Fifth Air Force should return home without first going by and personally seeing General Kenney. The General had never been known to be too busy to tell a private, sergeant, or officer goodbye regardless of how many generals happened to be in his office.
>
> On entering his office, his secretary indicates an anteroom for you to wait in until the general can interrupt his busy day to come

The open-air Jolly Rogers theater at Ward's Field, Port Moresby, in 1943. In the foreground is the projection booth. First-run movies from the States were shown weekly. Col. Rogers said goodbye to the Group here on December 17, 1943.

> in and pat you on the back and tell you how much he, the Army and the American people appreciate the job you've done. This is always a personal occasion, at which time you know it is sincere and not a mere ritual.
>
> General Kenney is one of the most understanding and loved Generals in our army today. His brilliant leadership inspires confidence, and his officers and men will unhesitatingly give up their lives to carry out any plan he sets forth. These great qualities of leadership are given to but few, and I thank God that he is leading our Air Force in our struggle against the fanatical Japanese.

Kenney remembered his farewell meeting with Rogers:

> By the time Rogers arrived I had his medals all laid out for the decoration ceremony—he had been awarded everything except the Medal of Honor. . . Rogers wouldn't admit it, but he was really tired and glad to go home for a while.[3]

It was true that Rogers was tired, his stamina worn down by both running the 90th Bomb Group and leading many of its missions, but what was really wrong with him would be discovered later, back in the States: amoebic dysentery and undulant fever (brucellosis). The microbes of the South Pacific had succeeded where the Japanese could not in putting Art Rogers out of action, and like so many Americans who served in the Pacific he went home with recurrent diseases that would plague him for the rest of his life.

Rogers told Kenney that the 90th Bomb Group was still short of nose turrets up at Port Moresby and suggested that the nose and tail turrets of "Connell's Special" be removed and put to use on other bombers before he flew it back to the States. Kenney agreed, and a few days went by while the turrets were removed and the resulting openings in the bomber's nose and tail closed over.

Rogers had the satisfaction of knowing that a new version of the B-24, the J-model, was now in the works and would be coming out of the factories with a nose turret installed, and many crewmen's lives would be saved by the additional firepower on the front of the plane. The first J-model B-24 would arrive at Port Moresby in the same month that Rogers was returning to the States, January of 1944.[4] In addition, B-24s would no longer be painted with camouflage paint, since he had demonstrated that unpainted airplanes performed better.

In January of 1944 Rogers flew his war-weary "Connell's Special" home to the States, taking his nose gunner Hal Pierce and his engineer Jake Seper with him. Most of the rest of his regular crew would remain at Port Moresby for a while longer to train replacements before also returning to the States. His copilot "Big Ben" Browder would be promoted to a first pilot and continue to fly bombing missions (he survived the war).

Rogers' flight back across the Pacific was made more exciting than it should have been by a combination of water in the plane's gas tanks and towering thunderstorms over the Pacific Ocean, necessitating engine shutdowns in flight and course diversions, but he finally landed at Hamilton Field near San Francisco on January 11, 1944. It had been a year, three months, and 27 days since the morning he had taken off for Hawaii and beyond on 14 September 1942, the same morning his squadron's doctor had accidentally set the wing of his airplane on fire with a cigarette lighter.

Rogers parked the tired old bomber for the last time, and he and the crew climbed out with their baggage. He knew the plane was too beaten-up to repair, and its next stop would likely be the scrapyard. As he walked away from the gallant old bird, he turned to take a last look at it:

> My battle-scarred old Liberator, after 17 months in active combat service, had many patches covering flak and machine-gun bullet holes. She had survived a bomb blast in which all the bulkheads from the bomb bay back to the tail were sprung, and had slid on her nose in a crash landing, tearing out the main structure of the fuselage in front. This had been replaced by steel in many places due to the lack of aluminum to make the fittings in the jungles.

> She certainly had proven her worth, and I hated to part with her, knowing that she was to be condemned for scrap. I also knew that very few airplanes could ever be loved as much as she was by her entire crew. You actually develop an affection for a sturdy old warrior of this type. An airplane develops a personality, and our affectionate name for her was "Susabella," even though she was officially known as "Connell's Special."
>
> In New Guinea, when my crew and I were forced to fly one of the newer planes while "Susabella" was getting some patchwork done for flak or machine gun holes, we actually dreaded flying in another airplane. In fact, we were all more or less superstitious to the extent of being jittery when each crewmember was unable to caress her many controls when in combat. The remarkable thing was that even though she was battered and beaten up at the end of over 500 hours on her weary engines, she would still cruise faster, longer, and climb better than any new plane we had.
>
> As I departed the field to go into San Francisco to board an airliner for my home of Greenville, South Carolina, I glanced back for one more glimpse, as I knew I would never see my plane again... She was still sporting the silhouettes of six definitely sunk enemy surface vessels and five possibles. Under this were four trim little Jap flags representing Zeros that had met their deaths by her guns, and a long chain of 46 bombs with stars above indicating successful missions completed...
>
> To many who looked at this plane she was merely an old, worn-out Liberator, but to me she was a real character, and symbolized the great productiveness and skill of the people of these United States. With a glint of sun on her shining fuselage, this is the picture that I took with me, a memory jam-packed with action and heartaches.

Rogers went home to his wife and young son in Greenville, and he would not return to the Pacific. However, he would be long remembered by the 90th Bomb Group. As the Group's historian, Wiley O. Woods, wrote:

> He had molded the 90th Bombardment Group into an outstanding war machine, and with only two heavy bombardment groups in New Guinea, Kenney had become more dependent on the 90th. Rogers had also lifted the morale of the men and it was a proud outfit. The men truly believed that they were "The Best Damn Heavy Bomb Group in the World."[5]

After Col. Rogers returned to the States in January of 1944, General Kenney placed Lt. Col. Harry J. Bullis in command of the Jolly Rogers, and Maj. Charles P. Whitlock became the Deputy Group Commander.[6]

"Moby Dick," a B-24D of the Jolly Rogers' 320th Squadron, gave its name to the entire squadron. Here the bomber is escorted by a pair of P-40 Warhawk fighter planes.

When the Jolly Rogers' 320th Squadron acquired an L-4 Piper Cub they named it "Moby Dick Jr." and painted it to look like its big brother, although it rather appeared to be eating its own engine.

Chapter Thirty-Seven

JAPANESE AIRPOWER IN NEW GUINEA SMASHED

By the beginning of 1944 the five Japanese airfields at Rabaul had been pummeled into near-obliteration by the Jolly Rogers and the other land-based bomb groups, as well as by Admiral Nimitz's carrier aircraft and the Marine planes based on Bougainville.* The Japanese at Rabaul had come to realize that when Japan had foolishly attacked America at Pearl Harbor it had grabbed a tiger by the tail. Japanese Staff Air Officer Masatake Okumiya confirmed the dire situation at Rabaul when he visited there on January 20, 1944 and wrote about the conditions he found among the Japanese air force commanders:

> I found on my arrival at Rabaul an astonishing conviction that the war could not possibly be won, that all we were doing at Rabaul was postponing the inevitable. Our executive personnel at Rabaul were not deluded by promises of future successes; they were experts in military aviation affairs and had personally undergone many combat engagements. As the months went by they watched the qualitative superiority of the Zero fighter fade before the increased performance of new American fighter planes which, by now, not only outfought but outnumbered the Zeros. There existed a growing feeling of helplessness before this rising tide of American might. Our men felt keenly the great difference between American industrial and military strength and the limited resources of their own country. Despite these convictions, they could only continue to send our pilots and air crews into combat and to their deaths. Who could blame them, then, for the mental regression into spiritual apathy and defeatism?..[1]
>
> And yet, absolutely nothing could be done to alleviate the situation. American air pressure increased steadily... The endless days and nights became a nightmare... Eventually some of our higher staff officers came to resemble living corpses, bereft of spiritual and physical strength... They lived under terrible conditions... Their sacrifices received not even the slightest recognition from the government.[2]

---

*Marine fighter ace and Medal of Honor recipient Major Gregory "Pappy" Boyington of "Baa Baa Black Sheep" (book and TV series) fame was shot down between Bougainville and Rabaul on January 3, 1944, flying out of Bougainville's Torokina airfield to attack Rabaul.

And yet the "great industrial strength" of the Americans in the Pacific that so impressed the Japanese on the front lines by the beginning of 1944 was only a small fraction of the war matériel that was being sent to Europe (and Russia*) to fight Hitler. Had the Japanese ever experienced the full industrial might of America right from the beginning of the war, it would have been a very short war indeed.

By 1944 a sensible Japanese government would have recognized that the war was unwinnable for them and sued for peace. Yet the delusional Japanese military cabal in Tokyo fought on, concealing the truth from their civilian populace (for example, after the Japanese ships that survived the Battle of Midway limped back to Japan, only six months after Pearl Harbor, the surviving sailors of the ships that had been sunk were isolated in concentration camps to prevent them from spreading the word of Japan's great defeat to the general population). The Japanese military continued to proclaim great victories over the Allies, claims with no basis in fact. The self-delusion of the Japanese would cost them (and other nations) millions more lives from 1944 onward, all wasted in futile and pointless resistance to America and her allies.

Rabaul eliminated as a threat

MacArthur's Operation Cartwheel, the operation to isolate and neutralize Rabaul, continued, and on the 12th of March, 1944, the Americans invaded nearby Manus Island in the Admiralty Group (see Map 37-1, opposite). As usual, the Jolly Rogers paved the way on January 26 and 27 by bombing the Japanese infantry defenses on Manus (as well as the two airfields there) practically out of existence—"Gloucesterized" them, in other words.

Then on March 20, a week after taking Manus, the Marine 4th Division occupied Emirau Island, 100 miles northwest of the Japanese airbase at Kavieng, also near Rabaul. The Jolly Rogers had no work to do on Emirau, since there were no Japanese on the island to oppose the landing. Kavieng itself was bypassed and left to "wither on the vine" along with Rabaul, but since aerial photography showed some Japanese aircraft still sitting on Kavieng's two airfields, the Jolly Rogers bombed them out of existence on the 11th, 13th, and 16th of February.

---

*Russian spy messages decrypted since WWII in the Venona Project prove conclusively that President Roosevelt's right-hand man (called by some his alter ego or co-president) Harry Hopkins was actually a Soviet agent who made many of the policy decisions of the Roosevelt administration, either unknown to FDR or with his approval. One thing that Hopkins made certain of (by order of Soviet dictator Josef Stalin) was that abundant American war matériel was "loaned" to Russia throughout the war under the guise of the Lend-Lease program, to the point of causing shortages of weaponry in the American armed forces, and certainly to the detriment of the Pacific theater of war. Hopkins also shipped secret American nuclear technology and Canadian uranium to Russia, enabling the USSR to assemble an atomic bomb shortly after the war.[3]

37. JAPANESE AIR POWER IN NEW GUINEA SMASHED   383

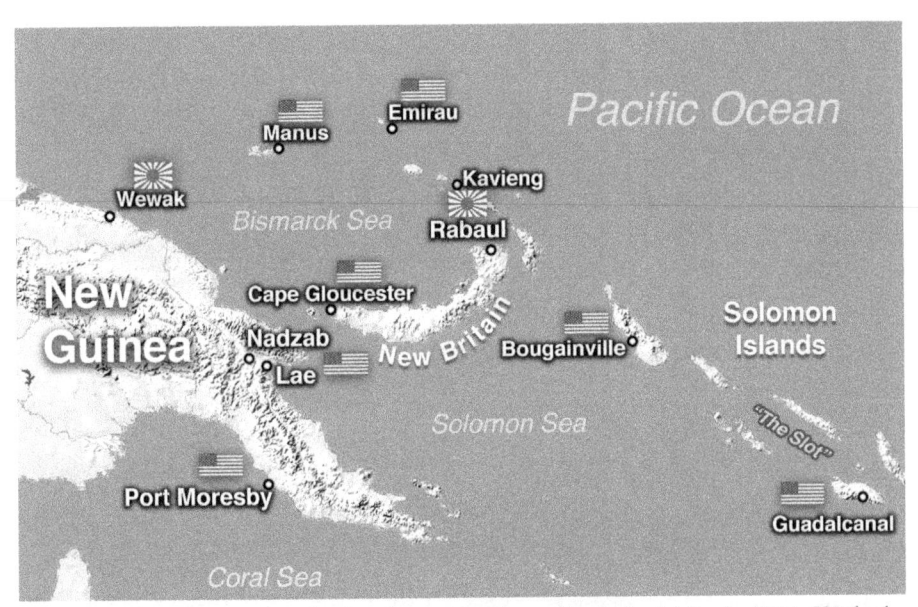

Map 37-1. The situation in the Southwest Pacific at the end of March, 1944. With the American occupation of Manus and Emirau Islands, Rabaul was surrounded and isolated, and General MacArthur's Operation Cartwheel was complete. Rabaul was then left alone to "wither on the vine" for the rest of the war. Next, Wewak would also be neutralized and bypassed. (Also on this map, note at lower right "The Slot" between the Solomon Islands where future U. S. President John F. Kennedy's PT-109 [Patrol Torpedo] boat was sunk.)

As a result of the bombings, the Japanese on Kavieng decided that an American invasion must be imminent, so they did what they usually did in such cases: they murdered all their Allied prisoners.* On 17 March of 1944, in what became known as the Kavieng Wharf Massacre, they took more than 30 Australians and other white civilians that they had captured in the area down to a wharf at the harbor and strangled them with ropes. Then they took the bodies out to sea, weighted them down with cement, and threw them in the ocean.

With the seizure of Emirau and Manus, the encirclement of Rabaul was complete, and the Japanese there were cut off from any possibility of resupply. They were thus forced to cease all air and sea operations, and what few intact aircraft remained at Rabaul were flown to safety 800 miles north to Truk Island. Any ships still above water in Rabaul Harbor also slipped away and fled to Truk.

---

* When the Japanese commander on Wake Island thought (also wrongly) that an American invasion was approaching on 5 October 1943, he quickly murdered his 98 American prisoners. Likewise the commander of a Japanese prison camp at Palawan, in the Philippines, seeing an American task force passing the island in December of 1944, immediately massacred the 150 Americans in his charge, that he had employed as slave laborers. And so it went.

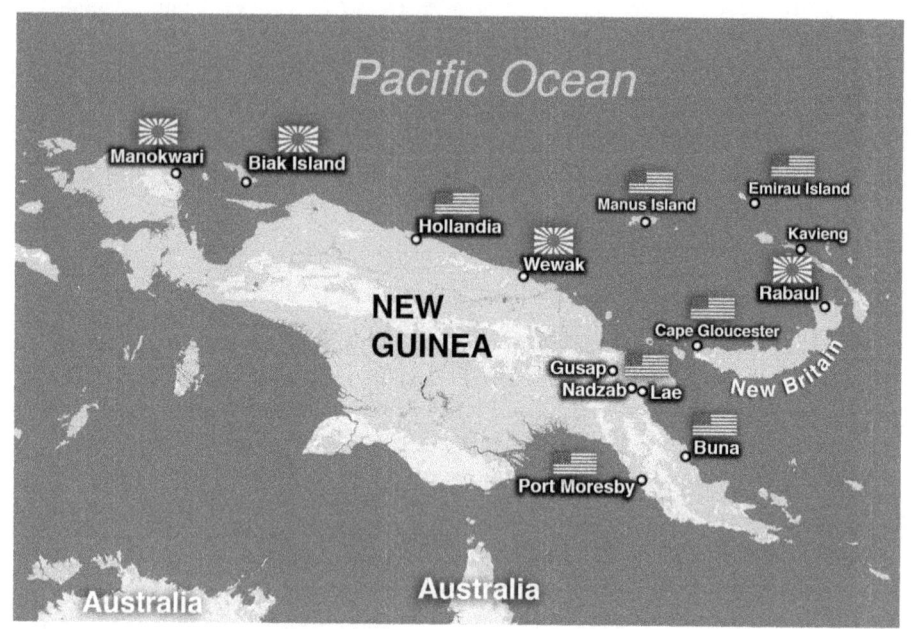

Map 37-2. After the destruction of the Japanese airbases at Wewak and Hollandia, and the American capture of Hollandia in April of 1943, the Japanese pulled their line of defense back to Biak Island and Manokwari (upper left).

Only Japanese ground troops remained at Rabaul, since they were surrounded and unable to get away. They prepared themselves for an American invasion that never came, and sat idle for the rest of the war, out of touch with Japan and "losing face," feeling dishonored for being ignored. Japanese military fanaticism was so strong that the Emperor's psychotic soldiers yearned for a chance to die in battle for their living god, and felt shame when they were denied the opportunity to do so.

Had the Allies actually invaded Rabaul, it would have resulted in a bloodbath that could easily have surpassed the murderous toll at places such as Iwo Jima, where the Americans suffered nearly 7,000 men killed. Iwo Jima was defended by 20,000 Japanese troops, while Rabaul had 90,000. As at Iwo Jima, the Japanese at Rabaul had had time to dig in and set up elaborate defenses.

However, bypassing Rabaul also meant that the Americans being held prisoner there, including Lt. James McMurria, would continue to endure brutal captivity until the end of the war. Most of them, including Medal of Honor recipient Maj. Ralph Cheli, would not survive to be liberated.

Final blows to Japanese airpower in New Guinea
In the spring of 1944, Wewak and Hollandia were the two biggest Japanese airbases in New Guinea, both of them on the north coast of the island,

blocking MacArthur's drive up that coast toward the Philippines (Map 37-2, opposite). Kenney had dealt the Japanese calamitous losses at Wewak six months before, on August 17 and 18, 1943, and then the Jolly Rogers had hit them again on Dec. 1, but they just kept taking the losses, filling in the bomb craters in their runways, and restocking the airbase with more airplanes. They were, in the words of *Saturday Evening Post* writer Charles Rawlings, a "busy little enemy," and in the words of General Kenney, "dumb." This dumb, busy little enemy was also unimaginative and predictable, which is why Kenney and MacArthur could keep dealing them decisive defeats with often inferior forces. As the Australian soldier Peter Pinney had noted, it was a good thing the Allies were fighting Japanese and not Germans.

As the new year 1944 opened, Hollandia, 200 miles up the coast from Wewak, was seeing an even bigger buildup of aircraft than Wewak, since the Japanese thought (erroneously, as they would soon find out—the hard way) that it was out of range of effective American airstrikes.

In early February of 1944 General Kenney decided to neutralize both of these troublesome Japanese airbases once and for all. Now that he had perfected the one-two punch of high-altitude bombing by B-24 heavy bombers, with their huge blockbuster bombs, followed by low-level attacks by A-20 Havoc and B-25 Mitchell light and medium strafer/bombers, with their devastating banks of machine guns and parafrag bombs, he had the means to do so. Wewak, the old nemesis of the Jolly Rogers, and the nearest of the two Japanese airbase complexes, would be dealt with first.

Wewak neutralized and bypassed

Once again, the Jolly Rogers were called upon to open the show. On February 3, 1944, their big bombs cratered Wewak's runways yet again, exploded supply dumps of fuel, bombs, and ammunition, and demolished barracks and headquarters buildings. Then the low-level B-25 strafers went in at close range and cleaned up what targets remained. At Wewak's two northernmost airfields, But and Dagua, the strafers caught a large group of Japanese airplanes on the ground just as they were preparing to depart on a strike against some Allied target. In Kenney's own words:

> Right behind the heavies and just over the treetops came sixty-two B-25s escorted by sixty-six fighters, which kept going and swept over But and Dagua. The strategy worked. The Nip behaved perfectly and had his planes lined up nicely, most of them with the engines turning over, crews in their seats and mechanics standing by, when the storm hit them. At But and Dagua alone, sixty Nip planes were destroyed on the ground while the fighters shot down another sixteen in air combat. We had no losses.[4]

A pair of Jolly Rogers bombers on the way to a target.

Wewak, even without aircraft, still had thousands of Japanese living on and around the four airbases, but MacArthur deemed them too isolated to do the Allies any harm, so he simply bypassed Wewak as he had done Rabaul, to become just another former Japanese stronghold condemned to "wither on the vine." Throughout the rest of the war Wewak was simply used as a dumping ground for any bombs that passing American bombers wanted to dispose of.

In May of 1945, near the end of the war, Australian troops would assault Wewak and capture it, battling against typically suicidal Japanese who fought to the death. It was a waste of life on both sides, however, since the Japanese Emperor would surrender all Japanese military forces only three months later in August. Most historians agree that the Japanese at Wewak should have been left alone until the war ended. As a result of combat with the Australians and the effects of MacArthur's "withering" strategy, only 13,000 of the 100,000 Japanese troops who had originally occupied the Wewak area survived.

Hollandia bombed and captured

After the four Japanese airfields at Wewak were obliterated, the Japanese High Command gave up on Wewak and pulled their surviving aircraft back to the three airfields at Hollandia, 200 miles further up the coast and nearly

Wewak's But airfield after the Jolly Rogers destroyed the runway with thousand-pound demolition bombs. The tremendous size of the bomb craters can be gauged by comparing them to the derelict Japanese truck at upper right. Some of the craters were over seventy-five feet across and twenty to thirty feet deep.

700 miles from the airfield from which the Jolly Rogers were operating at that time: Dobodura, near Buna. At Hollandia (a former Dutch town, as the name implies, a part of the Dutch East Indies) the Japanese thought, once again, that they were far enough away from the American airbases to be safe from such cataclysmic strikes. They knew the B-24s of the Jolly Rogers and Ken's Men could still reach them from Port Moresby and Dobodura, but they felt that they could defend themselves from the big bombers well enough with their many flak guns and numerous fighter planes. They thought that the distance was too great for the bombers to bring with them any Allied fighter escort, nor could the American medium strafer/bombers reach them with their limited range.

What they did not know was that "Pappy" Gunn's custom-made drop tanks for B-25s did give the strafer/bombers enough range to reach Hollandia. As for the fighters, Kenney received fifty-eight new long-range P-38s from the States in February, and he had large droppable fuel tanks made in Australia for his older P-38s. These fighters could fly all the way up from his new fighter base at Gusap (60 miles northwest of Nadzab, see Map 37-2 on page 384) to Hollandia and still have fuel to fight over Hollandia for a full hour.[5]

Tokyo Rose actually bragged over the radio that the Japanese airbase at Hollandia was beyond the reach of most American aircraft, and General Kenney did all he could to encourage that belief, hoping that the Japanese would feel safe enough to bring in a large number of aircraft, which he then intended to destroy on the ground as he had done at Wewak.

He sent only a few lone B-24s over Hollandia, and only at night, to drop a few bombs at random on the three Japanese airfields there, which were clustered around a lake named Sentani. He wanted the Japanese to think that he did not dare send unescorted bombers that far up the coast in daylight. Kenney wrote:

A Japanese fighter plane was left with nowhere to go after a bomb crater, likely made by a Jolly Rogers 1,000-pound bomb, separated it from the runway at Wewak.

> Hollandia now became the big Jap airbase to succeed Wewak... Sure that they were safe enough from our attacks, the Japs built up their air strength and parked airplanes almost wingtip to wingtip, with big gasoline and ammunition dumps on the edges of the fields. Tokyo Radio even boasted of the big air force they were building up at Hollandia in preparation for an early offensive that was to sweep the arrogant Americans out of the New Guinea skies...
> In the meantime, I said to keep on with small night attacks to lull the Nips into the belief that we did not dare to hit them in the daytime... Tokyo Radio jeered at us nightly for our futile bombing, and claimed that we were splashing the waters of Sentani Lake and messing up the scenery all over the place without hitting anything worthwhile.[6]

Photos of Hollandia taken by a high-altitude American reconnaissance plane early on the morning of March 30, 1944, showed nearly 300 Japanese aircraft parked on the three airfields, many of them wingtip-to-wingtip and in double rows. The trap was ripe for the springing, and that same morning Gen. Kenney pulled the trigger on his ambush. However, since antiaircraft guns were very numerous in the reconnaissance photos, Kenny decided to hold back his low-level strafer/bombers until the Jolly Rogers and Ken's Men had

37. JAPANESE AIR POWER IN NEW GUINEA SMASHED

This is Dagua, one of the four Wewak airfields, after the Jolly Rogers worked it over with thousand-pound bombs in the spring of 1944. Parked Japanese aircraft were shattered and tossed about like toys by the explosions. Photograph taken from a low-flying B-25.

either eliminated or greatly reduced the number of flak guns with clusters of fragmentation bombs (the non-parachute version of the parafrag bomb).

That day the Japanese at Hollandia were stunned to see sixty-five B-24s protected by eighty P-38 fighters come droning in over their heads in broad daylight. The bombers saturated the Japanese airfields with 14,000 fragmentation bombs, causing fuel and ammunition dumps to erupt in flames all over the airbase. Heavy black smoke rose to ten thousand feet, and most of the antiaircraft gun positions were wiped out, rendering the flak light and inaccurate. Forty Japanese fighters attempted to intercept the bombers, and ten of them were shot down by the P-38s without loss to themselves. In fact, the Americans lost no aircraft of any kind that day. As the American raiders departed, they could still see the smoke of the burning fuel dumps from 150 miles away.

The next morning the Americans were back with sixty-eight B-24s and seventy P-38s, and this time the bombers brought thousand-pound bombs that blew huge craters in the runways and made them unusable. Thirty Japanese fighters attempted to defend the field, but after fourteen of them were shot down they broke off the fight and fled westward up the coast. One P-38 was lost on this day.

The Japanese airfields at Hollandia got the treatment after Wewak. Seen here is a Mitsubishi Ki-21 "Sally" bomber seconds before it was blown to bits by American parafrag bombs released by a low-flying B-25, the same plane that took this photograph with its tail camera. Other Japanese aircraft in the distance are also being showered with parafrag explosives.

Bad weather gave the Japanese at Hollandia a respite for the next two days, but on April 3rd, after studying the post-strike photos, Kenney considered the Japanese antiaircraft defenses at Hollandia sufficiently reduced to allow the low-level strafer/bombers to go in behind the Jolly Rogers and clean up after them:

37. JAPANESE AIR POWER IN NEW GUINEA SMASHED 391

The effectiveness of Kenney's parafrag bombs can be seen in the burned-out remains of Japanese aircraft at Hollandia. At lower right more parafrags drift down to take care of another couple of parked Japanese planes.

Japanese planes caught parked in rows at Hollandia were destroyed wholesale. Note the ridiculous attempt to camouflage the bomber in the foreground by placing a few palm fronds on the wings and tail.

Closeup pictures taken on the ground after the capture of the Japanese airfields showed how the shrapnel of the parafrag bombs had riddled and shredded the parked Japanese aircraft.

> On April 3rd we completed the destruction of all the airplanes based at Hollandia. Sixty-three B-24s opened the attack, dropping 492 1,000-pound bombs on the antiaircraft positions. One hundred and seventy-one B-25 and A-20 strafers then came in over the treetops and swept up the pieces of what had once been a Jap air force. Seventy-six P-38 fighters escorted the heavy bombers. Thirty Jap fighters intercepted. The P-38s got twenty-four of them and the bombers got two more. We had one P-38 shot down. All the rest of our aircraft returned.[7]

Post-strike photographs showed 288 wrecked and burned-out Japanese aircraft. Tokyo Rose changed the subject, and went back to calling the Americans "gangsters." She said that Kenney and Whitehead were "[a] pair of gangster leaders of a gang of gangsters from a gangster-ridden country."[8] Obviously the Hollywood gangster movies of the 1930s had made a big impression on the Japanese.

Looking at the totals of destroyed Japanese airplanes at Hollandia, General Kenney commented:

> To occupy this base which Tokyo Rose had boasted was so safe had cost the dumb Nip 452 airplanes.[9]

Kenney's contempt for the Japanese high command was total:

37. JAPANESE AIR POWER IN NEW GUINEA SMASHED 393

Japanese prisoners at Hollandia being loaded aboard a C-47 for transport to a prison camp in Brisbane, Australia. The anxiety on the face of the second man from the right probably stems from the fear that he might be treated the same way the Japanese treated Allied prisoners. Far from it, these men were well cared for in Brisbane and were returned to Japan after the war.

> The Nip just did not know how to handle air power. Just because he knocked us off on the ground at the beginning of the war, when we were asleep at Pearl Harbor and in the Philippines, he got a reputation for being smart, but the way he failed to take advantage of his superiority in numbers and position since the first couple of months of the war was a disgrace to the airman's profession.[10]

On 22 April, 1944, the Americans landed the 24th and 41st Infantry Divisions at Hollandia and captured the Japanese airbase without much resistance from the disorganized Japanese defenders, who, as they had done at Salamaua, Lae, and elsewhere, fled into the jungle in disorder. Some trekked north to try to reach other Japanese bases higher up the coast, such as the one at Maffin Bay, and many starved to death in the jungle, or, as they had done on the Kokoda Trail and in other routs, resorted to cannibalism to stay alive.

At newly-captured Hollandia, the Seabees quickly bulldozed all the wrecked Japanese airplanes off to the side, where American troops dismantled them for souvenirs, and widened and lengthened the airfields to take American aircraft. Soon American planes flying from Hollandia were hitting other Japanese airfields as far west as Biak Island (See Map 37-2 on page 384).

The capture of Hollandia, along with nearby Aitape, allowed General MacArthur to vault 600 miles up the coast from Nadzab, leaving Rabaul and Wewak sidelined, stranded, and irrelevant in his wake, and throwing the Japanese high command into a state of confusion, as he had intended and expected. He had long asserted that the Japanese military mindset was an open book to him as a result of his long residence in the Orient, and these developments lent credence to his claim.

General Kenney, who had never been in the Orient before coming out from the States to take command of the 5th Air Force, had simply become scornful of Japanese air commanders through his own experience with them. He wrote:

> [T]he Nip was dumb to begin with and did not understand air warfare. He did not know how to handle large masses of aircraft. He made piecemeal attacks and didn't follow them up. He had no imagination. As long as his set plan went, he was a great boy, but if anything unforeseen interfered and upset the plan, he got confused. If ever anyone was a sucker for a left, it was the Jap. Our kids were better fliers and better shots than his were, and now that we had learned to use them properly, our airplanes were better. One big thing in our favor was that the Jap had no good heavy bomber that could fight its way to the target and back. We had both the B-17 and the B-24. When surface means of supply were lacking or insufficient, we had our air cargo planes and knew how to use them. The Nip had no air cargo service and would not have known what to do with it if he had. . . It proved once more that he had no business starting a war with the United States in the first place. He just wasn't good enough to play in the big leagues.[11]

The Jolly Rogers remain at Nadzab

To General Kenney's disappointment, Hollandia's soils proved too soft to support heavy bombers, so instead of moving up to Hollandia, the Jolly Rogers only moved 165 miles north, from Dobodura to Nadzab (see Map 38-2 on page 400), as detailed in the next chapter, and only used Hollandia for emergency landings during bombing missions.

General Kenney preferred hard coral-based runways for his heavy bombers, and the coral islands off New Guinea's coast fit the bill. Before long half of the Jolly Rogers' bombers (two squadrons) would move up the coast from Nadzab

General Kenney (center left) and Brig. Gen. Paul B. Wurtsmith of 5th Air Force Fighter Command chatting with fighter pilots after a medal presentation ceremony. Kenney had just presented 16 fighter pilots with medals. Kenney was in many ways the opposite of his boss, Gen. MacArthur. Kenney disdained pomp and ceremony. While MacArthur would travel in a staff car with his flags of rank flying, Kenney would often drive around in a beat-up jeep with no flag of rank at all on it, so that he sometimes appeared unexpectedly in the midst of a group of pilots or aircrewmen, to their shock, to chat with them and hand out a medal or two.

to Wakde Island at Maffin Bay. Only two squadrons would make the move because the island was so small that it wouldn't hold the entire Group, so the other two squadrons had to remain at Nadzab for a while. The move after that one would take the entire Group forward to Biak Island, another coral island but a much larger one. But we are getting a bit ahead of our story, for at this time both Wakde and Biak Islands were still under Japanese control.

Though not suitable for heavy bombers, the Hollandia airbase did serve well as a base for medium bombers and fighter planes. It was a lovely location visually, as well, with Lake Sentani surrounded by picturesque mountains. When General MacArthur finally moved his headquarters up from Brisbane, Australia to New Guinea, it was to Hollandia that he moved, in June of 1944, and his headquarters would remain there until the invasion of the Philippines five months later.*

With the loss of Wewak and Hollandia, the Japanese ceased trying to contest most New Guinea airspace with the Allies and drew back to defend Biak Island and Manokwari on the back of the New Guinea "buzzard's" head (Map 37-2 again, page 384). General Kenney had finally broken the back of Japanese airpower and achieved air superiority over New Guinea.

Deadly weather: Black Sunday

During the campaign against Hollandia there occurred a weather event that cost the Fifth Air Force more aircraft than were lost in any single air strike of the New Guinea campaign. Tropical bad weather remained the main enemy of all American fliers in the Southwest Pacific, but on April 16, 1944 the weather in the Allied area of operations was so bad, and the losses in aircraft and men so great as a result, that it would be remembered ever after as "Black Sunday."

On that day a deep, dark wall of storm cloud moved in behind hundreds of planes that had been out conducting combat missions in the Hollandia and Tadji areas and cut them off from their bases at Nadzab, Gusap, Finschaffen, and Lae. This huge, dense cloud began right at the surface of the sea and rose to 40,000 feet or more, altitudes that no World War II aircraft could attain. Laterally it extended for miles across the New Guinea jungle and mountains to the south and far out to sea to the north. No pilot trying to get home could go under it, over it, or around it—all he could do was try to fly through it and hope for better visibility within it, or on the other side of it, if it wasn't too deep to pass through. In many cases it did prove to be too deep, with fatal consequences for the pilots and crews.

Pilots on that day tried different methods of getting through the cloud front, and some were successful while others were not. The fighter planes were in the worst predicament, since many of them didn't have blind-flying instruments such as artificial horizons on their panels. Any pilot without visual orientation can experience vertigo and lose control of his aircraft in a matter of seconds. The pilots of the heavy bombers were experienced in the art of instrument flying and had the necessary equipment on their instrument panels to do it, but by not knowing their exact location over the land they could also fly blindly

---

*The American engineers built MacArthur a prominent residence on a hilltop at Hollandia with a grand view of the lake, the mountains, and Humboldt Bay. It was such a fine building, with a driveway lined with large white-painted boulders, that many soldiers pointed to it as an example of the general's vanity and taste for extravagant quarters. Actually, according to MacArthur's biographer William Manchester, MacArthur had nothing to do with the construction of the house and grounds since they were built before he arrived. The place is still called "MacArthur Hill" today.

into one of the many mountains just back of the New Guinea coast in that area. Some pilots did exactly that, and they and their crews were killed.

On that day, in front of the great, dark curtain of storm, aircraft of all types could be seen circling high up, low down over the sea or jungle, and everywhere in between, while the radios crackled with the voices of pilots desperately trying to figure out what to do, asking if anyone saw any gaps in the cloud, or reporting what they were going to try to do, or in some cases shouting that they were inside the cloud and out of control. Some pilots and crews bailed out and survived, but the Fifth Air Force could ill afford to lose the aircraft. General Kenney described it thus:

> **April 16th (1944) went down in the records of the Fifth Air Force as Black Sunday. We took a beating. It was not administered by the Jap. The weather did us wrong. Forty-five B-24s, Forty-nine B-25s, thirty-seven A-20s, and forty fighters raided the Tadji* area and put the final touch on the place. On the way home, however, they found that the low clouds and fog that had been hanging offshore for the previous three days had moved inland and blocked them off from their home airdromes. That night there was gloom in the Fifth Air Force. Of 170 airplanes that had left on the strike, seventy were unaccounted for. By noon the next day we had recovered thirty-six which had made emergency landings away from home and remained there until the weather cleared. Others were gradually accounted for, but the final cost was thirty-two kids and thirty-one airplanes. It was the worst blow I took in the whole war.[12]**

The Jolly Rogers were lucky; their Group lost no aircraft on Black Sunday, but the 43rd Bomb Group, Ken's Men, lost one B-24, and the 22nd medium bomb group (Red Raiders) lost a B-24 and three B-26 bombers, with the crews all killed.

In 2002, two B-24 bombers that had been victims of Black Sunday were discovered on a remote hillside in New Guinea only 700 yards apart: one nicknamed "Here T'is" of the 43rd Bomb Group, and an unnamed B-24J of the 22nd Bomb Group.† They had flown blindly into the jungled slope and both crews, twenty-one men total, had been killed instantly. The remains of the men were recovered and processed through the Army's Central Identification Laboratory in Hawaii, then returned to their relatives for burial in 2007, sixty-four years after the men had been reported missing in action.[13]

---

* Tadji was (and still is) about halfway between Hollandia and Wewak, where there was a small Japanese airfield that the Americans eventually captured and used for fighter planes.

† The 22nd Bomb Group was a former medium bomber group that was switching over to B-24s at the time of Black Sunday.

Chapter Thirty-Eight

THE JOLLY ROGERS MOVE TO NADZAB

After the capture of Lae and Nadzab from the Japanese in September of 1943, construction of a big American airbase was begun at Nadzab. However, the engineers could do little to prepare the field for heavy bombers until they could get the big graders, rollers, and other heavy construction equipment that they needed to the site. These were too big and heavy to be delivered in the C-47 cargo planes that had been landing at Nadzab from practically day one, bringing in equipment and supplies in a steady stream; they would have to be brought up to Lae's harbor in cargo ships, then unloaded and driven twenty miles up the valley to Nadzab, over a road that still had to be built.

In just about any other part of the world that twenty miles of road could have been constructed quickly; however, this was the hellhole of New Guinea, where the weather was so wet and the terrain so rugged and soggy that construction of the road would take months. In the meantime, the engineers working on the Nadzab airfields could only employ whatever machinery General Kenney could fly in to them by C-47. Jeeps and small bulldozers were no problem because they were small enough to fit into the planes (photo, p. 323). Some inspired mechanic (of which America had many in those days) discovered that the big ten-wheeled 2-1/2 ton Army trucks could be sawn in half at Port Moresby, loaded into the C-47s in pieces, and then welded back together at Nadzab.

General Kenney was delighted by this feat, and thereafter had many of the big trucks transported by air that way. On 13 December, 1943, some high-ranking officers from Washington, including General George C. Marshall of the Joint Chiefs of Staff, arrived at Port Moresby to look over the Pacific war situation and confer with Generals MacArthur and Kenney. Before the conference, Kenney gave these V. I. P.s an aerial tour of airfields in the area and showed them the progress being made at Nadzab. He wrote afterward:

> As we circled Nadzab, where the bulldozers and trucks were working for all they were worth, building strips and roads and hauling supplies from the constantly landing transport planes, the General [Marshall] remarked that we were lucky to have a road in from the coast. I replied that we not only didn't have a road but there probably wouldn't be one for another couple of weeks,

38. THE JOLLY ROGERS MOVE TO NADZAB 399

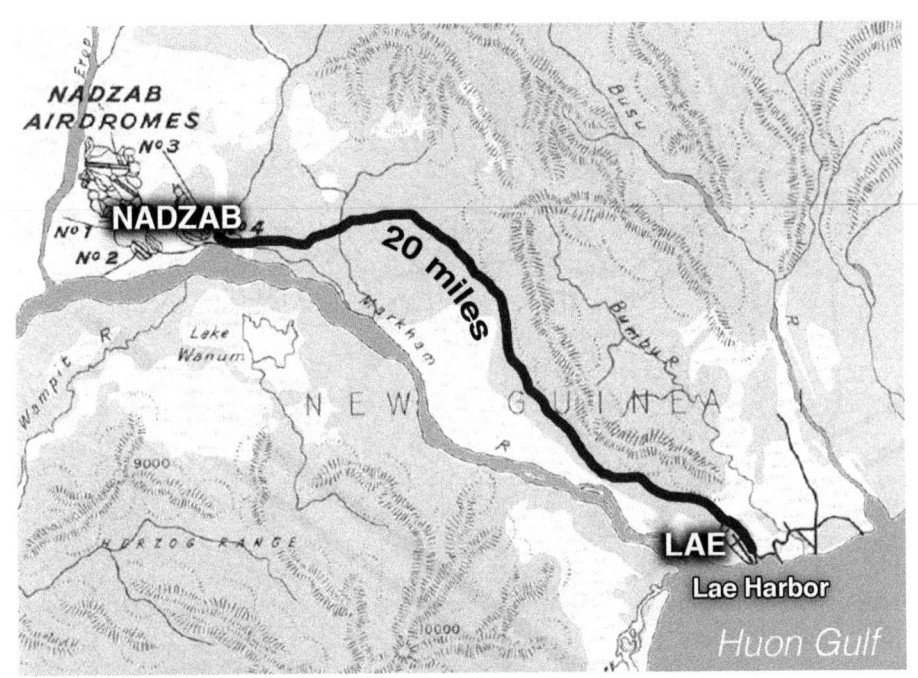

Map 38-1. The black line shows the 20-mile-long road from the harbor at Lae to Nadzab where the Army Air Corps was building its new airbase. Because of the rugged terrain, the road took nearly four months to build, and until it was completed no heavy construction equipment could be delivered to Nadzab for building runways suitable for heavy bombers.

although we had owned Nadzab for nearly three months.

"Those trucks down there," said General Marshall. "How did those get in?"

"We flew them in," I said.

"I don't mean the jeeps, I mean those two-and-a-half ton trucks, retorted the General. "You can't get those in a C-47."

"Oh, those?" I pretended to yawn. "We just sawed the frames in two, stuffed the pieces in the C-47s, and then welded them back together after we got them up here."

General Marshall got a great kick out of the story, especially when he discovered that it was true, and for years the episode was one of his favorite after-dinner anecdotes.[1]

The Jolly Rogers move across the mountains to Dobodura

As the new year 1944 dawned, the entire "tail" of the New Guinea "buzzard" belonged to the Allies. Although Nadzab was not yet ready to receive the heavy bombers, Kenney decided that it was time to at least move the Jolly Rogers and Ken's Men forward from Port Moresby. Dobodura, near Buna, was sufficiently developed by this time to take big bombers, and moving there would

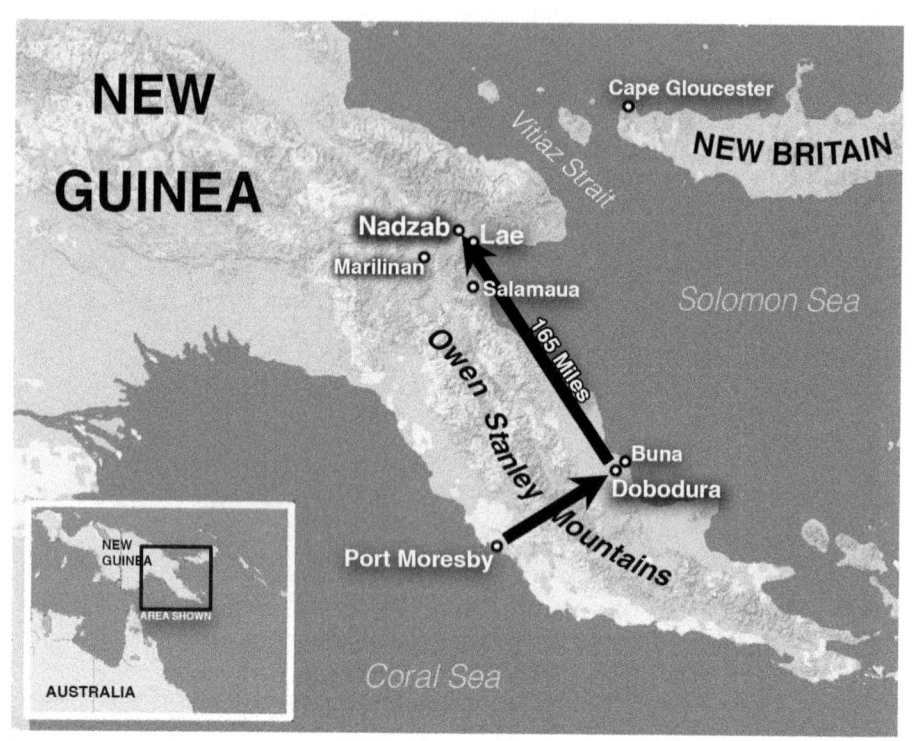

Map 38-2. In January of 1944 the Jolly Rogers moved from Port Moresby across the Owen Stanley Mountains to Dobodura, near Buna. In February they moved 165 miles up the coast to Nadzab, 20 miles up the Markham River valley from Lae.

put them on the other side of the Owen Stanleys, so that they would no longer have to deal with those towering mountains and their chronic thunderstorms on their way to and from bombing missions, as they had been doing ever since they first came out to the Pacific. Operating out of Dobodura would also put the bombers 90 miles closer to their Japanese targets.

However, getting closer to the Japanese obviously had its dangers: by moving the Jolly Rogers and Ken's Men closer to Rabaul and other Japanese airbases, Kenney was also risking getting them bombed by the Japanese while they sat on the Dobodura airfield. It was a calculated risk, just as it had been with the move from Iron Range to Port Moresby, but with the number of fighter planes Kenney had on hand by this time, and with yet more being promised by Washington, he thought that the Americans could defend the new fields well enough now.

Dobodura had started out as a small airfield ten miles inland from Buna Mission on the north coast of New Guinea. During the Battle of Buna (November of 1942 through January of 1943) General Kenney had improved the field and used it to fly in troops of the American 32nd Division in C-47 transport

38. THE JOLLY ROGERS MOVE TO NADZAB

The two longest of the Nadzab runways under construction in the Markham River valley in January of 1944. These were the runways that the Jolly Rogers would use.

planes, one of the first large airlifts of troops ever carried out, and certainly the largest up to that time. Thereafter he used the airfield to bring in supplies to the Americans and Australians who were fighting to eliminate the last of the Japanese invaders at Buna. After the battle was won, the Americans continued to improve the Dobodura airfield and used it as a base for fighter planes, as well as an emergency field for bombers or any other Allied aircraft operating in the area that were in trouble and needed to land.[*]

After the Seabees widened and lengthened the field until it was long enough to handle heavy bombers, the C-47s brought 150 tons of steel Marston matting "over the hump" (the Owen Stanley Mountains) from Port Moresby, and the runway surface was metalized just like Jackson Field at Moresby.[2] In January of 1944 the Jolly Rogers and Ken's Men said goodbye to Port Moresby and made the jump over the mountains once and for all, never again to be troubled by them on bombing missions.

From Dobodura in January of 1944, the Jolly Rogers struck Japanese airfields at Wewak, Hansa Bay, Alexishafen, Madang, and Saidor. They also hit enemy fields on New Britain.

---

[*]This was the "Buna airfield" that Col. Art Rogers referred to repeatedly as an emergency field in describing the big raid on Rabaul on October 12, 1943 (Chapter 33).

The Jolly Rogers move forward again
Meanwhile the road from Lae to Nadzab was finally completed, and heavy machinery offloaded from cargo ships at Lae's harbor was driven up the road to the new airbase and put to work. Construction then went into high gear, and by the middle of February the Nadzab airbase was ready to take the big bombers. The Jolly Rogers moved the 165 miles from Dobodura northwest to

Above: one of the tent "suburbs" of the Nadzab airfield complex. The group of tents in the foreground were occupied by the Jolly Rogers, who declared this to be the best airbase they ever had in the Pacific. The large runways of the airbase are out of the frame at the bottom of the photo. Below: a ground-level view of the tent city seen above.

Nadzab (Map 38-2 on page 400) on 23 February, 1944. The place seemed like a paradise after Iron Range and Port Moresby. If Iron Range was hell, and Port Moresby purgatory, then Nadzab was heaven, and was often described later as the best airbase that the Jolly Rogers ever had during the war.

Nothing could be done about New Guinea's heat, humidity, and endless rainfall, of course, but the gravel soil drained the rainwater away and cooling breezes swept across the open plain (photo, opposite). The hated jungle was far from the boundaries of the camp, the mountains provided scenic views, and a man could drive a jeep up into the foothills and find waterfalls spilling into cool, clear pools in which he could swim and take a bath.

At Nadzab the Navy engineers (Seabees) laid out a veritable tent city, a military town more orderly than most civilian towns in America, and every one of the hundreds of tents was provided with electric power. The long straight roads had posted speed limits enforced by the MPs. Liberty ships brought in prefab wooden buildings from the States that could be put together in ten-foot sections to create genuine wooden buildings that were delightfully not tents, and such buildings could be made as long as desired by just bolting on more sections.[3]

The big airbase eventually sprawled across so much of the Markham river valley that it astonished a B-24 pilot who was being ferried up to Nadzab from Australia in a C-47 transport plane. He wrote:

> On February 21, 1944, when I looked out the window of that Gooney Bird, I couldn't believe my eyes. I saw taxiways with hard stands to park airplanes curving every which way and half a dozen long runways abuilding. There were hundreds of heavy bombers, medium bombers, light bombers, transports, spotters, and fighters—P-38s, P-39s, P-40s, and P-47s—as far as I could see. Three of the heavy bomb groups were there, or were in the process of moving in—the 380th was still down in Darwin—and it seemed to me that most of the rest of Fifth Air Force was at Nadzab, too. . . The housing areas stretched from the hills that rimmed the northern side of the valley all the way south to the Markham River. . . The entire complex was twenty miles square. Nadzab was said to be the largest airfield complex in the world, and I believe it was.[4]

It was the sort of engineering feat of which the slovenly and ill-equipped Japanese military was utterly incapable, and was all the more remarkable in light of the fact that the Pacific war theater was receiving so little of America's industrial war output and manpower at this period of the war.

The Japanese made bombing and strafing raids on Nadzab on Nov. 6, 7, and 9 of 1943. They were intercepted by American fighter planes, including

P-38 Lightnings, P-39 Airacobras, P-40 Warhawks, and P-47 Thunderbolts, and several of the Japanese bombers and fighters were shot down. Still, a few Japanese planes penetrated Nadzab's fighter screen and by bombing and strafing managed to destroy several parked fighters and kill at least one man, the crew chief of a P-39, who took a direct hit from a bomb that rendered him, in the words of one eyewitness, a "soggy red bundle of clothes at the bottom of a bomb-scorched slit trench."[5] Another fighter pilot, Joe Potts, remembered:

> It was at Nadzab that I saw the Ki-61 Tony for the first time, and that was a sweet looking plane [photo on p. 357]. They came down and strafed us. We all dived into the nearest trench, all falling on top of each other. We could hear the bullets whistling by as they strafed, and they really did whistle, just like in the movies! They were sleek looking planes with that inline engine. They looked like our P-51s![6]

After General Kenney's devastating attacks on the Japanese airfields at Wewak and Hollandia in the spring of 1944, Japanese air raids on Nadzab ceased.

The Jolly Rogers would be at Nadzab for six months before moving on up the New Guinea coast again in August of 1944, as the war moved inexorably north toward Japan. In June a few new B-24 crews arrived at Nadzab from the States, after passing through Port Moresby, and the pilot of one of these crews was named James H. Horner. The Horner crew was assigned to the 320th ("Moby Dick") Squadron of the Jolly Rogers. In 2018 three surviving members of the Horner crew, including James Horner himself, related to the author their memories of their service in the Army Air Corps in the Southwest Pacific with the Jolly Rogers.

At this point we will pause the story of the Jolly Rogers and take up the story of the Horner crew from its formation through its training and its assignment to the Southwest Pacific. The story of how these young men entered the Air Corps, were trained to fly heavy bombers, were assigned to a crew, and found themselves in combat with the Japanese is representative of the experience of many of the young men who flew with the Jolly Rogers.

With the arrival of the Horner crew at Nadzab in Chapter 42, the story of the Jolly Rogers will resume, and continue with the Horner crew to the end of the war.

Part II

The Horner Crew

Back row, left to right: Lt. James Horner (pilot), Lt. Allan Cooper (copilot), Lt. Tom Theobald (navigator), Lt. Sylvester Ostafin (bombardier), Sgt. Ernest Eady (flight engineer).

Front row, left to right: Sgt. Doy Bruni (radio operator), Sgt. Edmund Rogalski (nose gunner), Sgt. Kenneth Carter (tail gunner), Sgt. J. W. Dale (left waist gunner), Sgt. Jaime Baca (right waist gunner). Photograph taken on Biak Island, 1944.

Chapter Thirty-Nine

INTO UNIFORM

The ten young men who made up the bomber crew of which James H. Horner was the pilot were typical of their generation. Jim Horner, Jaime Baca, and Tom Theobald, the three surviving members of the crew who have contributed their memories to this book, were living in different parts of the United States and going about their separate lives when they became caught up in the titanic whirlwind of events associated with the greatest war in human history. These young men would probably have never met each other had not the fortunes of war brought them together to crew a bomber in the U. S. Army Air Corps. But they did come together and they would fly hundreds of combat hours together in the Pacific against the fanatical military forces of Imperial Japan. Since bomber crews were referred to by the names of their pilots, this crew was known as the Horner crew.

Seven members of the ten-man Horner crew have passed away during the more than seventy years since the end of World War II and the time this book was written, so the stories of how those crewmen entered the Air Corps and chose, or were selected for, their crew positions are lost to us. Each man's MOS (Military Occupational Specialty) required a certain set of skills that he had to learn, individually, before being assigned to a bomber crew, and these skills were taught in specialized training schools all over the country.

While a man was being trained in one of these schools, whether he was learning to become a pilot, a gunner, a navigator, flight engineer, or bombardier, he had no idea what crew he would eventually be assigned to, nor did he know whether he would be sent to the European or Pacific theater of war, nor for that matter whether he would become the crewman of a light, medium, or heavy bomber. The Army Air Corps placed men where they were needed most at the time they graduated from their training schools. A pilot in the early stages of his training also did not know whether he would later be flying bombers, fighter planes, or transport aircraft.

An Air Corps trainee would only learn these things, and meet his other crewmen (if he happened to be assigned to a crew), after graduating from the school that taught him his MOS. The men assigned to a bomber crew would then train together (as described in the next chapter) for nine weeks to become a team that, barring illness, accidents, or other unforeseen circumstances, would remain together throughout their time in a war zone.

James Horner, Jaime Baca, and Tom Theobald have provided from their memories the details about their individual training which follow. Allan Cooper, who became the copilot of the Horner crew, died in 1981, but his son Michael has furnished us with his father's military records, his mission diary, and (since Cooper was a professional artist) his pencil drawings, and from these sources as well as what Michael remembers his father telling him, we have been able to piece together many details of his training.

America before the war: the situation at home

In the dozen years before the outbreak of the Second World War, America was in the midst of an economic crisis that has since become known as the Great Depression. After the stock market failed catastrophically in 1929, the American economy collapsed, banks and businesses across the nation closed, and jobs became scarce all over the country. To make things even worse, a drought struck in the 1930s, drying out the soils in the American Midwest, the breadbasket of the nation, accompanied by high winds that blew away millions of tons of fertile topsoil.

The giant soil-laden windstorms sometimes blotted out the sun and turned day into night, blowing from the Midwest to as far away as New York City, and this period, the entire decade of the 1930s, became known as the Dust Bowl Era. Thousands of farms withered up and disappeared along with their crops, and two-and-a-half million people were uprooted from their land and homes and migrated to the cities or anywhere they thought they might find work. The poverty of that time was real, not what is called poverty today, and many people simply didn't have enough food to eat. Hordes of destitute people set out by any available means of transportation for California, which was seen as a land of promise, where they hoped to find jobs and take up a new life.*

The young men who came of age during this time, and who went to war for America in World War II, came from many backgrounds, but one thing that most of them had in common was that they were living in hard times, and had to cope with the hardships and deprivation as best they could. They were "forged in the fire," so to speak, and developed qualities of endurance, self-reliance, and perseverance that served themselves and their nation well during the war years, as well as in the years following the war. It is for this reason many historians now call them the Greatest Generation.

America's hope for neutrality in the war

The Japanese had been moving toward creating an empire ever since their seizure of Korea clear back in 1905, but their program of conquest shifted into high gear with their invasion of China in 1937, and their military takeover and

---

*The exodus to California was chronicled in the novel *The Grapes of Wrath* by John Steinbeck, and the movie version of the book by director John Ford.

occupation of Southeast Asia and numerous strategic islands in the Pacific. In Europe, fighting had been in progress since 1939, when Hitler's armies invaded Poland as the prelude to his quest to conquer all of Europe. Both the Germans and the Japanese were determined to dominate their parts of the world, and Germany and Japan had formed an alliance to promote these goals in 1940. Fascist Italy under Mussolini had joined the alliance, and they had become known as the Axis Powers after Mussolini's claim that soon all European countries would "rotate on the Rome-Berlin axis."

Remembering the bitter sacrifices of World War One, many Americans believed that America could, and should, remain neutral and stay out of these wars on opposite sides of the world. The aviator Charles Lindbergh, who had become the most famous man in the world after his solo transatlantic flight in 1927, was the principal spokesman for an organization called the America First Committee, and he and other famous like-minded Americans traveled about the nation giving speeches advocating nonintervention and isolationism. Let Europe deal with German aggression on their own this time, they said, and as for the Japanese, who were slaughtering Chinese by the millions, that was China's problem, not America's, although America did place an embargo on American oil shipped to Japan to try to hamper the latter's military ambitions. The United States had large oceans separating it from both wars, and it could afford to simply stand pat and let them play out.

Millions of Americans agreed with Lindbergh. They felt that America had lost enough men (over 53,000) saving Europe from German takeover in the First World War only twenty years before, and no one wanted to go through that national agony again. America's debt to France for its help against Great Britain during its Revolutionary war, which was one of the justifications for going to war on the side of France in 1918, had been paid, in blood, and now America owed nothing to anyone.

America's forced entry into the war

Then, in the early part of December, 1941, the Japanese naval fleet moved stealthily, undetected, within 200 miles of the American Territory of Hawaii, and without warning, or any declaration of war, loosed a swarm of bombers, fighters, and torpedo planes on the American Pacific Fleet in Pearl Harbor. Its long-concealed intentions to dominate the entire Pacific Rim, and consolidate it into a Japanese Empire, were now out in the open. Suddenly over 2,400 Americans at Pearl Harbor were dead, the Fleet was crippled, and America was embroiled in the war as deeply as any combatant on either side of the world.

America immediately declared war on Japan, and Hitler and Mussolini, allies of Japan, responded by declaring war on the United States. We know now that in foolishly declaring war on the U. S. both Japan and Germany sealed their own fates, for if America had not been forced into the war, and had managed to remain neutral, Japan would likely rule Asia today, and Germany would probably dominate Europe. Once the industrial might and national resolve of America became organized and focused, Imperial Japan and Nazi Germany, two of the greatest evils ever to befall mankind, were doomed to defeat.

None of this was foreseeable as America entered the war in early 1942, however, and at that time the utter defeat of the Axis powers was not even considered possible by many Americans. When America suddenly found itself in a two-front war, it was woefully unprepared for war on even a single front. Once again, just as at the onset of World War One, young American recruits without equipment were drilling with fake wooden rifles and participating in war training exercises using automobiles with signs on them saying "Tank," since there were not enough real rifles or tanks to train with, while American industry figured out how to gear up to produce millions of real rifles and thousands of real tanks, small arms, artillery, warplanes, and ships for the navy.

Charles Lindbergh, who had joined the Air Corps Reserve before he flew the Atlantic, had been promoted to the rank of colonel after his historic flight, but after President Roosevelt had denounced him for his speeches advocating isolationism, Lindbergh had resigned his commission in protest. When war was declared, Lindbergh requested the reinstatement of his commission so that he could go to war as an Air Corps officer, but Roosevelt, shamefully and vindictively, refused to restore it. So instead Lindbergh went to work with Henry Ford at Ford's giant Willow Run plant in Michigan, helping to refine the design of a big four-engined bomber designated the B-24, and nicknamed the Liberator, that had been designed by the Consolidated Aircraft Corporation of San Diego, California. Ford would eventually build thousands of B-24s under contract.

The young men of America go to war

In Sept. of 1940 Congress, seeing war erupting and escalating on both sides of the world, and worried that America might eventually be drawn into the conflicts, had organized a system of drafting into the army all able-bodied American men between the ages of 18 and 36. This was the first peacetime draft in American history. Anyone drafted during this time was required to serve a year in the armed forces. When the U. S. entered the war, the enlistment period was extended to the duration of the war. By the end of the war in 1945, thirty-five million American men had registered for the draft and over ten million of them had been drafted into the military.

The Japanese had hoped that their sneak attack on America's Pacific Fleet at Pearl Harbor would have the same demoralizing effect on the Americans as their sneak attack on the Russian Fleet at Port Arthur in 1905 had had on the

Russians. However, there was a big difference between America in 1941 and Russia in 1905. Russia had been a decaying monarchy with an obsolete fleet built with 1800s technology. America was an up-and-coming republic with a vast, modern industrial base and the will and energy to use it.

Far from demoralizing America, the Japanese sneak attack on America galvanized the nation in a great surge of national outrage. Thousands of young American men didn't wait to be drafted, and voluntarily enlisted in America's armed forces with the goal of avenging the despicable attack, so that nearly 40% of American servicemen in WWII were volunteers.

James Horner, Tom Theobald, and Jaime Baca enter military service and train for specialties in the Air Corps

Today, in 2018, three of the men who would become part of the Horner B-24 crew, including James Horner himself, all in their mid-90s today, still retain clear memories of their entry into the armed forces and their experiences in the war. These memories include their training for their roles as bomber crewmen. Their individual stories follow, and will serve to illustrate the experiences of millions of other young American men who entered the U. S. Army Air Corps at this time under similar circumstances.

James H. Horner (pilot of the B-24 bomber crew) enlists in the Air Corps

The Horner family had been in America since 1608, when the first James Horner landed on the coast of Virginia from England. Since that time men of the Horner family had participated in nearly all of America's wars. Horners had fought in the American Revolution and had enlisted on both sides in the Civil War. James Horner's father had been a first sergeant in the regular army and had served in the cavalry patrolling the Mexican border against Pancho Villa between Brownsville and El Paso, Texas, from 1913 to 1917, then transferred to the artillery branch of the Army during the First World War. After the war, and his discharge from the army, James' father and his brother pooled their money to buy a cotton farm in Texas, and tried to make a go of farming.

James Hartley Horner was born on this cotton farm near the small town of

James Horner in 1943.

Celeste* in northern Texas on June 20, 1921. The bottom dropped out of the cotton market in 1922 and the Horner farm failed, possibly to the relief of James' mother, who hated living in Tornado Alley and had seen one twister after another threaten her family while they were living there. James' family left Texas in early 1923 and moved to Kentucky, where he spent three years with his mother and brother in a log cabin on another farm while his father traveled to Detroit, Michigan, to take a job doing construction work offered to him by a friend with whom he had served in the army. By the spring of 1926 he had saved enough money to bring his family there, settling in Hazel Park, a small city within the Detroit metro area. James started school there in 1927.

After James graduated from high school at age 18 in January of 1940 he took a job in a grocery store, where he was paid ten cents an hour, but after six months he found a much better job working in a Chrysler automobile engine plant for $32 a week, sometimes making as much as $35 a week with overtime pay. This was big money during the Great Depression, and James, who had never seen such money, went from driving a beat-up old 1931 Model A Ford to a snazzy '37 Pontiac Coupe. But this lucrative employment didn't last long; James was laid off after 4 months, and then took a job in the main Chrysler plant at a 40 percent pay cut, making $88 a month. He soon left Chrysler altogether to work in a small defense plant located only a half mile from his family's home in Hazel Park, near enough so that he could walk to work. This plant was housed in four or five buildings and manufactured parts for Pratt & Whitney aircraft engines, which were used in a variety of American warplanes, including the B-24 bomber. No complete engines were assembled at this plant.

With the plant operating under wartime pressures, this job entailed working 12-hour days, 6 AM to 6 PM, seven days a week. The only time off that employees were allowed during the entire year was a half-day at Christmas. Pay was earned two ways: by the hour and by the piece. James made 45 cents an hour during setup and tool sharpening, then he closed his time card and went on piecework, being paid for each engine part he made, and the parts were of various kinds. Under this system a worker might be paid anywhere from two to twenty cents for a finished engine part, and by the end of the day it usually averaged out to be about $1.20 per hour. James would hold this job from 1941 until January of 1943, running a variety of machine tools, including a metal lathe. The long 84-hour work weeks were tiring, but being young and vigorous, James would often get off work and go to a party somewhere rather than go home and sleep.

---

*The most decorated soldier of WWII, Audie Murphy, was born three miles south of Celeste in the town of Kingston, Texas in 1925.

On June 21 of 1942, all this activity and lack of sleep caught up with him. He was so drowsy on that day that he dozed off on his feet in front of his lathe, in the middle of building an engine part, and his cutting tool went clear through the part he was making and into the lathe itself, jamming it and doing some expensive damage to the machine. He decided that it might be a good idea to make himself scarce for the rest of that afternoon, so he closed out his time card and went to a movie. The next day, still worried that management might take him to task for damaging the lathe, he decided to skip work for the day and went out strolling with his brother Dennis and a high school friend named Wilburn Woody into the downtown area of Detroit.

This was on June 22, 1942, with America six months into the war, and two days after James' 21st birthday. With nothing better to do, the boys decided to take a self-guided tour of the Federal Building (which was ten stories high) in downtown Detroit. This building was the local nerve center for all the military services, Army, Navy, Marines, and Coast Guard, and during the war it was the liveliest place in town. Besides, with war raging around the world, military service was never far from any young man's mind, and the boys would be able to look into all the recruiting stations and see which branch of the service most appealed to them.

While wandering the busy hallways of the Federal Building, where all sorts of noisy and interesting activities were in progress, the boys came to a place where a crowd of young men were gathered outside a closed door, waiting for something. Asking what it was all about, they learned that in a short while a written exam would be offered to all comers, and if a man passed that test he would qualify for flight training in the Army Air Corps.*

The Air Corps had recently changed its requirements for becoming an "Aviation Cadet," as flight students were called. Previously, an applicant had to have at least two years of college before he could apply, but college experience was an uncommon thing in the 1940s, and the Air Corps needed a vast number of new pilots for its wartime expansion. So, by necessity, the college requirement was dropped, and by the spring of 1942 an applicant had only to pass a comprehensive aptitude test to qualify for flight training. This test was being made available to any young man who wished to take it, and this was the test the crowd was waiting to take in Detroit's Federal Building that day.

The boys were kidding back and forth all the while, and since taking the exam didn't cost anything, nor did it obligate one to join the army, they challenged each other to go in and give it a try. It would just be fun to see how they measured up. Thus when the door opened they entered the room with the rest of the boys and sat down to take the exam. As it turned out, the exam was not

---

*There was no independent U. S. Air Force at this time. The U. S. Army Air Corps would not become the U. S. Air Force until after the war, in 1947.

an easy one. It tested vocabulary, reading comprehension, mathematical skills, and one's ability to reason. For example, one math question was: If you had to make a 600 mile flight, and you flew the first third of it at 150 miles per hour, the next third at 180 miles per hour, and the final third at 200 miles per hour, how long would the flight take? Other questions were riddles that required logic to solve.

The boys finished their exams, turned them in for grading, and were told that the results would be posted outside in the hallway in an hour. To kill the time, they resumed their wanderings through the building, enjoying all the excitement of the hustle and bustle of wartime activity. When they returned to the room where they'd taken the exam, they found a list on the door of the people who had passed. James was the only one of the three whose name was on the list. That was interesting, but because he'd really only wanted to see how he would score on the test, not join the Air Corps, James didn't plan to sign up at first. He had no particular interest in becoming a pilot; in fact he'd never even been near an airplane.

But the other two boys pestered him to sign up, saying that if he did, they would sign up for military service as well. Dennis had been told that if a man failed the test, but still signed up for the Air Corps, he'd be allowed to retake the test every 90 days until he passed it. Their friend Woody had no interest in the Air Corps, but he liked the idea of becoming a Marine.

James also thought about how many people wanted to become pilots but couldn't qualify, and here the opportunity was his for the taking. He told himself that flight training had to be an easier job than the one that was wearing him down in the engine plant. In fact, almost any job in the military had to be preferable to that one. Flying seemed adventurous as well, and it definitely beat the walking army. He decided to go ahead and enlist as an Aviation Cadet, and all three of the boys signed up for military service before leaving the Federal Building that day. None of them had consulted their families beforehand—they simply did it.

James' brother Dennis signed up with the Air Corps to go to mechanics' school, planning to retake the aviation cadet school test until he passed it (and he did later pass the test and complete pilot training). The brothers' friend Woody went down the hallway and joined the Marine Corps, and only a few months later was involved in the vicious and bloody fighting for the Pacific island of Tarawa (he survived). Both Dennis and Woody left home for military service within three weeks of enlisting. Two weeks after enlisting, James received a notice instructing him to come back to the Federal Building for a swearing-in ceremony, along with a couple of hundred other young men who had passed the test in the intervening days. After he was sworn in, he was told to continue in his civilian job while he awaited orders to report for duty.

Weeks passed; then months. This was because even though only a small fraction of the thousands of men who took the Aviation Cadet exam passed it, there were still not enough training schools, instructors, or facilities to handle them all, so most men had to wait some months before they were called.

"After about a month," remembers Horner today, "in late August, it occurred to me that since I had already qualified for the cadet program, I should also be able to apply for West Point and get a regular army commission, and I could earn an engineering degree as well. My local congressman agreed, and approved my appointment for the next class at West Point. I was waiting for a resolution between my two applications when I received a letter from Congress pointing out that it was too late to join the current 1942 West Point class that had just started, and I would be 22 years old the following June of 1943, which exceeded the 22-year-old age limit before a class begins. So, with West Point out of the question, I was back to my Aviation Cadet enlistment."

James continued to work at his machinist's job while waiting for his call-up to the Air Corps, and finally, near Christmas of 1942, six months after he had enlisted, the long-awaited letter arrived. He was ordered to report to the Preflight Classification Center at Lackland Army Air Base at San Antonio, Texas on January 9, 1943. He was finally on his way to flight training. He was 21 years old.

Jaime A. Baca (waist gunner of the Horner crew)

Jaime A. Baca was born on January 30, 1923 into a large extended family that operated a farm along the Rio Grande river bottom near Santa Fe, New Mexico. Baca is one of the oldest names in America—a Cristobal Baca had brought his family up from Mexico City into the Santa Fe area in the year 1600, and was among the early colonizers of the territory north of Mexico that eventually became the state of New Mexico in the American Southwest. The town of Santa Fe was established in 1610, 165 years before the American Revolutionary War in which James Horner's ancestors fought. The area came to be called New Mexico Territory after the Mexican War in 1848, when Mexico ceded the region to the United States. The territory became the 47th state of the Union in 1912.

Jaime Baca's family lived in a little farming community called Pena Blanca (Spanish for "White Rock"), located on the east bank of the Rio Grande about ten miles south of Santa Fe. The town is adjacent to the centuries-old Pueblo Indian village of Santo Domingo.

Sgt. Jaime Baca in 1944 (from a hometown newspaper clipping).

Jaime's great-grandfather, a sheepherder, had been killed by nomadic Navajo

Indians in 1861, and whenever little Jaime misbehaved his parents told him that if he didn't mend his ways they'd let the Navajos get him. Thus, for little Jaime, the boogeyman was a Navajo Indian. While he was still a small child he saw some unusually dressed Indians on the train platform at Pena Blanca's railroad station, and when someone told him they were Navajos, he went screaming to his grandfather with the news that they were all about to be murdered and scalped. His grandfather calmed him down and told him that Navajos were friendly Indians nowadays and he had nothing to fear.

While growing up on the family farm along the Rio Grande, Jaime helped with his family's harvests of wheat, alfalfa, and apples, and helped tend his family's vegetable gardens. His father bought one of the first automobiles in the town, a Model T Ford. He remembers today that his grandmother's large old adobe home had earthen walls three feet thick, and gas lights powered by a carbide generator in the kitchen. New Mexico, a desert state, often has swelteringly hot daytime temperatures in the summer, but cool nights. Jaime's grandmother achieved a kind of summer air conditioning that cost her nothing: she would open all the windows of her home in the evening to let in the cool night air, then in the morning she'd shut the windows and trap the coolness inside. The thick adobe walls insulated the interior from the outside heat while preserving the interior coolness, and people who entered her house during burning hot summer days marveled at how refreshingly cool its interior was.

Since there was no mechanical refrigeration for food in those days, perishable goods were kept cool in a root cellar, and water was drawn from a well that provided cold water at any time of the year. Jaime remembers how on hot summer days he'd draw up some of this cold water and rush it to his grandmother's kitchen, where she'd use fresh lemons and sugar to make everyone lemonade.

At age 6 little Jaime was allowed to go out into the fields with the menfolk to do what chores he was capable of doing at that age, and he was proud to be counted among the men. Jaime Baca spoke only Spanish until he entered the first grade at the age of 5, in a school where the teachers spoke only English, and like most young children exposed to a new language he quickly picked up and became fluent in English. His grandparents, however, continued speaking only Spanish all their lives. In the 1930s, when Jaime was laughing at the antics of Amos & Andy on the radio, his grandmother kept begging him to please translate whatever it was he found so hilarious into Spanish for her, so that she could enjoy the jokes too. Jaime had to keep telling her, "Grandma, I'm sorry, but there is just no way to translate Black English into Spanish."

In 1932 Jaime's father moved his family 50 miles down the Rio Grande to Albuquerque so that one of his daughters could attend the University of New Mexico while living at home, and Jaime Baca attended St. Mary's Catholic School from 4th grade until high school graduation. He remembers today that the small city of Albuquerque in the 1930s was such a peaceful place that local policemen complained that they had practically nothing to do. Baca remembers a policeman telling him that he wished someone would at least report a lost dog so that he would have a case to work on. A gas station robbery along Route 66, which ran through town, was front page news for weeks.

In those days no one locked the doors of their homes, and Jaime's father parked his pickup truck at the curb in front of the house with the keys always in the ignition switch. "That's where those keys belong," he told his children, "so they won't get lost." Auto theft was practically unheard of in that time and place. About the only crime that Baca remembers today, besides the gas station robbery on Highway 66, was a case of mail fraud that had occurred in 1918, during the First World War. This was before he was born, but it was still being talked about. A classified ad in the newspaper had offered to tell men "How to Avoid the Draft" for a small sum of money, and provided the address to mail it to. Those who paid the money received an envelope containing a piece of paper on which was written: "Close the window." The sum of money paid was so small, however, that most of the victims considered it worth the laugh.

Jamie had only recently graduated from high school in 1941, and hadn't yet found a job, when a friend of his burst into the Baca home one Sunday with the shocking news that America had been attacked by the Japanese at Pearl Harbor. For New Mexicans, even worse news would come the next day, when it was learned that the Philippine Islands were also under attack. The Philippines had been an American protectorate since the Spanish-American War of 1898, and in September of 1941, over 1,800 New Mexican troops had been stationed in the Philippines as members of the 200th and 515th Coast Artillery units. Military leaders in Washington had reasoned that since so many New Mexicans spoke Spanish, they should get along well with the Filipinos, most of whom also spoke Spanish because the islands had been a colony of Spain for 300 years.

As a result, it seemed like nearly everyone in New Mexico had friends or relatives stationed in the Philippines, including the Bacas—Jaime had a second cousin named Benedito Baca there. For four months, from December of 1941 to April of 1942, these New Mexico soldiers, along with the other American defenders of the Philippines, under the command of General Douglas MacArthur (who would later command all U. S. Army and allied forces in the Pacific war) stubbornly held off the invading Japanese armies in desperate jungle fighting on the main Philippine island of Luzon. Owing to the vast distance between the Philippines and America, and the Japanese navy's domination of the Pacific, no reinforcement or supply from home was possible for the battling American forces, while the Japanese were close to their own country and continually received both, so that the outcome of the Japanese invasion was a foregone conclusion.

As the battle progressed, overwhelming numbers of Japanese troops backed the 75,000 Americans and their Filipino allies down into Luzon's Bataan Peninsula, until finally, out of food, ammunition, and medical supplies, they were compelled to surrender. It was the largest surrender of American forces in U.S. history. After their surrender, many of the New Mexico men were forced into what became known as the Bataan Death March, and were beaten, tortured, and murdered by sadistic Japanese guards while being herded 65 miles to prison camps along primitive roads without food or water. Many who survived the trek died under appallingly bad conditions in the camps.

From the time of the surrender, no knowledge of these men's fate would be forthcoming to America until after the war ended, and sometimes not even then. Many New Mexicans who were in the Philippines at the start of the war would never be heard from again. Benedito Baca, unfortunately, would be one of them. A survivor told the Baca family after the war that Benedito had been placed aboard one of the so-called Hell Ships, so named because of how the prisoners were treated, to be taken to Japan to become a slave laborer. However, he had become ill during the voyage so he was simply thrown overboard with other sick men to drown.

Of the 1,800 New Mexicans serving in the Philippines when the war began, only 800 would survive to return home. After the surrender of Bataan, some Americans, still under the command of Gen. MacArthur, were able to hold out a little while longer on the fortress island of Corregidor, a short distance offshore from the coastline of Bataan. MacArthur had his wife and son with him. The battle for Corregidor became known as the Alamo of the Pacific, and the outcome was the same as at the original Alamo, except that many Americans survived to become prisoners of the Japanese. But in March, just before the Japanese overwhelmed Corregidor, MacArthur and his family, along with some of his staff officers, escaped in a PT boat to the southern Philippine island of Mindanao by order of President Roosevelt, who did not want to lose what he considered his most competent commander in the Pacific. From Mindanao they were flown to Australia in a B-17 bomber. In Australia, MacArthur took command of all Allied army forces in the Southwest Pacific, and he would wage war against the Japanese until Japan was defeated.

After the Pearl Harbor attack, some of Jaime Baca's friends joined the Marines, wanting to do their part to avenge the Americans who had been killed and defeat the Empire of Japan. Jaime tried to do the same, but when he talked to the Marine recruiter in Albuquerque he was told that if he joined up he would have to leave for Marine boot camp that very day, or not go at all. Since he had not yet put his affairs in order at home, he told the recruiter he'd have to pass on joining the Marines and just wait to be drafted into the Army.

39. INTO UNIFORM

As America was gearing up its industries for the all-out war effort, jobs in war plants all over the nation became available to young men like James Horner and Jamie Baca. Unlike in World War One (1914-1918), when aviation was in its infancy, air power would play the primary role in the Second World War, and thus many factories were soon building aircraft and aircraft parts, operating around the clock with their workers on 12-hour shifts like James Horner's job building engine parts in Detroit. New Mexico had no significant industry of any kind to offer employment to young men, but Baca heard that practically any able-bodied man was being hired in California's defense plants. He rode out to California on the train and quickly found work in a factory making parts for B-25 bombers. Thus, at the same time that James Horner was building parts for airplane engines in Detroit, Jamie Baca was building parts for bombers in California. It wouldn't be long, however, before both these young men would be flying America's warplanes together instead of making parts for them.

Baca's mother loved to travel, and with her son working in California she took the opportunity to ride the Santa Fe train out there to visit him. While she was there with her son, Jaime's draft notice arrived. "Mama," he remembers saying to her, "it looks like I'm going into the army. We'd better go home now." They returned to Albuquerque, where Jaime reported to his draft board and received his enlistment instructions. Following his orders, on New Year's Eve, 1942, he took the train south to an army induction center at El Paso, Texas. The next morning all the draftees there were assembled and told that they would be shipping out to different basic training camps, and they would leave in two groups. The first group would board a train at 8 AM, the second one at 11, and the names of the men who would go in each group were read out. Baca's name was in the second group.

Having some time to kill, he went over to the PX (post exchange) to buy a few things, but he'd hardly gotten there when someone came running up to him and told him that he was supposed to be shipping out with the first group, and they were just about to leave. Baca told his friend that he had been assigned to the second group, not the first, but the friend insisted that they were looking for him and he had to go immediately. So he hurried back to the barracks and found that he was indeed expected to be shipping out right then. And he soon learned that this group would be going into the Air Corps.

Just as James Horner and his brother and friend had stumbled into the Air Corps exam in Detroit by chance, resulting in James Horner entering the Air Corps, a similar chance occurrence brought Jaime Baca into the aviation branch of the Army. Apparently someone in the first group had fallen ill, and Baca had been chosen to replace him, possibly because his last name began with B and was at the top of the list of names in the second group. By such quirks of fate were the destinies of so many men determined in the war.

Like James Horner, Baca had never flown in an airplane, had no special interest in the Air Corps, and could just as easily have ended up as an infantryman in the invasion of Italy in 1943, or wading ashore in the D-Day landings at Normandy in 1944, or as an artilleryman in the Battle of the Bulge. Instead he would become a crewman on a bomber flying in the Pacific war theater.

Everyone who entered the army was sent first to basic training, and Baca rode a troop train to the basic training camp at Sheppard Field near Wichita Falls, Texas. After he completed the eight weeks of basic training he learned that he was being assigned to the aviation armorer's school at Lowry Field in Denver, Colorado, where he would learn about the weapons and bombs carried aboard aircraft, and then he would go to aerial gunnery school at Laredo, Texas. Jaime Baca would become a gunner on bombers. He was 20 years old.

Tom R. Theobald (navigator of the Horner crew)

Tom Theobald was born in West Union, Iowa, on the 6th of May, 1921, the first of four children. His father was a butcher by trade, and his family moved from West Union to the nearby town of Oelwein, Iowa where Tom attended high school. After he graduated from high school in 1938, one of Tom's classmates joined the navy, and he persuaded Tom that it would be a good thing for him to do the same. It was a great way to see the world, Tom's friend told him, and all at government expense. No one could have known in 1938 that in three years America would be at war. So young Tom hitchhiked 70 miles north to the town of Decorah, where the Navy had a recruiting station, and enlisted. After signing his enlistment papers he went home to await his call-up.

Tom Theobald in 1944.

When the summons didn't come immediately, Tom took a job with a laundry company in Oelwein, and continued to wait. Months passed, then more months, until finally a couple of years had gone by, and still no word came from the Navy. Tom was perplexed. Had he somehow missed his summons? He began to worry that he might be arrested for desertion. In the meantime, he met a lovely girl named Shirley Streight, courted her, and they were married in June of 1942. By that time America was six months into the world war, and Tom still hadn't heard from the Navy. He wasn't sure what to do next.

Since his Navy enlistment appeared to have fallen through the cracks, and it seemed only a matter of time before he was drafted into the army, Tom decided to enlist in the Army Air Corps. Like most young men who joined the Air Corps, he initially had hopes of becoming a pilot, but after he reported to the Army Classification Center in San Antonio, Texas in January of 1943, he found that he couldn't pass the pilots' eye test. No one with imperfect eyesight was accepted for pilot training. Bombardiers were also required to have perfect vision, but Tom was told that he could still qualify to fly as a navigator.

When he subsequently applied for navigator training, a classification officer interviewed him to evaluate his suitability for the job. He asked Tom how much college schooling he'd had, and when Tom replied that he'd had none (unlike today, attending college was not common in the 1930s), the officer told him that in that case he would probably never make it through navigation school, since it required a level of competence with math that was usually only acquired at the college level. But Tom, who had always done well in high school math classes, took that statement as a challenge, and requested assignment to navigation school anyway. His application was accepted, and then he had only to worry about whether he could make the grade. He was 21 years old.

Allan Gordon Cooper (copilot of the Horner crew)

Allan G. Cooper died of prostate cancer in 1981 at the age of 64, but his war experience is recorded in his flight logbook and other papers that were preserved by his family, including a small diary in which he recorded every combat mission he flew. His son Michael, who made his father's records available for this book, has also provided details of his father's wartime experiences from what he remembers his father telling him while he was growing up.

Allan Cooper was born on November 24, 1917, in Los Angeles, California. From childhood he had a gift for drawing that bordered on genius, and he developed it throughout his school years. In his high school graduation yearbook he was described as a talented artist, which was a serious understatement—he was so skilled at drawing that he was easily

Allan Cooper in flight training, 1943.

able to land a job with the Walt Disney Studios as a cartoonist. In this day of computer-generated animation, many young people are unaware that cartoon animation was once done by hand, with each frame laboriously drawn by wonderfully skilled artists. At twelve frames per second, even the shortest cartoons required thousands of hand-drawn frames, and a full-length animated motion picture such as *Snow White* (1937) required hundreds of thousands of them. It took teams of artists to create all this artwork, and Allan Cooper was one of the many great artists who created everything from short cartoons featuring Mickey Mouse, Donald Duck, Pluto the dog, Goofy, and other Disney characters to Disney's feature-length films such as *Snow White*, *Dumbo*, *Pinocchio*, and *Fantasia*, all of which Cooper worked on.

Allan Cooper had another interest in life besides art: flying airplanes. In the spring of 1938 he began paying for private flying lessons in a 40-hp Taylor Cub[*] at the Ted Morton Flying Service at the Los Angeles airport. By August of 1940 he had accumulated nearly eight hours of dual instruction in three different light planes: the Cub, a Waco biplane, and a J-5 Piper Cruiser.

Being a Disney artist in the 1930s was not, unfortunately, a route to fame and fortune. It was not even particularly rewarding financially. Walt Disney paid most of his artists low wages, and he never even gave them credits at the end of a movie—all the animation credits went to Walt Disney alone. Thus the artists working for him toiled long hours in anonymity and with poor pay in the Disney studios in Los Angeles. Such working conditions were common for artists in any of Hollywood's animation studios at the time, not just at Disney (although the Disney Studio was by far the largest). In a bid to better their lot, a group of cartoon artists formed a union that they named the Screen Cartoonist's Guild, to negotiate collectively for better working conditions and pay. Many Disney employees joined the Cartoonist's Guild.

However, Walt Disney was intensely hostile to the idea of an artists' union, and he refused to recognize the Guild at first. This caused a great deal of bitterness between him and his artists. Even after he grudgingly gave in and accepted the union and its demands for better wages and working conditions, Walt found reasons to fire any Guild members who worked for him. As a result there was much bad feeling in the Disney Studio where Allan Cooper worked as a cartoonist in 1941, not only between Walt Disney and his artists, but between artists who had joined the Guild and those who had not. On May 29, 1941, two hundred of Disney's animators went out on a strike that lasted for five weeks. When non-member artists crossed their picket lines and continued to work, the strikers called them "scabs" and "strike-breakers," and the bitter feelings didn't go away when an agreement with Disney was reached and everyone went back to work.

What involvement, if any, Allan Cooper may have had in all this labor turmoil is not known, but we do know that in April of 1941, the month before

---

[*] Taylor Cubs were later called Piper Cubs after oilman William Piper bought the company founded by the plane's designer, Clarence Taylor. Taylor then went on to form the Taylorcraft Aviation Corporation, a rival to Piper. But it was the Piper Cub (Army L-4) that went to war.

the artists' strike, when all of the labor trouble in the Disney Studios was coming to a boil, Cooper left Disney and joined the Army. This was eight months before the attack on Pearl Harbor. He went to work in the Signal Corps, where he used his drawing talent to make training posters (pp. 424-5) and create architectural drawings, and a year later he was promoted to Staff Sergeant.

According to Army regulations, Allan Cooper did not qualify for Air Corps training at the time that he enlisted, nor for over a year afterward, but a cartoon drawn by one of his friends (below) shows Allan sitting in a latrine pretending to fly an airplane using a toilet plunger for a control stick, showing that he had hopes of being transferred from the Signal Corps to the Air Corps.

When Congress passed Public Law 658 (the Flight Officer Act) on July 8, 1942, which allowed enlisted men such as Sgt. Cooper to transfer to the Air Corps for flight training, if they could qualify, Cooper seized his chance and applied to become an Air Cadet. He took the same Air Corps entrance exam that James Horner had taken as a civilian in downtown Detroit, and passed it. Thus, in June of 1943, over two years after his enlistment in the Army, Allan Cooper entered flight training. He was 25 years old, well under the age limit of 27 for a flight cadet, but practically an old man to many of the teenagers and early twenty-somethings in the flight training program.

A cartoon drawn by a Pvt. Gallagher showing Sgt. Allan Cooper pretending to fly an airplane in the latrine. Cooper obviously was hoping for a transfer to the Air Corps.

Pilot training for James Horner

On January 7, 1943, James said goodbye to his parents and, like nearly all of the young men on their way into the army, took a train to the Army Induction Center specified in his orders. While he was standing in Detroit's Michigan Central Railroad Depot with his suitcase, waiting to board the train, he noticed around him on the platform about a hundred other young Michigan men from

(Above and right) some of the safety posters that Sgt. Allan Cooper drew for the Air Cadets who were undergoing fighter pilot training in P-38s.

all over the state waiting do the same thing. When the call came to board, they were all directed into two or three of the train's standard passenger cars.

The train then proceeded to Chicago, where more cars were added to it, also filled with young men in the same situation but from Pennsylvania, Ohio, western New York, Indiana, and Wisconsin. The train now contained many coaches filled with around 1,200 Air Corps Cadets, all with an average age of around 20. Once the cars were hooked together, and the boys could move freely between them, they all mingled and shared in the excitement of their grand adventure.

Many of the young men were leaving home for the first time, and were filled with all the fears, apprehensions, and excitement that accompany that situation, mingled in this case with the trepidation of going to war and facing possible death. In the America of 1943, just coming out of the Great Depression, many young men had never been on a train before, and most had probably never been more than 100 miles from home, so it was an exciting time for all. James found it stimulating to talk to such a diverse group of youngsters,

39. INTO UNIFORM

from such a wide area of the country, all of whom had the same goal: to fly airplanes in the U. S. Army Air Corps.*

Little groups of like-minded men soon formed, and the inevitable poker games broke out. The train arrived in San Antonio after midnight on the second night of travel, January 9, 1943. It was cold, raining, and everyone was hungry, not having had anything to eat since lunchtime owing to delays en route. At the San Antonio train station the men were loaded into waiting buses and transported into the huge Lackland Army Airbase complex, where amid much shouting and stumbling around in the drizzle and darkness they were herded into supply buildings and issued one set of worn-out fatigues each.

These Army work uniforms were ripped, missing buttons, and seemed to most of the men to be suitable only for rags, but that didn't matter—they were in the Army now, and they knew they had to do whatever they were told. Everyone changed his clothes on the spot and put his civilian clothes into his suitcase, which was tagged and set aside. The men were also given two blankets each and a sheet. Finally, around 2 AM, they were all escorted to the mess hall, thoroughly famished. The food consisted of a huge serving of hash and bread, with coffee or milk, and everyone wolfed it down eagerly.

After eating, the men were instructed to enter any of the two-story, eighty-man barracks buildings that lined the street outside the mess hall and search for an empty bunk. This would have been a difficult thing to do in daylight, considering that the bunks were already about eighty-percent occupied by tired, irritable, previous arrivals who shouted angrily if a light was turned on or a groping hand awakened them in the dark. The newcomers eventually all managed to find bunks, and most managed to get a few hours of sleep before whistles and shouts summoned them back out into the street again. There they were lined up and marched to breakfast, followed by a half-mile walk to the base theater for the first of many orientation lectures.

Inside the theater, the young officer on the stage had barely begun to speak when a hand shot up and a man asked to be excused to visit the restroom. A moment later another hand went up, then another and another, all for the same reason, until all order broke down and the aisles were filled with men frantically headed for the same destination. Somehow everyone in the hall had suddenly been stricken with diarrhea. The normally adequate four or five bathroom stalls in the theater were quickly overwhelmed, and then several hundred future army officers broke out of the building and started desperately searching for somewhere, anywhere, to relieve themselves.

---

*On the opposite side of the world, young Japanese men were experiencing the same thing. Tomokazy Kasai, age sixteen, remembered his first day of aviation training: "The boys were from all over Japan and spoke in different dialects. It was interesting to meet so many different boys from all across the country."[1] Their flight training, however, would be very different from that of the American boys, as will be described shortly.

The building next door was the base fire station, and the firemen quickly realized that the seething horde of frantic men surging toward them was a threat to their spotless facility and closed and locked their doors. It was too late anyway for the stricken young men. They dashed into the bushes, behind the buildings, or anywhere else they could find to relieve themselves. No official cause for this fiasco was ever acknowledged, but it was generally agreed that the most likely cause was soap residue left in the large army baking pans that had held the hash that the men had gorged themselves on during the night. Someone on KP duty had probably not rinsed the pans out well enough after washing them, and the result was that the men ingested soap along with their meals, and got cleaned out just like the pans. At least no permanent harm was done to anyone.

This was James Horner's introduction to the Army, and for him and the rest of the miserable, sleep-deprived young men wearing ragged, ill-fitting uniforms and suffering from diarrhea that morning, the experience established a baseline from which any further experiences had to be for the better.

Over in Japan, young Japanese men were also getting their first introduction to their military and flight training. This was done with wooden clubs wielded by their instructors, on which the slogan "bat to instill military spirit" was inscribed.[1] The trainees were beaten bloody with the clubs and by the fists of their instructors. This violence continued day after day during their training, so that they found it hard to sleep at night on their bruised backsides, and went to their classes with black eyes and swollen, bloody lips.[2]

The difference in training between the American military and the Japanese was the difference between a civilized nation and a nation that had renounced its humanity and descended into barbarism and savagery. This vicious treatment of its own servicemen, moreover, was the model on which Japan would base its empire and its relations with the peoples it conquered: nothing less than cruel, remorseless brutality.

James Horner is accepted for pilot training

Air Cadet Horner and the rest of the men with whom he arrived spent about eight weeks at the Army Classification Center, taking batteries of tests, both medical and psychomotor, while they sat through classes that would be equally relevant to bombardiers, navigators, or pilots as they waited to be assigned to one of those specialties. No one knew at the time what job he might be assigned to in the Army Air Corps, though most hoped to become pilots. The classroom instruction and related testing went on continually until every man was, by the end of the eight weeks, slotted into the job for which the Army decided he was best qualified, or else washed out of cadet school altogether and reassigned to other Air Corps duties. The final assignments were posted on the bulletin boards for everyone to note with either smiles or groans. Men who had hoped to be pilots were overjoyed when they received that assignment, while others with the same hopes were chagrined to find themselves classified as bombardiers or navigators.

Everyone then received his written orders. Those who qualified for pilot training were sent to primary flight schools, most of them being civilian flight schools operating under government contract. Men destined to be bombardiers or navigators were sent to military-run schools that taught those specialties. This being the AAF Central Training Command, most of these schools were scattered around Texas. The pilots had not yet been separated into fighter or bomber pilots—that would come in the second phase of their training, called the Basic phase. At this time they were all assigned to Primary flight school.

The four phases of Army Air Corps pilot training

An Air Cadet learning to fly airplanes in the U. S. Army Air Corps passed through four phases of training: Primary, Basic, Advanced, and Transition. Each of these phases lasted about nine weeks.

Primary Pilot Training taught students the most basic flying skills, using two-seater training aircraft. Primary training was usually provided by civilian pilot training schools operating under contract with the federal government through the Civil Aeronautics Authority (CAA). After he'd had enough dual instruction, a student was certified to fly solo. In Primary school cadets got about 60 hours of training in Stearman, Ryan, or Fairchild primary trainers, and then moved on to the second phase: Basic training.

Basic Pilot Training taught the cadets to fly cross-country to distant destinations and back, to fly on instruments alone, to fly in formation with other planes, and to fly at night. In this program cadets got about 70 flight hours in the Vultee BT-13 (or its variant, the BT-15) basic trainers. After completing Basic flight training, a cadet could move on to Advanced Training.

For Advanced Pilot Training, the cadets were placed into one of two categories: single-engine or multi-engine. Single-engine pilots, who would usually become fighter plane pilots, flew the AT-6 advanced trainer before moving on to the fighters. Multi-engine pilots, who would become the pilots of bombers or transport planes, learned to fly the twin-engined Curtiss AT-9, the Beechcraft AT-10, or the Cessna AT-17 advanced trainers before going on to the bombers or transports. Cadets got about 75 to 80 flight hours of advanced training before being awarded their pilot's wings and moving on to Transition training.

In Transition Pilot Training, the single-engine airplane pilots transitioned into fighters and fighter-bombers, while the multi-engine pilots transitioned into transports or bombers.

Primary training for Cadet Horner

James Horner was enrolled in Class 43-J (the 43 indicated the year, and J, the 10th letter of the alphabet, indicated that the class would graduate in the 10th month of the year, or October). He was sent to a primary school at Cuero,* Texas, a tiny town north of Houston that had a municipal airport with a single large grass landing field, with no outlined runway.† The flight school at Cuero was owned and operated by a man named Clyde E. Brayton. The Brayton Flying Service, like similar civilian-run primary schools all over the country, employed civilian instructors, but the training was supervised by military officers.

A PT-19 Primary trainer plane (PT stood for Primary Trainer).

The Brayton school could handle 290 cadets per class. After a cadet had completed the course under the civilian instructors, one of the Air Corps officers would give him a check ride and either pass or fail him. If a student failed his check ride, he was either washed out of the flight training program or, if he showed promise, was sent back to repeat the class.

For flight training the school used the single-engine Fairchild PT-19 (pictured above), a low-wing, two-seat monoplane of 200 horsepower. Its narrow inline engine allowed good forward visibility, and its wide-spaced landing gear made it very stable on the ground, making things a little easier for beginner pilots.

The students also had classroom instruction in meteorology, navigation, aircraft identification, and aircraft engines. Flight training included five hours in a Link flight simulator and about sixty-five hours of actual flying time, the total dependent on how much practice the instructor thought a student needed to be-

---

* Cuero means "leather" or "cowhide" in Spanish.
† The field is still in use today, but the runway is now paved.

come proficient at spins, aerobatics, landings and takeoffs, maneuvers over a road, and short-field work. Some students required up to ten extra hours of practice before they could demonstrate sufficient competence to fly solo. Few soloed in less than 7 hours.

When James Horner and the other flying students in his class arrived at Cuero,

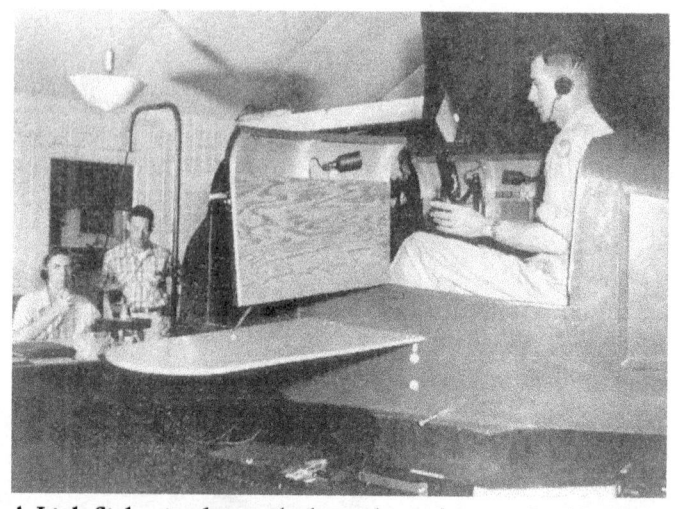

A Link flight simulator, which taught students to fly "blind" (by instruments alone). The simulators were made of plywood, and with the door closed and the lid shut, the student was isolated from his surroundings, could only see his instruments, and "flew" the simulator as directed by his instructor over an intercom. The student in this case is the author's father, Capt. Donald A. Baker.

they were pleased to find the food and accommodations excellent, if not wonderful, especially by Depression-era standards. They had dormitory buildings with single-level bunk beds on tile floors. The mess halls were set up like military mess halls with long tables, but instead of the men having to stand in a chow line, the food was served by waiters, just like in a restaurant. The food itself was great, including frequent steak dinners, and the cadets were encouraged to eat as much as they wanted. For boys from homes where food had been poor and scanty during the Great Depression, this all-you-can-eat banqueting was an unbelievable luxury. Horner soon gained about 15 pounds above his induction weight of 139 lbs, and most of the other boys had similar weight gains.

When payday came, the students got another pleasant surprise: they found that the Army was giving them a subsistence allowance. Since this was a civilian flight school, not a military one, the Army provided the cadets with a daily allowance for meals, laundry, and other civilian services. As James Horner remembers today, "For all the fine accommodations and food, it turned out that the school contractor did not spend all the money that the Army paid him for us, and he gave us what was left over. So now we were drawing our Army private's pay, which was $50.00 a month, plus 50% more in flight pay, or $25.00, and then a little more left over from our per diem allowance. That all added up

39. INTO UNIFORM

James Horner's Primary Flight School instructor, Mr. Clayton Moore (standing, center) and his four students. Parker and Tollet are standing at left and right, respectively, and sitting are Horner (left) and Hayden, who was killed during the training.

to something over $75 a month. With the great food and the good pay, this was the best of all possible worlds!"

Students were assigned four to an instructor. Horner was one of four students assigned to an instructor named Clayton Moore from Ohio, who was in his early forties and had a gorgeous, like-new Beechcraft Staggerwing biplane of his own. He also had a wife and a couple of kids back in Ohio. The other three students were named Parker, Hayden, and Tollet. Horner remembers that Tollet was part American Indian, had a great sense of humor, and was very athletic. He had played football in college, and he liked to play barefoot. Mr. Moore was a skilled and patient teacher, but only two of his four students graduated from the course. Parker showed little aptitude for flying and was soon washed out of the program, and Hayden was killed. The other students never learned all the details of Hayden's death, beyond the fact that he had somehow lost control of his PT-19 during a solo flight and had tried to bail out of it. But he had pulled his parachute's ripcord too soon, and his chute had snagged on the tail of the plane and he had been dragged down with it.

After seven-and-a-half hours of dual instruction from Mr. Moore, Horner soloed the PT-19. "I never had any trouble flying the airplane," he remembers, "and I did what I was told to the best of my ability. I found that I had enough mechanical aptitude that flying was not all that difficult for me. But some of the students, including another boy from Detroit named DeSlover, had considerable trouble. Once in a while DeSlover got permission for me to ride along with him on weekends while he put in some extra practice hours, so that I could help him with certain maneuvers that he was having trouble with. For the most part, this school was a very pleasant experience for me."

One part of the flight training that didn't work out so well for the class was simulated short-field landings, or so-called "carrier" landings (referring to an aircraft carrier). The objective was to land in as short a distance as possible. On the airfield the instructors set up two poles, five or six feet high and about 50 feet apart, with a string stretched between them at the top. The students were told to come in over the string (which would simply break harmlessly if they hit it) and then land as short as possible beyond it. The students soon discovered that instead of gliding the airplane down over the string to a landing without power, they could land shorter by "dragging" the plane in nose-high, holding it up with power, until they just passed over the string, then chop the power and drop quickly to the ground, flaring out just before touchdown to land gently. However, the flare-out took perfect timing, and until they got the hang of it, most of the students landed their planes with a decided thump.

This maneuver was also practiced at night, with the poles lit by flares. Students found that if they memorized whatever engine RPM got good results in the daytime, and used the same settings at night, things went well. However, they found it very difficult to judge their height above the ground in the dark, and if they chopped the power too soon, before they were close enough to the ground, or didn't get the nose up high enough to flare just before touching down, the plane would drop and "pancake" down hard against the ground.

After one night of doing this, about half of the planes were found to have puddles of gas under them the next morning. The PT-19 had a wooden beam or spar passing from side-to-side through the fuselage to which the wings were attached on either side. On some of the planes, the hard landings had broken that spar, and since the gas tank sat on top of it, some of the tanks had ruptured as well. This necessitated replacing the spars and gas tanks at considerable trouble and expense. Rather than continuing to risk damaging the aircraft, the school decided to eliminate that particular exercise from the training schedule.

Cadet Horner's Basic flight training

After the nine-week Primary course at Brayton Flying Service was completed, Flight Cadet James Horner and the other students in his class received orders to report to the Waco Army Air Base for the second phase of their training, known as Basic flight training. This training was conducted in a Vultee

The BT-13 Basic Army trainer plane.

BT-13 "Valiant" (BT stood for Basic Trainer), a large, low-wing single-engine monoplane powered by a big 395 hp radial engine (above).

The BT-13 was a much heavier and more powerful airplane than the PT-19 and required a lot more attention to fly, especially with the considerable engine and propeller torque generated by full power at takeoff. Since for every action there is an equal and opposite reaction, the big propeller spinning in one direction made the plane tend to veer off course in the opposite direction on its takeoff run. The pilot had to be prepared for this and make quick corrections with his flight controls. The BT-13 also had flaps for shorter landings and take-offs and a controllable-pitch propeller (i. e. the angle at which the propeller blades bit the air could be adjusted by the pilot).

As far as food and housing went, however, Waco was a considerable let-down for the students from the civilian Primary school they'd just left. The differences between the luxurious civilian living accommodations and great food they had enjoyed at Brayton and the spartan military room and board at Waco were striking. At Waco the students occupied stacked bunks in bare, drafty two-story military barracks, with 80 men crowded into each building, and most of the time the food was so poor that the students could barely stand to eat it. Why the food was so bad was explained when, near the end of the course, authorities arrested the school's commandant and his adjutant for theft of federal funds. It turned out they had been buying cheap, inferior food for the students with the government money and pocketing the cash they saved.

The Beechcraft AT-10 trainer plane introduced students to the management of more than one engine and a retractable landing gear.

The following class no doubt ate much better at Waco than Horner's Class 43-J did.

Cadet Horner's Advanced pilot training

While the students at Waco had been going through the nine weeks of Basic Flight Training in the BT-13, the Army had been evaluating and dividing them into fighter pilots and bomber pilots. Various factors went into assigning a student to one category or the other. The men were first asked which type of aircraft they preferred, and their choice was presumably given some weight in the decision-making process, and the various aptitude tests they took might also suggest that they were more suited for one type of aircraft than the other. It could also depend on whether the Air Corps needed more fighter or bomber pilots at any particular time.

Cadet Horner expressed a preference for multi-engine aircraft, feeling that he would rather have the company of a crew in flight, especially if he were being shot at, so he was happy when he was assigned to fly bombers. The boys who were accepted as fighter pilots were sent to Victorville, California (north of Los Angeles) or to one of the other fighter training schools, where they would train in single-engine AT-6s. The men chosen to be bomber or transport pilots went to the other side of Waco, to the Blackland Army Airfield, where they were introduced to twin-engine training planes, first the Beechcraft AT-10, and later the Cessna AT-17 (AT stood for Advanced Trainer).

Blackland was once again a different story as far as living accommodations for the students. Instead of the regular two-story army barracks the men had occupied at Waco, at Blackland they were housed in hastily built, single-story, tarpaper-covered structures with outside latrines. These buildings were barely adequate, and certainly not as good as the permanent facilities at Waco, but war demanded some sacrifices. The food was also decent, although of course nothing could compare to the extravagant fare the men had enjoyed at the Brayton primary school.

The AT-10 twin-engine trainer introduced the students to yet more new skills. Aside from learning to manage two engines, the planes had retractable landing gears. As at the previous two training schools, Cadet Horner's training at Blackland was uneventful, and his graduation from the Advanced school came at the end of October, 1943, at which time the students received their Army commissions and wings.

Since an Air Cadet in Primary, Basic, and Advanced training had a rank equivalent to an army private, along with an enlisted man's serial number, it was necessary to discharge him from the Army before he could be brought back in as a commissioned officer. On 2 November, 1943, the Air Cadets of Class 43-J, who numbered about 400 men, were issued honorable discharges (except for a few men who were already officers) for the purpose of being commissioned the next day. On 3 November they were sworn in as officers, most of them as 2nd Lieutenants, with about 10% of them being appointed as non-commissioned Flight Officers. The rank of Flight Officer fell somewhere between the highest enlisted rank and that of a 2nd Lieutenant.

The public was welcome to attend the swearing-in ceremony, and a large number of parents, wives, girlfriends, and other interested people were in the audience when the students received their wings. It was a proud day for all the young men who had made it through the more than ten months of flight training to reach this point, as well as for their families and other loved ones. Each man was handed his wings, and then many of the young ladies did the pinning job. Other advanced training schools all over the country graduated their own 43-J classes that same day, at fields on the east and west coasts, and at other fields in the Central Training Command, so there were thousands of new pilots, bombardiers and navigators graduating from school that month, as they did every month throughout the war.

After being awarded his wings, each student was given two weeks of leave before reporting for Transition Training, when he would begin taking instruction in the type of airplane he would ultimately fly in the war. Most of the students took the opportunity to go home for a couple of weeks to spend the time among family and friends. Lt. Horner returned to his parents' home in

Hazel Park, Michigan where he had his picture taken in his new officer's uniform (below).

Lt. Horner's Transition Training

The students of Class 43-J who were chosen for transition training to bombers received orders to report to Tarrant Army Air Base at Ft. Worth, Texas, where they would undergo nine weeks of training in the B-24 Liberator four-engine bomber. The students reported in from their home leave to Tarrant about the 1st of December, 1943, and since they were now "officers and gentlemen," they took up residence not in a "barracks" but in the airbase's bachelor officers' quarters (BOQ), which at many wartime schools was just a hastily-built barracks with a better-sounding name. The transition training generally followed the pattern of the three previous training phases, with the days divided between classes in weather, navigation, engineering, and flying.

Lt. James Horner as a newly commissioned 2nd Lt. and pilot in the U. S. Army Air Corps, November of 1943.

Out on the airfield, when Lt. Horner first walked up to a B-24 with his instructor and other students, he was nearly overwhelmed by the size and bulk of the huge plane. As he remembers it today: "The windows of the pilot's cockpit were eleven feet above the ground, and standing there gazing up at it, I wondered what I had gotten myself into. Could I ever learn to control such a huge piece of machinery? When I sat in the left [pilot's] seat and looked out along the 55 feet of each wing to the wingtips, I felt like I'd never be able to park this monster without hitting the wingtip of the next plane. It was hard to believe that this thing could actually get up in the air, even on jacks!"

However, his initial apprehensions proved to be unfounded, for as the training progressed he demonstrated an aptitude for flying the B-24 that developed into uncommon skill.

As had been the case in Primary flight school, the flight instructors, who were mostly 1st lieutenants (with an occasional captain), were assigned four students each. On most days all four students flew in the bomber with their instructor, and seats were provided for everyone. The four students could rotate through the pilot's and copilot's seats, spending about an hour every day in each section of the cockpit while practicing the subject of the day, such as takeoffs, landings, flight maneuvers, and emergency procedures. The only other person aboard the bomber during these flights was the flight engineer, the mechanic who was tasked with the maintenance of the plane, and who monitored its performance throughout the flight.

On one day in January of 1944, while shooting touch-and-go landings with their normal crew of the instructor, his four students, and the engineer, Lt. Horner's group of students got a landing lesson that wasn't in the curriculum. In a touch-and-go landing the pilot makes a normal landing on the runway, but then keeps rolling and takes right back off again, and goes around for another landing, and continues doing this for as long as the instructor directs. After an hour or two of raising and lowering the landing gear during these landings and takeoffs, they were suddenly unable to get a green light on the instrument panel for the right-hand gear, to indicate that it was down and locked.

They left the traffic pattern and spent some time cycling the gear up and down, trying to get both main wheels down and locked, but still could not get a green light for the right wheel. They tried bypassing the hydraulics and using an emergency hand crank, but the wheel still wouldn't lock down. Then they tried repeatedly diving the plane and pulling up suddenly to try to snap the gear down and make it lock, but nothing worked. There was still no green light for the right landing gear, which meant that there was a possibility that it would fold up on landing when the plane's considerable weight settled onto it (a B-24 weighed about 19 tons without bombs or a full fuel load).

The instructor pilot notified the airport control tower of the problem, but the people in the tower couldn't come up with any ideas that they hadn't already tried. It then became the instructor's choice what type of emergency landing they would make, wheels-up or wheels-down. Landing a B-24 with only one main wheel down, or with both wheels down but one gear leg collapsing, was not a welcome thought. With its high wing, the plane would immediately drop off toward the missing gear, and when the wingtip and propellers dug into the ground the plane would groundloop (twirl around in a circle). When a B-24 groundlooped it tended to break apart, due to its massive size, weight, and type of construction (by comparison, a B-17, with its low-mounted wing, had the potential to land gear-up without much harm, because even in the retracted position the wheels still protruded sufficiently below the wings to hold them up off the ground a little, reducing the chance of a wingtip digging in and the plane grouplooping). The tendency of a B-24 to break up during landings with only one main wheel down was just one more gripe about the airplane as far as its detractors were concerned.

The instructor pilot discussed the options with his students and took a vote, and the students all agreed to follow his suggestion to go for a gear-up or belly landing. They had been in the air for about three hours by that time, but they still needed to burn off another hour or so of fuel to reduce the danger of fire, in case any of the gas tanks ruptured during the landing, so they continued to circle around the airport for a while. To reduce the tendency of the heavy plane to dig into the ground on a belly landing, they decided to land on the paved runway rather than on the grass beside it, even though they knew that any sparks thrown up by the metal grinding against the pavement would increase the fire danger. They considered it better to risk fire with near-empty gas tanks, and go sliding down the runway intact, than take the chance of a violent break-up of the whole aircraft should it dig into the ground off the pavement.

After about four hours in the air, with the fuel supply dwindling, it was time to make the landing. With the instructor pilot in control, the gear was double-checked in the up-and-locked position, the flaps were lowered to reduce landing speed to the minimum, and the landing checklist was completed. After everyone in the plane was securely strapped into a seat, the pilot set up a slow, low-angle approach to the runway, and as the plane settled the last few feet to the ground, the instructor pilot slowly raised the nose. There was only a small lurch as the belly contacted the pavement, and then they were sliding along the ground at around 100 mph, with the pilot doing his best to keep the plane headed straight down the runway as the speed bled off. Without the wheels, he had no brakes, but he still had a fair amount of rudder control down to about 40 or 50 mph, and with that he managed to keep the plane on track and pointed down the centerline of the runway.

Under the plane's belly, the main center spar of the fuselage was being ground away against the pavement in a shower of sparks and a deafening roar, but the friction slowed their speed rapidly. When they had slowed to about 40 miles per hour, the right wing started to drop, and the plane drifted to the right side of the runway. Then the number four propeller (the one farthest outboard on the right wing) touched the ground, bent back, and also dragged on the runway, causing the plane to slew around to the right about 45 degrees as it came to a (literal) grinding halt.

After the plane finally came to a stop, a relieved silence fell in the cockpit, broken only by the whining of the gyro instruments on the instrument panel as they wound down. It had been a good landing under the circumstances—the aircraft was intact and no one was hurt. It had also been an interesting, if unplanned, demonstration of how to land a B-24 wheels-up. And of course, as the old saying goes, any landing that you can walk away from is a good one, and the men in the plane proceeded to do just that.

The instructor and his students climbed out the hatch in the cockpit roof above the flight deck, slid down the fuselage side onto the slanting right wing, and walked down the wing until they were near enough to the ground to hop off. The big plane was an interesting sight, sitting tilted at an odd angle and resting on one wingtip. Crash trucks quickly arrived on the scene and sprayed the hot belly of the plane with foam to cool it down, and a truck came out to pick up the men. As they were being driven away, they could see a long streak of aluminum residue on the pavement, stretching far back down the runway. As it turned out, the only damage to the bomber was the center (belly) beam of the fuselage and the one bent propeller. Later the plane was jacked up, towed in, repaired, and returned to service.

Aside from the wheels-up landing in the B-24, the only other notable experience at Tarrant AAB was a couple of mornings in January when they had to spray antifreeze on the wings of the planes to remove frost before they could fly. This was a common procedure in northern climes, but it was the only time the students experienced ice on their parked airplanes in Texas.

With Transition Training completed, in February of 1944 Lt. Horner received orders from the 4th Air Force Headquarters in Fresno, California to report to March Field at Riverside, California for Combat Phase training. In this part of his training a pilot was assigned a crew that would remain with him throughout his combat tour of duty. The orders included the names of four of the nine crewmen who would fly with him. He noted that someone named Lt. Allan G. Cooper would be his copilot, Lt. Sylvester Ostafin would be the bombardier, Sgt. Ernest Eady would be the crew's flight engineer, and Sgt. Doy E. Bruni would operate the radios. Along with himself, that would make five of the ten men of the crew. The other five, a navigator and four gunners, their identities as yet unknown, would soon join them.

Navigator school for Tom Theobald

As Tom Theobald had been warned, the Air Corps school for navigators was not an easy course. In a B-24, the lives of nine other crewmen would depend on the skills of their navigator, whose job was to plot a course to whatever target they had been assigned to bomb, and then get them back to base again, sometimes (as in the Pacific) across hundreds of miles of featureless ocean, including at night when no landmarks were visible. The grueling course of instruction was designed to insure that a navigator would be up to that extremely difficult task. Navigator School lasted 18 weeks, and consisted of 500 hours of ground instruction covering a great variety of subjects, along with practical navigation exercises in multi-engine trainer planes.

Aerial navigation included elements of trigonometry and plane geometry, as well as spherical trigonometry for celestial navigation (it was no wonder, then, in the era before electronic computers, when all this had to be done by hand, that good math skills were required). The student had to familiarize himself with aeronautical charts and compass bearings, and had to learn how to compute aircraft headings that would be accurate after taking into account adverse weather, wind drift, and variable airspeed and groundspeeds. A manual, circular calculator with rotating scales (the E6-B Flight Computer, familiar to every private pilot even today) had been devised for this purpose, and a navigator had to become expert in its use. To keep from getting lost when all else failed, a navigator learned the use of a sextant to locate his position and navigate by the sun and stars, just as if his aircraft were an old-time ship at sea.

Aerial navigation was difficult enough over the thousands of miles that a heavy bomber was capable of flying when all went well, but the exigencies of combat flying added a whole new dimension of complexity, and required the ability to cope with possibly desperate scenarios. For example, if a bomber got off course because of evasive maneuvering, owing to attacks by enemy fighter planes or antiaircraft fire, or if it became crippled by battle damage, or took refuge for an extended period of time in clouds, flying blind, or if it became low on fuel and had to get to the nearest airbase quickly, to mention just a few possibilities, the navigator had to be able to quickly figure out where they were and how best to proceed from that location to either their home base or to the nearest suitable place to land. This could be especially difficult at night, in the sparsely inhabited Pacific theater, where there were few (or no) lights on the ground to use for orientation, not to mention deliberate blackouts of towns and airfields because of air raids.

As it turned out, Tom Theobald's math skills and his native ability to handle complex problems proved equal to the challenges of navigator school, and after four weeks of classes on the ground, during which many other men dropped out of the course, he began the flying phase of the training. Students were flown in advanced navigator trainers such as the Beechcraft AT-7 Navigator, built especially for this kind of training, or the AT-11A Kansan, also built by the Beechcraft company. They carried out navigation problems during both day and night flights. Part of the training involved learning Morse code, in case the navigator ever had to take over for the radioman, since long-distance communication between a plane and its base was often conducted by Morse code instead of voice.

In the midst of all this training Tom learned that his wife Shirley, who was pregnant, had developed serious medical complications. Tom was given emergency leave and rushed back to his wife's side in Oelwein, Iowa, and he stayed with her until the crisis passed, but by that time he had fallen so far behind his classmates that he would have to start over again with the next class.

While he waited for that class to begin, Tom was sent to gunnery school, where he learned to operate the .50-caliber machine-guns that a bomber carried to defend itself, in the event that it ever became necessary for him to take over for a gunner. When the next navigation class began, he joined it and completed the course with no problems. He then received a commission as a 2nd Lieutenant and orders assigning him to one of the B-24 bomber crews that was forming at March Field, California at the beginning of February, 1944. He learned that his crew's pilot would be a Lt. James Horner.

Gunnery school for Jaime Baca

Jaime Baca was sent first to armorer's school, where he learned how to maintain the guns, bombs, fuses, and other hardware associated with bombers, and then went on to gunnery school at Laredo, Texas.

America's war factories were producing many thousands of light, medium, and heavy bombers by 1944, and hundreds of thousands of gunners had to be trained to crew them. A gunner's main job was to defend his bomber from enemy fighter planes, and less often he strafed targets on the ground or sea.

A .50-caliber Browning M2 machine-gun mounted in the right waist window of a B-24. This was the position that Sgt. Baca would occupy in combat.

Training at the gunnery schools evolved throughout the war, with new training aids and methods being developed all the time.

In most gunnery schools, following the lead of Art Rogers with his renegade gunners in the newly formed 90th Bomb Group at Barksdale Field in 1942 (as described in Chapter 2), students started out with skeet shooting, firing at clay pigeons with 12-gauge shotguns. Baca remembers that the shotguns had a considerable kick, and after a shooting session, all the student gunners sported multicolored bruises from the recoil against their shoulders. "All of us took to stuffing towels and other pieces of cloth into our shirts to try to cushion that kickback," he recalls today.

The student gunners learned that where they should aim at an attacking fighter plane varied with the direction from which the fighter was coming, because their bomber was also in motion. For example, in the case of a fighter plane that was flying in the same direction the bomber was headed, they were told not to aim directly at the fighter, nor to lead it (as in skeet shooting), but to aim between the fighter and the tail of their own plane, because the forward speed of their bomber was being added to the speed of the bullets. The amount the gunner aimed behind the fighter was called the deflection. In other words, gunnery from a moving aircraft, directed at another moving aircraft, was a complicated business, compounded by the fact that fighter planes often zipped by so fast that gunners only got a few seconds to shoot at them.

After the students had scored satisfactorily on the clay pigeons, they were introduced to the machine-gun that they would be using in combat, the .50-caliber Browning M2, a gun that could fire a heavy slug (1.6 ounces) at a rate of over 500 rounds per minute.

At some schools there weren't enough .50-caliber guns to go around, so the training was done with .30-caliber guns, also made by Browning, and the students later moved up to the .50s. These two Browning guns were the standard machine-guns used in both training and combat, which simplified things somewhat. Students learned all there was to know about the mechanical aspects of the guns, how to quickly load the ammunition belts and clear jams, and they eventually became so familiar with the .50 caliber gun that they could take it apart and put it back together blindfolded—and in fact were required to do so.

The students also learned to operate the power turrets used on the bombers, the B-17s, B-24s, and B-25s. Some gunnery schools had turrets mounted in the beds of pickup trucks, so that they could be driven parallel to a shooting range and fired at moving targets, with both the gunner and the target in motion as they would be in combat.

After training on the ground, the students were taken up in open cockpit AT-6 "Texan" two-seat trainer planes to shoot at towed targets, using .30

caliber machine-guns on flexible mounts. The pilot flew the plane from the front cockpit while the gunnery student occupied the rear cockpit with his machine-gun on a swivel. Several planes, each with a student gunner, took part in each training session, coordinating by radio, and the students took turns shooting at the target. The target was a large cloth sleeve, a tube something like a big windsock, towed on a rope by another plane. The rope was long enough (it was hoped) that the towplane pilot and airplane would be safe from stray bullets, and in fact it was rare for a student to hit a towplane.

During these aerial exercises each student took a turn firing at the sleeve, and the problem of knowing which students hit the sleeve, and how often, was solved by using bullets that had been dipped in different colors of paint. Each student shot bullets of a different color. Those that passed through the sleeve left traces of the color on the cloth. After the exercise was over the sleeve was brought back to earth and examined for hits, and the color around each bullet hole was noted.

The gunners were also given a course in aircraft recognition, studying the silhouettes of both enemy and Allied aircraft from various angles. Gunners were required to identify a plane from a photo that was flashed on a screen for only a second or less. In combat, knowing friend from foe very quickly could be a matter of life or death.

Young Baca proved to have a natural aptitude for accuracy with guns, and out of a class of 400 students he was rated in the top five. These five top-scoring students were offered the choice of remaining with the school as instructors or going on to join bomber crews. As an incentive to remain, they were offered a promotion, a furlough, and a pass that they could use to get off base anytime they were not on duty, not to mention that as instructors they would have safe duty stateside for the duration of the war.

But Jaime Baca, like most young men, craved adventure, and he turned down all the enticements to stay, and chose instead to go on to combat duty. He was careful never to let his mother know that he had been offered a safe job in the States but had turned it down, since, like any mother, she would have chastised him severely for choosing danger over safety. Like all the other parents of the men who went off to combat, Mrs. Baca was anxious for her son's safety during every moment of every day that her son was in the war. As a member of a devout Catholic family, she spent a good deal of time in church praying for his safe return.

Baca's trip to crew training is a train wreck

At the conclusion of his gunnery training, Jaime Baca was promoted to Staff Sergeant (S/Sgt.) and was authorized ten days of leave, followed by orders to report to March Field, California for assignment to a B-24 bomber crew. At Laredo, Texas, he bought a ticket on a passenger train headed for California, which would stop in Albuquerque where he would get off and spend several days with his family. He boarded the train on January 13, 1944 in Laredo. It was a cold, snowy day. The twelve-car Santa Fe passenger train included some very dilapidated old coaches. "With all the troops that had to be moved around during the war, the railroads had dug up every old obsolete passenger car they could find," Baca remembers today. "I was riding in this rickety old wooden car that probably should have been in a railroad museum, sitting near the front, and there were other people in the seats behind me, including women with children."

Baca remembers a little girl running up and down the center aisle of the car, laughing and playing. As the train made its way across Texas, it ran into a blinding snowstorm that slowed it down considerably, so that by the time it stopped at the little town of Novice, Texas to let off a single passenger, it was four hours behind schedule. For some reason, other westbound trains coming up behind it were not aware that this train was making such slow progress, and their engineers assumed that the track ahead of them was clear, creating a very dangerous situation. Before Baca's train could get started up again, the worst happened.

A four-car "extra" troop train bound for Camp Barkeley, Texas, southwest of Abilene, came barreling up behind the stopped civilian passenger train, and its engineer, with his visibility reduced to almost nothing by the snowstorm, failed to see the stopped train ahead of him and rammed the back of it at high speed. Several of the coaches in the stopped train were demolished, including the one in which Baca was riding. Seven of the passengers sitting right behind Sgt. Baca, including a mother with her infant, and the little girl that Baca had seen playing in the aisle, were killed. Eighty-three other passengers were injured. The train's metal coaches remained mostly intact after the crash, but the old wooden car that Baca was riding in shattered on impact, and Baca found himself trapped underneath it along with a lot of other people, both living and dead, in a great heap of tangled, splintered wreckage. "My arms and legs were sticking out in all directions," he remembers. "I was pinned, and I couldn't move a thing. I was really stuck. There were other people trapped all around me, and I knew that some of them were dead."

News of the wreck spread quickly, and ambulances from surrounding towns soon converged on the scene. Rescue crews went to work frantically in the bitter cold, trying to extricate people from the wreckage and get them to area hospitals before they died of their injuries or froze to death. Baca had to wait for over an hour, pinned in his painfully contorted position in the wreck.

"While I was under there [he remembers today], a steam pipe that was right near my face burst, and I was choking on the steam. I thought for a minute I was going to die. I pulled desperately hard on my left arm and managed to pull it partly free, scraping off my new wrist watch, a Christmas gift from my family, along with a lot of skin. But it gained me a little wiggle room and I was able to pull my face back far enough from the steam pipe to be able to breathe."

He remembers that just before rescuers reached him, they freed another man nearby who was severely cut up but still breathing. Then he felt rubble being pulled away from around himself, too, and soon hands were gently lifting him into an ambulance. In the ambulance, he remembers a voice close by saying, "The little girl is dead."

Baca was taken with two other injured servicemen to the nearby Coleman Army Flying School to be cared for by the army doctor there. However, he remembers, the doctor only gave him some painkiller pills and put him to bed, and then paid little attention to him. The doctor may have simply been too busy with other patients to attend to him, since there were hundreds of flight students at the school. After lying in bed for eight days, with no one paying much attention to him, Baca discovered that he was able to get up on his feet, painfully, and walk again. He asked to be allowed to resume his journey to California, and was sent on his way with no records of his injuries or treatment for later medical follow-up. Thus, Sgt. Baca's Army records make no mention of the incident.

One of the worst aspects of the whole episode, as far as he was concerned, was that he had used up most of his leave time in the hospital, eight of the ten days that he had planned to spend in Albuquerque saying goodbye to family and friends before his final phase of training and trip overseas. As it was, he only got a couple of nights at home before he had to proceed to California.

When he arrived at March Field, Baca found that he was the final addition to a ten-man B-24 bomber crew whose pilot was a Lt. James Horner. His sore back healed up well enough over the following months to enable him to carry out his duties, but he has never been completely free of back pain since. Today, in his 90s, this pain forces him to walk bent over with a cane. He considers it pretty ironic that although he ended up flying 48 dangerous combat missions in bombers, the worst injury he incurred during the war was not in combat but during a ride in a civilian railroad car.

Pilot training for Allan Cooper

Allan Cooper, after he qualified for flight training, was assigned to Class 44-A, which would graduate in January of 1944. Like James Horner, and all other Air Corps flight students, Cooper progressed through the usual Primary, Basic, and Advanced flight school phases, each phase being around nine weeks long. Since Allan Cooper is now deceased, we can only try to reconstruct his experiences from his military orders, his flight logbook, the cartoons he drew during his training, and a few things that his son Michael remembers his father telling him.

For his Primary training Cooper attended one of the civilian-run aviation schools supervised by military officers, just as James Horner and nearly all other aviation cadets did. Cooper's Primary training was provided by the Morton Flying Academy in Arizona, which used the same Ryan PT-22 low-wing trainers that most Primary schools were using. In an odd coincidence, Ted Morton was the same man who had run the civilian flight school at Los Angeles where Cooper had taken private flying lessons before the war. When the war began, Morton had contracted with the government to give military pilots their Primary training, and he set up his school on a flat, cleared piece of ground in the hot, barren desert near Blythe, Arizona. The airfield itself, which was just a large rectangular tract of desert, with adjacent barracks and classrooms, was known as Gary Field.* As in most such flight schools, the Commandant was an Air Corps officer, while most of the instructors were civilians, with Army check pilots testing the cadets at the end of their training to confirm that they were qualified.

Cooper began Primary flight training on June 28, 1943 and finished exactly two months later on August 28, having accumulated 66 hours and 20 minutes of total flying time. Each Primary class at the Morton Flying Academy published a classbook at the end of the training, something like a high school graduation yearbook that the cadets could take with them when they left the school, and the editorial staff were student volunteers. The classbook at the Morton Academy was called The Gosport.† Allan Cooper volunteered to be the staff cartoonist for Class 44-A's classbook, and he invented a cartoon character, an imaginary aviation cadet named Justun Conshus (just unconscious), who became involved in all sorts of comical situations during his training, as seen in the example on the opposite page. Cooper drew numerous Justun Conshus cartoons that were sprinkled throughout the classbook.

Cooper also drew a cartoon that he called the Class 44-A Hall of Fame (page 448), which illustrated some of the more memorable mishaps that befell some of his fellow flight students in this class. Cooper's extraordinary drawing ability is showcased in all these cartoons, and his masterful artwork gave the amateur-produced classbook a professional quality that probably surpassed any other classbook produced during the war.

Cooper moved on to Basic flight training on September 5, 1943 at Gardner Field, California, where, as Cadet Horner had done in his Basic class, he flew

---

* The field was named after Gary Falkin, the young son of the flight school's general manager Fred Falkin.

† A gosport was a flexible speaking tube used in trainer planes for communication between the instructor and his student, since they sat in different cockpits and had no other intercom.

39. INTO UNIFORM

Only on the flight line two days, A C Justun Conshus already has gotten a little behind in his work. Murgatroyd sweats it out in a fox hole, while Philbert is speechless.

Cooper invented Air Cadet Justun Conshus for his Primary class graduation book. This is one of several cartoons he drew for the book featuring this hapless character and his small animal friends.

BT-13s. He had no trouble with Basic flight training and graduated from this phase on 28 October with 136.5 total flight hours logged. It was then time to be classified as either a single or multi-engine pilot before moving on to the Advanced Training phase. According to his son Michael, Allan had no desire to become a fighter plane pilot, considering such small, extremely powerful aircraft to be too unstable and dangerous, and he requested assignment to bombers. He was approved for multi-engine training, and began Advanced flight training in twin-engine AT-17s at Douglas Army Airfield, a few miles north of Douglas, Arizona, in November of 1943. His flight logbook records that he had his first flight in one of these planes on November 11 and completed the training on January 2, 1944, with his total flying time now up to 210.5 hours.

After graduating from Advanced Flight Training, Allan Cooper was commissioned a 2nd Lieutenant in the Army Air Corps on January 7, 1944, and received the customary leave time that all new officers were given.

Allan Cooper illustrated some memorable moments in the Primary Flight Training of his Class 44-A in June through August of 1943.

    Lt. Cooper's next phase of training would normally have been Transition School, where he would have learned to pilot either a two- or four-engine bomber, as Lt. Horner had done. However, probably owing to the needs of the Air Corps at the time, Cooper was assigned to become a copilot rather than

Air Cadet Allan Cooper (circled) with his classmates in Advanced Training in twin-engine aircraft at Douglas, Arizona. The aircraft behind them is a Beechcraft AT-10 trainer.

a first pilot, and without further training he was attached to a newly forming B-24 bomber crew. He had never flown in a B-24 before, and thus did not know the duties of a B-24's copilot, but he would learn the necessary skills on-the-job, at the same time that the newly-formed crew was learning to work as a team.

Cooper received orders to report to Hammer Field, California, and upon arriving there he found that his pilot was another newly-minted Second Lieutenant named James Horner. At Hammer Field he and Horner, plus their bombardier Lt. Sylvester Ostafin, Flight Engineer Sgt. Ernest Eady, and radioman Sgt. Doy Bruni received orders to proceed together to March Field, ten miles southeast of Riverside, California, where they would meet the five other men who would be part of their crew. Then they would all begin their crew training together in B-24s.

Japanese flight training compared to American

In most cases, American Air Corps pilots retained pleasant memories of their flight training, and as Lt. Cooper's cartoons show, mishaps were often accompanied by a good deal of humor. By contrast, the flight training of their foe in the Pacific was nothing less than barbaric. Japanese flight students were brutally beaten at every turn, savagely and sadistically. Saburo Sakai, one of Japan's best fighter pilots, looked back after the war at his treatment as a Japanese navy recruit:

> It is still difficult, if not altogether impossible, for Americans and other Westerners to appreciate the harshness of the discipline under which we then lived... Whenever I committed a breach of discipline or an error in training, I was dragged physically from my cot by a petty officer. "Stand to the wall! Bend down, Recruit Sakai!" he would roar... And with that he would swing a large stick of wood and with every ounce of strength he possessed would slam it against my upturned bottom. The pain was terrible, the force of the blows unremitting. There was no choice but to grit my teeth and struggle desperately not to cry out. At times I counted up to forty crashing impacts into my buttocks. Often I fainted from the pain. A lapse into unconsciousness constituted no escape, however. The petty officer simply hurled a bucket of cold water over my prostrate form and bellowed for me to resume position, whereupon he continued his "discipline" until satisfied that I would mend the error of my ways...
>
> [W]henever one of us received a beating, each of the other fifty recruits in the outfit was made to bend down to receive one vicious blow... Let one single man moan in pain ... and to a man every recruit in the outfit would be kicked or dragged from his cot to receive the full course... Within six months the incredibly severe training had made human cattle of every one of us... We were automatons who obeyed without thinking."[3]

Sakai went on to an advanced training school, where he hoped the discipline would not be so severe. But in fact, it was even worse:

> Hardly had I arrived at the new school than I discovered that my prior experiences with naval discipline were minor ones... [T]he disciplinary customs [of basic flight training] were pleasant interludes in comparison...[4]

Japanese flight trainees—in fact all military trainees in either the Japanese army or navy—were routinely, viciously, beaten bloody, and their wounds usually left untreated. They limped about with bruises on their legs and backsides that prevented them from sitting down without great pain, or from lying on their backs in their cots, and often went through their training days with faces swollen and bleeding from blows to the head and face.

Sakai was right; no American, in fact no member of a civilized society, could have imagined such treatment of its military men by their own officers. This behavior placed the evil of Japanese military society on full display.

Western Civilization's emphasis on the importance, dignity, and freedom of the individual was incomprehensible to men from a historically feudal society, in which the vast majority of the population were peasants without rights, who farmed the land of their royal lords and masters and fought their wars for them unquestioningly.

The ordinary Japanese man at the time of World War II, under the militarism that the country had adopted, was seen by his superiors, by his society, and indeed by himself as nothing more than a useful drone to serve the purposes of his masters, the ultimate master being of course the allegedly divine Emperor in his palace in Tokyo. Unlike the Christian divinity, to whom is ascribed love and compassion, the Emperor had no consideration for the welfare or well-being of any individual who served him in his army and navy, beyond training, equipping, and keeping him alive so that he could perform his assigned function. The common Japanese serviceman, like the vassal or serf that he had historically been, had no rights beyond serving his masters, and indeed, when a Japanese soldier or sailor's usefulness was gone, he was abandoned without a thought. In a case where any able-bodied men could be evacuated from a hopeless battle to fight another day, the sick and wounded were abandoned as useless, and often encouraged to commit suicide.

But turning men into obedient automatons had its drawbacks. Beating independent thinking out of the men rendered them rigidly incapable of independent action, or of taking advantage of unexpected windfalls in battle. Like robots, they unquestionably did exactly what they were told to do and nothing else.

In a notable example of this mentality, during the Pearl Harbor attack, the Japanese planners foolishly overlooked the huge naval storage tanks filled with millions of gallons of fuel located right beside the harbor, holding all the fuel reserves of the American Pacific fleet. Many of the Japanese planes flew right over these big tanks, and although the pilots recognized them for what they were, they carried on with their orders to bomb and shoot up lesser targets, such as parked aircraft or the hangars on the American airfields.

One 92-year-old Japanese veteran pilot of the Pearl Harbor attack told an interviewer that as he flew over the giant fuel storage tanks he wondered why no one had been assigned to destroy them, since it would have been easy to do, but it obviously never entered his mind to use his own initiative to hit such a lucrative and vulnerable target. Instead, he blamed the planners of the attack for not assigning the target to any of the planes on the raid. The idea of a pilot hitting a target that he hadn't been assigned was unthinkable to him. This was discipline inflexible to the point of madness. Any American pilot, seeing such a high-value target, would have deviated from his original attack plan long enough to send some tracer bullets into the big tanks and blow them sky-high, recognizing them as a far more important target than an airplane hangar, a barracks building, or a row of parked airplanes.

Raymond Kerns, in his memoir *Above the Thunder*,* wrote of standing out in one of the quadrangles of Schofield Barracks with a Browning Automatic Rifle during the Pearl Harbor attack, trading shots with the backseat gunners of some of the Japanese planes. Shooting up a barracks building and wounding a few soldiers was evidently considered more important by the Japanese attack planners than blowing up the huge fuel tank complex nearby.† Later in the day Kerns' battalion moved out into the Hawaiian countryside to prepare for a possible Japanese invasion of the island and drove past the big storage tanks. He wrote later:

> Leaving the shoreline of Pearl Harbor, we passed a large number of huge storage tanks that I had been told held most, if not all, of the fuel reserve for the Pacific Fleet, and even I, in my massive ignorance of such things, wondered why the Japanese had not bombed them. Maybe they would be hit in further strikes later in the day. In fact, though, they were not, although it would have required small effort and would have been a truly devastating blow to the crippled fleet. Adm. Husband E. Kimmel later observed that destruction of the fuel reserve would have forced withdrawal of the fleet to the American West Coast. But it appears that high-level Japanese planners of the strike had failed to include the tank farm on the target list.[5]

So much for the "brilliant planning" of Admiral Yamamoto. His success at Pearl Harbor was primarily the result of having the extreme good luck to catch the Americans asleep at the switch that morning. American radar operators had seen the Japanese planes coming in, and reported them, but had been told that they were some B-17s they were expecting, and not to worry about them.

The rigid, robotic, unthinkingly obedient mentality that was beaten into Japanese aviators explains why entire squadrons of them enthusiastically embraced suicide bombing—kamikaze attacks—toward the end of the war, when it became obvious that Japan was defeated yet refused to surrender. As the world has seen many times, mass suicide is a common response of psychotic personality cults when their leader is threatened.

Defeating the malevolent Japanese Emperor-cult, which had set out with the goal of enslaving half the world, and which had attacked America without warning in the pursuit of that goal, would require four years and cost America the lives of many thousands of its finest young men.

---

*Raymond F. Kerns, *Above the Thunder*, Kent State University Press, 2009.

† Kerns wrote that the Japanese planes over Pearl Harbor "swirled and dived and zoomed like night bugs around a light."

Chapter Forty

CREW TRAINING AT MARCH FIELD, CALIFORNIA

Aerial view of March Army Airfield, California, in 1941.

In the first five days of February, 1944, the ten men who would comprise what their Air Corps orders termed "Crew 2-F" arrived at March Field,* California and were introduced to one another. For the next fourteen months, until May of 1945, they would be constantly in each others' company as a bomber crew. It's safe to say, considering what lay in store for them, that this would

---
* The field had been named in 1917 for 2nd Lt. Peyton March, Jr., the son of the Army Chief of Staff at the time, who had died in the crash of a Curtiss Jenny biplane only two weeks after he had been commissioned.

be the most exciting, and dangerous, period of their lives.

The young men of this crew, like most other bomber crews, were a cross section of America's young manhood, with their homes spread from San Francisco on the west coast to Charleston, West Virginia in the east, and seven states in between.

Once the crew was all present at March Field, the roster read:

The four officers of the ten-man Horner crew, clockwise from upper left: Lt. Sylvester Ostafin, bombardier; Lt. James Horner, pilot; Lt. Allan Cooper, copilot (this is the only picture of Lt. Cooper with a mustache); Lt. Tom Theobald, navigator.

2nd Lt. James Horner—pilot, from Michigan
2nd Lt. Allan Cooper—copilot, from California
2nd Lt. Sylvester Ostafin—bombardier, from Michigan
2nd Lt. Tom Theobald—navigator, from Iowa
T/Sgt. Ernest Eady—flight engineer, from Texas
T/Sgt. Doy Bruni—radio operator, from West Virginia
S/Sgt. Jaime Baca—right waist gunner, from New Mexico
S/Sgt. J. W. Dale—left waist gunner, from Missouri
Sgt. Edmund Rogalski—nose gunner, from Illinois
Sgt. Kenneth Carter—tail gunner, from Kansas

These ten men would train together as a crew for nearly twelve weeks at March Field, and then remain together throughout their year-long combat tour

40. CREW TRAINING AT MARCH FIELD

The entire Horner crew after the men assembled at March Field in February of 1944, standing beside one of the B-24s used in crew training. Front row, left to right: Lt. James Horner, Lt. Allan Cooper, Lt. Sylvester Ostafin, Lt. Tom Theobald. Back row: Sgt. Ernest Eady, Sgt. J. W. Dale, Sgt. Doy Bruni, Sgt. Edmund Rogalski, Sgt. Jaime Baca, Sgt. Kenneth Carter.

in the Pacific war zone. Since it was customary to refer to a crew by the name of its pilot, who was its commander, this was known as the Horner crew.

B-24 bomber crewmembers and their duties

Each crewman aboard the bomber had his own specialized role that contributed to the ultimate purpose of flying a B-24: to drop bombs on the enemy. Each man's duties were as follows:

The pilot (Lt. James H. Horner)

The pilot of a B-24, or any other aircraft with a crew, was the commander of the aircraft and responsible for the efficient performance of his crew. Like the captain of a ship, his word was law, although in emergencies bomber pilots often polled their crews as to what course of action they preferred to take, such as whether they should bail out, crash-land, or attempt to fly a crippled aircraft back to base, but the final decision was always the pilot's. Crew morale was best when the men knew they had a good pilot, since in the air their lives were in his hands. According to Mr. Theobald and Mr. Baca today, James Horner was one of the best. "Lt. Horner's flying skills are what saved us many times," says Baca today. Lt. Horner was 22 years old in 1944.

The copilot (Lt. Allan G. Cooper)

The copilot of a bomber crew was the pilot's assistant and backup man. He shared flying duties with the pilot and was ready to take over and assume command of the plane should the pilot become incapacitated. He also had specific duties to assist the pilot in the operation of the aircraft. For example, the copilot operated the wing flaps (used to slow the plane for landing), raised and lowered the landing gear, monitored the engine pressures and temperatures, and other such duties.

The copilot on the Horner crew was Lt. Allan G. Cooper, who at age 26 was considered one of the older crewmembers.

The navigator (Lt. Tom Theobald)

The navigator was in charge of determining the bomber's course to and from bombing targets or anywhere else the airplane might go. To accomplish this he used his maps, his (manual) flight computers, any available radio fixes, and he was also trained in celestial navigation using a sextant (there was a special glass dome above the navigator's station in the nose of a B-24 that allowed him upward visibility to take star or sun shots). The navigator provided the pilot with compass headings to follow and gave him advice related to the weather and visual checkpoints en route. The Horner crew's navigator was Lt. Tom Theobald. He was 22 years old in 1944.

The bombardier (Lt. Sylvester A. Ostafin)

The bombardier could arguably be called the most important member of the crew, or at least he was indispensable, since the entire purpose of a bomber was

Lt. James H. Horner, pilot.

Lt. Allan G. Cooper, copilot.

to drop bombs on an enemy target, and he was the man tasked with the job of putting them there accurately. Yet he was only active during the actual bombing run over the target. B-24s used the Norden bombsight, and the bombardier had to be expert in its use. During the bomb run, the bombardier's bombsight allowed him to temporarily take control of the aircraft's flight path, through an electrical connection with the plane's autopilot, in order to make any necessary adjustments to it before he toggled the bomb release.

Lt. Tom Theobald, navigator.   Lt. Sylvester Ostafin, bombardier.

The flight engineer (Tech/Sgt. Ernest L. Eady)

The flight engineer was the crew's mechanic, an expert on all mechanical aspects of the B-24 bomber, and he was the highest-ranking enlisted man on the crew. His wings emblem bore a radial engine and four-bladed propeller superimposed over the wings. When necessary the flight engineer also manned the top gun turret, so he had to attend gunnery school as well as mechanic's school.

Before a flight, the engineer removed the protective cloth sleeves over the bomber's pitot tubes, located on short arms or struts projecting from the nose of the bomber (see photo on p. 535); these tubes provided ram air to the airspeed indicator, which looked something like the speedometer in a car, and he checked to make sure that the gas tanks were full and that the gas caps were on securely (wind could siphon all the gas out of a tank in a hurry if its cap came off in flight). In general, he readied the bomber for flight.

T/Sgt. Ernest L. Eady, flight engineer.

During flight the engineer monitored the fuel consumption, and if gas had to be transferred between tanks, he operated the valves that did this. On take-offs and landings the engineer stood between the pilot and copilot and called out the airspeed as he read it off the airspeed indicator on the instrument panel, leaving the pilots free to concentrate on flying the plane. He had many other duties such as making sure the plane's landing gear was down and locked during a landing (or, if the hydraulic system wasn't working, he hand-cranked the wheels down). The engineer was the bomber's fix-it man, always available should the pilot call on him to deal with any mechanical problems.

The radioman (Tech/Sgt. Doy E. Bruni)

The radioman on a B-24 was the man who kept the bomber in communication with the outside world, including other bombers in a formation. The radioman had only one radio, but he had several boxes with different radio frequencies that he could use with it, and he could also reel out a long antenna cable that trailed behind the bomber to the length required, anywhere from 100 to 300 feet, to reach any given station. The length of the antenna determined the radio frequency.

The radioman on the Horner crew was Sgt. Doy Bruni, age 20, a quiet young man of Italian descent. His crewmates remember him as a rather shy, conscientious person who got along with everyone and was competent at his job. Horner remembers that

T/Sgt. Doy E. Bruni, radioman.

during missions Bruni never had a lot to do at his radioman job unless their plane was the squadron or group leader. The radioman in the lead bomber's plane was required to send back reports after the bombs were dropped on a mission, estimating the percentages of hits and misses on the target. He would send his report not with his voice but in Morse code, with a telegraph key. When he wasn't needed at his radio, Sgt. Bruni would make his way back through the bomb bay to the rear of the plane and join the gunners there, where he operated the twin machine guns mounted on a ring on the floor of the plane, pointed downward through the hole in the plane's belly where the ball turret used to be (belly turrets were not used on B-24s in the Pacific).

The nose gunner (Tech/Sgt. Edmond Rogalski)

40. CREW TRAINING AT MARCH FIELD

B-24s, beginning with the J model, had a powered turret on the nose with twin .50-caliber machine guns, and the nose gunner's job was to operate that turret. Sgt. Edmund Rogalski, the Horner crew's nose gunner, was 29 years old, which made him the oldest member of the crew (an old codger to the youngsters), and like Lt. Cooper he was married.

The waist gunners (Staff/Sgts. J. W. Dale and Jaime A. Baca)

The B-24 had two windows in the waist section of the fuselage, behind the wings and the bomb bay, one on each side. In each of these windows was mounted a single, hand-operated .50-caliber machine gun on a swivel. The two gunners who operated these guns had a field of fire between the bomber's wing to the front and the bomber's tail to the rear, and they had to be careful not to shoot up their own airplane while firing at enemy fighter planes. The waist gunners worked back-to-back, or, in bombers with slightly staggered windows (such as the B-24H), side-by-side. The left waist gunner on the Horner crew was S/Sgt. J. W. Dale, age 20, and the right waist gunner was S/Sgt. Jaime Baca, also age 20 in 1944.

T/Sgt. Edmond Rogalski, nose gunner.

The tail gunner (Sgt. Kenneth I. Carter)

S/Sgt. J. W. Dale, left waist gunner.

S/Sgt. Jaime A. Baca, right waist gunner.

From the very beginning of its production the B-24 had a power turret on its tail, since the danger of attack from the rear by fighter planes had long been a concern, and was remembered from the time of the earliest bombers in World War One. The tail gunner of the Horner crew was Sgt. Kenneth Carter, at age 18 the youngest member of the crew, eleven years younger than Sgt. Rogalski, the nose gunner.

The Horner crew's Combat Crew Training at March Field

The Horner crew's first flight together took place on the afternoon of February 6, 1944, in a B-24J (the model with a nose turret), when they were given an orientation flight by an instructor pilot, a captain. Under his direction they flew around March Field for about 30 minutes, seeing what the airfield looked like from the air and gaining familiarity with the local landscape. The captain pointed out landmarks, made sure the pilots understood the airfield's traffic pattern, and provided other useful information about the airbase. He then directed Lt. Horner to land and let him out. Having fulfilled his duty, the captain went off to dinner, leaving the crew in the bomber to do whatever they pleased on their own. It was about 6 PM by then, and evening was coming on.

Sgt. Kenneth I. Carter, tail gunner.

After the instructor pilot had departed, Lt. Horner took off again and flew around the area for another three hours. This was the first flight in which the complete crew were all together and at their duty stations. Except for Lt. Horner, who had already spent many hours in a B-24 during his flight training, everything about the big bomber was new and unfamiliar to the young men, and it was all rather exciting to them. Lt. Cooper had to learn the duties of a co-pilot from scratch, since he had never had any previous training at that job.

In the middle of their third hour of flying in the vicinity of March Field, after nightfall, around 8:30 PM, one of the gunners called Lt. Horner over the intercom to tell him that there were some small flames coming out of the number two engine (the closest one to the fuselage on the left wing). Lt. Horner, sitting in the pilot's seat on the left side of the cockpit, just ahead of that engine, twisted around in his seat to take a look at it and saw what the gunner was talking about: one of the engine's cylinders was spurting fire. The flames stood out clearly in the dark, and they had already burned a hole through the engine's sheet metal cowling. Lt. Horner instructed Lt. Cooper to shut that engine down, and he feathered the propeller.* The landing on three engines was uneventful, and after Horner parked the bomber he reported the problem.

It soon became evident to the crew that there were plenty of problems with the training bombers at March Field. Many of the planes were old and worn. Some had been flown back from the war zones in various states of disrepair, but since they still flew, they were patched up and considered good enough for training. "Good enough" is a subjective term, however; airplanes with significant defects were dangerous to fly, especially by new and inexperienced flight crews. The members of the Horner crew considered some of the dilapidated old bombers at March field to be nothing short of serious health hazards.

"They had some old wrecks there, for sure," Mr. Baca remembers today. "A lot of those planes were in terrible shape, and we hated to go up in them, but we had to."

"Some of those old bombers were really war-weary," Tom Theobald agreed recently. "Not only that, but they used a lower-octane fuel than was used at the war fronts. All in all, it didn't add up to a very good feeling about the training."

Mr. Horner remembers that four bombers crashed and burned on and around March Field on a single day; he was able to see the smoke rising from all four. Two had collided on the tarmac (one ran off the runway and clipped the tail of the other) and the other two had crashed close enough to the field for the smoke to be visible from the airbase. Aside from their age and condition, maintenance on the training bombers was probably not up to par. During Lt. Horner's earlier pilot training in B-24s in Texas, the crew chiefs in charge of bomber maintenance had flown with their airplanes on training flights, and monitored their performance in flight. Since their own necks were on the line, they'd had a personal stake in how the planes flew, and problems were dealt with promptly.

The crew chiefs at March Field, however, stayed on the ground. After a bomber was started up and rolled out for a day's training, they often went off to town for lunch. Any problem that cropped up with the bomber in flight was the crew's problem. In hindsight, the March Field training bombers were a disgraceful way to introduce young men to flying the B-24 as crews. Many were so dangerous to fly that one veteran pilot, Capt. Manville Heisel, formerly of the Jolly Rogers' 319th Squadron, who had been rotated back from the war zone to the States to become an instructor on B-24s, requested that he be returned to combat duty because, he said, combat flying was less dangerous than training. Heisel returned to the Jolly Rogers and became a pilot in the 400th Squadron.[1] He survived the war.

So many crews died flying the March Field training bombers that under peacetime conditions it would have been considered a scandal requiring a

---

* Feathering means turning a stopped propeller's blades edge-on to the wind, to streamline them so they don't drag in the airstream.

congressional investigation. But in wartime, when lives become expendable, apparently the training deaths were accepted just like deaths in combat, as something unavoidable in war.

Tom Theobald remembers that on the day he arrived at March Field, he looked out the window of his quarters toward the airfield just in time to see a bomber crash. It was a sobering introduction to crew training. In the enlisted men's barracks, Jaime Baca and his six comrades noticed six bunks near their own suddenly become vacant after another bomber crashed and its entire crew was killed. "I remember the supply people coming in and picking up their clothes and their blankets," he says today, "and then there were six empty bunks. That shook us up." The empty bunks conveyed to the young men the silent message that this crew training was a deadly serious business, and from now on death would always be looking over their shoulders.

The Horner crew's worst, and nearly fatal, training flight

In fact, the bunks occupied by the Horner crew also nearly became vacant when one of their night practice flights went seriously wrong. It was the night of March 26-27, 1944, and the crew was returning from some night bombing practice at the nearby Muroc Dry Lakebed, a 44-square-mile saltpan where gunnery and bombing were practiced on a realistic 650-foot mock-up of a Japanese heavy cruiser dubbed the Muroc-Maru (photo, opposite). The dry lakebed was only about a 20-minute flight north of March Field.

It was after midnight by the time the night bombing exercise was over, and Lt. Horner was bringing the bomber back to the field for landing. The plane was handling somewhat sluggishly, and seemed to lack power, but it was no worse than some of the other training bombers he'd flown. When he contacted the tower to report that he was inbound to land, the air traffic controller replied that thick smog had blown into the area from Los Angeles, reducing visibility to near zero, and the field was closed to takeoffs or landings. He was directed to fly east to the civilian airport at Palm Springs, where there were sleeping facilities for military aircrews. They could land there and spend the night, returning the next day after the smog had dissipated.

Lt. Horner therefore called his navigator, Lt. Tom Theobald, over the intercom and asked him for a compass heading to Palm Springs. Theobald's first plan was to tune the plane's radio compass to the Palm Springs radio station and take a bearing on it. This navigation instrument was a radio receiver with a 6-inch dial on the front that had an arrow on it. A plane's navigator could set the receiver to the frequency of any particular airport's signal, and then follow the station's CW (constant wavelength) beam to its source. However, when Theobald grasped the tuning knob, the arrow on the beat-up old device just fell off—the radio compass was useless. Then Sgt. Bruni, the radio operator,

40. CREW TRAINING AT MARCH FIELD

The "Muroc-Maru" was built on the dry lakebed for bomber crews to practice on (note the B-25 making a bombing pass above it).

reported that his communication radio had gone out as well; it was picking up so much static that he could neither transmit nor receive.

Sgt. Baca, back in the rear of the plane with the other gunners, remembers listening to the exchanges between the pilot, navigator, and radioman over the intercom system and thinking that everything seemed to be going wrong with this flight. But at this point he, and the other gunners and the bombardier, were only passengers, unable to do anything but sit tight and hope for the best. Remembering all the training bombers that had crashed from unknown causes, there was good cause for nervousness among the crewmembers.

Lt. Theobald had a rough idea where they were, so looking at his charts he plotted a course to Palm Springs, and he advised Lt. Horner to climb to a higher altitude immediately, since there were mountains between themselves and their destination. During the climb they encountered a lot of air turbulence. Unbeknownst to them, they were flying into a sandstorm. The bomber crossed over the mountains, unseen below in the dark, and flew out over the valley in which Palm Springs is situated, and the pilots soon spotted the rotating beacon of the town's airport.

With their radio out of service they could not communicate with the control tower, and since they had never landed at this field before, the pilots got out their airport directory to determine the local landing protocol. They soon discovered that the overhead cabin lights in the cockpit were also out of order, yet another defect in the old bomber, so they were forced to examine their directory and its Palm Springs airport diagram in the weak beam of a flashlight, all the while bouncing around in the rough air of the sandstorm.

Under these conditions it was difficult to read the small print on the directory's pages, but at least they could tell that the airport had a single runway running approximately north-south.

Without a radio they were unable to get verbal clearance to land from the control tower, so to alert the tower to their presence and predicament, they circled above the airport while Lt. Horner flashed the white light on the underside of the bomber to attract the attention of the controllers. The belly light of a B-24 could be used to flash messages in Morse code, the pilot operating it with a key.

Horner transmitted "SOS" repeatedly until the people in the tower noticed it and gave him a green light to land, using a hand-held light gun in the tower.[*] When Lt. Horner got the green light, his bomber was in a good position to make a standard left-hand landing pattern[†] to land from south-to-north, with the approach being made from the west side of the airport. What the pilots did not know, however, was that they were making what could well have been a deadly error. They had missed an important detail in their airport directory, and that was that all airplanes landing at Palm Springs were (and still are) supposed to make their approaches from the east side of the airport, so as to stay clear of the mountains that rise up close to the airfield on its west side. However, it was on the west side that Lt. Horner was now flying his landing pattern, and as he descended, he was dropping right in amongst the ridges and canyons of a mountain that he could not see in the dark.

But luck was with Lt. Horner and his crew, and they somehow made a successful approach pattern on the mountainous side of the field and landed safely at Palm Springs. They must have had some very close, unseen brushes with the high rocky ridges that crowd the runway on that side, but in the darkness, concentrating only on the lights of the runway, they were blissfully unaware of it. Once on the ground, as they were exiting the parked bomber, the crew stepped out into a screaming, stinging wind and realized that they had been flying in a sandstorm. In fact there was so much sand in the air that Lt. Horner decided to put the protective canvas covers over the engines, the first time he had ever done so, and it was not an easy task for the crew to accomplish in the darkness and wind. By then it was around 3 o'clock in the morning, and no one had had any sleep for 18 hours, but they managed to get the engines covered before locating their quarters and retiring for the night.

It wasn't until they got up the next morning and examined their surroundings that the crew discovered, with a shock, what a close brush they'd had with

---

[*] All airport control towers had [and still have] light guns to visually signal planes that either have no radio or whose radio is not working.

[†] "Left-hand pattern" means making all left turns in the rectangular landing pattern. A left-hand pattern is the default landing pattern for any airport unless otherwise noted in the airport's directory information.

death the night before during their landing approach. Mr. Theobald remembers today, "I got up the next morning and looked out the window, and it seemed like the mountain went right straight up from the west boundary of the airfield. We were very close to the mountains."

It took only a glance at the looming, rocky heights on that side of the field for the crew to realize how close they had come to smashing into them in the dark. "We must have nearly rolled our wheels across those mountains during our landing approach," says Mr. Horner today. "Actually, I don't know how we survived." One explanation may be that a good pilot, such as Lt. Horner would repeatedly prove himself to be, usually makes a tight landing pattern, staying in close to the airfield during his maneuvering, and this is probably why they didn't hit the mountain. Flying a wider, looser pattern would have taken them deeper into the mountains and would surely have resulted in disaster. Simple luck may also have played a role. Other bombers flying blindly around high terrain at night were not always so fortunate, which is why the mountains of America are littered to this day with the remains of World War II training bombers.

But the crew's troubles on this day were far from over, and actually, the worst was yet to come. They still had to get back to March Field, and the weather remained a problem. The wind was still blowing at practically gale force, making a safe takeoff questionable, but at least it was no longer full of sand. The crew waited around a while for conditions to improve, but if anything the wind grew worse. Lt. Horner had never flown in such a wind. Nevertheless, they saw a couple of DC-3 airliners take off, and then a Navy twin-engine plane also departed. The crew talked it over among themselves and decided that if the Navy could fly under these conditions, so could they.

They removed the canvas covers from the bomber's engines, a task once again made difficult by the wind, climbed aboard their plane, and cranked up the engines. Sgt. Bruni discovered that his radio was working again, and they were able to make contact with the tower and get clearance to depart. The takeoff to the north, heading into the wind, turned out not to be as difficult as Lt. Horner had imagined, and as they lifted off the runway and raised the landing gear, he began a left turn to leave the traffic pattern. But as soon as the wing dipped, the plane began losing altitude, and he had to quickly level the wings again. The engines were at full takeoff power, and the landing gear was up, so the bomber should have been climbing, but it was soon evident that not only was it not climbing, it was barely maintaining its altitude.

Lts. Horner and Cooper pushed the throttles farther forward until the engines were beyond normal takeoff power, but the plane still did not rise. The pilots knew that trying to force the bomber to climb by raising its nose any further would only have caused it to "mush," possibly stalling the wings, and then it would fall or spin to the ground. The airplane was either going to rise at its own pace, or not at all.

The valley in which Palm Springs sits is ringed by mountains, although there are gaps or passes in them through which an airplane can fly as it climbs or descends. But proceeding north from the airport, the direction they were heading, the valley rises toward a mountain range, and with the combination of the ground rising and the plane not doing so, they were getting closer to the desert floor, as well as the mountains ahead, with each passing second. They were soon miles from the airport, out over open desert, with the engines straining and boulders the size of houses passing just beneath the bomber's belly. It was a terrifying situation, and everyone in the crew could see the predicament they were in. They all held their breath as the plane staggered across the boulder-strewn terrain, just barely flying and struggling to rise.

"I felt like I could just reach out the window and touch those boulders," remembers Mr. Baca, who was watching tensely at his waist gun window. Lt. Theobald, up in the bomber's nose, could see the seriousness of the situation through the plexiglass windows on either side of his navigator's station. His comment today: "The ground was rising faster than we were!"

"I was frankly just looking for a place to crash," says Mr. Horner today, "but I knew that if I hit one of those boulders we'd all be sawdust." A B-24 needed a clear space as long as several football fields to land, and there was no such space below them, only a rocky landscape that would have been fatal to set down on.

"Our crew consisted of five Protestants and five Catholics," says Mr. Horner, "and I was told later that the Catholics were all praying and the Protestants were all swearing. I can't say whether that's true or not, because I was too busy dodging boulders to pay attention to anything else. In fact I was sweating so much that my flight suit was drenched with perspiration—sweat was even running down into my shoes. A crash-landing into those rocks would certainly have pulverized the plane and killed us all. Had any of the engines faltered in the least, that absolutely would have been our fate."

With all the praying and swearing that was going on amidst the roaring of the four engines, and with Lt. Horner concentrating hard on holding the plane's attitude on the fine line between climbing and stalling, the bomber finally began, very slowly, to rise. After they'd gained some altitude, to the immense relief of everyone aboard, Lt. Horner eased the plane, ever so gently, into a shallow left turn. Eventually he was able to complete a wide circle, with the plane all the while continuing to rise slowly over the valley, until finally they had enough altitude to clear one of the mountain passes into the next valley west and make their way back to March Field. But it still required extra power just to maintain normal flight, and the pilots noted that the bomber was flying with its controls slightly crossed. There was obviously something seriously wrong with the geometry of the aircraft. Later it was determined that hundreds of hard landings by novice pilots, or perhaps the stresses imposed by a severe thunderstorm, had actually twisted the wings out of alignment with the fuselage, with the result that it would not fly straight and true.

After they got back to March Field and landed, Lt. Horner wrote up all the problems with the plane and "red-X-ed" it, which meant that it could not be flown again until all of its problems were corrected. This led to a fight with the base's engineering officer, who was furious that a pilot had grounded one of his airplanes. But Lt. Horner stood his ground, fully aware that the bomber was too dangerous to fly again in its present condition.

According to regulations, a pilot had the right to "red-X" or ground any plane, and he could not be overruled, since it could be a matter of life and death. When the plane was inspected, Lt. Horner was vindicated; the bomber proved to be not only unsafe but beyond economical repair, and a decision was made to scrap it. Lt. Horner also had the satisfaction of knowing that by grounding the plane he may have saved the lives of the next crew that tried to fly it. Mr. Baca, commenting on the incident today, says "We all knew we had a bomber that should never have been flying to begin with."

The crew also knew that they had been blessed with a pilot who knew how to handle a B-24 under adverse conditions. Any airplane is easy to fly when all is going well. It's during emergencies that a pilot's skill (or lack thereof) becomes evident.

Training complete: moving on to the war

In the nearly twelve weeks (82 days) that the Horner crew trained at March Field, Lt. Cooper's flight logbook shows that they made 32 training flights, averaging one flight every two-and-a-half days. On these flights they performed exercises designed to hone the skills of every member of the crew. The final flight of the crew's combat training at March Field was on April 26, 1944. When they were not in the air, the crewmen got intensive classroom training on all aspects of flying the B-24 under combat conditions.

It was with great relief and no regrets that in the first week of May, 1944, the Horner crew bid an un-fond farewell to March Field and its dangerous, worn-out training bombers. Their stateside training, both individual and crew, was now complete and they were considered ready for combat. Their next orders, dated 8 May 1944, took them to Hamilton Field near San Francisco, the jumping-off place to the Pacific war. At nearby Fairfield-Suisun Army Air Base they would be issued a new bomber that they would fly halfway around the world, there to meet and do combat with the forces of Imperial Japan.

Chapter Forty-One

THE FLIGHT TO THE PACIFIC

After the completion of their combat crew training at March Field, California, the members of the Horner crew received orders to proceed to Hamilton Field, California, and thence to the Fairfield-Suisun Army Air Base and Departure Center. Fairfield-Suisun* is about 40 miles from the San Francisco Bay area, which served as the gateway to the Pacific war. At Fairfield-Suisun they were to prepare for travel overseas to Australia, and from Australia they would proceed north to New Guinea and into the active war zone. Their orders named two other bomber crews at March Field that were to travel along with them, the crews of Lts. Dale Holland and John Kremer. Thus, three new B-24s, complete with their crews, would be coming into the Southwest Pacific, something to warm the heart of General George Kenney, who was still having trouble getting Washington to send him aircraft and aircrews. Most of America's manpower and industrial output, as we noted earlier, was being sent to Europe and Russia. Only after Hitler was defeated would the Joint Chiefs of Staff turn their full attention to defeating the Japanese.

The three crews packed up their personal effects and left March Field on a train, arriving at the Fairfield-Suisun airbase early in May. There they were assigned gleaming new B-24 bombers, fresh from the Consolidated factory in San Diego. The tail number of the Horner crew's bomber was 44432, which meant that it was the 432nd B-24 built in the San Diego plant in 1944. The young men of the Horner crew were jubilant about being issued a brand-new bomber, and assumed that it would be their airplane to fly throughout the war and then bring home, just as the crew of the B-17 named "Memphis Belle" had famously flown their plane back from England in June of 1943, after flying 25 missions over Europe, to participate in a highly-publicized 31-city war bond tour. Mr. Baca remembers Lt. Horner saying, "When we come back, I'm going to fly this thing right under the Golden Gate Bridge!"

"How young and foolish we were!" Says Baca today with a chuckle.

Lt. Theobald, exploring the cockpit of the new bomber, found a factory invoice under the pilot's seat listing the cost of the aircraft to the U.S. Government: $137,000, or in today's (2018) money, $1,942,550. It is a measure of wartime

---

* Fairfield-Suisun is now Travis Air Force Base.

41. THE FLIGHT TO THE PACIFIC

necessities that many thousands of heavy bombers would be built at a modern cost of nearly two million dollars each, yet were considered expendable and placed in the hands of very young and inexperienced aircrews. It is even sadder that the lives of the young men who flew America's warplanes had to be considered expendable as well, but such is the nature of war.

The crew took their new bomber up for a two-and-a-half hour check flight on May 10th, 1944, found that all the aircraft's systems were working fine, and then left the plane to be prepped for its long flight across the ocean to Hawaii, while they themselves were given a week off from flying to rest and get their affairs in order in preparation for going overseas. Their departure date was set for the 19th, nine days away. During this waiting period they attended classes on such subjects as emergency procedures for flights over water and other topics relevant to their upcoming flight to the Pacific war zone. When they were not in class, they were given passes to go into San Francisco.

There was not enough time before they left for the Pacific for anyone to travel home to say goodbye to his family, except for the crew's copilot, Allan Cooper, who was practically home already, since his wife, Shirley, lived in San Francisco. During the training at March Field, Cooper had dashed to San Francisco one weekend to marry her, after courting her for several months. She and her mother shared an apartment, and the mother was an agent for theatrical acts, lining up choruses and entertainments for nightclubs.

A farewell party

When her son-in-law's crew arrived at the nearby airfield, Shirley's mother decided to throw a going-away party for Lt. Cooper and his three fellow officers. The venue she chose was the famous Top of the Mark Lounge on the top (19th) floor of the historic Mark Hopkins Hotel in San Francisco. This lounge had a dance floor, a band, a bar, and floor-to-ceiling windows that provided spectacular panoramic views of the San Francisco skyline, the bay, and the Golden Gate Bridge.

Top of the Mark was a place where many such farewell parties were held during the war years. According to a 1944 article in *Time Magazine*, as many as 30,000 service members a month from all branches of the armed forces passed through the lounge, many of them after standing for hours in the downstairs lobby waiting their turn to take the elevator up, since seating was limited. Men heading overseas had a farewell drink with friends and loved ones while watching the sun set over the Golden Gate Bridge, and many friends vowed to meet there again if they survived the war. They often left cards bearing their names on the walls and ceiling of the lounge to let any of their friends who might show up later know they had passed through.

During the daylight hours so many wives, girlfriends, mothers, and other family members went to the Top of the Mark to try to catch a last glimpse of a departing troopship with a loved one aboard that the northwest corner of the lounge became known as the "Weeper's Corner." Fate was not kind to everyone during the war, and many lovers who said goodbye to each other on the dance floor, hugging and moving to the music, or sitting at a table holding hands for one last night together, said goodbye there forever. The Top of the Mark lounge is still in business today, and an aura of history and heartache still lingers about the place.

On the evening of the farewell party for the Horner crewmen, the drinking began early in the apartment shared by the two women before the group set out for the hotel, and Lt. Horner had his share. However, not being accustomed to imbibing generous amounts of alcoholic beverages, Horner took aboard a bit too much, too fast, so that by the time they arrived at the hotel he had lost all interest in partying, his primary concern having become his upset stomach. Thus, while his fellow officers, Ostafin, Cooper, and Theobald went up the elevator with the rest of the partygoers to the Top of the Mark, Horner staggered off to a nearby Greyhound bus station where he occupied a bathroom stall for the duration of the party. He never did see the famous lounge.

Mr. Theobald remembers today that there may have been a little too much drinking during the party as well. He recalls getting up on the stage with the band and "doing a little dancing" to the music. The fact that the men would be off to war in a few days, headed toward an uncertain future, probably also contributed to the loosening of their inhibitions. At the conclusion of the party Ostafin, Cooper, and Theobald located and gathered up their indisposed pilot and they all returned to their quarters at Fairfield-Suisun, where Lt. Horner slept off a monumental hangover.

Final preparations to leave

As part of the preparation for flying overseas the crewmen were issued sidearms (the Colt-designed M1911A1 .45 service pistol), since airmen could have need of them for protection and survival after bailouts, but they were not given any ammunition for them, yet. This was because there had been incidents of men taking their pistols into town, having too many drinks at bars, and shooting the places up. The ammunition was placed inside their bomber, where they would have no access to it until the planes were safely in the air.

On the 12th of May, 1944, orders were issued for Lt. John Kremer, Lt. Dale Holland, and Lt. James Horner and their crews to fly from Fairfield-Suisun Army Airfield to Garbutt Field in Townsville, Australia, over seven thousand miles away on the other side of the world. From Townsville they would fly north to Jackson Field at Port Moresby, New Guinea, near the war front, for assignment to a bomb group and squadron.

The long trip across the Pacific to Australia would be done in stages, using various islands as stepping stones, just as the 90th Bomb Group had done in

October of 1942. The first jump would be the longest one, from California to Hawaii, 2,400 miles, in a flight that could take up to 14 hours over nothing but empty ocean.

Mr. Horner remembers, "Up until this time no one in the crew had ever flown over any body of water larger than the lake at Fort Worth, Texas. So we didn't really know what to expect when we were told that we were going on a flight across 2,400 miles of the Pacific Ocean, from the United States to Hickam Field on the Hawaiian island of Oahu." No one in the crew besides Lt. Cooper had even seen the Pacific Ocean before, and some of the boys had never seen any ocean. There was quite a bit of apprehension among the crews, but the men were all young and most of them viewed the flight across the Pacific as a grand adventure. It was for experiences such as this, after all, that they had all volunteered for the Air Corps, and the reason why Jaime Baca had turned down a safe stateside job as a gunnery instructor.

Farewell to the States

The takeoff from California was timed so that the bombers would land in Hawaii in daylight, and the fact that they would be flying west, racing ahead of the sun, would help by adding a few extra hours of light. Thus, on the 19th of May, 1944, in the twilight before dawn, with all the hopes and fears of men going off to war, the crews took off in their brand new B-24s and headed southwest out to sea.

Hundreds of bombers had made the crossing to Hawaii since the first B-24s of the 90th Bomb Group, with Art Rogers in the lead, had done it on the 15th of September, 1942, a year and eight months before, so it was considered a fairly routine flight by this time and there was no requirement for the planes to remain together. Therefore the fact that they drifted apart within the first hour and lost sight of each other didn't especially worry anyone. The navy had also established some radio navigation aids on stationary ships en route to make it easier to stay on course, providing extra peace of mind.

A fully fueled B-24 carried about 1,800 gallons of gasoline and could fly about 2,700 miles even without using any fuel from the 400-gallon auxiliary tank that had been installed in each plane's bomb bay. Thus there were no worries about running out of gas, as long as they didn't get lost. If they did get lost, those 400 gallons would buy them about three hours of time to search for Hawaii.

For the Horner crew, not getting lost was the responsibility of the crew's navigator, Tom Theobald, and he was feeling the pressure. As they passed over San Francisco's Golden Gate Bridge, with a magnificent sunrise in view on the horizon behind them, Theobald remembers thinking to himself, "Well, this is your first big test!" It would be up to him to plot the course that would get his plane and crew to Hawaii. Lt. Horner chose 9,000 feet as their cruising altitude, an efficient altitude for B-24s to operate, low enough for the men not to need their oxygen masks, but a bit chilly for the crewmen, who had to bundle up against the cold.*

Three radio navigation ships had been anchored between San Francisco and Hawaii, spaced out about equally along the route, each one sending out an omnidirectional CW (constant wave) signal at certain (variable) times of day (if they were to broadcast continually, the reasoning went, Japanese submarines might also home in on them and sink them) and on constantly changing frequencies. It was rumored that the ships were filled with lumber in an attempt to make them unsinkable. The navigator of an aircraft making the crossing could tune his radio compass into these broadcasts, and by taking two bearings on the source over a measured period of time, and using triangulation, could plot the position of his plane on a map.

In addition to using his charts of the ocean and various navigation tools to compute their compass heading, Lt. Theobald decided to try out the celestial navigation method that he'd been taught in school. He got on the intercom and asked Lt. Horner to hold the plane as steady as he could for a while so that he could take a fix on the sun with his sextant. Lt. Horner remembers seeing Theobald's head and sextant appear in the plexiglass navigator's dome on the nose of the plane out in front of him, then disappearing as he dropped down to record his readings. For a half hour or so Theobald took sun shots and plotted their position from them, but he was unable to get any consistent fixes.

That turned out to be the first and last time that Theobald ever tried to use celestial navigation. He found through experience that the dead reckoning method worked just fine, and the big footlocker that he and every other navigator had been issued, filled with star charts and expensive sextants and clocks, was never used again. Mr. Horner suspects that all this expensive gear may have later ended up beneath the floorboards of one of their tents in New Guinea, and it may be there still.

The gunners and the bombardier had little to do on this flight but sit and mark time. Sgt. Bruni monitored his radios, and Sgt. Eady, the flight engineer, kept an eye on the mechanical aspects of the flight, including monitoring the fuel consumption.

Just before takeoff, Lt. Horner and the other pilots had been handed a pouch of secret papers to be opened only after they were in the air. When this portfolio was opened, they found that it held a folder containing the transfer orders for each man in the crew. These orders assigned each of them to 5th Air Force in the Southwest Pacific, and they were to report to Bomber Com-

---

*Since the air temperature drops about 3.5 degrees per 1,000 feet of altitude, if the temperature on the ground at San Francisco was 60 degrees F. (typical for May), at 9,000 feet it was below freezing at 28.5 degrees. However the temperature grew warmer as they flew south toward the equator.

41. THE FLIGHT TO THE PACIFIC

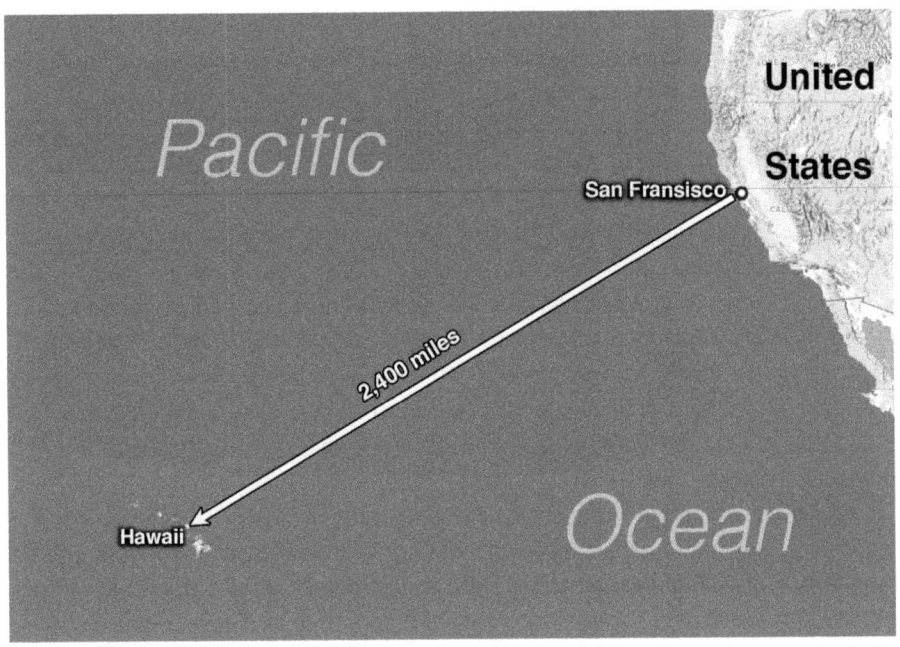

Map 41-1. During their flight from San Francisco to Hawaii, the young men of the Horner crew discovered that there is a lot of water in the world. J. W. Dale, the left waist gunner, nearly had a nervous breakdown before Hawaii came into view after 13 hours of seeing nothing but ocean all around him.

mand at Port Moresby, New Guinea. The pouch also contained a black binder whose pages provided such things as the locations of the navigation ships en route, the times of day that those ships would broadcast their signals, and what frequencies they would send on. The orders also provided the route and named the islands that the crew would land on as they made their way from Hawaii to Australia.

The hours passed, with nothing to interrupt the smooth, monotonous drone of the four big Pratt & Whitney engines out on the wings. Some of the men napped. The weather was fine, but the views out the windows monotonous. There was nothing to see but water, water everywhere, sparkling in the bright Pacific sunlight. The men in the bomber had never seen so much water in their lives. They might have learned in their high school geography classes that the Pacific Ocean is a 70-million-square-mile expanse of water that covers seventy percent of the earth's surface, but reading about it and seeing it for real were two different things. The ocean surrounded them clear out to the horizons in all directions, a fantastic sight. Sgt. Jaime Baca, the waist gunner from the desert state of New Mexico, was particularly amazed by the endless vistas of water he was viewing from the plane's waist windows, and he could imagine how easy it would be to get lost in such a liquid wasteland. However, like the other members of the crew, he trusted their navigator Tom Theobald to get them where they were going.

The other waist gunner, however, young redheaded J. W. Dale, was not so sure. The bomber seemed to be hanging motionless in an empty sky above an equally empty ocean, and all this isolation began getting on his nerves. They seemed to be all alone in the universe, and as time went by Dale grew more and more worried about being surrounded by nothing but water for as far as the eye could see in any direction. Dale, from Missouri, had had no idea that the world contained so much water, and now he found himself right in the middle of it. As hour after hour dragged by, with nothing visible anywhere but ocean and sky, he became increasingly rattled, until by the time a dozen hours had passed he was on the verge of panic. Baca could only keep telling him to calm down, take it easy, and everything was going be all right.

When finally, toward the end of the 13th hour of flight, Lt. Horner's voice came over the intercom letting everyone know that Hawaii had been sighted on the horizon, Baca remembers Dale going nearly wild with relief, jumping up and down and shouting for joy. "I guess he had decided that we were lost at sea, and we were all going to end up in the water," Baca says today. In the months to come, when bombing missions lasting as long as 15 hours over mostly ocean became routine events, Dale would become used to the sight of ocean all around him, but on this first flight over the Pacific it was all shockingly new.

After Horner's announcement, Baca, Dale, and the young tail turret gunner Kenny Carter leaned out of the bomber's waist windows and squinted ahead into the cold, roaring 150-mph wind to see a thin, reddish-colored strip of land up ahead, and soon the prominent landmark of Diamond Head rose up from the sea. Lt. Theobald's navigation had been dead-on—they were exactly on course.

Although it had been nearly two and a half years since the Japanese attack on Pearl Harbor, the military authorities in Hawaii were still jittery about incoming aircraft, to the point that no plane was allowed to simply fly directly in and land at one of the airfields on Oahu. An aircraft approaching the island was required to prove its identity before it would be given clearance to land, and it had to do this not only through radio communications but by performing certain maneuvers that were carefully watched on the Army's radar screens. These maneuvers were changed from time to time in case an enemy learned them.

The maneuvers in effect on the day the Horner crew approached Hawaii were specified in the classified papers in the pouch that Horner and Cooper had opened after taking off. It was made clear in the paperwork that if this

41. THE FLIGHT TO THE PACIFIC

process was not followed, an incoming aircraft would be considered hostile and would be fired upon. Lt. Horner would note later that Hawaii had the most elaborate approach procedure of any airbase in the Pacific, even though by 1944 it was far from the combat zone, and in fact the complexity of such approaches decreased the closer they got to the war zone, until right on the front line airfields, where there was a much greater chance of an enemy airplane approaching a field, there was no requirement at all for an Allied aircraft to maneuver for recognition by radar before landing.*

On their approach to Pearl Harbor that day, 19 May 1944, Lt. Horner was instructed to fly toward Diamond Head at a precise heading and altitude. When they were a certain distance out from that landmark, they had to circle to the right while dropping down 500 feet, then circle to the left, and so on. Mr. Horner's comment on all this maneuvering today: "You can believe I had a lot of back-seat drivers when we made this approach," since everyone knew what was at stake, and no one had any desire to be shot at. According to Lt. Cooper's pilot logbook, they touched down on Hickam Field after 14 hours and 5 minutes of flight from California, which works out to a respectable average of 171 mph for the 2,400-mile crossing. Since they had been flying west, ahead of the sun, they had gained about three hours on the clock, so it was still afternoon or early evening in Hawaii by the time they got the bomber parked. The other two bombers landed shortly after they did.

The men piled out and were shown to their quarters. After depositing their personal effects in their room, the Horner crew's four officers got freshened up and decided to visit the Pearl Harbor Officer's Club. However, when they arrived there in a taxicab, wearing their khaki uniforms, they were told that they were not properly dressed to be allowed inside. The club required that its patrons be dressed in whites, and since the men had no white uniforms, they were turned away and went back to their barracks at Hickam Field.

The crew spent that night, and the next day and night, in Hawaii, free of any duties, able to relax and enjoy having their feet back on the ground while their bomber was being serviced and readied to fly across thousands of more miles of water on its way to Australia. The men spent the 20th of May, 1944, sightseeing in their new, exotic tropical surroundings, the officers in one group and the enlisted men in another.

The officers decided to have a look at downtown Honolulu, so they caught a city bus and rode around for a few hours taking in the sights. At one stop the bus picked up five small people who seemed at first glance to be teenagers,

---

* The military had dealt severely with those who had failed to identify the Japanese airplanes approaching Oahu on Dec. 7, 1941, relieving many senior officers from their commands, and this may partially explain the elaborate procedures that were set up to identify every airplane that approached Hawaii during the rest of the war: a grim determination that it would never happen again.

but turned out to be adult native Hawaiians. One had a guitar, and as they rode along they sang familiar songs in an unfamiliar island accent. As the bus passed City Hall, the men could see rows of bullet holes that had been stitched up and down the walls of the building by the machine guns of strafing Japanese planes during the Pearl Harbor attack. Someone told them that those holes would not be repaired until Japan was defeated. They also passed the Royal Hawaiian Hotel on the beachfront, which had been leased by the Navy for the duration of the war as a rest and recreation center for sailors serving in the Pacific Fleet. They noticed that every balcony railing and every palm tree of this luxury hotel was draped with laundry hung out to dry. A stretch of Waikiki Beach in front of the hotel had been sectioned off with barbed wire and reserved for the use of the sailors alone.

The six enlisted men of the crew, meanwhile, were given a tour of the island on a military bus. One sight that caused some sober thinking was a great pile of wrecked airplanes at Hickam Field, left over from the Japanese attack two years and four months earlier. Baca thought that the wrecked planes should have been recycled by that time, but then decided that maybe the wreckage was being preserved (like the bullet holes in City Hall) as a symbol of why America was fighting the war. He remembers one of the other men speculating that this sight might be meant to prepare them for the realities of the war that they were about to enter. On a lighter note, they were later taken to visit a pineapple farm, and Baca still laughs today at the memory of a drinking fountain there that spouted pineapple juice instead of water.

Island-hopping to Australia

On the morning of the 21st of May, 1944, the Horner crew boarded their bomber again and set off on the next leg of their flight to Australia, along with the two other B-24s that were making the crossing with them, one of them being flown by Lt. Dale Holland and his crew. The Holland crew had gone through the March Field training along with the Horner crew, and many of the men had become friends. Now they were all going out to the Pacific together. Sgt. Baca of Horner's crew got along especially well with Sgt. John Barone of Holland's crew.[*] Both men were gunners, and Baca loved the way Barone, from Brooklyn, pronounced "girls" as "goils" and said that engines needed not oil but "erl." At the same time Sgt. Barone enjoyed Baca's slight Spanish accent, since Baca had spoken only Spanish until he had started grade school.[†] Members of the Horner and Holland crews laid bets on which of their planes would be the first to reach Australia.

---

[*] A picture of John Barone during the war is on p. 787.

[†] During the writing of this book, Jaime Baca and John Barone, both now 95 years old, became reacquainted with each other over the telephone (Barone now lives in New Jersey).

41. THE FLIGHT TO THE PACIFIC

From Hawaii, the next leg of their flight to the Pacific war zone was to the tiny speck of land known as Canton Island, actually a small coral atoll, only eight miles long and four miles wide, located 1,895 miles southwest of Hawaii. There the bombers would be refueled and the crews would spend the night. In 1942 the aircraft of the 90th Bomb Group had stopped at Christmas Island before going on to Canton (it was on Christmas Island, as you remember, that Col. Art Rogers had become stranded with an engine problem), but at this stage of the war Christmas Island was being bypassed as too much out of the way (see Map 41-2 on page 480) and the bombers flew straight to Canton. However, the great distance between Canton Island and Hawaii, and the tiny size of the island, presented the navigators with a formidable challenge. The Hawaiian Islands had been easy to find compared to Canton, and this time there would be no radio navigation ships positioned along the route to guide them—no radio aids of any kind, in fact. Once again there would be no formation flying, each bomber flying independently under the guidance of its own navigator, so again the Horner crew's safe arrival would be entirely dependent on the navigational skills of Lt. Tom Theobald. "Now, this was a *real* test of navigation," says Mr. Theobald today, and James Horner adds, "Finding Canton seemed harder than hunting for a needle in a haystack."

It is a tribute to the navigator training schools in the U. S. that the great majority of bombers en route to Australia and the Pacific War Theater during the war did find Canton Island, refuel there, and go on to their destinations in the war zone. Those few who did not find the island were usually never heard from again. The dire consequences of not finding Canton Island had been demonstrated earlier in the war when on October 21, 1942 a B-17 carrying one of America's most famous celebrities, Eddie Rickenbacker, a former race car driver and World War One flying ace, recipient of the Medal of Honor and a national hero, missed the island by 100 miles due to an error by the plane's navigator.

Rickenbacker had been on his way to the South Pacific war zone on a fact-finding mission for Secretary of War Henry L. Stimson. When the pilot of the B-17 realized they were lost, he searched for the island until the bomber ran out of gas, then ditched it in the sea. Back in the States, as soon as it became evident that Rickenbacker's plane had been lost, the news made headlines across the country. Rickenbacker and the others aboard the bomber spent 21 days adrift at sea on life rafts, during which time one man died, before they were spotted by a plane and rescued, again making national headlines.

But just as he had done from San Francisco to Hawaii, navigator Tom Theobald of the Horner crew steered his airplane directly to Canton Island, in a flight of a little over eleven hours, as recorded in Lt. Cooper's logbook. When the crew saw the miniscule size of the barren little atoll, a mere dot in the limitless emptiness of the Pacific Ocean, Mr. Baca remembers that they all felt renewed respect for their navigator. He remembers one amazed crewman saying, "How in the world did he ever find this tiny island way out here in the middle of nowhere? Have we got a good navigator, or what?" From this time onward, the nervous Sgt. Dale seems to have had no more worries about getting lost at sea.

There was not much to see on Canton Island besides a runway, a refueling station, a couple of hangars, and a barracks for overnight stay. Mr. Baca remembers that as soon as they landed and rolled to a stop, a ground crewman came running up to the airplane shouting, "Stay inside! Everyone stay inside! We have to make sure you haven't brought any mosquitoes with you!" The man hopped aboard the bomber with a bug bomb and sprayed the entire interior of the plane with it. He then told everyone that they had to wait at least 15 minutes before exiting, to give the poisonous vapors time to do their work on any insects that might be aboard (it probably didn't do any of the men's lungs any good either). After the quarter-hour quarantine was up, the crew was allowed to leave the plane.

Col. Rogers had noted during his stop here in the winter of 1942 that there was only one tree on Canton Island, and a guard was posted on it to protect it, since the crewmen on some of the bombers passing through had tried to take branches from it as souvenirs. Now, in the spring of 1944, the Horner crew found the situation unchanged.

"There was only one tree on the island," Baca remembers, "and they had placed a full time guard on it to make sure no one messed with it."

The island was home to a colony of gooney birds, who were also protected by the men who garrisoned Canton Island. One bomber pilot remembered:

> Lt. Fields also recalled one other peculiarity of Canton. [The] landing strip had numerous gooney birds on it . . . that could not fly; they ran and flapped their wings but could not become airborne. They [the men stationed on Canton] would have to shoo the gooney birds off the landing strip until the airplanes got in, and then they would let them back on again.[1]

In an interesting comparison of American and Japanese feelings toward local wildlife, Japanese fighter plane pilot Toshimitzu Imaizumi recalled the birds around his airfield on the island of Hainan:

> To break the monotony, the young men would head to a lonely part of the airfield near the water's edge to take potshots at seabirds with their service pistols. . . [It] helped pass the time.[2]

41. THE FLIGHT TO THE PACIFIC

The Americans protected their gooney birds while the Japanese shot at theirs, which may say something about the differences between the two cultures at the time.

The Horner crew got something to eat in the island's little mess hall and then took to the bunks in the barracks building to get a good night's sleep, while the resident ground crewmen of Canton Island refueled their plane and the other bombers that had landed there that day.

The third refueling stop on their itinerary would be Nandi Airport in the Fiji Islands, 1,235 miles to the southwest of Canton Island. Taking off on the morning of 11 May, the bombers covered the distance in about eight hours, making an average speed of around 160 mph. Here the crew spent another night, and that afternoon they decided to go into the town of Nandi about five miles from the airport and look the place over, having nothing better to do. However, they were told that servicemen were not allowed in the place. The people of that town didn't want any military men walking around in it, even though it was American military men who were preventing Japanese military men from walking around (and worse) in it. Gratitude was apparently not one of the virtues of the people of Nandi in the Fiji Islands.

Leaving unfriendly Fiji on the morning of the 24th of May, the sixth day out from California, the bombers reached the French-colonial island of New Caledonia, 860 miles away, after five and a half hours of flight. Since by this stage of the war the Allies had pushed the Japanese some distance to the north, after the original Japanese thrust into the South Pacific had been checked and turned back by the Americans in a prolonged battle on the nearby island of Guadalcanal (see Map 41-2 again, next page), none of these more southern Pacific islands was any longer under threat of invasion. Thus there wasn't much more on the airfield at New Caldeonia than there had been on Canton Island, just the refueling crews and a few mechanics to service airplanes passing through. The more active military presence had moved north with the war front. The bomber crews spent the night of the 24th on the island while their planes were being gassed up again.

Stuck in the mud

On the morning of the 25th of May, 1944, the bombers were ready to go once more, and they were taxiing from the parking area to the runway to take off when the Horner crew ran into its first and only real problem of the trip across to Australia—up to this point the island hopping had gone as smooth as silk. The blacktop taxiways of the New Caledonia airfield had been originally designed for fighter planes, not bombers, and they were narrow, only about twenty feet wide, or about the width of an ordinary city street. The main wheels of a B-24 were over fifteen feet apart, which meant that a bomber rolling along on these taxiways was a tight fit, leaving only two or three feet between the

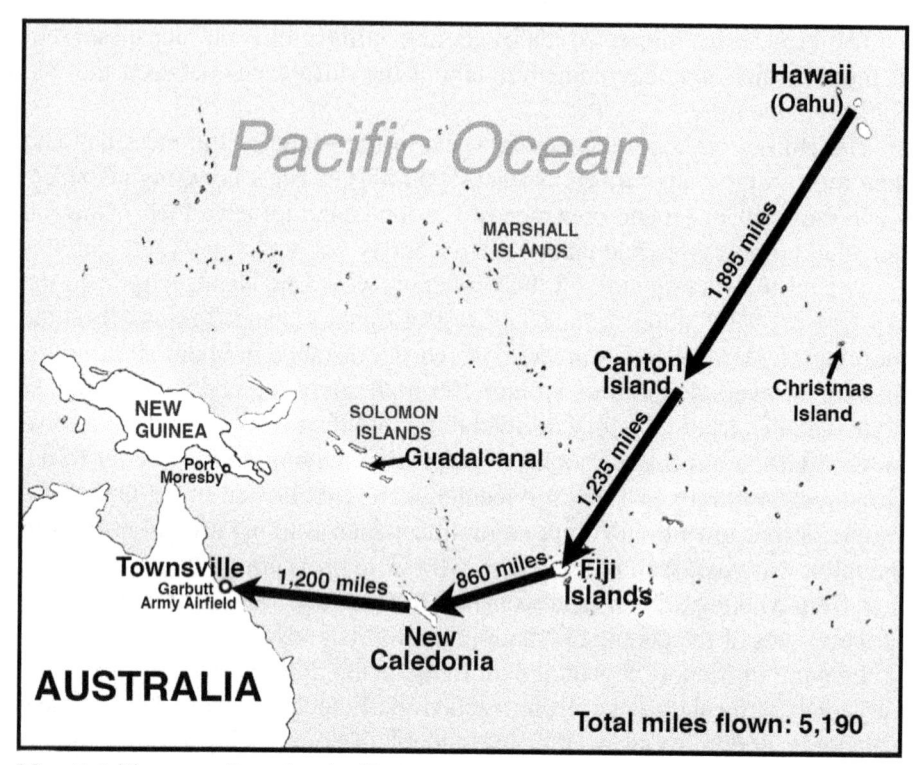

Map 41-2. The route flown by the Horner crew from Hawaii to Townsville, Australia, a distance of 5,190 miles. Adding the 2,400 miles from San Francisco to Hawaii, they had flown a total of 7,590 miles from the United States.

wheels and the edge of the pavement on each side. The shoulders of the taxiways were soft, gravel-covered soil, and beyond the gravel was swamp. To make things even more difficult for the pilots of wide-geared aircraft, these narrow roadways were not straight, but wound around through the trees.

Lt. Horner taxied his B-24 toward the runway on one of these twisting taxiways, steering with brakes and throttles, following the bomber of Lt. Holland. This is when he became aware of the rivalry between the two crews in the matter of getting to Australia first. He remembers: "I found out that Dale Holland's crew and my crew had been talking and razzing each other about who was going to get to Australia first. Then my crew got on me—'Don't let Holland's crew beat us to Australia!' Well, they were ahead of us in the takeoff order, and we were hurrying to catch up with them so that we could make a contest out of getting to Australia, and that's when we ran into trouble."

With the high-spirited young men of his crew urging him on to ever greater speed, Lt. Horner, in his haste, let his bomber's right main wheel get a little too close to the edge of the blacktop. The pavement crumbled away and the wheel went into the gravel and sank. A B-24 without bombs still weighed nineteen tons, and once the wheel went down through the gravel and into the mud beneath, the bomber was stuck fast. As the wheel sank, the right wing dipped down until it was nearly touching the water of the swamp. As the men piled out to examine their plane's predicament, Lt. Holland's bomber took off, and that was the end of the contest to see who would be the first to Australia.

Lt. Horner's was not the first bomber to get stuck in the mud on New Caledonia's taxiways; some of the first of the 90th Bomb Group's bombers to fly to Australia had had the same thing happen to them. It was simply one of the hazards of the place.

The crew's first move to free their bomber from the mud was to run back to the hangars and borrow a Cletrac—a small tractor with tracks instead of wheels that was used to tow aircraft around airfields—and attach it to the strut of the stuck wheel, but the little crawler couldn't budge it.

At that point the men heard a powerful roaring sound among the trees nearby, and upon investigation discovered a huge bulldozer, looking like a primeval dinosaur of the swamp, pushing down trees in preparation for widening the taxiways. The bulldozer operator, seeing a group of young men approaching him and waving their arms, paused in his work, throttled his engine down to an idle, wiped the sweat from his face with a handkerchief, and heard them out. Once he understood the problem, he obligingly drove his 'dozer over to the tilting bomber, where he took a heavy chain and attached one end of it to a clevis on the strut of the bomber's stuck wheel, and the other end to his bulldozer. Then he got back on his machine and pulled the wheel back up onto the taxiway with the greatest of ease. In the process, however, the tail of the plane dipped down and jammed the barrels of the twin machine guns sticking down through the belly of the plane into the ground, so that Lt. Horner worried that they may have been bent. However, later examination showed that they were still straight and undamaged.

With everyone back aboard, Lt. Horner taxied the bomber back to the hangar area and got out again to assess any possible damage the landing gear may have suffered. The right wheel and strut were so caked with mud that it was difficult to tell. They asked the mechanics on the field for their opinions, but found that they were not much interested. Mr. Baca remembers a mechanic taking a perfunctory look at the wheel and saying, "Oh, it's fine—go ahead and take off." Lt. Cooper, however, wasn't satisfied with this brush-off. "*You* don't have to fly these airplanes," he said to the mechanic, with some severity, "but *we* do. Clean it off and check it out." Thus officially ordered, the mechanics grudgingly went to work, and since the day was pretty far advanced by this time, and the prospect of arriving in Australia (the next stop) in darkness was not attractive, the crew went back to the barracks to spend another night.

Aerial view of Garbutt Army Airfield at Townsville, Australia, in 1944, where the Horner crew landed after their long flight across the Pacific.

Arrival in Australia

The next day, the 26th of May, 1944, assured that the cleaned-up landing gear was undamaged, the crew took off for Australia, about 1,200 miles away. This leg turned out to be an eight-hour flight, and the men passed the time by thinking up possible names for their bomber (one suggestion, based on the bomber's chubby profile, was the "Fertile Turtle"), and Mr. Baca remembers that he and the other gunners in the back rigged up a funnel and hose to use as a urinal, since no such convenience had been designed into their plane. They landed at Garbutt Army Airfield outside Townsville, a day late and the last of their group of bombers to arrive, and found that the crews of the other planes had gone off into town. There would be a layover of a few days while the mechanics at Garbutt Field, which was a repair and overhaul depot, made some modifications to the bombers, so the Horner crew, too, cleaned up and followed the other crews into town to see what diversions it had to offer.

As Mr. Horner remembers today: "Townsville at that time was a little town probably in the neighborhood of only 1,000 or 1,200 people. The local farmers would come to town with their families just like the folk back home in the Appalachians. They had rocking chairs in the back of the horse-drawn wagons, and the kids, and the whole family would go shopping. We went into town and discovered that they had farmers' markets along the street, and general stores that were a cross between our five-and-dimes and a regular country general store. So we bought a watermelon, some spoons, and a couple of table knives, and took the watermelon down on the beach by Townsville to eat it while our plane was being worked on at the depot."[3]

Sorry, but that is not your airplane

The next morning, at the airfield, the crew got some very unwelcome news when they were informed that the B-24 that they had flown over from America was not going to be their personal plane after all. "It was a terrible disappointment," says Mr. Baca today. "We had assumed that it was our bomber, and that we would fly it throughout our tour of duty and then bring it home. But at Townsville they told us, 'No, you were just flying it over. You'll get other bombers to fly when you get up to New Guinea—beat-up ones, too.' We were just so disappointed."

At least the Horner crew had not wasted their money having any custom nose art painted on the bomber back in the States, as some other crews had done. Carl Camp, a gunner in the 90th Bomb Group, wrote:

> [S]ome people, in the mistaken idea that the planes given to us were to be ours, had some pictures hastily painted upon them. Many crews that thought they owned their plane had paid out big bucks to have a picture and name painted on back at Topeka and then never saw their plane again.[4]

Mr. Horner remembers: "We found out that we were not going to keep the plane that we brought overseas, which we had begun to consider as ours. Instead we were given another one like it that had already been modified at the depot, and told that we were to deliver it to Port Moresby. As it turned out, planes did not belong to the crews as we had thought. Instead, it worked like bus drivers, where day-to-day each plane was assigned to any crew before a mission."[5]

And yet, this had not always been the case, which is why it was not unreasonable for a crew to think they would be assigned a specific bomber to fly.[6] In 1943, you will remember, Col. Art Rogers had flown the bomber named "Connell's Special" almost exclusively throughout his combat tour, and had then flown it home to the States. Col. Rogers had written of "Connell's Special:"

> An airplane develops a personality, and our affectionate name for her was "Susabella," even though she was officially known as "Connell's Special." In New Guinea, when my crew and I were

> forced to fly one of the newer planes while "Susabella" was getting some patchwork done for flak or machine gun holes, we actually dreaded flying in another airplane.[7]

It might be argued that since Col. Rogers was a high-ranking officer he had his choice of airplanes, and had claimed one for his own, but lowly lieutenants had also been accustomed to laying claim to and flying one particular bomber most of the time. The 90th Bomb Group's records show that in 1942 and -43 it was not unusual at all for any crew to come to view a particular bomber as their own, give it a name, and fly it nearly all the time.

In the European theater of war, 8th Air Force crews also consistently flew the same bombers. Maurice "Mo" Holmen, a friend of the author's, nearly always flew a B-24 that he named "Rugged but Right," and he and his crew had a dragon's head painted on the nose. They flew the bomber throughout their combat tour with the 448th Bomb Group of the 8th Air Force, based at Seething, England. And, as mentioned previously, the crew of the B-17 named "Memphis Belle" brought their bomber home to the States from England after completing their combat tour. As we saw in Chapter 29, Captain Lark Martin nearly always flew a bomber named "Mission Belle" except when it was undergoing repairs.

However, according to the historian of the 90th Bomb Group, Wiley Woods, in November of 1943 there was a change of policy and the Group's pilots were no longer allowed to claim any specific aircraft as their own.[8] The new policy stated that any available bomber would be assigned by operations officers to any pilot on the day of a mission. Nonetheless, in practice some squadron commanders and other officers with some rank found ways to regularly fly certain bombers that they preferred, and to which they gave special nicknames.[*]

By the time the Horner crew arrived on the scene in the spring of 1944, the "motor-pool" method of randomly assigning pilots to bombers for bombing missions had become the norm in the 5th Air Force. For whatever reason the policy was adopted, probably in the interest of efficiency, the result was that throughout their combat tour in 1944-5 the Horner crew never had any particular bomber assigned to it on a regular basis. And although many, if not most, of the 90th's bombers acquired nicknames and nose art, neither Mr. Horner, Mr. Theobald, nor Mr. Baca remembers the names of any of them today. They simply flew whatever aircraft they were assigned for a mission.

---

[*]As we will see in a later chapter, Lt. Cooper painted a bucking bronco on the bomber usually flown by Maj. Leland I. Harter, who hailed from a horse ranch near Boise, Idaho. Harter named the bomber the "Boise Bronc" (see pages 661-2).

41. THE FLIGHT TO THE PACIFIC

Armor removal

During the five days that the Horner crew laid over at Townsville, they watched the personnel of the Garbutt Field depot go to work modifying the bomber they had brought over. The factory in San Diego had installed hundreds of pounds of armor in the plane to protect the crew from enemy bullets and flak fragments, and all this was unbolted and removed to save weight. As Mr. Horner remembers: "There were half- to five-eighths-inch armor plated 'mummy cases' for the pilot and copilot, and other armor in other parts of the plane to protect other crew members. The so-called mummy case was a six-inch-deep steel box that fitted around the pilot and copilot's sides and shoulders and went up over their heads. The idea was that in combat you could pull back inside this case, and unless you were hit directly from the front you were pretty well protected from bullets and flak fragments. There was also a slab of steel in the floor, and armor plate in other areas of the plane to protect various crew members from shells and bullets coming through. What they did at the Townsville depot was to remove all this armor, around 3,500 pounds of it, and toss it out on the ground, to be disposed of. With all that weight removed, the plane could fly faster and carry a heavier payload—more bombs. These were the orders from our new commanders in the Pacific. So the Air Corps had spent all that money, fuel, and effort to fly all this armor overseas, only to have it torn out and tossed into a pile on the ground as scrap metal".[9]

The vast distances that had to be flown during bombing missions in the Pacific required more fuel to be carried than on European bombing missions,[10] and General Kenney, who as we have seen was continually finding ways to modify the aircraft he was sent, had decided that the ability to carry more fuel and bombs was more important than protective armor for the crew.

The flight to Port Moresby

The next step for the Horner crew was to report to Port Moresby, New Guinea, as specified in their orders, flying a modified B-24 that they were given at Garbutt Field to deliver there. On the 31st of May, 1944, after the crewmen were all aboard the plane and Lt. Horner was preparing to start up the engines and taxi out to the runway, a couple of women, who turned out to be Army nurses, ran up to the airplane and shouted up to Lt. Horner in his cockpit window that they needed a ride to Port Moresby, where they worked in a hospital. Then a P-39 fighter plane pilot trotted over and asked for a lift too, saying that he was familiar with Port Moresby's Jackson Field and could help them find it. Lt. Horner agreed to take all three along, and opened the bomb bay doors to let them climb aboard. Such informal hitchhiking was common on the airfields of the Pacific. Thus there were thirteen people aboard the bomber instead of ten when it took off. The hitchhikers stood or sat on the flight deck behind the pilots' seats.

The distance from Townsville, Australia to Port Moresby, New Guinea is 675 miles, around four hours of flight in a B-24, and the course was nearly due north across the Coral Sea (Map 41-3, opposite). Lt. Horner's instructions were simple: fly north until you come to the coast of New Guinea, then turn right (or east) and run down the coastline until you spot the Moresby Shipwreck, which was near the mouth of a river, turn left there and fly up the river to the airfield known as Jackson Drome (also known as 7-Mile Field because it was seven miles from the town and harbor).

Off they went, but halfway across the Coral Sea it began to rain. Then really foul weather began closing in. The cloud ceiling dropped lower and lower, forcing Lt. Horner to do the same, until they were flying only about 100 feet above the sea. Horner could have gone up into the overcast and flown on instruments, but in flying blind he wouldn't have been able to see the New Guinea coast when he came to it. Soon the rain was coming down so heavily that water started seeping into the plane (B-24s were far from watertight). The water was running along the floor of the flight deck, and it also dripped into and shorted out Sgt. Bruni's radios.

As if all this wasn't enough, one of the nurses announced that she had to "make water" herself, and right urgently at that. Lt. Horner told Sgt. Eady, the flight engineer, to take her to the bomb bay and show her the funnel and can that had been stowed there for such a contingency. Eady led her through the hatch door from the flight deck back to the bomb bay and showed her the arrangement, but she said that owing to certain differences between male and female anatomy it wouldn't do her any good. So then Eady opened the bomb bay doors a few inches and suggested that she climb down and squat on the catwalk, which she agreed to do. Then he closed the door from the flight deck to give her a little privacy. The nurse found this method of relieving herself successful, if awkward, but in the process a deluge of rainwater blowing up into the bomb bay from the storm outside soaked the poor girl to the skin, and she came back up onto the flight deck sopping wet. Noticing everyone on the flight deck eying her curiously, as she stood drenched and dripping, she said, "I don't care! I feel better!"

By the time they struck the coast of New Guinea, the cloud ceiling was down to less than 100 feet with only a quarter-mile visibility in rain. Lt. Horner turned right and flew down the coastline as per his instructions and shortly spotted the Moresby Wreck, where he hung a left into the mouth of the river and proceeded upstream, flying in a narrow gap between the cloud ceiling above and the tops of the jungle trees below, with everyone leaning forward and straining to see the airfield come into view though the streaming rain on the windshields. Suddenly, sooner than anyone had expected, the field

41. THE FLIGHT TO THE PACIFIC 487

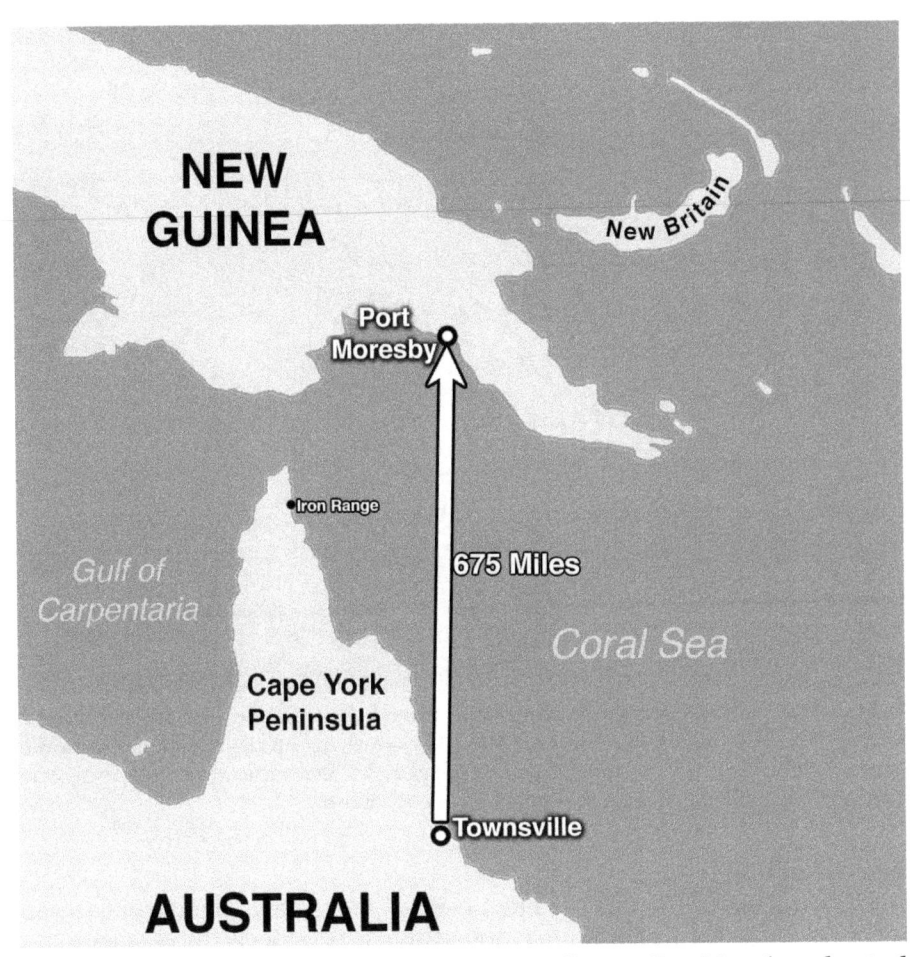

Map 41-3. The Horner crew flew a B-24J from Townsville up to Port Moresby and arrived there in a blinding tropical rainstorm that made landing extremely difficult.

appeared in front of them, but they were off to one side of the runway and going too fast to land, and the landing gear was retracted anyway.

Lt. Horner decided to go back to the river mouth and make another approach, now that he knew the location and layout of the field. He made a 180-degree turn to the left, which put his left wingtip down near the treetops, then leveled back out and ran back down the river to the sea where he turned around and set up another run. On the second try he came in at a slower speed and with the flaps and landing gear down, ready to land. Everyone in the cockpit was once again peering ahead through the rain when the field came into view again, and this time Lt. Horner was able to line the bomber up with the runway.

Jackson Field at Port Moresby, looking south toward the Coral Sea. Lt. Horner made a landing here in a driving rainstorm on May 31, 1944, flying up the river valley from the ocean, which can be seen in the distance at upper right. The white arrow shows where he skidded his bomber down the wet, slippery, metalized runway.

A slick landing

With the bomber's radios shorted out and inoperative, there had been no way for Lt. Horner to inform the airfield's control tower of his approach, so it was a surprise to the men in the tower when Lt. Horner's B-24 suddenly materialized out of the rain, just touching down on the end of Jackson Field's runway 32[*]. This caused quite a stir among the tower personnel because another aircraft, a C-47 transport plane (known as a "gooney bird") was also just touching down on the runway not very far ahead of the bomber.

Two airplanes landing on the same runway at the same time is never a good idea, but if it's going to happen, it's best to have them both going in the same direction and the fastest airplane in the front. In this case, the first condition was met but not the second. A C-47's landing speed was about 60 mph, while a B-24's was around 90, which meant that the bomber was about to run up behind the cargo plane and collide with it.

Mr. Horner still remembers quite vividly the scene from his viewpoint: "Suddenly the water-soaked radio came back to life and we could hear the

---

[*] Runway numbers are abbreviated compass headings. Thus an airplane landing on Runway 32 was heading 320 degrees on the compass, or nearly north (which is 360 degrees).

control tower yelling, 'Gooney bird! Gooney bird! Pick up your tail and run!' and there, only a few hundred yards ahead of us, was a C-47 touching down on the runway at about 60 mph. As the C-47 accelerated, desperately trying to get out of our way, I stood up on the brakes and locked them up, and we slid down the rain-slick runway for about a quarter mile. This runway was surfaced with the perforated, interlocking steel plates called Marston matting, and being wet with the rain it formed a slippery surface that we skidded along on with very little friction. We missed the C-47 and finally got stopped, and I turned off onto a taxiway. A jeep soon appeared with some officers in it, and after we got parked they told us that we were only the second B-24 to land there that day. The crews of other B-24s had given up trying to land in the storm, and some had run out of gas after circling in the clouds, and the crews had bailed out, while other bombers had ditched in the sea, not having enough fuel left to return to Australia. Several aircraft were lost that day in the area, as the storm was widespread. Only a few twin-engine C-47s had managed to get in, and the fact that many of these planes were flown by experienced civilian pilots, and the C-47 was a very agile airplane, may have had something to do with that.

"Only one other B-24 besides ours had made it down. I was practically a hero! I went up into the control tower, which was full of brass, all gathered around a radio, and somebody asked me, 'How much fuel did you have left?' I said that I had 1,100 or 1,200 gallons. In seconds I went from being a hero to being an ass. They told me that since I still had that much gas I should have turned around and gone back to Australia instead of risking a dangerous landing at Jackson Field. All I could say was, 'Nobody told me to come up here and then go back. My orders were to get here and land.' Nothing further was said about it."

When asked about the exciting landing today, Mr. Baca, then young Sgt. Baca the waist gunner in the rear section of the plane, says that he doesn't remember the bomber skidding down the runway. "It seemed like a normal landing to those of us in the back of the plane. We didn't know about all that excitement up front until later. I guess it's better sometimes not to know everything that's going on."

The crew was given tent accommodations on a hillside above the airfield, the four officers in one tent and the six enlisted men in another, in different areas, as usual in Army encampments. They had traveled 8,300 miles since they'd left California, and they were now on the opposite side of the world from their homes and everything that was familiar to them. Next they would have to become accustomed to living in the tropics, and prepare for their first combat mission against the Japanese.

Chapter Forty-Two

PORT MORESBY TO NADZAB

By the time the Horner crew arrived at Port Moresby on the last day of May, 1944, it was no longer a frontline airfield. The last Japanese bombing raid on Moresby had occurred eight months earlier, on Sept. 20, 1943. Japanese airpower in New Guinea had retreated, or rather been pushed, all the way back to the head of the New Guinea "buzzard," and Japanese bombers (the ones that remained after General Kenney demolished most of them on their own airfields) were no longer a threat to Port Moresby. American airpower now dominated the skies over New Guinea and nearby New Britain.

MacArthur's offensive drive toward the Philippines was in high gear in the spring of 1944, when the Horner crew joined the fight. Wewak, like Rabaul, had been neutralized and bypassed (see map on p. 384). Fifth Bomber Command was now headquartered at Nadzab, 200 miles north of Port Moresby, on the other side of the Owen Stanley Mountains. Hollandia, 500 miles up the coast from Nadzab, had been captured from the Japanese by amphibious assault on April 22, and American engineers were busy turning it into another American airbase. Wakde Island, a small coral island just off New Guinea's coast 125 miles beyond Hollandia, and 625 miles from Nadzab, had been captured from the Japanese on the 18th of May, and the Seabees had begun converting it to American bomber use even before the bullets had stopped flying.

Two hundred miles farther west from Wakde Island, U.S. troops had landed on Biak Island on May 27, three days before the Horner crew arrived at Port Moresby, and had begun a long battle to wrest it from the Japanese and turn it into another large American bomber base. Thus, although Nadzab was the center of Air Corps bomber operations in the Southwest Pacific at this time, MacArthur's ground forces were in action far up the coastline, paving the way for further advances, and Nadzab in its turn would eventually become a rear area like Port Moresby as the Allied forces moved relentlessly toward Japan.

After their nerve-wracking landing at Moresby in the blinding rainstorm on May 31, 1944, the Horner crew spent twenty days at Jackson Field before moving on up to Nadzab. The men occupied 16-by-16-foot pyramidal tents, the four officers in one and the six enlisted men in another. The tents had a center pole that held the canvas roof up 12 feet from the ground, and from there it sloped down to the sides, and the sides could be rolled up for ventilation. (photo at right)

Port Moresby's airbase complex was now calling itself the Fifth Bomber Command Replacement Center, meaning a rear supply base and reception center for crews coming in from the United States. Australian crews were also being trained to fly American aircraft at Jackson Field. The men of the Horner crew were informed that Fifth Bomber Command was going to review their qualifications as aircrewmen, and would test each man in his MOS (military occupational specialty) before sending him on to combat. The need for this retesting is questionable, since the men had just passed all their tests in the States, but that was the policy that had been adopted.

Pyramidal tents at Port Moresby's Jackson Field, with the sides folded up to allow any breezes to blow through to mitigate the stifling humidity and heat.

The Horner crew waited around for over two weeks before it was their turn to be tested, beginning on the 16th of June, 1944. During those two weeks the men began adjusting to the tropical climate and the dreary rehydrated food that was the staple fare in the mess tents. Since refrigeration was rare in the 1940s, all food sent from America to its fighting forces in the Pacific had to be dehydrated first to preserve it, then reconstituted before eating. The resulting fare was nothing to write home about (although many men did, bitterly).

Disease, the invisible enemy

The many tropical diseases in New Guinea continued to take a severe toll on the Americans working and fighting there; in fact, as stated in earlier chapters, diseases caused far more casualties than the enemy did. The Japanese fared no better, and usually worse because they paid less attention to sanitation. One war historian believes that a major reason the Allies prevailed over the Japanese was because the Americans practiced better hygiene:

> The reason that Europeans and Southeast Asians had more or less ignored the Solomons and New Guinea for centuries was simple enough: going to the South Pacific very likely meant death. The

populations of the Solomons and New Guinea had accommodated to nature's killing machine, but most outsiders could not. The great rainfall and heat of the tropics made a heaven for microbes of all types. Unlike areas north and south, there was no genuine dry season that forced microorganisms into some kind of natural cease-fire. Instead, the barrier between Australia and Indonesia was malignant terrain for humans, being rife with malaria, dengue fever, typhus, and dysentery. Ironically, armies and air forces could exist in this environment because of their numbers and the budding medical facilities behind them... No doubt one of the reasons that the Allies prevailed when they did was simply that they proved better able to confront nature's onslaught than were the Japanese.[1]

Masatake Okumiya, the staff officer with Japanese naval aviation stationed at Rabaul, confirmed that the Japanese suffered severely as a result of paying less attention to disease prevention than did the Allies:

> One of the major points which has been too often overlooked in an evaluation of fighting power, but which determined to a large extent the efficiency of air units, was that of hygienic installations. Japanese engineers paid scant attention to this problem, dismissing the pressing matter of mosquito protection by simply rigging mosquito nets in personnel quarters. Sanitary facilities were basically crude and ineffective...
> The Americans, by contrast, swept clean vast areas surrounding their ground installations with advanced mechanical aids. Through exhaustive disinfecting operations, they banished flies and mosquitoes from their air bases and paid similar attention to every phase of sanitation and disease.
> Some may consider this a prosaic matter, but it was vital to the men forced to live... in the midst of jungles swarming with disease and insect life. The inevitable outcome of such neglect was a tremendous difference in the health of the American and Japanese personnel who were assigned to these forward air facilities... It was a classic blunder, for which we paid dearly. Disease and insect plagues can hinder air operations as effectively as enemy attack.[2]

Still, despite the best efforts of American engineers to banish the causes of infections, diseases caused far more casualties among the Americans in the Pacific war than combat. One estimate is that for every two casualties caused by combat, five were caused by disease. Mr. Baca remembers that nearly every one of the enlisted men in the Horner crew came down with the "G. I.s," or diarrhea, shortly after arriving at Port Moresby. This was a common malady among Americans new to the tropics as they adjusted to the muggy climate and poor food.

Every American serviceman in the Pacific was also required to take atabrine tablets in an attempt to ward off malaria. Every mess hall table had a bottle of atabrine pills on it, and everyone was supposed to swallow one tablet a day. You could easily tell when a man had been taking his atabrine regularly because his skin turned a characteristic yellowy-orange color. As one of the Jolly Rogers' gunners, S/Sgt. Gordon Bixler, remembered about his own stay at Port Moresby:

> **Camp life was a succession of dateless days, one pretty much like another—hot, torrential thundershowers, battles against the mosquitoes, and everyone looking yellow from the atabrine.**[3]

Some men feared that the yellow skin color might be permanent, and there were also rumors that atabrine had a variety of serious side effects, including insanity, sterility, and impotence. Many men therefore didn't take their atabrine, despite orders to do so, if they could get away with it.

However, because the Army in the Pacific was losing so many men to malaria, in some outfits officers were assigned to personally see that every man took one atabrine tablet every day, and they would line the men up and stand in front of each one until he swallowed his daily pill.

The sallow skin color caused by taking the drug was mentioned in a poem written by Lt. Robert B. Logan, a pilot of the Jolly Rogers' 320th Squadron in 1944. Part of his poem reads:

Sign near a field hospital at Port Moresby.

> Here's to old New Guinea,
> It's the place that God forgot,
> Where the food will turn your stomach,
> And you'll catch the jungle rot.
>
> For your skin will turn deep yellow
> You'll have sallow, skinny cheeks,
> And you'll surely catch a fever,
> And lay in bed for weeks.
>
> Why the Japs would want to take it,
> Why they'd ever want this land,

> Why the hell we're fighting for it,
> I shall never understand.
>
> When my days on earth are over,
> And the death bell sounds its knell,
> If upstairs is like New Guinea,
> Then I'd rather go to Hell.[4]

It was estimated that over sixty percent of Americans in the Pacific combat zone contracted malaria at some point. Sgt. Baca came down with it in the course of his combat tour, and although the atabrine he took suppressed the symptoms well enough for him to carry on with his duties, he suffered from recurrent bouts of the disease for many years after the war.

Other tropical diseases ran malaria a close second, among them dengue fever, scrub typhus, jungle rot, yellow jaundice, and numerous others, some without names. "The doctors told us that there were diseases there that they had never even heard of," remembers Mr. Baca today. Later in 1944 Lt. Cooper, the Horner crew's copilot, would be hospitalized with dengue fever, also known as "breakbone fever" because the sufferer's terrible joint and muscle pains made him feel like his bones were breaking.

The oppressive, sweltering wet heat of the island also weighed heavily on most of the newcomers. Daytime temperatures commonly soared to above 100 degrees, and rain was incessant, sometimes continuing for days at a time. The heavy, moisture-laden air descended on the men like a hot, wet blanket. American uniforms consisted of long-sleeved shirts and long pants, and many Americans noted with envy the short pants and short-sleeved shirts of their Australian allies, which allowed the latter some degree of relief from the heat. A lot of Americans hoped that the U. S. Army would issue similar tropical uniforms, but General Kenney had already looked into the matter and decided against it. Mosquitoes were the main spreaders of malaria in New Guinea, and mites spread dengue fever. The mites clung to grass stems, and were picked up on the legs of men walking through grass, while mosquitoes feasted on the exposed skin of any part of the body. Kenney did not want his "kids" (as he called his airmen) wearing abbreviated uniforms which, although cooler for the wearer, gave the insects more places to bite. As he explained in his memoirs:

> When the Americans first came to New Guinea and saw the Aussies wearing shorts and shirtsleeves cut off above the elbow, it appealed to them as a smart idea for that hot, humid, jungle service. Just as an experiment, I put long trousers and long-sleeved shirts on one squadron of a fighter group and shorts and short-sleeved shirts on another squadron for a month. At the end of the trial period, I had two cases of malaria in the long-trousered, long-sleeved squadron

and sixty-two cases in the squadron wearing shorts. The evidence was good enough for the kids as well as for me, so I issued the order [to keep the long pants and shirts]. Later, in New Guinea, I noticed that Vasey's 7th Australian Division were wearing "longies."[5]

Masatake Okumiya would have seconded Kenney's mandate on long sleeves and long pants for all troops. While all the other officers around him became ill, Okumiya remained healthy, for which he partly credited his long trousers. He wrote:

> Incredibly, all during my stay [at Rabaul] I did not once become ill. Every last member of Rear Admiral Jojima's staff, including the admiral, suffered from either dengue fever or malaria, or both. Perhaps the reasons why I escaped illness were that, although I had had land duty longer than any member of the headquarters staff, and I was obliged to remain outdoors longer than usual, I always exercised the greatest care in selecting food and water. Further, I ignored the oppressive heat and wore nothing but long trousers and boots. These were not as comfortable, I admit, as the cooler short trousers, but they were preferable to fever and illness.[6]

Lt. Horner witnesses a fatal accident at Port Moresby

Accidents unconnected with flying occurred around the airbases, of course, as they do in any concentration of working men. Men crashed jeeps and trucks or were struck or run over by them. Men were electrocuted by faulty wiring from the generators that provided electricity around the airbase. And men were burned in the explosions of gasoline powered cooking stoves or other devices that used combustible fuels.

Lt. Horner witnessed an accident of the latter type one day at Port Moresby. The tent for the Horner crew's four officers was pitched on the side of a hill overlooking a mess tent that served several hundred meals a day on the busy airbase. Horner was sitting outside his tent, looking down at the mess tent, and saw one of the soldiers on KP duty trying to clean out one of the troughs that had been made by splitting 55-gallon drums lengthwise and then arranging them horizontally so that they could be filled with hot water for sterilizing mess kits. These half-barrel troughs had piping under them with holes drilled in the pipes so that when gasoline was run through them and ignited, the small flames kept the water hot. After eating, a soldier would dip his mess kit into the scalding hot water to clean and sterilize it. After a while, grease from the mess kits would build up in the troughs and had to be cleaned out.

The soldier on KP had been assigned to clean out this accumulated grease, and he decided to dissolve it in gasoline. He turned off the flames and dipped most of the water out of one of the troughs, and the rest quickly evaporated, since the metal was still very hot. The man should have waited for the metal to cool down before proceeding with the cleaning, but he immediately filled a bucket with gasoline and sloshed it into the trough. As Lt. Horner watched, horrified, the gas hit the hot metal, burst into flame, and splashed right back into the soldier's face. With his skin and clothing on fire, the man screamed and started running. By the time other men were able to grab him and put out the flames, it was too late, and he died of his burns.

Sgt. Baca encounters a dragon

The jungles of New Guinea do not harbor the large forms of wildlife that most people associate with the jungles of Africa. The largest animals in New Guinea are the crocodiles found in the many rivers and swamps. The island is home, however, to a great many kinds of birds, bats, and small mammals of the marsupial type, as well as reptiles smaller than crocodiles, and there are wild boars that are the feral descendants of domestic pigs.

One day Sgt. Baca, who loved to hike, went walking around the fringes of the Port Moresby airbase looking over the unfamiliar tropical flora and fauna. He found the tropics to be quite a different environment from the deserts of New Mexico, and there was a variety of interesting things to look at. At one point he heard a snapping sound behind him, turned around, and was startled to see a creature unlike any he'd ever seen before.

"It was some sort of a big lizard about four feet long, with a long tail," Baca remembers, "and it was snapping its tail at me." The animal looked similar to the lizards of his native Southwest, but most of those were only a few inches long; this one was huge by comparison. It was likely a monitor lizard, which is native to New Guinea and Australia. One version of this reptile, known as a Kimodo Dragon, can grow up to eight feet long. Whatever it was, Baca backed away from the ferocious-looking creature and left it alone.

New Guinea Natives

Baca also remembers encountering the New Guinea natives who hung around the airfields doing odd jobs. "We called them fuzzy-wuzzies," he says, "because of their big frizzy hairdos." Native women were banned from the American camps owing to their habit of wearing nothing from the waist up, which was considered too distracting to the young American men, who rarely saw such sights at home.

But the natives also rendered invaluable services to the Allies. During the fighting between the Japanese and Australians on the Kokoda Trail between July and November of 1942, the natives who lived in the villages along the trail had carried wounded Australians over some of the toughest terrain in the world back to aid stations and field hospitals at Port Moresby, and in so doing had saved many lives. They had become known as the Fuzzy-Wuzzy Angels, and today there are monuments and statues to their memory in New Guinea and Australia, erected by a grateful Australian people.

The Big Baloose Man

In pidgin English the natives called an airplane a "baloose," and since they thought General Kenney owned all the Allied airplanes, they called him the "Number One Baloose Man." One native chief presented a Captain Beck of V Bomber Command with a special gift for the Number One Baloose Man, of which Kenney wrote:

> He [Capt. Beck] said that the chief had a present for me—two fifteen-year-old virgins. I asked him what he did about it. Beck said, "Oh, I accepted them for you and then turned them over to the Australian commissioner, who put them to work around Government House. They're up there waiting for you."[7]

The New Guinea natives were called "Fuzzy-Wuzzies" by the Americans because of their big frizzy hairdos.

General Kenney was careful to avoid Government House in Port Moresby for a while.

Ancient vs. modern warfare

Some of the New Guinea natives had evidently seen, or heard of, the deadly effectiveness of General Kenney's low-level strafer/bomber attacks against the Japanese. Lt. Col. John P. Henebry, a pilot of the Third Attack Group, which flew these aircraft, remembered when the chief of a New Guinea tribe came to his Group headquarters with an interesting proposal:

> [A] delegation of local warriors, representing, said their chief, some 500 spearmen and bowmen, brought their war plans against a neighboring tribe to us. They wanted air support.
>
> These neighbors had raided their village some months previously, stealing away with untold numbers of pigs and women, two precious commodities in the jungle. The chief emotionally proclaimed his pro-American sympathies and assumed that his enemy was our enemy. Cooperation with air cover for his spear

and bow attack would not come without compensation, he promised. He was perfectly willing to split the booty—the enemy's women and pigs he would capture in retribution.

True, we hadn't had a more intriguing offer or more enticing rewards from General MacArthur, but we delicately declined the proposed mission and encouraged continued camaraderie with a formal pig roast and native dance in exchange for our gifts of costume jewelry, gold-lipped shells, and tobacco. The chief decided to forego combat if it wasn't to be backed with U. S. airpower.[8]

A war in which the Stone Age spear and bowmen of New Guinea went into battle with the support of General Kenney's strafer/bombers would have made an interesting picture indeed: the very oldest type of warfare combined with the very newest, but it was not to be. The native chief and Henebry agreed in the end to keep their wars separate.

The incident did illustrate, however, that men have always waged war and always will, using whatever technology is available to them, and that, as Plato wrote, "only the dead have seen the end of war."

The Horner crew's stay at Port Moresby

On June 6, 1944, everyone at Port Moresby, and in fact everyone in the world with access to the news, was electrified to hear that the Allies had crossed the English Channel in a great armada and landed at Normandy on the French coast. They had achieved a beachhead on Hitler's Fortress Europe and were pushing inland into France. This would be remembered in history as D-Day. A new and decisive phase of the European war had begun, and the newspaper headlines from Europe would push the reporting from the Pacific war onto the back pages for months to come. When Pacific war news did make headlines, it was more often about the activities of the Marines in their island battles in the Central Pacific, such as at Guadalcanal, Saipan, or Okinawa, than about the Army battling its way up the New Guinea coastline toward the Philippines. General MacArthur's war in the Southwest Pacific was poorly reported at the time and is nearly forgotten now, though it was as deadly as anywhere else.

Days passed at Port Moresby, and the Horner crew had little to do while waiting to be tested. To Mr. Horner today, looking back on it, it was time wasted; the base seemed disorganized and the activities confused and haphazard. He suspects that many of the people in command positions at Port Moresby had gotten their jobs through appointments by influential military and civilian authorities, and were only there in a now-safe part of the war zone to gain combat credentials without actually getting anywhere near combat, for use later in their careers, especially political careers.

One of the most famous such cases was that of Lyndon Baines Johnson, later the 36th President of the United States (1963-1969), who was awarded a

Silver Star, the military's third-highest combat medal for valor, for essentially doing nothing more than taking a ride in a bomber at Port Moresby. The truth is that he got the medal in exchange for promising to do a political favor for General MacArthur.

Lyndon B. Johnson's phony heroics at Port Moresby

In 1942 Johnson was a Texas congressman as well as an acting lieutenant commander in the Navy (he had enlisted in the Naval Reserve right after the Pearl Harbor attack to enhance his political prospects). Johnson had high political ambitions, and he knew quite well that MacArthur was anxious to receive more war matériel than he was getting from America due to the Allies' "Europe first" policy. Johnson struck a deal with MacArthur: in exchange for a combat medal from MacArthur that he could use to score political points with later, he promised to lobby President Roosevelt to provide greater resources for the Southwest Pacific war zone. It was a case of "you scratch my back and I'll scratch yours." MacArthur went along with the deal and provided a way for Johnson to look like he had been a hero and earned the medal.

MacArthur arranged for Johnson to ride along as a passenger in a B-26 Marauder twin-engine bomber* of the 22nd Bomb Group (Medium) on a raid from Port Moresby to Lae on June 9, 1942. Johnson was flown up from Australia in a B-17 that morning, and the mission was delayed an hour while everyone waited for Johnson to show up. After finally arriving at Port Moresby's Jackson Field, Johnson climbed aboard one of eleven B-26s going on the strike that day. The crew was told that their important passenger was on a "fact-finding mission." The Marauders then took off on their bombing mission to Lae, but a short while later the one in which Lyndon Johnson was riding reversed course and flew back to Port Moresby because of "generator trouble." It had turned back before getting within sight of Lae.

Since a passenger riding along on a bomber that aborted its mission, and who returned without ever having sighted the enemy, would hardly qualify for a medal for valor, a story was concocted in which the bomber, after "losing an engine," had been attacked by eight Japanese fighter planes and had engaged in a running gunfight with them on its way back to base. Johnson's contribution to the battle, according to his citation for heroism, was that he "evidenced coolness."

Johnson's late arrival at Port Moresby that morning had caused all the Marauders to take off an hour late on a mission that had been coordinated with B-24s and B-25s. The plan had been for all the aircraft to reach the target at the same time, flying at different altitudes, in order to confuse the defending

---

*Not many B-26s were assigned to the Pacific, and General Kenney didn't think much of them anyway. They were phased out in January of 1944 in favor of more B-25s.

Japanese fighter planes and antiaircraft gunners. Because of the delay, however, the B-26s got there late, after all the other American aircraft had come and gone, and attacked alone, so that the estimated two dozen Japanese Zeros that were still in the air after the other bombers had left had only the B-26s to concentrate on. One Marauder was shot down and its eight-man crew killed, and five other B-26s were damaged.

One of the pilots who flew on the mission later stated, bitterly, that the deaths of the crew that was shot down were a direct result of Johnson's delaying the mission and upsetting the attack schedule.

Nine days after the mission, back in Australia, Johnson was awarded the Silver Star by Major General Richard K. Sutherland, MacArthur's Chief of Staff. No one else in the bomber in which he rode received any kind of a medal. Johnson's award citation reads:

> "While on a mission of obtaining information in the Southwest Pacific Area, Lieutenant Commander Johnson, in order to obtain personal knowledge of combat conditions, volunteered as an observer on a hazardous aerial combat mission over hostile positions in New Guinea. As our planes neared the target area, they were intercepted by eight hostile fighters. When at this time the plane in which Lieutenant Commander Johnson was an observer developed mechanical trouble and was forced to turn back alone, presenting a favorable target to the enemy fighters, he evidenced coolness in spite of the hazard involved. His gallant action enabled him to obtain and return with valuable information."

The "valuable information" that Johnson gained was never revealed, but presumably it was the knowledge that if you go out on a bombing mission, it's safer to turn back before getting anywhere near the enemy than to continue to the target and risk encountering him. Johnson later requested that a copy of his citation be signed personally by General MacArthur and sent to him, and this was duly done, along with a cover letter written by one of MacArthur's other staff officers that read:

> Of course, your outstanding bravery in volunteering for a so-called 'suicide mission' in order to get a first-hand view of what our Army fliers go through has been the subject of much favorable comment since your departure. It is indeed a great government we have when members of the Congress take those chances in order to better serve their fellow men in the legislative bodies. You surely earned your decoration and I am so happy about your having received the award.[9]

Johnson framed his citation for bravery and displayed it on the wall of his congressional office, and for the rest of his life, including the time that he was President of the United States, he wore a lapel pin signifying that he had received the Silver Star for heroism in combat.

This is the sort of thing that makes real combat veterans such as Mr. Horner cynical about the activities of rear-echelon personnel like the ones he encountered at Port Moresby. There was no good reason why bomber crews coming into Port Moresby in the spring of 1944 should be tested all over again after just passing their MOS exams in the States, and it seems suspiciously like make-work for desk warriors who pulled duty in safe places such as Moresby had become by this time. These people took such jobs so that they could return home with war-zone credentials, even though, like Lyndon Johnson, they were never in any danger from the enemy.

The Horner crew's MOS tests at Port Moresby began on the 16th of June, and Lt. Cooper's flight logbook shows that the crew flew every day from the 16th through the 19th. Each flight took off from, and then returned to, Jackson Field, and was about three hours and 45 minutes long. Cooper did not record what went on during these flights, and they were so unnoteworthy that Mr. Horner cannot even recall them today.

Mr. Baca remembers that one of the flights took them out over the Moresby Wreck, where all the gunners took turns shooting at the old ship stranded on the reef.

The Horner crew moves to Nadzab

On June 20, 1944, having passed their qualification tests at Port Moresby, the Horner crew was given a B-24 and told to take it up to Nadzab, where they would be assigned to a bomb group and squadron. Lt. Cooper's flight logbook records the flight from Port Moresby to Nadzab as lasting three hours and forty minutes. That is a lot of time in the air to cover only 200 air-miles at 150 miles per hour, so obviously they did not take the most direct route across the Owen Stanley Mountains.

A more roundabout but safer route for a crew that was new to the area was to fly southeast from Moresby, down the southern New Guinea coastline to a well-known landmark called Hood Point, which is where the mountains flatten out as they approach the sea. There a plane could turn left (north) and cross the mountains at a low spot, passing over the Allied airfield at Dobodura, which made another good landmark for navigators, and then swing northwest up the northern coastline to Nadzab. This is the route that the Horner crew evidently took (see Map 42-1 on p. 503).

A shorter and more often-used route, but a riskier one because of the clouds that often obscured the mountains, was to fly northeast from Port Moresby across the mountains through what became known as "the Gap." This was the

8,500-foot high Kokoda Pass, the same pass that Japanese ground forces had used to advance across the Kokoda Trail from the north coast in their failed attempt to capture Port Moresby in 1942. Another look at Map 42-1, opposite, shows how much time could be saved by a plane "shooting the Gap" to reach Nadzab. This route could get a B-24 to Nadzab in well under two hours, but it was dangerous when clouds or bad weather hid the mountain peaks that rise up on either side of the pass, so that a pilot couldn't be sure whether he was really in the gap or off to one side of it.

Overconfident or impatient young pilots with little mountain flying experience sometimes came to grief trying to "shoot the Gap" when the mountains were clouded over. This is what happened to a Jolly Rogers B-24 named "Weezie" that tried to take this shortcut under unfavorable weather conditions in March of 1944.

"Weezie" fails to shoot the Gap; 22 men die

On 22 March, 1944, two months before the Horner crew arrived at Port Moresby, the B-24 named "Weezie" of the Jolly Rogers' 320th Squadron took off from Ward's Field at Port Moresby on a ferry flight to Nadzab and headed for the Gap. Aboard the bomber was a skeleton crew of three (pilot, copilot, and navigator) plus 19 hitchhikers from Port Moresby who had welcomed the chance for a quick lift to Nadzab. Hitchhiking on planes shuttling between airbases was common practice in the Pacific, as we have seen, but in this case it turned out to be a trip to eternity for all aboard. When the bomber didn't arrive at Nadzab, it was declared missing, and it remained missing for nearly forty years.

In New Guinea the Owen Stanley Mountains usually have big cloud build-ups above them every afternoon. As one Jolly Rogers pilot put it:

> The Owen Stanleys would be nice and clear in the morning, and obscured by clouds by afternoon. We couldn't go much beyond [above] 28,000, so flying over was usually impossible. If you could not find a crack, you simply took your chances and hoped there were no stray rocks around. Too often the crews weren't where they thought they were, and some rock fetched them a solid blow. End of mission.[10]

Don Johnson, an Australian transport plane pilot, wrote:

> In New Guinea, because of the humidity, the large cumulus clouds build up quickly, and it was always necessary to get over the Owen Stanley Range near the Kokoda area before midday if possible, else the cloud base lowered down to the tops of the mountains.[11]

42. PORT MORESBY TO NADZAB

Map 42-1. In June of 1944 the Horner crew took the longer, roundabout but safer route from Port Moresby to Nadzab, flying around the end of the Owen Stanley Mountains that had already claimed so many American aircraft. Three months earlier, in March, a Jolly Rogers bomber named "Weezie" had tried to "shoot the Gap" (the Kokoda Pass) and ended up crashing into Mount Thumb. Its wreckage would not be found for forty years.

Since "Weezie's" pilot, Lt. Robert Allred, took off in the middle of the afternoon, he almost certainly found the pass shrouded in clouds. In that situation a sensible pilot would have returned to Port Moresby and put the flight off until the next morning, or else turned southeast down the coast and taken the longer but safer route in the clear, going around the end of the mountains and their cloud cap, as the Horner crew would do in June.

Instead, Allred evidently decided to "shoot the Gap" blindly, right through the clouds, and unfortunately, the attempt proved fatal for him and everyone else aboard the plane. Allred had a reputation for boldness bordering on recklessness, and on this flight he finally pushed his luck too far. Sadly, twenty-one other men were trusting him with their lives that day, most of whom probably had no idea of the danger he was taking them into. Another youthful, inexperienced, impatient, and overconfident pilot came to grief, and in this case he took a lot of other people with him.

Allred had started to take off in the morning, when the Kokoda Pass was usually free of clouds, and he'd had even more hitchhikers aboard then—thirty of them in fact. However, he'd experienced an engine problem while taxiing

Here we have a deadly "hard-centered cloud" in the making. Rocks often lay in ambush for unwary aircraft inside the clouds that built up over the Owen Stanley Mountains every afternoon. The mountain peak above was typical, snapped by a photographer in a passing bomber as it was performing its daily routine of wrapping itself in its concealing clouds.

to the runway and turned back to the parking area to get it fixed. A mechanic told him that it was going to take a little time to remedy the trouble, so all the hitchhikers had gotten back out of the plane, and most of them had gone off to lunch while the work was being done. For one reason or another eleven of them had failed to get back aboard when the plane was ready to go again in the afternoon (and later, when the airplane was reported lost, were quite happy to have been left behind). "Weezie" took off at about 3 PM, and like many another aircraft that took off from Port Moresby and headed for the Owen Stanleys, was never heard from again.

In the early 1980s some natives hunting birds in the jungle on Mount Thumb noticed large pieces of metal scattered about the forest floor. They had found "Weezie." The wreckage was at the 8,800 foot level, 43 miles from Port Moresby and 14 miles east of the 8,500-foot-high Kokoda Pass. Lt. Allred had gained enough altitude to shoot the Gap, but he had drifted off course to the east in bad visibility, and instead of the Gap he had found the proverbial "rock-filled cloud." Slamming into a mountainside at 150 mph gave no chance of survival to anyone aboard. In 1982 a team from the Army's Central Identifi-

The wreckage of the bomber "Weezie" of the Jolly Rogers' 320th Squadron lies today on the side of Mount Thumb, north of Port Moresby, where it encountered a "rock-filled cloud" on March 22, 1944 while trying to shoot the Kokoda Gap. All 22 men aboard died.

cation Laboratory (CIL) in Hawaii was delivered to the crash site by helicopter and recovered the partial remains of all twenty-three people aboard (only about a fourth of the bones that were originally present could be found, probably because the rest had been washed down the steep slope of the mountainside by heavy rains over the years). After the remains were identified as well as possible in the CIL laboratory by the famous forensic identification expert Tadao Furue, they were returned to their relatives in the States for burial.*

In an interesting aside, a check of records shows that the B-24 named "Weezie" had formerly been flown on bombing missions by Capt. Morgan F. Terry, whom Lt. Horner would come to know well during his tour of duty in the Pacific. It was Terry's crew who had named the plane "Weezie" because of the peculiar sound of its engines.

Mr. Horner cannot remember today the exact route he flew from Port Moresby to Nadzab on June 20, 1944 with his crew, but it is certain that he didn't try to shoot the dangerous Kokoda Pass as Lt. Allred had done in "Weezie." The three hours and forty minutes the plane spent in the air, as recorded in Lt. Cooper's logbook, indicates that they took the longer route southeastward around the end of the mountains as Lt. Allred should have done.

This flight from the south to the north coast of New Guinea gave the Horner crew their first really good look at the mountains and jungles of the huge island,

---

*A book titled *A Missing Plane* by Susan Sheehan was written in 1987 about the discovery of "Weezie's" wreckage and the recovery and identification of the crash victims, along with personal stories of the men who died (see bibliography).

and they were a breathtaking sight from the air. This was a whole new world that most young men in America had never known existed. General Kenney had recorded his own first impression of the island when he flew from Townsville to Port Moresby in August of 1942:

> Soon after daybreak I got my first sight of New Guinea. The dark, forbidding mass of the backbone of the country, the Owen Stanley range, rising sharply from a few miles back of the coastline to nearly twelve thousand feet, and covered with rainforest jungle, was truly awe-inspiring. You didn't have to read about it to know that here was raw, primitive, wild, unexplored territory.[12]

Near the end of their flight, as Nadzab came into view, the Horner crew was met with another extraordinary sight: the American airbase, after eight months of development, was gigantic, spreading for miles across the grassy plain. Hundreds of tents were arranged in the usual orderly manner of an American military encampment, connected by a vast network of roads and streets. It was, in fact, a military city encompassing scores of square miles in what had once been the middle of nowhere, just a wide spot in the valley of the Markham River. In the center of this tent city were five long runways, three of them surfaced with steel Marston matting and capable of handling heavy bombers. The runways were connected by fifty miles of taxiways, larger than many international airports today. In the parking areas, hundreds of bombers and fighters sat lined up in long rows.

The Horner crew would remain at Nadzab for five days while their paperwork was being processed, before moving on to the most forward airfield in New Guinea at the time: Wakde Island, 630 miles farther up the coastline.

The Horner crew joins the Jolly Rogers

Shortly after their arrival at Nadzab on June 20, 1944, Lt. Horner was informed that he and his crew were being assigned to the 320th Squadron of the 90th Bomb Group, the group known as the Jolly Rogers. The 320th was the "Moby Dick" Squadron, which had as its symbol a whale with a wicked mouthful of sharp teeth, and like the bomber named "Moby Dick" (photo, p. 380) many of the 320th's B-24s had toothy mouths painted on them. Lt. Col. Harry J. Bullis was the squadron commander. Lt. Holland and his crew arrived shortly afterward and were assigned to the 319th ("Asterperious") squadron.

In their tents at Nadzab the men of the Horner crew, who only weeks earlier had been in California, were surrounded by veteran crews who had been flying bombing missions in the Southwest Pacific for a long time, some of them since the 90th had been based at Iron Range in Australia. A number of these crews had completed their combat tours and were waiting to be rotated back to the States, but had not been able to leave until their replacements arrived.

The arrival of the Horner and Holland crews thus allowed two veteran crews to go home.

Now that the Horner crew was getting close to flying combat missions, the men naturally became apprehensive about what lay ahead. Lt. Horner knew that they would soon be flying over a lot of water and jungle on long-distance strikes against the Japanese, and would also be meeting an enemy who would be doing his best to kill them. Had their training been adequate, he wondered, to prepare them for what lay ahead? All novices make mistakes, and in this business mistakes could easily prove fatal. In the interest of survival Horner decided to learn whatever he could from the pilots of veteran crews.

In the four days that they were at Nadzab, therefore, Lt. Horner tried to spend as much time as he could around experienced pilots who were either still flying missions or who had finished flying and were simply waiting for their orders to go home. He made a practice of hanging around any tent or mess hall where conversations were going on among such men, and just sitting down nearby to listen.

He remembers entering the tent of one veteran crew and the men politely moving over to let him sit down, but he was largely ignored. "I felt rather like a high school freshman among graduating seniors," he says today. He also felt as though he was, as he put it recently, "too dumb to even know what questions to ask." One useful thing he did manage to learn was that B-24 pilots in New Guinea were running their engines at higher manifold pressures and lower propeller rpms than he had been taught to do in training, in order to conserve fuel over the long distances that had to be flown. The slower the propellers turned, the less fuel the engines consumed.

Other members of the Horner crew were also listening to the chatter around them in the mess halls. They learned that a bombing mission was called a "strike" if bombs were dropped on a target, or a "sortie" if a plane was flown into enemy territory for any other reason, such as reconnaissance or to search for a lost plane. They learned that a point system was in effect for earning credit toward being rotated back to the States, and it took 100 points to complete a combat tour (more on the point system later).

The Horner crew moves up to Wakde Island

On June 25, 1944, the crew was ordered to take one of the B-24s at Nadzab and fly it over 600 miles up the New Guinea coast to tiny Wakde Island, there to join several other Jolly Rogers bombers and crews that had already been stationed there. It would be from Wakde Island that they would fly their first combat mission.

Wakde was the little coral island to which Col. Art Rogers had flown on the mission during which he had skip-bombed a Japanese ship (Chapter 27), which had been written up in a *Saturday Evening Post* article by war

Above and below: many of the bombers of the Jolly Rogers' 320th ("Moby Dick") Squadron, to which the Horner crew was assigned, had shark's teeth painted on their noses.

correspondent Charles Rawlings. Rogers had gone there to get photographs of the Japanese airfield on the island. Now, in June of 1944, the Americans owned the island and its airfield, and it would be the Horner crew's first combat duty station.

The Horner crew was assigned to the 320th or Moby Dick Squadron of the Jolly Rogers, the 90th Bomb Group. The 320th Squadron's symbol was a shark-toothed whale. Lt. Cooper, the copilot of the Horner crew and a former Disney artist, created this jacket patch for the crew's navigator, Lt. Theobald, by painting the symbol on a piece of leather cut from a leather case that formerly held a navigation tool. Theobald preserved the patch instead of sewing it onto his jacket, so that today, 74 years later, it is still in pristine condition. A black-and-white photo does not do justice to this colorful patch.

Chapter Forty-Three

WAKDE ISLAND

On the morning of the 25th of June, 1944, following their orders, the Horner crew took off from the big American airbase at Nadzab in a B-24D and headed for the tiny new forward airbase at Wakde Island, 630 miles up the New Guinea coast (Map 43-1, below). Although little Wakde Island, only 1.6 miles long by a half mile wide, with a surface area of only about 540 acres, was not large enough to hold the entire 90th Bomb Group, General Kenney had decided that at least some of the Group's planes could be based there, and the rest could stage through there on missions to the west (i. e. land on Wakde to take aboard fuel and bombs).

The Horner crew would be one of ten or twelve Jolly Rogers crews flying missions from Wakde Island. The first of the group's planes had landed there on May 27, and now, a month later, the Horner crew was joining

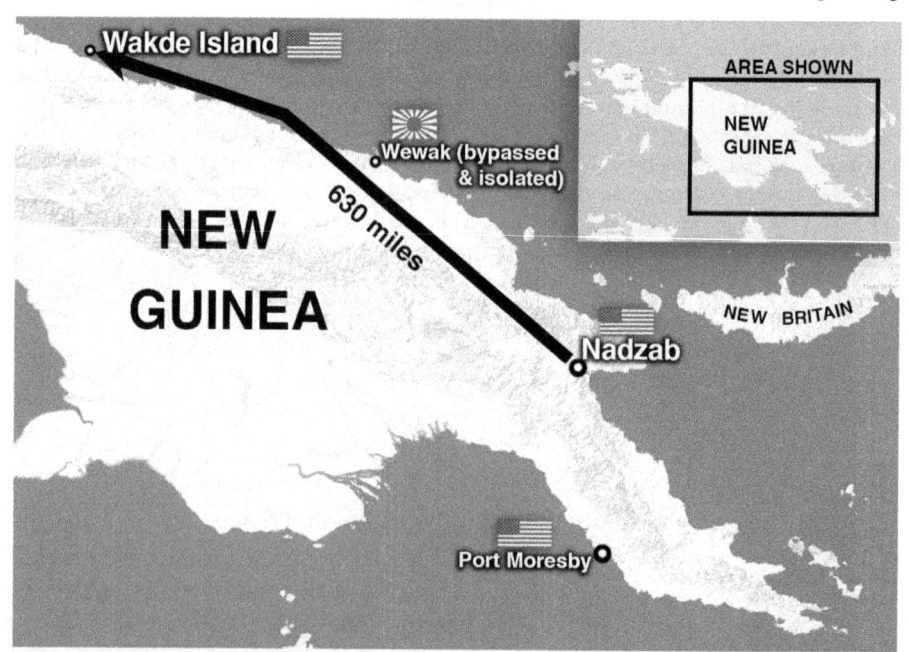

Map 43-1. On the 25th of June, 1944, the Horner crew flew 630 miles from Nadzab up to the forward airbase on Wakde Island, being careful not to pass over the flak guns at the bypassed Japanese stronghold of Wewak.

them. As soon as much larger Biak Island (200 miles farther west) fell to the Americans, the entire 90th Bomb Group would then move forward to Biak and be based there, so this splitting up of the Jolly Rogers was viewed as only a temporary measure.

The Horner crew's flight from Nadzab to Wakde Island

Lt. Cooper's flight logbook records that it took the B-24 a little over four hours to cover the distance from Nadzab to Wakde Island, giving it an average ground speed of 157 mph. After takeoff from Nadzab, Lt. Theobald, the navigator, was careful to keep the plane forty or fifty miles inland of the Japanese airbase at Wewak, which was on the coastline about halfway to their destination. Even though there were no longer any Japanese planes operating out of Wewak, and the place had been bypassed by the American advance, there were still Japanese troops there, and they still had some antiaircraft guns.

As they flew over vast expanses of jungle after leaving Nadzab, it became quite obvious to the crew why so many planes had vanished in New Guinea, and would continue to do so throughout the war (hundreds remain missing today). Any plane that went down into that endless rainforest would leave barely a nick in the jungle canopy to mark the crash site, and trying to find a downed plane in such a landscape would be like looking for a BB in a grassy meadow.

Fred Miller of the 38th Bomb Group (flying B-25s) recalled just how deadly these jungles were to downed airmen:

> "I'll give you an idea of how bad the jungle was. We had an engineer that flew with the pilot and copilot on testing an airplane after doing major maintenance on an engine—they don't take the unnecessary crewmen for that duty. They were up there and the plane started acting up and the pilot ordered the three of them to bail. So the engineer bailed out seven miles from the airstrip. The copilot bailed out three miles away. It took them seven days to rescue the engineer who was seven miles away. I was in a light search plane with an Aussie pilot and a native guide, and we flew over a native village probably less than a mile from where we could see the 'chute of the guy who'd gone down, the engineer. We dropped a gun and some food but he never got to them. They had to fly in one of their new amphibious jeeps or he'd have still been there. It took them three days to get the copilot. You just don't have any idea of what the jungle is like until you go back into it. Most U. S. soldiers never went inside the jungle because it was near suicide... So if you went down it was curtains. Except for those men we saved near our base, we never had a single P. O. W. or a single survivor from any of our men that went down."[1]

New Guinea has been described as a "green desert," and about the only animals available to eat in South Pacific jungles are bats, birds, and snakes, all very difficult to catch, and crocodiles that might eat a man instead of being eaten by him. Few jungle plants are edible. An airman who went down in New Guinea's jungles was in a very serious situation indeed, and his best hope was to be found by friendly natives (since unfriendly ones might eat him too).

As the Horner crew flew toward Wakde Island, the majestic peaks of the Owen Stanley mountain range that split New Guinea into north and south halves were passing by on their left, while to their right, in the distance, they could see the coastline toward which they were angling, and beyond the coast the limitless blue of the Pacific Ocean.

After passing Wewak they reached the coast and flew northeast along New Guinea's shoreline. The small towns of Aitape and Hollandia, which had been seized simultaneously from the Japanese by the U. S. Army's amphibious assaults on April 22, were the only friendly landmarks to be noted along the way, and they looked very small indeed against the backdrop of the endless jungle. Charles Lindbergh, after flying a fighter plane along this same coastline, wrote that American airfields along the way looked to him like "pin scratches in the great areas of jungle."[2]

New American airbases had been built at Aitape and Hollandia following their capture, but the runways were too short and too soft to handle B-24s, and thus heavy bombers did not land there except in emergencies. U. S. Army troops manned perimeters around the two towns and their airfields to keep the scattered Japanese in the jungle at bay. There were 120,000 Japanese in eastern New Guinea, and they still occupied the jungle all around these captured towns, but they were disorganized, cut off from supply, and unable to mount any serious counterattacks at this time. MacArthur, in planning his jumps up the coast, had picked his fights carefully, attacking and defeating the Japanese at selected locations, and he had expected this situation.

MacArthur maintained that when the Japanese were attacked at unexpected places and at unexpected times, as he had done at Aitape and Hollandia, their commanders were thrown into such confusion that they found it difficult to mount any effective resistance. The defeated Japanese milling around in the jungles after losing these battles had proved him right.

The Japanese 18th Army's Lt. Gen. Hatazo Adachi would attempt only one serious counterattack against the Americans in the Aitape-Hollandia area, and that would be in July. The Americans would repulse the attack, and then the Australians, arguably the best jungle fighters in the world, would chase the remaining Japanese, who were sick, starving, and cannibalizing their dead, all the way up to the north end of New Guinea where only a few would survive.

Of the 250,000 Japanese sailors, soldiers, and aviators sent to New Guinea during the war, fewer than 15,000 would remain alive by war's end.

The Horner crew saw no signs of human presence on the rest of their two-hour flight along New Guinea's northern coastline except for an occasional native thatched-roof hut beside its little garden. Lt. Theobald let the crew know when they were nearing their destination. Already, from miles away, they could see sunlight glittering on the canopies of the many airplanes parked on both sides of Wakde Island's runway, and flashes from the windshields of trucks and other vehicles moving around on the island.

Landing on Wakde Island

Lt. Horner got on the radio and called ahead to the Wakde control tower to let them know that he was inbound for landing, and asked for a traffic report, since Wakde Island was a busy place. The runway, about 6,500 feet long and a hundred yards wide, reflected back a bluish-white light in the hot sunshine as they neared it. Its surface was made of crushed coral, and it split the little island lengthwise, approximately east to west (see maps below and on next page).

Wakde Island, with the little islet of Insoemanai beside it, was only a couple of miles offshore from New Guinea's coast at Maffin Bay, and at Maffin Bay, as at Aitape and Hollandia, American troops were holding a salient in the jungle to keep the Japanese back away from the airfield. Wakde Island was

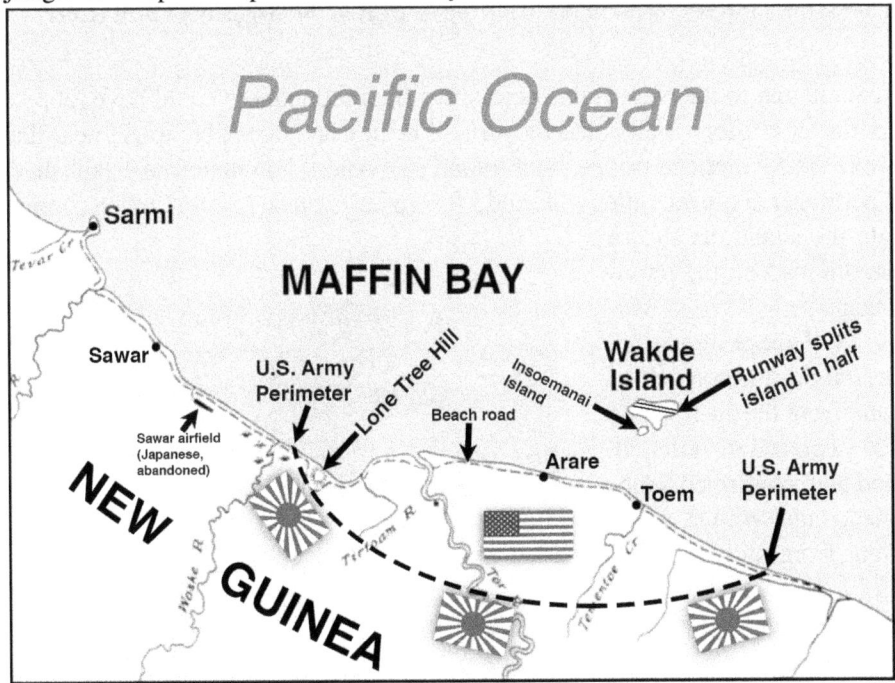

Map 43-2. Wakde Island was only two miles offshore from the New Guinea coast at Maffin Bay. The U. S. Army established a perimeter to keep the Japanese back away from the coast.

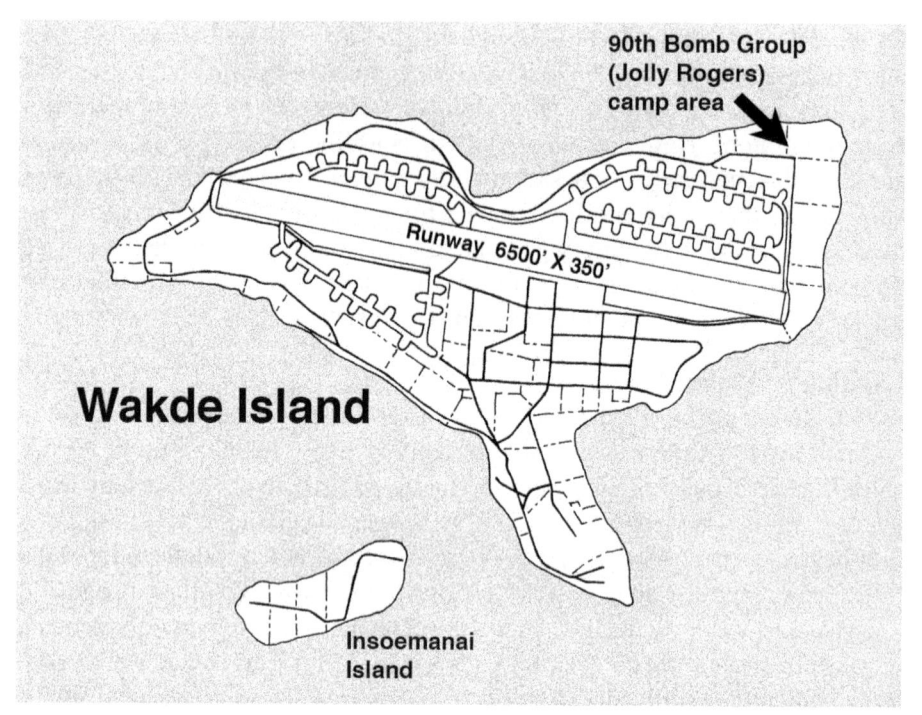

A 1944 Air Corps diagram of the layout of the Wakde Island airbase. The Jolly Rogers were allotted the northeast corner of the island (upper right in the diagram) for their camp.

near enough to the New Guinea coastline that the Japanese could have lobbed mortar or artillery shells onto the airfield if they had been able to get near the shore. The American troops (41st Infantry Division) had therefore established a perimeter about ten miles wide and a few miles deep on Maffin Bay just opposite the island, as shown on the map on the previous page.

Lt. Horner requested a straight-in approach to land from the east, which the controller granted, and then confirmed a moment later with a green light from atop the control tower, a somewhat crude structure made of coconut logs and pieces of lumber bolted together. The tower then ad-

Airfield control towers in the Pacific were rough-and-ready structures made of bolted-together coconut logs.

43. WAKDE ISLAND   515

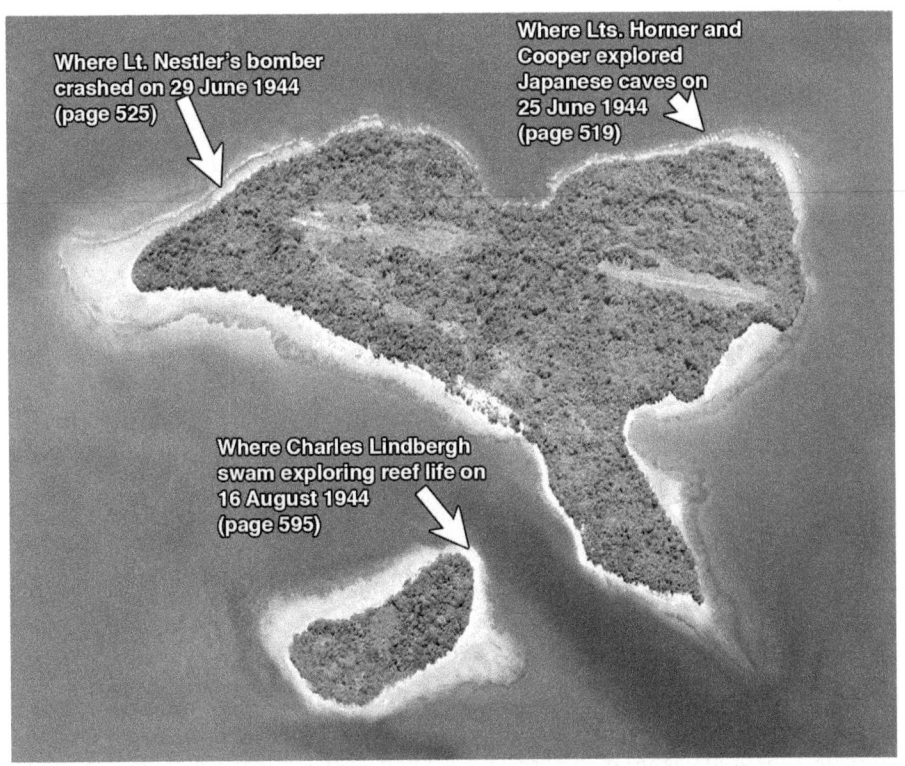

An aerial photograph of Wakde Island today (2018) shows it to be nearly all reclaimed by jungle, although traces of the runway that once split the island in half are still visible 74 years later. The wreckage of bombers that failed to lift off from the short runway still lies submerged in the sea off either end of it.

vised other aircraft flying in the vicinity that a B-24 was on final approach to land. Lt. Cooper, the copilot, set the bomber up for landing, throttling back to begin the descent, lowering wing flaps and landing gear. In the rear of the airplane the gunners, Sgts. Baca, Dale, and Carter leaned out the waist windows to get a better look at the island that they were now descending onto, which would be their home for the next couple of months.

The crew would fly their first combat mission from here, followed by a dozen more, before moving on in the middle of August to Biak Island a couple of hundred miles farther up the coast. But at the time they first landed on Wakde Island it was not known when American aircraft might be able to move up to Biak, since the battle to capture that island and its Japanese airfields, which had begun on May 27, was still in progress, being prolonged by stiff Japanese resistance. As usual, at Biak the Japanese were proving hard to dig out of their coral caves and camouflaged strongpoints in the jungle. The ground fighting on Biak was jungle warfare at its most ferocious, and the 90th Bomb Group

Wakde Island at ground level. This is the runway seen on the diagram on p. 514. The date is May 20, 1944, three days after American troops landed to capture the island from the Japanese. American engineers (Seabees) are grading a runway that runs from one end of the little island to the other, 6,500 feet long, using heavy equipment landed by LST. The Seabees began the work while they were still being shot at by the last of the 800 Japanese that the infantrymen of the 41st Division had to kill to take the island.

had been flying frequent bombing missions in support of the American 41st Division fighting there.

Bombers flying from Wakde Island would also carry out attacks on Noemfoor Island and the Vogelkop Peninsula (the "bird's head" of the buzzard-shaped island of New Guinea), Halmahera, Morotai, Ceram, and other island targets in the seas to the west, and would assist Admiral Nimitz's Central Pacific campaign by bombing Japanese positions on the Palau and Caroline Islands, and would also support the Marianas campaign. But because Wakde Island was so small, only parts of two heavy bomber groups, two fighter groups, and two reconnaissance squadrons could be based there.[3]

On that afternoon of 25 June, 1944, Lt. Horner set the B-24 down on the threshold of Wakde Island's runway, and by the time the plane had rolled out and slowed down to taxi speed it was about in the middle of the island, between aircraft parked on either side of the runway. Someone in a jeep drove out to lead him to the parking area. Following the jeep, he taxied the bomber to a parking spot alongside the runway between other bombers, and he and Lt.

Cooper shut down the engines and opened the bomb bay. As the four propellers slowed to a stop, the crewmen climbed out to investigate their new surroundings. Right away they could see that they were pretty bleak.

The pilot of another B-24, who arrived on Wakde Island a few weeks after the Horner crew did, recorded his first impressions of the place:

> Wakde resembles no island I've lived on or visited, only some I've bombed. It approximates the Hollywood version of a newly captured Jap base: the few palm trees still standing wear tattered crowns and shattered trunks; disused Jap foxholes and slit-trenches gape menacingly on all sides; piles of smashed guns, vehicles and other equipment—the detritus of war—have still to be bulldozed into the sea. Wreckage of one Zeke plane is of special interest to those of us who have only seen it at 20-thousand feet, trying to shoot us down. It's unusual to arrive at a base this soon, before it's been picked clean of "souvenirs."
>
> The place is still in bad shape from last May's invasion by U. S. troops. Rubble everywhere, bulldozed into large piles to make room for roads and campsites. The few trees left standing are stripped of their fronds.[4]

Most of the island's trees had been knocked over or damaged by either aerial bombing or artillery fire, and many were just stumps, or trunks without tops. Australian transport pilot Don Johnson said:

> On one occasion we had to land at Wakde Island while there were still shell craters in the runway. If there were 100,000 coconut trees on that island, only about 100 had tree tops left! It looked like an island of bare lamp posts.[5]

When Bob Hope's traveling troupe gave a show on Wakde Island in the summer of 1944, he started off his program by saying, "I love this beautiful island, with its magnificent palm trees . . . two of them with tops."

Today Mr. Baca remembers that the first thing the men wondered about as they set foot on the island was the source of some terrible smells that were wafting about the area. They were soon informed that the stink emanated from the rotting bodies of Japanese soldiers that had lain unburied all over the island since the battle to capture Wakde a month before. In their haste to enlarge and improve the former Japanese airfield, the American engineers had just shoved these corpses, along with wrecked Japanese equipment, broken tree trunks, and a lot of other junk, off to the sides of the runway with their bulldozers. This debris lining both sides of the runway was ten feet high in some places, and it had a lot of these month-old, decaying Japanese corpses mixed in with it. The stench of the bodies and the threat of disease posed by the millions of flies breeding on them caused some concern about a disease epidemic, so many of the corpses had been sprayed with DDT, a newly developed insecticide, but the flies and the smell persisted.

Usually, after battles in other island locations such as Guadalcanal, Okinawa, or Tarawa, the bodies of dead Japanese were disposed of by gouging out ditches or trenches with bulldozers and then scraping the corpses into the holes and covering them over with soil. No doubt some of the nearly 800 Japanese dead on Wakde Island had been pushed or dumped into some of the bomb craters in and around the runway before the craters were filled in and paved over with crushed coral.

But there were so many corpses scattered around that a lot of them had just been left to rot in the open. By this stage of the war, everyone was aware of the Japanese soldier's reputation for cruelty, fanaticism, and savagery, and Americans had heard many stories of how they tortured and murdered any allied soldiers or airmen who fell into their hands, so it was easy to consider the Japanese as something less than human and their bodies hardly worth burying except for sanitary purposes.

The stench of the putrid corpses was even more nauseating at close range, and the bodies themselves were crawling with maggots and engulfed in humming clouds of flies, but some of the men in the newly-arrived Horner crew held their breath long enough to peer down through the debris heaped up on the sides of the runway to get their first look at the enemy, in the form of these mangled and horribly grinning corpses. Any hope that anyone may have had of getting a souvenir off one of the bodies quickly vanished, since most of the corpses had already been stripped of their weapons and personal effects by the infantrymen who had killed them a month before. The macabre things would have been too disgusting to touch anyway.

Now that they were on the ground, the crew could also hear gunfire across the water on the New Guinea mainland, and they were informed that it was the American infantry expanding and defending their Maffin Bay perimeter. The Americans were also in the process of clearing the last Japanese troops off a coral knob jutting up from the beach known as Lone Tree Hill (see Map 43-2 on p. 513).*

The Battle of Lone Tree Hill had begun on June 8, and was still in progress when the Horner crew arrived on Wakde Island on the 25th, for the same reason the fighting was still going on at Biak Island: Japanese strongly entrenched in fortified caves and hidden jungle bunkers. Since from the top of Lone Tree Hill the Japanese could observe everything that was going on in the American beachhead on the coast, and on the Wakde Island airbase across the water,

---

*The hill was so named because on American maps it was marked with a single tree symbol, used to denote jungle.

the Americans had no choice but to evict them from it. This battle had been particularly vicious, since despite its name, the hill was densely covered with jungle, as well as being pocked with deep caves, and in the limited visibility of the thick forest the fighting was at close range and often hand-to-hand.

850 tough Japanese marines had defended the hill, many of them fighting from the caves, and the bodies of hundreds of them remain there to this day, sealed inside the caves, since the Americans had learned that the best way to eliminate a cave full of Japanese was to blow the entrance shut with explosives (though it took a brave man with a satchel charge to creep close enough under fire to do this).

The Battle of Lone Tree Hill, fought by the U. S. Army's 41st Division, is practically forgotten today, yet it was every bit as bloody as the better known Marine battles of Iwo Jima and Tarawa. 400 Americans died and 1,500 were wounded in the seizure of Maffin Bay, which included the Battle of Lone Tree Hill, and fifteen Americans remain missing on the hill.

The gunfire from the Maffin Bay perimeter never really ceased during the 53 days that the Horner crew was on Wakde Island, and Mr. Baca remembers that it usually increased at night, when the Japanese tried to penetrate American lines under cover of darkness. All the noise sometimes made sleeping difficult for the airmen on the island.[*]

On the day that the Horner crew arrived at Wakde Island the men were all directed to one large empty tent, and told that they could sleep there until they could erect their own tents. They dumped their personal belongings into this tent, set up a row of ten cots, and then scattered to check out their new surroundings. Being young men, and nearly always hungry, they were also anxious to locate the nearest mess tent.

Exploring a coral cave on Wakde Island

That afternoon, Lieutenants Horner and Cooper decided to take a look at the reef on the northeast corner of the island, where the Jolly Rogers were encamped (see diagram and photograph on pages 514-15). None of the airfields at Port Moresby or Nadzab had been adjacent to the sea, but the 90th's encampment on little Wakde Island was only yards from it, and the sound of the surf breaking on the shore was inviting. The 90th Bomb Group's tents were in the area where the Japanese had made their last stand at the end of the battle for the island.

Horner and Cooper walked out to the shoreline to find, not a sandy beach like the one on the southern side of the island (the side that faced the mainland), but a reef extending the full length of the north side of the island. This

---

[*]An excellent book giving the infantryman's perspective on maintaining the Maffin Bay perimeter against the Japanese is Raymond Kerns' *Above the Thunder, Reminiscences of a Field Artillery Pilot in World War II* (Kent State University Press, 2008).

was the side facing out to sea, where the coral had been worn and shaped by eons of wave action. The reef here rose six to eight feet out of the water and was split by many deep cracks and crevices. Some of the gaps were quite wide, with the waves washing in and out of them.

Looking down into some of the clefts in the reef, the two men were interested to see thousands of miniature crabs, from about the size of a dime up to a silver dollar, going about their business. They found that if they were very quiet, and moved slowly, they could watch all the little creatures moving around in the nooks and crannies of the reef, but if they dropped a pebble into the water, or made any sudden motion or sound, the little crabs would all vanish instantly.

But more interesting than miniature crabs were the numerous small caves that they found along this edge of the island. Most coral formations have cavities in them, some quite deep, and this reef was no exception. The Japanese had made the most of this and had burrowed back into some of the caves and created S-shaped entrances, roofed over with logs, and had then weighed down the logs with chunks of coral. The only way into these caves was from the ocean side. Horner was told later that during the battle to capture the island, American infantrymen had decided not to risk their lives trying to root the last of the suicidal Japanese out of these caves, so they had set drums of gasoline above the cave entrances, retreated to a safe distance, and then PT boats had run up and down the shoreline machine-gunning the barrels. Burning gasoline had run down into the caves and incinerated the Japanese inside.

Horner and Cooper found one of these fortified coral caves and decided to explore it, hoping there might be interesting souvenirs inside left by the former occupants. After they'd worked their way down into the cave, and were peering about in the dim light, Horner stepped on something that felt soft and squishy beneath his foot. It turned out to be the bloated, decomposing body of a Japanese soldier. Under his weight the balloon-like corpse popped and deflated, spraying stinking putrescence everywhere and causing the two men to quickly lose their enthusiasm for cave exploring. They made a hasty exit and decided that it was about time to return to camp anyway.

Actually, had they only known, there were plenty of war souvenirs in other caves nearby, along with (unfortunately) more Japanese corpses, but a number of these caves were never found while the Americans were there, and in fact remained untouched for nearly sixty years. On November 10, 2005, Japanese newspapers reported that the skeletal remains of numerous Japanese soldiers had been discovered in coral caves on the northeast side of Wakde Island, the same area that Horner and Cooper had been exploring.

Weapons, helmets, binoculars, and other equipment were found with the skeletons. Historians of the 41st Infantry Division recorded that during the

43. WAKDE ISLAND

Wakde Island, looking south toward the coastline of New Guinea at top of photo. Wakde was about two miles across the water from the mainland. This view shows how the runway ran the full length of the island. The coral caves explored by Lts. Horner and Cooper are at lower left in this photo, and this is also the area where the Jolly Rogers were encamped.

battle for the island some Japanese had been sealed into coral caves with explosives, just as had been done on Lone Tree Hill across the water on the mainland, and these may have been the same caves, perhaps reopened by wave action over the preceding six decades.

Oddly enough, according to one newspaper article, the skeletons of several New Guinea natives were found among the Japanese dead. What story lies behind the presence of natives among the Japanese during the battle for the island will probably never be known. The bones of the Japanese soldiers were collected from the caves and returned to Japan for cremation.

While jumping across one of the cracks in the reef on his way back to the bivouac area, Lt. Horner twisted his ankle and came limping back into camp in some pain.

The Japanese bomb the Americans on Wakde Island

After the Japanese had been ejected from Wakde Island, they retaliated in the only way they could, which was to bomb the Americans on the island as often as possible from their airfields farther up the coast and on some of the islands to the west of New Guinea. From these fields the Japanese sent one or more bombers to Wakde Island nearly every night. They had to bomb at night, since in daylight they would have been confronted by the American fighter planes based on the island, and would also have been visible to the American anti-aircraft gunners. Only in the dark, unseen, did they have a chance to approach Wakde Island and bomb it, at least until the Americans could bring up some of their new P-61 "Black Widow" night fighters (picture on p. 564, bottom).

The Japanese had no heavy bomber comparable to the American four-engine B-17 or B-24, but their two-engine medium bombers such as the Mitsubishi G4M "Betty" or the Kawasaki Ki-48 "Lilly" could carry enough of a bomb load to do some damage on an island that was as packed with targets as Wakde was. As Mr. Baca says today, a bomb dropped anywhere on Wakde was likely to hit something of value. General Kenney was well aware of the danger of basing so many aircraft on the little island, where there was no room to disperse them, but he considered it worth the risk in order to have a forward airbase with which to support the invasion of Biak, and to reach Japanese targets beyond Biak.

If things went as Kenney planned, American airplanes wouldn't be packed into Wakde Island for very long, but would soon be moving forward to new airfields. Huge Biak Island would soon be available (it was hoped), with plenty of room for longer runways, and small Owi Island, just offshore from Biak (at 5 miles by 1.4 miles still larger than Wakde), was also chosen to base some bomber and fighter groups on. There had never been any Japanese troops on Owi, so development of an American airfield was already underway there.

But for a couple of months in the spring and summer of 1944, Wakde Island was the most forward airbase the Americans had, and it hosted airplanes of every type, from the infantry's little L-4 Piper Cub spotter planes all the way up to the B-24s, and included P-38 and P-47 fighter planes, C-47 cargo planes, and light and medium bombers (A-20s, and B-25s). All these aircraft ended up parked on both sides of the runway practically wingtip-to-wingtip.

On the night of June 5-6, twenty days before the Horner crew arrived, two Japanese bombers took advantage of this situation to loose strings of bombs onto the parked American airplanes and damaged eighty of them, six beyond repair. Of Wakde Island General Kenney wrote:

> **Wakde had been put in shape and, within a week after its capture, was crowded with aircraft based there or refueling on the way to or returning from distant attacks. Our main heavy bomber strength was still back at Nadzab, as the Hollandia fields had not turned out as well as we expected and were only suitable for fighters and light bombers. The Maffin Bay Area was too soft to be practicable for quick airdrome construction, so we were crowding Wakde to the limit and hurrying development at Owi as fast as we could.**
>
> **I knew we were inviting trouble by parking aircraft almost wingtip to wingtip on Wakde, but we had to have our fighters for-**

ward to maintain cover over the shipping constantly unloading at Biak, and besides the flow of airplanes from the United States to the Pacific was now going along nicely. I no longer had to rebuild my wrecks from the ground up as I had been forced to do a few months previously, so we stacked them in and relied on attacking the Nip airdromes to keep the Nips from attacking us.

The Nip, however, refused to play the way I wanted him to and for a week, beginning on the 5th of June, until I got some night fighters operating at Wakde, he put over some mean night attacks. On the night of the 5th a Jap bomber blew up a bomb dump and had everyone on the island believing that an earthquake had hit the place. Between the Jap's bombs and our own we lost several hundred drums of gasoline and three P-47s.

Two nights later I lost ten more airplanes on the ground, and the night of the eleventh, the devils dug holes in the runway that took us all the next day to fill in and burned up another four airplanes. The Jap bombers came over at such frequent intervals all that night that the men spent nearly the whole time in their foxholes.[6]

The Horner crew's first Japanese air raid

On the day of their arrival on Wakde Island, the Horner crew had been warned about these almost nightly Japanese bombing raids, and since they were all sleeping in the same tent that first night, they were shown a slit trench just outside the tent that they could all jump into for protection if an attack occurred.

That evening, as the crew was getting ready for bed, they decided to keep their clothing on in case a dash to safety became necessary during the night. Then the question arose as to whether or not they should keep their shoes on as well. If they had to run to the slit trench they would need to have their shoes on to keep their feet from being cut up by the sharp coral surface of the island. Walking on coral, Mr. Horner remembers today, was like walking on broken glass, and even the leather soles of shoes became shredded after a week or two on the island. If an air raid occurred, having to put on their shoes in the dark before sprinting for the slit trench would waste precious time. The men decided it would be best to sleep with their shoes on, so as to be prepared for instant running.

However, the ankle that Lt. Horner had sprained that afternoon was hurting him, so he decided to take his shoes off after all. Mr. Baca remembers him commenting that surely there would be enough time for a man to put his shoes on if an air raid occurred. Everyone then went to sleep, and the next few hours passed peacefully.

Sometime after midnight, the stillness of the night was shattered by a tremendous blast that caused every man in the tent to leap from his cot and go sprinting for the tent door. This turned out not to be the explosion of a Japanese bomb but the muzzle blast of a nearby American antiaircraft gun that had begun firing at the sound of incoming Japanese bombers. The men stampeded out the tent door and dove into the slit trench, landing in a pile at the bottom. All but one of them, that is, for the men soon noted that Lt. Horner was not among those present. Between the explosions of the Japanese bombs, and the blasting away of the American antiaircraft guns, the men could hear Horner's muffled voice back inside the tent, shouting "My shoes! My shoes! I can't find my shoes!"

Lt. Horner had sprung from his cot like everyone else, but had landed on his sprained ankle, which had collapsed beneath him and left him sprawled on the floor. It took him a while to grope about in the darkness for his shoes, get them on, and go limping out of the tent. However, being the last man into the trench had its advantages, he discovered, since the first few who had jumped in had been bruised and battered by the others landing on top of them.

While the men waited out the air raid in the shelter of their trench that night, Lt. Horner had to endure some good-natured ribbing about the folly of a man on Wakde Island going to bed without his shoes on. That night was the crew's first real experience with the possibility of death at the hands of the enemy, and it served as their introduction to life on a front-line airfield in the war zone. Six days later they would also fly their first combat mission.

Lts. Ostafin and Cooper get the first taste of combat

Before the Horner crew flew a mission together, however, two of its officers, Lt. Cooper and Lt. Ostafin, each took a flight with other crews, filling in as substitutes for regular crewmen who were unavailable for one reason or another. On his flight, Lt. Ostafin dropped his first live bombs on an enemy target, and his bomber returned without incident.

Lt. Cooper's first combat flight, on 28 June, 1944, was more exciting. His bomber flew an eight-and-a-half hour mission to bomb a Japanese airfield at Samate, near the "beak" of the New Guinea "buzzard" (map, opposite). American intelligence suspected that Japanese bombers had been flying missions from that airfield against the Americans fighting on Biak, and the goal of the strike was to destroy as many of the enemy's aircraft as they could catch on the ground, as well as make the Japanese airfield unusable by cratering it.

Cooper's mission met with good results—the bombers dropped sixty-four tons of high explosive bombs on the Samate airfield and the Japanese aircraft parked around it. The Japanese were caught by surprise and there was no enemy opposition over the target, either from enemy fighters or flak guns on the ground. The excitement occurred as the returning bombers passed over the nearby town of Sorong. There the plane that Lt. Cooper was copiloting came under heavy and accurate fire from Japanese flak guns that American intelligence had not known were there, and consequently had not warned the crews about.

One flak shell exploded just beneath the bomber's nose and sent shrapnel flying up through the cockpit floor, making a large hole in the flight deck along with many smaller ones.* Luckily no one was hurt, but the parachute pack on which Lt. Cooper was sitting was peppered with bits of shrapnel, stopping them short of his skin, and the nearly spent fuse or nose cone of the shell went bouncing around inside the cabin before finally coming to rest on the floor. A crew member who tried to pick it up for a souvenir burned his hands on it and had to wait until it cooled off.†

Map 43-3. Lt. Cooper's introductory mission was to bomb a Japanese airfield at Samate.

Having lethal shrapnel flying around inside the cockpit on his first combat flight was a nerve-wracking introduction to combat flying for Lt. Cooper. Back at Wakde Island, he wrote down the facts of his first flight in a small leather-bound notebook that he would keep throughout his combat tour. It would eventually record 48 missions. Being an artist, on the first page he drew an impressive rendering of the Jolly Rogers skull with crossed bombs emblem.

The deaths of the Nestler crew

The next day, the 29th of June, the Jolly Rogers were scheduled to fly a mission against the Japanese airfield at Manokwari, located on the back of the New Guinea "buzzard's" head (see map 43-6 on p. 573). The Horner crew was not one of the crews scheduled to fly on this strike. However, Lt. Holland and his crew were scheduled to go, and their B-24 was second in line for takeoff.

---

* The armor plate that had been removed from the cockpit floor at Townsville to save weight would have been useful here.

† This information was furnished by Cooper's son Michael, who remembered his father telling him about the incident, and Mike also remembers as a young boy spreading the parachute out on the front lawn of their home and his father pointing out all the holes in it.

The first plane to take off was piloted by Lt. Joseph Nestler of the Jolly Rogers' 319th Squadron.

As Lt. Holland and the rest of the pilots watched, Nestler's bomber lifted off well before the end of the runway, but instead of continuing to rise, it sank back down and its wheels touched the runway again, causing it to lose speed. Then, to the shock of everyone watching, the plane ran off the end of the runway, across the reef, and into the ocean where it exploded so violently that almost nothing was left intact of either the plane or its crew.

Ten young men's lives had been extinguished in the blink of an eye. Debris flew high and wide and splashed down all over the area, while patches of burning high-octane aviation fuel floated on the sea. Killed in the crash were:

    2nd Lt. Joseph D. Nestler
    2nd Lt. Harold I. Severson
    2nd Lt. Edward C. Sprague
    2nd Lt. Clarence J. Sauer
    S/Sgt. Paul B. Schroeder
    S/Sgt. Lester R. Worthington
    Sgt. Louis T. D'Aliso
    Sgt. Clifford Fielder
    Sgt. Roscoe R. McCrea, Jr.
    Sgt. Alfred E. Schmitt

The bodies of the men were so fragmentary when recovered that only two of them, Schmitt and Sauer, could be identified. The remains of the rest of the men are buried today in a group grave at Fort Scott National Cemetery in Kansas.[*]

A witness in the control tower later speculated that when the plane lifted off, Lt. Nestler had tapped the brakes to stop the wheels from spinning, which was standard procedure in preparation for retracting the wheels up into the underside of the wings. But before he could retract the gear, the plane sank back down and touched the runway again on the stopped wheels. The drag as the huge tires skidded, and then began to spin again, slowed the plane down, and there was no room left to regain flying speed before running off the end of the runway. If this is indeed what happened, it would not have been a problem on a longer runway, but on this one of barely adequate length it was fatal. The combination of Wakde Island's dangerously short runway and heavily loaded bombers would claim more aircraft during this spring and summer of 1944.

---

[*] The remains of the crew were first taken back to Finschaffen for temporary burial, and after the war, in 1950, were returned to the U. S. Ft. Scott in Kansas was chosen as a central location for all the families attending the funeral.

LOUIS T D'ALISO CPL
CLIFFORD FIELDER SGT
ROSCOE R McCREA JR CPL
JOSEPH D NESTLER 2D LT
PAUL B SCHROEDER AVN CADET
HAROLD I SEVERSON 2D LT
EDWARD C SPRAGUE 2D LT
LESTER R WORTHINGTON S SGT
AIR CORPS
JUNE 29 1944   1621

Eight of the ten men of the Nestler crew are buried in a single grave at Ft. Scott National Cemetery in Kansas. After the explosion of their bomber, their remains were too fragmentary to be individually identified.

The explosion of Nestler's bomber just off the end of the runway resounded like a thunderclap all over Wakde Island, and it certainly did no good to the nerves of the men on the Horner crew, who were thinking about their first combat mission scheduled for the next day. As the fuel and wreckage of Lt. Nestler's bomber burned on the reef and in the water beyond the end of the runway, the control tower radioed Lt. Holland and the rest of the pilots waiting to take off that the mission would be postponed for a few hours while ground personnel cleaned up the wreck site. There were aircraft parts scattered all over the runway, and the men in the boats collecting the remains of the crew in the water off the end of the runway didn't need more bombers skimming just over their heads on takeoff.

Around noon, when Lt. Holland and the rest of the Jolly Rogers bombers did take off on the mission, the formation ran into bad weather trying to reach Manokwari and turned back. They found their secondary target socked in as well, so just before landing at Wakde they dumped their bombs on Hill 360 at nearby Sawar, on Maffin Bay, a Japanese strongpoint located on the New Guinea mainland only a few miles across the water from Wakde Island (see map 43-2 on p. 513).

Although bombing Hill 360 had not been on the schedule, the U. S. troops holding the perimeter against the Japanese there certainly appreciated the unexpected help. Referring to the short distance between Wakde Island and where the bombers dropped their bombs, the historian of the Jolly Rogers called it "the shortest bombing mission ever." Indeed, if the bombers had taken off, turned straight toward Hill 360, dropped their bombs, and landed again on Wakde, the entire mission would have been accomplished in a few minutes.

The first combat mission of the Horner crew

The next day, June 30, 1944, two days after Lts. Ostafin and Cooper had taken their first combat flights as fill-ins with other crews, the complete Horner crew undertook its first mission together. The crew had been alerted to the mission the day before on the bulletin board outside Group headquarters. There the twelve crews who were going on the mission, and the tail number of the bomber assigned to each crew were listed. From the memories of the three crew members alive today, and from the records of the 90th Bomb Group and other sources, this mission can be reconstructed in detail to show how a typical bombing mission in the Southwest Pacific was conducted.

Aircraft preparation

Before a mission, ground crews of various types: Maintenance, Ordnance, Armament, and Communications, went over a bomber thoroughly to prepare it for the flight. These crews all had specific duties to perform to get each plane ready to go.

A common and often nearly continuous sound from the flightline of any airbase occupied by the Jolly Rogers was aircraft engines being revved up and tested by the Group's mechanics. Each of a heavy bomber's four engines was a complex piece of machinery that required continual maintenance by highly skilled technicians to keep in peak condition. Four dozen bombers, the approximate size of the 90th Bomb Group at this time, meant nearly two hundred engines to keep in service, a never-ending chore that fell to the Group's Maintenance Section.

In the Pacific war theater the mechanics usually had to work outdoors in the open, standing on portable scaffolds, working in rain, dust, sun, and wind, as well as at night under the glare of work lights powered by portable generators. The tropical air was so humid that bare steel rusted in a matter of hours, even when it

More unsung heroes: the mechanics who kept the big bombers flying.

wasn't raining. The sun near the equator was so intense that anything made of metal, including the aluminum skins of aircraft, or a mechanic's tools, became too hot to touch after just a few minutes' exposure to it.

The men of the Maintenance Section had one of the most difficult jobs of the war in keeping sophisticated aircraft functioning under such primitive frontline conditions. Not only the engines but the entire aircraft and all its complex mechanical systems had to be kept in repair by these men. Since the B-24 underwent continual modifications at the factories that built it, and there were four major model changes, at one point mechanics had to consult four different manuals in order to work on the planes. The air war against Japan would not have been possible without the skill and dedication of these hard-working aircraft mechanics. Everyone associated with them, especially pilots and aircrews whose very lives depended on their work, remembers that they did a magnificent job despite the many hardships imposed on them by the Pacific environment.

The flight line of a heavy bomber group was an especially busy place on the morning of a mission. The mechanics, who had often worked through the night, made last minute adjustments to the engines, checked over the oxygen equipment in each plane (although oxygen was rarely used in the Pacific—the planes didn't usually go high enough for the crews to require it, but it had to be available in case it was needed)—and filled up each plane's fuel tanks with over 2,700 gallons of aviation fuel, pumping it from tanker trucks. They also checked to make sure the engines had the required 240 gallons of oil and the tires were properly inflated.

Meanwhile the Ordnance Section brought ten 500-pound demolition bombs for each plane, using small tractors pulling trains of bomb trailers (on Wakde Island the bomb and fuel dumps had been placed on the southeast corner of the island, across the runway from the Jolly Rogers campsite). After the bombs were delivered to the aircraft, the Armament Section men took over and installed fuses and tail fins on them, then hoisted them up into the bomb bays with hydraulic lifts and

Typical bomb storage dump on a Pacific island such as Wakde.

hung them on their shackles.

The armament crews also loaded the belted ammunition for the ten .50-caliber machine guns on each plane and checked the operation of the power turrets. Extra boxes of ammunition were placed near the machine gun stations so that the gunners could reload their guns if necessary. While all this was going on, the Communications Section was inside the plane checking out its transmitting and receiving radios, and making sure each crewman's microphone headset on the intercom system was working. Thirty minutes before the scheduled departure time of a bomber, its four engines were run up and checked by the mechanics one last time. The pilot would therefore be starting up warm engines.

An armament crew loading bombs onto the bomber "Twin Niftys" pauses to have their picture taken. "Twin Niftys" was later shot down in a raid on Wewak as described in Chapter 31.

Crew briefing

On the day of their first mission, the men of the Horner crew, as with all the crews going on the mission, were awakened and alerted before dawn by orderlies from headquarters, who came into their tents with flashlights to rouse each man from his cot and get him up and moving. At about 5 a.m., after dressing, the crewmen walked over to the mess tents for breakfast. After eating the tasteless rehydrated

Jolly Rogers crews at a pre-mission briefing. Getting all the information straight could be a matter of life or death, which explains the concentration reflected in the men's faces.

Map 43-4. The first bombing mission of the Horner crew, on June 30, 1944, was to bomb a Japanese radar station on the island of Noemfoor, 290 miles to the west of Wakde Island.

food, often flapjacks with marmalade or powdered sugar substitute on them, the Horner crew joined the eleven other Jolly Rogers crews assigned to this mission at the Intelligence tent for their pre-mission briefing.

The men took seats on folding chairs in the tent, and the Intelligence Officer stood on a small stage in front of them with a wall map behind him. On the map he pointed out the day's target: a suspected Japanese radar station at Cape Keretsbari, 290 miles west of Wakde Island on the small island of Noemfoor (Map 43-4 above). This was a small, nearly circular island about 8 miles in diameter. The radar station to be destroyed, along with some storage and barracks buildings, was near one of three airfields that the Japanese had built on the island.

Noemfoor had become a place of interest to the American high command. The battle to capture Biak's airfields was still raging, day and night, with the Japanese continuing to resist stubbornly, and MacArthur growing impatient. He wanted those Biak airfields badly, and in the middle of the battle he had dismissed the original commander of the 41st Infantry Division, Major General Horace Fuller, for allegedly moving too slowly, and replaced him with General Robert L. Eichelberger. The change of commanders made no difference; the Japanese continued to fight as hard as ever from their cave-riddled coral bluffs, the going was just as slow, and the Biak airfields had still not been captured by the end of June. Exasperated, MacArthur started looking around for other islands, including Noemfoor, where, as on Wakde Island, he could temporarily base some American bombers until Biak fell. Americans were scheduled to stage an amphibious and paratroop assault on Noemfoor to capture that island and its airfields just two days after this bombing mission, on July 2, so this strike was part of the preparation for that invasion.

MacArthur was trying hard to keep up with the advance of the Navy and Marines in the Central Pacific as they moved north toward Japan, island by island, in bloody battles that were making headlines in American newspapers (those battles, too, were fought to capture airfields, or the sites for them). If he could move his heavy bombers far enough forward, to the Biak area, he could support Admiral Nimitz's assault on the Palau islands, and after that the Marianas. But even more important than supporting Nimitz, to MacArthur, was not falling behind his rival in the race toward Japan. He was none too sure at this point whether the Joint Chiefs of Staff were going to approve his plan to liberate the Philippines, which had been his obsession ever since he'd been driven out of those islands in the first months of the war. The brass in Washington might yet decide that it would be best to bypass the Philippines and push on to Japan.

In fact the Washington planners did have a plan to bypass the Philippines and strike against Formosa instead, or against Japan itself. The ultimate decision whether or not to invade the Philippines would be President Roosevelt's, in his Constitutional role as Commander-in-Chief. On July 26, 1944, MacArthur and Nimitz met with Roosevelt at Pearl Harbor, and MacArthur presented his case: liberating the Philippines was a moral imperative, he said, to free the gallant Filipino people and expunge a defeat of American arms (his own defeat, the general might have added). It was evident to everyone that MacArthur's large ego was also involved. The head of the Joint Chiefs of Staff, Gen. George C. Marshall, reminded MacArthur that "personal feelings and Philippine politics" should not obscure the war's prime objective, the defeat of Japan.

To MacArthur, however, liberating the Philippines and defeating Japan were one and the same. "I shall return," he had promised the Filipinos when he left, and he had not meant "after the war." President Roosevelt ultimately backed MacArthur and authorized his invasion of the Philippines. Some historians now believe that the invasion was unnecessary, and the terrible American and Filipino casualties that resulted from invading the islands, not to mention the destruction of the great city of Manila, could have all been avoided if the islands had been bypassed. There were other places from which the invasion of Japan could have been staged, and the Japanese holding the Philippines would have been compelled to surrender after Japan had been defeated, just as they would do at Rabaul, Wewak, and every other bypassed Japanese stronghold. However, everything is clear in hindsight.

The Horner crew and the other crews preparing for their mission on June 30, 1944, knew nothing of this larger strategy, of course. They were absorbed in the matter at hand, which in the case of the Horner crew was staying alive and succeeding in their first-ever combat mission. In the briefing tent that morning, the Intelligence Officer provided the takeoff time, described the target, and pointed out on a large-scale map of the target area the locations of Japanese antiaircraft guns known to be arrayed around it. He told them that they would have no fighter escort on this mission.

He then dismissed all the gunners and flight engineers, while the pilots, navigators, radiomen, and bombardiers remained for further briefing. For them he assigned the position of each bomber in the formation during the bomb run, and gave the pilots their "base" altitude for the mission. In radio communications between planes, pilots could refer to this base altitude plus any deviations from it without giving away their true altitude to any Japanese who might be listening in. For example, if the base altitude was eight thousand feet, a pilot could radio to other pilots that he was flying at "base plus two thousand," or ten thousand feet. Many Japanese spoke English, and it had to be assumed that they were monitoring all American radio communications. If Japanese antiaircraft gunners could determine the exact altitude of approaching American bombers, they could set the fuses of their shells to explode at that altitude.

The briefing officer described the route and altitude to the target, waypoints (landmarks) along the route, the location of the Initial Point (IP) where the bomb run would commence, and the compass heading from the IP to the target. He prescribed how to break away from the target after the bombs had been dropped, and the route back to Wakde Island. In case the target proved to be obscured by clouds, he designated an alternate target, and if both primary and alternate targets were found to be cloud-covered, he directed the crews to jettison their bombs into New Guinea's Lake Rombebai on the way home. Bombers rarely brought their bombs back to base, and there was in effect at this time a rule prohibiting them from dumping bombs into the sea, probably because someone at MacArthur's headquarters with an overactive imagination considered doing so hazardous to American shipping or submarines.

For the radiomen, the Intelligence Officer provided the radio frequencies to be used during the mission, and in case a bomber was disabled and had to ditch, he gave the emergency frequency to use in calling for help from Catalina amphibious rescue planes or American submarines standing by.

The Weather Officer then took over and briefed the men on the expected direction and strength of winds aloft, weather fronts, and what cloud cover they could expect on the way to and from the target. While the briefings were in progress, the men penciled notes to take with them. When the briefing was over, the men all walked over to the supply tent and drew their parachutes, then returned to their own tents to pick up the handbags containing their flight gear, and since they knew it would be cold at high altitudes, they also took their flight jackets and gloves.

By this time one of the Horner crew's enlisted crewmen had run over to the mess hall to get a loaf of bread and a big can of Spam with which to make lunches to eat on the plane, and this was packed into a cardboard box to take along. Every crewman put on the shoulder holster that held his .45 pistol, for use in survival if his bomber went down. 2 1/2 ton trucks with bench seats in the beds pulled up to the tents and everyone threw their bags aboard and climbed in. The trucks took each crew to the bomber it had been assigned for the mission.

Getting aboard

No one recorded the tail number or nickname (if any) of the bomber that the Horner crew was assigned to fly that day. Lt. Cooper's flight log identified it only as a J-model B-24. After they were dropped off at the airplane, which was parked with its bomb bay doors open, the men threw their parachutes and bags up into the bomb bay and climbed aboard while the ground crews made their final checks. The canvas cover over the bomber's cockpit windows, which was kept on while the plane was parked to prevent the sun from turning the cockpit into an oven, was untied and removed.

Mechanics rotated the propellers of each engine by hand, six blades (two revolutions), to clear the lower cylinders of any oil or fuel that

The radioman's station in a B-24 was on the flight deck behind the copilot (the pilots' instrument panel and cockpit windows are visible behind him). On the Horner crew, this was Sgt. Bruni's station.

may have accumulated there during the half-hour since they had been test-run. Once he was aboard, each bomber crewman carried his parachute and bag to his crew station, stowed them, and checked the equipment he was responsible for. The bombardier, Lt. Ostafin, went into the bomb bay and looked over the bomb load, to confirm that the bombs were hung properly on their shackles and the safety pins were in the fuses. Up on the flight deck, radioman Sgt. Bruni sat down at his table and checked out his radios.

The pitot tube (circled) on its streamlined arm always had a cover on it when the bomber was parked. One of the duties of the flight engineer before a flight was to see that this cover was removed so that the plane's airspeed indicator on the instrument panel would function.

Before he got aboard the plane, the flight engineer, Sgt. Eady, went to the nose of the bomber and removed the canvas dust covers from the two pitot tubes, which were small-diameter metal tubes mounted on streamlined metal arms protruding from both sides of the aircraft's nose, with their ends facing forward (one is circled in the photo above). The tubing ran back to the airspeed indicator on the plane's instrument panel, the instrument that measured the bomber's forward speed through the air. The tubes were covered while the bomber was parked so that they wouldn't get clogged by windblown debris or insects. If the covers were forgotten and left on while flying, the airspeed indicator would be inoperative. A non-working airspeed indicator could make things difficult for the pilot, since many of his actions (such as lowering the wing flaps or landing gear) depended on knowing the bomber's exact speed.

After he climbed aboard, Eady went up on the flight deck and turned on the valves that supplied fuel to each engine. He then checked to make sure that the two main fuel gauges, which were sight gauges (with the actual fuel level visible in glass tubes) read full. These gauges were located on the bulkhead of the bomb bay at the rear of the flight deck, behind the pilots.

Before climbing aboard, Lts. Horner and Cooper walked around the aircraft giving it a quick preflight check, making sure everything looked normal. Once they were inside, up on the flight deck and in their seats, they adjusted the seats to a comfortable position (Lt. Cooper, at six-foot-three, usually had to move his seat back to gain some leg room) and set the rudder pedals so they could reach them easily. Then they strapped in and went through their cockpit pre-engine-start checklist. Lt. Horner removed and stowed the lock that prevented the controls from moving while the bomber was parked, then checked the controls for free movement, rotating the wheel right and left to move the ailerons, pushing and pulling the yoke fore and aft to test the elevators, and alternately pushing the pedals to operate the twin rudders. Sgt. Eady opened the hatch above the flight deck, stuck his head out, and confirmed for Lt. Horner that the control surfaces were all moving as they should.

Eady then went down through the hatch at the rear of the flight deck to the forward part of the bomb bay, where he started up the little gasoline-powered auxiliary power unit (APU) located there, commonly known as the "putt-putt." This little generator supplied enough booster power to the plane's batteries to start engine number three.[*] After #3 was running, its own generator would then power the starters of the other three engines. #3 also had the hydraulic pump on it that provided power to the brakes, wing flaps, and landing gear. Outside the bomber, ground crewmen stood by with fire extinguishers, a routine precaution during engine starts.

When it was time to start the engines, Lt. Horner, in the cockpit's left seat, called "Clear Left!" out his side window to warn anyone on the ground to get clear, or remain clear, of the propellers on the left wing, and Lt. Cooper did the same on the right side. Men outside on the ground called back "Clear!" Lt. Cooper turned on the ignition switches for all four engines, plus the master switch for the entire electrical system, which were located on the instrument panel on his side of the cockpit. He also made sure the cowl flaps on each engine were open to provide cooling air while the plane was on the ground, and he set the adjustable-pitch propellers to low pitch (high-rpm) for ease of starting.

With the little generator in the bomb bay now puttering away with a sound like a gas-powered lawnmower, Lt. Cooper hit the fuel booster pumps and primed engine #3 for starting, being careful not to overprime it, which could flood the engine and risk a fire (one reason why ground crewmen stood ready with fire extinguishers). Then he started the engines in the order 3, 4, 2, 1 (the two inboard, then the two outboard). Each engine's inertia starter revved up to a high-pitched whine, a sound that many men would remember all their lives, then the engine was engaged to the starter through a clutch. When the starter was engaged there was a sound like someone kicking a bucket of bolts, then the propeller began to rotate slowly, engine valves clanking, until the engine came jerkily to life with a cough and puffs of white exhaust smoke as some

---

[*] See the engine numbering diagram on p. 3.

of its cylinders began to fire. Then all the rest of the fourteen cylinders joined in with a roar and the propeller snapped into a blur that instantly blew away the smoke. Inside the plane the crewmen felt the airplane vibrate into life all around them.

After starting, each engine settled down to a steady rumble as Lt. Cooper adjusted the throttles to idle, and soon all four engines were purring smoothly with the subdued thunder of a combined 4,800 horsepower. The gunners in the rear of the plane, with nothing to do at the moment, watched the proceedings out the waist windows, smelling the pungent aromas of aviation fuel and exhaust smoke. The wind from the propellers blew into their windows and gave them a little relief from the heat. Sgt. Eady hoisted himself up halfway through the hatch above the flight deck, so that he was out in the open from the waist up, looking out over the top of the cockpit and wings with a fine view of the engines and everything else around him. Many of the flight engineers in the other bombers did the same, and stayed there until the plane had taxied to the threshold of the runway.

Lts. Horner and Cooper switched on their radios, and could then hear the tower talking to the pilots of planes that were already rolling, as well as other pilots talking to one another. After a brief warm-up of all engines, with Lt. Cooper monitoring the gauges on the instrument panel to confirm that each engine had good oil pressure and temperature, it was time to roll. Lt. Horner motioned to the ground crewmen to pull the wheel chocks, then advanced the throttles, revving up the engines to taxi the big bomber out of its parking space and join other planes lining up and moving down the taxiway. The nosewheel of a B-24 was not steerable—it only castered—so a pilot steered his plane with a combination of throttles and brakes. As the plane began to move, the men standing on the ground behind it squinted into the blowing dust kicked up by the propwash, and some turned their backs to the wind blast as it rippled their clothing.

Wakde Island soon became a very noisy place with the 48 big Pratt & Whitney R-1830 "Twin Wasp" radial engines of all twelve bombers rumbling and revving, their wheel brakes squealing intermittently as the pilots maneuvered them into position in line, headed for the takeoff end of the runway. Everyone on the island could tell by all the noise that another heavy-bomber mission was going out.

Airplanes always take off into the wind whenever possible, and because of the prevailing wind patterns on the island, which blew either toward or away from the mainland, depending on the time of day, most morning takeoffs on Wakde Island were toward the west, and most landings at the return from missions in the afternoon were toward the east.

Since the runway on Wakde Island ran the full length of the island, about 6,500 feet, its threshold was on the edge of the ocean no matter which direction a plane took off, east or west. From the cockpit of a bomber it looked as though a plane might be taxiing almost into the sea, until, right near the edge of the reef, it turned and swung onto the runway threshold.

When a green light flashed from the hand-held "biscuit gun" in the control tower, located halfway down the field on the south side of the runway, the first plane took off, and the others in line then began taking off at intervals of a few minutes each. An interval of a couple of minutes between takeoffs allowed time for the air turbulence stirred up by a plane's wings and propellers to settle down, and not buffet the next plane taking off. Small tornadoes are generated by the wingtips of heavy aircraft, and these whirlwinds can linger on the runway for a while after a plane takes off. The fact that these bombers were so heavily laden that they were barely flying anyway when they staggered into the air meant that it would be especially dangerous if they ran into severe air turbulence from a previous plane's takeoff at such a critical time.

As each aircraft took off, the remaining ones in line advanced one plane length, and the bomber at the head of the line checked its engines. After first swinging 45 degrees to the taxiway, so as not to blow its prop wash on the plane behind him, the pilot set the parking brake and then revved up each engine in turn to check its magnetos and cycle its propeller blades.[*] These checks completed, the engines were throttled back to an idle and the plane was ready to roll out onto the runway. The bombers ahead of Lt. Horner's took off one after the other with no problems, which was reassuring to everyone after what had happened yesterday to Lt. Nestler's crew.

When his turn came to take the runway, Lt. Horner swung the big plane around onto the threshold by revving up the two engines on the outside wing, at the same time holding the brake on the inside wheel. He stayed as close as he could to the end of the runway so as to make use of every foot of it, in keeping with the old pilots' adage that "you can't use the runway behind you or the altitude above you." Once the plane was pointed at the far end of the runway, he pressed the toe brakes to hold it in position. Lt. Cooper closed the cowl flaps to only 1/3 open, to streamline the engine cowlings, and set the wing flaps to ten degrees or 1/4 down (wing flaps give an airplane's wings more lift for takeoff). Sitting in takeoff position now with the engines idling, the two pilots watched the control tower for the green light. Sgt. Eady, who had been standing in the hatch above the flight deck since the airplane first began to roll, out in the open from the waist up, enjoying the breeze and the activity all around him from his elevated perch, now got down and closed the hatch.

---

[*] The adjustable propeller blades could bite the air either a little or a lot, depending on how the pilot set their angle.

Since only the pilots in a B-24 had seats to belt into, everyone else in the plane either stood or sat with his back to a bulkhead near his station, and braced himself against it to prevent being thrown forward in case of a sudden stop or jolt—not that it would have done much good if their bomber went into the sea as Lt. Nestler's had done. Everyone by now was aware of the B-24's tendency to come apart in water landings, and a plane fully loaded with fuel and bombs might explode as well as break up, as Nestler's had so tragically demonstrated yesterday. It only took a little spark from somewhere to ignite all the hundreds of gallons of high-octane gasoline that would spray from the ruptured fuel tanks.

Sgt. Eady stood between the two pilots' seats with a hand gripping each seat back, as all flight engineers did during takeoff. It was his job to call out the airspeed on the takeoff run, so that the pilot and copilot could concentrate on the situation outside the cockpit instead of watching the instrument panel. Everyone's lives were now in the hands of the pilot, and it was a comfort to the members of this crew to reflect that in Lt. Horner they had one of the best, as he had demonstrated on more than one occasion. In Lt. Cooper they also had a skilled and mature copilot—in fact Cooper, at 27 years old, was practically an old man to the younger crewmen. There was no reason for the men of this crew to worry about the competence of either one of their pilots.

What they did worry about, with good reason, was the shortness of the runway, and perhaps the mechanical condition of the airplane. And some of the crew were no doubt thinking that this is exactly what the Nestler crew had done the day before, and Nestler may have been a good pilot too, but everyone on that crew was now dead. The pilot's actions may have had nothing to do with that crash; it could have been caused by some mechanical fault in the plane beyond anyone's control. As with so many crashes without survivors, no one would ever really know the cause.

And what did the crew know about the airplane they were flying this morning, anyway; it had only been assigned to them at random. What condition was it really in? Most of the Jolly Rogers' mechanics were back at Nadzab; the ones on Wakde were short-handed, and some said that the 90th Bomb Group's B-24s on Wakde Island weren't getting maintained as well as they could be, owing to a lack of tools and spare parts, not to mention the fact that these planes were hard-used and often highly stressed under combat conditions no matter how well they were maintained. There were many things to worry about if a man allowed himself to think too much.

This would be the Horner crew's first takeoff from the dangerously short runway of Wakde Island, in a bomber fully loaded with bombs and fuel, and it was their first combat mission. Unlike all the training flights in the States, and the flights between airbases, this time they were heading into known danger: enemy airspace. Later on, these missions, and these takeoffs from Wakde, would become a familiar routine, but the worry of an overloaded bomber not lifting off from the short runway would always be present.

"On those takeoffs from Wakde Island," says Mr. Baca today, "we always 'sweated it up.' 'Sweating it up' meant just kind of forcing that airplane up into the air by sheer willpower. Every takeoff from that little island was dangerous. Sometimes it seemed like the wheels almost touched the water off the end of the runway."

Sgts. Baca and Dale, the waist gunners, closed their waist windows for the takeoff, because it streamlined the fuselage somewhat and lessened the air drag, allowing the plane to gain speed faster. The downside was that it made it even hotter inside the plane, and with the ambient air temperature nearly 100 degrees it was plenty hot enough to begin with. Their part of the fuselage, back behind the bomb bay, was a sweltering, claustrophobic place during takeoffs, and it would also have been pitch dark had there not been some light coming forward through the window of the tail turret. Young Sgt. Carter, the tail turret gunner, sat with the two waist gunners on the fuselage floor, their backs to the bomb bay bulkhead, just inches from all the tons of high-explosive bombs on the other side of it, and joked nervously. Sgt. Baca could see that the high-strung Sgt. Dale was getting jittery again, and made small talk with him to try to keep his mind occupied and calm.

Takeoff

Up on the flight deck, the pilots saw the green light flash from the control tower. While still holding the brakes, Lts. Horner and Cooper smoothly advanced the four throttles on the console between them up to full takeoff power, 29 inches of mercury and 2,700 rpm, the noise level rising until the four big, unmuffled engines bellowed out in a full-throated roar. Throughout the plane the crewmen's adrenaline levels rose with the sound. Nearly five thousand horsepower made the bomber shudder and tremble like a live thing. Then Lt. Horner released the brakes and the heavily loaded plane began to roll, slowly at first, but steadily gaining speed as it lumbered down the coral-surfaced runway, creaking and groaning, lurching a little from side to side.

Wakde Island's undulating runway had a big dip in the middle that made it a bit like a roller-coaster ride to an airplane taking off,[9] and when a plane approached flying speed, the pilot had to try to keep it from skipping across that low spot and running into the rise on the other side, which could slow it down. A bit of forward pressure on the control yoke kept the wheels in contact with the runway as they rolled through the depression. As the bomber accelerated down the field, Sgt. Eady called out the speed on the airspeed indicator as it rose: 60. . .70. . .80, and at 90 miles per hour Lt. Horner eased back the control yoke a little to lighten the weight on the nosewheel.

As Mr. Horner remembers it today: "On Wakde Island's runway, you had to horse an airplane off the ground sooner than you'd like to." The speed at which the pilot could raise the nose during the takeoff run varied with the individual plane and the load, but 88 to 98 mph was typical, and anywhere above 85 the nose began to feel light.

"Every plane was different," Mr. Horner recalls. "Some would be a few miles per hour faster or slower than others, and that could mean a difference of hundreds of feet of runway." With any bomber, however, at about 90 mph Horner would ease the control yoke back a bit to see if he could lift the nosewheel off the ground yet. If he could do so, and easily, then he knew the airplane was about ready to fly. If the nose did not come up, however, and still felt heavy, he would wait a little longer and then try again (and of course, all the while the end of the runway was approaching). Once the nosewheel was up off the ground, with the airspeed reading around 100 mph, the airplane would begin to fly, and Lt. Horner could roll back the elevator trim tab a little. He had become accustomed to lifting off with a certain amount of back pressure on the yoke, and he could adjust that pressure to exactly the feel he wanted with the elevator trim control.

Lt. Theobald, sitting up forward in the nose of the plane and looking out through the small plexiglass window on the left side of the fuselage, could see the usual orange exhaust flame trailing back from engine number two, and below that the landing gear strut bouncing up and down with the bumps in the runway. As the plane approached flying speed, he watched the strut lengthen, slowly, as the weight transferred from the wheels to the wings. The wings were flexible, and he could see them bend upward a little as they took the load.

After the nosewheel lifted, the main wheels slowly left the ground as well, with agonizing slowness, as thirty-five tons of airplane took to the air, with everybody aboard "sweating it up" on Wakde's short runway. The bumps and jars from the surface of the runway lessened until they finally ceased altogether, the end of the runway flashed past, and they were out over the water, beyond the place where the Nestler crew had died less than 24 hours before, climbing slowly but steadily. As the plane left the ground Sgt. Baca and the others in the rear of the fuselage felt the ride smooth out and heard the sound of the engines take on a different note. They were airborne. Everyone breathed a sigh of relief.

Once the plane was off the ground, copilot Cooper began slowly raising the wing flaps, a few degrees at a time, trading lift for speed. By around 120 mph he had them at only five degrees, and at 135 mph he brought them all the way up, at the same time raising the landing gear. As the gear tucked away into the underside of the wings with a thump, and the flaps came up flush with the wings, the crew could feel the plane accelerate as the drag of the wheels and flaps in the slipstream disappeared, as though someone had just let off an invisible brake that had been dragging. Now the plane was streamlined, climbing, and their first bombing mission was underway.

Climbing to cruise altitude

Still climbing at takeoff power, Lt. Horner banked the plane slightly to the left and took up the 282 degree compass heading that Lt. Theobald, the navigator, had given him, which put them on a direct course for Noemfoor Island, by cutting across the "shoulder" of the New Guinea "buzzard" (Map 43-4 on page 531). They angled in toward the New Guinea coast, crossed the shoreline, and then were flying over the dense jungle of the mainland, headed northwest. The bombers that had taken off ahead of them could be seen in the distance at a higher altitude. The planes would not assemble into a formation until they were near the target, and that was nearly two hours away.

The bomber continued to climb, in a nose-high attitude, until the altimeter read twelve thousand feet above sea level, the cruising altitude for this particular mission. Lt. Horner let the plane climb an additional 500 feet before he lowered the nose to level flight. As the plane leveled out and its speed built up, he eased back the throttles and set them to cruise RPM, letting the plane slowly settle down to the assigned twelve thousand feet. Lt. Cooper fine-tuned the RPM of all four propellers until they were nicely synchronized, so that the throbbing sound of the engines gave way to a smooth, steady hum, and they cruised along with 155 mph reading on the airspeed indicator. In pilot slang, the plane was "on the step," or flying smoothly and efficiently.*

"A B-24 actually flew like a big lump of coal," Mr. Horner says today. "If it slowed down and 'fell off the step' you could feel it. Then you'd have to drop the nose and build up some more airspeed. Otherwise it would burn gas like crazy. Every ship flew a little differently, but you could always feel whether one was 'on the step' or not. An indicated 155 mph would keep most any of them there."

In the back of the plane, Sgts. Baca and Dale swung up the hatch covers of their waist windows and latched them to the ceiling. With the windows open, cool air flooded in, flushing out the last of the steaming heat that had accumulated in the plane while it was parked on the ground. Now the gunners

---

* It could actually be dangerous to fly the B-24 "off the step" or too slowly. On a mission to bomb Wake Island in June of 1942, Maj. Gen. Clarence L. Tinker was in a B-24 flown by his aide, Capt. Coleman Hinton. Hinton decided to fly the plane slowly, near its stall speed, in an attempt to conserve fuel, despite being warned repeatedly by other B-24 pilots that it was a dangerous thing to do. Thirty miles south of Midway Island the plane was seen to stall and nose over into clouds, and it was never seen again, evidently crashing into the ocean. Tinker Air Force Base in Oklahoma is named in honor of Gen. Tinker, the first U. S. general to die in WWII, and he likely died because his pilot tried to fly his B-24 "off the step."

could take a look at their surroundings. Baca's eyes took a moment to adjust to the brilliant equatorial light, but after they did, he found himself gazing out over one of the most remote and primitive scenes in the world, the incredibly vast, dense, and wild rainforest of New Guinea (photo, p. 361). The green carpet of interwoven treetops stretched away for miles to the southern horizon, where the distant, hazy mountains of the Owen Stanley range raised their snowcapped peaks into the clouds.

"If you ever went down into those jungles," Mr. Baca says today, "you were a goner, that's all there was to it. Almost no one ever came out of those jungles alive." It was well known by this time that if an airman had to bail out, or survived a crash, and the Japanese didn't get him, the jungle almost certainly would.

In less than an hour they had passed over the shore of New Guinea again into the Pacific Ocean, and were once again over open water. Now they were crossing the open space between the "buzzard's" shoulder and the back of its head (see again map 43-4 on page 531). The next land they would see would be their target, the small island of Noemfoor, where they would drop their bombs on the Japanese radar station beside one of three airfields the enemy had built on the north end of the island.

While the scattered bombers droned on toward their target, everyone was able to relax for a couple of hours, or as much as anyone could relax on his first combat mission, with all the unknowns to worry about. Would they be met by the machine-gun and 20-mm cannon fire of defending fighter planes? Or ground fire? Or both? The answers would not be long in coming.

The air at 12,000 feet was refreshingly cool, around 55 degrees Fahrenheit, and it didn't take long for the men to actually feel cold. The chill at high altitudes is why some crewmembers would take extra canteens of water along on a mission, or a few cans of beer, so that after they got back to base they'd have something cool to drink. With no refrigeration on the island, it was one of the few ways for a man to get a chilled drink in the tropical heat. It was not uncommon to find cans of beer and other drinks stashed around the interior of a bomber by ground crewmen, who were also looking forward to a cold drink when their bomber returned.*

Twelve thousand feet was a typical altitude for Pacific bombing missions. A B-24 operated more efficiently at high altitudes, and ten to twelve thousand feet had been found to be a good trade-off between bombing accuracy and safety from ground fire. The higher the altitude from which the planes bombed, the less accurate was the enemy's flak, but also the less accurate the bombing. In Europe, Allied bombers flew from 20,000 to 30,000 feet, as high as the

---

* Other ways to cool a can of beer were to squirt it with a pressurized bug bomb before opening it, or let aviation fuel from a parked plane drip on it (from the gas overflow vent on a wing) and evaporate, and a few other tricks that clever soldiers came up with.

bombers could go, to try to avoid the highly accurate German flak guns. Flying at only twelve thousand feet over Germany's numerous and deadly flak gunners would have been akin to suicide. However, at 30,000 feet it was so cold, sometimes as low as 60 degrees below zero, that any exposed skin became frostbitten, and if a crewman lost his oxygen mask, or the flow of oxygen to it was interrupted for only a few minutes, it could mean death.

In the Pacific, where bombers rarely tried to attain such heights, flying any lower than ten thousand made a plane too easy a target for flak, while twelve thousand was about as high as humans could go without having to breathe supplemental oxygen. In other words, at twelve thousand and below, the crewmen didn't have to wear their oxygen masks. "I can't remember ever wearing an oxygen mask in the Pacific," says Mr. Baca today. Twelve thousand feet was a good all-around compromise.

Unlike the Germans, the Japanese were not, for the most part, good flak gunners, nor did they have as many antiaircraft guns as the Germans did. The best Japanese gunners were placed around high-value installations such as the oilfields at Balikpapan on the island of Borneo. Many airmen felt that the most accurate Japanese ack-ack gunners were the ones aboard their warships, since those ships depended on antiaircraft fire for their very survival against air attack.

On the way to the target at Noemfoor, Sgt. Eady, not having much to do up on the flight deck behind the pilots, opened the hatchway back to the bomb bay and walked across the catwalk to the rear of the plane, where he joined the three gunners, talking and smoking. Eady, Dale, and Carter all smoked, but Baca did not, so the clouds of smoke wafting around in the back of the plane always annoyed him. To converse, the men had to practically shout over the drone of the engines, just a few feet away from them out the waist windows, but they managed. About a half hour from the target, Lt. Horner's voice came over the intercom to tell Sgt. Baca, the crew's armorer, that it was time to arm the bombs. Baca then left the others and entered the bomb bay from the rear.

Bomb fuse with arming propeller and safety pin.

The bomb bay had a narrow (6-inch wide) metal beam, or catwalk, running down its length that a crewman could walk on, but his body was a snug fit between the bombs in their racks on either

43. WAKDE ISLAND

Jolly Rogers bombers headed to a target.

side of him. Below the catwalk were the closed clamshell doors of the bomb bay, but the doors were made of thin metal that would not likely support the weight of a man, so it was not wise to step off the catwalk.* Sgt. Baca went to each one of the ten 500-pound bombs hanging in the bomb bay and pulled a safety pin out of a small propeller on its nose. The propeller was part of the bomb's fuse, and the safety pin prevented it from turning (photo, left).

In order for a bomb to arm itself, the little propeller had to spin for a certain length of time, driven by the airstream while the bomb was falling. The propeller unscrewed itself while unlocking the firing pin of the bomb. After the bomb had fallen about 500 feet, the propeller dropped off and the bomb was armed—the fuse ready to trigger the explosive upon impact with the ground, unless it was a time-delay fuse, in which case its timer was activated.

In the bomb bay, even when all the safety pins were removed, the bombs were still prevented from arming themselves inside the airplane by a long piece of piano wire that was attached to the top of the bomb bay and threaded through

---

* Occasionally, in Europe, the bomb bay doors would freeze shut at the very high altitudes that the bombers flew, in which case the bombs were simply dropped right through the flimsy doors, and the doors replaced later.

all the propellers to prevent them from spinning. When the bombs fell from the bomb bay, the piano wire pulled out and remained with the plane, leaving the propellers free to spin. Thus, with both the safety pin and the piano wire in place, the bombs were doubly safe from accidentally arming themselves inside the bomb bay.

After he had pulled all the safety pins out of the bomb fuses, Baca returned to the rear of the fuselage and reported over the intercom to Lt. Horner and to Lt. Ostafin, the bombardier, that the job was done and the bombs were ready to drop.

Approaching the target

A short while later the gunners heard Lt. Horner tell them over the intercom: "Gunners, test your guns." Sgt. Eady stubbed out his cigarette and made his way forward through the bomb bay to the flight deck, which was his combat station, while Sgts. Baca and Dale pushed out the wind deflectors in front of their waist gun windows and latched them (photos above). These vertical strips of metal, angled outward to deflect the slipstream, diverted a good bit of the wind away from the waist windows to take some of the air pressure off the waist guns, making them easier to aim. Then Dale and Baca picked their machine-guns up off the

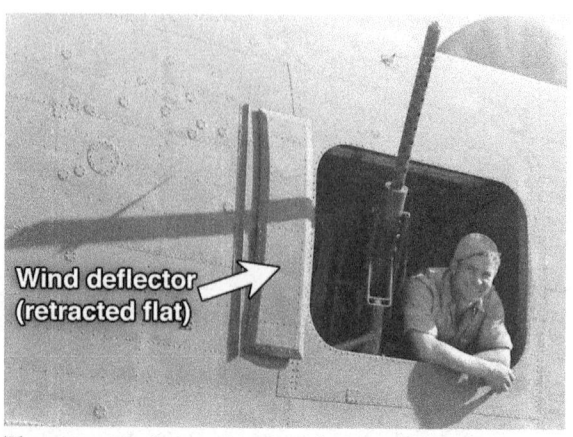

The waist windows of a B-24 had wind deflectors that could be pushed out to deflect wind away from the gun and gunner. In this picture the deflector is folded flat against the fuselage. In the picture below it is in the extended position.

At least one bomber in each squadron carried a camera to record the results of a bombing mission. Aerial cameras were very large because a large negative was needed to record all the details of a distant target. In this photo the right waist gunner's wind deflector is in the extended position, to take the wind pressure off the camera, or the waist gunner's gun.

floor of the fuselage and set them on their mounts on the bottom sills of the windows and locked them down (see diagram of waist gun mounting, right). They pulled on the guns' charging handles to cock them, pointed them down at the water, and rattled off a few test rounds.

Sgt. Carter crawled rearward through the tunnel behind the waist gunners to his tail turret, sat down in the seat, charged his twin guns, and fired a few rounds downward from them too. Up in the nose of the plane Sgt. Rogalski worked his way forward into his cramped nose turret and did the same, while on the flight deck Sgt. Eady hopped up into the seat of the top turret and tested that turret's guns. The turret gunners also swung their electrically powered turrets from side to side and ran the twin guns up and down, making sure the power was on and the turrets working.

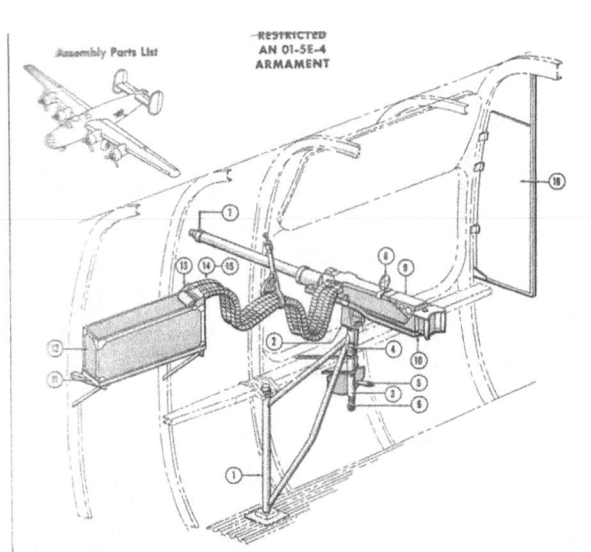

Diagram of the machine gun in the waist window of a B-24, showing how it was mounted and how the belted ammunition was fed to the gun.

All the gunners then took up watch, intently scanning the skies in all directions for enemy fighter planes. This was the first time the Horner crew's gunners had faced the real threat of enemy planes, and tension ran high.

The bomb run

As they neared the Initial Point (IP), Lt. Horner called the bombardier, Lt. Ostafin, down in the nose of the plane at his station just behind the nose turret, to confirm that he was ready to release the bomb load. Ostafin replied that he was on the job. At the Initial Point, which was always some easily recognized landmark, such as a cove on the coastline, or a small island, the twelve bombers assembled, took up the heading to the target, and began the bombing run. As they did so they maneuvered into three tight formations of four planes each, with the pilots taking up the positions they had been assigned at the pre-mission briefing that morning. Any enemy fighter plane that attacked the bombers now would be facing the massed guns of all the bombers, and the bomb pattern on the ground would also be tight.

However, this was also the time that a bomber formation was most vulnerable to ground fire, since it had to fly straight and level and could take no evasive action until the bombs were gone (the distance between the IP and the target was usually about twenty miles, or six minutes of flying time). But over Noemfoor, on this day, there was no ground fire, nor were there any fighter planes to be seen in the air.

Everyone in the crew could feel the slight vibration that passed through the plane as the two pairs of bomb bay doors opened, each door rolling up the outside of the fuselage like the cover of a roll-top desk. Ostafin would not be required to use his bombsight on this mission, nor would any of the other bombardiers in the formation except for the one in the lead plane, since they were all keying on the lead bomber. When the lead bombardier released his bombs, all the other bombardiers would do the same. Thus the bombardiers who could see the lead plane kept their eyes glued to it, while any bombardier who could not see the lead plane watched the leader of his own four-plane formation. The pilots concentrated on keeping the formation tight and steady. Then the lead bombardier let his bombs go, and an instant later all other bombardiers toggled theirs away as well. "Bombs away," reported Lt. Ostafin over the intercom.

Each bomber, suddenly lightened of its load of five thousand pounds of bombs, shot upward like an express elevator, and the waist gunners and anyone else who was standing up had to hang onto something to keep his balance. When their plane settled down again, along with their stomachs, waist gunners Baca and Dale couldn't resist looking downward and rearward from their windows to see where the bombs hit. "That was a bad habit we developed," says Mr. Baca today. "We should have been watching for Jap fighters all the time, not watching where the bombs went, but we always wanted to see where they hit."

On this mission the bombs had been released slightly early, and Baca saw the first of them splash and explode in the water just offshore from the island, throwing up great geysers of water, but the rest of them walked up the beach and right through the buildings of the Japanese radar station and other structures near the shore and blew them to bits.

Sgts. Dale and Baca, as well as Carter, who had an excellent view from his tail turret, saw flashes of light and circular shock waves blasting out as the bombs, sixty tons of them in all, detonated all over the target area. The ground boiled with great clouds of upthrown dirt and debris, and a few moments later a deep, thundering growl could be heard even above the drone of the bomber's engines. Fires broke out on the ground and long plumes of dirty smoke rose into the sky, visible for miles. The target appeared to be destroyed. One of the bombers on every mission had a big aerial camera aboard (p. 546), and the photos it was taking would be analyzed later to gauge the extent of the destruction. At any event, the Horner crew's first mission was a success. This was what all the training had been for.

The return to Wakde Island

After the bombing run, the bomber formation banked around and took up a heading for home. For a while the planes held their tight formation, in case they were attacked by fighter planes. But there would be no opposition from the enemy this day—no flak came up, no fighter planes attacked. In that regard this first mission turned out to be something of an anticlimax for the crew. As the target, and the danger, faded behind them, the pilots relaxed and the bomber formation loosened up. Japanese fighter planes only rarely attacked bomber formations very far away from their own bases. What fighters remained to the Japanese at this stage of the war were kept near their airfields to defend them, and in addition, owing to American submarines sinking their supply tankers, they didn't have enough fuel reserves to range out very far from their bases.

Halfway back home the gunners relaxed their vigil at their guns, and some of the men in the back of the Horner crew's bomber lit up cigarettes again, once more annoying Sgt. Baca with their smoke, as they discussed the flight and watched the ocean and jungle scenery pass by out the waist windows. Someone in the crew made sandwiches from the tin of Spam and the loaf of bread that had been brought along, and each crewman got one, washing it down with refreshingly cold water from his canteen. About two hours and 20 minutes after leaving Noemfoor, Wakde Island came back into view. The bombers lined up for landing, and one by one the twelve big airplanes touched down and taxied over to the parking area, where the crew chiefs and ground crews awaited them, and the pilots shut down their engines. Total time in the air for this first mission for the Horner crew, as recorded in Lt. Cooper's mission diary, was four hours and forty-five minutes.

The bomber crews climbed out of their planes through the bomb bays, back into the oppressive heat and humidity at ground level, and tossed their gear into the waiting trucks, then climbed aboard themselves, and the trucks took them over to the tents of the Group's Intelligence Section, where officers were waiting to question them about what they'd seen and done on the mission (this was standard procedure after all missions). After the interviews were concluded, on their way out of the tent the men met medics who dispensed an ounce of whiskey to each man, or, if the man preferred, dumped the liquor into his canteen to save for later. The men were then free to go back to their tents and sack out if they wished. Later the gunners would return to the plane to clean their machine guns, a chore they faced after every mission.

Japanese bombers hit Wakde Island again

On the evening of their first bombing mission, back in camp, the Horner crew and everyone else on Wakde Island found themselves under Japanese bombs again. The Japanese retaliated for the Noemfoor raid that same night,

Jolly Rogers bombers returning to Wakde Island after a bombing mission. The island and its runway are visible beneath the wing of the plane in the foreground. Note the wakes of small Army watercraft going to and from the island. Wakde was two miles offshore from the mainland of New Guinea, and there were regular shuttles constantly going back and forth.

their twin-engine Betty bombers arriving over Wakde Island around 11 PM. When the air raid warning sounded (usually someone firing a rifle or pistol into the air, Mr. Baca remembers today), the Horner crew had to jump from their cots (with their shoes already on their feet, of course) and race to cover again, along with anyone else who wasn't manning an antiaircraft gun, just as they'd done on their first night on the island.

The Japanese bombers did some damage on this night, which was not surprising considering the number of aircraft and the mountains of supplies of all types that the Americans had jammed onto the little island. One of their bombs hit a fuel dump, a collection of 55-gallon drums of aviation gas on the south side of the island, across the runway from the Jolly Rogers encampment. The fuel went up with a huge blast and a great flash of light, and other bombs destroyed a P-47 fighter plane and damaged an A-20 light bomber parked beside the runway, but no one was injured. Little sleep was to be had by the Americans for the rest of that night, for there were two more air raid alerts, one at midnight and another at 4 A.M., but both turned out to be false alarms and

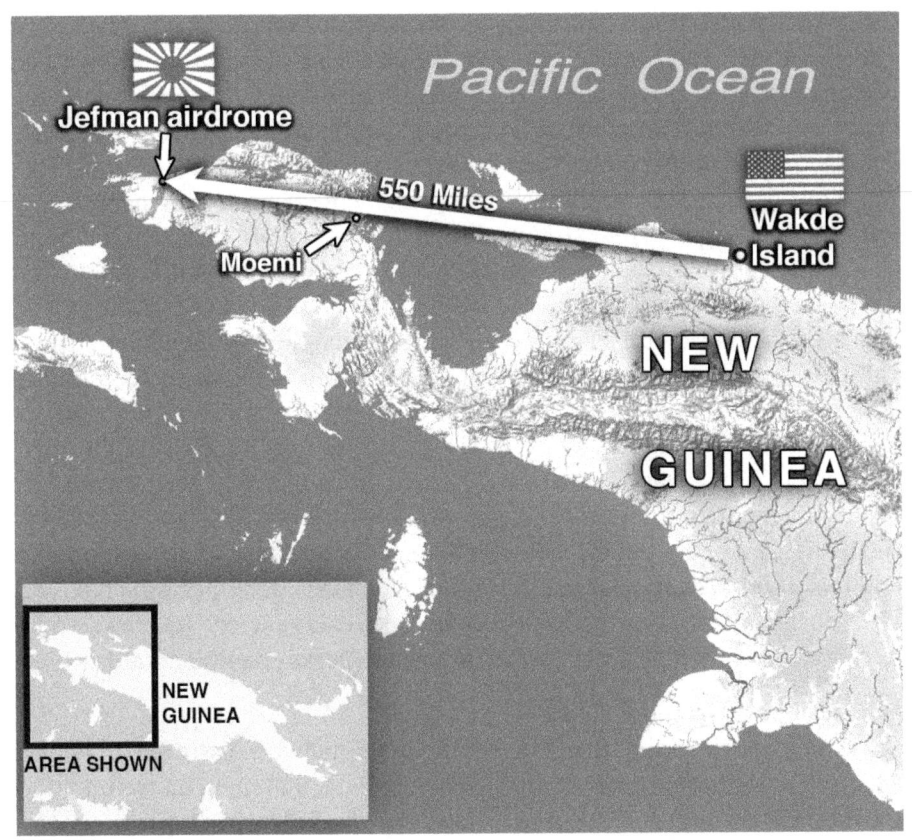

Map 43-5. The second bombing mission of the Horner crew, on July 4, 1944, was to bomb a Japanese airfield at Jefman, 550 miles west of Wakde Island. On the return trip the bombers passed over another Japanese airfield at Moemi and were shot at by flak guns.

no more bombs fell. With no mission to fly the next day, the men were able to catch up on their sleep after sunrise.

During this month of June, 1944, the Jolly Rogers lost five bombers with most of their crews, 48 men killed, the most recent deaths being the Nestler crew on the 28th. As usual, most of the losses were due to accidents and bad weather—only one of the five planes was lost to enemy action. The total number of deaths in the 90th Bomb Group up to this time, from the time the Group had been formed in the States on April 15, 1942, was 600 men killed.[7]

The second combat mission of the Horner crew

The Horner crew's second mission was flown four days after their first one, on the 4th of July, and this time it took seven and a half hours for the bombers to reach their target and return. On this strike they bombed a Japanese airfield on the shoreline of a small island named Jefman, just in front of the New

Guinea buzzard's beak, 550 miles to the west of Wakde Island (Map 43-5, previous page). Intelligence believed that Japanese planes from Jefman had been harassing the Americans fighting on Biak Island. Once again no enemy opposition was encountered over the target, but on the way back to Wakde Island the Jolly Rogers bombers passed over a Japanese airfield at Moemi. This was a mistake, for Japanese antiaircraft guns there opened up on them as they went by. Lt. Cooper wrote afterward in his mission diary that "Jap flak gave us [a] 4th of July celebration." Sgt. Baca also wrote home to his family to tell them that the only fireworks he had seen on the 4th of July were Japanese.

This mission saw the Horner crew's first experience with antiaircraft fire. Only Lts. Cooper and Ostafin had seen flak bursting in the sky before, during their first flights with other crews. As the black puffs of smoke blossomed out all around them, accompanied by the sharp crack of exploding shells, the highly excitable young waist gunner Sgt. Dale was at first startled, then terrified. In his fright he turned from his waist gun window, grabbed Sgt. Baca around the shoulders, and clung to him. Baca finally shook the frightened youth off and told him, "Get back to your gun!" None of the planes were hit by the flak, and Dale finally calmed down. Eventually he, like everyone on the crew, would learn to tolerate flak, if not ignore it, as just another on-the-job hazard.

Life on Wakde Island

As mentioned earlier, the 90th Bomb Group had been assigned a bivouac area in the northeast corner of little Wakde Island, and the men were told to set up their own tents there. First, however, the fallen trees, jungle undergrowth, detritus from the infantry battle in May, and other obstructions had to be cleared away. The quickest way to do that would have been with bulldozers, but when the Seabees were asked if they could come over for a short while and clear the Jolly Rogers tent area, they replied that they were too busy for such work just then—the smoothing of the runway and similar tasks had priority.

In the meantime a new and unexpected hazard appeared in the camp area: falling palm trees. Whenever the wind blew, some of these towering trees, up to fifty feet high, would come crashing to the ground, sometimes half a dozen at a time. A few of them fell onto tents, luckily empty ones, and flattened them. They could have killed any man they fell on, and in fact some Marines on Bougainville Island were killed by falling palm trees after a battle there. It was only luck that no one on Wakde Island had yet been hurt by them.

Examination disclosed that the trunks of many of these trees had been hit and weakened by artillery shells or bomb fragments during the American pre-invasion bombardment of the island. Some trees had toppled over immediately, but many others had only been damaged and remained standing, although only barely, and any significant puff of wind might bring them down.

Damaged trees could be identified by slashes across their trunks or by brown rust stains showing where metal was embedded.

The Seabees had grown skilled at knocking over palm trees with bulldozers, so taking down the weakened trees was another job for them, but whenever they were asked to do it the story was always the same: the airfield had priority, and they were too busy working on it to bring over a bulldozer anytime soon. However, the airmen soon discovered a method of temporarily altering the priorities of the Seabees, and that was simple bribery. And the best bribe of all was a bottle of liquor.

The value of a bottle of gin

Money was of little use on the island, which didn't even have a PX to spend it in, but a bottle of liquor had considerable trading value. In the diary that Charles Lindbergh kept during his six months in the Pacific, he described what a bottle of gin could accomplish (Lindbergh was on Owi Island at the time, up the coast from Wakde near Biak Island, but it could just as well describe the situation on any Pacific island occupied by Americans):

> "[A bottle of gin] was more effective than the signatures of all the stars [generals] on the island. We couldn't get a bulldozer when we needed it—none available for two weeks—but we got one immediately for a bottle of gin. There wasn't a foot of lumber to be had anywhere, but one bottle of gin brought 4,000 feet at once. The same way with cement and some cloth we needed. It's a disgusting situation, but you can't get anywhere at all on this island without a bottle of gin—and with one you can buy about anything."[8]

Lindbergh, a lifelong teetotaler and nonsmoker, thought that anything related to liquor was "disgusting," but a lot of other men, including those who ran the U. S. Army, disagreed with him. In fact the Army provided a liquor ration to all its troops, just as it did cigarettes, and a man who didn't smoke or drink could hoard his ration to use as trading material. Bottles of liquor were also brought back by airmen returning from leave in Australia. Mr. Horner remembers today that once a month he was allotted a fifth of rum and two bottles of wine, which, not being much of a drinker himself, he saved to trade with other men for things he wanted or needed.

However, a lot of the beer and liquor that the troops were supposed to receive never reached them. The distribution of a ration of beer at nearby Maffin Bay, just across the water from Wakde Island on the mainland of New Guinea, might give some idea why. There a young lieutenant named Raymond Kerns, who normally piloted an L-4 (Piper Cub) artillery spotter plane, was assigned to supervise the unloading of a cargo of beer that was supposed to go to the troops of the 33rd Infantry Division, which was maintaining the perimeter against the Japanese. A supply ship had pulled up to the dock and the beer was brought up from the hold. Of this experience Kerns wrote:

> There was some sort of a general plan, as I understood, to furnish one case of beer per month to each soldier in our division and, I suppose, other divisions in this hot, humid, and utterly uncivilized part of the world... But the 33rd had been down there now for several months without having received the first bottle of brew. It just so happened that two or three months' ration for our troops had arrived at Base F just in time to join our convoy for Maffin Bay, and now the small freighter was given priority at the solitary small dock to unload the beer and then to reload with cargo of the outgoing 31st Division. My job was to supervise the unloading and proper distribution of that shipload of beer...
>
> Some of the detail worked in the hold, filling the cargo net, while others were on the dock, loading the trucks. I moved about the ship and the dock, doing what I could to prevent the theft of the entire cargo. Members of the ship's crew would sneak cases into remote areas of their vessel; our own men would hide cases on the wooden bracing under the dock; men on the trucks, including the guards, would divert cases of beer to their own personal or their units' interests, and other cases simply vanished into thin air. This went on all night, and when all accounts were considered, it was estimated that the equivalent of one truckload of beer had failed to reach any known destination in the task force.[9]

In the Jolly Rogers bivouac area on Wakde Island, where palm trees crashing to the ground at odd times were making everyone jumpy, enough bottles of liquor were pooled among the airmen to strike a deal with the Seabees. A few bottles changed hands, and a bulldozer immediately came rumbling over to knock down all the trees in and around the camp area, and it also cleared away undergrowth and debris left over from the infantry battle. After that, the Jolly Rogers had a smooth, open area in which to pitch their tents and no threatening trees hanging over their heads.

After the Horner crew got their two separate tents, with the four officers in one tent in the officers' area, and the six enlisted men in a tent in their own area, life settled into a routine on the island. One of the most important elements of this routine, of course, was the meals served in the mess tents (no solid structure had been built to justify the term mess hall). However, the food served in these dining tents was a source of continuing disappointment, if not disgust.

Army chow, and other misfortunes

The quality and quantity of food available is always of prime concern to men anywhere, anytime, and especially to soldiers in a war zone, where pleasures of any kind are few.* Good food can lift morale, while bad food can send it into a tailspin. As the old saying goes, an army travels on its stomach, and during World War II that included the U. S. Army's Air Corps. However, the type of food that went into American Army stomachs during the Pacific war was the source of much grumbling by the owners of those stomachs.

The dehydration blues

Unfortunately for the aviators, as well as for most of the Americans fighting on the far side of the world near the equator, refrigeration was rare in the forties, so food had to be preserved before being shipped to the Pacific. That meant dehydrating it, since food with no moisture in it cannot rot. The dehydrated food was delivered to the war zone in cans, and then it had to be reconstituted by army cooks before it could be eaten. The process of taking all the moisture out of the food in the States and later putting it back in in the Pacific rendered it tasteless, or if it had any taste at all, it was bad, according to most of the men who had to eat it.

Meals were served three times a day in the mess tents on Wakde Island, as it was in all the American military organizations in the Pacific. Mr. Baca remembers that his breakfast was nearly always pancakes with some sort of powdered artificial sugar on them, something like today's sugar substitutes, and he was fed these flapjacks so often that he swore he'd never eat another one in his life after he got home. He remembers that when he did get home and his mother cooked him up a stack of pancakes, even though they were the real deal and not an Army imitation, he still could only barely touch them. He had to explain to his mom that he'd already consumed a lifetime supply of pancakes during his time overseas and was weary of even the sight of them.

Since Australia was within air transport range of the battle zones, and the Army could procure some food from there, for lunch and dinner the fare was often Australian bully beef supplemented with various dehydrated foods. The worst was probably the potatoes, which had been chopped into small cubes before being dried out. Dehydrated potatoes were shipped to the Pacific in gallon cans, and Mr. Horner remembers that the hard little cubes rattled around inside the cans like kernels of popcorn. The procedure used to rehydrate potatoes was to dump them into a half inch or so of grease in big army baking pans, heat the grease until it liquefied, and let the potato cubes suck up the goo like little sponges until the whole mass became (technically) edible.

Horner also remembers today that dried fruit, such as peaches, raisins, plums, and apricots, likewise came out to the Pacific in one-gallon cans. This fruit had a high sugar content, and after it was discovered that it could be used to make a type of applejack, or brandy, in simple home-made stills, the cans were

---

* Generations of mothers have taught their daughters that "the way to a man's heart is through his stomach."

often hijacked by moonshiners before they could reach the mess halls. Thus the cooks often had trouble getting any kind of canned fruit for their tables.

There was also something called "tropical butter" that was set out on most mess tables, and this butter substitute, which didn't taste very good either, wouldn't melt unless it was heated on a stove. In fact, if a cook didn't have some grease to reconstitute his potatoes with, he could substitute tropical butter, to get a slightly different bad flavor. But in solid form this butter wouldn't spread very easily on bread, not that it was really worth trying anyway. For drink there was powdered milk dissolved in water, which, like the imitation butter, was not very much like real milk.

Cooking as punishment

Such fare was unappealing to begin with, but it didn't help that the cooks in the Air Corps were either untrained or poorly trained in preparing it, and they were sometimes men who had been given kitchen duty as punishment for some breach of military regulations. Mr. Baca remembers that whenever a mechanic or enlisted air crewman incurred the displeasure of his superiors in the 320th Squadron, he was often sent to the kitchen to do penance by cooking. Needless to say, the food that was served up by such cooks was not especially savory.

Baca remembers one aircraft mechanic who was assigned to cooking duty because he forgot to put oil into a freshly overhauled B-24 engine, and the engine seized up during a test run. The ruined engine had hardly cooled before the mechanic was banished to the cookshack. Then there was the Chinese-American gunner who repeatedly irritated his bomber crew by shouting hysterically in Chinese over the plane's intercom whenever things became too exciting for him during a bombing mission. Since he couldn't seem to break the habit, he too ended up in the mess tent as a cook.

With poor food to begin with, and unskilled and often resentful cooks preparing it, the result on the men's plates at mess time was predictably dismal. Few men looked forward to meals in the Jolly Rogers mess tents on Wakde Island. The historian of the 90th Bomb Group mentions only one good meal served on the island during this time:

> Late in the month [of July, 1944] the mess hall on Wakde actually served fresh beef, fresh potatoes, and real creamy butter. One has to be denied these niceties to consider it a red-letter day when they are available.[10]

This rarely seen fresh food had been flown up from Australia (at high altitude to keep it cool during the flight) but it didn't last long.

Spam in the sky

As mentioned earlier, along with serving food in the mess tents, the squadron cooks provided take-out meals to the bomber crews to eat in their planes during missions. The B-24 crews had to take their lunches and sometimes their dinners along with them, depending on the length of the flights. Usually these meals were K-rations, which were imperishable food that came in tan-colored cardboard boxes. The boxes contained various kinds of meals, and were labeled as breakfast, lunch, or dinner. Today Mr. Horner remembers that scrambled eggs with ham was the favorite K-ration meal among most of the men, and it was his own favorite as well. Sgt. Baca preferred a meal that featured cheese. There was no way to heat any food in the airplane, but even cold scrambled eggs with bits of ham mixed into it tasted good to Lt. Horner in the middle of a long flight.

In addition to the K-rations, the aircrews also took along the makings of basic sandwiches provided by the mess hall cooks, and made available before the flights. On their way to the planes for a mission, one man on each crew would be designated to pick up a couple of loaves of bread and some Spam lunchmeat to spread on them (SPAM was an abbreviation for **SP**iced h**AM**). Spam came in rectangular tins sixteen inches long and four inches square on the ends. Mr. Horner remembers: "There were a couple of barrels outside the briefing tent with boards laid across them, and on these boards were set bricks of tinned Spam. The mess hall orderlies just took big meat cleavers and chopped off chunks of the tins and handed them out to the aircrews along with the loaves of bread. As a result, most of the Spam had strips of tin driven into it. It would have been better to leave the tins intact and open them with the key provided on each tin, and then slice the meat out, but that must have been considered too slow or too much trouble. During some portion of every flight, somebody in each crew would make sandwiches for everyone from the bread and Spam."

Lt. Horner gets a great meal from a daffy cook

Various types of amphibious vehicles and small boats were continually shuttling back and forth between Wakde Island and the New Guinea mainland, day and night. One was a tracked amphibious vehicle known as an "alligator" (officially an LVT, for Landing Vehicle, Tracked), which made daily trips between Wakde Island and the mainland carrying the mail. People often hitched rides on it.

One day a high school friend of Lt. Horner's named Bud Hall, who was a corporal in an artillery unit on the mainland, rode the alligator over to Wakde Island to say hello. Hall also had an ulterior motive: he had somehow gotten the idea that the Air Corps, like the Navy, served superb food, and he was looking forward to a great meal on the airbase. He was quickly disabused of that notion when he had lunch with Lt. Horner in the squadron mess tent. After a few bites of the pathetic meal the squadron cooks served up that day, Hall set his fork down and asked Horner, "Do you eat this stuff all the time here?"

When Horner assured him that unfortunately he did, the friend invited him to come over to the mainland for a much better meal if he ever got the chance, and he gave Horner directions to his camp.

One day between bombing missions, after a particularly tasteless lunch, Lt. Horner decided to take his friend up on the offer and rode the alligator over to the mainland, where he walked up the beach road toward Arare, as he'd been directed (see map 43-2 on p. 513). He could hear the sound of the big guns firing and their shells swishing over the treetops toward the Japanese somewhere in the jungle, and he soon located Bud Hall's artillery battalion in a clearing in the jungle, where it was firing in support of troops manning the Maffin Bay perimeter.

Looking around the camp, Horner noticed that each artillery battery had its own cook tent and cook, and the cook tent of Hall's battery was a particularly fine one, set up off the ground on corner posts, with a fine wooden floor. It was the best tent around, in fact, and Horner learned that good infantry and artillery cooks were commonly afforded such luxury, so highly valued were their services. Around the cook tent were set picnic tables for the men to eat on, and around the tables were pup tents in which members of the gun battery slept.

Horner learned that the infantry and artillery had true cooks, not just men appointed to the job with no prior experience at cooking, or enlisted men temporarily detailed to KP duty. A real army cook was trained for his job and had an MOS (Military Occupational Specialty) in cooking. Although a cook was an enlisted man, he was so highly regarded that he often ate with the officers and enjoyed considerable prestige. He could choose his own help and made sure they were competent.

Horner had reached his friend's artillery outfit at just the right time in the afternoon, when the men were getting ready for dinner. As Horner watched, the screen door of the cook tent opened and the cook, an elderly man perhaps 38 to 40 years old (quite geriatric by military standards) emerged with a pan of food and came down the steps whistling as if calling a dog. He put the pan of food on the ground for the dog and then went back into the cook tent. However, no dog appeared.

"Where's the dog?" Horner asked his friend.

"There is no dog," Hall said.

"I don't get it," said Horner. "Are you telling me you have a cook who feeds an imaginary dog?"

"That's right," said Hall. "He has an invisible dog. But don't say it too loudly. We don't want certain higher-ups to know about it. They might decide he's crazy and send him home."

"But he is crazy, and he should be sent home," Horner replied. "The poor man is out of his mind."

"Listen," said Hall, "that cook may be crazy, and he may have an invisible dog, but he makes the most wonderful pies and cakes you ever tasted. In fact, he serves the best food in this whole division. We'd do anything to keep him, and that means we have to keep the fact that he's nuts a secret."

Lt. Horner soon found out that Bud Hall spoke the truth—the dinner he got from the nutty cook was wonderful by Air Corps standards, a pleasant reminder that there really was still good food in the world, sometimes even in the war zone. After his fine dinner with the artillerymen, Lt. Horner rode the alligator back to Wakde Island and reluctantly resumed eating the miserable Air Corps fare.

Lindbergh's solution to bad chow

Even Charles Lindbergh, after he had spent some time flying with fighter squadrons in the Pacific (as will be told shortly), felt that something should be done about Air Corps food. Lindbergh brought up the subject when he met with Gen. MacArthur in Brisbane on August 22, 1944. He suggested that, at a minimum, Air Corps cooks should be better trained, and wrote afterward in his journal:

> We discussed the morale of the troops in New Guinea. I mentioned the great differences in the cooking at various squadron mess halls and suggested the possibility of giving some of the cooks better training. A good cook can make even the dehydrated food attractive. A poor cook often ruins fresh food on the infrequent occasions when it is obtainable, and makes such a mess of the dehydrated food that it can hardly be eaten at all.[11]

If Lindbergh's suggestion to give Air Corps cooks better training resulted in improved fare in any of the mess halls, it was never apparent to the Horner crew as the war went on. By and large, the men of the Air Corps simply resigned themselves to the terrible army food that was served on their Pacific airbases. Aside from small amounts of fresh food that might be procured by men flying back from leave in Australia, or planes sent there specially to buy some, which had to be eaten quickly before it spoiled in the tropical heat, there were no local means of supplementing their diet, since the jungles of New Guinea contained no edible game to shoot, unless crocodiles, bats, snakes, or parrots are considered game. The natives raised only yams and small pigs that Americans also didn't consider very good to eat.

Home-grown food fail

Attempts to grow their own fresh vegetables in little "victory gardens" like those being tended by civilians back home in the States didn't meet with much success either. Col. Art Rogers had tried to get a garden going at Port Moresby, on a hillside next to Ward's Field, but he noted, for one thing, that there were no bees in New Guinea to pollinate his corn, so he tried to do it himself using a little paintbrush, with indifferent success. He remarked that nothing seemed to grow very well in the soils of New Guinea, and finally abandoned the experiment.

Dynamite food

When Charles Lindbergh was on Biak Island in the summer of 1944, he and some other pilots went fishing in the ocean with dynamite, trying to add some fresh fish to their diet. They paddled around offshore on rubber rafts, tossing sticks of dynamite into the water, and after the underwater explosions they gathered up the dead or stunned fish that floated to the surface. Lindbergh wrote that on a typical outing they bagged about thirty pounds of fish this way, but were never quite sure whether some of the weirdly colored tropical fish were edible. Fearing that they might be poisonous, they ended up giving a lot of them away to the natives (who were always very happy to get them). They considered it safe to eat the larger ones, and cooked them in their mess kits, eating them with bread and tropical butter, washed down with coffee.

The Army's best cooks

The American Army of the Second World War was segregated, and many blacks who had been employed as cooks in civilian life carried their culinary skills with them into the Army. They were some of the few cooks who could make army chow palatable, but they remained with the black troops. Baca remembers walking past the mess tent of a black outfit on Wakde Island and inhaling some heavenly food aromas, and wishing he could get someone in there to invite him to dinner, but unfortunately he was not acquainted with any of them.

Sgt. Baca tries coconuts

Nearly all the Americans in the Pacific lost weight eating the poor Army food, and were always on the lookout for anything better to eat. Few men could procure dynamite to go fishing with, but one day Sgt. Baca, hungry all the time like most young men, found himself cocking a speculative eye at all the coconuts lying around on the island. He wondered if they had anything edible inside, perhaps even tasty. Coconuts were not something he'd encountered very often back home in the Rio Grande valley of New Mexico, but on Wakde Island they were scattered around everywhere, and he'd heard people speak of "coconut meat" and "coconut milk." He tried to break open a coconut with a screwdriver to see what was inside, but that didn't work, so he ended up chopping it to pieces with a big jungle knife. He didn't much like the taste of the watery liquid that spilled out, nor did he care for the taste of the white pithy material adhering to the inside of the shell, the so-called "meat." That one experience with a coconut was enough for Sgt. Baca. Thereafter he ignored them like everyone else.

Daily Routines on Wakde Island

James Horner, Jaime Baca, and Tom Theobald all recall today that Wakde Island was a very busy place during the summer of 1944, when it served as the 5th Air Force's most advanced airbase in New Guinea. Along with the continual takeoffs and landings of all kinds of aircraft were the comings and goings of many types of watercraft, mostly on its southern shoreline where a jetty had been built by the plantation owners who had operated a coconut plantation on the island before the war, and where there was a beach instead of a reef. Every sort of craft could be seen nosed up to the beach, from huge LSTs with their front doors swung open to disgorge supplies and equipment to the little "buffaloes" and "alligators" making runs to and from the mainland two miles away. Some of the boats brought wounded soldiers across from the mainland to be airlifted back to rear-area hospitals by transport planes (C-47s).

Angels from the sky

Army nurses from Nadzab or Port Moresby frequently flew into Wakde Island in C-47s to evacuate the sick and wounded, and to give men

Lt. Patricia Thompson, a nurse who arrived on Wakde Island in a C-47, receives a list of patients to be airlifted back to rear-area hospitals, who will be in her charge during the flight.

(Above) Nurses from the 5th Air Force Air Evacuation Unit arrived frequently on Wakde Island to evacuate the sick and wounded back to rear-echelon hospitals. The women had officer rank and were armed with .45-cal. pistols. (Below) an evacuation flight in the air.

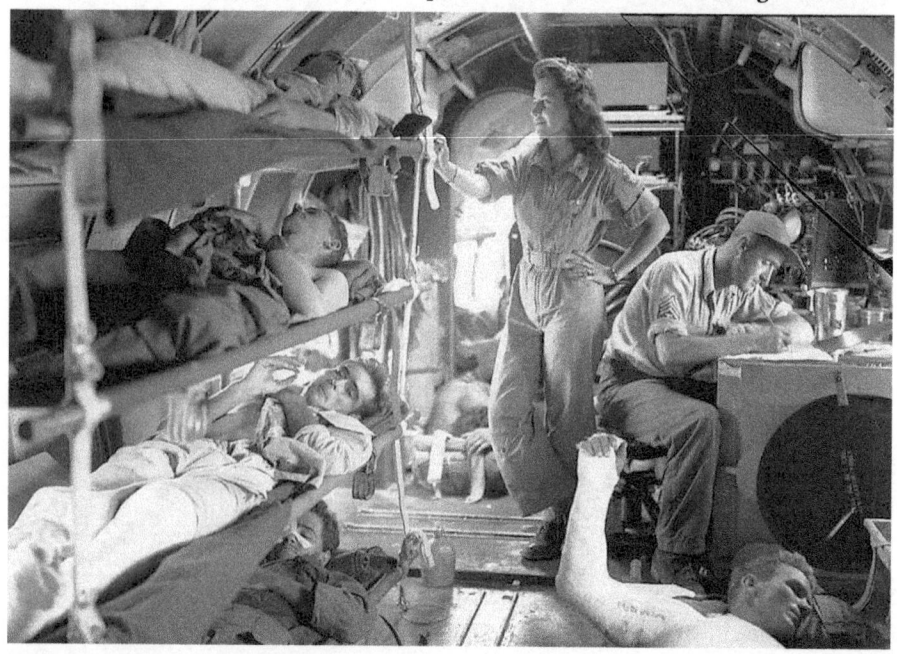

immunizations against disease. These were the only women to be seen on Wakde, and photos (such as the one on p. 561) show the men gaping at them as though they were creatures from another world, which, in a sense, they were. The planes left the island before dark because of the night bombings by the Japanese, since the Army of that more civilized time didn't believe in subjecting women to any dangers that could possibly be avoided.

With tropical diseases taking so many men out of action immunizations were of particular importance.

More night air attacks

The frequent nocturnal bombing attacks by the Japanese on Wakde Island continued clear up into the middle of August, and always made getting a good night's sleep difficult for the bomber crews. That, in fact, was the main intention of the Japanese. They deliberately unsynchronized the engines and propellers of their twin-engined bombers so that they throbbed irritatingly, like washing machines; hence the common name for them on any island that they afflicted: "Washing Machine Charlies." Often it was only one bomber on a harassing raid, but with each air raid alert, signaled by someone firing a pistol (if not an antiaircraft gun like on the Horner crew's first night on the island), everyone who was not manning a flak gun had to jump from their cots to take cover in a foxhole or slit trench.

Japanese bombs also continued to destroy American aircraft parked on both sides of the island's runway. Mr. Horner remembers a Jolly Rogers bomber that was reduced to junk by the direct hit of a bomb one night. A photograph of it (next page) shows nothing left intact but the right rudder bearing the Jolly Rogers skull and crossed bombs symbol. On that same night a P-38 fighter plane was also wrecked, and its pilot, who had been sleeping in a hammock strung between the twin tail booms, was killed.

There was no effective defense against these Japanese night bombing raids until the 421st Night Fighter Squadron, which arrived on Wakde Island in late June of 1944, gained enough experience to shoot down the intruders

A Jolly Rogers B-24 on Wakde Island was reduced to a pile of junk when a Japanese bomb made a direct hit on it during a night attack.

with their Northrop P-61 "Black Widows"[12] (photo below). These large, black-painted, twin-engine, two-seat night fighters, very sophisticated aircraft for their day, were equipped with onboard short-range radar to locate and stalk their prey, and were also aided by a ground radar station set up on little Insoemanai Island, next to Wakde Island. Mr. Horner also remembers that eventually the Navy stationed a destroyer with long-range radar just offshore to give the men living on the island early warning of a night attack.

On the night of 12 August, while the Horner crew were trying to get some sleep after a tiring 10-hour and 45-minute bombing mission they had flown that day, a Japanese twin-engine bomb-

Nothing much was left of the bomber except part of the right rudder with the Jolly Rogers emblem on it.

The Northrop P-61 Black Widow night fighter.

er came over Wakde Island on a typical raid to interrupt their rest. While the crewmen waited out the air raid in a slit trench as usual, one of the P-61s, nicknamed "Bright Eyes," took off and stalked the Japanese plane with its onboard radar, also receiving directions from the ground radar station. The Black Widow closed in behind the unsuspecting Japanese plane and blew it out of the sky at point-blank range. The crew of the Japanese bomber, no doubt thinking they were safe in the dark, probably never knew what hit them. It was one of the few times that one of these night air raids on Wakde Island had a satisfactory ending for the sleepy, grumbling men in the slit trenches.[12]

Night fighting on the mainland

Another killer of sleep, for which nothing much could be done, was the gunfire at night from the mainland at Maffin Bay, two miles across the water. The Japanese probing the American perimeter no longer had the manpower or weaponry to mount any major attacks, but like the "Washing Machine Charlies," their goal was to harass the Americans as much as they could. They were continually trying to infiltrate the American lines at night, and they often resorted to trickery.

One ruse was to shout for help in English as though a wounded American was lying outside the perimeter, hoping to lure out a medic to kill or capture. Some Japanese crept close enough to the American lines to listen to conversations and learn the names of American officers, then tried to shout orders to the Americans using the officers' names. Americans devised ways of telling whether a voice calling out in English in the night was American or Japanese. An American would shout back, "Say "lollapalooza!" or some other word with many Ls in it (Lucky Strike, Philadelphia, lollypop), which most Japanese couldn't pronounce.

Jungle fighting at night was a hellish kind of war, with Japanese creeping up to American lines to throw hand grenades, or crawling up to drop into American foxholes to try to knife the GIs to death. Mr. Baca remembers that the battle noise would often continue throughout the night, tapering off toward daylight.

Mr. Horner remembers a soldier visiting Wakde Island from Maffin Bay coming into his tent one day and offering to buy his .45 pistol from him.[*] It would give him an edge, the man explained, in the deadly hand-to-hand fighting that occurred when a Japanese soldier jumped into a man's foxhole at night. A rifle was useless at such close quarters, but with a pistol a soldier could defend himself. However, pistols were difficult for enlisted men to get, since they were usually issued only to officers. Lt. Horner declined to sell his handgun, since it was intended for his own survival use if he ever had to bail out over the

---

[*] Australian soldiers also liked the American .45 pistols and would trade the soft, fleece-lined flying boots that the Americans coveted for them.

jungle, and besides, he told the soldier, selling a government-issued weapon was illegal (not that it deterred anyone who really wanted to do it).

An artist's view of life on Wakde Island

In August some bombers of the 13th Bomb Group (flying B-24s like the Jolly Rogers) arrived on Wakde and took up residence in the northwest corner of the island. One of the pilots, Lt. David Zellmer, who had been a member of a New York dance troupe before the war, wrote of conditions on the island:

> **Life proceeds on a somewhat primitive (for us) level: meals are eaten from mess kits, drinking water, tepid and tasting of iodine, comes from hanging canvas Lister bags; showers are available only to those who wait in line for the one designated hour a day the precious sun-warmed fresh water is dispensed from a P-38 belly gas tank on a raised platform... There's no PX, no Officer's Club, no cigarettes... The tents are in rigid rows across a bleak, treeless peninsula jutting from the island's western shore. The runway... splits the island in half, is alive with the sight and sound of planes constantly landing and taking off.**[13]

Zellmer went on to describe his "unshaded, fly-collecting tent pitched over a floor of sand," lighted at night only by candles. With no other means of doing their laundry, the men washed their clothing in the ocean by a unique method:

> [S]ome of us tie our soiled clothes to the end of a long rope which we throw into the surf. After the clothes have rubbed along the sandy bottom a few days, we haul them out and hang them on a line, hopefully to be rinsed free of salt and sand by the daily rain showers. A half-hour exposure to the noonday sun takes care of the drying process. We wash and shave from steel helmets with tepid rainwater caught in the tied-off tent flaps.[14]

Lt. Zellmer wrote of some friction between the bomber crews and fighter pilots stationed on Wakde island:

> A P-38 outfit was already here on Wakde when we arrived. Those hot-shot pilots still act as if we B-24 drivers are intruding on their turf. First couple of days they delighted in blowing down our tents with the wash of their twin props. They'd fly in low over the camp, then pull straight up over the tents. Their wash would turn the tents inside out and scatter our personal stuff to kingdom come. Finally, our major talked to their major and the horseplay stopped.
>
> But not their showing-off. Whenever they return from a successful mission, they put on the best airshow in town. Today, for example, one of the returning '38s buzzed the runway at prop level. We ran over to the field from our nearby tent to see what was

coming next. The guy first pulled straight up and began arcing over into a big loop. At the top of the loop, directly over the field, he cut his two engines, feathered the props, dropping his landing gear as he plummeted down on the back side of the loop. He pulled out just in time to grease the plane in for a perfect dead-stick landing.[15]

Unburied Japanese bodies continued to be a nuisance on Wakde Island. Mr. Baca recalls leaving his tent one night to visit the latrine and stumbling over something in the dark which, when he shone his flashlight on it, turned out to be a human rib cage.

Baca, a Catholic, was unhappy that there was no Catholic chaplain on Wakde Island, and remembers today that more than one of the Jolly Rogers bases had no padre to say Sunday mass. With death a constant threat to the aviators, many of the young men attended whatever religious service was available, and the chaplains tried to accommodate all faiths as best they could. Some Christian chaplains learned to recite Jewish prayers at funeral services.

Lt. Zellmer recorded his impressions of the Sunday religious services held on Wakde Island:

> I awake mid-morning to the chime-like tinkle of a hanging Japanese brake drum being struck. It quickly stills the laughter-tinged chatter in the chapel tent across the way. The chanted monotone of a prayer holds the voices quiet. I can see rows of bowed heads from where I lie on my cot. The muted tone of a pitch pipe offers the first note of a hymn. I hear the young men singing, quietly, hesitantly—as if expecting, hoping to hear a soprano or a contralto joining them.[16]

The threatening tide (not)

Small incidents of a humorous nature that occurred on Wakde Island remain embedded in Mr. Baca's memory after nearly three-quarters of a century. The story of Lt. Horner's frantic search for his lost shoes in the dark during the crew's first air raid is a favorite. Another situation arose from the fact that Sgt. Carter, the crew's young (18-year-old) tail gunner, was both fascinated and frightened by the sea. Being from Kansas, he had never been near an ocean before, nor had he ever seen one until the recent flight from California to Hawaii, but on crowded little Wakde Island there was an ocean lapping at the shore dangerously close (he felt) to his tent. He noticed that, mysteriously, sometimes the water was closer to the tent than at other times. Someone then explained to him how the tide worked; how for twelve hours of the day the water sank away from the island, and for the next twelve it rose back up again. Young Carter pondered this mystery for a while, and then began to fret about it. He couldn't swim, and he wondered what would happen if the tide rose and didn't stop, but instead just kept on coming. If it should happen at night, they could all be drowned in their cots! One night, for some reason, Carter decided that the sea was in fact creeping up over the edge of the reef and heading for their tent. Baca remembers him frantically waking everyone up in the enlisted men's tent shouting "The tide is coming! The tide is coming!" They told him to go to bed.

More deaths on Wakde Island

Wakde Island proved to be a good emergency landing field for any aircraft that was in trouble in the area, or for bombers that had wounded men aboard who needed quick medical attention. The alternative was to fly 140 miles farther down the coast to Hollandia, the nearest airbase after Wakde, where the airfields were not well suited to B-24s, or go even farther down to Nadzab, the main B-24 base, 630 miles beyond Wakde. The island had no hospital, but it did have medical officers, doctors assigned to the squadrons, and if someone in a plane flying in the area needed basic medical attention in a hurry, Wakde was the logical place to get it.

One day the Horner crew's navigator, Lt. Tom Theobald, saw a B-24 land on Wakde's runway and a crowd of men gather around it as soon as it came to a stop. The plane was from a bomb group that was not based on Wakde Island, but it had made an emergency landing to get help for a wounded crewman. As Lt. Theobald watched, a man was taken out of one of the waist windows of the plane on a stretcher. As it turned out, it was too late for the doctors to help him; he was dead. In asking around, Theobald found out that the man was the crew's navigator, and that he had been hit in the head by a bullet from a Japanese fighter plane. This navigator had been standing on the flight deck between the pilot and the copilot when he was struck. Lt. Theobald made a mental note that he should not make a habit of standing between the pilot and copilot during missions in his own bomber.

Mr. Baca remembers another emergency landing that was made on Wakde by a B-24 that had wounded men aboard. After these men were taken off to the surgical tent, the crew left their damaged bomber parked beside the runway, empty. Sgt. Baca strolled over to take a look at it and saw that it was riddled with bullet and flak holes. Out of curiosity he climbed up into the waist area and looked around, and was sickened to see blood splattered around everywhere inside the fuselage. It was a grim reminder of what could happen when a crew's luck ran low.

Charles Lindbergh, who flew a P-38 fighter plane from Wakde Island on more than one occasion, was a romantic, and after some close brushes with death in combat with Japanese fighters he wrote in his journal:

Here in the lonely beauty of the sky one seems cleansed of the

> stench and bedlam of war, free of the suffering, the degradation, and the filth of surface armies. Here, even death is clean, like a steel dagger, swift, surrounded by the dignity of clouds and sky.[17]

In Lindbergh's imagination, death for an airman was "swift and clean." That's because he'd never seen it before, at least up close. Sgt. Baca, looking around him at the bloody mess inside the B-24 parked beside Wakde Island's runway that day, would have begged to differ with him.

Death in the bombers came from ways other than bullets and flak. Accidents also took their toll. Lt. Zellmer wrote about how his bomber squadron decided to practice night landings on the island's runway. Someone in authority had reasoned that the bombers would be able to stay out longer on missions if the pilots could return to the island after sunset and land in darkness. But Wakde's runway demonstrated yet again, tragically, that it was too short for B-24s to operate from safely:

> We lined up for takeoff a little off to the side of the runway and waited for the plane coming in to land. I watched the final approach: he was in a steep glide with full flaps, wheels down, landing lights sweeping the runway ahead. But the plane did not land, just leveled off and continued flying straight and level the length of the runway, finally disappearing from sight.
>
> We stayed where we were and waited for instructions from the tower. A few minutes later the tower said we were all to come in. Said that the plane we were watching had flown straight into the sea. There would be no more takeoffs and landings this night. Or ever, I thought to myself, for the three pilots, the co-pilot and flight engineer aboard that plane.[18]

Thus another bomber joined the remains of Lt. Nestler's B-24 and others on the sea floor just offshore from little Wakde Island. Someday, perhaps, archaeologists will explore the underwater aviation museum there.

Combat missions by the Horner crew from Wakde Island

The Horner crew flew a total of fourteen combat missions during the seven-and-a-half weeks they were on Wakde Island, in addition to some non-combat administrative flights back down the coast, before moving up to Biak Island on August 16th. The targets of the combat missions were mostly Japanese airfields to the west of Wakde, on and around the Vogelkop Peninsula (the "head" of the New Guinea "buzzard"), with the goal of preventing Japanese bombers and fighters from operating from those airfields. They flew combat missions every three or four days on the average.

Lt. Cooper recorded these bombing missions in the spring and summer of 1944 in his mission diary and flight logbook:

Mission #	Date	Target
1	June 30	Cape Keretsbari, Noemfoor Island
2	July 4	Jefman Airdrome
3	July 5	Sarmi, Maffin Bay
4	July 20	Manokwari
5	July 24	Moemi
6	July 26	Babo Airdrome
7	July 28	Manokwari
8	July 31	Ransiki Airdrome
9	August 2	Liang Airdrome, Ambon Island
10	August 5	Boela, Ceram Island
11	August 7	Galela airdrome
12	August 9	Boela, Ceram Island
13	August 12	Namela Airdrome, Boeroe Island
14	August 14	Babo Airdrome

In his mission diary he jotted down a few details about each one:

Mission 1—30 June 1944

Bombed radar units on Cape Keretsbari, Noemfoor Island, with 60 tons. No Ack-Ack or interception. Japs retaliated at 11:00 pm. Hit one small fuel dump, destroyed one P-47 and damaged one A-20. Had other alerts at 12:00 midnight and 4:00 am. No bombs dropped. 4:45 hrs. [flown on this mission]

Mission 2— 4 July 1944

36 tons on Jefman Airdrome. No A-A [Ack-Ack] or interception. Hit weather on return, passed over Moemi [airfield] by mistake & Jap flak gave us 4th of July celebration. (Another alert last nite.) 7:25 hrs.

Mission 3— 5 July 1944

Put six 1000 lb. bombs on Jap HQ and bivouac area at Sarmi. After bombing we strafed their camp area for an hour. 3:15 hrs.

Mission 4— 20 July 1944

Samate closed in. Hit secondary target, Manokwari, with 48 tons. Results poor. Expected heavy A-A—had none. 6:45 hrs.

Mission 5— 24 July 1944

Moemi and secondary targets weathered-in. Formation broke up in storm. Saw one fighter, no attack, no flak. Dropped 3 tons safe in Lake Rombebai. 4:35 hrs.

Mission 6— 26 July 1944

Plastered Babo drome with 96 tons. Clouds necessitated 4 runs - drew moderate Ack-Ack. Holed our wing ship (Nyre). 7:10 hrs.

Mission 7— 28 July 1944
Hit Manokwari drome with 66 tons after 3 runs. Persistent A-A fire. Accurate. Two planes observed taking off. 5:50 hrs.

Mission 8— 31 July 1944
Put 108 - 250lb. bombs on Ransiki drome through accurate flak. Our two wing ships (Charlton & Ketelhut) were well holed, Whatley shot down. Cats [Catalinas] picked up only 5 of crew. 5:00 hrs.

Mission 9— 2 August 1944
Knocked out at least 25 fighters & bombers on Liang drome, Ambon Island, with 3800 20lb. frag. bombs. Plenty of ack-ack from Kokas Bay, en route, from drome batteries, and from harbor gun emplacements; no hits. 9:20 hrs.

Mission 10— 5 August 1944
Hit fuel storage tanks, oil wells, power station and airdrome dispersal areas at Boela, Ceram Is., with approx. 5000 frag. bombs. Large fires. Ack-Ack inaccurate & few interceptors chased off by P-38s. 9:10 hrs.

Mission 11— 7 August 1944
Spread 630 one hundred pounders on Galela Airdrome & dispersal areas, damaging runway and more than 17 planes. Enemy fighters airborne too late. Heavy inaccurate A-A. 10:15 hrs.

Mission 12— 9 August 1944
Hit oil wells and tanks at Boela again, with 690 one hundred lb. bombs. Many fires, heavy ack-ack, no interception. 9:20 hrs.

Mission 13— 12 August 1944
Poor strike. Arrived over Namlea drome, Boeroe Is., to find it weathered over. Unloaded on secondary, Babo. Heavy, moderate, inaccurate flak. 10:45 hrs.

Mission 14— 14 August 1944
Hit Babo runway with 72 1000-pounders (supposed staging for Japs bombing Owi). Flew thru barrage of heavy A-A. 5:25 hrs.

A young Japanese woman under the bombs at Manokwari
The Horner crew's fourth and seventh missions were strikes against the Japanese airfield at Manokwari on the eastern end of New Guinea's Vogelkopf peninsula (see Map 43-6 on p. 573). Before the war the town of Manok-

wari had been a Dutch administrative center, and when the Japanese invaded New Guinea in April of 1942 they decided to establish their own civilian government there. Consequently about 500 Japanese civil service personnel were sent to Manokwari, including women who served as nurses and typists. In addition, two hundred academic researchers and 2,100 representatives of various Japanese trading companies joined the civil servants to scout out the natural resources in the area and develop industries. Thus, beginning in the spring of 1942, there were around 2,800 Japanese civilians in Manokwari in addition to the military personnel.[19]

One of the civilian women at Manokwari was 24-year-old Ayako Yoshida, known as Michi, a girl from a farming village in Japan's Tokushima Prefecture. In 1938, at age 19, Michi had left her family's farm and traveled to Tokyo, where she found work editing newsreel film. There she met and fell in love with a university student named Shibayama, and they became engaged to be married.

When the war began, Shibayama, like many young Japanese men, was conscripted into the military, and because of his superior education he was made an officer in the navy and sent to New Guinea, where he was stationed at Manokwari. Michi decided to follow him, volunteering to work as a typist with the civilian contingent at Manokwari, and traveled to New Guinea on a ship. At Manokwari the two lovers were reunited, and were able to meet as frequently as their work allowed. Years after the war, looking back on this time, Michi wrote:

> **We could not show our closeness too much, but people knew we were planning to get married. We could see each other after work. When one of us got ill, dengue fever in his case and malaria in my case, we looked after each other. We were happy to be in the same place at the same time.**[20]

However, as the Americans gained the upper hand in New Guinea, the B-24s of the Jolly Rogers and other bomb groups repeatedly pounded the Japanese airfield at Manokwari, and it became a dangerous place for military personnel and civilians alike.

The Horner crew's missions against Manokwari were typical strikes against the airfield there, which was suspected of sending bombers against Wakde Island and other American airbases, and according to Michi's memoirs, kamikaze planes were also sent out from Manokwari to strike American ships. Lt. Cooper wrote in his mission diary that on July 4, 1944, the Jolly Rogers dropped 44 tons of bombs on Manokwari, and on July 28 they dropped another 66 tons. Michi, who was under all the bombs dropped by the Americans up until the time she was evacuated, remembered:

> **We could sense the deterioration of the war, being in**

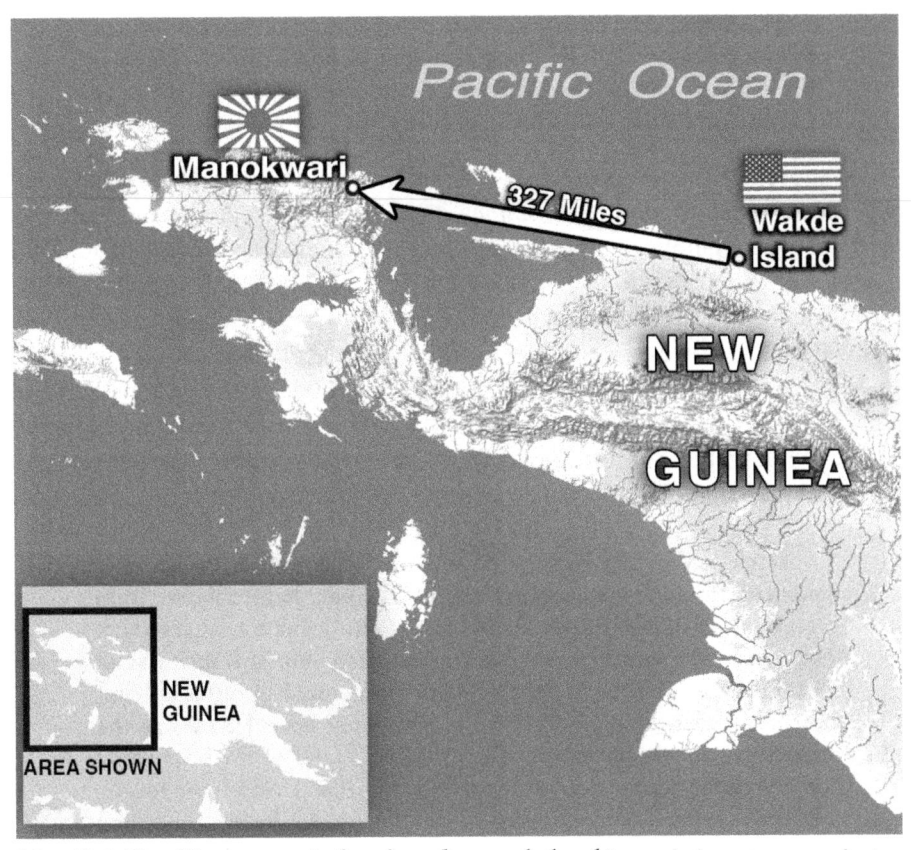

Map 43-6. The Horner crew's fourth and seventh bombing missions were against a Japanese airfield at Manokwari.

>Manokwari. By 1944, Japan started to lose the war and Manokwari was bombed heavily. Young pilots with white scarves started to arrive as members of Tokko-tai (Kamikaze Squad). Those pilots were to steer their airplanes to the target while they remained in the cockpits. At farewells before their sorties, I was asked by Shibayama to pour some saki into their glasses. One young pilot declined, and I asked him why. He said he could not drink. He was only seventeen years old. I felt so sad, and tears started to trickle down my face. Their planes left the airstrip whenever the planes could secure enough fuel, but none of us expected them to return.[21]

Along with the other civilian workers, Michi took cover in bomb shelters during American bomber raids, for the town was so close to the airfield that stray bombs fell into the town. Michi wrote:

>In one air raid on Manokwari, we were evacuated to a

> bomb shelter. My colleague who was sitting next to me offered to swap places, and the next moment a bomb hit the shelter. The colleague who was sitting in the position where I had been a moment before was killed instantly.[22]

As the Americans stepped up their bombing campaign against Japanese installations in and around New Guinea, the Japanese decided to evacuate the civilians from Manokwari, and the naval officers, including Michi's fiancé Shibayama, prepared to sail away from the nearby harbor. Michi and Shibayama once again said farewell to each other, planning to meet again and marry in postwar Japan. However, they would never see each other again.

Michi left New Guinea in a convoy of ships filled with civilians, headed back to Japan, while Shibayama's warship sailed for Ambon Island (another frequent target of the Jolly Rogers). Michi's voyage home was a dangerous one, for American submarines were active in the area between New Guinea and Japan:

> During the trip back to Japan, our boat was followed by a submarine which tried to torpedo us. The boat had to weave from left to right in order to evade the torpedoes. I was totally terrified. I thought the end had come for us. During this ordeal, I was in a cabin where bones of dead soldiers were stored in order to send them back to Japan. I clutched at a wooden box of bones as the fear was overwhelming me. The grinding sound of the boat while it was changing its course was something that I could not forget. When I realized that we had survived the attack, the box that I had been holding was almost shattered in my arms. Another boat in our convoy was not as lucky as ours. It was hit by torpedoes and sank in a very short time. While the ship was going down, its siren was going off all through it. Somebody must have been blowing the siren in the sinking boat. It was such a dreary sound and I can still remember it clearly.[23]

Back in Japan Michi went to stay with her fiancé's mother, and was with her when word came that Shibayama had been killed at Ambon. Michi's life and hopes were shattered, like those of millions of others who lost loved ones on both sides during the war. Michi wrote that for the rest of her life Shibayama visited her in her dreams. In these dreams he merely looked at her sadly, and said nothing. She always wondered what their life would have been like together.

The crash of the Whatley crew

On the Horner crew's eighth mission on July 31, 1944, their target was Ransiki, another Japanese airfield that, like Manokwari, was located on the back of the New Guinea "buzzard's" head about 340 miles west of Wakde

Island. All four squadrons of the Jolly Rogers contributed planes to the mission that day, and two targets were hit simultaneously: the 319th and 320th Squadrons attacked the Ransiki airfield, while the 321st and 400th dropped on another airdrome at nearby Moemi (see Map 43-7 on page 577). The Japanese were basing Oscar fighter planes on these airfields, and they were near enough to Biak and Owi islands to be a threat to the Americans there.

The Jolly Rogers bombers carried 250-pound demolition bombs on this raid, and Lt. Cooper's mission diary records that his formation dropped a total of 108 of them on the airfield. But the Japanese had a lot of antiaircraft guns defending Ransiki, and they threw up a thick barrage of flak at the American bombers. Cooper recorded that the planes flying on either side of them, piloted by Lts. Charlton and Ketelhut, were "well holed," but the Horner crew's bomber made it through unscathed.

Several of the bombers dropping on Moemi were also holed by flak, and one of them, piloted by 25-year-old Lt. Clifford E. Whatley of the 321st Squadron, sustained serious damage. The inboard engines on both wings of Whatley's bomber were hit. He tried to feather the propeller on engine number three but was unable to do so, and it just windmilled, causing a lot of air drag. Then engine number two lost oil pressure, so he shut it down and feathered it successfully.

Flying now on only the two outboard engines, the bomber was slowly losing altitude. Whatley called his crew over the intercom and told them to throw overboard everything loose aboard the plane, hoping to lighten it enough to arrest the descent. Out went the waist guns, ammunition boxes, personal gear, and the men even unbolted and jettisoned the bomb bay gas tank. This slowed the bomber's rate of descent somewhat, but it continued to sink. Two other Jolly Rogers bombers followed Whatley's crippled plane and stayed close to it. If it couldn't make it to land, at least they could radio its position when it ditched and drop survival equipment to the crewmen in the water.

The nearest American airfield was on newly-captured Noemfoor Island, about sixty miles from Ransiki, so Whatley headed in that direction. By the time they spotted Noemfoor they were down to 2,000 feet and still descending. Only ten miles short of the island, Whatley could see that he was not going to make it and was going to have to ditch. He spotted a boat leaving Noemfoor, which had to be American, and decided to set the bomber down as close to it as possible in order to get immediate help after they were down. He called back to the crew to take crash positions, and everyone except himself and the copilot, Lt. Jarvais J. Hudson, went back to the waist of the airplane and braced themselves against bulkheads there.

Later, Lt. Hudson could only remember the sound of breaking of glass in the cockpit and a terrific jolt as the airplane hit the water, and then he blacked out. When he regained consciousness he was underwater, still strapped into his seat. He managed to yank off his seatbelt and swim to the surface, where he found two other crewmen, S/Sgts. Daniel F. Hentscher and Kizzel Blakely, floundering around amid burning wreckage. Hentscher later said that as the plane contacted the water it hit a wave that stopped its forward motion so suddenly and violently that it caused an explosion and fire. He too lost consciousness and woke up underwater in a tangle of wires and cables, but, holding his breath, managed to free himself and make it to the surface.

As the three men floated in the sea, awaiting the arrival of the boat they had seen, and waving at the two bombers circling above them, the realization dawned upon them that they were the only ones who had gotten out of the airplane. Lt. Whatley and the other six men, to whom they had been talking only moments before, were gone, headed for the bottom of the sea in the wreckage of the plane.

Clifford Whatley said goodbye to his wife and baby daughter before leaving for the Pacific war. They would never see him again.

In about 15 minutes the boat arrived and took the three survivors aboard. Seven more families back in the States would soon get a War Department telegram bearing the news that they had all dreaded and prayed would never come. Lt. Whatley had a wife and baby daughter in Hope, Arkansas who would never see him again.

The men who died along with Lt. Whatley were:[24]

> 1st Lt. Howard J. Covich, navigator, from Illinois
> 1st Lt. Philip W. Brawn, bombardier, from Buffalo, New York
> T/Sgt. Cecil R. Hazel, flight engineer, from Texas
> T/Sgt. Joseph S. Blecha, radio operator, from Illinois
> S/Sgt. Clyde O. Wills, gunner, from Arizona

43. WAKDE ISLAND 577

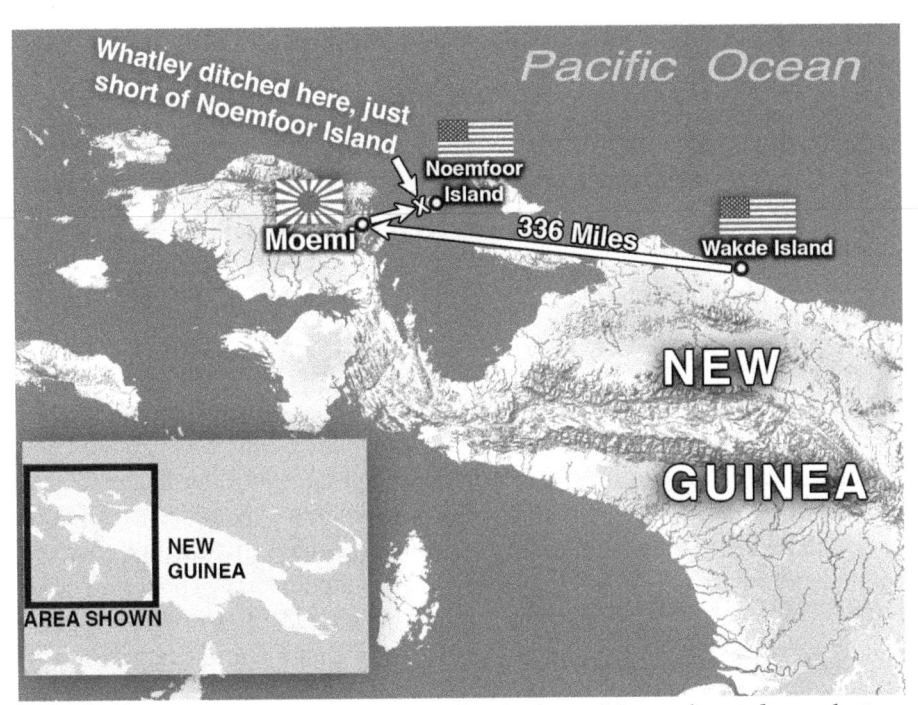

Map 43-7. After Lt. Whatley's bomber was damaged over Moemi, he tried to make it to Noemfoor Island, but crashed in the sea just a few miles short of it. Only three of the ten crewmen survived. This occurred during the Horner crew's eighth combat mission.

S/Sgt. Leon R. Younker, gunner, from Altoona, Pennsylvania

Today, somewhere within a few miles of the west coast of Noemfoor Island, the wreckage of this bomber and the remains of seven young American men rest on the ocean floor.

In 2018 two of Whatley's grandchildren contacted a nonprofit organization called Project Recover* about the possibility of locating the bomber and recovering the men's remains. They noted that Whatley's daughter and his niece and nephew (his sister's children) are hoping to bring his remains home for burial. Nothing has been accomplished as of this writing.

Whatley's bomber was the only plane lost that day. The plane flown by the Horner crew and the rest of the bombers on the mission landed safely back at Wakde Island.

---

* In September of 2017 Project Recover located and photographed the submerged wreckage of the Jolly Rogers bomber "Heaven Can Wait" under 200 feet of water in Hansa Bay. Hit by ground fire, the B-24 crashed into the bay on March 11, 1944 with a crew of eleven men (ten crewmen and a photographer). There were no survivors. Relatives of the crewmen are hoping that the men's remains can be recovered. More details are available on Project Recover's website.

Chapter Forty-Four

CHARLES LINDBERGH FLIES SHOTGUN FOR THE JOLLY ROGERS

In 1944 world-famous aviator Charles Lindbergh came out to the Pacific for six months as a civilian "observer," ostensibly to evaluate the performance of American fighter planes for the factories back home. By bending and skirting military regulations, however, he ended up flying the fighter planes on combat missions, later claiming that it was the best way to evaluate them.

Lindbergh's presence in the Pacific theater coincided with the first fourteen combat missions of the Horner crew, which was the time they spent on Wakde Island. On one bombing mission, Lindbergh piloted of one of the fighter planes that escorted the Horner crew's bomber formation to the target, and on several other occasions he flew protective cover for Jolly Rogers missions. At times both the Horner crew and Lindbergh were on Wakde Island at the same time, though they did not meet. Lindbergh always made a point of keeping a low profile, after years of being mobbed for autographs and photographs everywhere he went.

Lindbergh goes to the Pacific

In early May of 1944 Lindbergh flew out to the South Pacific on military transport planes as a civilian representative of the United Aircraft Company, whose Vought Aircraft Division built the F4U Corsair fighter plane that was in use by the Navy and Marines. He landed at Guadalcanal, from where Marine pilots were flying missions in the Solomon Islands. Officially he was there to observe the performance of the Corsair under combat conditions, and to report any problems back to the Vought company. He did this by flying Corsairs himself, in combat, right alongside the Marine pilots.

That a civilian should be able to fly military combat missions was extraordinary, but Lindbergh had learned from long experience that celebrity has its advantages. Described as the world's most famous man after his solo transatlantic flight in 1927, and then the kidnapping and murder of his infant son, and the sensational trial of the killer in 1932, he was welcomed and feted wherever he went in the Pacific war theater by star-struck privates and generals alike.

Everyone wanted to write home that he'd seen, spoken to, or been in the company of Charles Lindbergh. When he asked Navy commanders for permission to go along with their fighter pilots to "observe" how the planes performed under combat conditions, he was given fully armed planes to fly, and he shot up enemy targets and dropped bombs right alongside them. Some of these missions were flown to such dangerous Japanese strongholds as Rabaul.

Next Lindbergh wrangled Navy orders allowing him into the Southwest Pacific Command, which of course was the domain of General MacArthur and his air chief George Kenney. Since Corsairs were not used by the Army Air Forces, he adopted new justifications for being there: to study the performance of different types of Army fighter planes, and compare twin-engine fighters to single-engine ones, in order to develop better fighter designs in the States (at this time the Army used primarily the single-engine Republic P-47 Thunderbolt and twin-engine P-38 Lockheed Lightning).

He also told Army commanders that he could teach Air Corps pilots how to achieve better fuel economy, thereby increasing the range of their aircraft, a thing of tremendous value in a war theater where fliers had to cover long distances on nearly every mission. He knew that for this he had undeniable credentials, since he had flown the entire 3,600-mile width of the Atlantic Ocean from New York to Paris in a single-engine plane, and landed with fuel to spare. Not everyone knew that the *Spirit of St. Louis* was really just a big flying gas tank, and was never in any serious danger of running out of gas, but later on, Lindbergh really had learned a lot about flying with minimum fuel consumption during his long flights pioneering airline routes around the world in 1931 and 1933. In that regard, training pilots to fly farther on less fuel, Lindbergh really could, and did, provide a useful service to pilots in the Pacific.[*]

In his hopes of flying Army fighters in combat as a civilian, Lindbergh knew that he might not be so lucky with the Army as he had been with the Navy; therefore he simply bypassed MacArthur's headquarters in Australia and went straight to Nadzab, New Guinea, arriving there on June 15, 1944 (the Horner crew would arrive there five days later). General Whitehead, now Deputy Commander of the 5th Air Force, with his headquarters at Nadzab, was off at the front in western New Guinea on that day, so Lindbergh chatted with some of the colonels at the airbase headquarters, who were surprised, pleased, and honored that the illustrious Charles Lindbergh should suddenly drop in on them, literally out of the blue. He told them he'd like to study their aircraft for scientific purposes, and fly both single-engine and twin-engine fighters to judge their relative merits. He did not mention wanting to fly in combat.

Lindbergh was provided with a tent of his own, and on the day after his arrival he was allowed to take an hour's familiarization flight in a P-38. He

---
[*] Some pilots figured out for themselves how to save gas on long flights. Recall that Lt. Horner learned from experienced bomber pilots at Nadzab that they saved gas by flying with higher manifold pressure and lower propeller speeds than taught in training. This is the same thing Lindbergh proposed to teach pilots. To employ an automobile analogy, it was like driving a car slowly in high gear, with the gas pedal held well down to keep the vehicle moving.

quickly adapted to the management of two engines on a fighter plane. On the 18th General Whitehead arrived back at his headquarters, and Lindbergh had dinner with him, no doubt apprehensive that the general might question his presence at Nadzab and veto his request to fly Air Corps aircraft. He needn't have worried—everything worked out in his favor. Whitehead apparently assumed (or Lindbergh led him to believe) that Generals Kenney and MacArthur, at their headquarters in Brisbane, Australia, had authorized Lindbergh's study of Air Corps fighter planes. The truth was that neither Kenney nor MacArthur had any idea that Lindbergh was in the Southwest Pacific. Whitehead told Lindbergh to go ahead and do as he pleased—exactly what he had hoped to hear.

When the Horner crew arrived at Nadzab from Port Moresby on the 20th of June, Lindbergh was still there. Between the 20th and 25th, while Lt. Horner was trying to glean information from experienced bomber pilots about what it was like to fly in combat, Lindbergh was in another part of the huge camp in the company of the fighter pilots. The Horner crew left Nadzab on the 25th for Wakde Island in a Jolly Rogers bomber, and Lindbergh followed them the next day, headed for Hollandia in a borrowed P-38.

At Hollandia Lindbergh dropped in on the 475th Fighter Group, nicknamed "Satan's Angels," which flew P-38s. He told the Group's commander, Col. Charles H. MacDonald, that he was there by permission of General Whitehead, and that he had recently been flying along with Marine fighter pilots on their combat missions and would like to do the same with Army pilots. MacDonald went along with it and gave Lindbergh permission to fly with his squadrons. Everything had worked out precisely as Lindbergh had hoped.

The Jolly Rogers continue to bombard Biak

Meanwhile, many of the bombing strikes flown by the 90th Bomb Group in May, June, and July were in support of the 41st Infantry Division that was still fighting to evict the 11,000 Japanese from Biak Island and take over the site of the three airfields the enemy had begun building there. Unlike at Wakde Island, those fields could be made as long as desired and, also being coral-based, would easily support heavy bombers. American infantry had begun the amphibious assault on Biak on May 27, and the battle would continue until August 17 (and even then there would still be some Japanese hiding in caves).

The Japanese were as usual making full use of coral caves for defense. On Biak there was a massive coral ridge, practically a vertical cliff, 200 to 300 feet high and paralleling the shoreline about 1000 feet back of the beach. This ridge dominated the coastline and was honeycombed with caves, some of them huge interconnected caverns running deep into the ground, in which the Japanese were sheltering, stockpiling supplies, and from which they were launching attacks and shooting at the American troops with artillery and small arms. The Japanese would roll their artillery pieces to the mouth of a cave to fire them, then pull them back inside where they were safe from American bombs and artillery fire.

The Americans build an airfield on Owi Island

Since the battle for Biak was progressing so slowly, MacArthur decided to establish an airfield on Owi Island, three miles offshore from Biak (see map, p. 600). This was another small coral island, but at three miles long and a little over a mile wide it was a larger one than Wakde. Aircraft based on Owi could give close air support to the Americans fighting for Biak. Taking Owi was easy because the island was not inhabited, even by natives. When the Americans landed there, General Kenney soon found out why the natives wanted nothing to do with the place: it was a breeding ground for scrub typhus, and anyone who went to Owi Island was likely to get sick and die. General Kenney wrote:

> It was at Owi that I suddenly woke up to something that I should have realized a long while before. When we mentioned the place to the natives around Biak, they told us that no one lived there as the place was "taboo." We had heard that word many times ever since coming to New Guinea and had smiled and paid no attention to it. Just another silly native custom. In about ten days the troops on Owi began to develop scrub typhus. We had run into this disease several times before but now it suddenly dawned on us that in every case we had been warned by that word, but had been too dumb to understand what the natives were trying to tell us.[1]

One of the engineers building the airfield later wrote:

> By mid-July [1944], many of the first arrivals were getting sick with fevers of an unknown cause. Many had been bitten by ticks [mites] which carried a disease known as scrub typhus. The 864th Engineers had 15% of its men sick, most of them in hospitals. Three of their men died of the fever. Temperatures of as high as 107 degrees were not uncommon. The medical staff knew little about the disease or how to treat it... Once the cause was determined, as a precaution all clothing and blankets were treated with a solution of dimethyl phthalate soap which practically eliminated the problem. This seems to explain the natives' opinion that to go to Owi was to die! In the native tongue, Owi means "Island of Death."[2]

It was discovered that the mites that transmitted the disease lived mostly in the tall grass (scrub) on the island, so the grass was burned and bulldozed back away from the airfield and camp areas.

David Zellmer, the B-24 pilot of the 13th Air Force who was based for a while on Wakde Island wrote:

> One more disease has been added to our "worry" list—Scrub

Typhus. It's transmitted by the bite of a tiny mite found in tall grass hereabout. Those stricken experience a very high fever which, we are warned, can be fatal or cause permanent damage to the eyes, brain, or both. We were ordered to soak all our outer clothing in large vats of a liquid chemical, and to stay out of tall grass. The "worry" list already includes malaria, dengue fever, yellow fever, and elephantiasis. And homesickness.[3]

The Seabees began airfield construction on Owi Island on June 8, 1944, and such was their skill and speed by this stage of the war that the airfield was usable by aircraft in just six days. U. S. troops fighting on Biak cheered when they saw the first group of American airplanes land so near them on Owi. Charles Lindbergh arrived there on July 16th, in a P-38, and wrote in his journal:

> There is much concern about typhus on this island. Thirty new cases today, bringing the total to about 150. There has been too much rain to burn the brush and dead wood around the camp areas.[4]

On July 22 he wrote:

> Typhus cases now number about 200 on the island. For some reason there are very few on Biak, only three miles away... I have started rubbing my body twice a day with anti-bug oil.[5]

Also on July 22 Lindbergh watched eight B-24s, likely belonging to the Jolly Rogers, make a drop on the long coral ridge just back of the shore on Biak in an attempt to eliminate the Japanese fighting from the caves:

> The B-24s—eight planes in all—hit on the minute; first two bombers, then two more flights of three ships each—spread at sufficient intervals to allow the smoke from one flight to drift aside before the next was in position to release its bombs. Since there was no antiaircraft opposition, the bombers came over at the ideal altitude of 6000 feet. The bombs were perfectly placed, covering the entire length of the ridge. I could see them released with my naked eye—specks curving gracefully through the air—irretrievable death in flight. Then the flashing concussion waves as they hit, and the great column of smoke drifting slowly away to show the torn trees and battered coral ridge. Then the ground artillery began its bombardment, covering the ridge with smaller puffs. This afternoon, our infantry will attack.
>
> [Later] a report came in on the area bombed this morning. The infantry moved in following the artillery bombardment after the bombing. They occupied the area "without firing a shot"—found about forty dead Japs in one cave and "parts of quite a few more" scattered about. The few who were still living were sitting and

lying around in a dazed condition and made no move as they saw our soldiers.[6]

The Japanese who were captured alive after the bombing of Biak's coral ridges were in the same senseless condition, caused by bomb concussion, as those described by Col. Art Rogers after the Jolly Rogers bombed the Komiatum Ridge near Salamaua in August of 1943.

Charles Lindbergh flies escort for the Jolly Rogers

On July 3, 1944, twelve B-24s of the Jolly Rogers flew a mission from Wakde Island to bomb the Japanese airbase at Jefman (see Map 43-5, p. 551). This happened to be a day off for the Horner crew, who would fly a mission the next day. American intelligence had deduced that the Japanese nuisance-bombers that were keeping men awake on Wakde Island every night were probably flying from Jefman, so the mission on July 3 was to crater the Japanese airstrip there to make it unusable and destroy any enemy bombers that might be parked on the field.

At this time Charles Lindbergh was down the coast at Hollandia with the 475th Fighter Group, and a squadron from this group was assigned to fly fighter cover for the Jolly Rogers on this mission. The 475th sent up a dozen P-38s, and Lindbergh flew one of them. In fact, he took charge of a flight of four, creating the unprecedented situation of a civilian pilot in command of military pilots on a combat mission.

To fighter pilots in their late teens and early twenties, any 42-year-old man was considered geriatric, if not practically senile, but Lindbergh's reputation, and his demonstrated skill at flying any airplane, including the hottest fighter planes, had earned their respect. The young fighter pilots referred to Lindbergh as "the old man," but in truth they knew that Lindbergh's flying skills were at least equal to and probably superior to their own, since most of them were new pilots, trained during the war, while Lindbergh had been flying since 1922.

The fighters took off from Hollandia at 7:45 on the morning of the mission and flew up the New Guinea coast to land on Wakde Island at 8:05. Lindbergh and the other fighter pilots then attended a briefing about the mission. Meanwhile the Jolly Rogers, in four flights of four B-24s each, took off ahead of them and headed for the rendezvous point (their cruise speed was 100 mph slower than the fighters—150 vs 250 mph). The fighters left Wakde behind the bombers at 8:38 (all times are from Lindbergh's journal). Whatever the Horner crew was up to this day on the ground, they surely heard all the noise of the sixteen bombers followed by the twelve fighters departing, but these were normal sounds on busy Wakde Island and they probably paid scant attention to them. No one among them knew that Charles Lindbergh was one of the fighter plane pilots.

The fighters and bombers rendezvoused at ten thousand feet above the landmark of False Cape on the northwest coast of New Guinea, and then the whole formation headed for Jefman. It so happened that no Japanese fighter planes were encountered that day, so the American fighter planes had nothing much to do and ended up as merely spectators to the activities of the bombers. Lindbergh described the scene that evening in his journal:

> The bombers closed formation as they flew some 10,000 feet above the airstrip [Lindbergh was obviously watching the Jolly Rogers form up to make their bombing run from the IP to the target]. I brought my flight into position to see the drop. A single column of black smoke rose from the center of the strip below, and then the entire runway seemed to rise into the air, the delay-action bombs flashing like distant lightning amid the smoke and debris. It was a perfect hit. Hardly a bomb missed its mark. We circled overhead and followed the bombers back for a distance; then turned out to the coast for strafing.[7]

Col. MacDonald had told his pilots that rather than simply fly straight back to base on these escort missions, once they had seen the bombers safely on their way home they should spend their return trips shooting up any Japanese targets they could find on the ground or at sea, only being careful to make sure that they reserved enough gas to get home. MacDonald himself was leading the twelve P-38s on this day, and after the Jolly Rogers were well on their way back to Wakde Island and out of danger, he broke away from their formation and took his fighters down low along the coasts of some nearby islands to go barge hunting.

As mentioned earlier, after the Battle of the Bismarck Sea (Chapter 25), the Japanese no longer dared to try to resupply their garrisons with ships operating in daylight, and instead resorted to moving supplies along the coasts of New Guinea and other islands in barges or other small vessels that moved only at night. Each night, before dawn, the Japanese would run their barges in against the shore, beneath overhanging trees whenever possible, and camouflage them with palm leaves, vines, and anything else they could find to make them difficult to detect from the air. Then they would lay low during the daylight hours and resume their travel after dark. As a result, hunting and destroying barges hidden along the shorelines became a pastime of American fighter pilots, as well as for the crews of light and medium bombers such as A-20s and B-25s.

On this particular day, Col. MacDonald's squadron spotted a barge and a small ship, a "lugger," anchored close together in a small, deep cove of an island. The ship and barge were both so heavily loaded with supplies, and thus so low in the water, that the Japanese hadn't been able to drag them all the way up to the shore and they had grounded about 100 feet out. They had chosen this cove because it was surrounded by tall, steep hillsides that made it difficult for any strafing aircraft to get very close to them without danger of crashing into a hill. Since they had been unable to get their vessels up tight against the shoreline, they had tried to camouflage them to look like little islands.

The Americans were not fooled, however, nor were they put off by the looming hillsides. Forming a "strafing circle," they proceeded to take turns shooting up the Japanese vessels with the intention of sinking them. Lindbergh wrote later that it was indeed dangerous flying down among the hills lining the cove to get a shot at the barge and boat, and that he was only able to straighten out from a steep bank for a second or two to fire his guns before he had to pull up sharply to miss the jungled hilltops, which he was only clearing by a scant few feet. He also wrote that "the speed of the modern fighter is so great that you actually fly through [your own] ricocheting tracers as you pass over the target." All the American pilots proved skillful at dodging between the hills to strafe the ship and barge with their .50-caliber machine guns and 20mm cannon, and none of the fighters crashed into the hillsides as the Japanese had hoped. By the time the Americans were finished with them, the barge was on fire and the lugger so full of holes that it would never sail again.

Satisfied that none of the supplies carried by those vessels would ever make it to whatever Japanese airfield or troop garrison they had been intended for, the fighters resumed their barge hunting until their fuel began running low, at which time Col. MacDonald decided that it was time to follow the Jolly Rogers back to Wakde Island. Lindbergh, however, still had plenty of fuel left and wanted to continue barge hunting, so he stayed behind after the rest of the squadron left, and his wingman (whose name he did not record) stuck with him. They found more barges and strafed them before the wingman called Lindbergh over the radio to tell him that he was getting so low on fuel that he was not sure he could make it back to Wakde. Luckily, he was talking to the right man.

Lindbergh told the pilot to lean out his fuel mixture and lower the rpm of his engines, and together they flew at a reduced speed to the nearest American airfield, which was Owi. The pilot landed there with 70 gallons of fuel to spare, and Lindbergh, who had been conserving fuel all day, still had 260 gallons. After refueling at Owi they both flew back to Hollandia, arriving there around 5 PM. The experience dramatically underscored Lindbergh's points when he gave a fuel economy lecture to the squadron that evening.

Lindbergh is called to Gen. MacArthur's headquarters

Lindbergh had flown six combat missions with the 475th Fighter Squadron before General Kenney got wind of what was going on and called him back to Brisbane to explain himself. As Kenney wrote:

On July 4th [1944] one of the war correspondents just in from Nadzab came into the office and asked me if I knew that Col. Charles Lindbergh was in New Guinea. I admitted that I didn't. He laughed and said that GHQ [General Headquarters] didn't know it either... Without bothering to get permission or clearance from anyone, he had simply gotten a ride to New Guinea and checked in with Whitehead at Nadzab.[8]

Lindbergh wrote in his journal:

Just as we had finished supper Colonel Morrissey phoned me from General Hutchinson's headquarters. Said he had bad news for me; that a message had come in "from the south" (meaning Australian Army headquarters) saying a rumor was circulating to the effect that I was flying combat in New Guinea, and that, if true, there should be no more of it. Morrissey had been sent up from Nadzab to deliver the message to me... But Morrissey had no details. Decided to fly to Nadzab tomorrow and find out what happened; looks like politics.[9]

Lindbergh flew back to Nadzab and thence to Brisbane, where he was ushered into General MacArthur's headquarters. First he spoke to General Kenney, then to General Richard Sutherland (MacArthur's chief of staff), and finally to MacArthur himself. All three officers received him cordially and asked him what he was up to.

To all of them he pled his case for flying fighters in New Guinea and held out his fuel economy carrot: he could teach 5th Air Force pilots to dramatically extend the range of their aircraft using some simple fuel-saving measures that they had not been taught in their flight training, but that he could show them. Extending the range of American aircraft could mean a shorter Pacific war.

Lindbergh recorded his meeting with General Sutherland in his journal:

I outlined to General Sutherland the work I am doing and my reason for being in this area, i. e, studying pursuit operations in connection with the design of future fighters. Sutherland said that he would arrange the necessary papers for me for this area, putting me on observer status and that that would put me in a position to do about anything I wanted to do... [Then] the subject of fighter range came up. I said that none of the squadrons I had made contact with understood the subject of fuel economy, that they were wasting a large percentage of their gasoline by cruising their engines at too high an rpm and too low a manifold pressure, and that I thought a combat radius of 700 miles could be obtained with the P-38s after the pilots were properly instructed and trained [the standard range of the P-38D was considered to be 500 miles]. I told him that I believed the more experienced pilots could get a 750-mile combat radius from their planes...Sutherland said that if a 700-mile radius could be obtained, it would be of the utmost importance to their plans in this area.[10]

Sutherland then took Lindbergh to see Gen. MacArthur:

He ... [MacArthur] greeted me warmly, and spoke of the last time we had met, when he was Chief of Staff in Washington. He then turned immediately to the subject of combat radius for fighters... I repeated what I had told Sutherland, i.e. that I thought the average P-38 squadron, after a little instruction and training, could fly a 700-mile combat radius without much difficulty and with just as much fuel reserve as they are now coming back with from their present missions. MacArthur said it would be a gift from heaven if that could be done and asked me if I were in a position to go back up to New Guinea to instruct the squadrons in the methods of fuel economy which would make such a radius possible. I told him there was nothing I would rather do and that I could go back at once.[11]

Charles Lindbergh meets with General Kenney on July 12, 1944 at MacArthur's headquarters in Brisbane, Australia. Lindbergh wore a uniform, but since he was a civilian it carried no insignia of rank. He was addressed as "Mister Lindbergh."

Kenney told MacArthur:

If anyone could fly a little monoplane all the way from New

York to Paris and have gas left over, he ought to be able to teach my P-38 pilots how to get more range out of their airplanes. If he could do that, it would mean that we could make longer jumps and get to the Philippines that much quicker, so I wanted to take him under my wing, issue the necessary orders, and put him to work. Lindbergh nodded with that charming kid grin of his that is one of his best assets. General MacArthur said, "All right, Colonel [referring to Lindbergh's prewar rank]. I'll just turn you over to General Kenney, but I warn you. He's a slave-driver."[12]

Kenney then furnished Lindbergh with paperwork authorizing him to remain in the Southwest Pacific area as an "observer." However, Kenney told Lindbergh something that he didn't want to hear: he didn't want him flying combat missions:

> I got Lindbergh fixed up with enough pieces of paper to legalize his status and then we talked about the job. He was quite enthusiastic about its possibilities and thought that with a little training he could increase our operating radius of action nearly fifty percent. . .
> The first hitch came when I told him that I didn't want him to get into combat. He was actually a civilian, with a lot of headline possibilities. The headlines would not be good if he got shot down, and they would be still worse if by any chance the Japs should capture him. He thought that it would be hard to check on how well the pilots were absorbing his teachings if he couldn't go along to watch them, and besides, he wanted to observe the P-38 in combat to get the answers in regard to the comparison of single-engined versus two-engined fighters. I said . . . I'd let him go along with the fighter escort to the bombers . . . [but] I reiterated that I didn't want him to get into combat.[13]

After his conference with the generals in Brisbane, Lindbergh returned to the 475th Fighter Group and resumed his flying with them, escorting Jolly Rogers bombers as before, including, on at least one occasion, a bomber flown by the Horner crew. But as to General Kenney's instructions about staying out of combat, Lindbergh simply disregarded them.

Lindbergh recorded his experiences and observations on the Pacific war in a day-by-day war diary that was later published as *The Wartime Journals of Charles Lindbergh.** In his journal Lindbergh frequently waxed poetic about the beauties of the Pacific islands as seen from the air. A believer in the myth of the Noble Savage, he daydreamed about someday walking down some remote jungle path to encounter a village of picturesque natives who were as-yet

---

*Harcourt Brace Jovanovich, Inc., New York, 1970.

"unspoiled" by contact with the civilized world. Had he ever actually done so, of course, he might have furnished the picturesque natives with lunch, since so many of them in New Guinea, especially the "unspoiled" ones who had not come under the influence of Christian missionaries, were cannibals.

Lindbergh shoots down a Japanese fighter plane

On July 28, 1944, while the Horner crew was flying a mission to bomb the Japanese airfield at Manokwari, Lindbergh accompanied Col. MacDonald's squadron to the island of Ceram, flying one of their P-38s again. They took off at dawn from Mokmer Field on Biak Island (for by this time Biak had finally fallen into American hands) and headed south. This time the P-38s were not accompanying any bombers, but were acting as strafers, and their targets were some Japanese airstrips on the south coast of Ceram. Their intention was to shoot up the airfields and any aircraft that might be parked on them.

While they were looking over various possible targets, Lindbergh and the others pilots picked up the radio chatter of another fighter group that was engaged in a dogfight with Japanese planes somewhere nearby. This turned out to be a squadron of the 8th Fighter Group that had encountered two Japanese fighters. Both enemy pilots proved to be skillful fliers, avoiding the attacks of the American planes by making sudden, tight, evasive turns that the larger, heavier American P-38s could not follow. Lindbergh heard several of the American pilots report that they had used up all their ammunition without hitting either one of the enemy planes. One pilot griped over the radio that the Japanese were "making monkeys out of us."

Lindbergh and the other 475th pilots soon located the dogfight, and one of the Japanese planes, a Mitsubishi Ki-51 (code name "Sonia") two-seat ground-attack/reconnaissance plane, turned directly toward Lindbergh's P-38. The two fighters flew straight at each other with a closing speed of 500 mph, both firing. Lindbergh concentrated his tracers on the other plane's engine, saw hits, and saw its propeller slowing down.

At the last possible instant both pilots pulled straight up, Lindbergh hauling back on his control stick with all his strength, trying to avoid a collision. For an instant he got an extremely close-up view of the cooling fins on the other plane's engine cylinders,

A Japanese "Sonia" fighter/bomber like the one that Charles Lindbergh shot down near Ceram on July 28, 1944.

and felt a jolt that he feared was a collision but turned out to be only air turbulence from the close encounter. He estimated that the two airplanes probably missed each other by less than ten feet.

The Japanese plane then spun down out of control and struck the water, throwing up a fountain of spray. This would be Lindbergh's one and only aerial victory. After both of the Japanese planes had been shot down, the American fighters returned to Biak.

Lindbergh is nearly shot down by a Japanese fighter plane

On August 1, 1944, at Wakde Island, a large group of Jolly Rogers bombers (not including the Horner crew, who were again scheduled for a mission the next day) took off and were forming up over the island before heading for Ambon Island (just south of Ceram) for a strike at the Japanese airfields there. Before they were even all in the air, however, a report came in from a reconnaissance plane that Ambon was solidly socked in by clouds. The bombers were therefore recalled and returned to Wakde. The 345th Fighter Group that Lindbergh was flying with had been scheduled to take off from Mokmer Field on Biak Island to accompany the bombers to the target, but they too got the bad weather report and scrubbed the mission.

However, with their P-38s all fueled up, armed, and ready to go somewhere, Col. MacDonald and Lindbergh cooked up an alternate plan. Since the weather to the north was good, they decided to fly a fighter sweep in that direction, all the way up to the Palau Islands (map 44-1, opposite). They would take along with them two other pilots. The Palaus were 600 miles away, which according to conventional wisdom was too far for a P-38 to go, but Lindbergh viewed this as an excellent opportunity to once again demonstrate his fuel-saving methods, by flying there and returning with fuel to spare. However, this would be a dangerous flight, since Palau was a Japanese stronghold that was estimated to have 150 enemy planes on its airfield. In other words, it was a hornet's nest.

This, however, made it all the more attractive to the Americans, who had not gotten many chances to engage enemy fighters up to now and were spoiling for a fight. Off they went, and when they arrived over Palau they spotted some Japanese fighter planes on floats operating offshore and promptly shot two of them down. This took the American planes down near the surface of the sea, a bad place to be if jumped by enemy fighters, and that is exactly what happened.

A Zero dove on them from above and latched onto Lindbergh's tail. Normally a P-38 would simply dive away from a Zero, being a much heavier airplane and thus faster in a dive, but Lindbergh's fighter was already close to the sea and there was nowhere below him to go. He knew he couldn't outturn the agile enemy plane—even the Spitfires at Darwin hadn't been able to do that. All he could do was full-throttle his two engines and try to outrun the Zero, but the Japanese plane had gained a great deal of speed in its dive, making this impossible too. In short, the enemy pilot had him cold.

Lindbergh hunched down behind his armor-plated seat and waited for the bullets to hit him or his plane, thinking, as he wrote later, of his wife and children back home. But at that moment Col. MacDonald zoomed in from the side, and although he was too far away for accurate shooting, he sent a stream of tracers and cannon fire toward the Japanese plane in an attempt to distract the pilot. The trick worked, and the Japanese pilot veered off; Lindbergh was safe. Some of MacDonald's shells must have hit the Zero, too, for it was last seen headed toward a cloud with a smoking engine.

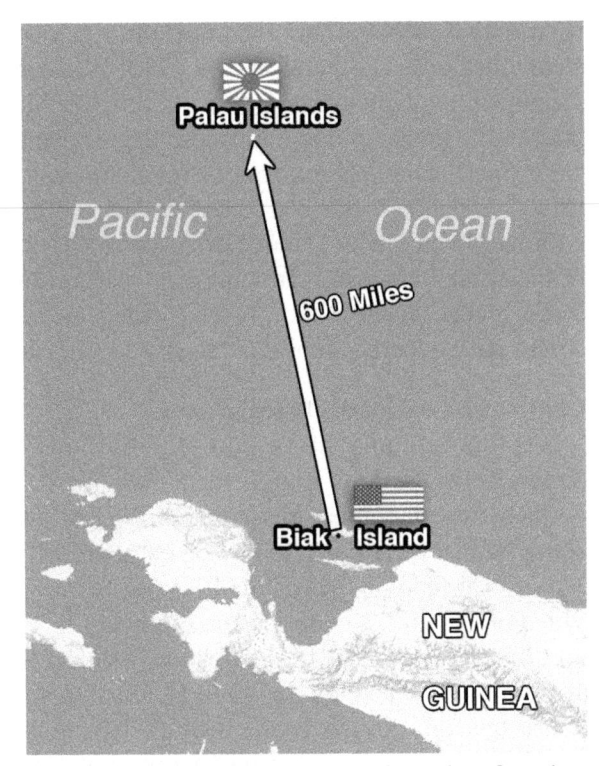

Map 44-1. Lindbergh and three other pilots flew their P-38 fighter planes about 600 miles north from Biak's Mokmer Field to the Japanese stronghold of Palau.

"Lucky Lindy" was the title of a song that had become a national hit after Lindbergh had flown the Atlantic in 1927,[*] and it referred to his luck in making it from New York to Paris, but Lindbergh was never more lucky than the day a Japanese pilot near Palau missed an almost sure opportunity to shoot him down.

With the hornet's nest at Palau now stirred up, the four American fighter pilots decided that they didn't have enough fuel for any further dogfighting and headed for home. They made it back to Biak with fuel to spare, as expected, but one of the American pilots must have spilled the beans, for word of the impromptu long-range mission, and of Lindbergh's close call, soon got around. Before long Col. MacDonald was called on the carpet by his superiors.

It seems that 5th Fighter Command had been turning down requests from Bomber Command for fighters to accompany the heavy bombers from Biak to Palau on the grounds that it was beyond fighter range, and so it had

---

[*]It was a terrible song (listen to it sometime and see for yourself).

been until Lindbergh and the three other pilots using his fuel-conservation techniques proved otherwise. But Col. MacDonald had embarrassed Fighter Command by demonstrating that not only could P-38s get to Palau and back but they could shoot down Japanese fighter planes there as well. Within days Col. MacDonald was relieved of his duties and sent back to the States "on leave." Lindbergh felt bad about it, but continued to fly combat missions with the 475th's new commander, Major Meryl Smith. That wasn't the end of the matter, however, for word that Charles Lindbergh had nearly been shot down by the Japanese soon spread widely in Fifth Air Force circles, and it would have repercussions for "Lucky Lindy" as well.

Lindbergh escorts the Horner crew

On the morning of August 9, 1944, over a month after Lindbergh accompanied the Jolly Rogers to Jefman in a P-38, the Horner crew took off on their twelfth combat mission from Wakde Island, flying a D-model B-24 along with several other Jolly Rogers bombers. This time their target was a Japanese airfield on the island of Haroekoe (now Haruku), south of the larger island of Ceram, 730 miles to the southwest of Wakde Island.

Lindbergh took off from Mokmer field on Biak Island in another P-38, along with fifteen others, and at 10:18 in the morning the sixteen fighter planes joined the Jolly Rogers B-24s over the Pisang Islands, the rendezvous point, and then escorted them to the target, keeping watch for enemy planes. Lindbergh and the other P-38 pilots wove lazy patterns above and around the slower B-24s, like cowboys herding cattle, and as always, the sight of protective fighter planes around them was a comfort to the crews of the bombers. Mr. Baca says today, "We always preferred P-38 fighters as escorts over other types of American fighter planes, because with their twin engines and tail booms it was easy to tell that they were American. As the P-38 pilots moved in close to escort us, they would always bank up sideways to show us their shape. They didn't want to get shot at by some trigger-happy bomber gunner." Gunners on bombers sometimes mistook American P-47s for Japanese Zeros, which they somewhat resembled at first glance, and had occasionally fired at them by mistake.

As the American fighters and bombers approached Haroekoe Island together, they could see that it was hidden under a solid layer of clouds, making it impossible to bomb. The bombers then turned back to their secondary target, an oilfield at Boela. Eight of the P-38s remained with the bombers, while the other eight fighter pilots, including Lindbergh, peeled off and went looking for a little action on their own. They spotted a small break in the clouds and spiraled down through it to find themselves over Piroe Bay, just off the north coast of Ambon Island. They flew over the island and examined a couple of Japanese airfields there, noting some enemy bombers on the ground and ships in the harbors to report to intelligence officers later, while drawing some ineffective antiaircraft fire from around the airfields.

The eight P-38s then turned out over the water of Piroe Bay, where they spotted a large sailing ship in the middle of Haroekoe Strait, between the islands of Ambon and Haroekoe. In these waters, any sort of boat, barge, or ship was assumed to be under Japanese control, so the American fighters lined up to attack it.

Lindbergh shoots up a sailing ship

Lindbergh considered it a shame that a magnificent sloop under full sail, a lovely sight to behold, had to be destroyed. War correspondent Charles Rawlings had felt the same way watching Col. Art Rogers skip-bomb a "clean, polished, smart-looking" little Japanese ship that displayed a lot of pretty brasswork (Chapter 27), and he had written afterwards, "Ships, like music and art, have no nationality." However, the picturesque sailing ship that the fighter pilots had spotted could have been delivering supplies to Japanese troops on these islands, so it had to be sunk. Lindbergh wrote that night in his journal:

> A ship with full sails set heeled over gracefully on the sea; a patch of clear blue sky above; freshening rain squalls in the distance. Mottling of sunlight. Rippling of wind. The jeweled setting of tropical land and sea. Those eternal seconds of stabbing clarity between life, peace, beauty, and the certainty of death.[14]

Other P-38s were lining up ahead of him to strafe the ship, and Lindbergh took his place in line as number four. He watched as the first plane opened fire:

> Spouts of foam rise up from the water. Splinters fly off the deck. A cloud of smoke veils the ship. Flashes mark where the 20-millimeters burst. . . The ship is wounded. The straight wake bends. The sails begin to flutter. . . The ship is in the center of another cloud of smoke. The wind haphazardly catches the sails, and it heels to the right again. It takes on the personality of a living, dying thing, as though it were made of flesh and blood instead of cloth and wood. It seems to be writhing in its agony like a wounded animal still trying to escape. . . There can be nothing left alive on deck. The ship is filled with dead and wounded men. Those who jumped overboard are swimming in the water a quarter mile behind. Probably a few of the crew are still unhit, crouching behind cargo and bulkheads in the hold.[15]

Then it was his turn to shoot as his fighter went racing toward the ship:

> "One thousand yards; 250 miles an hour . . . the 20-millimeters flash on the hull just above the waterline. Six hundred yards. I

> hold the sight on the center of the deck and clamp the trigger down. Flashes of the cannon bursts. Long streaks of tracers. Red balls of fire ricocheting off the hull. Bits of debris flying up into the air. All covered with a haze of smoke. Littered decks; shattered portholes; a fallen sail. Like a derelict abandoned in a storm.[16]

They left the sailing ship mangled and sinking. After firing at some other vessels nearby, leaving them also smoking and careening out of control, the American fighters climbed back up through the clouds and set course for home:

> The rolling white cloud layer has drawn together like a stage curtain. What happened underneath it now seems like a dream. We cannot fully realize how close we ourselves have brushed to death, that our guns have left ships sinking, on fire, with men dead and terribly wounded on their decks, with others drowning in the water, with rescue boats not daring to set out from shore. We throttle down our engines and take up our course for home, nearly 500 miles over enemy territory; but we feel as safe as though we were already there. A few years ago, in peacetime, such a flight would have been considered hazardous. Now, in war, we think nothing of it at all. We cross the sea, and the northwest neck of New Guinea, and land on Mokmer strip [on Biak island] at 1427 [2:27 PM].[17]

While the fighter planes were shooting up the Japanese shipping in Haroekoe Strait, the B-24s of the Horner crew and the other Jolly Rogers were dropping their bombs on the Japanese oil field at Boela, with antiaircraft shells bursting all around them. The flak was inaccurate, however, and no bombers were seriously damaged. Lt. Cooper recorded in his mission diary that a total of 690 one-hundred-pound bombs were dropped on Boela's oil wells and storage tanks that day, and as the bombers headed back to Wakde Island they left many fires burning on the ground, with smoke plumes rising high into the sky—yet another nail in the coffin of Imperial Japan.

Lindbergh is recalled to headquarters

Meanwhile word of Lindbergh's two close brushes with death from enemy fighter planes had reached the ears of General Kenney, who decided it was high time to rein in his celebrity civilian fighter pilot. Kenny felt that Lindbergh was pushing his luck too hard and too often, tempting fate, and too many pilots who had done that were dead. He sent Lindbergh an order to halt combat flying immediately and return to Brisban for a meeting.

Resigned to the fact that his wings had been clipped, Lindbergh prepared to head back to MacArthur's headquarters. General Wurtsmith requested that he give his lectures on fuel economy to all fighter groups that he passed by on his way back to Australia, and this he did, moving at a leisurely pace and writing about everything he observed as he hitched rides in, or borrowed, one aircraft after another. From Owi Island he caught a ride back to Wakde Island in a P-61 (Black Widow) night fighter, landing at Wakde a little after 2 PM on Wednesday, the 16th of August.

On that day the Horner crew was also on Wakde Island, busy loading their camp equipment into a B-24 to fly up to Biak Island with the rest of the Jolly Rogers, for Biak was now ready to receive them. The squadrons at both Nadzab and Wakde Island had begun making the move to Mokmer Airstrip on Biak on August 10th. The ground echelon of the Jolly Rogers was at sea, headed to Biak on transport ships. The Horner crew had already taken one load of equipment up to Biak that morning, and had returned to Wakde for a second one in the afternoon. This would be their last day on Wakde Island.

Lindbergh's P-61 landed near the crew, and since Lt. Horner admired P-61s he no doubt took note of this one as it rolled by toward the parking area, but of course he could have had no idea that world-famous aviator Charles Lindbergh was in the cockpit. After Lindbergh got out of the plane, keeping to himself as usual, he caught a ride to the south end of Wakde Island in a jeep. From there he took a boat across the 300 yards of water to little Insoemanai Island, where he was scheduled to meet with Major John T. Moore, the commander of the 348th Fighter Group (flying P-47s). The 348th was based on Wakde, and Lindbergh would give its pilots his fuel conservation lecture the next morning.*

Major Moore was not in his tent, so while waiting for him to return Lindbergh took the chance to relax a little on the nearby beach. He wrote in his journal:

> [S]ince his tent is only a few feet from the beach, I stripped, and after a half hour's sun bath, I waded out to the end of the reef and swam along watching the fish. The sea life is slightly different at every island where I have been—the starfish more purple here, and the "sea cucumbers" have different colored spines.[18]

Lts. Horner and Cooper could have told him that there were a lot of interesting miniature crabs to see among the coral reefs on the north edge of Wakde Island as well (Lindbergh would spend the later years of his life as a wildlife conservationist). But if the men of the Horner crew were even aware of the famous figure swimming nearby as they departed, they took no notice of him, and to Lindbergh their B-24 was just one more aircraft taking off from the busy airstrip nearby.

---

*When the 348th Fighter Group arrived on Wakde Island on May 22nd they found the island already so crowded that they established their headquarters on nearby tiny Insoemanai Island (see photo and diagram on pages 514-15) and set up a ferry service to and from Wakde.[19]

That afternoon the Horner crew happily bade farewell to Wakde Island and its miserable living conditions. The following day, after giving his lecture on fuel economy to the P-47 pilots, Lindbergh also left Wakde Island for the last time, flying a borrowed P-47, and headed in the opposite direction, back to Australia, to MacArthur's headquarters in Brisbane to explain himself. He was probably rehearsing his excuses all the way, in case rebukes awaited him.

Lindbergh departs the Southwest Pacific

On August 22 Lindbergh had meetings with Generals Kenney and MacArthur at Allied headquarters, and probably much to Lindbergh's relief they turned out to be cordial. Kenney had heard about Lindbergh shooting down a Japanese plane near Ceram Island, and then nearly being shot down by another one at Palau, and he asked Lindbergh for his version of the events. Kenney wrote later:

> [At Ceram] a lone Jap airplane suddenly loomed up directly ahead of Observer, Lindbergh's P-38. I had told him that, of course, if it came to a matter of self-defense, I could not expect him to refrain from shooting. How much elasticity his conscience suddenly acquired in regard to the business of self-defense I don't know and never asked him, but anyhow Lindbergh fired a burst and the Jap went down.
>
> I knew about the story shortly after the group landed, but as long as no one put in a claim for official credit for the destruction of an enemy airplane I pretended that I hadn't heard of the occurrence.
>
> [At Palau] Lindbergh gained the shocking information that a Jap airplane on his tail was something he could not get rid of. Luckily he had three experts at the art of handling such situations. They extricated him from his dilemma by the simple method of shooting down the Jap before the Jap shot down Lindbergh . . . The little episode over Ceram had made shooting down a Jap look easy. Lindbergh knew better now. He mentally filed the picture away somewhere in his brain. The next time he wouldn't get caught like that at low altitude by a Nip airplane that could out-maneuver him.
>
> There wasn't to be any next time, however. I told him he couldn't go out on any more combat missions and I wished he would go home. I was, and still am, exceedingly fond of Charles Lindbergh, but I was getting worried. I owed him a debt of real gratitude for increasing the combat range of our fighter planes. It was going to pay heavy dividends for the rest of the war and I appreciated what he had done, but I was getting worried for fear he would get shot down. If that happened it would hurt the Air Force and it would certainly bring down a lot of criticism on MacArthur

and on me for allowing him to go out on such missions.

Lindbergh agreed. He said that he had taught the kids all that he could, had learned the answers about fighter tactics that he had come out to get, and was ready to return to the United States. I asked him not to tell anyone back home about being in combat as long as the war lasted and said that, if the story leaked out, I would tell the newspapermen that there was no record of his ever having flown on combat missions, let alone having shot down a Jap airplane. Lindbergh said he had no intention of telling the story as he too was anxious not to have any publicity in regard to his activities in the Pacific, particularly while the war was on.[20]

Lindbergh next met with General MacArthur. He told MacArthur that the range of the P-38 fighter plane could now be considered to be 650 miles instead of the former 570, and that pilots well-trained in fuel conservation should be able to conduct combat missions to as far out as 750 miles from their bases. He did not mention any extension of the range of bombers, because he hadn't lectured any bomber groups on the subject. The truth was that Lindbergh wasn't really interested in bombers; he'd come out to fly fighter planes in combat and had done so, and had gotten away with it for as long as he could.

MacArthur asked Lindbergh about his flight to the Palau islands, and Lindbergh steered the discussion to the weather instead of the fact that he'd nearly been shot down. He wrote in his journal that evening:

> MacArthur asked me about our flight to Palau. I told him exactly what had happened and outlined the dangers of the tropical fronts which usually lie between New Guinea and the Palau Islands. I told him that pilots making such a flight should be well experienced in flying through weather. He asked me how many Japanese planes I had shot down. I told him, "One."
> "Where was it?"
> "Off the south coast of Ceram."
> "Good, I'm glad you got one."[21]

Two days later Lindbergh was on the first leg of his journey back to the States in a Pan American PBY flying boat.

Meanwhile, the Horner crew took up residence at Mokmer Field on Biak Island, their new base of operations, and they would remain on Biak, flying bombing missions, for the next four-and-a-half months, before moving on with the Jolly Rogers to the Philippines.

Chapter Forty-Five

THE MOVE TO BIAK ISLAND

From Wakde Island the Horner crew, along with the rest of the Jolly Rogers crews and their bombers, flew up to Mokmer Field on Biak Island, which had just been captured from the Japanese (Map 45-1, opposite). Biak Island is 200 miles up the New Guinea coast from Wakde Island, and thus 200 miles closer to Gen. MacArthur's obsession: the liberation of the Philippines.

Biak Island is a large, irregularly-shaped, upthrust fragment of the Pacific Ocean floor, 45 miles long and 25 miles wide (map, p. 600), thickly covered with jungle in most places like nearly all the tropical islands in this part of the world. Biak lies opposite the coast of northwestern New Guinea at Geelvink Bay, the deep indentation of the New Guinea coastline that divides the head and shoulder of the "buzzard."

The capture of Biak Island

The battle for Biak Island was, like the battle for Lone Tree Hill across from Wakde Island, one of the fiercest fights in the Pacific war, yet it is little remembered today. Like all these island battles, it was fought to gain airfields from which the Americans could operate heavy bombers on their march across the Pacific to Japan. As usual the Jolly Rogers and other bomb groups paved the way for the American ground troops who were tasked with the grim, grinding job of wresting the ground away from the Japanese, yard-by-yard.

In the spring of 1944 MacArthur wanted Biak Island badly, and like all his objectives, he wanted it fast, the quicker to liberate the Philippines, which were 800 miles to the northwest of Biak. The Japanese on Biak had already been at work constructing airfields on a flat, open area on the south coast of the island (photo, p. 601), and unlike on small Wakde Island there was plenty of room on Biak to lengthen runways to handle heavy American bombers safely.

Gen. Kenney also coveted an airfield on Biak for his big bombers, since it would give them a longer reach into Japanese territory, all the way to the southern Philippines in fact. Wakde Island had been intended to be only a brief stop on the way to Biak Island, but Biak proved to be a much tougher nut for the American infantry to crack than little Wakde had been.

45. THE MOVE TO BIAK ISLAND

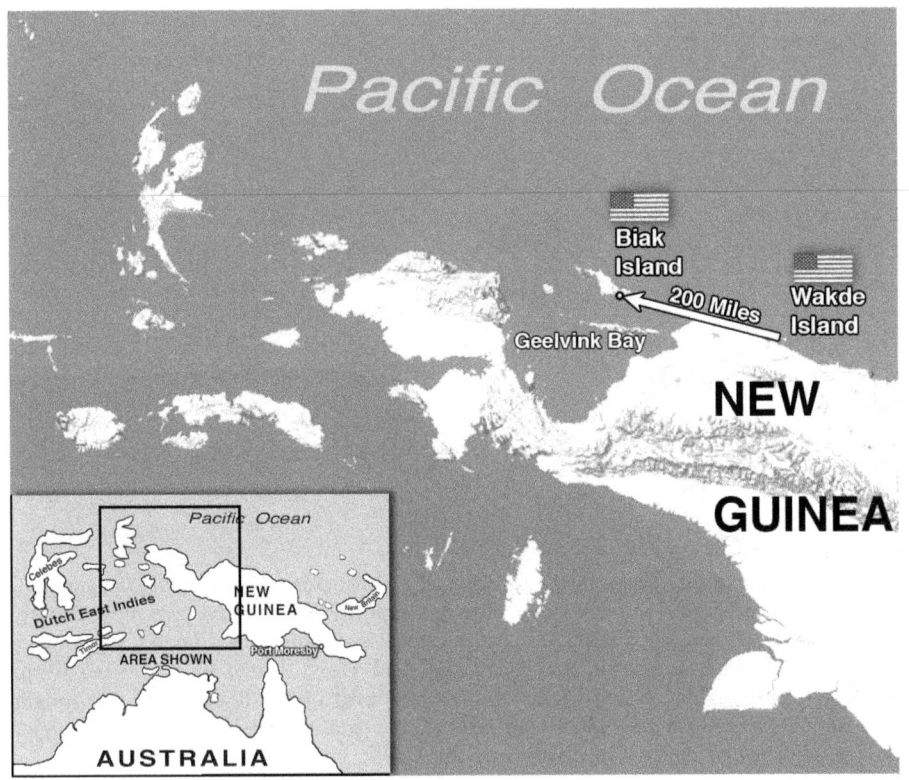

Map 45-1. In August of 1944 the Jolly Rogers moved from Wakde Island and Nadzab (they had been split up and based at both places) to Mokmer Field on Biak Island.

Both Wakde and Biak were attacked in May of 1944, but while Wakde fell in just three days (May 15-18), the capture of Biak would take over two and a half months, from May 27 to August 17. Wakde had been defended by only 800 Japanese troops, but Biak was occupied by 11,400 of them.

As with most battles in the Southwest Pacific, especially on New Guinea and other large islands, only a tiny part of Biak Island was contested by the belligerents, and as always the fight was over airfields. The Japanese airfields occupied only a small, open patch of ground along the southern coast of the island. Near those airfields, at a village called Bosnik, the American Army landed 12,000 troops (once again, as with Wakde Island, it was the Army's hard-fighting 41st Division).

As mentioned in the last chapter, along the southern shore of Biak Island are tall (200- to 300-foot) coral cliffs paralleling the shoreline just a few hundred yards back from the beach. These cliffs are riddled with caves, many of them massive caverns descending deep into the earth. Eons ago, when Biak Island was part of the sea floor, schools of fish swam through these caves; today

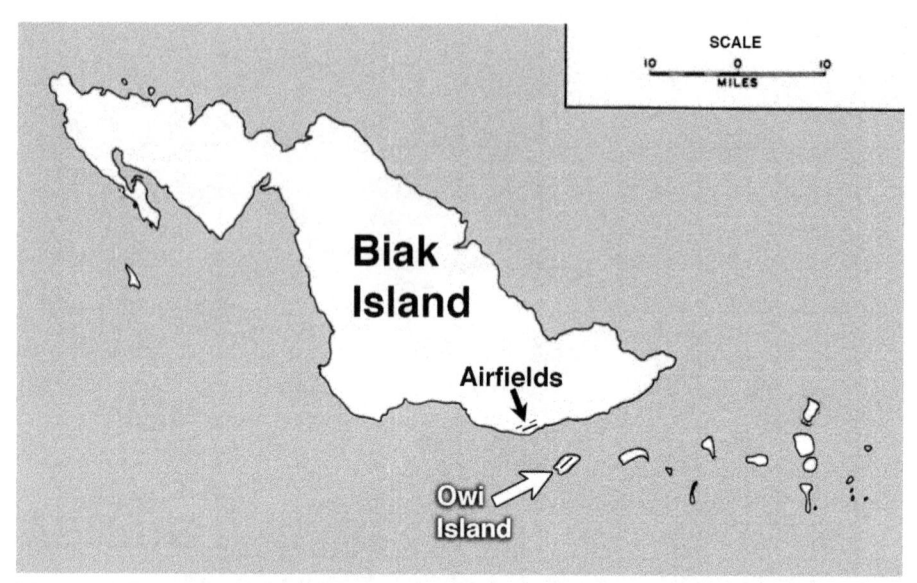

Map 45-2. Biak Island, showing the location of the airfields where the Jolly Rogers and other American air groups were based after the capture of the island (the main runway would be named Mokmer Field). The Americans also occupied Owi Island, three miles offshore from Biak, as shown, and based the 43rd Heavy Bomb Group (Ken's Men) there as well as fighter planes. Note what a small part of the Biak Island was fought over and utilized—just enough for an airbase, the area shown in the photo at right. This was typical of most island battles of the Pacific war.

they are above-ground catacombs. The entrances to most of the caves were obscured by jungle, and so well concealed that sometimes a man wouldn't recognize a cave even when he was standing right in front of it. The main airfield, near the village of Mokmer, was on a flat open plain near the sea, where the coral cliffs bent back to form a wide horseshoe around the plain, and those cliffs also were honeycombed with caves. The Japanese had developed most of these cavities, as they did on most Pacific islands, into strongholds from which to defend the island. Digging these suicidal "fighting insects" out of their holes would take much time and cost hundreds of American lives.

General Walter Krueger, commanding the Army infantry forces that invaded the island, had not considered it wise to land his forces on the open plain right in front of the airfields, surrounded as they were by the arc of cliffs with their labyrinth of occupied caves (dotted line on photo opposite), from which the Japanese could shoot downward on the invasion force from protected positions on three sides. He had therefore gone nine miles east up the coast, seeking a firm beach among the coastal swamps, and landed near the old Dutch town of Bosnik. From the landing beaches, the invasion force had turned left (west) and advanced down the coastline toward the airfields.

45. THE MOVE TO BIAK ISLAND

In this photo smoke rises from the main Japanese airfield on Biak (later named Mokmer Field) under aerial bombardment by the Jolly Rogers. Note the horseshoe of coral cliffs behind the airfield (dotted line). These cliffs were riddled with fortified caves. Rather than land on this beach under fire from three sides, the Americans landed farther up the coast near the town of Bosnik (out of this picture at upper right) and then fought their way down the coastline to the airfield (curved white arrow) between the cliffs and the sea.

However, this meant that the Americans had to proceed to the airfield location down a narrow corridor through thick jungle, with the cliffs on their right and the sea on their left (curved arrow above), with the Japanese hindering their advance every step of the way. In this corridor the Japanese could appear and disappear at will from their caves. The Americans landed without opposition, but this was actually by Japanese design.

The commander of the Japanese forces, Colonel Naoyuki Kuzume, had realized from studying earlier island battles that it was useless to oppose an American amphibious landing at the shoreline, since with American air and seapower pounding the beachhead beforehand, and on call during the landing, to do so was always very costly to the defenders.

Therefore he had developed a new strategy, one that would be used by the Japanese to defend islands from American invasions for the rest of the war. He would allow the Americans to land, and when they were concentrated on the beach, he would ambush them from cover. If he failed to drive the Americans back into the sea with his ambush and subsequent fighting, then at least he would extract a steep price in American blood as his forces retreated to the safety of their caves to continue the fight from cover.

On Iwo Jima, in February of 1945, the Japanese used this same strategy and allowed thousands of American Marines to establish themselves on the shore of the island before opening a heavy fire on them from caves on both ends of the beach and inflicting great slaughter. On Biak, Col. Kuzume had something similar in mind, but Gen. Krueger unwittingly spoiled his plans by landing before Kuzume had time to set up his trap, and thus the Americans massing on the Biak beachhead were not fired on after they landed. On the morning of 27 May, 1944, the U. S. troops went ashore and began their advance westward down the coastline. This trek soon devolved into more of the prolonged, nightmarish jungle fighting that characterized most island battles of the Pacific war.

The battle for Biak was another exclusively Army fight, with no Marines involved (the Marines, as you remember, were in the Central Pacific). Compared with the famous Marine island battles of Guadalcanal, Tarawa, Saipan, and Okinawa, the U. S. Army conquest of Biak Island is practically unknown today except to historians of the Pacific war. A search on the Internet for books about Iwo Jima brings up nearly a thousand titles, whereas fewer than half a dozen are to be found about Biak. The 41st Infantry Division, nicknamed the "Jungleers" for their many months of jungle fighting in the Southwest Pacific, suffered around 500 killed and 2,500 wounded in the protracted battle for Biak, while the Japanese lost a known 6,125 killed, with 460 Japanese and 360 Formosan slave laborers taken prisoner. The remaining 4,000 or so Japanese went unaccounted for. Many had been sealed in caves blown shut with explosives; others fled into the jungle and presumably died there. Typically, in this disease-ridden part of the world, about 6,000 American troops became casualties of scrub typhus and other illnesses.

The Americans fought their way down the coastal corridor to a location where the coral cliffs crowded even closer to the shoreline, leaving a narrow passage only 170 yards wide between cliff and sea, just before the bluffs swung inland to form the wide horseshoe around the airfields. This narrow strip of land (where the Jolly Rogers would later set up their camp) could have become a Japanese Thermopylae, holding up the American advance for a long time, had the Americans not had air and sea power to assist the troops. As it was, the Japanese had nine tanks hidden in this area that they threw into the battle on May 29, but the Americans had armor too—a dozen Sherman M4A1 tanks had been landed with the troops—and the result was a rare Pacific tank battle.

The Japanese tanks were their small "Type 95" with a crew of three, light armor, and only a 37mm main gun, while the larger Shermans had a gun twice the size: 75mm. These little Japanese tanks had terrorized Chinese and other peasant armies during Japan's advance through Asia, but they were no match for the Shermans. The armor-piercing shells from the American tanks passed right through the Japanese tanks, whose armor was not even thick enough to detonate them, so the American tankers switched to high-explosive shells

45. THE MOVE TO BIAK ISLAND

The little three-man "Type 95" Japanese tanks on Biak were no match for American Shermans. In a rare Pacific tank battle, the Shermans made short work of them.

and the Japanese tanks were soon demolished. Weeks later Sgt. Baca of the Horner bomber crew, walking around near the shore below his camp area, would examine the wrecks of these tanks.

Finally the Americans battled their way through the bottleneck and moved toward the horseshoe bluffs enclosing the airfields. By this point in the months-long battle, the bombs of the Jolly Rogers and other bomber groups, as well as naval gunfire from ships offshore, had been hammering the caves in the horseshoe for weeks, but many Japanese sheltering within the labyrinth of deeper caverns were still unharmed and full of fight. It took TNT, flamethrowers, and close-up infantry action to finally dig them out of or seal them within the caves. Towards the end of the battle, with his situation

"Those little Japanese tanks almost seemed like toys," says Mr. Baca today. Curious American troops examine a wrecked "Type 95" tank after the battle for Biak.

hopeless and surrender out of the question, the Japanese commander Kuzume burned his regimental flag to prevent its capture and committed suicide, just as the Japanese commander would do later at Iwo Jima.

As noted in the previous chapter, on July 22 Charles Lindbergh witnessed a Jolly Rogers bombardment of the coral cliffs on Biak from a vantage point three miles across the water on Owi Island, where the Americans had established an airfield. Sitting in his tent, Lindbergh wrote:

> The Japanese stronghold on the cliffs of Biak is to be attacked again in the morning. Several hundred Japs are still holding out in caves and crevices in an area about 300 yards wide and 1,000 yards long. So far, they have thrown back all of our attacks, and inflicted nearly one hundred casualties on our infantrymen. They have as perfect a natural defensive position as could be devised—sharp coral ridges overlooking and paralleling the coast, filled with deep and interlocking caves and screened from our artillery fire by coral ledges... The intense artillery fire has stripped the trees of leaves and branches so the outline of the coral ridge itself can be seen silhouetted against the sky. Since I have been on Owi Island, at irregular intervals through the night and day the sound of our artillery bombarding this Japanese stronghold has floated across the water. This afternoon, I stood on the cliff outside our quarters (not daring to sit on the ground because of the danger of typhus) and watched the shells bursting on the ridge. For weeks that handful of Japanese soldiers, variously estimated at between 250 and 700 men, has been holding out against overwhelming odds and the heaviest bombardment our well-equipped guns can give them.[1]

After the bombardment by artillery, air bombing, and naval shelling, the infantry moved in against the largely unharmed Japanese positions, and the fighting was as brutal and vicious as a land battle can get, frequently hand-to-hand. The battle proceeded cave by cave, a preview of what the Marines would encounter 8 months later at Iwo Jima. On both islands the Americans used flamethrowers and satchel charges in addition to their small arms, and were assisted at times by their Sherman tanks, naval gunfire, and air support. It was hellish work that cost the lives of many fine young American men, and maimed many others for life, both physically and mentally.

The island was officially declared secure on August 20. The Battle for Biak Island deserves to be better known. As the Marines are renowned for their heroism on Iwo Jima, so should the Army be remembered and honored for the valor shown by its troops on Biak Island.

The construction of Biak's Mokmer airfield

Just as at Wakde Island, American engineers immediately went to work grading and improving the Japanese airfields even while the last of the Japanese were still shooting at them, and on Biak the fields were soon in good enough condition to accept fighter planes, while still being lengthened and widened for the heavy bombers.

On July 24 Charles Lindbergh landed in a C-47 at Mokmer Field with members of the 475th Fighter Group, and he rode in a jeep with some officers up to the coral caves behind the airfield to look them over. Having watched the progress of the battle from Owi Island, he now wanted a closer look. He wrote in his journal that night:

The 863rd Aviation Engineers were on the job improving the airfields at Biak even before the shooting stopped.

> The west caves were down in a hollow beyond the hilltop... In the bottom of the hollow was a great pit in the coral, probably fifty feet wide, one hundred feet long, and thirty feet deep. A ladder, obviously of Japanese construction (poles lashed together), led to the bottom. At each end of this pit were the entrances to the west caves.
>
> We climbed down the ladder past the bodies of more [Japanese] soldiers and picked our way over to the entrance of one of the caves. The interior was dark and wet. We could hear water dripping down off the roof onto the floor. I threw my flashlight into the interior. The cave was large, with a number of side passages. The floor, some twenty feet below the entrance, was littered with boxes of ammunition, cases of food, sacks of souring rice and soybeans, and miscellaneous articles of clothing and equipment, all soaked by the water dripping down off the roof.
>
> I climbed down a ladder roughly made of poles... Inside the cave the stench was terrific—decaying food and decaying bodies... The cave at the other end of the pit was larger and a little deeper. A path ran steeply down into it over boulders and debris. Charred skulls and bodies marked the work of the flamethrowers. The inside of the cave was a mire of mud and filth, with the bodies of Japanese soldiers scattered everywhere... The far end of the cave opened into a second pit, also littered with dead bodies. We could

American soldiers examine one of the deep caverns that the Japanese occupied during their defense of Biak Island. Charles Lindbergh entered these caves after the battle but was soon driven back out by the odor of decaying Japanese bodies.

stand it no longer and turned back to our jeep.[2]

Even after the island was declared secure there were still Japanese hiding out in the catacombs and occasionally emerging to cause trouble for the Americans, including, as we will see, the Jolly Rogers in their encampment. But finally, on August 10th, 1944, after the usual fast and efficient work by both Army and Navy engineers (the Seabees) the longest of the three airstrips on the island, Mokmer Field, was declared usable for heavy bombers, and they began to fly in immediately. On that same day, in fact, the first of the Jolly Rogers' B-24s landed at Mokmer Field, and the entire 90th Bomb Group would soon follow.

For the Jolly Rogers, this would be another permanent change of base, after starting out at Iron Range on the north tip of Australia in 1942, then moving to Port Moresby on New Guinea's south coast in 1943, then to Dobodura and Nadzab on the north coast in 1944, then up the coast to Wakde Island, and now to Biak Island near the northwest end of New Guinea. In total, from Iron Range to Biak, they had moved 1,370 miles between 1942 and 1944 (the straight-line distance from Iron Range to Biak is about 800 miles).

As noted in earlier chapters, the Jolly Rogers had been split between Wakde Island and Nadzab, keeping aircraft from two squadrons at each place, since Wakde had been too small to take them all. The move to Biak brought the

45. THE MOVE TO BIAK ISLAND

The tents of the Jolly Rogers' officers on Biak, with raised floors made of dunnage wood from Liberty Ships. The Horner crew's four officers occupied the tent at upper left-center in this photo. The building at lower left is the camp's Post Exchange (PX). These amenities were a far cry from the crude conditions the Jolly Rogers had endured on Wakde Island.

entire Group back together again. The 321st and 400th Squadrons flew up to Biak from Nadzab, while the 319th and 320th Squadrons arrived from Wakde. With all four squadrons united again at Biak, and the ground contingent delivered to the island by ship, the 90th Bomb Group was intact once more. The Jolly Rogers would be based on Biak Island for over five months. The next move, in early February of 1945, would be a 900-mile jump to the island of Mindoro in the Philippines.

From the middle of August 1944 to the beginning of February 1945, the Jolly Rogers would operate against the Japanese from Mokmer Field on Biak Island.

The Horner crew moves to Biak Island

According to Lt. Cooper's flight logbook, the Horner crew made its first trip from Wakde Island to Mokmer Field on August 15th, and then made a couple more trips back and forth between Wakde and Biak islands bringing

Looking in the opposite direction from the previous photo, out to sea, as the scene appeared from Lt. Horner's tent. The men are lined up to get into the little PX. Owi Island, where the 43rd Bomb Group (Ken's Men) was based, and where Charles Lindbergh stayed with a fighter squadron, is faintly visible in the distance through the trees.

equipment forward. By the 16th they were established on Biak Island for good, setting up their tents and settling in, and the next day they would fly their first combat mission from Biak.

The Jolly Rogers' bivouac area was set up about a mile to the east of Mokmer Field, between the coral cliffs and the sea, in part of the corridor through which the American 41st Division had fought its way and won at such bloody expense. The camp area was connected to the airfield by a rough road surfaced with crushed coral. Unlike on little Wakde Island, there was room on Biak to disperse the tents widely to minimize the effects of Japanese night bombing.

The battleground had been cleaned up as the Jolly Rogers moved in, the Japanese tanks bulldozed down to the beach, the Graves Registration personnel gathering up the bodies of American infantrymen for temporary burial before eventually returning them to the States. The bodies of dead Japanese soldiers were buried in trenches scraped out by bulldozers, so that on Biak there

This Japanese staff car was among the spoils claimed by the Americans after the battle for Biak Island, and the Jolly Rogers appropriated it for use around their camp and painted their Group symbol on the side. Mr. Horner remembers it as a noisy rattletrap, but any sort of transportation was welcome around the sprawling airbase. The airfield was about a mile away from the bivouac area.

were no rotting Japanese corpses lying around everywhere to make the camp unpleasant as had been the case on Wakde. The trouble on Biak was not dead Japanese, but live ones. There were a number of them still hiding out in the caves in the cliff behind the camp, and they would cause the Jolly Rogers occasional trouble during their months on the island.

Docks and piers were constructed along the shore for use by supply ships coming in from the States—mostly Liberty Ships that carried large redwood planks in their holds as dunnage. This prized lumber was bought or bartered for and used to make flooring and porches for the men's tents (as seen on p. 607 and opposite). Portable generators provided electrical power throughout the Jolly Rogers' camp and other camps on the island, so that every tent had the luxury of an electric light bulb dangling on a wire from the ceiling.

Among the Air Corps ground personnel, the bootleggers set up their stills, and craps and poker games flourished. Bomber Command established a hospital to treat the sick and wounded, and staffed it with actual female nurses who could be invited to squadron parties, and the enlisted men and officers of the

Lt. Horner drives a jeep on Biak Island. Sitting to his right is Lt. Theobald, the crew's navigator, while Lt. Cooper, the copilot, hangs onto the back. Lt. Ostafin, the bombardier, was taking the picture.

90th Bomb Group built their own clubhouses out of Liberty Ship lumber and any other materials they could scrounge in the area.

Being only about one degree, or sixty miles, south of the equator, Biak was as hot as any island in the Southwest Pacific, with the noonday sun nearly straight overhead, but the trade winds cooled the air somewhat in the evenings, and freshwater showers were available in the camps. With all these luxuries and amenities, one could almost call life on Biak Island civilized, especially when compared to Wakde Island. Everything is relative, after all.

The fighter groups, bomber groups, and infantrymen all occupied their own separate camp areas. In addition, the infantry established and maintained a perimeter between the camps and the coral cliffs where an unknown number of Japanese soldiers were still hiding out, to keep them out of the camps. Aircraft of all types soon took up residence at the airfields, and once again, as they had done previously at Port Moresby and Nadzab, thousands of Americans of many specialties moved in to create another busy, temporary military city. This one would serve for about six months as the Air Corps' most forward airbase, from which the Jolly Rogers and other bomb groups would fly missions against not only Japanese bases in the region but clear up into the southern Philippines. Then, when the war front itself moved to the Philippines in January of 1945, Biak would revert to a rear support area like Nadzab and Port Moresby.

Life on Biak Island

After the Japanese had finally been evicted from Biak, they did the same thing they had done after they'd been kicked off Wakde Island: they bombed the new owners as often as possible from their airfields on other islands. Almost nightly at first they sent bombers over Biak to harass the Americans and deprive them of sleep, and to do what damage they could to the American aircraft parked around the airfields.* Their bombing of the airfields was usually so inaccurate, however, that some men felt that the safest place to be during these raids was the center of Mokmer airstrip.

With the American airbase spread widely across three airfields, and the camp areas well dispersed eastward up the Biak coastline, these raids were less effective than the ones on Wakde Island had been, and on Biak the Japanese bombing was more or less only a nuisance.

Nevertheless the Japanese managed to score a few lucky hits, and Mr. Baca remembers one night when five mechanics were killed beside the airfield when they took shelter in a bomb crater during an air raid. "They jumped into a crater made by a previous bombing, but lo and behold, a bomb dropped right on top of them and blew them all to pieces," he says today. "There was a burial detail the next day, and I remember one of the men on the detail saying afterward that all they could find of the five men was little scattered bits of flesh and bone. None of them could be identified."

During a typical night air raid, American searchlights would probe the sky for the Japanese bombers. Sometimes a searchlight would catch a Japanese bomber in its beam, and then the beams of several others would converge on it, and then all the antiaircraft guns around the airfield would cut loose and concentrate on it. Antiaircraft shells streaking up into the night sky and exploding made spectacular fireworks displays, and men would come out of their tents and shelters to watch the show. "Sometimes I actually felt sorry for those Jap pilots," Baca says today.

As the Jolly Rogers and other bomb groups struck Japanese airfields in the region and destroyed more and more enemy planes, the bombing raids on Biak diminished accordingly, until air raids became so rare near the end of the Americans' stay there that the airfield remained lit all night "like an international airport," Mr. Horner remembers today.

After the enlisted men of the Horner crew had established their tent in the Jolly Rogers camping area, Sgt. Baca continued his practice of hiking around the area near the camp whenever he got the chance during daylight hours, being careful to avoid the cliffs to the north where isolated Japanese

---

* There were P-61 Black Widow night fighters stationed on nearby Owi Island, but the author has been unable to find any record of them shooting down Japanese bombers over Biak.

soldiers were still hiding out. He walked down to the beach one day and came across the wrecks of the Japanese tanks that had attacked the American infantry three months before during the battle to capture the island. "Those little tanks were like toys compared to American tanks," he says today. The dead Japanese crewmen were still inside, their bodies blackened and decayed, and Baca didn't hang around there very long.

The wrecked Japanese tanks were bulldozed down to the beach where they became curiosities to hikers from the nearby camps, including Sgt Baca.

Milk runs

Bombing missions that turned out to be easy, with no Japanese opposition from either the air or the ground, were often described as "milk runs." However, there were also genuine milk runs, for real milk, as well as for fresh eggs, meat, and other food items that were hard to get in the war zone. The planes that made these runs from Biak down to Australia and back were called "Fat Cats" and were usually older bombers that had been retired from flying bombing missions. On Biak, men would pool their money and give it to the pilot of a Fat Cat before he left for Australia, along with a list of whatever items they wanted him to bring back.

Mr. Horner remembers a lot of men from camp running down to the flight line one day when a Fat Cat brought in some fresh milk. The milk wasn't going to stay fresh for very long in the tropical heat, and it had only remained cool on the way up from Australia because the plane had flown at high altitudes where the air was cold. Everyone grabbed his canteen cup and rushed down to where the plane parked to get a drink of the rare treat. On the occasions when fresh eggs were available in the mess hall, someone would invariably run through the camp shouting, "Eggs! Eggs!" which triggered a stampede to taste real food instead of rehydrated Air Corps fare. As Bob Hope said in one of his USO shows, "Army food is made to sustain life, not to encourage it."

Do-it-yourself refrigeration on Biak

Men received their beer rations on Biak, but with very few refrigerators available it had to be drunk warm. The only way to cool drinks without refrigeration was a method mentioned earlier: take it up to high altitude in an airplane for a while. In order to do that you either needed to be a pilot or the friend of a pilot. Any pilot could go down to the flight line, where the mechanics were constantly working on the bombers, and ask if there was a plane with a new engine or engines that needed breaking-in, or what was called "slow-timing," and usually there was. Lt Horner would load a case of beer into a bomber that needed some engine break-in time and take it up to high altitude, where he would cruise around slowly for long enough to both break in the engines and cool down the beer. When he landed there would be cold beer to drink for a little while. Horner wrote to his father back in the States, "With rationing, you get five gallons of gas a week for your car, while I just used 250 gallons of gas to cool my beer."

Bob Hope's USO show on Biak Island
Ten days after the Horner crew took up residence in the Jolly Rogers camp on Biak, on August 25, 1944, radio and movie comedian Bob Hope and his traveling USO troupe arrived on the island in a C-47 to give a show. Hope and his fellow entertainers, who included comedian Jerry Colonna, singer Frances Langford and dancer Patty Thomas, had their pictures taken beside one of the Jolly Rogers B-24s that had been nicknamed "Road to Tokyo" (photo, next page), a reference to the famous prewar Hollywood "Road" movies featuring Bob Hope, Bing Crosby, and Dorothy Lamour (*The Road to Zanzibar*, *Road to Mandalay*, *Road to Rio*, etc.). There were seven of these movies, all with similar plots, which were a combination of comedy, adventure, romance, and music.[3]

In some of the movies Lamour portrayed a lovely native of the South Pacific isles, with tropical flowers in her hair. This had given many young men in America the notion that there really were such native maidens in New Guinea and other Pacific islands. For American servicemen who had been hopeful of meeting a Dorothy Lamour look-alike among the natives, their first look at the real native women of the area was something of a letdown, to say the least, since Pacific Island women rarely conformed to Western ideals of beauty, and their near-Stone Age existence took a hard toll on their appearance (in addition, on Biak many of the native women were pygmies). The young men had to instead refocus their hopes of meeting appealing women on their leaves to Australia.

On Biak Island, Bob Hope's show of song, dance, and stand-up comedy was presented on an elevated wooden stage near the airfield. Sgt. Baca joined thousands of men who crowded around the area in front of the stage, some even climbing nearby trees. "I remember that in one tree there were about five guys sitting on a single branch," Baca remembers today. "The branch snapped and all five of them came crashing down. Fortunately no one was hurt."

Hope started out his show by saying, "Well, here we are on this beautiful, romantic Pacific Island!" After all the jeers and laughter from his audience subsided he went on, "Wait until I see that Dorothy Lamour! What a liar!" Hope

Bob Hope and his USO troupe pose in front of a Jolly Rogers bomber named "The Road to Tokyo," a reference to Hope's famous "Road" movies. The nose art was painted by Sgt. Arthur D. Hoffman of the 400th Squadron.

then introduced the members of his troupe. "I know you'll enjoy the girls," he said. "You remember girls?" This brought a tremendous roar of appreciation and whistles from the crowd.

Lt. Horner did not attend the show. He wasn't in the mood for it. The whole idea of entertainment in the midst of a war didn't much appeal to him. All Americans in the Pacific were homesick, he reasoned, and Bob Hope's show reminded the men of home, including pretty girls, so what was the point of making it worse? Besides, he expected that the high-ranking officers would get all the good seats near the stage, close enough to recognize the performers; most everyone else would be so far back, among thousands of other men, that those in the rear would barely be able to see the figures on the stage, and would have only the echoing loudspeakers to give them an idea of what was going on.

David Zellmer, the 13th Air Force B-24 pilot whose squadron had moved to Wakde Island shortly after the Jolly Rogers left there, felt the same way. In a letter home he wrote about the visit Bob Hope's troupe made to Wakde eleven days after their show on Biak:

Wakde, September 5 [1944]—Two so-called "big" shows recently found this tiny island. I avoided both. I find such entertainments ill-disguised attempts to make our life out here more tolerable. I resent that.

Life out here is meant to be intolerable. Nothing—no one—can make it otherwise.

Those who do not share my view—hundreds of them—waited two hours under the near-vertical burning sun to secure seats near the stage.[4]

However, thousands of other men took the opposite view and found the USO shows a welcome diversion from the daily grind and dangers of Army life in the war zone, and they appreciated the reminders of home. After seeing Hope's show at Hollandia, Donald Johnson, an Australian transport plane pilot, wrote:

Bob Hope's traveling troupe entertained the Jolly Rogers and other units on Biak Island on August 25, 1944. Hope is shown here singing with dancer Patty Thomas. "This is what you're fighting for, boys," said Hope when he introduced Thomas.

The highlight of that concert was, to me, when film star Frances Langford, one of Bob Hope's troupe of entertainers, sang to the large audience an old favourite song, "Whispering Hope." Hope for a brighter tomorrow, it meant, and if this wasn't a dream for the future, I don't know what else is; the troops gave her such a wonderful ovation [that] if there was a Japanese camp within twenty miles they must have heard the applause. It is still one of the highlights of my life...

I could sense that many of the American boys on that occasion really missed their homes and their brand of entertainment, and appreciated the fact of Bob Hope and his group of artists coming so far to entertain. War was proving to be a very ugly thing, and it's not until one is far from home and often in real danger that home is appreciated more than ever.[5]

After the show on Biak, the Jolly Rogers gave Bob Hope a tour of the area in the captured Japanese staff car that had the Group's skull and crossed bombs symbol painted on the sides (below). They also presented him with a captured Japanese flag. Hope thanked them for the flag and said that it would make a fine rag to blow his nose on, and proceeded to do just that for a photographer. In the 90th Bomb Group's history by Wiley Woods, the caption to the photo calls it "Bob Hope's salute to Tojo."[6]

More celebrities visit the Jolly Rogers

Besides Bob Hope and his troupe, other Hollywood stars visited the Jolly Rogers from time to time, including movie stars Gary Cooper, John Wayne, Joe E. Brown, Jack Benny, and Carole Landis. Many of them painted their signatures on bombs to be dropped on Japanese targets. Brown also signed the side of a Jolly Rogers bomber, and Benny had a bomber named after him, with a picture of him throwing a bomb painted on its nose. Carole Landis (photo, opposite) invited airmen to put an arm around her and pose for photographs.

Bob Hope takes a ride in the Jolly Rogers' captured Japanese staff car and displays a Japanese flag presented to him as a souvenir of Biak.

The Jolly Rogers capture a Japanese prisoner on Biak

The Japanese soldiers hiding out in the coral caves that riddled the cliffs behind the American camp on Biak Island occasionally managed to cause trouble, especially at night. Mr. Baca remembers today that some of them were able to penetrate the American infantry perimeter in the dark to attack airmen in their tents, or to hunt for food. He remembers incidents of grenades being tossed

Actor Gary Cooper autographs a 500-pound bomb destined for a Japanese target.

45. THE MOVE TO BIAK ISLAND

into American tents, and there were knife attacks on sleeping Americans in the middle of the night.

"We posted our own guards around our camp," Mr. Baca remembers today. "We also hung tin cans on strings stretched through the jungle with pebbles inside that would rattle and warn us if someone was sneaking around in the dark. It was dangerous to go outside your tent at night to relieve yourself, since you might be mistaken for a Jap. You had to keep shouting, 'I'm so-and-so, don't shoot!' You could hear the guards clicking their guns."

Sexy movie actress Carole Landis charmed the Jolly Rogers during a visit to Nadzab on August 1, 1944.

Actor John Wayne signs the plaster cast of a wounded man.

Comedian Joe E. Brown tries to imitate the Jolly Rogers emblem.

One night in his tent Sgt. Baca was awakened by the sudden rattle of machine gun fire from somewhere on the perimeter near the cliffs, and the next morning he learned that a group of Japanese had come rushing out of a cave towards the Americans in a suicide charge, screaming "Banzai!" before they were all cut down, thus fulfilling their obligation to die for their divine Emperor.

On the evening of November 11, 1944, some Jolly Rogers officers were playing poker in a tent when the edge of the canvas was lifted from the outside and a skinny brown hand reached in and snatched a pair of shoes. The poker players dropped their cards, ran outside, and blazed away in the dark with their .45 pistols at the shadowy form of the retreating Japanese thief.

Shoes were valuable items on a coral island where the razor-sharp coral could cut up even the most calloused bare feet. The next morning a couple of the Americans decided to follow the trail of the thief, and after a while they came upon two Japanese in the jungle. One tried to flee and was shot down; the other threw up his hands and, as Mr. Baca remembers the story today, shouted something like "Me father Chicago!," evidently trying to get across the fact that he had relatives in America and was willing to surrender.

The Americans marched their prisoner back to camp, where a crowd of bomber crewmen gathered to look him over. "Most of us had never seen a Japanese," says Baca today. "Oh, he looked terrible. His clothing was in tatters, and he was wretched and starving." The Americans gave the man food, clothing, and shoes and took some snapshots of him (right) before turning him over to the MPs to be delivered to Group Intelligence for interrogation. Eventually he was sent to a prisoner of war camp in Australia.

As time went on, the priority of the Japanese holdouts lurking around the fringes of American airbases in the Pacific changed from attack-

This Japanese prisoner, tall for a Japanese, was captured near the Jolly Rogers camp on Biak Island. Col. Wilson Banks (with hat), commander of the Jolly Rogers at this time, is visible in the background. The prisoner was provided with food, clothing, and shoes.[7]

45. THE MOVE TO BIAK ISLAND

ing their enemy to simply staying alive. Many Japanese in this hopeless situation committed suicide, either by ritually stabbing themselves, detonating a hand grenade against their bodies, or making a suicidal Banzai charge at some American position (such as Baca had heard one night).

Japanese prisoners were rarely seen by pilots or aircrews. This Japanese Zero pilot, flying from Rabaul, shot up and set fire to a parked Liberator beside the Milne Bay airfield before his plane was brought down by ground fire. He was unharmed in the crash.[8] The Australians appear to find him as big a source of amusement as the Americans did their prisoner at Biak.

Those less imbued with the Bushido warrior spirit, and who chose to try to stay alive, could only support themselves by clandestine scavenging off the Americans. This occurred not only at Biak but at other American garrisons where the Japanese had been defeated but not all killed or captured, and were eking out a bare existence in the jungle near the American camps. Pacific war historian Ian Toll wrote:

> Driven to desperation by hunger, many Japanese drew in close to the American encampments and looked for opportunities to steal food. Sentries often killed or captured these emaciated intruders around the edges of ration dumps, warehouses, or mess halls. In one often-related incident, a Japanese soldier was found sitting among a company of marines watching an outdoor movie. When discovered, he grinned broadly and raised his hands. Another surrendered to a marine sitting on a privy, later explaining that those circumstances seemed to offer the best odds of not getting shot.[9]

Back at Maffin Bay, across from Wakde Island, Lt. Kerns' artillery outfit actually caught a Japanese soldier in their chow line:

> It was still dark next morning as the men of Co. G filed sleepily through their chow line. One scrawny little guy with his fatigue hat pulled down over his face held up a canteen cup to the server, who withheld the ladle of powdered eggs and asked if the soldier didn't have a mess kit. There was no reply, just the lowered head and the thin hand holding the canteen cup out for food. The mess server

leaned over and looked under the brim of the old hat—into the frightened almond eyes of an Oriental.

"Hey! This here guy is a Jap!"[10]

The man had snuck into the American camp during the night, found and put on a GI uniform, and joined the breakfast chow line. He was taken into custody and fed in a different place.

As the war neared its end, some of these abandoned and destitute Japanese hanging around the American camps came to be considered harmless and were simply ignored. At the Bob Hope concert on Hollandia mentioned earlier, Donald Johnson realized that some of the men in the back row of the audience were actually Japanese soldiers:

> Sitting in a natural amphitheater, near the back row of perhaps ten thousand troops, it became apparent to us that a few Japanese troops were also enjoying the performance from the very back row! One American "guy" explained they were cut off from their units, and although not prisoners they were harmless, and [were] left to their own devices to survive. Indeed, they were known to raid the officers' mess during the night, and also raid the scrap bins to live off the land.[11]

Combat Missions of the Horner crew from Biak Island

After their first 14 combat missions from Wakde Island, the Horner crew flew 22 more bombing missions from Biak, the first one on August 17, 1944, the day after they arrived on Biak, and the final one on January 8, 1945, before the Group moved on to the Philippines. The following list of these missions does not include several administrative, ferry, and other non-combat flights:

Mission	Date	Target
15	17 Aug.	Liang airfield, Ambon Island
16	20 Aug.	Tobela, Halmahera Island
17	28 Aug.	Ambon town, Ambon Island
18	3 Sept.	Langoan airfield, Celebes Islands
19	6 Sept.	Davao, Philippine Islands
20	8 Sept.	Langoan airfield, Celebes Islands
21	10 Sept.	Tomohon town, Celebes Islands
22	13 Sept.	Kaoe airfield, Halmahera Island
23	16 Sept.	Kendari, South Celebes Islands
24	19 Sept.	Menado-Celebes fuel facilities
25	23 Oct.	Cotabato, Mindanao, Philippine Islands
26	25 Oct.	Warships in Mindanao Sea P. I.
27	28 Oct.	Recon search for Jap navy, NW P. I.
28	10 Nov.	Fabrica airfield, Negros, P. I.

29	15 Nov.	Libby airfield, Mindanao, P. I.
30	21 Nov.	Matina airfield, Mindanao, P. I.
31	24 Nov.	Sassa airfield, Davao, P. I.
32	27 Nov.	Daliao airfield, Mindanao, P. I.
33	29 Nov.	Matina airfield, Mindanao, P. I.
34	7 Dec.	Sassa airfield, Davao, P. I.
35	6 Jan. 1945	Warehouses, Davao, P. I.
36	8 Jan.	Storage dumps, Davao, P. I.

Lt. Cooper recorded each of the above strikes in his little mission diary, along with some comments:

<u>Mission #15</u>—17 Aug. 1944
Unloaded 132 thousand-pounders (and one can of Pabst beer) on Liang runway, destroying 5 planes, started fires. Intense barrage of medium ack-ack holed several planes, hit Holland and copilot Montague. 9:10 hrs.

<u>Mission #16</u>—20 Aug. 1944
Plastered Tobelo town, on the south end of Galela Bay in the Halmaheras, with one hundred forty-four 1000-pounders. Barracks and warehouses were demolished, & explosions and fires were seen. No ack-ack or interceptions. 8:10 hrs.

<u>Mission #17</u>—28 Aug. 1944
Wing formation of 90th, 43rd & 22nd Groups hit Ambon town, barracks, warehouses, dumps &, unfortunately a PW camp with 354 one thousand lb. bombs. My biggest raid to date. No int[erception]. Ack-ack fire intense but inaccurate. Universal Newsreel photographed. 8:15 hrs.

<u>Mission #18</u>—3 Sept. 1944
Dropped 110 thousand-pounders on Langoan Field, Celebes, destroying many 2-E. [twin-engine] bombers. P-38s didn't show up and 9 Zekes intercepted, shooting down Mahaney. Got 2 Zekes & three probables. 9:40

<u>Mission #19</u>—6 Sept. 1944
Philippines! 55 tons of thousand-pounders on ammunition factory and warehouses at Davao. Large explosions and fires observed. One Jap fighter, no interception, heavy ack-ack inaccurate. 11:20 hrs.

<u>Mission #20</u>— 8 Sept. 1944
66 tons on Langoan runway, 100% hits. No flak or interception. Few Zeros airborne but fighter cover excellent. 9:45 hrs.

Mission #21—10 Sept. 1944
   Hit the Sultan's palace at Tomohon (Jap HQ for northern Celebes) with 42 half-tonners. No interception or AA. 9:55 hrs.

Mission #22—13 Sept. 1944
   Pre-invasion strike on Halmahera (Kaoe Airdrome) turned back by weather. Dropped bombs in ocean. 6:20 hrs.

Mission #23—16 Sept. 1944
   216 500-pounders dropped on personnel area at Kendari, S. Celebes. 9 S. E. F. [single-engine fighters] observed taking off during attack. One uneager pass driven off by tail turret. 12:25 hrs.

Mission #24—19 Sept. 1944
   45 500-pounders on Menado-Celebes port fuel storage & refueling facilities. Fires and explosions. 15 P-38s strafed and blew up oil tanker in harbor. No interception; inaccurate flak. 9:55 hrs.

Mission #25—23 Oct. 1944
   120 1000-pounders on underground storage & personnel at Cotabato, north Mindanao. No fighters or flak. 11:30 hrs.

Mission #26—25 Oct. 1944
   Attacked two Jap cruisers & a destroyer attempting to reinforce Leyte, in Mindanao Sea. One cruiser crippled & many near misses on others. Heavy ack-ack, no hits. 14:15 hrs.

Mission #27—28 Oct. 1944
   Recco [Reconnaissance] for Jap navy around NW Philippines. No luck. Dropped 150 x 1000-pounders on Puerto Princessa drome, Palawan. No flak or fiters [sic]. Drew ack-ack from Zamboanga on return trip. 14:20 hrs.

Mission #28—10 Nov. 1944
   Primary target, Fabrica drome, Negros, P. I. [Philippine Islands] Weathered in. Dropped 780 Frags on Jap camp at Tagaloan, Mind[anao]. 12 Zeros airborne, no attack. 14:30 hrs.

Mission #29—15 Nov. 1944
   60 x 1000-pounders on Libby drome, Mindanao (supposed staging for Morotai raiders). Uneager pass by two Tojos were driven off. We led our first flight. 11:40 hrs.

Mission #30—21 Nov. 1944
   Our first as squadron leader. 40 tons squarely on Matina drome, Davao, Mindanao. No interception, but ack-ack fire heavy and accu-

rate. Holed 2 ships. 11:00 hrs.

Mission #31—24 Nov. 1944
Our 2nd as Sqdn. Leader, and all 19 x 1000-pounders on Sassa drome, Mindanao. No interception, ack-ack light. 11:20 hrs.

Mission #32—27 Nov. 1944
Led Sqdn. again but missed target, and lost #4 engine over target. Intercepted by 5-6 Zekes, Tonys & Tojos on bombing run. Saw my 1st phosphorous bombs. Target Daliao drome; no flak. 8:10 hrs.

Mission #33—29 Nov. 1944
Led sqdn. for 4th time over dispersal area at Matina drome, Davao. 100% on target with 80 x 1000-pounders. No ack-ack or fighters. 10:55 hrs.

Mission #34—7 Dec. 1944
Led sqdn. over dispersal area at Sassa drome, Davao. Dropped 70 x 1000-pounders, destroying one plane & rendering four unserviceable. No int[erception], ack-ack light, inaccurate. 12:30 hrs.

Mission #35—6 Jan. 1945
Missed Davao warehouses with 96 x 250 pounders, due to rack malfunction, while leading Group for 1st time. Nil int[erception]; only 4 bursts heavy AA. 11:30 hrs.

Mission #36—8 Jan. 1945
30 x 1000-pounders on underground storage dumps at Davao. No interception but flak very close on second run. Acting Command Pilot. 11:15 hrs.

The Horner crew's first bombing mission from Biak

The first mission that the Horner crew flew from Mokmer Field on Biak Island, which was their 15th combat mission overall, was uneventful as far as they were concerned, a strike at Liang Airfield on the northeast corner of Ambon Island, but Mr. Horner remembers it today because this was the flight on which his friend and fellow pilot from his Air Corps training days, Dale Holland, received a minor wound from flak.

Holland had been a 19-year-old draftsman in the Ford Motor Company's blueprints department, drawing up the plans for the B-24 bomber that Ford would produce at its Willow Run plant throughout the war. He'd had no idea at that time that he'd eventually be flying the bomber himself, but after he enlisted in the Air Corps in 1942 at age 21 and qualified for pilot training, that is just what happened. He had become acquainted with James Horner during their training because the names Holland and Horner were close together alphabetically and they often found themselves doing things together. They both ended up assigned to the Jolly Rogers in New Guinea, Holland in the 319th Squadron and Horner in the 320th, and they often flew together on Group missions, including the one in which Holland was wounded.

On the strike against Ambon Island on 17 August 1944 in which Holland was wounded, the Jolly Rogers bombers were carrying thousand-pound bombs intended to tear up the Japanese airfield at Liang and wreck any aircraft that might be parked around it, and this it accomplished. As Lt. Cooper recorded it later in his mission diary:

> **Mission #15—17 Aug. 1944**
> Unloaded 132 thousand-pounders (and one can of Pabst beer) on Liang runway, destroying 5 planes, started fires. Intense barrage of medium ack-ack holed several planes, hit Holland and copilot Montague.

Cooper provided no details on how or why a Pabst beer can came to be dropped along with the thousand-pound bombs, but Mr. Baca remembers that crewmen sometimes urinated into empty cans and defecated into empty cardboard ration boxes, then set them on the bomb bay doors so they would drop when the doors opened on the bomb run. It was a convenient way of both getting rid of waste and demonstrating a little scorn for the enemy.

No Japanese fighter planes intercepted the bombers that day, but the antiaircraft fire was heavy. One flak burst sent a piece of shrapnel though the right cockpit window of Lt. Holland's plane, narrowly missing the copilot, Lt. Robert Montague, and striking Holland on the arm, causing a cut. He was later awarded a Purple Heart for the injury.

The Japanese troops on the island that they were bombing that day, Ambon, like most of the Emperor's "Sons of Heaven" anywhere in the Pacific, richly deserved being bombed, but on Ambon Island especially so. There they had perpetrated one of the worst of their innumerable atrocities in what became known as the Laha Massacre. In February of 1942, after capturing the island from the Allied forces (Australian and Dutch in this case; the Americans were not yet in the Pacific in force), the Japanese had occupied Ambon Island's two airfields, Liang and Laha. When they landed on Ambon Island, they were opposed by a 1,100-strong Australian military contingent known as Gull Force, along with some Dutch troops.

The Australians and Dutch put up a valiant fight, but they were in the same situation that the Americans had been in the Philippines, outnumbered and with no hope of reinforcement, resupply, or evacuation. The Dutch troops were especially isolated, since their country had been seized by the Nazis. After it became evident that the defense of the island was hopeless, and 309 Australians had been killed in fighting around the Laha airfield, the Allies surrendered on February 2, making the mistake of thinking that they were surrendering to civilized human beings. They soon learned otherwise. As soon as the Australians and Dutch laid down their arms, their cold-blooded murders by the Japanese began. The prisoners were bound tightly and painfully, and ten of them were killed immediately, beheaded with swords and stabbed to death with bayonets, and another twenty to forty more were killed the same way between February 6 and 8.

On February 9, fifty-five more Australian and thirty Dutch soldiers were butchered and their bodies thrown into mass graves, and on the 24th two hundred and twenty-seven Australians were beheaded in an all-night orgy of ruthless killing beside a pit dug in the woods near the airfield. Flashlights were used to illuminate the necks of the prisoners for the swordsmen, and the Japanese drank saki (rice wine) and caroused as though they were at some uproarious party.

Some of the Australian soldiers were teenagers, hardly more than boys, but they were shown no more mercy than the Japanese showed any of their prisoners anywhere in the Pacific, man, woman, or child. Any youngster who pleaded for his life that night was ridiculed and given extra beatings before being butchered. The Emperor's despicable little men in many cases did not have the strength to cut their victims' heads completely off, so that many of the Australians lay moaning and twitching in agony in the mass grave with deep cuts in their necks, and were then buried alive. Only about 400 Australians were left alive on Ambon Island after the Laha Massacre, and they were only temporarily spared because the Japanese needed slave labor to work on the airfields. These prisoners were then worked to death or died from disease and malnutrition.

It can only be hoped that many of these sadistic savages of Nippon were blown to Hell by the bombs of the Jolly Rogers during the Group's several strikes against Ambon Island's two airfields in 1943 and -44. The first Jolly Rogers strike on Ambon was in February of 1943, carried out by the 319th Squadron flying from Fenton, Australia, and the last was on October 3 of 1944, when three planes from each of the four squadrons participated.[13]

Mission #18 and the loss of the Mahaney crew

On September 3, 1944, the Horner crew took off on their eighteenth mission, in a B-24J bomber from Mokmer Field on Biak Island, with three planes from each squadron participating again, twelve bombers in all. The Jolly Rogers were joined by two other heavy bomb groups, the 43rd (Ken's Men) and the 22nd (Red Raiders), all flying Liberators, which made this strike a large one by Pacific war standards—sixty bombers in all (for comparison, at this same time in Europe, raids were being made on Berlin with thousands of bombers at a time). They were all carrying one-thousand-pound demolition bombs, at their maximum load of eight bombs per plane, and their mission was to destroy a Japanese airfield at Langoan in the Celebes Islands,* 785 miles west of Biak (Map 45-3, below). This too was a former Dutch airfield that had been captured by the Japanese, in January of 1942, and just as at Ambon they had murdered many Dutch prisoners of war in cold blood.

After five hours of flight from Biak, as the formation approached the enemy airbase, they could see numerous Japanese twin-engine bombers parked around the runway. Directly over the field the sixty B-24s released their loads, and hundreds of giant bombs saturated the area, throwing up great founts of dirt and dust as the shock waves and bomb splinters demolished the parked Japanese planes, tore up the runway, and wrecked buildings.

But there were already some Japanese fighter planes in the air. Apparently the Japanese at Langoan had been alerted beforehand that American bombers were on the way, and had gotten some planes up to ambush them. Normally the Japanese only got a few minutes' warning of approaching American bombers, which was not enough time to get their fighters up, but since the large bomber formation's inbound course had taken it over the enemy-held Halmahera

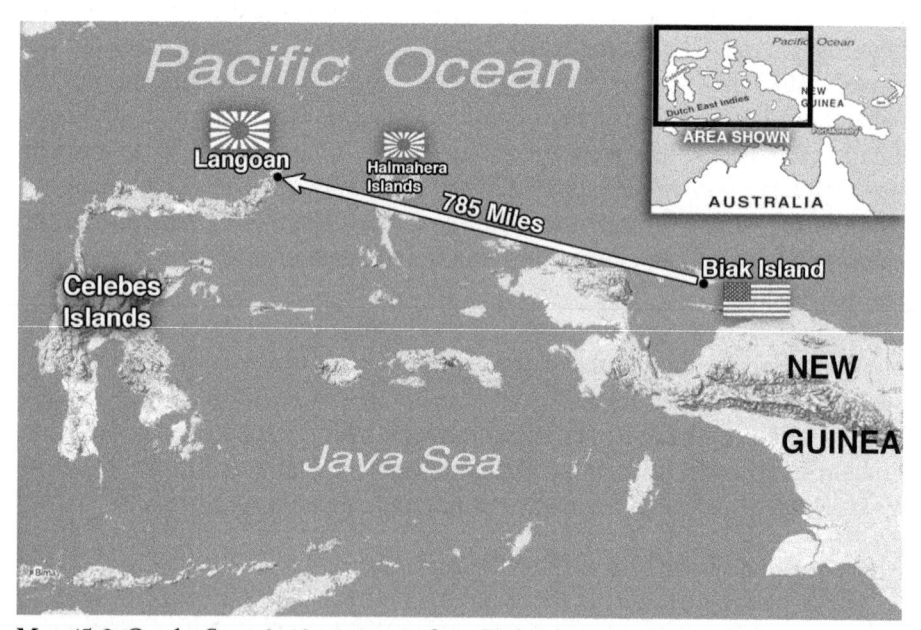

Map 45-3. On the Sept. 3, 1944 mission from Biak Island to bomb a Japanese airfield at Langoan in the Celebes Islands the Mahaney crew's bomber was shot down by a Japanese fighter plane.

---

* The "Celebes" is actually one large island that was mistaken for several smaller islands by early explorers because of its odd, sprawling shape, something like a pinwheel.

Islands on its way to the Celebes, it's likely that Japanese on that island had radioed Langoan that a raid was headed their way.

As the bombers completed their bomb runs and turned for home they were jumped by nine Zeke fighter planes, and they had no American fighter escort to deal with them. One of the planes flying that day was a B-24 nicknamed "Hay Maker," of the 320th Squadron, piloted by 2nd Lt. Edward J. Mahaney from Buffalo, New York. Mahaney was flying his plane just off the left wing of the Horner crew's bomber.

A Japanese fighter singled out Mahaney's plane and put a burst of machine gun and 20mm cannon fire into its left wing, causing the bomber's number two engine to catch fire. The waist gunners of the Horner crew, Sgts. J. W. Dale and Jaime Baca, saw "Hay Maker" turn away from the formation and start into a descending left turn, trailing smoke from its burning engine. "It was the first time I had ever seen a bomber going down," says Baca today.

What was going on in the Mahaney plane after its engine caught fire can only be guessed at, since no one aboard would live to tell the tale. The flames spread into the left wing, probably from a ruptured fuel tank, and it soon grew into a bigger fire than the crew could extinguish. Something also appeared to have gone wrong with the bomber's flight controls, which may have been the reason that the plane dropped

Nose art on the Jolly Rogers bomber "Hay Maker."

out of formation and began circling. As the crisis unfolded, things got worse by the minute for the Mahaney crew.

Perhaps the cables to the left aileron had been shot apart or burned through, causing a partial roll and turn. Nevertheless, it appeared to crewmen watching from the other bombers that Mahaney, or his copilot Lt. Donald Moore, or perhaps both of them together, regained control of the plane, leveled its wings, and then turned it back toward the formation. Seeing the bomber heading back toward them, apparently under control again, hope grew among the men watching in the other planes that Mahaney might yet be able to rejoin them, and perhaps, if the fire could be put out, might even make it home. While Mahaney and Moore struggled to control their bomber, their crew would have been fighting the fire.

But then something must have gone even more badly wrong with Mahaney's bomber, for the plane suddenly went into a steep left bank and nearly rolled over on its back, something that a four-engine bomber was rarely seen to do. Since the pilots of a B-24 were the only crewmen strapped into seats, the rest of the crew, along with anything else loose in the plane, must have tumbled about inside the fuselage when this occurred, adding to the chaos.

Somehow, once again, the pilot or pilots appeared to regain control of their plane. But by this time the fire on the left wing was out of control — and before long it had spread into the fuselage and was raging throughout the

Lt. Edward J. Mahaney, killed at Langoan, Celebes Islands, September 3, 1944.

plane from the bomb bay back to the tail. It was now a hopeless situation that could only end one way. If the intercom was still working, Mahaney would have been telling the crewmen to bail out, if they hadn't already done so. Men watching in other bombers saw two or three (there was disagreement later how many) parachutes blossom out in the wake of the plane. Finally, control of the bomber was lost for good, and the big plane nosed up steeply into a stall, then fell off into a spin and went down out of control, trailing flames and smoke. Thirty tons of flaming wreckage slammed into the ground and exploded in a wooded area only two miles west of the Langoan airfield.[12]

Sgt. Baca didn't see "Hay Maker" hit the ground because his eye had been caught by a group of four or five Japanese fighters approaching the bomber formation from above. He watched them peel off to make individual firing passes, and one of the Zekes turned toward his own plane. Baca, looking out the left waist gun window past Sgt. Dale, saw that the fighter was going to pass beneath his plane, from left to right, and realized that it would soon appear in the window on his side. He jumped to his gun and waited for it, aiming downward, his thumbs ready on the triggers. His exemplary gunnery skills, which had so impressed his instructors in Texas, were about to be put to the test.

As soon as the Japanese plane came into view beneath him, Baca caught it squarely in his gunsight and gave it a long burst. The big Browning .50-caliber machine gun fired over 800 rounds a minute, and the lightly-built enemy plane shuddered under the impact of the heavy slugs. Baca saw a big piece of the Zeke break off and fall away, and he knew he had done it some serious and maybe fatal damage. Lt. Ostafin, the bombardier, sitting in the nose of the plane, had been watching the Zeke approach, and as Sgt. Baca's bullets tore into it he heard Ostafin shout over the intercom, "You got him, Baca! You got him!" As Mr. Horner remembers it: "A Japanese Zero came up behind our right wing, and our waist gunner on that side, Jaime Baca, gave it a going over with his gun—he really raked him good."

When Sgt. Baca stopped firing, and the last of the hot empty brass casings rattled to the floor of the bomber at his feet, he kept his eye on the damaged fighter plane, expecting it to veer out of control and go down, but to his disappointment and disgust it continued on its original flight path as though nothing had happened, until it was lost to view behind the bomber's tail. But the Japanese plane or its pilot must have been disabled, for Baca was told later by gunners on following bombers that it had been an easy mark for them and they had finished it off and watched it go down.

The other Japanese fighters made several more passes at the bombers and received accurate fire from the gunners in return. According to Lt. Cooper's mission diary, the gunners definitely shot down two Japanese fighters that day, and probably got three more. As the bomber formation headed east out to sea toward home, the remaining Japanese fighters broke off the attack and turned back toward their airfield, now faced with the problem of trying to land on a runway full of large bomb craters. Two miles from their field, Mahaney's bomber was piled up on the ground and burning fiercely, sending up a thick column of black smoke. Residents of the island interviewed after the war said that the plane burned for two days, fed by the hundreds of gallons of fuel the plane had carried.

On the nearly five hour return flight to Biak, the crew members' adrenalin highs subsided, calm returned, and the men in the bombers who had friends on the Mahaney crew pondered their fate. Ten of their comrades were not coming home, that was certain, and some of them, at least the few who were seen to parachute from the plane, might still be alive. Most of the crewmen were probably dead, their bodies shattered and incinerated in the tons of burning wreckage, but some might be unhurt after reaching the ground, and even now might be running for cover in the jungle, hoping to evade the Japanese patrols that would soon be on their trail.

Those fugitives would be wondering, desperately, where they could go, where they could hide. If they were successful in evading capture, they would need food and water. Were there any friendly natives in the area? Without a doubt the Japanese would be racing to the scene of the crash. Was some crewman lying helpless on the ground near the crash site, crippled by broken bones and burns, holding his pistol ready for the first sign of the approaching

Japanese? Would he use his pistol on himself rather than be captured and tortured, as so many men claimed they would do?

Their friends in the bombers headed back to Biak could only speculate, but one thing was certain: whatever the condition of any survivors, there would be no help for them, for almost surely the cruel, savage enemy would find them sooner or later. If the Japanese didn't shoot the Americans on the spot, or hack or beat them to death as they'd done to other crews, they'd drag them back to some command post where they would be tortured for information and then bayoneted or beheaded. It was not a pleasant thing to think about.

The men who went down with the bomber "Hay Maker" that day were:

>2nd Lt. Edward J. Mahaney, pilot, from Buffalo, New York
>2nd Lt. Donald W. Moore, copilot, from Shively, Kentucky
>2nd Lt. John A. Gross, navigator, from Chicago, Illinois
>2nd Lt. Byron B. Luck, bombardier, from Dallas, Texas
>T/Sgt. Grady H. Richardson, flight engineer, Shreveport, Louisiana
>T/Sgt. Francisco J. Colunga, radio operator, from Nogales, Arizona
>S/Sgt. William A. Showers, gunner, from York, Pennsylvania
>S/Sgt. Robert T. Gates, gunner, from Shelton, Washington
>S/Sgt. Samuel H. Sikes, gunner, from Savannah, Georgia
>S/Sgt. Charles O. Smith, gunner, from Compton, California

To this day, no one knows what happened to the men of the Mahaney crew who parachuted to earth from their stricken plane. Some idea of what likely happened to them, however, can be gained from the experience of other crews that went down under similar circumstances, and whose fate became known either from crewmen who survived, or through examination of Japanese records after the war.

Among the Jolly Rogers, one such crew was that of 1st Lt. Bryant E. Poulsen of the 321st Squadron, who were flying a B-24 nicknamed "Hot Garters" on a seven-plane mission from Nadzab to bomb some Japanese antiaircraft gun positions at Hansa Bay on the north coast of New Guinea. The date was April 10, 1944. There were twelve men in Poulsen's bomber that day—the regular crew of ten plus a photographer and a radar expert. Poulsen, 22 years old, a native of Salt Lake City, Utah, was a veteran Jolly Rogers pilot flying his 51st mission and was near the end of his combat tour, looking forward to going home soon. On this day he was leading the formation.

What happened to Lt. Poulsen's bomber in many ways paralleled what would happen to Lt. Mahaney's plane five months later on Sept. 3. The seven bombers reached Hansa Bay at 10:25 in the morning and formed into a line to make individual runs on the Japanese gun positions. Poulsen's plane was at the head of the line and made the first bombing run. Before it could drop its bombs, however, a barrage of deadly accurate ground fire bracketed it. The Japanese flak gunners below were good ones, or perhaps on this day they were just lucky. The bombers were flying at twelve thousand feet, but the flak gunners had the range with their first shots. The bomber was hit in its number two engine, just as Mahaney's bomber was, and the wing was soon enveloped in flames.

Poulsen's plane began losing altitude and circling down. The bomber next in line behind Poulsen's on the bombing run, piloted by Lt. George R. Anderson, dropped its bombs on the target and then followed Poulsen's bomber as it circled down, with Anderson and his crew watching their friends' plight helplessly. Poulsen's bombardier, Lt. Bill Bernier, salvoed his bombs to lighten the bomber and improve its chances of staying in the air, but witnesses in other planes saw the fire from the burning engine spread into the fuselage, and before long the flames were streaming clear back past the tail of the airplane. A moment later the left wing came off, and as the burning bomber whirled toward the ground its tail broke off as well, falling separately.

Five members of the Poulsen crew managed to bail out before the bomber went into its fatal spin and while it was still high enough for their 'chutes to open, but the other seven men were still inside the bomber when it struck the ground in a clearing in the jungle and exploded, killing them all, including Poulsen.* As the parachutes of the five survivors floated down, two of the P-38 fighter planes that had been escorting the bombers circled them protectively, in case there were any Japanese fighters in the area, since the Japanese policy of shooting helpless men in their parachutes was well known. A PBY Catalina that had followed the bombers on this mission also remained nearby in case it could be of any help. The amphibious Cat could land on water, but it was the Poulsen crew's misfortune to crash on the land instead of in nearby Hansa Bay, so the men in the parachutes landed in the jungle instead of the water.

Witnesses in other bombers reported that two of the men who parachuted from Poulsen's plane landed in a clearing near the burning wreckage of their bomber and were seen walking around, while the parachutes of two others disappeared into the jungle canopy. The fifth man's parachute was seen to get stuck in a tree. The Catalina dropped some supplies to the men in the clearing, and all the American aircraft continued to circle until it was obvious that there was nothing more they could do.

The planes then headed back to their bases, and the survivors of the Poulsen crew were left to fend for themselves as best they could. This is the same

---

* The wreckage of the bomber was found in 2002, and the remains of six crewmen were recovered from the wreck site in 2014. The bodies of Poulsen and another crewman whose remains were not present were assumed to have originally been there, probably burned to ashes in the post-crash fire.

situation that survivors of the Mahaney crew would find themselves in a few months later, and that is where the latter's story ends, for nothing is known of what happened to them. With the Poulsen crew's survivors, however, it was different: the identities of the men and the details of their fate later came to light.

It was later determined, from native witnesses (speaking to Australians who occupied the area two months after the crash), and from captured Japanese records, that four of the five men of Poulsen's crew who parachuted to the ground were able to find each other and get together. They were Lt. Donald P. Greenman, the crew's navigator, S/Sgt. William N. Handleman, the photographer, S/Sgt. Donald C. Crotteau, a gunner, and S/Sgt. William T. Hyler, also a gunner. The identity of the fifth survivor of the crash was never established, and his fate remains a mystery. With his parachute lodged high in a jungle tree, he may have fallen to his death trying to get down (with the jungle canopy 50 feet high in most places, his predicament was the same as if he'd been hanging off the roof of a 5-story building), and his body was never found, or he may have made it to the ground but not made contact with the other men, and died trying to walk out of the jungle alone.

With any luck, the four other survivors of Poulsen's bomber might have been able to make their way through the jungle to friendly lines. However, as it turned out, the only luck they had was bad. After getting together and taking stock of their situation, they made contact with some local villagers, who were friendly and advised them to remain where they were for the time being, since there were Japanese patrols in the area and it wasn't yet known what was the safest direction to go. But the men decided to strike out immediately down the Ramu Valley toward friendly territory (Australian troops were known to be advancing up the valley toward them). Since they were suffering from burns and other injuries, they weren't able to make very good time through the jungle, and it wasn't long before Japanese troops got on their trail, caught up with them, and captured them.

The men all had painful burns on their hands, arms, and faces, and if these Americans had been shot down over occupied Europe, and had fallen into German hands, they would have been transported to a hospital where their injuries would have been treated and their pain relieved to the extent possible. Eventually they would have been sent to a prison camp to sit out the war.

But this was not Europe, and these were not Germans. Germans treated Allied prisoners humanely in the expectation that the Allies would do the same to their own men when they were captured. The Japanese, on the other hand, cared nothing for their own men if they were captured, and considered any Americans who fell into their hands to be dead men walking. These were the remorseless, murderous savages that Imperial Japan had loosed upon the world, who had been committing ghastly war crimes all over the Pacific since 1937. No humanity could be expected of them.

The captured Americans of Poulsen's crew were first tied up, and then despite their painful burns and other injuries were beaten brutally and sadistically with wooden clubs. Some natives who happened upon the scene, and later described it to the Australians, were ordered by the Japanese to beat the Americans as well, but claimed that they had refused to do so (what else could they say?).

The Americans, probably near death by this time, were kept alive in misery and mistreatment for a week while they were interrogated; then the Japanese decided to move them to another village. Lt. Greenman was unable to walk, so he was simply shot dead. Seeing this, Sgt. Handleman became enraged and struck one of the Japanese, with the result that he was beaten to death. The remaining two Americans, Sgts. Crotteau and Hyler, were marched to the village of Bogia, where after further interrogation, and probably more torture, both of them were shot also, and Crotteau had his head hacked off as well, probably because he was still alive after being shot.[13] Thus, as things turned out, Poulsen and the other crewmen who had died a quick death in the crash of their bomber were the lucky ones.

The members of the Mahaney crew who made it to the ground alive, if they were captured, likely suffered similar fates. There would have been no easy way for the Americans to get off the Japanese-held island, and even if they had somehow managed to do so, for example in native canoes, the surrounding islands were also occupied by the Japanese, for the Celebes at that time were deep in enemy-held territory. Death for any members of the Mahaney crew who survived the crash was nearly certain, one way or another. According to the historian of the 90th Bomb Group, Wiley Woods, no member of the Jolly Rogers who was captured by the Japanese during the New Guinea campaign was ever seen alive again, with the exception of Lt. McMurria, who was held prisoner at Rabaul, and the four members of his crew who were transported to a prison camp in Japan.[14]

A missing bomber crewman turning up alive after the war was a rare event. American prisoners who were considered useful or important, such as the world-famous Olympic runner Louis Zamporini, were sometimes kept alive for propaganda purposes (although Zamporini's family only learned that he survived the crash of his B-24, and subsequent mistreatment in a prisoner of war camp, after the end of the war). Zamporini's story of his imprisonment and torture at the hands of the Japanese was the subject of a book, *Unbroken*, which was made into a movie of the same name.*

---

* Book by Laura Hillenbrand, 2010, movie by Universal Pictures, 2014.

One captured American airman at Rabaul (who was not a member of the Jolly Rogers) managed to stay alive by claiming to have flown in the new B-29 bomber that the Japanese knew was under development. He invented such convincing technical facts about it that he was sent to Japan for further questioning, and survived the war in a concentration camp there. Americans who were sent to Japan to labor as slaves in mines and other Japanese industries were sometimes found alive after the Japanese surrender as well, including the famous fighter pilot Greg "Pappy" Boyington of VMF-214 *Baa-Baa Black Sheep* squadron fame, who was kept for a time in the same camp as Zamporini.

But the cold facts in the case of the Mahaney crew are that the men were never seen or heard from again, and like so many missing crews, they were finally declared dead when no information about them could be found.*

The bombers of the Jolly Rogers arrived back at Biak late in the afternoon of the day the Mahaney crew was lost. By the time they landed on Mokmer Field, the men had been in the bombers for nearly ten hours, and they were tired. They all filed through the intelligence shack for debriefing, and the intelligence officers recorded their eyewitness accounts of the shooting down of Mahaney's bomber, and used them to type up the Missing Aircrew Report (MACR).† Afterwards a medic dispensed the usual two ounces of whiskey to each man, and soon most of the weary men were back in their tents, and in their cots.

The two tents that had housed the Mahaney crew, one for the officers and one for the enlisted men, stood empty, just as the men had expected to return to them, and before long someone from the squadron's S-2 (Intelligence) section would enter those tents and begin sorting through the crewmen's possessions, boxing

---

*In an effort to learn the fate of the Mahaney crew, the author was able to acquire the service record of the crew's radio operator, T/Sgt. Francisco J. Colunga, 22 years old, from Nogales, Arizona. The record states that in January of 1948 a Dutch farmer near the town of Langoan found a skeleton lying in a field that he was preparing for cultivation. The skeleton was wearing tattered fragments of a U. S. Army Air Corps uniform, and dog tags identified the remains as those of Colunga. Since there was no trace of a parachute or any hardware associated with one, and most of the bones were broken, Colunga had presumably jumped to his death without a parachute to avoid being burned alive in the flaming bomber. After positive identification by the American Graves Registration Service, and notification of Colunga's parents in Arizona, the remains were taken to the American cemetery at Manila and interred there with "customary military funeral services." Recovered with the remains were some corroded coins: two American pennies, two nickels, an Australian 3-pence coin, an Air Corps signet ring, a telephone slug and a bus token from Sioux Falls, South Dakota (where Colunga had gone to gunnery school), and some bent sunglasses with their case. The Army sent Colunga's parents a letter asking if they would like to have these things, and his father wrote back, "Yes, please return to us these worthless items that to us mean a lot and are priceless. Thank you."

†The report is available from the National Archives as MACR #9017.

45. THE MOVE TO BIAK ISLAND

up their clothing and personal effects to mail back home to their families. At that moment, on the other side of the world, the missing men's mothers, fathers, wives, girlfriends and other loved ones were going about their day as usual, unaware as yet that today their men had, for all intents and purposes, vanished from the face of the earth, and would never be seen or heard from again.

Thousands of American families would experience this same anguish before the war was over, and many of them are still hoping for answers today.

In the officers' tent of the Horner crew, Lt. Cooper sat down, got out his little mission diary and a pen, and wrote:

> 3 Sept. 1944:
> Dropped 110 thousand pounders on Langoan Field, Celebes, destroying many 2-E [two-engine] bombers. P-38s didn't show up* and 9 Zekes intercepted, shooting down Mahaney. Got 2 Zekes & three probables. 9:40 [hours].

The nine hour and forty minute flight brought Cooper's total combat hours up to 149:40.

Air reconnaissance photos of Langoan airdrome a few days after the September 3 strike showed that the runway had been repaired and was back in operation again, although it had fewer planes parked around it, since some had been bombed into wrecks during the mission. To Fifth Bomber Command this meant that another strike on the field was warranted, so on 8 September, 1944, just five days after the 90th had bombed the field and lost the Mahaney crew, the Jolly Rogers, including the Horner crew, were back over Langoan again. It was the Horner crew's 22nd combat mission.

Once again the field was pounded with tons of high-explosive bombs and rendered unserviceable. If any of the Mahaney crew were still alive after the intervening five days, either on the run from the Japanese or in Japanese custody, they would have seen or heard the Jolly Rogers passing overhead, heard the detonations of the bombs, and wished mightily that they could be back up there with their comrades in the bombers. But the fortunes of war, ever cruel and arbitrary, had singled them out for death.

If the fighter plane that shot down the Mahaney crew had instead targeted the bomber flying just to the right of it, it might have been the Horner crew that was never heard from again.

A B-24 strike on the receiving end

The strikes on the Langoan airfield repeatedly churned it up in a boiling cauldron of powerful explosions, and yet, time and again, on this airfield and

---
* Since the target was nearly 800 miles away, beyond the range of American fighter planes, it's puzzling that Lt. Cooper expected them to show up.

Jolly Rogers bombers banking toward Mokmer Field on Biak Island (the runway is the bare strip visible among the vegetation at upper right) as American warships cruise offshore.

others like it, the ever-resilient Japanese filled in the crateers in their runways, repaired what aircraft remained to them, and rebuilt their installations so far as they were able, often working their slave laborers to death in the process, until finally the aerial bludgeoning by the Americans became so overpowering that surviving personnel were reduced to insignificant numbers and/or had no aircraft left to repair.

What was it like for the Japanese on the ground during one of these raids by American heavy bombers? Some idea can be garnered from the journal of Masatake Okumiya, the Japanese air staff officer quoted earler at Rabaul, who later described an American bombing raid as he experienced it on the receiving end. The raid Okumiya wrote about was on Buin airfield on the island of Bougainville, in the summer of 1943.

Before the attack that day, just as at Langoan on the day the Mahaney crew was lost, the Japanese had already gotten some of their fighter planes into the air before the American bombers arrived, and they were waiting in ambush at high altitude. Japanese observation posts on other islands had warned them that an American air strike was headed their way. The Japanese on the ground at the airfield hoped that their Zeros would intercept the American bombers, break up their formations, and disrupt their bomb runs. As usual it was a vain hope. They had not been able to do it over Langoan, when the Jolly Rogers did not even have American fighter escort, and they couldn't do it over Buin either.

In the raid on Buin, the bombers did have fighter support, which lowered even further the Zeros' chances of interfering with the raid. Commander Okumiya recorded it thus:

> Suddenly the lookout on our tower stiffens behind his binoculars; his voice carries to the ground. We see him pointing to the south. Yes... there they are; enemy planes, fast approaching the airbase. The siren screams its warning and the men on the field dash for cover, never too soon, as the enemy bombers close on the field with great speed.
>
> No one really stays down in the ditches and culverts. Hundreds of men stare at the sky, seeing the bombers and searching for the Zeros which should even now be diving against the enemy planes. Here they come, racing from their great height to break up the bomber formations. But even before they reach the slower, heavier planes the escorting enemy fighters scream upward to intercept the Zeros. No matter how determined the Zeros attack, the bombers maintain their formations. Even as the Zeros and American fighter planes scatter over the sky in swirling dogfights, we can hear the rapidly increasing shriek of the falling bombs.
>
> The earth shakes and heaves; great blossoms of fire, steel, smoke, and dirt erupt from the airfield as salvos of bombs 'walk across' the revetments and the runway. Sharp sound cracks against the eardrums, and the concussion is painful. Our own machine-gunners fire in rage at the droning bombers above even as the explosions come faster and faster. There is a rumble of bomber engines, the rising and falling whine of the fighters, the stutter of machine guns, and the slower 'chuk-chuk' of aerial cannon. The sky is filled with dust and flame and smoke. Planes on the field are burning fiercely, and wreckage is scattered across the runway, which by now is cratered with great holes.
>
> Through the smoke we can see the hurtling fighter planes, diving and climbing in mortal combat. Our men curse or only stare silently as we watch Zeros suddenly flare up in scarlet and orange flame and then plunge from the sky like bizarre shooting stars, leaving behind them a long trail of angry flame and black, oily smoke...
>
> Then, abruptly, the raid is over. The crashing, earth-heaving thunder of the bombs is gone.[15]

Mr. Horner remembers today that the Japanese could usually be seen filling in the bomb craters in their runways even before the American bombers were out of sight of the field. Since the ill-equipped Japanese had very little mechanized earthmoving equipment, this work could only be done by shovels and muscle, either by the Japanese themselves or more often by the Chinese, Korean, Indian, or Indonesian slave labor brought in from territories that the Japanese had conquered early in the war (photo at right). The book *The Approach to the Philippines** describes how the Japanese treated the slaves that they forced to build their roads and airfields:

> Over 3,000 Indonesians were shipped to Noemfoor late in 1943, mostly from Soerabaja and other large cities on Java. The shipment included many women, children, and teenaged boys. The Japanese, without regard to age or sex, put the Javanese to work constructing roads and airfields almost entirely by hand. Little or no clothing, shoes, bedding, or shelter was provided, and the Javanese had to supplement their very inadequate allowance of rations by shifting for themselves. Driven by hunger, many attempted to steal Japanese rations, but for their pains were beheaded or hung by their hands or feet until dead. Starvation and disease (the Japanese provided no medical care) took a steadily increasing toll. The dead were periodically collected for mass burial, and survivors alleged that many of the sick were buried alive. . . [O]nly 403 of the 3,000-odd brought from Java were found alive on Noemfoor Island [by the Americans] by 31 August. The physical condition of these survivors almost defied description—most of the others had succumbed to Japanese brutality within a period of eight months.[16]

The speed at which the Japanese could fill in bomb craters in their runways after an American raid is confirmed in Okumiya's account of what happened after the bombing raid that he described above. Even as the American bombers were still receding in the sky, the Japanese leapt to their shovels:

> As soon as the last bomb has expended its fury, the ground crews clamber from their air raid shelters, and with shovels in their hands race for the runway. They work frantically, sweat pouring from their bodies, ignoring the ever-present mosquitoes and flies, shoveling dirt back into the craters, rushing to patch up the field so that the damaged Zero fighters can land.
> The men jump aside as the crippled fighters, metal skin torn and holed by enemy bullets, stagger toward the runway. Most of them land safely, but every so often a badly damaged fighter spins under a collapsed landing gear or flips over on its back. As soon as it has stopped rolling, each arriving plane is surrounded

---

* Published by the Center of Military History, U. S. Army, Washington, D. C., 1984

Japanese officers supervise slave labor pulling a roller in the construction of an airfield. What the American engineers accomplished quickly with mechanized earthmoving equipment, the Japanese accomplished slowly with slaves from their conquered territories, literally working them to death.

> by the maintenance crews...
> The long day passes. The gathering dusk is a welcome sight, for it means some rest and, at least, respite from heavy raids. Neither we nor the enemy have the proper equipment to permit large scale night attacks...
> The maintenance crews are exhausted, but they drag their weary bodies about the field, heaving and tugging to move the planes back into the jungle. They pray for tractors such as the Americans have in abundance, but they know their dream of such 'luxuries' will not be fulfilled...
> And this is but one day, typical of the seemingly endless succession of day and night periods, filled only with work, exhaustion, the ceaseless enemy attacks, and the ever-increasing number of pilots and air crewmen who do not return.[17]

In the summer and fall of 1944, strike after strike by the Jolly Rogers and other bomb groups hammered the Japanese airfields in New Guinea and the Dutch East Indies, wore the Japanese down, and destroyed their aircraft faster than they could replace them. Eventually they were left with little or nothing to fly, and the American navy, both ships and submarines, patrolled the surrounding sea lanes to prevent the garrisons from being resupplied, so that even when they still had aircraft they often didn't have fuel or spare parts for them. Just as the last remaining Japanese soldiers of a defeated garrison would often end their lives in a suicidal banzai charge, pilots of the last remaining aircraft on a Japanese airfield would be sent out on suicide missions.

With their aircraft destroyed, and their usefulness gone, the remaining Japanese airmen and ground crews were callously abandoned by Japan, left on their own to survive or die. In truth, the "divine" Emperor that the Japanese served so faithfully and fanatically cared nothing at all for them when their usefulness was at an end. Their evacuation in the face of American air superiority was considered too risky anyway. In cases when an evacuation of Japanese troops was carried out, in order to use them elsewhere, only the healthy and able-bodied were taken to safety, the rest left behind and encouraged to commit suicide.[18] The inhumanity of Japan's military forces, even toward their own men, was never so clearly on display.

Japanese garrisons that were bypassed by the Americans but remained more or less intact, such as Rabaul and Wewak, were ignored by the Americans as well and left to "wither on the vine," as MacArthur moved on from New Guinea to the Philippines. As more and more isolated pockets of Japanese floundered in the backwaters of the war, the Australians sometimes moved in to capture them or their airfields, if the airfields were considered worth having; otherwise the Japanese were left alone to try to find some way to survive to the end of the war. They sometimes did so by growing their own food (many Japanese soldiers had been peasant farmers before the war), or by raiding the gardens and livestock of native villages, or even resorting to cannibalism, but untold thousands more simply perished under wretched conditions.

(Above and on opposite page): some Jolly Rogers nose artists managed to inject a little humor into the grim business of war. The bomber at lower right is named "Air Pocket."

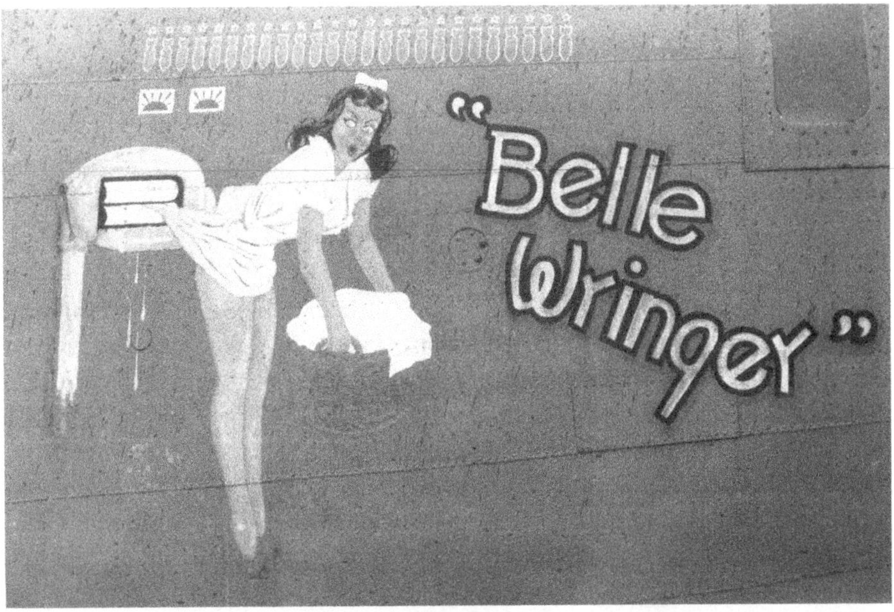
"Belle Wringer"

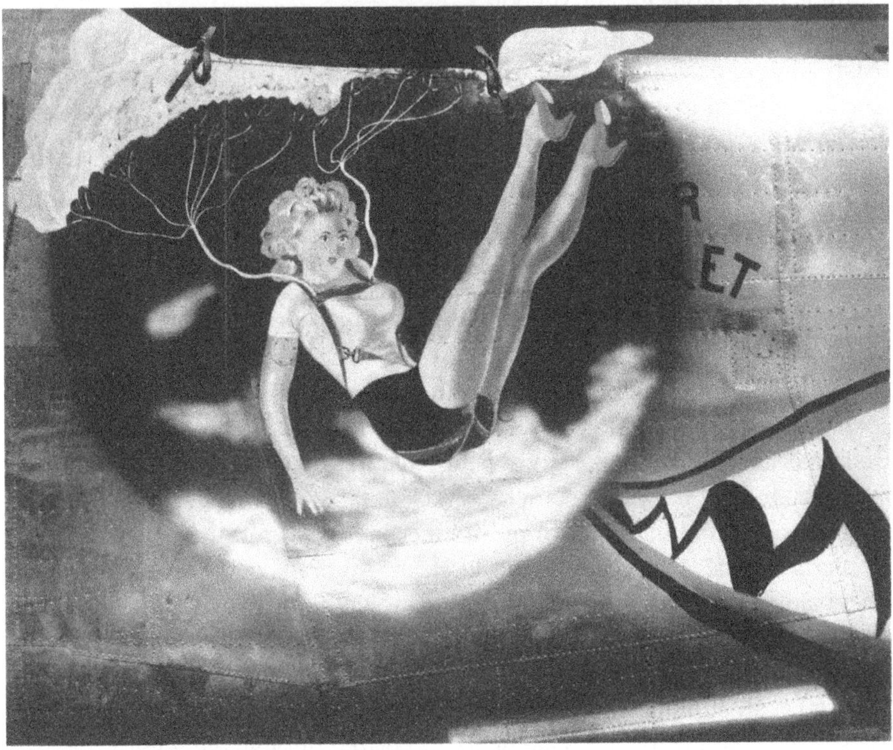

Chapter Forty-Six

LIFE ON BIAK ISLAND

Between the two missions to Langoan airfield in the Celebes Islands on Sept. 3 and September 8, 1944, the Horner crew flew its first mission to the Philippine Islands, to bomb a Japanese ammunition factory and warehouse at Davao on the southernmost Philippine island of Mindanao.

General MacArthur had been anxious to capture Biak Island for just this reason: the B-24s would finally be able to reach the Philippines from there. It was a long way to go, however, about 900 miles from Biak to Mindanao, and the missions would take from twelve to fifteen hours each, but the B-24 had the range to do it and so the strikes began. It was too far for fighter planes to go, so the bombers had to fly their missions to the Philippines without fighter support.

The Horner crew's first mission to the Philippines was on Sept. 6, 1944, (Map 46-1, opposite) and they would fly a total of fifteen more strikes to the islands between that date and January 15, 1945. The first mission took over eleven hours, and Lt. Cooper wrote afterwards in his mission diary:

> **6 Sept. 1944**
> Philippines! 55 tons of thousand-pounders on ammunition factory and warehouses at Davao. Large explosions and fires observed. One Jap fighter, no interception, heavy ack-ack inaccurate. 11:20 hrs.

The missions to the Philippines from Mokmer Field on Biak Island would soon develop into a routine. In order for the bombers to be able to return to Biak and land in daylight, they would have to depart Biak in the middle of the night and get back in the afternoon. On a typical mission, soon after their bomber took off at midnight from Mokmer Field, most of the crewmen in Lt. Horner's bomber would simply go to sleep. After all, only the navigator, Lt. Theobald, and the two pilots had anything to do on the way to the target, and perhaps the flight engineer, Sgt. Eady, if he was needed for anything, such as checking the fuel consumption. The gunners and the bombardier were not required at all until they neared the target, which was several hours away, after the sun rose. So the idle crewmembers just dozed through the night.

46. LIFE ON BIAK ISLAND

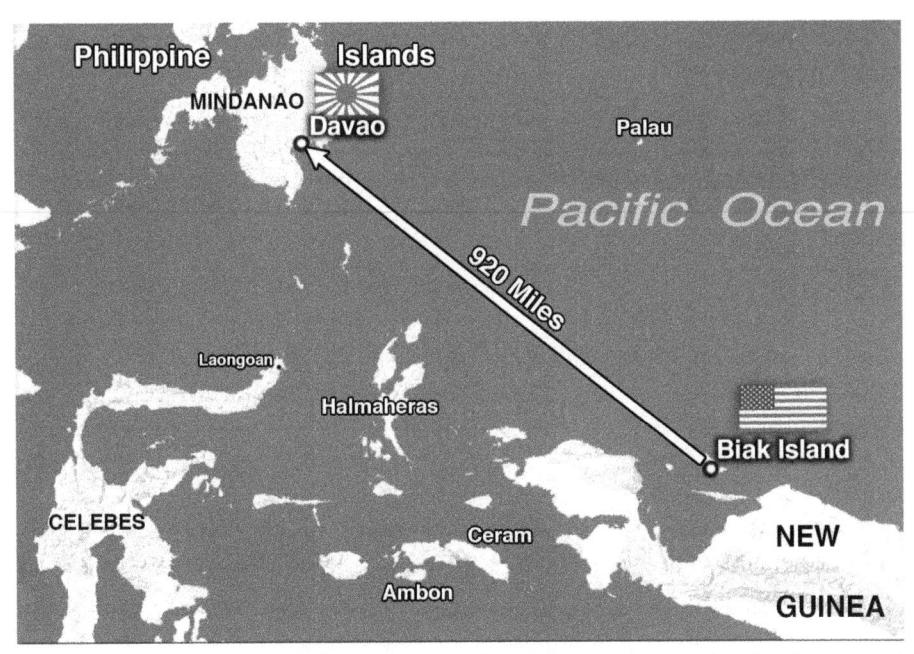

Map 46-1. The Horner crew's first mission to the Philippines was to bomb a factory and warehouse at Davao, on the Philippine island of Mindanao, over 900 miles from Biak.

"On those long missions to the Philippines," says Mr. Baca today, "we would leave Biak around midnight, and most of us would just go to sleep on the way out. As soon as the airplane took off and got up to altitude, and the pilot reported that everything was in order, it wasn't long before most of us guys were sound asleep. You just laid down on the floor of the plane and used your jacket or something for a pillow. It didn't take much for us to go to sleep."

Even the navigator, Lt. Theobald, would often hand Lt. Horner a compass course heading, say, "Wake me at daylight," and then go to sleep himself. There were no island landmarks for him to see in the dark anyway, and he wouldn't know for sure where they were until the sun rose and he could see things. In fact, Lt. Cooper, the copilot, sitting in the right-hand seat beside Lt. Horner, would often doze off as well, leaving Horner the only man of the ten-man crew awake in the airplane.

Horner had tried sleeping in his pilot's seat, after handing control of the plane over to Lt. Cooper, but found that if he was able to sleep at all it was only fitfully. He once dozed off only to awake suddenly with the feeling that something was strangling him, and found the cord of his throat microphone wrapped around his neck. After that he just decided to stay awake and let everyone else sleep.

"I'd tip my seat back," he remembers today, "and put my feet up on the instrument panel, and just relax and look out at the clouds in the moonlight. At night the temperature of the ocean was constant, and a smooth layer of clouds would form a few thousand feet above the ocean, and looking down at them from ten or twelve thousand feet was like looking out over a great white floor, from horizon to horizon. With everybody else snoozing, I had the whole world to myself."

To those whose only familiarity with World War II bombing missions comes from the movies and TV, and who thereby gained the impression that missions usually started out in daylight, with all the bombers forming up over their field before heading off toward the target in formation, with the gunners all at their guns and ready for action, this picture of a bomber cruising peacefully through the night toward its target, all alone, with everyone aboard sound asleep except the pilot, comes as something of a surprise.

The bombers were not really alone, of course; they just couldn't see each other in the dark, and radio silence was strictly observed to avoid alerting the Japanese that they were coming. But they were all alone as far as getting any help in an emergency. If a bomber went down into the sea for any reason, especially in the dark, hundreds of miles from any American airbase, the crew were probably as good as dead. They were trusting their lives to the reliability of the big Pratt and Whitney engines purring along out on the wings, and to the good craftsmanship of American workers, many of them women, in the bomber plants. And rarely were they ever let down by either one.

As the dawn approached, Lt. Horner would call his crew over the intercom to wake them up and let them know it was time to get to work. The gunners tested their guns, firing them downward into the sea, Lt. Theobald confirmed their position on his charts, and they headed for the rendezvous point, which might be an island or some prominent feature along a coastline, such as a bay. As soon as the sun was up the bombers began to assemble, circling over the rendezvous point until all were present and accounted for, and then they formed up into their squadron formations and proceeded to the Initial Point from which they would begin their bombing runs to the target.

As noted in Lt. Cooper's mission diary entry above, on the Horner crew's first mission to the Philippines on September 6, 1944, the antiaircraft fire from the ground over the Japanese airfield at Davao was heavy but inaccurate, and the single Japanese fighter plane that was seen did not attack. Lt. Cooper recorded that the bombs of the Jolly Rogers caused large explosions and fires in the ammunition factory they were bombing. This strike was a harbinger of things to come for the Japanese garrisons in the Philippine islands. For them, the handwriting was on the wall—things were only going to get worse from this time forward.

On the six- or seven-hour return flights from bombing missions to the Philippines, once again many of the bomber crewmen had nothing much to do. Whoever had been designated to make the sandwiches would do so, and move through the plane handing them out. In his station in the rear, Sgt. Baca whiled away the time sleeping, saying his rosary, or practicing his penmanship on pieces of cardboard that he'd brought along for the purpose (and he developed beautiful handwriting). Other crewmen smoked and chatted, speaking loudly in order to be heard over the steady hum of the four big engines just outside. Lt. Cooper, up in the cockpit, sometimes made preliminary sketches for cartoons that he would finish later in his tent in camp.

Everyone relaxed as the loose formation of Jolly Rogers bombers droned their way home across the seemingly endless watery wastes of the Pacific Ocean, passing islands here and there, until finally Biak Island and Mokmer Field came into view. Then Lt. Horner would set the big bomber down on the runway and taxi it to its revetment, where trucks would be waiting to take the crews to their debriefing in the intelligence tent. From there they would ride back to the bivouac area, where the men could relax in their tents for the remainder of the afternoon. Later the gunners would return to the flight line to clean their guns.

Each mission provided the crewman with a few more points toward the 100 total required for rotation back home, the ultimate goal of every American in the Pacific during the war.

A mission with a stop for gas

Someone at MacArthur's headquarters got the bright idea that if the heavy bombers could make a gas stop en route to the Philippines they could hit targets higher up in the island chain. The opportunity to try this came in October of 1944 when the Army captured one of the northernmost islands in the Halmahera group that had a small Japanese airfield on it, and the Seabees as usual started improving the field for American aircraft. At the time of the gas-stop experiment this airfield was barely adequate for Liberators to land and take off from, but whoever in headquarters had thought up this scheme figured it was worth a try anyway. After lengthening the coral runway, the army brought in 55-gallon drums of aviation fuel to top off the bombers' gas tanks with. Each bomber would take on about 10 barrels of fuel and then take off again with full tanks, with its range extended by about 800 miles. The bombers would be able to hit a target in the northern Philippines and still get back to Biak by dark.

Mr. Horner relates how well this experiment worked, or rather, didn't: "We took off about two AM in order to arrive at the island at daybreak, all loaded with bombs and most of our fuel. It was a scary thing landing a bomb-laden plane with a 110-foot wingspan in practically a ditch, where your wingtips were traveling over debris, dirt embankments, and tree trunks that had been hastily bulldozed aside to make the runway wider. To make it even worse, there was a crosswind blowing across the field at 15 to 20 miles per hour, which required landing in a crab* that had to be kicked out straight just before touchdown."

Still, everything went well until the fourth bomber came in, and its pilot was a second too late in straightening it out. When the plane touched down slightly sideways, the landing gear folded up under the side-stress and the plane skidded down the runway into a pile of debris. The bombs broke loose from their shackles inside the plane, tore through the side of the fuselage, and went tumbling down the runway—fortunately they were not armed. No one was seriously injured, and the wreckage was pushed out of the way and the mission continued as planned, minus one bomber.[1]

As far as Mr. Horner can remember, that was the first and last time that the Jolly Rogers ever tried refuelling en route to the Philippines. Landing with a full load of bombs and nearly full fuel tanks proved to be simply too dangerous. This is why bombs were always jettisoned at sea or dropped on some alternate target before the bombers returned to base.

The declining quality of Japanese fighter pilots

Mr. Horner remembers that by this stage of the war the pilots of many Japanese fighter planes seemed reluctant to attack the bomber formations. Lt. Cooper's mission diary describes them as "uneager." The fact was that by the fall of 1944 most of the best Japanese fighter plane pilots had been killed, and their replacements were often hastily recruited and inadequately trained young men, often little more than adolescents (the Japanese were taking recruits with an *average* age of sixteen—many just children)[2] who were less infected with the fanatical Samurai spirit that had animated Japanese pilots earlier in the war.

In fact, on some missions, Lt. Horner noticed that the enemy planes attacked the American bombers only when they were very close to the target, where the fighter pilots knew they were being observed by their superiors on the ground. They would make a big show of these attacks, but then did not pursue the bombers very far out to sea. Once they knew they were out of the sight of their officers, their aggression waned and they turned back to base.

One reason Japanese fighter plane pilots were not eager to take on a bomber formation, besides the fact that the gunners on the bombers could mass their fire from a tight formation, was that the .50-caliber machine guns of the bombers had a longer reach than the .30-caliber (7.7mm) guns of the

---

*An aircraft that is said to be "in a crab" has its nose angled into the crosswind as it descends to land, and is therefore not pointed straight down the runway, so that just before touching down the pilot must swing the plane into line with the runway ("kick out the crab") or risk landing somewhat sideways and skidding, as occurred here.

46. LIFE ON BIAK ISLAND

Japanese Zero (photo at right), so the bombers' guns could hit them before they could get close enough for their own guns to be effective. Japanese fighter pilot Tomokazu Kasai said that Japanese Zero pilots figured that the fire of B-24 gunners could hit them at 1,000 yards, while the Zero's machine guns only had an effective range of 650 yards.

Kasai called the B-24's .50-caliber machine guns "deadly," and described the bomber as being "prickly" with guns "like a porcupine."* He considered the nose turret so dangerous (Col. Art Rogers would have been pleased to learn) that he would never make head-on attacks. Kasai decided that the weakest side of a B-24 was its top turret, and would thus attack from above, diving almost vertically on a bomber at high speed:

> Diving down gave our 20mm ammo more range because gravity worked with us and not against us. There was less arching. I would get close enough to see the bomber crew's faces as I zoomed past. It was both exhilarating and terrifying.[3]

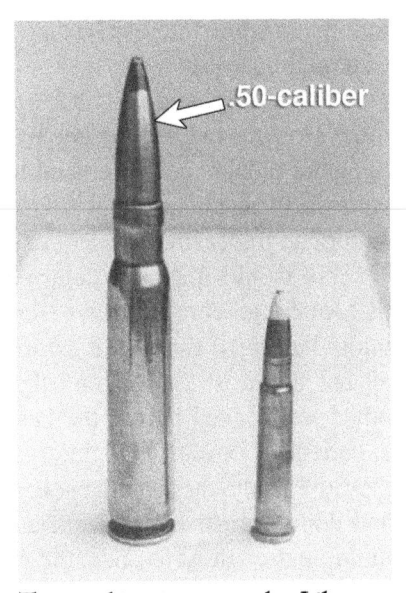

The machine-guns on the Liberator shot big .50-caliber bullets, while the guns of the Zeros fired smaller .30-caliber slugs. The American gunners could consequently hit the Zeros before the Zeros could hit them.

As a squadron leader, Kasai insisted that all the pilots under his command attack American bombers from above in this manner. But the dive-from-above approach allowed only a few firing passes per encounter, since after pulling out of the dive it took the Japanese pilots some time to climb back up above a bomber formation to make another dive on it.

Mr. Baca says today, "Our strategy against the fighter planes was to put up a 'wall of fire.' Every tenth round or so in our guns was a tracer, and you could see our fire going out. Those Japs saw it too, and it often kept them back. They were human, after all." Mr. Baca remembers that he and the other experienced gunners would begin firing at a Japanese fighter plane while it was still well out of range of their guns, just to let the enemy pilot see the tracers reaching out for him. This often had the desired effect of discouraging an attack.

He also remembers that new, eager bomber gunners sometimes got upset at him for keeping enemy fighter planes at bay this way—they wanted the

---

* Oddly enough, German fighter plane pilots on the opposite side of the world also compared a formation of American heavy bombers to a porcupine.

fighters to come in close so they could shoot them down and claim kills. Baca told them that they were fools—if they let a Zero get that close, it would also give the enemy plane a chance to shoot back at them. It was much safer and more sensible to keep the enemy planes at a safe distance, out of range of the fighters' guns, if possible. And many Japanese pilots near the end of the war were so inexperienced (or fearful) that all it took was a little warning from American tracer fire for them to steer clear.

This would not have deterred the skilled and aggressive Japanese pilots that American bomber crews encountered early on in the war, of course. Those pilots had been through a rigorous prewar training regime that weeded out all but the most skilled, and they had then gained experience in China and other places even before the Pearl Harbor attack. They were not only highly experienced but strongly motivated by their Bushido fanaticism, and when they made attacks in large numbers, especially on a single bomber, as they had done against Lt. McMurria's bomber at Wewak (Chapter 18), and from multiple directions at once, the American gunners could be overwhelmed and their bombers heavily damaged or shot down. But by late 1944 the number of such pilots, as well as the number of Japanese fighter planes, was shrinking, and Japanese training schools and aircraft factories could not keep pace with the losses. Nevertheless, as the shoot-down of Mahaney's crew over Langoan on September 3 demonstrated, Japanese fighter planes would remain a serious threat to American bombers to the end of the war.

The reduced quality of Japanese pilots in the last year of the war was also demonstrated in what became known as the "The Great Marianas Turkey Shoot" during the Battle of the Philippine Sea on June 19 and 20, 1944. In that engagement American carrier pilots had shot down over 600 Japanese planes with a loss of only 123 of their own, and many of the American pilots commented on the poor flying skills of their Japanese opponents. Japan's foolish policy of "fly till you die," never rotating its veteran pilots home either for a rest or to have them train new pilots as the Americans did, resulted in a steady decline in the quality of its fliers as the veterans were killed off and replaced with hastily-trained novices.

Mr. Baca remembers, however, that near the end of the war, when the Japanese began employing kamikaze attacks against ships, there were reports of Japanese fighter planes also deliberately trying to ram American bombers, as a Japanese plane had done to Capt. Roy Olsen's bomber in June of 1943 (Chapter 20). "To a suicidal pilot," Baca says today, "it must have seemed like a good deal—one of me for ten of them, and a little fighter plane for a big bomber." Whenever Japanese fighter planes were sighted, therefore, there was a certain amount of tension among the bomber crews. Would these pilots be

46. LIFE ON BIAK ISLAND

inexperienced youngsters, too timid to attack, or Bushido-crazed kamikazes who would come barreling in to ram?

Waist gunners had to be careful where they aimed

A gunner shooting from the waist window of a Liberator had a limited field of fire, bounded on one side by his aircraft's wing and on the other by its tail, as the pictures on this page show. With his gun on a swivel, and no limit to its side-to-side travel, it was easy for a gunner to shoot up his own plane if he wasn't careful. Under the stress and excitement of shooting at an enemy fighter plane, or under the G-forces of his own plane's evasive maneuvering, some gunners did just that.

On March 8, 1943, Lt. Paul E. Johnson's bomber came under attack by Japanese Zeros. One of them made a head-on pass and appeared to be about to ram the B-24, causing Johnson to make a sudden, sharp turn to avoid the collision. A waist gunner named "Pop" Sheridan, firing out of his plane's left waist window, was thrown off his feet by the sudden maneuver and his machine gun continued to fire as he fell to the floor, with the result that he did more damage to his own airplane than any Japanese fighter ever did. He shot the left aileron off the wing, put a hole in one of the engines, and blew out the left tire, which was in the retracted position under the wing. Luckily, Lt. Johnson managed to

Above: the view from the right waist window of a B-24, showing how easy it was for the gunner to accidentally shoot up the tail of his own bomber. Below: with the same gun swung to the left, the wing could get the same treatment—in fact, swung a little further, an incautious gunner could (and occasionally did) shoot out an engine.

land the bomber safely despite the damage.[4]

On 23 June, 1943, a bomber of the Jolly Rogers' 321st Squadron skidded off the runway on landing at Fenton, Australia (near Darwin), because its left tire was flat. The tire was flat because the left waist gunner had shot it to pieces when he slipped on loose shell casings under his feet while his finger was on the trigger of his gun. The plane skidded off the runway and came to rest with its tail protruding over the runway. Another B-24 that was attempting to take off struck the tail and both planes were wrecked. Two planes were thus lost because a waist gunner had shot out his own bomber's tire.[5] Fortunately no one on either crew was injured.

B-24 waist gunners had to be careful where they aimed to avoid shooting up their own aircraft.

On February, 24, 1943, Air Vice Marshal William Bostock of the RAAF (Royal Australian Air Force), along with a group of newspaper reporters, was examining a Jolly Rogers bomber named "The Nipper" at Fenton Field that had been nearly shot to pieces in an hour-long running battle with Japanese fighters, but had still managed to make it back to base. The plane was riddled with 7.7mm bullet holes from the fighters, but everyone noticed that it also had quite a few big .50-caliber holes in its rudders. Bostock "tactfully refrained from asking about their origin," wrote the Jolly Rogers' historian, but everyone knew that those holes had come from the bomber's own waist guns.[6] A waist gunner in a B-24 simply had to be very careful where he aimed.

Memorable Missions flown by the Horner crew

On Biak Island the Horner crew was flying three or four missions a week, and today, 74 years later, they tend to blend together in the recollections of the three surviving members of the crew. However, some missions do stand out in their memories, as related below.

Sgt. Baca is hit by a flak fragment

Mr. Baca doesn't remember today on which mission it was that a piece of shrapnel from a flak burst came through his waist gun window and struck him a glancing blow on the forehead, causing a cut. The impact stung, and he was startled and confused for a moment until he realized what had happened. He was able to stop the bleeding in a few minutes by holding a handkerchief to his head. He could have reported this wound and received a Purple Heart for it, but he didn't mention it to anyone except the other two gunners in the back of the plane, who saw him dabbing the blood off his head and asked him why he was bleeding. One of them urged him to report the injury and claim his medal, but he felt that to receive a citation for so small a wound would have been an insult to those who received the Purple Heart for more serious combat injuries. He says today that he's only glad that it wasn't a bigger and more lethal piece of shrapnel that hit him, since it might have gone right through his brain. Even the small piece that hit him could easily have put out an eye.

Mission #20: the Big Hole

On the September 8, 1944 raid on Langoan field, in a change from the usual practice of all bombers dropping on the cue of the lead bombardier, each bomber made an individual run on the target. The B-24s were loaded to their maximum weight-hauling capacity of four tons that day, hauling four monster 2000-pound high-explosive bombs each.

Lt. Horner set up his approach to the Japanese runway at a slight angle to it before handing control off to Lt. Ostafin, the bombardier, down in his "office" in the nose of the bomber. Experience had shown that bombing an enemy runway while flying across it at a slight angle produced the best results. It was hard for a bombardier to hit such a narrow target from ten or twelve thousand feet up while flying in line with it, and more often than not all the bombs would fall to one side or the other. But flying diagonally across the runway, and walking a string of bombs across it, gave a good chance for at least some of them to land on it.

Mr. Horner remembers that on a typical strike against an airfield, the runway being bombed would be approached at an angle of 15 to 20 degrees, and the bombs released "entrain," or sequentially, a fraction of a second apart, as the bomber crossed over it. In the ideal scenario, some bombs would fall short of the runway and some beyond, but most of them should hit right on it. Expressed in percentages, 20 percent of the bombs should land short of the runway, 60 per cent on the runway, and 20 per cent beyond it.

Thus, on this strike, carrying four one-ton bombs, if all went according to plan, one bomb would land just short of the runway, two on the runway, and one just beyond it. However, on this occasion, it accidentally worked out better than that—in fact, spectacularly better. Lt. Ostafin had carefully set his Norden bombsight to automatically begin dropping the bombs at just the right instant, beginning just short of the runway, and he was watching for an indicator light in the sight that would let him know that the bombs had begun to leave the bomb bay.

Up in the cockpit, the pilots would see a similar light flash on their instrument panel. There was always a chance of an electrical failure inside the bombsight, however, so Ostafin kept a close eye on it. If the little light didn't come on when he thought it should, meaning that no bombs were dropping, he could quickly toggle a salvo switch and let all them go at once.

On this day, that is exactly what happened; the light didn't go on in the bombsight, so as quickly as he could, Ostafin hit the salvo switch and all four of the one-ton bombs left the bomb bay simultaneously. The plane, suddenly four tons lighter, lurched and shot upward, rising hundreds of feet with everyone inside hanging on and hoping his stomach would eventually catch up with him. And because the cluster of bombs had been released just a tad late of the intended starting point, which would have been just short of the runway, as luck would have it they all hit together dead center on the runway.

The airplane hangar at the top of this picture gives some idea of the huge size of this crater in a Japanese runway. The Japanese would have a lot of work to do to fill this one in.

Eight thousand pounds of high explosives detonating on one small spot on the ground was bound to create quite a crater, and it certainly did, as shown on aerial photographs taken immediately after the raid. That evening, Captain Smith, the squadron's intelligence officer, while examining a photo of the day's results under a stereoscope (a device that causes photographs to appear in 3-D), was heard to shout, "Holy smokes! You could drop a whole hangar into that hole! That's one crater the Japanese won't be filling in anytime soon!"

As proficient as the Japanese were at filling in bomb craters, this one would present them with quite a challenge, for the hole was approximately 90 feet deep, twice that wide, and took out the whole center of the runway. The Japanese would not be using their runway at Langoan anytime soon.

Mission #24: Bomber Roulette: going around again

On 19 September [1944], the Jolly Rogers flew a Group mission to bomb a Japanese airfield near Menado,* in the Celebes Islands about 25 miles north of Langoan and 800 miles west of their base at Biak (Map 45-3 on page 626 shows the location of Langoan).

---

*The Japanese sank the U.S. submarine *Shark* just off Menado on February 11, 1942. A Japanese destroyer caught the *Shark* on the surface and sank her with gunfire from its main guns. Japanese records show that there were many survivors in the water but in typical Japanese fashion they were ignored and left to drown, and 59 Americans consequently died.

46. LIFE ON BIAK ISLAND

The 16-plane strike was comprised of four bombers from each of the Group's four squadrons, and each squadron had been assigned a different target on the enemy airfield. Major Leland I. Harter, Commander of the 320th Squadron, was flying in the lead of his squadron, and the Horner crew was flying one of the other three planes in the formation. Their target was a store of aviation gasoline on the Menado airfield. Blowing up a fuel dump for Japanese aircraft was nearly as effective as destroying the aircraft themselves, since the American navy was blocking all Japanese attempts to resupply their airbases, and the Japanese probably couldn't get any more gas to replace it. Airplanes without fuel were useless.

As usual in a squadron drop, the bombardier in the lead bomber, Major Harter's plane in this case, would lead the bomb run and the other planes would drop their bombs on his cue. However, as the formation passed over the target, no bombs fell from the lead plane, so the other three bombardiers, including Lt. Ostafin in the Horner bomber, held their bombs as well. As they passed over the Japanese airfield without dropping anything, everyone in the squadron wondered what was going on.

A radio message from Major Harter soon cleared up the confusion—he hadn't been satisfied with the bomb run, so he'd told his bombardier to hold his bombs for a second run. He didn't think the squadron had been properly lined up on the enemy fuel dump and the bombs would have been wasted. He informed the other three pilots in his squadron that they would all be going back to the IP to do it all over again.

"This would have been all well and good in a training exercise," Mr. Horner says today, "but this was a combat mission, and there was always considerable danger to bombers passing over a Japanese target, even once. Doing it twice doubled the danger." The flak on this day was sparse and inaccurate, but the gunners might always score a lucky hit on a bomber, and worse, there were Japanese fighter planes on the airfield below that were at that very moment scrambling to get airborne to attack the bombers.

The Jolly Rogers had caught the enemy's fighter planes on the ground, as they often did, but by circling back for a second bomb run they were giving them time to take off. The Japanese Zero had a rate of climb of over 3,000 feet per minute, and with the bombers flying at twelve thousand feet it would only be four minutes before they would be up level with the bombers and starting their firing passes at them.

As the four-plane formation flew back to the IP to start the second bomb run, anxiety among the crews was running high. "You only got one freebie pass over an enemy field," Mr. Horner says. "By the second one the air might be full of enemy planes. Doing two bombing runs was a risky business."

However, Major Harter was a conscientious commander, and he felt that a second bomb run had to be made in this case, danger or no. He wanted the strike photos to show that the squadron had done an effective job; otherwise their mission would have been a waste of time.

"We could see the Jap planes down there taking off, coming up like mosquitoes," Mr. Horner remembers today. "And here we were, going around again!" Mr. Baca, too, remembers the suspense felt by the gunners as they watched the Japanese fighter planes rising from the field below. On the second bomb run the squadron's bombs dropped squarely on the fuel dump, causing a huge explosion of orange flames, followed by thick plumes of black smoke. Maj. Harter had achieved his objective. Even as the bomb bay doors of the bombers were rolling shut he was turning the squadron for home, and fortunately the enemy fighter planes had not yet reached their altitude and chose not to pursue the Americans out to sea. But it had been a close call.

A number of crewmen were angry with Harter for flirting with disaster in such a manner, including Sgt. Baca. He laughs about it today, but at the time, he says, "We wanted to lynch that guy when we got back to base." But no harm had been done, except to the Japanese, and their anger soon subsided, to be replaced by satisfaction with a job well done. Major Harter had a reputation for being not only fearless but dutiful and demanding, and his men respected him for it. He had destroyed an important target that day, but he had been lucky to take his squadron away intact after two bomb runs.[7]

A rescue at sea

There was another story associated with the above mission, though the Horner crew was not involved in it. After the four planes of the Jolly Rogers' 321st Squadron had dropped their bombs and turned back over the sea, taking up a heading back to Biak, someone in one of the planes spotted an orange stain on the ocean below them. This could only be a dye marker deployed by some American in distress. Packets of orange dye were part of an American airman's ocean survival kit, to be released into the sea to make himself more visible to searchers in the air. After the news of the sighting had been radioed to the squadron's pilots, all four of the bombers circled back and dropped down close to the sea to investigate. What they saw was five men floating in their Mae West life jackets, waving at them frantically.

They turned out to be the crew of a B-25 strafer/bomber from the 345th Bomb Group (known as the "Air Apaches") piloted by 2nd Lt. Edward L. Reel, who'd been forced to ditch their plane in the water a short while before when one of their two engines had somehow lost all its oil, likely due to battle damage. The B-25s had been part of a coordinated attack on the Japanese airfield, and the strafer/bombers had gone in ahead of the heavies to shoot up parked planes and buildings while dropping parafrag bombs. Seeing the

46. LIFE ON BIAK ISLAND

B-24s coming their way after dropping their bombs, the men had released the brightly colored dye into the water, hoping it would be spotted, and thanks to a sharp-eyed Jolly Rogers crewman it was.

As we have seen, B-24s carried two large rubber life rafts for their own use in case of ditching, and one of the 321st's crews decided to toss one of theirs out to the men in the water. They heaved it out one of the waist windows, but the result was not what they had intended—the uninflated raft blew back and draped itself over the bomber's horizontal tail. Sgt. Joseph E. Sparks, one of the crewmen in the bomber, reported later that the fluttering and flapping of the raft against the plane's stabilizer caused it to fly "in quick, jerking, roller-coaster motions," which must have been an interesting sight to the men floating in the water, not to mention a source of extreme anxiety to the pilot fighting to keep the bomber under control.

As Sgt. Sparks' plane was galloping around the area with a raft draped over its tail, and its crew trying to figure what to do about it, the crew of one of the other bombers, piloted by Lt. Harry E. Pennington, tried to drop a raft also, but they too ran into trouble. Before they could get it out the window, the raft began to inflate inside the plane. The rubber monster grew larger and larger, filling up the fuselage and pinning the men to the walls, until one of them finally pulled his jungle knife and stabbed the thing into submission. A third bomber's crew had better luck dropping their raft, and it made it down to the sea, but once in the water it would only partially inflate. Nevertheless it was able to support two of the men in the water, with the other three floating around it, and the bright yellow raft would make the group easier to spot by a rescue plane.

Meanwhile the men on the roller-coastering bomber rigged up a knife on the end of a pole, and by leaning out a waist window they were able to cut the raft away from the tail of their plane and restore full control to the pilot (and then everyone in the plane no doubt had to wait a while for their stomachs to settle down from the wild ride). Radio messages had been going out all the while from the Jolly Rogers bombers in an attempt to make contact with a PBY Catalina amphibious rescue plane known to be in the area, and eventually a reply came back from a P-38 fighter pilot that the Cat had received the message and was on the way, escorted by two P-38s in case the Japanese tried to interfere with the rescue. Three of the four Jolly Rogers bombers then set out for home, but Lt. Pennington continued to circle the raft for over two hours, waiting for the Catalina to appear and keeping a close watch on the men in the water.

He had good reason to do so. Three months earlier, on a bombing mission from Wakde Island to the Japanese-held island of Pelielu, two men of a Jolly Rogers crew piloted by Lt. Leonard J. Hogland had survived a ditching and had also been floating in a raft, but after their comrades in the other bombers had reported their position to rescue planes, and departed, the men were never found and must have died at sea. The other eight men of the Hogland crew had gone down with the bomber when it broke apart upon contact with the water (the old story), but the two survivors, who could not be personally identified by the circling planes, were seen to be in good shape, sitting in the raft and waving at the bombers circling overhead. The men in the bombers had dropped survival supplies to them, including a radio, before they left, and were confident that a ship or Catalina would soon find and rescue them.

But in fact rescuers had never found them. A PBY and a Navy B-24 scoured the area where the raft had been reported, searching for hours, but failed to find it, and no trace of the men was ever found. Tragically, the radio that had been dropped to the men must have been defective, and their raft probably drifted away on the ocean currents into the endless wastes of the Pacific Ocean. The men must have died at sea from exposure, hunger, and thirst.[8]

Pennington was determined that the five B-25 crewmen in the water below him would not suffer that fate. He figured that he had enough fuel to hang around a while, flying slowly to conserve gas, and wanted to keep the floating men in sight until the Catalina showed up. As he circled, his crew shot flares into the air at intervals from the waist windows to attract the attention of the rescue plane, and he finally received a message over the radio from one of the P-38 pilots that they had spotted the flares and were headed in their direction. Finally the Cat arrived, landed beside the men in the water, and took them all aboard, so the story had a happy ending, and the tale of the wayward rubber rafts was told again and again with great hilarity back at Biak. General Kenney presented the men of Pennington's crew with letters of commendation for the part they had played in the rescue.[8]

All sixteen of the Jolly Rogers bombers that flew the mission to Menado that day made it safely back to Biak.

Sgt. Baca deals with a stuck bomb

On one of the Horner crew's missions from Biak, a 500-pound bomb got hung up in their B-24's bomb bay. The bombers had made their bomb run and dropped their bombs, and were on the way home when, as Mr. Baca remembers it today, Sgt. J. W. Dale looked into the bomb bay and came running back to him shouting, "Baca! Baca! There's still a bomb in there!" Baca took a look and saw a bomb hanging nose-down from one of the bomb racks.

As the crew's armorer, trained to service the bomb-dropping mechanisms, it was Baca's job to deal with the problem. He called Lt. Horner over the intercom to let him and the rest of the crew know that they still had a bomb aboard, asked Horner to open the bomb bay doors again, and told him he was going into the bomb bay to pry the bomb loose.

"Bombs would occasionally get stuck in the bomb bays of B-24s," Mr. Horner says today, "but this was the only occasion that it happened to us. It was not a good feeling, I can tell you that."

Sgt. Baca took a little toolkit that he kept handy down into the bomb bay to see what he would have to do to release the bomb. Lt. Ostafin, the bombardier, left his position in the nose of the bomber and came back to join him, in case he could be of any help. Both men had to stand on the 6-inch-wide catwalk beside the bomb. Normally when a man walked along the catwalk going forward or to the rear, the bomb bay doors were closed, giving him a sense of having a floor beneath him, but with the bomb bay doors open there was nothing under the catwalk but air, and in this case, thousands of feet below, the sea.

It was not a place for anyone with a fear of heights. To complicate matters, there was a 150-mph wind swirling up into the men's faces, tearing at their clothing and making their eyes water, and even by shouting they could barely hear each other over the roaring of the gale. The bomb bay was too narrow, and the space too tight, to allow them to wear their parachutes, so if either man's feet slipped off the narrow catwalk, it would have been him who dropped from the plane instead of the bomb. The men gripped the bomb racks on either side of them while they assessed the situation.

"It was a very tricky business," Mr. Baca says today. "We didn't know if that thing was going to explode on us or not." A bomb was held in the bomb bay of a B-24 by two shackles—U-shaped links closed by a pin—one near the nose of the bomb and one on the tail. The bomb itself had eyebolts built into it that were held in the shackles. When the bombardier activated an electric current over the target, the pins in the shackles pulled out and allowed the bombs to drop. On this bomb, however, only the front shackle had let go; the rear one had not released, and as a result the bomb was hanging nose-down from the rear shackle only.

After looking the problem over, Sgt. Baca took a screwdriver from his toolkit, and clinging onto a bomb rack with one hand to steady himself, he used the screwdriver to pry at the shackle pin until he was finally able to pry it out. This released the bomb, which dropped free and disappeared below, to the great relief of everyone aboard the plane. Lt. Horner then shut the bomb bay doors, Lt. Ostafin returned to his station in the nose of the bomber, and Sgt. Baca went back to his waist gun position. There he looked out the window and saw that his plane wasn't the only one with bomb bay trouble that day. On the bomber flying next to them, the bomb bay doors had somehow broken loose and were flapping in the wind below the plane. This would present a serious problem to the plane on landing, since there were only a couple of feet between the belly of a B-24 and the ground when it was on the ground (in fact, that was why the B-24 had bomb bay doors that rolled up the outside of the fuselage; the plane sat too low to the ground for any other kind of doors to work). If the dangling doors hit the ground on landing they might break off and create who-knew-what kind of mischief. Those doors would have to be secured before a landing could be made.

Doing this required somebody in the plane to lay face-down on the catwalk, likewise without his parachute, and reach down to somehow fish up the broken doors and secure them to the catwalk with a piece of wire or something. As Baca and the other crewmen in the Horner bomber watched, this was successfully done, and the bomber was then able to land safely.

Lt. Cooper's art

Allan Cooper, the former Disney artist, continued drawing cartoons after he entered the Army, first creating the series of humorous safety posters for fighter plane training schools shown in Chapter 39, and then after he joined the Air Corps to become a pilot himself, filling one of his student pilot classbooks with cartoons. When he went out to the Pacific as the copilot of the Horner crew, he continued drawing whimsical sketches for the amusement of his fellow crewmen and other friends in his squadron.

Judging from the drawings that survive, which were saved and later brought home by Lts. Horner and Theobald, Cooper enjoyed poking gentle fun at his fellow crewmen in some of these cartoons. In the first sketch reproduced here, at right, we see Lt. Theobald, the crew's navigator, holding a map of the South Pacific along with his sextant, but obviously he has made a slight error in his computations, because he has taken his

Allan Cooper cartoon showing that Lt. Theobald, the navigator, has made a course error. Despite holding a map of the South Pacific and a sextant, he has made a miscalculation and taken the bomber to Nazi-occupied Europe.

crew to Europe instead of whatever Pacific target they may have been headed for. While Theobald peers in confusion from his navigator's dome, the windmills of Holland appear below the plane, and above it is the separated tail of a B-17 bomber, whose tail gunner is spitting in the eye of a German fighter plane pilot.

In the next cartoon (right) we see Lt. Horner leaning out the cockpit window to observe his bombs hitting a Japanese outhouse, and on the next page he gives us his own copilot's view of Lt. Horner during a Japanese fighter plane attack.

Lt. Cooper's artistic genius went beyond cartoons. He was quite as capable of creating realistic art, as can be seen in the pencil portrait at right of Lt. Horner that he drew when they were sitting around in their tent one day. Cooper had aspirations of becoming a serious oil painter after the war, and this drawing suggests that he certainly had the potential to become a fine portrait painter.

When news came that on June 22, 1944 President Franklin D. Roosevelt had signed into law an act known as the G. I. Bill, which would provide veterans with funds for attending college or other

In this cartoon Lt. Cooper imagines his bomber destroying a Japanese outhouse with a bomb, with Lt. Horner leaning out the cockpit window to confirm the hit. The outhouse also happens to be occupied. A nearby Japanese flak gunner is so overcome by the odors from the wrecked latrine that he cannot fire his gun.

types of schooling after their discharge from the service, Cooper told members of his crew that he hoped to use that opportunity to study art in Europe.

Lt. Cooper also used his amazing talent to decorate the nose of at least one Jolly Rogers bomber, and probably others. This was Major Harter's plane, that he named "The Boise Bronc" after his home on a horse ranch near Boise, Idaho. Cooper painted a bronco on the side of the bomber bucking off a Japanese soldier (opposite page). A black-and-white photo does not do justice to this masterfully done color cartoon. Fortunately someone with a roll of

In this cartoon Cooper gives us his right-seat copilot's view of Lt. Horner, the pilot, who appears a bit tense as he watches a string of Japanese Zeros streaming past his cockpit window.

color film took a picture of the painting and thereby preserved it for posterity. Like nearly all B-24s, the "Boise Bronc" was broken up and melted down for scrap after the war, and the painting by Allan Cooper vanished with it.

Jolly Rogers nose art

The Army Air Corps, in both Europe and the Pacific, was unique among the services in allowing pilots of fighter planes and the crews of bombers to decorate their aircraft with custom artwork. Navy and Marine pilots were only rarely allowed to do this. Many of the bombers of the 90th Bomb Group thus had artwork painted on their noses, and of course from the time the 90th decided to call itself the Jolly Rogers (July of 1943) it also had tail art: the huge skull and crossed bombs painted on the rudders of all the Group's planes. As noted earlier, in the early part of the war in the Pacific a bomber crew was allowed to practically claim a bomber as its own and personalize it with a nickname and artwork. Later on, when bombers were assigned to crews pretty much at random for missions, many bombers still acquired nose art unique to

46. LIFE ON BIAK ISLAND

Lt. Cooper's nose art on the B-24 "Boise Bronc." An American bronco bucks off a bewildered Japanese soldier, sending him and his samurai sword flying (Biak Island, 1944).

The crew of the "Boise Bronc" relax beside their plane, with Lt. Cooper's artwork on the side of it behind them. This is the bomber shown on the cover of this book. Major Harter, the pilot, is standing, second from right.

themselves, even though one plane might be flown by many crews.

If the slab sides of the B-24 did not contribute to its beauty, they were at least well suited to the application of artwork,* although the artist might be hampered a bit by having his "canvas" marred by hundreds of protruding rivet heads, and he was required to leave all Army markings and placards in place (thus any artist who did not care to

The "Boise Bronc," like most bombers of the Jolly Rogers 320th Squadron (the Moby Dick Squadron) had a shark's mouth painted on its nose. Lt. Cooper's artwork can be seen beneath the cockpit window.

A Disney-quality cartoon on another Jolly Rogers bomber was almost certainly painted by Lt. Allan Cooper, although no one can be sure because he didn't sign his nose art.

*The photos on page 12 show how much easier it was to paint nose art on a B-24 than a B-17. The sides of a B-24 were nearly flat compared to the round fuselage of a B-17.

have "Fire Extinguisher" written across his painting would have to plan its positioning accordingly).

The quality of the artwork painted on Air Corps aircraft varied from professional to abysmal, depending on the level of skill that the artist brought to his task and the complexity of his composition. The art skills of most nose artists were mediocre to poor, although there were some with real talent. Few were as skilled as Lt. Cooper, but some were good enough to achieve a degree of fame for their work. At Nadzab, Sgt. Al Merkling (right) painted quite a few excellent examples of nose art on B-24s, and is still remembered for it today.

Since the 320th Squadron of the Jolly Rogers was known as the Moby Dick Squadron, and its squadron symbol was a whale with a mouthful of nasty teeth, many of the 320th's bombers had toothy shark's mouths painted on their noses similar to the ones made famous by the AVG (American Volunteer Group)'s Flying

Sgt. Al Merkling at work painting nose art at Nadzab in 1944. Many of Merkling's figures were life-sized, like this one he's painting on an often-repaired bomber nicknamed "Patched-Up Piece." Unlike Lt. Cooper, Sgt. Merkling signed his artwork.

Merkling's finished painting on the nose of the bomber "Patched Up Piece."

Tigers in China on the noses of their P-40 fighter planes. Many other Jolly Rogers aircraft had other emblems, names, slogans, portraits, cartoons, and alluring women painted on their noses. A sampling of these is on the opposite page.

Often, once a squadron had identified a good artist in its midst, he would be paid or bribed in some manner to paint whatever name or picture a crew desired on the nose of their bomber, and was thus able to profitably exploit his talent when he wasn't too busy with his regular Army duties. Mr. Baca remembers that Lt. Cooper was kept busy with his paintbrushes down on the flight line, and although Cooper never signed his nose art, some very professionally done Disney characters that appeared on the sides of Jolly Rogers bombers were almost certainly his creations. One of these shows Donald Duck with a sledgehammer chasing a miniature Japanese soldier around (p. 662).

We may never know the motivation behind some nose art.

Since the bomber crews were made up of mostly young men in their late teens and early twenties, many of the pictures painted on the bombers were predictably "pin-up girls" in varying stages of undress, or nude. The latter were known as "chaplain shockers" and weren't popular with everyone (besides chaplains), including Charles Lindbergh. Lindbergh may have been a superb airplane pilot and a courageous man, but he was also something of a snob and a prude with regard to bomber art. After driving a jeep past long lines of parked bombers and fighters at Nadzab, he sneered at the nose art on the aircraft and claimed it made him "nauseous," writing in his journal:

> Drove to Topline strip [one of the runways at Nadzab] with General Wurtsmith and brought his jeep back to Fighter Command after he took off, through the long lines of planes parked in revetments. The cheapness of the emblems and names painted on the bombers and fighters nauseates me at times—mostly naked women or "Donald Ducks"—names such as Fertile Myrtle" under

46. LIFE ON BIAK ISLAND

a large and badly painted figure of a reclining nude.[9*]

Women being the most popular subjects of artwork painted on bomber noses, squadron artists often copied the calendar girls and centerfolds produced in America at this time by artist Alberto Vargas, who must to this day hold the record for the number of ways the female figure can be posed. Copies of the same Vargas paintings can be seen on the sides of many bombers in both the European and Pacific theaters of war. Although the "Vargas Girls" on the calendars and magazine pages wore clothing, many of the nose artists abbreviated it or removed it entirely in their copies. In one instance recorded by the historian of the Jolly Rogers, the nudes had to have some minimal clothing hastily painted on them when some female celebrities were known to be on the way to visit the Group in a USO show, since the women were likely to be given a tour of the flight line.

Other women painted on bombers were portraits of the actual wives or girlfriends of pilots or crewmen, and there were some children's portraits as well (viz: "Little Queen Mary" on the previous page). Any subject, in fact, was fair game for the nose artists, and the result was many interesting examples of folk art painted on Jolly Rogers aircraft and those of other bomber and fighter groups throughout the war, and remembered today in several collections of nose art photographs in books. The actual artwork itself all vanished when the aircraft were scrapped after the war.

A failed takeoff experiment at Mokmer Field

One night on Biak Island Lt. Horner took a jeep down to the airfield to watch an experiment that was conducted to see how fast a squadron of B-24s could get into the air. A number of B-24s was taking off on a mission that night, likely to the Philippines since they were departing around midnight, and it was planned for the bombers to take off only sixty seconds apart instead of the usual interval of a few minutes.

Horner had heard that this was going to be tried and wanted to see how it worked out. The reason for attempting this accelerated takeoff sequence was never made clear, and may have been arranged by some operations officer just

---

* Lindbergh, who once lectured an inebriated woman at a party on morality and told her that she was "a poor example of American womanhood," turned out to be a poor example of American manhood, at least with regard to the morals that he paid such lip service to. He became a secret polygamist after the war, with his one legitimate family in America and three more secret ones in Germany. The number of children he fathered was possibly as many as seven in Germany with his three mistresses there, and six children with his real wife, Anne Morrow, for a total of at least thirteen. Three of the known German offspring were confirmed to be his through DNA testing and by the love letters that he wrote to their mothers, while the rest prefer to remain anonymous. None of Lindbergh's dozen or so well-known biographies mentions this double life, since it was only discovered in 2003 (Lindbergh died in 1974).

to see if it could be done, in case a situation ever arose that required getting all the bombers off the field with the greatest possible speed, such as an imminent heavy Japanese air attack. Under normal conditions there was no reason for bombers to take off at such an accelerated pace, and in fact there was good reason not to.

Normally at least two or three minutes were allowed to pass between takeoffs so that the air disturbed by the wings and propellers of each airplane had some time to settle down before the next plane passed through it. Anyone who has watched an airplane flying through fog or smoke has seen the miniature tornadoes spinning off its wingtips, a byproduct of generating lift, and a large and heavy airplane such as the B-24 could produce some very large and powerful vortexes of that type. In addition, the air stirred up by the prop wash from the bomber's huge propellers added to the turbulence. All this wildly churning air tended to linger above a runway for a while after an airplane had departed, and it could endanger the next plane as it lifted off.

It had always been deemed wise, therefore, to let two or three minutes elapse between takeoffs. An exception might occur if there happened to be a significant crosswind on the field, since it would blow the disturbed air off the runway. The pilot of a plane about to take off always had the final say in such matters, and if he saw the wings of the airplane ahead of him dipping and wobbling after it lifted off, indicating dangerously turbulent air, he could play it safe and wait a little longer before starting his own takeoff run.

The planes taking off from Biak's Mokmer Field that night were all carrying full loads of gas and bombs. Mokmer was a long strip, somewhere in excess of 8,000 feet, but the trees at the end of the runway were forty to fifty feet high. These trees normally posed no problem for airplanes taking off, since the planes were usually well above them by the time they got that far, but tonight things would be different.

Lt. Horner got out of his jeep and climbed the stairway to the control tower to get a better view of the field. It was about 3 o'clock in the morning, with some spotlights illuminating the runway. As each plane thundered by on its takeoff run, sixty seconds apart, Horner could see the effects of the air turbulence building up over the runway. The wings of the bombers were rocking back and forth as they lifted off, and the churning of the air was getting worse with each takeoff. The pilots stuck to the program, however, and dutifully started their takeoff runs every sixty seconds as they got the green light from the tower.

By the time half a dozen planes had taken off, the air turbulence had become critical. The next bomber to lift off was thrown nearly out of control by the roiling air, and it had hardly climbed at all by the time it reached the end of the runway. Its left wing clipped the trees, and the left landing gear and the lower part of the left rudder also plowed through the branches and were damaged. The propeller of engine #2 hit a branch thick enough to bend the blades and stop the engine. As the crippled aircraft lurched into a left turn out over the bay, its pilot found himself in a desperate situation, with a dead engine on his left wing, his rudder control impaired, and very little altitude to work with.

He quickly feathered the propeller on the dead engine, but now he was flying a sluggish, fully loaded bomber with very little airspeed or altitude, and the flight controls were not responding properly. He realized that a crash was imminent, but he had to get up to an altitude where it was possible for his crew to bail out.

The plane continued in a sweeping left turn, climbing slowly as the pilot struggled for control. As soon as he reached three or four hundred feet, the minimum altitude needed for parachutes to open, he ordered the rest of his crew to bail out, and they quickly complied. The plane continued its left turn until it had completed three quarters of a circle and was headed back toward the land.

After all the rest of the crew had jumped, the pilot cut the throttles, yanked off his seat belt, and quickly made his way back to the bomb bay where he threw himself through the open bomb bay doors and pulled the ripcord on his own parachute. He, along with the last couple of crewmen who had jumped, came down on the shore, while the others landed in the water offshore. The ones in the water were soon picked up by patrol boats that had been alerted by radio from the control tower.

These boats were always on standby during mission takeoffs for just this purpose. Their searchlights could be seen probing the water until all the men had been located and picked up. Lt. Horner and other pilots watching this drama felt that the pilot had pulled off a miracle in getting all his crew and himself out of the disabled bomber so fast. In less skilled hands the plane might have crashed into the sea and killed everyone aboard.

The pilotless bomber glided on and crashed into the hills back of the airfield, near an area where some infantry troops were encamped. Fortunately no one was hurt, but the commanding general of the Army division was furious and wanted the pilot prosecuted for endangering his men. Lt. Horner and the other pilots who had witnessed the incident thought that the pilot (whose name is not recorded) deserved a medal instead. The general finally dropped the matter.

Later in the day, when the sun was up, Lt. Horner went up on the hillside where the bomber had crashed to have a look at the wreckage. He was interested to note that the flames from the hundreds of gallons of gasoline in the bomber's full fuel tanks had burned so hot that they had even melted the plane's engines. Not only had the softer aluminum parts melted and run down into cracks in the rocks, but even steel parts had liquefied, flowed, and fused into the surrounding coral.*

Leave to Sydney, Australia

All bomber crews looked forward to leave in Australia for R & R (rest & recreation). Sydney was the city to which most Americans were sent on leave, and most of the young men were starved for the comforts of civilization that it offered, such as sleeping in a normal bed between real sheets, eating fresh food, and enjoying the company of women. Men going on leave pooled their money and rented rooms together. The names and phone numbers of Australian girls who had shown Americans a good time were passed around between men coming back from and those going on leave, so that many men coming into Sydney already had phone numbers to call, and the same apartments and hotel rooms were turned over to groups of new occupants every week or two. As one member of the Jolly Rogers 320th Squadron remembered it:

> Each squadron probably had its covey of girls [in Sydney]. I know we got names and addresses before going, looked them all up, and then passed the names and addresses along to the next crew. The Aussies were terribly hospitable and showed us a great time.[10]

American servicemen got about double the pay that most Australian troops did, the British were paid even less, and many Australian girls were happy to help the young Americans spend their money. The city had many nightclubs with bands and orchestras for dating couples to enjoy, and there were restaurants, amusement parks, and swimming beaches. Sydney was a place where the war could be put aside and forgotten for a little while. Wartime romances bloomed in abundance, and there were marriages between Australian girls and American servicemen, some of which outlasted the war.

The attitude of many Americans on leave from the war front, some of whom had seen their comrades killed in battle, was "eat, drink, and be merry, for tomorrow we (may) die." That was the reason why squadron intelligence officers, when gathering up the effects of men killed in combat to send home to relatives, carefully read men's diaries and letters before sending them home, in case they contained any evidence of uncharacteristic behavior that might distress family members. It would not be well, for example, for a wife or fiancé in America to find letters from an Australian girlfriend among an airman's effects. Any such embarrassing material that was found was destroyed before the men's belongings were sent home.

---

* Hiking is a popular activity for tourists on Biak Island today, after they arrive on airliners at Mokmer Field, which is now paved. Perhaps some hikers have come across this interesting geological feature—metallic coral—and wondered about its origin.

Americans on leave in Sydney found the Australians to be extremely grateful to them for the defense of their country, and they were accordingly treated well. Art Rogers remembered:

> At this time the Australians were receiving the Americans with open arms as saviors of their country, and we were treated grandly where ever we went. In fact it was jokingly being said by many that Australia would like to become the forty-ninth state of the Union...
>
> The Australians whom I came in contact with . . . were very bitter toward the British, and felt as though they had been left to be gobbled up by the Japs while their able-bodied men were fighting in Africa and England. Many people would remark that they had lost a son, brother, or husband in the fall of Singapore and I realized that this was a nation depleted of most of its young men.[11]

On Biak Island, among the Jolly Rogers bomber crews, there was no definite number of missions required before a crew was eligible for leave to Sydney. Mr. Horner remembers today that whenever a crew thought they might be close to getting leave, they kept an eye on the squadron bulletin board hoping to see their names listed for it. After they were alerted for leave, they would be given orders containing the exact time, destination, and other details of the leave. Often more than one crew would go on leave at the same time.

No one among the crews knew exactly when or why leave was granted at the times that it was. It could have just been at convenient times for the Group, or perhaps the Squadron Medical Officer had been noting signs of fatigue in a crew and sent the men on leave when he felt they needed a rest. Before the Horner crew went on its first leave, someone mentioned to Lt. Horner that he'd been seen taking off on a recent mission with the cowl flaps of his bomber's engines open (the flaps were kept open when the bomber was on the ground to provide cooling to the engines, but were supposed to be closed on takeoff to reduce drag), and Horner didn't know whether the man was just ribbing him or pointing out that he was starting to get tired and make mistakes. At any rate, his crew's first leave came shortly afterward.

During the five months the Horner crew was on Biak Island (August of 1944 to January 1945), they were given two leaves to Sydney, one in September and another one in December. Each leave was to be of ten days' duration, not counting travel time going and coming. The first leave came after the crew had flown 24 missions, and the second one after only eleven missions more, perhaps reflecting the fact that fatigue was building up in the men along with the mission count. The crew's first leave began on September 22, 1944. The Fifth Air Force's Air Transport Command (ATC) operated a shuttle service between Biak and Australia, and on the day designated for their departure the crew rode a truck from their tents in the camp area down to the airfield to board

46. LIFE ON BIAK ISLAND

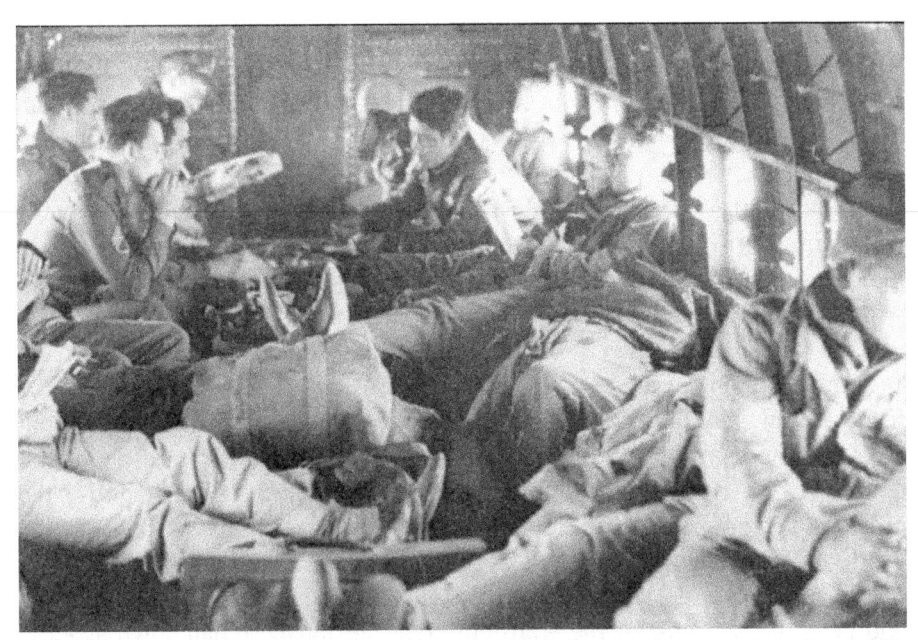

The 2,500-mile flight from Biak Island down to Sydney in a C-47 may have been dull, with little to do but read, smoke, sleep, or watch the scenery pass by out the window, but the prospect of spending some time back in civilization more than made up for the boredom of the ride.

a C-47 that had been equipped with canvas seats for passengers. It took about two days of flying to cover the 2,500 miles from Biak to Sydney, with fueling stops at Nadzab and Townsville, Australia.

There were about 20 other men aboard the plane going on leave with the Horner crew the first time, and some of them were part of a Navy B-24 crew. Lt. Horner struck up a conversation with one of the Navy officers and found out that they were going on leave because they had survived a ditching, and it was standard practice for the Navy to grant leave to a crew that had been through a forced landing in the water. The man told him they'd lost a couple of men in the crash. Horner was amazed that so many of the crewmen had survived.

"When we ditch," he told the Navy pilot, "usually we're dead. How do you do it?" As it turned out, Navy pilots received extra instruction on the best ways to land a B-24 in the water. "We may lose a man or two," the Navy pilot said, "but it [a successful ditching] can be done if you know how." Lt. Horner reflected that most Army Air Corps pilots definitely did not know how.

Life in wartime Sydney, Australia

In Sydney, young Americans who had never traveled much in their own country, mostly owing to the Great Depression of the prewar years, entered a vibrant, bustling foreign city that seemed to thrive despite wartime shortages and rationing. It was a place where cars drove on the "wrong" side of the road and all the young women had intriguing British accents. As Art Rogers had noted, the average Australian was very grateful to America and her military men for warding off the Japanese threat to their country. The Japanese had intended to capture Port Moresby and then use it as a springboard for an invasion of Australia itself. Had it done so, the horrors of Nanking and Singapore would likely have been repeated in Sydney and other Australian cities, especially with the Japanese military's demonstrated hatred of Caucasians.

But the American Navy had put paid to that threat by driving back the Japanese fleet, including its Port Moresby invasion force, at the Battle of the Coral Sea in May of 1942. Up to that time the Japanese had had everything their own way in the war, but the Battle of the Coral Sea showed them, and the rest of the world, that they were not invincible and set the stage for the crushing defeat of the Japanese navy a month later near Midway Island. The Battle of Midway, which was the beginning of the end for Japan, occurred only six months after the Pearl Harbor attack. The Battle of the Coral Sea had been the first gust of the whirlwind that the Japanese had sown at Pearl Harbor, which would soon develop into a hurricane of destruction that would envelop them and lead to their utter defeat in 1945. To this day the Battle of the Coral Sea is commemorated annually in Australia, and American Navy veterans of that battle are encouraged to travel to Australia to be honored and feted as heroes.

In 1944, while Americans such as the Horner crew were on leave in Sydney, Australia's mother country, Britain, was still preoccupied with Hitler and the war in Europe, and had no naval or ground forces to spare for the defense of its Australian commonwealth. The two great British battleships that had been in the Pacific at the outset of the war, the *Repulse* and the *Prince of Wales*, had both been sunk north of Singapore, off the east coast of Malaya, three days after the Pearl Harbor attack by Japanese dive bombers (which also settled the debate over whether warships could operate safely without air cover).

Australia did not even have its own soldiers at home to defend it at first, since early in the war it had sent its men to join the British in the fight against the Germans and Italians in Europe (the European war had started with the German invasion of Poland in 1939, and at that time Japan had not been seen as an imminent threat). Britain had promised the Australian government that it would defend Australia if the Japanese attacked, but when the war came, the British forces in Asia were as severely mauled as the Americans in the Philippines were in the opening days of the war, leaving no British troops in the area to defend anyone or anything.

Australian Prime Minister John Curtin had sought to bring his divisions home from Europe to protect Australia, but British Prime Minister Winston Churchill strove mightily to keep them in the European theater. Nevertheless in January of 1942 the Australian 6th and 7th Divisions had been withdrawn from North Africa, where they had been battling Rommel, and brought back home where they went into action in New Guinea, driving back the Japanese invasion force that had tried to advance on Port Moresby across the Kokoda Trail over the Owen Stanley Mountains. Men fresh from the deserts of North Africa were soon fighting in the steaming jungles of the Southwest Pacific. It is no wonder that they were considered some of the best fighters in the world.

But it was primarily the Americans who had thwarted the Japanese designs for an invasion of Australia, and Australians knew it and loved them for it. However, the American/Australian relationship wasn't always sunshine and roses. By 1944 there were so many thousands of American servicemen in Australia, either working there or on leave from the war front, that the Australians' gratitude was occasionally mingled with resentment over the sometimes unpleasant effects of so many American men in their midst. The same thing occurred in England, where many British soldiers and civilians alike were complaining that the "Yanks are overpaid, oversexed, and over here."

Lt. Horner witnessed this friction firsthand one day as he rode an Australian streetcar. There were several other American servicemen on the crowded car, and at one stop an Australian woman boarded who did not immediately see a place to sit down. "Everywhere you go," she said testily, to no one in particular, "these damn Yanks are in the way. They take up all the space, everywhere!" A veteran Australian soldier sitting nearby heard this. "Lady," he said to her, "if these Americans weren't here, you'd probably be a sex slave in the tent of some Japanese officer right now. Think about it." The woman sat down and said no more.

On his way into the Pacific theater, on May 17, 1944 Charles Lindbergh had discussed the situation in Australia with an Army colonel on Funafuti Island, and recorded the conversation in his journal:

> [W]e discussed the situation which is building up in Australia as a result of the presence of so many American soldiers, sailors and Marines. American pay is much higher than Australian, and Americans spend freely. Morals in Australia are considered low (by all the officers I have talked to who have been there). The result is a thriving black market, loose women, and a rising resentment toward Americans, mixed in with gratitude for our protection against Japan. Most of our men go to some place like Sydney for their vacation, if possible, trade cigarettes for gasoline and liquor when they cannot buy it with money, and expect to sleep with about any girl they can get to go out with them. The Japanese are

using this situation as a part of their propaganda, dropping leaflets with verses and cartoons to remind the Australians of what is going on at home. "Thinking you diggers will never come back alive, the blacks and the Yanks are raping your wives, your daughters, your sweethearts... They're helpless without your protection," etc.[12]

Mr. Horner remembers that the members of his crew split up on arrival in Sydney and went their separate ways for the ten days of leave, and all three men who are still alive today remember how happy they were to enjoy the sights, sounds, and fresh food of civilization after so much deprivation at the war front. Sgt. Baca, a devout Catholic, remembers searching for a Catholic church so that he could attend Mass. Mr. Horner remembers falling by chance into the company of a nice girl who was the daughter of the female owner of a pub he visited, while he was enjoying a beer in their establishment. The mother voiced no objection to her daughter dating "an officer and a gentleman," so the girl agreed to accompany him around town, acting as his guide to the local attractions, and they rode around on buses together enjoying the sights, chatting, and also attended a dance. It was a world away from air combat and Mr. Horner still remembers it fondly to this day.

Pay differences and resulting problems

As mentioned earlier, the pay discrepancy between Americans, Australians, and British that Lindbergh spoke of was considerable: Americans received $100 a month overseas pay, Australians got $50 per month, the British only $25. In fact, the British could buy so little in Sydney with their meager pay that there was a fenced-in area reserved for them at a park in Sydney's famous King's Cross district, where prices were reduced to accommodate their pay. British military men on leave spent their time inside the fence, where no Americans were allowed. Some British sailors hung around an amusement park on Luna Pier hoping to get dates with Australian girls, but there was such high feeling against the British navy in Sydney that Australian girls were insulted if someone even suggested they date a British sailor. Americans didn't much care for the British either. On Luna pier there were almost nightly fistfights between the British sailors and Australians allied with Americans, and the sailors frequently got tossed off the pier into the water, which was a bit worrisome for those tossed since there were known to be sharks in the water.

Admiral Bruce Fraser of the British navy, the Commander-in-Chief of the Home Fleet, angered most Australians by sending British ships to Australia long after the threat of Japanese invasion had passed, and then behaving like a conquering hero, acting as though the Australians owed him gratitude. He filmed a speech that was shown in Australian movie theaters, in which he announced pompously that "Your saviors are now in your cities!" causing enraged moviegoers to shout unprintable epithets at the screen and hurl their popcorn and candy wrappers at it. The British navy had been nowhere to be seen when the Japanese were bombing northern Australian cities and threatening invasion—it had been the Americans who had traveled across the Pacific and driven them back.

Funny money and anonymous shops

Mr. Horner remembers today that the streets of Sydney were not like those in America; there were few signs above the restaurants or shops to tell passersby what sort of establishments they were (he visited Australia again in recent years and says that nothing much has changed in that regard). The shops reminded him of speakeasies back home during Prohibition—you had to go to the door and look inside or ask what kind of a place it was.

Americans on leave also had to learn to deal with the complexities of Aussie money. With the paper money, the size and color of a bill could give you a clue as to its relative value: a half pound note (worth about $3.20 American at that time) was orange, and was smaller than an American dollar bill, while a one pound note was green and much larger, a five-pound note was larger still, and a bright purple fifty-pound note was so large—twice the size of an American dollar bill—that it would not fit into any American's wallet without first being folded up.

There was also the matter of Australian coins, some of them called florins and bobs (a bob was half a florin, and was worth one shilling, and there were twenty shillings to the pound). To add to the confusion, shop windows didn't display the price of goods in pounds and shillings, but used symbols instead, with the result that Americans could frequently be seen standing in front of store windows doing mental arithmetic trying to figure out whether they could afford to buy something they were looking at.

Fresh food!

One thing available in Sydney was something that all American servicemen coveted: fresh food, of many kinds. You could order just about anything you wanted to eat in a Sydney restaurant, although since food was rationed in Australia just as it was in America, you couldn't get everything on the menu in one sitting. If you ordered certain things, because of the rationing you were prohibited from ordering certain other things. The restrictions were all explained in the menus.

There were other differences from restaurants back home, as Art Rogers remembered:

> **My entire sixteen months in and out of Australia I have yet to sit down to dinner in any of their eating places, restaurants, or big hotel dining rooms, and be served water along with the meal.**

When you ask a waiter or waitress for a glass of water along with the meal, they always look at you as if they think you're a little 'touched.'

Mr. Horner remembers a nice restaurant in Sydney where, if you ordered a bottle of wine, the owner of the restaurant popped the cork against the wall, and if he failed to catch it before it hit the ground you got the wine for free. He was so good at it that only rarely did the patrons get free wine.

Among other memories of the men who went on leave in Sydney was the sight of cars and trucks with large gas bags mounted on their roofs. Because Australia had no oil wells, gasoline was scarce in the city and was strictly rationed. However, in both Europe and Australia it had been discovered that car and truck engines would run, after a fashion, on the combustible gas byproducts of burning wood or charcoal.

(Above and below): cars and trucks in Sydney often sported bags of combustible gas during the war, gasoline being scarce.

Other Australian automobiles simply reverted to the original kind of horsepower for the duration of the war.

The the gas produced this way could not be compressed, so large balloon-like cloth envelopes had to be mounted on the vehicles to store it and deliver it to the engines.

A woodburning car or truck often had a stove grafted onto to it somewhere with pipes running up to the gasbag, and more pipes running from the bag down to the engine. Some of these vehicles looked like plumbers' nightmares with the piping running all over them, but oddly enough they ran. The engines could be started up on regular gasoline, then switched over to the gas in the bags to run. Since the gas didn't produce much power, engines running on it could not rev up very high, and if the vehicle encountered a hill where more power was required the driver would just switch back to gasoline until he got back on the flat again.

The black market

There was a lively black market in Sydney, in which goods and services could be bartered for, and Americans could trade for just about anything they wanted with American cigarettes. American servicemen were issued regular cigarette rations, and those who didn't smoke hoarded their cartons of cigarettes to take to Australia on leave, where they were as good as money and often better.

Mr. Horner remembers filling up an Army B4 garment bag with cartons of cigarettes on Biak before going on leave, and in Sydney he found a plating company that was willing to nickel-plate his .45 service pistol for twenty cartons. He got the pistol plated so that it looked as shiny as chrome, but then found that the plating had thickened up the parts so that it was too stiff to shoot. He had to work the action a while until it loosened up, but when it did become loose enough to shoot again, it was tighter and better-shooting than before.

Cigarettes thus traveled from America to the active war zone and thence south to Australia, while Australian liquor went the other way, moving north to the war zone with men returning from leave. Just before the Horner crew had gone on leave, Lt. Horner, unaware that he would soon be getting leave, had lost all his pocket money, about $150, in a poker game in the officer's club. He had to borrow $200 from the squadron adjutant to be able to go on leave, but in Sydney, he purchased enough bottles of Australian whiskey to pay the adjutant back and then some.

A dangerous mission missed

Before the Horner crew had gone on leave, there had been some worry among the Jolly Rogers crews over the news that they would soon have a new and especially dangerous target to bomb: the Japanese oil refineries at Balikpapan on the island of Borneo. This oil refinery complex was sometimes called "the Ploesti of the Pacific," referring to the Ploesti oilfields in Romania, 30 miles north of Bucharest, that provided Hitler with sixty percent of his oil.* One hundred and seventy-eight American Liberators flying out of Libya had

---

*Winston Churchill called Ploesti the "taproot of German might."

attacked the Ploesti installations in a famous all-out raid on August 1, 1943, and fifty-three of them had been shot down with the loss of 530 bomber crewmen. Most of the planes were shot down by hundreds of antiaircraft guns that the Germans had arrayed around the refineries.

As Ploesti was to the Third Reich, Balikpapan was to Japan, an important source of oil upon which its war machine depended heavily, and Balikpapan, like Ploesti, was defended by the best antiaircraft guns and gunners the Japanese had. As Mr. Horner puts it today, "The flak gunners at Balikpapan could shoot your eyes out. They could hit a B-24 so accurately that nothing came down but the wingtips." An attack on Balikpapan could be expected to result in high losses of bombers and men, and no crew among the Jolly Rogers was looking forward to going there.

As it so happened, the Horner crew missed the first mission to Balikpapan, and oddly enough it was the unwitting doing of a young woman in an office at the leave center at Sydney's airport. This girl processed the paperwork of American servicemen coming and going from the city on leave. She happened to be dating one of the enlisted men of the Horner crew (no one can remember who it was now, nor the name of the girl) and she had grown quite fond of him. When the men reported to the processing center at the end of their ten days of leave, ready to board a plane back to Biak Island, the girl devised a way to get a few more dates with her boyfriend: she simply stamped their paperwork "No Transportation Available." She did this three days in a row, and each time the crewmen turned around and went back into Sydney to spend another day there, and the girl got another date. After the third day, she probably figured that she'd gotten away with about as much as she could and sent the men on their way back to Biak.

The result was that when their ATC plane landed at Biak on Sept. 29 [1944], the Horner crewmen saw a line of Jolly Rogers bombers rolling toward the runway to take off on the first strike on Balikpapan, and they were too late to participate. Had they gotten back from leave on the day they should have, they probably would have been in one of those bombers going out.

On that mission to Balikpapan the Jolly Rogers were attacked by Japanese fighter planes, endured accurate flak, and had phosphorus bombs dropped on them by the fighters. One plane of the 319th Squadron, nicknamed "Silas Marie II," piloted by 1st. Lt. Warren M. Kofsky, of Rochester, New York was shot down by the Zeros. Five parachutes were seen to open as the bomber lost a wing and spun down to the sea. Seeing the parachutes, the Japanese fighter plane pilots followed their usual practice and machine-gunned the helpless crewmen as they floated down, then strafed them again after they landed in the water. No one from Kofsky's crew survived.

The battle between Japanese fighter planes and the American bombers over Balikpapan raged for half an hour, and many of the other Jolly Rogers planes were damaged and some of the crewmen wounded. Three other B-24s from the 13th Air Force that had joined the Jolly Rogers on this raid were shot down and their crews killed.[13]

Forty American fliers were lost on this first mission to Balikpapan. The girl at Sydney who had delayed the return of the Horner crew to Biak, which prevented them from participating in the mission, may well have saved their lives.

A mission with concrete results

In August of 1944 Major Harter decided that the bombardiers of his squadron needed more practice with their bombsights. A training device had been developed at bombardier schools back in the States, a tall scaffold-like contraption made of steel tubing that rolled around on three wheels on a concrete slab (picture below). The bombardier and his bombsight were positioned on a platform at the top of the scaffold, and the bombsight was connected to controls that operated an electric motor driving the rear wheel, so that it could be steered. This imitated the way a bombsight actually worked in a B-24 during a bombing run, when the bombardier controlled the flight path of the plane by turning his bombsight. The trainer allowed the bombardier to

Biak Island: bombardiers practicing their bombing technique on a bombsight trainer, rolling around on a concrete slab built with cement flown in from Finschaffen by Lt. Horner and a skeleton crew in a B-24.

make practice approaches to a mark laid out on the concrete slab to represent a bombing target.

A couple of these bombsight trainers had been delivered to Biak on a supply ship from the states, and Major Harter was determined to put them to use. However, there wasn't enough cement in the 90th Bomb Group's camp at Biak to pour the large concrete slab that the trainers required. At least a couple of tons of cement would be needed. Making inquiries, Harter learned that there was plenty of cement available at a supply depot at the port of Finschaffen, about 900 miles back down the New Guinea coast near Lae, and he was told that he could have all he wanted if he'd send a plane down to get it. A B-24 could haul 8,000 pounds in its bomb bays, and the weight could just as well be cement as bombs, so Harter had the squadron's maintenance shop install some heavy oak planks (more dunnage from the holds of supply ships) in the bomb bay of an old B-24 to lay the bags of cement on, and then he only needed to choose a crew to fly the plane.

At this time the Horner crew had been flying combat missions about three times a week, and were about due for a break from the strain of combat, so Harter delegated to Lt. Horner the relatively stress-free task of picking up a load of cement. Thus early one morning Lt. Horner, with a skeleton crew of four other crewmen, set out on the 1,800-mile round trip to Finschaffen, planning to arrive back at Biak with the concrete before dark.

Lt. Cooper was the copilot as usual, and the navigator Lt. Theobald went along to plot the course. Radio operator Sgt. Bruni, and the flight engineer, Sgt. Eady rounded out the crew. All the gunners were left behind at Biak, since by this time no significant Japanese air power remained from Biak eastward down the coast of New Guinea to Finschaffen, and it was highly unlikely that they would be bothered by any Japanese fighter planes. And of course there was no need for Lt. Ostafin, the bombardier, on this flight, so he too got a day off from flying.

The flight down to Finschaffen was uneventful, Lt. Horner following the coastline all the way but staying a ways offshore, since isolated pockets of Japanese still held some of the areas that they passed and might have been tempted to take pot shots at any American aircraft that came within range of their guns. They gave Wewak an especially wide berth. After they landed and parked at Finschaffen's airfield, labor gangs at the supply depot loaded one hundred eighty-pound bags, or four tons, of cement into the B-24's bomb bay.

Mr. Horner remembers that every airport in the war zone had people hanging around wanting to hitch a ride to somewhere, and Finschaffen was no exception. Three young men approached Lt. Horner's bomber while the cement was being loaded and asked him where he was going. From their appearance and speech he judged them to be Dutch sailors, possibly from one of the merchant marine ships in the nearby harbor. When he told them he was headed to Biak, they said that they wanted to go there too and asked if they might ride along. These boys may have just wanted to go somewhere, anywhere, and Biak was as good a destination to them as any. Traveling the 900 miles from Finschaffen to Biak by surface ship would have taken the men weeks, whereas the B-24 could get them there in hours. Lt. Horner consented to give the men a ride, so they climbed up into the vacant waist area of the plane and stood at the windows, waiting for the plane to take off. Being alone in the rear of the plane, back behind the bomb bays filled with cement, they had no way to communicate with the bomber's crew up front.

When the cargo and passengers were all aboard, and everything was ready for the return trip, the two engines on the old bomber's right wing refused to start. The electric starters on both engines had blown their fuses. Since this B-24 had electrically powered Emerson gun turrets, Sgt. Eady borrowed fuses from the turrets to replace the ones in the starters, and once again they tried to start the engines. This time engine #4 fired up, but #3 continued to blow fuse after fuse until there were none left. Turret fuses were evidently too weak to work effectively in engine starters.

There was no longer any aircraft maintenance shop at Finschaffen, nor any engine mechanics for Lt. Horner to ask for help with the balky engine. It had been months since the Finschaffen airfield had seen any heavy air traffic; the war had moved on, and now the field was little used, although the tower was still operating. Why cement was even stored there is a question; perhaps there was a warehouse there capable of protecting it from the rain and high humidity, since powdered cement will soon turn to stone if allowed to absorb any moisture.

Stuck with an engine that wouldn't start, Lt. Horner decided to try another way of getting it going. By taxiing the airplane down the runway at a brisk speed, the relative wind caused by the plane's forward motion would cause the propeller to windmill and turn the engine over until it fired up. Other pilots had started engines this way. It would be like pushing a car in gear to get the engine started, and it was at least worth a try.

Lt. Horner called the Finschaffen control tower and asked for clearance to fast-taxi the bomber down the runway, and since there was no other traffic on the field at the time, the tower gave the OK. Horner took the bomber down to the takeoff end of the runway, turned it around into the wind, and then ran it down the runway at only about half its takeoff speed, 40 to 50 mph. As he had hoped, the propeller on the dead engine began to rotate in the breeze, then smoke puffed out the exhaust pipes as the cylinders began to fire, and the engine roared to life. With all four engines now running, Lt. Horner braked the plane to a stop, turned around, taxied back to the downwind end of the runway, and made a normal takeoff with his cargo of four tons of cement and three hitchhikers.

Since they'd lost so much time fooling around with the balky engines, and he wanted to reach Biak before dark, Lt. Horner chose the most direct route, which was 60 to 100 miles inland from the coast. This took them across the central part of New Guinea and over the Owen Stanley Mountains, which necessitated climbing to an altitude of around 11,000 feet to clear the mountain peaks and remaining that high for an hour or so. They arrived at Biak before dark as planned, and after the plane was parked and the engines shut down, the three passengers in the rear of the plane climbed stiffly out, looking miserable, shivering with cold and mysteriously covered with scrapes and scratches. It was obvious that they had not had a pleasant trip.

When they were asked what had happened, they said that when the bomber had made its three-engine run down the runway at Finschaffen, they thought Lt. Horner was trying to take off with a dead engine. Although they were admittedly not well versed in aviation matters, they considered a pilot who did not make use of all the engines available on his airplane to be reckless and unsafe to fly with, so they had decided to abort their ride with the maniac and exit the airplane through the waist windows.

Halfway out, however, they saw how fast the ground was going by below them, changed their minds and scrambled back inside, so that all they achieved was to give themselves a lot of scratches and scrapes on the sharp metal edges of the windows. It was fortunate that they had not tried to jump, because if they had dropped the ten feet or so to the ground while the plane was going 40 to 50 mph they probably would have been killed.

Then while the bomber was flying over the mountains, the passengers had nearly frozen in the icy cold wind blowing in through the open waist windows. It had been 80 degrees on the ground when they took off, but at 11,000 feet the temperature had dropped into the 40s, and felt much colder with the wind chill, and the three passengers had had to endure this cold in their shorts and T-shirts for over an hour. Had they known how to shut the windows they could have done so, but they didn't. They might also have made their way forward to the front of the plane where it was warmer, but that would have required climbing over the big pile of cement bags in the bomb bays, a daunting prospect, so they stayed where they were and simply shivered. The three young men thus arrived at Biak cold and scuffed up, but otherwise all right.

Major Harter soon got his concrete slab poured, and the squadron's bombardiers were able to get on with their practice bombing using the bombsight training devices.

The Big Storm

When asked today what he considered the most dangerous mission he flew during the war, Mr. Baca without hesitation names one in which the crew encountered a huge, deadly storm that very nearly caused the pilots to lose control and could easily have proven fatal to them all, underlining Mr. Horner's statement the Pacific weather was a much more dangerous foe than the Japanese. "We lost two or three times as many planes from the weather as we did from the enemy," Mr. Horner says today.

During the crew briefings before the long missions from Biak to the Philippines, the forecast of the weather on the way to the target could only be an educated guess made by the squadron's weather officer, unless an American aircraft had recently sent in a report from that area, but even then the tropical weather could change so rapidly that there was no guarantee the report was still accurate. A weatherman could also never be sure that the bombers' targets would not be covered over by clouds, preventing bombing them, which is why secondary and even tertiary targets were designated for each mission, and sometimes all three targets would be found to be shrouded in cloud. Above a cloud-covered target, the bombs could sometimes be dropped through the overcast if the lead bomber had one of the new onboard radar systems installed. The radar could read the invisible terrain through the clouds, but just as often the bombs had to be jettisoned at sea if no target were visible.[14]

Tropical typhoons could be rough on a B-24, and some planes even became permanently warped and unserviceable from the stresses imposed on the airframe by the violently turbulent air. The wings of a B-24 were designed to be somewhat flexible, like those on modern airliners, and its wingtips could flex up and down as much as two feet on landings and takeoffs without harm, but a fully loaded bomber weighed thirty-five tons, and in extremely turbulent air it was easy for something that large and heavy to get permanently bent or twisted, so that the wings ended up out of alignment with each other. A warped bomber could be difficult to control, as the Horner crew had learned first-hand during their training at March Field, California, when they flew a bent bomber to Palm Springs and nearly crashed it on the return trip (Chapter 40).

The Horner crew encountered the giant storm referred to by Mr. Baca on one of their missions to the Philippines in the fall of 1944, which typically required twelve to fourteen hours of flying. This one began like all the others, with a takeoff after midnight, followed by six or seven hours of monotonous flight over the sea, unseen below them in the dark. Each bomber of the Group flew independently, as usual, since it was impossible for the planes to see each other at night. Also as usual, at daybreak the bombers formed up over the rendezvous point and continued toward the target together. But on this day, the weather was such that the bombers were in for a very rough ride, for there turned out to be an unforeseen, and unforecasted, typhoon between them and their target.

"First we saw a wall of cloud ahead of us," Mr. Horner remembers today, "and it was black." There was no way around it, so the bomber formation would have to pass through it. This is why B-24s had blind-flying instruments and the pilots were trained to use them, so this in itself was not a big deal. In such a situation there was an established procedure for opening up some maneuvering room between the planes before entering clouds, just in case rough air tossed them around some while they couldn't see each other, and that is what the formation did in this case. The bomber in the lead continued straight ahead, but those to either side of it altered their courses outward from the center a few degrees and held that heading for one minute before taking up the original course again. Thus spread out, the formation entered the cloud.

Immediately the wild ride began. "Suddenly we were rising at 5,000 feet per minute," Mr. Horner says, "and the next thing we knew we were going down just as fast. Sometimes a big shadow would go past us, either up or down, and that would be one of the other bombers in the same situation. Of course, that scared the hell out of you." The threat of collisions under such circumstances was dire, but there was nothing anyone could do about it now. The big planes were all helpless in the grip of a monster storm, a typhoon. In the back of the plane, all that Sgt. Baca and the other two gunners could do was cling to some part of the plane's structure and hope for the best.

"That plane was going up, down, sideways, and every which-way you can imagine," Mr. Baca recalls today. "We all just hung on for dear life. And water was coming in everywhere. I figure we must have been flying through a nearly solid wall of water." To make things worse, Sgt. Baca and the others were experiencing this terror in near-darkness, since the waist windows were closed and what little light they had was filtering in through the tail turret.

"Water was running along the flight deck," remembers Mr. Horner. It was coming in through the openings around the cockpit windows, and from many other leaks. Everybody was wet." Down in the nose, water was blowing in from around the nose turret and coming up from the nosewheel well, and everyone down in that part of the plane was soaked as well.

In addition to being sopping wet, the pilots had to fight with all their strength to maintain control of the big bomber as it was hurled about in the storm. A B-24 had heavy flight controls to begin with, since they had no hydraulic assistance and were all cable-operated, but under the stresses of the storm and the wild gyrations of the plane, the control yokes became almost too stiff to move. Whenever the plane's nose dropped, both Lt. Horner and Lt. Cooper would brace their feet against the instrument panel and haul back on the yokes with all their combined strength to pull it back up again, and the next moment

The cockpit of a B-24. During the wild gyrations caused by the typhoon, Lts. Horner and Cooper were alternately pushing and pulling on the control yokes together with all their strength, struggling to maintain control. The other men of the crew could only hang on and pray.

the plane would pitch up nose-high and they'd have to put both feet on the control yokes and push them forward with all the strength in their backs and legs trying to get it back down again. Everyone else in the bomber could only hang on and pray for survival. "There were no atheists in a bomber crew when their plane got into trouble," Mr. Baca remembers.

Lt. Bill Martin, a pilot with the Jolly Rogers' 321st Squadron, described being in a storm like this:

> It wasn't uncommon for my copilot and myself to be holding the wheel all the way forward, watching the altimeter climb two or three thousand feet a minute, sometimes higher . . . hit the top, a tremendous crash, the wings would almost break off and down you'd start. It took the strength of two of us to keep the thing level. . . So it was a tremendously trying psychological experience. . . I'm sure my crew must have been horrified to sit in the back and be thrown around, praying the pilot knew what he was doing, because there just wasn't any rescue if we went down. . . Accidents and weather got more American crews than the Japs

ever did.[15]

"After we had been thrown all over the sky for a while," says Mr. Baca, "Lt. Horner's voice came over the intercom and he said, 'I don't think I can control this airplane much longer. Get your parachutes on and I'll let you know when to jump.' So we snapped on our parachutes and waited, scared to death." They all knew that their chances of survival from a bail-out into a typhoon were practically nil. For one thing, all the water in the air might make their chutes too soggy to open, and even if they made it safely down to the sea, they would be in for another wild ride in gigantic storm-tossed waves, floating around in their Mae Wests with no life raft, no provisions, and no idea where they were, in an ocean infested with sharks. Nor would anyone else know where they were, so rescue was unlikely. But bailing out would at least provide some slim chance to live, whereas riding the bomber down and slamming into the water with it would undoubtedly be fatal. "I was never so scared in my life," says Baca today. "It seemed like the end for all of us."

Ferocious 100-mph-plus winds such as the ones in this storm, in this same area east of the Philippines, actually capsized three destroyers of Admiral Halsey's Task Force 38. The howling winds and 70-foot waves just rolled the ships over and sank them, with most of their crewmen trapped inside. 790 sailors drowned. Other ships in the task force survived after rolling from side to side as much as 70 degrees. The aircraft carriers in this task force managed to stay afloat, but they were hurled about so violently by the sea that the aircraft belowdecks crashed into each other and into bulkheads and caught fire, while 146 aircraft up on the flight decks were either blown overboard or wrecked.*

Admiral Halsey feared that his flagship, the giant battleship *New Jersey*, might also roll over and sink in the huge swells. He later wrote:

> No one who has not been through a typhoon can conceive of its fury. The 70-foot seas smash you from all sides. The rain and the scud are blinding; they drive you flat-out, until you can't tell the ocean from the air. . . At broad noon, I couldn't see the bow of my ship, 350 feet from the bridge. . . This typhoon tossed our enormous ship as if she were a canoe. . . We ourselves were buffeted from one bulkhead to another; we could not hear our own voices above the uproar. . . What it was like on a destroyer one-twentieth the New Jersey's size I can only imagine."[16]

Today the three destroyers *Hull*, *Spence*, and *Monaghan* lie on the bottom of the sea 300 miles east of Luzon in the Philippine Sea, each one the tomb of hundreds of American sailors.

---

*One of the firefighters who battled a fire raging aboard the carrier *Monterey* that day was Lt. Gerald Ford, who would become the 38th President of the United States in 1974.

A typhoon that could toss a 45,000-ton battleship around "like a canoe" could hurl a mere 35-ton B-24 about within itself like a bit of confetti. Lt. Horner's bomber was whirled, spun, flipped, and tossed all over the sky, while inside the plane the crewmen clung to the bucking plane with all their strength, waiting in terrible suspense for Horner's order to bail out, if they could even manage to. Minutes that seemed like an eternity passed until finally, to the enormous relief of all aboard, Lt. Horner's voice came back over the intercom to say, "It's all right! It's okay! I've got control of the airplane again. We won't have to jump."

By the time the bombers tumbled out the other side of the storm and regained stability, they were so scattered, and the crews so shaken, that they felt unable to continue the mission—they were merely happy to be alive. They jettisoned their bombs into the sea and flew back to Biak, making a wide detour around the center of the storm. To the best of Mr. Horner's memory today, no Jolly Rogers bombers were lost that day, which is nothing short of a miracle in itself.

No doubt many of the Jolly Rogers bombers that simply vanished on missions fell prey to such vicious storms. Only if there happened to be survivors would anyone ever know what happened to these planes. Such was the case of a bomber flown by Lt. William F. Courtney of the 22nd Bomb Group. On January 18, 1945, while flying at ten thousand feet on a bombing mission to Formosa (today's Taiwan), Courtney's bomber entered a storm. What happened inside the storm was nearly identical to the Horner crew experience, but the ending was not so happy. The pilots fought to maintain control, but the nose of the bomber rose up almost vertically and then the plane stalled and fell off into a dive. It fell 8,500 feet before the pilots managed to regain control and arrest the dive, but by then they were only 1,500 feet above the sea. The plane then entered a spin and the pilots lost control again. At such a low altitude they didn't think they would be able to recover before they hit the water, so the pilot gave the order for everyone to bail out immediately.

However, only two men managed to get out of the plane before it crashed. By that time the plane had been blown over land, and the plane didn't crash into the sea but hit the ground on the Philippine island of Catanduanes. No one in the bomber survived the crash, but the two who parachuted out landed in the ocean offshore, then swam to the beach, where natives found them and gave them food and shelter. They later returned to their base and reported the fate of their bomber.[17]

Japanese aerial phosphorus bombs

The Horner crew's 32nd mission, flown on November 27, 1944, was another strike on the Japanese airfield at Daliao on the southern Philippine island of Mindoro. Lt. Horner was flying the lead plane of the 320th squadron on this day. As the Japanese airfield came into view and the bombers started into their bomb run, there was no flak from the ground, but suddenly four Japanese fighter planes appeared above and ahead of them. These fighters did not attack, however, and it soon became apparent that they were not interested in engaging the bombers in a gunfight—not immediately anyway. They were up to something else, and had obviously prepared a different kind of reception for the Americans. What it was became evident when several phosphorus bombs blossomed out above the bomber formation, with long streamers of burning phosphorus spreading out and downward from the explosion of each bomb, reaching for the American planes.

Mr. Horner says of this experience, "Japanese fighter planes used a frightening new weapon against us: phosphorus bombs. They would fly straight at you, then roll over, and as they put their belly to you they would release one of these bombs. When it exploded, long white tendrils of burning phosphorus went out into your path. Since bombers in formation cannot turn or take any evasive action, we could only fly straight ahead and hope not to be hit by one of these chunks of phosphorus, which could stick to the skin of a bomber and burn right through it, or even melt through an engine."[18]

Two Japanese aerial phosphorus bombs explode over a formation of B-24s. Although spectacular, the explosions rarely harmed the bombers.

46. LIFE ON BIAK ISLAND

A pilot's view through his windshield of a pair of Japanese aerial phosphorus bombs detonating in front of his formation.

"To me they looked like spiders," Baca says today. The fragments of burning phosphorus, spreading outward and downward from the big initial puff of the explosion, created a visual effect similar to the body and legs of a spider. But the legs of this spider were deadly. If one of the chunks of burning phosphorus stuck to a wing, and burned through the gas tank to the fuel, the result would be a fire or explosion.

Japanese Zero pilot Tomokazu Kasai, interviewed in his 90s, remembered that the fighters he flew carried two of the 66-pound phosphorus bombs. According to Kasai,

> We approached from the high side, head-on. The key was to release the bombs the moment the bomber was blocked from view by your own engine cowling... If a Type 3 cluster bomb is dropped at the right spot in the middle of an enemy formation, you can damage three or four planes at once. The burning phosphorus will start fires that can eventually bring a bomber down. However, this is quite difficult to accomplish.

Fortunately, on this day none of the Jolly Rogers planes ran into any of the phosphorus fragments and the bombing run proceeded as normal. According to the historian of the Jolly Rogers, the Japanese fighters engaged in another

A Japanese phosphorus bomb explodes harmlessly behind an American B-24, in a view from the plane's left waist window past its tail. One Japanese pilot compared the shape of the airburst to that of an octopus, and this photo seems to bear him out, although this deadly octopus has many more than eight legs.

unusual bit of deviltry on this particular day in addition to the phosphorus bombs: they dropped long cables with weights attached to each end, hoping to entangle the propellers or flight controls of the bombers. These, too, were poorly aimed and did no harm.[19]

However, on Lt. Horner's bomber, there was a problem unrelated to the enemy. Engine #4, the outboard engine on the right wing, began losing oil pressure. Since Lt. Horner was leading the squadron, and all the other squadron's bombardiers were cueing on his plane, he didn't want to slow down and drop back by shutting down an engine. He had Lt. Cooper watch that engine's oil pressure gauge carefully and allowed it to continue running until the pressure was nearly down to zero. By that time the squadron had dropped its bombs, and he told Lt. Cooper to shut down #4 and feather the propeller. The squadron's bombing was accurate—the strike photos showed that two Japanese aircraft on the ground were destroyed in addition to damaging the runway.

As the bomber formation swung away from the target and headed back toward Biak, Lt. Horner's aircraft was flying on three engines. A B-24 could do this safely, but at a reduced speed. The Japanese fighter planes were not aggressive on that day and did not pursue the bombers, but that might have changed if they had spotted a lone cripple with a dead engine. A big cumulus cloud appeared ahead, and Lt. Horner carefully eased his bomber into it, then radioed the pilot of one of the other bombers to take his place in the formation as squadron leader. He was careful not to mention having an engine out, since many Japanese pilots spoke English, listened in on American radio transmissions, and might immediately have begun searching for the straggler.

For five hours the Horner crew flew on toward Biak alone, with a dead engine. They were in no serious danger, unless another engine failed. Lt. Theobald, the navigator, suggested that since their route home would take them directly over an American airfield at Morotai, on one of the Halmahera Islands, which had been constructed two months earlier in September, they should land there and have the defective engine repaired. Lt. Horner agreed, and they landed on Morotai's airstrip where mechanics were shortly able to correct the oil pressure problem. They made it back to Biak on the same day.[20]

As they climbed out of the plane, Sgt. Baca noticed a group of bomber crewmen and mechanics gathered in front of one of the other Jolly Rogers bombers, looking up at one of its engines, and he walked over to see what it was all about. He found them all examining a ragged, blackened hole in one of the propeller blades. "A piece of phosphorus had hit a propeller on that bomber," he remembers today, "and it had stuck to it and burned all the way through. And those propellers were made of metal several inches thick."

A courier mission to Tacloban, Leyte Island

In September of 1944 General MacArthur was preparing to launch his long-anticipated invasion of the Philippine Islands, with the help of Admiral Chester Nimitz's Pacific Fleet. During October of 1944, while the Horner crew was flying bombing missions out of Biak, Mr. Baca remembers looking down at a vast American fleet assembling south of the Philippines in preparation for the invasion. It was, he says, a truly breathtaking sight to see the ocean covered for miles in every direction with hundreds of American warships of all types. Generals MacArthur and Kenney were traveling together on one of those ships, the cruiser *Nashville*, and Kenney described his view of the armada from sea level:

> The whole ocean looked full of ships as far as the horizon on all sides. It was a sight that I wouldn't have missed for anything, although just before dark when we suddenly changed course to avoid hitting a floating mine, I wished I were on an airplane instead of a ship.[21]

On October 20, 1944, the invasion began. Over a hundred thousand American troops landed on the Philippine island of Leyte, in the first stage of the operation. A few hours after his troops landed, MacArthur waded ashore from a landing craft with his staff.* That day, MacArthur made a radio broadcast in which he declared, "People of the Philippines, I have returned!" Finally, two years, seven months, and nine days after he had fled the island fortress of Corregidor in a PT boat and been flown to Australia, he had kept his promise.

As the Americans gained a foothold on Leyte and began moving inland, a landing strip of steel Marston matting was laid down parallel to the beachhead and about a hundred yards inland. The Jolly Rogers were called upon to make a series of courier flights between Biak's Mokmer Field and this new strip, dubbed Tacloban Airdrome, hauling supplies, personnel, and messages to MacArthur's headquarters from Fifth Bomber Command. The bombers that made these flights tried to spend as little time as possible at Tacloban because the place was experiencing sporadic Japanese air attacks.

On the night of Nov. 14, four Jolly Rogers bombers flew a courier mission to Tacloban together, and as they passed the island of Mindanao they were attacked by a Japanese night fighter, which fortunately failed to hit any of them with its fire, although the streams of tracers that it sent toward them in the dark were nervewracking. After the four planes landed at Tacloban, the crews had to endure three Japanese bombing raids plus a strafing by a Japanese fighter plane that damaged one of the bombers and wounded three passengers that they had delivered there.[22] They took off and returned to Biak as soon as they could.

On 17 November, 1944, Lt. Horner made one of these courier flights, taking with him the same skeleton crew that he had used to retrieve the cement at Finschaffen. The purpose of the flight was to deliver a pouch of dispatches from Bomber Command on Biak to Leyte. In company with another Jolly Rogers bomber, he flew up to Leyte and landed at Tacloban in the afternoon, where he and his crew were interested to see fifteen or twenty U. S. Navy fighter planes and torpedo bombers scattered up and down the nearby beach for about a mile, many of them upside down after nosing over in the soft sand while trying to land. This was part of the aftermath of the Battle of Leyte Gulf, in which the Japanese fleet had tried to attack the American invasion forces, and had sunk three small American escort or "jeep" aircraft carriers before being turned back. The planes that had been launched from those carriers had found themselves with nowhere to land after their mother ships were sunk, and since the Tacloban airfield was not yet serviceable at the time, they had been forced to try to land on the beach, with varying degrees of success.

While Lt. Horner and his crewmen were on the ground at Tacloban, word was received from reconnaissance planes that the Japanese were attempting

---

* MacArthur had not intended to wade ashore, and was initially angry to have to get his feet wet, but it made such a great photo op that he did it all over again for the newsreel cameras.

to land a force at Ormoc Bay on the opposite side of the island. This was a serious development, for if the Japanese could put enough troops ashore they could oppose or even reverse the American landings. Lt. Horner had checked in at the Army headquarters, a concrete building, and had delivered his bag of messages, in the process getting a glimpse of a lot of high ranking general staff officers milling around in a rather animated manner, no doubt related to the news of the Japanese landing on the other side of the island.

Of this day Gen. Kenney wrote:

> **During the night the Japs sent the first of a series of convoys into Leyte with reinforcements, landing them at Ormoc on the west side of the island. From five to nine destroyers and five barges made up the convoy. It was estimated that 1,000 troops were put ashore. We didn't have anything to stop them.**[23]

Lt. Horner returned to his bomber to get it ready for the flight back to Biak. Mr. Horner recalls today: "As we were getting ready to leave, a jeep pulled up, and we were told that the Japanese were counterattacking, and that there was a large contingent of barges loaded with troops coming up on the back side of Leyte. We were put under orders to stand by for a bombing mission to take out these incoming barges. We really weren't prepared for this; we had only a skeleton crew, without bombs or bombardier. They told us that they could get bombs for us off some of the navy planes that had crashed on the beach. I don't know why they thought that those planes would have any bombs on them. I would never have thought that any pilot would try to crash-land with live bombs. But anyway, they were going to procure bombs for us from somewhere, they said, and load them on our plane."[24]

However, with darkness coming on, and rain beginning to fall, conditions were not favorable for a bombing strike, so the idea was dropped and Lt. Horner was ordered to leave, to get his airplane out of the way of any other operations on the field that might be conducted against the Japanese, and return to Biak.

Horner took off from the Tacloban strip and pulled up into the rain, and as he did so he realized that the airspeed indicator on his instrument panel was not working. Looking through his cockpit windows out to the sides of the bomber's nose, he could see that the canvas covers were still on the pitot tubes. "It was Sgt. Eady's responsibility to see that those cloth covers were removed," Mr. Horner says today, "and he hadn't done it. So I told him to do it now, any way that he could. So Eady took a fire ax and chopped holes in the airplane's aluminum skin just behind the pitot tubes, reached out through the holes, and took the covers off." The airspeed indicator then came back to life on the instrument panel. Back at Biak, mechanics had to patch the holes in the sides of the airplane, but they were experts at that from repairing flak damage.

The Horner crew completes its combat tour

In September of 1944 the 5th Air Force adopted a point system to determine when bomber crewmen were eligible to rotate back to the States, and this system remained in use to the end of the war. An airman would have to accrue 100 points before his combat tour was considered complete. Points were awarded for bombing missions as follows:

> **1 point for every five hours of combat flying.**
>
> **1 point if any aircraft in the squadron was hit by flak on a mission.**
>
> **1 point if the squadron was intercepted by enemy fighters but had American fighter cover.**
>
> **3 points if the squadron was intercepted by enemy fighters and had no American fighter cover.**
>
> **5 points for a crash or a bail-out.**
>
> **5 points for any crewman who received a combat wound.**[25]

No new crews had joined the Jolly Rogers since the preceding June. The invasion of Europe by the Allies had resulted in all the new crews being sent to the European theater, so the crews on hand at Biak were worked hard, sometimes flying three or four missions a week. It was an exhausting pace, but the upside of it was that by flying that often the Horner crew was able to rack up combat hours and points in a hurry. Lt. Horner soon had 48 missions and over five hundred hours of combat flying logged, and by early January he had amassed the necessary 100 points to complete his combat tour and was taken off flight status to await transportation back to the States. Most of the rest of his crew had also accrued their 100 points, but both Lt. Cooper and Sgt. Baca still needed a few more flights to get their totals up to 100. This was because they had both spent a few weeks in the field hospital on Biak, Cooper with dengue fever and Baca with malaria, and thus had missed some flights. They would need to fly a few more missions as fill-ins with other crews to complete their point total.

Because there were no replacements immediately available for Jolly Rogers crewmen on Biak who had completed their combat tours, and the Group's Table of Organization required a certain number of personnel to be continually on hand, regardless of flying status, the entire Horner crew made the move to the Philippines in early February of 1945, there to await replacements so that they could go home, and for the two men still short of 100 points to make them up.

46. LIFE ON BIAK ISLAND

One crew of the Jolly Rogers' 321st Squadron was proud that their pilot, 22-year-old (in 1943) Captain Leaford Bearskin (front, right), of Oklahoma, was a full-blooded member of the Wyandotte Indian Tribe.

The Bearskin crew named their bomber "Big Chief," and flew 46 combat missions before returning to the States in late 1944. Leaford is at front left in this picture. Later in his life he really was the Chief of the Wyandotte tribe, up to his death at age 91 in 2012.

Chapter Forty-Seven

THE MOVE TO THE PHILIPPINES

MacArthur's forces had landed in the Philippines on October 20, 1944, but it would be over three months before the Jolly Rogers would move forward from Biak to join them. It took hard fighting by American troops, and a lot of aggressive flying by General Kenney's 5th Air Force pilots, as well as by Navy pilots flying from aircraft carriers, to beat down Japanese airpower in the Philippines to the point where it was considered safe enough to base heavy bombers in the islands. Until that time, the Jolly Rogers continued to operate from Biak Island, off the coast of New Guinea, nearly a thousand miles from the fighting front. It was a long way to fly on missions to the Philippines, but they continued to do it routinely.

In December of 1944 Kenney was hammering Japanese airfields in the Philippines with his now well-proven one-two punch of B-25 strafer/bombers hitting them at low altitude, often at treetop height, destroying aircraft and anything that moved on the ground, while the Jolly Rogers and other B-24 groups struck from higher up, saturating the runways, barracks, headquarters, ammunition and fuel dumps with large bombs. Meanwhile American fighters flown by now highly-experienced pilots took on any Japanese fighters that rose to defend their bases. It was clear that the Japanese were fighting a losing battle to hold the Philippines; in fact it was clear to everyone, including the Japanese, that they were losing the war, but the Emperor and his fanatical cabal of military advisors, the so-called Supreme War Council, refused to entertain any idea of surrender. Eventually their desperation would drive them to order their pilots to conduct suicide attacks on American warships with what few planes and pilots remained to them, and these kamikazes, flying from the Philippines, Formosa, and Japan itself would do a lot of damage to the American fleet. All, of course, without affecting the inevitable outcome of the war.

Clark Field, the prewar American airbase sixty miles northwest of Manila, was one of the targets of the returning Americans. Over three years earlier, on December 8, 1941, most of the American fighters and bombers in the Philippines had been based at Clark Field, and beginning on the day after the Pearl Harbor attack Japanese air raids had destroyed many of them on the ground. Now, in December of 1944, it was the Japanese who were based on Clark Field and the tables were turned. Kenney wrote:

47. THE MOVE TO THE PHILIPPINES

> By the 22nd [of December 1944] there were no longer any worthwhile airdrome targets left south of Luzon. That afternoon, with over 200 bombers, strafers, and fighters, we opened the campaign on the big Jap air base sixty miles north of Manila, at Clark Field. Nearly 100 planes were destroyed on the ground and eight of the nine Nips that intercepted were shot down. We had no losses...
>
> Sixty Jap fighters intercepted our attack on Clark Field on the 24th. It cost the enemy thirty-three airplanes in combat and another fifty-eight on the ground. We lost a P-38.
>
> On Christmas Day we plastered the Jap airdrome at Mabalacat, about ten miles northeast of Clark Field. Seventy Nip fighters rose to intercept. It cost them thirty-nine. We lost five P-38s but recovered three of the pilots. Tommy McGuire, leading his squadron of P-38s, shot down two Jap fighters to bring his score to thirty-four...
>
> On the 26th we raided Clark Field again. Only twenty Jap fighters contested this time. Our escorting fighters shot down thirteen of them. Four of the victims fell to Tommy McGuire, back in there still leading his squadron. His record now stood at thirty-eight, only two behind [Richard] Bong's forty.[1]

During the first month of 1945 General Kenney finally began moving his B-24s from Biak Island to the Philippines. They would be used to support the American ground troops advancing toward Manila and to suppress the Japanese airbases 650 miles farther north on the large island of Formosa. The Jolly Rogers would not be bombing mainland Japan. That task was placed in the hands of the new 20th Air Force, flying the giant new long-range Boeing B-29 Superfortresses, which had a 1,500-mile operational radius, from airfields in the newly captured Mariana islands, principally Saipan.

The 46-square-mile island of Saipan, 1,300 miles from mainland Japan and 1,450 miles from Tokyo, was captured in July of 1944 and put to use as a B-29 airbase beginning in October. The first B-29 bombing mission against Tokyo was flown from Saipan on November 24, 1944, and produced banner headlines in American newspapers: "TOKYO BOMBED!" B-29 raids of ever-increasing size and frequency followed. The fact that over sixty Japanese cities would be targeted, and hundreds of thousands of Japanese civilians would die in the bombing raids, left the Emperor and his advisors unmoved. The lives of their own countrymen, civilian or military, meant as little to them as the millions of people who had died at their hands all over the Pacific in their quest for an empire. These men were evil personified, and they were determined to fight to the last.

While B-29 raids were destroying Tokyo and other mainland Japanese cities, General MacArthur's assault on the Philippine Islands continued, assisted by the Jolly Rogers and other elements of General Kenney's 5th Air Force. The American Army landed on Luzon Island, at Lingayen Gulf, on January 9, 1945, and began a drive south toward Manila. The day before that, on January 8, 1945, the Jolly Rogers were informed by 5th Air Force Headquarters that toward the end of the month they would be moving from Biak Island to a newly constructed airfield on the southern end of the Philippine Island of Mindoro, near the town of San Jose (Mindoro is the large island just south of Luzon. See Map 47-1 on p. 701). Fifth Bomber Command's headquarters would move to the San Jose airfield along with them.

This would place the Jolly Rogers only 150 miles south of the capital city of Manila, so that their bombers would easily be able to support the American troops battling in that area, or anywhere else in the Philippines for that matter, while at the same time bombing the Japanese airfields on Formosa. However, bombing Formosa, one of the last Japanese strongholds, would be no picnic. It was, like Balikpapan, defended by many antiaircraft guns and well-trained gunners, and the Jolly Rogers would lose planes and crews to their flak.

The best place to base heavy bombers in the Philippines would have been Clark Field, with its long bomber-friendly runways, its hangars, barracks, and other prewar facilities, and in fact that is where the Jolly Rogers had expected to be sent, but that airfield would remain in Japanese hands until late February. By that time most of its hangars and other buildings would be bombed into rubble and unusable.[2]

San Jose airfield, the Jolly Rogers' new base, would soon be renamed McGuire Field in honor of P-38 fighter pilot Major Thomas McGuire (the "Tommy" McGuire of General Kenney's quote above) who was killed on January 7th in a dogfight with Japanese Zeros over Negros Island in the central Philippines. As noted in the previous chapter, Charles Lindbergh had flown with Tommy McGuire and his 475th Fighter Group out of Owi and Biak Islands from June 1944 through the middle of August, and McGuire and Lindbergh had flown fighter protection together for the Jolly Rogers on various occasions, as detailed in previous chapters.

McGuire, 24, from Ridgewood, New Jersey, was the second-highest scoring American fighter pilot of the war, with 38 aerial victories, only two short of Richard Bong's 40. McGuire had been out to beat Bong's record, but was killed during a desperate attempt to drive a Japanese fighter plane off the tail of another plane he was flying with. In so doing he banked his P-38 fighter too steeply a turn at low altitude, causing it to stall and spin to the ground, killing him instantly.

McGuire, like all American fighter pilots, knew better than to try to engage Zeros in close dogfights, since the nimble, lightweight Japanese fighters, although delicately built and outclassed in nearly every other way, could still

47. THE MOVE TO THE PHILIPPINES

Major Thomas McGuire (left) with Charles Lindbergh in front of a P-38. The men have just returned from a bomber escort mission. Major McGuire was only 24 years old and grew a mustache to try to look older. Photo taken on Biak Island in July of 1944.

out-turn any American fighter at close quarters. However, the fight had begun at low altitude, which prevented the American fighters from diving away to safety. To try to save his friend, McGuire took the gamble of making too tight a turn in his big, heavy twin-engine fighter, and he lost. As Kenney told it:

> [McGuire] said that the next morning [January 7, 1945] he and Major Rittmayer, a visiting P-38 pilot from the 13th Air Force, who had four [aerial victories] to his credit were planning to take along a couple of youngsters, who had just arrived in the squadron, for a sweep over the Jap airdromes on Cebu and Negros to see if they could stir up something...
>
> On the morning of the 7th McGuire and Rittmayer and the two new lads took off on the mission as scheduled. At 2000-feet altitude over Negros they sighted a lone Jap fighter plane, flying at about 200 feet off the ground. McGuire led his flight to the attack. The Nip turned sharply to the left and quickly maneuvered into position on Rittmayer's tail. Rittmayer called for help as the Jap fired a quick burst into him.
>
> McGuire pulled around in a frantic effort to get his guns on the Nip and save Rittmayer. He pulled his turn too tight in the attempt, and the airplane stalled and crashed to the ground. The Nip poured another burst into Rittmayer's already crippled P-38, and Rittmayer

went down in flames. The Nip ducked behind a hill and got away. The two youngsters, who had gone on the flight to gain experience, in trying to stay with their two leaders had gotten out of position and couldn't catch him before he disappeared from sight.

Once again an accident had deprived me of a great aviator and leader. No Jap had shot him down. I don't believe there was a Jap in the world who could have shot down Tommy McGuire, but his loss was one of the worst blows I took in the whole war. I wrote to his father that night. It was not an easy letter to write.

We named a field on Mindoro after Tommy, and later he was awarded the Congressional Medal of Honor posthumously.[3]

The field named after McGuire on Mindoro Island was the one to which the Jolly Rogers would move from Biak Island in late January of 1945, the same month McGuire was killed.

McGuire's death was a blow to American morale, since the exploits of fighter pilots were avidly followed by the American press and public, despite the fact that fighter planes did much less damage to the enemy than bombers. Bombers were, of course, the primary Allied offensive weapon, while fighter planes played a mainly defensive role. The saying of those who really knew the score was, "Fighter pilots make headlines, while bomber crews make history."

Nevertheless, America eagerly followed the achievements of its glamorous fighter pilots, and nearly anyone who read the newspapers could name America's top aces in the Pacific: Dick Bong, Joe Foss, "Pappy" Boyington, Tommy McGuire, but rare indeed was anyone who could name a bomber pilot or crew. Even Col. Art Rogers, who had given his name to the famous Jolly Rogers Bomb Group, was practically unknown as an individual. All the fame and glory went to the fighter pilots.*

After the word went out to the Jolly Rogers that the move to the Philippines was on, they began dismantling their camp on Biak Island and getting everything ready to go north. At this time the Jolly Rogers had 49 flyable B-24 bombers (one more than they had brought out to the Pacific in October of 1942), thirty-seven of them J-models and twelve B-24Ls. The Group had 610 officers and 1,916 enlisted men, making a total of 2,526 men who had to be moved with all their equipment and aircraft from Biak Island across nearly 1,400 miles of ocean and islands to Mindoro. The last bombing mission flown by the Group from Biak was on January 22, 1945. All the Group's attention from that time forward was on the move to McGuire Field.

---

*McGuire's fame and prestige were such that, after his body was recovered from the wreckage of his plane in the jungle in 1948, General Kenney was one of the pallbearers when he was laid to rest in Arlington National Cemetery.

47. THE MOVE TO THE PHILIPPINES 701

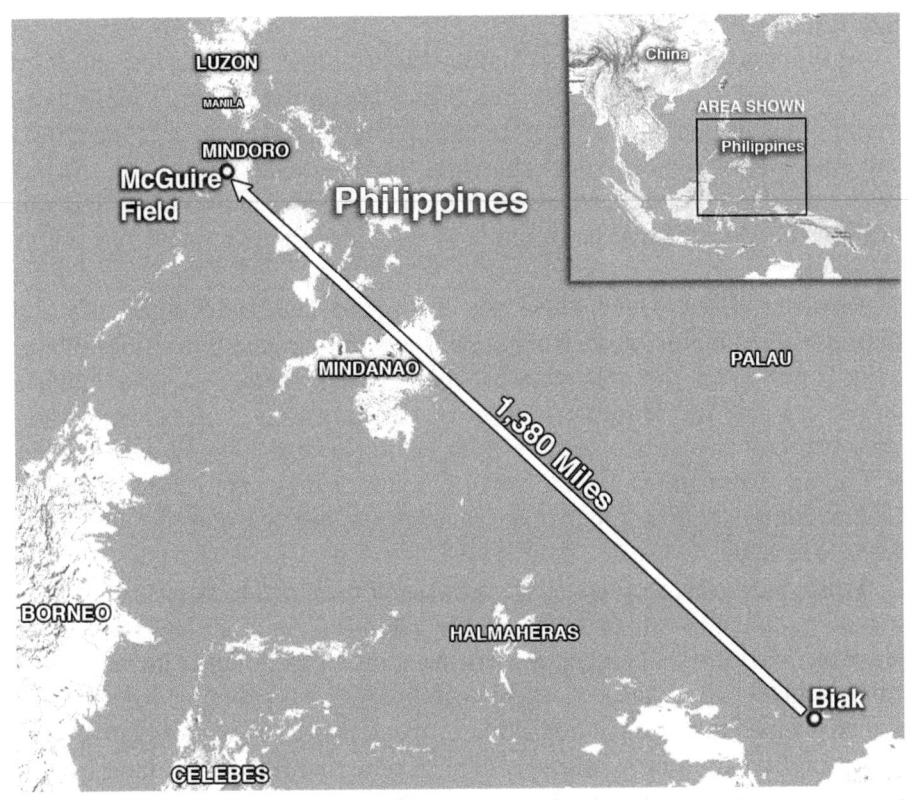

Map 47-1. In January of 1944 the Jolly Rogers moved from Mokmer Field on Biak Island to McGuire Field on the Philippine island of Mindoro.

As usual, most of the ground echelon and heavy equipment, such as trucks, jeeps, and other vehicles, would go by transport ship, an eight-day voyage, while the bomber crews could get there in around nine hours, carrying whatever camp equipment they could pack into their planes, giving priority to items that would be needed immediately by the crews such as tents and cooking equipment.

On January 26, 1945, more than half of the Group's planes, thirty Jolly Rogers bombers, set out from Mokmer Field on Biak Island headed for McGuire Field on Mindoro in the permanent change of base. Lt. Horner flew his crew to Mindoro in one of the planes, even though he had been officially taken off flying status and would fly no more combat missions. Each bomber navigated to the new airbase independently. All but one of the thirty planes taking off that day would arrive at McGuire safely.[4]

Sgt. Baca loses a friend

At the conclusion of the final Sunday Mass on Biak Island before the Jolly Rogers moved to the Philippines, Sgt. Baca was surprised to spot a highschool friend of his named Duilio Sei from back home in Albuquerque in the crowd that was leaving the little field church at the end of the service. He tried to catch up to Duilio but lost sight of him in the camp area and couldn't find him that day. He decided that he would look his friend up as soon as they got to Mindoro.

However, Baca would never see his friend Duilio Sei again. Of the thirty bombers that took off from Biak Island and headed to McGuire Field, Sei's bomber was the only one that didn't arrive there. Sei was a gunner on the crew of Lt. Charles R. Trusel of the Jolly Rogers' 400th Squadron. Trusel's bomber and another one flying along with it, piloted by Lt. Earle B. Earhart, encountered a thick bank of clouds as they approached Mindoro. Earhart elected to go up and over the weather, and he made it to McGuire Field without incident.

Trusel, however, decided to try going under the cloud bank instead of over it, a decision that would cost him his life, and the lives of all but one man on his plane. He took his bomber down to what his altimeter told him was about a thousand feet above the sea, where visibility was still poor in cloud and rain, and he decided to remain at that altitude, apparently believing, or hoping, that conditions would improve ahead of him. A thousand feet should have been a safe altitude when the plane made landfall, but it proved not to be so. There is a good chance the plane's altimeter was not reading accurately.*

Nearing Mindoro, Trusel felt the need to relieve himself, but the urinal near the flight deck (a simple funnel and can) was unusable, so he handed control of the bomber over to his copilot, Lt. Jack Liscum, and left the cockpit to make his way back through the bomb bay to the rear of the plane to use the urinal back there.

Sgt. Vernon J. Strawn, a passenger who was acting as an assistant flight engineer on this flight, was also in the back of the plane, and since it had begun to rain heavily, and the rain was coming in through the waist windows, Strawn decided to close them. As he was doing so, he looked outside and was startled to see the plane suddenly cross over onto land, then shocked to see that it was flying among trees, lower than the treetops. Lt. Liscum, up forward in the cockpit, must have seen the same thing at the same time, for Strawn heard the engines suddenly go to full power to begin a climb. The last thing he

---

* Aircraft altimeters are essentially just barometers, and before each flight they must be set to current barometric pressures, which are always changing. During flights, especially long flights like this one, if a plane flies into an area of lower barometric pressure, the altimeter can show the airplane to be hundreds of feet higher than it actually is.

remembered was Lt. Trusel saying, "What's wrong now?" an instant before the bomber smashed into a mountainside.

Hours later, only one man woke up amid the wreckage. Sgt. Strawn slowly regained consciousness to the sound of birds chirping and the babble of a brook flowing somewhere nearby. The bodies of the men who had been in the rear of the plane with him were scattered around in the debris, all of them dead. Through some miracle Strawn alone had survived, although he was badly injured. Fortunately the bomber had not caught fire in the crash. Following the sound of the water, Strawn dragged himself to the stream for a drink. The plane had crashed in territory held by the Japanese, but luckily some Filipino guerrilla fighters found him before the enemy did.

The guerrillas were under the command of Col. Wendell Fertig, an American officer who had been stranded on the island three years before when the Japanese took over. Fertig had never surrendered, instead going up into the hills to organize guerrilla resistance. Fertig took Strawn into his camp and tended his wounds, and when an American ship came in bringing supplies to him and his Filipino fighters, he put Strawn on the boat and sent him back to the American lines and a hospital.[5]

After Sgt. Strawn reported the crash of his bomber, all the other members of his crew were listed as missing in action, and would remain officially in that status until their deaths could be confirmed. But since the wreckage was in enemy territory, as well as being in a remote mountainous area, confirmation of their deaths would not be possible anytime soon. Sgt. Baca, however, had heard Sgt. Strawn's account of the crash and had no doubt that his friend Duilio Sei was dead. Months later, after Baca had returned home to Albuquerque, Sei's family invited him to their home to ask him what he thought were the chances

Sgt. Baca's friend Duilio Sei is buried in a group grave with seven other members of his crew at the Jefferson Barracks National Cemetery in Missouri. Sei was 21 years old, the same age as Baca, when his bomber crashed on the Philippine island of Mindoro.

that their son might still be alive. Might he be a prisoner of the Japanese, they asked him hopefully, or could he possibly be staying with Filipinos in some remote village, waiting for the Americans to reach him? The heartbroken family was clutching at straws.

Baca had been ordered not to divulge any information about his friend until his death had been officially confirmed, so he felt obliged to say nothing, even though he was certain that Duilio was dead. He could only mumble something about hoping for the best. It was a heartrending situation. He felt very sorry for the Sei family, and very bad that he could not resolve their anguish, so that when he left them that day the parents still, pathetically, had some hope that their son was alive. They would not know for sure that he was dead until 1950, when the wreckage of the plane was finally found and the remains of the crew identified, or at least the bodies counted, for by that time the remains were mostly just scattered bones, and individual identification of most of the men was not possible in that era before DNA-testing. Duilio Sei and seven of his crewmates now rest in a common grave in the Jefferson Barracks National Cemetery in Missouri (picture of gravestone on previous page).

The Jolly Rogers settle in at McGuire Field

Jolly Rogers bombers parked along a taxiway at McGuire Field on Mindoro, Philippine Islands, in February of 1945. Lack of Japanese airpower in the Philippines at this time allowed close parking rather than the widely spaced revetments of earlier airbases.

47. THE MOVE TO THE PHILIPPINES

Aerial view of McGuire Field, Mindoro Island, Philippines, looking west. The 7,000-foot-long metal-planked runway has parking pads on either side of it, where the bombers in the photo on the opposite page are parked. This picture was taken in the spring of 1946, ten months after the end of the war, after McGuire had been abandoned and was just an empty ghost airfield. Today it is San Jose municipal airport, surrounded by dense neighborhoods of Filipino homes.

All Jolly Rogers bombers were in residence at McGuire Field by the end of January, 1945. McGuire had a 7,000-foot-long runway planked over with metal Marston matting. It was built on the shoreline, like most of the island airfields, and one end of the runway ran right off into the sea (photo, above). Double rows of parking pads were built on either side of the runway on which to park the Group's bombers, with taxiways connecting them to the runway. The planes were parked close together on this airfield, and there were no built-up protective revetments, reflecting the fact that Japanese airpower was so weak at this point in the war that there was little chance that they would be bombed or strafed. The desperate Japanese, with what planes remained to them, were now flying suicide missions against American warships, not aircraft sitting on airbases.

The Jolly Rogers' tent encampment was set up on the southeast side of the airfield, on the sandy soil of the beach, where it was hoped the sand would provide sufficient drainage during the coming rainy season. The metal matting on the runway would provide a non-muddy surface to land on and take off from, although as usual rain would make it slick. Once established at McGuire Field, Lt. Horner and the rest of his crew, with the exception of Lt. Cooper and Sgt. Baca, had little to do, since they had completed their combat flying back on Biak Island and been taken off flying status. Now they were just waiting for orders to go home, which would not come until their replacements arrived.

This was the same situation that Lt. Horner had encountered eight months earlier when he and his crew had reported to Nadzab in June of 1944, before they had begun flying combat missions. At that time there had been many veteran crews sitting around idle at Nadzab, their combat tours finished, waiting for their replacements to arrive. The arrival of the Horner crew at Nadzab had released one veteran crew to go home. Now the situation was reversed, and it was the Horner crew, most of them anyway, who sat marking time waiting for a new crew to replace them.

Back at Nadzab, as you will remember, Lt. Horner had visited veteran pilots in the camp to learn whatever he could from them about flying combat missions, and he had acquired some useful information. At McGuire Field it was Horner who was the veteran, having flown 48 missions, and he was ready and willing to share his knowledge with any incoming pilot who might seek his advice. However, he found that new crews, when they finally began to arrive, had little interest in learning from him or any other experienced pilots. "They seemed to think they knew everything already," Mr. Horner remembers today, "and they actually resented anyone who disagreed. The result was that they didn't get the benefit of our experience, and during early 1945 some crews were lost making mistakes that we could have warned them about."

Life at McGuire Field on Mindoro

Lt. Horner and most of his crew ended up sitting pretty much idle for two months at McGuire Field. This would have been hard to endure at some hellhole such as Iron Range, or Wakde Island, but fortunately, living conditions at McGuire Field on Mindoro were relatively good for a military camp. This was largely due to the people and culture of the Philippine Islands, and their

47. THE MOVE TO THE PHILIPPINES

historical ties to America and the West. Filipinos were not the primitive, near-naked Stone Age people of New Guinea and other South Pacific islands; indeed, except for some tribes in the remote interior mountains, they were a civilized people, many of whom had interbred with Spanish and Latin American colonists during their nearly four centuries under Spanish rule.

First the population had benefited from those hundreds of years of European colonialism (the Philippines were named for King Philip II of Spain), and then, after the Spanish-American War of 1898, when Spain ceded the Philippines to the United States, the population experienced nearly a half century of American influence, as inhabitants of an American territory (America had planned to grant the Philippines independence in 1946). As a result, Filipinos felt more of a bond with the West than with the Orient, and they understood Americans and their ways. Most of them spoke English, and to this day the Philippines remain the only majority-Christian nation in the Pacific, with over 80 percent of the inhabitants of the archipelago being Roman Catholic.

To the historic bond with America was added profound gratitude to the Americans for deliverance from three years of unspeakable barbarism under the Japanese, who had killed at least a million Filipinos either by outright murder or by enslaving and working them to death. For all these reasons, the Jolly Rogers and all other Americans who liberated the Philippines were welcomed with open arms by a friendly and civilized people, and treated very well indeed.

In the Philippines the Americans saw a great improvement in their diet, with fresh foods of various kinds available from local sources to supplement the always-poor Army chow. The Army cooks were able to get fresh meat from nearby towns and villages; they could buy or barter for chickens and pigs, as well as fresh eggs, and from the extensive farm fields in the region came corn, tomatoes, rice, sweet potatoes, and beans. The Filipino people themselves went to work for the Americans and relieved them of various kinds of drudgery. As the historian of the Jolly Rogers wrote:

> **The people were pleasant and good company. Fraternization was not discouraged [as it had been in New Guinea]. . . The Filipinos were hired for KP [kitchen chores] and this pleased every soldier who lacked the rank to avoid it. The women did a beautiful job on the GIs' laundry, but the men spoiled them by overpaying them. . . Some of the crews hired houseboys who ran errands, filled canteens from the Lister bags and swept out the tents. Most of the Filipinos spoke English. . . Sgt. Dan Rahal entered in his diary, "I sure am going to like this place." Most of the men did.**[6]

Many Filipino women were skilled seamstresses who could mend uniforms, and could often be seen through the windows of their huts busily pedaling away on their Singer sewing machines.

With little to do, and being off flying status, Mr. Horner's memory of this time period is vague today. He does remember Filipino traders moving through the American camp, and of these he recently said, "I do remember Filipino traders called 'sharpies,' very educated, who came around with duffel bags full of trading goods and helpers to carry them. The porters were usually 'Huks,' natives from the mountainous backcountry. The traders would come into your tent and try to buy or trade you out of things. One thing that they wanted very much were the .45 cal. pistols that the aircrews had, which I refused to sell, and they also bought khaki shirts or anything else you had. I bought a few things from them as souvenirs to take home: a Samurai officer's sword, a bolo knife, and a sniper rifle with a sawed-off barrel."[7]

And he remembers a Filipino girls' baseball team. The game of baseball was another thing that Filipinos had in common with Americans. Baseball games were always being played around American camps, and the encampment of the Jolly Rogers was no exception. One day some tiny Filipino girls from the nearby town of San Jose, who couldn't have weighed more than 100 pounds each, shyly offered to play the Americans a game, saying that they'd had some prewar experience with baseball. The Americans agreed to play them, intending go easy on the girls so as not to embarrass or hurt them. On the day of the game, the girls showed up in gorgeous, professionally made uniforms, and proceeded to beat the pants off the astonished Americans, winning every game they played by a large margin.

The Jolly Rogers help American troops retake the Philippines

Although the main targets of the 90th Bomb Group operating from McGuire Field would be Japanese airfields on the west coast of Formosa, the 230-mile-long island that was the last Japanese stronghold in the Pacific before mainland Japan itself, the Jolly Rogers also gave tactical air support to the American troops battling the Japanese only a short distance to the north on the island of Luzon. The American 6th Army under the command of General Walter Krueger that had landed at Lingayen Gulf on Luzon Island on January 9th had advanced steadily southward toward Manila, pushing the Japanese out of their jungle and mountain redoubts as it went. On January 31, 1945, the American 8th Army landed in southern Luzon and advanced north toward Manila, so that Americans were approaching the capital city from two directions. On February 3 American troops began what would become the month-long task of driving the Japanese out of the capital city itself.

The Japanese holding Luzon were a formidable force of over a quarter of a million troops, grouped into three areas: 80,000 men in the mountains east of

Manila, 30,000 in the hills north of Manila, and over 150,000 in northeastern Luzon. The Jolly Rogers, with no Japanese airfields left to bomb in the Philippines, began giving close air support to the American armies that were fighting these groups of Japanese in the mountains and jungles, dropping their bombs directly on Japanese troop positions, as they had done on the Komiatum Ridge in New Guinea during the drive toward Salamaua and Lae in August of 1943 (Chapter 30). These were short missions compared to what the airmen were accustomed to, lasting only a few hours each, so that they often flew two missions a day from Mindoro to Luzon and back. With Japanese airpower in the Philippines now mostly eliminated, interceptions by Japanese fighters were rare.

Both Lt. Cooper and Sgt. Baca, during their bombing missions from McGuire Field, got bird's-eye views of the destruction of Manila, the once-beautiful city of over a million people that had been known before the war as the "Pearl of the Orient." As was their practice, the Japanese army was maliciously wrecking the city and slaughtering its inhabitants in a spiteful scorched-earth policy as American troops drove them out. They dynamited historic architectural treasures and set fire to famously beautiful city districts.

Great columns of smoke from the burning city rose over eight thousand feet into the air.[8] The 17,000 Japanese troops occupying Manila could have simply headed for the hills and lived to fight another day with their comrades in the mountains. Instead, filled with hatred and vindictiveness, they staged a replay of the Rape of Nanking, destroying everything they possibly could and killing thousands of Filipinos whom they dragged out of their homes and businesses and murdered in the streets. They did this for no other reason than that they wanted to—there was no military advantage to it. As a result, over 100,000 Filipino civilians were massacred. General Kenney wrote:

> That afternoon [3 Feb. 1945] the 37th Division arrived in Manila and the clean-up began. It had been hoped that the Japs would evacuate the city without destroying it, but the Nips decided that if they couldn't have the place, they would cause as much destruction as possible before they left. Practically every building in the city was dynamited or burned during their retreat west across the Pasig River to the old walled city, where part of them made a last stand, and southeast through the suburban district to escape to the mountains. Bridges, churches, government buildings and office buildings were destroyed or damaged beyond hope of repair. Water lines, sewer lines, and power lines were blown up with land mines, and a city of nearly a million people left without water, electricity, or food—to stare at their once beautiful capital city.
>
> The wanton destruction of Manila was bad enough, but the Japs earned the undying hatred of the Filipinos for all time by

Map 47-2. Once the Jolly Rogers had settled into McGuire Field on the Philippine island of Mindoro, their bombing targets became primarily Japanese installations on Formosa (today's Taiwan), from which kamikaze planes were attacking the U. S. fleet. They also gave close air support to U. S. troops fighting on Luzon. The bombing of Japan itself was left to the new B-29 Superfortresses.

47. THE MOVE TO THE PHILIPPINES

> their senseless orgy of pillage, murder, and rape of the civilian population as they evacuated the city and suburbs. People in the houses were called out and shot in the streets, the houses searched for liquor and loot and then set on fire. Crazed with alcohol, Japanese officers and men raged through the city in an orgy of lust and destruction that brought back memories of their conduct at the capture of Nanking several years before, when their actions had horrified the civilized world.[9]

In 1942 the Japanese had killed hundreds of Americans in the Bataan Death March, and paraded American prisoners through the streets of Manila to demonstrate to the Filipinos the superiority of Japan over America, and over Westerners in general. Now that the bill for these crimes was coming due, and the reality of Japanese military inferiority was setting in, the Japanese in Manila reacted with raging malevolence and violence, like children throwing a tantrum, and went on a rampage throughout the city, determined to destroy everything within their reach and kill anyone they could get their hands on.

Once again, as in China and everywhere else in the Pacific since the beginning of the war, the pure evil of Japanese militarism was on full display. One historian wrote:

> The devastation of Manila was one of the great tragedies of WWII. Of Allied cities in those war years, only Warsaw suffered more. Seventy percent of the utilities, 75 percent of the factories, 80 percent of the southern residential district, and 100 percent of the business district were razed. Nearly 100,000 Filipinos were murdered by the Japanese. Hospitals were set afire after the patients had been strapped to their beds. The corpses of males were mutilated, females of all ages were raped before they were slain, and babies' eyeballs were gouged out and smeared on walls like jelly... the uniforms of Japanese sailors and marines were saturated with Filipino blood.[10]

The Manila Massacre and the Rape of Nanking were identical bookends to the Japanese cruelty and barbarism of World War II. American soldiers finally put a stop to it in Manila by killing all the Japanese in hand-to-hand fighting, singly and in groups, advancing city block by city block, house by house, room by room, but it cost the lives of over a thousand young American men, with over 5,500 more wounded. The Americans had never been trained in urban warfare, but they learned fast.

Sgt. Baca witnessed the fighting in Manila from the air, in Jolly Rogers B-24s. "We could see all the smoke hanging over the city, and the flashes of the guns," he remembers today. "We didn't know exactly what was going on there, but we could tell that something really bad was happening."

Out in the countryside, U. S. troops continued to advance toward Clark Field, and finally captured the airbase on January 29, 1945. It was found that because of American bombing and strafing raids the Japanese had dispersed their aircraft and spare parts widely around the airfield, and even out into the surrounding villages, hiding propellers and other large items in native huts. Some aircraft parts were buried in the ground. This led General Kenney, who had a low opinion of Japanese air commanders to begin with, to comment:

> The Nip had dispersed his stuff, all right, but how he ever expected to find it and use it to keep his air force going is still a mystery to me. His method of refueling his airplanes was evidently by hand. The only refueling gasoline tanker truck that I saw on a former Jap field in the Philippines was one at Clark Field which still had stenciled on its sides the words "U. S. Army Air Force." I was beginning to feel annoyed that it was taking us so long to defeat so ill-equipped and stupid a nation.[11]

Lt. Cooper and Sgt. Baca help retake Corregidor

In February of 1945 both Sgt. Baca and Lt. Cooper, separately flying their final few bombing missions with the Jolly Rogers, participated in the liberation of Corregidor, the fortress island two miles off the coast of Bataan on Luzon at the entrance to Manila Bay (Map 47-3 opposite). Cooper, who by this time had been promoted from copilot to first pilot, led a formation of Jolly Rogers bombers over Corregidor on February 9, 1945, and that night wrote in his mission diary:

> Mission 45, Feb. 9 [1945]. Led my 1st flight over Corregidor Island. Dropped 48 tons of 1000-pounders on A/A [antiaircraft] positions. 2:25 hours.

Sgt. Baca was one of the gunners on a bombing strike against Corregidor on February 16, the day that American troops invaded it. His bomber formation dropped its bombs at dawn on the 16th of February, only hours before American paratroopers landed on the island in the first stage of the American assault to retake it.

As Mr. Baca reminded the author, the word "corregidor" means tadpole in Spanish, and the name accurately describes the island's shape (right). The island is only a mile-and-a-half wide at its head and three-and-a-half miles long from head to tail. It contained an extensive system of large, deep American-made tunnels of reinforced concrete to protect its defenders from bombardment. When the Americans were in possession of the island, one tunnel had housed a 1,000-bed hospital. Corregidor had been fortified for hundreds of years, from Spanish colonial times, since it guards the entrance to Manila Harbor, often described as the best deepwater harbor in the Far East.

47. THE MOVE TO THE PHILIPPINES 713

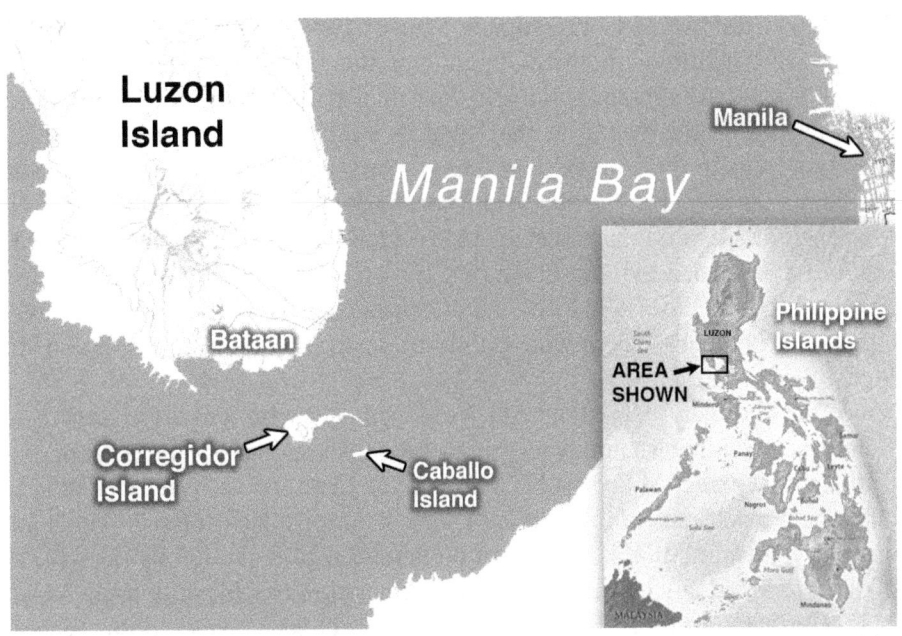

Map 47-3. The fortress island of Corregidor guarded the entrance to Manila Harbor. The Japanese seized it in May of 1942; the Americans retook it in February of 1945.

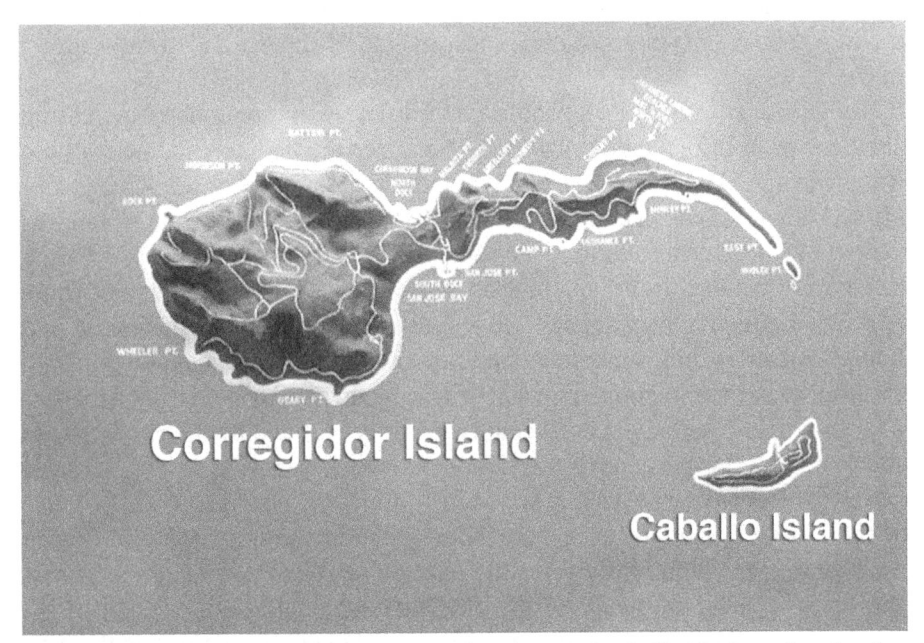

Map 47-4. Corregidor ("Tadpole" in Spanish) is three-and-a-half miles long from head to tail, and a mile-and-a-half wide at its head. Both Lt. Cooper and Sgt. Baca participated in bombing missions against Corregidor in February of 1945, and Cooper also bombed the Japanese in the fort on Caballo Island.

Flashback: the loss of Corregidor in May of 1942

It was on Corregidor, the "Gibraltar of the East," also known as "The Rock," that the Americans had made their final stand in the Philippines at the beginning of World War II, as the Japanese overwhelmed the American and Filipino forces in the islands. The Japanese assault on the Philippine Islands had begun the day after the attack on Pearl Harbor.

General MacArthur had been in command of the American forces and their Filipino allies when the war broke out. His army was called the U. S. Army Forces in the Far East (USAFFE), and it consisted of 135,000 troops, although eighty-five percent of them were poorly trained Filipino soldiers armed with World War I rifles.

Before the war MacArthur had lived with his wife and small son in a penthouse suite in a Manila hotel, but as the Japanese invasion progressed, on Christmas Eve of 1941 he sent his wife and son to safety on Corregidor Island, while he himself moved into the field with his troops. He declared Manila an open city, meaning that it would not be defended or contested by the Allies, in order to avoid any harm to the civilian population or to the city itself. Most of MacArthur's air force, based at Clark Field, had been quickly destroyed on the ground by Japanese airpower operating out of Formosa, and the inadequate forces of the American navy in the area, known as the American Asiatic Fleet, abandoned MacArthur and the Philippines to the powerful Japanese navy, leaving behind only some submarines, a few PT boats, and some support ships.

By March of 1942 the Japanese ground forces, in continually increasing numbers as reinforcements came in from Japan, had forced the battling American and Filipino defenders down into the mountainous southern part of Luzon known as Bataan (see again Map 47-3 on p. 713). MacArthur's plan was to hold off the Japanese as long as possible and disrupt their timetable for the conquest of the Pacific, hoping to keep them preoccupied while America came up with an effective war strategy. He was also hoping that America might find some way to send him some relief and support. Although he was able to tie up the Japanese army for some time, he was unable to get any help from America. The American Pacific fleet had been temporarily crippled by the Pearl Harbor attack, and the Japanese navy was in control of the area.

In late December of 1941 MacArthur moved his headquarters two miles offshore from Bataan to Corregidor Island and directed the defense of Bataan from there. MacArthur's move to the relative safety of Corregidor's tunnels had been resented by many of his men fighting on Bataan, and led to his being referred to by many soldiers as "Dugout Doug" for the rest of the war. MacArthur's biographer William Manchester, however, claims that MacArthur chose to remain outside of Corregidor's tunnels, living with his family in a cottage out in the open in order to share the dangers of the men on Bataan. According to Manchester, during Japanese air raids on Corregidor MacArthur would stand outside the cottage with a walking stick, smoking a cigarette and watching Japanese bombs drop all around him, while his wife and child waited out the attacks in a nearby bomb shelter.[12]

On February 23, 1942, two months after his move to Corregidor, MacArthur was ordered by President Roosevelt (by coded radio message) to escape from the island in order to take command of Allied forces in the Pacific from Australia. It was thought that MacArthur was too famous and competent a general, and his loss too severe a blow to American morale, to allow him to be captured. A submarine was made available for his escape, but MacArthur, who had a tendency towards claustrophobia, chose to leave Corregidor by surface vessel instead. At the time there were still a few American PT boats operating in the islands.

Thus MacArthur, along with his staff officers, his wife Jean, his 4-year-old son Arthur, and his son's Chinese nanny (called Ah Cheu), 22 people in all, boarded four PT boats and ran the gauntlet of the Japanese blockade through stormy seas on the night of March 11, 1942. Although many of the party suffered from seasickness in the rough waves, the PT boats managed to evade the Japanese warships in the area and make it the 600 miles to the southern end of Mindoro Island (where the Jolly Rogers would be based three years later when the Americans returned). From there MacArthur and his party were flown to Australia in two B-17s that had flown from Australia into Mindoro through Japanese dominated skies to bring them out. Altogether it was a daring and successful rescue.

Finally, on April 9, 1942, out of ammunition, food, water, and medical supplies, the remaining 78,000 American and Filipino troops on Bataan had been compelled to surrender to the Japanese. It was the largest American force in history to surrender to an enemy. The American and Filipino prisoners were then marched over 60 miles to a concentration camp, and it was during this trek that the Japanese victors exhibited the barbarous behavior that characterized them throughout the war. Many of the men in the marching column were sadistically tortured and killed in what became known as the Bataan Death March.

Around seventy thousand men started the march, and sixteen thousand of them died along the way, with about 650 of the victims being Americans and the rest Filipinos. The marching men, many of them sick and wounded, were not allowed food or water, and their Japanese guards killed them on the slightest of pretexts, or for no reason at all. Anyone who straggled or dropped out of the marching column was summarily shot, bayoneted, or beheaded.

Meanwhile, on Corregidor, 13,000 American and Filipino troops under the command of Gen. Johnathan Wainwright held out under siege for nearly another month. The Americans on The Rock fought to the last, surrendering only when Wainwright decided that further resistance was useless and would only waste lives. The story of the siege of Corregidor, often called "The Alamo of the Pacific," and the heroic American resistance against hopeless odds, should be commemorated and remembered with pride by every American.

It was MacArthur's humiliating loss to the Japanese, who had defeated his army and forced him to flee to Australia, that resulted in his fierce resolve to return to the Philippines and settle the score. The first public thing he had said upon reaching Australia was, "I shall return." He viewed his and America's return to the Philippines as a moral imperative as well as a personal crusade. Some historians of World War II now think that it would have been better to bypass the Philippine Islands as the American forces surged north across the Pacific toward Japan in 1944-5, and concentrate on the defeat of the Japanese homeland, but MacArthur would not even consider it. General Kenney agreed with his boss and wrote:

> The suggestion that we bypass the main Philippine island of Luzon and go to Formosa before liberating the Filipinos was unthinkable to me. That people belonged to us and had fought loyally on our side. If we blockaded them and left a half million or so Japs in their country to steal their food and subject them to misery and starvation, I felt we would not be keeping faith with them. The Japs certainly would live off the country and let the Filipinos starve rather than go hungry themselves. From a purely military view we would have a large landmass, with a lot of airfields and a lot of airplanes, right in our midst; it would offer much more of a problem than the bypassing of some small island or an isolated place like Wewak on the edge of a comparatively uninhabited place like New Guinea.[13]

However, had the Philippine Islands been bypassed and isolated until the surrender of Japan, so that the Japanese in the islands would have been compelled to surrender bloodlessly, as they did at Rabaul, the destruction of the great city of Manila could have been avoided, along with the deaths of more than sixteen thousand American troops and seven thousand U. S. sailors, not to mention over a million Filipino civilians (out of a total population of 18 million), all of whom were killed in retaking the Philippines. But MacArthur had been able to persuade the American Chiefs of Staff to go along with his wishes, and in hindsight it's always easy to come up with better strategies than the ones that were actually employed.

47. THE MOVE TO THE PHILIPPINES

After the American surrender of Corregidor on May 6, 1942, it would have been quite in character for the Japanese to massacre all their American and Filipino prisoners, but there were 11,000 of them, which represented quite a lot of useful slave labor to their captors. The Japanese triumphantly paraded hundreds of the American prisoners through the streets of Manila to demonstrate to the Filipinos the superiority of Japan over America, and the Oriental race over Caucasians, then dumped them into Bildad Prison in the city, where only a few would survive the war.

The rest of the Americans were transported to slave-labor camps all over the short-lived Japanese Empire on what became known as Hell Ships, on which many died under truly hellish conditions. Sgt. Baca's cousin Benedito Baca was killed on one of these ships, thrown overboard because he had become sick and therefore useless as slave labor. General Wainwright was sent to Manchuria, where he suffered from malnutrition and mistreatment until the end of the war. In 1945, at the Japanese surrender ceremony on the *USS Missouri* in Tokyo Bay, MacArthur made sure that Wainwright, thin and weak though he was, stood right in front of the surrendering Japanese.

There were also 65 American Army and Navy nurses in the hospital on Corregidor during the siege of the island, and under the ordinary circumstances of capture by the Japanese these women would have been sexually assaulted and then murdered. Five months earlier, in fact, that was exactly what happened to a group of British nurses that the Japanese had captured in their invasion of Hong Kong. On Christmas Day, 1941, Japanese soldiers had entered a hospital in the city which was flying the Red Cross flag. Their first action was to throw hand grenades into the hospital wards that killed many of the patients in their beds, then they entered and bayoneted to death anyone still alive. Three British doctors who tried to intervene were shot dead, and then the Japanese began raping the British and Chinese nurses and female orderlies, and continued to gang-rape them throughout the night. Two nurses who tried to fight back were dragged outside and beheaded.[14]

Next twenty-two Australian nurses whom the Japanese captured south of Singapore were massacred. After hearing what had happened to the hospital staff and patients in Hong Kong, these Australian nurses, along with some wounded British soldiers, had been fleeing the Japanese attack on Singapore, but their ship had been spotted by Japanese planes, bombed, and sunk. The surviving soldiers and nurses took to lifeboats and washed up on the shore of Banka Island, where the nurses hoisted a Red Cross flag on the beach and were tending to the injuries of the soldiers, ten of whom who were lying on stretchers. There were also some walking-wounded soldiers helping the nurses.

On February 16, 1942, fifteen Japanese soldiers discovered this group of people on the beach, and the British soldiers surrendered to them. After the surrender, the Japanese bayoneted all the walking soldiers to death, then did the same to the wounded men lying helplessly on the stretchers. Finally they murdered the 22 Australian nurses, who were wearing their nurse's uniforms and standing under the Red Cross flag. They forced the women to wade out into the surf until they were all waist-deep in the water, then machine-gunned them in the back. All but one of them died. Nurse Vivian Bullwinkel, although badly wounded, survived by floating motionless in the water amid the bodies of the other women, feigning death. After the Japanese had left, not considering their victims worth burying, she was able to make it to shore and escape into the jungle, and lived to tell the tale—otherwise this massacre would probably have gone unrecorded, as many other Japanese mass murders without survivors undoubtedly did.[15]

Thus the American nurses on Corregidor were fortunate not to be assaulted and butchered immediately following the American surrender, and the only reason they were not was probably because Gen. Masaharu Homma, the man who had presided over the Bataan Death March and the surrender of Corregidor, was aware that the American public, and in fact the news agencies of the world, were closely following the fate of Corregidor's defenders. Under this scrutiny he evidently decided to put up a civilized front and leave the American nurses unharmed. They were shipped to an internment camp near Manila, where for two-and-a-half years they managed to survive on very little food, losing an average of thirty pounds each by the time the war ended, while they continued to nurse the sick and wounded civilians who were also interned in the camp. Among the civilians were the wife and children of Paul "Pappy" Gunn.

The retaking of Corregidor, 16-26 February, 1945

Fast-forwarding from the surrender of Corregidor by the Americans in May of 1942 to the early months of 1945, the Japanese now in possession of Corregidor found themselves in exactly the same situation the Americans had been in, under siege by superior forces and cut off from any help or resupply. The swaggering, triumphant Japanese troops who had hauled down the American flag on Corregidor's parade ground and burned it for newsreel cameras in 1942 were now hiding in the underground tunnels of Malinta Hill, under a near-constant American barrage from land, sea, and air. Surrender was never an option for the fanatical Japanese; as usual they would fight for their divine Emperor's "honor" until they were killed, while trying to take as many Americans with them as they could.

Beginning on the 23rd of January, 1945, the Jolly Rogers joined other bomb groups to give the Japanese on Corregidor a daily pounding to soften up their defenses for the American invasion. On the 10th of February, a Jolly Rogers bomber flew a couple of paratrooper officers over Corregidor to study the area on the island onto which they would parachute on the invasion day.[16]

A week before the invasion, on February 9, Lt. Cooper flew his pre-invasion strike on Corregidor that destroyed some of the Japanese antiaircraft gun positions on the island. Two days later, on the 11th, Cooper was back in the air again, flying a bomber substituting for a weather reconnaissance plane that had crashed on takeoff, killing the crew. Cooper stayed aloft for nearly eight hours that day, reporting the weather in the Manila Bay area for other aircraft coming and going, and before returning to McGuire Field he also made a bombing run on Japanese positions on little Caballo Island, only about a mile square, which was located in the bay about a mile south of Corregidor (see maps on p. 713). Like Corregidor, Caballo was part of the harbor defenses of Manila Bay, and there were Japanese holed up there too.

Caballo Island featured a former American fortification known as Fort Hughes, which, like Corregidor, housed some large coastal gun batteries. During the siege of Corregidor in 1942 there had been 800 Americans on Caballo Island, firing the big guns of Fort Hughes at the Japanese forces on Bataan. When Corregidor surrendered on May 6, 1942, the Americans on Caballo were forced to give up also. Now, in 1945, Caballo was occupied by the Japanese, and the Americans were poised to take it back along with Corregidor.

Corregidor under the bombs of the Jolly Rogers. Lt. Cooper flew a strike on the island on Feb. 3, 1945. Over 4,000 tons of bombs were dropped on an area about one mile square. The Japanese took refuge in the complex of deep tunnels, just as the Americans had done in 1942.

Lt. Cooper wrote in his mission diary:

> **Mission 46**   **Feb. 11 [1945]**
> Flew as sub. for weather recco plane which crashed & burned on takeoff. Observed fighting in Manila & bombing of Corregidor and Bataan. Dropped 20 X 260 lb. frags on Cabola [Caballo] Is. 7:40 hours. 414:30 [total hours flown to date]

On the morning of the invasion of Corregidor, February 16th, Sgt. Baca was assigned to fly as a gunner on one of the bombers that would make a final bomb drop just before the paratroopers went in. On this mission he manned the nose turret of his bomber, giving him a panoramic view of the proceedings. At sunrise on the invasion day Baca's bomber dropped its bombs on Corregidor, the last to be dropped before the landings, and then the plane remained on location, circling over the island to provide weather information to the C-47s that were on their way with a thousand American paratroopers aboard.

This was the 503rd Parachute Regiment, the same tough troops who had dropped on Nadzab in New Guinea, and later on the island of Noemfoor to capture a Japanese airfield there. Now they were dropping on the upper part of Corregidor known as Topside, the head of the tadpole-shaped island and its most dominant feature. Their assignment was to seize and hold this hill, since if the Japanese occupied it they could fire down on the lower areas of the island where the American amphibious landings would be made.

Knowing the wind strength and direction was important that morning because the landing area, the former parade ground of the American post on Corregidor, was a very small target, and the paratroops would have to jump upwind whatever distance was necessary to compensate for it. The men in the bomber could only provide a rough idea of the wind by watching the smoke and dust rising from the island, but it was better than nothing.

As Sgt. Baca and the other crewmen in his bomber watched from above, the paratroopers jumped from only 500 feet above Topside in order to minimize their time in the air. However, the wind was blowing fairly strongly that day, something over 20 mph, and some of the paratroopers were blown over the side of the island and landed in the sea, where they were picked up by waiting boats. A few of the paratroopers died when their chutes malfunctioned, just as had happened back at Nadzab; others were killed when they crashed against the ruins of the old concrete barracks buildings on Topside, while still others landed down the hill behind the Japanese lines and had to fight their way back into the American perimeter.

At the same time that the 503rd's paratroops were landing on Topside, infantrymen of the American 24th Division made amphibious landings on the lower (eastern) end of the island, which put Americans on both the head and the tail of the tadpole, so that the Japanese were faced with attacks from two

Topside on Corregidor as it appeared just after the American paratroopers (the 503rd Regimental Combat Team) landed on the island on the morning of 16 February 1945. The white objects are deflated parachutes, and the row of buildings at upper left is the barracks and administrative buildings of the prewar American army garrison.

directions. The battle for Corregidor would pit about 7,000 American troops against an approximately equal Japanese force of 6,700.

The battle to retake Corregidor was a typically ferocious Pacific island battle, as was any fight with the mindlessly fanatical Japanese. The defenders of Corregidor this time were some of the Emperor's best troops, known as "special landing forces," or what we would call marines. During the battle the Japanese repeatedly staged mass "banzai" attacks, as well as sending out suicide squads with explosives strapped to their bodies. All these frenzied attacks failed, and the charging Japanese were shot down. Over 250 Japanese bodies were counted after just one of these suicide charges.

As usual, toward the end of the battle, when the Japanese realized that the game was up, they began committing suicide rather than surrender. They detonated huge caches of ammunition deep inside the tunnels of Malinta Hill, some of which erupted like volcanoes on the surface.

Other Japanese barricaded themselves in the tunnels. After American engineers repeatedly called for surrender down the ventilator shafts, and were reviled and rebuffed in return by the enemy shouting up from below, they poured gasoline down the ducts and ignited it to suffocate or incinerate the Japanese underground. Numerous cave and tunnel entrances were also blown shut with explosives, sealing the Japanese inside, as had become standard practice in Pacific island battles by 1945.

At the beginning of the war, in 1941 and 1942, it had taken the Japanese four months to take Corregidor from the Americans, but in 1945 it took the Americans only twelve days to take it back from the Japanese. The cost to the Americans was about 200 men killed 700 wounded. Of the 6,700 Japanese defenders of Corregidor, all but about 50 were killed or committed suicide.

Corregidor Island was declared secure by American commanders on February 26, although more underground explosions would be heard for days as Japanese holdouts continued blowing themselves up in the tunnels. On March 7, 1945, General MacArthur returned to the island that he'd been forced to leave on the night of March 11, 1942 in a PT boat with his family and staff, and he presided over a ceremony to restore the American flag on the old parade ground at Topside. "I see that the old flagpole still stands," he said to the color guard. "Have your troops hoist the colors to its peak, and let no enemy ever again haul it down."

Mrs. MacArthur had rejoined her husband in Manila the day before, on March 6, and as the ship on which she was sailing passed Corregidor on its way into Manila Harbor, the island didn't look the same to her. The last time she'd seen its profile was when the General had sent her and their son there for safety in 1942. When she met General Kenney in Manila she said, "George, what have you done to Corregidor? I could hardly recognize it as we passed it! It looks as though you've lowered it at least forty feet." Kenney replied that if the island seemed lower in the water to her, it could only be the result of the more than four thousand tons of bombs that his bombers had dropped on it in the previous few months.[17]

Meanwhile on tiny Caballo Island (the name means "horse" in Spanish), a mile south of Corregidor, on which Lt. Cooper had dropped his bombs on February 11, the Japanese continued to resist. On March 27, just before an American invasion force landed on the island, more bombs were dropped on Caballo by the Jolly Rogers, and it was also shelled by the guns of American destroyers offshore and American artillery set up on Corregidor.

After the bombardment ceased, and the smoke drifted away, an American amphibious force landed and soon captured two of the three fortified hills on Caballo. A Sherman tank that was put ashore ran over a mine and was disabled, and it still sits there today, rusting among boulders on the shoreline. About 200 Japanese in large concrete mortar pits and associated tunnels refused to surrender, and all attempts to dislodge them from the surface failed. Unwilling to sacrifice any more American lives, on April 5 and 6 combat engineers laid a pipe into one mortar pit from a ship offshore and pumped thousands of gallons of gasoline and diesel fuel into the position, gave it time to sink into the tunnels, then ignited it with explosives. The fire burned for hours, and caused

47. THE MOVE TO THE PHILIPPINES

The entrance to the Malinta Tunnel complex on Corregidor, a few months after the end of the battle in February of 1945. The sign says: "Attention! Souvenir hunters, for a quick death, pick up ammunition on this island." The man on the right is Capt. Donald A. Baker, the author's father. Capt. Baker and his friend landed in an L-4 artillery spotter plane on Corregidor's small airfield and explored the tunnels for a few hours before flying back to Manila. Later they learned that there were still Japanese inside the tunnels. In an extremely uncharacteristic example of Japanese soldiers surrendering, twenty Japanese marines came marching smartly out of Malinta Tunnel on January 1, 1946, with a white flag and surrendered to an astonished American Graves Registration Officer. The Japanese had found and read a wind-blown newspaper that convinced them the war was over.

some huge underground explosions when ammunition that the Japanese had stockpiled blew up.

However, after the flames had died down there were still some Japanese alive in the tunnels, still refusing to surrender, so the operation was repeated. Finally a solitary Japanese soldier, badly burned, emerged from a hole in the side of the hill with his hands up and was taken into custody. American troops then entered the tunnels beneath the mortar pits and found all the Japanese inside dead, either incinerated or suffocated.[18]

The Malinta Tunnel as it appears to tourists today.

The Jolly Rogers accidentally give U. S. troops a scare

Close air support of American troops fighting on Luzon by the heavy bombers of the Jolly Rogers continued, but it was a risky business for those on the ground, especially in the jungle where the opposing lines were hard to identify from above. In Europe, an attempt by B-17s and B-24s to provide tactical support to U. S. troops in July of 1944 had resulted in the deaths of Lt. Gen. Lesley McNair and a hundred or so American soldiers, when bombs of the Eighth Air Force fell short of the German lines. Gen. McNair was the highest-ranking American officer killed during the war, and he was killed by bombs dropped by American bombers. The Jolly Rogers were determined not to make any similar deadly error.

However, Sgt. Baca flew as a gunner on a close support mission on February 22, 1945, in which the Jolly Rogers accidentally dropped bombs closer to American troops than had been intended, and although no one was killed, the result was a shake-up in the Group's chain of command. The goal of the bombing that day was to try to blast some of the 30,000 Japanese troops in the mountains west of Clark Field out of their entrenched positions. The battle was in rough terrain that made it especially difficult to determine from the air exactly where the American and Japanese lines were. The American troops marked their front lines for the bombers with ground panels and smudge pots that put out orange smoke, but these were not easy to spot in the jungle. The Jolly Rogers had done the same thing the day before, twice in fact, once in the morning and again in the afternoon, and all had gone well.

On these missions the bombers were flying in a right echelon formation, meaning the 24 bombers were staggered back in a long line to the right of the lead bomber, and the Group's bombardiers were keying on the lead bombardier. Each bomber was carrying six 1,000-pound demolition bombs, so that 144 one-thousand-pound bombs tore up a huge piece of the landscape, annihilating any Japanese in the target area and concussing into insensibility any others within a wide radius around the blasts, just as had happened on the Komiatum Ridge back in New Guinea, 18 months earlier in August of 1943.

The morning mission of Feb. 22 went well, and the Jolly Rogers' bombs hit Japanese positions accurately and effectively. However, the bombardier who had led the bomb run became ill with dysentery after he landed, and an inexperienced substitute took his place in the afternoon for the second mission of the day. The new bombardier, through some error, released his bombs in the wrong place, dangerously close to the American lines, and of course all the rest of his flight, keying on him, did the same. The American troops were surprised and shocked by such big blasts so close to them, but despite rumors of fatalities, no record exists of any Americans being killed or injured by these bombs. The crews of the bombers had no idea that a mistake had been made until they returned to McGuire Field, where an irate Lt. Gen. Lesley Crabb, Chief of Staff of Fifth Bomber Command, was on the phone asking to speak to the Jolly Rogers' commander, Lt. Col. Wilson Banks, to demand an explanation.

Lt. Horner happened to be in the Jolly Rogers headquarters when the call came in, and he overheard the conversation. When Gen. Crabb asked to speak to Col. Banks, the aide who had answered the phone tried to stall the General off by saying that he wasn't sure where the colonel was just then. The truth was that Col. Banks was not anywhere on the airfield, nor even on Mindoro Island. Col. Banks was all the way back down at Hollandia, nearly 1,700 miles away on the coast of New Guinea, where he was rumored to have a girlfriend. He had apparently developed a habit of flying off to visit her without informing anyone at higher headquarters of his absences.

Gen. Crabb must have been aware of these rumors, however, because Lt. Horner heard him say, "Never mind, I think I know where he is. Have him call me when he gets back." Crabb then immediately issued orders relieving Col. Banks from command of the Jolly Rogers and replacing him with Lt. Col. Ellis L. Brown, a highly respected leader who had been with the Group for a long time and had led many bombing missions.

Sgt. Baca and other crewmen who had flown the mission, meanwhile, were not so much bothered by the change of command than with the rumor that they may have killed some American troops on the ground that day. "We felt terrible about it," he says today, and for over seventy years Mr. Baca continued to feel badly about that mission, thinking that Americans may have died on the ground under his plane's bombs. Recently the author was able to tell him, after examining the records, that there is no mention of any U. S. soldiers being killed by the bombing that day. It was 70 years in coming, but the relief felt by Mr. Baca when he heard this news was considerable.

The rescue of American prisoners in the Philippines

While the Jolly Rogers were providing close air support to the ground troops retaking Luzon, other American soldiers, whom we would call today Special Forces, were rushing to rescue Americans held captive in Japanese prison camps before the Japanese could massacre them. The Japanese made a practice of spitefully murdering the Americans in their prisoner-of-war camps whenever American forces approached. One such incident had occurred on Wake Island (not to be confused with Wakde Island), where the Japanese had captured a number of American civilian construction workers when they took over the island in December of 1941 following their Pearl Harbor attack.

The Japanese had kept 98 of the Americans on the island alive as slave laborers and treated them brutally for nearly two years. On October 5, 1943, an American naval task force passed by Wake Island and planes from its aircraft carriers bombed the airfield in passing. Wake Island was just another of those places that the Americans had left to "wither on the vine," but the Japanese commander thought that the bombing was the prelude to an invasion. As a result he had his American prisoners bound hand and foot and lined up beside a trench, where they were all shot in the back with machine guns and rifles before their bodies were shoved into the ditch and covered up.

Another such massacre occurred in a prison camp on Palawan, the most western of the Philippine Islands, on December 14 of 1944 when the Japanese who ran the camp saw an American convoy approaching. They, too, decided that an American invasion was imminent, although the convoy was actually only passing by on its way to Mindoro. The Japanese herded all their American prisoners, about 150 of them, into three covered trenches, filled the trenches with gasoline from 55-gallon drums, and ignited it with torches and by throwing hand grenades. Their intent was to burn all the Americans alive, and any who tried to get out of the trenches were machine-gunned, bayoneted, or clubbed down.

Nevertheless some of the Americans did get out, dashed at their Japanese executioners, and managed to kill a few of the loathsome "Sons of Heaven" with their bare hands before they were shot down. Others who got away were hunted down, and when caught were tortured, sadistically set afire, or stabbed. Any who tried to swim away were shot in the water. When the Japanese buried the American bodies in a mass grave, some were still alive but were smothered under the dirt. Eleven Americans who escaped in the confusion of the killings lived to tell the tale.

To prevent more of these mass murders of American prisoners, General MacArthur ordered American Army commandos to penetrate Japanese lines wherever possible to make surprise raids on the P. O. W. camps and rescue the prisoners before their captors could act. On February 3, 1944, during the Battle of Manila, a fast-moving armored column charged into the Santo Tomas internment camp near the city, rammed open the compound's gate with a Sherman tank, and rescued the nurses who had been captured on Corregidor island in April of 1942, as well as other civilians held there, before the Japanese camp guards could take any action to harm them. On the same day another raid liberated prisoners in Manila's Bildad Prison.

In the most famous of these rescue raids, staged on the night of January 30, 1945, a hand-picked unit of American Rangers and Filipino guerrillas penetrated 30 miles behind Japanese lines to ambush and kill the guards of the Cabanatuan concentration camp on Luzon and bring out 500 American pris-

47. THE MOVE TO THE PHILIPPINES

Freedom! The date is 12 February 1945, and the American nurses that the Japanese had captured on Corregidor Island in 1942 are being rescued after nearly three years of imprisonment. A Sherman tank at the head of a flying column smashed open the gates of the Santo Tomas internment camp near Manila, the Japanese guards were overpowered, and the jubilant nurses climbed aboard trucks to be transported back to American lines. They were soon flown home to the States. "Pappy" Gunn's wife and children were also in this camp and were rescued along with the nurses.

oners who had been held there ever since the Bataan Death March at the beginning of the war. A book was written about this operation that was made into a movie, *The Great Raid* (poster at right). Minutes before the raid began, a P-61 Black Widow night fighter flew in circles above the camp to distract the guards as the American commandos crept toward the compound in the dark, while the Filipino guerrillas heroically held off a large Japanese force that tried to intervene during the rescue.

Yet another raid, this one on Los Banos prison camp on 23 February, 1945, rescued 2,147 Allied soldiers and civilians and killed the 250 Japanese who ran the camp. In the closing phases of the war, the same haste was made to liberate Allied

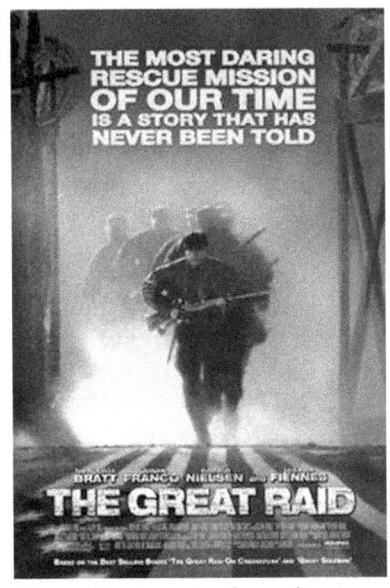

Poster for a movie about the rescue of Americans from the Cabanatuan prison camp. The movie was released by Miramax Films in 2005.

prisoners in slave labor camps all over the former Japanese Empire, and later within Japan itself, before the Japanese could slaughter them.

"Pappy" Gunn is reunited with his family

"Pappy" Gunn had been wounded and hospitalized when on October 30, 1944, Japanese fighter planes strafed and bombed a front-line airfield that he was helping to construct at Tacloban, on the Philippine island of Leyte. He and General Kenney, who had been standing together on the field, had dived under different jeeps as the strafing planes came in, but Gunn had been hit in the left arm by a piece of phosphorus from an incendiary bomb. It was a serious wound, and Kenney had sent him back to a hospital in Brisbane, Australia for treatment. As soon as Kenney learned that "Pappy's" wife and children had been rescued in Manila and were unharmed, he put them aboard a plane and flew them to "Pappy's" bedside. "Pappy's" wife Polly seems to have been as much a character as he was, for as soon as she saw him, she said, "All right, where have you been for the past three years? And this better be good!"[19]

The Horner Crew receives orders to go home

In February of 1945, with the war in Europe coming to an end, replacement bomber crews began to arrive in the Philippines, at first a trickle, and then a flood with three or four new crews coming in every week. Some of the crews joining the Jolly Rogers were veterans who had flown in Europe until they were no longer needed there as the war against Hitler wound down. When these new crews flew missions to Formosa, they reported that the Japanese antiaircraft fire there was as accurate as anything they had experienced over Germany. The crack Japanese gunners on Formosa could send five-inch shells into an American bomber formation at 30,000 feet, and several Jolly Rogers crews were lost to this deadly flak.

Since a veteran pilot such as Lt. Horner was worth two or three new pilots fresh from Stateside training with no combat experience, Horner and other pilots who had completed their combat tours were offered enticements to stay on and continue flying. In exchange for a second tour they would be given promotions, better jobs such as squadron commanders or operations officers, and other perks. Lt. Horner was not interested in remaining in the Pacific, however, and declined the offers, but some pilots that he knew accepted the deals. Later, when he heard that some of them had been lost on bombing missions over Formosa, Horner decided he had made the right decision.

During the last week of February, Lt. Horner and all of his crew except Lt. Cooper and Sgt. Baca received their orders to return to the States, and Cooper and Baca finished up their combat flying in early May and got their orders to go home as well. After more than nine months of combat flying in the Pacific war theater, the Horner crew was finally going home.

Chapter Forty-Eight

THE HORNER CREW RETURNS HOME

By early May of 1945 all ten of the young men who had comprised the Horner bomber crew had accrued enough rotation points to complete their combat tours and received orders to go home. They had entered the war in May of 1944 and they were leaving it in May of 1945. When they had left the States in a brand new B-24 they had thought, naively, that they might come home the same way, in the same plane. Lt. Horner had even declared that he would fly it under the Golden Gate Bridge to celebrate their homecoming.

However, the reality was that they wouldn't even be coming home together, much less on the same plane. After the men were taken off flying status, they were given orders that authorized them to return to the U. S. individually, on any military ship, plane, or combination of the two that was headed for San Francisco and had room for them. Thus, depending on whether a man made the final leg of the journey home on a plane or a ship, he would arrive home by passing either over or under the Golden Gate Bridge.

When a man applied for transportation home, at whatever place he happened to be in the Pacific war theater, his name went onto a waiting list, and whenever a ship or plane passed through going in the right direction with space available, it took men on the list in the order they had applied until it was filled up. If it was not going all the way back to San Francisco, a man rode it as far as he could, usually to one of the other Pacific island bases, and then put his name on another list of men awaiting transportation to go further. Battlefield casualties always had priority, and during battles many of the ships and planes headed back to the States were too full of wounded men to take anyone else.

At McGuire Field on Mindoro Island, the men of the Horner crew said their goodbyes to each other, signed each other's "short snorters" (paper currency on which servicemen collected signatures), and went their separate ways home. At this time, unarmed Jolly Rogers bombers were ferrying men who had finished their combat tours back to Mokmer Field on Biak Island, which at least got them 1,300 miles closer to San Francisco, and there they could await further transportation. Near the end of February, 1945, this is what Lts. Horner and Ostafin did. The ferry bombers were flown by skeleton crews, with no bombardier or gunners, since there was no longer any danger from Japanese aircraft between the Philippine Islands and New Guinea, and this made more room for passengers.

However, the Japanese had never been as great a danger to American aircraft as the tropical weather, and the storms, not to mention mechanical failures or navigation errors, remained a threat no matter where an airplane flew in the Pacific. From the southernmost Philippine Island to Biak is 900 miles of open water. On February 24, 1945, pilot Capt. Carl E. Peterson of the Jolly Rogers' 320th Squadron took off from McGuire Field with his skeleton crew of copilot, flight engineer, navigator, and radio operator, to ferry to Biak five of the Group's men who had completed their combat tours and were on their way home. Like most men in the Pacific, Peterson's thoughts were about what he was going to do after the war, and he had decided that with his experience at flying four-engine aircraft he would qualify to become an airline pilot.

But after Peterson's plane left McGuire, it was never seen or heard from again—one more Jolly Rogers bomber that took off and just disappeared. Tragically, no immediate search for the plane or survivors was made because Peterson had been so blasé about what he considered a routine ferry flight that he had not bothered to file a flight plan. Even today, it is normal procedure (though not always mandatory) for a pilot to file a flight plan prior to a flight. Had Peterson done so it would have advised authorities of his takeoff time, his route, and his estimated time of arrival. On arrival at his destination a pilot closes his flight plan, or his failure to do so triggers an immediate search for the plane.

Since Peterson had not filed a flight plan, several days passed before anyone realized he had gone and not shown up at Biak. If the men had ditched the plane and managed to get into life rafts, they would therefore have been at sea for days with no one even aware that they needed rescue. Before the belated search was begun, ocean currents could have taken the rafts far away from the plane's flight path, out into the wastes of the Pacific where the men would have perished from exposure, hunger and thirst. Regardless of how they died, there was bitter irony in the fact that the five passengers aboard the plane had survived hundreds of hours of combat flying and had been on their way home to rejoin their families and take up their postwar lives when they were lost on a routine ferry ride.[1]

Another simple ferry ride that went fatally wrong turned out to be the most catastrophic single loss of men that the Jolly Rogers ever suffered. On May 6, 1945, a B-24 piloted by Capt. Hans H. Williams was taking a group of men on leave from Mindoro up to Manila. Aboard the plane were four crewmen and twenty passengers. They took off from McGuire Field at 2 p.m. in abysmal weather and headed for Clark Field, 200 miles to the north, and were never heard from again. The clouds were right down on the ground at McGuire Field that day, with poor visibility in heavy rain, but better weather was reported over the sea to the west, so Capt. Williams took off on instruments and headed west, expecting to shortly be in the clear. He did not have a navigator aboard, probably figuring that he didn't need one on such a short flight, and one that he had likely made several times before. Williams did file a flight plan, though, and when the plane did not arrive at Clark Field by that evening, PBY Catalinas began searching along Williams' most likely route, and they continued to search for five days without finding a trace of the plane. Like the B-24 named "Weezie" (Chapter 42), which lay on a mountainside north of Port Moresby with the remains of 23 men for 37 years before it was accidentally discovered, perhaps someday Capt. Williams' plane will also be found.[2]

Lts. Horner, Ostafin, Theobald, and Cooper return home

No such disaster befell the ferry rides of Lts. Ostafin and Horner back to Biak Island, when they rode separate aircraft from McGuire near the end of February and arrived safely at Mokmer field. This was the airfield from which they had flown so many combat missions in the five months between August and the end of 1944, but by this time Biak, like other airfields left behind in the advance on Japan, such as Nadzab and Port Moresby, had become a supply and replacement depot, and a stopover place between Australia and the Philippines. Now that their combat tour was over, Horner and Ostafin were just two of hundreds of transients at Biak on their way home. They added their names to the list of men awaiting transportation to San Francisco, and settled into tent quarters near the airfield to await developments.

After a week, a ship headed for San Francisco appeared in Biak's harbor that had some space aboard, and Lt. Ostafin was able to get a place on it. Lt. Horner had to wait another three weeks for a ride home. During his wait he noticed several Jolly Rogers bombers sitting idly around the airfield,[*] apparently retired from combat, and offered to fly one of them back to San Francisco and take ten or fifteen men with him. However, he was told that his orders stipulated no further flying duty, so the idea was dropped.

One evening Lt. Horner was killing time by attending an open-air movie in the camp area near the airfield, and while the show was in progress a lone Japanese bomber came over the field and dropped a few bombs. This was a highly unusual event at Biak by this stage of the war. The bombs hit nothing of importance, and no one was hurt, but the movie was halted abruptly, all the lights in the area were switched off, and a near-panic ensued among the movie audience in the darkness as men collided with one another in a mad dash to get to air raid shelters that they couldn't see. A number of men fell down in the confusion and were cut up by the coral ground, since falling on coral, as Mr. Horner puts it today, "was like falling on broken glass and razor blades." The medics had quite a bit of work to do stitching up cuts and treating abrasions after the all-clear was sounded and the lights went back on.

---

[*] The bombers that Lt. Horner saw sitting around the airfield later became part of a huge collection of abandoned aircraft that eventually was sold to scrap metal dealers.

An inexperienced young major was in charge of all the transients waiting for rides home, and this insignificant bombing raid, probably the only one he had ever experienced, made a strong impression on him. Lt. Horner and other veterans figured that the raid had probably been the last-gasp effort of some isolated group of Japanese on a bypassed island somewhere, who cobbled together a flyable airplane from the wrecks of several and used it to make one final suicidal bombing raid on the Americans. The plane had no doubt ended up in the ocean after it had dropped its bombs, and neither it nor its crew would ever be seen again.

Nevertheless, the agitated young major was all for sending out reconnaissance planes to try to discover the origin of the bomber and retaliate against the Japanese responsible for the raid. He called for volunteers among his transient pilots, but none of them, including Lt. Horner, displayed any interest, and in fact Horner reminded him that he (the major) himself had previously emphasized that they had been taken off flying status, when he (Horner) had offered to fly a bomber home. In any event the matter was dropped, and no more bombing raids ever occurred.

After Lt. Horner had cooled his heels on Biak for a month, a modified B-24 being used as a courier plane passed through Mokmer Field on its way to San Francisco, and it had room aboard for three passengers. Lt. Horner was lucky enough to get one of the spaces. This was no ordinary B-24, as Mr. Horner recently recalled: "One of the air couriers from MacArthur's headquarters came through Biak, and I along with two others were able to get a ride home on it. This bomber had been converted to fly passengers, and was specially set up for General MacArthur, with many luxuries including reclining leather seats, and the pilots were civilian airline pilots. MacArthur always made sure he had the best of everything. While we were flying along I chatted with the pilot and found that he was making $800 a month, and the copilot almost as much. They were grousing because they hadn't been home in 2 weeks. I told them that I had been making $220 per month as a pilot while being shot at, and I hadn't been home in a year.[3]

The bomber arrived in San Francisco on Easter Sunday, 1945, the same day that the transport ship carrying Lt. Ostafin, which had set out from Biak Island three weeks earlier, pulled into the harbor. The ship had spent those weeks plowing through heavy seas, in storms, which had made everyone aboard including Ostafin miserably seasick.

Lt. Theobald, the Horner crew's navigator, was able to catch a ride from McGuire Field all the way to San Francisco on a C-54, a four-engine transport, arriving in the States a week before Lt. Horner did, and on the same day that Franklin D. Roosevelt died.

It is not known by what means Lt. Cooper returned home, but his flight logbook shows that he was back home in California by the middle of May, 1945.

Before Cooper left Mindoro he had all the members of his crew sign his "short snorter," a Filipino dollar bill, which his son still has. Short snorters were common souvenirs among servicemen in the Pacific, and some men collected so many signatures on their paper notes that they had to tape the bills together into a roll, and would then compete to see who had the fattest roll.

Nor is it known, since the rest of the Horner crewmen are now deceased, by what means the other members of the crew returned home—we can only say that one way or another they did so, and went their separate ways back to civilian life.

Sgt. Baca returns home

Lt. Horner left Mindoro for home before Sgt. Baca did, and Baca remembers Horner coming into his tent late one night and waking him up to say goodbye. They would not see each other again until 1950, when Baca was passing through Detroit and stopped by Horner's home to visit with him for a few minutes.

When Baca got his orders to return home, his experience was different from Lt. Horner's. He expected many delays en route, but somehow ended up getting space on one transport plane after another in rapid succession, hopping eastward from island to island to Hawaii, and then right on through to San Francisco with no delays whatsoever. He remembers riding in planes filled with wounded Marines from the recent battle for Iwo Jima, and yet every time he reached an island and began settling in for what he assumed would be a wait for the next ride, it seemed that a plane would immediately appear on the airfield headed west with room for him on it.

He was at a loss to explain it. When he got home, his mother told him that she'd been praying daily to St. Joseph, the patron saint of travelers, for her son to reach home as soon as possible, and the prayers seemed to have worked, or at least it's as good an explanation as any for the speed of his return.

After Baca got home he was not immediately discharged from the Army, but was sent to the Pacific Northwest to fight forest fires. Beginning in 1944 the Japanese had launched thousands of balloons into the jetstream from Japan to America, each balloon carrying an explosive firebomb, hoping to ignite the forests of the U. S. west coast. In May of 1945 a pregnant woman and five children on a picnic in a forest in Oregon were killed by the explosion of one of these balloon bombs, after they discovered it in a meadow and fooled around with it, trying to figure out what it was. The forest fires fought by Sgt. Baca and other servicemen may have been ignited by these devices.

After fighting several of these fires, Sgt. Baca was discharged from the Army and returned to his family in Albuquerque, where his extended family was overjoyed to welcome him home.

Chapter Forty-Nine

THE END OF THE WAR

When the Horner crew completed its combat tour and went home in the spring of 1945, the war still had three more months to play out, and the Jolly Rogers would fly bombing missions almost to the last.

As the American navy closed in on the Japanese home islands, and the B-29 Superfortresses were flattening Japanese cities, flying from island airfields ever closer to Japan, the Emperor became increasingly desperate. As Japan's ability to make war diminished, he approved the use of suicide or "kamikaze"* pilots, many of whom were little more than children who had only barely been trained to fly an airplane. They were placed in bomb- or torpedo-carrying aircraft and then led out in groups of several planes like sheep to the slaughter, following more experienced pilots to concentrations of American warships, where they had been instructed to crash into the ships, aiming primarily for the aircraft carriers.

Fewer than 20% of kamikaze attacks managed to hit an American ship, but they were still able to kill around 7,000 American navy men and damage dozens of ships, at the cost of about 3,800 Japanese pilots. However, the kamikazes were not effective in stopping, or even slowing down, the American juggernaut that was bearing steadily and relentlessly down upon Japan.

Corporal Yukio Araki, a child kamikaze pilot, died in a suicide attack on American ships near Okinawa on 27 May, 1945.

By this time it was patently obvious to everyone including the Japanese themselves that Japan was finished, beaten, yet Japan's delusional military

---

* Kamikaze means "divine wind" and refers to a typhoon that scattered and destroyed a Mongolian invasion fleet that was on its way to attack Japan in AD 1281. In the same way, the suicide pilots were supposed to scatter and destroy the approaching Allied fleet.

leaders refused to give up, and in fact welcomed a fight to the death for not just its military but for all Japanese, as some sort of transcendent sacrifice to demonstrate their spiritual superiority to America and the West. By the spring of 1945, under the bombs of the American B-29s, Japan's six largest cities were in ruins, its industrial base was wrecked, its navy mostly destroyed, and nothing left of its air force but poorly trained pilots and suicide bombers. Low-flying American reconnaissance planes reported seeing Japanese civilians amid the ruins of their cities waving white flags at them.

Nevertheless the Emperor was determined to continue the fight. He approved the conscription and training of all able-bodied Japanese women, children, and elderly to fight the American invaders to the death, using whatever weapons came to hand, even if they were nothing more than sharpened bamboo sticks. In his delusional thinking, perhaps there would even be enough of them, along with the remaining military forces, to stave the Americans off or fight them to a draw. One historian wrote:

> **Hirohito's generals, grimly preparing for the invasion, had not abandoned hope of saving their homeland. . . Allied troops, they boasted, would face the fiercest resistance in history. Over ten thousand kamikaze planes were readied for "Ketsu-Go," Operation Decision. Behind the beaches, enormous connecting underground caves had been stocked with caches of food and thousands of tons of ammunition. Manning the nation's ground defenses were 2,350,000 regular soldiers, 250,000 garrison troops, and 32,000,000 civilian militiamen, a total of 34,600,000, more than the combined armies of the United States, Great Britain, and Nazi Germany. All males aged fifteen to sixty, and all females aged seventeen to forty-five, had been conscripted. Their weapons included ancient bronze cannon, muzzle-loading muskets, bamboo spears, and bows and arrows. Even little children had been trained to strap explosives around their waists, roll under tank treads, and blow themselves up. They were called "Sherman carpets."**
>
> **This was the Japan that the Pentagon had learned to fear and hate—a country of fanatics dedicated to hara-kiri, determined to slay as many invaders as possible as they went down fighting.**[1]

An invasion of Japan would have been a bloodbath of unimaginable proportions for both sides, but that didn't trouble Japan's leaders. The Emperor was perfectly content to have his nation's children blowing themselves up beneath American tanks in his name, or its women charging Allied soldiers with bamboo spears. If anything exemplifies the pure evil of Japan's military culture and its emperor, it is this callous willingness to cast away the lives of the nation's innocents to delay inevitable defeat. Suicidally insane to the last, the Japanese leaders were willing to commit national as well as personal suicide,

Japanese schoolgirls being taught by military instructors to lunge at opponents with bamboo spears. Japanese leaders had no qualms about sending young girls armed with sticks into battle should the Allies invade Japan.

and, despite the few white-flag wavers amid the ruins of their homes and cities, the obedient Japanese people would follow their orders and fight until they were annihilated. As historian M. G. Sheftall put it:

> The entire nation would go down in flames, standing on its feet, with its gene pool intact, its women pure, and its civilization unsullied. It would die unconquered and unbowed, steadfast in its resistance to the white man's juggernaut of world domination and soulless rationalism. Perhaps other non-Anglo-Saxon nations would take up the struggle in the future, and Japan's historical example could inspire other races of color to fight on. It would be a good death.[2]

As always with the Japanese militarists, it was death over surrender, based on the same twisted notion of honor enshrined in their Bushido code that the Americans and their allies had encountered everywhere in the Pacific that they had fought the Japanese. Everyone in Japan should die this "good death," thereby "saving face" and remaining heroically steadfast and "honorable." It would be glorious suicide for all as mandated by the death cult of the divine Emperor. If one reason for Japan's leadership going to war had been to prove their nation's equality to, or superiority over the West, then in that quest it had failed miserably. The cruelty and sadistic brutality of Japan's military forces toward the peoples of the countries that it conquered only mirrored the supreme evil of the military cabal that had taken control of the Japanese nation

49. THE END OF THE WAR

and led it to ruin. On the other side of the world, Hitler's Nazis had done the same thing to Germany, with the same results. In both cases it took the lives of hundreds of thousands of Americans to rid the world of these twin evils.

The end nears; the Jolly Rogers fly their final bombing mission

The strategic island of Okinawa, only 350 miles south of the Japanese island of Kyushu, had been captured in a bloody series of battles by the U. S. Army and Marines between April 1 and June 22, 1945. Both the Marines and the Army had joined forces to capture Okinawa, and the battle therefore represented the convergence of General MacArthur's drive up from Australia with Admiral Nimitz's thrust up the central Pacific. They had now come together on the doorstep of Japan.

The Japanese fought as suicidally as ever for Okinawa and had lost at least 100,000 killed, by actual body count. Kamikaze pilots had made about 2,000 attacks on American shipping during the battle, sinking eleven destroyers and damaging several aircraft carriers and other vessels. American losses on Okinawa were 12,000 dead and 36,000 wounded. This battle was so viciously fought and so costly in lives that it figured strongly in the American decision to use the atomic bombs on Japan, since it was reasoned that the Japanese could be expected to fight every bit as fiercely for their home islands and on a much larger scale.

The goal of the Americans taking Okinawa was, of course, to gain yet another and still more advanced airbase from which to bomb mainland Japan, and from late June of 1945 onward, the American B-29s were busily engaged in doing just that. The five airfields that the Americans established on Okinawa put Japan within range of even General Kenney's B-25 strafer/bombers.

By this time, with the war in Europe ended (VE Day was May 8, 1945), and with all of America's attention now pivoting toward the defeat of Japan, America would no longer find it necessary to fight the Pacific war with one hand tied behind her back. With war supplies now starting to flow exclusively toward the Pacific, the Empire of Japan's time was short. The Jolly Rogers shared in the matériel largesse and soon grew rich in aircraft and crews. Had the war continued, the Jolly Rogers might have swelled to the size of the huge bombardment groups that had flown against Germany. As it turned out, however, the war had less than two months to go after the capture of Okinawa and no more planes or crews would be needed.

On July 13, 1945, the Jolly Rogers flew their 10,000th sortie, and on July 24th, 1945, they flew what would turn out to be their last bombing mission of the war.[3] The target was Kiangwan Airfield near Shanghai, China, which had been sending out kamikaze planes against the U. S. fleet. The mission was flown out of McGuire Field on Mindoro, but staged through Okinawa, 900 miles to the north (see Map 49-1, next page). Forty Jolly Rogers planes, ten

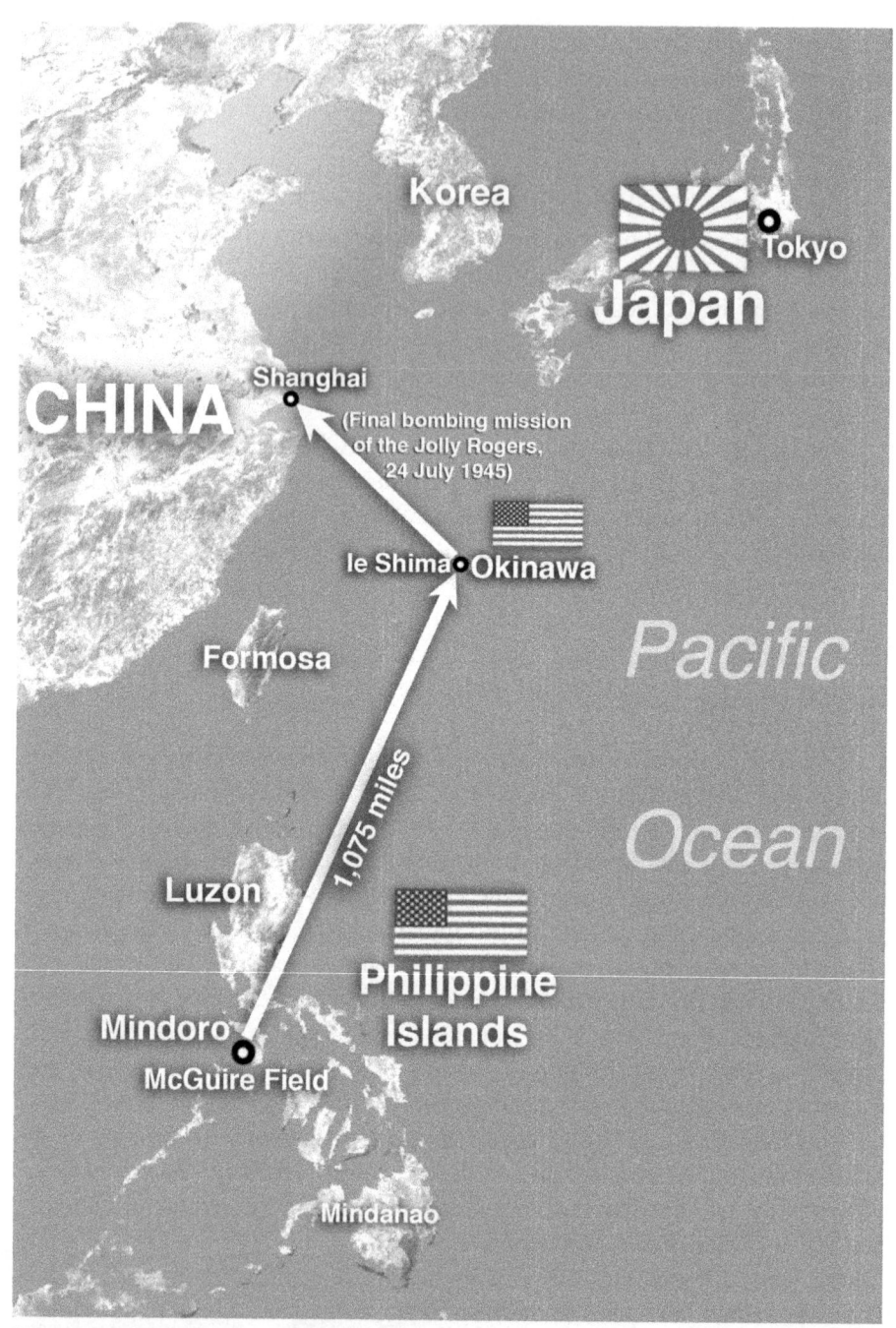

Map 49-1. The final move of the Jolly Rogers in the war was from McGuire Field, on the Philippine Island of Mindoro, to little Ie Shima Island, 1,075 miles closer to Japan and just offshore from Okinawa, at the beginning of August 1945. From there they would be able to support Operation Olympic, the code name for the American ground invasion of Japan. The dropping of the atomic bombs made the invasion unnecessary by ending the war.

from each squadron, arrived over the target to find it covered over by clouds, as so often happened, so the lead bombardier made the drop by radar, and there was no way to observe the results through the undercast. All bombers returned safely to base.[4]

At McGuire Field the men resumed their preparations for moving on to their next base. Word had gone out that they were moving north again, and they wondered how soon they would begin bombing the Japanese home islands. No one knew how soon the war might end, but all expected that an Allied invasion of Japan would be necessary, supported by Jolly Rogers bombers as usual.

Map 49-2. The Jolly Rogers' final move was to Ie Shima (circled), three miles across the water from Okinawa, and they were on Ie Shima when the war ended.

The Jolly Rogers make their final move forward, to Ie Shima

Generals MacArthur and Kenney, along with Admiral Nimitz, now began advancing their chess pieces again, setting up the checkmate of Japan. The eighth and final move of the Jolly Rogers would be another long jump, comparable to the move from Biak Island to the Philippines. This time it would be 1,075 miles from McGuire Field on the Philippine Island of Mindoro to the little island of Ie Shima, two by five miles in size, located three miles off the western shoreline of Okinawa (see Map 49-2, above, and the aerial photo on the next page). The Jolly Rogers would occupy Ie Shima from the 10th of August until the war ended.

The Group by this time consisted of about fifty bombers and around 2,500 men, along with their various kinds of support equipment. As usual with a change of base, the combat crews flew their planes to the new location while the mechanics and everyone else boarded troopships and LSTs to be transported by sea. It would take the seaborne contingent several days to arrive at Ie Shima, and some men were left behind temporarily to dismantle and clean up the old camp. As usual the Army cleaned up after itself so thoroughly as to leave practically nothing behind, even burning the wooden floors of the tents to ashes.

Ernie Pyle's death on Ie Shima

One of the things that the Jolly Rogers found when they arrived on Ie Shima was the grave of the world-famous war correspondent Ernie Pyle, who had been killed during the battle for the island. U. S. troops had landed on Ie Shima on 16 April, 1945, as part of the three-month battle to seize nearby Okinawa. Pyle, a small, thin man with graying hair, 44 years old, was with them as what is today called an "embedded correspondent," covering the Pacific war after accompanying American troops for four years through North Africa, Italy, and France. His hundreds of reports from the front lines, based on interviews with individual soldiers, and stories about their endurance and heroism, had been carried throughout the war in over 200 American newspapers and made him one of the most beloved writers in American history.

The little coral island of Ie Shima (ten miles square) as it appeared to the Jolly Rogers aircrews when they moved there in August 1945.

Collections of Pyle's battlefield reports have been published as books: *Here Is Your War* (1943), *Ernie Pyle In England* (1945), *Brave Men* (1945), and *Last Chapter* (1946). They were best-sellers in their day and are still well worth reading today. Every morning, throughout America, people sitting down to breakfast scanned their newspapers for Ernie Pyle's latest article from the war front.

On Ie Shima Pyle went ashore with the U. S. Army's 77th Division and set about doing what he always did, collecting interviews with soldiers and adding his observations of the battle in progress, which he would then type up on his portable typewriter, sitting in his tent, or if he had no tent, sitting outdoors on anything handy. The reports would then be sent back to his newspaper syndicate in the States.

On the 18th of April [1945], two days after the landing, after chatting with some soldiers (picture at right) and signing their "short snorters" for them, he climbed into a jeep with a colonel from division headquarters and they headed down a dirt road to a command post near the front lines. What they didn't know was that there were Japanese behind the American lines. At a bend in

49. THE END OF THE WAR

the road they suddenly came under Japanese machine-gun fire, so they jumped out of the jeep and took cover in a ditch. After a few minutes, Pyle raised his head a little to take a look around. More shots rang out. The colonel said something to Pyle, but Pyle didn't answer. His body had gone limp. He had caught a bullet in his left temple, just under the rim of his steel helmet, and had died instantly.

A couple of years earlier, when Pyle had been with Allied troops in North Africa, a German Stuka bomber had dived on them, and he'd leapt into another ditch along with a soldier. After the plane flew off, Pyle had said to the man, "That was a close one, wasn't it?" but the soldier didn't answer—he was dead. Now the same thing had happened to Pyle. He was seven thousand miles from his wife and their cottage in Albuquerque, New Mexico (which was just a couple of miles from the home of Sgt. Jaime Baca's family). In some of his last articles he had written about how weary he was of war and how much he was looking forward to going home to his wife. Now he had joined the more than one hundred thousand Americans who would never return to their homes and families from the Pacific war.

Ernie Pyle, America's favorite war correspondent, was killed on Ie Shima before the Jolly Rogers arrived there.

Back in the States, as the news of Ernie Pyle's death spread, fourteen million regular readers of his newspaper column were plunged into sorrow, and this was only six days after the nation had been shocked by the death of President

Ernie Pyle (center) interviews a Marine on Ie Shima Island shortly before he was killed.

Franklin D. Roosevelt at Warm Springs, Georgia, from a cerebral hemorrhage. Pyle was buried in a little cemetery on Ie Shima along with some of the other 172 Americans killed in the six-day battle for the island.* The Americans also had 902 wounded and 46 missing on Ie Shima for a total of 1,120 casualties.

A small monument was raised to honor Pyle, and since it was near their camp many of the men of the Jolly Rogers visited it and had themselves photographed beside it (above). The loss of Ernie Pyle was one of the lowest points of the war for America.

Three members of the Jolly Rogers pose beside the monument to Ernie Pyle on Ie Shima, in August of 1945. The inscription says: "At this spot the 77th Infantry Division lost a buddy, Ernie Pyle, 18 April 1945."

The first thing the Seabees did with the captured island of Ie Shima was, as usual, to improve the Japanese airfields to make them usable for U. S. bombers. After the Jolly Rogers arrived in the first days of August, they settled in and waited to be assigned their first bombing missions from this base. Meanwhile, there were momentous things afoot, of which neither they nor most other Americans knew anything, but would soon find out.

The Atomic Bombs

Faced with the problem of a country that was obviously beaten but refused to surrender in the face of conventional warfare, America, under its new president, Harry Truman, resorted to the new and unconventional: the atomic bombs developed at the secret laboratory of Los Alamos in the mountains of Sgt. Baca's home state, New Mexico, and tested one time in the southern part of the state, a desolate desert area known as White Sands. The hope was that the stunning power of this weapon would have what is nowadays called the "shock and awe" effect on the Japanese leadership, and its sheer irresistibility would provide the Emperor with a way to surrender while "saving face." If the Emperor and his cabal still hoped to fight the Allies to a draw during an invasion of their home islands, it was calculated that using this bomb would demonstrate the futility of that plan. The Emperor's palace

---

*After the war Ernie Pyle's body was exhumed and reburied in the National Memorial Cemetery of the Pacific (the "Punchbowl") in Honolulu, Hawaii.

could easily have been obliterated by one of these bombs, of course, or even by conventional bombing, but it had been declared off-limits as a bombing target. Allied thinking was that the death of their emperor would harden the will of the Japanese people to resist, whereas if Hirohito could be made to surrender, his people would do the same.

First the Americans dropped five million leaflets over Hiroshima warning the populace that an extremely powerful bomb would soon be dropped on the city, capable of wiping it (and them) out, and that they should immediately abandon it. However, no one seemed to take the message seriously. And, as it turned out, the first atomic bomb, dropped on the city of Hiroshima on August 6, 1945, was not convincing enough to Emperor Hirohito and his Supreme Council. The city was flattened and utterly destroyed, but some of the Emperor's advisors assured him that the Americans could not possibly have another one of these super-bombs. It would still require, they told him, an invasion by the Allies and massive American casualties to subdue the Japanese people, blood the Americans may not be willing to shed. The Allies might yet be driven to the bargaining table to negotiate a truce, an armistice such as the one that ended World War One, and that had left German institutions and culture intact.

The second atomic bomb, dropped three days later over Nagasaki, put an end to that notion and provided Japanese leaders with a strong dose of reality. It proved that Americans need not risk their troops in an invasion at all—Japan could be leveled from afar, using as many of these new super-bombs as was necessary. Japan was now looking at total annihilation without any means of resistance whatever. Two Japanese cities had just been obliterated by only two bombs, whereas it had taken hundreds of B-29s dropping thousands of bombs to burn down Tokyo on the night of March 9-10, 1945. In the face of such awesome destructive power, even the fanatical Japanese leadership, or at least most of it, realized that it was time to throw in the towel. Promised "prompt and utter destruction" if he did not capitulate, the Emperor at last accepted the Allied demand of unconditional surrender. The near-extinction of the Japanese people, including their emperor, did not, after all, seem like such a noble and glorious end to the war.

The Japanese surrender

On August 14, Japanese radio stations played a recording made by the Emperor in which he addressed his people directly, something no emperor had never done before. It was the first time they had ever heard his thin, reedy voice, and he was telling them that he was surrendering their country to the Allies. Many Japanese fell prostrate before their radios and wept in veneration of their living god and the news of his and their country's defeat. In what had to be the understatement of the century, the Emperor told his people, in all seriousness, that "the war has not necessarily gone in Japan's favor. . . "

Some of Japan's military diehards refused to go along with the surrender, however, and attempted to storm the royal palace and destroy the recording before it could be played out over the airwaves. The coup failed, and the rebels were driven off by the palace guard. Other fanatics vowed to sabotage the surrender proceedings and continue to fight. Some high-ranking Japanese officers committed ritual suicide in protest.

Fighting ended on August 15, 1945, and preparations for the formal surrender began with an exchange of messages between the Japanese government and General MacArthur. Today the world remembers the elaborate surrender ceremony aboard the *USS Missouri* on Sept. 2, in Tokyo Harbor, but little known is that the Japanese actually surrendered before that, on August 19, at MacArthur's headquarters in Manila. MacArthur sent a radio message to Japanese officials in Tokyo stating that he wanted a delegation sent to him in Manila to sign preliminary surrender documents and to plan a more formal ceremony of surrender later, in the presence of all the Allies, to be held aboard an American warship in Tokyo Bay. He told them to send the delegation from Tokyo to Ie Shima in two Mitsubishi G4M "Betty" bombers painted white with green Swedish crosses on their wings and fuselages (reflecting the fact that messages between the Japanese and American governments regarding Japan's surrender had been passing through the Swedish embassy).[5] At Ie Shima the Japanese emissaries would be transferred to an American C-54 four-engine transport plane and flown down to Manila.

The two Betty bombers were duly painted, although someone later noted that they weren't very good paint jobs, done sloppily by hand with paintbrushes, and the red "meatball" insignias were bleeding through the white paint. The pilots of the two Bettys were instructed to rendezvous with American aircraft shortly after leaving the southern coast of Japan, off Kyushu, and the American planes would then lead them to Ie Shima. Upon sighting the American escort planes, the Japanese were to identify themselves over the radio as "Bataan 1" and "Bataan 2," and indicate that they were ready to follow their American guides. The Japanese in Tokyo protested the choice of the code word and wanted to substitute something else, but MacArthur would have none of it. He wanted to rub their noses in his return to the Philippines. "You will say 'Bataan,'" he ordered.

The two Betty bombers with their peace envoys aboard set out for Ie Shima on August 19, 1945. Rumors had circulated that there were renegade Japanese pilots opposed to the surrender who would attempt to intercept and shoot down the two Bettys, so the Japanese planes did not start out on a direct line toward Ie Shima, which would have been southwest, but instead flew northeast to throw off any pursuit. As they flew out over the water, a formation of fighter planes came into view above them, and one of the Japanese delegates commented that this looked like the end for them—they were about to be shot down. However,

49. THE END OF THE WAR 745

as the fighters neared, it became obvious that they were American P-38s, not Zeros, and they were merely taking up escort positions. They had been sent out to provide top cover for the Japanese planes and their B-25 guides.

Since the sky is a big place, and it's easy to miss a rendezvous over open water, three pairs of American B-25 bombers had been sent out, to bracket the expected course of the Japanese planes so that at least one group would be sure to intercept and guide them in. One of these groups found the Bettys shortly after the P-38s did, and after exchanging the code word "Bataan," the Japanese

The two white-painted Japanese Bettys photographed from one of the escorting American B-25s. With a formation of P-38 fighters forming a protective umbrella above them, and a B-17 rescue plane following along behind with a droppable lifeboat slung under its belly, the entire formation headed for Ie Shima where a C-54 Skymaster was waiting to take the Japanese delegation further south to MacArthur's headquarters in Manila.

The B-25 strafer/bombers leading the Japanese planes to Ie Shima had the angry, scowling goblin faces of the 345th Bomb Group, the Air Apaches, painted on their noses, a fitting representation of the fury that Americans had felt toward the Japanese from their Pearl Harbor attack onward through three years and eight months of vicious and bloody warfare.

planes fell in behind the B-25s and the whole formation took up a course for Ie Shima, about 350 miles away.

The lead B-25 was piloted by Major J. C. McClure, and after a few minutes McClure noticed that the two Japanese planes had tucked themselves in snugly beneath his wings. The Japanese pilots had decided that the best insurance against being shot at, either by rogue Japanese planes from above or by American warships below, was to stick tight to their escort. The formation was also joined by a B-17 that had been modified for rescue work, with a boat attached to its underside that could be dropped by parachute to men in the water.

Thus, for nearly four hours, the two Japanese surrender planes were led southwest by a pair of General Kenney's strafer/bombers with angry goblin faces painted on their noses, seeming to symbolize American fury at being forced into nearly four years of a war that had killed over a hundred thousand Americans. The formation arrived over Ie Shima this way, and all the planes landed in sequence on the dazzling white crushed-coral runway that was lined on both sides with thousands of American servicemen, including members of the Jolly Rogers, who had come out to watch the proceedings.

The Jolly Rogers bombers were parked along the sides of the runway with their tails pointed toward it, so that the Japanese surrender planes, fittingly, arrived under the baleful gaze of the Jolly Rogers skulls and crossed bombs emblems. There were nine men aboard each Betty, six crewmen and three envoys, making nineteen Japanese in total, with the delegation led by Lt. Gen.

Thousands of American servicemen watch one of the two Japanese surrender bombers park on the airfield at Ie Shima, 18 August 1945. It's easy to see why Japanese pilots nicknamed this airplane "the Cigar." Not only was it shaped like one, but it lit up (caught fire) easily in combat.

49. THE END OF THE WAR

Torasirou Kawabe, the Vice Chief of the Japanese Army General Staff. After their planes had been directed to a parking place and come to a stop, the Japanese disembarked and were transferred from their rather shabby looking bombers to a huge, gleaming silver C-54 Skymaster four-engine transport plane that took them 900 miles farther south to Clark Field on Luzon.

From Clark Field they were driven to General MacArthur's headquarters in Manila where Gen. Kawabe signed the surrender papers, and the plans for the formal surrender ceremony in Tokyo Bay were provided to him. While the Japanese delegation was in Manila, back on Ie Shima a crowd of Americans including some members of the 90th Bomb Group, the Jolly Rogers, climbed up on one of the Japanese bombers and had their pictures taken standing on it (p. 749 below). It had taken the deaths of 820 members of the Jolly Rogers over a period of three years to bring them to this time and place, from Iron Range to Ie Shima.

The next day the Japanese were flown back to Ie Shima where they reboarded their own bombers and flew back to Tokyo with their instructions. The formal surrender ceremony, which was attended by representatives of all the Allied powers, and was photographed for the world, was held aboard the battleship *USS Missouri* in Tokyo Bay on Sunday, September 2, 1945, four weeks after the atomic bombings.

General Johnathan M. Wainwright, who had surrendered the American forces in the Philippines to the Japanese in 1942, and General Arthur E.

In this still frame from an Army newsreel movie can be seen some of the men who lined the runways on Ie Shima to watch the arrival of the Japanese surrender delegation. Parked with their tails toward the runway were the bombers of the Jolly Rogers, with their crews standing nearby. The Japanese thus stepped down from their planes under the baleful glare of the Jolly Rogers' grinning skulls. The symbolism was apt.

Percival, who had surrendered the British forces at Singapore in the same year, had both been liberated from a Japanese prison camp in Manchuria, and although they were thin and weak from Japanese mistreatment, General MacArthur made sure that they were standing nearby as the Japanese signed the documents of surrender.

Above the surrender ceremony, framed on a bulkhead wall, MacArthur displayed the same 31-star American flag that Commodore Matthew Perry had flown on his warship when he had sailed into Tokyo Bay in 1853, to open Japan up to the world (and in an amazing coincidence, MacArthur was related to Matthew Perry). After 92 years and millions of deaths from Japanese aggression, the flag had returned to Japan on another American warship.

In the time since Perry's visit, airplanes had been invented, and in the sky above the surrender ceremony on the *USS Missouri*, 1,200 American warplanes of all types, in V-shaped formations symbolizing victory, thundered past at low altitude in wave after wave, in the mightiest display of airpower ever witnessed. It was a fitting conclusion to a catastrophic war that had begun with an attack on America by Japanese bombers at Pearl Harbor, and was ended by American bombers delivering terrible retribution in the form of the atomic bombs dropped on Japan. From start to finish, airpower had played the major role.

Lt. General Torasirou Kawabe, the Japanese Emperor's representative, scowling in the foreground, is clearly not happy being where he is or doing what he's doing, which is heading down to Manila to meet General MacArthur and sign the preliminary surrender papers. He and the rest of the Japanese delegation are about to board the four-engine C-54 Skymaster whose wing towers above their heads.

49. THE END OF THE WAR

While the Japanese surrender delegation was in Manila meeting with MacArthur, Americans back up at Ie Shima, including members of the Jolly Rogers, took the opportunity to pose for photographs on top of one of the two Betty surrender bombers.

September 2, 1945: General Douglas MacArthur, in front of the microphone at left, watches a Japanese diplomat sign the surrender documents aboard the USS Missouri in Tokyo Bay. The Pacific war had lasted three years, eight months, and 26 days, but it was finally over.

Chapter Fifty

THE JOLLY ROGERS DISBAND

When the men of the Jolly Rogers, along with all other Americans, heard of the dropping of the first atomic bomb on August 6, 1945, and the fact that it had leveled a large Japanese city, they could scarcely believe the power of such a weapon. The largest bombs carried and dropped by the 90th throughout the war were 2,000-pounders, very powerful bombs as conventional weapons went, but it still took many of them to "Gloucesterize" a target. This was a single bomb, and it had destroyed a city!

On August 9, when the Japanese government did not respond to the dropping of the first bomb, a second one devastated the city of Nagasaki. The next day the Japanese government finally capitulated, and with that news the Jolly Rogers camp became a scene of wild rejoicing.

That day, and on into the evening, guns of all types were fired into the air, hoarded bottles of liquor were broken out and passed around, and a night fireworks display was put on by the local antiaircraft batteries. Some of the more prudent men remained in their quarters and celebrated more quietly, not caring to be out and about among inebriated men discharging firearms. Fortunately, there were no injuries.

The war was over, and there would be no more bombs dropped by the Jolly Rogers. However for the rest of the month there would still be routine weather reporting missions and reconnaissance flights to fly in the area.

The Jolly Rogers get one flight over Japan

One recon flight in particular generated a great deal of interest around the Jolly Rogers camp, and that was an armed reconnaissance over mainland Japan scheduled for August 25. This would be the Jolly Rogers' only mission flown over Japan.

It would be an armed reconnaissance because the Japanese had not yet formally surrendered (the ceremony would be held eight days later on September 2), and for all anyone knew, considering the fanaticism for which the Japanese military was so well known, the American bombers might still be fired upon by flak guns. Accordingly, each of the eighteen bombers, chosen from three of the four Group's squadrons (only the 400th Squadron's planes didn't participate) carried three 500-pound bombs, but the crews were warned

50. THE JOLLY ROGERS DISBAND 751

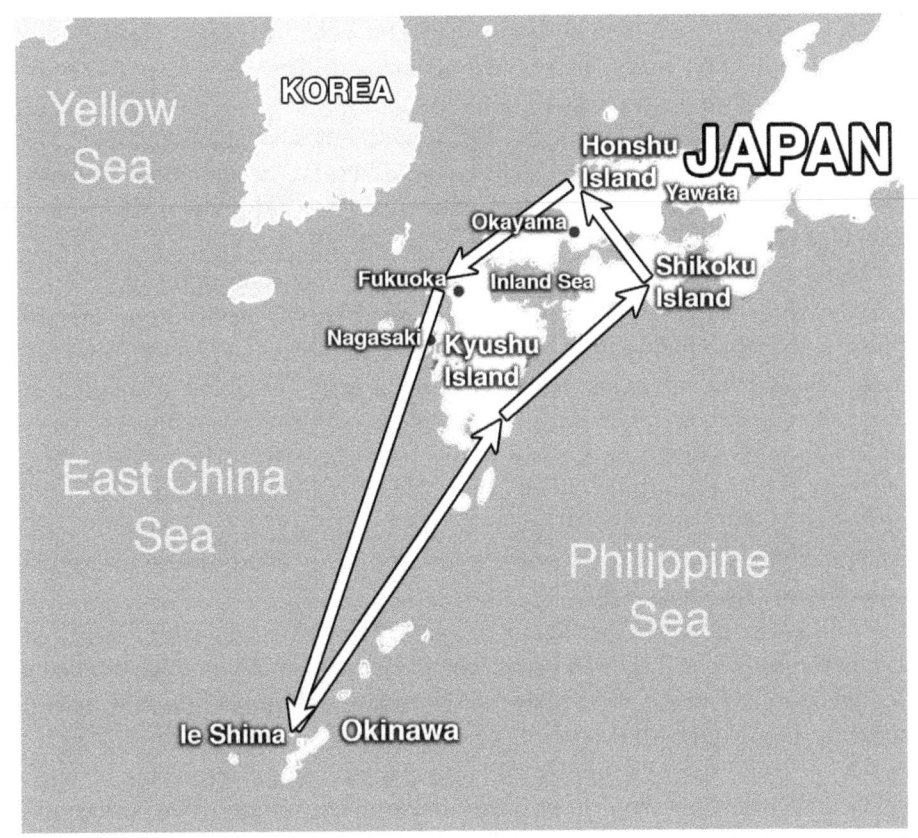

Map 50-1. The final mission flown by the Jolly Rogers (not a strike but an armed reconnaissance) on August 25, 1945. This was the 90th Bomb Group's one and only flight over mainland Japan. The crewmen viewed the awesome destruction of American bombing, including the city of Nagasaki, which had been flatteneed by an atomic bomb.

not to drop them unless they were shot at, and even then only if the guns doing the shooting were in an area where it was unlikely that any civilians would be harmed.

The airmen were aware that, with the formal end of the war only a week away, this might be their one and only chance to get a look at mainland Japan, toward which the Group had been slogging across the Pacific ever since they first set up operations at Iron Range in northern Australia in November of 1942. Therefore, in addition to the flight crews, many ground crewmen, mechanics, and administrative staff also crammed into the planes as sightseers. Col. Ellis Brown, the Group Commander, led the mission.

The planes took off from Ie Shima, assembled above the little island, and then headed northeast for Japan in a loose formation. Col. Brown led them along the southeast coasts of the Japanese islands of Kyushu and Shikoku (map, previous page), then northwest across the Inland Sea, where they saw Japanese warships riding peacefully at anchor. Then they crossed to the northwest side of Honshu and continued along the west coast of Kyushu, passing over numerous towns and cities, including Okayama, Fukuoka, and Yawata. Men crowded at the waist gun windows, the cockpit side windows, took turns in the nose and tail turrets, and looked down from anywhere else in the planes that allowed them a view of Japan's landscape.

Many of the towns and cities they saw below them were completely burned out, showing the effectiveness of the B-29 raids over the previous nine months (the first B-29 raid had been on Nov. 24, 1944). There were no Japanese aircraft in the air, and the only ones they saw on the ground were lined up motionless along the sides of the airfields. They spotted prisoner-of-war camps, or more accurately slave labor camps, recognizable by the large white letters painted on the roofs of the buildings to identify them for American cargo planes that were dropping food, clothing, medicine, and other supplies to the prisoners until American troops could reach them (most prisoners had been on starvation rations under the Japanese).*

Nothing had prepared the men for the sight of the devastated city of Nagasaki as it came into view. This was what General Kenney would truly have called a "Gloucesterized" city. Only a few of the strongest masonry buildings were still standing, though gutted; everything else was blackened and flattened for as far as the eye could see. One strange thing, to men accustomed to seeing bombed landscapes, was the complete lack of bomb craters, since all this destruction had been the result of a single bomb, and a bomb that had not even reached the ground before exploding. It was a shocking scene and a sobering one, and it gave the men food for thought as the bombers turned back for Ie Shima, and after they got back to their base. Warfare was never going to be the same with bombs like that available to warring nations, and there was a real possibility that humanity itself could be eradicated in future wars.†

The Jolly Rogers' final mission, flown over Japan on August 25, 1945, was the culmination of all the efforts of the 90th Bomb Group since the days of its inception in the spring of 1942, after the Japanese had bombed Pearl Harbor. It had been two years, nine months, and ten days since the Group's first mission to bomb Rabaul on November 15, 1942, and since that time the men of the Group had fought their way from Iron Range on the northern tip of Australia up across the back of the New Guinea "buzzard" to Biak Island, thence

---

* The Japanese had been warned that if any harm came to Allied prisoners in these camps the perpetrators would be harshly dealt with. In most cases the Japanese who ran the camps fled into hiding and left the prisoners in charge.

† Especially true since the bombs that obliterated Hiroshima and Nagasaki were quite small ones compared to current atomic bombs.

50. THE JOLLY ROGERS DISBAND

up into the Philippines, and finally all the way to Japan itself, arriving there along with all the other American Pacific forces as victors over a supremely evil enemy. They had finally flown over a defeated and subdued Japan. With the surrender ceremony in Tokyo Bay on Sept. 2, 1945, their job was done, and the process of disbanding their Group and going home began. V Bomber Command directed that the 90th Bombardment Group, the Jolly Rogers, be deactivated by November 1, 1945.[1]

But the Group's work was not yet quite finished. The flight crews took up one final and most satisfying task: ferrying men rescued from the prison camps in Japan back to Manila on the first leg of their return home to the States.

The Jolly Rogers transport former American P. O. W.s

As soon as American ground troops landed on mainland Japan, they dashed inland to the Japanese prison camps and liberated the Allied captives, providing them with food, clothing, and medical attention. The men were then airlifted down to Okinawa, from where they were flown to Manila for more extensive hospitalization if needed, and all were processed to go home. Since there were not enough regular transport planes available to get all the former prisoners—some 32,000 of them from around 160 prison (slave-labor) camps—from Okinawa down to Manila in short order, all available Jolly Rogers bombers were pressed into service as transport planes.

With their guns and upper turrets removed, and with makeshift wooden benches installed in their bomb bays, Jolly Rogers aircraft made 138 flights between Okinawa and Manila transporting Americans who had been prisoners of the Japanese. The crewmen reported that there was nothing so gratifying as welcoming back Americans who had been abused for years in Japanese concentration camps, whom they were now sending on the first leg of their joyous journey back home to their families.

Of the Jolly Rogers themselves who had been taken prisoner by the Japanese, only six survived the war. Four of them were members of the crew of Lt. James McMurria, who had been shipped to Japan from Rabaul (Chapter 18), the fifth was James McMurria himself, still held at Rabaul until September 7, 1945, when the Japanese there surrendered, and the sixth was Lt. Michael C. Sherdon, from a crew shot down over Takao, Formosa. Other members of Sherdon's crew had survived the crash, but, as usual, they had been murdered by the Japanese after they parachuted to the ground. Why Sherdon was spared is unknown, and he was too traumatized by his treatment at the hands of the Japanese to even talk about it.

Jolly Rogers records discarded

On August 26, as part of the disbanding of the Jolly Rogers, through someone's shortsighted and foolish orders a tremendous collection of photographs, mission reports, and other records of the Group that had accumulated throughout the war, records that modern historians would give much to have today, were all disposed of—destroyed. Photographs of targets, photomosaics of target areas, maps, intelligence reports, records of mission results, all were simply piled up on the ground and burned, not being considered worth the trouble of shipping back to the States. We are fortunate that the Group's Headquarters Intelligence Section on Ie Shima, which carried out this work, did not have all Jolly Rogers photographs or reports in its possession, or this book and others like it would have precious few illustrations, and details of many missions covered in this book would not have been available. Nevertheless, most regrettably, a large amount of historical information was deliberately discarded and lost on Ie Shima.[2]

29 Jolly Rogers bombers return to the States

During September, V Bomber Command came up with something it called the Sunset Project, a plan to let the bomber crews fly twenty-nine Jolly Rogers planes back to the States. Besides the flight crews, each of the planes would carry three passengers who were also members of the Group. The route home for these bombers was from Okinawa to Guam, thence to Kwajalein, Hawaii, and finally Sacramento, California.

The bombers set off from Ie Shima on October 17. A new system of radio navigation called Loran (for **L**ong **R**ange **A**id to **N**avigation) had just come into use, employing strategically placed radio transmitters all across the Pacific sending out long-range signals that were picked up by new receivers in the bombers. The navigators marveled at the ease of navigating with this new system, which told them exactly where they were at all times, and they wished they'd had something like it during the war—it could have saved a great many lives. Loran was a sign of things to come in aviation, a forerunner of today's GPS navigation systems.

All twenty-nine B-24s made it safely to California, where the crews parked them at the Sacramento Air Depot, climbed out of them for the last time, carrying their travel bags, and went their separate ways home.* Back in September of 1942, three years before, the original forty-eight bombers of the 90th Bomb Group had left from here headed to Hawaii on the first leg of their journey to Australia to enter the war. Twenty-nine returned in September of 1945 to complete the circle. From Sacramento, ferry crews flew the bombers to the storage yard at Kingman, Arizona, where they were parked in long lines, wingtip-to-wingtip, waiting to be cut up and melted down for scrap metal, still wearing their nose art featuring mostly pretty girls, and with scores of little

---

*A wonderful movie about men returning from the war and taking up their civilian lives again is *The Best Years of Our Lives*, Sam Goldwin Productions, 1946.

50. THE JOLLY ROGERS DISBAND

The Jolly Rogers bomber "Form 1-A" in flight. This plane racked up 161 combat missions, more than any bomber in the entire Air Corps. It was then flown back to the U. S. and scrapped.

symbols painted below their cockpit windows—rows of bombs recording their number of missions flown, and silhouettes of planes and ships counting enemy fighter planes shot down and Japanese ships sunk. It was all history now.

Only one of the Jolly Rogers bombers failed to reach Kingman from Sacramento, and that was one named "Form 1-A" (pictures above and right). This bomber held the all-time record for number of bombing missions flown in the entire Army Air Corps—161, more in fact than any bomber in any country's air force. The plane made an emergency landing in a pasture near Long Beach, California, with mechanical trouble. Historians and aviation buffs today can only dream about what it would be like to have this historic old warhorse in a museum somewhere, such as the National Air and Space Museum in Washington, D. C., exhibited among other history-making aircraft. But alas, "Form

Nose art on the bomber "Form 1-A." In selective service (draft board) jargon 1-A meant "Fit for duty." The artist is unknown.

1-A" was disassembled where she sat and the pieces trucked away for scrap. America was sick of war, and these were warplanes, worn-out and obsolete, and most Americans now only wanted to forget the war, mourn the dead, and try to return to normal life after the long national nightmare that had begun with the bombing of Pearl Harbor.

Meanwhile, back on Ie Shima, letters and packages for members of the Jolly Rogers were still pouring in from their families back in the States, for men who were no longer there because they were on their way home. At the last, only a cleanup crew remained on the little island. The mail piled up until it ultimately filled several buildings. Rather than try to redirect it all back to the men to whom it was addressed, it was decided to just bulldoze it all into the sea, along with vehicles, buildings, tents, equipment, and everything else belonging to the Group (evidently on the theory that if it was underwater, and out of sight, it no longer existed).

Anything deemed worth keeping after the cleanup was loaded into an LST and taken away. Finally, the Americans left Ie Shima, and all vestiges of the Jolly Rogers camp disappeared. Today, only the airport runways are still there, two of them still in use. The 90th Bomb Group was removed from

One of the smelters at the Kingman, Arizona aircraft storage and scrapyard. Here the Jolly Rogers bombers that were flown back to the States were melted down into aluminum ingots like those stacked in the foreground (each B-24 contained 15 tons of aluminum). In June of 1946 there were 5, 553 aircraft stored at Kingman, and by the end of 1948 all of them had been melted down. Of the more than 18,000 Liberators built during the war, just fifteen survive today, and only two are still flying.[3]

50. THE JOLLY ROGERS DISBAND 757

active duty on the Air Corps books. On January 27, 1946, the Jolly Rogers officially ceased to exist.

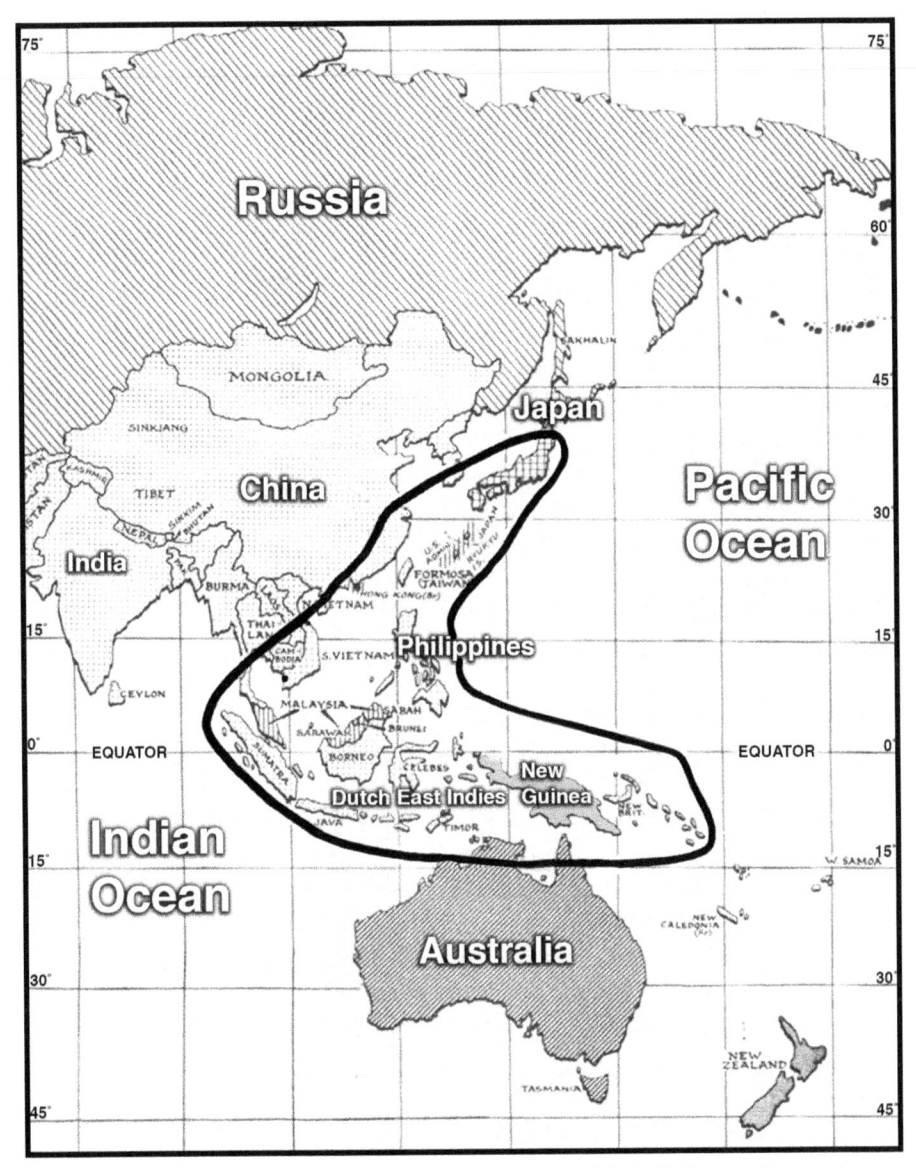

The black line on this map encloses the area of operation of the Jolly Rogers during the war.

Epilogue

AFTER THE WAR

Jaime Baca returned home to New Mexico after the war and used his GI Bill education benefits to earn a teaching degree at a Colorado college, then became a highschool history teacher in New Mexico. He taught history for thirty years, and never married. For years after the war he suffered recurring bouts of the malaria he contracted in New Guinea. After retiring from schoolteaching Baca became a deacon in the Catholic Church and today lives in an assisted living home in Rio Rancho, New Mexico.

Deacon Jaime Baca at age 95.

James Horner accumulated over 500 hours of combat flying during 48 combat missions before returning to the States. He estimates that he and his crew flew 100,000 miles during their nine months of combat flying (mid-May of 1944 to mid-February of 1945), about 75% of it in combat and the rest in search-and-rescue and other non-combat missions. He was awarded the Air Medal with four oak leaf clusters, as well as the Philippine Liberation Medal with star. He returned to Detroit where he became a materials manager for the Ford Motor Company. After 36 years with Ford he retired to Florida, where he lives today. He has two daughters and a son.

James Horner at age 96.

Tom Theobald returned from the war to his young wife and baby daughter in Oelwein, Iowa and resumed his job at the city laundry. As the years passed his family grew to two girls and three boys. He continued working in the laundry plant for 45 years, and by the time he retired he was its general manager. Today Theobald lives in a retirement home in Oelwein.

Allan Cooper, the former Disney cartoonist, pursued his dream of becoming a serious artist, a painter in oils, after the war and used his GI Bill benefits to travel

Tom Theobald at age 96.

to France to study painting. However, Cooper soon realized that his beautiful, realistic art was no longer in demand by a corrupted art world. Cooper, like other gifted artists of the day, was unfortunate enough to live at a time when artwork of beauty and genius was disregarded in favor of so-called "modern art," a term covering anything from random splatters of paint on canvas (Jackson Pollock) to oversized reproductions of soup can labels (Andy Warhol). The result was that despite his phenomenal skill and talent Cooper could not support himself with his art, and he gave it up and returned to California.

For reasons unknown, Cooper did not return to the Disney studios as a cartoonist, possibly because the pay was still low and the working conditions poor. Married and with a growing family to support, Cooper took a well-paying job as a designer of neon signs for commercial businesses, a job which still employed his artistic skills, but in a different way. He never again painted or drew cartoons, and the world is the poorer for it. He also showed no further interest in flying after the war. Cooper died of prostate cancer in 1981 at the age of 64. He raised a son and two daughters.

Arthur H. Rogers returned to the States in December of 1943 and was assigned for a short time to the Elgin Field Proving Ground in Florida where he was involved in evaluating a new General Electric radar-directed bombsight. Then he was given command of the Experimental Station at Pinecastle Air Force Base, also in Florida, where captured German V-1 and V-2 rockets were studied, and where the first jet fighter plane, the Lockheed P-80, was tested and flown.* By that time, a year after the war had ended, Rogers' health had deteriorated from blood diseases that he had contracted in the

---
*Maj. Dick Bong died in a crash while test-piloting a P-80 in California on Aug. 6, 1945. Bong, 24 years old, was America's highest-scoring WWII ace, having downed 40 Japanese planes.

Above left: Dec., 1943: Col. Arthur H. Rogers (at left) shakes hands with Col. Harry Bullis as he transfers command of the Jolly Rogers to Bullis at Port Moresby just before returning to the States. At right, 36 years later the two men, both retired, met again at a Jolly Rogers reunion in 1979 at Colorado Springs, Colorado (Rogers is on the right). They were standing beside a restored B-24 flown to Colorado Springs for the occasion. (Photo by John S. Alcorn).

Pacific, and he entered a hospital at Coral Gables, Florida where he remained hospitalized for months. The maladies did not respond to treatment, and in March of 1947 he was given a medical discharge from the Army, ending his promising military career.

In the early 1950s Rogers and his wife Elsie took up ranching in Florida on 3,000 acres of land reclaimed from the Everglades. There they raised three sons.[1] In his early 70s Rogers was diagnosed with incurable lung cancer. On November 10, 1983, eight months before his death, Rogers attended a Jolly Rogers reunion in Cheyenne, Wyoming and saw many of his comrades whom he hadn't seen since the war. Before he died on July 12, 1984, at age 72, Rogers left a final message for his men: "To the Jolly Rogers: I have been assigned the longest and greatest reconnaissance mission that has ever been given to the organization. You will also have to make it someday, and I will be waiting for each and every one of you on the other side of the bridge."

Rogers' grave is in Arlington National Cemetery.

James McMurria was rescued from the prison camp at Rabaul on September 7, 1945. After Japan's emperor had announced his surrender on August 14, the Japanese troops on Rabaul realized that they were going to have to submit to the victorious Allies. McMurria and six other prisoners, the only men left alive of the original 120 military captives, were not aware that the war had ended when, on the same day as the emperor's radio announcement, they were released from their prison cell and given medical attention and decent food and clothing. Having endured years of brutal treatment and deprivation by their captors, they were astonished and mystified by these actions.

The truth was that their Japanese overlords, who had never believed that Japan could lose the war, now feared the punishment they might face if their seven prisoners were found in the wretched, starving condition in which they had been kept. They had decided to clean them up, feed them, and make them look as presentable as possible to the Allies who would arrive at Rabaul to accept their surrender. They also feared answering for their war crimes and had begun covering up the evidence of their many massacres of white civilians and prisoners of war, destroying all prisoner records and inventing cover stories for having directly murdered or otherwise caused the deaths of all but the seven men still alive in their custody. Their main claim was that all their other prisoners had been killed by Allied bombing.

When Australian ships arrived in Rabaul's harbor to accept the Japanese surrender and rescue the Allied prisoners, McMurria and the six other survivors were struck by what seemed to them to be the "huge" physical size of the Australians. He wrote in his book *Fight for Survival*:

> **In unison we exclaimed, "My god, they're a bunch of giants!" That impression is indelibly etched in my mind. After living with the Japanese for so long we were appalled at the physical difference in the two races. The Aussie sailors looked enormous by comparison.**[2]

McMurria had been so long in association with the barbaric minions of the Emperor that he had forgotten how small they really were.

James McMurria had somehow managed to survive over thirty months of Japanese captivity. During all that time, back in America, his family and his fiancé Mary Francis Smith had had no idea whether he was alive or dead, and knew only that he had been declared missing in January of 1943. They were overjoyed when they received a telegram from the Army in September of 1945 telling them that James had been discovered alive, though severely malnourished, in a Japanese prison camp on Rabaul.

McMurria and the six other prisoners were flown back to the States where James slowly regained his health. He married Mary Francis and in the years that followed they raised four children. He took up a career as an accountant and banker in Greenville, South Carolina. McMurria recounted his experiences as a prisoner of war at Rabaul in *Fight for Survival: An American Bomber Pilot's 1,000 Days As a P.O.W. of the Japanese*, published in 1991. After 57 years of marriage to Mary Francis, McMurria died in 2003 at the age of 85.

General Douglas MacArthur was appointed Supreme Allied Commander at the end of the war and remained in Japan as the commander of the occupation forces. MacArthur was given authority to remodel the Japanese government and redirect the considerable energies of the Japanese people toward peaceful pursuits. He accomplished this with a series of decrees: the Directive for the Disestablishment of State Shinto (1945), The Imperial Rescript Renouncing [the Emperor's] Divinity (1946) and the Post-War Constitution (1947), which gave the Japanese a Western-style republic: a parliamentary system with the emperor as its ceremonial head (a so-called "constitutional monarchy").

At the outbreak of the Korean War in June of 1950 General MacArthur once again assumed command of U. S. forces, and after initial setbacks he outflanked and drove the North Korean invaders back, but ended up being sacked by President Truman for acting independently of his orders. On April 19, 1951, MacArthur made his famous farewell speech before Congress, which ended with a phrase from an old military ballad: "Old soldiers never die, they just fade away." MacArthur died of liver disease at age 84 on April 5, 1964, and he and his wife's remains are interred in the Douglas MacArthur Memorial at Norfolk, Virginia.

Gen. Douglas MacArthur and Emperor Hirohito at Allied Headquarters in Tokyo on September 27, 1945. Japanese who saw this photo in newspapers were shocked at the emperor's small stature, since the Japanese press had previously only photographed him from angles that made him look tall and imposing.

General George Kenney after the war became the first commander of the newly-formed Strategic Air Command in 1946, then the commander of the Air Force's Air University until his retirement to Florida in 1951. He wrote three books: *General Kenney Reports* (1949), *The Saga of Pappy Gunn* (1959), and *Dick Bong, Ace of Aces* (1960). He died in 1977 at the age of 88 and is buried in Arlington National Cemetery.

Emperor Hirohito, although a war criminal, was not prosecuted and was retained as a figurehead of the Japanese government and a symbol of Japanese social continuity, although his cabal of military ministers were tried and imprisoned or executed (those who had not committed suicide) for their crimes against humanity. His title was changed from Imperial Sovereign to Constitutional Monarch after General MacArthur outlawed emperor worship. MacArthur issued his decrees on the changes in Japanese society through Hirohito in order to make them more acceptable to the Japanese people. Hirohito functioned as a government figurehead for the rest of his life and died on January 7, 1989 at age 87.

Paul I. "Pappy" Gunn returned to the Philippines after recovering from his war wound where he resumed operating his aviation company, Philippine Airlines. He died in a crash on October 11, 1957 while maneuvering a twin-engine aircraft at treetop level over the jungle trying to avoid a tropical storm. He was 57 years old. His family buried him in the Barrancas National Cemetery in Pensacola, Florida.

Rev. James Benson of the Anglican Church, after being freed from Japanese custody at Rabaul in 1945, returned to his mission station at Gona village, near Buna, New Guinea, on August 23, 1946, and was welcomed with great joy by the villagers. He resumed his missionary activities, rebuilt his church and school buildings, filled in bomb craters, and found and buried in the churchyard numerous skeletons of soldiers killed in the Battle of Buna-Gona in January of 1943. Near the end of his life, in the mid-1950s, he was recalled to England to become a pastor at St. Paul's Church in Knightsbridge, where he died in 1956. His superior, the Rev. William Wand, wrote that Benson was "supremely happy" at the time of his death.

Bob Hope continued making comedy movies and entertaining American troops with his USO shows in succeeding wars. He entertained the younger brothers of the WWII soldiers during the Korean War, their sons during the Vietnam War, and their grandsons in the Persian Gulf War. He died in California in 2003 at the age of 100.

Charles Lindbergh had his military commission restored by President Dwight Eisenhower and in 1954 was promoted to the rank of Brigadier General in the Air Force Reserves. His book, *The Spirit of St. Louis*, describing his solo transatlantic flight from New York to Paris in 1927, was awarded a Pulitzer Prize in 1954. Lindbergh never really settled down after the war and traveled almost continually in support of conservation causes, making numerous trips to wildlife preserves around the world promoting the World Wildlife Fund and the International Union for Conservation of Nature and Natural Resources. He campaigned for the preservation of dozens of endangered species. He also secretly visited his three mistresses in Germany and fathered seven children with them. He and his wife Anne built a home on the Hawaiian island of Maui where he spent the last years of his life, and where he died of lymphoma on August 26, 1974, at the age of 72. His grave is on Maui.

The Jolly Rogers' aircraft

The production of B-24 Liberator bombers was halted in April of 1945, even before the war had ended, as the larger and better-performing B-29 Superfortresses took precedence. By that time over 18,000 B-24s had been built, more than any other military aircraft ever made.

When the Americans left the Pacific at the end of the war they simply abandoned most of their aircraft on the airfields where they sat. A few bombers were flown home, as convenient transportation, but at Biak Island, Nadzab, and Port Moresby, New Guinea thousands of American planes of all types were just left sitting where they were parked when the war ended. Many of the Jolly Rogers bombers were among them. Each B-24 had cost today's equivalent of millions of dollars to build, but they were warplanes, obsolete ones at that, and after the war ended were only considered good for scrap metal. The B-24s, along with medium bombers, fighters, transport, and liaison planes, were bulldozed into piles, ready to be disposed of.

These aircraft graveyards, sitting around the former Air Corps airfields in the Pacific, were eventually bought by Australian and Dutch salvagers who chopped the planes into pieces small enough to fit into portable smelters and melted them into lumps of marketable metal. Stockpiles of gasoline and oil on the former Pacific airfields were also sold to civilian dealers.

In the U. S., many of the now-obsolete WWII aircraft were flown to a desert graveyard near Kingman, Arizona where they too were eventually chopped up and melted down. The last B-24s produced by some of the factories were flown directly from the assembly lines to the scrapyards. Mr. Baca remembers reading a newspaper article in the 1960s in which B-24s were being offered for sale to the public for a few hundred dollars each from the Kingman, Arizona storage facility, to be flown away, or disassembled and trucked away, by the buyer, and he thought at the time that it might be interesting to own one. The problem was where to keep a 19-ton airplane with a 110-foot wingspan, so he quickly shelved that daydream. Of course, anyone who had been able to buy and store a B-24 would now own a rare, historic aircraft worth millions of dollars.

The Southwest Pacific today

Many of the Southwest Pacific island battlefields remain today just as they were left when the Americans moved on toward Japan. New Guinea,

EPILOGUE 765

The end of the line for the Jolly Rogers B-24 named "Hangover Haven," with its colorful nose art painted by Al Merkling. At top it is seen in its prime during the war, and below as a sun-bleached derelict, just one of the many Jolly Rogers bombers awaiting the scrap dealer's torch in this photograph taken after the war at Nadzab, New Guinea.

along with its surrounding islands, is still a remote and sparsely settled part of the world, and many of the battle locations remain practically untouched, as well as largely forgotten. What Pacific battles Americans do remember are mainly those that were fought by the Marines in the Central Pacific, such as Okinawa, Saipan, Iwo Jima, etc. The Army's war in New Guinea has faded from public memory.

The monumental waste of war. This was only one part of a B-24 scrapyard on Biak Island after the war. Over 18,000 B-24s were built, and nearly all of them that survived combat ended up as scrap metal, many of them abandoned in the Pacific, as seen here, beside the airfields where they were parked when the war ended.

The remains of one of the last Jolly Rogers bombers, just before it disappeared into the scrap dealers' smelters at Nadzab. By the time this picture was taken, the Americans who had flown it were back in the States pursuing their peacetime lives. Aside from the remains of some of these skull-decorated rudders moldering in the jungle at remote crash sites, the only example of the skull-and-crossed-bombs symbol on a B-24 rudder that can still be seen today is one that was transported by helicopter from the crash site of "Weezie" (picture on p. 505) to a small war museum at Port Moresby, New Guinea.

Hikers from Australia visit Port Moresby today to walk the Kokoda Trail, which has monuments and markers at various places along its sixty-mile length commemorating notable phases of the protracted battle (July through November of 1942) between the Australians and the Japanese. However, the marshy, malarial, thickly jungled Buna battlefield on the coast at the north end of the trail is rarely visited.

Iron Range, in the wilds of northern Australia, the Jolly Rogers' first Pacific War airbase, is now Lockhart River Airport, a small paved runway surrounded by jungle that serves as a link to civilization for the nearby small town of Lockhart River, which is inhabited by around 700 aboriginal people. A plaque on the airfield commemorates Lt. Paul Larson's takeoff crash that killed twelve men on the night of November 16, 1942 (pp. 86-89). Small, scattered artifacts protruding from the forest floor, and rusting 44-gallon drums in the jungle surrounding the airfield mark where the 90th Bomb Group was once encamped, and on the beach a few miles to the east still sits the hulk of the bomber named "The Condor," where Capt. Dale Thornhill crash-landed it on November 15, 1942, after it ran out of fuel trying to return to Iron Range from a strike on Japanese warships near Bougainville Island (picture, p. 77).

Wakde Island, which once had a wide coral runway running the full length of the island, and was used by the Jolly Rogers as a forward airbase in the spring and summer of 1944, is today almost completely overgrown by jungle. It is difficult, looking at aerial or satellite photos of Wakde today (p. 515), to imagine that it was once packed with aircraft, people, and supplies, with ships nosed up to jetties unloading cargo and the air filled with aircraft of all types constantly coming and going. Today the island is practically uninhabited, with only a few native shacks on the southern shore, where Charles Lindbergh once crossed the short water gap between Wakde and the islet of Insoemanai to visit an Air Corps officer, and where he snorkeled just offshore examining the local fish and sea life. And beneath the sea off the east and west ends of Wakde Island, forgotten now, lies the wreckage of the B-24 bombers that failed to lift off the too-short runway and crashed into the sea, along with the remains of some of their crewmen.

Opposite Wakde Island, three miles across the water at Maffin Bay on the New Guinea coastline, the site of the extensive American infantry encampment is also overgrown by jungle, and on Lone Tree Hill, only the calls of parrots and the patter of rain are ever heard over the bones of the Americans and Japanese who died in battle there and were never recovered. It is a battlefield without visitors or memorials, unremembered by anyone but war historians. Hundreds of Japanese bodies remain entombed in sealed-off coral caves that now blend into the landscape, and the bones of fifteen Americans who went missing still lie somewhere on the hill.

Bougainville Island, the Komiatum Ridge on New Guinea, and many other once-fiercely contested Pacific battlefields are also forgotten and unvisited today.

A few of the former Air Corps airfields in New Guinea and the Philippines are still in use as local or regional airports, since airplanes are still the easiest (and sometimes the only) way to get around in this vast and remote part of the world. The great American airbases at Port Moresby, Nadzab, and Biak, with their multiple runways, no longer exist, but at any former airbase where there were several runways in use during the war, sometimes one is still maintained today for local aircraft. Jackson Field at Port Moresby is now Jackson International Airport, the only one of the former seven military airfields at Moresby that is still in use today, and pavement has replaced the Marston matting on which Lt. Horner skidded his bomber during a rainstorm on May 31, 1944 (pp. 488-9).

Only one of the six runways at Nadzab, New Guinea is still in use, although traces of the others, and the many miles of taxiways connecting them, can still be seen in satellite imagery such as the computer program Google Earth. The military tent town that occupied twenty square miles adjacent to Nadzab's runways has long since vanished. Perhaps archaeologists of the future will study the organization and layout of this huge military encampment of WWII, whose site has remained undisturbed since the war.

Biak's Island's Mokmer Field is still being used, but the other military airfields that once existed near it are gone, and Owi Island offshore, from which Charles Lindbergh flew fighter planes is, like Wakde Island, almost entirely reclaimed by jungle and nearly uninhabited. McGuire Field on the Philippine Island of Mindoro, where the Jolly Rogers took up residence after leaving Biak Island in January of 1945, is now San Jose Airport, and all the bomber parking pads which once surrounded it (picture, p. 705), once occupied by Jolly Rogers bombers, have vanished, replaced by Filipino housing developments.

The fortress island of Corregidor in Manila Bay is now a tourist attraction, offering guided bus tours, and visitors can walk through the tunnels of Malinta Hill, where General MacArthur and the last survivors of the American surrender at Bataan held out under siege by the Japanese in the spring of 1942. During the tour the tunnel's lights are switched off, and in the intense darkness, visitors are treated to an audio-visual presentation about the events that took place on "The Rock" and in the tunnels during the war.

The Cargo Cults

For years after the war, the primitive natives of New Guinea tried to bring back the Americans and their supply planes filled with bountiful food and useful objects by forming "cargo cults" that they hoped could magically recall them. They built replica airplanes around which they danced and performed magical ceremonies, replica headquarters with desks containing papers to shuffle around, imitation telephones to call back the Americans and their airplanes, and they marched around in military formations just as they had seen the Americans do, but nothing worked. General Kenney's great fleet of cargo planes, along with the extensive American installations where the natives found plentiful work to earn what were to them exotic foods and a wealth of manufactured goods, have never returned.

Modern-Day Japan

Today Japan, with its pacifist government and Constitution designed by Gen. MacArthur, has prospered under its capitalist economy and energetic population; in fact Japan now has the third largest economy in the world, after the U. S. and China. The status of its women is substantially better than it was before the war—MacArthur gave Japanese women the right to vote, commenting that women do not vote for war. Japan today has a population of over 125 million, of which 70 percent claim no religious affiliation. Japan's postwar constitution prohibits it from forming any military other than the Japan Self-Defense Forces, whose stated purpose is "to preserve Japan's peace, independence and safety." The JSF is most often involved in international peace-keeping missions.

However, recent Chinese threats toward the Japanese, specifically China's occupation of small islands in the East China Sea claimed by Japan, have rekindled the idea in the U. S. of allowing Japan to develop a more powerful military, but nothing has changed as of this writing. Ironically, America remains the main protector of the Japanese nation, a nation whose criminal aggression caused the loss of over 100,000 Americans lives between 1941 and 1945.

No apologies from Japan for its WWII atrocities

It should not be required that the sins of the fathers be visited upon the sons, but a country that wreaked so much horror, misery, and death on the world during World War II has a moral obligation to at least acknowledge its wrongdoing and to vow never to repeat it, as Germany has done. Occasional weak

Cargo cultists of New Guinea wait in vain for the return of the American airplanes of WWII that brought them bounty and prosperity such as they had never experienced before, and haven't since.

statements of regret by Japanese officials are usually viewed as inadequate or insincere, and in fact in 2006 Japanese Prime Minster Shinzo Abe (a successor to World War II Prime Minister Hideki Tojo) said, "There is no definitive answer either in academia or in the international community on what constitutes aggression. Things that happen between countries appear different depending on which side you're looking from." Japanese schoolchildren today are not taught any of the details of the Pacific war—it is simply glossed over in their textbooks (not to say that American students are taught much more about it in their dumbed-down curricula under the U. S. Dept. of Education).

It is ominous for Japan, however, that Oriental memories are long, and for the Chinese, the Rape of Nanking and the wanton torture and murder of millions of their people by the Japanese during World War II are recent events.

Because the attack on Pearl Harbor was an ambush carried out in peacetime, killing thousands of Americans without any declaration of war, it was declared a war crime at the Tokyo War Trials held between 1946 and 1948, but Japan has still not formally admitted to any wrongdoing.

In December of 2016 Prime Minister Abe visited Pearl Harbor with American President Barack Obama. Obama took Prime Minister Abe to a monument near Pearl Harbor erected by the United States as an apology to Japan for the deaths of nine Japanese men who were killed when an American submarine, the *USS Greenville*, accidentally surfaced beneath a Japanese fishing boat named the *Ehime Maru* on February 9, 2001, wrecking and sinking it.

The memorial of apology to Japan for the accidental sinking of a Japanese fishing trawler by a collision with a U. S. Navy submarine in 2001.

This incident was, let it be stressed, purely an accident. The Japanese trawler was sailing in American waters about ten miles south of Oahu, Hawaii, when the *USS Greenville* unintentionally came up underneath it. Two days after the accident, on February 11, 2001, President George Bush formally apologized to the Japanese nation on national television. The American ambassador to Japan also personally apologized to both the Japanese prime minister and to the Emperor.

Following an investigation into the accident, the skipper of the submarine was relieved of his command, discharged from the Navy, and sent to Japan to also personally apologize to the families of the nine dead men. He laid a wreath on a monument to the ship, bowed his head, read aloud the names of the dead, and wept. The families of the dead were paid 16 million dollars in compensation by the U. S. government, and the U. S. taxpayer also bought the Japanese a new fishing boat. Sixty million (that's *sixty million*) more U. S. taxpayer dollars were spent to recover the bodies of the nine dead men from the deeply submerged wreck.*

At the request of the Japanese government, the U. S. constructed the expensive marble monument of apology to Japan (photo on opposite page), with the ship's anchor as a centerpiece. President Obama made sure that Prime Minister Abe got a good look at this monument for his approval.

Abe and Obama also visited the *Arizona* memorial where more than 1,000 American sailors and Marines still lie entombed in the submerged hulk of the battleship, and there Prime Minister Abe laid a wreath, but offered no apology for the sinking. Finally he was taken to the National Memorial Cemetery of the Pacific in Honolulu (the "Punchbowl"), where many of the Jolly Rogers dead are buried among over 34,000 other Americans killed during the Pacific war, and there he laid another wreath. A reporter for the *U. K. Telegraph* on 27 December 2016 (online) wrote: "Mr Abe will not apologise [sic] for the attack but will ... pay his respects to the victims and encourage historical reflection." Since he declined to apologize for the Pearl Harbor attack, he thereby tacitly condoned it, along with all the other atrocities and massacres committed by Japan during World War II.

There is something seriously amiss here, and some American veterans of the Pacific War and their families have pointed it out. The nine men of the Japanese fishing boat were killed accidentally, in American waters, yet America groveled to Japan in abject contrition, paid out many millions of dollars in reparations, and built a monument of apology to the Japanese at Pearl Harbor. Japan's Pearl Harbor sneak attack of Dec. 7, 1941, in peacetime, killed over 2,400 Americans and was no accident, but was carried out with the expressed

---

* Flashback: Before dawn on May 14, 1943, the Japanese submarine I-177, commanded by Hajime Nakagawa, spotted the Australian hospital ship *Centaur* off the coast of Queensland, Australia. Despite the fact that the ship carried prominent Red Cross markings on its hull that were illuminated by spotlights, Nakagawa fired torpedoes that sank the *Centaur*, killing 268 people, including many doctors and nurses, most of whom were asleep belowdecks when the torpedoes hit and had no chance of escape. Only 64 people survived the sinking. They later reported that the Japanese submarine surfaced near them but ignored their plight and sailed away (they were lucky, however, because after Nakagawa sank another ship, he surfaced and fired on the survivors). Commander Nakagawa survived the war but refused to comment on his sinking of the hospital ship, and was never charged with a war crime. He died in 1991. In 2008 the *Centaur* was located on the sea floor at a depth of 6,755 feet, its hospital markings still clearly visible in photographs taken by a remote undersea vehicle. Australia has declared the site a protected war grave. Japan has never acknowledged the sinking of the hospital ship *Centaur*, much less apologized for it or built a monument of remembrance to the victims.

goal of killing every American it possibly could while destroying the U. S. Pacific Fleet. Japan has never shown any consideration whatever for the families of the Americans it murdered that morning, yet it demanded (and got) apologies and reparations for the *accidental* killing of nine Japanese on a fishing boat.

Japan should long ago have built a monument of apology to America not only at Pearl Harbor but at the site of the Bataan Death March, along with another great marble monument in Manila, the city it senselessly ravaged, to apologize for the millions of Filipinos it terrorized, brutalized, and murdered during the war. At the place on Wake Island where the Japanese lined up 89 American civilians beside a trench and shot them all in the back, afterward burying some of them alive, there should be another well-maintained stela of regret and contrition.

Bayoneting babies and beheading civilians by the thousands was typical Japanese behavior in the countries that it invaded during World War Two.

A colossal Japanese shrine of remorse should now be standing in Nanking, China, but in fact there is nothing of the sort there at all. There should be a Japanese monument of apology to Australia on the island of New Britain, at the site of the Toll Plantation Massacre where the Japanese tricked 160 Australian soldiers into surrendering and then slaughtered them with bayonets and swords (p. 82). There should be another marker of commemoration at Buna village on the north coast of New Guinea where the Japanese bayoneted and beheaded British missionaries, men, women, and children; another memorial on Ambon Island apologizing to the Dutch and Australians at the spot where drunken Japanese soldiers caroused all through the night of February 24, 1942 while beheading scores of helpless young Australian and Dutch prisoners in the Laha Massacre (pp. 624-5). There should be a cenotaph of apology to the British on the beach at Banka Island where the Japanese machine-gunned a party of British nurses and their patients and left their bodies to rot. There should be another one to the murdered Allied prisoners at Rabaul. . . but this could go on and on. The point is that to this day the government of Japan has never formally expressed any regret or remorse for any of its heinous war crimes of WWII.

According to the same *U. K. Telegraph* article quoted above, there were "Japanese nationalists" who objected to Prime Minster Abe's visit to Pearl Harbor, just in case he might express regret for the attack. The fact that there are Japanese today who vehemently oppose any apologies for Japan's war of aggression, which resulted in more than a hundred thousand American dead and millions of victims of other nationalities murdered, is troublesome indeed, enough to make one glad that the American military still has a significant presence in Japan: 23 military bases with over 50,000 Army troops and more than 10,000 Marines, along with the headquarters of the Navy's U. S. 7th Fleet. Under these conditions any attempted revival of Japanese militarism can be quickly checked, and the The U. S. needs keep its gun to Japan's head.

The 90th Bomb Group Association was formed to perpetuate the memory of the Jolly Rogers, and it held its first reunion in 1970, with hundreds of veterans of the Group attending. There have been reunions every year since, each time in a different city. Time has been taking its toll on the Greatest Generation, however, and even the youngest of the men who fought in WWII are now (2018) in their 90s.

At the 2017 reunion there were only five Jolly Rogers veterans among the 48 people who attended; the rest were family members of veterans both living and deceased. Robert J. Tupa, the treasurer of the Association, who puts out its newsletter, estimates that the number of remaining Jolly Rogers veterans is well under 100 as of this writing.

At a 2015 reunion sponsored by the 90th Bomb Group Association, 100-year-old Earl C. Butterfield, a former Jolly Rogers pilot (320th Squadron) dances with a member of a troupe that reenacted a Bob Hope USO show that he had seen 71 years before, in 1944, on Biak Island.

At the 2015 reunion the group visited the World War II museum in New Orleans and was treated to a re-creation of one of Bob Hope's USO shows, as the Jolly Rogers saw it on Biak Island in August of 1944 (pages 613-167). Afterwards Jolly Rogers veteran Earl Butterfield, 100 years old, put on a mop wig and coconut bra and danced with one of the female performers (photo, previous page).

Remembering the Jolly Rogers airmen who did not return from the war

820 members of the 90th Bomb Group died fighting the Japanese in the Pacific War. Scores of the Group's dead remain missing in action today.[3] Maj. Robert H. Mericle, U. S. Air Force (retired), formerly of the Jolly Rogers' 321st Squadron, wrote a eulogy to all the Group's dead several years after the war:

> In our hearts we will say: I surely appreciate it men. I know you were red-blooded, clear-eyed young fellows. I know that you would have enjoyed living on as I am living on today. I know that you would have liked to see your little boy and girl grow up as children of today are growing up. I know that you longed to come home at night as we long to come home when we are tired. But your country called and you went to answer that call. By your bravery, your wounds, your heartache and your sacrifice, you made it possible for us to enjoy life and liberty, and with every living fiber of our hearts and bodies, we thank you and WE SHALL NOT FORGET, no matter what the day.[4]

None of the Jolly Rogers veterans would ever forget their fallen comrades-in-arms, but the 90th Bomb Group has faded from the consciousness of the American nation as a whole, along with the war in the Pacific itself. With students in American schools being taught little about WWII today, it my well be only historians who remember anything at all about the air war.

For the airmen of the Jolly Rogers who never came home, and indeed for all the Americans who fought in the Pacific war and whose remains have not yet been found, and may never be recovered, there is the inscription on the Pacific War Memorial on Corregidor Island. It is a round structure with a skylight in its dome, and under the skylight is a circular marble altar on which is engraved the following:

> Sleep, my sons, your duty done
> For Freedom's light has come
> Sleep in the silent depths of the sea
> Or in your bed of hallowed sod
> Until you hear at dawn the low
> Clear reveille of God

CHAPTER NOTES

Introduction:
1. Benson, *Prisoner's Base and Home Again*, pp. 60-1.
2. Sheftall, *Blossoms In The Wind*, pp. 30-1.
3. *Sea of Thunder, Four Commanders and the Last Great Naval Campaign, 1941-45*, pp. 17-18.
4. Ibid., p. 20.
5. Ibid., p. 18.
6. (from <https://www.yahoo.com/news/pearl-harbor-why-japan-attacked-150000811.html>.
7. Bergerud, *Touched With Fire*, pp. 13-14.
8. Ibid., pp. 11-12.

Chapter 1: In the Beginning
1. *The Legacy of the 90th Bomb Group, the Jolly Rogers*, p. 5.
2. Ibid.
3. *Under the Southern Cross*, p. 8.
4. *Zero*, pp. 157-8.
5. Ibid., pp. 158-9.

Chapter 2: Art Rogers
1. Rogers memoir, which has no numbered pages. All Rogers quotes are from his manuscript.
2. *The wartime Journals of Charles Lindbergh*, p. 697.
3. *The Legacy of the 90th Bomb Group, the Jolly Rogers*, p. 6.
4. Ibid.
5. The estimates of the materials that made up a B-24 is from *Under the Southern Cross*, p. 9.
6. Rogers memoir ms.
7. *The wartime Journals of Charles Lindbergh*, p. 613.
8. *Fire in the Sky*, p. 553.
9. *The wartime Journals of Charles Lindbergh*, pp. 690-1.
10. Ibid, p. 699. The names of all the crewmen killed are on p. 7 of *The Legacy of the 90th Bomb Group*.
11. *The Legacy of the 90th Bomb Group, the Jolly Rogers*, p. 7.
12. *The wartime Journals of Charles Lindbergh*, p. 699.
13. Ibid., p. 627.
14. Rogers memoir ms.
15. Ibid.
16. *The Legacy of the 90th Bomb Group, the Jolly Rogers*, p. 7.
17. Ibid., p. 8.
18. Ibid.

Chapter 3: The 90th Moves to Hawaii
1. *The Legacy of the 90th Bomb Group, the Jolly Rogers*, p. 8.
2. Ibid.
3. Quoted in *Letters from the Greatest Generation*, pp. 3-4.

Chapter 5: The 90th Joins the 5th Air Force
1. *The Legacy of the 90th Bomb Group, the Jolly Rogers*, p. 15.
2. Kenney, *Air War in the Pacific*, p. 25.

3. *The Conquering Tide*, p. 218.
4. *American Caesar*, pp. 469-470.
5. Kenney, *Air War in the Pacific*, p. 23.

Chapter 6: Iron Range
1. *Under the Southern Cross*, p. 50.
2. Ibid.
3. Ibid.
4. *The Legacy of the 90th Bomb Group, the Jolly Rogers*, p. 99.
5. Lord, *Tales of the Jolly Rogers*, p. 149.
6. Ibid., pp. 15-16.
7. Rogers, memoirs ms.
8. Lord, *Tales of the Jolly Rogers*, p. 149.
9. McMurria, *Fight for Survival*, p. 14.
10. Ibid., p. 19.
11. Ibid.
12. Ibid., p. 16.
13. Manchester, *American Caesar*, pp. 454-5.

Chapter 7: The 90th Enters the War
1. General Kenney is quoted in Woods, *The Legacy of the 90th Bomb Group, the Jolly Rogers*, p. 15.
2. Quoted in *Under the Southern Cross*, p. 53.
3. Lord, *Tales of the Jolly Rogers*, p. 16.

Chapter 8: The 90th's First Bombing Mission
1. *The Legacy of the 90th Bomb Group, the Jolly Rogers*, p. 18.
2. The spotting of the wreckage by a helicopter pilot in 2005 is from the Pacific Wrecks website.
3. The fact that the plane is mostly now buried under sand is reported on the Pacific Wrecks website.
4. *The Legacy of the 90th Bomb Group, the Jolly Rogers*, p. 18.
5. *Fight for Survival*, p. 15.

Chapter 9: The 90th's Second Bombing Mission: Rabaul
1. *Invasion Rabaul*, pp. 35-37.
2. Ibid., pp. 74, 123.
3. Ibid., p. 227.
4. *Tales of the Jolly Rogers*, p. 10.
5. Ibid.
6. Personal communication to the author from former bomber pilot Maurice Holmen of the 448th Bomb Group, 8th Air Force.

Chapter 10: More Missions for the 90th.
1. Kenney quoted in Woods, *The Legacy of the 90th Bomb Group, the Jolly Rogers*, p. 15.
2. *Air War in the Pacific*, p. 79.
3. *General Kenney Reports*, pp. 126-7.
4. Ibid., pp. 142-3.
5. *Tales of the Jolly Rogers*, pp. 303-4.
6. *The Legacy of the 90th Bomb Group, the Jolly Rogers*, p. 29.

Chapter 11: Art Rogers arrives at Iron Range
1. *The Legacy of the 90th Bomb Group, the Jolly Rogers*, p. 23.
2. This and subsequent quotes are from Rogers' unpublished ms.

Chapter 12: Rogers first combat mission
1. The fact that tight formations caused pilot fatigue and used up extra gas was communicated to the author by James Horner.
2. Witnesses gave varying numbers of fighter planes. Lt. McMurria's diary mentions 30, and Woods wrote that the number of Japanese fighters was 15.

CHAPTER NOTES

3. *Fight for Survival*, p. 18.
4. Middlebrook, *Air Combat at 20 Feet*, p. 30
5. Ian Toll, *The Conquering Tide*, p. 101.
6. Saburo Sakai in *Samurai*, p. 105.
7. *The Legacy of the 90th Bomb Group, the Jolly Rogers*, p. 23.

Chapter 13: Crosson's Odyssey
1. *The Legacy of the 90th Bomb Group, the Jolly Rogers*, p. 23.
2. *Fight for Survival*, pp. 19-20.
3. information from the Pacific Wrecks website.

Chapter 14: Casualties Mount
1. Gamble, *Target Rabaul*, p. 85.
2. *The Legacy of the 90th Bomb Group, the Jolly Rogers*, p. 28.
3. Ibid.
4. Ibid., p. 29.
5. Ibid., pp. 41-2.
6. *Tales of the Jolly Rogers*, pp. 278-9.
7. Gamble, *Fortress Rabaul*, p. 295.
8. Ibid.
9. *The Legacy of the 90th Bomb Group, the Jolly Rogers*, p. 28.
10. Ibid. p. 29.
11. Ibid, p. 32.
12. Pacific Wrecks website, John F. Heyn webpage.
13. *Tales of the Jolly Rogers*, pp. 107-8.
14. Ibid., pp. 126-7.
15. Ibid., 51.
16. Cundiff, *Ten Knights in a Bar Room*, p. 81.
17. *Tales of the Jolly Rogers*, p. 163.

Chapter 15: Taking Turns at Port Moresby
1. *The Legacy of the 90th Bomb Group, the Jolly Rogers*, p. 31.
2. The website Pacific Wrecks provided details on the seaplane "Camilla."
3. Bradley, *Flyboys*, p. 256.

Chapter 16: General Walker Lost
1. *General Kenney Reports*, pp. 166-7.
2. *The Legacy of the 90th Bomb Group, the Jolly Rogers*, p. 32.
3. *Fight for Survival*, p. 20.
4. *The Legacy of the 90th Bomb Group, the Jolly Rogers*, p. 32.
5. The ship straddled by bombs is described on the webpage www.afhistoricalfoundation.org, Volume 61, Number 3, Fall 2014, p. 12.
6. From the Rutgers Oral History Archives, online at: Wesche III, Frederick, <http://oralhistory.rutgers.edu/component/content/article/30-interviewees/interview-html-text/76-wesche-iii-frederick>.
7. *Air War in the Pacific*, pp. 160-1.

Chapter 17: Another Convoy Attack
1. *The Legacy of the 90th Bomb Group, the Jolly Rogers*, p. 33.
2. *Fight for Survival*, p. 20.
3. *The Legacy of the 90th Bomb Group, the Jolly Rogers*, pp. 33-4.
4. Ibid., p. 34.

Chapter 18: Lt. McMurria Shot Down
1. *The Legacy of the 90th Bomb Group, the Jolly Rogers*, p. 21, and *Fight for Survival*, pp. 14-15.
2. Ibid., p. 21 and Ibid., p. 20.
3. *Fight for Survival*, p. 20.

4. Ibid., p. 38.
5. Ibid., p. 43.
6. Ibid., p. 44.
7. Sakai, *Samurai*, p. 111.
8. Lord, *Tales of the Jolly Rogers*, pp. 17-18.
9. Tanaka, *Hidden Horrors*, pp. 175-8.
10. Manuel, *70,000 to One*, p. 47.
11. Benson, *Prisoner's Base and Home Again*, p. 87.
12. Ibid., p. 51.
13. Ibid., p. 47.
14. Ibid., p. 151.
15. *Retreat From Kokoda*, p. 51.
16. *70,000 to One*, p. 64.
17. Bradley, *Flyboys*, pp. 245, 288.
18. *Prisoner's Base and Home Again*, pp. 93-4.

Chapter 19: The B-24 Gets a Nose Turret
1. All quotes from Rogers are from his unpublished ms.
2. Kenney, *Air War in the Pacific*, pp. 135-6.

Chapter 20: The 319th Goes to Darwin
1. Livingston, *Under the Southern Cross*, p. 62.
2. Lord, *Tales of the Jolly Rogers*, p. 27.
3. *Under the Southern Cross*, p. 63.
4. Ibid., p. 59.
5. *The Legacy of the 90th Bomb Group, the Jolly Rogers*, p. 48.
6. *Under the Southern Cross*, p. 9.
7. *Tales of the Jolly Rogers*, pp. 26-27.
8. *The Legacy of the 90th Bomb Group, the Jolly Rogers*, p. 62.
9. Ibid.
10. Ibid.

Chapter 21: The 90th Moves to Port Moresby
1. *The Legacy of the 90th Bomb Group, the Jolly Rogers*, p. 94.
2. Livingston, *Under the Southern Cross*, p. 53.
3. *General Kenney Reports*, p. 38.
4. Ibid., pp. 70-71.
5. Ibid., pp. 39-40.
6. *The Legacy of the 90th Bomb Group, the Jolly Rogers*, p. 58.
7. Ibid., p. 84.

Chapter 23: No Rest for the Weary
1. Middlebrook, *Air Combat at 20 Feet*, p. 249.
2. *The Legacy of the 90th Bomb Group, the Jolly Rogers*, pp. 55-6.
3. Lord, *Tales of the Jolly Rogers*, p. 285.
4. Ibid.
5. Alcorn, *The Jolly Rogers*, p. 120.

Chapter 24: Cannibals
1. Lord, *Tales of the Jolly Rogers*, p. 18.
2. Alcorn, *The Jolly Rogers*, pp. 76-78.
3. From a transcript of a recording made by Capt. Frank McLaughlin and transcribed by Wiley O. Woods.

Chapter 25: The Battle of the Bismarck Sea
1. *The Legacy of the 90th Bomb Group, the Jolly Rogers*, p. 43.
2. Birdsall, *Flying Buccaneers*, pp. 51-53.

CHAPTER NOTES

3. *General Kenney Reports*, p. 144.
4. Bergerud, *Fire in the Sky*, p. 592.
5. Middlebrook, *Air Combat at 20 Feet*, p. 154.
6. Manuel, *70,000 to One*, pp. 59-60.
7. *General Kenney Reports*, p. 204.
8. Manuel, *70,000 to One*, pp. 7-8.
9. Gamble, *Fortress Rabaul*, p. 310.
10. Manuel, *70,000 to One*, p. 62.
11. Middlebrook, *Air Combat at 20 Feet*, pp. 169-170.
12. Hastings, *Retribution, the Battle for Japan*, p. 49.
13. *General Kenney Reports*, p. 204.
14. MacArthur's comment is quoted in *Under the Southern Cross*, p. 63.
15. *Fire in the Sky*, p. 592.
16. Ibid.

Chapter 26: Rogers' Flight to Prove the Nose Turret
1. *The Legacy of the 90th Bomb Group, the Jolly Rogers*, p. 94.
2. Ibid., p. 91.

Chapter 28: The 90th Becomes the Jolly Rogers
1. Lord, *Tales of the Jolly Rogers*, p. xiii.
2. *The Legacy of the 90th Bomb Group, the Jolly Rogers*, p. 69.
3. Ibid., p. 84.

Chapter 29: Capt. Lark Martin Lost
1. All quotes from Rogers are from his unpublished ms.
2. All Rawlings quotes in this chapter are from his article in the *Saturday Evening Post*, Aug. 19, 1944.
3. *The Legacy of the 90th Bomb Group, the Jolly Rogers*, pp. 76-77.

Chapter 30: The Drive on Salamaua and Lae
1. Middlebrook, *Air Combat at 20 Feet*, pp. 311-12.
2. Ibid., pp. 407-409.
3. Pinney, *The Barbarians*, p. 109.
4. Ibid., pp. 120-1.
5. Ibid., pp. 124-5.
6. Ibid., p. 136.
7. Ibid, p. 116.
8. Ibid, p. 104.
9. Ibid, p. 209.
10. Ibid, p. 217.
11. Ibid, p. 209.
12. Ibid, p. 136.
13. Ibid, pp. 124-5.

Chapter 31: Wewak Attacked; Lae and Nadzab Captured
1. Gamble, *Target Rabaul*, pp. 98-100.
2. Crash details provided by the Pacific Wrecks website, on its "Twin Nifties" webpage.
3. *The Legacy of the 90th Bomb Group, the Jolly Rogers*, p. 73.
4. The information on the ditching of Lt. Pariah's bomber. His from the Pacific Wrecks website.
5. *General Kenney Reports*, pp. 12-13.
6. *Target Rabaul*, pp. 100-104.
7. *General Kenney Reports*, p. 278.
8. *The Legacy of the 90th Bomb Group, the Jolly Rogers*, p. 74.
9. Ibid., pp. 278-9.
10. *Target Rabaul*, pp. 111-112.
11. *General Kenney Reports*, pp. 288-9.

12. Ibid., p. 288.
13. Ibid., p. 37.
14. *The Legacy of the 90th Bomb Group, the Jolly Rogers*, p. 79.
15. *General Kenney Reports*, pp. 292-4.
16. Rogers memoirs ms.

Chapter 32: Bridge Busting
1. Gamble, *Target Rabaul*, pp. 98-100.
2. *General Kenney Reports*, p. 308.
3. *The Legacy of the 90th Bomb Group, the Jolly Rogers*, p. 184.

Chapter 33: Big Strike on Rabaul
1. *The Legacy of the 90th Bomb Group, the Jolly Rogers*, p. 82.
2. Rogers memoirs ms.
3. *The Legacy of the 90th Bomb Group, the Jolly Rogers*, p. 83.
4. *General Kenney Reports*, pp. 313-14.

Chapter 34: More Losses at Wewak
1. Cundiff, *Ten Knights in a Bar Room*, p. 66.
2. Ibid. p. 76.
3. *The Legacy of the 90th Bomb Group, the Jolly Rogers*, pp. 89-90
4. *Ten Knights in a Bar Room*, p. 78.
5. Quoted in *Ten Knights in a Bar Room*, pp. 76-77.
6. *Ten Knights in a Bar Room*, p. 77.
7. Ibid., from the *Missing Aircraft Report*, p. 74.
8. Ibid., p. 81.
9. Ibid., p. 82.
10. *The Legacy of the 90th Bomb Group, the Jolly Rogers*, p. 90.

Chapter 35: Cape Gloucester
1. Birdsall, *Flying Buccaneers*, p. 109.
2. *General Kenney Reports*, pp. 76-77.
3. Ibid., pp. 272-273.
4. Ibid., pp. 214-15.
5. Ibid, p. 244.
6. Ibid., pp. 329-30.
7. *The Legacy of the 90th Bomb Group, the Jolly Rogers*, p. 91.

Chapter 36: Col. Rogers leaves the Jolly Rogers
1. *General Kenney Reports*, p. 382.
2. Rogers, unpublished ms.
3. Kenney, *Air War in the Pacific*, p. 288.
4. *The Legacy of the 90th Bomb Group, the Jolly Rogers*, p. 94.
5. Ibid., p. 91.
6. Ibid., p. 92.

Chapter 37: Japanese Airpower in New Guinea Smashed
1. *Zero*, p. 225.
2. Ibid., p. 224.
3. Diana West's book *American Betrayal* thoroughly documents the extent of Russian infiltration of the Roosevelt administration and its subsequent cover-up. To this day it is one of the greatest stories never told.
4. *General Kenney Reports*, p. 351.
5. Ibid., p. 374.
6. Ibid., pp. 373-4.
7. Ibid., pp. 380-81.
8. Ibid., p. 162.

CHAPTER NOTES

9. Ibid., p. 393.
10. Ibid., p. 234.
11. Kenney, *Air War in the Pacific*, pp. 178-9, p. 347.
12. *General Kenney Reports*, pp. 387-88.
13. The recovery of the two B-24s lost on Black Sunday is detailed on the Pacific Wrecks website.

Chapter 38: The Jolly Rogers Move to Nadzab
1. *General Kenney Reports*, pp. 332-3.
2. Ibid., p. 189.
3. *The Legacy of the 90th Bomb Group, the Jolly Rogers*, p. 101.
4. Sheehan, *A Missing Plane*, pp. 161-2.
5. Park, Edward, *Nanette*, pp. 180-82.
6. Potts, Joe, on the Nadzab No. 1 Strip webpage of the Pacific Wrecks website.

Chapter 39: Into Uniform
1. King, *The Last Zero Fighter*, p. 244.
2. Ibid. p. 7.
3. Saki, *Samurai*, p. 7.
4. Ibid., pp. 10-11.
5. Kerns, *Above the Thunder*, p. 51.

Chapter 40: Crew Training
1. Alcorn, *The Jolly Rogers*, p. 155.

Chapter 41: Flight to the Pacific
1. Salecker, *Fortress Against the Sun, The B-17 Flying Fortress in the Pacific*, p. 94.
2. King, *The Last Zero Fighter*, p. 204.
3. Letter to the author from James Horner.
4. Carl Camp is quoted in *Ten Knights in a Bar Room*, pp. 52-3.
5. Letter to the author from James Horner.
6. *A Missing Plane*, p. 149.
7. Rogers, unpublished ms.
8. *The Legacy of the 90th Bomb Group, the Jolly Rogers*, p. 85.
9. Letter to the author from James Horner.
10. Personal communication with the author.

Chapter 42: Port Moresby to Nadzab
1. Bergerud, *Fire in the Sky*, p. 97.
2. Matasake Okumia, *Zero*, pp. 167-8.
3. *Tales of the Jolly Rogers*, p. 280.
4. Alcorn, *The Jolly Rogers*, p. 53. There are actually fifteen stanzas in the poem.
5. Kenney, *Air War in the Pacific*, pp. 93-94.
6. *Zero*, p. 230.
7. Kenney, *Air War in the Pacific*, pp. 131, 133.
8. Henebry, *The Grim Reaper's At Work in the Pacific Theater*, p. 150.
9. From *LBJ's Silver Star: The Mission That Never Was*, by Barrett Tillman and Henry Sakaida, PDF file at <http://tinyurl.com/jrsnney>.
10. *Tales of the Jolly Rogers*, p. 279.
11. *Autobiography of Donald A. Johnson*, 1997, from the webpage: https://familysearch.org/photos/stories/1809223.

Chapter 43: Wakde Island
1. Bergerud, *Fire in the Sky*, pp. 108-9.
2. *The Legacy of the 90th Bomb Group, the Jolly Rogers*, p. 124.
3. *The Pacific War: The Strategy, Politics, and Players that Won the War*, p. 222.
4. Zellmer, *The Spectator*, pp. 92, 97.

5. *Autobiography of Donald A. Johnson*, 1997, from the webpage: https://familysearch.org/photos/stories/1809223.
6. Kenney, *Air War in the Pacific*, pp. 304-5.
7. *The Legacy of the 90th Bomb Group, the Jolly Rogers*, p. 124.
8. *The Wartime Journals of Charles Lindbergh*, p. 906.
9. Kerns, *Above the Thunder*, p. 142.
10. *The Legacy of the 90th Bomb Group, the Jolly Rogers*, p. 128.
11. Ibid, p. 907.
12. *Northrop's Night Hunter: the P-61 Black Widow*, p. 100.
13. Zellmer, *The Spectator*, p. 97.
14. Ibid., p. 72.
15. Ibid., pp. 98-99.
16. Ibid., p. 101.
17. *The Wartime Journals of Charles Lindbergh*, p. 907.
18. *The Spectator*, p. 103.
19. *Michi's Memories*, p. 20.
20. Ibid., p. 19.
21. Ibid., p. 20.
22. Ibid.
23. Ibid., pp. 20-21.
24. *The Legacy of the 90th Bomb Group, the Jolly Rogers*, p. 128.

Chapter 44: Charles Lindbergh Flies Shotgun for the Jolly Rogers
1. Kenney, *Air War in the Pacific*, p. 302.
2. Bob George, *Owi, An Island of Death*, from the webpage <http://engineersvietnam.com/engineers/WWII/owi.htm>.
3. Zellmer, *The Spectator*, p. 76.
4. *The Wartime Journals of Charles Lindbergh*, p. 877.
5. Ibid., p.881.
6. Ibid.
7. Ibid., p.863.
8. *General Kenney Reports*, pp. 411-12.
9. *The Wartime Journals of Charles Lindbergh*, p. 868.
10. Ibid., p. 872.
11. Ibid., p. 873.
12. *General Kenney Reports*, pp. 412-13.
13. Ibid.
14. *The Wartime Journals of Charles Lindbergh*, p. 899.
15. Ibid.
16. Ibid., p. 900.
17. Ibid., pp. 900-1.
18. Ibid., p.908.
19. *The US AAF in the Pacific*, p. 629.
20. *General Kenney Reports*, pp. 413-15.
21. *The Wartime Journals of Charles Lindbergh*, pp. 911-12.

Chapter 45: The Move to Biak Island
1. *The Wartime Journals of Charles Lindbergh*, p. 879.
2. Ibid., p. 883-4.
3. *The Legacy of the 90th Bomb Group, the Jolly Rogers*, p. 131.
4. Zellmer, *The Spectator*, p. 102.
5. *Autobiography of Donald A. Johnson*, 1997, from the webpage: https://familysearch.org/photos/stories/1809223.
6. *The Legacy of the 90th Bomb Group, the Jolly Rogers*, p. 131.
7. Ibid., p. 143.
8. *Under the Southern Cross*, p. 34.
9. Toll, *The Conquering Tide*, p. 521.

10. *Kerns, Above the Thunder*, p. 189.
11. *Autobiography of Donald A. Johnson*, 1997, from the webpage: https://familysearch.org/photos/stories/1809223.
12. *The Legacy of the 90th Bomb Group, the Jolly Rogers*, p. 134.
13. Ibid., pp. 111-12.
14. Ibid., p. 75.
15. Okumiya, *Zero*, p. 207.
16. *Approach to the Philippines*, pp. 421-2.
17. *Zero*, pp. 207-9.

Chapter 46: Life on Biak Island
1. James Horner in a letter to the author.
2. King, *The Last Zero Fighter*, p. 8.
3. Ibid., p. 258.
4. *The Legacy of the 90th Bomb Group, the Jolly Rogers*, p. 47.
5. *Under the Southern Cross*, p. 62.
6. *The Legacy of the 90th Bomb Group, the Jolly Rogers*, p. 40.
7. Ibid., p. 135.
8. *The Legacy of the 90th Bomb Group, the Jolly Rogers*, p. 121.
9. *The Wartime Journals of Charles Lindbergh*, p. 853.
10. *Tales of the Jolly Rogers*, p. 280.
11. Rogers, unpublished ms.
12. *The Wartime Journals of Charles Lindbergh*, pp. 808-9.
13. *The Legacy of the 90th Bomb Group, the Jolly Rogers*, pp. 135-6.
14. Ibid, pp. 136-7.
15. *Under the Southern Cross*, p. 74.
16. From the *Warfare History Network* online: http://warfarehistorynetwork.com/daily/wwii/two-typhoons-crippled-bull-halseys-task-force-38/.
17. *The Legacy of the 90th Bomb Group, the Jolly Rogers*, p. 151.
18. *The Last Zero Fighter*, p. 257.
19. *The Legacy of the 90th Bomb Group, the Jolly Rogers*, p. 144.
20. Ibid. p. 144.
21. *General Kenney Reports*, p. 446.
22. *The Legacy of the 90th Bomb Group, the Jolly Rogers*, p. 144.
23. Kenney, *Air War in the Pacific*, p. 350.
24. James Horner in a letter to the author.
25. *The Legacy of the 90th Bomb Group, the Jolly Rogers*, p. 137.

Chapter 47: The Move to the Philippines
1. *General Kenney Reports*, pp. 497-8.
2. *The Legacy of the 90th Bomb Group, the Jolly Rogers*, p. 155.
3. *General Kenney Reports*, pp. 503-4.
4. *The Legacy of the 90th Bomb Group, the Jolly Rogers*, p. 151.
5. Ibid., pp151-2.
6. Ibid., p. 154.
7. James Horner in a letter to the author.
8. *The Legacy of the 90th Bomb Group, the Jolly Rogers*, p. 156.
9. Kenney, *Air War in the Pacific*, pp. 388-89.
10. Manchester, *American Caesar*, pp. 482-3.
11. *Air War in the Pacific*, p. 386.
12. *American Caesar*, pp. 254-5.
13. *General Kenney Reports*, p. 371.
14. Tanaka, *Hidden Horrors*, pp. 82-3.
15. Ibid., pp 85-6.
16. *The Legacy of the 90th Bomb Group, the Jolly Rogers*, p. 157.
17. *American Caesar* p. 494.
18. Pacific Wrecks website.

19. Kenney, *The Saga of Pappy Gunn*, p. 90.

Chapter 48: The Horner Crew Returns Home
1. *The Legacy of the 90th Bomb Group, the Jolly Rogers*, p. 160.
2. Ibid., p. 182.
3. James Horner in a letter to the author.

Chapter 49: The End of the War
1. Manchester, *American Caesar*, pp. 510-11.
2. Sheftall, *Blossoms in the Wind*, pp. 30-31.
3. *The Legacy of the 90th Bomb Group, the Jolly Rogers*, p. 187.
4. Ibid., p. 188.

Chapter 50: The Jolly Rogers Disband
1. *The Legacy of the 90th Bomb Group, the Jolly Rogers*, p. 193.
2. Ibid., p. 192.
3. The numbers are from Veronico, *Hidden Warbirds*, p. 8.

Epilogue
1. Alcorn, *The Jolly Rogers*, p. 121.
2. McMurria, *Fight for Survival*, p. 165.
3. *The Legacy of the 90th Bomb Group, the Jolly Rogers*, pp. 195-201. The names of every man who died are listed, both alphabetically and chronologically.
4. Alcorn, *Tales of the Jolly Rogers*, p. 126.

ACKNOWLEDGMENTS

Thanks are due first, of course, to the three men who furnished first-hand information about flying Jolly Rogers bombers in the Pacific: Mr. James Horner, Mr. Jaime Baca, and Mr. Tom Theobald. Mr. Baca got the ball rolling by giving a talk about his experiences in the war to one of our home school history classes, and then helped us locate the other two surviving members of his bomber crew. He also came up with the book's title, after I told him that we didn't have a title for it but whatever title we came up with should probably include some reference to the Jolly Rogers. After thinking about it for a minute he said, "Well, I can tell you one thing: it wasn't so jolly over there. Could that be the title?" It is.

Mary Doherty could be said to have planted the seed for the project when she suggested that Deacon Baca come to our class to tell the students what it was like to be a bomber crewman during the war. That was when I met him for the first time, and things developed from there.

Thanks to Robert J. Tupa for most of the photographs that illustrate this book. Bob's grandfather was Capt. Norman Lawler, the adjutant of the Jolly Rogers, who had a connection with the Group's photo section. Capt. Lawler (photo on page 195) preserved hundreds of photos after the war and passed them down to his grandson Robert, who made them all available to me for this book. Bob is also the treasurer for the 90th Bomb Group Association, puts out the Association's newsletter, and organizes the annual reunions. As I was writing this book, there was rarely a question about the Jolly Rogers that Bob couldn't answer, and he would often illustrate an answer with a useful photograph, which probably makes him the world's leading authority on the Group.

Col. Art Rogers' grandson, Eric, put me in touch with his father, Col. Rogers' oldest son, Buck. Buck provided me with a copy of his father's unpublished war memoir, along with permission to quote extensively from it, which I have done. Buck's younger brother Bill found the manuscript among their mother's effects, transcribed it, and then put it into PDF form so that it could be e-mailed to me. Buck also loaned me his father's copy of Andrew Lord's book, *Tales of the Jolly Rogers*, when I had difficulty finding a copy.

Thanks are due to Mrs. Beatrice Holmes, who read, corrected, and critiqued the original manuscript, and stressed the need for more maps.

James Horner's daughter Cindy Kruczynski typed up many of her father's reminiscences for me; his son, Dick, furnished some photos and videotaped his father speaking about his war experiences, and his daughter Pam assisted tremendously by locating Michael Cooper, the son of the crew's copilot, Lt. Allen Cooper. Dick, Cindy and Pam offered continual encouragement throughout the writing of the book.

Mike Cooper, or "Coop," made an invaluable contribution when he mailed me a box containing all of his father's wartime military papers and memorabilia. This was a real treasure chest. Among the items in the box were his father's mission diary and his flight logbook (neither Mr. Horner nor Mr. Theobald still have their logbooks). Using Lt. Cooper's flight log, I was able to put dates on each of the crew's flights, beginning from the time that Lt. Cooper joined the Horner crew in the spring of 1944. The mission dairy identified the target of each bombing mission along with Lt. Cooper's comments on what happened during that mission.

One item in the collection was a "short snorter," a Filipino dollar bill that had been signed by each member of the crew when they were in the Philippines. One of the names on the bill was Jaime Baca's, and when I showed it to Mr. Baca recently he said he did not remember signing it, and with his declining vision he could not make out his signature, but he said it was very interesting to hold that bill again after an interval of over seventy years.

Cynthia Lundry, the daughter of the crew's navigator, Tom Theobald, provided me with information about her father, and Rochelle Kane, who works at the assisted living facility where Mr. Theobald resides, interviewed him with a video camera and sent me the footage.

The nephews of Mr. Baca, Tom and Jim Baca, were also helpful; Jim provided a transcript of an interview he did of his uncle in which they discussed his war experiences, and Tom furnished the picture of Sgt. Baca at the time he joined the Air Corps from an old newspaper clipping (p. 415). Both provided encouragement along the way. Since Mr. Baca's poor vision prevented him from driving a car, Mr. Jerry Miller and Mr. Art Vandereedt drove him to my home at different times for dinner and chats about his war experiences.

Bob Nelson contributed photos left to him by his father, John Nelson. John had been a gunner and photographer with the Jolly Rogers' 319th Squadron and was credited with shooting down two Japanese fighter planes. Ray Cervantes e-mailed me, in PDF form, the diary of Lt. George Pracher, the navigator of a Jolly Rogers bomber named "Double Trouble." John Brown, the son of the Jolly Rogers' last commander, Col. Ellis L. Brown, offered support and encouragement. Others with whom I corresponded about the Jolly Rogers were Randall Nave, the nephew of Sgt. Fred Diggs, who died in the ditching of the Jolly Rogers bomber named "Crosair" (pages 137-41), Mrs. Beejay Butterfield, wife of Jolly Rogers pilot Earl Butterfield, and Leigh Holland, daughter of pilot Dale Holland. The Horner and Holland crews frequently flew missions together and the crewmen were friends.

John Barone, a gunner on the Holland crew and a good friend of Jaime Baca when their crews were flying bombing missions together, contacted me through his son Joe to let me know that he was from Brooklyn, not New Jersey as I had originally written—in fact he was known on his crew as the "Brooklyn Kid," and he had that nickname written on both his leather jacket and field cap (photo at right). John and Joe together also reviewed the video version of the Jolly Rogers story for me.

I was very fortunate that my daughter Mary Baker is an editor, artist, and graphic designer. Mary proofread and edited this book, did the page layout, designed the cover, and then put the manuscript into the electronic form required by an online publisher. Mary's services are available to other writers; she can be contacted at her website: Quills, Nibs, and Keyboards Editing and Design Service (qnkediting.com). My wife Lee created most of the book's maps in a computer graphics program and also spent many hours working on the index, while my brothers Don and John reviewed and made suggestions for improving the manuscript, which makes this book something of a family effort. Mary is also a student glider pilot, and her flight instructor, Stan Roeske, took an interest in the story of the Horner crew and arranged for the 90-minute video version of the crew's story to be shown to a large audience at an adult education center, where it was so well received that I was spurred to finish the book at a time when my energy was flagging from all the research required.

John Barone, known as the "Brooklyn Kid," posing with his bomber crew in 1944. Today he is 96 years old.

Without the assistance of all the above people, to each of whom I give sincere thanks, this book could not have been written.

BIBLIOGRAPHY

Ambrose, Stephen E., *The Wild Blue, The Men and Boys Who Flew the B-24s Over Germany 1944-45*, Simon & Schuster, 2007.

Ardery, Philip, *Bomber Pilot, A Memoir of World War II*, Kentucky, 1978.

Arnn, Larry P., *Churchill's Trial, Winston Churchill and the Salvation of Free Government*, Thomas Nelson, 2015.

Astor, Gerald, *Crisis in the Pacific, The Battles for the Philippine Islands by the Men Who Fought Them—An Oral History*, Donald I. Fine, 1996.
Semper Fi in the Sky, Marine Air Battles of World War II, Ballantine, 2005.

Barker, Rodney, *Hiroshima Maidens*, Penguin, 1985.

Barrie, Alexander, *War Underground*, Ballantine, 1961.

Beevor, Antony, *The Fall of Berlin 1945*, Penguin, 2002.

Bendiner, Elmer, *The Fall of Fortresses, A Personal Account of the most Daring— And Deadly—American Air Battles of World War II*, G. P. Putnam's Sons, 1980.

Benson, James, *Prisoner's Base and Home Again*, Badger Books, 1959.

Belote, James H. and William M., *Corregidor, The Saga of a Fortress*, Harper & Row, 1967.

Bergerud, Eric M., *Fire in the Sky, The Air War in the South Pacific*, Westview, 2000.
Touched with Fire, The Land War in the South Pacific, Penguin Books, 1996.

Birdsall, Steve, *Flying Buccaneers, The Illustrated Story of Kenney's Fifth Air Force*, Doubleday, 1977.
Log of the Liberators, The iIllustrated combat record of the B-24 Liberator and of the men and units that flew them in the Second World War, Doubleday, 1973.

Blair, Clay, *Hitler's U-Boat War, The Hunted 1942-1945*, Random House, 1998.

Bowman, Martin W., *B-24 Combat Missions, First-hand Accounts of Liberator Operations over Nazi Europe*, Metro Books, 2009.

Bradley, James, *Flyboys*, Little, Brown, 2003.

Bryan, III, Lt. Comdr. J., USNR & Reed, Philip, *Mission Beyond Darkness*, Duell, Sloan & Pearce, 1945.

Campbell, James, *The Ghost Mountain Boys, Their Epic March and Terrifying Battle for New Guinea—The Forgotten War of the South Pacific*, Crown, 2007.

Cass, William F., *The Last Flight of Liberator 41-1133, The Lives, Times, Training and Loss of the Bomber Crew which crashed on Trail Peak at Philmont Scout Ranch*, The Winds Aloft, 1996.

Childers, Thomas, *Wings of Morning, The Story of the Last American Bomber shot down over Germany in World War II*, Addison-Wesley, 1995.

Claringbould, Michael John, *The Forgotten Fifth, A Photographic Chronology of the U.S. Fifth Air Force in the Pacific in World War Two*, Aerothentic Publications of Australia, 1997.

Connolly, Bob & Anderson, Robin, *First Contact, New Guinea's Highlanders Encounter the Outside World*, Penguin, 1987.

Crumpton, Kit, *Raiding the Empire of the Sun: Tinian 1945*, Ro Bar Romaani, 2011.

Cundiff, Michael J., *Ten Knights in a Bar Room, Missing in Action in the Southwest Pacific, 1943*, Iowa State University Press, 1990.

Curtis, Richard K., *Dumb But Lucky, Confessions of a P-51 fighter Pilot in World War II*, Ballantine, 2005.

Davis, James M., *In Hostile Skies, An American B-24 Pilot in World War II*, UNT, 2006.

Dorr, Robert F., *B-24 Liberator Units of the Pacific War*, Osprey, 1999.

Duffy, James P., *War at the End of the World, Douglas MacArthur and the Forgotten Fight for New Guinea, 1942-1945*, NAL Caliber, 2016.

Eden, Paul, and Soph. Moeng, *Aircraft Anatomy of World War II*, Amber Books, Ltd., 2007.

Edsel, Robert M., *The Monuments Men, Allied Heroes, Nazi Thieves, and the Greatest Treasure Hunt in History*, Center Street, 2009.

Evans, Richard J., *The Third Reich at War*, Penguin, 2009.

Francis, Devon, *Mr. Piper and His Cubs*, Sentimental Journey, 1987.

Gallagher, James P., *With The Fifth Army Air Force*, Johns Hopkins, 2001.

Gamble, Bruce, *Invasion Rabaul Book One of the Rabaul Trilogy*, Zenith, 2006.
    Fortress Rabaul, the Battle for the Southwest Pacific, Zenith, 2010.
    Target: Rabaul, Book Three of the Rabaul Trilogy, Zenith, 2013.

Gann, Ernest K., *Blaze of Noon*, Holt, 1946.
    In the Company of Eagles, Simon & Schuster, 1966.

Griffith, Jr., Thomas E., *MacArthur's Airman, General George C. Kenney and the War in the Southwest Pacific*, Kansas, 1998.

Hammer, Joshua, *Yokohama Burning*, Free, 2006.

Henebry, John P., *The Grim Reapers, The Third Attack Group of the U.S. Fifth Air Force*, Pictoral Histories, 2002

Hillenbrand, Laura, *Unbroken, A World War II Story of Survival, Resilience, and Redemption*, Random House, 2010.

Holland, James, *Dam Busters, The True Story of the Inventors and Airmen who led the Devastating Raid to Smash the German Dams in 1943*, Grove, 2012.

Hylton, Will S., *Vanished, The Sixty-Year Search for the Missing Men of World War II*, Riverhead, 2013.

Hyman, Nat, *Eyes of the War, A Photographic Report of World War II*, Tel-Pic Sales, 1945.

Idriess, Ion L., *Gold Dust and Ashes, The Romantic Story of the New Guinea Goldfields*, Angus & Robertson, 1947.

Imparato, Edward T., *Into Darkness, A Pilot's Journey Through Headhunter Territory*, Howell, 1995.

Jasper, Joy, Waldron/Delgado, James P./Adams, Jim, *The USS Arizona, The Ship, the Men, the Pearl Harbor attack, and the Symbol that aroused America*, St. Martin's, 2001.

Johnson, Forrest Bryant, *Phantom Warrior, The Heroic True Story of Pvt. John McKinney's One-Man Stand against the Japanese in World War II*, Caliber, 2007.

Johnston, George H., *The Toughest Fighting in the World, The Australian and American Campaign for New Guinea in World War II*, Westholme, 2011.

Kenney, General George, *Air War in the Pacific, The Journal of General George Kenney, Commander of the Fifth U.S. Air Force*, Duell, Sloan and Pearce, 1949.
   General Kenney Reports, A Personal History of the Pacific War, Office of Air Force History, 1987.
   The Saga of Pappy Gunn, Duell, Sloan and Pearce, 1959.

Kerns, Raymond C., *Above the Thunder*, Kent State University, 2009.

King, Dan, *The Last Zero Fighter, Firsthand Accounts from WWII Japanese Naval Pilots*, Pacific, 2012.

Kolln, Jeff, *Northrop's Night Hunter: the P-61 Black Widow*, Specialty Pr Pub & Wholesalers, 2008.

Kowalik, Ernest E., *Alone and Unarmed, An Army Pilot sharing the skies with

Artillery Fire in WWII Italy, Glenn Curtiss, 1968.

Krueger, General Walter, *From Down Under to Nippon, The Story of Sixth Army in World War II*, Battery, 1989.

Lamont-Brown, Raymond, *Kamikaze, Japan's Suicide Samurai*, Rigel, 1997.

Lindbergh, Charles A., *The Wartime Journals of Charles A, Lindbergh*, Harcourt Brace Jovanovich, 1970.

Livingstone, Bob, *Under the Southern Cross, The B-24 Liberator in the South Pacific*, Turner, 1998.

Lord, Andrew M., Lt. Col., USAF *Tales of the Jolly Rogers*, Andrew M. Lord, 1985.

Makos, Adam, with Larry Alexander, *A Higher Call, An Incredible True Story of Combat and Chivalry in the War-Torn Skies of World War II*, Berkley Caliber, 2012.
with Marcus Brotherton, *Voices of the Pacific, Untold Stories from the Marine Heroes of World War II*, Berkley Caliber, 2013.

Manchester, William, *American Caesar, Douglas MacArthur 1880-1964*, Dell, 1978.
Goodbye, Darkness, A Memoir of the Pacific War, Back Bay, 1979.
The Last Lion, Visions of Glory 1874-1932, Dell, 1983.

Mayo, Lida, *Bloody Buna, The Grueling Campaign in New Guinea that Thwarted the Japanese Invasion of Australia*, Doubleday, 1974.

McAuley, Lex, *MacArthur's Eagles, The U.S. Air War Over New Guinea, 1943-1944*, Naval Institute, 2005.

McManus, John C., *Deadly Sky, The American Combat Airman in World War II*, Presidio, 2000.

McMurria, Captain James Austin, *Fight for Survival!, An American Bomber Pilot's 1,000 Days as a P.O.W. of the Japanese*, Honoribus Press, 2005

Merridale, Catherine, *Ivan's War, Life and Death in the Red Army, 1939-1945*, Metropolitan, 2006.

Middlebrook, Garrett, *Air Combat at 20 Feet, Selected Missions from a Strafer Pilot's Diary*, Authorhouse, 2004.

Miller, Donald L., *Masters of the Air, America's Bomber Boys Who Fought the Air War Against Nazi Germany*, Simon & Schuster, 2006.

Moore, Jack I., *We Never Said Good-Bye, Memoirs of a Bombardier from World War II*, CGM, 2011.

Morris, Eric, *Corregidor, The American Alamo of World War II*, Cooper Square, 1981.

Nason, Joseph G., *Horio You Nezt Die!*, Pacific Rim, 1987

Okyumiya, Masatake, and Jiro Horikoshi, with Martin Caidin, *Zero!*, Ballantine, 1956.

O'Reilly, Bill, & Martin Dugard, *Killing the Rising Sun, How America Vanquished World War II Japan,* Henry Holt, 2016.

Park, Edward *Nanette, Her Pilot's Love Story,* Smithsonian, 1989.

Parshall, Jonathan, and Anthony Tully, *Shattered Sword, The Untold Story of the Battle of Midway,* Potomac, 2005.

Paull, Raymond, *Retreat from Kokoda, The Austrlian Campaign in New Guinea 1942,* Heinemann, 1958.

Peckham, Howard H., and Shirley A. Snyder (Editors), *Letters from the Greatest Generation: Writing Home in WWII,* Indiana University Press, 2016.

Pelander, Colonel Jack H., *Combat Pilot B-24 World War II*, Jack H. Pelander 2002.

Pinney, Peter, *The Barbarians, A Soldier's New Guinea Diary,* University of Queensland, 1988.

Ralph, Barry, *Savage Wilderness, the Epic Outback search for the Crew of Little Eva,* University of Queensland, 2004.

Rees, Laurence, *Horror in the East, Japan and the Atrosities of World War II,* Da Capo, 2001.

Reynolds, Quentin, *70,000 to One*, Pyramid, 1960.

Rogers, Everett M. and Nancy R. Bartlit *Silent Vioces of World War II, When the Son of the Land of Enchantment met the Sons of the Rising Sun,* Sunstone, 2005.

Rutter, Joseph W., *Wreaking Havoc, A Year in an A-20,* Texas A&M, 2004.

Sakai, Saburo, with Martin Caidin and Fred Saito *Samarai!, The Autobiography of Japan's World War II Flying Ace,* Uncommon Valo.r, 2015.

Salecker, Gene Eric, *Fortress Against the Sun, The B-17 Flying Fortress in the Pacific,* Combined, 2001.

Scearce, Phil, *Finish Forty and Home, The Untold World War II Story of B-24s in the Pacific,* UNT, 2011.

Serling, Robert J., *When the Airlines Went to War, The Dramatic, Never-Before-Told Story of America's Civilian Air Warriors,* Kensington, 1997.

Sheehan, Susan, *A Missing Plane,* Putnam, 1986.

Sheftall, M. G., *Blossoms in the Wind, Human Legacies of the Kamikaze,* NAL Caliber, 2005.

Sides, Hampton, *Ghost Soldiers, The Epic Account of World War II's greatest Rescue Mission,* Anchor, 2001.

Siegal, Craig, *Righteous Might, One Man's Journey through War in the Pacific*, Rochelle, 2011.

Sloan, Bill, *Brotherhood of Heroes, The Marines at Peleliu, 1944—The Bloodiest Battle of the Pacific War*, Simon & Schuster, 2005.

Smith, Larry, *Iwo Jima, World War II Veterans Remember the Greatest Battle of the Pacific*, Norton, 2008.

Smith, Robert Ross, *The Approach to the Philippines, The War in the Pacific*, The National Historical Society, 1994.

Taaffe, Stephen R., *MacArthur's Jungle War, The 1944 New Guinea Campaign*, Kansas, 1998.

Tamura, Keiko *Michi's Memories, The Story of a Japanese War Bride*, Australian National University, 2011.

Tanaka, Yuki, *Hidden Horrors, Japanese War Crimes in World War II*, Westview, 1996.

The 33rd Infantry Division Historical Committee, *The Golden Cross, A History of the 33rd Infantry Division in World War II*, Battery Press, 1948.

Thomas, Gordon, and Max Morgan Witts, *Ruin from the Air, The Enola Gay's Atomic Mission to Hiroshima*, Scarborough House, 1997.

Tillman, Barrett, *Clash of the Carriers, The True Story of the Marianas Turkey Shoot of World War II*, Caliber, 2005.

Toland, John, *The Last 100 Days, The Tumultuous and Controversial Story of the Final Days of World War II in Europe*, Random House, 1965.

Toll, Ian W., *The Conquering Tide, War in the Pacific Islands, 1942-1944 Volume II*, Norton, 2015.

Veronico, Nicholas A., *Hidden Warbirds, the Epic Stories of Finding, Recovering and Rebuilding WWII's Lost Aircraft*, Zenith, 2013.

West, Diana, *American Betrayal, The Secret Assault on Our Nation's Character*, St. Martin's Press, 2013.

Whiting, Wayne B., and Jerry W., *I'm off to War, Mother, But I'll be Back, Reflections of a WWII Tail Gunner*, Tarnaby, 2001.

Woods, Jr., Wiley O., *Legacy of the 90th Bombardment Group, "The Jolly Rogers,"* Turner, 1994

Zellmer, David, *The Spectator, A World War II Bomber Pilot's Journal of the Artist as Warrior*, Praeger, 1999.

Zuckoff, Mitchell, *Frozen in Time, An Epic Story of Survival and a Modern Quest for Lost Heroes of World War II*, Harper, 2014.

INDEX

Numbers

1st Marine Division 366, 368, 374
5th Air Force xviii, 1, 48-52, 81, 142, 173-4, 207, 224, 232, 235, 239, 240, 311, 367-8, 376, 394-7, 403, 472, 484, 561-2, 579, 586, 670, 694, 696-8
  table of organization 49
7th Air Force 41
7th Australian Division 56, 90, 317, 322, 324, 495
"8-Ball" (B-24) 64, 72
9th Australian Division 321-2
13th Air Force 581, 615, 679, 699
13th Bomb Group (B-24s) 566
19th Bomb Group (Heavy) 7, 53, 84, 96, 103, 174
20th Air Force 697
24th Infantry Division 393, 720
32nd Army Division 90, 219, 401
33rd Infantry Division 553
38th Bomb Group (Medium) 200, 303
41st Infantry Division 90, 219, 393, 515-16, 519-20, 531, 580, 598-9, 602, 608
  at Battle of Biak Island 531, 580
  at Battle of Hollandia 393
  at Battle of Wakde Island 515, 520
43rd Bomb Group (Heavy) 7, 84, 87, 92-3, 95, 130, 143-5, 190, 203, 224, 228-9, 233, 235, 237, 269, 308, 368, 386, 397, 600, 608, 621, 626
54th Troop Carrier Wing 211, 317
77th Infantry Division, U. S. 740, 742
90th Bomb Group (Jolly Rogers) xix, 1-3, 5, 13-15, 24-5, 27-9, 31-5, 40-5, 47-50, 53-60, 63-6, 68-73, 77, 79-80, 84, 87, 89-93, 95, 97-101, 107-8, 113, 116, 118, 127-7, 142-6, 148, 151-3, 156-7, 164, 174, 176, 178-81, 183, 188-91, 193, 196, 201-3, 206, 208-9, 211, 220-1, 223, 228-9, 232, 239-41, 247, 251, 253-4, 269-70, 274-5, 277, 318, 325, 328, 331, 333, 343, 364, 368, 375, 377-9, 442, 471, 476, 480-1, 484, 506-7, 510-11, 516, 519, 528, 539, 551-2, 556, 563, 580, 606-7, 610, 616, 621, 633, 635, 660, 680, 706, 708, 751-4, 756, 767, 773-4
  at Willow Run 27
  first combat mission 66, 69-71
  flies to Australia 44
  flies to Hawaii 37
  four squadrons of the 90th 2
  second mission 78, 84, 86
319th Squadron 2, 37, 40, 63, 70, 73, 95, 99, 101, 108, 137, 145, 155-7, 164, 180-1, 183-5, 187, 270-1, 274, 318, 353, 461, 526, 574, 607, 624-5, 678
320th Squadron 2, 70, 84, 88, 91, 130, 152-3, 188, 203, 223, 270-1, 278, 304, 324, 348, 350, 380, 404, 493, 502, 505-6, 556, 574, 607, 624, 627, 653, 662-3, 669, 679, 687, 730
321st Squadron 2, 117-18, 148, 151, 156, 188, 209, 221, 228, 232, 270-1, 295, 305, 328, 340, 356, 574-5, 607, 630, 650, 654-5, 685, 695, 774
400th Squadron 2, 64, 144-5, 164, 188, 205, 270-2, 304-6, 318, 462, 574, 607, 702, 750
162nd Regimental Combat Team 299
345th Bomb Group (Medium) 189-90, 332, 590, 654, 745
348th Fighter Group (P-47) 188, 332, 595
380th Bomb Group (B-24s) "Flying Circus" 180, 183, 368, 403
421st Night Fighter Squadron 563
475th Fighter Group "Satan's Angels" (P-38s) 188, 332, 580, 583-5, 588-9, 592,

INDEX

605, 698
503rd Parachute Regiment 316, 319, 720-1

A

A-20 Havoc, Douglas 94, 189, 227-9, 231, 239, 318-19, 360, 368-9, 385, 392, 397, 522, 550, 570, 584
A-24 BD Dauntless dive bomber 192
Abe, Shinzo (Japanese Prime Minister) 769, 770-1
Aborigines, Australian 63, 122, 128
Above the Thunder (book) by Raymond Kerns 452
Acetylene Annie 26
Ack-Ack See Flak
Adachi, Gen. Hatazō 322, 512
Adair, Sgt. Uhland S. 358-9
Adams, 1st Lt. Harold M. 131
Adams, 1st Lt. Richard A. 131, 305, 353-5, 362
Adams, Sgt. Rupert W. 305
Adler, 1st Lt. Irving 328
aerobatics by Japanese fighter pilots 108
Affeld, Sgt. Freddie K. 154
Ah Cheu (MacArthur's son's nanny) 715
air superiority xvii, xviii
Air Transport Command (ATC) 670
Air Apaches (345th Bomb Group) 745
Aitape, New Guinea 394, 397, 512-13
Akikaze (Japanese destroyer) 166
Akikaze massacre 166
Alexander, 1st Lt. Alonzo D. 138
Alexishafen, New Guinea 131, 402
"Alley Oop" (B-24) 185-7
Allred, Lt. Robert 503-6
Altman, 2nd Lt. Dayton S. 152-4, 173
Amberly Field, Australia 44
Ambon Island 180, 204, 570, 571, 574, 590, 593, 620-1, 623-6, 627, 718
America First Committee 409
American Manila Cemetery 150
American Pacific Fleet xvii, 2, 409
American Graves Registration Service 150, 307, 608, 635
American Volunteer Group (AVG) 270
A Missing Plane (book by Susan Sheehan) 505
Anderson, Lt. George R. 631
Angel Island, San Francisco Bay 41
Approach to the Philippines (The) (book) 638

Araki, Yukio (child kamikaze pilot) 734
Arawe, New Britain 365-8, 371, 373
Arlington National Cemetery 129
armor of B-24s discarded in Australia 484-5
Army Air Corps xviii, 13, 22, 48, 50, 207, 407, 411, 413, 421, 426-7, 436, 447, 635, 660, 671
Arnold, General "Hap" xviii 42, 318, 370-1,
Ashai Shimbun (Japanese newspaper) vi
Asterperious (319th Squadron nickname) 270-1
AT-6 Texan (North American) trainer plane 428, 443
AT-7 Navigator (Beechcraft) trainer plane 440
AT-9 Curtiss advanced trainer plane 428
AT-10 Beechcraft advanced trainer plane 428, 434-5, 449
AT-11A Kansan (Beechcraft) trainer plane 440
AT-17 Cessna advanced trainer plane 428, 435, 447
atabrine tablets for malaria 61, 206, 493, 494
atomic bombs xviii, 382, 737-8, 742, 751-2
atrocities, Japanese 624, 718
    Akikaze massacre 166-7
    Banka Island Massacre 717-18
    Bataan Death March xvi, 235, 418, 711, 715, 718, 770
    Buna Mission Massacre 167-9
    eating prisoners' livers 170
    Harvey family murdered 83
    Hong Kong hospital massacre 717-18
    Kavieng Wharf Massacre 382
    Laha Massacre 82-3, 171, 382, 624-6, 718
    Manila Massacre 711
    Palawan Massacre 382, 624, 726
    sinking of hospital ship Centaur 771
    shooting men in parachutes 233, 285, 678
    Rape of Nanking xvi, 709, 711, 769
    Talili Bay Massacre 171
    Tol Plantation Massacre 82-3
    torture of nuns at Rabaul 168
    Wake Island Massacre 382, 771
Austin, Lt. Louis 168-9
Australia xi, xii, xviii, 2, 33, 35, 42, 44-5, 48-9, 53-4, 56-7, 63, 78, 82, 92, 98, 112, 122, 136-7, 146, 155, 167, 176, 181, 186-7, 188, 198, 201, 206, 219, 277, 288-9, 299, 311, 366-7, 370-1, 376, 388, 396, 403, 418, 468, 470, 473,

477, 480-1, 485-6, 489, 492, 499, 555, 579, 594, 606, 612, 669-77, 699, 715-16, 728, 731, 737, 751-2, 754
Australian 22nd Battalion—see Lark Force
Australian money 675
Australian:
    nurses 717-18
    pilots 699
    troops 56, 58-9, 210, 219, 223, 238,
    allied with Americans 288-90, 292-3, 296, 298, 320, 322-3, 386, 669, 692, 708-9
Australian 7th Division 56
Axis Powers 14, 409

B

B-17 Flying Fortress, Boeing xviii, 1, 5-7, 9-13, 27, 29, 37, 42, 53-4, 87, 92-3, 132, 142,-7, 152, 189-90, 197-9, 224, 228, 233-5, 237-8, 240, 303, 315, 317-21, 333, 418, 437, 442, 452, 468, 477, 484, 499, 659, 715, 724, 745-6
    durability of 5
    wing differences from B-24 5
B-24 Liberator, Consolidated xviii1, 1-34, 36-7, 41-4, 47, 53-4, 63-4, 67-9, 71-6, 84-88, 92, 94, 96, 100, 109, 113-16, 118, 120, 124-5, 129, 131, 133, 137-139, 143-4, 146, 152-4, 158, 160-1, 164, 173, 175-9, 181, 183-6, 189,191-6, 198, 220-1, 223, 225, 228, 232, 240, 243-5, 248, 250-1, 253-4, 250, 255-6, 260, 269-70, 273-4, 280, 282, 287, 292, 294, 303, 308, 319, 323-4, 329, 331-4, 340, 345, 350, 355-6, 360, 368, 378, 380, 385, 387-9, 390, 392, 394, 397, 403-4, 410-12, 436-9, 441-3, 445, 449, 454-61, 464, 466, 471, 476, 479-80, 483-9, 500-2, 505-7, 510-12, 515-17, 522, 525, 529, 534, 537-9, 542-3, 556, 564, 566, 568-9, 572, 577, 581-3, 592, 594-6, 606, 613, 615, 624, 626-8, 630, 634-6, 647-51, 654-7, 660-3, 666,-7, 671, 678-81, 683-5, 687-90, 696-7, 700, 712, 724, 729-32, 754, 756, 760, 764-7
    flying range 10
    fuel capacity 4

Model 31 Flying Boat 7
nose turret 18, 29, 30, 33, 43, 65,116, 160, 173, 176-179, 240-1, 243-4, 247, 249, 250-2, 254, 331, 339, 378, 460, 547, 647, 651, 684, 720, 722
origin of name Liberator 4
specifications 2-4
B-25 Mitchell, North American 94-5, 108, 222, 225-9, 236-9, 291-3, 296, 303, 310, 312-14, 318, 322, 332-3, 349, 368-71, 385, 388, 392, 419, 654, 656, 696, 737, 745-6
B-26 Marauder, Martin 1, 163, 397, 499,
B-29 Superfortress, Boeing xviii, 9, 10, 634, 697, 710, 734-5, 737, 743, 752
Baa Baa Black Sheep (book and TV series) 381, 634
Babo Airdrome, New Guinea 570-1
Baca, Benedito 417
Baca, Tom and Jim (nephews of Jaime Baca) 786
Baca, Jaime ii, 134, 405 (crew picture), 407-8, 411, 415-20, 441-5, 454-6, 459-63, 466-7, 473, 476-8, 481-4, 489, 492, 494, 496, 501, 515, 517, 519, 522-3, 540-6, 548-9, 552, 555-7, 560-1, 565, 567-8, 592, 602, 611-12, 614, 617-19, 624, 627-9, 643, 645, 647-8, 650, 654, 656-8, 664, 674, 683-6, 689, 691, 694, 702-4, 706, 709, 712-13, 720, 724-5, 728, 758, 764
    Baca family history 415-16
    drafted into army 419
    goes to gunnery school 441-3
    in train wreck 443-5
    near-crash at Palm Springs 465-7
    flight to Hawaii 473-4
    at Port Moresby 496, 501
    encounters Kimodo Dragon 496
    first combat mission 539-49
    tries to open coconut 560
    sees blood-splattered B-24 568-9
    shoots up Japanese fighter plane 629
    long missions to Philippines 643
    hit by flak fragment 650-1
    deals with stuck bomb 656
    goes on leave to Sydney 670-8
    flight through big storm 683-7
    sees phosphorus bombs 689, 691
    bombs Corregidor 712

INDEX

witness air assault on Corregidor 720
witness to Battle of Manila 722
returns home from war 733
life after the war 758
"Bad Penny" (B-24) 274
Baer, Sgt. Max 269
Baggett, Sgt. Sidney L. 350
bagpipe 196
Baibara Island, New Guinea 75, 77
Baker, Capt. Donald A. 430, 723
Baker, Don 787
Baker, John 787
Baker, Mary (book editor) 787, back cover
Baker, Elise (Lee) 787
Baker, Sgt. William 313
Balikpapan, Borneo xiv, 544, 677-9, 698
Ball, Sgt. William D. 354
Balut, Sgt. Mitchell E. 354
Bandy, Lt. 211
Banka Island Massacre 717
Banks, Lt. Col. Wilson 618, 725
barges, Japanese 142, 152, 238-9, 322, 368-9, 584-5, 693
Barksdale Field, Louisiana 2, 13, 15, 32, 68, 242-3, 442
Barone, Sgt. John 476, 787
Barone, Joseph (son of John) 787
Bassman, 2nd Lt. Herbert R. 88
Bataan Peninsula 235, 418, 712, 714-15, 719-20, 744-5
Bataan Death March xvi, 235, 418, 711, 715, 718, 770
Batchelor Field, Darwin, Australia 180
bats, Australian, at Iron Range 60
Battle for Biak Island 602
Battle of Leyte Gulf 692
Battle of Lone Tree Hill 518-20, 598
Battle of Manila 709, 727
Battle of Midway xv, 382, 672
Battle of Rabaul 82
Battle of the Bismarck Sea 11, 94, 190, 219-20, 222, 226-7, 232-3, 238-9, 254, 292, 302, 310, 323, 340, 366, 368, 370, 584
Battle of the Coral Sea xviii, 10, 55, 672
Battle of the Kokoda Trail 56, 74, 90, 209, 394, 497
Battle of the Philippine Sea 648
Battle of Tushima Strait xi
Bearskin, Captain Leaford 695
Beaufighter, Bristol (heavy attack fighter plane) 228, 333, 345
Beaufort (twin-engine British fighter-bomber) 185, 224, 228
Beeby, William H. (chaplain) 196
beer 553-4, 543
beheading by Japanese xvi, 82, 143, 168-70, 314, 625, 630, 638, 716-17
belly turret, B-24 36, 42, 72
Bena Bena, New Guinea 165, 210-11, 216-17, 308, 325
Benny, Jack (comedian) 616-17
Benson, Rev. James (missionary) vi, 167, 170, 171, 763
Berkowitz, Sgt. Marvin 198
Bernier, Lt. William 631
Berry, Capt. Alexander R. 171
Best Years of Our Lives, The (movie) 754 (footnote)
"Betsy" (B-24) 1 (picture)
Betty bomber (Mitsubishi GM4) 54, 522, 549, 744-6, 749
Biak Island 384, 394-6, 490, 511, 515-16, 518, 522-4, 531-2, 553, 560, 569, 574, 580-3, 589-92, 594-5, 597, 601-2, 604-20, 623, 626, 629-30, 634, 642-3, 645, 650-2, 654-6, 666-7, 669-71, 677-83, 687, 690-704, 729-32, 739, 764, 766-8, 773
"Big Chief" (B-24) 695
"Big Emma" (B-24) 64, 86-7
Bildad Prison, Manila 717, 726-7
birds 14, 63, 77, 194-5, 234, 259, 263, 478, 496, 504, 512, 703
Bixler, S/Sgt. Gordon 130, 493
black market in Sydney, Australia 676-7
Black Pirates (400th Squadron nickname) 270
Black Sunday (weather-caused crashes) 396-7
Black Widow (P-61 night fighter) 522, 563-5, 595, 611, 727
Blakely, Sgt. Kizzel 576
Blanche Bay, Rabaul 143
Blaney, 1st Lt. Fred H. 353
Bleasdale, Maj. Jack 146
Blecha, Sgt. Joseph S. 576
Blessing, Sgt. John M. 307
Blossoms in the Wind by M. G. Sheftall ix
Bobbora, Sgt. Rocco W. 358
Boela, Ceram Island 570-1, 592, 594
Boes, Sgt. Stephen K. 342
Bogadjim Road, New Guinea 326, 328
Bogucki, Sgt. Francis H. 154

"Boise Bronc" (B-24) 484, 660-1 front book cover
bombsight training device 679-80
Bombs Away (321st Squadron nickname) 270
"Bombs To Nippon" (B-24) 87
Bong, Maj. Richard I. 697-8, 700, 759, 762
Booroojy, 1st Lt. John K. 85
Borneo xii, xiv, 49, 544, 677
Bosnik village, Biak Island 599-601
Boster, 2nd Lt. Charles F. 137
Boston (RAAF A-20 light bomber) 228
Bougainville Island xv, 70-1, 77, 136, 139, 330-1, 367, 381, 552, 637, 767
Bowen, Sgt. William H. 340
Boyer, Sgt. Clarence W. 218
Boyington, Maj. Gregory "Pappy" 381, 634, 700
Branchley, Margaret (missionary) 169
Brawn, 1st Lt. Philip W. 576
Brayton Flying Service 429, 432-3, 435
Brett, Lt. Gen. George 50-1
Brigham, Sgt. Francis H. 153-4
Brisbane, Australia 44, 50, 53, 57, 98-100, 127, 142, 173, 207, 222, 225, 242, 251, 331-2, 369, 376, 393, 395, 559, 580, 585-8, 596, 728
Britain, Great 10, 299, 409, 672
Browder, Lt. Bennet "Big Ben" 241-2, 246, 249-50, 258-9, 262, 264, 336, 378
Brown, 2nd Lt. Eugene B., Jr. 218
Brown, John (son of Col. Ellis Brown) 787
Brown, Capt. (later Col.) Ellis 304, 725, 787
Browning, Lt. Archie B. 223-4
Brown, Joe E. (comedian) 616-17
Brown, John (son of Col. Ellis Brown) 787
Bruni, Sgt. Doy E. Pat II, 439, 449, 454-5, 458, 463, 465, 472, 486, 534-5, 680, 692
BT-13 (Vultee) trainer plane 422, 433-4, 447
Buddhism vi
Buin-Faisi anchorage, Bougainville Island 70-1
Bullis, Harry, Maj. (and Col.) 40, 70, 269, 379, 507, 760
Bullwinkel, Nurse Vivian 718
Buna village, New Guinea xviii, 55, 90-1, 95, 100, 167, 169, 219, 223, 236, 256, 267, 288-9, 296, 342-4, 353, 387, 400-1, 763, 767, 772
Buna Mission Massacre 167-70, 772
Bundy, Sgt. William H. 350

Burketown, Australia 122-3
Burnette, Sgt. Leslie H. 158, 161, 170
Bushido warrior code v, 619, 648-9, 736
Bush, Lt. George H. W. (later President) 141
Bush, Sgt. James A. 307
Butterfield, Beejay (wife of Earl Butterfield) 786
Butterfield, Lt. Earl 773, 786
Butterfield, Beejay, 787
Butterfield, Sgt. Albert L. 74-5
Butt, Sgt. Lewis B. 354

C

C-47 cargo plane, Douglas 211, 217, 219, 276, 316-19, 322-3, 368, 393, 398-9, 401-3, 488-9, 522, 561, 605, 613, 670-1, 720
C-54 four-engine transport plane 732, 744-5, 747-8
Caballo Island, Manila Bay 713, 719-20, 722
Cabanatuan concentration camp 727
Calise, Sgt. Vincent H. 154
camera viii, 120, 216, 231, 262-3, 265, 268, 272, 285, 307, 333, 351, 355, 390, 546, 548, 784
Camilla (flying boat) 140, 775
Camp, Sgt. Carl 134, 363, 483, 779
Camp Stoneman, California 34
Canady, Sgt. Carl A. 350
cannibalism by Japanese 209, 235, 394
cannibals 209-10, 213-17
Canton Island 44-7, 476-9
Cape Gloucester, New Britain 224, 365-74, 778
Cape Keretsbari 531, 569-70
Cape York Peninsula, Australia 56-7, 97, 120-1, 123
Cargo cults 768-9
Carlson, Lt. Howard F. 129
Carter, Sgt. Kenneth I. 454-5, 460, 474, 515, 540, 544, 547-8, 567
Casale, 2nd Lt. Joseph M. 304-5
Catalina See PBY Catalina flying boat
catwalk, in B-24 bomb bay 87, 260, 262, 486, 544, 657-8
Cayten, Sgt. James W. 360
Cecilia, Mother (Catholic nun) 168
Celebes Islands 180, 183-4, 620-2, 626-8, 633-5, 642, 652

cement transported by Horner crew 679-82
Centaur (hospital ship, sunk) 770
Central Identification Laboratory, Army, in Hawaii 505
Ceram Island 516, 570-1, 589-90, 592, 596-7
Cervantes, Ray 786
Chaffin, Lt. Colonel Harold N. 198
"Change O'Luck" (B-24) 64
charts, navigators' viii, 37, 68, 71, 119, 257, 261, 267, 440, 463, 472, 644
Chase, Major "Kip" 254, 258, 260,-4, 268, 333, 338
Chattanooga, Tennessee 25
Cheli, Major Ralph 313-14, 384
Chennault, Brig. Gen. Claire Lee 270
Chesterton, G. K. vii
Chichi Jima 141
China v, vii, x, xi, xiv, xvii, 9, 159, 185, 270, 409, 648, 663, 711, 739, 769, 770
Chinese v, x, xvi, 11, 78, 277, 409, 556, 602, 638, 715, 717, 769
Chovanec, Lt. Henry 145, 209-11, 215, 217-18
Christianity vii 451
Christian missionaries vii, 167, 589
    Benson, Rev. James vi, 167, 170-1, 763
    Branchley, Margaret 169
    Cecelia, Mother (Catholic nun) 168
    Hayman, Francis May 168-9
    Holland, Rev. Henry 169
    Lashman, Lilian 169
    Redlich, Rev. Vivian 168-9
    Manion, Fr. (Catholic priest) 166
    Wendling, Fr. A. (Catholic priest) 274-5
Christianity, influence of vii
Christmas Island 44-7, 98, 476
Churchill, Prime Minister Winston S. 48, 52, 672, 677
cigarette lighter 38, 205, 276, 378
Civil Aeronautics Authority (CAA) 428
Clark Field, Philippines 50, 53, 696-8, 712, 714, 724, 730-1, 747
Clay, Sgt. Maston "Harry" 206, 208
Clipper Ships (flying boat airliners) 45-6
Clyer, Capt. John 198
coastwatchers 140, 154, 169, 210, 213
cobra (snake) 60
cockatoos 194-5, 308
Coggin, Cpl. Chester O. 218

Collier, M/Sgt. James D., Jr. 198
Colonna, Jerry (comedian) 613
Colt .45 Army service pistol viii, 470, 478, 534, 549, 563, 565
Colunga, Sgt. Francisco J. 631, 635
Congressional Medal of Honor 146-7, 314, 700
Connell, Brig. Gen. Carl W. 173
"Connell's Special" (B-24) 177-9, 241-2, 245, 249-54, 257-9, 265, 269, 333-4, 376, 378-9, 483
Consolidated aircraft factory 25, 468
Constitution, American iv
Conti, Lt. Philip 206, 241, 244-5, 248, 250, 258-61, 264, 267-8, 337, 342
convoys, Japanese xv, 10-11, 58, 95, 100-4, 106, 109-11, 113, 115, 118, 127, 129-31, 143, 148,-9, 151-3, 156, 165, 219-29, 231, 236-9, 250, 282-3, 366, 693, 727
Cooper, Gary (movie actor) 617
Cooper, Lt. Allan G. 193, 405, 408, 421-8, 439, 445-9, 454-6, 459-61, 467, 469-71, 474-5, 477, 481, 484, 494, 498, 501, 506, 509, 511, 515-21, 524-5, 528, 534-42, 549, 552, 569, 572, 575, 594-5, 608, 610, 621, 624, 629-35, 642-6, 658-64, 680, 684-5, 690-2, 694, 706, 709, 712-13, 719-20, 722, 728, 731-3, 759, 786
    hired by Disney studios 422
    joins the Army 423
    transfers to Air Corps 423
    draws training posters 424-5
    "Justin Conshus" cartoons 447
    flight training 445
    explores cave on Wakde Island 519-20
    first combat mission 524-5
    nearly hit by flak fragment 524-5
    paints Jolly Rogers Moby Dick patch 509
    draws cartoons of his crew 658-660
    paints nose art on the "Boise Bronc" 660-662
    draws portrait of Lt. Horner 659
    bombs Caballo Island 719
    bombs Corregidor 712, 719
    life after war and death 759
Cooper, Michael (son of Allan Cooper) 408, 525, 785-6

Coral Sea 10, 54-6, 70, 84, 91, 96, 105, 112-13, 119, 123-4, 129, 136, 188, 191, 486, 488, 672
  Battle of xviii, 10, 55, 672
Corregidor Island 49, 53, 418, 692, 712-23, 726-7, 768, 772
Corsair F4U (Vought) fighter plane 137, 578-9
Courtney, Lt. William F. 687
Covich, 1st Lt. Howard J. 576
"Cowtown's Revenge" (B-24) 64, 148, 150-1, 221, 223
Crabb, Lt. Gen. Lesley 725
crabs, miniature, on Wakde Island 520, 595
Crandall, Sgt. Donald 285
crocodiles 58, 63, 122, 496, 512, 559
"Crosair" (B-24) 137-40, 150, 786
Crosson, Lt. Norman R. 116, 118-23, 153, 155, 775
Crotteau, Sgt. Donald C. 632
Cundiff, Michael J. (book author) 362, 363
Currie, Lt. Alden 185
"Czech'em" (B-24) 209-10, 212, 218

D

Dale, Sgt. J. W. 440, 455, 459-60, 473-4, Part II, 478, 627-8, 656, 785
Daliao airfield, Mindoro, Philippine Islands 621, 623, 687
D'Aliso, Sgt. Louis T. 526
Dam Busters, The (movie) 92
Daniel, Capt. Benton 146
Danks, 2nd Lt. Lester K. 342
Darwin, Australia 180-1, 183, 186, 204, 243, 368, 403, 650, 776
Davao, Philippine Islands 621-5, 642-4
Davis, Lt. John 40, 42
Davis wing on the B-24 7, 258
DC-2 Douglas cargo plane 58
D-Day in Europe (Normandy) 420, 498
DDT (insecticide) 518
Death March, Bataan xvi, 235, 711, 715, 718
Declaration of Independence, American iv
Dee, Sgt. William J. 88
DeFreitas, Lt. Edward R. 96-7, 118-19, 121, 155
dehydrated food 491, 555, 559
DeLoach, Ralph K. 130
Dempster, 1st Lt. George M. 348

dengue fever 191, 492, 494-5, 572, 582, 694
Devine, 2nd Lt. Edward J. 73, 75, 77
Diamond Head, Hawaii 40, 474-5
Diggs, Sgt. Fred T. 138, 140, 786
Diotti, Cpl. Lewis A. 88
Directive for the Disestablishment of State Shinto 762
"Dirty Gertie" (B-24) 181-3, 185, 187
diseases, tropical 204-5, 491-2, 494, 563, 759-60
Dobodura airfield, New Guinea 188, 267, 296, 308, 318, 322, 355-6, 387, 394, 399-403, 501, 606
Dodson, 2nd Lt. Richard T. 305
Doherty, Mary 785
dogs 194-6
Domer, Sgt. Carol E. 138, 140-1, 150
"Double Trouble" (B-17) 232, 235
"Double Trouble" (B-24) 786
Dowd, Sgt. John F. 328
Dowie, Lt. Frank D., Jr. 148-9
Doyle, 2nd Lt. Thomas F. 116, 158-62, 170
Duffill, John (missionary) 169
Dunmore, Lt. George "Ace" 241, 244-6, 250, 258, 264-5, 336
Dust Bowl Era 408
Dutch East Indies 33, 49, 180, 386, 640
Dyer, Lt. John D. 118-19, 123, 125
dynamite fishing 560
dysentery 61, 122, 191-2, 378, 492, 725

E

Eady, Sgt. Ernest Part II, 439, 449, 454-5, 457, 472, 486, 535-40, 544, 546-7, 642, 680-1, 692-3
Earhart, Amelia 288
Earhart, Lt. Earle B. 702
Early, Sgt. Glynn R. 307
Eaton, Sgt. Jack W. 305
Eckert, Lt. Clarence A. 72
Egypt iv
Ehime Maru (fishing boat) 770
Eichelberger, General Robert L. 531
Elias, Sgt. Theodore N. 138, 140
Elkins, Lt. Col. Red 39
Emirau Island 382-3
Emperor, Japanese (Hirohito) iv, v, vi, viii, x, xiv, 82, 141, 167-8, 183, 297, 384, 386, 451-2, 618, 624-5, 640, 696-7,

INDEX

719, 721, 734-6, 742-4, 748, 760-3, 770, (picture, 762)
Empress Augusta Bay, Bougainville 331, 367
Engel, Sgt. Fred Stephen 158, 161-2
engineers see Seabees
Enlightenment, Western iv
Erskine, Pfc. Walter R. 158, 160-1
Essen, Sgt. Jock 211, 213-14, 216
Eta Jima (Japanese naval academy) ix
Europe iv, vii, xii, xiii, xvii, 4, 48-9, 60, 136, 143, 170, 201, 222, 304, 409-10, 468, 498-9, 543-4, 626, 632-3, 658-60, 672, 676, 694, 706, 724, 728
evil v, vi, xi, xvi, 141, 238, 266, 297, 450, 711, 735-6, 752
eyeball sockets (for machine guns) 14, 20

F

Fairfield-Suisun airfield, California 467-8, 470
Faisi-Buin harbor, Bougainville Island 136
Farnell, Sgt. Raymond J., Jr. 158, 170
Faulk, Sgt. Leo D. 307
Fenton Field, Darwin, Australia 180, 182-5, 187-8
Fertig, Col. Wendell 703
Fielder, Sgt. Clifford 526
Fight for Survival by James McMurria 761
Fifth Air Force xviii, 1, 48-52, 81, 142, 173-4, 207, 224, 232, 235, 239, 240, 311, 367-8, 376, 394-7, 403, 472, 484, 561-2, 579, 586, 670, 694, 696-8
  table of organization 49
Fiji Island 44, 478-9
Filipinos v, 417, 532, 703, 707, 709, 711, 715-16
Fillmore, President Millard viii
Finschaffen, New Guinea 158, 225, 270, 396, 526, 679-82
fishing with dynamite 560
Five-Mile Field. *See* Ward's Field
flak 5, 7-8, 68, 77, 103, 110-12, 115, 118, 135, 137, 141, 149, 152, 155, 157, 159, 204, 206, 224, 233, 242, 246-8, 260, 263, 281-2, 294, 304, 313, 336, 338, 343, 346-8, 351, 354, 363, 373, 378-9, 387, 389, 483-5, 510, 524-5, 543-4, 548, 551-2, 563, 568, 570-1, 575, 594, 622-4, 631, 650, 653, 659, 678, 688, 694, 698, 728, 750

flash bomb (for aerial photography) 307
Fleet, Reuben H. 4, 452, 674, 714
fleet, American 691
  British 674
  Japanese 692, 726
Flight Officer (rank, explained) 436
floatplanes, Japanese 72, 185, 590
Flugge, Sgt. Eldon M. 340
flying fatigue 201-2, 205, 284, 286, 375
Flying Fortresses. *See* B-17 Flying Fortress
Flynn, Errol 78, 300
Ford, Edsel 28-9
Ford, Lt. Gerald 686
Ford, Henry 28, 30, 410
Ford Motor Company 20, 25, 30
Ford, Sgt. John L. 342
"Form 1-A" (B-24) 274, 755
Formosa Island 532, 687, 696-8, 708, 710, 714, 716, 728, 753
Foss, Capt. Joe 700
Foss, Maj. Joe 108
Fraser, Admiral Bruce 674
Freas, Lt. Charles 306
Ft. McDowell, San Francisco Bay 41
Fuller, Major General Horace 531
Furue, Tadao (forensic ID expert) 505
fuzzy-wuzzies 496 (photo) 497
Fuzzy-Wuzzy Angels 497

G

Galela airdrome 570-1, 622
gangsters 392
Garbutt Field, Townsville, Australia 470, 482, 485
Gardner, Lt. Herbert 153-4
Gasmata, New Britain 102, 130, 221, 365-6, 368
gasbag automobiles 676
Gaston, Sgt. Grady 123, 125, 126
Gates, Sgt. Robert T. 631
Gaudet, T/Sgt. Neil J. 148-50
Gebbie, 2nd Lt. James A. 358, 360
Geelvink Bay, New Guinea 598
genocide by Japan v, xi, xiv, 297
George, 2nd Lt. Jason V., Jr. 305
Germany iv, vi, xii, 2, 10, 14, 48, 78, 92, 143, 409-10, 543, 666, 706, 728, 735, 737, 764, 769
Geydos, Cpl. John 120

GI Bill 660, 759
gin, value of a bottle of 552, 553
Glenn, Cpl. John J. 75
Golden Cross Division (33rd) 553
Golden Gate Bridge 35, 39, 41, 468-9, 471, 729
"Golden Voice" Vial, Flt. Lt. Leigh Grant 210, 218
Gona village, New Guinea vi, 256, 342, 763
Goodenough Island 149, 151
gooney bird 478
Gooney Bird (C-47 cargo plane) 403, 488
Gori River Bridge 324
Gormley, Sgt. John E. 342
Gotcher, Sgt. William C. 350
Gottke, Lt. Paul W. 152
Grandolfo, Pfc. Patsy F. 158, 160-1
Gray, 2nd Lt. Lucien B. 342
Great Depression 90, 408, 412, 424, 430, 671
Great Raid, The (movie and poster) 727
Greece, ancient iv
Green, Frances (WASP pilot) 27
Greenman, Lt. Donald P. 632
Greenville, South Carolina 13, 24-5, 31, 64, 68, 116, 153, 157, 379, 761
Greenville, USS (submarine) 770
Gregory, Sgt. William 74-5
Griffin, Capt. James R 198
Grimes, Lt. Dale V. 123
Gross, 2nd Lt. John A. 631
Guadalcanal, Battle of 222
Guadalcanal Island 11, 222, 330, 366-7, 479, 498, 518, 578, 602
Gulf of Carpentaria, Australia 120-3
Gull Force 625
Gumaer, Lt. James E. Jr. 128-9
gunboat diplomacy by Admiral Perry viii
Gunn, Paul I. "Pappy" 94, 175, 225-7, 292, 308-10, 332, 369-71, 387, 718, 727-8, 762-3, 782
    adds machine guns to B-25s 225-6, 370
    adds gas tanks to B-25s 308-9
    shoots up Japanese destroyer and transport plane 369-70
    reunited with family 728
    picture of, 371
    death of 763
Gunn, Polly (wife of "Pappy") 727-8
Gunther, Lt. William R. 41-2
Gusap airfield, New Guinea 387, 396

H

Haggerty, Sgt. John J. 358
Hale, Maj Gen. Willis H. 41-2
Halgren, Sgt. Axel J. 88
Halmahera Islands 516, 621, 627, 645, 691
Halsey, Admiral William F., Jr. 141, 367, 686
Hamilton Field, California 36, 40-1, 378, 467, 468
Handleman, Sgt. William N. 632
"Hangover Haven" (B-24) 765
Hansa Bay, New Guinea 309, 358, 401, 577, 631
Hansen, 2nd Lt. Henry C. 218
Hansen, S/Sgt. Ernest E. 218
Haroekoe Island 592-4
Harrow, James L. 130
Harter, Maj. Leland I. 484, 653-4, 660-1, 679, 680, 682
Harvey family murdered 83
Hastings, Michigan 30
Hatcher, Sgt Joseph H. 354
Hawaii 35-47, 57, 63-4, 88, 98-9, 115, 152-3, 155, 176, 178, 195, 362, 409, 469-77, 480, 505, 567, 733, 742, 754
"Hay Maker" (B-24) 627, 629-30
Hazel, Sgt. Cecil R. 576
Heath, 1st Lt. John H. 186-7, 318-19, 353-5
"Heaven Can Wait" (B-24) 577 (footnote)
Heck, Sgt. Kenneth E. 307
Heisel, Capt. Manville 461-2
Hell Ships 717
Helzer, S/Sgt. Harold H. 138, 140
Henebry, Major Jock 368-9, 497-8
Hentscher, Sgt. Daniel F. 575
"Here 'Tis (B-24) 397
Hermerding, Sgt. George H. 272, 274
Herry, Capt. Robert L. 314
Hess, Lt. Charles 185
Hevener, Lt. Harold G. 181, 185, 187, 196
Heyn, Sgt. John F. 132
Hickam Field, Hawaii 36, 40-3, 471, 475-6
Higgins, 1st Lt. Walter E. 148-52, 156, 221, 223
Hilton, Sgt. James B. 120
Hirohito, Emperor iv, v, vi, viii, x, xiv, 82, 141, 167-8, 183, 297, 384, 386, 451-2, 618, 624-5, 640, 696-7, 719, 721, 734-6, 742-4, 748, 760-3, 770 (picture, 762)
Hiroshima 743, 752

INDEX 803

Hitler, Adolf iv, 5, 48, 136, 409, 410
Hobson, 2nd Lt. Earl M. 24
Hodges, Sgt. 243
Hogland, Lt. Leonard J. 656
Hollandia, New Guinea 50, 255, 324, 384-97, 404, 490, 512-13, 522, 568, 580, 583, 585, 615, 620, 725
Holland, Leigh (daughter of Dale Holland) 786
Holland, Lt. Dale 468, 470, 476, 480, 525, 624, 787
Holland, Rev. Henry (missionary) 169
Holliday, Capt. Henry C. 133
Holmen, Maurice ("Mo") 484
Holmes, Beatrice 785
Holmes, James xiii
Holt, Capt. Robert S. 87, 152-3
Homma, Gen. Masaharu 718
Hong Kong hospital massacre 717
Honolulu, Hawaii 35, 153, 475, 742
Hood Point, New Guinea 501
Hooper, Lt. Leroy 285
Hope, 1st Lt. Dean P. 307
Hope, Bob, and USO show 517, 613-16, 620, 763, 773-4
   on Biak Island 613
Hopfield, Pfc. George T. 198
Hopkins, Harry (Roosevelt advisor and secret agent for Russia) 382
Horner crew 404-5, 407-8, 411, 415, 420-1, Part II, 454-6, 458-62, 464, 467, 470-1, 474, 476-85, 490-2, 494-5, 498, 501-4, 506-10, 512-13, 563-4, 567-70, 571-2, 574-5, 577-80, 583, 588-90, 592, 594-8, 602, 607-8, 612-13, 620, 623, 626-7, 635-6, 642-4, 650, 653, 656, 658, 670-2, 677-80, 683, 687, 691, 694, 706, 728-9, 732-3, 786-7
Horner, James H. 4, 134, 193, 404-5 407-8, 411-15, 419-21, 423, 427, 429-32, 434-7, 439, 441, 445-6, 448-9, 454-6, 458-68, 470-88, 495-6, 498, 501, 505-9, 513-14, 516, 519-21, 523-4, 535-41, 546-7, 553, 556-9, 561, 580, 595, 608-10, 612-14, 623-4, 629, 638, 642-6, 651, 653-4, 656-60, 666-8, 670-1, 673-8, 680-94, 701, 706-8, 725, 728-9, 731-3, 758, 768, 783-4
   Horner family history 411-12
   works in machine shop 412-13
   enlists in the Air Corps 414
   flight training 423-39
   belly-landing in a B-24 437
   near-crash at Palm Springs 465-7
   flight to Hawaii 471-5
   flight to Canton Island 476-478
   bomber gets stuck in mud 479-81
   difficult landing at Moresby 487-9
   sees fatal accident at Moresby 495-6
   assigned to Jolly Rogers 506-7
   explores cave on Wakde 519-20
   can't find shoes during air raid 523-4
   first combat mission 509, 515, 524, 527-43
   blows big hole in Japanese runway 651-2
   gets a meal from a crazy cook 557
   goes on leave to Sydney 670-8
   flies mission to get cement 679-82
   flies through typhoon 683-7
   sees Japanese phosphorus bombs 688-90
   loses an engine on a mission 690-1
   courier mission to Tacloban 691-3
   completes combat tour 694
   returns home 732
   life after the war 758
Horner, Pamela (daughter of James Horner) 785
Horner, Richard (son of James Horner) 785
Horn Island, Australia 197
hospital ship Centaur sunk 770
"Hot Garters" (B-24) 358, 630-33
Hoyt, Lt. William 153-4
Hudson, Lt. Jarvais J. 575
Hull, USS (destroyer) 687
Humboldt Bay, New Guinea 255, 261-2, 267, 396
Hunt, Elsie 13
Hyler, Sgt. William T. 632

I

Ie Shima (island) 738-42, 744-52, 754, 756
Imaizumi Toshimitzu (fighter plane pilot) 478
Imperato, Maj. 211
Imperial Japan v, 1, 77, 82, 301, 407, 410, 489, 633
Imperial Rescript Renouncing Divinity 762
Indochinese v

Indonesians v, 638
Initial Point (IP) on a bombing run 533, 547, 644
Insoemanai Island 513, 564, 595, 767
instrument flying 4, 67-8, 111, 196, 246, 272, 338, 396-7, 428, 430, 438, 486, 534, 536-7, 684, 694
Iron Range, Australia 54, 56-66, 69-71, 76-9, 84-100, 104-6, 112-22, 128-9, 131-2, 136, 143-5, 152, 155-7, 173, 178, 180, 188-9, 191, 193, 197, 201, 206, 400, 403, 507, 606, 706, 751-2, 767
Irving, Sgt. Ernest I. 88
Islet Island 150, 152
Iverson, Lt. Leroy C. 86-7
Ivie, Sgt. Marvin I. 340
Iwo Jima 141, 384, 519, 601, 602, 604, 729, 733, 765
Izzo, Sgt. Louis C. 148, 149

J

Jackson Field, Port Moresby 70, 138, 144, 158, 190, 192-3, 197, 244, 316, 401, 470, 485, 488-91, 499, 501, 767
Jacoby, 2nd Lt. Lawrence D. 285
Japan Self-Defense Forces 769
Japanese navy xv, 11, 324, 418, 450, 672, 714
Jasper 789
Java 180
Jaynes, S/Sgt. James F. 285
jeep 117, 323, 374, 608, 610 335, 395, 398-9, 740-1
Jefferson Barracks National Cemetery 307, 359, 363, 703-4
Jefman, New Guinea 551, 569-70, 583, 592
Johnson, Donald 503, 517
Johnson, Lt. Paul E. 164-5, 649
Johnson, Lyndon Baines (later President) 499-501
Johnson, Sgt. Charles L 359
Johnson, Sgt. Harry A. 198
Johnson, Sgt. Lawson M. 354
Joint Chiefs of Staff, U.S. 48, 136, 190, 207, 398, 532, 691
"Jolly Roger Express" (B-24) 662
Jolly Rogers (90th Bomb Group) 73, 77, 79-80, 84, 87, 89-93, 95, 97-101, 107-8, 113, 116, 118, 127-7, 142-6, 148, 151-3, 156-7, 164, 174, 176, 178-81, 183, 188-91, 193, 196, 201-3, 206, 208-9, 211, 220-1, 223, 228-9, 232, 239-41, 247, 251, 253-4, 269-70, 274-5, 277, 318, 325, 328, 331, 333, 343, 364, 368, 375, 377-9, 442, 471, 476, 480-1, 484, 506-7, 510-11, 516, 519, 528, 539, 551-2, 556, 563, 580, 606-7, 610, 616, 621, 633, 635, 660, 680, 706, 708, 751-4, 756, 767, 773-4
Jolly Rogers nickname & emblem, origin of, 269
"Joltin' Janie" (B-24) 294-5 (pictures)
Jones, Capt. Charles, E. 181-3, 185
Jones, Mary Ann (wife of Capt. Jones) 182
Jordan, Sgt. Oscar R. 305
Jordan, Sgt. Vico W. 85

K

Kairiru Island 166
kamikazes 649, 696, 734
Kane, 2nd Lt. Valentine B., Jr. 305
Kane, Rochelle 784
Kasai, Tomokazu (fighter plane pilot) 426, 647, 689
Kavieng 250, 382, 579
Kavieng Wharf Massacre 382
Kawabe, Lt. Gen. Torasirou 747-8
Kawa Island 139, 140
Kay Army Airfield 2
Kelly, Cpl. Cephas L. 171
Kendall, Capt. Paul C. 232
Kendrick, Lt. Roy A. 131
Kenney, Major General George C. xv, xviii, 48-54, 56, 65, 67, 70, 81, 83, 89-90, 92-5, 100, 132, 136-7, 142-3, 146, 152, 173-5, 178-9, 188-93, 198-9, 202, 208, 219-20, 222-8, 234, 237-9, 250-1, 253-4, 257-8, 268-9, 290-1, 296-7, 299, 302, 308, 310, 312-18, 321-4, 328, 331-47, 368-72, 374-9, 385, 388-9, 391-98, 400-1, 404, 468, 485, 490, 494-5, 497-9, 506, 510, 522, 579-81, 585-8, 594, 596, 598, 691, 693, 696-700, 709, 712, 716, 722, 728, 737, 739, 746 (pictures of xviii, 51-2, 81, 174, 395, 587)
Kenny, T/Sgt. John J. 285
Kerns, Lt. Raymond F. 452, 553, 620

Ketsu-Go (Operation Decision) 735
Keystone B-6 (American bomber) 13
Kimbe Bay, New Britain 221
Kimodo Dragon 496
Kimura, Admiral Masatomi 222, 224-5
Kindelberger, Dutch (aircraft designer) 370
King, 2nd Lt. Eugene B. 30
Kingman, Arizona aircraft scrapyard 754, 764
Kinsella, 1st Lt. Robert I. 85
Kirchner, Margaret (WASP pilot) 27
Kiriwina Island 140, 337
Kruczynski, Cindy (daughter of James Horner) 785
Kofsky, 1st Lt. Warren M. 678
Kofukuda, Lt. Commander Mitsugu 29
Kokoda Trail Battle 56, 74, 209, 394, 497
Kokoda Pass 304, 502-5
Kokoda Trail 56, 90, 209, 219, 496, 502-5
Komiatum Ridge 289-91, 294-7, 301, 583, 725, 767
Konoe, Prime Minister ix
Koon, Col. Ralph E. "Zipper" 89, 95-6, 98-9, 114-15, 164, 173-4, 178, 240-1, 244-7, 249-50, 269
Korea 409
Koreans v, 769
K-rations 556
Kremer, Lt. John 468, 470
Krueger, General Walter 600-1, 708
Kuhl, Maj. Philip J. 137-40, 150
Kutcha, Sgt. Walter E. 342
Kuzume, Col. Naoyuki 601-4
Kwajalein 754

L

L-4 (Army Piper Cub) 28, 323, 380 (photo), 422, 522, 553, 723
"Lady Be Good" (B-24) 123-6
Lady Be Good movie and song 123 (footnote)
"Lady Beverly" (B-24) 64, 73-6
Lae, New Guinea x, xviii, 54-5, 100, 113, 118-19, 137, 148, 152, 155, 163, 189, 210, 219-21, 223-5, 228, 236, 238-9, 257, 288-9, 296, 299, 302, 314-18, 320-4, 328, 365-6, 394, 396, 398-400, 403, 499, 680
LaGarde, Sgt. Philip J., Jr. 354
Laha Massacre 624-5
Lamour, Dorothy (actress) 613

Landis, Carole (actress) 617
Langford, Frances (singer) 613
Langley Field, Virginia 13
Langoan airfield, Celebes Islands 621-2, 626, 627-9, 635-7, 642, 648, 651-2
Lark Force (Australian troops) 80
Larson, Lt. Paul R. 86-9, 131, 152, 178
Lashman, Lillian (missionary) 169
Lavedan, 2nd Lt. Albert J. 340
Lawler, Capt. Norman 195, 785
Leave to Sydney 669-70
Lenaghan, Sgt. John H. 350
Lend-Lease program 382
Leonard, Sgt. Edward A. 148-9
Lewis, S.Sgt. Rowland M. 285
Leyte Island, Philippines 65, 623, 691-3, 728
Liang Airdrome, Ambon Island 570-1, 621, 624-5
Liberator, Consolidated B-24 1, 4-6, 11, 20, 24, 29, 36, 42, 98, 100, 106, 137, 252-3, 378-9, 410, 436, 645, 647, 649, 677
Liberty Ships 188, 327, 398, 403, 609, 610
Libyan desert 125
Lief, 2nd Lt. William 198
Lifaba Island 150-1
Lindbergh, Charles A. 20, 22-4, 28-34, 41, 68, 313, 409-10, 512, 553, 559-60, 568, 578-80, 582-97, 604-6, 664, 666, 673-4, 698-9, 763, 767-8
 at Willow Run B-24 plant 20, 28-9
 critical of B-24 29
 flies Navy Corsairs 578-9
 fishes with dynamite 560
 goes to Southwest Pacific 578
 escorts the Jolly Rogers 592
 shoots down Japanese fighter plane 589-90
 nearly shot down by Japanese fighter plane 590-1
 escorts the Horner crew 592
 shoots up a sailing ship 593
 leaves the Pacific 596-7
 visits caves on Biak Island 605
 secret family of 666
 pictures of 587, 699
Lingayen Gulf, Luzon 697, 708
Liscum, Lt. Jack 702
"Little Eva" (B-24) 64, 118, 121-3, 125-6, 153-4, 169, 173
Little, Lt. Homer F. 328

Lockhart River Airport (Iron Range) 87
Loewenberg, Capt. Stanley A. 198
Logan, Lt. Robert B. 493
Lone Tree Hill (Battle of) 518-20, 598
Loran (Long Range Aid to Navigation) 754
Lord, Andrew 164
Los Alamos National Laboratory 743
Los Banos prison camp 727
Lowther, Sgt. William C. 218
Luck, 2nd Lt. Byron B. 631
Lucky Strike cigarettes 565
Lundry, Cynthia (daughter of Tom Theobald) 786
Luzon Island, Philippines 417-18, 686, 696-7, 708-10, 712, 714, 716, 724-5, 747

M

MacArthur, Gen. Douglas xv, 48-53, 65, 83, 129, 136, 142, 146, 208, 219, 222, 239, 283, 288, 296, 302, 314-18, 320-1, 323, 365-8, 372, 374, 382-6, 394-6, 398, 417-18, 490, 498-500, 512, 531-3, 559, 579-81, 585-8, 596-7, 598, 640, 642, 645, 691-2, 696-7, 714-17, 722, 726, 732, 737, 739, 744,-5, 747-9, 762-3, 769
  escapes from Corregidor 715
  returns to the Philippines 692
  Comdr. of Occupation Forces 762
  Commander in Korean War 762
  death, 762
  (pictures of 49, 52, 317 320, 749, 762)
MacArthur, Jean (wife of General) 715, 722
Makassar, Celebes Islands 180, 183-4, 187
MacDonald, Col. Charles H. 580, 584-5, 589-92
Madang, New Guinea 112, 257, 314, 322, 324-6, 328, 402
Maffin Bay, New Guinea 254, 394-5, 513-14, 518-19, 522, 527, 553-4, 558, 565, 569, 602, 620, 767
Maggio, S/Sgt. Joseph J. 285
Magness, 2nd Lt. Thomas M. 325, 328
Mahaney, 2nd Lt. Edward J. 621, 626-37, 648
Maher, 1st Lt. George T. 324, 328
malaria 61, 192-3, 203, 301, 494, 572, 758
Malaya xvii, 672

Malinta Tunnel, Corregidor 714-15, 718, 723
Manchuria x, 717, 748
Manila Massacre 711
Manila, Philippine Islands 50, 150, 305, 369, 532, 635, 696-8, 708-9, 711-14, 716-20, 722, 726-8, 730, 744-5, 747-9, 753
Manion, Fr. (missionary) 166
Mannoccir, Cdr. Ferdinand D., II 198
Manokwari, New Guinea 180, 384, 396, 525, 527, 569-75, 589
Manson, Sgt. Harry M. 305
Manuel, Sgt. Gordon 233, 235-7, 776-7
Manus Island 382, 383
March Field, California 439, 441, 443-5, 449, (picture) 453-5, 460-2, 468-9, 476, 525, 683
Marines, U. S. 330, 372, 374, 381, 578-80
Markham River 296, 302, 317, 400-1, 403, 506
Marshall, General George C. 398-9, 532, 650
Marston matting 316, 401, 489, 506, 692, 704, 768
Martin, Capt. Lark E., Jr. 164-5, 279-87, 484
Martindale, 2nd Lt. Robert R. 158, 170
Martin, Lt. William 685
Massacres by Japanese
  Akikaze massacre 166
  Banka Island Massacre 717
  Buna Mission Massacre 167-70, 772
  Harvey family murdered 83
  Hong Kong hospital massacre 717
  hospital ship *Centaur* sunk 770
  Kavieng Wharf Massacre 382
  Laha Massacre 82-3, 171, 382, 625-6, 711, 718
  Manila Massacre 711
  Palawan Massacre 382
  Rape of Nanking xvi, 709, 711, 769
  Talili Bay Massacre 171
  Tol Plantation Massacre 82-3
  Wake Island Massacre 383, 772
McCalmont, T/Sgt. Howard V. 328
McClellan Field, Sacramento, Cal. 33
McClure, Major J. C. 746
McCrea, Sgt. Roscoe R. 526
McCullar, Capt. Kenneth 92-3, 133
McGuire Field 698, 701-2, 704-10, 719, 725, 729-30, 732, 737-9, 768
McGuire, Lt. Thomas B., Jr. 697-700 (photo on 699)

McKeen, Sgt. Edward J. 120
McLaughlin, Capt. Frank 211, 213, 216, 776
McMurria, Lt. James A. 40-1, 63-5, 77, 108, 116, 122, 145, 151, 155-66, 169-72, 244, 247, 282, 314, 324, 348, 353, 362, 384, 633, 648, 753, 760-1, (photos on 156-7, 172)
McNair, Lt. Gen. Lesley 724
McNamara, Sgt. Thomas D. 358, 361-2
McNaughton, Cpl. Edwin B., Jr. 325, 328
McNeff, Flt. Officer Donald K. 342
McWilliams, Lt. Robert N. 91
Medal of Honor 144, 146, 147, 314, 377, 381, 384, 477, 700
Meding, Sgt. Edward S. 305
Mediterranean Sea 124
Meehan, Col. Arthur W. 42-5, 70-1, 84-9, 99, 127, 142, 197
Meehan, Lucy (wife of Col. Meehan) 85 (photo on p. 43)
"Memphis Belle" (B-17) 468, 484
Menado airfield, Celebes Islands 621-2, 652-3
Merauke, New Guinea 197, 199
Mericle, Maj. Robert H. 774
Merkling, Sgt. Al (nose artist) 663, 765
Michi (Ayako Yoshida) 572-4
Middlebrook, Capt. Garrett E. 108, 200, 229, 237-8, 292-3, 295-6, 312, 775-7
  pictures of, 292-3
Midway Island xv, xviii, 10, 71, 85, 382, 672,
Milder, Lt. Fran G. 186-7
militarism, Japanese v, vi, 279, 452, 711
military culture, Japanese v, xvi, 735
  brutality 427, 449-50
  fanaticism 384
Miller, Jerry 786
Miller, Lt. Fred 511
Mills, Lt. H. C. 351
Milne Bay, New Guinea 74, 138, 140, 149, 152, 224, 228
Mindanao Island (Philippines) 418, 621, 623, 642-3, 692,
Mindoro Island (Philippines) 607, 687, 698-704, 707, 709-10, 715, 725-30, 733, 737-40, 768
"Miss Deed" (B-24) 221-3
missionaries, Christian
  Benson, Rev. James vi, 167, 170-1, 763
  Branchley, Margaret 169
  Cecelia, Mother (Catholic nun) 168

Hayman, Francis May 168-9
Holland, Rev. Henry 169
Lashman, Lilian 169
Redlich, Rev. Vivian 168-9
Manion, Fr. (Catholic priest) 166
Wendling, Fr. A. (Catholic priest) 274-5
"Mission Belle" (B-24) 165, 280-3, 484
Mitchell, Captain (medical officer) 38, 205
Mitchell, Maj. Gen. William "Billy" xvii, 222
Mitsubishi Ki-51 "Sonia" fighter plane 589-90
Moby Dick (320th Squadron nickname) 270
"Moby Dick" (B-24) 304
Moemi, New Guinea 551, 569-70, 574-5
Mokmer Field in Biak Island 589-92, 597-601, 605-8, 623, 626, 636, 642, 645, 666-7, 669, 692, 701, 729, 731-2, 768
Monagahan, USS (destroyer) 687
Montague, Lt. Robert E. 625
Moore, 2nd Lt. Donald W. 628, 631
Moore, Lt. Woodrow W. 232-4, 237
Moore, Maj. John T. 595
Moore, Sgt. Hugh F. 359
Morobe, New Guinea 154
Morse, Maj. Raymond S. 84-5, 88
MOS (Military Occupational Specialty) 14, 407, 491, 501-2, 558
mosquitoes 60-1, 122, 193, 201, 478, 492-4, 639, 654
Moss, 2nd Lt. Frank L. 340
Muething, 2nd Lt. David D. 88
Muric Swamp 362 (map)
Muroc-Maru (artificial practice bombing ship) 462, 463
Murphy, Audie 412
Murphy's Law 86, 247
Murray, 2nd Lt. William K. 342
Mussett, Lt. Col. Eugene P. 2, 17, 37-9, 42, 44
Mussolini, Benito (Italian dictator) 409-10

N

Nadzab, New Guinea 132-3, 296, 302, 314-23, 387, 394-6, 398-404, 490, 501-3, 505-7, 510-11, 519, 522, 539, 561, 568, 579-80, 585-6, 595, 599, 606-7, 611, 617, 630, 663-4, 671, 706, 720, 731, 764-8

Nagasaki, Japan 743, 750, 752
Nakagawa, Cmdr. Hajime 770 (footnote)
Nambu (Japanese machine gun) 298
Namela, airdrome, Boeroe Island 570
Nassau Bay, New Guinea 289
Nate (Japanese fighter plane) 183-5
National Memorial Cemetary of the Pacific (the "Punchbowl") 742
Nations, 1st Lt. Glenn E. 353
Nave, Randall (nephew of Sgt. Fred Diggs) 787
Nayfa, Sgt. Jimmie M. 85
Naziism v 735, 737
Nelson, Bob (son of Sgt. John Nelson) 786
Nelson, Sgt. John 786
Nestler, 2nd Lt. Joseph D. 525-9, 541, 550, 569
New Britain Island 56, 78, 80-1, 83-4, 96, 100, 102, 104, 130, 137-8, 147, 148, 151, 156-7, 169, 213, 220-1, 224, 239, 256, 270, 288, 296, 317-18, 336, 338, 365-6, 370, 402, 490, 718, 772
New Caledonia Island 44-5, 479, 481
New Guinea vi, x, xi, xviii, 11, 33, 49-50, 53-8, 74-78, 84, 90, 96-7, 105-6, 129-32, 135-6, 138-9, 143, 148-9, 154-5, 158-9, 164, 166-9, 178, 180-1, 190-4, 196-200, 202, 209-10, 213, 215, 218-222, 238-40, 254-7, 260-1, 267, 276, 281, 283, 288, 290, 297-8, 300, 308, 314, 323, 327-9, 330, 337, 350, 355-6, 360-2, 364-8, 379, 381, 385, 388, 395-99, 401, 403-4, 468, 470, 472-3, 483, 485-6, 490-8, 500-3, 506-7, 509-15, 518, 521, 524-5, 527, 533, 542-3, 550-1, 553, 557, 559-61, 569, 571-4, 579, 581, 584, 586-7, 589, 594, 597-600, 602, 606, 613, 624, 630, 633, 639-40, 671, 673, 680, 682, 696, 707, 716, 720, 724-5, 729, 752, 758, 763-5, 767-8, 772
New Mexico, USA 34, 415-19, 454, 473, 496, 560, 741-2, 758
Nimitz, Admiral Chester W. 222, 381, 516, 532, 691, 737, 739
Nix, Sgt. Robert P. 218
Noemfoor Island 516, 531-2, 542-4, 547, 549, 569-70, 575-7, 638, 720
Noonan, Fred 288
Norden bombsight 92, 149, 457, 651
Norris, T/Sgt. Robert W. 285
North Africa 124
North, Lt. Alexander F. 285
nose art 660-6
"Not In Stock" (B-25 of Pappy Gunn) 371
Novak, Sgt. Stephen J. 254, 265, 307
nuns tortured by Japanese at Rabaul 168

nurses (U. S.) hitch ride with Horner crew 485-6
    airlifting casualties 561-2
    captured on Corregidor 717-18
    liberated at Santo Tomas 561-3, 726-7
    British, massacred in Hong Kong 717
    massacred on Banka Island 717-18
    killed in sinking of hospital ship *Centaur* 770

O

Oahu, Hawaii 40, 471, 474-5
Obama, President Barack Hussein 769
Okada, Seizo, war correspondent vi
Okinawa 498, 518, 602, 734, 737-9, 753-4, 765
Okumiya, Masatake 9-10, 239, 381, 492, 495, 637, 639
Olsen, Capt. Roy W. 181, 183-5, 187, 236-7, 333
Operation 81 (Japanese convoy) 221, 239
Operation Cartwheel 330, 366, 382-3
Operation Chastise 92
Orient, the iv, ix, x, 394, 707, 709
Ormoc Bay, Leyte Island, Philippines 693
Osborn, Blanche (WASP pilot) 27
Oskamp, 2nd Lt. Clifford G. 307
Ostafin, Lt. Sylvester L. Part II, 439, 449, 454-7, 470, 475, 524, 528, 535, 546-8, 552, 610, 629, 651-3, 657, 680, 692, 729, 731-2
Owen, 2nd Lt. Daniel B. 285
Owen Stanley Mountains 54, 56, 84-5, 91, 96, 105-6, 119, 129-31, 138, 157-9, 166, 169, 188, 191, 210, 212, 217, 223, 244, 248, 254, 272, 281, 304, 306, 308, 318, 347, 400-1, 490, 501-

INDEX 809

4, 506, 512, 543, 673, 682
Owi Island 522, 553, 571, 574, 581-2, 585, 595, 600, 604-5, 608, 611, 698, 768
Ozawa, Masaji 141

P

P-38 Lightning (Lockheed) fighter plane xv, 152, 175, 189, 227-8, 232, 234, 238, 284, 308, 312-13, 332-3, 337, 368, 370, 387, 389-90, 392, 403-4, 424, 522, 563, 566, 568, 571, 579-80, 582-4, 586-93, 596-7, 622, 632, 636, 655-6, 697-9, 745
P-39 Airacobra (Bell) fighter plane 192, 368, 403-4, 485
P-40 Warhawk (Curtiss) fighter plane 368, 380, 403-4, 664
P-47 Thunderbolt (Republic) fighter plane 188, 332, 368, 403-4, 522-3, 550, 579, 592, 596-7
P-61 Black Widow (night fighter) 522, 563-5, 595, 611, 727
Pacific War Memorial, Corregidor Island 772
Palau Islands 515, 532, 590, 597
Palawan Massacre 382, 623, 727
Palm Springs 462-66, 683
"Pappy" Gunn (see Gunn, Paul I.)
parafrag bombs 176, 310-11, 368, 385, 389-92, 655
paratroops, 503rd Parachute Regiment 302, 315-20, 531, 712, 720
  at Nadzab 315, 720-1
  at Noemfoor 720
  at Corregidor 720-1
Parran, Lt. John T. 308
Parsons, Sgt. Jay B. 91
"Patched Up Piece" (B-24) 663
Patterson Field, Ohio 41
Patterson, Lt. Elmo L. 131
Patty, Cpl. Harold L. 88
Paul, Raymond (war correspondent) 168
Paviour, 2nd Lt. Robert 148-9, 222
Paw, 2nd Lt. Joseph 307
PBY Catalina flying boat, Consolidated 7, 141, 152, 223-4, 308, 356, 533, 597, 632, 655-6, 731
Pearl Harbor 28
  attack vi, viii, xii, xiii, xiv, xv, xvii, 2, 9, 13, 31, 35, 42, 53, 66, 80, 220,

239, 288, 299, 344, 373, 382, 409, 417-18, 423, 451-2, 474-6, 499-500, 648, 671-2, 696, 714, 725, 745
Pelander, Capt. Jack 347 (picture)
Pennington, Lt. Harry E. 655
Perakos, 2nd Lt. John 138
Percival, Gen. Arthur E. 747
Perry, Admiral Matthew vii, viii, ix, 340, 748
Pete (Japanese fighter plane) 185
Peterson, Capt. Carl E. 730
Peterson, Sgt. Roland M. 307
"Pete the Carrier" (B-24) 285
pets 194-5
Philippine Islands xii, xiii, 417-18, 532, 620-2, 642-4, 648, 687, 691, 697-8, 701, 703-4, 707, 710, 714, 716, 726, 728-30, 738-9, 758, 763, 768
Phillips, Sgt. Raymond M. 358
phonographs 65, 196
phosphorus bombs, aerial 678, 687-90, 728
Picker, Cpl. Lester L. 88
Pierce, Sgt. Harold (Rogers crew) 243-4, 247-8, 258-9, 264, 266, 378
Pinney, Pvt. Peter 297, 385
Piroe Bay, Ambon Island 593
Pisang Islands 592
pistol 243, 470, 478, 534, 549, 563, 565, 630, 677
"Pistol Packin' Mama" 340-1, 352-4
pitot tube 87, 457, 535, 694
Ploesti oilfields, Romania xiv, 677-8
"Pluto" (B-17) 197
Podesta, Sgt. Alfred A. 305
point system for rotation home 202, 694
Portland Roads, Australia 56, 58, 188
Port Moresby, New Guinea xviii, 10-11, 54-6, 58-9, 65, 70-2, 74-5, 81-2, 84, 88, 91-2, 105-6, 109, 112-13, 115, 129-32, 136-40, 142-50, 154, 157, 164, 166, 169, 179-80, 188-95, 197, 199-201, 208, 210, 217, 219, 221-4, 235, 240, 244, 247-9, 251, 253-4, 256, 272, 275-7, 288-9, 302-4, 308, 313, 316-18, 321, 323-5, 331-2, 342-5, 347, 354, 356, 363, 367-9, 373, 376-8, 387, 398, 400-1, 403-4, 470, 472, 483, 485-8, 490-3, 495-506, 519, 559, 561, 580, 606, 611, 672-3, 760, 764, 764, 766-8
Post, Sgt. Earl T. 340
Potter, Lt. Lionel B. 304

Potts, Lt. Joseph 404
Poulsen, 1st Lt. Bryant E. 358-9, 631-4
Pracher, Lt. George 786
Pratt & Whitney R-1830 "Twin Wasp" B-24 engines 4, 128, 537, 644
Prince of Wales, HMS xvii-iii, 672
Project Recover 577
PT-19 (Fairchild) trainer plane (picture) 429, 431-3
PT-22 (Ryan) trainer plane 446
PT boats 53, 222, 418, 520, 692, 714-15, 722-23
"Pudgy" (B-24) 348, 350-1, 362
Punchbowl see National Memorial Cemetery of the Pacific
"Punjab" (B-24) 64, 84-5
Purple Heart medal 85, 202, 625, 650-1
Pyle, Ernie (war correspondent) 740-2
   books by Ernie Pyle 741
Pyron, Cpl. Albert J. 85

Q

Quaal, Sgt. Ortis L. 198
Quills, Nibs, and Keyboards Editing and Design Service 787

R

RAAF See Royal Australian Air Force
Rabaul, New Britain 53, 78-90, 93, 95, 100, 132, 137-9, 142-8, 152, 166-72, 197, 200, 219-21, 228, 239-40, 256, 272, 281, 284, 288, 309, 314-15, 318, 322, 330-5, 337, 337-9, 341, 343-5, 348, 365-8, 381-4, 386, 394, 400-1, 490, 495, 533, 579, 619, 633-4, 640, 716, 752-3, 760-1, 763, 767, 772
Rafferty, Lt. John 129
Ramey, Brig. Gen. Howard K. 147, 164, 197, 198-9, 240, 279, 320
Randal, Lt. Alan 58, 60
Ransiki Airdrome, New Guinea 570-1, 574-5
Rape of Nanking xvi, 709, 711, 770
rationing of food and fuel
   in America 613
   in Australia 675
Ratliff, Sgt. John F. 154

Ratliff, Sgt. Robert A. 218
Rawlings, Charles A. 195, 254-6, 265, 281-2, 286-7, 307, 327, 384, 509
Rawson, 2nd Lt. Wendell P. 358, 360
Reagan, President Ronald xvi
Redlich, Rev. Vivian (missionary) 169
Red Morning (movie)
Red Raiders (22nd Bomb Group, Medium) 397
Red, Sgt. Claude D. 87
Reel, 2nd Lt. Edward L. 654
Regan, Lt. Scott L. 164-5, 247, 282, 348
Rendon, Sgt. Mercy, Jr. 350
Republic, U.S.A.T. (troopship) 35
Repulse, HMS xviii, 672
Rhodes, Sgt. Ernest R. 138, 140
Rich, 1st Lt. Hampton E. 340
Richardson, Sgt. Grady H. 631
Rickenbacker, Eddie 477
Riley, Sgt. James (Rogers' crew) 242, 259, 265, 268
Rittmayer, Maj. Jack B. 698-99
"Road to Tokyo" (B-24) 613
Robertson, Sgt. (Rogers' crew) 248-9
Rockefeller, Governor Nelson 217
Rodenberg, Capt. Joseph H. 351
Roebeck, Lt. Stanley 355
Roeske, Stan 787
Rogalski, Sgt. Edmund 454, 459-60, 547 Part II, 459, 547
Rogers, Bill, Buck (sons of Col. Arthur H. Rogers) 785
Rogers, Col. Arthur (Art) 13-19, 24, 29, 30, 32, 37, 40-1, 43-4, 46-7, 58, 88, 94, 98-102, 104-6, 109-17, 119, 127, 136, 142, 153, 156, 160, 173-4, 176-8, 190-1, 193-6, 201, 204, 206-9, 225, 240-59, 269-70, 273, 275, 282, 284-5, 287, 290-1, 293, 295-7, 303, 307, 322, 325, 331, 333-4, 340, 343, 345, 347, 364, 373, 375-9, 401, 442, 471, 477-8, 483-4, 509, 559, 583, 593, 647, 670, 672, 675, 700, 759-60, 785

   recruits turret gunners 15
   skeet shooting with turret 16
   gets idea for nose turret 24
   promoted to Deputy Group Commander 37
   delayed on Christmas Island 46
   mission to prove nose turret 240

INDEX 811

skip-bombs a Japanese ship 261-6, 593
   leads Group attack on Rabaul 334-45
   postwar career and death 759
Rogers, Eric (grandson of Art Rogers) 783
Rolph, Lt. Charles 133
Rome, ancient iv, 14, 409
Rommel, Gen. Erwin 56
Roosevelt, President Franklin D. 28, 48, 146-7, 206, 208, 382, 410, 418, 499, 532, 660, 715, 733, 742
Rose, Lt. George M. 143, 145-7, 151
Rosie the Riveter 26
Rothenberg, 2nd Lt. Joseph 340
Rothwell, 2nd Lt. Robert J. 358, 360
Royal Australian Air Force 184-5, 211, 228
Rufe (Japanese fighter plane) 185-6
Russia ix, xii, xvi, 382
Russo-Japanese War of 1904-5 ix, xii

S

Sacramento Air Depot 34
Sacramento, California 33-4, 36, 754
Saidor, New Guinea 355, 362, 402
Saint John's Catholic Mission 166
Saipan 498, 602, 697, 765
Sakai, Suburo 108, 163, 450, 775-6
Salamaua, New Guinea 210, 219, 221, 288-91, 294-301, 366, 393, 583, 777
Samate, New Guinea 524-5, 570, 572, 583, 592
San Antonio Rose (B-17) 143, 145-7
Sanderson, Dr. Richard J. "Doc" 201, 205-7, 286
San Diego, California 36, 410, 468
San Francisco, California 31, 33-7, 40-2, 74, 137, 152, 155, 195, 205, 305, 378-9, 454, 467-9, 471-3, 480, 729, 731-3
Satan's Angels (see 475th Fighter Group) 188, 332, 580, 583-5, 588-9, 592, 605, 698
Santo Tomas internment camp 726-7
Sanxter, Lt. Donald L. 96
Sarmi, New Guinea 257-8, 569-70
Satterfield, Sgt Henry W. 148, 150
Saturday Evening Post 94, 254-6, 281, 307, 327, 384, 509
Sauer, 2nd Lt. Clarence J. 526
Schmitt, Sgt. Alfred E. 526
Schoenaue, 2nd Lt. Lyle 148

schoolgirls, Japanese, trained for war, 736
Schooler, Cpl. Forest C. 85
Schouten Islands 598
Schroeder, Sgt. Paul B. 526
Seabees (construction engineers) 56, 62, 190, 192, 205, 323, 337, 342, 396, 398, 401, 403, 490, 492, 516-17, 533, 537, 552-4, 581, 605-6, 639, 721-2, 742
Seidel, 2nd Lt. Walter C. 74-5
Sei, Sgt. Duilio 701-4
Sellmer, Lt. George W. 148-50, 221
Semler, Pvt. Claude J. 75
Sentani lake at Hollandia 388, 395
Seper, Sgt. Jake 242, 247-50, 260-3, 266, 268, 378
Sepik River, New Guinea 169, 306, 357, 360, 362
Seven Mile Field See Jackson Field
Severson, 2nd Lt. Harold I. 526
Shaffer, Lt. George W. 223
Shanghai 739
sharks 122, 130, 163-4, 205, 238
Shark, USS (submarine) 652
Sheehan, 1st Lt. Oliver 356-60, 363
Sheehan, Susan (author of "A Missing Plane") 505
Sheftall, M. G. (historian) ix, 736
Sherdon, Lt. Michael C. 753
Sherman Carpets (child suicide bombers) 735
Sherman Tank M4A1 602, 722
Shinto religion v, vi, 762
shorts snorter 133, 729, 733, 741, 786
shotgun 15, 17, 30, 259
Showers, Sgt. William A. 631
Sikes, Sgt. Samuel H. 631
"Silver Streak" ("Connell's Special," B-24) 252-3, 333
Simons, Sgt. Henry S. 218
Simpson Harbor, Rabaul 78-80, 143-4, 221
Singapore xi, xii, xvii, 299, 670, 672, 717, 739
Sipple, 2nd Lt. William F., Jr. 88
skeet shooting 15-18, 32
skip-bombing Japanese ships 92-4, 133, 174, 189-90, 210, 225, 227-9, 236
"Sky Lady" (B-24) 272
slave labor 626, 638, 717, 727, 752
Slazas, Cpl. Raymond J. 75
Slim, General William 238
sloop, sailing, shot up by Lindbergh 593-4
Smeltzer, Lt. Warren H. 270, 272, 276-7
Smith, 2nd Lt. Edwin B. 218

Smith, Capt. Lawrence N. 348, 351
Smith, Lt. Norman D. 153-4, 169
Smith, Mary Francis 41, 64, 157, 761
Smith, Sgt. Charles O. 631
Smith, Sgt. George J. 328
Smith, Sgt. John A. 342
snakes 60-3, 512, 559
Solomon Islands 49, 56, 222, 367, 578
Solomon Sea 84, 100, 102, 105, 138, 149-50
Sonia (Mitsubishi Ki-51) fighter plane 589-90
Sorensen, 1st Lt. Wallace S. 85
Sorong, New Guinea 524
sortie 507, 572
Southwest Pacific (Area) xvii, 2, 45, 48-52, 69, 79, 127, 135, 175, 223, 227, 239-40, 254, 302, 330, 365-7, 383, 398, 404, 418, 468, 472, 490, 498-500, 507, 579-80, 588, 599, 602, 610, 673, 764, 774
    (Command) 579
Spam (spiced ham) 47, 61, 534, 549, 556-7
Spanish American War xiii, 417, 707
Sparks, Sgt. Joseph E. 655
Speltz, 2nd Lt. Arthur N. 119, 123, 125
Spence, USS (destroyer) 687
"Spirit of St. Louis" 28, 579, 763
Spitfire, British Supermarine (fighter plane) 181, 368
Sprague, 2nd Lt. Edward C 526
Stalin, Josef 382 (footnote)
"Star Duster" (B-24) 232
Stephens, Sgt. (Rogers' crew) 242, 248
Stewart, Flt. Officer Daryl M. 350-1
St. George's Channel, New Britain 138
Stalin, Josef, Soviet dictator, 382
Stith, Sgt. Robert R. 198
St. Jeor, Sgt. Raymond L. 305
Stoecklein, Lt. Bernard 269
Stoll, 1st Lt. Harry M. 348
Stoneman, Camp 34
storage tanks for fuel 451-2, 594
strafer/bomber 175-6, 189, 225-7, 239, 291-3, 308-14, 320, 322, 333, 349, 368-70, 385-7, 389, 392, 497-8, 655, 696, 737, 745-6
Straw, Lt. Eugene W. 131-2, 211
Strawn, Sgt. Vernon J. 702-3
strike (U.S. workers) 422-3
    (attacks) 452, 499, 507, 524-5, 532, 551, 554, 571-2, 580, 590
Stuka (German dive bomber) 741

submarine xv, xvi, 35, 44, 141, 239, 336, 472, 533, 549, 574, 640, 714
Sugden, 2nd Lt. Alston F. 158, 161, 170
suicide xvi, 166, 184, 451-2, 500, 511, 543, 604, 618-19, 640, 696, 705, 721, 734-6, 744, 763
Sumatra 678
Sunset Project, the 754
"Susabella" (B-24) a. k. a. "Connell's Special" and "The Silver Streak" 379, 484
Sutherland, Gen. Richard 51, 500, 586-7
Swanson, Lt. Dustin "Dusty" 357, 360, 364
SWPA. See Southwest Pacific Area
Sydney, Australia 128, 157-8, 172, 206, 270, 337, 614, 669-79

T

Taberfane Island Japanese seabase 184-5, 187
Tacloban, Leyte Island, Philippine Islands 65, 691-4, 728
Tadji airfield, New Guinea 396-7
Tales of the Jolly Rogers by Andrew Lord 785
Talili Bay Massacre 171
tanks American (Sherman M4A1) 602, 722
    Japanese Type 95 602-3, 612
Tarzan of the Apes 58
Task Force 38 686
technology, Western superiority viii
telegraph viii
Telegraph, U. K. (newspaper) 770
telescope viii
"Ten Knights in a Bar Room" (B-24) 355-60, 363
tents, pyramidal, U. S. Army 490
Terry, Capt. Morgan F. 506
The Approach to the Philippines (book) 638
The Best Years of Our Lives (movie) 754 (footnote)
"The Butcher Boy" (B-24) 223-4
"The Condor" (B-24) 64, 75-7
The Dam Busters (movie) 92
"The Dude" (B-24) 307
The Gap (Kokoda Pass) 502-6
The Great Raid (book and movie) 727
Theobald, Tom 407-8, 411, 420, 439-40, 405, 454-7, 461-6, 468, 470-5, 477, 484, 511, 513, 541-2, 561, 568, 610, 642-4, 658, 680, 691-2,

731-2, 759, 785-6
  enlists in the Air Corps 421
  goes to navigator school 439-41
  sees crash at March Field 462
  navigates to Hawaii 471-4
  navigates to Canton Island 477
  navigates to Wakde Island 511
  sees dead navigator on Wakde 568
  life after the war 759
Third Attack Group (B-25 strafer/bombers) 368, 497
Thomas, Patty (USO dancer) 613
Thomas, Sgt. Ellis G. 340
Thompson, Lt. Patricia (nurse) 561 (picture)
Thornhill, Capt. Dale J. 76, 284-5
Thusgaard, Carl (war correspondent) 269, 325, 327-8
Tiger Moth (British biplane) 276
Tinker, Maj. Gen. Clarence L. 542
Tojo, Prime Minister Hideki v
Tokyo Radio 65, 388
Tokyo Rose 387, 392-3
Tol Plantation Massacre 82-3, 772
Tony (Japanese fighter plane) 313, 324, 356-60, 404
Top of the Mark Lounge 469-70
Torokina airfield, Bougainville 331, 381
Torres Strait 197-99, 308
torture of nuns by Japanese 168
Townsville, Australia 58-60, 127-8, 470, 482-7, 506, 525, 671
Trainor, Lt. Barney E. 187
Tripartite Pact 14
Trobriand Islands 139, 337, 341-2, 344
Truk Island 281, 383
Truman, President Harry S. 85, 742, 762
Trusel, Lt. Charles R. 702
tunnel gun in B-24 belly 36, 248, 481
Tupa, Robert J. 195, 773, 785
Turner, Sgt. Eugene V. 328
Turrentine, Pvt. M. D. 325
"Twin Niftys" (B-24) 305-7
Twitty, 1st Lt. Kenneth E. 348
typhus 191, 195, 492, 494, 581-2, 604

U

Unbroken (book and movie) 634
Unruh, Lt. Col. Marion D. 30, 40, 43, 176
Uraga Harbor viii, ix
uranium for atomic bombs, 382
U.S. Army Air Corps xviii, 13, 22, 48, 50, 207, 407, 411, 413, 421, 426-7, 436, 447, 635, 660, 671
Utne, Sgt. Clarence S. 152

V

V (Fifth) Bomber Command 1, 142, 147, 197-8, 211, 217, 240, 303, 320, 347, 373, 490-1, 636, 692, 697, 725, 753-4
Vandereedt, Art 786
Venona Project (decrypt Soviet messages) 382
Versailles Treaty of WWI vii
Vial, Flt. Lt. Leigh Grant "Golden Voice" 210, 218
Vineyard, Lt. Carl. H. 363
"Virgin III" (B-24) 324-5, 328
Vitiaz Straits 158, 221, 224, 239, 365, 366
Vunakanau airfield, Rabaul 138

W

Waddle, Cmdr. Scott 769
Wainwright, Gen. Johnathan 716-17, 748
Waist gunners shooting up their own planes 649
Waite, Sgt. Paul D. 350
Wakde Island 254-7, 395, 490, 506-7, 509-33, 537, 539-41, 548-57, 559-69, 572, 574, 577-8, 580-1, 583-85, 590, 592, 594-6, 598-9, 602, 605-11, 615, 620, 655, 707, 725, 767-8
Wake Island xviii, 46, 71, 85, 383, 542, 643, 726
Wake Island Massacre 383, 771
Waldner, Ann (WASP pilot) 27
Walker, Brig. Gen. Kenneth N. 94, 142-48, 151-2, 197, 279, 331, 775
Walker, Sgt. Francis E. 342
Wall, Sgt. Richard D. 358
Walpole, 1st Lt. Edward J. 75
Walrus (British amphibious biplane) 186
Waltzing Matilda (song) 156, 366
Ward's Field (Drome), Port Moresby 129,

188-9, 191, 194
Washing Machine Charlies 563, 565
WASPs (Women's Airforce Service Pilots) 27
Wau, New Guinea 289, 298, 320
Wayne, John (actor) 617
"Weezie" (B-24) 502-6, 731, 766
Weissmuller, Johnny (Tarzan actor) 58
Wells, Lt. "Spiffy" 211
Wendling, Fr. A. (missionary) 274
Werner, 1st Lt. John H. 73-7, 138-9
Wesche, Fred 145, 775
Western Civilization iv, vii
Wewak, New Guinea 129, 157, 159, 162, 164-5, 169, 189, 210, 239-40, 244-5, 247-50, 257, 260, 264, 267-8, 282-5, 302-4, 306-15, 318, 324, 326, 328, 346-53, 355, 357-8, 362, 368, 370, 383-90, 394, 396, 402, 404, 490, 510-12, 530, 533, 640, 648, 680, 716, 777-8
    Boram airfield 257, 302, 304, 311, 349, 352
    But airfield, 302, 311, 385
    Dagua airfield 257, 267, 302, 311-14, 385, 389
    Wewak Central airfield 302, 304, 309, 311
whaling ships, American vii
Whatley, 1st Lt. Clifford E. 571, 574-7
Wheeler Field, Hawaii 36
Whitacre, Lt. William L. 144-5, 183
Whitcomb, Russell 34
Whitehead, Gen. Ennis C. 95, 127, 142, 198-9, 201, 204, 224, 240, 316, 347, 375-6, 392, 579-80, 586
Whiteman, S/Sgt. William J. 85
White Sands, New Mexico 743
Whitlock, 1st Lt. Charles P. 36, 152, 379
Wilde, Lt. Norman 211
Willcoxon, Lt. John B. 324-6, 328
Williams, Capt. Hans H. 730
Williams, Cpl. Harold L. 75
Willow Run, Michigan B-24 factory 22, 25-31, 33, 36, 43, 68, 410, 624, assemblyline picture on p. 26
Wills, Sgt. Clyde O. 576
Wilson, Sgt. Loy L. 122
'wither on the vine' (MacArthur's island bypass strategy) 171, 382-3, 385, 640, 726
Wolf, Cpl. Ralph N. 148-50
Women's Airforce Service Pilots (WASPs) 27

women in war industries 26
Wood, 1st Lt. Everett 127
Woods, Wiley O. (historian of 90th) 34, 68, 73, 118, 137, 183, 195, 287, 364, 379, 484, 527, 556, 633, 650, 666, 690, 707
Wootten, General G. F. 321
Workman, Sgt. Charles B. 120-22
World War One vi, vii, xvii, 50, 174-5, 292, 322, 409-10, 419, 460, 477
World War Two iv-vi, x, xvi, xvii, 1, 28, 101
Worthington, Sgt. Lester R. 526
Wurtsmith, Maj. Gen. Paul V. 395, 595, 664
Wu, Sgt. Jack C. 277
Wyandotte Indian tribe 695
Wynne, Sgt. Frank O. 158, 170

Y

Yalch, S/Sgt. John 285
Yamamoto, Admiral Isoroku xiv, xv (footnote), 220-1, 239, 366
Yamanaka, Akira 309-10
"Yanks From Hell" (B-24) 305
Yaple, Lt. Karle W. 307
Yasukuni Shrine to war dead 202
Yoshida, Ayako (Michi) 572-4
Younker, Sgt. Leon R. 576
Ypsilanti, Michigan 25

Z

Zalic, Sgt. John P. 328
Zamporini, Louis (Olympic runner) 634
Zeke (Japanese Zero) 165, 313, 622-3, 629, 636
Zellmer, Lt. David 566-7, 569, 581, 615
Zero (Mitsubishi A6M Japanese fighter plane also called Zeke) 9-11, 29, 54, 96, 100, 103-4, 106-113, 116, 131, 145, 148-9, 152-4, 160, 163-5, 173, 178, 185, 189, 223-5, 227-8, 232-3, 235, 240, 243, 245, 247, 250, 257, 261, 264, 267, 282-5, 298, 313, 326-7, 338-340, 354, 357, 379, 381, 388, 500, 590-2, 619, 622-3, 629, 637-9, 646, 647-9, 653, 660, 689-90, 698, 745, 773, 778-9, 781

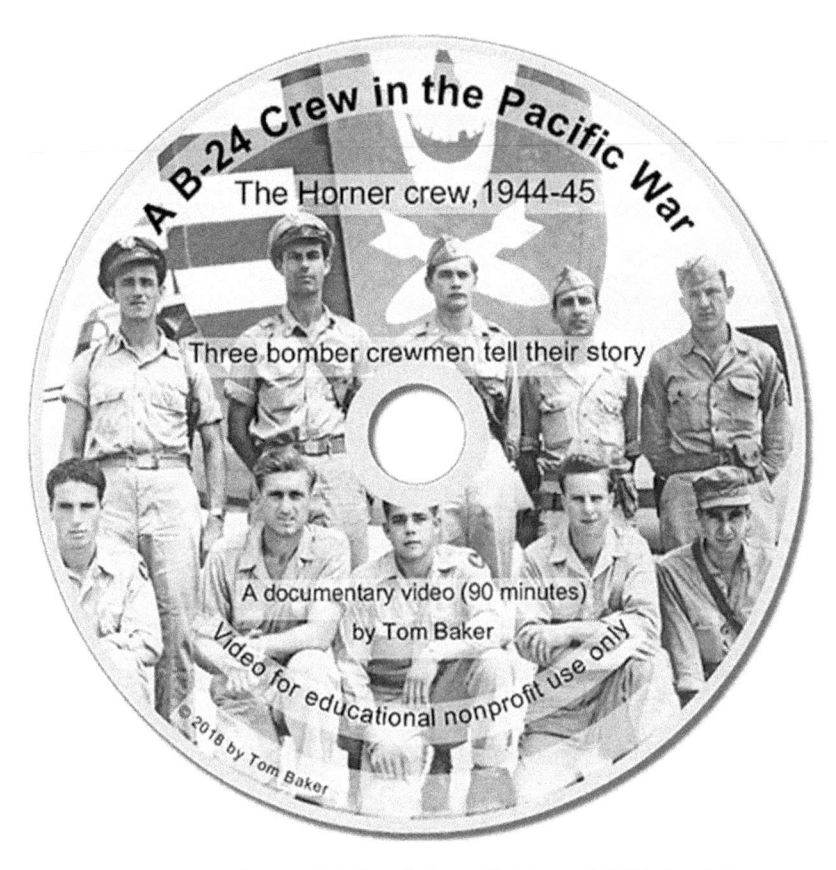

A companion video to this book is available on DVD. In this video documentary, the three surviving crewmen of the Horner crew, Jim Horner, Jaime Baca, and Tom Theobald, tell their own stories about the events covered in this book. Tom Baker narrates the story of the Jolly Rogers within the context of World War Two, with photos, movie clips, and music of the time. 90 minutes, NTSC format.

Available at https://tbaker137.wixsite.com/itwasntsojolly

Lightning Source UK Ltd.
Milton Keynes UK
UKHW021445090921
390292UK00013B/999